Folio

PSYCHOMENTAL COMPLEX
OF THE TUNGUS

Psychomental Complex
of the Tungus

BY

S. M. SHIROKOGOROFF

LONDON

KEGAN PAUL, TRENCH, TRUBNER & CO., LTD.

1935

Made in China
Printed by the Catholic University Press, Peking

FOREWORD

At first it was not my intention to write a foreword to the present work. I therefore included some questions, usually treated in a foreword, into Chapter III of the Introduction. However, after reading, in proofs, the whole of the book and especially the Introduction, I deem it necessary to add some explanations, in order to be well understood. In fact, my remarks concerning "Theories affecting investigator's work" (Section 3, pp. 6-10) may produce the quite wrong impression that I altogether disagree with all my predecessors and contemporaries and with all theoreticians. My intention was not to write about ethnography in general and to find out "theories helping investigator's work". The whole of the science of ethnography is of course helpful for a collector of original data, and I need not emphasize it. It is clear, at least for those who are engaged in the collecting and analysing of original materials. A great number of original investigations among the various ethnical units and groups, now carried out in all parts of the world, a great number of theoretical works, and very rich ethnographical collections found in the museums put the modern investigator into a new position, very favourable for both the theoretical result of the work and the collecting of new data. However, this favourable position also imposes great obligations on the modern investigator. Ethnography is no more a new field: the observer cannot be a naive romantic who is looking for exotic facts and situations unforeseen by the European complex; he cannot let himself to be carried away by imagination for heaping artificial constructions, perhaps satisfying one's aesthetic feeling, but perfectly useless, even dangerous, for the science; he also cannot become a collector who has no other aim but "collecting", for this attitude will soon lead to an unproductive waste of energy, which is now much needed for the passing through the coming, perhaps already going on crisis; moreover, he cannot refuse to face life, such as it is, as a historian often does, for Ethnography has ceased to be a "science about primitive tribes" which has nothing to do with "civilized mankind". The old ethnography of the nineteenth century is dead. The ethnographer-historian is nowadays working at the restoration, as far as possible, of the complexes of the past; the field ethnographer, armed with all possible theoretical knowledge, is describing and analysing "living" complexes, as *complexes* in their functional and historical aspects. In this respect the ethnographer comes near to the historian and all those specialists who are dealing with various aspects of culture (i.e. Ethnography) among the so-called civilized ethnical groups. In fact, the study of cultural complexes is not of yesterday. But it was confined to special manifestations of the complexes. The study of the common law, stimulated by a practical need of its codification, or merely of comprehensive recording for practical use; the study of the social organization, language, art, various aspects of technology, etc. stimulated by various reasons; even the study of the technical and, naturally, economic processes imposed by their functioning—all these special studies actually dealt with the same phenomenon of "cultural adaptation in man" which called to life the *ethnographer* and stimulated the organization of the new science of ethnography. We can now leave aside the question as to the practical stimuli which undoubtedly were greatly responsible for the existence of ethnographers and ethnography, but the philosophical premises are of importance for our present treatment. The almost general theoretical conception, even among the most clear-thinking people, was, firstly, that all cultural complexes, besides those with which the Europeans were familiar, were relatively simple and primitive, so that any educated man could understand and describe them and, secondly, that by studying them it was possible to write the history of the present civilized mankind. At the first contact with the realities it appeared, almost at once, that the culture of supposedly primitive peoples was not as simple as it had originally seemed and, a curious fact, a great number of ethnographers "specialized" in "material culture", "social organization", "religion", "language", even "folk-lore", "decorative art", "family", "primitive economics", etc. to such a degree that they easily could have degenerated into an inferior class of technologists, philosophers, philologists dealing with "primitive phenomena". However, the pressure of life was strong enough and the ethnographer has successfully survived by cutting his ties with the old philosophical premises and by creating, by means of facts, the necessary basis for Ethnology (in my sense). Another effect of the increase of knowledge was that the idea of reconstituting history appeared to have been inadequate for doing this work by simple means of scaffolding of hypotheses. There was one still more important effect, namely, the ethnographer has realized that he must not only pay attention to the "primitive people", but his attention must also be attracted by the ethnical groups to which he is indebted for his original education and methods of thinking. The objection to such an extension of ethnography comes at once, namely, that the field of ethnography is so vast that no human being is able to fathom it. However, this objection is not based upon a scientific reasoning, but on the fear of being unable to master the task. It is perfectly true that *to know all cultural complexes* is impossible, but as I shall now show, it is not even needed. Whether we deny the fact of the existence of ethnography, as here defined, or not, it does not change the situation. Such situations happened in other fields of human knowledge. For instance, there was a time when a botanist might have known *all plants known at his time*, nowadays he may know only a section of the botanical classification. There was a time when a chemist *knew all organic combinations known at his time*, nowadays no human being can know all chemical organic combinations, of which new ones are moreover discovered every day. However, nobody will say that Botany or Organic Chemistry cannot exist, or even that they do not exist, as it happens with timid people when they face a really enormous quantity of ethnographic facts known and, especially still to be known.

We must acknowledge that such a state has already been reached by Ethnography, and this implies a new attitude on the part of ethnographers.

Now, I must make another step in order to approach my goal. There was a time when a botanist needed no special training in general biology, chemistry, physics, microscopic technique and even applied mathematics, but nowadays he must have this training before he may become a modern botanist. There was also a time when a chemist needed no special training in physics, chemophysics and mathematics and could go ahead with his discoveries. The inference is evident: to be a botanist or a chemist (organic) nowadays is much more difficult than it was before, if one wants to make discoveries in these fields and not to remain a qualified servant in a botanical museum or a chemical laboratory, where such specialized and qualified workmen nowadays are needed, just as on board of a man-of-war a high percentage of skilful specialists is needed, even with a high (equivalent to the European university) education. Why should it be different with Ethnography?

However, there is another aspect of the same situation. In the beginning of the nineteenth century it would have seemed impossible for a young man to have done in physics what nowadays is done by a pupil of a middle school before his entering the university; and the modern student of a university is busy with problems which were beyond the reach of professors a century ago. The inference, often forgotten when Ethnography is discussed, is that the method of work is perfected and therefore shortened. A great number of problems are no more problems and the field is clear for further steps, because of the formulation and verification of *general principles and generalizations*, and, in so far as the technique of observation is concerned, because of working out of new *methods of investigation*. No modern physics can exist one day without its theoretical foundations. The same is true of Ethnography. Thus, in Ethnography two sides must be distinguished, namely, the first one is the collecting of new facts, which presumes a certain theoretical training and a perfect possession of modern methods for collecting facts, and the second one is the direction of investigations which presumes a broad theoretical preparation, knowledge of the factual side and a perfect mastering of methodology. In so far as the collecting is concerned it must, of course, not be based upon the trial-error method, as it was practised before, but special methods justified by and based upon certain theoretical foundations must be worked out, and so it will be, if Ethnography is not doomed to perish. There is nothing impossible in it, for we have such instances in some special branches of ethnography. For instance, in olden days it would take many years to record the common law of an ethnical unit, with the present knowledge of theoretical jurisprudence it takes a few weeks; a description of a dialect (including vocabulary, phonetics and morphology) in olden days would take years of work, with the familiarity with general linguistics it does not take more than a few weeks. The same holds good for social organization, also economics and technology in general, but on the condition that one be familiar with the theory. However, even when one is technically prepared to do the gathering of facts, one may easily remain automatic in collecting new facts, which sometimes may perhaps become quite superfluous if one is not sufficiently versed in the theoretical side. In fact, the ethnographer is only a collector of facts and even not always an analyst. The cases of collecting facts which cannot be analysed and published because of their volume are well known. Therefore, to know how many facts are needed is not less important than to know how to make it within a short time. The collecting of facts may easily degenerate into a "mania of collecting". Although the facts may be quite curious and artfully presented, they are often superfluous, if the trend of Science in general is disregarded. I shall give now an absurd example of an insane botanist who is measuring one by one the leaves of all trees which he meets on his way. The work may be accurate, painstaking, almost heroic, but it is useless, since the biometrical methods may shorten this work. One may spend one's life on the most accurate record of individual phonetic variations, but it will not contribute anything to the knowledge of the nature of language, the fundamentals being already discovered. In the same way, to follow up all possible dialectal variations, going from village to village, and from house to house, will not differ very much from the work of the botanist measuring leaf by leaf. Of course, one may find *pleasure* even in collecting stamps, used pens and musical records for gramophone in a number surpassing the physical possibility of enjoying them. But, I have never heard of any contributor to finances, steel work and music among the people who were affected by the mania of collecting stamps, pens and musical records. One sometimes finds pleasure in folklore, as such, and in general ethnography, as such, but if it turns into a mania of collecting, I greatly doubt that such a condition may be considered as completely harmless, should it occupy too many people in the ethnical unit (or group). The refinement of amateurs of cock fighting, flea racing and that of various gamblers, all of whom have pleasure in their occupations, is not sufficient for a social (ethnical) justification of their activity. Under ever increasing interethnical pressure these seemingly harmless and seemingly aesthetic passions may paralyse the ethnical unit, if the *thinking layer* of the unit is affected by them. Thus, this kind of justification of an aimless ethnographic collecting of facts cannot be regarded as satisfactory, and such a collecting cannot be considered as useful for the science and completely harmless for the ethnical units to which the collectors belong, if they still can be useful members of the society; but, of course, such a passion may be utilized by those who direct the Science. By pointing out these seemingly paradoxical parallels, I intend only to show that the overgrowth and further "degeneration" of a useful cultural phenomenon, such as an ethnographical collecting, may occur, if there is no directing science behind the ethnographers. Just as behind the qualified workmen in botany, the systematists, and the qualified workmen in chemistry, the experimentators in organic chemistry, there are the general biology and general chemistry which direct these skilful workmen, behind the ethnographer-collector there must be a science which is able to direct him. As a matter of fact, the history of ethnography always reflected this situation. On the one hand, there was a tendency of specialization in the sense of further dissection of ethnography, as stated above, and "specialists" intended to simplify in this way their work and to remain beyond control; on the other hand, there was an open protest against an interference of theoreticians and a marked tendency to become "specialists—ethnographers". The first tendency needs no explanation, but the second one needs some remarks. It must be admitted that the tendency to eliminate the interference of theoreticians, as shown before, was greatly due to the failure of the theoreticians to show a right direction to the collectors who soon appeared to be ahead of them. The latter were not so much familiar with the actual facts. This was a period of trial-error in theory, and the same in practice of collecting material. However, apart from it, the protest and tendency of specialization were in the same line of other phenomena left without a real theoretical guidance. The fundamental problems, such as where the unit is to be investigated, where the dialect is to be recorded, what the mechanism of formation of complexes (and "complexes" have appeared only lately) is; how the elements spread, what to record, etc. were left without answer, whilst the theoreticians were arguing about the promiscuity, the origin of everything, the matriarchat and patriarchat, the totemism, the evolution of primitive mentality, without seeing any "primitive man", and hundreds of other things interesting for the philosophical trend of the last century. Lately introduced discussions as to the "psychological method", diffusion and parallelism, "soma" and "noos" and other "problems" cannot at all satisfy the ethnographer's demand for guidance.

Naturally, all these answers may be given only by a general science—Ethnology—i.e. the theory of ethnical and ethnographical variations and that of ethnical unit, with a special part dealing with the definition of the present state of ethnology in the system of knowledge (science), and principles of classification, which covers all manifestations of human existence and treats them not in abstractions, but in complexes and individuals, as they are observed in life. Thus the physical conditions of ethnical bodies and their cultural complexes will not be artificially dissected for the reason of difference in the form of biological adaptation. Of course such a science requires much more preliminary work than any specialized branch, but it may be remembered that there was a time when for the same reason General Biology, Chemophysics, even General Linguistics were misdoubted and the possibility of their existence was questioned. Sooner or later such a general science will be created or else the depending sciences, such as anthropology, ethnography, including folklore, linguistics and others, will grow into a malignant tumor and suffocate under the piles of unanalysed, unclassified and perhaps useless facts. The signs of such an overgrowth are now already visible. On the one hand, self-restriction in the analysis can be observed, such as the tendency to make of ethnography a simple "historical" discipline, or to build it on the basis of some internal mechanisms of culture, e.g. the functionalism, as a new wording for the old "utility", the famous schematization of "instincts", such as "hunger", "sex" etc. which idea is closely connected with that of Elementargedanke, and ethnography of "internal evidences" or to make of it a kind of "applied ethnography", at the service of the administration, and still narrower, at the service of political parties.

Ethnography has of course its historical aims, but to identify it with "History" is impossible, for, first of all, history is not the only aim of ethnography, and for some specialists-historians it is not yet clear what they have to do: to record fact by fact, to record what seems to be important, to create a kind of "philosophy of history", to analyse the facts, to operate with the "values", to analyse "geography" and "races" in action, or to make of it a kind of "applied history" for the use of political propaganda.

History has its own problems of technique, such as verification of the authenticity of documents, operation with the sequence of facts, chronology, classification etc., like any other branch of knowledge, which *collects* and *describes* facts, has its own technique. But the historians have failed to create a general science (perhaps owing to the complexity and complexal character of historical facts dealt with) which could direct the historian in his work; and his position does not differ from that of the ethnographer who looks for guidance. However, in so far as technique is concerned, the experience of the historians is great enough and useful for any science dealing with a sequence of facts. Naturally the technique of the historians of the past century cannot be used nowadays—the historian cannot be indifferent e.g. to the fact of a change occurring in a population, from the anatomical (anthropological) point of view, at two different historical moments; he cannot be indifferent to the conclusion of an ethnographer, when the latter gives his analysis of the ethnical composition of a population, and he cannot be indifferent when the palaeontologist analyses extinct and living species of animals found in the archaeological strata, although the methods of the anthropologist, ethnographer and palaeontologist are not those of a historian of the nineteenth century. The historian of our days, if he wants to be at the level of modern science, must be competent in his judgement as to the methods used by the "scientists". Actually it means that the scope of the modern historian's work is much wider than that of the historian of the nineteenth century. In fact, the historian cannot confine himself to the "historical methods" alone. The dividing line, that was intended to be created between "history" and "science", has now disappeared, and this idea is now maintained only by those who did not master the methods of "science" and who do not want to see that there are Science and various techniques proper to the nature of facts dealt with by specialists in differently specialized branches of knowledge.

Undoubtedly, to understand the internal mechanism of any cultural complex is the primary task to be fulfilled by the ethnographer. True, it may be only "functional" or "interno-evidential", gedonistic, materialistic, historical, i.e. the light may be thrown only from one side, but it will be done, for it is now realized that one can no more disregard the *complex* of culture. It is also clear that such a specialized approach to the internal mechanism of complexes is not sufficient, for the "causes" of processes, which are going on in the cultural complexes, sometimes lie far from the internal mechanisms. In this respect the attempts at calling attention of ethnographers to "human biology", "geographical environment" and "history", i.e. external and not "cultural" conditions, must be regarded as a vital necessity. It is interesting to note that even in this case the above mentioned tendency of "specialization" takes hold of ethnographers.

I need not dwell long on the trend of "practical value" of ethnography, so much emphasized nowadays when the ethnographer wants to get the support of rulers who do not know how delicate the mechanism of psychomental complex is which produces, amongst others, the cultural element of science, functionally bound to *cognize* without any practical aim. This stimulus of cognition has ever existed and is only an element of the working mechanism, but should this stimulus restrict the activity of the ethnographer, it would be only pernicious for the ethnographer and ethnography. In fact, no sane man can think of using a learned engineer for driving in nails, and a physicist for repairing type-writing machines. As soon as ethnography becomes an instrument of "practical value" it ceases to function as Science, and thus its inferences cannot be reliable. Moreover, such a "practicism" unavoidably leads to a narrow specialization of an ethnographer who ceases to be ethnographer. As shown, such an ethnography existed for a long time without being called ethnography. To revert to this type and trend of investigation is nothing but a manifestation of a conscious or unconscious desire to stop the too fast growth of ethnography. This is the same attitude which is manifested in the narrowing of the "point of view", and in the making of ethnography a simple "history".

Such a state of things is not typical of the ethnography alone. A great number of other "humanities", such as e.g. sociology, history, even partly economics and others, are in search for an issue out of the entanglement in the forest of theories of imaginative theories which were created owing to an artificial approach to new facts and methods of investigation. It is not an impasse, as some writers suppose, but it is a real crisis: the old methods of analysis and generalization cannot cover all facts acquired by the special and specialized branches of knowledge. We have a very good example in the psychology which has already severed connexion with "philosophy" and in this movement has made even a too great swing which, it is true, may also result in an artificial narrowing and "specialization". Of course, it is only a temporary reaction.

Should such a state of things be maintained in Ethnography, it will remain in the imaginary impasse. Moreover, if Ethnography does not fortify its theoretical rear and does not organize itself, it will suffocate under the weight of facts. We have also the very interesting instance of sociology in America. The thin body of theoretical sociology, i.e. the theory of social organization and function, can hardly be increased by means of old methods, while its body is now stuffed with theories, which may have only a historical interest, and with an enormous collection of facts concerning all those phenomena which are an effect of the contact between two and more individuals. Catch-words—"social", "society", etc.—happened to be stronger than simple good sense. All the practical problems imposed by the functioning of "modern society" were covered by the "social sciences", and "sociology" has tried to treat all of them. Such functions as those of policemen, inspectors of mores, municipal clerks, sales-agents for contraceptive apparatuses, advertizing agents, labour inspectors, even modest teachers, etc. have been transformed into "social workers" whose activity must be put into a "sociological frame". Owing to this the really horrible mixture of "applied sociology", and its theoretical justification in the form of "Principles of Sociology" completely submerged the meagre theory. With this overgrown appendix,—a malignant tumor of "practicism" of half-educated people,—the "theory" should be, at least in volume, enlarged by including all theories which were ever produced—from Plato up to the last year's productions. Of course, they are quite interesting from the historical point of view, but one must be historian and ethnographer for being able to treat them. There are excellent chemists who do not know theories of various alchemists of the XVIIth and XVIIIth centuries. What importance for Science of our time can have abberrations of Rousseau, Montesquieu and others, by accident selected "thinkers" of the past, when they are treated ad nauseam by "social sciences" which impose them on the young generations, instead of giving a simple Sociology. Here, as in Ethnography, we meet again with the same paucity of theory, the same tendency to an early specialization and the same "practicism" which have brought modern "sociology" to an impossibility of mastering, without any solid theory, an ocean of facts. Perhaps for a long time sociology will be handicapped by all these conditions and perhaps it will even not come out at all of the present entanglement.

It is not yet too late for ethnography to avoid such a situation. First of all, during the last decades a great number of ethnographical methods has been tried and proved to be useful. The technique of ethnography is far advanced: the ethnographer uses his technological knowledge, linguistical analysis, psychological analysis, statistical approach when needed, historical methods, etc.; he has no more prejudices as to the choice of his facts and ethnical groups, he has become objective, he does not approve or disapprove, he observes all cultural complexes, including ethnography itself. But what ethnography needs is theory— Ethnology—as it has been defined above. The filling up of the gap between the physical conditions of human existence and a special functional adaptation created in ethnical bodies—the cultural (ethnographical) adaptation—is beyond the power of Ethnography, as such, but it is one of the aims of Ethnology.

The relationship between the sciences may thus be formulated, if Ethnology is taken as the central point.

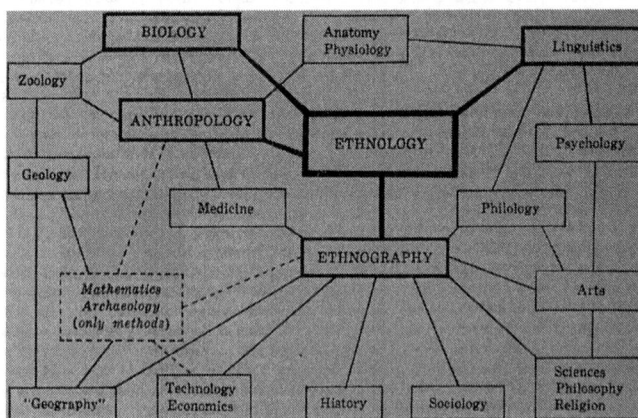

Unfortunately it is impossible to represent in a simplified scheme, in two dimensions, instead of the needed three, all sciences and their special branches, as well as their relations. I therefore give here only an idea of these relations. Any science here indicated may be taken as a centre.

From the scheme it can be seen that I reserve for Anthropology the place of a specialized branch of zoology, while to the *Ethnography*—a descriptive science—I assign that of a specialized study of secondary adaptation going on and preserved only in groups—the *ethnical* unit. But the "history of human races" which at some time constituted the old *Ethnology* must be partly reserved for Palaeontology and for History of Mankind. Naturally, the methods of classification of human groups, the ethnical and interethnical equilibria, the physical and functional (especially cultural) changes, and in general the system of equilibria (which cannot be separately solved by the anthropologists and ethnographers), the behaviour of moving populations and the spreading of cultural elements and complexes, etc. are referred to Ethnology. If this had been done earlier, a great number of "problems", such as the "influence of environment", "anthropogeography", "heredity versus milieu", "diffusion versus parallelism" and others would never have arisen. The very important generalizations and analytical descriptions of ethnographical phenomena have already been made, so in this sense Ethnology exists without being recognized. In fact, various problems are answered in Anthropology, Ethnography, Linguistics, Archaeology, History and even Ethnology as it was known in the nineteenth century. I am in favour of a strict demarcation, for the old Anthropology—the Science of man —like the Naturphilosophie of the beginning of the XIXth century has overgrown itself. There is, at least now, no better name than Ethnology. Of course, the main objection to such a science is that it requires too much preliminary work of an ethnologist, but this cannot be helped. As stated above, the same objection was made when General Biology appeared. Theoretically it may be foreseen what kind of objections will be raised by the persons specialized along particular lines, but it will not stop (it may only retard) the growth of Science, for life is stronger than any individual effort, and Science is life. I do not think that in future there will be a very great number of *ethnologists*, but by analogy with what is observed in other scientific fields it may be supposed that there will be, as before, specialists in anthropology, linguistics and ethnography, even specialists in crania, Eskimo grammar, and social organization, whose contributions to the science will be of the greatest importance.

It is evident that a further growth of Ethnology into a science, to some degree similar to General Biology, is postulated as a particular manifestation of the general growth of Science. If the latter declines, together with the whole cultural complex, or if the cultural complex is entirely modified and science is substituted by something else, there will be no question about Ethnology. However, the number of ethnographers, anthropologists and linguists is now on the increase, because of the inclusion of new ethnical units, at least partially, into the same cultural cycle,—the Japanese, Indian and Chinese contributors are coming and they must be satisfied with the answers that may be given only by Ethnology.

Looking back at the work accomplished during the period when Anthropology, Ethnography and Ethnology formally existed, it must be definitely recognized that the present advancement in all these branches of knowledge is due to the brilliant past. Within four generations profound investigations in all directions were accomplished. A summary description of almost all ethnical units of the Earth, from the point of view of their physical and cultural characters, is possible; a great number of facts concerning physical and cultural history of man relieves us from the worry about the unknown; the methods of investigation are perfected; the foundation of Ethnology is laid down. Among the figures of the past those who collected new facts and those who tried to decipher their meaning were great men. Of course, the facts collected remain as they are, and their contributors will remain for ever great men, but the greatness of those who attempted deciphering should not be minimized. They might be right or wrong, but their efforts created the milieu in which every new generation felt more and more confidence in its work. Queer as it may now seem, the construction of evolutionists of the nineteenth century has helped in its way; narrow as they are the systems of the end of the nineteenth and the beginning of the twentieth centuries, still surviving, have cleared up the field of theory. It is only for the sake of saving time that I express in the brief manner of a wholesale rejection my disagreement with certain theories of the past, and for the same reason my remarks about the epigones of the great men and uncritical imitators may assume the form of "polemics". However, I must point out that the class of imitators and vulgarizers in theory who influence the young generation of ethnographers is a real social burden.

In the present Foreword I need not repeat what I have said in the forewords to my "Social Organization of the Northern Tungus" and "Social Organization of the Manchus". Now I want to stress the fact that my approach to the cultural phenomena is not of yesterday and that it was formulated during and just after the investigation had been carried out. However, in my earlier works I could not touch upon this question so much as I can do it now. The reason is threefold, namely, the space allowed for theoretical excursuses is now much larger; the facts are presented; the reader is more prepared by my former publications to meet opinions which are not common and which often are only my own opinions. In some remarks concerning my former publications I have noticed a tendency to bind me up together with some "schools". I deem it necessary to say that as an ethnographer I consider myself to be of the "ethnological (in my sense) school". Of course, in Ethnography there can be no "points of view"; there can be only one possible treatment of facts—the ethnological one.

During the last proof-reading I have met with some misprints. Unfortunately, under the actual conditions of printing, they could not be avoided. Some of them I have corrected in the Glossary and Indexes, but some of them, when they were evident, I have left without corrections. This time I had greatly to abbreviate my glossary and indexes, because of their possible dimensions. I must also appeal to the indulgence of the reader for my English. In this sense I was helped by Professor R. D. Jameson who made some polishing of the first 48 pages, by recommended by him Miss B. Wingfield who did pp. 49-240 and by Mr. W. O. Klemm, who went over the rest of the work. I am greatly indebted to these persons. Any one who is familiar with the conditions of printing of such works as the present one, may realize that Mr. B. A. Romanovsky who, being manager of the Press, supervised the printing, deserves my best thanks.

This work was prepared for publication during a long time. After the completion of the collecting of the material the latter could not be used before the linguistical analysis had been completed. Yet the writing had to be still more postponed because I condsidered it necessary to publish other works dealing with other aspects of the Tungus cultural adaptation and especially with the classification of the Tungus groups. So, when all preliminary steps had been made and the material had been analysed, in 1932-1933, I proceeded with the writing. During that time I consciously avoided any reading of recent publications connected with the subject. In fact, the freshness of new publications may sometimes lead astray. However, after completing my writing a perusal of some new publications, such as those by R. Marret, P. Radin and some others, has convinced me that I need not introduce any new additions and interpretations. This is the reason why the reader will not find references to some very recent works, my general attitude towards them being clear from the present Foreword and the Introduction.

After reading this work I have regretted that I had too much abbreviated the whole of the Part One, dealing with the positive knowledge, and Chapter XV dealing with the various hypotheses. However, it was necessary to shorten the exposition for the work had already assumed a length by far surpassing the usual size. For this length I must apologize to the reader. Once I had the idea to recommend to the reader some chapters and sections of general interest, but after the last reading of the work I gave up this idea because *the Tungus Psychomental Complex can be understood only as a whole, as a complex, and reading of isolated chapters and sections may give a distorted picture of the Tungus and of the author.*

The Author.

Peiping, China. June 1935.

TABLE OF CONTENTS

PSYCHOMENTAL COMPLEX

OF THE TUNGUS

INTRODUCTION

CHAPTER I

DIFFICULTIES OF AN INVESTIGATION INTO THE PSYCHOMENTAL COMPLEX

1. PSYCHOMENTAL COMPLEX At present there may be no differences in opinions as to the nature of ethnographical phenomena in general, nor as to their complexes and elements. They are observable manifestations of acquired knowledge, practices, and behaviour. These are either transmitted from one generation to another, or borrowed from neighbours, or even created by the individuals who compose ethnical units, which, like any other *populatio*, possess a series of inherited physio-psychological complexes, the latter leaving possibilities for and putting limitations on creation of ethnographical phenomena. They are thus of a purely psychological and mental character, being a form of human adaptation as the latter is observed in the human units resulting from the process which I call *ethnos*. Ethnographical phenomena, in complexes and in elements, are functions and as such they cannot be understood in their static abstractions, so that description of an ethnographical complex, and consequently elements, forming the complex, presumes necessity of penetration into the *mechanism* of this function.

Since the ethnographical complexes cover a great number of cultural elements they must be classified in some way, for their description and even for their observation. The classification of the ethnographical elements and complexes into groups of material (or technical) culture, social organization, and "psychomental" complex is strictly technical; as I have already pointed out in my work dealing with the social organization of the Northern Tungus, the phenomena of material culture, social organization and psychomental complex form a certain system, a well balanced complex, in which all elements are more or less "adjusted" and thus they cannot be treated independently one from another. In this aspect of the problem we may consider complexes as *interacting* which expression cannot be taken literally for the cultural elements as such do not *act*, but the populations are acting. These remarks may suffice for showing my point of view, namely, in the treatment of the psychomental complex the grouping of ethnographical

elements into these three headings, is done only in view of the exposition of facts which must be classified in some way.

By the term "psychomental complex" I name here those cultural elements which consist of psychic and mental reactions on milieu. Milieu as a whole and in its elements is a changeable or stable, dynamic or static. For convenience of treatment these elements may be classified into two groups, namely, (1) a complex of reactions of a permanent and definite character, though they vary within a certain range, and (2) a complex of ideas which define certain mental attitudes and which may also be regarded as a theoretical system of the given unit (or even person). The psychomental complex of a unit as it is a function is also responsible for the functioning of the population unit as a whole. The functioning of this assures, or better, merely manifests existence of the unit. In fact, the psychomental complex as a function of adaptation to the *variable* milieus, makes the unit sensitive enough, both by rigid resistence and a flexibility, for production of reactions.

Indeed, the ethnographical facts gathered and presented here are phenomena of a special character. In the case of the material culture there are physical objects to be described, photographed, recorded, and analysed; in the case of the social organization there are relations which may be described as a fixed complex of practices; while in the case of psychic and mental elements, which form the psychomental complex, the description is confined to the attitudes and ideas, and only partly to the description of behaviour, customs and practices, which may be recorded and rarely photographed. So as material they greatly differ from other ethnographical groups. This is one of the additional reasons for treating them separately although I shall always refer to their connexion with the material culture and the social organization. The elements of the psychomental complex, as compared with those forming the complexes of material culture and social organization, are sometimes less stable; and at the same time — when taken separately — they are more numerous and of lesser importance. In

1

fact, the elements which constitute, for instance, the present theory of posthumous life may change, even the entire complex may change and not affect other elements of the ethnographical complex. Also, the acquisition of knowledge held responsible for the change of some elements of the material culture may be easily accepted or rejected and not produce any harmful effect on the whole. The same may be stated with reference to æsthetic manifestations. However, these remarks cannot be spread over the phenomena of a purely psychic order in a narrow sense of the phrase.

Variations and instability of the elements of the psychomental complex are very general, — they are very often borrowed from neighbours, especially when they are not in a crying contradiction to the existing complexes. For instance, European science, which has become almost universal, is one of cases of instability of the psychomental complexes amongst the ethnical units bound by the interethnical pressure of the European ethnical complex. Under the condition of restricted intercourse between the ethnical units and lesser interethnical pressure, the stability of complexes in general, and psychomental complexes in particular, is much higher than in the case of groups living beyond a strong pressure. This may also be shown from the general principle of impulsive variations.

2. DIFFICULTIES OF INVESTIGATION DEPENDING ON THE CHARAC-TER OF MATERIAL   The importance of the studies of the complexes was realized long ago; but we are still far from forming exact ideas as to these complexes among different ethnical groups. There are, it is admitted, excellent descriptions of various aspects of these complexes, e.g. the folklore, "religions", etc. but the attempts at the reproduction of systems of psychomental complexes of non-European groups have not yet been successful. One of the chief causes of this failure was lack of adequate investigations, but cause of no less importance was a methodological fallacy, namely, a postulate of the existence of a difference between the methods of thinking observed amongst the "primitive", "savage", and "barbarian", as opposed to the "civilized man". Certainly, after the failure in constructing these theoretical types according to which the existing psychomental complexes might be classified, the position of the investigators became somewhat better, for they now know that they must, as far as possible, eliminate the influence of their own complex on the inferences made from the facts observed; and especially they must eliminate a conscious and unconscious selection of the facts to be dealt with. Indeed, the psychomental complex is an extremely difficult matter for an observer. First of all, the investigator must forget, if it is possible, his own complex and record the facts without making selection, like a mechanical apparatus, if such a comparison may be allowed, without permitting his own positive and negative reactions on the facts observed, and the facts which may be observed, to interfere with the process of observation and record. Such a requirement may seem to be phantastic, for human beings cannot be abstracted from their ethnical milieu and they cannot be mechanized. When I formulate such a requirement, I mean it as a certain ideal for the investigator and not as condicio sine qua non, — the investigations (observations) have already been carried out, and they will be carried out even by persons who have no idea how they must

approach this kind of work or of what is required from them.

In the process of gathering preliminary information, before reaching the goal of the investigation, the investigator has to go through the difficulty presented by an unknown language. Of course, the study of a language, as a complex of grammatical rules, including phonetics, and the memorizing of the lexical material, does not present great difficulties,—it is only a question of time and memory; but a real difficulty comes with the semantic variations, in a superficial view,—minor shades of meaning of words,—and syntax which make manifest the most delicate elements of the psychomental complex. As a matter of fact, there is, for instance, many a piece of literature which cannot be translated into other languages. The difficulty of this task is well known from the treatises dealing with the Indian, Chinese and Greek philosophy, where the notions like nirrhwanna, dao (道), logos (of Plato) need long explanations requiring space and time, and still remaining difficult, if not incomprehensible to the people who are not familiar with the subject in the language in which these notions were originally treated. The difficulty of comprehension consists, of course, not in the complexity of these notions in their native complex, but in the fact of their belonging to alien, different, complexes. Even in the same language the meaning of words changes with the current of time so much that texts need long commentaries. There are languages, for instance, the Chinese written language, the perfect knowledge of which is almost impossible, if one does not live from childhood amongst the creators of this complex. Yet, in reference to the literary Chinese language, which exists apart from the Chinese spoken languages and has grown, so to speak, above the composite Chinese complexes, at the same time deeply rooted in them, becomes more difficult for understanding and assimilation than, for instance, the complex of European science for the non-European groups, although the complex of European science is chiefly based upon the complex of formal logic. Indeed, in a lesser degree, the same may be said with reference to other non-European languages when they are studied by Europeans. This is well known from the science of general linguistics and philology; but simple and important conclusions do not always reach ethnographers. Again the reason is that the "words" belonging to an alien language belong to an alien complex and when they are translated in the mind they go straight along the existing "channels" of the translator's mind (complex). The same idea may be better expressed in terms which I have proposed in my publication "Ethnological and Linguistical Aspects" (1931). In fact, if we consider the psychomental complex, in so far as the method of thinking and the reactions are concerned, as a system of conditioned reflexes; and language as a complex of "starters" in the sense that the function of language is to "start" corresponding reactions in the hearer (they may be produced by different methods, — the sounding starters, visual starters and others) by the speaker, then it will be obvious that when we "translate" words, they produce a different chain of reflexes, when the psychomental complexes are different. The "meaning" of translated words may thus become wider or narrower than that in the native complex. Moreover, this process is only partly controlled and it proceeds chiefly in the pre- and sub-conscious complexes (strata), where it is often affected by the well known hindrances of the subconscious complexes of a purely psychological even some times physiological character in a narrow sense of the phrase. Therefore we may very often hear an inference from practical experience, namely, — it is impossible to understand people (language) without loving it. The love for the people under the investigation at first may appear as one of the conditions of success, for in the process of understanding an alien complex those who hate (amongst the ethnical units this is a somewhat prevailing attitude towards each other) the object of their studies, they meet with the hindrance which resides in their own complex of a sub-conscious character, such as the fear, disgust, aversion and the like. The farther the complexes are distinct and the farther physical ("racial") differences are, the smaller is the chance of carrying out a successful investigation. However, love may not be recommended as a means of eliminating the psychic hindrance for approaching an alien complex. As such it cannot help the investigator. More than this, the sympathy-complex may affect the result of the investigation even carried out by those investigators who are scientifically absolutely correct and honest. In fact, many investigators who "loved" the object of their investigation (especially in the field of ethnography*) have contributed a large amount of wrong description, which in extreme cases turns into a sentimental naïvety of a European complex**. At the basis of this complex the results of sympathy are that the elements of an alien complex, which are in conflict with the investigator's complex, are rejected or justified by a mind-soothing rationalization. Since the love for one's own complex is typical of the mechanism of maintaining the existence of one's own ethnical unit (or merely group), the complex of sympathy is very likely to affect the investigator when he deals with the groups with which he is bound, either by the similarity of the complex or by the personal connexion or dependence. Therefore, as the result of the observation of investigators, we may say that the nearer the complexes and the nearer the physical (racial) characters, the less is the chance of carrying out a successful investigation. It may also be noted that in the case of the sympathy-complex, the investigator carrying out his work amongst very distinct groups is not in a better condition; for he falls into sentimentality without even being able to record the fact.

These difficulties in the preliminary study of the language spoken by the groups under investigation are not yet all to be overcome in ethnographical work. When the meanings, terms and notions are clear in the complexes they must be translated into the language in which the matter is treated; and in the investigator's mind they must be presented in terms of scientific complex. The choice of ways of translation and that of terminology depends, of course, on the investigator's art and knowledge, also on the degree of advancement of science. The difficulty of translation sometimes is so great that even the best dictionaries

of the European languages, which have in common most of the elements of the European cultural complex, can give only approximate meanings of "words" and have to give reference to a series of synonyms. Yet, such complete dictionaries do not exist, so the foreigners must use the famous Oxford, Webster's, Larousse's, Meyer's and other dictionaries.

With the languages of non-European groups it is still more difficult (for a writer in one of European languages), and is not easier with the languages in which the dictionaries have not yet taken the form of the above indicated "great dictionaries". Is it really possible to give an absolutely exact translation of all terms and "notions", especially those related to the psychomental complex, met with within an alien complex? I do not think so. There may be given only very rough approximations which to some readers will seem to be flat and thoughtless, just as some jokes and witticisms when translated lose all their flavour and even sometimes produce on the people just an opposite effect.

Thus, from the point of view of language, even with a good knowledge of it, the gathering of the material and its treatment is very difficult, but not absolutely impossible, especially with reference to some particular subjects. One of the conditions of success is that the investigator or his reader must not treat the alien complexes from the point of view of his *own ethnographical complex.*

We have just seen that the observation and recording of the facts regarding the psychomental complex of other ethnical groups present great difficulties. However, this is not the opinion of some observers who take for granted that observation is simple and easy. In this case they are misled by the fact that they accept, i. e. understand, as "observation" the process of their own reactions, positive and negative. When one needs to have a real understanding as, for instance, in international relations, the difficulties become evident. As a matter of fact, understanding even between nations of the same, or nearly the same cultural complexes, presents great difficulties for the practical activity of diplomats* on account of the difficulty of understanding an alien complex; but when the difference in cultural complex is great, the difficulty of understanding becomes absolutely impassable. This is the position of many a traveller amongst the "primitive" and "barbarian" ethnical units (and groups) when the traveller looks at the groups investigated from the point of view of superiority and inferiority of the cultural complexes. Yet, in the case when the investigator has no such an idea as to inferiority and superiority and looks at the other complexes simply as distinct from that with which he is familiar, the difficulties are not yet overcome for there remains the problem of choice of facts to be recorded. It is physically im-

---

* The reason why the ethnographers are most affected is simple. —the ethnical units are in the state of struggle (it is not necessary for it to be a bloody and tragic one). Yet, the distant "races" of man are natural competitors. The zoologist is in a much better position than the investigator of human groups for he does not "hate," nor "love", the mollusks and even mammals, except perhaps the domesticated animals and rarely monkeys, when their mentality is investigated. However, the superiority, and competition-complex very often affect the work of the zoologist, too.

** This is the case of some missionaries who live amongst the so called "primitive peoples", also among the Chinese and other very distinct groups,

* It is here understood that the "understanding" and "misunderstanding" are not mere forms of diplomatic ways of acting, but they are actually cases of adjustment, successful and unsuccessful. One of the interesting facts pointing to the sincerity of good diplomats in their relations as representatives of common interests of different nations is the use of languages for talking over the problems. In such a case they choose that language which can be understood by both parties regardless of the fact whether the given language is their native language or not. Here I have in view the cases when diplomats are "honest".

possible to record everything which is seen and heard, so that a choice of facts is inevitable. Therefore, the observer has to pay more attention to some facts and less attention to other facts. Owing to a multitude of conditions he pays attention to a selected group of facts which may enter into the range of his personal complexes, for in every particular case the starting point is the investigator's own complex. With certain experience in observation the investigator may attain a relative independence from his own complex; but it is not in the reach of all observers for it requires long experience, personal will power, and great effort on the part of the observer*. Theoretically we may say that if there is preferential selection of facts recorded, if the ethnographer has his own strong reactions on the facts, and if he has his own complex (or that of the unit to which he belongs) which conditions his inferences, the work may have only one value, namely, the value of a document reflecting the author's complex and not that of ethnical groups discussed. As an ethnographical work, it has no value at all; but as ethnographical material it may be used by other ethnographers who are studying the ethnography of the unit or group of units to which the author belongs. This class of works is the most numerous in the ethnographical literature.

The problem of time and equipment needed for a thorough investigation into the psychomental complex now requires consideration. It is evident that this work cannot be carried out in a few weeks, as it was by great number of investigators in the past. Indeed, the term "time" needs certain corrections. In fact, other conditions influence the amount of the material gathered: namely, preparedness of the investigator from the point of view of his personal power of observation, — an individual character, perhaps inherited complex, — his familiarity with ethnography which, let us add, does not consist only of memorizing various theories and hypotheses, and his ability of establishing good relations with the populations. I do not need to quote cases when investigators stay for long years among a group and remain absolutely ignorant as to the culture of this group and incapable of understanding the most simple attitudes of the people. Perhaps I should not speak about it, for it is evident. Yet lately this problem was discussed in the sense that the investigator must spend a very long time (in terms of years) among the same peo-

ple to be able to know them; while the question of the quality of the observers was put aside as of no importance. As a matter of fact, the idea of carrying out scientific investigations by means of enrolling large numbers of persons was lately quite fashionable and somewhat in accordance with the idea of substituting quantity for quality, — an idea which may have very limited practical application, namely, when no brain is required for the field work. Indeed, there also exists a minimum limit of time, even for the most endowed observers, however even this limit is variable. In fact, the volume of culture of groups is not the same, and when going from one to another group of more or less similar complex one may see much more than when one remains for a very long time at the same spot. The minimum is that which is needed for studying language (this also depends on the investigator's ability) and the gathering of a sufficient amount of facts for giving description of the complex. I think that for the same investigator in some cases a few months may suffice while in some other cases long years would be needed. Thus no definite limit as to the minimum may be formulated, but the investigator himself must decide whether he feels himself to have mastered the psychomental complex or not and he must also feel how much more he can produce. As a matter of fact, sometimes it is hopeless to remain even a minimum of time for the group cannot supply the needed material. For instance, when a group is found in a state of complete ethnical disintegration, the investigation should be directed along quite different lines. This question must be decided at the spot by the investigator himself, for nobody can help him to find a practical solution*.

It is sometimes believed that the first condition of scientific success in ethnographic work is financial funds. The persons who are not familiar with the character of ethnographic work believe that, — the more funds, the better. This opinion is absolutely wrong. The excess of funds used in such work may be quite pernicious to the result of investigation. What is actually needed is a good equipment. The latter depends on the conditions of travelling. For instance, travelling in a steppe region requires a different type of equipment as compared with travelling in the mountains or along the rivers, or as compared with "settled life" in villages. The work may be more successful if the equipment does not become a burden, and an equipment which consists of very expensive and seemingly up to date devices and scientific paraphernalia may become as useless toys if it is not adapted to the *practical needs* of work. So that even in this sense there are limits put by the practical conditions of work: a heavy equipment sometimes may greatly affect the outcome of the work. Yet, money will not gather ethnographic material, as unfortunately is sometimes practised by investigators. Even an abuse of gifts may produce bad effect by attracting a selected group of people unscrupulous enough to use this opportunity. In fact, if the group or the individuals under

---

* In order to facilitate the first steps of the observer there have been made, in different countries, lists of questions to be answered by the observer. Such lists are good, when the observer has an independent mind and when he continues his investigation even after answering all the questions on the list and all questions resulting from the answers received; but for the beginners whose minds may be paralyzed by the limits put by the questioner, such lists of questions have the most disastrous influence as to the amount of facts gathered and conclusions made. Since the observers who have independent minds may do the same work without a list of questions, and since the other observers may lose their ability to increase the power of observation, if they rely upon the list of questions, the latter have a somewhat negative influence on the increase of our knowledge as to alien ethnical groups. Moreover, when one deals with such a delicate matter as the psychomental complex a list of questions is out of discussion. Thus they may be good only for the studies of simple phenomena chiefly considered from the static point of view and especially for the study of their geographical distribution.

* For this reason, the itineraries and time schedules worked out by those who send young investigators, or merely investigators who are not independent, show only one thing, namely, the theoretical unpreparedness of the authors of itineraries and schedules. This is usually closely connected with the complex of limitless selfconfidence and impregnation with various theories intimately associated with general ignorance. It is evident that if the investigator cannot decide for himself his itinerary and schedule, he usually is not able to carry out the investigation. This is the error of his superiors who charge him with a work which is beyond his ability.

investigation are paid or get appreciable benefit from the ethnographer there would be an almost inevitable flow of wrong information invented by the persons inclined for gain.* On the other hand, the making of a scientific investigation into kind of exploit for the investigator may also greatly affect the outcome of his work. In fact, I have met with some naïve investigators who professed that the smallest possible funds must be spent, for scientific work is an heroic action which requires heroic means. Therefore, the investigator must abstain from food, comfortable sleep, even medical assistance, and so on**. Indeed, the conditions of travelling must be adapted to local conditions and the individual tastes of the traveller and the latter must be ready for submitting himself to certain hardships and privations.

Another important condition is that the investigator, at the same time, must not make his investigation into a kind of profession, for as a professional he runs the risks of losing the greatest impulse of work: his love for the investigation. This is one of reasons why a great number of persons owing to their lack of resignation cannot become efficient travellers, and a great number of them are not investigators but professionals living on easy works of travelling. So if there are too many funds for investigation, there is always a great influx of professionals who cannot become scientists at all, but who like an "easy life"***.

These ideas, namely, that the work of investigation may be carried out by any one, provided he is supplied with sufficient funds for equipment, travelling, and "buying" information, are greatly responsible for the impoverishment of investigation carried on according to these principles. In fact, these principles attract a great number of lovers of the easy life and their "work" needs to be covered by great advertising, good pictures, popular lectures which should produce an impression on an ignorant crowd. Indeed, this system will not last a long time and at the end of this period there will remain only doubtful, scanty material, millions of dollars spent, some private fortunes made, while the real

investigators' works will remain as a basis of further scientific investigations*.

After the material is gathered there is another step to be taken, namely, the analysis of the facts and their classification. At this stage ethnographical work is handicapped by still more serious obstacles, — the pre-existing theoretical conceptions to which the facts are adapted. These conceptions cannot be regarded as something different from the existing ethnographical complexes of the ethnical units amongst whom the science of ethnography is cultivated. In fact, variations of ethnographical theories are parallel to those of other branches of knowledge in which the theoretical part dominates that of the facts and scientific laws, as in physics, chemistry, and even natural sciences. On the other hand, the sciences dealing with the phenomena of cultural complexes are closely found with the *prevailing* cultural complexes and thus, as a part of them, they reflect the advancement of scientific knowledge in a lesser degree than the changes in the psychomental complex of the units in general. When the ethnographer comes into conflict with the prevailing ethnographical complex of the unit, he always risks of being misunderstood, and for this reason rejected. Owing to this particular position of ethnographers, and the science of ethnography prevailing theories ought to be chiefly considered as ethnical reactions on the facts observed, just as, for instance, the cosmogonic theories of Middle Ages were reflecting the folklore of local groups and their adaptation to the ethico-philosophical systems. It is thus natural that when the observer approaches the ethnographical facts from the point of view of one of the existing theories, he greatly endangers his success in establishing the scientific meaning of the facts observed**. Naturally the theories like that of evolution, that of Durkheim, that of Freud, and others, in spite of their scientific appearance, may be responsible for a failure. Indeed, the best result may be obtained by application of the methods used by the behaviourists, provided the method is not used for proving pre-existing theories***. So here we have to make dis-

---

* Even the purchase of ethnographic collections may introduce an undesirable spirit of "business" and "profit". Owing to this, most of my collections were bought in the last days of my living among the groups. Yet, if the purchase is very important, then the news about the investigator's buying ability may spread too far and affect further investigations. Therefore the investigator must not turn his work into that of a collector of specimens. Thus although my buying capacity was rather high I always avoided making large purchases of collections.

** During my travelling I once met with such an investigator whose name I do not want to mention, and whose intention was to investigate a certain group living in the mountainous taiga region. Since he had this conception of scientific work he took with him only some lard and dried rye bread as food, no tent, no sleeping accommodations, except his sheepskin overcoat,—very cheap but extremely heavy and uncomfortable for travelling,—only one horse for loading, and a man, a real rascal who was supposed to go on foot. After wandering in the neighbourhood for three or four weeks the investigator had to turn back, without seeing the people whom he wanted to investigate, because both of them, the traveller and guide, were exhausted by improper food and housing ("tenting").

*** I once met with a "prominent" archaeologist who confessed to me that he joined a richly equipped expedition with a good remuneration for the participants, because he wanted to have a rest from his life in a certain big city. There is no wonder that the outcome of his participation in the expedition was of a little scientific value.

* Indeed, this point of view as to the technique of investigation is not dangerous at all for nations which have experience, but this point of view is really dangerous for nations which have not yet reached the stage when they may carry out their investigations. In this case, as in all cases of vulgarization, the European complex appears in its worst modification.

** Here the difficulty of the treatment of ethnographical phenomena comes out which requires not only thorough knowledge of facts, but which also requires thorough knowledge of the existing theories and their analysis from the ethnographical point of view, in the ethnographical complexes in which they have been "created" and to which they have been adapted. As a matter of observation of the history of ethnography, this is a very rare occurrence. Perhaps the best way of shortening the process of self-education of ethnographers is the accumulation of facts and very broad general education in sciences which have already reached the stage of formulating definite scientific "laws", have long history, and have a well developed methodology.

*** In many recent publications on ethnographical subjects one may often see this interesting case of adjustment. The essential of the behaviouristic method consists in the recording of the facts without the presumption that they are selected. However, the authors very often seem to use this method; actually they select facts to suit their pre-existing theories and bring them forth under a behaviouristic cover, so that the reader cannot see how far correctly the method is used.

tinction between methods and theories. This inference from the above discussion is evident, — the path of the ethnographer is hard when he gathers material; it is still harder when he proceeds to the analysis of the facts gathered.

3. THEORIES AFFECTING INVESTIGATOR'S WORK As stated the difference between the ethnographical complexes of the observers and that of ethnical groups observed produces great difficulties in carrying out investigations and in the analysis of alien complexes. This is especially true for beginners. But even the investigators who are advanced in their work are often found in a difficult position owing to the assimilation of ready-made theories. Some of these theories produced an effect on investigators and in many instances were responsible for an arrest in the ethnographical studies.

I shall not now repeat what has been stated in reference to the theory of evolution and its influence on the investigators of languages and all inevitable consequences which may affect results and lead to erroneous hypotheses*. Yet, monistic interpretations of ethnographical phenomena, e.g. economic, geographical, all have already left the place, for a while occupied by them, to other systems; but their revival is still possible and their effect upon the investigators from time to time reappears**.

The theory of animism as proposed by E.B. Tylor, and further developed by A. Lang, and especially by Sir J. G. Frazer was one of theories which had great influence on investigators. However, it was represented in such a manner that instead of bringing facts together it separated

---

* Cf. "Aspects", Chapter III.

** In spite of the fact that these theories are out of use, they do reappear. From the ethnological point of view one of interesting cases is that of "economic interpretation", in its further modification of "class struggle", as it is nowadays revived among the ethnographers dependent upon the communistic party which has taken control of Russia. Speculative in its nature, historically by-product of German scholastics of the beginning of nineteenth century, after an assimilation of early pre-Darwinian theories of "struggle" and "catastrophic" changes, it became a modernized form of a pseudo-scientific justification of the politicians of a new formation who needed it for opposing themselves to their predecessors in "reforming" the European social system. The relapse of this theory among the present ethnographers is due to two causes, namely, a general lowering of cultural complex in Russia (seen, for instance, in the decrease of food and clothing supply, reduction of the number of educated people, simplification of the social organization, etc.) resulting in a lowering of scientific criticism, and in an excessive political pressure of a party which, as elsewhere, cannot be competent to direct science. Indeed, such a theory greatly reduces the scientific outcome of the work; but it is, so to say, an abnormal phenomenon which has occurred within a desintegrated unit (group of units) and it is not characteristic of modern scientific trend. Moreover, it has no chance for survival,—it may now occur only in the conditions of disintegration of present cultural complexes and ethnical units (and groups), in which condition ethnography would become quite a superfluous luxury, as a special branch of knowledge, moreover quite impossible owing to the requirements of a preliminary theoretical training of ethnographers. Together with other cultural elements it will also perish, as well as ethnographers, without producing any effect upon ethnography as a science cultivated in other ethnical complexes. I do not need to pause on geographical monism which is observed among those who, owing to their defective general education, fail to become real geographers (extensive naturalistic knowledge), and ethnographers. (In addition to the general education special training in linguistics, "humanities", etc.),

some into a group of "primitivism" and on the other hand made of the theory a too broad conception. In fact, animism is a universal conception which forms the background of various complexes. These complexes show an enormous range of variation and local interpretation. The fact of recognition of "animus" (spirits) is thus too general. This may be illustrated by any number of instances picked up from different complexes. However, if animism is accepted as a finished system of thinking, as a kind of philosophy, it may overshadow other theories accepted and used by the ethnical units. As a matter of fact, animism may exist by the side of the theories and systems grown on the ground of a critical study of milieu. Yet, the spirits (animus) may have different origins and different properties, — e.g. the "spirits" of different branches of Christianity, those of the Buddhism amongst the Mongols, the spirits of the Australians. These spirits are essentially different; yet all of them are based upon a hypothesis.— the existence of spirits, which man, even perhaps the human ancestor, made in time immemorial.* In spite of this, the theoreticians of the last century by accumulation of facts concerning "animism" among various groups have constructed hypothetical systems of animism which as such were mere by-product of the European complex. Indeed, such systems do not exist beyond the European scientific complex. Apart from the fundamental hypothesis of "animus", no one of actually existing complexes can be put into the framework of theoretical animism. Nevertheless the European ethnographer when meeting new ethnical groups tries, with the help of these theories, to find new proofs for supporting them. The facts are not lacking, so that after a selection he naturally increases the old amount of "proofs". The Tungus, Australians, American natives and others who would like to find new proofs from the study of European complex, for supporting their own "animistic" theories, are in the same position. One of the curious manipulations of this type has recently been made by the theosophic writers who, taking the facts which they needed out of "scientific complex", have found new support for their own animistic system. However, either they do not want or they cannot adopt the scientific complex as a whole which absolutely deprives them of the possibility of penetration into the complex of science. In

---

* From the fact of burial ritual observed in the period of old stone culture we have to infer that the idea of spirit was known to the men of the Neanderthal "race" so that the origin of this idea is lost for ever. The theories regarding the origin of "animism" are naturally confined to the hypothesis based upon reasoning and not upon facts. The man of Neanderthal is not considered, by the anthropologists, as an animal of the same species as Homo Sapiens. We cannot postulate that the hypothesis of spirit did not exist in the complex of still earlier ancestors of present man. The ethnical groups which exist at present time are as modern as European groups, so that without another postulate,—the survival of old ethnographical complexes amongst the "primitive" groups,—it is impossible to believe that the investigation of these groups may give us the key for establishing the origin of this conception of spirit. An understanding of the weight of this element in the psychomental complexes does not require a finding of the "origins" so that the search for the origin of this hypothesis is rather useless for we have no means to establish and restore the complex in which the hypothesis of "animus" has made its first appearance. Without knowing the complex it is impossible to find out how and why it was created and what was its original function and meaning. Since that time the hypothesis of "animus" was transmitted from one to another generation, from one to another ethnical unit, and perhaps from one to another animal species.

the same position are those who begin their investigation into alien psychomental complexes with the help of the theory of animism as it has come out of science of the last century. They naturally remain faithful to their beliefs, again supported by the facts picked up from an alien complex, for they always remain in their own complex. No understanding, no penetrations into the alien complex is possible, just as a theosophist cannot understand the fact that the science-complex may do well without the hypothesis of "high spirits".

Another theory, perhaps yet more dangerous for the investigator, is that of the existence of "primitive mentality," and more generally, mentality which is postulated to be different from that of the investigator and especially of the theoreticians. Mentality can be understood only after a careful study of the whole complex, which has been produced by it, and after an absolute understanding of the mechanism, — the logic, — is reached by the investigator. As in the case of the theory of animism, facts may be picked up from the records of travellers and investigators for supporting a new theory of "primitive mentality" but this theory will remain with and within the European ethnographical complex. In accordance with evolutionistic postulate it has been supposed by L. Bruhl that mankind had passed through the period of pre-logic and from a mosaic work he has produced his hypothetic reconstruction. His position was more difficult than that of his predecessors who did the same kind of work to build up their theory of "animism", for the number of facts which he could use was not so vast as that in the case of "animism". Therefore he had to use some facts from doubtful sources, some facts which were misunderstood, at last some facts which were merely mistaken. Yet, a large number of facts were dismissed from the discussion although these facts could be used for building a theory just opposite to that proposed by L. Bruhl. It is not surprising that the tendency to show an absolutely similar mentality amongst all peoples of the Earth, with all consequences resulting from it, was continuously to gain many followers. Indeed, the new theory may bring, to maintain itself, as many facts, as the opposite theory; for the chief condition of the success lies in the theoretical premises, namely, the recognition of the theory of the evolution of cultural phenomena and this presumes that mankind went through a series of successive stages, so that the ethnographical facts, taken in abstracto, may be used just as those used by the biologist when he traces the evolving series of animals by the comparison of a series of homologous bones of the extinct and the living. Such a scaffolding of hypotheses and theories based on an analogy may be better understood from the comparison of such a reasoning with the reasoning by analogy characteristic of the "primitive mentality," as it is described by the writers on primitive mentality. The reasoning by analogy with the organic and thus physical phenomena is especially dangerous, for in the ethnographical phenomena no analogous nor homologous elements may be distinguished, for the complexes are still very little investigated and we know nothing about various "missing links" which might bind the isolated complexes as sequence series. However, if we are successful (which is very doubtful) in building up such a series it will prove nothing regarding the "evolution" of these phenomena for they are not organic, physical phenomena; but they are a function. It is evident that the ethnographical elements may form any complex, if the internal equilibrium of the complex is preserved and if the complex may serve as a good form of adaptation. However, the importance and meaning of different elements in different complexes may be different, — an element may be borrowed from the complexes which have nothing to do with that which incorporates the elements into its body. Yet, the same element may entirely change its function in a new complex. It is clear that in the case of the discovery of such an erratic element one may fall into an error as to its function, meaning, and origin. It is thus evident that the elements taken out of the complexes can be used only when they are checked up every time as to their present, as well as their former, meaning in the complexes, their rôle, and origin. In other words the complex must be first investigated and its elements carefully defined. When L. Bruhl was constructing his theory he was picking up the facts which might suit his theory. From the methodological point of view there is no great difference between his modus operandi and that of his predecessors. However, the influence of the theory on investigators is still more dangerous than the simplicist theory of animism, because the theory of primitive mentality looks more "scientific" than the old theory of "animism", it operates with the facts better adjusted to the theory, and it is more up to date with reference to the ethnographical shape of modern science. Although the theory proposed by L. Bruhl, according to the conviction of many authors has never been accepted, nor seriously discussed by ethnographers, it cannot be so easily dismissed for it is only one of manifestations of the conceptions originally proposed by E. Durkheim in a series of works at the end of the last century and at the beginning of the present century for whom society (alter ego of culture, etc.) was a supra-organic phenomenon with its own life, history, mechanism, etc. but immaterial in its nature. A whole generation of ethnographers was living on this new modification of the old conception of ethnographical phenomena considered as an entity disconnected with the physical bearers and physical conditions which presumes the existence and "life" of the ethnographical complexes. So that, if the theory of L. Bruhl is rejected it will not mean that the method of treatment will be rejected. As a matter of fact its new modifications may now be seen in the works of historians, ethnographers, and sociologists sometimes artfully presented in new forms*.

A new approach is made by S. Malinowski who under the influence of a new psychological school attacked the problem from another point of view, namely, the "complexal" aspect of the elements, interpreted in terms of their psychological mechanism. First of all, this approach does not help to disclose the origin of ethnographical elements which is put by S. Malinowski as one of important aims of his ethnography and, in so far as these attempts are made, the constructions become mere hypotheses which do not essentially differ from the hypotheses proposed by "animists", "evolutionists" and "primitivists". In fact, to know the psychological mechanism of society does not yet mean that one will know the "origin" of the elements of the psychomental complex. Yet, when the complex is dissected into its elements and these elements are separately analysed the psychological analysis will not help in the understanding of the mechanism regulating the variations of the complexes as a whole. Those ethnographers who will follow this new trend of ideas either will lose them-

* Vide e.g. M. Granet's publications.

selves in theoretical and hypothetical constructions, as has already happened with the creators of psychoanalysis, particularly, S. Freud, who has made attempts at the treatment of enigmatic ethnographical problems such as exogamy, customs of avoidance, etc.; or in the best cases of application of this method, they will present new and old facts in a new wording, little helping to understand the complexes as whole, but greatly emphasizing *certain* aspects—just as light effects in theatrical performances are produced when, with different colours of light, experienced artists make different pictures come out of the same stage.*

I do not mean to say that this psychological method should not be used by ethnographers; but I want to say that its practical application must be reserved to the special aspects of the ethnographical work in which it must be recognized as a good and successful method, — it is only a technical method par excellence and it must not be abused**.

I have dwelt on the "psychological" method for it has already produced its harmful effect on the ethnographers who treated the problem of shamanism among the Tungus. In the chapters dealing with it I shall analyse the attitude of an ethnographer in this case, but now I want only to point out that by applying psychological method, L. Sternberg has come to the idea that shamanism at its basis has a sexual complex. As a defense of this proposition is difficult when one deals with the totality of facts treated in the complexes in the manner of Sir J. G. Frazer, L. Bruhl, and other mosaicists. Indeed, the sexual complex cannot be excluded from the consideration of the psychomental complex in general, however it is not alone responsible for the existence of shamanism and origin of shamanism among various ethnical groups. This trend of ideas is also one of the components of the European complex and in its application to ethnographical investigations it may turn the attention of the investigator from the analysis of the alien complex as a whole and particularly from the analysis of its elements.

The historico-cultural method (also historico-ethnographical, and "Kulturkreise" method) chiefly created by E. Gräbner, W. Schmidt and W. Koppers, being quite useful for the investigation of special problems, particularly historico-ethnico-cultural problems, may also produce an undesirable effect upon the investigator if he wishes to confine his methodology to this method alone. The internal mechanism of complexes and their "functioning" may be easily overshadowed by a formalistic reconstruction of complexes which perhaps never existed. So that in this case as in the case of modern psychological trend the investigator must not forget that there are other aspects of ethnographical complexes.

Attempts have been made at the creation of new systems from the pieces of old theories which have not yet been totally rejected. Such is the case of F. Boas who partly rejected the theory of evolution and who substituted seemingly new hypotheses for its weakest points at the same time preserving the theory of progress and some other attributes of the theory of evolution*. Another case is that of R. H. Lowie who had decidedly rejected the old theory of evolution, but did not go further than a simple enumeration of various forms of "religion" and "social organization", but who preserves the old conception of "primitivism". His own theory is that which may be called a theory of all possibilities. Yet, he goes as far as to recommend that no new material be gathered, for, according to him, no such material is needed any more** in spite of the fact that the analysis and investigation, even simple description of the complexes, have not yet been begun, while the facts previously gathered badly need revision. The theory of R. H. Lowie deserves special attention for it revives the early "rationalistic" school. In fact, he brings forth the idea of "utility" of institutions which defines their existence***. One more instance of theoretical eclecticism may be quoted, namely, that developed in publications by A. Kroeber who tries to bring back ethnography to an organic conception of culture****, but who at the same time and with good reason raises the problem of culture in other animals.

Perhaps the greatest theoretical hindrance to a successful investigation is a series of theories concerning classification of human groups into primitive, civilized, superior, inferior etc. Indeed, there are deep ethnographical reasons for existence of these theories, which reside in the European complex. Still, ethnographical studies take their own course. Investigations among different ethnical groups have already brought so many facts which destroy the idea of "primitiveness", that many investigators have changed their behaviour. Similarity of some ways of thinking and behaving observed among distinct groups has shadowed dissimilarities which had been formerly dismissed from the consideration. As a matter of fact, the method used for proving this proposition is the same as that for disproving the opposite proposition, — a picking up of facts for a mosaic picture, and a regrouping of facts*****. Of course, both theories are accepted by

---

* Cf. F. Boas "The Mind of Primitive Man", 1918, also his article "Anthropology" in "Encyclopaedia of Social Science", 1930. Indeed, F. Boas' "critical method" is a technical method of preparing material for analysis, which has made him still more sterile in so far as the orientation in the ethnographical phenomena is concerned.

** Cf. R. H. Lowie "Primitive Society", also "Primitive Religion".

*** Rationalization of ethnographical phenomena is characteristic not only of the investigators, but also of the units when they are undergoing a process of variation at a rapid tempo. In fact, when the process is going on very fast the unit has no time for perceiving the elements of the complex as stable ones, given by the high spirits, or established by the semi-deified ancestors. Then the unit is inclined to explain all phenomena as product of a rational calculus. This is the case of some modern ethnical groups which undergo the process of change at a rapid tempo. The rationalization of the ethnographical phenomena amongst the ethnical groups observed by the investigators is also very common. One of forms of rationalization is the utilitarian interpretation of these phenomena. This attitude is also closely connected with the prevailing ethnographical complex characteristic of a unit to which the investigator belongs. Indeed, such a unit may be one of the groups which forms the ethnical unit (vide infra, Section 5). I will not stop longer on this theory for its methodological defectiveness is evident.

**** Cf. A. Kroeber, "Historical Reconstruction of Culture Growth and Organic Evolution", in American Anthropologist, Vol. 33, No. 2, pp. 149-156, 1931.

***** Cf. for instance, O. Leroy, "La Raison primitive. Essai de refutation de la théorie du prélogisme", Paris, 1927.

---

* e.g. vide recent publication by A. I. Richards, "Hunger and Work in a Savage Tribe. A functional study of nutrition among the Southern Bantu", London, 1932.

** It is clear that my use of the term "functional" is much wider than that adopted by S. Malinowski and his followers. I must emphasize it because the same "sounding" starter—function, functional, etc,—may be used as starters of different chains of conditioned reflexes, to have different "meaning". A full "meaning" of my use of these terms will be clear after the reading of this work.

different groups of readers, including the investigators, according to their own complexes, as was the case with the followers of different theories regarding the "animism".

The evident deficiency of the theories which recognize superiority and inferiority of ethnical groups´and "civilizations" has brought new conceptions of distinction. In fact, the old schemes of relative position of the ethnical groups in the scale of "progress", "development" and "evolution", which unfailingly were crowned by the ethnical group to which the authors belonged, were compromized, but since this complex always survived it was given a new, and seemingly scientific appearance. The difference between the ethnographical complexes was expressed not in the form of the denial and refutation of the culture of other groups, but in their quantitative aspect in which the old presumption remained untouched, — the greater the quantity, the better. Yet, there has also been given dynamic conception of difference in culture. J. Deniker in the second edition of his work "Les races et les peuples de la terre" (1926) reproduces his naïve classification of groups according to the tempo of change, namely, — the groups·à progrès exclusivement lent, the groups à progrès appréciable, mais lent, the groups à progrès rapide. According to this scheme, the Chinese, together with the Malays, Mongols and ancient Egyptians, belong to the middle groups of semi-civilized. His classification was a pure and simple hypothesis for nobody had measured the tempo of variations among different groups discussed, and the tempo itself without consideration of the population and interethnical pressure means very little. Naturally, the Western Europeans occupied the first place in this classification. According to this classification, ethnical groups (peuples et nations) were put about in the same order of the hierarchy as they were in the old classification of Morgan and Vierkandt, also other authors who based themselves on the lack of some cultural elements which defined in their mind the relative place of the groups. Indeed, a desire of being "first" (an interesting psychological complex!) is the condition which leads to the idea of such a classification. So it is not a scientific classification, but it is a *reaction rationalized in pseudo-scientific forms*. It may be supposed that a careful study of other complexes will probably result in finding similar attitudes among other groups beyond Europe, e.g. in India and China.

In spite of all good will to build up a new method, the old European complex with its element of the consciousness of immeasurable superiority shows its face. In such special studies as that, for instance, of F. H. Hankins[*]

also in R. H. Lowie's works the idea of "primitive" and "civilized" peoples occupies the place of importance.

The question of superiority and inferiority closely connected with the ideas of progress etc. supposes a movement from inferiority to superiority, from simple to complex, from barbarism to the civilization, as it is commonly understood from "bad" to "good". This conception is still narrower than the idea of "evolution" and it is always supposed that the early stage is worse than the later one in the minds of "optimistic" people, and vice versa in the minds of "pessimistic" people[*]. This complex is very deeply rooted in the European and other complexes. It probably has its roots in the "subconscious strata," — the growth of the child, the "instinct" of accumulation (food, etc.). Let us take some instances. If the stature of the given ethnical unit or of a group of units is changing positively (the increase of stature very commonly observed) this gives great satisfaction to the unit; if it changes negatively it produces a kind of fear of "degeneration". However, we do not know what is better for the self-preservation of the unit. Biologically every change points to some process which the unit is undergoing; so that at this moment the unit is in the state of relative instability and we cannot say which end will ensue in the process. As a matter of fact, the positive and negative changes may result both in the survival and decline of the unit for the question is: in which condition is the unit better adapted for survival or decline? The same may be referred to any other change, both static, physical (morphological) and functional (cultural and physiological). The only objective way of judgment is whether the process results in the preservation or decline of the unit, and from this point of view it may be "good" or "bad" for the unit and individual who undergo the process[**]. If it is possible to prove that the over-growth of stature gives certain preference in the struggle for existence then it is "good", but from the instance of the giant elephants and giant ·deer of quaternary period it may be seen that the size may result in difficulty of adaptation. On the other hand a decrease of the size may be "good" especially under changing conditions of the struggle for existence, but we also

---

[*] Cf. F. H. Hankins, "The Racial Basis of Civilisation". This work is interesting for it reflects the ideas of a certain group in America which has not yet completed the process of ethnical formation and where the ethnical elements which form this new unit greatly feel the difference of their complexes. However, the title of this work, as well as its contents, show that neither "racial" nor "prejudice" are clear to F. H. Hankins, and these elements he takes in good faith as elements against which he is called to fight. This work is not isolated. Lately there have·been published many pamphlets, articles and even books ·the authors of which manipulate these ideas pro and contra, under the cover of science, but actually with a practical aim of strengthening the position of the units to which they belong or believe themselves to belong, or with a practical aim of weakening the position of their actual or imaginary enemies (ethnical, and even merely professional). All these publications may give good material for an ethnologist who would devote his time to the study of ethnical reactions, both aggressive and self-defensive. I hope to come back to this problem in my future publications.

[*] The change of attitude chiefly depends on the general trend of behaviour of the ethnical unit. In fact, if the unit is in the state of growth and may hold its position among other ethnical units an "optimistic" behaviour is very likely to appear, while the units which lose their internal equilibrium (particularly after the flexion of the curve of cyclic growth of population) are inclined to show "pessimistic" behaviour, which in certain conditions of interethnical pressure may lead to a complete loss of vital resistance and collapse (internal). Indeed, since the masses of population are built up of individuals, the individuals are affected by the change of behavior which is also correlated with the individual reactions and general conditions (of individuals). Therefore a purely psychological and psychopathological approach to this problem cannot help in the analysis of the origin of the change of the ethnical attitude.

[**] The "pessimistic" point of view: the first step of the child is that to death, which is quite true, for life is limited. This is "pessimism" of a man on his decline. It is different with the young people who never think about death, the idea of which does not yet come to their minds if they are "normal." The same is true with reference to the mass psychology observed in the ethnical units which, if they are biologically strong, believe in their eternal existence and this psychic attitude assures the necessary tension of their reactions. As a matter of fact, the observation of the psychic behaviour and the tempo of variations, under a known interethnical pressure and at the known moment of the population cycle, may suffice for giving hints as to the near future of the unit.

know the case of the quaternary elephants the reduction of the size of which was associated with their extinction in Malta. Who can say whether a change really assures existence of the unit, if the latter complicates its culture and refines its psychomental complex, or leads the unit to its decline and extinction? If such a definition of the process as "good" may be used in reference to the units which have their own history, which begin from small size, grow, overgrow, and usually sooner or later die, then it cannot be used in reference to "mankind" as the present species of man. Gradual extinction of some ethnical units leaves the place for other units which may grow better (faster) and in this way they may assure the existence of the human species as opposed to other animal species. One may continue this reasoning further and the result will be the same: a relativity of the meaning of the change of physical and cultural adaptation. So the complex of "progress", "development" etc. cannot be justified as terms of an exact language in reference to the ethnographical phenomena. Their introduction into our scientific terminology may also hinder the analysis of the ethnographical (and ethnological) phenomena.

One of the particular cases of theories dangerous for the investigators is the complex of superiority in the form of belief in the "mysticism" of the non-scientific mentality. The theory of spirits in some complexes is quite a satisfactory working hypothesis for solving certain problems. However, as such it does maintain the equilibrium of the psychomental complex and thus the unit may peacefully continue its existence. Science will change later, so its present state will be as much "mystic" as the theory of spirits seems to be to the "anti-mystic" scientists of our days. Since the terms "mystic", "mysticism" etc. are introduced into the terminology of an ethnographer it is almost certain that this ethnographer will not be able to penetrate into the essential elements of the "primitive" complex. This label enables him to hide from himself and from the readers his own lack of understanding of an alien complex. Therefore, it is very common that such a naïve investigator puts in this box everything which is beyond his understanding. In fact, even in recent years, the phenomena of self-suggestion, mass hypnosis, even mental and psychic maladies were classified under this heading. It is not the label which is dangerous but the power of observation on the part of the investigator which is inevitable since a simplicist solution of difficult problems is found. It is not surprising that in the writings of poor observers and thinkers the "accusation" of mysticism of "primitive" and "religious" people, also their own colleagues is common.

The history of the theories of totemism, of late years occupying attention of all ethnographers, shows quite clearly* how this phenomenon might be modelled in the midst of the European groups with their ethnographical complexes. After a series of attempts at the solution of this relatively simple problem the theoreticians have come to the conclusion of giving up the idea of creating a general theory. Indeed, it is quite natural for totemism (in a narrow sense, as a theory of other ethnical groups) can be

* Cf. A. van Gennep "Le totemisme".

understood in every case when taken separately, within the complex only. It may be compared with the theory of animism and it may be treated as one of theories resulting from the wide-spread theory of *animus*. Under the influence of current fashions, many investigators have tried to disclose totemism everywhere where hints to animals and plants were found. The zeal of ethnographers brought them to the unintentional distortion of facts actually recorded, in order to suit them to the theories. Yet, in its greatest development it has reached the summit of imagination when treated by E. Durkheim and his followers as a social system in the scale of "human evolution". Indeed, totemism as W. H. Rivers suggested might migrate very easily as such and in the complexes and thus might now be found in many a place where it could be accepted as an element which created a better equilibrium with the other elements of the psychomental complex.

In order to conclude this short enumeration of difficulties created by the recent increase of scientific theories which may greatly handicap the investigators I want to point out that these difficulties at present can be better realized, if we remember that the process of thinking, according to some psychologists, is going along the channels of previous practice, and according to the physiologists either as a chain of conditioned reflexes, or as physically existing connexions of the brain tissues. Since the process (proceeding in the "channels" and through the system of association, proceeding as a system of reflexes or in the "engrams") is fixed in everyday thinking, still more supported by the complex of European ethnographical milieu, the young investigator will always go along these "channels" for combining the newly acquired facts concerning other ethnical groups (alien complexes), if his own critical spirit (method) is not strong and is inclined to the stabilization and petrification of theories received from the milieu. Such a conservatism, as I have already shown on different occasions, is one of the conditions of the transmission of existing ethnographical complexes (including "culture," "civilization", "Science"), so its existence is conditioned not only by the individual character of persons, but also by the mechanism of the continuity of the secondary milieu in general. Under the existing conditions it is quite natural that the exceptionally brilliant young pupils endowed of talents and appreciated by their teachers often fail in their own investigations. The cases when the teachers of genius also leave no pupils are well known in all branches of knowledge. In such cases the pupils may be too oppressed by the grandeur of their teachers. The same is true of the musicians—performers who very often show their geniality in childhood after passing through the "good school" of the best teachers later become mediocrities. More than that, many scientific discoveries have been made by persons who had not been originally specialized in the field of their discoveries. All these cases are of a purely psychological order. It ought to be added that the liberation from the mechanical movement along the channels or system of conditioned reflexes acquired during long life in the midst of the given ethnical unit and supported by the complexes of an unconscious order (Freudian) is extremely difficult for the beginners when they begin their observation of alien complexes and almost impossible for the persons of a certain age and previous training along the special lines.

CHAPTER II

METHODS OF APPROACH TO AN ALIEN COMPLEX

4. OBJECTIVE METHODS. I have devoted almost all of Chapter I to the problem of difficulties met with by the investigator and this also permitted me to indicate by the way the negative sides of the methods discussed, and what I admit as recommendable conditions, namely, (1) as far as possible to avoid approaching an alien complex from the point of view of the ethnical unit to which the investigator belongs; (2) to have sufficient general theoretical preparation; (3) to have sufficient time for observation and technical facilities, including language; (4) to be free of the influence of theories which do not result from the investigation and which bear the original fallacy of being based upon unchecked hypotheses and postulates; (5) to record if possible all facts; (6) to be an ethnographer*. Although these conditions may at first appear obvious it is not so in fact, in support of which there may be brought forth a great number of facts from the history of ethnography. However, the ethnographer is not in a hopeless position for he finds great help for carrying out his difficult task in the perfection of methods of invesigation. Here I have in view chiefly those methods which as far as possible eliminate the investigator's personal feelings and opinions. They are technical methods and theoretical approaches to the functional phenomena in ethnical units which help in gathering the facts and analysing them. These methods we may call "objective" ones**.

Naturally in the present chapter I cannot give a complete treatement of ethnographical methodology, so I shall now confine myself to giving a general idea of what I understand as "objective methods".

To this class of technical methods I will refer the study of associations, reactions, errors in using words and names, also the analysis and record of dreams and other methods well known from the experience of modern psychology. The simpliest methods used for the study of psychology and mentality of the apes can also be used*. Very good material may be obtained from folklore, as well as every day simple expressions and conversations, and particularly the order in which they occur. The real difficulties met with here are interpretations on the part of the investigator. Yet, the grammar and selection of the vocabulary are direct documents for a correct approach to the psychomental complex**. The semantic study of the language, change of meaning in time, and adaptation of the alien elements is an inexhaustible source of evidence. The same is true in reference to logical constructions.

The physical objects on which one may see the psychomental activity, as for instance various implements, instruments and devices, methods of breeding of domesticated animals and man, the objects used in the medical and shamanistic performances are also good documents when properly interpreted. The same may be said with reference to the actions of individuals and groups of individuals in their social manifestations when they may be described in terms of behaviour. No doubt, the chief source for a description of the psychomental complex and

---

* Mentioning of "ethnographer" may produce a surprise, so that I shall at once explain what I understand as "ethnographer." It is a complex. Not every one who is interested in cultural adaptation of ethnical units is an ethnographer and not every one may become an observer-ethnographer. Besides physical and physiopsychological and mental fitness for this work, as for instance, high power of special and general perception, also high power of self-analysis and self-control, the ethnographer must have special inclination-interest and ability of general and special observation. Yet the ethnographer must have a necessary knowledge of ethnographic phenomena as they are observed in different ethnical units and groups. Indeed, this knowledge may be learnt, but there will remain still more which cannot be learnt and which must be inborn in the ethnographer. However, among layman it is believed that every one may become an ethnographer after reading ethnographical works, although even for driving public cars one needs special examination of fitness. It is not surprising that there are so few ethnographers.

** Indeed, my use of the ambiguous term "objective" may raise a needless discussion as to the existence of "objectivity" in general. Therefore I deem it useful to point out that such a "philosophical" discussion nowadays would be quite superfluous for no abstraction of the thinking process is possible, the process being physically bound with the cognizing individual and all his cognition is a mere reaction on the milieu. More than this, the individual is not only bound by his physiopsychological complex but also by the populationes in which he has been born, has been living, and mentally growing. He cannot be abstracted from his milieus, as his thinking process cannot be abstracted from his physiopsychological complex. When I oppose "objective" to "subjective" I have in view only a relative elimination of rude feelings and now quite evident theoretical aberrations which are still prevailing in the young sciences.

* Cf. investigations into the mentality and psychology carried out e.g. by R. M. Yerkes, W. Koehler and N. Kohts, on gorilla and chimpanzee.

** This method has already been used for a long time. However, it ought to be pointed out that in inexperienced hands and with the presumptions of theories discussed above, this material may become absolutely misleading. In fact, so many sweeping conclusions have already been made regarding the mentality and psychology of alien groups that this method has become somewhat compromised. For instance, some European writers supposed and believed that the only languages, good for correct and exact expressions of ideas, are the European languages, and mainly the language in which the authors were writing. The lack of knowledge of languages might be an excuse for such an opinion, but at the present time when the study of non-European languages is rather advanced such opinions (they are still met with from time to time in the publications of prominent writers) ought to be regarded as a sign of real ignorance and thus used not as scientific opinion, but as material for European ethnogarphy. This opinion received very heavy blows when the European scientific works were successfuly translated into the so-called Ural-Altaic languages and the sciences professed in the university (Finland, Hungary, Turkey). The last blow to the old conception was that when the Japanese and even Chinese languages, at least partly, overcame this difficulty. All languages with some additions and borrowing of technical terms, may be adapted for the needs of European science, which is also true of the European dialects. It may be also remembered that among the early linguists it was believed that the "primitive" languages possessed no morphological system (inferiority as opposed to the European superiority). Under the pressure of facts this opinion changed into an opposite opinion,—the "progress" of language consists in the loss of morphology which was again a new variety of the old complexes. However, under the pressure of new facts the opinion of linguists changed once more,—the change from simple to a complex morphology, and vice versa are met with, so the modern linguists begin to investigate the complexes and recognize that all forms are possible. Still, these old conceptions under new and slightly different forms from time to time appear even in the writing of the linguists.

its understanding are the opinions of the individuals and groups investigated when they are textually recorded, and not the interpretations of these opinions.*

Another important source of objective data concerning psychomental complex, ought to be mentioned, namely, nervous, psychic and mental disturbances. The study into the behaviour of the persons affected by these disturbances, also the attitude towards them of the persons who are not affected sometimes may give a right key for the understanding of the "normal" psychomental complex**.

I will not now speak of the instrumental methods of investigation for under the conditions of field-work, especially for ethnographers, these are out of the question. Yet, the investigation into the physiological conditions of the units, which theoretically must have a definite influence on the ethnical psychomental complex, may be quite convincing as an objective method, but since this investigation requires special laboratory conditions it is also out of the question. However, some observations of this kind are possible and they may be used for the purpose of an analytical description of the psychomental complex.

I have here enumerated some of the objective methods of investigation which have been used for gathering and describing the psychomental complex as it had been observed amongst the groups here treated. However, the question as to how far these methods may be used and practically applied depends on the investigator and the mode of life of the groups investigated. In fact, the Northern Tungus who live chiefly on hunting have no settlements. They gather in large numbers very rarely, only on the great occasions of weddings and annual markets, and rarely in small groups for shamanizing. Furthermore, since the number of population in these groups is not large the mass material generally is very limited. For an exhaustive investigation of a group it would take several months before one could start a special investigation into the psychomental complex. Yet, when a group is investigated this cannot suffice, for the investigator must have some comparative material without which the conclusions and even the description cannot be carried out. This involves the investigator in other similar inquiries which again take a long time. Practically one needs several years of assiduous investigation before being able to make an approximate idea of the complex. However, such a diligent work leaves little time for analysing the material and preparing it for publication. In fact, we have many instances of investigators who become so specialized in one of the directions of these investigations that they lose their ability of having a general

outlook on the phenomena. Yet, some other investigators are so overloaded by the material gathered that they become unable to analyse and publish it*. However, it is not enough to collect and analyse, even with the help of the best methods, the material concerning psychomental complex for these phenomena cannot at times be fully understood from the point of view of their internal mechanism, their causes of changes being beyond this complex. The psychomental complex becomes much clearer when it is investigated in connexion with the concrete ethnical units in which it is found and in connexion with other ethnographical phenomena. It is common that the causes of changes in the psychomental complex have only secondary origin. Therefore, in this setting of the problem one must approach the psychomental complex in its functioning within the ethnical units and thus we must stop on the problem of ethnical unit in general as formulated by me in the theory of ethnos. As a matter of fact, I might now confine myself to a reference to my previous publications dealing with the theory of ethnos, but I consider it desirable to make an addition in the present work for some of publications to which I might refer may not be available, while others are not sufficient for an introduction to the psychomental complex.

5. AN OUTLINE OF THEORY OF ETHNOS. There are many units with which the scientists are dealing according to their specialization, e.g. (1) ethnical groups by ethnographers; (2) populations by biologists; (3) nations by historians, and students of political science; (4) regional groups by geographers; (5) social groups by sociologists; (6) religious and generally cultural groups by psychologists, historians of culture, and especially "philosophers" of the old sociological and ethnographical schools. These groups do exist as *realities* covering a certain mass of population which are the actual subjects of these investigations.

The study of a great number of ethnical units leads us to the conclusion that the units are very numerous, their size is variable, they are conscious of their existence, they possess means for mutual understanding, they are culturally more or less homogeneous, and they intermarry within themselves, i.e. they are endogamous. These are units in which the process of cultural adaptation takes place, where it is transmitted, and in which hereditary conditions are transmitted and modified, i.e. in which the process of biological adaptation, in the broadest sense of the phrase, is carried on. However, there are also very numerous

---

* Description and interpretation of shamanistic and other "religious" and "magic" implements meet with great hindrances when the investigator is imbued with the European (or other) ethnographical complex. These objects are very often regarded as "fetishes", "idols" etc. while in reality they may be simple symbols and "placings for spirits". Description of the shaman's costume is, for instance, a very important item, but one very often forgets that the same elements may have entirely different meaning in different complexes or even have no "meaning" at all, being preserved as simple marks of distinction. The use of these objects becomes reliable only on condition that they are correctly defined in the given complex.

** The question is how to make a definition of the limits of "normal" and "abnormal" which sometimes present some difficulties. Since in the hospital conditions the specialists very often find themselves in a difficulty to label the intermediary cases, in the conditions of field-work it is sometimes altogether impossible. Yet, there are some disturbances so frequent in the ethnical units and even territorial units, that they cannot be regarded as "abnormal" in the given groups.

* It is very common that the persons who are not familiar with field-work make their suggestions to the field-workers, even propose their programs of investigation, sometimes attracting attention of the investigators to the questions which are difficult only for the people who confine their work to the study of the existing literature. Yet, the influence of these people is sometimes more dangerous for the investigator than the theoretical aberrations discussed in the previous section. Practically the investigator must adapt himself to the complexes under the investigation. Indeed, if he is unable to do this, it may be supposed that even with good programs he will produce no useful work and will burden the existing publications with a new failure. In the eyes of critics and persons patronizing such an investigator his publications very often become more valuable than the original investigations which bring up new material and a new treatment. But since this question is one of the questions connected with science as an ethnographical phenomenon of the European complex, I shall come back to it in my other publications.

cases which cannot be called "ethnical units" for the above conditions of adaptation are lacking: they are not sometimes homogeneous, they do not preserve a perfect endogamy and they possess no consciousness of their existence. Therefore, the ethnographer sometimes begins to operate with the regional groups, cultural groups, social groups and even mere abstractions when e.g. cultural groups are abstracted from the populations. It is thus evident that the ethnical units in the definition given above are not stable units, and yet sometimes they cannot be perceived. We can take, for instance, discussions regarding Gypsies, Jews, Manchus, Irish, and other cases. Yet, difficulties met with by the ethnographers, when they try to make up ethnographical maps, may be remembered here.

Still looser are *populationes*, studied by the biologists, when they are not differentiated into, for instance, ethnical units and regional groups. The populations have become units of biologists after the failure to prove the hypothesis as to the existence of sharply differentiated races. Owing to this the biologist is looking for a new unit. Sometimes he may happen to deal with the ethnical units, other times with the nations, rarely with the social, cultural and even religious groups. Generally, the tendency is that he is looking for a concrete group in which there are found similar physical conditions and in which transmission of hereditary conditions takes place.

When historians and students of political science are dealing with the nations they meet with the bold fact: these units may have very short existence, without passing over a period of a few years. Yet, up to the present time to my knowledge, nobody could give a clear definition of what "nation" actually is. The historians turn themselves to the ethnical units which again very often escape them as seizable realities. However, there are "nations" which last for a very long time although their composition by the process of biological substitution may change altogether. So a "nation" may become a simple abstraction in so far as the aim of investigation is to deal with the populations, concrete groups.

Sometimes regional groups can be easily separated, but since in a great number of cases these groups are all the time shifting, and there is influx of new elements and loss of old elements, the region may become the same as a passenger train which crosses a great country in which the population of the train is always changing. Indeed, there are permanent conditions influencing selection in coaches of distinct classes or trains of different speeds according to the ticket price per mile, and direction of the train, while the movement across varied regions is also responsible for the character of the selected population of the train at different moments. So one may very soon be misled by these permanent conditions. Such investigation will not actually deal with the concrete units in which the processes are going on, but it will deal with the selective conditions as they are manifested in the ever changing populations. By this remark I do not want to say that the occurrence of stable populations in regions is out of question; I only want to point out that the geographer very often and sometimes first ought to study conditions of populations, and thus the regional unit as such cannot always be used as a unit of investigation. Indeed, there are regional groups which for long generations stay at the spot, and these may be studied both ecologically and in their adaptive manifestations as concrete units.

Social groups formed on the basis of economic activity and functional division of work in general are realities, but a sharp differentiation of social groups exists only in theory. The social groups actually are all the time shifting and there usually remains a large percentage of the population which cannot be classified at all. Therefore, if so far as the study of populations in social groups is the sociologist's aim he cannot seize it as a permanently existing unit. So the study of social groups leads us to the same study of selective factors. We are sometimes misled by the groups which have differentiated themselves to such a degree that they have become endogamous and homogeneous units, e.g. casts, "privileged" groups etc. which as I shall later show are merely new ethnical units the existence of which was stimulated by a social differentiation.

Religious groups are also realities, but in some cases they are still less stable than the social groups. In their psychomental aspect they are observed by the psychologists and historians of culture as realities as long as they are formed of the same populations, but when the religious groups are abstracted the investigation turns into an operation with a series of hypotheses the principal of which is that the psychomental condition may be identified with a population. The intra-ethnical political grouping in principle sometimes does not differ from the religious grouping, but their potentiality in covering a shifting population is so well known that we do not need to dwell on them. Still there may occur a perfect coincidence of population with religious grouping practising endogamy and naturally becoming a culturally homogeneous unit.

At last I want to mention cultural groups or groups which possess similar complexes of secondary adaptation. They may be realities as regional, social, and religious groups are, in so far as they cover the same population which is not differentiated by other characters, but when the cultural similarity is taken for that of populations, the philosopher permits himself to be carried on by a series of hypotheses which, may be quite ingenious and attractive, but they are imaginary in their nature. Still, when the "philosopher" wants to remain near to the realities he comes to the populations, bearers of cultural complexes, or to the ethnical units, nations, regional groups, and even social groups. Still here there may be cases when common cultural complexes would coincide with the differentiated populations.

From the review given above of units dealt with by the specialists we may see two facts, namely,—first, these groups are created when the problem of unit is discussed from a static point of view, i.e. when the investigator believes that these are units which exist by themselves, as individuals exist, and when he postulates their continuity; second, they are different in their character for the investigators consciously or unconsciously approach them from a certain point of view, namely, that which is supposed to be their speciality. However, the deeper the investigator goes, the looser becomes the unit, fixed in static terms, and the more he has recourse to the aspects of units uncovered by his speciality*.

---

* I shall not now go into the details of the problem as to how it happened that a static point of view was assumed and an artificial narrowing of the angle, under which various aspects of the units were considered, was created but I want to point out that they were conditioned by the trend of the science of the last century which attempted simplifications, classifications, and generalizations without be-

Evidently the unit must be given a different character if it is intended to be used as a scientific tool.

All the above indicated units result from a similar process, in so far as we can see from its final manifestations: more or less similar cultural complexes, speaking the same language, believing into a common origin, possessing group consciousness, and practising endogamy. This is a definition which corresponds to our definition of *ethnical unit*. However, not all of them are "ethnical units." In fact, we have seen that such a crystallization may occur in any group: groups implied by the environment, economic activity, psychomental complex, and especially peculiar conditions of interethnical milieu about which I shall speak later. Yet, such a crystallized state is not always observed and in some groups it rarely occurs, as for instance, in groups based upon religious and economic differentiation. This is a *PROCESS which only may result in the formation of ethnical units, and this process I have called ETHNOS.*

This process may be recognized in its different aspects, namely,

1. Ethnographical aspect,—as seen in similarity of cultural adaptation (secondary milieu), discovered by the ethnographers.
2. Psychomental aspect,—as seen e.g. in the similarity of language, disclosed by the linguists, and ethnographers.
3. Continuity aspect,—in so far as it is reflected in the existing conviction and tradition discovered by the historians.
4. Psychological aspect,—as seen in the fact of self-cognition as unit.
5. Biological (in a narrow sense) aspect,—as seen in the fact of confinement of the process of transmission of hereditary conditions and further physical changes discovered by the biologists.

I do not need to enumerate other signs of the process, but I want to point out that since we treat the unit from the dynamic point of view the process may be understood with certainty only being observed in time, i.e. whether at two moments there is the same situation or not. If different aspects of units are preserved during this period we may assert that they do exist as characters which are at least correlated with the process of crystallization of units and their opposition to other units. If there is noticed intensification of characters studied we may suspect that there is a process of further crystallization and thus this process may be characterized by its centripetal movement in the population affected by it, resulting in a gradual consolidation of the units. However, such a process may be also established by a combined analysis of social, psychological, economic, ecological, biological and other conditions of the units. If there is disclosed a parallelism of differentiation in several aspects there may be suspected a deep centripetal movement which may result in a complete differentiation of groups into new ethnical units. The difficulty of diagnosis here consists in the fact that the causa prima may lay far from these conditions and their similarity may be due to a single but very "powerful" condition e.g. specific ecological

ing supplied with a sufficient amount of facts and which relied upon philosophical premises more than might be admitted. As a matter of fact, there is nothing new in this situation. It has happened before, and, it may be supposed, will again happen with the phenomena imperfectly investigated.

condition, special biological condition, or even their similarity may be due to the effect of interethnical pressure.

In observing these processes in a great number of instances, and in their various aspects, we soon come to the discovery of a general fact, namely, that the similarity of elements of adaptation, conditions of environment, and biological adaptation are not always correlated and even one of them may result in a strong centripetal movement, however, without producing a final effect of ethnical differentiation. Yet, they may have a quite opposite effect upon the existing group formed on the basis of centripetal movement. In fact, let us suppose a group with very strong internal centripetal movement conditioned by the similarity of language and established as a fact by historic and analytical methods. Within this group there may appear centripetal movement, as an effect of further cultural adaptation, in its turn conditioned by the discovery of local ways of adaptation, among smaller groups differentiated on the basis of difference of primary milieu. In reference to the former group the new groups will act as a desintegrating factor. So these forms of cultural adaptation ("progress") will result in an opposite, centrifugal movement.

If we take any form of differentiation, be it individual, family, clan, professional, economic, or any other form of adaptive differentiation implied by the need of new forms of general adaptation, they would appear within the groups, where they exist, as elements of centripetal movement, and thus in reference to the larger units they would act as centrifugal force. The change of adaptation is a permanent condition of all living organisms and groups, for the environment does not remain invariable. There are seasonal variations, solar periodicity, and still longer periods of fluctuations, and perhaps gradual changes which require continuous re-adaptation. The living organisms by their morphological and functional adaptations (including cultural) create special conditions of centrifugal movements.

If we have a very strong centripetal movement annihilating centrifugal movement, there will be loss of power of local adaptation to the changing conditions of environment and thus a loss of vitality especially under the conditions of interethnical equilibria; on the other hand if the centrifugal movement is too strong there will be no more cohesion between the newly formed units and thus the larger one will also lose its vitality[*].

If we now return to our definition of the unit we may express it as a dynamic effect of equilibrium which exists between the centripetal and centrifugal movements within the units. The unit may safely exist only on one condition, namely, equality of tension of these movements which may be symbolized as

$$\sum_{1}^{n} a = \sum_{1}^{n} b \, . \quad \text{But if} \quad \sum_{1}^{n} a > \sum_{1}^{n} b$$

there will be loss of adaptive elasticity (e.g. physical and cultural), if

$$\sum_{1}^{n} a < \sum_{1}^{n} b$$

[*] Vide some more details as to centripetal and centrifugal movement in "Aspects", sections 5 (pp. 19-26) and 15 (pp. 56-60).

there will be loss of total resistance (e.g. lack of resistance to the interethnical pressure and even biological "degeneration").

The origin of these movements may be different too. Ecological conditions and interethnical milieu are permanent,—but variable conditions,—which are not residing in the units, but most of the centripetal and centrifugal movements within the units are conditioned by the elements created within the units, and new elements are always created. This is, by the way, the reason why the classification of forms of centripetal and centrifugal movements may have only very relative theoretical interest*.

Let us now take another step and approach the process here called ethnos from another side, namely, that of internal ethnical equilibrium. Under this term I understand a constant relation which exists between the quantity of population, territory occupied by it, and biological adaptation, the cultural adaptation being considered as one of special forms of biological adaptation. So we will have

$$\frac{q}{ST} = \omega$$

which I call *constant of ethnical equilibrium*.

This simple relation between the indicated phenomena was formulated (1912) by myself after theoretical studies into the problem of population, analysis of thousands of cases seen in ethnical units, and direct observation of a great number of ethnical units (first published in 1922). Several investigators have approached the same idea; but none of them formulated it in the above indicated expression and they did not take the next step; namely, to formulate consequences resulting from this constant. I may mention, e.g. names of Schmoller and others who calculated density of population for different types of economic organization; Lippert's and Sumner's ideas on land-ratio; R. Pearl who in 1924 put it at the basis of his investigation as a postulate (my "S" was regarded by him as cultural adaptation which point of view cannot be shared) ; A. Lotka in his treatment of equilibria makes a very near approach to the same idea: I do not now speak of those who gradually begin to follow this approach to the problem of ethnical unit.

I have in mind, when operating with this formula, that sooner or later the functional adaptation may be expressed as a certain *quantity*. At present we may only suppose that this element of the equation is of an energetic nature, —the consumption of energy and production of energy. So that theoretically we may continue with the differential treatment of our equation. Yet, it is evident that the quantity T and q must not be understood in a simplicist manner. Indeed, the square kilometre of territory in the

* When there is incidental coincidence of elements covering the same population, it is very likely that a new unit will be formed. However, in some conditions even one element may suffice for forming such a unit and several elements may have no such effect. From this point of view there may be compiled a scale of elements according to their importance, as factors of lesser or greater importance in creation of centripetal movement. However, in carrying out analysis of this aspect of elements one is liable to an error; namely, to accept the elements of secondary origin for those of primary origin and thus to take the effect for the cause. Since our methods of analysis are not yet very certain, it is much safer to leave this classification for the future. But it ought to be pointed out that the element of self-cognition may be lacking altogether.

Sahara and in France, in the Mongolian plateau and in the Yangtse valley are not equivalent. A million of population with certain distribution of age groups is not equivalent to another million of a different population with a different distribution of age groups without speaking of energy production. Therefore, there ought to be introduced corrections for bringing T and q to certain standards.

The change of one of the elements of the equation on the condition of constancy of equilibrium, produces a corresponding change of two or at least one of the elements,

$$\frac{\Delta q}{\Delta S \Delta T} = \omega$$

whence we may see that the change of population may act as impulse of variation of culture and territory, and vice versa. So we have *impulses of variations*. Naturally, they must be taken relatively, as to the former quantity and as a factor affecting the system of equilibrium. Thus we have

$$\pm i_{\pi} = \omega \frac{\Delta q}{q} \; ; \; \pm i_{\epsilon q} = \omega \frac{\Delta T}{T} ; \; \pm i_{\epsilon q} = \omega \frac{\Delta S}{S} ;$$

It is evident that there may be positive and negative impulses. When they are positive and strong we may say that the unit is in the process of growth,—numerical, or adaptive, or in territory; when the unit shows negative impulses of variations it is indicative of a declining state. Zero impulses are indicative of stagnation and in given conditions of interethnical pressure, usually growing, being also indicative of a relative ethnical decline. In these cases we do not need to make ingenious explanations and justifications of the situation, but we have only to state the facts.

Since the impulse of variation produces a corresponding change of one of two of the other elements, the impulses and their effects will be equal. Thus if

$$\pm i_{\pi} = \omega \frac{\Delta q}{q} \quad \text{and} \quad \pm i_{\epsilon q} = \omega \frac{\Delta T}{T}, \quad \text{where} \quad i_{\pi} = i_{\epsilon q} ,$$

so

$$\omega \frac{\Delta q}{q} = \omega \frac{\Delta T}{T}, \quad \text{whence} \quad \Delta q = q \cdot \frac{\Delta T}{T}$$

on the supposition that the culture remains the same.

By the same reasoning we may thus formulate,—

$$\Delta T = T \frac{\Delta S}{S} \quad \text{the population being the same; } \quad \Delta S = S \cdot \frac{\Delta T}{T}$$

the population being the same. I cannot go into the very interesting details as to the effects of the same impulses on different initial quantities, which in some combinations bring us a quite new light as to the history of some ethnical units, their growth and decline, also limitations for potential growth, etc. But I want to show some interesting situations. Let us take

$$\Delta T = T \frac{\Delta S}{S}$$

with a constant population. Since in the system

$$\omega = \frac{q}{ST}$$

the increase of S results in the decrease of T and vice versa, the process is analogous (perhaps even in its nature similar) to the loss of heat with the reduction of pressure in gases, and vice versa. In the case of absolute saturation of territory, which is a theoretical proposition, and thus constant q, there will be created a situation when cultural growth will be zero for since the increase of T is zero, the increase of S will be also zero.

However, this may be considered as a condition of perfect stagnation which, as shown before, under varying conditions of environment is impossible. Then the cultural adaptation may be produced on account of essential morphologo-physiological changes, or in other words formation of a new species. This is just the process which we seem to observe in the substitution of animal species in the same territory. So, in a near future, perhaps, it will be possible to calculate in which conditions and approximately at which moment there may appear an entirely new species of man.

———

A special aspect of impulsive variations is growth of population according to the logistic curve of Verhulst-Pearl. In fact, we have such occurrences when there appears a new impulse of variations. For instance, there may be opening of a new territory, e.g. empty bottle for drosophila, territory taken from the ethnical groups of low resistance, like America, and Siberia, or introduction of an important adaptive condition, e.g. a new source of energy production, like steam, agriculture, etc. A complete consummation of the new territory or integral exploitation of a new form of adaptation cannot possibly be carried out at once for there are biological conditions of reproduction with their limitations, as period of gestation, and process of growth; and, in so far as cultural changes are concerned, there is a very delicate mechanism of re-adaptation of the psychomental complex for which there is also a limit to tempo of variations. Therefore the process will last a certain period of time covering at least several generations. The greater the impulse of variations, the longer the process. Yet, it will naturally proceed as it is with the autocatalytic chemical reactions expressed in well known Ostwald's formula

$$\frac{dx}{dt} = k_x x(a-x) - k_x x^1 \quad \text{and after integration:}$$

$$\frac{x}{A-x} = k(t-t_o), \quad \text{or as a well known formula}$$

$$\frac{dx}{dt} = ax + bx^1, \quad \text{of autocatakinetic growth.}$$

The process of population growth *when it is not disturbed and when it is forced by the impulse of variation of population* proceeds in the same way. In fact, the formula of growth

$$x = \frac{q}{1 + e^{-at}}$$

is the same. It is interesting to note that a mathematician, Verhulst, came nearly a century ago to the same idea, as biologist experimentator, R. Pearl, which naturally greatly impressed students of population growth, and also produced a strong negative reaction. Naturally, I have put aside the question of mathematical expression of the process,—the facts are facts,

but the formula does not cover, and cannot cover, all cases of growth, which ought to be emphasized. The process of growth is not as simple as it was first represented by W. Ostwald, and quite successfully applied to the cases such as growth of flies and infusoria confined to a limited space, or to the small and rather simple organisms. After the publication of T. B. Robertson's work on growth of organisms this has been noticed by his critics, and several attempts were made to introduce corrections. There was introduced, for instance, volume of the body, a quantity variable during the growth. Yet, even with this important correction the formula of growth cannot be regarded as representing the actual process, for there are conditions which were originally overlooked, namely, the constructive limits, a variable condition since the composition of the materials of construction does not remain the same during the process of growth. Therefore this formula can represent only a part of the phenomenon. Particularly, in the human organism during the growth there are formed different limits which actually result in a sequence of unachieved logistic curves, and as a whole the process of growth cannot be represented in a scheme. Whether there are two, as suggested by C.B. Davenport, or three cycles as suggested by T. B. Robertson and his followers, or even more cycles now has no more importance for we are facing a different problem,—a changing system of equilibria[*].

I have dwelt upon the process of individual growth for the growth of population in principle does not differ, from it. Yet we meet with the same kind of difficulties which are met with on the way in representing growth of population in a simple and general form of logistic curve. These are volume of growing units, change of the constructive possibilities, and substitution of components of a differentiated population. But even a successful solution of these difficulties will not permit us to generalize the process. Personally I think that for some simple cases corrections may be found,—and it will soon be done,—and in these cases the process of population growth will be represented as a series of interrupted logistic curves, but there is one more variable condition residing outside the growing units, namely, the interethnical milieu from which the growing ethnical units cannot be separated to be studied in abstracto. At last, it is very questionable whether in general it is possible to carry out this investigation since the units of man, as shown before, are not individuals, but only effects of a certain process (ethnos), and as such they cannot be identified with the populations, especially populations of functionally and morphologically homogeneous infusoria and drosophila. This is an old story,—the analogies are taken for identity: a common methodological error. However, by these remarks I do not reject the facts and their short formulation by Verhulst-Pearl, so I shall now return to this phenomenon in its special aspect.

Without assuming that the process of population growth is generally represented as a completed logistic curve, or that it may be a series of incompleted curves, let us take a special cases of growth expressed in a logistic cycle which will help us to approach some other and even more complex problems. At the beginning of a cycle, as well as at the end of it the tempo of variations, which

———

[*] Application of the theory of ethnos to the problem of growth is found in may publication "Process of physical Growth among the Chinese", Vol. I. Shanghai 1924 and especially in "Growth and Ethnos" in which I treat new Chinese material.

$$\frac{f}{t} = \tau$$

$$r\frac{\omega_{\Delta}q}{qt} = \rho_{,r} \quad (\text{`tension'})$$

is slow, while in the middle period it is fast; during the first half of the process it is always increasing, while during the second half it is decreasing. From the point of view of adaptation to the tempo there is enormous difference between the behaviour of the ethnical unit during the first and second halves of the cycle, as well as at its beginning and at its end. Since different tension of adaptation at different periods is required we may ask ourselves a question of theoretical and practical importance: are there limits of the tempo? The answer is positive and we do not need to go into rather doubtful reasoning as to ethnical psychology, racial adaptability and other usually imaginative speculations. In fact, in respect to S in its cultural manifestations, the tempo cannot exceed that of an integral use of a new element which has required certain expenditure of stored energy in the ethnical unit. I now give a rough example for illustration. The change of method of production is practicable, as a system of adaptation, only after the amortization of the capital spent on the innovation. When a railway is built up for using steam power, the latter cannot be re-organized into electrical power two years after the completion of construction,—it would mean loss of all locomotives, expenditure on additional creation of electrical plants and system of transmission of energy, without speaking of a complete change of technical staff*.

For the same reason the system of social organization which presumes certain specialization (in technique) of social groups cannot be changed before the former system is integrally used. In fact, in the matter of social changes the limitations of tempo are still greater, for a new social system, to be efficient, must be balanced with the psychomental complex, which is extremely slow in its variations, and seems to involve physiological conditions of units as well. In fact, every change in the form of adaptation requires a certain psychomental reaction, the intensity of which will be greater when there is rapid tempo of variations,—

$$r\frac{f}{t} = \rho$$

Thus, e.g. the tension of reaction during the change of cultural phenomena, implied by the impulse of growth of population, the formula will be:

* This is, by the way, the reason why in the countries with a very complicated industrial system, when the tempo of variations is very rapid, industrial reconstruction is practically impossible, while it is very easy in the countries of low industrialization. It may also be remarked that in such countries in this condition there appear a series of interesting phenomena, like self-limitation in reproduction of species, obstinate conservatism, and tendency to propagate the same ideas among other ethnical units in view of their weakening. This may be understood or it may go on unconsciously as it is with most of similar phenomena. Indeed, when I am speaking of this limitation I do not mean to say that it is never transgressed by the ethnical units. Such an occurrence is common especially under the conditions of changed interethnical pressure (vide infra) but if it is repeated too often the consequence is evident,—the ethnical unit becomes weaker, so that it cannot resist interethnical pressure and perishes or it is desintegrated owing to the military action or owing to the increase of centrifugal movement within the former unit chiefly stimulated by the interethnical pressure. Therefore, this limitation is not an absolute one and it becomes effective only in the system of interethnical and ethnical equilibria.

Indeed, in different ethnical units this potential tension has its limits, and is partly conditioned by the existing tempo (the existing inertia), partly by the physiological conditions of the units which are not alike, and at last partly by the impossibility of an essential change of the psychomental complex during the same generation. All these conditions are responsible for the creation of certain limits of potential tension of reactions, or limits of psychomental efficiency in the process of variations of ethnical equilibrium. After these remarks I shall now give some illustrations as to new aspects of the situation during the process of impulsive variations.

In the first half of the cyclic process we have thus gradual increase of tempo and together with it a gradual increase of psychomental tension. If this tension passes over the potential limit, typical of the unit, it may break down and this may assume various forms of disfunction or even a complete collapse of the unit may occur. When the point of flexion is passed another and quite special form of adaptation is required; namely, decrease of tempo of variations and various limitations resulting therefrom, such as regulation of birth, marriage, etc. which do produce a new tension in the psychomental complex. The psychomental complex at these periods usually shows signs of instability which may result in the loss of internal equilibrium of the unit. Here, we touch upon a delicate problem of the psychomental complex which may be treated from the pathological point of view. However, such a treatment approached from the point of view of individual pathology cannot be successful. In the best case it would be possible to describe its mechanism, but the causes lying beyond the phenomena of "pathology" will remain hidden. Indeed, the range of normal variations of the normal and abnormal individuals is also affected. Therefore the psychiatrist may greatly help in the diagnosis and analysis of the condition of instability in units, but a pathological approach to the masses of population and individuals cannot explain the phenomena as a whole. A very great tension may result in its breaking and the functional collapse of the unit. Such collapses rather often occur in ethnical groups and they may produce what in popular language are called "revolutions"*.

I have mentioned these cases of the breaking down of the ethnical equilibria because of the breaking of the tension of the psychomental complex which we approach with the theory of ethnos; but the same can be done empirically in every case, if there are keen persons who may take into account all details of the process. This may be com-

* In this connexion I want to point out that in the history of ethnical units "revolutions" are of great and vital importance, so I shall pause to discuss this phenomenon. There are three kinds of revolutions, namely, those implied by the maladjustment in the process of variations which may require a sudden change; those which are caused by the interethnical pressure; and those which are mere reactions of the psychomental complex on the change of existing inertia of variations. The last case practically is much more frequent than the first two types. The effect of the first one is that the process of growth is not affected and a readjustment can take place while in the second and the third cases the unit usually pays a high price with the loss in tempo, very often with the loss of population, and even a loss of territory taken by other units. The revolutions of these two types are sometimes like the effect of a sudden arrest of movement. Energy is transformed into the heat and the body may explode.

pared with a driver who before using a new road empirically studies whether his horses can climb up the hill with the full load, or not; and if not, he either harnesses one more horse or puts down a part of his load, or he may look for another road. The engineer after calculating, may tell beforehand which angle of elevation is possible and he will not need to carry out experiments in which a common driver may lose his horses and load. The engineer's work becomes quite indispensable in modern methods of transport,—railways and motor-roads,—so that without his theoretical work the keeping of roads is practically impossible. Seemingly we come to the same condition in the life of ethnical units within which the tempo of variations becomes more and more accelerated.

I shall now return to the problem of interethnical milieu which, as I have pointed out, may change process of growth and affect ethnical equilibrium up to producing a complete collapse. For this reason the treatment of ethnical units in isolation is impossible, and the interethnical milieu ought to be studied with a special care. We have already seen that the centripetal movement in groups, differentiated on the basis of forms of adaptation, may result in the creation of ethnical units. In studying a great number of facts we may see that there exist great a number of units of different size, big and small ones, which form what I called *interethnical* milieu. The relations between the units are defined by a peculiar system of equilibrium which exists between the given unit and other units. So the greater the power which is possessed by the unit the stronger may be the pressure sustained by the unit. It is evident that the power of the unit consists in the number of the population (q), its adaptive power (S), and territory with which it is bounded. The power of the unit becomes $qST=f$, or if we substitute for ST $\frac{q}{\omega}$ from the equation of ethnical equilibrium we shall have

$$f=q\frac{q}{\omega}, \quad \text{or} \quad f=\frac{1}{\omega}q^2.$$

However, the actual power of the unit may be valued only when all pressures produced by other units are considered. Let us suppose that the unit is surrounded by a group of other units each of which has impulses of variations as to the population, adaptation, and territory, we may write the sum of impulses produced by the unit as

$$\sum l=\omega\frac{dq}{q}+\omega\frac{dS}{S}+\omega\frac{dT}{T};$$

and if there are several units, we may symbolize as

$$\sum l=\sum_{1}^{n}l_{q}+\sum_{1}^{n}l_{sr}+\sum_{1}^{s}l_{t_q}$$

The unit opposes the sum of pressures by its resistance which is naturally equal to the pressure, for otherwise the unit will be either swallowed by other units, or it will swallow other units. Thus the actual value of the unit will be

$$f.\sum l=\epsilon \quad \text{or} \quad \epsilon=\frac{1}{\omega}q^2\sum l.$$

This is a new expression of the ethnos in the system of interethnical equilibrium in terms of potential energy of interethnical milieu.

If we consider the internal conditions of a unit found in the relation between the centripetal and centrifugal movements we may have a complete characterization of the unit in reference to its internal structure and system of existing equilibrium.

We have seen that the stronger the centripetal and centrifugal movements, the stronger adaptive resistance of the unit which may be symbolized as

$$\frac{1}{\omega}q^2\sum i\left(\sum a+\sum b\right)$$

but since the outcome of the process may go along the lines of further centripetal and centrifugal movements which depends on the difference between

$$\sum a \quad \text{and} \quad \sum b$$

we may thus express the equilibrium of the unit as

$$\beta=\frac{1}{\omega}q^2\sum i\left(\sum a+\sum b\right)\left(\sum a-\sum b\right)$$

where $\left(\sum a-\sum b\right)$

may be O and there will be reached an absolute stability of the unit in the system of moving interethnical and ethnical equilibria[*]. In the case of difference between two movements the process of "petrification" of the unit may begin when there is excess of positive movement; and the process of "disintegration", if there is excess of negative movement. The stronger the unit, and the stronger the original centripetal and centrifugal movements, the stronger the process of always increasing disequilibrium, for

$$\left(\sum a+\sum b\right)\left(\sum a-\sum b\right)=\left(\sum a\right)^2-\left(\sum b\right)^2.$$

In the units which possess a numerous population and which are under a strong interethnical pressure the process of "petrification" and "disintegration" proceeds with an enormous and always increasing speed; when the reactions of the ethnical units on the interethnical milieu are considered, different situations are created. So if the internal movements give a positive excess, the power will be positive, and aggressive behaviour will be natural, while if they give a negative excess the power and behaviour will be recessive. This also gives us an idea how the process of disintegration of units may proceed under the pressure of interethnical milieu alone, and that the process of disintegration of large units may proceed with a greater speed than that of small units[**].

When we do not abstract ethnical units from their natural milieu it becomes then evident that the impulses of variation may come out as effect of the interethnical pressure, and thus all the internal power of the unit for self-

---

[*] It may be pointed out that a continuous survival of very small ethnical units in the midst of very strong and aggressive units loses its startling enigmatism, if we have before our eyes the relations shown above, expressed in formulae. As a matter of fact, interethnical stability of the smallest units may be very definite.

[**] I now leave aside the very interesting question of variability of these conditions, implied by distance and topography for this would take too much space. I shall only remark that the relations which are established between the units may be better compared with the principles deduced from phenomena of physics. Some of them may be directly applied. As a matter of fact, it is not surprising at all for in the body of ethnical units we have phenomena analogous to liquids: populations bound by psychic cohesion.

adaptation may be spent producing equilibrium in the midst of other ethical units and there will be left no more impulses for the internal benefit of the unit in the sense of its further growth and stabilization. Therefore it is also clear that there may be changes of S (bio-cultural adaptation) and there will be no effect on q and T. Yet, the process of population growth, according to the logistic curve, may be altered and even interrupted by the interethnical pressure, so that the practical application of this principle is possible only in the exceptional cases of isolated units, and perhaps leading ethnoses*. In spite of this, in a great number of cases its application is important, even as revealing the character of disturbing factors.

The theory of ethnos may be easily applied to plants and other animals, in which the phenomena in some respects are more obvious and in some other respects may become more difficult for understanding. They are simpler because of relative paucity of secondary functional (cultural) adaptation, but they are more difficult because of the slowness of the process of change of adaptation. We hope that a careful and wise application of the theory of ethnos to the other animals and perhaps plants will permit us to dismiss a series of postulates and hypotheses which are no more needed for understanding the process of physical changes. So the theory of ethnos brings our ideas near to the realities, as to phenomena of both cultural and physical adaptation, and at the same time it formulates the nature of changes in a simple, although purely theoretical form, of modern functional thinking dealing with the differential processes. The naive nominalism, so called laws, teleology, evolution and other products of the last century's science are now no more needed. I hope that in a relatively near future it will be possible to treat these phenomena in terms of energy-matter conception, the problem of matter in so far as it is expressed in the populations being left to the applied science and the latter may grow from "driving" mentioned above, to a real "engineering"**. Yet, I think those who first will master it, will have more chance to become a new leading ethnos which at present seems to be absent.

6.　PARTICULAR PROBLEMS:　The above outline of the
　　ILLUSTRATIONS OF THE　theory of ethnos as it is
　　PRACTICAL APPLICATION　here expounded may ap-
　　OF THE THEORY OF ETHNOS.　pear as "pure theory". It
may refer to my description of the Northern Tungus groups, given in my work "Social Organization of the Northern Tungus", which has

* Vide infra Section 6.
** When I am mentioning "engineer" it should not be taken for a hint to the so-called technocracy lately discussed. It is common that political, social and professional groups have an ambition of taking the control of the governmental apparatus. Any of them may become good after a certain experience in governing and any one may fail, but as soon as they become professional "rulers" they lose their former character. From this point of view it is of no importance whether they originally were engineers, lawers, bankers, liberals, conservatives. The practical question is how costly may be for a nation to change the groups should it be actually needed. The engineers, as well as other specialists, are needed by a good government for consultation only. The need of having good specialists, including engineers, is evident, but it cannot suffice for convincing nations that these special professional groups must become government. Indeed, one of reasons of this "movement" is that a great number of unemployed engineers are seeking for work.

been done with the application of the theory of ethnos to the analysis of ethnical groups. I shall now give some cases of analysis of complex phenomena, as illustration of practical application of the theory.

First I shall discuss the problem of social differentiation. We have seen that a population may assume a very strong centripetal movement which may result in the formation of an ethnical unit which would oppose itself to other units. If a unit occupies a large territory with variable regions, but does not create any common organization, except the government functioning chiefly for organizing resistance to the interethnical pressure, the long adaptation to the local conditions of regions may result in a differentiation (centrifugal movement) of local groups which in their turn may grow into ethnical units. Indeed, after such a differentiation the unity of the former group may be chiefly and sometimes solely maintained by the interethnical pressure. However, such a situation could not occur if the unit would create a complex system of economic organization which would also imply specialization of non-territorial groups of population. In such a case the process of differentiation proceeds along the lines of social structure i.e. so to say in horizontal direction. The mechanism of this differentiation, as a form of centrifugal movement, is the same as that in regional differentiation. Both of them are imposed by the need of adaptation and in so far they are beneficial for the unit, but when this process is too intensive the new social units when formed and well organized may elaborate all traits typical of ethnical units. For instance, there may be elaborated a special language (in fact in socially differentiated units languages are numerous and so distinct that the social groups do not understand one another); there may be elaborated a complex of cultural adaptation including special literature, art, and what may be called "philosophy", there may be formed "class consciousness", and at last marriage limitations, confined to the newly formed units,—the merchants, workmen, peasants, intellectuals, very specialized groups such as priests, naval officers, and so on. So that there will be actually formed new ethnical units with all characteristics typical of them. The cohesion between them may be maintained only by a very strong centripetal movement, expressed in a special common language, strong government, etc. chiefly imposed and justified by the strong interethnical pressure. We have some instances of perfect stabilization of such units into legally recognized units, the endogamous castes.

When the centripetal movement is weak, the former unit split into new units may lose its ability of resistance and either be conquered by the stronger ethnical units or perish in the so called "class struggle". I say "perish in the class struggle" because the reason of existence of differentiation was adaptation of the units as a whole, so that when differentiated units destroy each other (in this respect there is no essential difference between the ethnical and class struggle) the former unit as a whole is not able to function, and thus it perishes. It may be noted that the formal disintegration of the socially differentiated units is very often observed when the interethnical pressure is temporarily removed, so that the centripetal movement stimulated by the outside pressure does not work any more.

However, occurrences of purely social disintegration are very rare, for the big units which are affected by the social differentiation usually comprise several half-disintegrated ethnical units and, occupying a large territory, they may include a certain number of regionally differentiated groups. Great numbers of historic cases are combined cases of social, regional differentiation and ethnical secondary integration. Such are cases of Roman collapse, Russian collapse, and perhaps the approaching collapse of some other units of the same type of empire. It may be also pointed out that the similarity in the justification and rationalization of ethnical and class struggle is remarkably great, although sometimes the class and ethnical struggles being simultaneous and proceeding on parallels, exclude one another and thus two centres of crystallization may be formed. Yet, after the victory, the victorious social and ethnical units sometimes assume the same ideology and practices, as those of the former unit. There are usually introduced only new phraseology, new justification and new rationalization of the status. Naturally, the revolutionary appearance is lost very soon and a new process of differentiation begins. Indeed, it cannot be otherwise, for this is the only mechanism of adaptation which exists. However, in a great number of cases the groups affected by these processes, especially if they are very large, are almost automatically swallowed by other units, and their survival is possible only on the condition of partial breaking of interethnical pressure.

Thus, I may conclude these remarks on social differentiation by stating that social groups are potential ethnical units and at the basis of the process we have the same process of ethnos. Indeed, as in the case of "racial", regional, cultural and other units, the process of formation of ethnical groups from social groups is arrested by strong centripetal movement, and so the completion of the process is observed only *in the cases of collapsed units.*

Another problem is that of the nation. I do not want to repeat here that the attempts at giving a clear definition of nation have failed. The cause of this failure resides in the fact that two different things were mixed and identified as one, namely, the process and the physical populations. The problem of nation may be approached from two sides, namely, from the historic-comparative and from the analytico-functional. Both approaches are good if we keep in mind that this *is a process affecting populations.*

Three classical cases are clear in the formation of nations.

(1) A group of ethnical units (differentiated either on regional or functional principles, or both) may come into relations of cooperation based upon division of work in the larger aggregation of several units. As soon as this new form of adaptation is organized, even without being understood, a single unit cannot carry on its struggle for existence. Then a temporary colony of units will be formed and connected by a system of common interests. If such a colony meets with the opposition of the other ethnical or similar combined units, and thus is found under a direct pressure of interethnical milieu, a strong centripetal movement may appear. It is very likely that there will be formed either a federation of these populations or a new larger ethnical unit.

(2) Another case is that of a fast growing ethnical unit, usually biologically very strong, which spreads over the territory thinly peopled or even empty. Such a unit may attain large size equalling that of the preceding case of colonies. It is merely a large ethnical unit.

(3) An ethnical unit, usually very much inclined for warfare, gradually spreads and overcomes neighbouring units. Owing to the fact that a large number of people may carry out the function of centripetal activization of the unit formed out of subjugated units, the latter begin to lose their centripetal movement in favour of the larger unit. So a conquest may result in the formation of a colony of units headed and forced to stay together under the pressure of the conqueror. This colony of units with the course of time may become an ethnical unit.

However, survival of all these units is possible only on the condition of existence of a particular interethnical milieu and equilibrium created partly because of newly formed units. In fact, we have many instances of this kind when peopled regions cannot be occupied by the large groups and are left alone. Such regions may have very mixed populations consisting of one or several ethnical units and they will not be taken over by the larger units for the existing equilibrium will not permit it. Modern terminology gives them the name: "nations". On the other hand well defined ethnical units may receive no recognition as "nations" and they will not exist as factors influencing *international* relations.

My enumeration will not be complete if I omit another case, namely, when the new colony of ethnical units or merely population is formed owing to the peculiar conditions of relations between the existing units-nations. Some regions may be left without direct interference of "nations" and placed under the control of one of the ethnical units. As soon as this ethnical unit is in control it may gradually spread its influence over the other units or population of the region and begin to play the part of centripetal factor. Thus an actually functioning unit may gradually be formed.

In all these cases we have large units which originate owing to the existing interethnical equilibrium. When they are recognized, they become "nations". A nation may exist for a few months or for long centuries. It may grow into an ethnical unit, and yet, it may remain heterogeneous being composed of different ethnical units. However, in all these cases it will be a by-product of interethnical equilibrium,—a unit recognized by other similar units.

For these reasons a nation cannot be identified as an ethnical unit and even the process which I called "ethnos", must be well established before ethnological identification is given to a nation. I may here point out that in the hands of Sir A. Keith, the application of the theory of ethnos to nations was a source of some defects in his outline of the process of evolution of human races. When one wants to use theory of ethnos, the distinction between the ethnical units and nations must be very sharp.

The third problem is that of the cultural complexes and elements in their relation to ethnos. The effect of spreading of cultural phenomena is most important in the process of ethnical differentiation. First, the wider the area of the cultural complex or elements the less important they are in the process of differentiation of ethnical units. Second, it must be pointed out that every cultural complex and every cultural element possesses a certain *potential of diffusion* which is different for different complexes and elements, and which is different in different ethnical milieus. This aspect is of great importance. There are some elements, for instance, matches which possess very great power of diffusion for they are needed by all human groups. They are cheap, and their adoption does not imply any great modification of the existing cultural complex. On the other hand there are some other elements the potential of diffusion of which is almost none, e.g. such is the case of the syntax of the French language, which, let us point out, is a cultural element of a large cultural complex,—the French language. The potential of diffusion of this element is confined only to the territory with populations speaking the French language. I have taken these two examples as instances, but there may be given thousands of other instances. Spreading of elements of complexes in different ethnical (culturally different) milieus: modern composers' works easily spread among the ethnical groups of Europe, but they meet with great hindrance as soon as they leave these groups; new fur, used for winter coals, may spread only among the ethnical units possessing complex of winterfurcoats, evidently to some degree limited by the climatic conditions and existing "fashions".* The leading ethnoses (this problem is discussed below) which bring with them new forms of cultural adaptation have great influence on the spreading of complexes and elements. Together with their spreading,—and this is one of characteristic features of leading ethnoses—these complexes and elements of adaptation lose their differentiating function. However, together with their spreading and loss of differentiating function they do not always remain so, but within other ethnical units they may undergo secondary differentiation and thus become an effective condition of chemical differentiation. Such is the fate of many religious systems, also philosophical and political teachings. So in these cases we have the same phenomenon of ethnos reflected in the cultural phenomena. The field of languages in this respect is especially rich in reliable and well checked material**. I now point it out for the nature of these phenomena was very often taken for independent, supernatural and metaphysical existence of functional phenomena. The theory of ethnos solves this enigma quite successfully together with the solution of the problem of dynamic processes in the populations which result in the formation of various groupings, as ethnical, national, social, regional on the one hand, and in the creation of necessary conditions for human physical changes (evolution). Thus the latter cannot be regarded from the teleological point of view, but as a peculiar effect of variable equilibria in man working through the mechanism of ethnos.

_____

Under the technical term leading ethnos which is very important as mechanism of adaptation and remodelling of cultural complexes and as mechanism of changes in the interethnical milieu, I understand a process which results in the appearance of ethnical units or groups of ethnical units which at different historic moments become models for other ethnical groups. There is great analogy between the animal species and ethnical units. In fact, in the classification of geological strata, palaeontological remains are used as character of distinction. Indeed, if a certain animal

appears in a stratum and thus at certain historic period in a great number of individuals and very often in a great number of varieties, we may be allowed to suppose that in the given milieu there were particularly favourable conditions for growth of the species and groups of species which were better adapted than other species and related species. Such species may remain, survive, during the subsequent periods when there may appear other species which will be characteristic of the new conditions of existence, and such species may perish altogether without leaving any offspring. So the geological periods may be characterized by appearance of different species which may be considered as typical and well adapted at the given geological time; from Palaeontology we know that duration of continuity of species is very variable,— some species appear for a very short time while other species survive for a very long time. I shall not enumerate all characteristics of the conditions of their appearance, variations and extinction, but I shall now point out only two important conditions, namely, before extinction the animal species shows great adaptive specialization and it usually produces great number of varieties and new species.

We must account the fact that the biological adaptation of the ethnical units is following the line of functional adaptation in connexion with which no morphological changes may occur. These functional adaptations are relatively simple and may be carried out during a relatively short period, for, as shown, they are essentially a function of the density of population and the latter—as we know from biology—possess an enormous potentiality of increase when the animal is in "favourable" conditions. Every new form of cultural adaptation may open this possibility. Therefore existence of _leading ethnical units_, i.e. units which appear as better adapted at the given historic moments, as compared with palaeontological species is very short* and differentiation of ethnical units may proceed in a more extensive manner.

In a great number of cases the important condition of appearance of a new leading ethnical unit is the discovery of a new form of cultural adaptation, be it a new technical discovery, new form of social system, or essential change in the psychomental complex, be it a single cultural element or a new complex. Such a new adaptation may permit the ethnical unit to grow numerically and become more powerful than the units which surround it. Naturally, this will result in the increase of interethnical pressure which would stimulate further adaptation (cultural) and usually further complication of the existing complex. In such a state the leading ethnical unit will become a model for other ethnical units, and it will become culturally _leading_. In the conditions of interethnical disequilibrium such a unit may overgrow its former boundaries and form a unit (nation, empire) which at a certain moment may appear in the conditions of zero of interethnical pressure. As soon as this condition is created the newly formed unit will collapse under the pressure of ever increasing centrifugal movement. This is the most common case of collapse of leading ethnical

* Here I point out that when we are dealing with the palaeontological species we cannot penetrate the problem of minute functional adaptations of extinct animals, for these functions might have no effect on the morphology of these animals. However, the animal ethnoses formed within the species morphologically distinguished and "functioning" as mechanism of changes were of the same "functional" type, as in human ethnical units, the difference being that of quantity of physiological adaptation.

* I shall return to this problem in the concluding part of this work.
** The nature and function of language is treated by me from the point of view of theory of ethnos in my "Aspects" (1931)

units which overgrow in the conditions of heterovelocity of change of cultural adaptation in a heterogeneous interethnical milieu. However, when there is interethnical equilibrium the leading ethnical unit will produce its influence and it may even remain in this conditon for a long time, as inventor of new forms of adaptation. There may be two cases: the ethnical unit may become parasitic on other units and, naturally, perish with the first essential change in the interethnical milieu, and in its high specialization it may lose elasticity of adaptation and its inventive power will not be used by itself, but by the other ethnical units which are not so much specialized, In this case the new adaptation permitting further increase of population would open new series of variations (it may be supposed usually cyclic), breaking of former interethnical equilibrium and ethnical clash, usually in the form of war. The former leading ethnical unit will thus become either highly specialized in the newly created interethnical milieu or it will even leave its territory to the other aggressive units. Then a new leading ethnical unit will occupy its place as leader. Indeed, the forms in which leadership is expressed depend upon the character of cultural adaptation, typical of the historic period and given interethnical milieu, and concurrently on the biological character of the unit, as for instance, psychomental elasticity, potential power of reproduction, character of metabolism, physical strength, and so on. We may theoretically suppose that if there is some essential change in the physiological and even morphological characters of the unit, it too may become a leading unit. Remodelling of the interethnical relations in this case will take form of physical extinction of the units which cannot compete with the new physical modification of the old type. However, such instances cannot be very numerous in man, although this constitutes an important item in the dreamy philosophy of all times.

It is remarkable that on looking back on the history of European groups, one may see that almost every important change in the system of material culture is connected with the change of leading ethnical units every one of which brings something new to the preexisting complex, particularly psychomental complex. Indeed, it would be quite artificial to regard these changes as due to the single factor, like "material culture", economic system, war technique, etc. for behind these changes there is change of leading ethnical units which are changing substrata. In the same manner we may see subsequent substitution of ethnical units in their function of leading ethnos among the populations of parts of the world, the history of which is better known, as Eastern Asia, India, Western and Minor Asia. We may suppose from the study of cultural sequence and "racial" changes in prehistoric time that the same phenomenon of leading ethnos was a "working mechanism" of changes.

Before leaving this problem I want to point out that there are periods when no definite leading ethnos is seen, when the struggle for supremacy is not yet finished and the interethnical milieu appears to be in a state of confusion. Second, there is enormous difference in the psychomental attitude of the leading ethnical unit as compared with other ethnical units. However, here there ought to be kept in mind that peculiar conditions of psychomental complex at different periods of cyclic growth must not be overlooked. The leading ethnical unit usually believes in its perfect superiority, "right" to direct other units, when necessary to destroy other units in the name of "progress", justice,

God, and other justifications the choice of which exclusively depends on the existing psychomental complex. Such a unit does not believe in its temporal existence, but it believes that the existing position will be maintained for ever. These self-assertions, self-confidences, self-justifications, deep ethnocentrisms, and limitless egoisms form the complex of mechanism which permits the unit to overcome all difficulties in functioning as a leading ethnical unit. When this mechanism is destroyed the unit loses its functional ability of leading ethnos. History gives us a great number of examples of decline due to the destruction of this mechanism. Again, the period of cyclic process here must be especially considered.

It may be also noted that the attention of other ethnical units is always attracted by the leading ethnical units, and the attention of the ethnical unit itself is also absorbed by its own activity[*]. Owing to this in the historic records we have great disproportion of information as to the ethnical units existing simultaneously. This is also a very interesting condition which puzzled historians to such a degree that they could not see the causes of the collapse of leading ethnoses which naturally themselves are only one of the complex manifestation of interethnical milieu and beyond this milieu cannot be understood.[**]

The struggle between the leading ethnical units and candidates constitutes the romance of history which attracted much more attention on the part of historians than the real history of mankind.[***]

From the point of view of the spreading of cultural complexes the existence of the process here called *leading ethnos* is of primary importance. In fact, when an ethnical unit begins to play the part of *leading unit*, the cultural complex created by it begins its spreading, as a whole or as elements. As pointed out in the section dealing with the problem of cultural complex and ethnos, spreading of the elements and complexes will naturally meet with certain hindrances, thus they will not spread equally on the territory, and yet they may be subject to a secondary re-adaptation in which form they may lose their former function which prepared the ground for further penetration of the leading ethnical unit. Existence of some cultural cycles, so called linguistic "families", spreading of some philosophical and religious systems, and other similar phenomena are usually connected with the spreading of the influence of leading ethnical units. I say "spreading of influence" and not "spreading of ethnical units" for the influence may proceed without a spreading of populations constituting leading ethnical units. It may be here noted that in the

* In some cases it may turn into real ignorance. However, when such a leading ethnical unit begins to pay too great attention to other units this may be considered as a sign of coming decline,—disfunction of psychomental complex.

** It is common to meet the most phantastic explanations of collapses of ethnical leading units which may be explained as punishment of superior powers, degeneration, especially liked by the biologists, "exhaustion of creative power" and other hypotheses, while the reality is variations of the system of equilibria in a differentiated milieu, sometimes stimulated even by the factors lying beyond the earth.

*** There are two great reasons for this situation, namely, emot'onal condition,—puzzle of change; and utilitarian stimulus,—to learn how to become a leading ethnical unit and get even though temporary benefit of this position. Among the "candidates" the belief into an ever-continuous existence is still stronger than among the declining leading ethnical units. The question as to how far the process of becoming leading ethnical unit may be regulated if at all, is beyond the present subject.

regions where there were alternations of leading ethnical units, there are usually found traces of cultural cycles, and "families of languages". So, for instance, in Europe at the present time so called "Indo-European family" with its layers corresponds to the changes of leading ethnical units with subsequent spreading of their languages. However, it was preceded by another "family" (Japhetic "family") which is now overlapped by the Indo-European group of languages. The most interesting case is that of Turkish, Mongol and Tungus "families" which had no time for continuous spreading because of very intensive alternation of leading ethnical units of a short duration by the side of the Chinese written language which covered enormous territory. In Africa we have very instructive instance of Bantu "family" and Arabian "family"; in North America, Algonquin, Athabaskan and Uto-Aztecan; in South America, Arawak, Carib, Tapuya and Tupi all of which probably were used to be leading ethnical units of their time. About some of them we have quite definite historic evidences. A puzzle for ethnographers, linguists, and ethnologists was the existence, by the side of these "families", of a great number of languages which could not be classified at all, as the famous "about seventy smaller families" in South America and "nearly seventy smaller families" in North America, indefinite number of "smaller families" in Central Africa, "Palaeasiatic languages" in Asia and mosaic picture of languages spoken in China and Indo-China which only with all possible liberty could be quite arbitrarily grouped into "Sino-Tibeto-Siamese family", just to sooth minds which require "families". However, the process of leading ethnos gives us a perfect understanding of the situation without any postulates and hypotheses, as to the "evolution" of languages and their "genetic relations." The same method may be applied to the analysis of cultural complexes and their relations in cultural cycles, greatly limited by the conditions of milieu and density of population among the ethnical units, without speaking of the pre-existing complexes. A consideration of the fact of the existence of leading ethnos in the analysis of existing complexes in a great number of cases leaves aside heated discussion about "diffusion", "parallelism", Kulturkreise, evolution, "race-language-civilization problem", and many others.

Although the problem of application of theory of ethnos to the anthropology in a detailed manner is discussed in my work devoted to the process of growth mentioned before, and though the physical changes in man, as well as classification of human populations, at first may seem to have no direct connexion with the psychomental complex, I deem useful to give here some remarks in order to avoid possible misunderstandings should the differentiation on the basis of cultural adaptation be opposed to the physical differentiation. As shown before, an opposition (in function and nature) of the cultural adaptation, particularly psychomental complex, to the physical adaptation, particularly physiological complex, is a permanent source of misinterpretations of phenomena of human biology. In fact they are only different aspects of the same phenomenon*.

* A very curious behaviour is observed among the investigators: when the social and generally cultural adaptation of "animals" is discussed,—e.g. the family and group organization, tradition, etc.— they are approached as special aspects of animal biology, while when

Physical differentiation of animals is also a process which proceeds first in individuals, in so far as mutation and ontogenetic formations are concerned; then in small groups,—they either may be or may not be cognized,—when a new modification multiplies, or when a group of individuals are affected by a similar change; at last, in numerous *populationes*. This process may affect a large number of individuals, but it may also affect a very limited number of them. Further numerical increase of a new modification depends on a multitude of conditions, particularly on the degree of its adaptiveness under the conditions of ever varying primary, secondary (cultural) and tertiary (interethnical) milieus, and especially on the stability ("dominantness") of the complex of characters (even single characters) in the process of crossing. Indeed, the formation of new modifications is the most common, and probably very frequent phenomenon, especially when the human *populatio* is migrating and when it is found under the process of change of cultural adaptation*. When newly formed modifications are not perceived their crossing is going on parallel to the formation of new modifications. When they are perceived, a selected crossing may take place. As it has already been shown by the anthropological analysis of some populations, quite "mixed" offsprings may be produced from such crossings owing to a segregation of heterozygous characters and these offsprings may have certain stability.

Here it is timely to point out that with the present knowledge of physical characters we are confined only to phenotypic rough characters, such as forms of the head, body, limbs and hair, also pigmentation, while perhaps the most important characters,—the chemical functional complex and physical constructive complex**,—remain beyond the observation, without speaking of the chromosomes and

human cultural complex is treated it is opposed to the human "biology." Such an opposition is deeply rooted in the European ethnographical complex,—the body and the spirit, "soma" and "noon", etc.—on the one hand; and functionally it depends upon specialization of investigators, in their preliminary education, in artificially separated groups of knowledge,—humanities and natural sciences,— on the other hand. Of course, the body of knowledge in the socially differentiated groups is not the same, and the specialization in different branches is conditioned by the need of professional education, and naturally professional interests. So that such an opposition is one of the particular effects of the process of ethnos in populationes (ethnical units and their colonies) which result in social differentiation.

* Experimentally (chiefly on plants and insects) it is known that the mutations are very common and can be produced. From the observation of facts the same is found in the realm of "uncontrolled" nature. A great number of anthropologists and general biologists observed effects (probably both hereditary and ontogenetic) of very strong factors such as deviations of the food, air, sunlight, humidity (in migrations also ethnical and social differentiations), also a supposedly new factor,—the so-called "domestication". Naturally, the above mentioned deviations and their effects must be special group of phenomena, distinct from the secondary and tertiary milieus. "Domestication" of animals, as well as "domestication" of man, merely means a complex interspecies relation (it also exists between e.g. man and micro-organisms, man and some insects and animals which are not domesticated) under the pressure of ever growing population and consequently (or alternatively) ever changing cultural adaptation. As shown, it is only a particular aspect, which ever existed, of the process of ethnos, easily understood if we do not accept an anthropocentric and ethnocentric attitude in the approach to the problem, and if we do not postulate an opposition of "soma" to "noon", etc.

** Analysis of the last complex is given in my last work on the Growth.

plasme, about the differences of which in human groups we have only vague guesses. Anthropology and particularly classification of human populations was going on along the same line as zoology, especially mammalogy. This was an imitation, while the material and aims of anthropology and zoology were not exactly the same*. Owing to this there were advanced the ideas of species, sub-species and race which were not needed at all for the analysis of human populations and the whole discussion for more than a century went astray**,—a search for "species" and "races" kept busy several generations of anthropologists. The second consequence was that the attention was attracted by the static differences, again by analogy with other animals, while functional side was sometimes consciously banished***, although biologically the differentiation of human groups (and individuals) is more essential in its functional aspects than in its static aspect. With a considerable advancement of general and human biology, the problems of crossing and inheritance have come to the first plan and together with it a real crisis of old anthropology has begun, so that a definite tendency to change the name of this science has appeared desirable to some anthropologists. Of course, it is only a temporary reaction.

The existence of species and races has never been inferred from the facts, but it was postulated. However, long time ago P. Topinard pointed out that "race" was only a theoretical abstraction which did not exist as a tangible reality, a real human unit where the process of changes is going on. Some similarity between the individuals undoubtedly is a fact, so that I admit that when anthropologist is dealing with a *populatio* he must distinguish the types without any presumptions as to their inter-relations and origin. Indeed, with the help of a fixed group of selected characters, or only with the help of "physical" characters, all the types cannot be distinguished, while even a single character may sometimes suffice for distinguishing a type from another type, in spite of similarity in other characters. Practically, distinction of such types is needed for an elimination of confusion of characters, for a restoration of continuity of populations, when the same type (or types) is met with among distinct ethnical groups, and especially for the analysis of variations of characters, both single ones and in complexes. Naturally, new anthropological types are always found as result of spontaneous

modifications (chiefly mutations) ; but not all of them become numerous and many of them become extinct within a generation, and yet not all of them are noticed*. It does not mean that anthropologically no uniform populations are formed. Although historically they may be composed of different types (and quite different ethnical groups), the process of crossing may go as far as to form a really homogeneous and little varying groups observed, for instance, among endogamous small regional groups, endogamous social and ethnical units (also "families" and "clans"). However, the fusion of different types may not occur at all, if there is no fusion of populations of which ethnical, social and regional groups are composed, and if there is a strong process of adaptive differentiation in these groups and formation of new mutations. On the other hand, theoretically it must be admitted that in a population which consists of different types a gradual selection of some types may occur, so that at the conclusion of this process a homogeneous monotypic population may also be formed.

An exclusion, à priori, of various adaptive characters from those which are taken as characteristic of the anthropological types is absolutely arbitrary. This becomes especially evident when physiological (and thus potentially psychological) characters are not excluded**. Moreover, entirely to neglect cultural adaptation in the matter of biological (physical) selection is as much arbitrary as to neglect, for instance, primary milieu. Of course, the situation is greatly complicated for the investigator who wishes to define what is the cause and what is the effect,—whether the cultural adaptation (especially psychomental complex) underlies the psycho-physiological complex, or vice versa. Naturally without postulates or mere presumptions this question cannot now be answered, and it seems to be of no importance should the populationes be considered from the ethnological point of view. It is plain, no individual can be abstracted from the ethnical milieu in which he was born and lived, for the individual functional power, in the sense of adaptation, is not that of an isolated individual, but his own power multiplied by that of the ethnical unit (potentially it may be an uncompleted process of ethnos) to which he belongs de facto, i.e. what he "receives" from the milieu***.

* Indeed, the difference is not that "men" is Man and "animals" are Animals, but the difference is that historically a rough and approximate classification of animals was needed as such for recording facts, while in man the question of interest was minor (as compared with other animals) differences confined not only to the "physical characters."

** This movement astray was not naturally fruitless. The human populations, at least in some respects, have been thoroughly investigated and a new approach to the problem of human classification has become possible. But this indirect approach to the problem has greatly delayed the reaching of the goal. Of course, as it is characteristic of the European complex, unchecked postulation of hypotheses and acting by analogy are always retarding the process of cognition of milieu.

*** Physiological investigations of human groups is a quite new branch of anthropology. Indeed, the attention to it was attracted long time ago, but the information was incidental and covered only a small group of phenomena. Some anthropologists have even excluded physiological anthropology from the scope of anthropology. In the same way the process of growth for a long time was neglected and only in recent years it deserved attention of investigators as a means to penetrate the functional differences of populations.

* Statistical operation with samples of population may sometimes dissimulate presence of newly formed and relatively rare types. The same holds good for an arbitrary choice of geographical areas, and socially selected groups. Sometimes only a direct observation of variations may lead to the discovery of such types.

** The history of classifications of human groups is rather instructive even from this point of view. In fact, an increase of units (types, varieties, races, etc.) is typical, and it is due not only to the detailed observation of formerly unknown populations, but it is also due to the fact of increase of the number of characters selected by the anthropologists,—the more the characters in play, the more the units likely to come out. Should there be no theoretical presumption of a limited number of races, conditioned by the evolutionistic theories of the last century, and should there be no desire to "generalize", the number of "races" would be still larger. Another purely psychological condition,—a fear of complicating the problem,—also was an important check of an increase of the number of "races".

*** An interesting aspect of the situation comes out in the ethnical reactions on the aliens. Here the individual attitudes are conditioned not only by the actual power of the individual to be "valued", but also by the individual psychomental complex of the "valuer", in its turn connected with his ethnical complex. Here resides the reason why a "valuation" of an individual by the aliens (I must point out that "aliens" may be found within the same ethnical unit which is affected by a strong centrifugal movement) chiefly has importance for the ethnologist who is studying reactions,

Thus, we now may say in a more general form: the characters of an individual are product of *mass of populatio* bound by the centripetal movement, regardless what is its nature, and since the cultural adaptation is a function of the *mass* of the unit in the system of interethnical equilibrium, the specific characters of the *mass* must not be neglected when individuals are considered. In this formulation the *hereditary, ontogenetic, and post-growth adaptation*, both in the static and functional aspects, are comprised.

Thus in its essential the process of formation of new types, their numerical growth, extinction and fusion, is the same as that of the ethnical units (particularly, social groups) and this process is only one of the aspects of ethnos. As soon as the idea about the anthropological differentiation is precised, amongst others the importance of anthropological-typological analysis, as much detailed as possible, for further investigations into the human biology, entirely overshadows the old aims,—a philogenetic classification of "races" and various "origins". Naturally, an analytical description of anthropological types gives us some documentation (when very carefully applied) for the study of continuity of *populationes*, but a complete restoration of history of types and populations probably is as much impossible, and even methodologically fallacious, as operations with "nations" by historians, "cultures and civilizations" by historians of culture, "cultural complexes" by ethnographers, "social classes" by sociologists. These static pictures of the process, as a representation of realities, are still less tangible than the individual organism in its continuity which is possible to accept only within very strictly defined limits and for special purposes.

The psychomental complex as shown before, is only a group of elements of functional adaptation separated by us only for technical reasons of treatment. As a complex, it comes into the complex of ethnical equilibrium here designated as S. It is thus evident that the principles of impulsive variations, tempo and intensity of variations, and naturally tension of reactions ought to be applied to the psychomental complex. Indeed, the influence of physical, and especially physiological, conditions of the ethnical unit has the greatest importance for the functioning of the psychomental complex. Even minor changes or a defective functioning of the physiological complex may be responsible for changes in the psychomental complex. Yet, the formation of the psychomental complex and its further variations especially in the accumulation of ideas greatly depends on the numerical power of the unit, and selective mechanism of the individuals best adapted for mental work—i.e. the contributors of the new ideas. So that the psychomental complex is intimately connected with the biological (in a narrow sense) conditions of the unit and numerical power of the population. In so far as the psychomental complex is a complex of cultural elements it is subject to the conditions characteristic of the cultural complex in general, i.e. continuous re-adaptation of the complex to the system of moving ethnical equilibrium and pressure of interethnical milieu. In the system of ethnical equilibrium the rôle of the psychomental complex is especially important; for the

but in so far as "finding of an actual value" is concerned, these reactions have no significance of documents. Let us remark that "recognition" and "non-recognition" have only ethnographical importance.

cohesion of the unit,—interrelation of members constituting the unit,—is achieved through the medium of this complex, yet the reactions of the unit expressed in the re-adaptation of the technical culture and social organization must first pass through this complex. At last, the influence of the interethnical milieu on the unit is also produced through the psychomental complex. The influence on this complex, its disbalancing, its disintegration are primary objectives in the interethnical pressure. By these means consciously or unconsciously the struggle between the units is operating only in serious cases resulting in a clash between the physical bearers of the complex.

Especially important in this complex is the existence of a very influential self-regulating mechanism of the automatism which permits the unit to readapt itself without cognition of this process. Destruction of this mechanism may mean for the unit loss of ability of maintaining equilibrium without even being affected by physiological disfunction, so that it can not be understood from a pathological point of view, while a minute analysis of the complex may give us quite a clear picture of internal causes of disfunction. In this respect the mechanism of acceleration and retardation of the variations of the psychomental complex cannot be understood without a minute analysis of the tempo and intensity of impulsive variation and that of the internal equilibria of the ethnographical complexes as a whole.

This importance of the psychomental complex in the life of populations grouped into ethnical units is greatly responsible for shadowing other aspects of the ethnical equilibrium and its abstraction. However, such an approach to the psychomental complex, cannot be justified when one wants to penetrate its functioning and on occasion its contents. In fact, the psychomental complex is conditioned, as shown, not only by the inherited psychophysiological complex, but also by the social organization, technical culture and primary milieu, from which it cannot be separated. Changes in the primary milieu, and secondary milieu produce changes in the psychomental complex, or they may produce disturbance of the psychomental complex.

We have seen, under a varying condition of impulsive variations assuming form of logistic curve of population growth for a cyclic period, the psychomental complex does not remain the same, either as a form of adaptation, or as its character, e.g. hopefulness, aggressiveness, relative tranquility, hopelessness, passiveness, etc. Such changes in the psychomental complex are conditioned by the character in movement of population,—they actually are functions of movement of population,—and they cannot be understood without consideration of conditions of population in its dynamic aspect. Such phenomena as sudden collapses, shown above, may not be understood from only the psychological point of view, but the external state of the unit ought to be considered in respect to the causes of change of tempo of the variations.

From the above remarks as to the relation between the psychomental complex and remarks concerning the theory of ethnos and cultural complex in general, it may be seen that a detailed description and analysis of the psychomental complex are possible only when the latter is considered in a totality of relations existing within the ethnical unit and these created by the interethnical milieu, and therefore the theory of ethnos must be made the theoretical basis of a treatment of the psychomental complex.

7. SCHEMATIC REPRESENTATION OF THE ETHNIC PROCESSES In order to give a concrete idea as to the above discussed phenomena of the process of ethnos, I present here six series of schemes; namely, 1 - Formation of ethnical units and interethnical pressure; 2 - Integration and disintegration of the units; 3 - Migration of an ethnical unit under the pressure of interethnical milieu; 4 - Social selective differentiation; 5 - Parasitizing and migrating of an ethnical unit; and 6. Growth of a linguistical "family" and diffusion of cultural complexes. It is evident that these schemes are only generalized schemes of phenomena taken in abstracto. However, all cases here shown may be illustrated with the facts from history of ethnical units of our time and those of the past.

In the first series,—Ethnical units and interethnical pressure,—I show how the interethnical pressure increases together with the growth of population. This series requires no special explanation.

———

In Series II I show a gradual incorporation of several units into a new larger unit due to the influence of a strong (central) unit which first culturally influence its neighbours, afterwards penetrates their territory and unites them into a larger unit. Owing to the interethnical pressure, which increases, the newly formed large unit is affected by a process of disintegration. The new centres of centripetal movement are formed, the centripetal movement of the large unit gradually becomes weak, and after a continuous increase of the pressure, the large unit collapses. The *populatio* is distributed between the newly formed units and their neighbours.

———

In Series III I show the process of breaking of boundaries by a strong fast-growing unit, here shown in red colour, which gradually forces for itself a passage into the territory of its neighbours. The latter cannot resist this pressure and after absorption they are gradually incorporated into a new large unit. However, some groups (lower part of the schemes) cannot be assimilated and so they preserve their ethnical characters. With the increase of population of the central unit, it strongly presses upon its right neighbour and finally breaks a passage. A flow of the migrating and fast-growing mass proceeds as far as territory permits. The effect of this movement is that the former territory is partly abandoned and the former pressure upon the neighbours decreases. The remainders of the former units begin numerically to grow and after a series of fusions they form larger units. After receiving cultural stimulation from the larger unit, the other units, a passage through which was forced, begin to grow and fuse into a large unit sufficient enough for separating the migrating unit into two groups,—one in the former territory and another in the newly acquired territory, where still numerous remains of the old, half-destroyed, units are shown. A continuation of the process, in a different aspect, is shown in Series VI.

———

In Series IV I schematically show a social differentiation as a form of cultural adaptation. In Table 1 four functionally distinct types are symbolized by different signs. With an increase of population there appears a need of division of work, as an effect of change of cultural adaptation. Since the new differentiation of groups is based upon functional characters of population, the new social groups are physically and psychically selected groups. However, a differential natality and a differential mortality in the social groups produce their effect upon the composition of the socially undifferentiated population,—some types become less and less numerous owing to their exhaust on in the social groups which cannot reproduce themselves and receive supply of population from the undifferentiated population, while other groups in which other types are selected show an increase of population, and supply not only the needed population for themselves but also for the undifferentiated population, which is shown by arrows. With a further increase of population there appears a need of a further social differentiation (division of work),—new social groups are branched. Some of them can reproduce themselves and even give a surplus to other groups, chiefly those which are functionally related, while other groups are continuously pumping their members from the common source. Owing to a great differentiation (cultural) some groups discontinue their intermarriage with the other groups (centripetal movement is indicated) and isolate themselves from the common stock, with further effects, —either their numerical decrease and extinction, or their further growth which may result in an overgrowth and parasitizing. In Table VI a special case is shown,—a particularized group falls under an heterethnical influence, begins to intermarry with the foreigners, and finally incorporates them. As soon as the functional types, needed for the differentiated social groups A and B, become exhausted, the other functional types, less adapted for the particular social functions, begin to penetrate as substitutes of the properly adapted types, which naturally results in a functional weakening of the ethnical unit as a whole. In this way, without any internal disturbances and without any change of the primary and tertiary milieus, nor any formation of new "mutations", the process of change of the average population may occur. However, practically such a process is usually followed by a secondary re-adaptation of the ethnical unit as a whole, with its natural effect upon the interethnical equilibrium.

———

In Series V I show a special case of interethnical relations,—a parasitizing ethnical unit (it may be a socially differentiated unit as well)[*], here shown in red colour, first appears among the upper right unit. Under favourable conditions it multiplies rather fast. However, it produces strong negative reaction on the part of the object of parasi-

———

[*] As I have shown (vide "Etnos", 1923, pp. 100-105 and mentioning in "Ethnical Unit and Milieu", 1924, p. 24) the relations between ethnical units living in the same territory, may assume three forms, namely, those of co-operation, commensalism, and parasitism. In the last case the effects are evident. The parasite is living on account of another ethnical unit, thus it cannot multiply beyond a certain limit which depends on the size of the unit on which the parasites live, and forms of adaptation of both subject and object of parasitism.

I. FORMATION OF ETHNICAL UNITS AND INTERETHNICAL PRESSURE

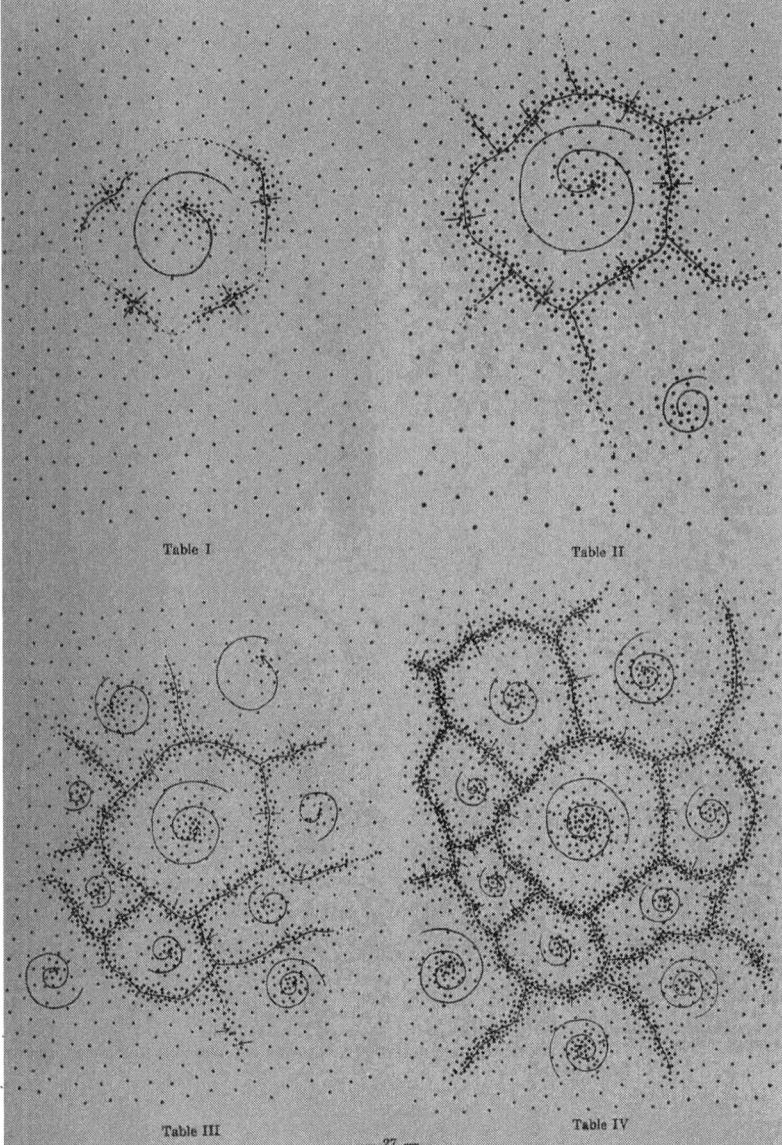

Table I

Table II

Table III

Table IV

II. INTEGRATION AND DISINTEGRATION OF ETHNICAL UNITS.

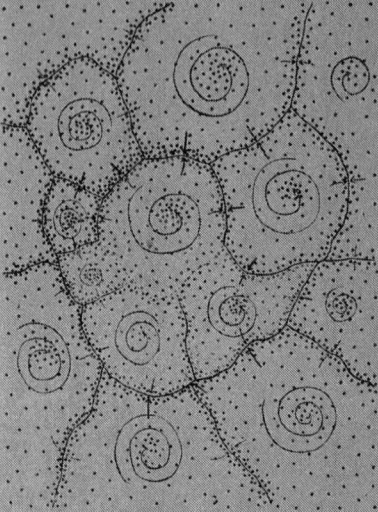

Table I

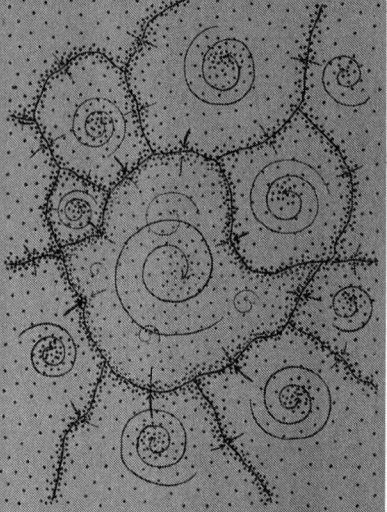

Table II

Table III

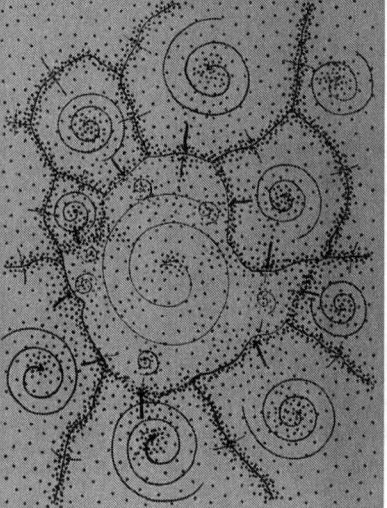

Table IV

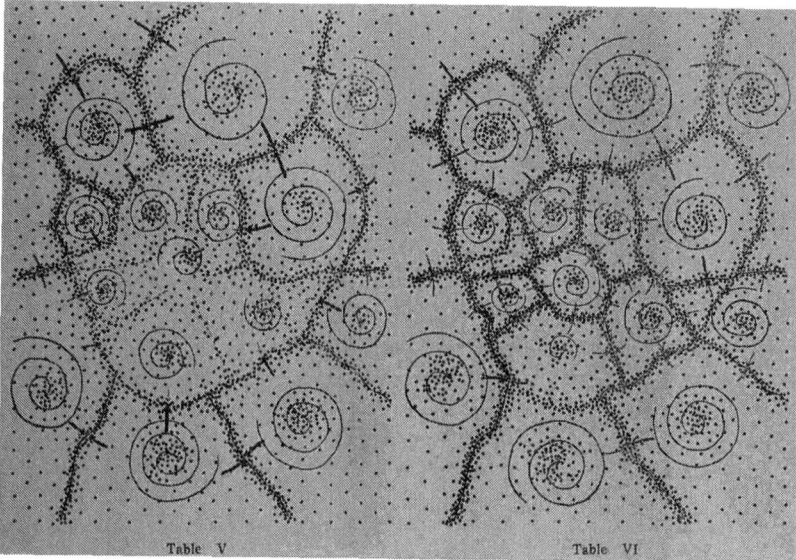

Table V   Table VI

tism which "surrounds" it and pushes out. The parasite spreads among the neighbouring units which do not allow it to settle and assimilate it. But the parasite succeeds in settling among the upper left unit which produces no strong negative reaction, in spite of a marked ethnocentric behaviour of the parasite. Owing to a non-resistance, the parasite begins to increase which finally affects the unit-object to such a degree that it loses its power of increase of population. Decrease of population and consequently increase of the interethnical pressure, even partial occupation of the territory by the neighbours, ensue the process. Then the parasite leaves the territory by breaking a passage into the territory of the neighbouring unit, numerous and strong, but possessing no sufficient power of resistance to the penetration of the parasite. This may be due to a disfunction of the psychomental complex, special interethnical pressure and other "causes". The other units by this time are strongly consolidated, even though the upper-left one with a loss of population and territory, and they produce a very strong pressure on the lately affected unit owing to the change of the system of interethnical pressure (new equilibrium).

Mutatis mutandis the same scheme may be applied to a single ethnical unit in which a social differentiation is found in such an advanced stage that the centrifugal movement takes over the centripetal movement and from social groups, typical ethnical units may be formed. Practically this is the case of over-growth of an ethnographic element which loses its functional weight in the system of cultural (adaptive) equilibrium* and results in the formation of a parasitizing social group. Doubling of social functions is especially harmful for both object of parasitizing and social parasite.

———

Series VI deals with the spreading, and its consequences, of influence of a leading ethnical unit (or a group of them). The initial conditions of units are shown in Series III, Table VI. The process is effectuated through a continuous and always peaceful penetration of individuals and groups of individuals into the regions of neighbours who imitate the invaders. Gradually the invaders' lang-

* For instance, an over-growth of social groups such as those attending to the legal matters (lawyers), to the government ("politicians"), to the exchange and credit (bankers), to the aesthetic needs ("artists"). An over-growth may affect any branch of cultural differentiation, e.g. advertizing, "research work", police, newspapers, etc. It may be pointed out that such an over-growth is only rarely associated with the governmental apparatus which is too evidently seen. However, in the normally functioning units the process of over-growth of social groups is usually checked up. In a contrary case a collapse of the unit in the system of interethnical milieu or an internal collapse are very likely to occur. Naturally one of the first sufferers is the parasite which either may be or may not be perceived.

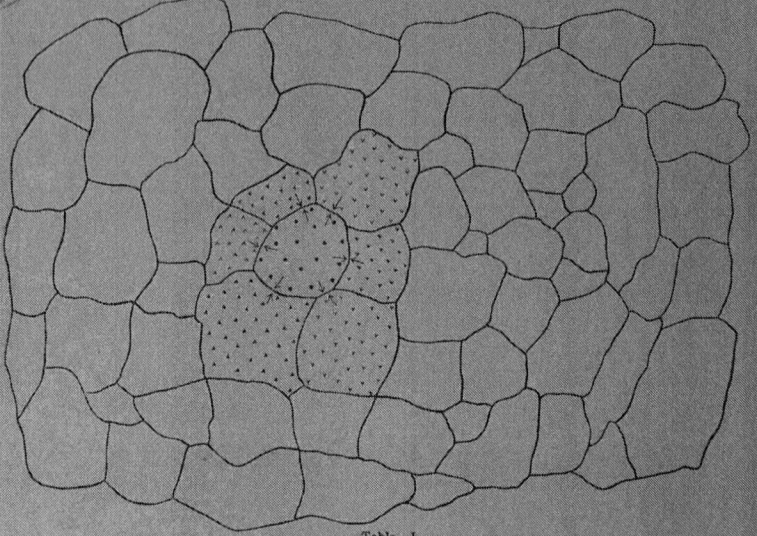

Table I

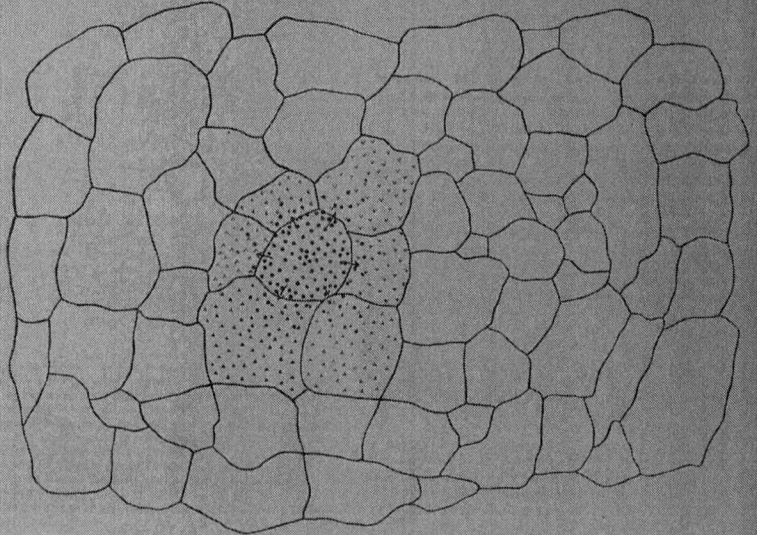

Table II

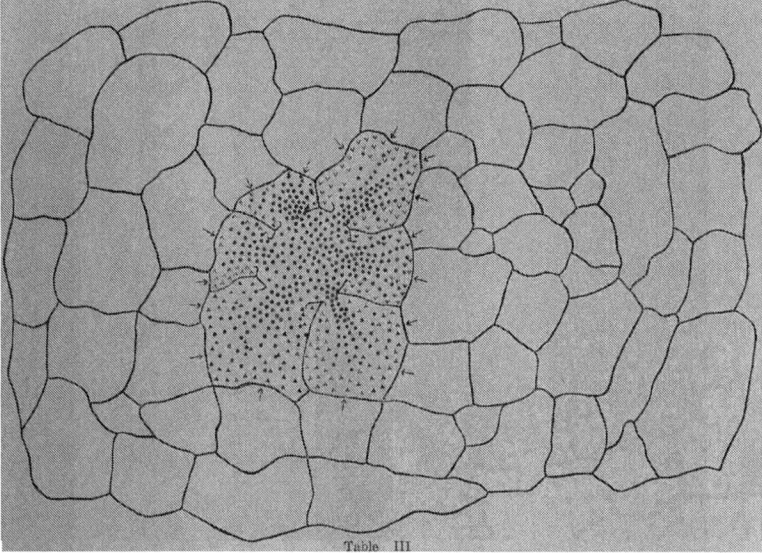

Table III

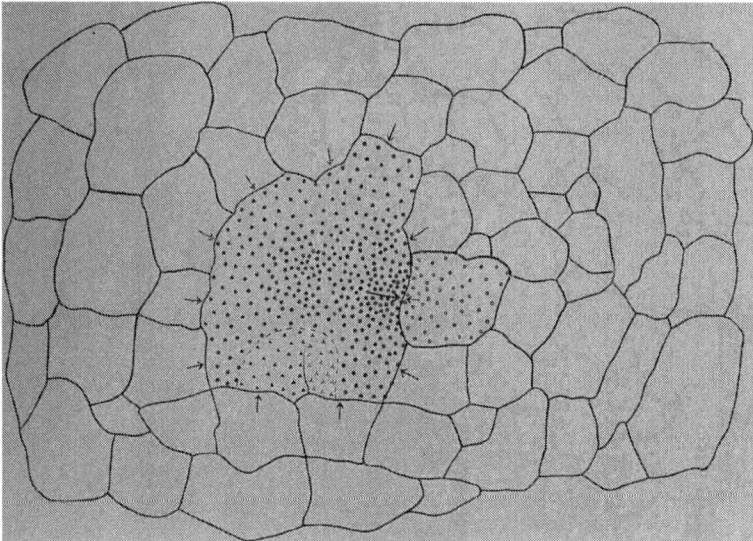

Table IV

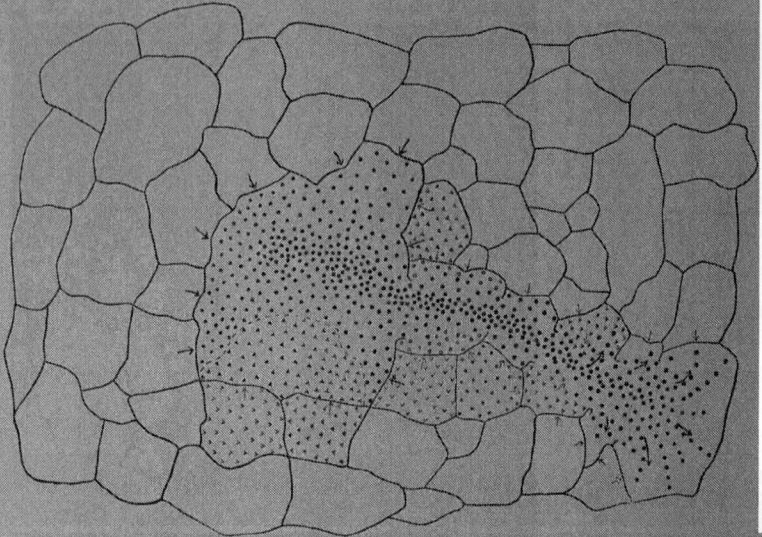

Table V

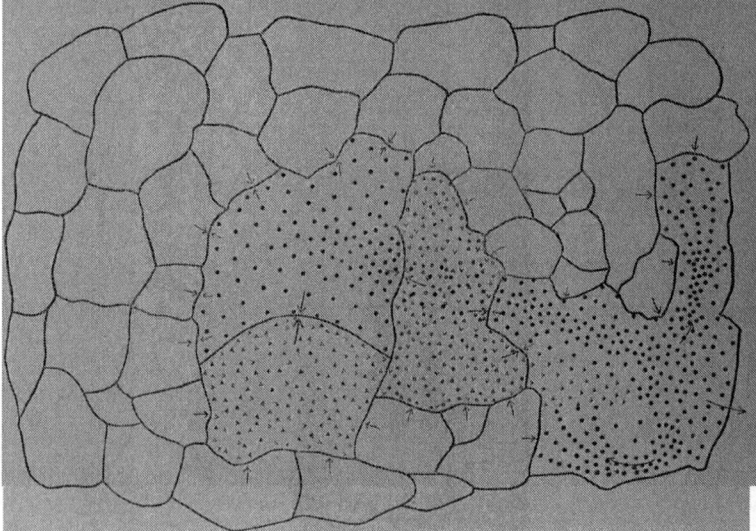

Table VI

IV. SOCIAL SELECTIVE DIFFERENTIATION

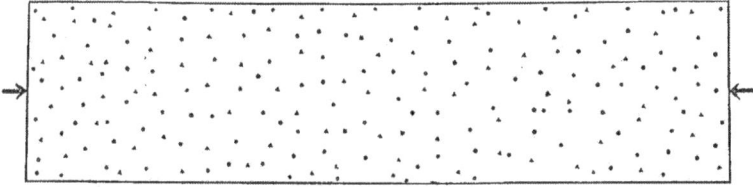

Table I

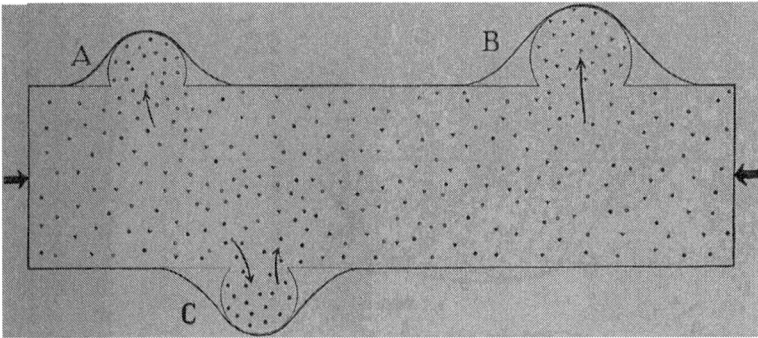

Table II

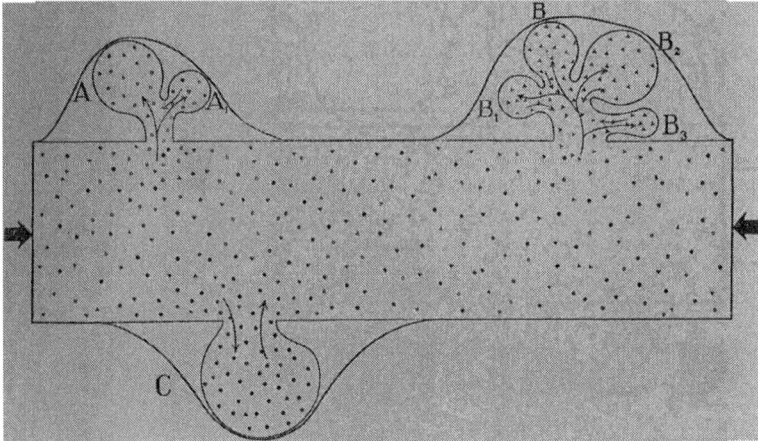

Table III

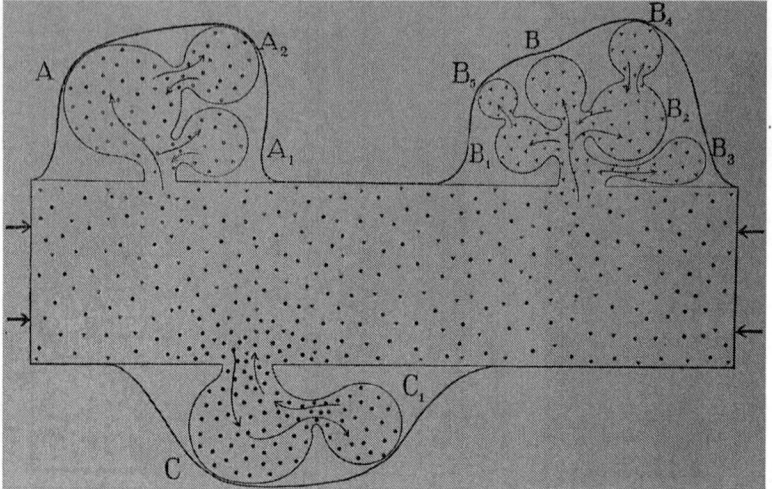

Table IV

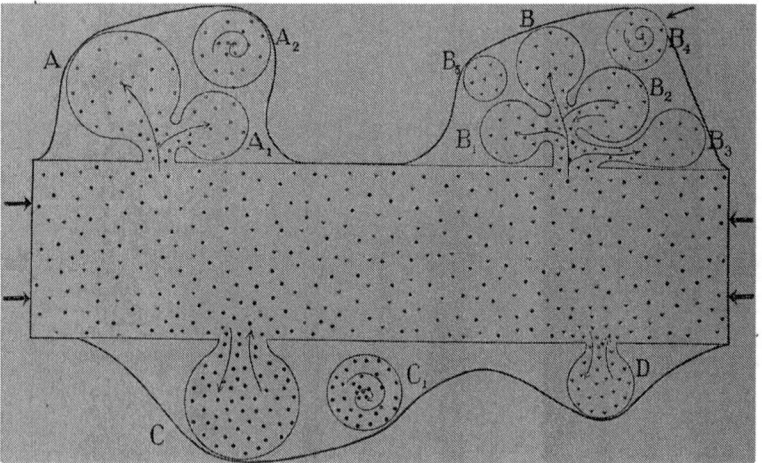

Table V

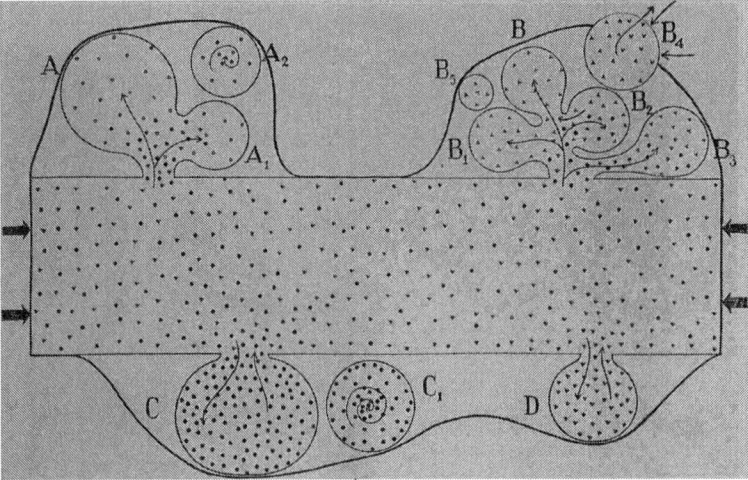

Table VI

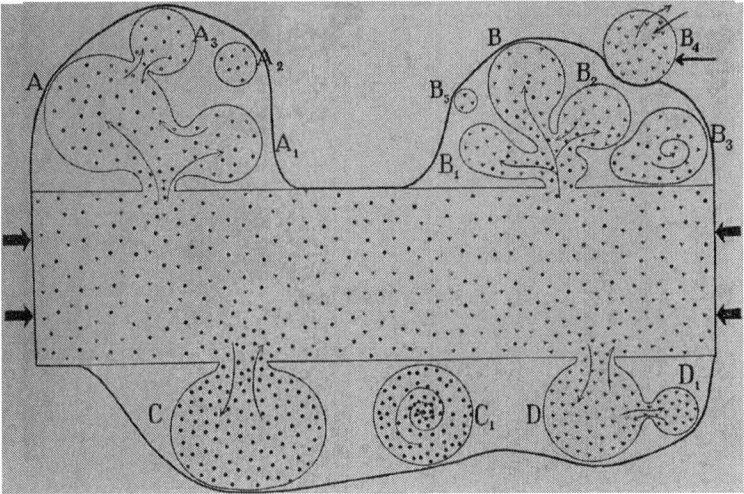

Table VII

V. PARASITIZING AND MIGRATING ETHNICAL UNIT.

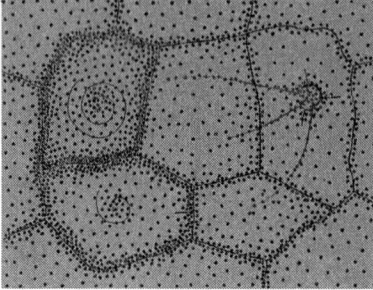

Table I

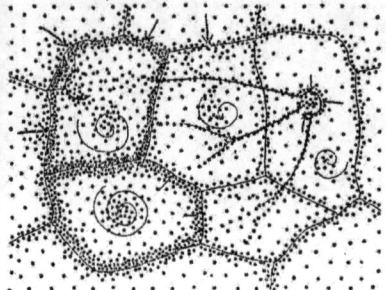

Table II

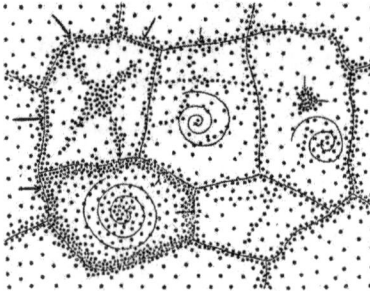

Table III

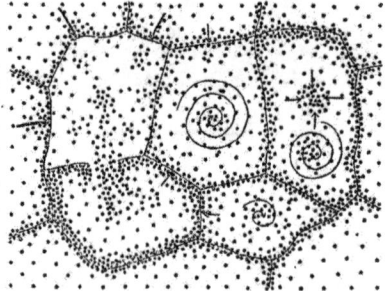

Table IV

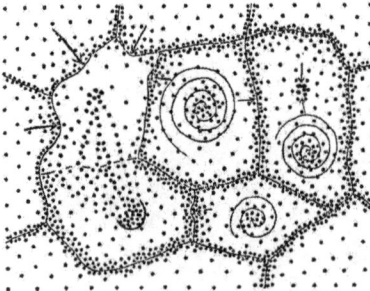

Table V

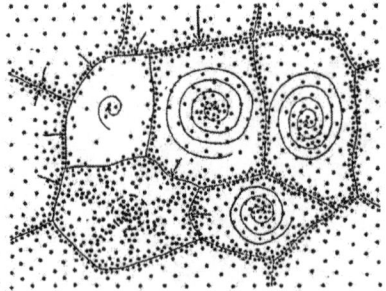

Table VI

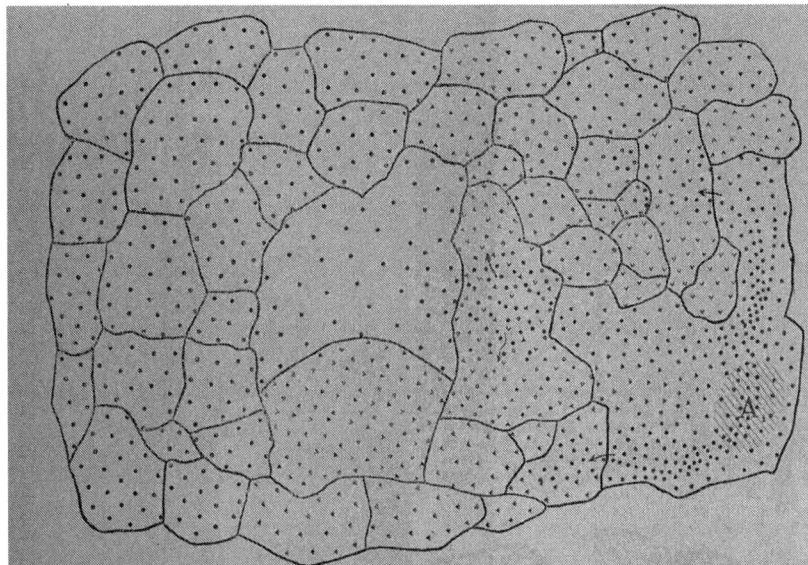

Table I

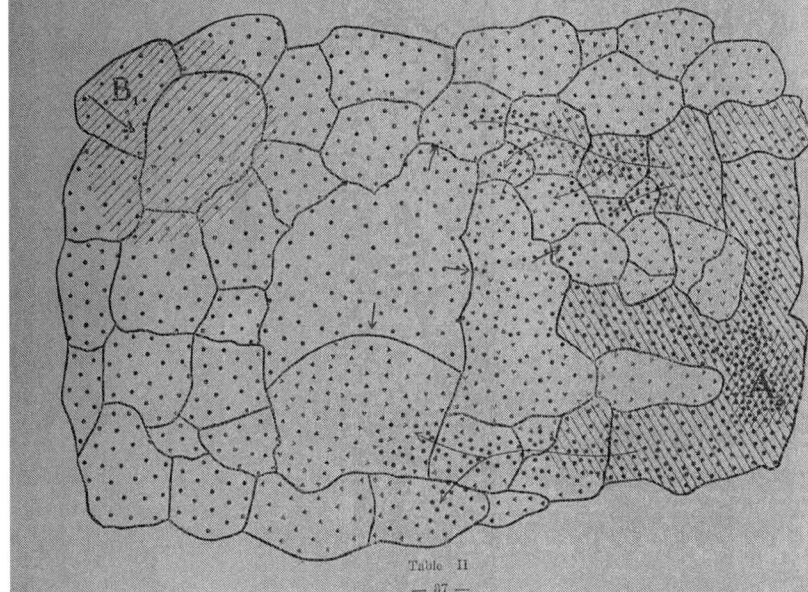

Table II

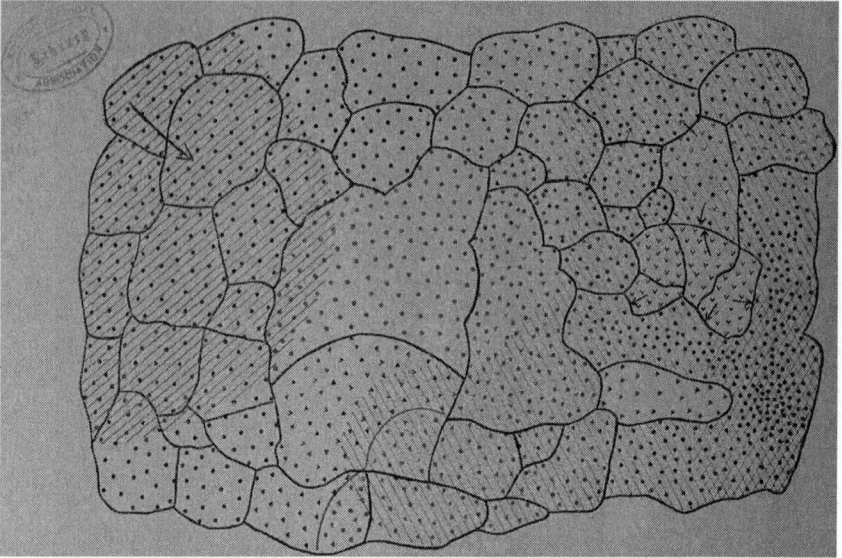

Table III

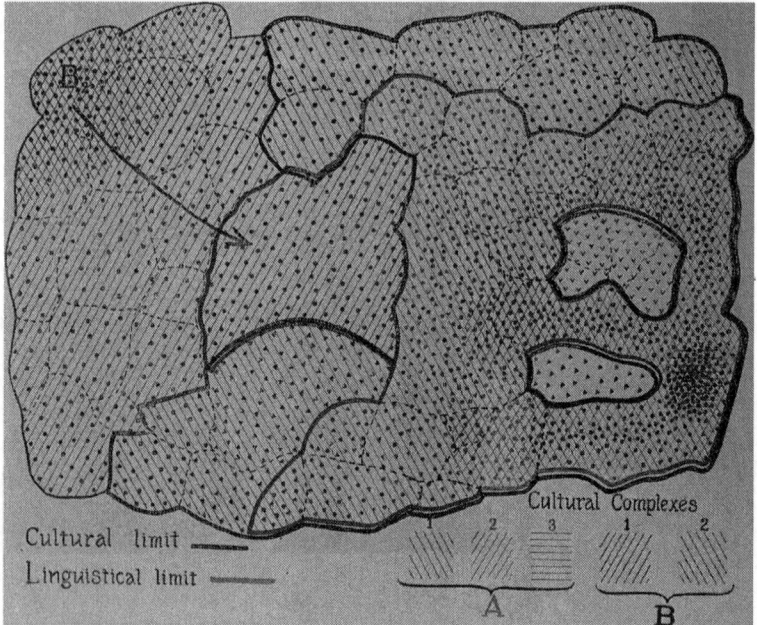

Cultural Complexes

Cultural limit ————
Linguistical limit ————

Table IV
— 38 —

usage in its pure and modified forms is adopted and adapted, which here is shown by change of the colour (red instead of black). In this way the groups and dialects are formed as a "linguistic family"[*]. The leading ethnical unit creates its own cultural complex (first shading in red, Table I) which gradually spreads over neighbouring groups and sometimes passes far over the linguistical limits of a "family". However, some groups (units) cannot be linguistically assimilated and they cannot accept the new cultural complex (it may be due to the conditions of primary milieu, a better local adaptation, a strong opposition to the pressure, etc.) here designated in black and without red shading. A group which originally was the initial point of growth and migration (Series III) of the leading ethnical unit, remains beyond the cultural influence of its own offsprings, bearers of the process of leading ethnos. This group gradually falls under a strong cultural influence of another "cycle" which approaches it from the upper-left corner here designated as black shading. In the last Table IV, I show a final result of these processes, namely, an overlapping of cultural complexes, including languages, covering populations which greatly differ as to their physical origin, in some cases remaining rather "pure.' (anthropolo-

* Of course, this is not the only way to form a "family".

gically), while in other cases being mixtures of quite distinct types.

The above given schemes of ethnical phenomena naturally are abstractions. What we commonly observe are combinations of the processes, such as for instance, integration and disintegration connected with a differential growth of population, change of centripetal and centrifugal movements under variable interethnic pressure, sometimes overlapped by a diffusion of cultural complexes, affected by the internal social differentiation and not rarely by the parasitizing ethnical and social groups. Therefore it is evident that these phenomena must always be investigated as complex realities of equilibria. Social phenomena, various cultural movements, political clashes, wars, internal collapses etc. cannot be functionally understood unless one considers biological (in a narrow sense of the word) conditions of populations involved, primary milieu, interethnical milieu, internal equilibria of centripetal and centrifugal movements within the units which, let us point out, do not sometimes complete the process of "crystallization" and even cannot reach such a state, for the achievement of a perfect "crystallization" often means collapse of the whole system. These are processes.

CHAPTER III

MATERIAL GATHERED AND ANALYSED

8. AUTHOR'S APPROACH TO THE INVESTIGATION The Tungus and Manchu psychomental complexes in so far as their general character is concerned do not differ from what may be observed elsewhere. These are differences in the forms and systems. However, in so far as gathering of facts and analysing are concerned perhaps they are still more difficult to comprehend for they are greatly influenced by the systems which are very distinct as compared with the European complex, e.g. the Chinese and Mongol complexes. Not very much has been done up to the present time in their description. The facts are rather scarce. Although the Manchus were known for centuries we have only some translations of "religious" texts by Ch. de Harlez, L. Langlès and very few facts recorded by the travellers, e.g. R. Maack who visited the Manchus on the banks of the Amur River. The greatest part of the Manchu literature consists in translations from Chinese and thus as such they do not belong to the original Manchu complex. There are some other publications on the Manchu "religious" system, but since these deal with the Manchus living in Peking who were for a long time under Chinese influence they cannot be considered as reliable material for giving a picture of the Manchu complex. As to other Tungus groups we are richer in the material related to the psychomental complex. These data were gathered by travellers and special investigators who made their important contributions during the XVIIIth and XIXth centuries. Here we may point out several names: S. Brail-

ovskiĭ published his observation on the Udehe; V. P. Margaritov and I. A. Lopatin on the Oroči; P.P. Šimkevič and I.A. Lopatin on the Goldi; K.M. Ryčkov on the Enissy Tungus; L. von Schrenck on different groups of the Amur River region; and at last W. Jochelson on Tungus groups of the Yakutsk Government, living in contact with the Yukagirs. A scattered number of facts are in the works of travellers and investigators as J. G. Georgi, P. S. Pallas, J. G. Gmelin, and especially M. A. Castrèn, A. Th. von Middendorff, and R. Maack. However, the facts published do not form detailed descriptions of the psychomental complex, but they are brought by these investigators rather like illustrations of differences between the complexes of the observers and those of the groups observed. The facts are not systematized except in the works by P.P. Šimkevič and I.A. Lopatin, and only partly by L. Sternberg who was not familiar with the Tungus language. In these works the Goldi system of spirits is treated, but the theoretical premises did not permit these authors to have represented the system of spirits in the Goldi complex.

Generally one of the great difficulties of these investigations was the fact that the investigators did not know the native languages.[*] The works here mentioned

* In so far as I know, K. M. Ryčkov was familiar with the Tungus dialect of the group investigated by him. However, his theoretical background was not solid enough to enable him to carry out an extensive and scientific investigation. I.A. Lopatin possessed some knowledge of the Goldi language but it was not sufficient for a

were not all published at the moment when my own investigations began (1912). So, for instance, those by I. A. Lopatin, K. M. Ryčkov, and W. Jochelson have been published much later. Owing to the character of the previous publications as well as those which have appeared since completion of the field-work, and owing to the scarcity of the facts, I shall not use these publications as a basis and shall refer only in the cases of evident reliability of records. I shall refer to these publications chiefly for the illustration of the reactions of observers*.

In so far as familiarity with the Tungus complex was concerned my own position at the beginning of my investigations among the Tungus was nearly the same as that of any other investigator. However, after coming into close contact with the Tungus and especially after mastering Tungus language, when I could understand and speak Tungus, my position was entirely changed for I could directly penetrate into the Tungus complex. Still, I had to overcome another difficulty, namely, to enter into the Tungus complex for looking at the facts from a Tungus point of view. It was not easy before the fundamental conceptions became familiar to me; the gathering of the facts was done in such a manner that the facts might be received by the observer without any conclusions at the spot, and without approaching the Tungus mentality as "inferior" and "primitive". So the facts, the opinions and ideas, were recorded without commentaries, but the cases of possible misunderstanding were checked up several times and usually recorded in Tungus: all Tungus notions were understood in the Tungus system and mind, in the Tungus complex.

Here I feel that I need to pause on the problem of my own attitude towards the material investigated, and the way how I have come to the study of Tungus in general, which will be historic in its nature, and partly autobiographic in form.

My original scientific interests were directed to the general problem which at that time might be called "philosophy of history", i.e. what much later came out in my formulation as mechanisms of ethnical and ethnographic variations. Beginning from the study of sociology, economics, and history, in a narrow sense, I have gradually shifted to the problems of population, ethnography, "prehistory", and at last anthropology ("physical") which also involved on my part a special preparation in biological sciences. After extending the scope of my interest, I came to the idea of working as a trial on two problems,

thorough investigation into the psychomental complex of the Goldi. M. A. Castren, whose knowledge of the language could be easily extended, did not remain a long time amongst the Tungus.

* There are some recent publications indirectly concerning Tungus psychomental complex. Some of them have reached me, but most of them I know only from the reviews. In spite of the fact that they are recent and from the theoretical point of view they might be up to date, they are carried out with a practical view,—to turn the Tungus from their "superstitions" to the credo of "scientific socialism", "dialectic materialism" and other elements of the non-Tungus complex and thus to denationalize them as few decades ago the Orthodox missionaries did by converting the Tungus to Christianity. Another aim of these investigations is to find new support for the theory of evolution of human society which according to the theoreticians of socialism must fatally come to the economic and social system which is preferred by these theoreticians. Owing to these unscientific conditions the recent publications, which are as a rule carefully revised by the governmental agents, can be used only with great caution.

namely, (1) the problem of parallelism of Magdalenian art and culture in general with that of Palaeasiatic groups of Siberia; (2) the problem of forms and material of arrows in correlation with the material used and technical purpose of this weapon. Those problems brought me into the Museum of Anthropology and Ethnography of the Imperial Academy of Sciences at St. Petersburg, the director of which, W.W. Radloff, after some four to five months of my work in this museum proposed to me to begin some field work and to study some languages according to my choice, namely, Samoyed, or Dravidian, or Tungus. Although I did not think of myself as a field worker, especially in a new branch of languages, in principle I accepted W. W. Radloff's proposition trusting him that I could try myself in a field work and particularly in the little known languages. Yet, by that time this idea responded to my desire of coming into direct contact with some living material in order to receive new facts and especially a concrete idea of non-European groups. I did not hesitate as to the choice between three groups, the most interesting being in my eyes Tungus, according to my knowledge at that time, less influenced by other ethnical groups of the so called "civilized mankind", and less known than Samoyeds and Dravidians who had been already studied by a great number of investigators*.

The first contact with the ethnographical realities greatly supported my earlier critical attitude as to the methods of investigation and primarily as to the methods of observation and recording what was seen and heard. I very soon found by practically ascertaining myself that various theories, with which I was familiar, went to pieces in touch with realities; that the pictures of "primitive people" were quite artificial, that the only way to investigate Tungus was to gather material without selection of facts, to try to understand the people investigated, and to adapt myself to the Tungus milieu by becoming friendly, i.e. to look at the things from their point of view and not from the point of view of protective behaviour, of feeling of immeasurable superiority. The practical consequences were enormous in the sense of remodelling my own attitude and my own behaviour,—I soon discovered that these Tungus in some respects were much superior to myself in so far as local adaptation was concerned. Yet, my lack of knowledge of their language was not in my favour as a representative of a "superior" culture. I had to learn; and this could be done only with the help of the Tungus themselves. The best way was thus to explain the real purpose of my living among them, to show them the practical importance of studying their life, and conditions, as well as language, as a way to show to the Russians that the Tungus must not be disturbed,—to make them understood by the Russians.** In this sense I was successful,—I was never

* I shall not here repeat what has been already written by me, in the Foreword to my SONT, as to the order of investigations, persons and institutions with which I was connected at that time. The "field work" began in 1912 and continued with interruptions up to 1918.

** As a matter of fact, such was the attitude of the local superior administrators who wanted to have more accurate knowledge of these groups in order to preserve them, as a useful economic factor of the little-peopled regions. This humanistic approach to the non-Russian population was not something new, but the local high administration could not easily find the investigators at the spot, while a great number of "scientific investigators" were chiefly interested in two things, namely, criticism of administration and scaffolding of hypotheses with the facts picked up here and there.. I had heard such

lacking various kinds of information and the good will of the Tungus to teach me. For them it was evident that I had no bad intentions as to them and I was not treating them as "savages", so that I could understand them. Indeed, such an attitude towards myself implied a change in my behaviour and also that of my wife,—we should observe their customs and avoid any personal or group offense, e.g. with taking notes in the society meeting, to "investigate" them, and especially to torture them with "questions".* When such relations were established, the rumour about our travelling among the Tungus spread far away and the Tungus groups were waiting for our arrival. Owing to this we did not need to repeat every time from the very beginning our behaviour for establishing good relations. The same was repeated in Manchuria but in more difficult conditions. In fact, at our first meeting with the Tungus of Manchuria I had to find out new ways of explaining to them the purpose of our visit. In spite of the fact that we were foreigners on Chinese territory, I succeeded in explaining to them, as I would do with any "civilized" people, and I was understood. Since it was so, the work went on quite smoothly. More than this, the Tungus carefully reported to me all gossip about ourselves picked up from the Chinese and Mongol petty authorities, and even local petty officials among the Russian settlers.** In this way we could avoid a great number of difficult situations and gather a great number of facts as to interethnical relations. In fact, one of the interesting items of Tungus confessions were their relations and attitudes towards other ethnical groups, naturally including Russians.

I do not need to add that owing to the character of the Tungus (vide SONT Ch. VIII) it was not difficult to create not only socially good relations, but also in some cases very friendly personal relations which permitted, in some cases,

quite intimate and very personal inquiries, without producing any harm to the friendship.

Indeed, these conditions of work made it difficult from another side, namely, I could not regulate the flow of facts for keeping immediate record of them, and naturally I could not refuse to accept the facts since they were coming to me from friendly behaving people. However, this difficulty for a field-worker was a pleasant one.

The conditions of work among the Manchus were different in the sense that with their experience in "politics" the Manchus had many more difficulties in understanding my attitude towards themselves. So for establishing perfectly convenient relations there was needed a much greater number of people and with the Manchu complex natural attitude of distrust and cautiousness, it was still more difficult to extend necessary relations over all Manchus met.* Even under these much less favourable conditions, after a certain readaptation, it was possible to gather the material needed.

This description of the history of investigation on the one hand explains the large (for a relatively short period of field work) body of facts recorded, and on the other hand it shows how owing to the creation of close contact with the populations investigated, I have come to the idea of a different approach to these populations needed for the investigation itself.

9. MATERIAL   Naturally Tungus mentality and psychology is strongly manifested in the folklore understood in a broad sense of the term. Since I am introducing distinction of "folklore in a broad sense" opposed to that "in a narrow sense," I need to explain myself. Once I had occasion to express my point of view as to the folklore** in the sense that folklore of an ethnical group, as a functional phenomenon, is the psychomental complex as it is cognized and reflected in a system of symbols (and starters) in the form of: (1) explanation of milieu (including myths), (2) recorded historic facts (annals, epic poems, anecdotes etc.), (3) short formulation of experience (sayings, proverbs etc.), (4) stories and other forms (riddles etc.), satisfying the need of mental work, (5) creations satisfying the creative complex (e.g. poetry, fairy stories, etc.). The subjects of folklore are

"A. The complex of encyclopedic knowledge regarding the facts and mechanisms of the

1. Primary milieu: animals (including man), plants, inorganic world, the world-as-whole, etc. (later, anatomy, botany, astronomy, meteorology, etc.).

2. Secondary milieu: organization and functions of society, technology, psychomental complex as a whole (and in its elements).

---

complaints on the part of high administrators, the full meaning of which became clear to me only when my own work was completed. Some of these administrators told me that they were asking for practical advice as to what should be done to these populations; but most of the investigators could formulate nothing except meaningless impractical general statements. Here it may be noted that many of these administrators greatly encouraged local research societies. Such were e.g. several governor-generals of Eastern Siberia (in Irkutsk) beginning from Count Muraviev-Amurskiĭ, governor-generals of the Far East (in Khabarovsk) ending with N.L. Gondatti, who himself was known by his ethnographical and anthropological works; a great number of governors and vice-governors, whom I personally knew, were greatly interested in these problems, e.g. in Transbaikalia, Amur and Maritime governments.

* Some travellers with great pride say how many hours they spent pressing their victims with stupid questions learnt from "questionnaires" and books. Cf. e.g. L. Sternberg "Divine Election". He naturally had a great number of imitators of his "school".

** As a matter of fact, the most amusing stories were told to the Tungus, so they had to explain what I was actually doing; sometimes they wondered how these petty officials could not understand. When we were living in a Tungus Birarčen village on the Amur River, the local authorities told the Tungus that our aim was to gather Tungus together, to form from them a Tungus regiment under my command for Russia needed (1916) many troops for fighting Germans. As an example of Tungus attitude another fact is curious: in 1917 when the revolution broke out we were arrested, in a train of the Amur Railway on our way to Transbaikalia, as "bearers of old regime"; the Tungus who travelled with us (a Birarčen) refused to leave us alone with the new authorities and as final conclusion as to their activity he told us: "In fact, these new authorities are more stupid than the pettiest officials of the new Chinese Government" (that of Chang Tso-lin). Indeed, I could not defend new authorities and I did agree with the Tungus.

* The work among them may be better compared with that carried out among the groups of European complex. Here, by the way, I may point out that the methods of approach of European groups naturally must be different. Generally, the method of approach, in my eyes, is not something absolutely fixed; there are different methods. I admit that in some cases the only way of investigation is the method of negative reactions. So that the above description is not a kind of an ethnographic panacea. The ethnographer must adapt himself to the individual characters of the units under investigation.

** Cf. my notes to R. D. Jameson "Three lectures on Chinese folklore", Peking 1932, pp. 146-149, on "Function of Folklore" and "Science of Folklore".

3. Tertiary milieu: phenomena of interethnical milieu and relations between the groups and the given unit.

4. Phenomena of the psychomental complex.

B. Complex of functions manifested:

1. Previous ethnical experience (narrative and formulae).

2. Manifestations of emotive complex

    a. Mental exercise.

    b. Rhythm in all forms.

    c. Complex of the so called instincts.

Naturally, the complexes of knowledge and of manifested functions overlap each other."

Such a definition of folklore is deprived of its subjective condition; namely, how the ethnical unit behaves in reference to its own creation, how it uses it and what is the investigator's attitude towards the folklore of the given unit. In fact, if we introduce this element then there will be no possibility of comparing folklore of different groups and there will be introduced a quite arbitrary selection of facts by the investigator. From the European point of view some observations as to the animals, gathered among non-European groups, for a long time seemed to be a product of mere imagination of "primitive mind" and they were classed as "folklore." However, with the extension of knowledge into the field of psychology and mentality of the animals among the Europeans, a great number of these "stories" appears in a new light,—they are a record of facts and quite sound generalizations, and as such they cannot be included into the "folklore." So that the behaviour of the European mind towards the "primitive people" and its ultra-scepticism were ethnographic in their nature, they were "folkloristic" themselves.

Here is another case. The theory of creation of species by God and subsequent geological catastrophes developed by Cuvier, at his time was quite logical and simple as to the formulation of accumulated facts. However, in the eyes of the present generation this theory now begins to come out as a form (not always cognized) of European interpretative folklore of the beginning of the nineteenth century; while, for instance, cosmogony of the Middle Ages is already fixed as mediaeval folklore regardless of whether it was created by the most learned scholastic scholars or by the ignorant farmers. We may say that the theory of evolution with its teleological background as it was practised, professed, in the European universities in the middle of the nineteenth century, in the eyes of the present generation being styled a "scientific theory," in the eyes of later generations will appear in its real form of European folklore of a given period. Yet, we may say a priori that the same attitude will be that of the further generations towards the most advanced science of our days. However, no mediaeval scholar would admit that his theories were folk-stories, just as Cuvier would not do so, and the biologists of the nineteenth century would be reluctant to admit their work as folkstories, but they will be so understood by younger coming generations. The basis of this attitude is a strong belief in the difference between "science" as knowledge of realities and method, on the one hand, and "folk imagination" crystallized in "folklore" (used in a common sense).

Here is a third case. The scaffolding of the theories of primitive mentality, prelogism etc. as they come from the pen of talented Europeans is accepted as scientific operation but the coming generation who will be more familiar with the "primitive people" will regard these theories as a European reaction on alien complexes, interpretative folklore serving as justification of European aggressiveness, bringing light of civilization to the people living in darkness of ignorance.

The given instances are sufficient for illustrating my idea, although I have not touched still more striking instances. Some of these are "economics"—a post factum justification of realities; and especially some "philosophy"— a particularly ethnographic and folkloristic (in my sense) reaction, both individual and ethnical, on the conflict between the existing ethnical cultural complexes on the one hand, new facts and suppositions, guesses as to the existence of other facts, on the other hand. However, neither "economists", nor "philosophers" would agree that they are creators, bearers of folklore,—they believe that they are doing something which is far out of range of mere and simple ethnographical functioning in an ethnical complex; most of them are speaking not less than in the name of God, Eternity, Absolute Spirit, Scientific Truth etc.

However, as soon as we introduce reaction of the ethnical unit on the existing folklore into the definition of what is folklore and what is not folklore the situation changes,—in the eyes of mediaeval scholast his conception of the world was a scientific truth or at least a scientific hypothesis. Biblical history was taken as a fact, while the stories about the gnomes and fairies were rejected as pagan "superstitions" and folklore.

The ethnical units always differentiate their folklore into the groups of the above indicated five forms with various degrees of truthfulness as reflexion and explanations of realities. When a story is told for satisfying action of the emotive complex it would not be always considered as "truth", just as great number of symbols are treated merely as symbols and not as realities, but sometimes they may be treated as "truth". A love song which cannot be excluded from folkloristic manifestions, unless we adopt quite an artificial classification, is never regarded as "truth", but is regarded in absolutely the same manner as among the so called "civilized nations". So that in so far as the reaction on folklore is concerned, the attitude of the creators of this folklore ought to be considered; thus a fairy story, love song, etc. should not be regarded as reflexions of "naturphilosophie" of the people, and their conception of the world.

As to the outer form in which the folklore is inserted, whether it is a rhymed and rhythmed poem, or rhythmed prose, a history-like "story", or story-like history, it is of secondary importance, but there is an important character in folklore which distinguishes it from individual creation, it has ethnic character, i.e. it is adopted by the ethnical unit and *it has thus more or less stabilized forms in which it is* transmitted. Indeed, the existence of written language, which contributes to the preservation of authors' names, makes this formal distinction quite elusive, but the negative sign, i.e. loss of the inventor's name, cannot be taken as a distinctive character of folklore, so that when an author's creation becoming a folkloristic piece is recorded, it does not lose its folkloristic character. Here the investigator must rely upon his familiarity with the complex for distinguishing where he deals with a personal creation which did not receive and cannot receive ethnical recognition and where he deals with a personal creation which is incorporated into the folkloristic complex.

Here thus I introduce two limitations for "folklore in a narrow sense of the term" mentioned at the beginning of the present section, namely, the folklore is not recognized as representing truth by the owner (ethnical unit) and it is preserved in fixed forms. However, from the European point of view there will be included everything in the folklore which in European eyes may appear as folklore as opposed to the "true knowledge" and "science".

Since in gathering material we cannot put a sharp line of demarcation between what is considered as "truth" and "imagined story"—the opinion of owners being sometimes uncertain—I shall now express the Tungus point of view as to the material recorded, and gathered.

Among the Manchus there are very sharply distinguished two cases,—namely, the true story *wuneyi baita* (Man. Sp. corr. *unengi baita* Man. Writ.),—"true case (affair)"; and *fūyu* (Man. Sp.),—the "fairy" stories, an imaginative story. Indeed, historic books like the well known novel *"Ilan gurun bitxe"*—the "Book of Three Kingdoms" translated from the famous Chinese work,—the histories of Great Leao, Kin etc. are considered as *wuneyi baita*, but the term *suduri*,—"the history",—is rarely used. On the other hand, the books like those translated from Chinese as for instance (聯齋合壁) *lao-ji-jy-i*, are considered as doubtful and half-true. It is very interesting that *Nišan Saman*, a description of a case (*vide infra*) under the Ming Dynasty is considered as *wuneyi baita* only by those Manchus, who preserve their faith in the shamans. "*Teptalin*", an enormous epic poem, which I have recorded from the mouth of an old woman, is considered as *fūyu*, although it deals with the facts supposed to be historic, of war between the Manchus and Northern Tungus. The Birarčen assert that *Teptalin* is not *fūyu*, but a true historic record. Indeed, all translations from Chinese as to the geographical and naturalistic descriptions, in spite of their occasional "phantastic character" are believed to be *wuneyi baita*. Indeed, the lists of spirits of different clans are considered as a true reflexion of the reality. In dealing with this material one must thus find out the Manchu attitude towards these sources.

Indeed, besides the above mentioned epic poem the Manchus are very rich in "true affair" and "stories" orally transmitted and preserved. In a great number of these specimens of their folklore it sometimes is impossible to say what may be the Manchu attitude, and they themselves after listening to a story may ask the question; *èr wuneyi baita? fūyu?*, i.e. "It is a true story or a fairy story?" The teller's answer sometimes satisfies the questioner, sometimes not, so the listener often establishes his own attitude.

The analysis of the stories not recorded in written form shows that in a great number of them there is a reflexion of the Chinese complex. But there are also stories, like that of the man with three wives quoted by R. D. Jameson (*vide* op cit. p. 124.) in which the subject of the tale is a persecuted mother and her child. This story is met with far from the Manchu area. The circumstances accompanying the story,—for instance, three wives' promises to the husband are well known e.g. in Russian folklore (three sisters!),—are not "Manchu", and the whole construction is only one of combined variations in elements met with among other ethnical groups. Here, as in similar manifestations we have a complex which consists of elements of various origin,

agglutinated by the Manchus, and maintained because of deep psychological reasons, or mere amusing character of the stories, mental exercise, meeting of new situations, wit, etc. There are also stories of local origin built upon the original ground and in an original shape or shaped according to the known patterns.

The same "folklore in a narrow sense" may be approached from a psychological point of view, i.e. how far does it reflect specific Manchu psychomental complex and common "human" psychic conditions?

The Northern Tungus attitude towards their folklore is the same as that of the Manchus: they distinguish the imaginative story—in Birarčen called *ulāyir ~ uliyir*, which ought to be connected with *ulgar ~ uliyer* (Mongol),[*] and historic stories—*n'opti*, i.e. "what was in earlier time". The same distinction is made by the Reindeer Tungus of Transbaikalia. Songs, sayings and true stories [*toyyolkon* (Bir.) *nimnakawn* (Ner.)][**] are separated into special groups.

In the foregoing sections we shall see how the Tungus explain the structure of the world, and here I give a Birarčen *ulāyir* as to the same subject, told to children. This is a translation of a summary of several stories grouped together, and given to me by a Birarčen.

"A long time ago people lived on the earth. They had no *burkan*, nor *malu*, nor shamans. All of them went to heaven. One can now see them in the constellations. The constellation of Orion is called *mayi*. There three large stars form his belt, three small ones are his penis and testes. *Mayi* wants to catch the seven girls (*nadan unil*)—the Pleiades, but on his way there is the wild boar's jaw which bars his way. Near *Mayi* there is an arrow and several bows. Venus, the evening star is a female, and the morning star a male, called *čolpon* is considered *ejan* ["the khan", "chief", "master".] If the morning star cannot be seen it shows that the khan has died. These supposed two stars are khans of all stars. The Polar star—*togolgan*—"the pillar, post", was put on by *buga*. *Buga* blew in a bladder so that the earth remained down and he fixed the pillar in order to support the inflated bladder. The stars are roots of a tree. Between *owlan*[***] and Orion (*mayi*) there were small and big elks (Alces). The small one was killed (by man) and remained on the earth, while the big one is still in the heavens. If the big one should be killed, elks would stay on the earth. On the heavenly lake there is a swan. Formerly swans were not shot. But since this swan was killed it fell down to the earth. When it (swan) makes rounds over the campment and sees men, it cries. It also cries in the heavens. It was shot by *bèjä osekta* ("man star") who was in a canoe. If a man should be ill one prays to *bèjä osekta*. If the star is seen the sick man will recover, if not, the man will die. The people learnt to make bows and arrows, also birch bark canoes by copying what is seen in the sky. The milky way is the road of *mayi*. It is in the middle of the waters in which are found the whole world and earth. According to another version, it is a river with several small tributaries (or channels). The sun starts slowly on horseback; after midday it rides faster on the dog. Accord-

---

[*] However, these Tungus give their own etymology, namely, from *ulôki*-"to lie"-in modifications met with in a great number of Tungus dialects.

[**] P. P. Schmidt gives for Neg. tölungü, tälum compared with tölungu (Olča), telingu (Goldi), tälumučï (Oroč.), but it is not stated what kind of "stories" these are.

[***] Also *dolowon* (from Dahur).

ing to one version, the sun is male and moon is female; they meet once a month. The falling stars mean: *sus'i tiktan* "the souls fall". If it is a big star, it means that an important man (chief) dies. The comets are arrows sent by Venus (two stars),—the khan. *Mayi* and Three Brothers formerly were in the moon."

The adult people do not believe it as a "true story" or real explanation of the sky, but they use the same names for the stars as those in the above given *uläyir*. Indeed, these stories cannot be used as characteristic of the Tungus ideas as to the relations between the celestial bodies.

All Tungus groups have different "moods" when different types of stories are told. If there is a serious mood, the Tungus would not allow the telling of *uläyir*, but they would listen to a teller of *toyyolkon* or *n'opti*. More than this, among the Manchus it is said that those who would tell *jüru* (corr. to *uläyir*) and even listen to them during the day will never be rich. In the same way and for the same reason the telling of *uläyir* is prohibited among the Tungus. There is no need to look for a complex explanation: the true reason is that the telling of such stories is merely considered an idle pastime. The same people during the day time would listen *toyyolkon* of practical importance, and they would not consider it quite useless to listen to a teller of historic stories (*n'opti*). Another attitude will be when the Tungus and in a lesser degree the Manchus, amuse themselves in salty stories and various forms of witticism etc. In this mood the common fairy stories will not satisfy the audience.

The difference in kinds of folk production, grouped as folklore in general, becomes quite evident when there would be considered composition of the group of listeners. In fact, some stories (chiefly, fairy stories) attract only children; others attract women; third attract middle aged people ("natural history", history, hunting etc.); fourth the young men (especially hunters' experiences); fifth all groups except small children, but approaching from different points of view (shamanistic experience.) It is thus evident, that the value, as evidence of the psychomental complex, is not equal in all forms of folklore.

Considering the Tungus and Manchu attitude as to their own folklore it would be perfectly absurd to use folkloristic material in its unclassified form for picturing Tungus ideas in general. So that first what I had to do was to separate what was accepted by the Tungus themselves as expression of their ideas as to the various phenomena of milieus and their own psychomental complex. In the present work I shall use this part of Tungus and Manchu folklore (in my sense), leaving aside what is considered by the Tungus and Manchus as *uläyir* and *jüru*, i.e. "imaginative stories."

The value of the latter is great for a detailed analysis of the psychology of the groups investigated and forms of literary creation, but I shall not at present use this material for it may have only secondary importance for picturing the psychomental complex; as an ethnographical phenomenon it only confirms Tungus and Manchu cultural connexions, both direct and indirect, with various ethnical groups and cultural complexes: the use of this material presumes that it must be first published and supplied with translations and notes. Although this material has already been put in a state for being used by myself, but it has not yet assumed the forms which are needed for publication, so that this material will be later used only for completion of the psychomental complex here treated, let

me add, chiefly from the point of view of psychology of the "unconscious," as it may be sometimes disclosed after a minute analysis of folklore. Before leaving this question I want to give some idea as to the folkloristic material which I have gathered and used for the present work.

The Tungus of Transbaikalia and Manchuria gave me altogether 114 stories of different kinds (fairy stories, history, hunting experience etc.) in English words, about 85,000. In addition to this, twenty stories, 6400 words, were recorded for me by a Birarčen whom I had taught to write his own dialect in transcription; the record is so good that the material can be used; twenty five Tungus and Manchu "shamanistic" texts (prayers etc.) with about 1200 rhythmed lines; certain numbers of Tungus songs; twenty two Manchu stories, about 25,000 words; Manchu poem *Teptalin*, about 20,000 rhythmed lines; also a certain number of shamanistic Manchu written texts, and especially *"Nîsan Saman"* which alone contains over nine thousands Manchu words, without speaking of Manchu written stories (recorded for me by the Manchus) and Manchu literary sources which, it is true, are not of great value for my purpose. More detailed discussion as to this material may be found in the last chapter of Part I.

10. DIRECT ETHNOGRAPHIC OBSERVATIONS Rich as it is, this material is far from including the actual gathered material. The latter consists of direct ethnographic observations. I include here all stories which cannot be formally incorporated into Folklore for either they were individual communications made by the Tungus and Manchus, or they were not always transmitted, or they did not assume one of folkloristic forms. For instance, only a very small part of facts regarding Tungus ideas about milieus could be found in the records of folklore. Indeed, the same is true of spirits, hypotheses and shamanism, the stories about which do not usually assume a definite, or more or less fixed form good for transmission. From the point of view of record, these observations are especially numerous and at the same time the most difficult for I have tried to record in so far as possible every fact. However, a great number of them could not be recorded at all because of (1) shortness of statement confused with other statements; (2) unreliability of the informers; (3) very commonly, impossibility of immediate recording; (4) their character as my too personal "impressions".

The shortness of statement, as for instance, "the wolf is cleverer than the fox", found in a text of a conversation dealing with a different subject may be easily omitted, but if it is repeated several times in similar conditions it is remembered. Some Tungus generalizations ∶ assume a short form of truths well known to the Tungus which do not need to be supported by evidence, and which at the same time perfectly coincide with the "good sense" of the European complex. Indeed, this group of statements is very large and they constitute the main body of acquired knowledge and thinking, but usually they remain unnoticed by the observers because the latter have the same ideas, which seem to be natural, like the air, the breathing of which is not perceived until a different mixture of gases is substituted. When the observer is .looking for exotic elements he naturally does not pay attention to "air". As a matter of fact, the record of all these facts is physically impossible, but it is possible to keep in mind that on specific points no difference was found in approach or in statement which may be noted from time to time*.

In carrying observations one very often finds that a statement is not worthy of record owing to its individual character, personal opinion conditioned by an aberration, wrong information etc. In fact, among the Tungus groups the individuals are not equally equipped with the knowledge of their own complex, and there is also a certain specialization among them, i.e. degree of competence is not the same. Moreover, in some cases one meets with conscious or unconscious liars whose information may have only special interest. However, when the investigation into the essential elements of the complex is completed then it becomes possible and instructive to record the cases of liars. In the same class there may be also included information received from "abnormal" persons, e.g. affected by neurotic and maniacal conditions. The latter are interesting only when one masters the "normal" complex, i.e. practically after a certain period of work in the population investigated**, while these cases must be carefully avoided at the beginning of investigation.

Physical impossibility of immediate record is a very common occurrence in the field work. In fact, a great number of observations are gathered e.g. during travelling when it is physically impossible to write, during darkness, when no light can be used, as in night performances***. The impossibility of recording is especially common when the material is gathered from the conversations. In fact, if the investigator during such a conversation pulls out his note-book to write, the effect would be about the same as that in Europe at a social gathering if one of the guests should pull out his note-book and take notes on the conversation.

Indeed, owing to rather rough manners of Europeans he would be asked as to his notes, would receive a well deserved reprimand, and probably would never be received again, while among the Tungus his tactless behaviour would be observed, probably the subject of conversation would be changed, and the Tungus would in the future abstain from selfexpression in his presence*. Indeed, if the investigator is not merely a "guest," but an official person, his position would not become better, for the Tungus would hesitate to be absolutely frank, and in some cases they would try to be pleasant to the investigator and supply him with the supposed facts**.

I have also mentioned a group of records which I made only in rare cases, i.e. my own personal impressions which in olden days used to form the bulk of travellers' records. I do not deny the value of such impressions. In fact, even in the case when they give no real picture of groups investigated they may be used as an ethnographic picture of the author seen from his reactions on an alien group. Such documents are of interest, but from the point of view of the investigator himself they are of little value, for he cannot directly use them. In spite of this in my diaries I have made some remarks of this kind, their chief purpose being a comparison of impressions received at different periods of investigation. Indeed, some of those "impressions" were subject to the changes which did mark the stages in the process of penetration into the essential of the Tungus complex, which greatly helped a critical analysis of the records themselves.

To the thousands of facts recorded there must be thus added a much greater number of facts which have not formerly been recorded but observed and some groups of which could even be put in the form of generalizations.

The facts contained in documents such as collections, designs, ornaments, photographic and phonographic records, and specimens of materialized manifestations (ethnographical collections) form a special group of materials for the psychomental complex. As a matter of fact, a detailed technological analysis of some specimens of the so called material culture may bring important light as to the mentality of the manufacturers; the specimens of "placings for spirits" (including pictures) may give very important hints as to the Tungus ideas about the spirits; a detailed comparative study of complexes, as for instance, shamanistic paraphernalia, may give important facts, as to the diffusion of some elements and complexes. However, since these collections are beyond my present reach,—all of them being in the Museum of Anthropology and Ethnography of the Russian Academy of Science at St. Petersburg,—I can only partly use this source, viz. in so far as it has found its reflexion in the diary and in so far as I can rely upon my memory. This hindrance in presenting material at first had seemed to me greater than it appeared after the other material from diaries and folklore was brought into a form ready for writing. The amount of facts being at my disposal seemingly is quite sufficient for giving a detail-

---

* Among the field workers, and especially among the beginners, the looking for "differences" results in relative paucity of diaries. Days pass sometimes during which no "facts of interest" as to the psychomental complex are recorded, while the observer actually misses the most essential elements of the complex only because those elements do not differ from his own. When the material is submitted to the description, the observer completely forgets what he observed and comes to the formulation of "primitiveness", "paucity", "simplicity" of psychomental complex even in the cases when he understands all the cultural elements of the groups under the investigation, which let us add, is a rare occurrence amongst the investigators. Still worse is the situation when the material gathered is not presented by the investigator himself. In this case the most essential part of the complex observed, but not recorded and even very often not perceived, rema'ns hidden and the whole picture is perfectly artificial and unreal. As shown still worse is the situation when the observer is supplied with the selective apparatus in the form of theories. It may be pointed out that another peculiarity is also observed among the investigators, namely, they become "blind" as to the differences. This case is especially common among investigators poorly equipped with general knowledge, and impressed by the idea of similarity.

** Cf. infra Part 4, where difficulties of investigation of these conditions are pointed out. However, a great number of investigators begin from this point, e.g. by attacking the problem of shamanistic practices with "abnormal" cases. Indeed, the most extraordinary pictures may be constructed with the facts of this kind.

*** A particular case is that of shamanizing. When the shaman is asked to reproduce his "songs" etc. for being pleasant to the investigator he may do it, but how reliable will be this record is another question. As will be shown, the shamans are not sometimes even conscious of what they are doing and singing. What may be recorded in this way is a small part of the performance, i.e. the incantations, formalized and stylized, a kind of prayer, which from the point of view of shamanism have a very secondary importance.

* Indeed, it is possible even publicly to take notes, but this ought to be arranged very carefully and under some decent pretext. All depends on the investigator's sense of tact.

** From this point of view investigation of groups like Manchus is still more difficult, for the Manchus, in accordance with the Chinese ideas of politeness, and under the stimulus of gaining sympathy of the investigator may supply him with imaginary facts by adapting themselves to the investigator's complex.

ed picture of the psychomental complex. I do not think that the facts based upon the collections would be superfluous for the present work, but their lack does not affect my analysis of the complex; it chiefly affects the outer form of the work which would be better if illustrated. Perhaps, in the future, it may be possible to give additional illustrations with special explanatory notes.

11. PRESENTATION OF THE MATERIAL The material discussed in the previous section was analysed, checked once more, partly rejected for the reasons indicated above, and classified for writing the present work. It may be pointed out that some problems have appeared better investigated, sometimes the amount of facts exceeded what was actually needed for the exposition, while some other problems have remained obscure. In the exposition we shall meet with both cases. There are three reasons for this situation, namely, (1) problems sometimes arise on the ground of European complex without being actual problems in the Tungus complex; (2) the Tungus themselves cannot give their own solutions of some problems actually existing in their complex and there is no means of explaining them from the Tungus point of view; (3) the conditions of work sometimes do not permit insisting upon certain questions for such a pressure upon the Tungus may produce quite an undesirable effect and, as shown, the investigator may lose the Tungus as voluntary informers.

I have constructed my treatment according to the structure of Tungus complex, which will be sometimes responsible for an unusual form of exposition. However, I considered undesirable an adaptation of the Tungus complex to the European complex, or to a conventionalized form found in a great number of publications. Still in the arrangement of the material my own analysis of the Tungus complex is also responsible for the form of this work. In fact, the technical ways of exposition will not be the same as those used by other authors, so for convenience of exposition I have described the psychomental complex in its relation to the milieus, namely, the primary, secondary and tertiary milieus as they have already been defined in my earlier publication, while "customs", some ideas, and practices are described together in a special part. Moreover, I have divided my work into four parts dealing with (1) positive knowledge; (2) hypotheses; (3) practical methods resulting from hypotheses; and (4) shamanism. However, in the first part I had to include sections on language, folklore, decorative art and education which are important manifestations of the psychomental complex, but at present they cannot be separated into a special part and they are not conditioned by the hypotheses to be treated in Part 3. On the other hand, I have written an introductory chapter on some Tungus conceptions without which the reading of Part I might not be clear. My original idea was to include shamanism in Part 3, as one of the practical methods resulting from hypotheses, which is the real character of shamanism, but the latter is too voluminous to be included in Part 3, and it has its own conditions which required special chapters on "Psychic conditions of groups" and "History of Shamanism". Owing to this, and against my original intention, I have separated shamanism under a special heading, which is not, however, indicative that I regard it as something different in nature from other various practical methods treated in Part 3.

In order to avoid possible misunderstandings and in order to be clear to my readers I shall now dwell a while upon the terms used in this work. Some of the terms are already evident from the previous discussion of difficulties of investigation and theory of ethnos (Chapter 1 and 2). Since some terms as "evolution", "development", "progress", "starter" and others have been discussed by me in other works (namely,—"Social Organization of the Northern Tungus", 1929 and "Ethnological and Linguistical Aspects of the Ural-Altaic Hypothesis", 1931,), I shall not again repeat this discussion. However, in the present work I shall use some new terms which will be in due course explained and I shall omit altogether some old terms for which omission I must give reasons. But first of all, I must justify my preference for the term "psychomental complex" which is likely to meet with opposition. It is evident that we shall deal with a complex. I call it *psychomental* because the phenomena designated as *mental* may be regarded so only abstractly, while they are actually connected with the whole psychic complex of the ethnical units and individuals. This complex is functional complex which is created as an outcome of adaptation of the given (and variable) physiological complex to the totality of conditions of units, which may be transmitted as inherited potentiality and as a pattern of imitated behaviour learnt from the ethnical milieu. I call it not only *psychic*, but also *mental* because the group of phenomena which are called *mental* being easily observable manifestations liable to an easy recording and analysis, do influence psychic functions in units and individuals and thus "psychic" and "mental" phenomena cannot be separated. These considerations have brought me to the compound term "psychomental".

In the existing ethnographic works one meets with different terms e.g. "spiritual culture", "religious culture", "religion", even "superstitions" and "shamanism" as a "religion". None of these terms is good for such a phenomenon as the psychomental complex. Indeed, the term "spiritual", has the specific contents of "spirit", yet a great number of phenomena of the psychomental complex in their nature are not "spiritual" at all, and such a specification of these phenomena puts them into opposition to the "material" phenomena which is in crying contradiction with all modern scientific thinking. Terms like "religious" and "religion" presume comparison of opposition with the cultural phenomena such as Christianity and Buddhism. However, to include elements like regulation of psychic life, as it is observed among the Tungus, into the complex of religion would mean to oppose this "religion" to the complexes like Christianity which does not include medical art. Indeed, these terms ought to be reserved to special well known phenomena in order to avoid always undesirable confusion of different cultural complexes put into the form of a pseudo-scientific generalization.

Indeed, the terms "superstitions", "predjudices" etc. still surviving in the ethnographical literature may have no more place in the scientific publications for they presume an absolute certainty of holding in hand *TRUTH* the existence of which no serious European scientist may now accept. In fact, a great number of such truths announced during the last century have since appeared as errors due to in-correct postulates some of which were of a supernatural order, i.e. the constructions were not cognized superstitions. The term "shamanism" is still less convenient for as I have already shown in my previous publications* shamanism is not a phenomenon which may cover the whole psychomental complex. Indeed, shamanism is well adapted to the existing complex and it can hardly exist in a different complex, but it forms only one of the elements of the existing complex. On the other hand, the shamanism may exist in association with different complexes, and the Tungus complexes may include no shamanism at all. So that such an identification of Tungus psychomental complex is erroneous in principle**. Indeed, shamanism is not a religion even on the ground that it is not a fixed, stabilized system, and also absolutely lacking ethical element***.

In this work the reader will not find the term "medicine man" sometimes applied to the shamans, for as I have already pointed out shamanism is not a "medical art" only. I have also banished from my terminology terms like "magic", "mystic" etc. with their derivatives. In fact, these terms presume, on the part of the speaker, a definite attitude towards the complexes and elements designated by these terms, the essential of which is that they are opposed to something "rational", "scientifically proved" etc. while they actually designate and cover elements and complexes which are either not yet understood by the investigators, or belong to distinct complexes when compared with great religions and modern science.

Owing to deep psychological reasons, into the discussion of which I cannot enter here, the introducing of new terms and giving of new "meanings" to the old ones is almost always met with a kind of hostility. As a matter of fact, such an introduction of new terms is not often required by the situation, and these terms are introduced because of reasons lying far away from the needs of science. However, when new ideas are introduced or new phenomena are described, i.e. phenomena which have not yet been described, or phenomena which have not yet been separated, the need of new terms becomes quite imperative. In fact, I find it necessary to introduce such terms as "ethnos", "starter", "olonism", and I insist upon my understanding of "shamanism", as it is here described, for otherwise the reading of the present work will be difficult, perhaps impossible. I was reluctant to introduce new terms and to be persistent in my use of some other terms given new meanings, but I do it because these terms are needed. The same may be stated in reference to my avoid-

ance of some old terms. Naturally it is not for reasons of giving this work an "original" appearance, but for giving it more clearness and more independence on the European complex, for in fact, as shown in the present work, *it is possible to describe an alien complex without making re-course to an ambiguous terminology*. Therefore there is on my part neither pedantism, nor pretention to origina-lity.

By introduction of a few new terms and rearrangement of the meanings of some common terms I do not cover all existing needs of a new terminology for description and analysis of alien complexes, and I am certain that on this ground there will originate some misunderstandings. Still greater is the chance of misunderstanding because of the language as I have already pointed out in speaking about the difficulties of translating (*vide supra* pp. 2-3) Tungus texts and rendering Tungus ideas in terms of European complex.

———

This work at the last stage of its preparation for pub-lication has been carried out as above described, but it cannot satisfy all the requirements which I demand in such an investigation. The main reason is that the mate-rial at my disposal still is not sufficient, according to my ideas, for an exhaustive treatment, especially in so far as the psychological side of the investigation is concerned.—Nothing can compensate for the lack of a laboratory.

In spite of these objections, I give below my observa-tions and conclusions as they have been formed at the end of my work, on all material which I have. Indeed, in some cases,—and they will be numerous,—I shall abstain from interpretations and conclusions confining myself to state-ments of facts. I will abstain not because of the impossibi-lity of finding *some interpretation*, but I will do so because these interpretations may be uncertain and conclusions wrong, and therefore they are useless for my chief aim which is to give a picture of the psychomental complex. For the same reason I will leave without interpretations and conclusions some facts which I shall quote from other authors. As may be seen from the previous sections these facts are in some cases brought forth by the investigators as isolated facts, and without their connexion with the complex as a whole.

Although a great number of parallels found in the descriptions of psychomental complexes among other and sometimes distant ethnical groups are strikingly similar to what is observed among the Tungus, and in writings of comparatists they would certainly be included, I shall not include them in the present work except in those cases when the presentation of parallels may be instructive as an indica-tion of possible source of borrowing. These will be those groups chiefly living, at present and in the past, in direct contact with the Tungus groups described, and others which although indirect were a certain source. Indeed, the groups like Chinese, Mongols and northern neighbours, as the Yakuts and various Palaeasiatics, might supply an enormous amount of facts, but for a profitable use of these facts there is needed space to be occupied by quotations, their interpretation and critical analysis of theoretical value of such parallels which would actually require a special critical and comparative study; an incidental quota-tion of parallels, in my eyes, cannot be justified. First of

———

* Cf. "Essay" in Russian (1919) *also other publications*, as "What is Shamanism" (1924), "Šramana-Shaman" (1924) (in collaboration with N. D. Mironov), also "SONT", Supplem. Note VIII pp. 364 et seq.

** This term has been widely used as a term equivalent to "pagan", "heathen", in the official records, as opposed to Christianity, Buddhism and Mohammedism. Cf. e.g. S. K. Patkanov's work on Tungus. In these cases shamanism was regarded as a "religion".

*** Indeed, one may find "ethical" elements in "shamanism" when one would include in shamanism all spirits and the ethical complex. But this would be equivalent to an arbitrary treatment of shamanism. The Tungus ethical complex may be free of spirits as well. The same is true of the establishment of the existence of a "religion", as does e.g. W. Jochelson, "The Yukaghirs" etc. (pp. 135 et seq.), on the ground that some ethical prescriptions are connected with the spirits, while among the Christian populations there are some "spirits" too.

all, most facts are accessible for the specialists, while their quotation may still occupy too much space needed for other purposes—i.e. the facts which have not before been published and their interpretation, as well as the establishment of a theoretical basis of the present work. Second, quite involuntarily the facts taken out of complexes on the background of a distinct complex may easily happen to appear in a distorted form, functional and even sometimes factual when curtailed. Moreover, I do not believe that such facts can be safely used without a perfect knowledge of the whole complex, in which they are included. Yet, even with the best investigated groups, this cannot be always done, without a personal acquaintance with these groups. This difficulty is well known to all ethnographers who are familiar with distinct groups, and who know that the essential character of any cultural complex is its functional aspect which is difficult to show in a "description",—it ought to be seen, heard, and "felt". A misuse of ethnographic facts may thus result in wrong inferences; this chance is very great for behind the choice of the facts compared, there are always some preconceived ideas and hypotheses.

In the present work besides the Northern Tungus groups investigated I will also treat the psychomental complex as it was observed among the Manchus and for this reason the present work is entitled "Psychomental Complex of the Tungus". As a matter of fact the Manchus have been responsible for many ideas concerning the shamanism and many other elements of the psychomental complex observed amongst the Northern Tungus groups, so that the Manchu psychomental complex must be treated here. Since the social organization among the Northern Tungus and Manchus is closely connected in my treatment with the psychomental complex, I will often refer to my publications devoted to the description of the social organization. I have already given a general and very brief description of the Northern Tungus mentality and behaviour in order to make clearer the functioning of the Tungus social organization. So in the present work I shall not repeat what has already been discussed as to the classification and general characteristics of the Tungus groups. If I should succeed in showing the Tungus complex in terms of functions, and if I should succeed in tracing some elements to the sources of their ethnical origin, i.e. to establish some facts as to the sequence of variations or merely hints as to history of changes, at last, if I should succeed in my ethnological inferences, from the facts observed, although quite tentative and perhaps temporary, I shall consider my task fulfilled.

PART ONE

POSITIVE KNOWLEDGE

CHAPTER IV

SOME FUNDAMENTAL CONCEPTIONS

12. PRELIMINARY REMARKS In order to prepare the reader for a treatment of the Tungus psychomental complex first I must introduce some general and fundamental conceptions found among the Tungus. In this introduction it will be impossible to give an exhaustive treatment; this will be done, in so far as possible, in special chapters.

The fundamental Tungus ideas are here represented in a systematic manner, which is not that of the Tungus. The facts and inferences are much more fragmentary amongst them than it is in my schematization based upon an investigation of several Tungus groups, and many individuals forming these groups. A formulation of their ideas meets with the difficulty of distinguishing between what is not essential in the system, and what is essential, what is common opinion and what is individual opinion, what can be adopted by all Tungus, and what may be adopted only by some of them. This is the work of the investigator and I must show how I arrived at my generalization.

Regarding the problem of fundamental ideas it must be emphasized that not all Tungus are interested in these problems the discussion of which is a privilege so to say of mentally superior individuals. The average Tungus receives his education not in philosophical formulations but in the form of accumulation of knowledge regarding the facts of milieu taken one by one and always in the light of the existing philosophical conception. Indeed, there are some Tungus who are unable to form any general conception, so they accept a "vulgarization" presented to them by people whom they trust. This is true of highly differentiated groups as well: if one confines one's work to the farmers and factory workmen, one cannot naturally find out which are the essential elements of the psychomental complex of the European ethnical groups as a whole.

Moreover, amongst different Tungus groups there are some differences as to the details of these conceptions. For this reason I do not now give details, observed amongst different groups, but I confine myself to the general formulation of this system which may be admitted by all Tungus groups. It is true, I was sometimes unable to check up, directly amongst all groups investigated, conception of "*animus*" as it is here presented. So, for instance, amongst the Kumarčen I was able only indirectly to check up in the particular cases analysed. Since the conception was found to be valid in particular cases and since no signs of other general conceptions have been found, I have considered it safe to spread my formulation over the psychomental complex of the Kumarčen.

In my further treatment of the psychomental complex

of the Tungus, I will follow the same method. When the fact is referred to the Tungus it will mean that it is referred to all Tungus groups either as perceived by them as such or as lying at the basis of their system. In case there are special references to particular groups it will mean that I can make no generalization, either because of the lack of facts or because of existing differences, which will be pointed out.

The objection which may be raised at once is that it will not be the complex described and analysed in the individual, but a concentrated and condensed picture. However, my intention is not to give the mentality of an individual Tungus, but to give a description of the mechanism of the psychomental complex which may help to understand the behaviour with included ideas of an individual and groups of individuals in the ethnical units.

It has now become usual that instead of general formulation of phenomena investigated and described authors give rough material, almost untreated. In my particular case I might do the same, i.e. to bring up all individual cases, ideas and attitudes, and confine my effort to the publication of these facts. However, I think this cannot be done when the material is too voluminous and it is useless when the formulation of general conclusions is possible; rough material is published in case the investigator wants to publish something but is not sure of being able to draw conclusions or is not considered able to do it by his readers. Some time ago the same situation existed in the field of anthropology when the anthropologists were not yet familiar with the methodology and used to publish only individual measurements and the work of critics chiefly consisted in checking up arithmetical calculations. With the improvement of methodological training the need of publishing individual measurements disappeared, which by that time had become so numerous that their publication was practically impossible. This is true of "some humanities" in which the methodological training is still in its childhood; investigators are not trusted and therefore they have to publish their original data. Sometimes this way is stated to be a genuine scientific method; actually it shows that science does not yet exist, but there exists some data the collectors of which ought to be checked at their every step.

There are, thus, reasons for my considering useless and impossible the publication of all the data I have, and I shall now confine myself to the description and analysis of inferences without reproducing here the total amount of facts gathered. In further chapters when necessary facts will be given.

49

13. ANIMUS Before the Tungus, as before any ethnical group which observes the milieu, there arises the problem of the matter with its aspects in time and changes, and human reactions on it. The fundamental idea of the Tungus, including the Manchus, is that matter in so far as it may be perceived in certain forms distinguished by them, consists of two elements: the material substance and the immaterial substance; for convenience I shall call them *matter* and *animus*.

Every thing which may be touched and felt, seen, heard, and smelled as a physical body is matter. So a stone, wood, or a piece of skin etc. are simply *"matter"*. They may be distinct and classified as such. The Tungus language, in so far as I know, possesses no general term for it, and designates "matter" by specified terms: "stone," "wood," "iron," "skin." The further classification of the various forms of the matter is based upon their practical utility, e.g. ʃoʃo—"stone"—may be used in referring to any mineral, not possessing characteristics of any pure and composite metal, as iron and brass, and being in the solid state, not reduced to powder or solution. However, the stone reduced to powder is recognized to be "the stone reduced to powder". The rocks are built up of stone. If the stone has some particular application, e.g. for painting—*davik, davuk* or *daviksa* (of several dialects)—the "ochre"; as medicine *ʃoʃo amun'in* (Ner.)—the stone "purgative",—it will have a proper name (*davik*) or with specification (*amun'in*, from *amun*—to evacuate.) If the stone is considered as a characteristic feature of river deposit—the "pebble"—it will have a special term, e.g. *iŋga, gʲa, iŋa* (in various dialects), but it may also be called *ʃoʃo* (*biran'i ʃoʃo*—the river pebble). Thus *ʃoʃo* is "stone-matter," and "stone."

The same may be seen in the conception of "wood"—*mo*. The wood may be specified as we have seen in the case of "stone". However, it is different with the metals which are known to the Tungus from other and different ethnical groups and are called by different names: "iron", "brass", "copper", "silver", "gold" etc. which show no uniformity amongst different groups and in most cases they may be traced back to their linguistical source. As far as I know there is no term for "metal" (common language) but it does not mean that the Tungus have no such a conception. When a Tungus wants to designate "metal" he would distinguish it from other and different forms of *matter* by negative definition; it is not "stone", nor "wood", nor "meat" etc. and he would be surprised if one should not understand that there is something in common in all metals which has no general name. Let us remark that the Tungus did not yet need to have such a general term, but the notion of "metal" does exist.

Now it will be clear that the Tungus may have no term for "matter" but they do possess such a notion.

Let us now suppose we have a wooden stick, about 110 centimetres long, ornamented and with a handle, used as a special instrument by women for maintaining their equilibrium when riding reindeer back, called *tijavun*. It may even now be replaced by a simple piece of wood with a natural handle. As long as it preserves its integrity, is not broken, it may be used as *tijavun* and so called. However, when it is broken into two pieces it is no more *tijavun*, but—two pieces of wood (*mo*), it is "broken *tijavun*". The *tijavun* loses something which is proper to it and becomes simple matter—"wood matter". This "something" is the im-material substance which is liberated when the piece is broken. This is the *animus*.

The evidence of the existence of the *"animus"* is seen in Tungus practice, at least among some groups, of breaking the articles placed in the coffin with the corpse. Their idea is that the *matter* will not follow the *animus* of the dead, but the immaterial substance will follow the immaterial substance of the dead, and in this way the dead will have everything he needs. The liberation of the *animus* may be attained by leaving wooden and other perishable materials to decompose. As will be later seen the Tungus do not accept this conception without criticism. There are some. Tungus who would doubt in some cases whether animus is present or lacking; for instance, naturally formed phenomenon, the pebble, which when broken may be regarded by some Tungus as "stone" while by the others as "a broken pebble". The same question arises with the broken *tijavun*, which after repairing may be again used as *tijavun*. The controversy amongst the Tungus originates but usually it is left without further considering the question. So that the conception of animus is subject to variations among the groups and individuals which form the groups. Indeed, such deviations in opinion are conditioned by the conception itself and flexibility of Tungus mind, as well as by tolerance characteristic of the Tungus.

The conception of "animus" has no special term, just as "matter", for the Tungus does not need one. In fact, the process is like this: a wooden piece made with definite purpose is *called* by a certain *name* (sounding starter) which produces a certain process of conditioned reflexes; when the piece is broken it cannot be defined by the same name, while potentially, as a complex of conditioned reflexes, does exist.

It may be compared with the "idea". However, this identification is not complete for the Tungus suppose that the continuity of the existence of "animus" is not interrupted and it has certain "reality", when we look closer at their conception, even a material reality. Perhaps, the Tungus point of view may be compared with that of European dualistic complex which opposes the "matter" to the "spirit". However, as shown there are some essential differences too. So I do not intend to identify these conceptions and still less do I intend to bring the Tungus conception into a diffusional dependence on the European complex. We do not need this hypothesis, for the conception seems to be very old, older than the existing ethnical units, bearers of the European ethnographical complex.

It is very likely that a more careful investigation amongst the other ethnical groups, not only in Asia, but in other continents as well, will show great similarity in this fundamental conception, which results from the fact that the existing milieu is conceived through the psychomental complex and the "animus" actually is the perceived cognition of the elements forming the milieu. The further complications and "explanations" of the fundamental conception are responsible for the varieties of the philosophical conceptions observed among different groups, because the psychomental complexes are different and approach one another in spite of their varieties, the fundamental conception being the same.

From this broad point of view the Tungus philosophical conception may be called "animism", but this term loses its value for such an "animism" is characteristic of almost all ethnical groups, including the European groups.

It may also be noted that this Tungus conception has sometimes been mistaken by the investigators for the idea of spirits. As will be later seen the animus and spirit are different conceptions. The source of misunderstanding is that the Tungus when they speak to foreigners use Russian terms *dux*, *duša* ("spirit", "soul" etc.) having no term *animus* in their own language. However, I have many a time experimented to find out the Tungus and alien reactions. The result always was the same if my experiment was correctly arranged. In the cases when I intentionally used the method of checking through the wrong identification of "spirit-soul" and *animus*, the Tungus smiled at my naivety and tried to explain to me the difference between them. When an investigator does not speak the language of the people investigated, the Tungus leave him alone with his erroneous identification, for they are not able to explain the matter in terms of an alien (e.g. Russian) complex. The same would happen in case the investigator, even speaking their language, should approach Tungus with his own ready made conceptions. In their eyes it would be hopeless to explain to him the Tungus idea of animus as it would be hopeless in the case of explaining to an European farmer the idea of totemism, logos, tao etc. So it is not surprising that the ethnographical descriptions abound in the most extraordinary absurdities ascribed to the ethnical units which possess non-European complexes.

In this short section I have thus shown that the Tungus possess abstract conceptions for which they have sometimes no corresponding terms. The lack of terms cannot be treated as indication of a lack of conceptions. We have also found that the Tungus recognize existence of *matter* and *animus* the latter being independent of the *matter*. The animus cannot be identified with the *idea*, nor spirit.

14. LIFE When the Tungus approaches phenomena of plants which do not behave in the same way as the minerals do, i.e. the plants grow, change their leaves, die out etc., the Tungus see certain similarities between the plants and animals which make the plants distinct from the mineral realm. The Tungus opinions about this matter are not uniform, but most of them agree that the plants possess "*life*" which is present in all animals and which is lacking in the mineral realm.

The life in Tungus is called *èrga* (Bir. Kum. Mank.), *ergan* (Lam), *erge* (Tum), *öigön* (Neg. Sch.), *ōrgō* (Goldi) (Sch.), *èrgen* (Manchu Wr. and Sp.)*. It may also mean "breathing", "to breathe", and in a wrong translation it may be rendered as "soul". However, this translation may be accepted only in the largest sense of "soul". Among the Manchus the life *èrgen* is identified with "breathing" and "living power", so that the *èrgen* is located in the body on the height of sternum. It is also identified with air exhaled by living people.

It is difficult to say what is the original meaning of *èrgen* and whether it can be connected with the verb "to breathe",—*or*, with variations,—or not. It seems to me that this is an independent stem, in so far it has received the meaning of "life". However, in Manchu *èrge* also means "to breathe". It is possible that *èrgs* being of same origin as *or* (*Vr*) had received a special secondary meaning and

spread over the Tungus groups. In Bir. we have *èreγaī* (Bir.) which is "living" as opposed to "dead" and "who does not breathe". The breathing seems to me only a sign of *èrga* and it is *ori* (Khin. Ner.), *or'i* (Bir. Mank.), *äri* (Ur. Castr.), *ör'i* (Bir.), *eji* (Neg. Sch.)—"to breathe", consequently "to be alive"*. I find no parallels in Turk and Mongol dialects. In a broad sense it may be referred to plants and animals, including man. There is another stem, namely *in* (and *in'*) which is used in Ner. Khin. Bir. in the sense of "living" as opposed to "dead" and "spirits" (Bir.) and only in reference to the man (Bir.). This stem is interesting for it is met with in RTM in the sense "to live", "inhabit" *inji* (RTM) (also in Enis.) where *ji* is a suffix. It ought to be pointed out that this group uses a Russian term for "life" and "soul". In Lam. I find another meaning of *inji* (Lam.)—the "arteria", "pulse"**. In Ang. (Tit.) the stem *in* is used in the sense of "life", opposed "to die", also in a broad sense "to exist". In so far as I know there are no parallels in other languages. It is possible that in the pro-Tungus language in the sense of "life" there was used only one stem.

It may be thus stated that the Tungus possess the stems *èrga* and *in*, which have nearly the same meaning, but *èrga* is nearer to the idea of "breathing—life".

When one asks a Tungus to give a definition of life he would point out pulse as the most essential evidence of life after breathing. This is the active *èrga—sudala* (Bir.)— "the life, blood vessel (arteria),"—*majin* (Bir.) (the etymology is not clear.) [cf. *sudala* (Manchu), *sudal* (Mongol, Kow.)—"blood vessels", "pulse"].

One of definitions of life of animals is movement. However, it is sometimes rejected for the reason that plants have *èrga*, but they do not move. For the same reason the activity of the heart is not considered as characteristic of life, for insects, and worms have, according to the Tungus, no pulse, but they have *èrga*. Even, the breathing is not characteristic of "life" for many animals have no breathing, e.g. the fishes have no lungs. In the dialects like Bir. where *èrga* and *in* exist side by side, *in* cannot be referred to plants, not moving, not breathing animals. I do not know the actual meaning of *in* and *inji* in other dialects.

From the above shown facts it is evident that the best translation of *èrga* is "the life" in a broad sense of the word, as perceptible activity, referred to plants and animals, which grow and multiply. Thus in addition to "animus" the Tungus also have *èrga* which must not be taken for "soul"***.

15. SOUL The activity of the animals,—and as such only moving animals are considered,—convinces the Tungus in the existence in animals of another element lacking in plants. The Tungus have no generally accepted conception about the nature of this element. This element may be understood as a manifested functioning of the

---

* This conception of "life" has become familiar to me only after the analysis of my Transbaikalian data, so that I could not directly establish the term in Ner. and Barg.

* In the dialects of the Enisay Tungus I find *arikša* (Enis.) and in another collection *rikša* (*urikša*) in the sense of "life". [cf. *ärikšan* (Ur. Castr.)—"breathing"]. They are connected with a series of words of the same stem Vr and used in the sense of "to come to life" etc. e.g. ar (Bir.) (Sam. Tit.), eru (Enis.).

** *Iyir* (Yakut, Pek.) the "sinew"; sometimes the "sinew" and "blood vessels (pulse)" are called by the same Russian term—*žila*. In the small dictionary like that of Lam. dialect which I have, an error is possible.

*** I think that the corals would not be recognized as living and the holoturia would be taken for plants, for some of them do not move.

nervous system, including the central nervous system,—the brain. However, in order better to understand the difficulties met with by the Tungus I shall now give the Tungus idea of how man differs from non-living phenomena and then the place of animals will be better seen in the Tungus system.

According to the Manchus the human being consists of the material element and elements which cannot be seen, but which make the man live and act as man does. These elements are called *fajanga* (Manchu Writ.), usually *fojeyo* (Manchu Sp.), which may be translated "soul". This is not, however, a good translation, for *fojeyo* is composed of three elements; namely, (1) *wuneyi fojeyo* (*unengi fajanga*)— the "true soul", as the Manchus understand it, which is considered as a principal component of *fojeyo*; (2) *čergi fojeyo* (cf *čargi fajanga* Manchu Writ.)—the "soul which precedes" which is near the first (cf. *čargi*); (3) *olorgi fojeyo*— the "external soul". These three elements are not understood by the Manchus as independent one of another, but according to their explanation the three-fold aspect of the soul is the same as that of a finger which has nail, bones, and "meat". The soul is received from *oyos'i mama* who supplies all children with souls. The second soul after death returns to *oyos'i mama* for being given to other children, while the third soul goes to the spirit of the lower world *i̯munxan*, after which it may be incarnated into other people and animals, thus it is received from *i̯munxan*. According to some Manchus, the second soul may be identified with the power of continuation of the species, i.e. it is a biological power of continuity which is characteristic of the man and all animals, but which, according to the Manchus, is lacking in plants. The second "soul" seems to be also responsible for all physiological functions of a higher order. After death it remains in the body for some time. The first or "true soul" is that which may be compared with "consciousness", "self-cognition". However, the "thought" is not the same as "true soul" for "thought"—*gonin*—is a result of the activity of all "souls" which is produced in the heart and is in some relation to the liver[*].

The controversy among the Manchus is about the question whether the first "soul" exists in animals or not: some of them would deny it, some of them would recognize it. From a further description the particular characteristics of these components will be clearer. The three "souls" must be well balanced in a system of permanent movement which will be described later.

Thus, this theory of "soul" may be represented in the scheme: the soul, which is the principal one, is the individual consciousness; the second is the reproductive power; the third one is the migrating "soul" which is the soul familiar to Europeans; all three together form *fojeyo*—the "soul" characteristic of man. Indeed, this conception of soul is not originally a Tungus conception,—it is one of numerous modifications of the vulgarized Buddhistic conceptions which reached the Manchus through the Chinese and Central Asiatic groups.

Among the Barguzin and Nerčinsk Tungus the idea of a complex soul is also adopted. I cannot assert how many elements it comprises, for I was unable to receive any definite statement. These Tungus call the soul *an'akan*, the etymology of which will be discussed later. The soul may

partly leave the body which is called *ulda*,—the "meat", as opposed to *an'akan*. The spirit *om'i̯an* is sending souls and is looking after the souls, but this spirit seems to be controlled by another one *dayačan* (a generic term for all "masters"). Also all animals have souls.

The system adopted by the Tungus of Manchuria, with exception of the Reindeer Tungus of Manchuria, is similar to that of the Manchus. *Sus'i sus'e* (Bir. Kum.) consists of three elements which have no special names. The etymology of this word is not clear. Amongst the Birarčen (*vide supra*) the soul given by *um'isma ～ um'i ～ om'i* is called *om'i*. They say that *om'i* is given by the spirit to a child when it is in the mother's womb. If it is not given by the spirit the child will not grow. As without *om'i* it cannot grow, so without *èrga* it cannot live. In this conception the soul *sus'i* is independent of *om'i* and *èrga*. The Birarčen go so far that they assert that *om'i* is not even given to the children but to the parents and those who have no *om'i* may have no children. In this conception *om'i* is merely "reproductive power" and growth. However, this opinion is in conflict with the Manchu system but it is in entire agreement with the Birarčen opinion as to the third *sus'i* which remains in the family. The usual expression amongst these Tungus in reference to children is *om'i yalaren*, instead of *sus'i yalaren* when they want to say "the child is afraid". From a certain moment the child is not considered having *om'i* but as having *sus'i*. Before that time his soul is not yet established in the body, and there is a special placing for it which is called *an'an*[*].

The difference between Birarčen conception and that of the Manchus is that after death one *sus'i* does not have the place and looks after the children, another *sus'i* goes into the animals and third one remains in the world of dead people. One of *sus'i* is given by *um'isma* (corresponding to *oyosi mama* of the Manchus) and for some while it remains near the tomb (corresponding to *čergi fojeyo*). According to the Tungus themselves, this theory is borrowed by them from the Manchus and particularly from Manchu books. All animals which can move have also *sus'i*. However, the human being also possesses *dō* (Bir.), *doy* (Khin.), *don* (Ner.), which may be defined as "the complex of mental and psychic activity", which results in a certain "moral" and "intellectual" aspect and value of the person. It must not be understood as "thought" or "wish" for which conceptions they have special terms, borrowed from the Mongols—*jalåva* (Bir.), *jalva* (Ner.) [cf. *jalwår'i* ‖*jalbari*, Mong. Rud.]; and they have another term *jon* (Bir. Kum.). Together with the destruction of the body *dō* naturally disappears altogether. Etymologically it ought to be connected with *dō* (Bir.)—the "inside", the "internal organs" [cf. *dō* (Manchu), *dosi* also *doso* (Buriat, Castr.) and *dotor* (Mong. Rud.]. According to the Birarčen, some animals have *dō* in the sense of the psychomental complex.

---

[*] The Manchus say that the man uses his head for "eating" and "looking" and not for thinking.

[*] *An'an* is "the soul", and etymologically it may be compared with fan a of Goldi and fajanga of the Manchus, where an'an is bilabialized. We know another modification kapan—the placing for special spirits for children amongst the Tungus of Manchuria which looks like an aspirated form of the same an'an—*kayan*. However, this is not sure, for it supposes that the word was recorded with x perceived and reproduced as k (this is a common case) and that a—y (also common, but we have no connecting links). In Tungus *anjan ‖ kapan* is used in reference to the "placing for spirit-soul" and "the shadow".

Amongst the Nomad Tungus of Man'kova the conception of "soul" is borrowed from the Buriats together with the term which is *sunusun* (Mank.), also *sunäsun* (Ur. Castr.) [Cf. *hundyu* (Buriat, Shirokogoroff), *sünesün* (Mong. Xalxa), *hünehen* (various Buriats) (Podg.)]. At the present time the Man'kova Tungus are under a strong Russian influence, so that this term does not cover the original conception. The Reindeer Tungus of Manchuria have a Russian conception of "soul", which is a variation of the European complex. Since it does not recognize the existence of "soul" in animals, this Tungus group finds itself rather in a difficult position for rearrangement of the general conception of "life" etc.

Amongst the Tungus there seems to exist another conception of "soul" which is related to the term *om'i* (Ur. Castr.), *om'i* (Nerr. Barg.) [cf. *amin* (Buriat. Castr.) where it is connected with the stem used for "to breathe"] found in children and with which the activity of the spirit *um'is'i* is connected. The term used by the Enissy Tungus belongs to the same stem—*omugda*. Amongst the Reindeer Tungus of Manchuria *om'i* is equivalent to *sus'i*. At the present time it is impossible to restore the old Tungus conception of "soul".

In the records of Lam. dialect I find two terms which in P. V. Olenin's translations are the "material soul" *han'inn'i* (Lam.) (indeed, it is an aspirated form of *an'an*) corresponding to the Yakut *kut*, and the "immaterial soul" *muyonn'i* (Lam) corresponding to the Yakut conception of *sür**. Both Tungus terms do not seem to be free of suffixes, and the second cannot be connected with the terms for those conceptions found in other languages. If the record and translations are correct the conception of "soul" is different amongst this group. The conception of *kut* and *sür*, as they are given by the specialists, is essentially different as compared with those above described.

Conception of "soul" amongst the Goldi who are living in the neighbourhood of the Birarčen and Manchus is very close to that of the Manchus and Tungus of Manchuria. I.A. Lopatin has given some facts which are interesting. He says that the Goldi distinguish "three kinds of soul", which are *omija*, *ergeni* and *fan'a*. We have already observed all three among other groups. *Omija* is the "soul" sent by the spirit *eyosi mama* (Manchus), *om'is'i* (Tungus Birarčen-Kumarčen etc.). I.A. Lopatin gives the same fact when he relates how the shaman may get the soul for a child. *Ergeni* is *èrga* above discussed and it cannot be called "soul", —among the Goldi it is "life" as it is among other groups**.

---

*. cf. E. Pekarski's Dictionary under the words kut and sür, kut is a "complex of physiological processes" while sür, according to another authority [cf. V. M. Ionov (Publ. M.A.E. R.A.S. Vol. V. p. 188)], after death šör, continues to exist. As a matter of fact, kut is not "soul". The Yakuts naturally use a full definition kut-sür for "human life-activity".

** What is related by I. A. Lopatin in reference to ergeni may be understood much better if we do not mix the idea of soul with that of ergeni ("life"). As shown, the human body possesses "animus" as other things and living beings. Indeed, when a Goldi has to explain it to a foreigner he must have a term for designation of the idea of integrity of the body "animus" which he may designate as ergeni. When the question of the relationship between physical body and "animus" is discussed it will be better seen what the Goldi may mean when they speak of separation and moving of ergeni. The reason why I. A. Lopatin was unable to represent to us the Goldi idea in a clear manner and why he misunderstood the nature of "animus" [he asserts that every thing has its "soul"—animals, mountains, rivers,

I will not go further into the analysis of the material published by this author for it is distorted and cannot be relied upon.

In conclusion it may be thus formulated that the Tungus of all groups have a conception of "life" which distinguishes moving animals and man from the plants, the latter being recognized only by some Tungus as being "alive". Men and animals also possess "soul" which may be of different complexity varying with the different groups. The "soul", according to some Tungus, is a characteristc feature of all moving animals, but it is lacking in plants. Some Tungus believe that human beings have a special "soul",—the first *sus'i* and *fojeyo* (of the Manchus), —as to the existence of which in animals they are not sure. The phenomenon of "thought" and "will" is not the same as "soul" and it is also characteristic of the animals (*vide infra*, reindeer "soul" of Barguzin Tungus).

What we actually have in the Tungus conception of the "soul", "animus", "life" etc. is an attempt at the solution of the problem of human psychomental and biological activity and relationship which exists between the body as a physical phenomenon, an organized matter, and its functions. The problem is solved by putting forward a hypothesis which is that of the existence of matter and a certain immaterial substance, both of which have an objective existence. The hypothesis becomes a well established theory when the Tungus begin to bring facts in its support. Together with the observation of new facts the theory may receive certain modifications, e.g. in the form of splitting of the "soul", fusion of the elements into a complex, e.g. the conception of "life", the conception of "thought" sometimes designated even with foreign terms. The theory may be increased by the incorporation of new hypotheses and theories accepted by the Tungus as facts ("reliable conclusions"), so forming an eclectic theory, a syncretic complex. The new complex may spread over other groups. It may be totally or partially accepted or rejected, in every particular case being adapted to the existing ethnographical complex. In this respect the Tungus are not "conservative" at all and if you were to bring them some new facts or mere theories they would accept them on condition that the new theories better suit the existing complex and explain some newly perceived facts. In this respect the Manchus who have written records of their own (and Chinese) theories are more "conservative" for they have fixed them in a written

---

sun, winds, plants etc. (cf. op. cit. p. 198), while actually these may become placing for spirits (vide infra) without having their own "soul"] is that his starting point was that the Goldi are "animists" as they were pictured by the theoreticians of the last century and that according to this theory they must recognize the "soul" in the phenomena enumerated. Owing to this he begins his account of the Goldi's "beliefs" in the section of "Mythology" and sub-section of "Animism" (a ready made scheme which presumes the *contents of the* Goldi complex) by the statement; "The religion of the Goldi is very primitive". However, after reading his report one may see that their complex is not as simple as that, and it is not "primitive" at all for it contains elements of the Chinese complex overlapping the Buddhistic conceptions, intermingled with the shamanistic complex and what may be supposed or merely named as the old Tungus complex. The idea that the Goldi "religion" is primitive is a postulate of the European complex (ethnography of the nineteenth century) and the picture given by I. A. Lopatin is an adaptation to this complex. I have dwelt on this case for it repeats itself in many other instances of other authors, e.g. P.P. Šimkevič, L. von Schrenck and others. The case of I. A. Lopatin is more demonstrative for his work appeared in 1922.

form which as we have already seen produces certain effects on the stabilization of the complexes among the Tungus familiar with Manchu.*

For the same reason the Tungus may rather easily accept new theories professed by the missionaries and foreigners in general, and they would do it with readiness if new theories bring a new light to the facts observed. In the farther treatment of the problem of the Tungus mentality I shall return once more to this peculiarity of the Tungus, who do not particularly differ from other ethnical groups who are under favourable conditions of environment from the point of view of their being able to observe variations of natural phenomena.

The Tungus theories may be perhaps better understood if we remember that the same fundamental principle, i.e. the opposition of the matter to its functions, is also characteristic of the European complex. In fact, the conception of the matter and spirit, soma and noon, and other variations of the same conception are still reigning even in scientific circles. Descartes located the human "soul" in the epiphyse. The time when the fate of the human soul was seriously discussed (and is still discussed) is not far from us. The modern sociologists still make an abstraction of the psychological nature of society from the bearers of the psychological complex. The modern jurists operate with the abstract conceptions like "state", "normes" etc. discarding physical conditions of the individual and ethnical (also compound ethnical) mass which produce the "state" and juridic "normes". The historians of human culture still speak of the culture as a super-organical phenomenon which has its own life,—birth, childhood, youth, etc. The historians cannot distinguish when they deal with populations and their abstractions of the processes in the form of "nations", "state" etc. And the modern writers would try to convince themselves and their readers that they may have immortality of their own in the form of the proposed hypotheses and theories and will be perhaps worshipped and deified by the coming generations**. If one goes still further into the analysis of these complexes one would find the old conception of matter as opposed to its functions, which is the same hypothesis which is the basis of the Tungus theory. Thus the difference between the Tungus conception and that produced in the European complex is that of quantity of facts covered by the hypotheses and their adaptation to the existing complexes. It may be stated that if one approaches the Tungus from the point of view of some of the existing ethnographical complexes one would not be able to group the essentials of the Tungus complex and the latter will appear as a distorted image, merely as a reaction, of the observer himself.

In the case of I. A. Lopatin we have seen how an European complex may be responsible for the creation of

non-existing conception of the "soul". As a matter of fact, this case is not an isolated one. If one puts together all the phenomena of functional activity of the organism and groups of organisms including mental, psychic, and physiological manifestations under the generalized name of "soul" (it may be actually so translated by the groups investigated who are not familiar with the modern scientific terminology), there may appear descriptions of complex "soul" which are not so when they are reduced to the actual conceptions accepted by the ethnical groups. For this reason from the complex "soul" I have excluded "animus", "life", "thought", "will", and I have preserved under the term "soul" the complexes above described as for instance, *fojeŋo* of the Manchus *suˀi* of the Tungus of Manchuria, understood by them as compound complexes forming a unit in a living, normal human being, and some simple conceptions as that of *suŋusun, omiŋa*, etc. Indeed, I might gather under the title of soul other conceptions mentioned before and even include the phenomena like "pulse", "breathing", etc. I believe that in some instances of very multiple "souls" like that of the Gilaks we have the ethnographer's complex, his creation and not that which exists in the Gilak mind. As a matter of fact, sometime ago it was quite fashionable to discover multiple souls.

16. SPIRIT In the previous section we have already seen that the Tungus recognize the existence of an immaterial substance which actually is the thought, the reaction-idea of the observer produced by physical objects, as it is with the immaterial substance of "animus" which, in Tungus eyes, has an objective existence and which may be thus "exteriorated". The exterioration is merely a logical inference from the first proposition. Yet in the analysis of the functional manifestations of animal beings and particularly man, as physical complexes, the Tungus arrive at the formulation of the idea of other immaterial substances, as "life", "reproductive power", and "soul" as a complex of functions. These immaterial substances also may be exteriorated. However, the opinions of the Tungus in this question are not alike,—some of them do not accept the idea that "life" may be exteriorated and thus it is regarded as mere function which cannot be separated from the physical body. In this case their idea is near to that of some Europeans who consider the life as "condition of the matter". Indeed, these are minor details. But what is essential is that the immaterial substances as they are manifested in the different functions of the animal (and human) organism may be exteriorated and thus returned to the bodies in which they were originally placed, or remain exteriorated for ever, or place themselves for a time in any other physical body. For the convenience of explanation I will call the body, in which the exteriorated immaterial substances of this type may be placed, *placing, or loculus**. When they are in such an exteriorated state and the former loculus is destroyed, e.g. by the decomposition of the body after the death, burning, any mechanical destruction etc. they may choose any other new loculus. In such a state they become a special group of phenomena which have no

---

* It ought to be pointed out that even amongst the Manchus the written records of theories do not assume the function of "Sacred books", which is rather characteristic of the European complex: the holding to the written document as to a more trustworthy basis. The place of the Bible may be occupied by the "origin of the species", and "Das Kapital", the reference to which may suffice for putting an end to discussion, and for stopping a critical reaction on the newly acquired facts.

** The anecdotes (such is the form of treatment) gathered among the European groups by Sir J. G. Frazer, A. Lang, L. Bruhl and many others are numerous and need not here be reproduced.

* This term I have already used in my previous publications on this subject. In the original Russian work (1919) I used term vm'estilišče—the "receptacle."

general name in Tungus languages and which may be called *SPIRITS*.

We cannot restore the history of this Tungus theory unless we allow ourselves to be carried on by a stream of hypotheses. Since the problem of "origin" of the spirits has already been discussed by a great number of theoreticians and since these theories are not in our eyes convincing I prefer to leave it without discussion. Indeed, it ought to be pointed out that the "origin", in the sense of the first creation of this idea, may be supposed to be very old since the idea of soul was known to the hypothetic ancestors of the present man—Homo Neanderthalensis, who did practise burial. However, Homo Neanderthalensis is not regarded by the anthropologists as an animal of the same species as Homo Sapiens, and thus the idea of soul is going out of the range of Homo Sapiens. We may now go one step farther. The Homo Neanderthalensis in Europe possessed the so-called Mousterian cultural complex. However, the Sinanthropus Pekinensis who is somewhat related to the Pithecanthropus Erectus, both of which cannot be directly connected with Homo Sapiens and ought to be regarded no more than *hominidae*, was using the same type of implements as Homo Neanderthalensis. This shows that the highly differentiated cultural complex of Mousterian type was known to other hominidae as well. On which ground can we suppose that other elements of the cultural complex of Mousterian culture were not known to other hominidae? If it is so, then the origin of the idea of soul and its possible exteriorition ought to be brought back to the animals which are now extinct. The scientist is thus in the position of being unable to restore either the complex in which this idea has made its first appearance, or the first forms of these ideas. The scaffolding of the hypotheses will not help the investigator; it may relieve him of the burden of unknown and it may easily become not the truth but a justification and rationalization of the investigator's own ethnographical complex. For this reason I shall not venture to propose any new hypotheses or support any one of those previously proposed*.

The analysis of the spirits' characters shows first of all that the spirits possess characters in greater or lesser degree similar to these observed in man. Yet these characters may be increased with the elements that result from the further complication of the original conceptions. The spirits are thus supplied with the human characteristics, human desires, human thoughts, human will, etc. Again

---

* Some authors are now inclined to the idea that there existed at least two "stages" of animistic and preanimistic complexes (Zelenin and his predecessors). In the Tungus complex we shall see both forms of building up hypotheses and theories which imply the complex of other cultural elements. They are thus, at least now, synchronous. However, their sequence in time cannot be shown unless one postulates several hypotheses. For understanding functional value of the theory of spirits and positive knowlege one must consider them as they are found in the existing complexes and never as an abstraction. Indeed, the theories of Mana, and others like it, are still more phantastic than that of the distnction of "animistic" and "preanimistic stages."

the analysis of different types of spirit bring us to a generalization as to the nature of spirits. According to the Tungus idea, the spirits are immaterial, they cannot be seen unless they take special form, they may influence physical bodies, they produce various sounds, they possess all human characters, including feeling of temperature, hunger, anger, gratitude, emotional excitement, and so forth. Thus the spirit is like the human being, only it cannot be perceived with sight, touch, smell and taste. Since the spirits are supplied with all these characters they may be treated in the same way as human beings are treated. On the other hand further observations of the spirits' activity have brought the Tungus to the limitations of the spirits' similarity with man and sometimes to a reduction of their complex to simple manifestations of certain human characters and those created by the Tungus theoretical thought. Since the spirits possess immaterial nature they may assimilate physical phenomena only in their immaterial substance. Owing to this the spirits may consume, e.g. the sacrifice, in its immaterial manifestations. It ought to be noted here that the Tungus regard smell, evaporation, smoke, etc. as immaterial in their nature and thus as "substances" which may be easily assimilated by the spirits. So it is very important to analyse what is regarded by the Tungus as "material" and "immaterial", if one wishes to understand their system.

As soon as the theory of spirits was created many confused questions of nature and relations originating between man and milieus might be easily explained as result of spirits' activity. Many groups of natural phenomena which could not be covered by a naturalistic generalization in this cases began to act as a scientific hypothesis explaining phenomena of milieu, the Tungus psychology and mentality. In this respect the Tungus did not and do not show great differences as compared with other ethnical groups. In fact, if the Tungus happen to learn something new about the spirits already existing they would not hesitate to increase the spirits' character or their potential activity with a new element. If they learn that some of the characters were wrongly referred to the spirits they would introduce some corrections or they would reject the spirit as a mistake on the part of the earlier producers who might make a mistake. If they should learn about some new spirits previously unknown to them they would accept these as we would accept a hypothesis looking credible and not being in a conflict with the whole of the existing complex.

Therefore the number of spirits is always changing; they increase, decrease, and change their characters. The elasticity of this system permits the Tungus to give up their spirits which are not thus *petrified in a fixed* system of a religion with its tradition, sacred books, etc.

I will not now enumerate the spirits which will be treated in a detailed manner in the special chapters, for the above remarks regarding spirits will suffice before we reach the Tungus theories based upon the hypotheses of spirits.

CHAPTER V

PRIMARY MILIEU

17. EARTH AND CELESTIAL BODIES Under the term primary milieu I shall understand the milieu with which ethnical units meet when they arrive at a new territory not occupied by other ethnical units. Such a milieu is beyond a direct control of human units. Thus, the cosmos, with the solar system, the Earth, the conditions of topography, geology, soil, climate' flora and fauna, also all physical and chemical phenomena are the elements forming the primary milieu. The ethnical unit which consists of individuals through their accumulation of observations regarding primary milieu and through making inferences from the facts observed, also accumulation of facts and inferences made by other human units, all of which are transmitted through the tradition, forms the complex of natural science. It is not here presumed whether the observation of facts and inferences made correspond to what is found by modern science or not, whether this knowledge is extensive or not, whether the inferences made from the point of view of modern science are correct or not. The differences will be that of quantity of facts known and correctness of inferences, but as to the essential of science, i.e. the cognition of the nature (primary milieu), it is the same among all ethnical units. Therefore this chapter could be titled as one dealing with the natural sciences.

In the Tungus system, among all groups, the Earth is regarded as a stable and flat body. Over the Earth there is sky which is of solid consistence. The nature of the sky material is left out of discussion, but it is believed that it, may reflect the sun-light. The sun, moon, and stars are moving on the sky according to their own paths. The path, or place occupied by them as well as by the stars is called in Ner. *koklon**. The sun and moon rise and set back after their daily or nightly running along their paths. The stars are small as compared with the sun and moon and they are not alike for some of them change their relative place according to the periods (planets), while others regularly keep the same position in reference to other stars. One of them, the Polar Star, possesses its constant position and does not move at all. The terms for Polar Star are different. It is called *toγolga* (Bir), *bugadulin* (RTM), *ogdeu ošikta* (Ang. Tit.) *gátá* (Kum). The terms for "star" in all known Tungus dialects are of the same stem—*osi* which is subject to the variations owing to the alternation $o \sim u$;

$$i \sim e; \; z \sim \check{s} \Big\langle \begin{matrix} h \to x \to \gamma \\ \check{z} \end{matrix} \quad \text{and increase of the initial}$$

vowel with bilabialization and aspiration. The stems are usually supplied with the suffixes (*kta*, *ža*, etc.), so that the most distant forms are *mužiya* (Manchu Sp.) and

oγekat (Lam)*. Thus, the stem *osi* seems to be very old and Tungus which has no parallels in other languages. True, this stem with a certain imagination may be connected with the words known from other languages but it will not be sure. It is different with the name for Polar Star. In spite of the fact that Birarčen and Kumarčen have a dialect in common** the names for Polar Star are different *gáta* (Kum) and *toγolga* (Bir). In RTM it is *bugadulin* which is composite one and must be translated: "the middle of universe", while *toγolga* (Bir) is "the pillar" which supports the universe. So that at the basis of this conception is the same idea of a revolving world about a pillar. The pillar would not be understood as a physical pillar, but in sense of "axe" of European languages. This conception does not seem to be of Tungus origin. In Aug. (Tit.) we have again a different term *ogdeu ošikta*, which is either "great star", if *ogdeu* is a Tungus word or it is an alien word. In Kum. we have *gátá* the etymology of which I do not now propose***.

These facts may suffice for showing that the Tungus have accepted various theories and changed the name of the Polar Star in the process of adaptation to the new conceptions. The essential for us is that the Tungus know that the sky is revolving according to a definite principle, there are stars which change their place (*koklon*)**** and there are stars which remain fixed in relation to other stars and in relation to the revolving system; and last the Tungus have accepted various ideas from or through their neighbours.

The constellations are known to the Tungus under various names and almost all of them are connected with explanatory myths. Mythology is very rich and consisted in elements of various ethnic origin which may be seen from the names and myths. For instance, we meet with the myth of the Pleiadae referred to as the seven-stars constellation—*nadan unit* or *unat*—" the seven girls"; the Great and Little Urses, Orion and others are connected with different myths. There are other stars and constellations as for instance, the Wild Boar's Jaw—(Hyades) ; the Dog —(Regulus) ; the Hero; the River Boat, etc. It should be noted that Venus has lately received special attention of the Tungus, it may be supposed, in connexion with the recent spreading of some Mongol cultural elements amongst them. It is called by a term which is met with in Mongol *čolmon* and Yakut *čolbon*, e.g. *čolpon* (Bir. Khin.), *čalbon* (Kum. Man. Ner. Barg.), *čolbon* (RTM), *čalbon* (Ang. Tit.). However, it may also be called "evening" and "morning" star.

The milky way of the sky naturally attracted attention of the Tungus. There exist at least two sets of myths: the

---

* Cf. Ang. (Tit), where *osikta bijeren umu koklo* is translated by E. Titov as "the Polar star remains at the same place". Indeed *umu koklo* cannot be written, as E. Titov does, together, as one word. Here it may be pointed out that the place and path are designated by the same term *koklo*. What is the etymology of *koklo* I do not venture to guess.

* cf. Aspects, p. 105.
** The Birarčen have two dialects (cf. SONT).
*** The Manchu system is under the influence of the Chinese astronomy which itself in its form known at the moment of meeting of the Manchus with the Chinese was already connected with the astronomical notions of other (western Asiatic) groups. (cf. L. de Saussure and others) therefore I will not now compare the Manchus.
**** In Manchu it is *oron*,—the "place", "throne", "bed",'etc.

Manchus call it the "Sungari River" and the Northern Tungus usually call it the Birds' Way. The Tungus of Manchuria sometimes accept the Manchu name. As far as I could see the Tungus do not understand it as a river or as a birds' way, but regard it as a peculiar accumulation of stars which they cannot explain. If they are asked as to the nature of Milky Way they reply:—"Certainly, these are stars". If you insist upon the explanation they tell you that "Such is the name!—the people say so".

This is true of all names of stars and constellations except those names which are not Tungus names, as for instance *čolbon* ("Venus").

The comets are called (Bir) *čirda*,—the war arrow,—and their appearance is connected in some way with the Venus (*čolbon*.)

The description of the Tungus mythology at present time has no importance for us, for the Tungus do not believe that the myths reflect their ideas as to the organization of the universe. In the eyes of the Tungus these myths are mere literary creations, pure and simple myths, and they treat them only from the point of view of art. No conception of reality is connected with these myths. The Tungus mythology will be dealt with in special publications on the Tungus Folklore*.

* To distinguish where is literature (folklore in a narrow sense) and where is an exposition of the scientific theories accepted by the ethnical unit is not an easy task even for an experienced ethnographer. It is evident that the body of facts known to ethnical units possessing a culture of the same volume as that of the Tungus is rather numerous. Owing to the fact that the scientific knowledge is transmitted by oral tradition their record must be done by the ethnographer. So before the ethnographer there stands the task of distinguishing where is an artistic creation and where is a positive scientific record of facts with their analysis and conclusions. It requires not only a good knowledge of the language and many branches of general knowledge, which is rare amongst ethnographers, but also a keen analytical mind for tracing the line of demarcation, if there is any, between the scientific knowledge and artistic creation, and first of all a perfect knowledge of the psychomental complex. However, when the ethnographer first visits the ethnical group as a rule he approaches it either with no knowledge at all, or with a series of ready-made patterns, for which he has only to select the facts. On the ground of European psychomental complex and ethnocentric complex the groups of the "inferior" complex are considered à priori as possessing the most "queer" and "strange" conceptions which must strike the imagination of the readers (psychology hominis avidi rerum novarum) by something which is not usual and common, particularly "prelogic" and lacking of common sense. If the ethnographer cannot satisfy this requirement of the "market" and "crowd" he is considered, as a rule, with suspicion, while those ethnographers who are able to produce a required mosaic picture will be recognized as "real" and very learned authors. The ethnography is thus one of the elements which constitute the European complex. What happens practically is that the ethnographer visits the groups for a short time; he cannot distinguish the elements of folklore (in a narrow sense) (art!) from positive knowledge, which is so accepted by the groups, and he confuses everything which he collects. After coming to his own milieu he produces a kind of heterogeneous composition agreeable to his readers. Indeed, the European ethnographical complex is richer than that of some "primitive" groups, so the "folklore" and "science" of Europeans contain more elements (and facts). To become familiar with them requires more than a human life, but the amount of knowledge amongst the "primitives" is not so small that it may be recorded during a short visit. Let us suppose that an ethnographer who does not belong to the European cycle passes a long period of two years (I increase proportionally the period) among the Europeans, he will not be able to analyse and know the complex and he will record together as a whole of cosmogonic theories Wagner's Tanhäuser, Kant-Laplace's theory, and Madame de Taibe's predictions. If the readers of the groups to which

The sun is a very large body which runs along his path (*koklon*). It rises up, goes up the summit of the skies, and descends, falls down, in order to continue his path tomorrow. The sun has at least three different names in different dialects. So he is called *dilačá* (Bir. Kum.), *dilača* (Ner. Barg.) (Ang. Tit), *dèlača* (Man.), *delača* (Ner.), *delačá* (Czek.); also another series: *s¹ivun* (Khin.), *s¹i̯ĥun* (RTM), and contracted forms, e.g. *s¹iun* (Neg. Sch.) (Goldi, Gr.), *siu* (Oroč. Sch.), *sun* (Neg. Sch.), *šun* (Manchu Writ. Sp.) and others; and a third series,—*n¹ultin* (Lam. Tum.) *n¹últan* (Lamut). There are thus differences which reveal at least three groups of dialects. It seems to me that the forms of *dilača* type are perhaps of secondary origin*. These stems cannot surely be compared with the stems of other languages.

The moon moves in the same way as the sun but does not appear during a certain period at all. The phases of the moon are not understood and the Tungus suppose that the moon is periodically "born". Whether it is a metaphor or a physical conception I cannot say, but there is no doubt that the "birth" is not the same as that in man and other animals. The word for "moon" in all Tungus dialects is derived from the stem *bega* with variations in contracted form being *b¹a* (e.g. Manchu). No connexion with other languages is possible.

The sun and moon eclipses are known as natural phenomena, but according to custom the Tungus produce noise and shout in order to frighten the heavenly dog which swallows the sun and moon. However, when the Tungus say so they do not accept it seriously and regard it rather as a joke, for, they say, one may see the sun and moon during the eclipse. The "heavenly dog" is not of Tungus origin, but of Chinese origin, which is also known to some Tungus groups (Birarčen). Amongst the Bargusin Tungus the function of the dog is performed by the spirit—*jarajarguči*—which seems to belong to the non-Tungus complex.

18. YEAR AND ITS SUBDIVISIONS The seasons are distinguished according to the position of the sun and their sequence is connected with the sun's movement**, so that four or more seasons form a year. The year in Tungus is *aygan¹i* (Khin, RTM, Bar), *ayyani* (Bir. Kum. RTM), *ayani* (Bir) (Mank. Castr), *ayyini* (Lam), etc. *anyn* (Oxot. Klaproth), *anan* (Lamut, Klaproth), *an¹a* (Manchu Writ. Sp.), *an¹e* (Nuichen, Grube). The Manchu form is also used among the Tungus who are in contact with the Manchus. The beginning of the new year is not fixed among all groups, which depends on the calendar in use. Groups which have adopted Manchu-Chinese system begin the new year according to

the ethnographer belongs show a negative reaction towards the European complex and consider it as "inferior" his publication will be accepted as a clever and learned work, and carefully reviewed by competent critics. This may give the picture which is often produced by the ethnographers visiting for a short time "primitive" groups.
* It is very attractive to connect them with dil,—the "head",
** The Birarčen would say the sun is Buga which creates the seasons. However, it will not be an identification of the celestial body with the spirit buga (vide infra). The sun is only one of the manifestations of buga. The summer is the mother, the winter is the father, the spring and autumn are daughter and son respectively. The Spring covers itself as a girl with flowers. The mother feeds all of them. Indeed, these are poetic metaphors and probably of not Tungus origin.

this system, while the groups influenced by the Russians begin it much earlier. What was the original Tungus system and when they used to begin the new year is difficult to say.

The months are known and counted according to the moons. There are different arrangements of calendar. Amongst the Tungus of Manchuria—the Birarčen, Kumarčen and Khingan groups,—the Manchu names for months are adopted with a slight phonetic adaptation. This is a Chinese system translated into Manchu, i.e. the first moon, second moon, and so on. The "month" is *b'a* as in Manchu, and not "*bega*".

The system of the Reindeer Tungus of Manchuria is evidently borrowed from the Yakuts. It consists of twelve months beginning from the end of January:

1. *Toksun'u*—understood as "the cold weather is over"—cf. *toxsun'u* (Yak. Pek.) (Pek. etymology: *Toyus*,—"nine", the ninth month).
2. *Olon'o*—the meaning could not be established—cf. *olun'u* (Yak Pek.) (Pek. etymology: "ten", the tenth month,—February—March).
3. *Kuluntutar*—understood as "to keep the kolt"—cf. *kulun tutar* (Yak Pek.) (Pek. etymology: *kulun*,—the kolt; *tutar*,—to keep off. *vide* p. 1210).
4. *Omija*—understood as "the grass appears"—I do not venture to compare with Yakut words. It does not sound like a Tungus word, and it cannot be understood as a Tungus word.

   Another term is *Buyustar*—understood as "the ice (river) breaks"—cf. *mus* (*bus*) *ustar* (Yak. Pek.) (Pek. etymology: "ice broke",—April—May).
5. *Boy'ija*—understood as "the pine bark can be separated" (formerly used as a food stuff)—cf. *büs* (Yak. Pek.)—the pine. In Yakut (Pek.) it is *yamyja*, *balykyia* ("May—June").

The meaning of the following four months could not be established:

9. *Boy'in'i* cf. *bäsin'i* (Yak. Pek.) (Pek. etymology: "five");
10. *Alin'i* cf. *alyn'y* (Yak. Pek.) (Pek. etymology: "six");
11. *Satin'i* cf. *sättini* (Yak. Pek.) (Pek. etymology: "seven", the seventh month);
12. *Aksinn'i* cf. *axsyn'y* (Yak. Pek.) (Pek. etymology: "eight").

From the comparison of RTM names with those of the Yakuts it is evident that RTM terms are merely borrowed from the Yakuts. This Tungus group formerly was under a Yakut influence (*vide* SONT). However, some considerations are of interest. First of all, the Tungus understand the names of months not in their etymological meaning (vide E. Pekarskii's analyses) but as various characteristics of the months. In some cases, like *kuluntutar* the meaning in Tungus and Yakut coincides. *Olon'o* is not understood at all. The names *Omija* and *Boyija* are seemingly lacking (?) in Yakut and have quite concrete meanings. I do not know how the names of the months are now understood by the Yakuts, and whether the Tungus interpretations correspond to that of the Yakuts or not, but the fact that there are names which are not met with in Yakut is indicative that in the Tungus (RTM) mind the names of the months have certain meaning in which there are included characteristics of the months as seasons. I have been told by some Tungus, e.g. in Transbaikalia and in Man-

churia (Birarčen) that they formerly used to have different names of the months by which they characterized the seasonal conditions. Perhaps the spirit of RTM names is a secondary adaptation of the Yakut names to the old complex. The counting of the months as "first", "second", etc. in RTM seems to be an adaptation to the Russian Church year cycle, which begins in January (14th of Gregorian calendar). I was unable to establish when these groups used to begin their year cycle.

The system used among the Tumynxyn Tungus recorded by P. V. Olenin is quite different. When they count months they sometimes touch the head and articulations of the upper limbs as shown.

1. *Xeja*—the top of the head; (cf. *ojo*, etc. also Mongol and Manchu, ibid., the top of the mountain, head, etc.) which seems to fall on January (end?).
2. not recorded. Probably *m'ir'i*—the shoulder.
3. *Iečän*—the elbow; (cf. *ičan*, etc. the "elbow"); the elbow of the right arm is meant or touched.
4. *B'ilän*—the wrist; the wrist of the right arm is touched.
5. *Neun'in'i* so is called the first summer month which seems to be merely "the spring" (*vide infra*).
6. *Kulin* elann'i*—the second summer month.
7. *hunni elann'i*—the third summer month [The etymology is not clear. *Elan* (Tum) *elann'i* (Lam), according to the record, means "the month"] is not clear].
8. *Mont'ahii*—the fourth summer month [The etymology
9. Marked but not recorded.
10. *Eur'i m'ir'i*—the left (arm) shoulder.
11. *Eur'i iečän*—the left (arm) elbow.
12. *Eur'i b'ilän* the left (arm) wrist.
13. *Eur'i unm'i*—the left (arm) finger root.

To this system may be related the system given by Rev. Popov (?) [cf. op. cit. 33] who translated the Lamut system as shown.

January—*Xeja*
February—*M'ir*
March—*Eča*
April—*Bilen*
May—*Onma*
June—*N'ëng'in'i*
July—*D'üpun'i* [The etymology is not clear; perhaps it may be connected with "summer" (*vide infra*)]
August—*čoka* [the etymology is not clear].
September—*Tótti onma* [*tótti*—seems to mean "rising", from the stem *tot*—to rise, climb, going from the finger root up to the shoulder.]
October—*Tótti b'ilen*
November—*Tótti ečan*
December—*Tótti m'ir*

This system is a variation of the Tum. system. Indeed, the identification of *Xeja* as January must be accepted with great caution, for it is not likely that these Tungus (Lamut) counted according to the old Russian style—the first of January prior to 1900 falling on the 13th day of the Gregorian January. The Lamut system seems to be an adaptation of the Tungus system to the needs of the Church. Yet, according to Lam. system there are thirteen months while according to the Lamut system there are only twelve. It may be pointed out that the names of summer months are different in the two compared dialects.

* Kulin is it not "snake"?

In a small dictionary of an Enissy Tungus dialect compiled by a missionary I find the names of "January" and "February" *gildena*, which seems to be the name of a season; "April" *noɡen'i*, which seems to be the name of the season (*vide infra*); June—*manman'i*, and July—*xum'in'i*, which may be compared with the name for "third summer month" of Tum. dialect. Perhaps this dialect still preserves some old Tungus names. However, it must be pointed out that these names may also be new names (for the months) introduced under the pressure of missionaries.

In order to complete the variety of existing systems it may be noted that the Tungus groups in Transbaikalia use either Russian names (modification of Latin names) in a Tungus phonetic adaptation, or they use Buriat names when the Buriat influence is strong.

So, in so far as it may be seen from the facts, the Tungus at the present time use different systems: (1) Chineso (in Manchu modification and Tungus adaptation); (2) Yakut (perhaps fused with the old Tungus system) (based on the counting of months as it was amongst the Uigurs); (3) the mechanical counting of months, with the names of uncertain origin and meaning; (4) the Russian system; and (5) the Buriat (Mongol) system. These four cultural influences may be observed in all phenomena of Tungus complexes. All these systems are not of Tungus origin, and even the system (3) cannot be considered as Tungus, for it seems to be a translation of an alien system. In fact, the Tungus as many other ethnical groups count by bones and articulations (cf. amongst the Europeans the counting of months with 30 and 31 days). However, in the RTM system, as well as in Tum. and Lamut system for summer months we find some traces of the old Tungus system which was based upon the essential characteristics of the regions of Siberia, e.g. *Om'ija*—"the grass appears" (in May), *Boɣija*—"the juicy pine bark" (in June), *kulin elann'i* the "snake (?) month" (in June) If these hints may be accounted as an evidence, the inference may be made that the Tungus prior to the appearance of the above indicated influences possessed a certain calendar based on the lunar months named according to the local characteristics of the seasons. This was a Northern Tungus system but in so far as it may be seen the old Pro-Tungus system cannot be restored. The Chinese system has received great diffusion through the Manchus and it has been adapted, conventionally "translated", to some distant groups (e.g. in Lam. and Lamut). The Uigur-Yakut system has also influenced the Tungus. The Buriat-Mongol and Russian-Latin system are recent influences.

The Tungus complex recognizes *seasons* which do not cover definite months.

SPRING. There seems to be no definite period or starting moment of the "spring". There are two words in some dialects (RTM) for designation of a period which may be called "spring". The stem *nVl*+suff. *ki*: *nulki* (Khin), *nälki* (Mank), *nälki* (Ur. Mank. Castren), *nelki* (Tum.) (Neg. Sch), *nilki* (RTM), *nöltki* (Neg. Sch.) designate the season when the snow begins to thaw. The stem *noɣ* (ja): *noɣja* (RTM), *nöuɣi* (Lam), *n'onɡn'on*, *nönɡn'ön* (Neg. Sch.) *n'önɡn'ŏ* (Goldi. Sch.) *n'epn'er'i* (Manchu Writ.) etc. designate the period when the grass appears. The stem and word *or'ilasani* (Ner.) [*ovilassa=or'ilašani=ov'elakšani*. (Ang. Ner. Tit.)] designates early spring, when the snow is part-

ly melted and the earth begins to be seen. Indeed, these are designations of the *periods of the spring*, but they are not "spring". In the records these names were sometimes identified as names of different months. So e.g. it was done by the missionaries, E. I. Titov referred *nilki* to "March", but *nongnŏn'i* (Ang. Tit) to "June-July", which does not seem to be correct, for this period is called "summer" (*vide infra*). Such an identification is not correct. The etymology of these stems is difficult to find. Some parallels are probable but they are not at all sure. Naturally the beginning of the seasons greatly depends on the local climatic conditions and these cannot be referred to definite months of the year[*]. SUMMER. In so far as I know all Tungus dialects have the same stem for designation of the summer—season: *juɡa* with the suffixes—*ni* (*n'i*) and r'i (Manchu). The modifications are numerous: e.g. *juɣani* (Ner. Bir.) *juven'i* (Manchu Sp.) [cf. also *juvemb'e*—"to spend the summer" (Manchu Sp.)], *jua* (Goldi, Sch.), *duɡan'i* (Neg. Sch.)[**]. This season covers a varying number of days depending on the local conditions. AUTUMN. In so far as I know there is only one stem used—*Bolo* with suffixes *n'i* and *r'i* (Manchu). The variations are not interesting[***]. WINTER. In so far as I know there is only one stem—*tuɡa*, with variations similar to those of *juɡa*, "the summer", the most contracted form being found in Goldi *tu*.

Amongst the Birarčen the characteristics of the seasons are as shown:

The Spring—*nŏlk'ini*—begins when the snow begins to melt. There are two periods: the first one *nŏlk'ini ineɣi iren* [the spring day comes out (proceeds)]; *kois'i* (the period when the snow is off); *dèɣi èmèrèn* (the birds arrive); *olo kačin činaka turaren* (all kinds of small birds speak). The second one: *orokto čotorgaran, abdanna ollarɡaran* (the grass begins to become green and the leaves begin to come out); *birakama ollo soloron* (small river fish go up stream).

The Summer—*juɣani*—begins with appearance of the insects during the first period when *manmâkta jüren, irɡâkta jüren* (the mosquitoes come out, the gad flies appear); and the second period when *orokto isŏmi ogdi ŏdan, monin napčin isŏm ogdi ŏča* (the grass in reaching big become the tree leaf in reaching big became), *älla kačin kulikan jüren* (all kinds of "worms and snakes" are coming out), *čokomokta jüren* (the midges are coming out).

The Autumn—*boloni*—begins when *bolor ineɣi iren* (the autumnal day proceeds); *s'iliksä ɡ'iliɡdi ŏdan* (the dew cold becomes); *abdanna sillären* (the leaves change colour); *bojeɣɡa büɣčeran* (the Cervus Elaphus cries); *orokto olɡoron* (the grass becomes dry). The second period is when *jukä jüren, tur tuksären* (the ice comes out, the earth [soil] becomes cold). The third period is when *emana tukillan* (the snow falls down).

The Winter—*tuɣan'i*—which begins about the middle of November, when *ɡ'iliɡdi odinji emanava doɣilifkanen* [with the extremely cold wind the snow is made to fly (like a bird)]; the second period is when *turtan iren* (the coldest period comes) [there are distinguished: *ilan turtan odin*

[*] In the dictionary compiled by the missionaries in Enissy region, Spring (as adjective) is figured as *bolen'i*. I believe it is a mistake of the recorder.
[**] In Lam. there has been recorded *ireldu* as "the summer", but I am not sure of this record.
[***] In Lam. the autumn is recorded as *mont'ahli*, cf. also the name of the fourth summer month. I am not sure about the record.

(the three coldest winds)]; the third period is when *buya n'amallan* (the world becomes warm), *dilaĉa okugdi ōdan* (the sun hot becomes), *ineyi gonom ōdan* (the day becomes long.)

As seen in this system the periods are distinguished with great detail, and are referred to the lunar months of the Chinese—Manchu system. I do not need to point out that this classification satisfies two requirements,—the correct characteristics of the seasons and periods and the aesthetic feeling of the Tungus.

From the above facts it may be seen that the distinction of seasons is well preserved amongst the Tungus groups and it is rather uniform. There are some other minor distinctions of the seasons, but they are not uniform, and one may see in them the influence of the change of vegetation and economic activity of the groups*. It may be supposed that in former days the Tungus groups possessed different system of designation of smaller units of the seasons but how far they coincided with the calendar, it is difficult to say. Yet, we have no data regarding the old Tungus calendar in the sense of counting years and months.

As shown the Tungus language possesses the word for "the year" (the stem *anga*, contracted in Manchu to *an'a*) but for counting age all Tungus groups have different terms, borrowed from the Manchus, Yakuts and Mongol-Buriats; for counting age of animals, they have distinct names for all important age groups of reindeer, and even *wild cervines*, as well as for horses and cows amongst the Tungus living on horse and cattle breeding. Indeed, such a particularism is not incidental. Among all Tungus groups it is common that the people do not know their exact age. The distinction of persons according to their social position and according to their, shall I say, physiological condition,—children, young people, adult people, elderly people, old people and very old, —suffice the Tungus for establishing their relations. The age in terms of years is not so much needed as it is in the European groups. Certainly it does not mean that the Tungus do not know the method of exact record and do not count years, months and days. They are very strict, and do it without mistake, when it is necessary. For instance, they sometimes make arrangements for meetings to take place several months after the agreement. To aid memory they would make a mark on a device, usually a wooden piece with the marks of days, months and years. Some of these are very complex but nevertheless can be read easily by the Tungus. The days of the new moon and Winter and Summer soltices are carefully observed.

19. MEASURES Since we have mentioned the subject of the exactness I shall add some facts in order not to return to this question. The Tungus have sometimes been described as people who do not know how to count. This is a great misunderstanding,—they easily manage within the limits they need for counting their herds, days, months, and hunting spoils. Indeed, they do not need to operate with the numbers which exceed a few hundreds**.

When they do not count their debts to the merchants it is not because of their ignorance, but because they know perfectly well that they are not in position to bargain with the merchants. Moreover, in the Tungus mind, minuteness in the matter of money is something which is not permitted by their pride. I have observed it very often amongst all groups. Amongst the groups which are now under a strong foreign influence, and when the old complex is lost, the Tungus make their accounts as well as other ethnical groups, e.g. the Chinese, and Russians.

In the previous section we have already discussed measurement of time and we have seen that the Tungus do have the units for measuring time, i.e. the solar and moon movement, of which the day is perhaps the smallest unit. However, besides the unit—day [the stem is *inan*, with suffixes and modifications (sometimes contracted e.g. *in'i* Goldi, Sch)] which consists of the day time (*inan*) and night (*dolbon*) the Tungus divide into two parts: from midnight (*dolbondulin*, i.e. the night middle) to midday (*inandulin*, i.e. middle of the day) and from midday to midnight. There are distinguished the moments of sunset and sunrise, and special periods: the morning, the period between the morning and midday—*ogdi dulga* (Bir.), the moment about three hours before the sun set —*xyalayin* (RTM); the moment about one hour and a half before the sunset—*s'ikĕĝyi* (Bir.)*, the period after the sunset—*boror* (RTM), that about sunset—*luyur* (Ner.) and others. Such a division of the day permits the Tungus to give, with a good approximation, time in their relations and for appointments. Every Tungus knows how to judge the time by measuring the direction and length of the shadow. Indeed, they would not express it in the terms of hours, which they do not need, but they know the principle**. It may be added here that the Tungus know rather well the time even during cloudy days and in the night***. Also, they know perfectly well how long a time (in terms of periods) is required for traversing a certain distance. Let us remark that the idea of a smaller unit of time does exist. This is that of the winking of the eye, the pulse, and breathing. However, these units are rarely used.

We have touched upon the problem of the methods of measurement of time which brings us straight to the problem of measurement of length in general. Referring to the unit-distance of travelling we shall see that the Tungus measure both time-unit (the travelling distance)**** and

---

* For instance, the seasons distinguished are: turlan (Bir)—the period of the most intensive cold weather (according to the Chinese complex containing 9.3 days); siyilaya (RTM)—the season of the hunting of squirrel; ĉukalaya (RTM)—the season of the intensive growth of grass. I need not multiply instances.

** As a matter of fact the Tungus dialects possess no Tungus words for "thousand". It may be borrowed from the Manchus,

Mongols, and Russians, while in some dialects it is replaced by "ten hundreds" e.g. ĵangrin'ama (Lam.). In some dialects n'ama—"hundred" is replaced by the Manchu word tangu which also means "the number" and "great number".

* From a common Tungus stem s'ikaä (with modification) "the evening", met with in many dialects. There ought to be added x'ieyedin (Tum), x'eyedin (Lam.), ayiltana (RTM) with the same meaning.

** In connexion with this it may be noted that they also know how to estimate the length of a tree by measuring its shadow, which shows that they have the idea of proportion. I do not need to bring more facts to show that this simple principle is known to them, which will be evident when we go through other details of their psychomental complex.

*** Amongst all the groups I have made many experiments by asking day periods and checking their statements with my watch. This is quite common amongst the Tungus, almost general, while a "good feeler of time" is rather rare amongst the Europeans.

**** This may be used as a pretext for endowing the Tungus with the idea of relativity. The reader will not expect me to do so for the reasons why I rejected a similar attempt on the part of an eth-

absolute measure are not practically expressed in numbers of same unit.

The Tungus have the following units:

1. The fathom which will be understood as the distance between the fingers of the outstretched arms. As known from the anthropology it is subject to the variations depending on the stature and relative length of the arm and bi-acromial diameter. Practically amongst the Tungus it may be expected to be 165 centimetres. It is called *dar* (Bir. Khin.) [cf. *darambi* (Manchu),—to "stretch the arms"] *da* (Neg. Sch.) (Manchu Writ.) [cf. *dari* (Goldi),— to measure] *alda* (Man) (Ur. Castr.) [cf. *alda* Mong. Writ and Sp.]

2. The "half fathom". It is called by a term *delim* (Bir.) borrowed from the Mongols (cf. *delim, aldadelim*. Mongol, Rud.).

3. The distance between stretched thumb and little finger,—*toyor* (Bir.).

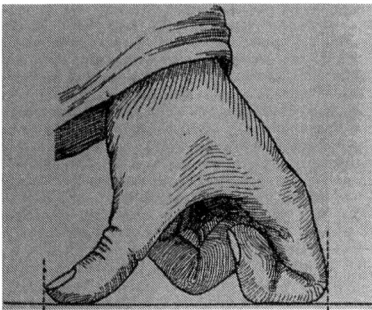

4. The distance between the stretched thumb and the articulation of the first finger, *sum* (Bir.).
5. Four fingers together—*angá* (Bir.).
6. The finger—*unaka* (Bir.) (there may be one, two, and three fingers).
7. The elbow (foot)—the distance between the elbow and root of the fingers—*ičá* (Bir.).
8. The inch, the length of the middle part of the index (first finger)
9. stride, *g'irás'ikta* (Bir.).

The smaller lengths have divisions into 8 and 16 parts, of *unaka*, also divisions of all other units. All the measurements are considered as of average man. They cannot be considered as very exact, but they are sufficient for the needs of the Tungus[*]. They have also a system of measures for volume, but they are rarely used. The units are e.g. rein-

nographer. Cf. "North Tun. Migr." where the case of W. Bogoras is discussed. This author did not confine his explanation to the Chukchi and published another work "Einstein and Religion" (in Russian, Moskaw—Petrograd, 1923) which in the eyes of ignorant people may look as it would be a very learned ethnographical treatise.

[*] The Manchus possess very detailed standards of measures and weight which were copied from the Chinese system.

deer bags (for loading), handful, hollow of two hands, etc

As it may be seen the units are found in human body and they are met with amongst other ethnical groups in different parts of the world.

It may be noted that the Tungus distinguish geometrical elements such as the sides of right angled triangle, hypotenuse, diagonal, triangle, square, circle, ellipse, cylinder, etc,—for which they have special terms[*]. For drawing they also use callipers for making circles. Indeed, those of the Tungus who have become familiar with s'andard measures as used amongst the Russians and Chinese use them without any difficulty. In such a case the terminology is borrowed or the old one is adapted.

Indeed, the Tungus, when necessary, can give good approximation in "fathoms" or "strides", e.g. for the distance of the arrow effectiveness, which is perfectly known; also for modern fire-arms the use of which requires a very exact estimation of distance,—even a minor mistake in the elevation of the rifle for a long distance may cost to the Tungus a day of work. So the greater distance, like that between two geographical points may be expressed in the same unit. However, for practical purposes in the conditions of Tungus life they do not need the unit like "kilometre", or "mile". However, under the influence of an alien complex they do adopt such units. For instance, the Tungus of Trans-baikalia use a Russian term—versta (about 1065 metres)[**], while the Tungus of Manchuria use *bo* (Bir. Kum.) which, according to the Tungus, is a contracted form of *buya*,— the "territory, place, distance", and which is used in Manchu as term for the Chinese unit *li*[***].

20. WORLD AND ORIENTATION The observation of the stars, planets, sun and moon leads the Tungus to the idea of the structure of the world. These ideas amongst the Tungus are subject to great variations because of the intrusion of alien complexes. What was their own conception, I believe, it is now impossible to say.

We have already seen that the earth is considered as a flat solid body, of very large size. The idea that the earth approaches the round form is unknown to the Tungus if we omit the case of the Tungus who receive their education in Russian and Chinese schools.

Amongst the Tungus of Transbaikalia including the Mankova Tungus the most common conception of structure is that the universe, which is called *turú*, consists of three parts: the upper world—*uyidunda*, the middle world—*dunda*, which consists of the solid earth *jorko*[****], and the sea—*lamu* in the middle of which is the solid earth *jorko*; at last, the lower world—*orgidunda*. The names are interesting. The name for "universe" *turu*, and *tiru* in some dialects, is

[*] Indeed, many terms of such special meanings are mere adaptations of the Tungus stems, e.g. triangular is ilan kirēi (Bir.) which means:—having three "peaks" or "tops"; they may be borrowed as it seems to be in the case of the cylinder bumbo (Bir.) from Mongol; they may be descriptive, e.g. like "ellipsoid"—tuporin—which is derived from tupo—to bend, etc. However, these terms as they are used, now have geometrical meanings.

[**] Cf. in Yakut biäristä (Pek.)

[***] In Buriat (Podg.) we find the term modo, modon, which mean the "wood", i.e. the wooden post, the mark of versta used by the
[****] I do not venture to give the etymology of this word.
Russians.

used in the sense of "soil" "earth", so we have *tur* (Kum. Bir. Khin.), *tor* (Oxotsk.), *tui* (Neg Sch. where *r→i*). It is very likely that *turu* in the sense of universe is of secondary origin, the original being "the earth—soil". The meaning of the word *dunda* does not seem to be of Tungus origin, but it looks a Buriat conception of the world*. As a matter of fact this meaning has rather limited geographical distribution amongst the Tungus. The additions *uyi* and *orgi* have a very definite meaning "upper" and "lower". So these "three worlds" are reflecting the Lamaistic system. If the Tungus are pressed with additional questions they give explanations of minor subdivisions of the upper and lower worlds. This conception finds new support from Christianity.

The system of the world among the Tungus of Manchuria in the main lines is the same as that of the Tungus of Transbaikalia. There are three worlds the names of which reflect directions, e.g. *uyillan* (Bir. Kum.),—"upwards", and the idea of human life, e.g. *buni* (Bir. Khin. Kum.),—"the world of dead people". The Manchus are seemingly responsible for this system. Among the Tungus of Transbaikalia there is also a system of worlds of "living" and "dead" people.

These systems seem to overlie an older system in which the universe was called *buya*. The same term is used in the sense of "locality" and even "mile"; *buya* is used for designation of the highest spirit [also "weather" and "sky" (Neg. Sch.) which will be discussed later]. It is impossible to assert whether we have here the same original conception or several conceptions and fusing of different "meanings" owing to the similarity of the starters. In the Tungus dialects *buya* is subject to variations and in some dialects it has been reduced (or preserved) to particular meanings, e.g. we have in Manchu the contracted form *ba* [cf. *boa* (Goldi), *bua* (Bir.)] used only in the sense of "locality", "place". I believe it is now impossible to restore the old complex.

The original system of orientation in so far as it may be restored from the analysis of the terms of orientation amongst the Tungus** is not connected with their ideas as to the structure of the world, but it is based upon the orientation with regard to the local course of rivers and position of the mountains in reference to the sun. So that if we do not connect in our minds their orientation with regard to the sun with our own system of orientation, their system will appear as pure and simple local orientation. In fact, the "South" and "North" are recognized and called: the southern slope—*ant(a)*—of the mountain which is characteristically distinct from the point of view of vegetation and insolation (an essential condition for the Tungus), when compared with the northern slope—*boso*— of the same mountain. These two terms have no other meanings.

The travellers amongst the Tungus and investigators have recorded a great number of terms of orientation with regard to "West" and "East". The analysis of these terms brings us to the conclusion that they are only designations of the courses of the rivers, usual directions of migrations,

well known geographical places, e.g. Lake Baikal, the sea and great rivers, e.g. the Lena, the Amur. This system of orientation might suffice for small local groups of which the Tungus originally consisted. For practical orientation they would use indication of the locality, position of the sun and at night, position of the Polar Star. In fact, there are terms for both "West" and "East"—*soloki* and *ajaki*,—which in different groups are used in opposing senses and mean: the upper course and the lower course of the rivers or more literally,—upwards and downwards, against or with the river current. There are terms like *bargila*—"the opposite side of the river",—also names of local winds, etc. However, *soloki, ajaki, bargila*, etc. may also be locally used in the sense of "North", and "South" as well. The case of the Tungus is not an isolated one. The same system is observed among the Lolos who have their orientation according to the course of a river*. Theoretically, the same system may be expected to be found amongst other ethnical groups in Asia and elsewhere. The difficulty of its discovery consists chiefly in the investigator's attitude who "translates" from and into his own language.

The old Tungus system has been covered by other systems of orientation. So we may distinguish at least two systems, namely, the orientation with relation to the East, viz. when the speaker faces the East and finds on his left the North and on his right the South. Such a system existed among the ancestors of the Manchus,—the Nuichen. Whether this system was their original invention or borrowed from their southern and western neighbours is not important for us. The early Mongols, according to the supposition of W. L. Kotwicz**, also had the orientation with relation to the East and the groups of Middle and East Asia, like the Uigurs, and Kithans, had their orientation with regard to the East***. The recognition of the mode of orientation (points of orientation) in most of cases may be based only on the analysis of the terms, for we have no direct evidence regarding theories. This system of orientation is often found amongst some Northern Tungus groups which term the East "front", "in front", "frontwards" etc. It may be found in amalgamation with the old system of terms of local orientation. As the basis of this system amongst the Tungus is taken the movement of the sun which "rises" and "falls" when the meridian is passed (the midday). The same idea, i.e. orientation according to the movement of the sun seems to be found in the Buriat system. This is a new conception of orientation according to the Tungus *koklon* (*vide supra*). The second system which covers the original one and the above discussed is orientation in which the principal point is "South". It spread amongst the ancestors of the Manchus and Mongols and at last reached the Tungus who borrowed it together with the Manchu and Mongol terminology. Perhaps there

---

* Dunda in the sense of "earth" is met with chiefly in western groups of dialects e.g. Barg. Ner. Ang. and only rarely used in the sense of "earth-ground" (Enisey) (missionaries).

** Vide my study: "Northern Tungus terms of orientation".

* cf. A. F. Legendre, T'oung Pao, Series II. Vol. X, p. 605.

** cf. W. L. Kotwicz. "Sur la mode d'orientation en Asie Centrale", R. O. Vol. V, pp. 68-91.

*** The two different things must not be confounded, namely the orientation of habitations and that of the points of orientation. The dwellings can be oriented according to the local conditions, e.g. topography, winds, etc. while the points of orientation chiefly have their importance for migrations and location of neighbours and regions of interest. So I maintain my opinion as to the orientation amongst the Manchus in spite of considerations brought forth by W. L. Kotwicz (cf. op. cit. p. 82.).

existed other orientations as well, but in so far as I can see no traces can be surely established[*].

The orientation with relation to the East is particularly interesting because it is connected with the theory of the three worlds which as stated above, is also connected with the spreading of Buddhism (Lamaism) also adapted by some Tungus groups. Let us point out that the orientation with regard to the East is that which prevails in India and regions being under a strong Indian influence. It must not be inferred that the whole complex of Buddhism (even in the form of Lamaism) has influenced these groups, but it is much safer to consider the incorporation of the orientation with relation to the East as one of elements which might be useful for the ethnical units which began to spread their influence over small ethnical groups living within restricted regions. In other words, the complex of the three worlds and the orientation with regard to the East must not be regarded as a complex which as a whole penetrated among the Tungus; the system probably penetrated element by element, one after another, as is usually observed in the spreading of complexes.

21. NATURAL PHENOMENA The Tungus take for granted that there are mountains and rivers. They do not ask themselves how the mountain ridges were formed, which may be explained by an inoffensive "explanatory myth", but they observe how the rivers were formed and how through the activity of the water the process of destruction of mountain ranges proceeds. The river deposits in the form of pebbles and sand, as well as clay and organic products, are understood to be the result of natural processes. The possibility of changes in the orographic system due to the destruction of mountains is understood in the same way as it is understood by European science[**]. The phenomena of active volcanoes (e.g. the group of twelve volcanoes in the region of Mergen), hot springs etc., have no satisfactory interpretation. Caves attract attention of the Tungus, but in so far as I know the Tungus have no satisfactory explanation of this phenomenon. However, a naturalistic point of view is not hostile to the Tungus even in these questions. For instance they call the Gobi Desert, which has been visited by some Tungus, olgon lamu, i.e. literally "dried out sea"; thus it is considered to be the bottom of a sea (the Birarčen). In the same way they sometimes explain the presence of shells in the mountains. However, in the case of the Tungus of Manchuria, it is not likely that they have become familiar with the modern geological theories (e.g. from the Russian source). Yet, the destructive influence of vegetation, particularly that of the roots of large trees, on rocks is well known among the Tungus.

The Tungus as stated (vide supra Chapter IV) distinguish different kinds of "stones" when this distinction is essential for them e.g. peculiar conditions of denudation of

[*] As to the details of terms vide my study "Northern Tungus terms of orientation."
[**] From many instances of the kind I may quote a case when a Tungus explained to me how the system of the upper course of the Bystraia River (in North-Western Manchuria) might change its present connexion and instead of running into the Argun River, run into the system of the Nonni, if a low range were gradually washed by the streams until the upper course of the Bystraia were on a higher altitude than a tributary of the Nonni.

granites and porphyres, as compared with the lime formations and sandstone. They may be distinguished by colour and character of structure—small grained, large grained, etc. When the rocks may be used for practical purposes, e.g. as for colours, as grinding stones, whetstones, stones used for medical purpose ("black and white stones",) etc. they receive special name. The names of some rivers are connected with the particular characters of the local geological formations, e.g. daviksa, is applied to the rivers where ochre is found; ingali is applied to the rivers particularly rich in pebbles, etc. Elementary geological knowledge is very essential,—water, wood, and shelter depend upon the character of the local geological deposits. Also the palaeontological remains do not escape attention of the Tungus, e.g. well preserved ammonites, and some bivalves. The explanations are variable and very often they are connected with the activity of rivers.

Let us remark that since the Tungus know how the rivers begin, by gathering water from the small valleys and springs into the streams, then changing from streams to the small rivers and at last to large rivers, they know perfectly well the natural causes of the change of the water level, and they do not need any hypothesis of spirits for understanding the behaviour of large rivers. The explanations with the spirits is typical of the populations confined to limited areas, near the courses of big rivers, as for instance the Manchus.

The phenomenon of rain is explained as due to the condensation of the water in the clouds,—from fog (the fog, clouds and heavy rainy clouds are sometimes designated by the same word tuksu) to a cloud, and to a heavy cloud. So if the wind brings the clouds together (e.g. the clouds cannot pass over the high mountains) the rain may fall. The phenomenon of lightning and thunder is clear to the Tungus and they accept it as a fact of nature in some cases venturing to propose various hypotheses chiefly based upon the activity of the spirits. These hypotheses are numerous for the ethnical groups differ in this respect and propose various solutions.

The phenomenon of hail is explained as freezing of the rain in the upper strata of the atmosphere. That the changes of temperature depend on the altitude, is well known to the Tungus who visit high peaks. The phenomenon of snow is also understood in the same manner. The winds are not understood as movement of the air, for the existence of the air and atmosphere is not clear. However, the wind is accepted as a physical phenomenon compared with the movement of the air when one blows. No inference is made as to who is blowing. The difference in the climate of various regions and seasons is explained as due to the sun, which may be nearer or farther from the earth, to the length of the days and altitude.

The above given description of the Tungus attitudes in reference to the conditions of topography and natural agents is characteristic of the groups which occupy large areas and live on hunting which imposes migrations and a perfect knowledge of the local geography. It is not so with the groups which have no such an experience. The populations, like the Manchus on the banks of the Amur River and even some Tungus groups (also the Dahurs) who have settled and live on agriculture, or fishing have different conceptions, in which the place of natural treatment of the phenomena is occupied by the hypotheses as to the spirits. However, these populations are more familiar than the hunting groups with the behaviour of big rivers, change of seasons and other facts of importance for their economic activity. The sum of facts, regardless as to whether causes are explained by the theory of spirits or otherwise, is large and the people adapt themselves not to the existing theories but to the facts. The knowledge of small details goes so far that e.g. the Manchus know the day of ice breaking in big and small rivers with an approximation of four or five days, which they may predict several months before the fact takes the place*. Of course, such knowledge of local conditions is possible only for a population which lives for a long time in the given locality, accumulates facts, classifies them, and makes correct inferences as to the probability of occurrence and correlation of the changes of weather.

Indeed, no exact formulae can be given by these populations and the finding of "causes" may be beyond their reach, but the practical inferences are sufficient for facilitating their economic activity and at least for reducing the harmful effects of seasonal or accidental changes. It is difficult to restore, in all its details, the logical process of reaching conclusions and generalizations, but the fact of their correctness is indicative that the process is good in respect to the aim. Indeed, since the facts are not statistically recorded but usually transmitted through the mechanism of tradition it is evident that (1) the facts cannot be kept in the mind and that the conclusions are accumulated by the generations who transmit them through tradition, and (2) the conclusions are reached by the method of repeated correction. This is possible only on the condition of non-repulsive reaction to the new inferences and a certain degree of scientific objectivity. Thus as a process and as a method of building up the system of conclusions the ethnical groups here discussed do not differ from the real scientists who have not yet mastered modern statistical methods**.

In so far as knowledge of minor variations of seasons is concerned the Northern Tungus are inferior to the Manchus, but still they also have accumulated a great mass of facts regarding seasons. As a matter of fact, the hunters do not depend in such a degree as agriculturists and fishermen on the variability of the seasons and for this reason less attention is paid to the variations. As to the change of weather the Tungus are quite experienced. They base their plans for hunting on the *possible* changes of weather. In some cases this is absolutely necessary, for certain kinds of hunting may be done only under certain conditions of

---

* I have used all opportunities for recording their predictions as to the breaking of the ice, appearance of frost etc. and in my collection of these predictions I find very small deviations from the facts.

** Indeed, this is not typical of the Tungus alone,—it is typical of other ethnical groups as well. There may be a difference of the correctness of inferences, which in its turn is greatly conditioned by the body of facts gathered and practical utility of the knowledge. The experience of the fishermen living along the Chinese coast goes so far that they know the character of typhoons, their seasonal variations, signs of their approach etc. The fishermen's movement back to shelter is always considered by the experienced European seamen. On the other hand, the latter do not know how these humble fishermen know of the approach of typhoons and in their eyes this movement may be as much mysterious as the behaviour of birds before a typhoon. On the other hand among the educated Europeans, living in cities, the idea persists that on certain days, e.g. Christmas, etc. the weather is always the same. This is a survival of approximations regarding the regulations of Europe worked out by the farmers (many of which are new settlers in the regions occupied by them) and meteorologists. The self-confidence of the latter as to their possessing the truth depends upon the same mechanism as that of the farmers and the Tungus.

---

weather, e.g. to be able to see foot prints, to find animals in certain kinds of weather feeding themselves on grass, salted soil, etc. Should the Tungus not know, at least approximately, the possible variations of the weather, they would not be able to hunt because of the risk of useless spending of energy. The hunting sometimes requires several days of a certain type of weather which the Tungus must foresee. Moreover, the effect of heavy snow fall and the degree of danger from it to the migrating family, as well as the length of stormy weather, especially miscalculation of danger may cost life to the hunter and his family. Again here the Tungus must have correct observations and inferences, and he transmits these to the growing generation. This is not scientific knowledge, but it is a body of very elaborate and detailed knowledge, which is rarely properly understood and valued by superficial observers*.

22. PLANTS The Tungus are in great dependence upon the *vegetation* of the regions occupied, so their attention is turned to the problem of plants, as one of the conditions of the milieu.

The Tungus distinguish plants from minerals and animals. According to some Tungus, the plants possess a certain quality which is lacking in the mineral realm. The distinct character of the plants is that they grow. However, this opinion among different groups and among the individuals of the same group, is far from being generally adopted.

The Tungus accept the idea that all plants have "animus" in the sense given in Chapter IV, e.g. a tree possesses "animus". When it is cut down it becomes simple wood, good for making fire and manufacturing, so that the tree loses its animus. Besides the animus, the plants possess elements which may be called "life" manifested in growth, production of flowers, fruits etc. Therefore when the tree is cut into pieces of wood it loses its "animus" and "life". The nature of "life" will be discussed in the next section, so that now I shall confine myself to the general remark that the Tungus opinion differs as to whether the "life" of plants and animals is the same or not. Usually the Tungus abstain from speculation regarding this question. If one presses them with questions they give *some* reply to satisfy the persistence of questioner, but this will not mean that they are sure of what they say.

Plants in general have no designation in the Tungus dialects. They are classified according to the scheme: the

---

* Among the ethnical groups who possess the art of keeping written records, and especially among the Europeans, there is a curious ethnographical phenomenon, namely, they believe the science to begin with written records, so that science is not science until it is recorded in the form of treatises. Therefore the actually acquired scientific knowledge such, for instance, as the climatic changes and variations which permit the agriculturist to divide his work into regular periods, would not be considered as scientific knowledge, while a collection of anecdotes about "meteorological phenomena" explained with the most phantastic hypotheses as to their nature, published in book form commonly found till recently in Europe, would be considered as "science", Yet, the most accurate observations and conclusions made without following ethnographical features of European scientists would not be considered as science while the most unscientific treatise, lacking exact facts and filled with wrong inferences, if the outer forms of "science" be preserved, would be considered as a serious scientific work. The ethnographer when analysing these phenomena must be free of his ethnocentristic complex, which indeed is not easy.

trees—*mo* (all dialects), the same term being used for "wood", "stick" of no special use etc.; shrubs—*sekta* (RTM. Bir. Kum. Ner. Barg. Khin.), the same term referred to special kinds of shrubs, e.g. willow shrubs, and even to the thin branches of trees unknown to the Tungus; grass—*èuka* (Ner. Barg.) (Neg. Sch.), *èoka* (Bir. Kum.) (Neg. Sch.), *còka* (Mank.), *cùka* (Ur. Castr.) ; all kinds of green grass is so termed but if the Tungus is asked about the kind of grass he will give a special name if there is one; the mushrooms are named according to the special kinds of mushrooms, there being no general name unless *mògo* (Bir.), *moko* (Khin.), *mègè* (Manchu Writ.) [(cf. *mògu*(n), *mùgu* (Mongol, Rud.)] is such one; the hydrophites, known under different names, are distinguished from the grass.

The Tungus may produce the impression that they are indifferent to the flowers for which they have very few names, and with which they do not embellish their wigwams. However, it must be noted that they name flowers which may have practical importance for them, e.g. the iris which is used for manufacturing the lilac colour. In connexion with this it may also be noted that they know the colouring properties of several plants, as for instance, the alder-tree bark, leaves of some other plants etc. They know different flowers which they may describe and of which they may very often make a good picture. The reason why they do not cut the flowers is that the flowers are "homes for ants and other insects". However, they have no special ideas as to ants and other insects, but they simply believe that it is useless to destroy the flowers since they may be admired growing and since they may be needed by other populations of the taiga. This Tungus attitude will be better understood when the Tungus point of view as to the exploitation of the taiga is discussed.

The above given classification is based chiefly upon the size and partly upon the character of plants. Therefore a young willow tree may be classified as *sekta*. However, the Tungus would distinguish a young shrub-like birch-tree, or larch-tree as small *mo* ("tree"). The Tungus have special names for all trees which are found in their territory. Some of these names may be of non-Tungus origin, or confined to a limited group of dialects. So we meet with several tree-names borrowed from Mongol, and perhaps reintroduced into the Northern Tungus dialects from Manchu. Also it is very likely that some names are not Tungus at all but were borrowed from the local populations when the Tungus occupied new regions. The trees are very well known to the Tungus from the point of view of their utility, as fire-wood and as material for implements. The most useful of them are especially appreciated and attract special attention, such as the white birch, and larch-tree. However, for fire they prefer the ulmus, the wood of which gives more heat than any other fire wood. The same is true in reference to the shrubs which are named when they have special importance, e.g. the shrubs producing berries, colours, and those used for incense. The Tungus distinguish trees according to the form of the leaves and seasonal changes of the green cover, e.g. the larch-tree is regarded as a tree similar to the fir-tree, and pine-tree, i.e. as coniferous trees which are covered with needles [*èiga* (Bir.), *dèkta* (RTM)] and not with the leaves [*avdanda* (with variations in all dialects)] but since it changes the green cover, it is regarded as a tree of special type. The plants of grass type are also named when have some particular value for the Tungus, e.g. as kinds of pasturage, as hygroscopic material for the shoes, kinds re-

markable by their structure e.g. euphorbia, spurge etc., or those supplied with organs of selfdefense like nettle, thistle, and others. The names of these plants are very often borrowed from the neighbours. Yet there is a very detailed classification of all kinds of grass which may be eaten—leaves and roots*. The same is true in reference to the mushrooms, which are also classified, according to the needs of the Tungus and the animals. Indeed, the Tungus know very well which mushrooms may be eaten without harm by the man and the animals.

Indeed, to give a complete list of botanical terminology is impossible for an investigator who has to pay attention to all branches of special terminology, but as conclusion it may be formulated that the Tungus have their rough classification of groups of plants; they have special terms for the plants of importance, from their practical point of view; and they have special terms for those plants which attract attention owing to their peculiar character.

It may be also noted that the Tungus know that the plants may grow in a "normal" and in a "abnormal" way, in the sense of the unusual. They know, for instance, that the larch-tree sometimes revolves around a longitudinal axis and the trunk of such a tree is very good for certain implements. They have a special term for it. They know that the tree may be affected by overgrowth of wounded parts, which they produce artificially for industrial purposes. They know the anatomy of plants in the sense of the structure of the trunk covered with different layers of bark, special structure of roots and organs of supply. Yet, they also have certain ideas regarding the physiological processes going in the plants which they compare with that in animals. The physiological function of plants in reproduction is not beyond their attention and naturalistic explanation. (I will return to this question). They know that the roots possess great power of destruction of rocks, which they illustrate with well selected examples. Moreover, they know the particular characters of most of the plants in respect to their survival in different environments. They observe how the plants grow, how the rate of growth varies at different seasons etc. When a Tungus observes these facts he is not only stimulated by a utilitarian result of his observation for his own benefit, but he observes plants as he would observe animals. However, the interest in the plants is inferior to that in the animals.

The interest as to the life of plants and their classification, is certainly stimulated by the practical needs of the Tungus, for conditions of life in the midst of nature require a good knowledge of plants too. In fact, for the sake of survival the Tungus must know geographical distribution of plants, as trees, grass etc. and the character of these plants. Also he must know degree of danger when, for instance, he is going across a forest in which the trees being rotten or burnt may fall down at any moment. He cannot exaggerate degree of danger for otherwise he would lose his time in making useless turnings. He must know the difference of danger when the wind is strong or not. Sometimes the Tungus would recommend avoiding a forest during windy weather, and not during the calm weather. If one insists on the explanation of the difference, the Tungus will refer

---

* Among the Tungus this terminology is not as rich as it is among the Manchus (in Manchu Sp.) for this kind of food is rather limited among the Northern Tungus but it is very important among the Manchus. I have recorded over fifty names among the Manchus and about twenty amongst the Tungus.

to the wind, but if the questioner does not understand, perhaps, the Tungus will not be able to explain in a foreign language, very few travellers being familiar with the "native" languages, and the traveller by putting more and more questions may easily come to the conclusion that there are special spirits which may kill a man during the windy weather. Yet, if the investigator is ready to collect facts as to primitive "illogism" and "prelogism" he may always find some ambiguities in the Tungus speech which may be reworked by the investigator and suggested to the Tungus who would not wish to say that the forest is not peopled by the spirits, the meeting of which is undesirable for the Tungus. I now wish to point out that many of the spirits of investigators and many conceptions of this kind have their origin in the misinterpretation of the Tungus ideas and behaviour, which is due to the defects of investigators and not to a confusion reigning in the Tungus mind.

23. GEOGRAPHY AND MEANS OF COMMUNICATION. The conditions of topography and direction of the rivers as shown, played and still play a very important part in orientation. Yet, the conditions of life characteristic of all Tungus groups are such that the Tungus must know topography, orography, climatic conditions and generally physical geography much better than the average city dweller. Yet, here, it ought to be pointed out that the Tungus live in the regions crossed by numerous mountains and rivers.

The Tungus, not only the men but also the women, know very well the system of mountains and rivers of their regions, so that almost every one of them is able to make a schematic map of the region with which he or she is familiar. After the publication of several works on the geographical maps made by the "primitive" peoples* the idea that the "primitive" people are not able to represent on plan the facts observed decidedly must be given up.

When the Tungus is making a map he does not always represent all the details that he knows. He may give some selected details which may be useful for the traveller, and they will be emphasized on the map. Yet, the sinuosities of a river may be omitted altogether which will not mean that the Tungus does not know them. All Tungus very well understand detailed printed maps which they can read without knowledge of the language,—by the directions of the rivers and mountain ranges only. If there should be found some errors, the Tungus would be able to make corrections. I have seen this in a great number of instances. However, some special remarks must be made as to the Tungus maps. First of all the Tungus idea of the locality may be represented in two forms,—the distances may be expressed in the unit of time i.e. how many hours (day divided into portions, as shown before, in Section 19) ; and the distances may be shown in the approximate values of measure of length which is indispensable when the Tungus wish to connect a series of known points into a system. In the first case they would represent on the map (usually the routes of caravan) an irregular line with the distances between the points of importance designated in time. Such a map is useful for the traveller's orientation. It is very common that they do not practically need to know how many miles there are, but

* Cf. e.g. Adler's, Bogoras's, Jochelson's works also some other recent publications.

they want to know in *how long a time* they may reach a certain point. On such a map one sometimes finds the change of direction of the line due to the lack of space (on a piece of birch bark, for instance). It is different when they wish to show the relationship between the points and the distances between them. In such a case they would employ the same method as do others, i.e. using angular orientation, showing the direction of the line which may lead to the point to be reached or mapped. Every Tungus has seen the region from some mountains or peak. So when the Tungus wishes to represent the relationship of several points he will place himself in the centre from which he will show the direction of various points, adapting the distances between the points in terms of certain units of absolute measure of length. Then he will proceed to another point, from which he will make a new centre for making another angular system connected with the first. Indeed, such a work requires great effort for connecting these systems and almost surely the Tungus would not be able to put on the map a very large territory. It ought to be remembered that the Tungus *have no material* for making a map on a large scale,—we must consider that. Yet such maps have no great practical value for them and the Tungus have no leisure for making them.

In so far as making of maps is concerned the Tungus does the same work as any topographer, the difference being that he does it approximately and often with the practical view of travelling,—the symbolization of the itinerary in line and unit of time of travelling. This may be compared with the railway schedule, where the distances are indicated in hours, and not with the map. On some maps, again for the purpose of travelling, the Tungus combine both methods. These facts cannot be used for showing that the Tungus have no exact physical conception of the country where they live.

If you ask them to put on the map the regions that they do not know personally it is almost sure that they will represent them in such a manner that the known region will occupy the centre in a certain scale, then the regions less known will be represented with less details and in a smaller scale, and last the regions about which they have only a vague idea will be represented in a very reduced scale and without any details. Such a map will be of the same type as that of Europeans when the latter did not know other regions and did not use astronomical methods.

The only possible inference from the above shown facts is that the method of approach to the problems of topography and map-making amongst the Tungus does not differ from that of ethnical groups which put at the basis of this work geometrical conceptions. The difference is that of quantity of facts known and refinement of mathematical methodology.

As compared with other ethnical groups the Tungus differ also in another respect, namely, the geographical knowledge and art of orientation and potential mapping amongst the Tungus is not restricted to the limited number of people, but almost every one of them knows at least local geography and methods of orientation. Indeed there is nothing mysterious in it. The conditions of life, namely, the hunting, migrations, and the lack of communications, requires the Tungus to be "geographers". Naturally, the men must know locality, and modes of orientation, but also it is not rare among the women who very often are left to travel alone, sometimes distances of several days. In fact the usual manner of Tungus migration is that the women with their children and loaded animals go along one way, while the men are going along another way where they may happen to meet game. Children, even as young as twelve years old, are sometimes charged with scouting and bringing messages, and used for communicating with other groups at distances passing over that at which the aim of travelling may be seen. Both the boys and girls do it perfectly. The women sometimes go hunting alone (vide SONT pp. 262 et seq.) and sometimes migrate very long distances. I know a case of a Birarčen woman who left her husband's clan which lived in the region of the Zeïa River (the Amur Government) and travelled alone by boat for several days in order to reach the Birarčen settlement on the banks of the Amur River. The distance traversed was not less than 250 miles. Indeed, among the Tungus there are some individuals who know better while others know much less the locality and there are some individuals who are not endowed with the ability of drawing maps, but a case of a complete lack of ability of orientation has never been encountered among the Tungus. In this respect they are far superior to the average Europeans, including those who dare speak about the "primitive peoples"[*] without being familiar with the subjects of this mentality and the mentality itself.

Among the Birarčen as well as among other Tungus groups it is believed that the man cannot lose his power of orientation or his way unless he is led astray by the spirits[**] while the Russians and Chinese can suffer such loss "because they do not know the region and are not accustomed to living in the taiga", according to their very clear objective explanations.

As stated, the topography of the region occupied by the Tungus is required to be carefully observed by the children beginning from when they are very young. The Tungus gradually visits all the regions of the territory occupied by the unit. Since their profession—hunting—requires a perfect knowledge of the topography the Tungus are compelled to acquire this knowledge for the sake of safety and survival. In fact, the Tungus first of all must know in which direction the animal[***] which he is hunting may go and in which direction it is useless to look for it. So that the Tungus must have in his mind the map of the region with all possible details, including the character and altitude of the mountains, the depth of the rivers, and so on. Since the regions visited by the Tungus are very large,—sometimes covering

nearly hundreds of thousands of square miles,—the knowledge of the region requires a good memory, experience and still more, ability of orientation in the system of usually very crossed country. Therefore the Tungus have the idea of the systems of ranges and their general direction, and in going to an unknown portion of the region any one of them would easily find his own location and possibilities of further movement along the valleys and mountain ranges. He is found, let us add, in a much more difficult position than the traveller who has instruments and theoretical knowledge of topography, for he usually is not supplied with even food and very often carries his family with him. However, the cases of a Tungus lost in an unknown region are extremely rare: They do occur but only in case where the Tungus is "attacked by the spirits", and loses his power of orientation and of critical analysis of a new situation.

Indeed, the orientation in an unknown country is not an easy task. So the Tungus before going to such a country has to become familiar with the methods of reconnaissance, must have information on a region known to other people and from tradition. In other words a certain education, in the sense of assimilation of previously acquired geographical knowledge and some general principles, is quite necessary. There are old men who possess this knowledge and they transmit it to the younger generation and so there is just one step for formulating general principles which may be seen for instance in Tungus names for rivers. In fact the Tungus have the most elaborated classificatory terminology for the rivers which may be seen in the names. The Tungus names are usually conditioned by the character of the river, its direction, character of the vegetation, character of the valley, character of the water and thus they are essentially descriptive which greatly help in the orientation. I will give some instances.

Amasar—the river which has its sources coming from the direction opposite the lower course, i.e. returning back (*ama*).

Dobkur—the double, when the chief stream is split into two minor streams (*dobkur*—the double walled.)

Silkir—the stressed (river is stressed between the gorges)

Uyikta—the river which is stressed (*uyi*—narrow etc.)

Olgokta — the river which periodically dries out (cf *olgo* — "dry").

Suŋkoit — the river which has some places with very deep bottom (*suŋkta*—the depth).

Munuči — the river which has water with a bad smell (*muni*—to become rotten).

Takači — the river with numerous fallen trees (*taka*—the tree trunk).

Amuǰia — the river in the valley of which there are many lakes (*amuǰi*—the lake).

Mar'ikta — the river the valley of which is covered with shrubs (*mar*—the forest of shrubs).

Tala — the river the valley of which has salty soil (*tala* — the salty soil).

Amnuunali — the river, in the course of which there may be easily found unfrozen water during winter (*amnuli*—the source).

---

[*] In spite of the fact that geography constitutes one of important items of the scholastic program in European schools, the lack of geographical knowledge far exceeds the limits of what may be allowed after a long training in geography. European ladies are famous for their lack of ability of orientation and sometimes even statesmen show ignorance of illiterate people. These facts should not be interpreted as cases of "primitive mentality", but merely as due to the lack of practical need of extensive geographical knowledge and a certain inability, characteristic of city dwellers, in operating with the special conceptions and geometry.

[**] What is the nature of "spirits" will be discussed later, but now it must be pointed out that there is nothing particularly mysterious about the nature of the spirits and that their intervention into the Tungus travelling has nothing to do with the change of topography. According to the Tungus themselves, the trouble is with the Tungus mind and not physical conditions of topography.

[***] It is here supposed that he is familiar with the habits of the animals; vide infra Chapter VI.

Kulinda — the river in the valley of which there are many snakes (*kulin*—the snake).

Arbukakta — the river with dry sections or which has a dry bed at certain seasons (*arba*—the dry river).

S'ivak — the river with fresh water hydrophites which the elk likes (*s'ivak*—the water grass).

Sivartu — the river the valley of which is very marshy (*sivar*—the marshy places).

There are hundreds of names which may be understood in the same way and which are indicative of the character of the rivers from the point of view of practical needs of the Tungus. Sometimes it is sufficient to know the names of the local rivers for forming a relatively good idea of the character of the region.

Since we have touched upon the problem of names of rivers it may be added, that the Tungus sometimes name their rivers according to the events of travelling, e.g. *g'ida*— the "spear", which was lost, etc. or to some other signs, e.g. *g'iramk'iči*—the one having a coffin, etc. Yet the old, sometimes foreign, names are also preserved, e.g. *gän*—a river in Manchuria so named probably by the non-Northern Tungus populations. The number of rivers with the names which have no meaning in Tungus is rather small. It may also be noted that some rivers remain unnamed the reason being that they are not interesting and little visited by the Tungus. Such rivers for purpose of orientation may be called either by number, or with the suffixes of diminutivus—*kan, čan* etc. of the names of neighbouring rivers of greater length or importance. The Bystraia River in Manchuria has over sixty tributaries amongst which only a half are named. However, in a region peopled by the same group during long time every tributary would be called by some name. In the Tungus territory many rivers have more than one name, known to the Tungus, and one of them may be a Tungus name. For instance, the Amur River is called *Šilkir* in Tungus, *Karamur* in Dahur, *Saxalan ula* in Manchu and *Xeize* in Chinese[*].

The Tungus also give names to the important lakes, mountain ranges, and important peaks. All big mountainous masses may also have their names. However, sometimes a general word is used in reference to the large ranges. So, for instance, the Khingan Mountains are called *d'idin*, and under the same name is known the Yablonov and Stanovoi ranges. It is not a proper name but it may be referred in Tungus to any important watershed dividing the systems of large basins, e.g. the Amur river, the Nonni River, the Lena River, etc. Mountains of different size may be termed by different classifying designations. For instance, a large tree-less peak is called *jay* (Ner.), *kumá* (Khin.) *kumay* (Bir.); a mountain covered with a good forest—*toksoko* (Ner.); an isolated mountain—*toloyei* (Mank.) (probably of Mongol origin, a phenomenon typical of steppe regions); low with slight slope—*vălu* (RTM) (Bir.); mountain of middle size—*uru* (Ner. Bir. Kum. Khin.

[*] Historico-ethnographical and historico-geographical values of the names of rivers is very great. However, before these names are used as evidence they must be carefully checked up. The Tungus names sometimes lose their original form (e.g. *Šilka* of the Russians, instead of Šilkir) or the foreign name is adopted and adapted by the Tungus as a Tungus-like name. Without a thorough knowledge of the history of the names and Tungus language the operations with the names of rivers may lead to errors. Cf. the case of V. B. Šostakovič (vide SONT.)

Barg. etc.); the mountain with rocks—*kadar* (almost all dialects) (cf. *kada* Buriat Cast.)

kamniya (RTM. Khin.) — a narrow valley (gorges) of a river which leaves but small passages.

koltoko (Kum.) — narrow line laid between the river and its former bed periodically under water.

čuɳeka (Bir.) — a land surrounded by sinuosities of a river and its former bed.

kočo (Bir.) — the same, if it is covered with good but not very thick forest ("cozy").

suɟen (Bir.) — the narrow space, near the river, covered with the sand and pebbles.

tăm (tiyan) (Bir.) — a place under the high bank of a river.

čuɳuka (Bir) — a place, near the river, covered with good pasturage.

čilčalkuma (Bir.) — a place rising up in a valley, or steppe and not covered with forest.

saɟa (Bir.) — a flat place before the mountain pass.

This list may be still increased with other terms.

There are also special terms for characteristics of the vegetation. Sometimes they may be identified with the names of trees or shrubs, but sometimes they are special terms designating a complex, e.g.

mar (most of the dialects know this term)—the place covered with small shrubs, very often marshy;

saɟaka (Bir.) — treeless space in the taiga;

kulura (Ner.), *kulla* (RTM) — a place where there was a fire (the next year there may be good grass for horses.)

buarin (Bir.) — a place on the high mountains covered with the burned cedar.

Yet, there are special terms which designate characters good for hunting and breeding, or bad or good for travelling, for instance,

t'yʰika (RTM) — a place good for horseback riding (not marshy, not stony but with good firm soil).

samnakon (Ner.) — a place with grass destroyed and shrubs cut off (cf. *samna*—to wear out).

foliɳgra (RTM) — a place in a river good for hunting the fish taimen, Salmo taimen (cf. *foli*—the taimen).

jamku (Kum) — a river place visited by elk (rich in hydrophites) [cf. *jam*+Suff. (RTM)—the hydrophites].

jaworaltan (RTM) — the river good for using birch bark canoe (cf. *ja*—the birch bark canoe.)

As a matter of fact on condition of good knowledge of the region one may distinguish every mile by something characteristic of it, and with such a specialization as is found in Tungus terminology one may give a very good characterization not only of the river or region, but also all of other details designating particular places even without giving distance in units of length.

———

The Tungus for reaching the goal of their travelling choose a direction which would satisfy two requirements, namely, shortness, according to the axiom—the shortest distance between two points is a straight line—and convenience for travelling. When the Tungus live at one spot for a long time and use the same directions it is very likely that there will be formed, little by little, paths. However, the Tungus paths are not alike and very rarely are they straight.

Although this question is very simple for every one who is familiar with the conditions of virgin regions inhabited by hunters, in the hands of some "theoreticians" it has been greatly confused, so I will now give some details.

The paths used by the Tungus are not alike, because some of them are used only for going on foot, others are used for both horses and reindeer, and still others are used only for reindeer riding. Some conditions of regions render them so difficult for horse back riding that horses cannot be used for riding at all. These are marshy spaces, regions without grass (for horses), sometimes very stony spaces [e.g. the broken masses of rocks on the slopes of mountains,—*oroĉo* (Ner. Barg.) *joloy* (Bir.) (RTM), *ivay* (RTM),—usually covered with lichens, shrubs, and fallen trees], very narrow space for a path, and so on. Reindeer can be used under these conditions. However, if the space is covered with small hard angular stones and the soil is firm the reindeer is not good for riding. Owing to the peculiarities of the horse and the reindeer two paths may go parallel along a valley but they will be different. For instance, the path for horses may go over the slopes of the hills, on firm, stony, ground, while that for reindeer may go below that for horses on the slightly soft soil of the valley, or much higher almost on the crest of the mountain range, so the paths made by wild cervines may be used for riding on the reindeer. However, these cervine paths are sometimes misleading for the aim of some cervines is to attain isolated peaks from which there is no egress.

The paths as a rule are not straight, and they go with slight deviations from a straight line which may be due to the above mentioned various conditions. However, even in a locality with soft soil and without stones or marshes to be avoided the path still is rarely straight. The reasons are manifold and so-to-say historic in their nature, e.g. sometimes after heavy rains deep pools are formed which must be avoided; during this time the new path for avoiding the pool is formed and later used, for the old path is not at once even and the soil is not firm: if the new sinuosity is not great and the consequent loss of time is of less importance than loss of energy for overcoming the difficulty of returning to the old path, the new path with its sinuosity will be used.

Fallen trees may often produce the same deviations of the path. When the fallen tree is rotten and reduced to nothing after being reduced to nothing the new path may persist while the deviation of the path cannot be understood from a "rationalistic" point of view. However, the old path may be restored if the deviation of the new path is essential and if the making of a new path would not require too much energy. Indeed, the same is true of the paths going along the stony and marshy regions. The sinuosity and deviations from the straight line have nothing to do with the "primitive mentality", fear of spirits and other phantastic hypotheses*. The "rationalistic" point of view alone cannot always explain such cases.

The whole region inhabited by the Tungus and those which are very often visited by them are covered with a net of paths which are real means of communication. The path is adapted to the needs of travellers not only in regard to facility of movement, but also in regard to finding water (not everywhere is the water good!), good fuel, and pasturage for the horses and reindeer. Yet, the path sometimes makes a deviation for reaching a place good for erecting a wigwam. A wigwam requires special material (wood) and the Tungus like to have their wigwams protected against the winds in winter and autumn, and open for winds in summer, against the insects. Moreover, the Tungus like to have before their eyes "good scenery". For finding such conditions the paths make either a deviation or a branching. Sometimes one can see no reason for such a deviation if one does not know that the place may be good and is sometimes used as a summer or winter station, or just to spend a night on the way. Possibly no traces of a station are seen.

However, if the Tungus need to produce a new path for a short cut or when occupying a new place, they would not hesitate to change the old system, or a section of it. It is especially natural with the change of draught animals, e.g. when the horse is substituted for the reindeer, a change is necessary and it takes place.

The Tungus perfectly well know to where the path leads, for what reason it changes its direction and even how long ago it was used last, who passed on it, with how many animals, etc. They read the past so easily that th's was ascribed to a special and distinct character of primitive mentality. Means of communication, as a system of paths, for the Tungus is very familiar and important.

The system of paths is so well adapted to the topography, to the draught animals used, and to the needs of the Tungus that the same system may be used by other people as well, if they are equipped in the same manner as are the Tungus. As a matter of fact one can feel oneself safe if one does not lose the Tungus system of communications, for these communications are the best under the given conditions and one may meet the Tungus in their stations. It is different when one does not know this system; one may pass at a distance of a few miles from a large campment, and a few hundreds yards from a small campment without seeing the Tungus. A single person might not be noticed at a distance of a few yards should he not wish to show himself.

With the Tungus knowledge of the regions,—i.e. minor details of the character of the localities,—with their ability of orientation in a new region, which is based upon the orientation with regard to the sun and stars, and with their general knowledge of topography, they feel themselves absolutely sure and safe in what, in the eyes of a city dweller, may appear as the frightening wilderness of a primitive forest. The Tungus behaves there with the same feeling of security and self-confidence as a city dweller behaves in a big city with its thousands of streets and uniform houses, etc. again on condition that he is familiar with it. For

---

* Cf. L. Bruhl, op. cit., where he points out this peculiarity of primitive mentality. Indeed without a hypothesis might be produced only by the "thinkers" who know very little of actual conditions of life and topography. This calls to my mind those ignorant people

who criticize the constructors of railways and suggest making the line "more straight", without considering the cost of building. The usual explanation given by these ignorant people is that the constructors are not clever enough, or that they are dishonest. Such a method is not far from that of L. Bruhl and others who analyse similar phenomena without being competent in judgment as to the actual causes of supposed deviations from their own logic. The theory of spirits is very often used as a justification.

understanding the Tungus behaviour in respect to the vast regions one must not build up a reasoning based upon the impression produced by the primitive forest, or wilderness on one self, when one is not familiar with it. Indeed, the Tungus have also their fears but these are not produced by the wilderness, but are produced by the psychic instability of the Tungus themselves, which will be later dealt with.

The same knowledge of conditions and the same considerations of practical utility and economy is characteristic of the Tungus when they use rivers as a means of communication. The Tungus are very careful in this respect. Before using a river they carefully investigate its course. Before approaching a dangerous waterfall, or dangerous sinuosities, they learn the course and they would go about to see the degree of danger. They know perfectly well the effect of flood, when rivers become dangerous for navigation because of floating trees of the size of mast pines which are carried down by the rivers, danger of swift current, and other conditions. Under such circumstances the Tungus must know in every particular case degree of real danger for navigation. Indeed, some of these rivers are not dangerous at all when in flood: only some of them become so. If

the Tungus do not know a river they will not use it. In this case the surest way of travelling is that of following Tungus advice*.

Owing to these conditions the Tungus do not use all rivers which may be used. In fact if the river may be used at a short distance or its direction does not correspond to that of the Tungus migratory tendencies it is very likely that the river will not be used and even the art of navigating it will be forgotten. In the eyes of a superficial observer this may wrongly appear as "primitiveness", "conservatism" and adherence to the custom.

---

* Most of the accidents with travellers,—and in the history of the scientific exploration of the region occupied by the Tungus these cases were very frequent,—were caused by the travellers' lack of knowledge of the conditions of rivers and underestimation of the Tungus ability of orientation and their knowledge. Many of these travellers believed that the Tungus were frightened by "nature" and did not know the degree of actual danger. Indeed, in a single case one may successfully pass a dangerous place, but the Tungus who have to do it every day cannot naturally take risks. The daring of such a traveller in the eyes of the Tungus would appear as due to the lack of experience.

CHAPTER VI

THE PRIMARY MILIEU (continued)

24. CLASSIFICATION OF ANIMALS. A Tungus when meeting animals first of all observes them and either classifies them according to the existing classification or makes of the newly observed animal a special group. We have already seen that a Tungus finds himself in difficulty when he traces the line of demarcation between the mineral realm and plants, and when he traces it between the plants and animals.

Both plants and animals possess "life",—erga,—for they first of all grow and die, and react on seasonal changes. But since the animals move, they also possess what may be called a "soul". From this point of view the Tungus will be misled in classifying animals which do not move and show no striking features of the living organism. They will surely be put together with plants with an explanation that they are like some given plant, but still different. Similar to plants the animals are classified in groups according to their appearance. There is no general term, in so far as I know, for all animals, which does not mean that the Tungus have no such a conception. They do have it which may be seen on different occasions.

The animals like mollusks, especially those supplied with shells and living in the water, where their movement is not well understood by the Tungus, are regarded as a special kind of "living" matter naturally possessing "animus" and even perhaps erga—"life", but the physiological functions of these animals remain unknown to the Tungus. This class is called in different dialects, by different terms, e.g. tak'ira (Bir. Kum.), taxura (Manchu Writ.), kětta (Khin.), the "river bivalves". But there are also special terms for special kinds of mollusks, e.g. čuk'ita (Bir.)—the "snail";

kaikari (Manchu Writ.)—the "ammonite"; kākta (Tung. Sch.), k'axta (Oroči, Goldi, Olca, Sch.)—the "shell fish". The Manchu terminology in this respect is very rich for the Manchus had to give Manchu names to the animals known to them from the Chinese zoological treatises and encyclopaedias. However, the mollusks do not interest the Tungus very much for they are not much as food.

The insects also have no general name, but the Tungus distinguish many genera, and even species. However, there is a special name for all small insects, particularly harmful for the Tungus, like midges, and mosquitoes, different kinds of which they also distinguish by special names, e.g. in Ner. unm'ikta, monmaktá, nănmakta, nunm'ikta, etc. in Bir. čokomukta, manmakta etc. not to mention terms borrowed from Mongol as bargosun, buyutuna, etc. The same is true, for instance, for the names of tick and related insects which are in Bir. daktá, upilivla—one moving forward with its back; one which deeply penetrates the skin—tiyir'ifki; also in the gadflies Bir. distinguishes one with white head— n'aigda; small black—komčoki; large brown-yellow—ōmulc; white hairy—gèdènèkta; with a general name ìrgaktá. The same may hold good for the insects which are not very harmful for man and animals e.g. the grass-hoppers, different kinds of bugs, etc. The Tungus observe insects, especially those of large size, with all possible details as to their habits and as far as possible their anatomy. The Tungus spend much time in observing the life of ants, amongst which they distinguish several species. They observe among them wars, relation with other insects, migrations etc. Also, they try to distinguish whether ants can hear and see, by experiments similar to those of the behaviourists etc. In the insects the Tungus would see how the insects use their legs for softening food, how they fight with other insects; the Tungus try to find the eyes, sexual organs, the rectum and they make all possible minor observations regarding anatomy and simple physiology. They know how the insects are produced from the eggs and they distinguish males and females.

The fishes are called by a general name *oldo*, (with modifications, in all North Tungus dialects), *n'imaxa* (Manchu) (Goldi modification—*imaxa*) and there are names for different fishes of importance and even for those which are not used as food. The Tungus know habits of fishes, their geographical distribution, the egg-laying periods etc. Here a Tungus is already an anatomist and a comparatist.—He has names for different anatomical parts, he knows how the internal organs are made, and to which organs they correspond in other animals. In different kinds of fishes the Tungus know the number of teeth and the distribution and functions of fins. In the same group the Tungus include also the crayfish.

The snakes are classified together with worms which according to the Tungus conception, may be of different size,—from the size passing visual capacity of the human eye up to the largest snakes. The kinds of snakes and worms have no special names, except in a few cases of the most remarkable snakes and worms, e.g. *sirg'idika kulikan* (RTM) (where *sirg'idika* is from *sirg't*—the sand),—the worm formed in the river sand*. The lizard and turtle have names as well as the toad, but the Tungus do not usually distinguish species. It is different with the frogs among which the Tungus distinguish some species too. In the same group, but under a different name, are included the boaconstrictor, unknown in the regions here discussed and the dragon, the idea of which is borrowed from neighbours; a very few of these are believed to live in the region of Manchuria. I shall return to this question. It ought to be added here that *kulikan*—the "worm"—of very small size are supposed to infect man and animals, which is inferred by the Tungus from the overgrown parasites which may be observed in animal tissues, wounds and fecae. The Tungus go still further and they say that there are some worms of such a small size that they cannot be seen. Some diseases are explained by the Tungus of Manchuria as due to small "worms". Indeed, it is a hypothesis and not all the Tungus know which diseases may be ascribed to this cause. Since no traces of alien origin of this idea were found and since this idea is merely a logical development of Tungus ideas I am inclined to see that the Tungus, perhaps locally, created this hypothesis.

The birds are classed together as *dog'i* (with modifications all North Tungus dialects). I do not bring here the Manchu classification which is an adaptation of the Chinese classification**. The classification of birds is very detailed and they are grouped into related species, e.g. the ducks are considered as a group *n'ik'i* (with the modifications Bir.

Kum. RTM. Tum. Manchu) (Ur. Castr.) and there are distinguished, e.g. in Manchuria, at least over thirty kinds. Indeed, my observations could not be complete for not all ducks could be observed, and their names recorded on the spot. One of the peculiarities of the Tungus classification is that the males and females of the same species may have different names as it is, for instance, in European classifications of ox, horse, dog etc. In the same way there are classified the geese, the number of names being naturally smaller for the number of geese species is rather limited (e.g. four names in Bir.), with a general name goose *n'uyn'ak'i* [with variations: Ner. Bar, Bir. Kum. Khin. RTM. (Neg. Sch. Oroči. Sch.; Goldi, Grube), Manchu, perhaps Gilak *n'ön'i* (Grube)]. The birds of prey are also classified in a detailed manner, as well as night birds of prey, the grallae order, and even the birds of small size and of no practical importance for the Tungus are also distinguished. Thus the birds are classified according to their morphological characters, habits, and more attention is paid to those which are of practical importance or of peculiar character.

The classification of the mammals is still more elaborated, and there are no animals which have no names. However, as far as I know there is no general name for the mammals. They seem to be grouped according to size *bojun* also *boigga*, etc. (Man. Bir. Kum. RTM.) (Neg. Sch.)— may be called large sized animals including cervines, bears, wolves etc.; according to the character of the fur, i.e. good or not for hunting, e.g. *ëiya* (Bir.) (these must not be confounded with the terms for "fur" and "fur-animals".) There are still more detailed classifications of these animals according to sex, and age. It may be noted that among different groups the name of the one year old Cervus Elaphus may be referred to the one year old elk etc. Less important animals have no specified names according to the age, e.g. wolves. This method of classification thus greatly varies amongst the groups. The domesticated animals are not *bojun* for they are not "wild". So the domesticated reindeer—*oron**; the cattle—*adun, abdun, adasun* etc. (loanword from Mongol); the horse—*morin* (with modifications cf. Mongol) also the sheep—*konin* (cf. Mongol); the dog—*n'inakin* [with modifications, e.g. *indaxun* (Manchu)]; the cat—usually borrowed from the Manchus, Mongols, and directly from the Russians. All these animals have their own names, very often borrowed from the Mongols (Buriats), directly and through the Manchus, also from other alien groups. In the names of the animals like "the cow" one may see very clearly various overlapping influences. So we have the stems met with: *ukur* (Mongol), *ixan** and *ynax* (of Yakut language) perhaps connected with (Manchu) *ïnen*, whence one may follow all the modifications of terms found in Northern Tungus dialects. The sex and age distinctions are worked out in a detailed manner in the dialects spoken by the groups living on cattle breeding or familiar with it. The terminology as a rule is borrowed from the original source of cattle breeding***.

The distinction of age in wild and domesticated animals is very important for the Tungus. In fact, among the animals every age is characterized in reference to their weight, possibility of loading, sexual activity, etc. I have shown it

---

* It does not mean, however, that the Tungus do not see the difference between the snakes and worms. They know that the snake is more like lizard, but has no legs. The Tungus very well know the habits of snakes, also that they change the skin, etc. (For explaining that man's skin is renewed the Tungus bring evidence of the snake which changes it at once, while in men this process is slow.)

** In Manchu *gasxa* (in Goldi *gâsa*, etc.) is applied to birds in general, but it is usually understood as a bird of large size, and especially a bird of prey.

* All dialects with the modifications. Vide SONT, p. 27, and Aspects, p. 184.
** Vide Bilabialization, p. 249; and Aspects.
*** Vide SONT, p. 38 et seq.

in the instance of the Reindeer Tungus of Manchuria who have introduced new terms for the reindeer which is not strong enough at the age of four years and so they had to distinguish one year more as compared with the Transbaikalian Tungus. The reason for this new term is quite practical.

The man is *bojo* (with modifications; all Northern Tungus dialects) but *bèje* in Manchu and Mongol is "the body", while for "man" Manchu has *n'alma* (*nijalma*—transliterated.) This term has been reduced to *n'i* met with in Goldi and neighbouring Tungus dialects. The same stem seems to be known in other semantic variations amongst the Northern Tungus groups; namely, *n'irai* (Bir. Kum.), *n'iravi* (Mank.), *nejavi* (Neg. Sch.), *n'ari* (Tung. Sch.) for *l — r* is very common, in the sense of "male" and opposed to the "female"—*as'i*. Beside these there are also terms indicating the age of individuals in terms of "childhood", "maturity", "adult" and "old" ages. The social importance of relationship terms and long duration of childhood might have compelled Tungus to put stress on social relations, so that the age classification has not such a great importance as in domesticated animals.

The large hunting animals, as for instance, the elk and Cervus Elaphus, also Cervus Tarandus, may be called by the same name *bojun* which merely means "wild animals or beasts". We have seen that this may be referred even to the tiger. However, among the groups who hunt both elk and the Cervus Elaphus this name would be referred only to one of them. The Cervus Elaphus in general is called *kumaka* (Bir. Kum. RTM. Ner. Barg.) (Ang. Tit.) (Neg. Sch.) (Goldi, Oroči. Sch.); the elk in general is called *tòki* (Bir. RTM. Kum. Barg. Ner.) (Ur. Castr.) (Ang. Tit) (Neg. Goldi, Oroči, Sch.), *toxo* (Manchu), *to* (Oroči, Sch), *'tox* (Gilak, Grube) [cf. *toxi* (Mongol)]. The male Cervus Elaphus is called *buɣ, buɣu, boɣu*, etc. (Bir. Kum Khin. Ner. Barg.) (Ur. Castr.) (Ir. Ang Tit.) *buxu* (Manchu) [cf. *buɡu* (Buriat), *bòx ‖ box* (Mongol, Rud)—"the bull"] which seems to be a substitute name, perhaps borrowed from cattle breeders. The female is called *onin* (the "mother") (RTM. Bir. Kum.) *on'in* (Khin.) (cf. *enen buxu*—the mother *buxu*—Manchu); also e.g. *ner'igači*—one which has an embryo (*ner'iga*)—the "pregnant one"—referred to females (animals). The same terms may be referred to the elk female [additions: *ènin* (RTM) *enen* (Manchu Lit.), *n'inanan* (Kum. RTM)—the one with a fawn (*n'inan*)]. The females of Cervus Elaphus are also called *soyon* (RTM) (Ang. Tit.), *soɣonon* (Ner.) [cf. *xoɡon, soɡon* (Buriat Tunk. Podg.—ibid.)]. The male elk is called *anam* (RTM. Bir. Kum Khin. Ner.) (Ang. Tit.) *anami* (Manchu Writ) ; it may also be called by various names, e.g. *tuku čon* (RTM. Ner.),—during the period of early spring when it is thin; *kandaya* (Bir.) [cf. *kandaxan* (Manchu Writ.), *xandaɡai, kandaɡai* (Buriat Podg.)] rarely used in the "religious" texts; *k'ira* (RTM)—during the period of mating (also thin); *halanjan*—"the one with the antlers forked in a special way"; there may be added two names more which are interesting, namely *dandakka* (Lam), which is not clear, and *soxatyi* (Mank) borrowed from the Russians [in this dialect the Cervus is also called by a Russian tern *olen'* which is not used by the Russian hunters who prefer *zv'er'* (the beast, animal)].

This long list of names by which these animals are designated shows that there are names borrowed from the neighbours as substitutes for some of the original names; there are substitutes like "mother" and there are particular names for the distinction of seasonal peculiarities. However, there are at least two terms which may be perhaps included in the original Tungus stock, namely *kumaka*, the Cervus Elaphus in general; and *anam*—the elk-male, while the third one *tok'i* perhaps will remain as one of local names adapted by various groups which appear in the region, and conventionally it may be regarded as "Palaeasiatic".

It may be added that the elk and Cervus Elaphus are also distinguished according to the age. So we have the elk of less than one year old—*n'inan* (RTM. Kum.); over one year old—*monnaɣa* (RTM.); over two years old *čiran* (Bir.). The Cervus Elaphus is cal'ed when less one year old, *nar'iɣačan* (RTM.), *neir'iyä* (Bir.); over one year old—*moɣyojin* (Bir. RTM.); with two, three, four and five branches of the antlers *jurmájen, ilanmájen, díyinmájen tunyanmájen* (Bir.) respectively. Such a secification of age is essential from the point of view of commercial value of the animals of these ages. As will be shown the Tungus very often abstain from killing females, young, and very "thin" male animals, so they must have special terms for designating them. For this purpose they use sometimes general terms for distinguishing the age and the form of the antlers (as in the case of Birarčen), and also numerous alien words. The same is true of the terms regarding other cervines*.

Thus the essential characteristic of the Tungus classification of animals is that the Tungus base their classification on the morphological characters, the habits of the animals and their practical utility for the Tungus. Indeed, as compared with the existing European classifications it is different, but does not differ to such a degree as it is usually supposed. The Tungus put, for instance, the crayfish into the class of *oldo* (fish), but they recognize the difference as the English speaking people do when they use terms like fish, shell-fish, jelly-fish etc. In the same way the snakes and worms seem to be classed together under the same name, but they are not so in the Tungus mind. The animals are also classed according to the mode of reproduction. The chief difference between the Tungus and *modern* European classifications is that the Tungus in their classification do not presume genetic affiliation of the groups, as in the European conception of evolution, which itself is scrutinized by the most advanced biologists. However, the idea of relationship between the different animals in principle is accepted by the Tungus. For instance, the Reindeer Tungus recognize that the domesticated reindeer is connected with the wild reindeer (Cervus Tarandus). Amongst the Birarčen I have recorded the idea that the wolf, the dog, the sable and Canis Procinoides are of the same origin (*umun kala*—one clan, of the same clan). Besides the morphological similarity one of the interesting evidence is that their meat has the same smell. The bear and badger are also classed as relatives of a group different from that previously mentioned. One of the interesting peculiarities of the Tungus zoological classification is that man is recognized to be an animal which is much nearer to the

---

* These remarks may suffice for showing that the conclusions approaching these terms from the point of view of "hunting superstitions", "religious meaning" etc., as well as the using of this material for comparative linguistic studies, are very undesirable before we have a complete analysis (in the complexes) of the terms.

mammals than the wild mammals are, for instance, to the birds. For experimental purposes I have tried, on several occasions, to explain to the Tungus the European idea of "evolution" and "genetic affiliation" between the animals. In no case did I meet with difficulties or objection on the part of the Tungus. They grasp the idea very easily and for supporting it they bring forth facts of their own observation and all of them repeat the hypothesis, well known amongst them, which is as follows: formerly man was like a wild animal; he was living without wigwams; he was naked and the body was covered with hair; the hair was lost owing to the use of salt; yet there also occurred some other physical changes too, e.g. the reduction of number of teeth, weakening of the physical strength etc. As a matter of fact, this point of view, quite well adapted to the Tungus mentality, puts the Tungus very near to the idea of "evolution". Indeed, many other so called primitive peoples do recognize physical evolution of man's ancestors and many of them connect man with other animals. However, it ought to be pointed out that the folk-stories, and religious poems cannot be taken as evidence of Tungus ideas regarding natural phenomena,—the folklore and "religious" complex have their own history of diffusion and formation and they cannot be identified with the general positive knowledge of the ethnical units which may not always find its reflection in the poetry and folklore. In fact, as will be shown, the Tungus literature as seen in the fairy-tales, poems, etc. does not even pretend to reflect Tungus naturalistic conceptions,—they are transmitted from generation to generation in oral form, while the ethnographers as a rule pay no attention to this class of Tungus cultural elements forming their psychomental complex, because of their own idea, namely, that scientific knowledge may have only that form which is known amongst the Europeans and if one wants to form an idea as to the "scientific" conceptions one must look for facts in the fairy stories, poems, etc. No one would believe that it is possible to formulate the idea of the Englishman of the XVIIth century about natural phenomena by studying Milton's poetry. Why shall we do it with the Tungus? When we go through the details of the Tungus psychomental complex this idea will be still clearer.

In connexion with this remark it may be noted that the Tungus information regarding the animals not found in their territory very often has a mythological shade. Such ones are e.g. lion, elephants, monkeys, boa-constrictors crocodiles etc. Yet, it may easily happen that the Tungus would include into their classification of animals pure imaginative animals existing in the Chinese (chiefly received through the Manchus and Mongols) books, e.g. dragon, licorn, etc. The Tungus would look at them as real animals not met with in their region.

The Tungus information regarding the local animals is sometimes very scanty. I have been told by them that in the basin of the Sun River (a small left tributary of the Amur River, about 120 miles from the mouth of the Zeja River) there is a snake six or seven feet long which has tail supplied with rattles, like the rattle-snake. It lives chiefly on large birds, wood-cocks. In the same locality there is found a giant turtle. The Tungus proposed to me to take me to this locality for showing me these rare animals which many of them saw. There is a series of stories relating to the existence of the boa constrictor *tabjan* (also *jabjan*)

which is pictured as an animal living in the water, having a white abdomen and dark back.*

It may be noted here that recently among the Tungus of Manchuria the idea of the dragon appeared from another source, namely, from the Russians, many of whom assert that they have seen it in the taiga. The Tungus (Birarčen) are very sceptical about it, and say: "Perhaps, they have seen it on the Russian side, but not on this side (of the Amur River)". There is one important condition in the accumulation of zoological and generally naturalistic knowledge amongst the Tungus, namely, they have no written records, so that the animals which are not met with in their territory are very often forgotten, if the source of information does not continue to supply new information. On the other hand, the same condition is also responsible for the loss of accurate observations regarding the animals which become extinct or which they do not meet any more. This has already been pointed out in previous exposition.

25. ANATOMY, PHYSIOLOGY AND HEREDITY. When killing a new animal a Tungus is first of all interested in finding the anatomical peculiarities of this animal. Indeed, it is very essential, for he must skin and sometimes dissect the animal without breaking the skin and bones. Here the Tungus appears before us as anatomist. As a matter of fact, the skinning and dressing of the animals is one of the essential elements of the Tungus education. The man who does not know how to do it, will not be able to carry out this industry. A fact may help us to understand the Tungus attitude in this matter. A man amongst the Birarčen did not know that the articulation of ribs of the bear is not like that in some cervines with which he was familiar. In fact, when the breast bone is taken off the ribs in cervines must be turned outside, while in the bear they must be pressed inside. He did try to dissect the animal and he could not do it. Then he tried to break the chest with a heavy piece of wood. This did not solve the problem, but the meat was reduced to pieces, and thus could not be transported and used. This man's name was always repeated as an instance which must not be followed. Every body laughed at him. However, the Tungus is not only a butcher, he is an anatomist. He is interested in the comparative study of bones and soft parts of the body and he comes to form a good idea as to the anatomical similarities and dissimilarities in animals and even man. Let us remark that the occasions of studying human anatomy present themselves rather often, especially, in former days, for the Tungus at least those of Manchuria did interfere in the traumatic cases and they did practise the cleaning of bones after a certain period after death and thus could and must know the skeleton, also soft parts of the body.

---

* I have heard two stories: a Manchu fishing for pearlshells in the Sungari River discovered the animal in the water and gave it some light dry wood reduced to small pieces which the animal swallowed and was brought up dead to the surface of the water. Another case of a Tungus woman who discovered such an animal in a lake and gave it a basket of burning coal. The animal swallowed this and was also brought up to the surface. The Tungus believe in the possibility of the existence of such an animal, but they do not assert its existence. It is one of cases of uncertainty of the Tungus themselves which they do not hide from outsiders.

The Tungus, therefore, pay great attention to the bones of animals and they know passably well their number, location, articulation, form and function. So the Tungus may give the definition of any bone, sometimes indication whether a small bone belongs to the left or right limb, and certainly to which animal, if the animal is a common one. Anyhow even in animals which they do not know they may guess fairly well as to the right position and function of the bone. Indeed, the bones which they have no occasion often to see they do not know as well as the bones with which they are familiar. For instance, the bones of the human hand which cannot be examined—ossa carpalia—they do not know, but they know the small bones in animals. Certainly the small bones of the human skull also remain unknown. The Tungus dictionary possesses anatomical terms for bones, but some of these names are really descriptive e.g. the small bone of the lower part of the leg.—*n'iǯikun* (small) *ilguka* (both tibia and fibula). Yet, the anatomical terminology includes many terms borrowed from the Mongols and Manchus. It is difficult to say why the Tungus did it, for as I shall have occasion to show later, the Tungus language sometimes preserves both Tungus and Mongol terms. Perhaps this phenomenon is analogous to the substitution of the Latin anatomical terms for the terms of Anglo-Saxon origin in common and professional (medical) speech*.

One of the time distraction occupations amongst the Tungus is the showing of the bone and asking of its name, location.** Yet, if they have bones, after boiling meat, they would put them together.

The Tungus form an idea of similarity and dissimilarity of bones in different animals of the same species and they make a further step,—they compare the analogous and homologous bones of different mammals, also reptiles and birds. In fact, the Tungus (e.g. Birarčen) use the same word *čaka* for designation of the same articulation of the leg (calcaneus and tibia) in the horse although their positions are different in the posterior and anterior limbs. The names of the bones in most of instances are the same in all animals and man. Their attention was also attracted by the bats, which according to them are not birds, but have long arms like man. Indeed, they compare them with other "flying" animals. They did pay attention to the facts like the fifth rudimentary toe in dogs.

The soft parts of the body are carefully investigated. The Tungus distinguish the principal muscles, and their fixing, and they can carefully separate these muscles from the other anatomical units. The system of blood vessels is known fairly well, although there are no names, in so far as I know, for the principal branches. They distinguish the arterial system as e.g. *èrga*. (the life) *sudala* (Bir.) from

* e.g. In Mank. dialect instead of **ilguka** a Mongol term is used **šilbe** (Buriat, Castr.); instead of **gurgakta**—the beard, used in Northern Tungus dialects, **sakal** (Mank.) (from Buriat), **xuse** (Manchu) (from Chinese **xudze**) and **salu** (from Mongol). The same is true in reference to the brow, the eyelashes, even the arm, the hand, the leg etc. This phenomenon misunderstood by the comparatists-philologists was a source of extensive linguistical aberrations in the problem of common languages etc. Some remarks regarding this problem have been made in my "Aspects."

** I have carried this experiment with many Tungus in order to find how far they are familiar with the small bones and for gathering data for my dictionary. Indeed, I was unable to exhaust this branch of their knowledge as it was impossible to do with all the plants and animals, known to the Tungus.

the venal system *sudala* (Bir.). The peripheral nervous system remains rather unnoticed, but the sinews are well known, and some of the most important have special names e.g. that of the legs, toes, neck, and vertebral column. The reason why they are so well studied is that they are used by the Tungus for making thread. The internal organs are all known under different names, the most important glands as well, some of them being particularly appreciated as dainties. The Tungus also know the difference of morphology of the internal organs in different animals, as e.g. the kidney in bear, the stomach in the herbivorous and carnivorous animals, the brain in birds and mammals, the matrix in different animals, particularly dogs and reindeer, the relative length of the intestines and bowels etc. The number of teeth and their form are well known. Naturally, the Tungus know that some organs, e.g. the heart, are very complex while other organs, e.g. the bladder, are rather simple. The Manchu knowledge of anatomy is much more limited than that of the Tungus.

The Tungus ideas regarding physiological functions in some respects are not very clear, but in some other respects they are very definite and correct. The function of the nervous system as a whole is not known. However, some mental troubles are explained as the result of injury of the brain. In this respect the Tungus who are under the Manchu influence have accepted Manchu ideas which produced some arrest in the perfection of the knowledge. The Manchu conception of "high nervous work" being produced in the heart in some respects satisfies the Tungus inquisitiveness, for in the reaction of the heart during mental and psychic activity the Tungus find a strong support to the Manchu theory.

The function of digestion is referred to the system of stomach- intestine -bowels, but the process how the urine is produced remains unknown. However, the Tungus know that kidneys have something to do with this process. The blood circulation is connected with the heart, but how it goes on, they do not know. The Tungus know and do not explain by any hypothesis the physiological effects of food and alcoholic drinks. The phenomenon of sleep is accepted as a fact, but the explanations of this phenomenon differ amongst the Tungus. The most common explanation is that the "soul" is not active and therefore the animal (or man) sleeps. Yet, the soul may leave the body during sleep. However, the loss of consciousness may also happen owing to the physical cause of loss of the ability of "thinking", e.g. when the head of the individual is injured. He does not sleep but he is unconscious, and yet the soul may remain untouched, and potentially active. The observation of the hibernating animals has brought the Tungus to distinguish three conditions; namely, animals which are frozen and preserved in this way, e.g. the frogs, insects; animals which hide themselves from the cold, as e.g. the snakes which remain half active having grouped themselves together; and the animals like the bear, badger, and canis procinoides which survive by suckling their paws. Owing to the suckling of fat from their own bodies they become very thin in the spring. The Birarčen Tungus recognize that the man also may fast for a limited period, namely seven days for male and nine days for female. The Tungus recognize that the hair and skin in man are subject to change.* In man this process takes a long time and is gradual while in the snakes the skin comes entirely off at one time. The hair is also removed gradually, not like in other animals. The Tungus know very well which tissues can be restored and which cannot e.g. skin, muscles, bones, hair, etc.

The function of reproduction is very clear to the Tungus. The act of fertilization of the female by male for the Tungus is clear. According to some of them, the male sexual cell is contained in sperma produced, according to them, by the testes** in the form of very small *kulikan*, i.e. "small worms" of microscopic size, which is introduced into the female's matrix where it grows in an embryo***.

Some of Tungus of Manchuria are familiar with the Chinese ideas and say that the bones are from the father, the fleshy parts and blood—from the mother. However, this hypothesis is not generally accepted because sometimes the similarity between the children and mother, even in stature (size of bones), is greater than that between the father and son, and sometimes the children resemble more their father than their mother in respect to flesh and blood complex. All Tungus accept the idea that physical and psychomental characters are inherited. As to the physical characters they have no doubt for it is evident to them when they observe men and domesticated animals. The selection of a good male—e.g. reindeer, horse or dog—is largely practised. Yet, the Tungus believe that the psychomental complex is also transmitted. So, for instance, a Birarčen woman told me with many details the geneological history of her husband and systematically pointed out the same characteristics, e.g. the cleverness, the sexual inclination, bad temper etc. In the Tungus conversation the expression that a certain character is from the father and some other character is from the grand father is very common. The moral qualities are usually inherited at least by one of children, in explanation of which a Tungus (Birarčen) told me, "it is the same as it will be with a piebald stalion or mare which will have sooner or later a piebald colt". This opinion is shared by all Birarčen****. It is not surprising at all for the Tungus are familiar with breeding.

The physiological act of coitus according to the Tungus results in pregnancy which may last different periods of time in different animals. Their knowledge of period of

gestation in animals goes so far that they know about all of them with good approximation. The period is counted in lunar months. In my work "SONT" I had occasion to speak about it in reference to the human kind (*vide* SONT, pp. 273-274), where I have shown that the keen Tungus observer knows that in woman the pregnancy may normally have different periods of gestation which is conditioned by the fact whether the women is primiparous or is giving birth to the second, third and more children. This observation has been recently confirmed by the European biologists (cf. e.g. SONT). Thus the Tungus give their estimate of duration of pregnancy either from the day of coitus or from the last menstruation. Indeed, this is a scientific approach of the problem. Yet, as I have shown (SONT) the methods of definition of pregnancy are such that they have in view possibility of interruption of the menstruation without pregnancy and signs of pregnancy including increase of the size of the abdomen are not yet sure until the fetus shows signs of heart work and movement. Again, this fact shows that the Tungus are very careful observers and they foresee possibility of making a wrong inference.

They spread their observations on other animals, especially the domesticated animals the sexual life of which the Tungus know very well. Yet, their observations also cover the wild mammals. The process of fertilization of directly females or their eggs, is carefully observed by the Tungus, so they know that in some animals like fishes there is no act of copulation. If a Tungus does not know these particulars about some other animals, like mollusks, he would reply, if asked, evasively suggesting some conclusions by analogy, e.g. with the fishes, but without being sure of it.

Thus the general characteristic of the Tungus ideas as to the physiological functions is that they are based upon the facts observed and the inferences are made with more or less success which depends chiefly on the quantity of facts observed and their importance for the Tungus daily life. In this respect, as in the case of observation of anatomy, the Tungus are good naturalists, and in making their conclusions they are usually very careful and cautious. As we have seen before, when the conditions of topography and plants were discussed, a Tungus cannot permit himself to commit too serious a methodological error of reasoning for sometimes it may cost him his own life and that of his family. The same is true of their behaviour in reference to the animals which will be particularly clear when we go through the next section.

Amongst the Manchus who are not such good observers as are the Northern Tungus there are some theories which contradict a naturalistic approach to this question. According to them, the woman asleep may become pregnant through the intercourse in her dream with one of spirits of the group *enduri* (*vide infra*)*. The fertilization of the

---

* Yet, the Birarčen have an explanatory theory showing how the hair was lost by man. Formerly the man was covered with long hair but after beginning to use salt he began to lose the hair which all went off and he had to cover himself with clothing and to prepare fur. The salt and hot food are also held responsible for the loss of formerly good olfactory function, which was as good as amongst other animals. Thus as pointed out the Tungus are not hostile to the idea of evolution and have their own explanations.

** The castration of the reindeer, horses and bulls is well known among the Tungus and they do not make of it any "magic" idea. According to them man may also be castrated. Indeed, the Manchus who were informed of Chinese castration of palace servants now themselves know this practice in men.

*** I was unable to find out whether the process is understood as the fertilization of the female egg, or not. It seems to me that it is understood as growth of the male element.

**** Amongst the Tungus of Manchuria there is a belief that if one wants to find one's father's bones amongst the bones of other people one must drop one's own blood on the bones. The father's bones will absorb the son's blood. However, this idea has no general recognition. They told me that it would be very interesting to check up this saying which is not one of the Tungus complex. Seemingly, it has been received from the Chinese.

* However, this theory has rather relative importance when the case of the girl's pregnancy is under the discussion. I have shown (SOM) that the girl who happens to become pregnant usually enters into the difficulties with her clan and the case cannot be dismissed under the pretext of the enduri's responsibility. The same would be in the case of a widow or a woman who becomes pregnant in the absence of her husband. Indeed, pour sauver les apparences, they would maintain the woman's or girl's version as to the spiritual origin of her pregnancy, without sincerely believing in it. Among the European groups there are also some explanations of incidental pregnancy due to the using of bath which was used before by man, to the wind, etc. at last the parthenogenetic hypotheses serving for justifica-

eggs of the turtle is produced by the turtle female when she looks at the eggs*. Generally speaking the Manchus have incorporated into their complex many ideas of Chinese origin. One of chief sources of their ideas being the Chinese book 兒 婦 科 浸 附 記 which is translated into Manchu**. In spite of these theories the Manchus know as well as the Northern Tungus the natural ways of conception etc. They do not leave the female mule to pair with a stallion for the fruit may be so large that it would be necessary to cut the abdomen—since the male cannot be delivered. This is one of reasons why they do not breed the mules, and asses as the Chinese do. They are good breeders of chickens and select the cocks, as they do with the other domesticated animals. If may be also noted the Manchu practice of artificial incubation of chicks in which they succeed quite well***.

Indeed, the theories like the above mentioned may also spread among the Tungus, but after a critical analysis the Tungus usually reject them when the question is of importance. I shall return to this subject when the theory of spirits is discussed.

26. PSYCHOLOGY AND MENTALITY · A Tungus as we have OF THE ANIMALS.   already seen is a very good observer and he is also a good analyst and generalizer. However, in some cases of observation of the animals when looking for explanation of phenomena observed he himself turns to the hypotheses. Such hypotheses are that of soul which is possessed by animals, put on the same footing as man, and the second is that of spirits which may introduce themselves into animals as they do with man. Here, however, the distinction of the natural phenomena, so understood by the Tungus and European biology, and the phenomena due to the agents of an imaginative order, presents certain technical difficulties for the investigator. First of all the Tungus sometimes are more familiar with the animals, and their psychomental complex, than the European biologists, so that the latter may sometimes mistake natural phenomena observed by the Tungus for hypothetic explanations of an imaginative order. Second, natural phenomena are very often expressed in terms borrowed from the hypotheses regarding the spirits and in the eyes of the investigator they may seem to be mere variations of the hypothesis of spirits, while actually they are not so****. In my exposition of the Tungus ideas regarding the psychomental complex in animals I shall try to represent them as they are functioning in the Tungus complex.

tion of complex cases. However, as among the Manchus, no one sincerely believes in these explanations.

 * The Manchus have such an expression of abuse "she looks like a turtle looking at her eggs." The abusing meaning of this expression is mere convention of the Chinese origin.

 ** There are many other books of this class; some of them are mentioned in A.V. Grebenšćikov's sketch.

 *** The eggs are put into a basket which is filled up with the millet and put on the heated bed (k'ang). Only a small percentage of eggs fail to produce chicks.

 **** As a matter of fact, even European scientific terminology is not free of enigmatic expressions borrowed from those old conceptions in which the hypothetic spiritual factor occupied an important place. Most of controversies regarding teleologism, vitalism etc. are based on the poverty of terminology and its ambiguity due to the semantic extensions and variations.

The Tungus like to observe without any direct practical aim. It is very unlikely that the Tungus would miss the occasion of observing animals when it is possible. In fact, when a Tungus sees a new animal he will observe its behaviour before making his conclusions. If he may observe for a long time the life of animals, even those which are well known to him, he will do it regardless the loss of time, hunger and the hardship of such observations. When the animals cannot notice a Tungus he will spend hours observing them undisturbed. I have been told by one of them that he happened once to discover a female bear with two cubs. Since he approached the den located in a tree, without being noticed, he climbed up to a neighbouring tree and spent there the whole day from early morning until dark, so he might see how the bear mother behaved with her young ones. For a part of her time she was busy in the den, but she did not fail to look out of it when the young bears produced unusual noise. Also she descended from the tree several times for giving food, and once for punishing one of them. During the whole time of observation she was "talking" to the young from her den and in some cases they obeyed her, e.g. responding to her call they climbed back into the den. She taught the cubs how to climb, and to do other things. This Tungus was so much interested in observing them that he did not notice the fall of night.

I have just given this example which might surprise the reader, but it did not the audience of Tungus who added some other facts and they were not surprised at the fact that the man had spent such a long time in the observation of animal family life. It was absolutely natural for them and every one of them would do the same under similar circumstances.

Here is another fact of interest. An old man amongst the Birarčen asserted that there was a bird muduje (one in the water) č'inaka (small birds, chiefly passerers) which dived into the holes in the ice and came out through other holes. The Tungus were a long time looking for an opportunity to catch such a bird. When they succeeded they attached it to a string for observing, how it dived, what it ate etc. A group of Tungus observed it very carefully at least half a day. The bird was then killed and examined anatomically; the skin was examined still more closely in order to verify the saying that it had many insects (a kind of louse). In connexion with the fact concerning the insects the Tungus have communicated to me at which seasons the animals have these insects. So, for instance, the sable has fleas the year round.

Indeed, every new fact is communicated to other Tungus and in this way the natural history of animals is created as a body of knowledge. When the facts are not sufficient, the Tungus under this stimulus keep near themselves the animals which they do not yet well know. Sometimes one may see near the Tungus wigwam young birds of different species which may happen to have been caught alive. They are not immediately killed, but are left attached to a post by a string. In the same way the Tungus keep other animals but in justification they explain that the animals are kept for amusement of the children, yet the adult people spend their time observing these animals*.

 * The experiments of the domestication of wild animals is very clearly connected with these experiments. I shall return to this question.

The Tungus observe all the animals which are met with in the region. However, their knowledge is not equal'y good of all animals. There are four conditions which are responsible for it; namely, the Tungus pay more attention to the animals on which they are living; not all animals allow man to approach them very closely; the number of animals is different for different species; the animals behave differently towards man and those which are dangerous attract more attention.

A good knowledge of the psychology and mentality of the animals is *condicio sine qua non* of the Tungus survival. In fact, a hunter who does not know the habits of the animal, degree of the sharpness of ear and eye and keenness of smell, who does not know how strong is the animal, whether and in which conditions it attacks or not, he is doomed to perish either because of his inability to get the animal, or because of the animal itself which very often attacks the inexperienced hunter. Hunting based upon the calculation of incidental meeting and killing of the animals is not dependable and man cannot live on it. Hunting is first of all a difficult profession and when the Tungus goes hunting he always has a definite plan and purpose of killing, in a certain definite locality and even an animal sometimes met before, or to meet a group of animals which may be surely found there. If the professional hunter wants to live on hunting he must know what he wants to kill, and instead of a meat animal he will not kill the fur animals incidentally met on the way, supposing of course that the fur animal is not exceptionally valuable. Yet, he will not kill a wolf incidentally met on his way or any other animal which he is not intending to hunt. I have already pointed out in SONT that the Tungus very often specialize in various forms of hunting and in certain kinds of animals. One of the causes of such a specialization is the knowledge of the animals, which may be acquired by personal experience and by hearing from other people.

Indeed, such a knowledge cannot be based upon the imagination. It must be, as it actually is, very realistic and correct, for mistakes of this kind cost dear to the Tungus. No exaggeration of danger or easiness of the animals' character for the hunter, or lie is permitted by the Tungus. As a matter of fact the Tungus never lie, nor give full freedom to their imagination when they relate the facts and observations regarding hunting or animals*. In the society which is not living on hunting "hunting stories" have become synonymous with imagination of not ill natured liars. And most of such hunters a priori are classed so. It shows only one thing, that the life of cities does not impose knowledge and accuracy regarding wild animals. If such a comparison may be allowed, I should say that for a Tungus to lie regarding the hunting and animals is equivalent to a lie of a railway company in its schedule of trains,—it is merely impossible. The Tungus liar, or merely a man who imagines stories, would lose his social position and would be looked upon as an abnormal person.

When I describe the Tungus as excellent observers and men of discipline, I do not intend to say that they never mistake, never over-or underestimate animal character, never propose wrong explanations of the phenomena observed. Certainly, they do. Later on we shall see that in some respects the Tungus cannot solve problems without help from

* The fairy stories concerning animals form a special branch of folklore, but every Tungus knows that these are fairy stories, and not the facts.

the hypotheses, but what they know about the animals far surpasses what is known to people who do not live on hunting.

First of all the Tungus recognize that animals possess certain mental abilities which may sometimes be superior to those of man, but which are usually inferior, and at least in some animals reduced to such a minimum that the Tungus are not sure whether or not these animals have any mental activity. However, those animals which possess a high mentality, even superior to that of man, are not like man, for their mentality is different. For instance, the tiger in Manchuria is considered by the Tungus as a very intelligent animal. In fact, this animal may easily lead the man on a false track and when the hunter loses the tiger from his sight it may follow the hunter and kill him at any moment. Therefore when hunting this animal the Tungus are very careful. It will be later shown what they do in order to escape the tiger's attack. The leopard also is considered as very clever animal, especially owing to its method of attacking by jumping from the trees, but the Tungus do not know this animal as well as they know the tiger. However, if one asks the Tungus which is cleverer: the Tungus or the tiger, they would say that the Tungus are still cleverer than tigers for they kill the tiger and in some respects the tiger is "stupid".

The bear is considered as an intelligent animal but not to such a degree as the tiger, for the bear has some habits and certain psychological characters which make it very easy for hunting. However, the Tungus recognize that the bear is more intelligent than the tiger e.g. as it would be seen from the above mentioned female bear. Different species of bears possess different mentality, so that for instance the small Tibetan bear is considered more intelligent than the brown bear.

The cervines, except the domesticated ones, are considered as much less intelligent than the tiger and bear. The wolf together with the badger on the contrary are considered as stupid animals. The horse is not so intelligent, as the reindeer; and the cow, where it is know, is considered as a stupid animal, while the mentality of the dog is equal to that of man, at least in some respects. Amongst the fur animals, the sable is considered as very clever animal, while the squirrel is much inferior to the sable; however, the Tungus do see a sign of high mentality of this animal in the fact of its storing food for winter. The birds are classed too,—some of them are considered as inferior, e.g. the eagle, while the others are considered clever, e.g. the raven, for the latter may cooperate in hunting*.

Yet, the Tungus recognize that animals have certain individuality, and some of them are more and some others are less clever. For instance, if the tiger does not show its usual ability of "cheating" the hunter, it would be considered as "stupid", so as in the case if the tiger does not understand that the hunter does not intend to interfere with the

* According to the Birarčen bears, elk and the Cervus Elaphus without antlers are not clever, while the Cervus Elaphus with the antlers and tigers are very clever. The elk and bears recognize man's presence by his smell. The tiger has perfect sight, hearing and sense of smell. However, it runs rather badly. The bear is a perfect runner, which is never tired. The sight is very good in the raven and wolf. The wild bear has poor sight, so he can see only on a short distance, but his sense of smell and hearing are very good.

tiger's affairs (vide infra). The same is true of other animals, especially dogs, reindeer and horses. It ought to be here noted that the Tungus do recognize that the animals may become placings for the spirits. If it is so, then also the animal may become "stupid", "unreasonable", or being actually directed by the spirit it may become as clever as the spirit itself.

When one wants to understand the Tungus attitude towards the animals it is important to keep in mind, that the animals which are not well known to the Tungus are very often supplied with imagined characters. Here folklore in the narrow sense of the term (vide supra Chapter III) may be a source of enlightenment, especially alien folklore, which sometimes may be understood as a reliable source of information. In this respect the Manchu ideas regarding the animals' psychomental complex are very typical. In fact, the Manchus being chiefly agriculturists have already lost their connexion with the hunting complex and the knowledge of animals amongst them plays the role of passtime or distraction. Into their complex they adopt all kinds of information and particularly from the Chinese books and novels. So generally among the Manchus one may find the most extraordinary stories about the animals which the Manchus accept as true stories. For instance, the famous fox-stories of the Chinese folklore and literature are accepted as facts. The same is true of the Tungus groups which become disconnected with the groups living on hunting. This is the case of the Birarčen settled in villages. In the same position are found the Northern Tungus of Transbaikalia who now live on cattle breeding.

The observations of the life of the tiger and bear have brought the Tungus to the idea that these animals may in some respects be treated in the same manner as man. The Tungus recognize that these animals would not attack the man if he does not want to harm them. So in order to make the tiger understand that the hunter does not intend to interfere with the tiger's hunting, the man must leave his rifle, putting it on the ground, and address the tiger with a speech in which he states that he will not interfere with the tiger's interest in the region that he only visits it on his way to his own hunting region etc. The tiger is supposed to understand not word by word because the tiger cannot speak, but by a special method of penetrating into the sense of the speech.

The facts of speaking to the tiger are known from other regions too. So, for instance, V.K. Arseniev relates about it and under similar circumstances in his records (cf. "Darsu" etc.). Here it ought to be pointed out that the speaking to the animals is observed amongst almost all peoples of the earth. However, the purpose and ideas are not the same. If one takes all formally similar cases together, then one may confound the facts of different origin and function. I will not now go into the details which may take us very far, but it must be pointed out that the same Tungus do speak sometimes to themselves (psychologically this is the case of monologing), they do speak to the implements although they do not believe in the existence of soul or mentality in the implements and the latter have no special spirits. Yet, the Tungus would speak to an inanimate placing for the spirit (which may be especially made, or may be a tree or a rock),

but he will speak to the spirit and not to the placing for the spirit. These are different cases of "speaking". However, in the case of speaking to the tiger he actually speaks to the animal with the intention of being understood. The ethnographers very often, if not usually, take for granted that the "primitive" people believe that the animals understand human speech as men do. It is not so, at least in reference to the Tungus in the case of their speaking to the tigers. According to the Tungus, the animal does not understand word by word, but it grasps man's speech in the sense of the man's behaviour. In fact when meeting a tiger without any intention of fighting it, the Tungus must speak something and with a certain sincerity in order to be trusted by the tiger. Naturally in a similar case he would remember what he had heard from the experienced hunters and he would repeat more or less exactly the sense of the speech heard by him. Under certain circumstances it may take the form of pure convention and even degenerate into a "magic" trick. Thus, one cannot take this case as evidence of the fact that the Tungus believe in the tiger's ability to understand human speech in general. The other facts mentioned above and to which we shall return, have entirely different meaning and function in the Tungus complex. I think that all similar facts must be carefully analysed before being used for generalization like that of a recent writer on this question who trusting himself to the scientific reliability of Sir J. Frazer inferred "the primitive man attributes to the animals the understanding of human language" which he needs for developing his own variation of Sir J. Frazer's theory of taboo[*]. I do not deny the possibility of such an attribution amongst some ethnical groups and in certain conditions, e.g. as a special theory or as a magic method etc. but I cannot agree that this is a typical "primitive" character. Indeed, it is a late and secondary inference, perhaps a new adaptation of badly understood cultural elements borrowed from the original inventors.

If the tiger is not "stupid" he will leave the man alone and the man does not longer need to think about the tiger,— the tiger will not attack him. The Tungus believe that the tiger is not friendly to the man, but the tiger does not dare to fight man for the latter is well armed. Yet, the fact is that the Tungus when behaving unfriendly towards the tiger may be attacked by the tiger,—what happens rather often with inexperienced hunters. Owing to this the man must demonstrate before the tiger his peaceful intention as shown. The Tungus believe,—and it seems to be a matter of observation,—that the tiger recognizes his RIGHT ON A CERTAIN TERRITORY which cannot be harmlessly visited by the man, or large bears as well as other adult tigers. The tiger would not attack the man or large bear outside of his own territory and he will not attack the man or bear on his own territory if they do not show hostility. The tigers, bears and many other animals, according to the Tungus, know perfectly well the meaning of the fact when the man is armed with a gun, or with a spear. The same recognition of territorial right is supposed to exist amongst the large bears. The Tungus of Manchuria are inclined to see the idea of property amongst the small bears too, when they put their marks on the trees (by biting them) located at the radius of 25 or so metres from the den. They do the

---

[*] Cf. D. K. Zelenin, "Taboo," etc. p. 10.

same with the entrance to the den if it is located in a hole of a tree. So the Tungus find the bears when they want to hunt them. A recent biting is recognized by the freshness of the bite which becomes gray after the period of summer rain. Other bears do not disturb the bear which already hibernates. However, if marks are put on the trees for indicating the region occupied by the bear, a fight between the two bears is possible. Again, as I have pointed out (SONT), this is used as a method of finding animals. The Tungus also recognize such a distinction of ownership of territory and they would not go into war with their neighbours,—the tigers and bears,—unless they are forced to take away the territory occupied by them. In the Tungus mind it is a war. According to the Tungus, such a war is very dangerous because the bears or tigers may destroy the family of the hunter and his domesticated animals during his absence, while he cannot stay all the time watching his family and household. The ownership of territory and nonattacking policy, are recorded in different parts of the world—e.g. in Africa, Canada, also in the Marit'me Gov.— so they seem to be a fact. The complexity of relations between the man, tiger and bear, as I have described in SONT, is thus only a particular case of local adaptation of these animals, in the midst of which the Tungus does not underestimate and probably does not overestimate his own power of control of the territory and thus he remains a realist. The methods of arranging relations with these animals are gradually worked out, and they are effective as an empiric solution of the problem. Yet, when a Tungus speaks to the tiger, he leaves his gun down etc. and does not believe the tiger to be a being endowed with supernatural power. He hopes to be understood but if he fails he has to fight.

It is different with the BEAR which cannot understand speech. However, if the Tungus is not armed—which is usual with the women and they are not afraid to go alone —the bear would not attack him. Yet the bear may be frightened by something unusual and may lose his ordinary way of acting. So, for instance, a Tungus (Nerčinsk) meets a female bear with a young cub, and since he knows that the female is dangerous and he has no cartridge in his gun, he takes his gun in both hands and begins to beat a tree with it and to cry with a harsh voice. The female bear is surprised at his attitude and retires, while according to her usual behaviour she would attack. Therefore the Tungus say that the bear is not as intelligent as the tiger which cannot be surprised by such a simple trick. The bear cannot be killed at once unless it is hit in the heart. Practically it is almost impossible to do this unless the bear stands upon its hind legs and leaves the chest exposed. The bear as a matter of fact does this when it approaches the man for attacking him with its paw. But some of them rise up too late for enabling the hunter to shoot, so the hunter has to do something unusual to make it stand up at a certain distance. Sometimes the Tungus begins to dance and cry which produces the necessary effect on the bear. The intelligence of the bear is seen by the Tungus in occurrences which happen from time to time with some Tungus, when they are attacked by the bears. After a successful attack when the man is down the bear considers first by smelling and carefully looking whether the man is alive or not. If it believes that the man is dead it will bury the man supposedly killed, under a pile of the trunks of trees, of shrubs, leaves and earth; then it will

again return and verify whether the man is there or not and at last it will leave the place. Naturally the man under such circumstances must do his best not to show he is alive.

The intelligence of the bear and tiger is seen in their ability to know those people who were touched by them. Here the theories and observation of facts and inferences cannot be surely distinguished so I will confine myself to the statement of facts. The Tungus of Manchuria assert that these animals, especially the bear, as a rule attack the people who were once attacked by them. On my question how these animals know it, I received a definite reply:— by their smelling. The things which have been touched by them are also recognized in the same way. The term used by the Tungus of Manchuria is *gálegda*, and the act of touching *galenk'i* [they may be found in other dialects as derived from the stem *ɣale*]. The stem is *gale* (*ɣale*)— to fear, to be frightened. In reference to the man they say *s'i gálegda boje b'is'in'i*,—i.e. "you *galegda* man are"; and the hunting rule is: *gálegda jakava osin gada*,—the *galegda* things one does not take (with on going to hunt) (Bir.).* In its further extension the idea of *gálegda* resulted in the hunters' avoidance of persons touched by bear. Yet, as a rule (amongst the Birarčen), the things touched once by the bear must be buried with the man who was touched by the bear. Yet the Tungus avoid touching the trees bitten by bears. The hunter who did not succeed in killing the animal and who was touched by it, is recommended not to hunt these animals any more, for he is not fearless, he is *gálegda*. Perhaps in this case the chief reason is that the hunter possesses no special ability for hunting these dangerous animals, or even perhaps he becomes unable to do it owing to his previous unfortunate experience.

When the bear attacks the hunter and if it succeeds in taking possession of the spear or gun, it immediately breaks the arms. This fact is also considered as an indication of a special intelligence of the bear. In such a case when the Tungus are informed of the bear's attack they go well armed and with the dogs immediately to meet the animals aggressors. This attitude could be compared with the custom of vendetta, but I do not want to insist upon it. In the same way the Tungus recognize the intelligence of the bear in the fact that bears store food in the earth and carry it from one place to another until it is finished. However, they say that the bears are not good to their young for which they do not leave food (meat). So that some Tungus call bears "dirty", "bad-natured" animals, for the bear finishes all its food alone, and it is often found overburdened with the food, and asleep, at just the place where the food is stored. Similar facts incline some Tungus to the idea that the bear is not very intelligent but the other facts convince them that the bear is not a bad hearted animal, and under certain conditions can be trusted, e.g. the bear very often collects berries at a short distance from the women also gathering berries. Thus according to the Tungus the bear is intelligent enough to understand the real danger for himself. The Tungus know that the bear is fearful when surprised which may result in spontaneous

---

* As it will be later shown the term gálegda has still greater use, namely, it may be referred to the localities and things touched by certain spirits. It must not be, however, inferred that in this term and behaviour of bears and tigers as described, there is something connected with the "religious" conceptions.

excretion of fecae which makes the animal very weak. They know the peculiar character of the bear when it hibernates. It may be stated that the Tungus know all the steps in the life of this animal which they recognize as possessing certain rights of life and territory, which they consider as a more or less intelligent being, possessing a soul as man does, possessing certain peculiarities of character. Naturally when the Tungus needs to have a bear skin, and meat he would not hesitate to kill it, but if he does not need them he would not do it, for according to the Tungus idea of hunting—as it is a professional po.nt of view—there is no need to kill an animal if one does not need the meat or skin. The abstaining from killing the bear is based upon this practical consideration and lack of experience of hunting this powerful and intelligent animal.

The behaviour of this animal shows to the Tungus that the bear has a soul, which will leave the body after the bear's death and as any other soul it may harm the man if he was wrong. Hence there are complex customs connected with the managing of the bear's soul. This complex is increased with the other elements borrowed from various groups. If we add to this the aesthetic side of performance and its justification, then we will have the complex of ceremonial eating of the bear, its funeral in the form of exposing the bones (as the Tungus did with man's bones,) cutting off the furred skin on the legs, prohibition to the women to sit on the bear's skin and at last prohibition to the women to eat bear's meat, some dancing and singing, which formerly followed the human funeral perhaps. The partial abstaining from eating the bear's meat in the conditions of Transbaikalia and Manchuria is not of great economic consequence for the bear is rather rare and cannot become an essential component of the daily food*.

Amongst the Birarčen and Kumarčen, bear hunting is no more professionally practised. Formerly the hunters used to preserve the bones and skin from the head and also paws, on a special platform, and to ask pardon to the bear's soul. At the present time the Tungus usually cut off the head and leave it on the platform or hung up in a tree but they do not practise other customs and they bring back everything which can be carried. Sometimes only the skull was painted in black and fixed on a post. Yet many Tungus do not observe even this custom and they throw away the head, while the heads of other animals are brought home. Owing to this it is difficult to buy complete skins of this animal. However, the Tungus give up even this custom and on special request they may bring the whole skin. The Tungus folklore is very rich in stories concerning this animal. The Tungus accumulate them from the Chinese books and also other ethnical groups, e.g., for instance, the Goldi. Yet, the Tungus do appreciate the bear's meat, but they are somewhat reluctant to eat it as well. However, the introduction of prohibitions may be due to considerations which have nothing to do directly with the special aspects of the Tungus psychomental complex, in so far as it is connected with various hypotheses. Since the Tungus make a kind of sausage of the blood of animals, as Cervus Elaphus, reindeer, and other big animals, they formerly used to make

* However, among the Birarčen the women are now allowed the posterior part of the bear.

the same of the bear's blood;—it was considered a good dish. However, the taste changed and now e.g. the Birarčen make no sausage of bear's blood, so this abstaining is quite modern, while the explanation is that during the summer the blood of bear has a bad smell wa (Bir.), which the old people did not notice before. If one now eats such a sausage "the people will laugh". Indeed, in the eyes of some observers this "prohibition" would appear as one of "religious" prohibitions.

Here I give an illustration of how the ritual complex is built up and maintained. The Birarčen when the bear is killed during the hot weather, after the animal is skinned and dissected into large pieces, cut off the sublingual bone and throw it away. The reason is that if the bone is not cut off, worms about 10 or 12 centimetres long, will infect the meat (the meat is preserved). If the bone is cut out, the worms will concentrate in the cavity and may be easily destroyed. According to the theories, the people who do not know that this must be done only during the summer months sometimes do the same during the cold weather. Indeed, first of all this practice must be carefully investigated and it must be found out how far the Tungus explanation holds good, whether it is a "rationalization" or is based on the facts observed, whether it is connected with some special theory regarding this bone and soft tissue attached to it, or is a mere meaningless rite.

The bears are called by different names. So we have in Manchuria three species: the tibetan bear—vayana (Bir.) ; the common small brown bear—moduje (Bir.) ; the large grisly-like—turni (Bir.). The etymology of the first name is not clear. The second moduje is mo—the tree + du (locativus) + je (suffix commonly used for making of a similar combination a "noun")—it may be thus translated: the one living on the tree, which is characteristic of this species. The third one is of the same type: turni —"of ground", or living in a den in the ground which is also typical of this animal. It is evident that in these cases we have names for different species, but there is no special term "bear". Yet, both moduje and turni may be referred not only to bears. It seems that the term "bear" is now out of use amongst the Tungus. Yet, we meet with the same situation in other Tungus dialects in Manchuria. In Manchu it is lefu, and in Goldi it has different names of the same type as amongst other Tungus groups discussed below. In Transbaikalia, the general name for bear is mani (Ner. Barg.). This term is sometimes confounded with another one, namely, mapi which means the mythological class of heroes and perhaps spirits. Besides these there are numerous other terms, which may be classed in two groups: names in which there are pointed out some humiliating traits of these animals, e.g. soptaran (RTM)—the one who empties himself of berries ; koguor'jo (Mank.),—the "blacky" ; hobai (RTM)—the one who has an ugly (hideous) appearance; urgulikkan (Bir.)—the "heavy" one etc. ; and the names referring to the honourable persons, e.g. sagdikikan (Khin.)—the old (man) (a diminutive form from sagdi—old) ; ätirkän (and atirkan if it is referred to a female) (also atirkaya) (Bir. Kum. Khin. RTM. and others) whence atirku (Ner. Barg.) which is a term referred to honourable persons compared by me (SONT) with "madame", "monsieur." Yet the bear may be called ama (Bir.)—the father (or the grandfather) and on'o—the mother (and the grandmother) which are terms referred to very honourable persons. There are many other terms e.g. *satimar* (RTM)—"the bear male" which seems to be a Tungus adaptation (*mar*) of the Yakut term; *ayakakun* (RTM)—the father, which is a Tungus adaptation (*-kakun*) of the Yakut term *aga*—the father; and several other terms which I do not venture to interpret, e.g. *derikan* (Tum.); *keɣapti* (Lam.); *ɣukata* (Neg. Sch.); *säpsäku* (Ur. Castr.); *bakaja* (Neg. Sch.) (perhaps from *baka*—to "find", i.e. the one who is found by the hunter); *n'on'oko* (Bir. Kum. Khin.) which is perhaps "the great baby" (*n'on'o*—the baby) [cf. R. Maack op. cit. p. 49.— *n'ayn'ako* (Kum.)—the interpretation is wrong.] E. I. Titov ("Some data on the cult of the bear among the lower Angara Tungus of Kindigir clan", Siberian Živaja Starina, 1923, p.p. 92-95.) gives *šatimar* (Ner.) which he compares with *šadamar* (Buriat)— "alert- strong" (Podg.), which does not look likely, considering RTM *satimar; taktikaydi*—one who lives in a cedar forest; *oboči*, which cannot be connected with Mong. *ebei* and translated as "terrible" owing to the suffix *či* which means "having", in this case it would be "fear" [cf. also *abači* (Eniss.) and *ebiko* (Eniss. Ryčkov) which are terms of kinship (cf. Mongol *aba*—the father) ; the form *ebiko* is a term translated "the grandmother"—the female bear], *ɣaleɣa*—cannot mean "four armed" for it means "fearful", etc.; *säpkäku* (cf. M.A. Castren's *säpsäku*)—is a doubtful record and translation. For this reason, other terms translated by E.I. Titov such as *boborowki, nataragdi, uč'ikan* for which there are no corresponding words in E.I. Titov's dictionary and which I cannot justify by my own dictionary, I refrain from discussing. As it is common amongst most of ethnical groups familiar with the bear, the names used during the hunting and the travelling in the taiga are different from those commonly used and they are not direct names for the bear, e.g. *sagdi, ama, atirkan* etc., and yet the names sometimes are of an ironical and even offensive character. Naturally the bear in the Tungus complex cannot be considered as a "sacred animal", or "ancestor-animal". The styling of the bear as "father" etc. is merely a "polite form." Yet, the Tungus have no fear to speak or to joke about it.

The question as to why the Tungus have such a long list of names for the bear, and why the original names sometimes disappear, just as it is observed e.g. in some European languages, may be explained by several possible hypotheses. I think that there are different reasons. For instance, some terms used in the joky stories about the bear are not naturally used when the hunter goes for a serious work such as a dangerous hunting. This behaviour is characteristic of all peoples and not only in reference to the hunting animals. Another case may be that of a special language used in hunting, and not because of fear of spirits but because of the existence of such a custom in general. What was the original cause of the existence of such a language may also be answered by several hypotheses which may be more or less satisfactory to explain the fact but they will remain mere hypotheses, for the original discoverers of special language are unknown. The practice of distinct language in the special professional work might be discovered once or more than once and spread over various groups. In this spreading among different groups it may be explained by different reasons. Let us suppose that amongst some groups it was due to the fear of spirits which

might interfere with the economic activity of the hunter if the animals, implements and arms are named by their names. Since it was found that the non-naming brings "luck" in hunting the other groups naturally might imitate the discoverer, especially if the change of language did not present great difficulties and especially if such a new language became a source of interesting experiments and distraction, a case which is actually observed. If the ethnographer would insist upon the reason, the questioned hunter might reply, as the Tungus do,—"there will be no luck in hunting", or "the spirits so and so must not know about it", or even "the animal must not know it" etc.. My experiments with the Tungus convinced me in fact that they may give various reasons when they are pressed, especially if the answer is already included in the question, which is the usual way of getting data. But if one does not press them they simply reply "such is our custom", or "such is the regulation of hunting."[*] As a matter of fact in an average case a Tungus does not bother himself with the question as to why he uses these customs and he does not need their justification.

According to the Tungus statement in former times they did not hunt the TIGER and at the present time many of them still abstain. The reason given is that the tiger is the same as *bajanam'i*—the taiga spirit (cf *infra*). However, this is not a prohibition, and it may be a simple justification of their attitude of fear conditioned by the actual danger which may result from the hunting the tiger. Yet, the tiger is considered as a good-natured animal too, which is seen e.g. in the fact that the tiger always brings food to its young.[**]

The cleverness of the tiger is also seen in its very good knowledge of the habits and possibility of hunting other animals. The Tungus suppose, I think with a good reason, that the tiger knows that alone it cannot fight a big bear. which sometimes takes the tiger's spoil; it knows that it cannot attack the wild adult boar unless the latter is surprised in a sleeping state; it also knows that it cannot fight man when the latter is armed, and it does this only in the case of being very hungry or excited and frightened, i.e. when it becomes "stupid".

About the same complex of ceremonialism as with the bear is found when the tiger is killed. However, this com-

---

[*] The same reply would be received from any European when he is asked for the reasons of prohibition of terms for sexual organs. Perhaps if he is pressed still further he may give some moral justification to the existing prohibition. Moreover, it must be considered that the so called primitive peoples do possess certain conceptions of social politeness which implies satisfaction of the questioner, especially one of a superior ethnical group, and under the insistence on the part of an influencial group well equipped with arms and power, even sometimes soldiers, foreigners; they would not dare to resist in their mutism,—if they have nothing to say they would find any handy explanation. So there must be used evidences checked up by cross examinations, and the place of folklore in this matter must be very modest. Yet, every evidence must be taken in its relative complexal meaning.

[**] It ought to be pointed out that the Tungus inference regarding parental feelings needs perhaps some correction. As a matter of fact, young bears have a different kind of food as compared with the tigers and in the given description we have the booty consisting of meat.

plex is not as rich as that connected with the bear. Indeed, here it ought to be considered that the geographical distribution of tigers is rather limited, and this animal is known only to the Tungus of Manchuria, chiefly amongst the Birarčen (*vide* SONT). The Tungus hunt the tiger for it is a rather valuable animal for its skin, its bones used as Chinese materia medica, even its moustaches used for teeth cleaning etc. However, the Tungus are very sceptical as to the medical effects of the bones. When they happen to eat tiger they do not like its meat which is hard and sour to taste. Although among the Tungus the tiger is not surrounded by special prohibitions, these spread owing partly to the same condition as that with the bear, and partly to the alien influence. In fact, lately amongst the Manchus the using of rugs made of tiger's skin has developed into a prohibition. At a certain moment the tiger's skin as a seat became a privilege of high officials (amban), and the Tungus of Manchuria obeyed their superiors of the military organization and the prohibition came into the existence. However, the Tungus themselves believe that there is no prejudice in using tiger's skin as a seat and treat this custom as a "Manchu law". Naturally with the complex mythology and stories found in the Chinese books the meaning of this prohibition may grow still further and become justified by new considerations. I think this is the case of the Goldi and their neighbours who fell under the Manchu-Chinese influence earlier than other groups. Amongst the Tungus of Manchuria the women must abstain from eating tiger meat.

The folkloristic aspect does not now concern us, so I will leave this question to my further publications. Among the Tungus groups the tiger is called by different names. It is called *bojuja* (Ner. Barg.) but it is very little known amongst these groups (*vide* SONT); *lavu* (Kum), *lawda* (Bir.) which according to the Tungus, is borrowed from the Chinese; *m'er'ir'in* (Bir.)—"stripped"; *yalaya* (Bir.)—"fear exciting"; *tasiya* (Khin.)—from Manchu *tasxa; utači* (Bir.) (e.g. in combination *m'er'ir'in utači*)—"one who has children" (great father, father); yet it may be called merely *amba* (Goldi and their neighbours)—"great", also by honourable terms like that used for "bear", e.g. *mafa* (cf. Manchu term), *ama* etc. So in the terms used for the tiger we may see the same phenomenon as in the case of the bear, so I do not need to repeat what has been stated in reference to the terminology.

Regarding the family life of the tigers the Tungus information is not complete; amongst the Tungus of Transbaikalia it is very poor.

Among the little known animals, the leopard may be mentioned as one which, according to the Tungus, is very intelligent. It is called either "the beast"—*bojuja* (Khin) or by a special term,—*megdu* (Khin), *muyan jarya* (Manchu Sp.).

DOMESTICATED ANIMALS interest the Tungus. The REINDEER is considered as a very intelligent animal. Its intelligence is seen by the Tungus of Transbaikalia and Reindeer Tungus of Manchuria in the whole complex of relations which have been established between man and reindeer. The Tungus recognize cleverness of this animal which they see in the fact that the reindeer

obeys the human voice, knows many commanding words, also their personal names given by the Tungus, carefully behaves when carrying loaded bags and especially children in their cradles, knows how to defend itself against wolves and knows that the best protection for it is the human beings, to whom it runs when in danger and whenever possible. The Tungus recognize that the reindeer possesses a soul which may exteriorate like that of man and other animals, and a mentality which is not, however, equal to that of man; at last, according to the Tungus, the reindeer does understand the change of mood in man, as do e.g. the dogs. The intimacy of relations makes the Tungus love the reindeer nearly as human members of the family and when a Tungus is alone he may talk to the reindeer which, according to the Tungus, can understand. Again, this understanding of man can be admitted not too literally, but about in the same manner as we have seen in the case of the tiger. However, with the supposition that the reindeer may become a placing for spirits, the Tungus may address his speech to the reindeer in view of speaking to the spirits which naturally can understand human speech. Naturally the Tungus are very familiar with the behaviour of the reindeer during different periods of their life. When they are left in the herd the functions of the male as protector of the herd are interpreted by the Tungus as one of the manifestations of the reindeer intelligence. The same is true also of horses which in the herd show still better organization, especially when they are attacked by the wolves and when females form a circle turning their heads toward the center where the colts are grouped and their strong back legs outside, and when the stallion is running round the formed circle and is the first to maintain order and to meet the attacking wolves. The Tungus know very well the behaviour of the female reindeer towards the males at different periods, also towards the fawns. So the Tungus recognize the feeling of love for the young and in this respect they say that there is no great difference between the reindeer and man. Such an inference is naturally made as a result of long observation of the life of this animal, which the Tungus must know if they want to be successful in breeding. Thus, the Tungus idea is that the reindeer is very intelligent and is frequently used by the spirits. In further discussion I shall come back to the problem of the reindeer function in the rites and ceremonies, also in the shamanism.

DOGS are considered as very intelligent animals too. This opinion is shared by all Tungus, but not in reference to all dogs. As regards the mentality of the dogs, the Tungus infer from the observation of this animal, as seen e.g. in the fact that, within certain limits, the dogs can understand human speech, particularly simple sentences and their own names; they can understand the change of mood in man, as is also true, according to the Tungus, of the reindeer; they know their right on the campment when, for instance, they do not touch the hunting spoil or food left without men in the wigwam, but take possession of food reserved for them; the dogs know their functions in the reindeer breeding and watching the campment and the herd; the dogs in case of danger look for protection from man; dogs are specialized in their functions, e.g. for different kinds of hunting in which the dog actually cooperates with man. The high mentality of the dog is also seen in the fact of storing food if it cannot be consumed by the dog (especially females). Naturally the dogs possess souls, as reindeer do. However, dogs as a rule are not eaten by the Tungus, the reason being that their meat is not good, especially at old age, while the dog is more valuable for watching, hunting and simple companionship (e.g. the man must treat the dog like his companion in hunting giving the dog a good portion of the hunting booty, etc.). The dog plays a very unimportant part in the ritual complex and its part in the folklore is rather limited. Indeed, this attitude towards the dog has no reason in so far as the Tungus idea about the mentality of the dog is concerned. I shall return to this question later. Naturally, the Tungus distinguish between intelligent and non-intelligent dogs as they do in reference to other animals.

The Tungus recognize a certain mental ability in HORSES. However, their knowledge of this animal, even amongst the Tungus who have no other riding or draught animals, is much inferior to that of the reindeer. The Tungus also recognize that the horse has soul, individual character and varied mental ability. So they say that there are clever horses which after getting experience know conditions of taiga and do not waste their energy on useless jumping, unreasonable fear etc. These horses spare their energy, eat the berries, hydrophites etc., Such a horse can be used for two or three weeks even during the season when the usual food is not available for the horse.* However, the mentality of the horse is inferior to that of the dog. CATTLE, the cows and oxen, in reference to their mentality are put by the Tungus as inferior in the scale. However, the Tungus do not know these animals as they know the reindeer and dog. Some facts of interest, as for instance, the reaction of these animals on slaughtering, are noticed by the Tungus,—when doing it (e.g. amongst the Nomad Tungus, also amongst the Tungus formerly reindeer breeders in the Nerčinsk group) usually send the cattle away as far as possible.** The same preventive measures are taken when reindeer are slaughtered. The explanation given by the Tungus is that the animals do not like to see how one of them is slaughtered.***

---

* The case of accustoming the horse to eat meat (SONT p. 39) is considered as a product of human cleverness.

I do not make reference to the opinions of the Reindeer Tungus who are sometimes familiar with the horse, but since they do not like it, their opinion may be influenced by their hostility towards this animal.

** Once in 1912 in the Tungus village Akima (Nerčinsk district) I observed a kind of "rebellion" of cows and oxen when one of them was slaughtered before their eyes. This case gave me a good occasion for carrying out an interesting observation as to the Tungus ideas on this matter and methods of preventing "rebellions". Let us remark that the fact of non-reaction amongst the animals as observed in slaughter houses perhaps needs some additional verification. The seeming lack of reaction expressed in the docility, is also observed in men when they are slaughtered in a large number, as it is observed among the civilized nations during the revolutions when the changing parties slaughter each other. The penetration into the animal psychology is greatly hindered by the fact of lacking speech in domesticated animals, very limited knowledge of animal psychology in general, and repulsive reaction of "seeing" on the part of those who are connected with the profession of slaughtering.

*** If these observations of the Tungus are correct, the case of human sacrifice, and cannibalism for which the populations practising them have no aversion, as well as the cases of public capital punishment ought to be understood as peculiar cases of the adaptation of

In reference to the Tungus knowledge of animal psychomental complex amongst the animals which are not dangerous for man and which are not domesticated, the first places are occupied by the CERVINES and fur bearing animals, which the Tungus must know for their hunting.

The Tungus collect and transmit from generation to generation the facts regarding animals' mentality and psychology, so that at last the body of facts becomes enormous and the conclusions are rather good. In most of the animals the Tungus recognize certain mental power, which however, is not the same in different animals, as we have already seen before. The Tungus do not believe the cervines, such as the elk, Cervus Elaphus, reindeer, and musk-deer to be clever animals and they recognize in addition that these animals may be intelligent and stupid individually. The Tungus (Birarčen) quoted to me an evident instance of the stupidity in animals. A Tungus on horseback approached a male reindeer. Instead of running, the animal looked and went slowly round the horse. The animal was naturally killed. Such a stupidity, according to the Tungus, is rare. However, they know rather well the character and degree of the attention, development of smell, auditory, and visual power. According to the Tungus these animals know how dangerous man is and they run away from him as soon as they can smell, see or hear him. Amongst the Tungus of Manchuria hunting on the roe-deer is very often practised by hiding under a special dress made of roe-deer skin, so that the skin from the head of the animal together with the small antlers is put on the hunter's head. The roe-deer allows the hunter to approach the herd of roe-deer to within a short distance if the wind does not bring the human smell to which all animals are very sensitive. The hunter may then easily kill the animal.* On the same knowledge of animal psychology there is also based the hunting of the Cervus Elaphus challenged by the hunter by imitation of male's voice calling him to fight. The imitation is perfect. ** In the same way the Tungus exploit the maternal feeling of the female roe-deer and musk-deer to attract them near to the hunter by imitating the cry of the fawns (only during the period when the fawns are small).

The Tungus names of these animals show some interesting features which may be pointed out as characteristic of the Tungus psychomental complex. We have seen that in their classification the Tungus give no hints as to the mystical and supernatural character of these animals. Their terminology is a pure and simple zoological and industrial specification of the animals. Again if these animals may become particularly powerful, more powerful than man, it is due to the spirits which may locate or place

human (ethnic) psychology to the special conditions in which the complex of "religious ideas", as well as "social ethics" take special forms, and the practice becomes a common phenomenon.

* Naturally this method is well known amongst other hunters e.g. the Bushmen who simulate the ostrich. Perhaps the quaternary painters did represent such a hunter, who has become known, chiefly as "magician" and even "shaman".

** The horn is made of a wooden piece of birch bark and it was known centuries ago (vide SONT) which is indicative that this practice is very old. It may be noted here that, according to the Tungus of Manchuria, the tiger also knows this method, but the tiger cannot exactly reproduce the last note (cf. E. Shirokogoroff, Folk Music No. 38) so that the hunter may recognize whether it is a cry of deer or a tiger's imitation. This fact is also quoted by the Tungus of Manchuria as showing a great mental ability of the tiger.

themselves in these animals. Here it may be noted that the Tungus very often say that some animals are good and bad, even clever or stupid, intelligent and unintelligent which is misunderstood by the travellers and then a very mystic interpretation is given. For instance, the animal which does not allow itself to be killed, runs away etc. is called stupid etc., but in the Tungus complex this does not mean to say that the animal individually taken is stupid; it is "stupid" for the hunter who cannot kill it. Therefore sometimes the Tungus say that a "good animal", "clever animal" goes straight under the hunter's shot, or in the hunter's trap, while a "bad" "stupid" animal does not. It is a judgment from the point of view of Tungus aim of hunting, but they have no such a term like "difficult to be hunted" or "easy to be hunted". So that when the Tungus say about squirrels that they are "clever" and "like" the hunter it does not mean, as it is interpreted, that they want to be killed by the hunter in order to be pleasant to him. It is one of those metaphors in which all languages are rich. However, since the souls of these animals may be influenced by the human soul,—direct or through the intervention of other spirits,—there may be a certain evaluation as to the animals' soul, and this may become again a source of a misleading inference regarding the mysterious character of the animal psychology and mentality.

The Tungus consider the SABLE (Mustela zibellina) to be a very clever animal which is not easily taken. The method of misleading the hunter practised by this animal is quoted (by the Birarčen) as one which I will now give in detail. When the sable wants to leave the night shelter it does not leave it at once but by making several loops (from thirty metres to two kilometres) and returning to his starting point, after which he runs straight to the new place. If the hunter does not know this behaviour of the sable and follows the foot prints of the animal he will spend many days and perhaps will not be able to find the actual direction of the animal. Yet sometimes the hunter loses his mind. Therefore the Tungus use a simple rule: *never cross the sable's single track* while the fresh double track can be crossed which is shown in the figure. In con-

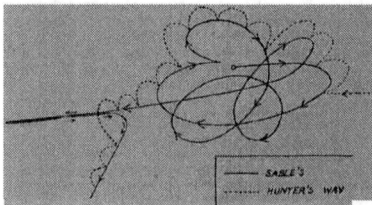

nexion with this it may be noted that the Tungus know very well, and professionally they must know, the character and meaning of the tracks of different animals. For instance, the bear usually makes two parallel tracks in opposite directions, so that it is difficult to know the actual direction in which the bear has gone. The steps must be counted.

The horse goes a long way during every night so that finding it is difficult. All mustelidae leave the same type of tracks, as the sable.

Amongst the Tungus there is a strong conviction that animals sometimes commit suicide. There is a small bird which puts its neck in between two narrow branches of shrubs and trees and suffocates; the same is observed amongst the forest mice. The analysis of the situation convinces the Tungus that there is no purpose of protruding the head between the branches, so that the cases are regarded as suicide. The "old men" used to say that the animals did this because of missing the sunrise, which interpretation is undoubtedly connected with a complex of folklore. These cases are often observed. As to other animals the Tungus know of no cases. The cannibalism of the salmon, in the autumn in the small rivers, when the teeth overgrow in old fishes (five years old, the last year of the cycles) is considered as having the purpose of destruction, for otherwise the fishes which do not die in this way will die owing to the destruction of their bodies by a kind of worm.

The WILD BOAR is considered as the strongest animal, which possesses a certain intelligence and a very strong sense of smell but is defective in some respects, e.g. its sight is not good and it cannot easily change direction when running. The intelligence of this animal is seen, for instance, in the method of fighting the tiger*. The mother's feelings as a sign of high intelligence are seen by the Tungus in the wild boar when the female accumulates leaves, dry grass, small branches and other material into a heap, goes under it and by turning herself round forms a nest with an entrance in which she gives birth to the young well protected against mosquitoes and midges.

Yet the Tungus do not deny certain intelligence of the BIRDS. I had occasion to relate the way of co-operation between the hunter and raven, when the raven from its high position notices the animals and flying in their direction leads the hunter forward. As soon as the animal is killed the raven receives the bowels and intestines as a natural compensation. According to the Tungus (Birarčen), the raven would pay no attention to them if they go out without the rifle or with a stick instead of the rifle.** Yet the ravens usually express their emotion, when the animal is killed, by a cry and "dance" around the hunter when he

* Here I want to relate a case which has been quoted by the Tungus for showing the mentality of this animal. An old and strong boar was chased by three tigers. The tigers were weak, perhaps, already starved which sometimes happens with them, and which was later confirmed by the examination of their bodies. The hunter followed the boar and the tigers for seeing what would happen to them. At a certain moment in a place good for fighting the boar stopped in such a position that it was with its back to the tigers but it could see them. It was attacked by one of them. The boar in a second changed its position and cut the abdomen of the tiger, when the latter approached at a short distance; when the tiger was killed the boar occupied its former position and showed that it wanted to continue on its way. The second and third tiger subsequently attacked the boar and both of them were killed in the same way. Then the boar changed its behaviour and carelessly considered the dead bodies of its enemies. At that moment the hunter killed the boar so he brought back four big animals.

** They say the same of the crow.

skins the animal. As a matter of fact, the Tungus do not understand the mechanism of this co-operation and many of them refuse to believe that the ravens may bring "luck." Should the man not believe and fail to follow the raven, the raven would not show the way.*

The eagle is considered by some Tungus as a stupid bird. They are inclined to see this manifested in the over eating of the eagle when it may have its prey. Yet, according to the Tungus, the eagle's stupidity may also be seen in the fact that when it attacks the roe-deer it pounces on the back of the roe-deer which runs in the forest. The eagle tries to stop the animal by grasping a tree with one leg. The leg is sometimes broken off and the eagle perishes.** The Tungus see the cleverness of the cuckoo in the fact that they observe the migration of this bird on the back of the large goose. The birds' languages are also known to the Tungus who sometimes may understand what the various cries of birds "mean". Naturally, the birds-imitators, like some thrushes, are greatly admired, but the Tungus know perfectly well that these imitators do not always "know" the meaning of imitated words and phrases.

I will not quote other facts of this group of my observations. The facts here quoted may suffice for showing that the judgment of the Tungus regarding mental and psychic characters of the birds is also based upon the observation of the behaviour of the birds which the Tungus first describe, and after which they draw conclusions and if necessary give names to the birds many of which, it is true, are onomatopoetic. I will abstain from the linguistic analysis of these names which may be used as good basis for making up the idea of the Tungus conceptions regarding birds in general. However, such an operation is extremely dangerous for those who are not familiar with the language and psychomental complex of the ethnical groups discussed. Since this method will not bring too many new facts I will not give my analysis which may be disastrously imitated by other writers on this subject.

I have not recorded any facts or opinions regarding the snakes, frogs, toads, turtles and lizards. These animals are known to the Tungus chiefly from the alien folklore, while their idea as to the mosquitoes, gad flies and midges is not very high. However, the Tungus also recognize that some INSECTS possess some mental ability. So, for instance, the Tungus believe that the ants are clever, and perhaps for this reason they do not like to destroy the constructions of the ants and do not want to deprive them of their "houses" (i.e. flowers, *vide supra* Section 22). The wasps are also considered as clever animals.

* Such a case of co-operation between the hunter and raven may be easily understood, but the Tungus are inclined to see in it something different. They go even so far with their hypotheses that they suppose that this bird may predict. The Tungus reasoning may be seen from the given example below. "There was a company of seven with 13 horses (going for hunting). One of horses was very weak (sick). The raven cried at the moment of their leaving. The owner of the bad horse killed (an animal). The raven again cried. The next night one of the good horses perished in the marshes. The sick horse became well." The interpretation is that the raven predicted the success in the hunting and recovery of the horse. However, not all Tungus would agree with such an interpretation, and the reasoning based on simple post hoc propter hoc will not satisfy them.

** The Tungus hunt the eagle for selling the feathers to the Chinese. When they abstain from killing it the reason is that the Tungus do not need it, while useless killing is not practised as a rule.

The insects fight between themselves. For instance, the drones attack the gad flies. They perforate the abdomen and suck the liquid contained in the heart which is "like sugar". The drone steals the honey from other insects. In order to see the behaviour of the insects the Tungus make them fight, e.g. wasps and spiders. The spider's bite is considered very poisonous for man, while that of wasp is only painful.* When the spider attacks other insects it seizes them with "arms" and covers them with a network. Two spiders are believed to be very fierce. If one puts even a large spider into the web of a small spider the owner will attack and the large spider will fall down from the web in order to leave the field. The reason is that a spider does not go to the web belonging to another spider. The spider is "fishing" when it examines the string by touching it with the "arm" in order to see whether there is any booty or not in the net. If the string is heavy then the spider pulls it up to catch the booty. The ants preserve their eggs deep in the earth, protecting them against the frost. Ants fight with other groups of ants, maintain the same roads and repair very quickly the damages in their constructions.

———

This description of the Tungus ideas regarding the psychology and mentality of animals might be increased with a great number of facts taken from the folklore. As I have already pointed out I do not want to do this, for in the eyes of the Tungus the folklore is not the source of exact knowledge and the Tungus, when they need facts, are not inclined to use the folklore as a source of information or references. The information gathered by the Tungus from other ethnical groups (e.g. the Chinese, Manchus, Dahurs and Russians) is not rejected by the Tungus but it is also not blindly adopted. It may be very often heard from all other groups that the Tungus knowledge of the local animals is superior and that the Tungus are critical. In fact they spread this scepticism even with regard to the animals unknown in their territory. However, this does not mean that the Tungus do not reproduce in their folklore stories which are not believed by them to be "true".

If we summarize what has been expounded in the present section, we may say that the Tungus as observers do recognize certain psychomental characters in the animals. This description of the Tungus opinion regarding the mentality of the animals is near to that given by Sir J. G. Frazer (cf. "The Golden Bough", Part V, vol. II, p. 310).

"It has been shown that the sharp line of demarcation which we draw between mankind and lower animals does not exist for the savage. To him many of the other animals appear as his equals or even his superiors, not merely in brute force but in intelligence."**

* For the bears who like the honey the sting of bees is not effective. The same is true for some people.

** Here, Sir J. G. Frazer's opinion as to his scientific ideas and superstitions of savages is of interest. He says: "For whereas the order on which magic reckons is merely an extension, by false analogy, of the order in which ideas present themselves to our minds, the order laid down by science is derived from patient and exact observation of the phenomena themselves" (op. cit: Part VII, Vol. II, pp. 305-306). However, he comes to a somewhat pessimistic con-

Indeed, it is not exactly what may be formulated in reference to various groups. It is safer to say that *the ethnical groups of non-European complex in reference to some animals admit their physical and in some respects their mental superiority*, which is conditioned by their experience and adoption of certain theories. The idea of Sir J. Frazer is however deeper, namely, he proves with all his work that the "primitive man" is oppressed by this superiority and spirits which people the man's environment, while he, Sir J. Frazer, is free from this belief. This complex of superiority becomes one of the important causes of misinterpretation of the animal mentality, common even amongst those who have devoted themselves to the study of animals, and being the fundamental characteristic of the low class of city dwellers who do not know the animals and are convinced of their own immeasurable superiority, even as compared with the villagers. L. Sternberg who followed the ideas and method (i.e. picking up of facts and making of them mosaic pictures) of Sir J. Frazer has gone still further when he asserts that "the animals . . . are pictured as perfectly human-like beings as to their physical nature and mode of life, but who like at the same time to appear to man in forms of one or another animal" ("Gilak Folklore" p. XIV). This inference is made chiefly from the folklore in which, according to this author, "the Gilaks do not see the product of imagination but real events", for they take for real the facts, that which seems to be facts, the dreams and hallucinations (l.c.). This statement cannot be accepted under any conditions for if such be the Gilak he could not survive under the pressure of this psychosis. This picture of the Gilaks is done with the colours more vivid than those used for the same subject by Sir J. Frazer, e.g. in the following broad generalization: "The speaker imagines himself to be overheard and understood by spirits, or animals, or other beings whom his fancy endows with human intelligence; and hence he avoids certain words and substitutes others in their stead, either from a desire to soothe and propitiate these beings by speaking well of them, or from a dread that they may understand his speech and know what he is about, when he happens to be engaged in that which, if they knew of it, would incite their anger or their fear." (Op. cit. Part II, pp. 416-417). And furthermore: " . . . . man's first endeavour apparently is by quietness and silence to escape the notice of the beings whom he dreads; but if that can-

clusion as to his science by formulating: "We must remember that at bottom the generalizations of science or, in common parlance, the laws of nature are merely hypotheses". . . . . and "In the last analysis magic, religion, and science are nothing but theories of thought." (ib. p. 306). I do not need to especially stress that "tha sharp line of demarcation" never was a hypothesis advanced by science, but it was one of elements of extension, by false analogy, of an ethnocentric and anthropocentric behaviour.

not be, he puts the best face he can on the matter by dissembling his foul designs under a fair exterior, by flattering the creatures whom he proposes to betray, and by so guarding his lips, that though his dark, ambiguous words are understood well enough by his followers, they are wholly unintelligible to his victims" (ib. pp. 417-418).

As a matter of fact this picture may be referred to a schizophrenic who is affected to the last degree of mania of persecution. These are artistical images, but they are not reality. There are two sources of these creative achievements; first, the complex of superiority which guides the writer, and second, an artificial selection of facts taken out of the complexes in their formal aspects (very often misunderstood and badly rendered) so to say functionless. What happens with such authors is that they concentrate the facts gathered amongst several persons and refer them to an ideal "Gilak" or "primitive man" which never existed and never was thinking as they make him seem to do. The method of gathering facts from diverse ethnical groups and their concentration is still more productive of strongly expressed images. In order to make the picture still more expressive the complex as a whole is not given, but there are selected those facts which may particularly impress the reader affected by the same complex of superiority and avidity for reading a "real", but frightening story, the reader whose psychomental complex cannot be any more satisfied with the detective stories and cinematographic melodrama. In addition such a picture of primitive man gives a moral justification of his psychical destruction, or ethnical absorption. Ethnologically, these creations are a very rough product of modern ethnocentrism. I will not here speak of the technique of this class of work which actually can be carried out even with no great personal effort,—by assistants who read, and put facts on the cards and make a card catalogue. It shows still better the modern type of serial manufacturing.

I do not need here to bring foreward the ideas of the writers like Levy-Bruhl and his numerous followers. From the description of the Tungus knowledge and methods of observation we have seen that the process of mental work does not differ from that of any other observers of natural phenomena, if the observers need to have an exact idea as to the phenomena observed. In this respect their method gives more security of scientific proceeding than that of Levy-Bruhl who bases himself chiefly on selected facts and whose aim is to prove (justify) certain pre-existing assumptions without worrying about the disastrous effects of such a work. Indeed, the disastrous effects do not spread very far and they do not affect those of his readers who have practically to deal with the groups of non-parisian complex. Their effects sterilize only those young men who follow the ideas and methodology of their leader, which fact perhaps has only personal importance.

CHAPTER VII

TECHNICAL ADAPTATION

27. MIGRATIONS In the previous Chapter V, I have already shown how the Tungus mind behaves in reference to the natural phenomena of primary milieu. In accordance with the acquired knowledge of the primary milieu the Tungus have worked out their system of migrations, also imposed by their chief industry of hunting and reindeer breeding, and the substitutes for the reindeer-breeding. We have seen that the Tungus have created a system of communications, the paths. Indeed, in the eyes of the people accustomed to the railways and artificially erected high-roads with bridges, dams, the system of Tungus paths would not seem to be a technical achievement, a cultural adaptation. However, it is not so when one looks more closely at the phenomenon.

The Tungus roads are made with quite concrete aims, namely, to reach certain points, e.g. the hunting region, the pasturage for reindeer or horses, the best localities for the campment etc. The choice of the directions is also conditioned by consideration of the ability of the draught animals, in carrying the loads, anatomical characters of the animals as the form of the leg seen e.g. in the reindeer and horse, their psychomental characters, and their power of resistance to the hardships of travelling. Indeed, the Tungus must know perfectly well the degree of danger from natural agents such as the rivers changing their water level during different seasons, fire in the forest, the falling of trees under the pressure of strong wind etc. If a Tungus is not familiar with these conditions he may sometimes lose his own life, those of the members of his family and exhaust the energy of the animals, that of his family members and his own when terrified by the non-existent or wrongly overestimated danger. So in nomadism the system of roads is created in the same manner as that of the railway which is cut into the sections with stations, where the fuel and water may be supplied and the servants changed (in the Tungus conditions they take rest) ; the roads are adapted to the least loss of energy of the animals and men. Yet, this system is also correlated with the needs of hunting and others, as for instance, the hay storing, pasturage etc. When one is familiar with the actual conditions one may see that this system is the best one in the given conditions and it shows that the Tungus are very keen observers, people who arrive at perfectly good conclusions and the best forms of practical solutions of the problem.

As one of the interesting facts it may be pointed out that in the creation of the system of communications there are engaged not only men but also the women. In fact, the Tungus women very often, if not to say usually, perform duties of the leaders of the caravans. During the travelling they very often have to change, at least slightly, the local variations of the direction, and thus they also take their part in the improvement of the system of communications.

Sometimes it happens to the Tungus to meet on their way the spirits which may very often lead the people astray. These cases are considered by the Tungus as due to the weakness of the people and illnatured character of some spirits. Since according to their ideas, the spirits are particularly dangerous at night and when the people are drunk, after heavy drinking they avoid travelling during the night, especially when they are not familiar with the locality. Yet, some localities are almost permanently either visited or even inhabited by the spirits and these places are avoided, especially during night travelling. So that with certain preventions, and when the migrating groups are numerous, this factor affecting the rational system of communications is not of great importance, amongst the Tungus who are using the system. There are many reasons for that. Let us suppose that a Tungus brings in evidence that a certain locality is affected by bad spirits. This information may be accepted and the Tungus will avoid this region until some other Tungus happens to visit it. If nothing happens and no confirmation of spirits' activity is found the first idea will very likely give place to the restoration of the idea of the original safety of the place, according to the Tungus, perhaps, temporarily affected by the spirits. The need of having as much as possible of the territory free of spirits will bring them to the "cleaning" of the territory from the spirits. Yet sometimes the spirits may be removed by special methods, which will be later discussed. It is, however, different with the Tungus who do not very much depend upon their migrations. Such groups of the Tungus who do not hunt extensively and live on cattle breeding or some other trade practised in a limited region, believe much more in spirits located in different places, which they do not want to visit. It is very likely that in this case the peopling of these regions by the spirits is one of the forms of justification for the Tungus for abstaining from the hunting and preferring the quietness of life in the settlements, (e.g. some groups of Birarčen, the Nomad Tungus in Transbaikalia and others). It is interesting to note here that the Manchus who live on agriculture refer as one of the reasons for their abstaining from hunting, to the numberless Tungus (orončun) spirits which people the taiga, and whom they are afraid to meet. According to the Tungus living on the taiga, the Manchus are wrong.

If a Tungus were asked the cause of misfortune, for instance in the case of a tree falling on a traveller, he might give the reason as the activity of a certain spirit. He might choose the road across a forest, where there are many half-rotten trees, in fair weather, but he would avoid it during the stormy weather; he would know perfectly well that the forest in which there are no half-rotten trees even during a storm is not dangerous. The conception of spirit in this case would approach very near that of the "luck" and "bad chance". Thus the record of similar explanations of accidents must be always carefully checked up and analysed.

For protecting themselves against different accidents the Tungus must know exactly what they must do in various conditions. For instance, if a Tungus is surprised by the snow and rain, which is typical of Manchuria and Transbaikalia during transitory periods (sometimes in

August and September which depends on the altitude), he must stop immediately, make a big fire and not become chilled. This is practised by all Tungus groups. In spite of relatively high temperature,—zero centigrade,—a Tungus, after his clothing is wet, little by little begins to lose his ability of controlled movements and dies very soon. In the case of heavy cold and snow storm a Tungus must take off his shoes, lie down bringing together as nearly as possible the head and legs, and cover himself with the snow. He must remain in such a position up to the end of storm which may last several days. If there are two men, they must do the same and lie down together. It is impossible to enumerate various methods of self-protection which may seem to be strange when the observer is not familiar with the conditions. Naturally, all these methods have been formulated after long experience and they are the best solution in the given conditions. * Indeed, this is also one element of the cultural adaptation.

In connexion with the migrations it may be pointed out that the Tungus have arrived at great achievements as to the form and material for the harness, saddle and loading bags. They are adapted to the animals, to the character of the loaded goods, and the material used. Only after long experience in travelling does one arrive at the idea how rational and clever are the people who have invented and perfected this cultural complex through the long transmissions from generation to generation.** In my SONT I had the occasion to give a detailed description of the cradle loaded on reindeer back, so I will not repeat it here.

The Tungus are great specialists in choosing the place for campment. As I have already pointed out they select the places which may suit different requirements and seasons. Thus the character of the locality, seasonal direction of winds, potable water, and fuel are accounted before the choice is done. Again one begins to realize the practical value of their choice only after detailed investigation of the reasons. Sometimes the Tungus will give an explanation which may joyfully be taken by the ethnographer inclined to the search for mystic conceptions amongst the "primitives". Once in the upper course of the Kumara River we stopped at a long distance from the river, under the shelter of a rock. The choice seemed to be at first strange. The reason why we stopped there, and evidently the place was frequently used by the Tungus, was that "This is a good place; no bad spirits around". However, the reason became quite clear when a very strong wind began to blow. Under the shelter, in the cold season of the middle of October, we were safe, while in an open space near the river the Tungus sometimes perish, especially if the wind is combined with the snow mixed with the rain. Indeed, in the phrase of an old woman "bad spirits" indicated the accumulated knowledge of the region and the need of preventive measures and the "spirits" were not so concrete as they are when the Tungus deal with them. Yet, from further acquaintance with the same old woman I discovered that in her speaking she might give this reason as an

abbreviated explanation of her behaviour instead of giving to an ignorant (of local conditions) man the actual reason for her choice. Such explanations are very often given by parents to young children when they learn from their parents the art of safe migrations.

Considering the conditions of roads at different seasons, the animals used and purpose of travelling the Tungus have gradually created different systems of partially overlapping roads good for various purposes, and their abstaining from using some of them at certain periods would be explained in the same nature as the old woman made her explanations.

I have mentioned in the foregoing lines that the Tungus choose places which have good fuel. As a matter of fact, if the Tungus very often visit the same locality and if the forest is fresh, they will prepare fire wood by cutting trees which they may use perhaps several months and even years later. This is one of numerous instances of their foresight, which is directly opposite to the theoretical conceptions of "primitive mentality".

The Tungus canoe made of birch bark is one of the remarkable inventions of the populations living in the regions rich in birch bark. In fact, most of rivers in the regions inhabited by the Tungus are not good for navigation. They are very often interrupted by cataracts the crossing of which is out of the question. However, with the exception of short distances where the cataracts are found the rivers may be quite good for shallow canoes. The birch bark canoe is so light that one capable of carrying three men and some cargo may be easily transported on the shoulders of two men when it cannot be used. The Tungus who know perfectly well all conditions of the rivers, the rapids, the cataracts etc. may thus quite safely use the birch bark canoe. In spite of possible great age of this type of canoe it has perfectly survived amongst the Tungus groups living in the regions where other methods of communication are difficult. For instance, the Kumarčen use the birch canoe along the rivers, such as the Kumara and the Taga rivers, but their neighbours the Birarčen do not use it because the Amur River is too big a river for such a canoe. The Reindeer Tungus of Manchuria use birch bark canoes only for hunting, crossing rivers and when they go to visit the banks of the Argun and the Amur rivers, in which case they go on, leaving the reindeer behind. Yet many groups prefer the birch bark canoe for hunting elk often found feeding on the hydrophites. The hunter may approach very near the animal without any noise in a very small canoe for one person. The survival of this form of the canoe is conditioned thus by considerations of utility and it may appear again as observed amongst the horse-breeding Kumarčen.

The Tungus are very careful in using fire. The fire must be carefully extinguished before the caravan leaves the campment. This regulation is very strictly observed in general and especially during the season when dry grass and leaves are found. Since the fire is a placing of a special spirit (vide infra) the explanation of the extinguishing the fire may be given in terms of possible activity and mischievousness of spirits. However, what the Tungus do is merely prevention of accidental fire in the forest. The policy of prevention is the chief element of the Tungus economic system. They know and mention that the useless burning of the forest will affect the hunting, for many animals may live only in the forest, and feed on the product

---

* The non-Tungus travellers have to follow these practices too, e.g. cf. V.K. Arseniev's report of his travellings.

** The new arrivals in the region inhabited by the Reindeer Tungus very often criticize the methods of saddling and loading. However, after some personal experience and consideration of the expence connected with the change of this complex the new arrivals usually come to the idea that these methods are the best.

of forest, as e.g. squirrels, some cervines etc. The burning of the forest may result in spreading of the fire over the area whither they migrate and thus the people themselves may greatly suffer from it. Thus, this policy is based upon previous experience and upon foresight. However, the Tungus especially those living on horse breeding, e.g. the Tungus of Manchuria, very often burn the areas covered with the dry grass in early spring and late autumn in order to have better grass the next season. However, in such a case they would choose a good day in respect to the wind and possibility of avoiding a big fire in the forest. It may be noted by the way that the carelessness on the part of Russians (in Transbaikalia) and Chinese (in Manchuria) in dealing with fire is a constant source of Tungus dissatisfaction with these people whom they call "stupid" and "ignorant".

28. HUNTING. The Tungus consider hunting as their principal profession which must be learned by every one of their hunters. We have already seen that this profession requires first of all a perfect knowledge of the habits of the animals hunted, which may be acquired both from direct observation of these animals and from tradition. Therefore the transmission of traditions in this case is one of primary conditions of this profession. Beside the knowledge of the animals, the hunters must know special methods of hunting for every particular animal. Long experience in hunting has brought the Tungus to very elaborate methods of hunting. There exists a great variety of snares and traps, a great variety of weapons, and with the introduction of fire-arms, a great variety of the guns used. The hunter must know those which can be used for hunting of particular animals. Naturally, the Tungus were used to the bow and arrow before the arrival of the Russians in Siberia, following which the Tungus began to use flint guns. During the XIX-th century they changed their arms soon after the change of the arms in the Russian army. So the modern rifle of the latest model introduced after the Russo-Japanese war was already known in 1915 in Transbaikalia and Manchuria. Also the Tungus of Manchuria know very well the rifle of German type (Mauser with 10 cartridges), and also the Japanese rifle, without speaking of old types as the Berdan, Winchester, and others. No hint as to the conservatism in this respect could be observed in the Tungus behaviour. However, one might meet with the old flint-gun, with the percussion cap gun, and other old types. The Tungus prefer these guns for some particular reasons and use them for special hunting, e.g. the squirrel was hunted with the gun of small size and very small round bullet to avoid as much as possible destroying the skin. Also the charge of this gun was small and thus economical. The flint gun was preferred for hunting very large animals like the elk, bear and tiger which must be hit with a very large bullet. In some cases the Tungus refrained from using fire-arms against the bears. In this case the reason was the difficulty of killing the animal with a small bullet of the modern rifles. They preferred the old method of bear hunting with a spear, or hunting knife fixed on a long wooden shaft. The choice of arms depended also on the cost of the charge and the effectiveness of the shot. In fact, the very best fire-arms in some cases could not be used at all by the Tungus because

of the very high price of the cartridges and because of the impossibility of repeatedly recharging them as with the Berdan cartridges. In spite of the modernization of arms the Tungus up to recently continued using the cross-bow, and produced different types of arrows adapted for various kinds of animals. Some of these arrows were even very recently supplied with wooden and bone points not because of the lack of the iron, but in view of the particular qualities of these points. So, for instance, an obtuse wooden point was used for hunting large birds. Formerly the using of poisoned arrows was common. For instance, among the Kumarčen even in recent times a poison was used which was prepared from decaying liver. * They also used some plants for manufacturing poisonous substances. This art is now forgotten. Among the Birarčen there has been found a new method of preparing poison which, according to them is good for a few effective shots. A small snake is put into the hollow of the gun and left there to decay. After its destruction the gun is charged and the bullet which hits the animal produces a wound the edges of which soon become dark and animal succumbs soon after being even slightly wounded. The meat of the animal killed in this way cannot be eaten for the reason of being poisonous.

I point out these details for they show how practical reasons may cause the survival of certain old forms which from a superficial point of view may appear as manifestations of conservatism, obstinacy and poverty of these hunters, and which in some cases may appear in the eyes of the ethnographers inclined to see mysticism and "religious" reasons, as "sacred methods" of hunting. Indeed, one may imagine perhaps more effective methods of capturing animals and killing them but here two important considerations appear, namely, the economic side, whether the capital spent on the "improvement" may give higher benefit or not, which does not require any special explanation, and the self-limitation in the hunting, which is a systematic policy of the Tungus.

The living on hunting for very long centuries in the same regions has convinced the Tungus of the necessity of regulating hunting. At the present time some of these regulations are often broken. The chief rules are as shown: (1) no animals must be killed if the hunter cannot carry the spoil; (2) animals which are not needed by hunter must not be killed; (3) the animals especially cervines of certain age and sex must not be killed at certain periods; (4) the animal wounded must be followed by the hunter until it is killed. The practical meaning of the first rule is evident,— the preservation of the animals. The second rule produces the same effect and also prevents useless spending of energy on hunting and killing of useless animals like, for instance, wolves (vide supra). The third rule is composed of several particular rules. For instance, the females especially when pregnant must not be killed at all,** the very young

---

* Cf. R. Maack, op. cit. This has been confirmed by the Kumarčen. I am not competent to judge as to the chemical conditions of production of poison which is not destroyed by the heat of explosion. However, the Tungus themselves compare this method with the poisoning of arrows. It may be pointed out that the Chinese chronicles frequently mention the use of poisoned arrows among the populations of Manchuria, particularly the Sushen.

** The pregnant female bears must not be killed. The killing of the bear-female the Birarčen suppose may result in death of one of the members of the hunter's family. This prohibition is strongly supported by the peculiarity of the pregnant bear which may

fawns of elk, Cervus Elaphus, Cervus Tarandus must be spared too. (The fawns of Cervus Capreolus—roe-deer—may be killed; as a matter of fact they are very numerous); all fur bearing animals must be spared at the periods when the fur is not good, all animals whose skins are used for manufacturing must not be killed during the period when the skin is perforated by the insects. The list of regulations may be increased, but what is stated will suffice for showing that these regulations have in view an economical use of the natural wealth represented by these animals. The regulations of pursuing the wounded animals has in view the avoidance of useless destruction of animals.

Indeed, these regulations may receive a certain explanation in the form of reference to the spirits who "send" the animals to the hunter. They would sometimes say that the spirit of the taiga (it may have different names, *vide infra* Ch. XI) will not send the animals if they are uselessly destroyed, it will not give *mahin, mayin* (Barg. Nerč. Bir.) *mahin, majin* (RTM. Bir. Kum.)—the hunting "luck".* The luck is given by the spirit of the taiga. Even a good, skillful hunter may have no *mayin* in his hunting. Yet, he must not transgress the regulations of hunting in order to have *mayin*. As a matter of fact in this conception of *mayin* there is concentrated the experience of hunting in which there is always certain play of probability of meeting the animals and missing them, and when they are met to hit them or to miss the shot. On the other hand the actions of the hunter may reduce the number of animals, e.g. in the case of non-observation of the regulations regarding their preservation, when the animals become rarer, and the breaking of some prohibitions and customs, the practical meaning of which is not perhaps clear, may warn the animals of the hunter's presence. Indeed, in so far as the conception of *mayin* is concerned, it is a mere "chance" which may be increased or decreased by the hunter's acts, but as to the spirit giving the *mayin*, it is a hypothesis. However, the hypothesis of spirit has a secondary importance when the hunter considers the practical side of the hunting and the Tungus, especially experienced old hunters, give quite clear and rationalistic reasons even in the explanation of some customs avoiding a useless killing of the animals and preventive methods regarding the hunter's smell perceived by the animals.

The hunting complex has also gradually incorporated several other regulations all of which I shall not describe here, but I shall give only some instances. While hunting the Tungus use some restrictions as to the production of useless noise, laughing, useless talk, sometimes making a fire, abstaining from using certain words (special language, or better a special vocabulary). There are several other special prohibitions, as for instance amongst the Barguzin and Nerčinsk Tungus, the hunter must not give to the dog or throw away the head and testes of the musk dear, the

liver and heart of the Cervus Elaphus, and so on. Among the Birarčen the hunter must not start hunting on odd days of the month. However, such regulations exist only among the groups which keep an exact calendar. Some of these prohibitions may be understood as measures for preventing animals from being disturbed, while some other phenomena such as the use of *galegda* objects which may be recognized by the animals by their smell,* or the managing the animal's soul, or specific professional terminology may grow since the fashion receives a certain recognition. I think the abstaining from laughing and idle talk is connected with the importance, the seriousness of the hunting, to the Tungus. ** During the hunting, the oesophagus, the wind pipe, and the principal arteries and veins of the neck must not be cut; these organs must be taken out together and carefully separated one from the other. If this rule is broken there will be no luck in hunting —*mayin obdowča* (Bir. Kum.),—"the luck was broken." Finally some of these customs cannot be explained by the Tungus themselves and they follow them as with other rules and customs already described, the violation of which may reduce the *mayin*—the chance of killing the animal.***

So amongst the Tungus there was little by little formed a complex of rules concerning hunting. This complex might be created only on the condition of its transmission from one generation to another. Naturally, it was worked out owing to the continuous increase of experience and correct inferences made of the observations of facts and change of the Tungus and of the animal population of various regions, and yet more generally, of the regions occupied by the Tungus living on hunting. As a code of rules, many of which could not be justified by practical reasons, it needed therefore support of the higher authority which was that of taiga spirit. It may be noted that even during the last century, there were introduced new ideas of hunting for the market which required more than the old regulations permitted. On the other hand, the needs of the Tungus also increased owing to the change of weapons and increase of the goods used by the Tungus: e.g. regular supply of the alcoholic drinks, manufactured tissues, and even food-stuffs (*vide* SONT, pp. 26-28). This conflict between the old system of regulations and new requirements has resulted in change of the idea as to the spirits regulating the hunting, and even *mayin*. The change of this complex was greatly assisted by the missionaries who did their best to destroy "old beliefs" in the spirits. This conflict involved the young and old generations in the continuous discussions in which the old generation was sure of the necessity of keeping to the old self-limitations, while the young generation insisted upon the technical changes and quick enrichment of the Tungus.

---

* Once among the Birarčen I heard a complex explanation (a theory) of the fact that the animals recognize the things galegda namely, every animal, the man as well, has a kind of micro-organism (kulikan) which say to the animal about the presence of galegda. These kulikan are especially sensitive as to the presence of iron. Therefore an inexperienced hunter as far as possible must avoid having iron with him. The iron brings some animals into the state of excitement, e.g. bear.

** However, some Tungus believe that the bear may understand human speech, as the men understand it, at a distance (vide infra).

*** Here it may be especially pointed out that the hunters must be very careful about producing noise, rmells and showing themselves to the animals. Most of the animals possess well developed senses. For the beginners these customs are sometimes taught in the form of absolute and unexplained rules.

---

give premature birth to the cubs leaving them to the hunter and herself running away, which is a common occurrence, according to the Tungus. This produces very strong psychological effect upon the Tungus.

* The same word has received a new function, with the introduction of Christianity. So in Enis. main is translated as God, master; main (Transb. Tit.)—the god, Jesus Christ [the etymology given by E. I. Titov—mangi—(vide infra) is certainly wrong.] It is very likely that main was used by the missionaries. Owing to this among some Tungus there appears a new term for mayin (main) this time borrowed from the Russians hunters,—fart—the "luck".

Indeed, such an enrichment could not be possible under the conditions of the system of economic exploitation by the Russian and Chinese traders, which was realized even by the older generation.

The older generation knew that the increase of hunting spoil was possible if the fire arms were changed, but in the system of equilibrium existing between the increase of wild animals and Tungus consummation of them, the fire-arms as they were first used and strict observation of the regulations were in a complex relation to the reproduction of animals and to the Tungus needs. From the point of view of individual wealth these restrictions of hunting were not beneficial but they permitted the Tungus to have preserved their ethnical existence. This consideration was a decisive moment in their behaviour. The innovations in the form of modern fire arms, non-observation of regulations, intrusion of foreign traders, reflexion on the hypotheses regarding the spirits meant for the old generation, destruction of the Tungus integrity and finally loss of their independence. The change of "old faith" [*fè doro* of the Manchus, *n'opti* or *sagdi ón* (Barg. Nerč. Kum. Khin. RTM. Bir. Mank.), also *sagdi dorоyon* (Bir.), *sagdi joso* (Khin) (Ur. Castr.) cf. Mong. Rud. *jos* || *joson* cf. also *joso* (Manchu Writ.)] was thus equivalent to the destruction of the Tungus. Indeed, in this case I show the process of reasoning which was not expressed exactly in the terms here used, but which was that of their idea. The old generation did accept the new situation for in their eyes it was impossible to oppose the penetration of the alien (Russian and Chinese) influence and the young generation was not yet versed in the problem of the methods of keeping the equilibrium,—as shown they did not know all the consequences which might result from the change of the old regulations and increase of the hunting spoil.

As a characteristic element of Tungus behaviour it may be also noted that the Tungus are not atrocious in the sense of causing useless suffering to the animals. They do not kill animals which are not needed for the reasons already indicated and yet they would consider it "bad" should one kill them without any aim. As a matter of fact, they recognize killing of the animals as a necessity and they avoid making the animals suffer. If the animal is wounded and cannot move the Tungus immediately kill it by introduction of the narrow hunting knife into the brain through the basal aperture of the skull. For the same reason they do not kill the animals by methods of slow action. The explanation given may be that the animals will be angry with the hunter. However, this may be a simple rationalization of their dislike of atrocity conditioned by some different causes (*vide* SONT, Ch. VIII).

We have seen above that the Tungus do object to change methods of hunting and customs connected with it on the ground of preservation of the existing equilibrium. So that in this case if there was certain opposition to the innovations in technique of hunting it was not always based upon the psychological condition of sticking to the existing complex, and mental laziness but it was based upon practical considerations as to the *possibility* of changes in view of preservation of the ethnical integrity and independence. In the system of hunting the element of tradition and understanding of the practical possibility of changes was not of lesser importance than theoretical knowledge of

economic relations. These have formed the theory of economics and economic policy of the Tungus, as one of the elements of the material complex in its reflexion in the psychomental complex of the Tungus. Indeed, the contents of this branch of Tungus knowledge is not very voluminous for the body of facts and relations to be dealt with is not large. Yet, the method of investigation of economic relations, as we have seen, based upon the collecting of facts, and their analysis from which the Tungus make their conclusions and generalizations, only in some particular cases and individuals is supported or explained by the hypothesis of spirits' activity which in its turn is based upon dualistic treatment of the phenomena.

From the above analysis of the facts observed amongst the Tungus we may thus see that they have come to the creation of what may be called the elements of economics. Being an element of the psychomental complex it may be regarded as a derivative function of the material culture. The contents of the Tungus economics thus might increase together with the quantitative growth of the material culture and complication of the relations resulting from it, if the Tungus should be left as an independent group of ethnical units.

Together with the tendency of preservation of the existing complex we meet with a peculiarity of the Tungus psychomental complex, already pointed out on several occasions, namely, the Tungus are anxious to learn new methods of hunting and fishing. In fact, in the Tungus complexes of these industries we meet with the elements quite commonly borrowed from the neighbouring groups. If the new element of technique may be thus adapted to the existing complex, if it is good, and if it does not disturb the functioning of the whole complex, it is adopted immediately. Otherwise the Tungus would hesitate to incorporate it. So the Tungus complex may consist of elements of various origin, ethnically and chronologically. As to the technique used by other groups, as for instance an unregulated destruction of the animals in the regions, practised by the Chinese and Russians, it may be severely criticised by the Tungus. They consider in the same way any new weapon or method of hunting.

Those who are not familiar with the complex conditions of Tungus industry of hunting very often believe them to be conservative and backward. However, before making such a generalization, one must carefully investigate the causes of preservation of certain forms of hunting, of preference for oftentimes very "primitive" methods and of general policy of keeping the hunting spoil at a certain level. In fact, the hunting of some animals by modern methods, as e.g. squirrel, could not pay back the expenses, considering the market prices, while the "primitive methods" sometimes better preserve the skin. The Tungus policy of control of hunting can be understood only after a very detailed study. There are people who advise the Tungus to introduce changes, but such incompetent advisors in the Tungus eyes look childish. Should these advisors insist upon their innovations and the Tungus should accept them the whole complex would be destroyed.

The process of disintegration of the Tungus hunting complex, as stated, began during the nineteenth century. In most of the localities occupied by the Tungus the living animals are becoming more and more rare, so that the former equilibrium has been shaken. * In so far as it may be seen from the recent reports of the travellers, since the destruction of the old social organization produced by the governmental policy in Siberia, the Tungus have gone still farther in the process of their disintegration**. The loss of this complex in Manchuria is chiefly conditioned by the increase of population consisting of newcomers,—Chinese hunters,—who do not care to preserve the animals and destroy as many as they can. The loss of the former equilibrium and the loss of the old complex have ruined the Tungus of Amgun regions (cf. I.I. Gapanovich). In the Sixota Alin (Maritime Gov.) region many animals have gradually disappeared (cf. S. Brailovskiĭ) which brings the Tungus towards an ethnical disintegration justified by the idea of accepting a "superior" form of culture (Chinese).

It is evident that the loss of the complex of hunting and that of the knowledge of extinct animals produces great changes in the psychomental complex in general. This is especially evident in the groups which have discontinued their regular nomadism, like the settled group of Birarčen, e.g. in the village Čelu (vide SONT), the Nomad Tungus of Mankova, and naturally all Tungus groups which adopted fishing (especially in the regions of the Amur River) and agriculture. Amongst these groups the positivistic method of thinking shows marked decline, and the overgrowth of the spirit complex, chiefly due to the alien influences, begins to take the place of the former familiarity with the natural phenomena.

29. SOME OTHER ELEMENTS   I will not go into the de-
      OF THE COMPLEX   tails of the description of
                                the breeding of domesticat-
ed animals which has been already discussed in my work dealing with the social organization. Here it may be noted that the existence of the complex of reindeer breeding is possible only on the condition of very good knowledge of the reindeer. Indeed, the accumulation of positive knowledge of this animal has required very long time, and the time during which it was possible to domesticate, not only tame this animal, could not be short either. The methods of taking care of the animals and improvement of the species as seen in the selection, are worked out through the series of experiments and inferences made from the facts observed. The scope of this industry is so voluminous that one must study it rather a long time, so it constitutes one of the important items of Tungus education.

The reindeer breeding is believed by the Tungus to be of human invention, and its perfection comes within the

human reach. * Indeed, in Transbaikalia and Manchuria, as I have shown (in SONT) reindeer breeding cannot attain the importance of an industry on which, solely, the Tungus might live. The family needs only a limited number of reindeer for carrying members of the family with their belongings, for these people live on hunting. For this reason, the Tungus of these groups do not need to have very many reindeer and they may slaughter the excess. However, they impose certain limitations; the slaughtering of the reindeer is practised by the Tungus only in the case of great need in meat; the slaughtering ought to be justified by some reasons, e.g. the social function, like the wedding ceremony, or the sending of the reindeer's soul (the meat is eaten) to some spirits or as riding animal to the souls of dead people. The Tungus would slaughter the reindeer in the case of great famine. The slaughtering must be done according to the special rules described in SONT. It is strictly prohibited to kill the reindeer with the gun. The man who would do it will have no more mayin in hunting other animals.** In further discussion I will describe the medical methods some of which may be "magic". The methods of similia similibus type are used by the Tungus for increasing the milk. They also carry with them the dried bear's paw with claws and scratch the udder with it.*** As I have already pointed out, the reindeer is believed to possess the soul and thus it may be used for managing the spirits' activity.

Dog breeding among the Tungus does not require so much knowledge as with the reindeer. However, selection is also practised. The dogs are intentionally educated for special kinds of hunting. Indeed, among the Tungus using the dog as draught animal, as e.g. the Goldi and others, more attention is paid to its breeding. The dog which possesses soul may be used for sacrifice, but this is never practised among the groups here described. However, the placings for spirits in the form of dogs are used for carrying on souls of dead people and the souls of dead people are supposed to eat dog's meat (among the Birarčen). In the Manchu complex the dog has similar functions when they deal with special kinds of spirits. In the case of some very bad disease the Manchus sometimes bury a dog and cat, both alive near the entrance of the house. The dog or cat may move, which may be seen a certain time after the burial when the earth is re-opened; it is considered as very bad sign, if they should go away altogether.****

Horse breeding amongst the Tungus is borrowed from the Manchus and Mongols. However, the Tungus have introduced a new method, namely, the adaptation of the horse to eat meat (vide SONT). This interesting experi-

---

* e.g. already in the XVIIIth century the local Tungus groups of Manchuria could not find sufficient number of sable skins for paying their tribute, so they began to buy them from the Tungus living in the Russian territory. In 1915 there were no more sables in the mountains of Khingan. The decrease of the sable in Siberia in 1912 compelled Russian government to prohibit its hunting for a certain number of years. In some regions, e.g. in the Oxotsk region, no animals are left for hunting except the squirrel. (cf V.N. Vasiliev, op. cit. pp. 29-30.)

** The governmental policy seeks the support of young generation which is neither competent nor willing to maintain the old system, while there is no more chance of building up a new hunting system.

* The Tungus practise selection by pairing the best reindeer and buying good reindeer from their neighbours. Also they know perfectly well the effect of pairing with the wild reindeer (Cervus Tarandus).

** I know a case of a Barguzin man who by mistake killed a reindeer, after which he could not kill anything except the squirrel. It is evident that here is a case of self-suggestion due to certain pre-existing theory.

*** I am not sure whether we have here a form of massage, as a form of stimulation of udders, or merely a "magic" method. I have not been able to find any other connexion between bear and reindeer.

**** It was asserted to me that in a similar case a dog was found more than a metre away from its original place of burial and that there are cases when the dogs and cats run away.

ment goes well together with other experiments showing the trend of Tungus ideas.

The Tungus do not confine their breeding to the animals used at the present time. In the previous chapter I have already pointed out that the Tungus like to keep for experimental purposes all small animals and birds. Some of them are used to attempt domestication. I know a case of a Tungus in Manchuria who wanted to domesticate and use wolves, and to cross them with dogs. The experiment failed and the wolves were killed by him.*

The reasons differ as to why the Tungus do not sometimes carry on the breeding of some animals such as swine in Manchuria, oxen, and sheep. Sometimes breeding like that of the cattle involves the Tungus in great reorganization of the whole system which does not recompense for the energy spent; sometimes they have to introduce some changes which are of doubtful practicability. For instance, swine and sheep breeding meets with the danger from the dogs. As a matter of fact, the dog is a much more important animal (in hunting) than the swine and sheep the breeding of which requires isolation of the dogs and requires a settled life. Therefore one cannot say that the Tungus have aversion for adopting the breeding of other animals than the reindeer, dog and horse. Such an aversion is not characteristic of the Tungus. Abstaining is imposed by the Tungus economic system and the whole ethnographical complex. The same is true of the Tungus mentality in the case of introduction of agriculture. We have many instances which show that the Tungus very often refuse to carry on the agriculture not because of their "laziness," "conservatism" etc, but because they do know that to become an agriculturist one must learn it, and they may become agriculturists only on the condition if the benefit from it would be superior to that of hunting. They would adopt agriculture on condition if benefit of it should not make of them a lower kind of citizen, both in Manchuria and in Siberia. They realize that the adoption of the agricultural complex by the Tungus will soon be followed by their absorption by the stronger, more numerous, and more experienced agriculturists,—the Chinese and Russians.

The elements of the Tungus complex of clothing and household, beginning from the wigwam, are indicative of two facts, namely, that the Tungus gradually and regardless of origin have accumulated knowledge of using the materials found-at-hand in the most economical way in the given conditions and that their complex of the clothing and household with a few exceptions is well adapted to the local conditions and needs of a hunting mode of life. The process of readjustment of the elements in the case of the partial change of the complex may be observed among almost all Tungus groups. Here I have in view the changes like substitution of horse breeding for the reindeer breeding and readaptation of the elements to the

new condition of the limited possibilities of migrations during the dry-grass seasons.

The Tungus conical wigwam, as we have seen (SONT), is made of a wood frame which consists of simple young trees, cleared of the branches, which can be found everywhere in the taiga, and a cover made either of skins for the cold season when the rain would not destroy them, or of an especially prepared birch-bark for the seasons when the rain is possible, or finally of different kinds of material when the above mentioned materials are lacking. These may be the tissues* of alien origin, dry grass,** or earth.*** The preparation of the skins, in general, requires good experimental knowledge of the methods and personal skill which are transmitted from one generation to another. In dependence upon the season and kind of skin, also its individual thickness, the skin is treated with some chemicals**** and by various mechanical methods for reducing thickness and hardness of the dry skin. The variety of types of perfect chamois and skins in different degrees of preparation is such that for almost all kinds of clothing, household and nomading accessories and wigwam covers there is a special kind of skin material. The covers for the wigwams may be made either of skins of the large cervines (except the elk whose skin is too heavy) sewed together, or the small skins of roe-deer (amongst the Tungus of Manchuria) sewed together in large pieces carefully ornamented. Indeed, such a wigwam during extremely cold weather cannot produce a warm shelter but it may protect against the winds and serve as a good screen for the fire in the centre of the wigwam. From the point of view of ethnical units accustomed to the warmed houses such a housing would appear very imperfect. However, the Tungus opinion is different. First of all, they point out that their wigwam must be light enough to be easily transported during their migrations; second, they believe that the sudden change of the temperature, when they have many a time during the day to leave the wigwam, e.g. for supplying wood and water or looking after the animals, may have bad effects on them; third, since they often have to spend their nights and whole days without warm shelter and even without fire, they believe that the living in a very warm winter shelter might make them unable to go out without suffering harm to their health; fourth, the children must be accustomed from their young age to the hardship of living and hunting in any season of the year. Owing to this they do not adopt the

---

* The reason why the Tungus do not domesticate wolves is that the latter have a "bad heart". For showing it they relate a story. A Birarčen Tungus had educated a wolf together with his dogs. The grown wolf hunted very well. However, when the man was on hunting trip, his dog and wolf were for long a time without food: the wolf attempted to kill his master while the latter was half-asleep. The dog defended his master. Then the Tungus after observing the struggle between the dog and the wolf decided to kill the wolf and did so.

* In Transbaikalia the Tungus used to have tissues made by the Russians, in Manchuria those manufactured by the Chinese. They liked very much waterproof tissues manufactured by the Russians, but their objection was their weight, especially after the rain.

** The dry grass and bushes are used e.g. by the Birarčen for their wigwams erected for a long period. In fact, the birch-bark covers cannot be easily manufactured in their region owing to the relative rarity of this tree. They would have to buy the birch-bark from their own people permanently living in the taiga.

*** The earthen wigwams (in this case instead of light poles they use thick planks) are erected by the Reindeer Tungus of Manchuria for their long campments during the winter when they have to stay for their regular visiting of the traps. This kind of wigwams, as further adaptation of the same conical type, is also known in the Tungus regions in the Yakutsk Gov. and amongst the Yakuts.

**** Organic ingredients in the process of decomposition, rarely the ashes, and tanning ingredients, such as bark of some trees and shrubs, also smoking.

system of transportable iron stoves* as a further improvement of their winter shelter, and other suggestions proposed to them by the people who stick to their own ethnographical complex and who know no actual conditions of the Tungus life. Such are the opinions of the Tungus who themselves do not practise living in well heated houses. However, we have the opinion of these Tungus (e.g. in Manchuria and partly in Transbaikalia) who use the Chinese type of house with heated stove-bed (*k'ang*) and winter dwellings of Russian type. They say that although these types of houses are more comfortable, several maladies occur directly owing to the fact of their living in heated houses which they have to leave from time to time even in the conditions of half settled hunting groups. The same observation is made by the Tungus regarding the Mongol type of semispheric well heated felt tents.

In this instance of the Tungus cultural adaptation we may thus see that their dwelling is perfectly well adapted to the needs of the hunting groups, both from the point of view of biological (in a narrow sense) adaptation and from the point of view of integral use of the material locally produced and manufactured. So in this case the general characteristics of the Tungus psychomental complex may be applied to the description of these particular aspects of their activity.

One of difficult problems in the conditions of ever wandering groups and even incidental travellers in the regions inhabited by the Tungus is the material of which the loading boxes, utensils etc. are made. Taking into consideration the fact that the reindeer cannot be overloaded, and the number of reindeer used by the economic and social unit,—the family,—cannot pass over a certain limit,** the materials used for the manufacturing of the commonest things must satisfy several requirements, namely, they must be light, not fragile, they must be easily found in the region inhabited, resisting the changes of temperature, and convenient for handling. The chief materials are found in the forests, namely, wood and especially birch-bark. The wood used for various utensils, hunting implements and weapons is carefully selected from the great number of local varieties. Yet, the abnormally grown trees are used for various purposes, e.g. the larch-tree turned round its axis is used for the bows, the abnormal formation on the trunk of the birch is used for carving cups. But the chief material is the birch-bark which is used for making summer covers for the wigwams, loading bags, and a great variety of boxes for different purposes, e.g. for utensils, implements, sewing boxes, special women's boxes, hunting boxes, boxes for placings for spirits etc. The Tungus language possesses very elaborate special terminology for these boxes and vessels, in every dialect covering at least twenty varieties. The birch bark can be used only when it

is very soft, i.e. about in the middle of June. It is worked out by a long process of steaming in a specially made apparatus. When it is sufficiently steamed it may be again softened by some supplementary operations. Then the bark is reduced to the thickness required by the particular use of the boxes and vessels. The latter may be ornamented with stamping, cutting, by coloured designs and leather. The pieces of birch bark sewn together are used as covers for the wigwams. The loading boxes are made of birchbark and covered with the little worked reindeer skin or with chamois and usually very carefully ornamented. Such a box is waterproof and very light; it cannot be broken even when the reindeer falls, together with its load. As a matter of fact, there is nothing as good as the material and form of the reindeer boxes, and those who have to use the reindeer for carrying loads, sooner or later come to the same conclusion.

The system of loading of horses is different. The Tungus have partly preserved their reindeer boxes and adapted the forms borrowed from the Mongols. In addition to this they have invented a practical new form of bags made of elk skin from the legs.

At the present time all Tungus groups use iron kettles and large iron and brass tea-pots,* which are carried on reindeer and horse in specially made nets, or leather bags. However, this is an innovation. In former days, and sometimes at the present time, the cooking is done with help of hot stones. Very rarely can one now meet with metallic cups. Indeed, in these conditions it is almost impossible to think of the possibility of having any kind of pottery or crockery. Thus the seeming obstinacy of the Tungus in respect of their preserving the old forms and materials used for the nomading and household things is conditioned by the whole adaptive complex of the Tungus, what we have already seen in all other cases.

The Tungus clothing is adapted to the needs of their migrations, hunting, change of weather, sex and age. The forms and material are subject to great variations owing to the difference in quality of the material and under the influence of neighbours, such as the Russians, Mongols, Manchus, Chinese and Yakuts, as well as sometimes the Palaeasiatic groups. When the Tungus do not need "professional" dress for the hunting they will not refuse to adopt any new form of dress or new materials as, for instance, the manufactured tissues, if they prove to be suitable for their needs. Owing to this we have a great variety of forms and materials in Tungus clothing. So we have different styles in Transbaikalia and Manchuria, as well as in different interethnic surroundings. However, it is not so with the professional hunting dress. As stated this is made of different kinds of leather, so that, for instance, the shoes and moccasins, may be sometimes made of different skins. ** The same is true of the parts of the costume. It is well adapted to the needs of the hunter so that the other ethnical groups which live occasionally on hunting accept

* This was suggested by some Russian travellers who used the stoves in their tents, and the local Russian population who are accustomed to very warm houses, well adapted to the conditions of their life in the cold climate and their professional work.
** The number of loaded reindeer cannot be very large for it will take too a long time for loading them almost every day, and even twice a day during the seasonal migrations. With the increase of individually needed clothing, vessel, etc. there must be increase of the loads, reindeer, and the persons who look after the animals, load them, and so on. This puts a certain limit to the increase of the things personally used, and implies a careful choice of the materials used for their manufacturing.

* It may be remembered (cf. supra, p. 50) that the names of the metals are borrowed from various neighbours.

. ** Generally there is a great variety of moccasins adapted for different seasons, sexes etc. Cf. very interesting work by C. Hatt "Moccasins and their relation to Arctic Footwear," Mem. of. Am. Anthr. Ass., Vol. 3, pp. 194-250, 1916. Actually among the Tungus variety is still greater and this work schematizes too much the problem.

the Tungus shape and often buy from the Tungus women whose work cannot be equalled by that of other ethnical groups.*

There is a peculiarity in the Northern Tungus costume which remains somewhat enigmatic. Amongst the Tungus during the last century and earlier there was in use a coat made in the shape of European morning coat, cut in a very complex manner and carefully ornamented.** It was used all the year round. At the present time it has survived only in some instances of the western Tungus groups and in the shaman's coat which will be later described. As a matter of fact, this coat cannot be considered as very protective during the cold weather. It is open, so that the breast and abdomen must be protected by a special apron.*** Indeed, such a coat is convenient for riding and perhaps for hunting. However, its existence amongst the Tungus remains enigmatic. I have supposed it to be a survival of the Tungus formerly living in a mild climate. This is one of the cases which I cannot understand from the point of view of usual Tungus rationalism in the matter of the technical culture. However, I do admit that perhaps something of particular practical value in this form of the coat remained unnoticed by me.

The methods of cooking amongst the Tungus could not exhibit great variety. First of all they have limited cooking possibilities, and second, they have a limited variety of food. However, the Tungus have developed to the highest degree their taste and ability of distinction of various kinds of meat which I have pointed out in my study of the social organization (vide SONT, Ch. VIII). They pass far beyond that of other ethnical groups. It may be noted that their taste is so refined that they do not need and do not like very much the seasonings such as salt, pepper, mustard etc. According to them these seasonings are gosi—bitter, harsh on tongue etc. The Tungus especially like the fat, also classified according to the animals and parts of the body which invariably is considered ala—"tasty", "sweet", etc., and yet there is a more special term for the taste of fat—daligdi (Bir.), which is usually lacking in other language. So that in so far the available food is concerned, the Tungus have highly refined their taste and the perception of difference in taste is reflected in their consciousness and language. As in other ethnographical phenomena the Tungus are not hostile to the food of different styles, that of alien origin. In observing their reactions in this respect I find that with their refined taste for meat and fats they are not people easily satisfied (cf. SONT). The Tungus reaction on Chinese cooking is generally positive, while the same cannot be stated in reference to simple in respect to the taste, and little varied, food of the Russian low class people of neighbouring regions. However, all Tungus very much like fresh butter.**** I do not need to treat this pro-

blem as it stands amongst the Manchus, who have adopted Chinese type of cooking. The above shown facts which I have selected for showing the psychomental attitude of the Tungus may suffice for making a conclusion analogous to that which I have made after the description of other forms of Tungus activity.

30. MEDICAL ART In the present section I will not deal with the phenomena concerning the regulation of the nervous and psychic life and disturbances common amongst the Tungus. In connexion with other questions I shall treat it later in a detailed manner in Part Four of this work. I shall now confine myself chiefly to the use of surgical methods and practical use of medicines. However, some remarks are needed before giving facts. The Tungus distinguish different groups of cases which are usually treated in a different manner,— surgical intervention required by the injury of the bones, skin and soft parts of the body are considered as cases of "breaking" and "repairing", as natural as any other "breaking" which may be "repaired"; surgical intervention for giving an outlet for the accumulated products of a local pathological process (various abcesses); individual slight physiological and pathological disorders; infectious diseases; the obstetrical cases; and the psychomental disturbances.

Different troubles requiring intervention, according to the Tungus, may be due to accidents (breaking of tissues), to infection with the microorganisms (kulikan), or to activity of the spirits, and naturally child birth. The first group does not require any special explanation. If something is "broken" it may be "repaired," so the Tungus, for instance, stop bleeding with hygroscopic materials, e.g. rotten wood, ashes etc. Yet, they may press the blood vessels above the wound. In the case of breaking bones they would fix the broken edges and strongly bind the broken limb. No essential intervention will be made in case of breaking small bones or the skull. In the case of cutting sinews of the hand the Tungus (Birarčen) kill a partridge, take out the sinews of the leg and with a piece of it connect the separated ends of the sinew fixing them with a long hair. This is a case of transplantation of tissue. With the animals (reindeer and horses) they would go still further and would carry out more complex operations, as extending the skin for covering wounds and "repairing" the wound with the skin taken from other parts of the body, always sutured with horse or human hair. In the case of falling out of the organs due to rupture of the external covers of the abdomen, which is a common occurrence with the animals, they would put them back and

* It is so in the regions of Manchuria and Transbaikalia visited by the Russian hunters, and professional Chinese hunters in Manchuria.

** The excellent specimens of this coat are preserved in the Museum of Anthropology and Ethnography of R.A.S. first described by Georgi. (Cf. W. Koppers, op cit.).

*** This is still in use amongst the children and women, also more rarely men. It is known amongst the Manchus and all Chinese groups, especially among the children.

**** The reindeer Tungus do not produce butter from the reindeer milk. The reason is that they have very limited quantity of milk

which is used for small children and as addition to the tea of poor quality to make it tasty. V.L. Sieroszewski (Yakuts, etc. p. 147.) was surprised that the Tungus did not know how to make butter from reindeer milk. The Tungus, whom I knew, learnt or discovered the process of manufacturing butter. (This might be achieved by the observation of the process of producing sometimes butter from the milk carried by the Tungus in the birch bark vessels on the reindeer. Yet, it might be learnt from their butter producing neighbours). I think the Tungus surprise in the case of V.L. Sieroszewski was either a form of politeness characteristic of the Tungus, or a surprise at seeing a gentleman doing woman's work.

sew the wound. * In case of hopeless wounds and breaking of the bones they would cut off the fingers, even the hands, and even other fractions of the limbs. A hot iron is used to stop the bleeding**. In the case of supernumerary teeth in horses the Tungus of Manchuria extract them, for the horse with such teeth is thought to be doomed to perish. However, sometimes it is impossible to carry out a successful operation. The operation of castration of the reindeer is made by biting but some disinfection and arrest of bleeding is made with hot iron. The operation of sawing antlers is carried on with the same precautions. The cases of abscesses are first diagnosed and different cases of "swelling" are distinguished. They distinguish, for instance, the swelling of the thyroids, according to the Tungus Birarčen, very common amongst the young people (which is well known from the observation on other ethnical units) and characteristic of some localities amongst the adult persons, especially the Dahurs. In this case they say that it is due to the water, e.g. the upper course of Sun Bira (i.e. the Sun River, a tributary of the Amur below Aigun) is particularly bad. The abscesses sometimes must be cut as soon as possible, but in some cases one must wait until the matter is accumulated. The perforation and squeezing of the matter from the abscesses is also widely practised. In the animals it is always done. The operations on abscesses of the throat in man as well as those on the neck are done, although they are considered dangerous. In domesticated animals, the Tungus also use perforation of the bowels, reached from the back, when they are filled with gas.

The idea that the diseases may be due to the microorganism has been reached through the observation of the wounds in which the worms are sometimes growing and attain a size sufficient for being visible by the naked eye. The inference made is that there were very small *kultikan* (worm) which could not be seen by the eye but which have gradually grown into large worms. The next idea is that there are various diseases due to the micro-organisms. Here the Tungus would not agree one with another as to the causes of disease. Some of them would recognize diseases as due to infection while the others would suggest the spirits' activity.

For instance, amongst the Tungus of Manchuria, smallpox as a rule is considered as a disease sent by the spirits, but they recognize that it is contagious. Therefore they are very strict in avoiding families affected by it. The owner of the house, or of the wigwam places outside a post with a piece of red cloth. The Manchus observe the same custom. These houses cannot be entered by the outsiders. Indeed, the announcement of smallpox is considered as a custom connected with the spirits, but the Tungus act as though they know the infectious character of the disease. Therefore all Tungus groups accept with pleasure vaccina-

tion as a preventive method. * Chickenpox and measles are regarded in the same manner and so they are announced. As to the explanation of origin of these diseases the Tungus, as in many other cases, use Chinese theories. Amongst the Birarčen the method of vaccination has become so common that when they cannot get vaccine they take the secretion from freshly vaccinated persons. However, the Birarčen say that such a vaccine is not sufficiently effective, which they see in the fact that the process is not virulent. So in this case they become experimentalists. Hydrophobia in dogs is regarded as a special disease which may also affect man if the dog bites the man. ** However, even if there is no wound the bitten man must carefully cut out and throw away the parts of the. clothing bitten by the dog. The hydrophobia is recognized from the behaviour of the dog when it stands against the wind with the hair up. No spirits are responsible here and no method of curing is known. ***

The diseases thus may be classified according to their genesis. In dependence on the diagnosis there may be chosen various methods of treatment. In the case of infection they would use all kinds of medicine and physical intervention, while in the case of spirits they would confine themselves to prayers and sacrifices. We shall see later that the shaman's activity is very limited and is chiefly confined to the psychotherapeutic disorders and only partly to the management of other spirits producing physical troubles.

The methods of curing diseases are thus varied. They use very largely the treatment with the hot springs,**** the effectiveness of which, however, may disappear in case, for instance, a woman *akipču* (*vide* SONT), i.e. prohibited, should enter the spring.* They would use hot tea, hot melted fat, hot bandages etc. The Tungus materia medica, as far as I know, are not numerous, and they sometimes contain the ingredients like the hair of the bear etc. which, it may be supposed, have no therapeutic effect. ** The organs of animals are also used. However, whether they have any organotherapeutic effect or are used as "magic" methods I cannot definitely state. Together with the extension of their relations with the Russians and Chinese the Tungus have introduced several medicines of foreign origin, some of which they greatly appreciate and particularly those which produce some external and noticeable effect, such as local inflammation and irritation on the skin. Some

---

* Amongst the Kumarčen a man in the state of intoxication cut his abdomen, so that a part of omentum came out. He could not put it back. Next morning he carefully cut it off and sewed the wound. In a few days he recovered.

** Amongst the Birarčen after a strong attack of a bear the man's skull was badly broken. The bones were fixed as far as possible, the edges of the broken skin cut off and what remained was stretched and connected with the hair.

---

* This is practised by the wandering Chinese "doctors", and specialists,—Russian doctors and trained nurses amongst the Tungus of Transbaikalia.

** Some Tungus believe that if the dog should bite a tree or any other unanimated thing the latter may move (Birarčen).

*** The Dahurs use a powder prepared from an insect (beetle). According to them the person bitten by the mad dog will not fall ill if this powder is used within a certain time. Amongst the Chinese, according to the Tungus, the man bitten by the dog is put in a dark room away from the sun, for one hundred days, so no disease would occur.

**** The Tungus have discovered a great number of springs in different parts of known territories and outside of their territories which they visit only for the purpose of taking cure.

* e.g. this was the case with the hot springs near the twelve volcanoes near Mergen (vide SONT).

** I find in my records very few facts as to this matter. In fact, I have noticed only two minerals used as laxatives,—"white stone" and "black stone" used by the females and males respectively. The same stones may be used for relieving cough, or pain in the stomach. It does not, however, mean that the Tungus do not and did not know other medicines.

materia medica and methods have reached the Tungus through the Mongol lamas. Amongst very numerous methods which may be conventionally called "magic" methods and which have in view the protection of man from the activity of spirits and various pathogenic agents there are some methods which may be classed so only with great reserves. Indeed, the local irritation of the skin with friction, pinching, etc. which has been known from time immemorial as a result of experiment, also from the Chinese, cannot now be regarded as magic for the effect of these methods on the course of some maladies must be considered as positive. However, even in recent time these methods as distinct from those used in European medical art, and sometimes misunderstood, were regarded as pure and simple magic. The same is true of some Chinese materia medica often used in coloured paper with written characters on it. The attention of the observer may be attracted by the colour and characters which have sometimes no intended magic function at all. Moreover, the self-suggestion stimulated by the swallowing of a paper with characters written upon it, or by swallowing a quite inoffensive medicine perhaps must be accounted as one of common positive methods of medical art. To a superficial observer they would appear to be magic as well. *

In the case of the help to women in labour there are methods of special kinds which have already been partly described in SONT.

There are distinguished different diseases due to the infection resulting from the living together, e.g. in the villages. Amongst the Birarčen and Kumarčen they are grouped under the names of various burkan (vide infra Ch. XIII) and sometimes they are directly connected with the presence of soldiers, Mongols etc. as it is with the

* The medical art of the last century in Europe with its bleeding on various occasions, inoffensive materia medica (aqua distillata with various syrups), septic surgery, peculiar classification of diseases etc. would now appear as built up of the "magic" and empiric methods based upon coincidence of taking medicine and relative improvement of the health (very often not correlated at all,—post hoc propter hoc). But the medical art of our time is also far from being free from the same characters. The fashions of operating tonsils, cutting appendices, abuse of "antisepticism" without speaking of some medicines of strong effect but doubtful result, at last uncertainty in diagnosis and "naming" of diseases reveal a picture which in the eyes of further generations will appear in the same light as the medical art of the beginning of the XIXth century appears in the eyes of our contemporaries. However, the medical art of our day cannot be described ethnographically for it will produce a storm of indignation on the part of professional and industrial groups of ignorant populations. Such an investigator will be declared as a dangerous and undesirable individual who in some way must be isolated or reduced in his social activity. This is one of the curious instances of functioning of the so called "civilized nations", and in this matter the so called "primitive peoples" are more tolerant and less conservative.

venereal diseases and syphilis. Yet, a series of diseases which I could identify as typhoid fever, typhus, influenza, pneumonia, pleuritis, malaria (I have never observed it amongst the Tungus) etc. altogether numbering seventy two are known under the name of ain'i burkan. Indeed, in this case burkan is not exactly the same as burkan with which the shaman can deal. In disease the Tungus take medical measures or await the end of the process. They do not understand burkan in the sense of spirits but in the sense of infectious diseases, almost like general name "influenza" which may cover the most different diseases and their causes. The ain'i burkan is especially "active" in the places where many people live together. This is the reason why the Tungus very often avoid the visiting of such places.

We have already seen that in the case of measles, smallpox, and chickenpox the Tungus use no medical intervention. They place the person affected in a separate room, when possible, or isolate in a large sleeping bag in the wigwam. They try to avoid noise, sometimes keep dark, try to make a child pleased, and from time to time make sacrifice and pray. No medicines may help. The same method is used in the case of some diseases due to ain'i burkan. This is a recognition of the impossibility of helping the sick people. One may see and hear very often discussion as to the cause of disease and kind of burkan which is responsible for it. After the experiment with the shamanistic intervention they come to the conclusion that there are other burkan which cannot be controlled by the shamans, or to the conclusion that there is a wearing out of the organism or some defect as it is e.g. in the case of some woman's troubles. The treatment is to leave alone the person affected to go through the disease with no further intervention.

Here it may be pointed out that the Tungus recognize the ageing, wearing out of the organism, which they would compare with the senescence of the animals, trees, and manufactured "unanimated" things. In their eyes this is a natural process which cannot be controlled. So that all diseases, according to them, due to old age are considered as natural phenomena in which nobody and nothing can help. In the same way they treat death, as will be seen, but it does not make it better in the eyes of the Tungus who lose the people whom they love.

Indeed, the opinions of the Tungus regarding various diseases and defectiveness of the organism are subject to the great variations both amongst the groups and amongst the individuals belonging to the same group. We have seen that in this respect the new ideas come from various sides, from the alien groups, and from their own investigation of facts, and they may be due to correct or wrong generalizations. Therefore the same pathological condition may sometimes be explained in different ways.

CHAPTER VIII

SOCIAL ORGANIZATION

31. COGNITION OF THE SOCIAL ORGANIZATION The systems of social organization a m o n g t h e Northern Tungus and Manchus have been described and analysed in two monographs previously published. In these two studies I have shown that amongst the groups here treated there are great varieties of the forms of social organization based upon two variable institutions, namely, the clan in the sense of the exogamic unit and the family. Yet, it has been shown how these forms are adapted to the other elements of the Tungus cultural complexes, and to the needs of self-reproduction of the Tungus groups. The elements of which the complex of the social organization is built up may be of various origin in the sense of their pre-existence amongst other and distinct groups.

The attitude of the Tungus groups towards their social organization is neither simple nor uniform. The social organization, which naturally existed amongst the Tungus and their ancestors longer than any other cultural complex, * was based upon the distinction of social position of the individuals as in any other ethnical group.** The latter was connected with the bearers of certain classificatory terms of relationship. So the Tungus naturally had their social organization functioning in so far as the differences of relationship,—terms and the rights and obligations connected with them—were understood. However, the fact of the existence of the *social organization* did not reach the Tungus mind, and thus they did not need to explain it. Such was the situation as long as the existing organization, as a whole, remained untouched and unchanged. When it began to change in a noticeable manner, attention was attracted to it. Such a change occurred under the influence of a slowly changing system of rights and obligations connected with the bearers of classificatory terms of relationship and also under the pressure of other ethnical groups which compelled the Tungus to change their organization not from the bottom but from the top.

When a Tungus used a certain term of relationship in his mind the terms, rights and obligations were the same; e.g. *gusin* is the mother's brother and as such he is in a certain relationship to the speaker (ego), or he who was in such a relation to the speaker that was *gusin*. Owing to this the man conventionally called *gusin*, even without being physically the mother's brother, *eo ipso* appropriates all the rights and obligations. Therefore the persons who are not bound by the relations of their respective origin when named by certain terms, assume a certain social (relationship) position corresponding to the names, so the children of the widowers belonging to different clans cannot intermarry when their parents are again re-married; the persons who are bound by the relationship of *aki-noku*

---

* This is a fact hypothetically restored. The complex of the material culture amongst the Tungus has changed several times, but in so far as it is logical to think, there was no such a state amongst the Tungus when the material culture was lacking altogether. Such a state in reference to the Tungus would be a purely imaginary condition which cannot be considered as one to be taken into account in our investigation of the Tungus.

** I think this is not a proposition to be proved. The social organization presumes that there is a distinction as to the position of members forming the unit which possesses a social organization. The latter may be based only upon the distinction of sex and age groups but it will exist if such a distinction is made in the unit. The human unit deprived of the social organization is an abstraction. Such a unit has never been observed living and capable of surviving. Indeed, the cases of ethnical disintegration as well cannot be taken as evidence of the possible and historic existence,—i.e. as a reality,—of the human ethnical units. Thus, when I say that the social organization existed longer than any other cultural complex, I mean that the existing cultural complexes, as e.g. the reindeer breeding, the horse breeding, the hunting etc. are more recent (the elements can be traced either historically or ethnically) than the social organization as a method of adaptation and regardless of the forms of the organization.

and belonging to different clans (seemingly a recent practice) cannot intermarry their children; and so on. Indeed, the relation at one time was based upon the actual relation which existed between man or woman and their parents, also other persons from the point of view of their physical connexions of origin. This does not presume that all the terms met with in the original Tungus system have originated from the blood relationship, but there is no doubt that at a certain moment this point of view was prevalent. Later on together with the formation of the complex of social organization, i.e. the fixed relations between the persons forming the unit, the relation began to be understood as an element of the complex which existed by itself and independent of the actual relation. This may still be observed in the Tungus language in its secondary manifestations. So the Barguzin and Nerčinsk Tungus for designation of the mother's husband who is not the speaker's father use the term *amiran*—i.e. *ami* (father)+ *ran* (instead of) (SONT p. 182), while amongst the Tungus of Manchuria there is now in use simply *ami*, and even *ama* (the grandfather, as a term of honour).* In the last case the present meaning is that of a social relation based upon the idea of observation of the relations. There is only one step to be taken to introduce the practice of general abstraction of the formal relations,—and this will be the present system found amongst the Tungus of Manchuria. Such a state of things is not a primitive state and it does not reflect the original Tungus attitude in this matter. As will be later shown, the process of disintegration of the older forms is responsible for the change of the Tungus attitude.

The Tungus did not understand the fact of existence of the clan which was, in their eyes, merely a group of persons connected by a certain complex of rights and obligations, bearers of terms, and they could not intermarry. In this way they were connected with the previous generations, whence came the idea of continuity and theoretical inference: The original founder of the group must have been a man, an earlier ancestor.** One of the reasons is that the clans now included in the same ethnical units were numerous and it is likely that the tendency was to include only two intermarrying clans which were distinguished by the proper names. It is not surprising that amongst the Northern Tungus we find no Tungus term for such a fundamental unit, as "clan" is in the Tungus social organization. I have analysed this situation amongst the Tungus and found that they had to adapt some terms of alien origin either at the moment of change of the social organization, with the transition from the matrilineal system to the patrilineal system or even perhaps under

---

* Suffix -ran here understood as "instead of", may have other functions as well, e.g. "equal to", "acting as", "even as", etc.

** There is no little doubt as to the renewing of the blood in the clans which adopt members of other clans (with the patrilineal system, the male line being continuous) and thus the theory of a single ancestor responsible for the existence of the clan cannot be admitted. As a matter of fact in some cases it is possible to trace back to a certain historic person the origins of the clan, its formation, but the Tungus go much further and very often suppose that clans have originated in this manner and probably (here they are not always sure) all of the clans. Indeed, since the change of the original matrilineal system into a patrilineal system is very likely, if not sure, the whole construction of the Tungus as to the clan origin remains a foundationless hypothesis.

pressure of their powerful neighbours. In fact, many Tungus groups, as for instance the Tungus of the Barguzin and Nerčinsk taiga, and the Enissy Tungus say that before they had no clan organization and the latter was established by the Russians,—they lived as "wild animals"*bojūja*. The same idea is characteristic of the Tungus of Manchuria, e.g. the Birarčen who assert that they were first organized by the Manchus in the seventeenth (or even eighteenth) century. These Tungus ideas as to the origin of their organization may be understood either as a confounding of the administrative organization, which actually was the aim of the Russians and Manchus, with the clan organization, or as a simple *naming* and clear perception of the phenomenon of clan organization as a unit until that moment not understood and not noticed. In this respect the Manchus give an exactly opposite picture, for they all the time, perhaps beginning from the sixteenth century, changed the term for the exogamic unit "clan" which was subsequently designated as *aiman, xala, gargan*, at last *mokun*. This might be due, as I have shown, to the fact that the Manchus already had written records and intensively migrated and multiplied in connexion with their particular interethnical position. Yet, the Chinese cultural complex had also its influence in the sense of association of the exogamy, as a legal institution, with the clan names (*s'in* 姓) very often violated owing to the spreading of the bearers of clan names and their disassociation. So that amongst the Manchus the idea of "clan" as a social institution was clearly understood and used as a basis for their administrative and partly military system. Amongst the Northern Tungus of Siberia the situation shows a different aspect,— the "establishment of the clans" was associated with the establishment of the administrative units, so that together with the disintegration of the clan organization and preservation of the administrative units the term clan borrowed from the various groups was referred to the administrative units only.

We have just seen that the phenomenon of social organization in its form of the clan was not noticed and understood. This case is not isolated in the Tungus psychomental complex and it is not characteristic of the Tungus only. In fact, when the process of changes proceeds at a very slow tempo the living generations do not perceive it for the changes are so insignificant that there is nothing to be compared and thus perceived as a change. The attention of the unit is not attracted to the phenomena which remain so to say beyond the consciousness, as grammar is lacking in the consciousness of illiterate people. When the change is going rapidly it may be noticed and the phenomenon is perceived. In this way understanding of the existence of the social institutions depends on the tempo of their changes, variations.

Amongst the Tungus we have thus different attitudes towards the existing institutions. Questions as to the origin and reasons for some institutions are not asked; these things are taken for granted and even not perfectly perceived. If they are designated, named and understood, with the help of alien terms, their origin and establishment may be referred to the alien groups, as it is with the "clan" amongst the Tungus of Manchuria which is connected with the Manchus. Yet, the reasons that are given in explanation of existence, may be different. So it may be explained as an institution imposed by powerful neighbours (Manchus, Russians, Buriats) or it may be explained as one which has always existed and beyond human control. In this case there actually is no explanation for the fact is accepted, taken for granted. Therefore, the interference of higher spirits in the life of the clan is rarely met with amongst the Tungus. This is true among the Tungus of Manchuria (Birarčen and Kumarčen and whether or not this is true among the Khingan group, I cannot say) so that they make appeal to the spirit of world—*buya*—(*vide infra*) only in the case of the clan division.

The FAMILY is found to be nearly in the same position. Although the family exists amongst all Tungus groups it is not actually named. However, what is named is not the family but the complex wigwam-economic unit. Owing to this in Tungus the term for "family" in the sense of social-biological-economic unit seems to be borrowed from different neighbouring groups, and perhaps especially from the Chinese. The Tungus formed their idea of the family from the fact of this unit living in the wigwam, which is also perceived in its economic functions, also from the fact of the biological function of the family, namely, reproduction of the species. These two aspects of the family come to the Tungus mind when the family is observed. However, the family as a social unit has escaped their attention altogether. So it is natural that the Tungus believe that before their going under Manchu, Mongol and Russian influence, they had no family as a social institution and lived as wild animals. In fact, we have already seen that in the Tungus mind the animals may have family for self-reproduction, as for instance the bears, and thus the family in a biological sense is not a particularly human institution. With the intrusion of alien ideas and influences the existence of the family as a social institution was perceived, named with alien terms, and thus understood.

The organization of the family amongst the Tungus is based upon the economic efficiency of the unit which must contain at least a person supplying skins, and meat, and another person who makes the skins and looks after the household. As a matter of fact such relations may be established between the persons who might not be husband and wife. However, the Tungus recognize that the real family must consist of the male and female who may be potentially able to reproduce the unit, i.e. might have children, for there is no other place for rearing children except the family. The relations within the family, as it is with the clan, are recognized by the terms of kinship. So that since there is a father, mother, the sons and daughters, who need not be connected by the actual relations of husband and wife, progenitors and progeny,—the family exists. The adoption of children is based upon this mechanism of perception of the family as a biological and economic unit.

Since the clan and family as social units of the Tungus are not understood as such, the whole complex of relations which exists between these institutions must be regulated by a system of relations which are not understood as social relations, but which are understood both as economic and as biological. The first are seen in the clan intervention in the life of the family when the latter shows inefficiency; the second, in the clan control of marital relations of the family members. Owing to this no conflict exists between these two distinct units. Such a smooth functioning of these two units may produce on the travellers an impression of the human relations which may exist only as an ideal norm: they are perfect from the point of view of adjustment. It is not so actually, at least amongst the Tungus who merely do not perceive these units as distinct social institutions and groups of people who are conscious of the existence of such distinct groups. From this point of view one cannot speak of actual adjustment as an act of consciousness and will. So peace between the clan and family reigns not because of an ideal adjustment but because of the lack of these relations in the psychomental complex of the Tungus.

The situation entirely changes when these units are understood by the Tungus as distinct social groupings, i.e. as the family which is opposed to the clan. This is the case of the Tungus who may have a strong organization of the clan as well as of the family, clearly distinguished by the names, but the conflict would be frequent and strong, sometimes resulting in the separation of the family from the clan. In such position are found the Birarčen and the Kumarčen. This process usually coincides with the disintegration of the clan organization, which as a matter of fact on Tungus soil is only a different aspect of the process of self-determination of the family as a unit. The ideas borrowed from alien groups in this case have very great importance as a pattern which may be imitated.

The institution of EXOGAMY is not understood in its function and it is accepted as a condition taken for granted. Indeed, without exogamy, the existence of the clan is impossible. The Tungus who do not perceive the clan as a social institution do not naturally understand exogamy as connected with the clan, but as a prohibition of intermarriage between the bearers of certain classificatory relationship terms (names). Therefore the existence of the clan is possible even when the name of the clan does not exist; so it is e.g. amongst the Manchus where *mokun* as a rule does not possess its own name* and it is opposite amongst the Tungus who may have exogamy confined to the small units which preserve their original names by the side of the new ones. Yet, the exogamy may survive still longer even after the dissolution of the former units. It is likely that it would take, in this case, the form justified by the imitation of alien groups, e.g. the Russians.

The Tungus ask themselves no question as to the existence of the MARRIAGE as an institution. They accept it as a matter of fact which must not be transgressed. The reasons of non-violation may be different, e.g. they would make reference to the tradition which is accepted as practically verified, or they may refer to the intervention of the spirits in the case of transgression. Marriage for them consists of the complex of customs and acts which must be performed in a certain sequence, and which under the pressure of circumstances and alien influences may be modified. The lack of some elements may annul the validity of the customs and acts performed. Owing to this, marriage as a whole is not named. As a whole, it is designated by a descriptive expression, namely *asiva gadan*, i.e.

* The lack of names of mokun in this case may depend upon the fact of existence of the written records in which the names of old exogamic units are jealously preserved.

the woman (wife) (he) takes, but the person who takes may be either the marrying person or his relatives who "take" her for him. In case the bridegroom joins his wife's parents they would say *kurakanma gadan*, i.e. the son-in-law he or they take, the persons who take may be senior relatives or the parents of the woman. However, the customs and acts are named, and many of them are designated by terms borrowed from the alien groups. Under the pressure of alien groups the Tungus may accept some innovations which would not change anything in their cognition of the marriage. For instance, the Reindeer Tungus of Manchuria are supposed to be baptized and to be Christians and are required to celebrate their marriages in the Russian churches. Since the legal minimum age of the bride is eighteen, the Tungus bring the couples, married sometimes several years before, according to the Tungus complex of customs and acts, to the church for legalizing the marriage in the eyes of Russian authorities. So this act now becomes a necessary component of the complex of marriage.*

The analysis of the elements of which the complex of marriage consists shows that all of them may be explained by the Tungus with elementary reasons. The taking of a woman into the family as wife of a young son would be understood and explained as an act aiming to get a working woman in the family. The limitations as to the choice and preferences again would be explained either by the need of maintaining good relations with another clan which supplies the women, or by the lack of women in other clans except one of them, or even by a simple reference to the impossibility of violation of an old custom, which would be opposed by the seniors. The carrying out of the ceremony of wedding which consists of different elements would be explained as a desire of the clan and members of the families involved to have an occasion of having unusually good food, and remain on good terms with the other clans and persons. The sacrifice made by the bride would be explained as a preventive measure for avoiding a hostile attitude of the family spirits towards the new member of the family. The act of prima nox preceding the day of the wedding ceremony would be explained as no objection against the love pleasure at the moment of a near celebration of the wedding. In this way all the acts are "rationalized" and then they receive recognition as acts worthy of being done. So they may not exist in the Tungus mind as a whole, as a complex, which we designate here as marriage. When the "rationalization" becomes impossible the element may be dropped altogether, or be replaced by some newly introduced and "rationalized" practices. Indeed, the empoverishing of the complex may lead to its disappearance which will not be perhaps noticed at all. Again in the case if alien groups interfere with this institution and a sudden change of the whole complex takes place and in the case of mixed marriages with other ethnical groups, the complex may be understood as a whole, and it may receive recognition and name. In this position are found those Tungus groups which have recently changed their complex, as for instance the Nomad Tungus who have adopted the Mongol (Buriat) complex, also perhaps, if not totally then partially, the Tungus of Manchuria.

----

* The consummation of marriage nowadays takes place after this ceremony (vide SONT p. 213).

The complex of the customs and practices concerning the RIGHT of property, inheritance, also judicial functions of the clans, the rights of the seniors and juniors, and generally all particular forms of right as it has been shown, are accepted by the Tungus either by tradition as institutions existing among the previous generations and thus imitated together with their rationalization, or they are accepted as imposed by the authorities of alien groups. Yet, there are some regulations which are implied by the new conditions of life and introduced into the existing practices on the same basis as any other cus'oms, i.e. by practice and establishment of a tradition. The Tungus mind would be satisfied with a simple reference: "such is the custom." As a rule the Tungus do not appeal to the authority of the spirits, although such an occurrence is possible when there is no other way of rationalization. *

The existing relations between the members of a clan are regulated and there is no question amongst the Tungus as to the nature of these regulations,—they are not explained and very often, if not usually, connected with the positions of the members in the system of relationship. More than this, the rights and obligations in the Tungus mind cannot be separated from the name by which the person is designated in the system of the clan organization. The inequality in the Tungus organization depends upon the inequality of age and origin fixed in the terms of relationship. Usually the age and the social position correspond one to another for which there are special reasons **, but in rare cases it may happen that socially the person younger in age is senior, and this will result in an adjustment, both conditions being considered by the Tungus. They would not break down observation of formalities designating the inequality of persons.*** The woman's position greatly differs from that of man and the woman is prohibited in many respects. There are different reasons for these prohibitions. The limitation of her movements in the wigwam which is erected by her and where she is living, is conditioned by the theoretical considerations regarding the spirits, while some other prohibitions and avoidances, as for instance that connected with her economic and physiological activities, are based upon the physical and psychic differences which exist between the sexes amongst the Tungus. Although she is bound by these regulations she does not occupy a position subordinate to her husband. The Tungus have no idea of "equality" or "inequality" between the sexes. The men are also bound by a complex of prohibitions and avoidance customs, and in the case of senior-junior relations they must obey the women as they obey

the men. In family life the direction of affairs belongs to the one who is able to direct, either man or woman. However, owing to the peculiarities of the woman's functions (physiological and psychological) the chance of her becoming the chief of the family is smaller than that of the man. These differences in the position of the men and women are not fixed by any conception of "right" which may exist independently of the concrete cases of particular relations and may influence the establishment of relations. Naturally such a situation may exist only on the condition of its recognition on the part of both men and women.

In respect to the transgressors of the existing customs the Tungus recognize an absolute right of the clan to punish the CRIMINAL by any means at hand, including capital punishment. Naturally such a decision may be taken by the clan only on the condition of recognition of the clan authority, for individually any criminal may run away and leave his clan. Running away actually occurs, as we have seen, in the cases when the runner may have protection of alien groups. This, however, means at least partial disintegration of the Tungus organization and therefore is not typical of them. Criminality is understood by the Tungus as it is by any other ethnical group, i.e. as a breaking of the existing relations which may have importance for the Tungus, i.e. for clan. In the class of serious offenses are included those which in the eyes of representatives of other ethnical groups may appear quite unimportant, while some acts looked upon by the Tungus as minor misconduct may be held by other units to be heavy crime. If we make an abstraction of the qualifications of crime and consider only the spirit of penal practice amongst the Tungus we may consider it severe, and criminality a frequent phenomenon. Indeed it ought to be taken into consideration that the Tungus have limited facilities as to the choice of methods of punishment and, on the other hand, all Tungus groups which may be now observed are found in the state of intensive variation, chiefly under the influence of reduction of territory and important changes in the system of cultural adaptation. The last condition is greatly responsible for the increase of criminality. For understanding of the psychomental complex among the Tungus, two facts of importance may be pointed out. The first is the principle of conditioned punishment when the criminal is sentenced, better to say, when the crime is qualified, and thus the punishment is understood and execution is not carried out unless the criminal again falls into the hands of clan justice. This time the punishment is increased as it is with the recidivists. By these practices the clan policy becomes elastic and leaves to the criminal a chance to change his criminal inclinations. Second, another characteristic of the Tungus mentality is that in their qualification of crime they consider the mental and nervous state of the offender. In such a case the diagnosis will receive the form of an explanation of the mental and nervous disorder produced by the spirits. To this aspect, I shall return in further chapters. Thus, the Tungus justice is not formalistic and the Tungus experts are important witnesses in judicial procedure.

In the above given instances we have seen that the Tungus did not originally suspect the existence of these institutions, did not name them, and in many a case, did not notice the process of changes especially when these were proceeding at a slow tempo. Indeed, in the eyes of

---

* In my experience I have not met with such a justification of Tungus justice.

** First of all the Tungus clans are not numerous. Second, the period during which a father may have children by his wife (the remarrying of widowers is rather rare) is limited so that the ages of the children do not differ so much as among other groups. The distinction of only two groups aki and nokun also simplifies the problem.

*** Observation of these practices is possible for the Tungus consider it useful to preserve the existing organization. Yet, this is not difficult for the Tungus, for such cases as shown are relatively rare. The attitude of the Tungus in this case would be something like that of the so called civilized groups when the old statesmen express their obedience to the young hereditary monarch, or when honest statesmen do the same toward the chief of the state who may be dishonest, etc. This attitude is not characteristic of the "primitive" psychomental complex.

those who know these institutions and who understand them the attitude of the Tungus would appear as one characteristic of primitive mentality, while what is observed amongst the so called civilized groups does not differ from the Tungus complex. In fact, the "structure" of the present societies, as they exist among the "civilized" groups, is far from being clear to their members and the problem of description of this society still stands before science of sociology. Many phenomena are far beyond the understanding and even cognition,—the new phenomena appear in the process of adaptation and so remain unnoticed. The fact of the existence of various "points of view" from which the society is discussed, is indicative of the lack of understanding.* However, only theoretically may we assume that sooner or later there will be found methods for cognition of the social organization beyond this ethnocentric attitude. Furthermore, we may theoretically also foresee that this goal will be beyond reach until the phenomena of social organization are understood as functions which cannot be described in terms of static thinking. Indeed, the new social phenomena, which with impulsive variations, are always created, perhaps will never be cognized immediately but will remain unnoticed for a certain period, as it was before and as it is now. An exhaustive cognition of the social phenomena perhaps is possible only on condition of a complete arrest of variations or that of a reduction of the social organization. However, the first supposition is a mere abstraction in fact never observed, while with reduction of the social organization it is very likely that the sociologists will disappear altogether and there will be no specialists to cognize the process of reduction, and the social organization thus existing at any given moment.**

The revision of other elements of the social organization within the clan and family will bring us no new aspects of the Tungus psychomental complex, therefore I shall proceed to other forms of relations which originate between human groups.

32. GROUP CONSCIOUSNESS From the previous exposition we have seen that the Tungus individual is under the control of his own clan. However, he comes into contact with the other clans of the same ethnical groups and with the other ethnical groups. At the present time amongst most of the Tungus groups there exists preferential intermarriage between two clans. With great probability we may suppose that originally the ethnical Tungus groups always consisted of two intermarrying clans only. In the Tungus mind there were thus aki—nokun (his own clan besides his own father, and grandfather) and the world outside of them and particularly the clan from where his mother, his wife and all women were taken as wives. So that even in this case the Tungus needed no conception of the clan as a social unit. The

relations between these two units were established and continued on the principle of exogamy, the cognition of the clans not being responsible for the preferential intermarrying between the two clans. This practice may be maintained even when the aki-nokun (clan) might come into contact with other clans. In this case the maintenance of the relation would be based upon the connexions of personal relations established between the aki-nokun and the group of guisin-ina, who are aki-nokun of their wives and mothers. An extension of the marital relations over other groups of aki-nokun,—potential guisin-ina,—is not obstructed by the obligatory dual organization which has never been cognized but which in spite of that was maintained prior to the formation of larger Tungus ethnical units.

For the Tungus mentality it is typical that members of a clan, even those living in the other clans, do preserve their relations with and dependence upon their native clan owing to which there may originate special problems concerning the interest of both clans. It is evident that in case there are only two clans in the unit, the questions actually will be brought for discussion to the whole unit, although there will be no cognition of the fact of existence of such a unit. The relations with the mother's clan and cognition of these relations are based on the same classificatory terms of relationship which in their turn are based upon the blood relationship between the group of guisin-ina of "my mother's clan", and that of aki-nokun of "my father's clan".

In so far as my observations are advanced, I may suppose that the cognition of the clan as an exogamic unit may come from another source; namely, the disequilibrium between the sexes in one of the clans bound by the marital relations, and disequilibrium between two clans one of which may become more numerous than the other and thus a large portion of young men will not be married. I do not know cases when the cognition of the clan existence was due to this condition, but since the Tungus give, as the reason of divisions of clans, the above mentioned difficulties in marital relations, it is possible that such occurrences might have taken place before and in this way the existence of clans was discovered. It may be noted that the cognition of the fact of existence of the clan as a social unit has greatly helped the Tungus in the regulation of marital and other relations. They might divide the clan into new exogamic units as is now practised by all Tungus groups. Indeed, since such an act must be justified, the Tungus have found a good way of doing it by referring the whole matter of division to the highest spirit buya (vide infra). It is interesting from the point of view of Tungus mentality, that in spite of the fact that this matter concerns other clans as well, the overgrown clan would make its decision with no intervention on the part of other clans.

With the inclusion of other clans in the marital sphere, which does not depend on marital relations and does not depend on the fact of existence of the clans, there comes the cognition of the clans as units opposed one to another. In such a "pluriclanal" unit the process of cognition of the individual clan is facilitated by the fact that there are different names of groups of aki-nokun needed first for regulation of the relations between the clan and the world and afterwards between the clans which maintain marital relations in the dual system. From the fact of relations which may originate between two clans on the ground of

---

* Indeed, the conviction that from a certain "point of view" one may understand society and the conviction that one knows it greatly handicaps the process of cognition of the actual social organization.

** Here I do not have in view the "applied sociology" which may exist and does exist under pressure of practical needs of society and thus is functioning as any other ethnographical complex. This may have no connexion with the science of sociology.

preservation of the dependence on the native clan even after the marriage, especially with the women, also with the man who stays in the wife's family, there is formed no complex of relations cognized as those of the ethnical unit which is actually formed by two clans. Such two clan units bound by regular marital relations would not make any further increase of relations cognized as those of the new unit formed of two clans. These relations would be understood as exclusively marital relations. The relations perceived as internal, ethnical relations would not appear even in the case of the pluriclanal system although the complex of the relations such as, for instance, cross-marriage between four clans, would be in function. Together with the cognition of the clan, its name assumes great importance in the Tungus system for the individual belonging to the clan is identified by the clan name. We have seen how this problem is solved by the Tungus when they have to create new exogamic unit-clans. But the case of partial migration of the clans is also common, so that the survival of the same names even amongst the Tungus ethnical units which at the present time do not know each other is also common. In case two Tungus groups should discover similar clan names in different ethnical units they would suppose that there was an earlier separation of the clans in question. And they would try to compare different clan names for showing their common origin.

In fact the Tungus ethnical units cognized by themselves owing to some other functions, for instance, the administrative functions of alien origin, as seen when the Kumarčen oppose themselves to the Birarčen, which are Manchu administrative units, or when the Barguzin Tungus oppose themselves to the Nerčinsk Tungus on the same ground, created by the Russians. Yet when the unit is opposed by other similar units, or by the alien groups the cognition of the ethnical unit may be achieved. Here the interethnical pressure coming from the related Tungus groups or from entirely different groups is responsible for the appearance of a new idea, a conception of the ethnical unit.

Naturally there is no special term for designation of ethnical unit in general, for the number of such units in the vicinity is not large. The Tungus dialects (of Manchuria) may use the Manchu term *gurun*, already assimilated by some Northern Tungus which may be referred not only to the ethnical units but also to distinct groups of animals in the sense of "animal kind", particularly species, race, also political units, nations etc. However, this term is familiar only to those Tungus who are familiar with Manchu, i.e. the educated group, while the other Tungus groups are satisfied with *naming* particular groups by their names, e.g. *Nerčugan* (the Nerčinsk Tungus), *borel* (the Buriats), *kitat* (the Chinese) etc.

I have shown in SONT the very interesting phenomenon of the names by which the Tungus designate themselves, and I have shown that the original name *evenki* used by the Northern Tungus may disappear altogether if there are several Tungus groups living side by side and differing in some cultural respects. As a matter of fact, this is a general phenomenon. In many cases we may trace from historic evidences how and why the name *evenki* was lost. Yet, we have also seen that some Tungus deny the right of other groups to name themselves *evenki*. These facts are indicative of the Tungus ethnical consciousness.

The discovery of the groups which style themselves by the name *evenki* may meet with two reactions; namely, (1) mutual denying of the correct use of this name which very often happens in the case of great difference in cultural complex, and (2) the recognition of the correct use. From the latter the inference is made that the groups are of the same origin, for they call themselves by the same name. The Tungus would proceed furthermore in their establishment of the relationships between the groups as would the ethnographer; namely, they would compare the language, by comparing words, and compare other cultural elements within reach of their cognition. There the Tungus are liable to commit error for in the most of the cases they would be inclined to consider their own complex to be the genuine one, while that of all other groups, in so far as distinct elements were perceived, would be looked upon as borrowed from the other ethnical and very distinct groups. In many instances they make absolutely correct inference by comparing the complex of another group in its distinct elements with that of other ethnical groups. Yet, aberrations are also possible and common.

Let us take examples. The Kumarčen who call themselves *evenki* believe that their present cultural complex is the genuine *evenki* complex. When they speak of the Reindeer Tungus of Manchuria they admit that they may be *evenki* too, but not very well preserved owing to the Yakut influence and a late, at least partial, Russianization. The differences in dialects they would explain by the same influences. However, the situation is not quite so. The Reindeer Tungus of Manchuria would admit that the Kumarčen are *evenki*, but they would also point out that the Kumarčen have fallen under a strong Manchu (more exactly *bogdo*—the Manchus and Chinese ruled by the Manchus) influence, whence there have originated a new type of ornamented clothing, Manchu words, habits, manners, inclination for robbery (which is a wrong statement) ; this is connected with the fact of their serving in the Manchu military organization and pressure on the part of the government; the Reindeer Tungus would not deny that they themselves were under the Yakut influence, and that they have adopted some Russian elements, of which two influences they are proud; but they would strongly protest against the Kumarčen's opinion as to the reindeer breeding, some types of clothing etc. which according to them are genuine Tungus elements. The conflict of these two opinions cannot be amicably solved in their discussions and will serve as a new support for distinction of the groups in question.

The Nomad Tungus of Mankova recognize in the Tungus of the Urulga a related group which, however, was so much influenced by the Buriats that they are no longer Tungus, but like the Buriats themselves. In some instances even minor differences may suffice for justifying a distinction. Such differences may be isolated words, a special clothing, even shoes, etc.

The Tungus also pay attention to the physical type and they are quite sensitive as to the alien admixture which they recognize as well as do the European populations accustomed to certain anthropological and physiognomic types met with in their area. The admixture of the Chinese and Russians is very easily recognized. The same is true of the Yakuts. The Tungus would use these characters for nicknames of individuals. Indeed, these questions put in an awkward manner may be embarrassing. In fact, the cases of Tungus women who come into contact with alien men are not rare but are usually disapproved. So in some instances one may receive a reply concealing the actual well.

opinion. This may hold good for other ethnical groups as

The distinguishing of the Tungus, by themselves as compared with other ethnical groups, is based on the same principle. The alien groups are recognized by their external appearance as seen in the clothing and general physical attributes of the material culture, in manners and in physical features. Indeed, in the eyes of the Tungus, language is an essential character. The Tungus are very familiar with the characteristics of the neighbouring groups for which they may have general names and even slight regional differences are noted. For instance, the Tungus of Manchuria who are living near the Russian frontier distinguish the groups such as the cossacks, and non-cossacks, the workmen, peasants etc. Among the Manchus, they distinguish those speaking Manchu and those who do not speak it. The Barguzin Tungus distinguish the Russians from the Jews, the Buriats of Barguzin district—from those of the Amalat River (tributary of the Vitim River). These distinctions are based upon the minor differences in manners, clothing, behaviour, and language.

Their interest in other ethnical groups goes much further than that of the neighbouring groups. They collect their information from various sources which sometimes supply them with very inaccurate information and oftentimes, the products of imagination. Naturally, the groups whose representatives are met in Tungus territory are better known, while the groups which are known only by report are often conceived in a distorted picture. The field of their knowledge, however, spreads over all Asia, excluding the populations of India and the South Sea Islands about which they know very little, to America through the Tungus groups who have encountered Eskimos and American whale-hunters, to Europe through contacts with Russians and Chinese who give them this information although the Europeans are rarely met. The well known groups are the Russians, the Chinese, the Buriats and Mongols, also Manchus, Dahurs, Yakuts, Koreans and Japanese and less frequently encountered Tibetans. It is interesting that the Tungus living in Transbaikalia and in Manchuria know very little about such groups as Chukchis, Gilaks, Ainos, Koriaks and other groups in the adjacent territories.

The Tungus as any other ethnical group believe their own people to be the best—they like themselves. Most Tungus would admit their superiority at least in so far as their professions are concerned, i.e. the hunting and reindeer breeding. They would also be positive in their preference for the Tungus beauty.

However, they would also admit that in some respects the other ethnical groups may be superior and yet those Tungus who have already fallen under a strong alien influence may prefer the foreigners to their own people. Indeed, these are cases of ethnical disintegration and thus they are not typical of the Tungus complex. The experience of personal intercourse with various groups and the information regarding the present (1912-1918) position of various groups have convinced the Tungus of the fact of their relative weakness. The Tungus did not at once accept the policy of resignation. At the beginning, when the Russians penetrated their area in small numbers, the Tungus fought them with all available means and the Russian records of early meetings with the Tungus are unanimous as to the Tungus bravery, military skill and cunning in warfare.[*] The same experience convinced the Tungus of the Yakut superiority after which wars with the Yakuts were discontinued.[**] In so far one may rely upon the folklore, the Tungus fought the Manchus also before accepting their political rule.[***] Owing to this submission the power of the ethnical resistance is greatly reduced amongst all Tungus groups including the Manchus. Nevertheless, they have not lost their hope as to the possibility of Tungus revival. In my SONT I have given some facts which may characterize the Tungus attitude and so I shall not repeat them here. In this respect the Tungus have quite realistic ideas and therefore do not allow themselves to be lulled by unreasonable hope of resistance to the enormous interethnical pressure.

From the description and analysis of the Tungus ideas and attitudes towards the phenomena of social organization and ethnical relations it may be seen that the Tungus treat them as other natural phenomena. They observe the facts, some of which are cognized while others escape their attention and thus are beyond their complex. In this respect the Tungus mentality does not differ from that of others with which we are familiar. As a matter of fact, the social phenomena may exist and function without being cognized. After an analysis, the Tungus classify the facts perceived in a way which responds to their needs. In this respect the Tungus reveal the characters already pointed out, namely, inquisitiveness and ability to draw correct inferences. So we may now state that they possess a certain objectivity, in so far as it is not affected by the ethnocentric complex, in their judgment as to other ethnical groups; the result of their analysis of the relationship between the ethnical groups, which requires rather complex operations with the historic, ethnographic and particularly linguistic evidences, is very close to an objective representation of the actual relations.

---

[*] cf. e.g. Miller op. cit.

[**] cf. V. L. Sieroszewski's Yakuts, p. 223.

[***] The Manchu epic poem written down by me contains description of the wars between the Northern Tungus groups and the Manchus.

CHAPTER IX

VARIOUS MANIFESTATIONS OF THE PSYCHOMENTAL COMPLEX

33. LANGUAGE Language gives us facts for forming an idea as to the mentality. I will not here go into the details of the Tungus language, which would require too much space, but I shall point out some characters which may give some light as to the Tungus mentality.[*] In the previous exposition, as well as in my previous work on the social organization, we might see that the Tungus language is very rich in special terms. As to the geographical and topographical terminology I have pointed out that the Tungus dictionary is rich in those terms because the Tungus need them for their economic activity, migrations, etc. This may hold good for other sections of the dictionary. It is difficult to say how voluminous is the Tungus dictionary in different dialects. Such statistical observations would be beyond our present possibilities. Of course, in so far as I can see from my own material, a Tungus dialect includes at least several tens of thousands of words, produced from at least several thousands of stems. So that from the point of view of volume of the dictionary one must leave to the Tungus language a position which cannot be considered as inferior to that of other languages. Indeed, the Manchu language which possesses some literature is also very rich. Of course, the number of words (sounding starters) of a language (or dialect) is not yet indicative whether this language generally is rich or not in starters, for the same sounding starter may be used as starter of different chains in dependence upon the complex starters (combination of several sounding starters). Here it must also be considered whether the language is a written one or only spoken. In written languages the increase of starters and the secondary semantic variations are met with as well. Moreover, the longer the language is used, the richer the cultural complex is, the richer the starter content becomes. Owing to this, inferences made from a simple statistical calculation of number of "words" are quite risky.

The dictionary naturally is rich in the words used for designation of the phenomena important from the Tungus point of view. These elements may be lacking in other languages. Here I may quote, for instance, special terms for all ages and sexes of some wild and domesticated animals, very rich topographical terminology, extensive group of "verbs" for designation of different special forms and methods of hunting, in some dialects detailed classificatory system of relationship terms etc. On the other hand, as shown, for some phenomena which remain unnoticed there may be no terms. As compared with other languages, for instance, of the ethnical groups living on industry of modern type based upon the modern science, the Tungus language will show a lack of special terminology of this type.

All Tungus languages possess a well developed section of terms for the abstract notions,[*] which they may have. Again the number of these words will be more limited than in the languages amongst the ethnical groups which possess particular inclination for formation of this group of notions. This may be conditioned by the special ways of ethnical adaptation, and sometimes incidental growth of particular branches of knowledge. However, in so far as the theory of spirits and regulation of the spirits' activity is concerned the Tungus language is richer than many other languages.[**] Perhaps the process of logical thinking may be better seen in the analysis of the etymology of words which represent abstract notions. Let us take an example: *aja* (all dialects) is a starter (*vide* "Aspects", p. 39) for "particular property of the object (things and relations) which produces positive reaction in the subject." This starter may be used alone when the Tungus mind is interested in defining the attitude in general, which ought to be shown to the hearer, or to oneself (in the case of monologue). The expansion of the stem with specific starters (suffixes) may permit the formation of a series of new and particular relations of *aja*.

aja + suff. personal — "to like"

ajaba + suff. personal — "to be good, prosperous, healthy," etc.

aja + (suff. instrumentalis) *ji*—(in) "good" (manner, way) (suff *ji* may be substituted by its equivalent, *t.*)

ajaka + suff. personal—"to perform something" (in reference to the children and to the dogs when they are asked to show some of their amusing tricks, cf. "faire le beau".)

ajakan'ji — the farewell greeting

ajama— "good" (possessing the property "good")

ajama+ suff. personal—"to recover, to proceed from «bad» to «good»".

ojat + suff. personal—"to want, to desire, to envy".

njav— "to love, to like in such a manner that the liking will affect the object of liking."

ajarin— "good (actions), the property of producing «good»".

With the increase of suffixes of diminutive and others for showing degree of *aja*, e.g. *ajakan*— "slightly good, pretty", etc.; *ajakakan*—further diminution; *ajakïn*—highly good, etc. one may give shades of *aja* in its intensity, e.g. *ajatkukakun*—"the best of all". With the agglutination of suffixes of relation in space and time, one may produce a still longer series of new starters.

In so far as one may logically give new shades of meaning by using a primary starter with addition of specific starters the increase of new shades of meanings is possible. The limitations come from the logical impossibility of combining a primary starter with other starters. Yet, the position of the starter may also be used for giving it a new function. Thus, one may see that the process of formation of the new starters is strictly logical.

The sources of the new starters are different. The Tungus as well as any other ethnical unit in this particular form of cultural adaptation do not hesitate to borrow from the existing milieus* and sometimes they may invent some new starters by using the old starters and again they may substitute new starters for their old ones borrowing these new starters from the neighbours should these prove to be better in any respect, e.g. in "sharpening" the meaning, in shortening the process, etc.

The analysis of the Tungus dictionary shows that the Tungus groups use various methods of increase of the lexical contents. The number of "words" borrowed from different ethnical sources is very large as in other languages. The chief sources of words are the people, in the neighbourhood of which the Tungus are living. The borrowing of 'isolated "words" may thus proceed from one group to another without any direct contact by the particular group investigated.

It is not easy to restore the complex of starters which existed amongst the Tungus before their last migrations, for the substitution of some starters might take place at different periods and in different degree amongst the groups. Yet, such a restoration cannot help us to restore the psychomental complex which existed at that time, and from this point of view this question is beyond the scope of the present work.

For showing how the mental process goes on in Tungus system of thinking let us take some instances: *b'i s'in'jun gĕnĕldilĕaf b'iradulāvi ollovan butam'i*—I thou with started together to go to the river fish to harpoon, or "you and I went to the river for fishing." *s'inĵun* is *s'in* ("thou") and suffix of comitativus which may be rendered "together" or "with"; *gĕnĕldilĕaf* is *gĕnĕ*—stem "going"; since we went together it is indicated by the suffix—*ldi*—used in the action undertaken collectively with respective influence of one on another person (here "going together"); there is indicated the time when this event took place—*ĕa*—in the past, an accomplished action, and this action took place, was started —suffix-*l*—before the act of "going" had place; suffix *f* depends upon *bi* for showing that *gĕnĕldilĕa* is referred to *bi* ("I"). Thus, there is no ambiguity in this form, but a clear and logical description of the act of "going". *Biradulavi* is still more expressive; it may be dissected into *bira* (stem) "river"; *du* the suffix by which there may be designated the idea of "dativus" and "locativus", e.g. *sindu*—to thou (e.g. to give), and *ĵudu*— at home; *la* is the suffix of "directivus," so that combined with *du* it will give a more definite idea of direction towards

*cf. Aspects, p. 64 et seq.

the river for the purpose of staying; yet we have the suffix *vi* which is the suffix of "transitiveness" and thus when the river is reached it will be affected here by the speaker and his companion (*s'i*); so altogether it will mean the direction to the river in view of remaining in it. This is clear but the purpose of remaining in the river is explained *ollovan butam'i*. *Ollo* is the fish; *va* is the same suffix as *v'i* i.e. here designating the object *ollo;* the suffix *n* shows that the fish belongs to the river; thus it may be translated "(to act on) its (river) fish"; *butam'i*—is *buta*,—the idea of "harpoon",—which is increased with the suffix *m'i* for rendering the idea of action with the harpoon, although neither the time nor the persons and conditions of the action are designated.

The order of words may be changed within certain limits so that the sense will not be affected. The limits are defined by the rhythm of speech, musical contents of the sentence and sequence of logical moments. The whole sentence is built up in such a manner that there may be no other meaning even in the case of inaccuracy in the sequence of "words". Every suffix has its strict function designating the complex relations between the actors objects, actions with the emphasis as to the time and mode of actions. Thus a sentence is like a complex mathematical formula. Indeed, such a structure of language requires a strong analysis of relations at every given moment, for otherwise the functions of the starters would never be established and speech would become impossible. The Tungus languages thus have been gradually formed, being based upon the minute determination and designation of relations and starters for various ideas, so that the formal parts of the language have reached the highest possible degree of specialization, and at the same time they possess a perfect flexibility.

In the above analysed instance of *aja* we may see that the stem with the increase of some suffixes may play the part of subject, object, action, property, etc. The same is true of the stem *buta* which depending on suffixes, may become any logical conception connected with the idea "harpoon". The analysis of the Tungus "words" show that a Tungus actually operates with the mere hints to the ideas. The case of suffix *vi-va* (with variations) is used with different degrees of emphasis as to the transitiveness. The same suffix used in starters can be used for designation of actions when one needs to give transitive meaning to the starter of action, e.g. *kara* the idea to "look out", etc. but *karavu*—"to look out for", the idea "to watch after"; *mu ujuren*—" the water is boiling"; *muva ujuvren*—" (he or she) is boiling the water". The suffixes used for designation of the relations between the actors, objects and subjects, and the suffixes used for developing in the particular meanings of actions may be supplied with the same phonetic contents and these will be the same suffixes,—specific starters. * The number of suffixes which are potentially

* The analysis of the suffixes, their history of changes, their origin, in so far the borrowing may be suspected, constitute one of difficult tasks of the philologist. As a matter of fact, suffixes which are borrowed from other groups are met with. Yet, the common phonetic variations of the same suffix may give the idea of the existence of independent suffixes. For instance, in some Tungus dialects, the Chinese suffix *ja*, quite meaningless in Tungus is used merely for emphasis. It is also used (spoken Northern) for keeping the rhythm of the speech. Yet phonetically the same *ja* may be a reduced form of *va* (the suffix of transitiveness), so that for instance Bir. *muĵa* may have two meanings, namely, the emphatic *mu* (the starter is short and very often cannot be rhythmed) and *muĵa*

used in both senses is not small, but there are also some suffixes which may be used only with the starters for subjects and those which may be used only in the starters for actions. These facts, however, do not suffice for tracing a sharp dividing line between the categories of the Latin grammar which distinguishes nomen, adjectivus, verbum etc. These categories would entirely distort the actual structure of the Tungus language. The Tungus operate with the original starters for ideas and directing starters (suffixes) in which system the "nouns", "adjectives" and "verbs" are formed only for the moment of their function in the given complex. Therefore we cannot approach the Tungus language with the formal categories which would mean the application to the Tungus psychomental complex, the scheme of the European complex which cannot cover the contents of the Tungus complex. * Owing to this the approach to the Tungus language with the frame-work of European grammar will lead to the most elementary blunders and the "spirit" of the language will not be understood. To the persons incompetent in the nature of language, the Tungus language may appear as "strange" and "primitive", this time owing to its complexity. **

Construction of sentences opens new possibilities to the Tungus for perfecting their method of the exact expression of relations. I shall give, in addition to the above case (vide supra, footnote) a simple case of such a construction. The sentence is s'i gĕnĕksa m'inova omoča unakan(a) oji, which means literally: "you (thou) when being in the process of going me have come to speak do not" or "when you don't say that I have come". Here it is interesting to note that m'inova is m'in ("me")+va (transitiveness). Yet, there would be no mistake and more sharpness to say instead of omoča, omočava. I meet with some cases when

—muva. The suffix va may change by the process of assimilation into ma in which form it may be confused with the suffix of possession of property of the one designated by the starter-stem: e.g. uldä (meat), üldävä ("meat" + transitiveness), but we may also have üldän ("his, her, its meat"), whence üldänmä (ibid + "transitiveness"), while üldämä will be "possessing the property of meat", and üldänmä may become üldänmä→uldäma. (Here with the above dots, I designate the height of the musical tone, where one dot means low, two dots mean higher and so on). In this case the suffixes mä and mä phonetically may be absolutely identical for the tonality depends on many conditions, and thus theoretically mä and mä may be mä. By these remarks I want to point out that the operation with the suffixes requires very great ability and knowledge on the part of the investigator of Tungus languages, especially when the suffixes of relations are met in the starters for objects and actions.

* Here I give an instance when a "verbal" construction is subject to "declension." The "verb" sa—to "know; the negative form is oɛin sara, or osin sar'i ("he or she or it does not know). The speaker wants to express the idea "there is anything to be known". The "there is anything" is ejakat (anything) dĕin (there is not), the whole expression will be ejakat osijan sar'ija äčin in which oɛin sar'i are supplied with the suffix of transitiveness, for cjakat äčin expresses a negative possession (transitiveness). The question is about the insertion of ja between os'i and n; n is a personal suffix, the stem being o, s'i—the suffix (corresponding to si in b'is'in, logically equivalent to r'i). This case is from Bir. dialect "declension".

** It is true that the framing of languages into the scheme of Latin grammar, which is constructed on the principle of static formalism, is greatly responsible for the difficulties of studying any European language from the books. In spite of great reaction against schematization, no scientific approach is yet found to the grammar, i.e. a general approach which would permit expressing the grammar in short and simple formulae. Indeed, it will be done in the future, when the problem of grammar is not approached from

the long sentences are put into indirect form. More than this, if the directing action requires the idea of giving or directing, the whole sentence including "verbs" which depends on it may be turned into "locativus-dativus". In a simple case it will run as s'i m'indu goro buyaduk bojedu omočadu ullavas bukol—"you (thou) to me far place from to man to whom has come thy meat give;" in this sentence bukol— "give" has implied the use of the suffix of "dativus" not only in m'indu but also in the whole sentence. In the Tungus mind goro buyaduk bojo is a complex the particular elements of which, except the last one, do not naturally need du. These sentences are as logical as mathematical formulae and they leave no place for misunderstanding. This is achieved through the preferential use of the directing starters. It reveals keen analytical ability and skill of the Tungus in putting their ideas into a clear, although difficult, form.

Indeed, when Tungus children begin to speak they have to go from simple to complex constructions. In their speech, as well as in that of some adult people, especially the women when they speak to the children, we meet with simple constructions and rather limited use of suffixes. In my records I find that the style of women's stories is much simpler than that of the authors of stories told to the adult persons. Yet, the complexity of expression greatly depends upon the person,—some people like complexity, so they would build up a series of linked sentences of the above shown type. In using the directing starters they accumulate them and produce more and more relations and "interactions" of the original starters. On the other hand, there are persons whose speech is simple. Naturally the persons who cannot use and understand all the operation with the original and directing starters are considered as mentally inferior. The Tungus are very sensitive to the errors of the thought which their grammar with its original and directing starters demonstrates perhaps better that the grammar of a language poor in these elements and especially of those languages which have symbolized too far the complex of meanings, consciously or unconsciously classified in formal categories.

The Manchu language as to its Tungus characters is different in many respects. First of all this language is not so rich in the directing starters; second, it uses the order of words in the function of directing starters; third, this language uses in a limited manner the accumulation of suffixes. The same is true of the Goldi dialects (vide "Aspects", Section 32). At the present time it is impossible to say whether the Southern Tungus languages are in a state of reduction of the original morphological complexity, or whether in the Northern Tungus languages we have a relatively recent increase of the morphological elements. The true fact is that if we examine the Northern Tungus dialects comparing one with another, we may see that some dialects have probably quite recently borrowed new suffixes; e.g. in the Birarčen dialect, there are suffixes borrowed from Manchu, Chinese and Dahur. On the other hand, in the same sense the Buriat language produced its impression

the professionally traditional philological point of view. Since the Tungus language has not yet been put into the frame of Latin grammar that must not now be done. It must be pointed out that in case of "mixed" languages, in which different grammatical system may overlap each other, perhaps no grammar expressed in short and simple formulae is possible. Seemingly, such is a case of some European languages.

on the Transbaikalian Tungus dialects. These facts seem to indicate a continuous and recent process of increase of the directing starters in Northern Tungus. However, it is very difficult to say what was in this respect the pro-Tungus language, i.e. the language which was common to the ancestors of the Northern and Southern Tungus.[*]

34. FOLKLORE From the classification and degree of development of Tungus folklore given in the Introduction it may be seen that folklore in a narrow sense is relatively rich and varied but as material for our main subject it may supply only a small part of what is needed. Moreover, the folkloristic material is not yet published so its analysis will be difficult here. Therefore I shall confine myself to general remarks only. Yet as shown the existing Tungus folklore cannot always be regarded as one reflecting exactly the Tungus complex for a great part of folklore is formed of recent borrowings from neighbours. Indeed, I now see no possibility of separating Tungus elements which I could accept as Tungus invention and to operate with them, for a great number of undoubtedly alien elements are perfectly assimilated and adapted by the Tungus, so that they are included in the Tungus complex and can be abstracted only for historical purposes.

However, besides these elements there are many recently borrowed elements which are not yet fused with the complex and which play no great part as conditions of the existing psychomental complex. Such elements are, for instance, Russian elements introduced together with a certain influence of missionaries and schooling (*vide infra*). These elements may be easily distinguished for in a great number of cases Russian terms are preserved and the elements are found in an evident conflict with the formerly existing complex. The imaginative creations have also been greatly increased with Russian elements, as for instance, the whole series of fox stories connected with common European motives, sparrow stories which may have no ground in Tungus complex etc. Indeed, these stories are also interesting as documentation of the process of diffusion and adaptation of the adopted elements.

Another important source of borrowing is to be found in the Buriat and Yakut complexes which may be held responsible for a great number of elements of Tungus complex. Owing to my lack of intimate familiarity with these two complexes in a great number of cases I do not dare to take on myself responsibility for asserting that these elements are of Buriat or Yakut origin, but there is no doubt that such important cultural complexes as the cattle-breeding complex, cosmogony, orientation, and as we shall see later on, the shamanism are impregnated with the Buriat and Yakut elements. Sometimes, one may ask the question: "How numerous are genuine Tungus elements in these complexes?" and one comes to the conclusion that in some of these complexes the hand of the original Tungus is seen only in the adaptation of alien elements and in their

arrangement in a new complex. Indeed, this is true not only of Tungus cultural complexes.

In the folklore of Tungus of Manchuria there are seen two strong influences responsible for a great number of elements, namely, Mongol complex as it is observed among the Dahurs and Barguts, and Manchu complex which as will be shown is itself a composite one. As we have already seen a great number of hypotheses, and summarized facts have been assimilated and incorporated into the complexes by the Tungus of Manchuria. So that it would be legitimate to ask the same question as to the alien elements in the complexes of these Tungus, as I did this in the case of Transbaikalian Tungus, the difference being that of sources of borrowings. Distinction between the Dahur and Manchu sources is sometimes very difficult for the Dahurs have undoubtedly borrowed a great deal from the Manchus. In addition to these two influences in folklore we may also speak of a late Chinese influence received without intermediary transmission by the Manchus. Amongst the Reindeer Tungus of Manchuria we find chiefly Yakut and recently borrowed Russian elements. However, it must be kept in mind that the Russian population of the Argun River and Amur River, with which this Tungus group came into contact, culturally include some Tungus-Buriat elements received by this population from the Nomad Tungus incorporated into the cossack organization, so that together with this Russian influence some Buriat-Mongol elements are also introduced.

The Manchu Folklore essentially differs from that of the Tungus Folklore owing to (1) a long existence,—already for three centuries,—of Manchu writing, (2) very strong Chinese influence, and (3) different complex of environment and technical culture.

Existence of writing is responsible for the fact that some elements are preserved longer than if they were orally transmitted. Yet, the written records in general receive more credit, for in a great number of cases they are supported by the authority of the authors whose names are preserved, or by the name of the emperor who ordered the translation or composition of the works, a quite common occurrence in Manchu literature. I shall later on show what effect the existing writing has produced on some phenomena of the psychomental complex. The second character of difference,—the Chinese influence,—is still more important. We have already seen that the Chinese knowledge as to the milieus and ideas, as summarized in theories regarding the milieus, have deeply penetrated into the Manchu psychomental complex. At last, the Manchus being agriculturists and a politically influential group in China needed the more to pay attention to the village—city—agriculture complex than to mountain—taiga—hunting complex. Owing to this the Manchu folklore is poor, in so far as knowledge of primary milieu is concerned, but it is rich in various theories borrowed from the Chinese. In fact, for instance, many zoological and botanical terms have been borrowed or translated from Chinese [*] and there are very few geographical and historic facts which have not been received from the Chinese. The imaginative creations

_____

[*] Here I leave aside the discussion of theories proposed for explaining the existing differences between these two groups of Tungus languages. Most of those theories were implied by the postulates and hypotheses which were the basis of investigation into this complex problem. Therefore they have no importance for the present study. Cf. my "Aspects".

[*] Cf. P.P. Schmidt "Chinesische Elemente im Mandschu" in Asia Major, 1932, Vol. VII pp. 573-628, and Vol. VIII pp. 233—436. In this work one may find a great number of other facts of the same order. However, it ought to be pointed out that some parallels from Chinese given by P.P. Schmidt cannot be accepted without reserves.

of Chinese origin have been introduced in the function of historic facts and confused with statement of facts in the Manchu folklore. The Manchu stories of imaginative character are greatly influenced by the Chinese literature from which Manchu story tellers borrow their material, but sometimes only with slight modifications. Yet, a great number of sayings and witticisms are mere translations from Chinese.

Owing to these special conditions of Manchu folklore Manchu literature, which is not enormous, ought to be studied. In fact, the Manchu literature was chiefly created in the eighteenth century there was already a great decline of the Manchus as an ethnical group as well as decline of their literature. The existing literature in hand-made copies and in printed form, according to W. L. Kotwicz who recently (1928) touched upon this problem, amounts to 705 (of which 442 were printed) works*. A more detailed survey perhaps will bring this number to a higher level, but as compared with other literatures it will still be very low. Yet, many of the works known still cover subjects such as Chinese classics, Buddhism, Taoism, Christianity (32.6 per cent), languages (13.6 per cent). If we add to these subjects other subjects such as government and administration, military art, translations of Chinese dramas and novels, also poetry there will remain very little which may be regarded as genuine reflexion of the Manchu complex. Here, it ought to be pointed out that the greatest part of this literature is not accessible for the humble population of Aigun where the number of educated Manchus was always small. In this respect the lists of books and MSS. found by A. Grebenščikov in Aigun and Tsitsihar regions are very demonstrative. In fact, A. Grebenščikov has pointed out paucity of books at the time of his visit (1908) of the Aigun district which I may fully confirm by my observations (1916). By pointing out this fact I do not want to say that the Manchu literature known in other parts of the Manchu territory did not penetrate the most remote regions in oral form or in form of books which undoubtedly perished during the Boxer movement.

With a few exceptions the Manchu literature is Chinese literature translated into Manchu, and it was not only the literature which brought the Chinese complex, for a great number of Manchus even in the Aigun district could read and write Chinese, and Chinese books were much more numerous than Manchu books. It must also be added that the school education in Chinese introduced already under the Manchu Dynasty has played its rôle in the remodelling of the Manchu complex. In fact, a great number of Manchus did not differ from n'ikan (Chinese incorporated into the military organization), who themselves had been formerly influenced by the Manchus.

I shall not enumerate here all forms of Manchu folklore, but I shall only make some remarks as to the oral forms observed among the Manchus.

Apart from the Chinese complex of "positive know-

ledge" passed into the oral tradition, the Manchus have their own elements especially regarding local phenomena which Chinese complex does not cover. Here it ought to be mentioned the record of N'išan Saman (vide infra Part Four and supra Ch. III).

The group of imaginative creations among the Manchus is well developed, but a great part of these are merely Chinese elements translated and remodelled by the Manchus. As material characteristic of the Manchu psychomental complex these stories have rather relative value for the reasons already indicated. However, there are some stories, such as "Teptalin", which give a picture of Manchu life as it was reflected in the folklore. The same may be stated in reference to a great number of imaginative stories (juyu) which give pictures of spirits. Perhaps among the Manchus this class of stories is richer than among the Northern Tungus.

35.	DECORATIVE ART AS ONE	Artistic manifestations
	OF MANIFESTATIONS OF	of the Tungus may give
	PSYCHOMENTAL COMPLEX	us some light as to the
		psychomental complex

of the Tungus. However, I now find myself in a rather difficult position for the ethnographic collections needed for illustration are beyond my reach, while my diary notes are not quite sufficient to treat this side of the Tungus complex. For instance, the musical manifestations are of great demonstrative interest for they show the cultural character of groups and they also reflect the physiological complex, in so far as the latter determines the choice of forms of musical self-expression. Moreover, the musical manifestations, like other cultural phenomena, permit other groups to establish cultural influences over the Tungus. * Yet there is another quite special function of the musical complex, namely, that connected with shamanism. The latter will be discussed in Part Four, while I now give up the idea of representing musical manifestations in general, since the principal material is recorded on phonographic rolls which are beyond my reach. The dancing is closely connected with the musical manifestations. But this branch of Tungus artistic manifestations is very poorly represented in general. I have already made some remarks in my previous work (vide SONT Ch. VIII) and I shall touch upon this problem in discussion of shamanism. Owing to this I shall confine myself only to remarks and some illustrations of the decorative art among the Tungus.

Ornaments and play of colours are important artistic manifestations, seemingly closely connected with the physiological reactions.

Amongst the Tungus groups one may distinguish three ornamental complexes, namely, (1) the Northern Tungus complex, (2) the Nomad Tungus complex which is an adaptation of the Buriat complex, and (3) the Manchurian complex closely connected with the Manchu-Chinese complex. I shall shortly describe them for they complete the

---

* Cf. "Sur le besoin d'une bibliographie complète de la littérature mandchoue" in R. O. VI pp. 61-75, Lwow, 1928. A paper which was to have been read at the XVIIth Congress of Orientalists at Oxford. In previously published lists of Manchu works by P. G. von Möllendorff ("Essay on Manchu Literature" in R.A.S.N.C. Br. XXIV pp. 1-45), B. Laufer ("Skizze der manjurischen Literatur" in Keleti Szemle, IX.), A. Grebenščikov (1909) and others the number was much smaller, less than two hundred works being known.

* For instance, there are some Mongol musical elements and some Chinese elements which have been assimilated by the Tungus groups. There is a problem of musical instruments, very limited among the Northern Tungus, and a problem of method of singing, also other aspects all of which may bring interesting light as to the cultural influences.

picture of influences and they may also give some additional light as to the existing complexes.

The ornamental motifs of the Northern Tungus usually consist of combinations of the following elements: (1) simple straight lines; (2) double lines; (3) short lines —dashes; (4) points; (5) cercles; (6) rectangles. These geometric elements may be combined into various designs of more or less regular geometric appearance. There are different methods of their expression, e.g. carving of bones, wood, rarely metals (e.g. shamanistic paraphernalia); painting with different colours; cut work of skins and cloth; stamping, especially birch-bark and skins (very rarely); sewing of designs particularly with white reindeer hair; mosaic work with pieces of coloured skins, birch-bark and various kinds of cloth and fur, trimming with beads of different colour and size; and others. In one and the same piece there may be a combination of different forms, e.g. carving and inlaid work, embroidery of designs and combination of coloured skins, and so on.

As specimens of bone carving the most frequent are found in *gilbaun* (RTM, Ner. Barg.) which is an important element of reindeer harness and leading. It is made from fifteen to twenty centimetres long of a piece of bone, in the form as shown below. With two thongs fixed at and passed

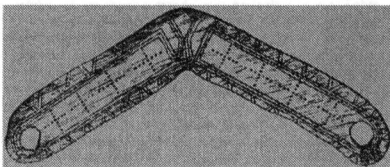

through the holes it is fastened to the back part of the reindeer saddle, so that the following reindeer is attached by its bridle in this way to the first reindeer. Among the Tungus of Enissy region the bone piece of the reindeer harness usually is also a piece to be carefully ornamented. The best specimens of wood carving are wooden parts of the reindeer saddle which, as a matter of fact, present still more

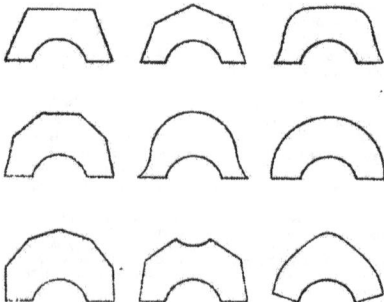

varieties as ornamental motives. Since the form of saddle has its ornamental function, I give these forms as well. The carved ornamentation of the saddle may be emphasized with colours.

From the specimens of ornamentation it may be seen that the form of objects sometimes implies variations of the ornaments. This may be seen in the *gilbaun* in which there may be found triangles for ornamental connexion between two parts. I give here below a specimen of ornamentation of a saddle which is particularly interesting. It may be seen that the central design is conditioned by the outer form of the saddle and this form is not a common form. There are five elongated circles partly covered with the central design, and two lower circles are connected so that they make a wavy line, a motif rarely encountered in Tungus ornament. As a matter of fact it is found, for there

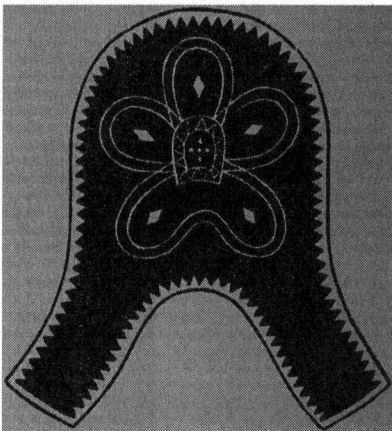

is a combination of semicircles which may easily result in a wavy line as an ornamental motif. This motif is also

met with rather frequently but usually preserving a point in the centre of the segment which is a little more than half-circle.

Great variety of forms, material, and colour combinations is observed in the boxes made of birch-bark which as a rule are always ornamented. In former times the coats and especially the women's coats, were very richly ornamented with strips of skin, beads of different colours, and reindeer white hair. Specimens of old costumes are now preserved only in the museums but I could see some pieces of old costumes and a coat made for a special occasion. Among the Yukagirs and Yukagirized Tungus they were met with at the end of last century and perfectly described by W. Jochelson to whose work I may refer the reader.

The combinations of colours are well represented in the ornamentation of birch-bark boxes, covered with the reindeer skin (usually with fur), loaded on the reindeer, and that of the woman's coat. However, at the present time the complex ornamentation has given place to combinations of strips of coloured tissues,—the Tungus of Transbaikalia and other regions now use tissues of Russian production.

Ornamentation is encountered on almost all instruments, utensils, and weapons, used by the Tungus, e.g. handles of knives, powder horns, wooden parts of guns, long hunting knives (used as spears), staves for reindeer riding etc. The parts of dress, especially women's moccasins, headdress covering the forehead, various bags and other things made of skins are also ornamented. Ornamentation may be lacking on man's clothings, also common bags and, of course, on those things which cannot be ornamented because of the material used.

On the whole the Tungus belongings even now produce the impression of being purposely made for delighting Tungus eye, and attract the aesthetic attention of other people. When a Tungus group is in the process of travelling it produces an impression of people who know no hardship of living under the conditions of the taiga,—everything seems to be done for pleasure.

Sometimes, one may meet with ornaments of Yakut type, but this is only observed and then very rarely, chiefly among the Reindeer Tungus of Manchuria. Indeed, the things of Yakut origin rarely met with in Transbaikalia have different ornaments. The Buriat ornaments, especially on moccasins also rarely on coats, begin to penetrate among the Reindeer Tungus, by the side of rare manifestations of Russian motifs. However, both Buriat and Russian motifs are very rare,—they become important only among the Nomad Tungus and settled Tungus living on agriculture. In spite of prevalence of Buriat and Russian ornamental complex one may also very rarely meet with the old Tungus motifs.

There is no little doubt that amongst the Tungus who use Northern Tungus ornaments, as described here, the art of ornamentation is in a state of decline. As shown, the best specimens known from historic records of early travellers and collections are no more found among the present Tungus groups. The Russian dress which had already penetrated among the Tungus greatly impoverished application of ornament to the costume. Yet, introduction of tissues has put great limitations as to the ornamentation. The greater the Russian influence, the poorer the ornament. This may be seen in studying Tungus groups in Transbaikalia, where the ornament used to be better developed among the Barguzin Tungus, much less among the Nerčinsk Tungus, and preserved only in traces among the Reindeer Tungus of Manchuria.

The Buriat complex is quite different both in the sense of motifs, method of execution, and colours. There are two important characters of this complex, namely, "sun and moon", and "sheep-horn". The "sheep-horn" as a term is translation of the Buriat term (xusín ĕbĕr) for this orna-

mental motif. This motif is a more or less complicated imitation of horns, always in pairs. It may be combined with the "sun" and "moon" also with the "geometric ornament" consisting of lines, triangles, squares etc. * Again, the penetration of the Russian complex reduces even this relatively simple ornamental complex, so that among the Nomad Tungus it is found in a simplified form as compared with the Buriats. It may be also noted that combinations of colours are not so daring as among the Reindeer Tungus in dresses,—black and blue colours prevail, while red, yellow, green are only moderately used. However, in utensils, boxes, bags etc. red colour is still common. Some variations of colours are introduced by the bright coloured dresses of Buddhist priests and monks, but on the whole the Nomad Tungus complex does not produce an impression of gaiety and joyfulness of character of the people. Yet, it is much poorer than that of the Tungus of Manchuria who use the same motifs.

The ornamental complex of the Tungus of Manchuria is quite different as compared with that of the Reindeer Tungus. Although these groups are living under conditions similar to those of the Reindeer Tungus, with the only exception that they use horses instead of reindeer, they have adopted a different shape of coat, seemingly borrowed from the early Manchus in their dress influenced by the Mongols. Together with the new cut of dress new ornamental forms intimately connected with the dress, were introduced. These ornamental motifs probably come from a still further area, namely, China. ** However, the Tungus of Manchuria have at least partly preserved some early ornamental motifs.

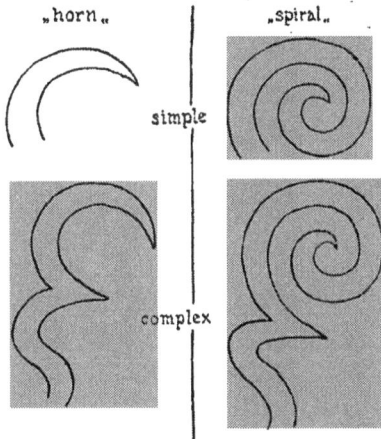

simple   „horn„   „spiral„

complex

* The chief characteristics of this complex may be seen in the work by B. E. Petri "Ornament of Kuda Buriats" (in Russian) in Publ. of Mus Anthr. and Ethn. Vol. V, pp. 215-252. St. Petersburg, 1917-1925. Indeed, there are some differences among Buriat groups, but they are not essential.
** Cf. B. Laufer "The decorative Art of the Amur tribes" (vol. IV, The Jesup North Pacific Expedition, Memoirs of the Mus. of Nat. History, 1902) dealing especially with the Goldi ornament.

The most essential ornamental elements are those already indicated as characteristic of the Northern Tungus and some others,—(1) combination of lines produced by pressing with a special instrument,—a stamp made of bone or hard wood,—skins, and especially birch-bark; designs of stamps are different: there may be, for instance, forms as shown ▼ ▨ ∿ ▨ and other variations,—this is quite an individual invention; (2) dots (usually of double lines) made with stamps and treads; (3) simple and complex spirals and horns; I call "simple" the form, as shown above, which may be further complicated by giving elongated and angular forms; (4) swastika with its variations, especially "endless swastika" of Chinese type; (5) meander; and (6) varia as for instance "bat", "butterfly", "flowers" etc. chiefly of Chinese origin.

Besides the ornamentation of birch-bark, widely used for various boxes, receptacles etc. the chief application of ornament is seen in clothing, the ornamentation · of which is made with ready made patterns of different colours or of the same colour but emphasized by stitches, dots, etc. It may be noted that the Khingan Tungus much more than other groups use line ornamentation of birch-bark utensils and much less ornamentation of their clothings, which on the contrary is especially rich among the Kumarčen. Yet, in so far as general characteristic of colour combinations is concerned the latter are neither rich, nor bright and daring as in the Northern Tungus complex. There are even introduced colours like gray, green-brown, light brown and others which can make no sharp design.

The ornamental motifs have special names only in rare cases and usually they are designated with the names of objects with which they are associated or with the material used for ornamentation. However, there are a few terms some of which I shall now give. The ornament in general is called *ilga* (Bir. Kum.) [corr. *ilxa* (Manchu Writ.) *ilγā* (Man. Sp.)] ; a circle with a point in the centre—*ěsači ilga* (Bir.)—"the eye having ornament", which in other groups may also be "the sun" as well; four points distributed thus ⁖ are called *lawda ujá*—the tiger's footprints; encircled swastika (used on the cradle)—*deliksan* (Bir. RTM); swastika in general *amsakan dèγ'i* (Bir.),—*amsakan* (could not be identified) birds; swastika on shaman's coat —*saman'i g'evan'i ilga*,—"the shaman's headdress ornament"; an ornament commonly used among the Manchus ↓ is called *čoko fatka* (Manchu Sp.)—"the chicken's foot"; *s'ilpä* (Bir.), *salpa* (Bir. Khin), *selpe* (Kum) [cf. *selfe* (Manchu Writ.)—"slash in the side of a coat" (usually ornamented), perhaps cf. *salätě* ‖ *salayatal* (Mong.) *salal* ‖ *salayala* (Mong.)—"branched".]—the ornament on the slash on the side of the coat; ᴄᴐ —*n'anj'an* (Kum.), the etymology of which is not clear; *on'o* (RTM)=*moritin* (Ner.)—"the ornament on the reindeer loading boxes." To the above terms there ought to be added terms like *n'iriptun*,—an ornament on the shaman's coat; *ormu* (Khin.),—"the ornament on the moccasins (cf. *orumus*)" evidently connected with the parts of the dress; terms like *torgadan* (Nerč.) (cf. *targa*—"a tissue")—the strips sewn upon the coat in general; *monγavdaptin* (Nerč.) [cf. *moygoraku* (Manchu Writ.)—"ribbon, strip facing the edges of a dress"]—in general ornaments on the clothings made of different material; *s'irinan* (Ner.),—the ornament sewn with threads (*s'ira*, etc. "the threads") which merely designate the material used. It may be here noted that the

"sheep-horn" is lacking, and the names of a great number of motifs are merely conventional "starters",—the names of motifs are of a late "origin". However, among the Manchus it is called *goxon ilxa* (Man. Writ.) or *koγoγ ilγa* (Manchu Sp.), i.e. the hook.

The finding of a hidden meaning in ornaments, and their "mysterious" functions etc. are very common in ethnographic literature. Without denying such a possibility in some and perhaps rare cases, I shall now give some considerations as to the complex ornaments met with among the Tungus.

Almost every complex ornament may be dissected into the elements and then there appears a very interesting phenomenon, namely, the elements grouped are usually simple, but their complexity and variations originate from geometrical manipulations with the elements. The most common geometrical manipulations with an element or with a group of elements are,—(1) simple repetition along the lines; (2) repetition by rotation about a point; (3) mirror-like reproduction and repetition by rotation, both alternating. In the case of repetition along a straight line, the ornament may change its direction owing to the shape of the material ornamented, so that a circular line, broken line, all kinds of curved lines etc. are met with, the principle of ornamentation being the same. Mirror-reproduction may be repeated twice and even thrice, which naturally will produce very complex design. The repetition by rotation about a fixed point may give varieties depending on the angle, e.g. which may be 180°, 120°, 90°, 60° which will produce a corresponding number of repetitions, two, three, four, and six. I have not observed more than hexagonal complexes. There may be also noted a special technical method of varying ornaments, namely, using of positive or negative patterns, and yet even combination of positive and negative patterns in the same complex. Such a complex may receive a special name if it is used as a conventionalized unit connected with a definite cultural element, as it seems to be in the case of the swastika in a circle (*deliksan*, *vide supra*). A much more complex case is that of the swastika repeated endlessly and mirror-like by means of a continuation of lines at right angles. This ornamentation complex has been borrowed from the Chinese together with the cultural element *jambol*,—a tobacco pouch.

By the side of these motifs and their combinations there may also be, though rarely, stylized animals such as the bat, the butterfly and the "dragon" borrowed from the Chinese. These patterns of Chinese decorative art are met with on Chinese and Manchu articles in great numbers so there is no need to go to the Goldi to seek for patterns, as will be later shown. It may be noted that lately a new movement has made its appearance; namely, the use of assymmetrical ornament which includes birds and flowers undoubtedly of Chinese-Manchu origin. The objects so ornamented greatly differ from all others. The choice of colours for these ornaments has also been influenced by Chinese taste.

I have just rejected the supposition that the Tungus of Manchuria have been influenced by the Goldi. In fact, the Goldi ornament as it was known in the XIXth century and even later, when the Goldi were visited by B. Laufer,

L. J. Sternberg and I. A. Lopatin included no typical Northern Tungus elements, but it used very largely "spiral", "horn" and other curved motifs, and it was especially rich in animals and plants which were not evidently introduced under pressure of the recent Chinese-Manchu complex. The same is typical of the Gilak ornament. However, there is no need to suppose, as I.A. Lopatin does (op. cit., p. 335), that the Goldi ornament is their own invention which has "evolved" from stylization of animals and plants. Indeed, bats, butterflies, dragons, fish etc. were essential components of the Chinese-Manchu complex; to make addition of lizards, toads, cocks (indeed this fowl is not geniune Goldi element!), reindeer, etc., perhaps also met with in Chinese patterns, would be quite natural. The problem of interest is that this art has grown in Goldi soil in so far as I could see more than, for instance, among the Manchus, which, however, does not yet prove that the Manchus had not before a better represented decorative art. Yet another point of interest is that among the Gilaks the original forms—the Chinese-Manchu patterns—are better preserved, as for instance the dragon, two fishes, etc. which seems to indicate that the Gilaks did not add much adaptation of the original patterns.[*] This re-adaptation and other complications of the Chinese-Manchu complex make of the Goldi complex something distinct as compared with the original Tungus forms and forms used by the neighbours.

Analysing one by one the elements, and complexes, especially in connexion with the objects ornamented, one may clearly see that the decorative art of Tungus of Manchuria has been borrowed from the Chinese-Manchu complex, partly directly, and partly through the Dahurs, but some elements of the old Northern Tungus complex are preserved, especially in the ornamentation of birch-bark, wood and bones.

Near to the problem of decorative art is that of design and sculpture if one is allowed to speak in these terms of small artistic manifestations observed among the Tungus. As a matter of fact, I have met very few specimens of this kind. It is true that the Tungus have occasion to manifest it, for instance, in carved wooden placings for spirits representing different animals (vide infra Ch. XVI), but they are executed in a conventional manner in which form they are transmitted from generation to generation. However, I was impressed by the fact that with a few cuts made in a few minutes on a piece of wood, the Tungus arrive at representing not only the kind of animal needed, but they supply it with certain expression: movement, rigidity, anger, smile, etc. In looking for pictures made by them I could not discover them, but I frequently saw the Tungus with help of charcoal or other colouring matter, reproduce by hand the most complex designs for patterns of ornamentation. This has revealed another side of the problem of

design manifested in complex ornaments, namely, before making an ornament the Tungus has it in a mental picture (imagination!) and then he (or she) may make a pattern which would be adjusted to the idea. So that, if the design as a whole may be dissected into the elements and repeated by rotation and mirror-reflexion, there will be made only the necessary unit of the complex. By this I do not want to say that the complex forms do not sometimes result from the operation based upon the principle of simple trial. In fact, the small children, especially among the Tungus of Manchuria, like very much to play with birch-bark (or lately paper) and scissors or knife, making patterns. The same may be also observed among the adult persons. Yet, when the ornament is finished, they make sometimes additions for "embellishing" the design, to make it fuller, even sometimes with asymmetrical elements. These cases are indicative that the outcome of technical effort sometimes does not correspond to the existing taste. However, in the greatest number of cases of creation of a new pattern, the design undoubtedly is in the mind of the artist. The fact of absence of design of realistic specimens of the milieu has compelled me to experiment by asking the Tungus to reproduce from memory various animals and plants. These reproductions in most cases are clear and represent characteristic features of the objects, so that there is no doubt as to the understanding of the picture. For instance, in representing different kinds of deer, the form of the antlers, the form of the anterior part of the head or the high, curved nasal bone of the alces with its spade-like antlers will be accentuated. In representing the wild boar, the peculiar distribution and form of the bristles and teeth will be indicated. These pictures are realistic, sometimes being simple reproductions and sometimes impressionistic pictures pointing out distinct peculiarities. The same is true of the representation of plants.[*] Indeed, the Tungus are not reluctant to represent realities by which they are surrounded,—for this there is no "religious" reason,[**] no prohibitive reason,—but, seemingly, the Tungus are not attracted by these forms of artistic self-expression. They are more impressed by and they merely like better the rhythm, of geometrical design than the faithfulness in reproduction of the milieu, although they are not devoid of feeling of realities and necessary technique for their reproduction. Perhaps, this constitutes a very essential difference between the art of such groups as the Chukchis, Koriaks, Eskimos, whose artistic effort is chiefly directed to the expression of movement of animals, to a realistic representation of the milieu. At the same time it constitutes an essential difference between the Northern Tungus decorative complex and particularly that of the Tungus of Manchuria and that of the recent modern Chinese complex, the elements of which may always be very easily distinguished in a Northern Tungus complex.

---

[*] Indeed, the Gilak cultural complex included a great number of elements received from the Manchus and Chinese, so their "primitiveness" is extremely doubtful. First, L. von Schrenck, and later L. J. Sternberg believed them to be romantically primitive, which was implied on the one hand, by the trend of ethnography of the last century,—to find "primitive peoples",—and on the other hand, by the fact that none of these investigators were familiar with the groups of Manchuria and the Chinese complex of pre-Manchu period, the chief cultural source of Manchuria after the downfall of Yuan Dynasty. It is natural that this group, which lived on the big commercial road, such as was the Amur River for centuries,—was under the strong influence of their powerful neighbours.

[*] The above given characteristic of Tungus ability is not one which may be generalized over all Tungus individuals. As among other ethnical groups, and as in reference to other cultural characters the individuality is of great importance: There are individuals who are good artists and there are individuals who are very poor artists, in general. Yet, there are some Tungus, especially women, who make very fine ornaments, but they are unable to make any good picture representing plants or animals.

[**] In this and similar ways a great number of facts of this kind among other ethnical groups was "explained" by ethnographers who have usually been wrong.

36. ACCUMULATION OF THE FACTS. In the previous chapters we have seen that the Tungus accumulate the facts cognized into complexes of knowledge. The facts naturally must be first cognized and the Tungus succeed rather well because of their habit of observing animals and nature in general. Indeed, the cognition of facts depends on the one hand on the extension of their knowledge which facilitates the approach to the new unknown phenomena and on the other hand, on the practical need of the facts for carrying on their cultural routine.

Naturally among the people who have no writing, as among the Northern Tungus, * the only way to accumulate the facts is to record and transmit them in oral form. Indeed, this form may be reliable only on the condition of accuracy of statement of facts and accuracy of their further transmission. It may be here noted that the

---

* Although some Northern Tungus groups have begun to learn foreign languages and writing, practically no serious attempt has been made for using the Mongol and Manchu alphabet for recording their own language. However, some Tungus words and especially the clan names have been transcribed in Manchu for the practical needs of administration. During my stay among the Tungus, I attempted to show them the method of phonetic transcription, formerly used by the linguists of the Russian Academy of Science. In several instances, I succeeded to the extent that some individuals themselves recorded some stories. In due time, these records will be published, I hope. The Soviet authorities have also attempted to adapt phonetic transcription to the Tungus language in form of "latinization".

There is a large group of specialists who, it may be supposed, even against their will, have to compose a new alphabet for Asiatic groups including the Chinese and in the future for all languages which do not use the Latin alphabet. Since the fact is interesting from the ethnological point of view I shall digress to mention some details. The stimulus of this reform is the simplification of the methods of disseminating communistic propaganda in view of spreading the languages into areas open to the political influence of the Soviets. It is hoped that after the standardization of the alphabet, there will be a fusion of all languages into a single language of mankind which, it is supposed, will be communistic. This linguistical pseudo-scientific justification was adapted by N. Marr. It may be thus noted that this attempt at the creation of Tungus writing is only a step toward the destruction of the Tungus language which by these steps would soon be led to absorption (fusion with other languages). In this footnote we cannot go into the interesting details of this ethnological process. Indeed, since there are many Tungus dialects which differ one from the other the creation of a single system of writing will result in the creation of a new written language, for the basis of which there will be selected perhaps one of dialects better known to the inventors of this language. Furthermore, since the Tungus themselves are not numerous at all and there is a very small probability that they would produce broad minded linguists, it is to be expected that this will be taken by some of those ignorant and audacious persons who do not find any other way of earning their living and become specialists of the assimilation and economic exploitation of ethnical groups of Siberia. In these hands the Tungus written language will be modified according to their taste and ideas as to the language in general and particularly the Tungus language. Such a language if it ever becomes of general use (personally I do not think it will for the Tungus will soon know other languages) may create in the future great confusion in the mind of the linguists who will not know the origin of this language. There is already a practical step made by J. P. Alkor (Koškin) who in 1930 published (in Russian) "Projet d'alphabet pour la langue des evenkis (toungouses)". The attempt is rationalized and justified by the theoretical considerations. Also vide "Materials of the First All-Russian conference for development of the languages and writing of the peoples of North," edited by J. P. Alkor (Koškin) and J.D. Davydov (1932, Moskow—Leningrad), which is a document of a great ethnographic interest for it greatly reflects an ethnocentric complex, yet quite unconsciously.

Tungus as a rule are very strict when they relate hunting events, or facts concerning other animals and other ethnical groups, also in general any fact to be communicated to other people. The Tungus may make involuntary mistakes and may give an involuntary misinterpretation of the facts which depend on their familiarity with the subject and degree of clearness of the original statement, but they would not believe the people who are not able to relate clearly and without distorting the facts. Such a man would be known for ever as an unreliable person. In this respect, the Tungus possess a special intuition which helps them to define their attitude towards the speaker. The liars are considered as the worst possible people. This particular element of the Tungus complex is conditioned by the need of having exact information as to the animals and people met with, which is necessary for successful carrying on hunting and maintaining social relations. Indeed, the fact that the Tungus have to transmit their knowledge through the mechanism of oral transmission is greatly responsible for the fact of their strictness in the relation of the facts and inferences. Indeed, if the Tungus would be inclined toward distortion of the facts and conclusions, their technical knowledge could not be preserved at all. There is one more condition which greatly helps the Tungus in maintaining tradition and principle of truthfulness in their daily practice. We have seen that a Tungus preserves his connexion with his clansmen throughout his life. The common interests of the clan in which the facts are accumulated and transmitted are very important, for a member of the clan cannot live beyond the clan. The latter interferes with his family life, it assists the clan member if he needs it, which may be in form of food supply, marriage etc. Owing to this a Tungus would not mislead clansmen, and he would not try to hide something from clansmen and use it in his personal interest. In fact, if he would do so his personal gain might become subject to the redistribution, direct or indirect, among the clansmen.

From the above remarks it is evident that the Tungus preference for truth is not that of a particular moral complex, but it is imposed by the conditions of life and practical consideration of the usefulness of truth from both personal and social point of view. This peculiarity of the Tungus behaviour spreads over all Tungus attitudes, so that in general they are the people who are not inclined to the lie even in those cases when the lie might be useful for personal gain, as it is true of the relations originating beyond the clan, family and even beyond the ethnical unit, i.e. with the foreigners. This particular trait of the Tungus "character" has been very often noticed by travellers and neighbouring groups who greatly appreciated it together with the Tungus principle of keeping their word in the case of obligations taken on even by the previous generations (father and even grandfathers). These facts are so well known that I do not need to repeat them here.

Together with the destruction of the existing social organization and assimilation of the alien complexes by the Tungus the above indicated trait of the Tungus "character" is subject to changes. Such changes may be observed among the groups which are in direct contact with the alien groups in Transbaikalia, e.g. the Nomad Tungus, in Manchuria some groups of the Birarčen and Khingan Tungus who have already fallen under a strong alien influence.

In connexion with this it may be noted that the facts

and news are immediately communicated to the members of the unit,—every one is conscious of the need of communicating to other members of the unit. Owing to this the news spread over the Tungus groups with a marvellous speed which greatly surprises travellers amongst other ethnical units as well.

In this respect the Manchu complex is quite different, at least at the present time. First of all, the Manchus who already for several centuries had their written system are not compelled to be very careful with the transmission of their knowledge through the oral method, so their memory and accuracy of statements need not be very strict. Second, the Manchus for a long time have already been in touch with several ethnical groups who ruled them (the Mongols) and whom they ruled (e.g. the Mongols, the Chinese, the Northern Tungus and palaeasiatic groups), which does not help to maintain frankness and truthfulness. Third, the field of Manchu activity—agriculture—does not require so many new facts as with the hunters who depend upon the migrating animals. Fourth, the long living in a state of organized large political units greatly reduced the need of practising the principle of maintaining and seeking truth. The government naturally took on itself the task of defending the common and private interests, so that the moral obligations in the consciousness of the Tungus were replaced by the legal regulations and administrative initiative. At the present time the Manchus cannot be characterized as a people particularly "honest" and seeking for truth. The individual adjustment within the clan and especially in the midst of the foreigners, pushed the Manchus to the adoption of a perfectly elaborated system of individual adaptation in which the lie is admitted as a legal method of self-defence and self-determination. This condition was greatly responsible for general weakening of the Manchus who gradually lost their faith in the loyalty of their own clansmen. It is impossible to say what the Manchus were before being involved in the complex political relations which brought them to the position of conquerors and rulers. However, it may be supposed that they were not like the Tungus were even in recent time. In fact, the Manchus,—agriculturists and people surrounded by their strong neighbours,—have been since long ago, in an entirely different position.

_____

One has naturally to ask oneself the question as to how the Tungus transmit their knowledge without any written records. The methods of transmission are chiefly oral and only in small part based on the imitation of the products of the culture represented in physical objects and sequence of actions. In the description of the social organization, I have given some facts regarding the education amongst the Tungus. The knowledge of the facts and different methods of industrial and social technology is gradually transmitted to the coming generation by the experienced women and men of the clan. If such ones are not found in the family the young people may be transferred to another family or they may temporarily join the neighbours or hunting companies. It is thus evident that the need of and process of education are understood by the Tungus and they designate it by the starter _tat_ used in majority of present dialects and

in Manchu (_taĕi_) which may be rendered as "to teach", "to learn" etc. *

In the preceding chapters we have seen that the amount of Tungus knowledge to be transmitted is not small. Moreover, the approximate knowledge which may be received in the regular schools (among the so-called civilized groups) is not absolutely indispensable for the pupils and it may be acquired in a small part, while the knowledge of facts regarding the geographical conditions, animals, and methods of nomadizing and hunting are absolutely indispensable and must be correct and very good, for otherwise the men will not be able to carry on their profession and gradually the knowledge acquired by the previous generations will be forgotten altogether. Naturally, the teachers are the experienced old men whose opinions and knowledge are appreciated. Such an experienced man would teach his young men by telling them what they have to accept as a "truth" and what they may accept as "doubtful", at last what they do not need to know. In the last group are included fairy-stories, jokes etc. which are regarded as a mere pastime. One may hear the Tungus ask: "Is it true or it is just a story?". If it is a simple story it would be accepted as such. As a matter of fact, there are Tungus who are interested in true stories (history and experience) and in the account of facts, but they would not listen to a story-teller. Yet, there are old men who perfectly well know the facts, but who are rather indifferent to stories of all types. Sometimes the men of middle age would become authorities as to the facts to be acquired, and sometimes very young men, even young boys may become famous story-tellers. It is not very frequent that both inclinations are found in the same person.**

Such a distinction of two types of "educators", perhaps even of two distinct psychomental complexes, may be observed among all ethnical groups of Tungus. It is thus natural that these types cannot be regarded as one type and their complexes fused. Yet, still less can one regard the Tungus folklore, in a narrow sense, as reflecting the system of their positive knowledge,—the Tungus themselves make a sharp distinction between the two. Indeed, some of the Tungus "true stories", as they are transmitted by tradition, may be an erroneous approach to the facts, and some of their theories ("hypotheses") which are believed to be "truth" may be erroneous. However, the Tungus themselves would sharply distinguish two groups of which the folklore in a narrow sense cannot be criticized for it is not "true" but consists of "stories", while the second group

_____

* In Bir. by side of this stem there is used another one—tan—which is "to stretch", "to pull", etc.
** Unfortunately most of the travellers among the so-called primitive peoples are looking for exotic facts which would appear interesting to simple-minded readers. The facts which are similar to those existing in the European complex are very often omitted altogether. In case the observed "primitive man" does not know the "folklore" of his people he receives no attention on the part of the investigator for he cannot supply any "striking" fact well suited to the idea of what the primitive men should be. In witness of my statement I may take numerous lists of questions prepared for inexperienced travellers, from which it may be seen what the traveller is expected to bring. It is not surprising that there was gradually created the conception of primitive man based chiefly on his folklore. It would be equivalent if the "primitive" man would form his idea of the psychomental complex of "civilized" man by studying fiction and the theatre, and accepting, for instance, "Le Chantecler" of Rostand as a biological conception of Europeans.

covering facts and hypotheses can be criticized, and increased with new facts or their interpretation. Sometimes amongst the Tungus the question may be raised as to how the story must be regarded as a "true" one or a "fairy-story". They would sometimes disagree. Such is the fate of many epic stories which are very often differently accepted by the listeners. * When we proceed in the second part of this work to the discussion of various hypotheses we shall better see the difference that exists in the Tungus psychomental complex between the facts accumulated, the hypotheses and folklore in the narrow sense.

Indeed not all Tungus may succeed in mastering the existing complex of knowledge. Some of them would not be able to learn everything and they would become specialists of a certain limited group of knowledge. Such is, for instance, the case of the hunters specialized in hunting of squirrels, or specialized in hunting sable. These people would not know very much about the hunting and characters of other animals, such as the bears, and tigers. On the other hand, the men do not always know details of woman's work, especially, the making of the chamois. However, there are some men, and also women who do not confine their interest to a limited field of knowledge and who may accumulate and may transmit to the other generations all of the existing knowledge. Yet, the Tungus have their own measure of intelligence and general equipment of individuals and they establish different attitudes depending upon the individual.

The loss of acquired knowledge may interest us in not a lesser degree that the acquisition of the knowledge and its transmission. The loss of knowledge amongst the Tungus is easier than among the groups which are numerous and which have written records. In fact, since the tradition is based chiefly on its oral form and since the stimuli for acquisition of certain groups of knowledge may disappear there is very little chance that some of the knowledge will be preserved. Indeed, the acquisition of knowledge of the behaviour of the sable and working out of the methods of catching this animal's skin unbroken has required the effort of many generations. At last, the Tungus knew how this animal might be taken with the minimum effort. When this animal became extinct the stimulus of transmitting the complex "sable-hunting" ceased to be effective. Three or four generations would suffice for a complete oblivion of the complex. True, it may be preserved for a longer time as historic record, but it will

* As a matter of fact I could see no difference in this respect between the Tungus and the so called civilised groups. Amongst the latter may imagination may sometimes be accepted as a scientifically established fact although later on it will be given up as an erroneous conception. The history of different sciences abound in such examples, so without leaving the ground of ethnography (and linguistics) we may quote, for instance, "the evolution of cultural phenomena"; minute description of the history of Indo-European languages and peoples with their hypothetic migrations, divisions, origin etc.; the uralaltaic hypothesis, and many others which a few decades later will be understood by the most backward professionals as the latter now understand the futility of calculations how many devils may be placed on the point of a needle. However, scholastics who worked on these important hypotheses were considered great thinkers and scientists of their time. In their time there existed special literary creations and folklore which were never regarded by them as "true", while their calculation of the devils were regarded as a scientific truth.

not be restored, if no sable re-appears. In such a condition I have observed the Khingan Tungus who do not remember how they used to hunt the sable, a fact historically known. The Birarčen begin to forget it, as well. However, the methods of sable-hunting are still well preserved amongst the Reindeer Tungus of Manchuria in whose region the sable is not yet entirely extinct. Such instances are common among the Tungus groups. Together with the change of primary milieu (e.g. extinction of animals, deforestation etc.) the corresponding complex may disappear. Yet, still in a greater degree it is true of the cultural complexes which may be partially lost and together with their loss (e.g. the hunting complex) the corresponding elements of the psychomental complex may be lost too. I have already quoted the case of loss of the hunting complex and, together with it, of the complex of knowledge of the animals, c.g. amongst the agriculturists-Tungus, amongst the Nomad Tungus and amongst the Manchus. In this way the whole psychomental complex may be substituted and former profound knowledge of certain branches forgotten altogether, so that the same (physically) ethnical unit if continued, under the pressure of new needs may again rebuild the knowledge of a certain branch of facts formerly known and afterwards forgotten. In this condition there were found some Manchu groups which after the downfall of their political rule in China returned home and restarted their relations with the Tungus from whom they relearned the hunting and the complex connected with it.

As to the Manchus in respect to education, they were in an entirely different position. In fact, their complex of agricultural knowledge was transmitted in the usual oral way, while the existence of the books permitted them to transfer a part of this function to the shoulders of professional teachers. Together with the teaching of Manchu there was also introduced Chinese language owing to which the Manchu complex began to give way to the Chinese complex. The process was especially activized because of the lack of the original Manchu books,—most of Manchu books are translations from Chinese. The oral tradition, which might be a genuine Manchu tradition, in the conditions of the Manchus as a ruling group of China could not be carried on for the younger generations were depending on their success in the assimilation of the Chinese complex. Thus, what originally was the Manchu method of teaching and transmission of the Manchu cultural complex in general we may only suppose with more or less great probability. The only exception should be the transmission of the tradition regarding the clans and shamanism. The Manchus after introduction of written records of the clans created a different condition for the preservation of the clan tradition and, as we have pointed out, a new need of re-adaptation of the term for the exogamic unit (vide supra Section 31). Owing to the existence only of the oral tradition among the Northern Tungus the latter did not meet with this peculiar need of new terms for "clan". On the other hand, the keeping of very voluminous clan records has become a great burden for the social function of clan, which is also a curious aspect of the maladjustment of the method of tradition in social organization. Something similar occurred to shamanism where the written records deprived shamanism of its plasticity in adjustment and formalized it. To this question I shall return later.

PART TWO

HYPOTHESES

CHAPTER X

NATURE OF THE TUNGUS HYPOTHESES

37. GENERAL CHARACTER-ISTIC OF HYPOTHESES In the present Part Two, I shall deal with various hypotheses met with among the Tungus. Indeed an exhaustive account of all existing hypotheses would be impossible. First of all it was not my intention to record all hypotheses, as well as all facts known to the Tungus; second, to give all the hypotheses recorded, as with facts, would be useless for most of them being based upon some fundamental propositions thus are their mere consequences; third, the variety of hypotheses is rather extensive but the variations are not very interesting from the point of view of giving a general idea of the psychomental complex. Therefore, in the present part I shall follow the same method of exposition as in Part One. However, there will be an essential difference; namely, I shall dwell at greater length on some hypotheses for we shall need them later.

The Tungus build up their hypotheses as do other peoples. If the Tungus cannot connect a group of facts into a system by a simply formulated law and if such a connexion is needed owing to the psychological condition, they will find an explanation based upon a supposition which in their eyes may look as a probable one. Degree of confidence in the hypothesis depends on a series of conditions, namely, (1) how far the new hypothesis is correlated with the existing complex; (2) how far the new hypothesis may cover the facts known; (3) how far does the hypothesis not come into the conflict with the new facts observed; (4) how reasonable is the source of the hypothesis i.e. whether or not it is created by the clever people or whether or not it is received from the ethnical groups known as reliable and superior groups; (5) how critical is the individual who accepts the hypothesis. It is thus evident that the hypotheses are accepted and rejected by the Tungus in dependence upon these conditions. So their simple probability becomes certainty and the hypothesis is considered as a fact, if it perfectly suits the existing psychomental complex, covers all the facts known and is confirmed by newly-acquired facts, if its source is reliable and if the individuals are not particularly sceptical. On the other hand, if the new hypothesis is in conflict with the existing complex, does not cover the facts known, comes into conflict with the newly acquired facts, originates from a doubtful source and the individuals are extremely sceptical, the hypothesis has no chance of being accepted. The degrees of acceptance of hypotheses are thus different. This might be illustrated by hundreds of instances, but I deem it useless in view of further dealing with the hypotheses. For illustration of the process of building up hypotheses I will now give some instances.

We did not discuss the problems concerning Tungus ideas as to the phenomena of psychic and mental activity with the exception of the remarks concerning language and transmission of cultural complexes. This has been done in view of avoiding the repetition of facts and discussion.

Let us now take the problem of the soul. We have seen that the existence of the soul is accepted as a fact, although its existence cannot be proved as a fact. Thus the existence of the soul may be regarded as a hypothesis. This hypothesis is now accepted by all Tungus groups because the fundamental element of the complex, i.e. an opposition of material substance and immaterial substance, is laid down at its basis. The soul is only a particular case of existing immateriality of the phenomena. Thus it suits the complex. The observation of facts shows that they may be easily understood in the light of this hypothesis and no facts are left which cannot be covered by it. This hypothesis does not come into the conflict with the experience,—the newly acquired facts. Yet, the source is the previous generations whose experience is considered as reliable; it is supported by authority of other ethnical groups.

In fact, the Tungus may observe the presence of soul and its exterioration on themselves and on the other persons as well as animals. The man during his sleep may "go" to a long distance for seeing his friends or some region. The visit would appear a reality for after the "travelling" the dreamer may be "tired", yet the physiological effects and behaviour after the dream may be quite real. These inferences are confirmed by the observation of animals, e.g. the dogs who during their sleep sometimes move their legs, as though running, they bark, move the tail, nose etc. The inference is that the dog's soul was absent and was running etc. These facts of importance are confirmed by people who relate of their travelling, visiting distant places and persons, also of various events taking place in the dreams. The evidences are confirmed by still more decisive facts. The Tungus in the dream may have a talk with other persons and those persons would know about it. It is true not all men can do it, but many of them, and particularly shamans can do it easily.

Since this group of facts is not very well investigated I shall relate what is known about them among the Tungus. In the state of great concentration the shamans and other people may come into communication with other shamans and ordinary people. Among all Tungus groups this is done quite consciously for practical needs, especially in urgent cases. What is the mechanism of this process may now be only hypothetically supposed. For practical use to achieve such a communication, the person must *think* about another person and formulate the desire, e.g. "please, come here" (to a given locality). This must be repeated until one "sees" the person called or until one "knows" that the person perceives the call. One can "see" the person called as a physical person in the natural surroundings. Afterwards when the person called is met he may be asked to confirm the surroundings and location at the moment of call. The person may also reply in the form of a bird or animal which would speak with the person's voice. The same animals cannot do it in their ordinary state.* So these animals are not understood as physical animals.** The Tungus who are connected by close relations, e.g. the children and parents, friendship, and mutual understanding (e.g. the fighting shamans may be hostile one to another but they would understand each other), may communicate easier than the people who do not know each other. Yet, some people cannot do it at all. About such a people the Tungus would say "they do not know how to do it", but they would not be able to explain how they do it themselves. The shamans use this method in their common practice when they want to meet some people or other shamans. Sometimes they do not realize the motive as to why they leave one place and go to another where they meet the person who called them,—they go because *they feel they must go*. The best period for such a call is calm weather and night. V.K. Arseniev related to me a case in Maritime Gov., when under his observation a shaman invited the other two shamans from distant places on an accidental occasion (sudden illness of a young man) and they arrived within such a period that they could not have physically done it if invited by a messenger. The Tungus speak about such cases as a common thing, and do it when they have no time for sending a messenger.***

* Let us remark that, according to the Tungus conception, the animals do not speak by themselves; as to the "speaking" vide supra Chapter VI.

** Cf. SONT p. 274, where prediction of the sex of children is discussed.

*** Transmission of thought at a distance was observed by several authors and interpreted in different manners. However, the experiments have confirmed the possibility of such a transmission of thought. V.M. Bexterev was particularly interested in this problem so he and his assistants have carried out their experiments on the dogs and men, in conditions which exclude possibility of mistake. The experiments have shown that at least in some conditions, the transmission is a fact (cf. "Collective Reflexology" where the other publications are given, p. 122). In 1921 I carried out several experiments with a dog which although isolated in another room could easily find objects (e.g. watch, notebook, crystal top of an inkstand, purse etc.) transferred from one place to another by one of the persons present (There were five persons present.) or even from the pocket of one person to that of another. These facts may now be understood in the light of modern theories and on condition of general positive approach to this problem,—not possible even a few years ago. Indeed, the question will be solved very soon. Let us remark here that the scepticism due to the ignorance and prejudice did not permit collection and publication of facts. In fact, some time ago any one who dared to discuss these questions or to publish the facts met with criticism from the "scientists" who said that these were "superstitions", "folklore", "immaterial approach", "lack of criticism" etc., while they themselves were merely impressed by the existing theories and hypotheses accepted as "truth". As a matter of fact such a behaviour of scientists is as much ethnocentric as that of the Tungus and it is as much "folklore" as that designated as such

This series of observations is interpreted in the sense that there is an element which exteriorates as an immaterial substance,—the soul,—which communicates with the souls of other persons. In the same group of evidences of the existence of the soul, the Tungus include the cases of "vision on distance" the mechanism of which is perhaps the same as that of "telepathy". * According to the Birarčen, the soul of a dying man enters into the body of one of the young near-relatives. The young person may feel this. In addition to the above enumerated evidences confirming the existence of the soul, there must also be included a large number of coincidences. In fact distant communication may sometimes be only the mutual desire of meeting on the part of two people connected by common interest, especially when the periods of relative freedom are short which greatly increases the chance that two persons will think about the matter and dream about it at the same time. Such coincidence would be, of course, interpreted as an evidence of the activity of the soul.

This point of view is still more supported by the fact of the soul's travelling, according to the will of the bearers of the soul. In fact, before falling asleep the Tungus express their desire of seeing distant places and people. If the dream occurs the fact is interpreted as a voluntary direction of the soul. The practice of conscious loss of consciousness practised by the shamans and candidates to become shamans gives hundreds of facts which confirm the hypothesis of the existence of soul. In the same line are found all cases of hypnotic actions.

The new facts are presented by further observations of psychic functions cognized and interpreted as new evidences of the existence of the soul. The second source of evidence is that of the other ethnical groups which also have the same conception of soul. So these authoritative opinions would be quoted for supporting the existing complex idea of the soul. The Tungus would increase their knowledge of the soul with the new aspects discovered by other groups which, as modus operandi, would not very much differ from the modern investigators who would look for support of their ideas into the sources, with which they are not in conflict, without giving themselves any trouble of finding how far the premises of these sources are reliable.

In this way the idea of soul is always confirmed and it becomes in the Tungus psychomental complex one of fundamentally established truths. In this function it will be made the basis of further Tungus investigations into the particular questions, where the soul may explain the complexity of phenomena. .

by the scientists. "Science" is not so much accumulated facts, as method of approach to the facts.

* Some illustrations given by the Tungus are that in general when some misfortune to the people occurs, one may know it at a distance by a peculiar feeling perceived by the heart. On the third day after the grandfather of my communicator arrived, a nephew (or brother) had committed suicide by hanging himself. The grandfather had not been able to stay away for he had felt an uneasiness which compelled him to return. He was not surprised at the suicide. When people die the young members of the clan may know it and relate what has happened and the circumstances of the death. The Birarčen say that this is also true among the Manchus and the Dahurs. Such a statement may be taken as a starting point for an investigation. An instance for illustration is that of a small boy who "saw" his grandfather's uncle kill his father and predicted that the murderer would return after three days with the antlers of a Cervus Elaphus, killed by his father. The man came as had been

Let us take another instance of hypothesis which cannot be accepted. This time I shall take the hypothesis of the spirits responsible for various diseases known amongst the Tungus of Manchuria under the name of *ajin'i burkan*. This *burkan* has seventy-two manifestations many of which may be identified with the infectious diseases. This complex was seemingly received, through the medium of the Manchus, from the Chinese. As a source in the eyes of the Tungus it is quite reliable, but it is not "genuine" Tungus for its origin is partly remembered. The entire seventy-two kinds of diseases are not met with amongst the Tungus, but only a few of them. This objection is rejected under the pretext that probably these diseases are known amongst other groups (Chinese) and not amongst the Tungus, which naturally is a case of adaptation. So that the hypothesis will be only partially accepted. There will be no objection for accepting it on the ground of its complexity for the Tungus previously possessed the idea of complex spirits. However, there are difficulties: in the theory of the spirits there is a postulate, namely, that the spirits cannot be managed by medicines if they are real spirits, while the Chinese themselves use various kinds of medicines, which fact brings the Tungus into conflict with the general conception of spirits. Furthermore, the success in medical treatment of some of these seventy-two diseases brings another doubt into the Tungus mind. For this reason the hypothesis is not accepted by all Tungus but only by a part of them particularly by those who are not critical and inclined to recognize the authority of "superior" ethnical groups.

Between these two extreme instances one may put all other hypotheses in the respect of their admissibility by the Tungus. We have seen that the theory of spirits was a logical consequence of the originally accepted hypothesis as to the existence of soul and "animus". To find when the first spirit made its first appearance amongst the Tungus is, of course, impossible. Yet, such a question would bring us to the slippery ground of groundless hypotheses. Of course, we may establish the origin of many spirits, but some of them will remain quite mysterious, and on this ground it will be impossible to consider them as original Tungus spirits. What is really important is that such an idea of spirit did appear after which it might receive its further complication and further increase as formed by the method of analogy. Indeed, the moment of the appearance of the first idea of spirit must be brought to the time when no Tungus as an ethnical unit existed, for theoretically it is but a short step from the idea of managing the souls of dead people to the idea of their free post-mortal existence, which makes absolutely hopeless the search for establishing the origin and sequence of hypotheses regarding the spirit complex.[*] Yet, the problem of origin, in the present state of ethnography, is not even important for without this knowledge one may still form an idea of a functioning complex and its components.[**]

The existence of the new spirits may be suspected in phenomena up to a certain moment unknown amongst the Tungus. For instance, the settlement of the Chinese in the Mergen region brought among the Tungus of this part of Manchuria some venereal diseases. The new disease was attributed to the special spirit supposed to be brought by the soldiers. Indeed, this hypothesis will exist up to the moment when the modern treatment of these diseases will disprove the conception of this new spirit. Psychic troubles were known for a long time, but the shamanistic method of their treatment brought a new hypothesis, namely, the hypothesis of a particular kind of spirit which is responsible for the trouble.

If a new hypothesis satisfies the Tungus, they accept it. However, there must be all of the necessary elements for its being accepted. First of all the original fallacy of postulating the existence of spirits must be there. Second, the new phenomenon, or the phenomeon just cognized, must not be explained by any other hypothesis, nor "natural" causes. If there are no such two conditions the hypothesis cannot be accepted. Thus at the basis of all hypotheses of spirits there is always present the original fallacy. However, the hypotheses may be rejected after subsequent observation of new facts which can be explained without the original postulate, but the latter will persist till the whole complex is little by little substituted or the original postulate compromised. In one of the stages of the process, as I have recorded amongst the Birarčen, the reasoning is as follows: "if there is soul, there is spirit; if there is no soul, there is no spirit; but *burkan* (a special spirit, *vide infra*) must not be admitted if the soul is admitted". This fact shows that among the Tungus even the fundamental postulate of the soul may be subject to essential scrutiny by some individuals. As a matter of fact, those of the Tungus who may change their ethnical milieu and may receive the school education among the Russians become free of this postulate, if they do not happen to be influenced by the Russians who themselves are not free and retain the postulate either in a religious form or in its philosophical justification, a dualistic conception of phenomena. In so far as knowledge of newly acquired facts permits, a Tungus in his conclusions will scrutinize the most fundamental conceptions. Owing to this trait of the Tungus psychomental complex,—the criticism and inclination for the observation and analysis conditioned as we have seen chiefly by the professional needs[*],—the hypotheses received from other ethnical groups are subject to the adaptation, if they can be used, or to rejection. Here the source of the hypotheses for the Tungus is of importance. If it comes, for instance, from the educated Manchus who are familiar with the Chinese books, the hypothesis has more chance to be accepted, at least for temporary use, while the hypotheses received from both uneducated Chinese and uneducated Russians are not at once accepted. In such a case they would say: "the Russians (or Chinese) believe so, but we do not know whether it is true or not". More than

---

predicted. He was immediately taken before the boy who repeated his sayings. The man then confessed, the body was found and sentence of death for the criminal passed at the clan meeting

[*] vide supra p. 55.

[**] I now leave aside the historical aspect of ethnographical phenomena. Should we approach it we must follow modern methods used in historical research.

[*] I do not want to involve the problem of innate character of the Tungus psychomental complex, for it would mean to bring the problem to the slippery and misleading ground of hypotheses. Although it is possible that such a correlation does exist, but since this line of investigation is not yet scientifically explored, it is safer to keep the problem in its functional aspect. Yet, the case of the Manchus who perhaps originally did not differ very much from the Northern Tungus is also instructive; the lack of criticism and sticking to the hypothesis is rather typical of the Manchus.

this, the Chinese zoological and anatomical treatises (in book form!) are not blindly accepted as "truth", for the Tungus sometimes meet with errors which they explain as due to the fact that the Chinese are not hunters, and thus cannot know the animals and anatomy. *

The hypotheses used by the Tungus may be classed into two groups, namely, the hypotheses based upon the postulate of the spirit; and hypotheses free of this postulate. The first group of hypotheses can be easily classified and described in the analysis of particular spirits, while the second group cannot be treated in the same systematic manner for the basis of these hypotheses is not uniform. In order to be clear I shall give an instance of Tungus theory based upon a hypothesis which was accepted as a postulate. This is the case, already quoted, of loss of hair by man owing to the use of salt. It runs as follows:

1. *The man had incidentally discovered the white stone, which was salt, and began to use it for seasoning the raw meat* (a proposition which may be theoretically accepted as one of probabilities!) ; (2) *owing to the salt consumed, the hair began to fall out* (a proposition which cannot be accepted without proofs and which is a mere hypothesis accepted as a truth; the Tungus themselves use salt for the reindeer and horses, and they know that the wild animals largely use salt if they can have it; the fallacy of reasoning is not noticed) ; (3) *since the hair began to fall out man needed protection with animal skins* (a proposition based on the present human behaviour which cannot be extrapolated into the past) ; (4) *and fire* (ibid.) This theory of human evolution and change of culture is told to the children. However, the adult Tungus may sometimes notice the fallacy of the proposition (2) by pointing out the cervines which are fond of salt but still covered with hair. In such a case they would say: "it is a story for children", and it is not accepted by all the Tungus as an established fact.

As another instance of hypothesis I may quote that of *kulikan* as the male element in the heredity and embryological process which disregards the female element. Such hypotheses have already been mentioned in previous chapters in the course of exposition of the facts regarding the positive knowledge of the Tungus. I shall now leave them unclassified and I shall return to some of them which may be particularly interesting in the last chapter of the present part.

38. COMPLEXES OF SPIRITS AND THEIR CLASSIFICATION

The hypotheses based upon the spirits postulate will be now discussed first from the point of view of their classification. The spirits as they appear in the Tungus complexes cannot be treated in abstraction. They must be treated in the complexes where they are found. In fact, if we have a spirit like the Chinese *n'jaɲn'jaɲ* its Chinese form must not be taken as that found amongst the Tungus. Amongst the Chinese· this complex spirit,—a series of spirits,—is due to the reflexion of the Chinese complex of child birth and child education. Many elements of the Chinese education are entirely lacking in the Tungus system. Therefore, the Chinese *n'jaɲn'jaɲ* in the Tungus

*. I do not know what was the Tungus reaction toward Russian books for in my time the Tungus were not yet much familiar with them.

complex appears in its shortened form. Another instance,— the spirit of the lower world *irlinkan* in the Tungus complex is figured as a partial representation of the *erlik xan* known amongst the Uigurs who themselves modified it from the original Ahriman (Buddhic—Yama) of Iranians where it had an entirely different function.

With all these spirits the Tungus would operate in such a manner that the elements of the spirit which are formally discovered in the spirit imported are preserved in so far as they may suit the existing complex. The elements which do not suit will be omitted and those which are neutral may be either preserved or rejected. In this process the formal elements would be naturally given a new function corresponding to the existing complex. The spirit may be thus accepted only when· it is needed in the complex, i.e. when it explains something essential, and if it may suit in its original, or modified form the existing complex.

From the study into the history of the process of the formation of Tungus ethnical units we have seen that their cultural complexes are different owing to the conditions of local adaptation and interethnical pressure. There is one more condition to be accounted; namely, the Tungus groups do not react in an absolutely identic manner on the alien groups and they do not equally well know the languages of the foreign groups, so we do not meet two Tungus complexes absolutely similar.

Since it is so the flood of alien elements produces different reactions and different elements are differently accepted in their original or modified forms. It is especially true of the spirits which do not depend upon the conditions which impose similar cultural elements, as for instance in clothing, hunting, etc. The spirits have no such limitations as that presented by the primary milieu. It is therefore natural that under the given conditions, amongst the Tungus groups we have very distinct complexes of spirits. Although many elements may be found to be common in several complexes, as a whole the complexes are different, and thus there is always a slight variation of the spirits found in different complexes. However, the spirits are grouped in the complexes with a certain regularity due to the character of the existing complexes which accept easier the elements suitable for them. So we have, for instance, two neighbouring groups,—Manchus and Tungus of Manchuria who are rather closely connected. Amongst the Manchus we have the complex of spirits *fučixi* (received from the Buddhist complex, perhaps through the Chinese), while among the Tungus this complex is unknown in its Manchu form. The complex of spirits among these Tungus is quite different from that found amongst their neighbours —the Nomad Tungus whose complex is borrowed chiefly from the Buriats. Yet, among the Reindeer Tungus of Manchuria the old complex of shamanism is now lacking, while it is well formed among their neighbours,—the Kumarčen and Khingan Tungus with whom they frequently meet. From these remarks it may be seen that the variety of spirit complexes is very extensive,—even the nearest neighbours may have entirely different complexes.

It is impossible to give a complete and synchronous list of spirits. The facts which we have were recorded prior to 1917, which is the date of my last field work among the Tungus. Yet, for some groups we have still earlier records. However, the Tungus, as shown, are inclined to change their ethnographical complex, especially the complex of the spirits. If they learn something new along this line they will not hesitate to include the new facts and hypotheses in their complex. In this case they greatly depend upon the neighbours who supply them with the new facts and hypotheses. The last decades, especially after the increase of the interethnical pressure connected with the Russian and Chinese migratory spreading, were especially favourable in this respect. In fact, the Tungus of Siberia have met with the strong influence of the Orthodox Christian Church in Siberia and even partly in Manchuria, while in Manchuria the pressure of the government, after the revolution of 1911 in China, compelled some groups to give up shamanism, if not in their conviction then in practice, which greatly affected preservation of the complex. Some Tungus groups, especially those of Transbaikalia living on agriculture and cattlebreeding, gave up altogether the system of spirits which had previously existed, and adopted the Russian complex. The Tungus of the Maritime Gov. known under the name of Udehe, adopted the Chinese complex from the trappers and merchants. This process went still further after my investigations were carried out. In fact the new authorities in Siberia declared a merciless war on all kinds of "religious beliefs". Although the war is supposed to be carried on with help of almost academic methods of "enlightenment" and "anti-religious propaganda", the practical ways of doing it are different,— the Tungus are not free to continue their customs and methods connected with the beliefs in the spirits. This is done with the help of organized groups selected amongst the young people and older people who want to adapt themselves to the new policy of their masters ruling ethnical units. These new Tungus authorities disregard the academical ways and act so as to obtain maximum results by pressing their fellow men with their authority which they have as members of the ruling strata (communistic party). The result is evident,—the Tungus lose the remains which have been left after the first Russian cultural attack carried on by the missionaries. However, there is now a new condition. Under the national government the natives of Siberia were put in such a position that in so far as possible the groups were not allowed to oppress one another. With the disintegration of the old organization some ethnical groups have received "autonomy". Such groups in the territories occupied by the Tungus are the Yakuts and the Buriats. The immediate effect was that the Tungus, who had no autonomy and were everywhere in the minority, also in a certain economic dependence upon these groups, found themselves under strong and unregulated pressure. The effect of this pressure is evident,—the Tungus are losing their former complex which includes the spirits. In this respect the position of the Tungus in Manchuria is not different for they find themselves under the pressure of other groups and are not protected by the central government.

Considering the present conditions of the Tungus groups it may be expected with great probability that the spirits which were on my list in 1912-1917 now are not the same,—some of them may have been dropped, while some others may now be included.

CLASSIFICATION OF SPIRITS The spirits which are
l found amongst the
Tungus groups are numerous. In so far as I can see there

are five ways to present them to the reader; namely, according to (1) alphabetical order, (2) origin of spirits, (3) importance of the spirits in the complex and in the Tungus mind, (4) ethnical groups, and (5) character of the spirits.

The alphabetical order is very convenient for the reader, but since at the end of the book I give the index of spirits this order can be dropped. The classification of spirits according to their origin might be quite convenient. The Tungus themselves sometimes notice the alien origin of their spirits, e.g. the Birarčen and Kumarčen call the foreign spirits *dōna;* a great number of foreign spirits preserve their non-Tungus names; some spirits bear such evident traces of their alien origin that there can be no hesitation in classifying them as foreign spirits; and there are spirits which now have no traces of their alien origin, actually may be so. Such a classification would be misleading in all the cases which are not definitely established.

The classification of spirits according to their importance in the complex and in the Tungus mind might be also good if it were possible to establish some objective scale of importance, e.g. the frequency of occurrence in practice. This, however, cannot be done for among different groups the frequency will be different, and some spirits frequently used may have very small importance in the complex, e.g. the spirits like *areŋk'i* are very common and very often mentioned, but they occupy no important place in the complex,—in the Tungus mind they are rather insignificant. True, in some cases it is possible to speak either of the importance or of the lack of importance, of their "weight" in the complex, and in the Tungus estimation.

The classification and description of spirits may be referred to the ethnical groups. However, if we review the groups in this respect some groups may appear to be very poor in spirits while others may appear very rich. This may be due to two conditions; namely, some groups really have a very limited number of spirits owing to their loss and substitution of the Russian complex for the Tungus complex, as is e.g. with the Reindeer Tungus of Manchuria, while other groups will appear here poor because regarding the spirits my data are not complete, as is e.g. the case of the Kumarčen whose complex is nearly the same as that of the Birarčen and amongst whom I did not carry out an exhaustive investigation into the complex of spirits. Moreover amongst the Tungus in this respect there may be distinguished four groups which are more or less similar, viz. the Reindeer Tungus of Transbaikalia, the Nomad Tungus of Transbaikalia, the Tungus of Manchuria and the Manchus. However, such a grouping may lead to a certain misinterpretation of facts which unintentionally will be referred *in toto* to the above indicated four groups.

The classification of the spirits according to their character seems to be the best, if one adopts no artificial differentiation of the characters. In fact, the Tungus spirits cannot be classified according to the scheme of evil and good, malevolent and benevolent spirits, as it is often done by authors adapting the spirits of other ethnical groups to that of their own or to that with which they are the most familiar. The Tungus actually do not distinguish such two extremities,—any spirit may be malevolent, benevolent or neutral which depends chiefly on the human attitude and human art of managing the spirits. Perhaps some of spirits are particularly malevolent or benevolent or neutral, but in the Tungus mind there is no such a grouping as "evil" and "good" and the most benevolent spirits may become malevolent, and the most malevolent spirits may become neutral and even benevolent. The Tungus distinguish the spirits according to their power, but this classification may bring us to the conflicting evidences from different groups, which are not unanimous as to their opinions regarding the power of spirits,—some spirits may be less powerful in a group, as e.g. with the little known spirits *fuéxi* among the Tungus of Manchuria, while the same spirits become the most powerful spirits among the Manchus.

I will now give a description of the spirits according to their characters as seen amongst different groups, pointing to origin, the relative position in the complex, and ethnical connexions. As scheme first I shall take the primary milieu and spirits connected with it; afterwards I shall proceed to the spirits connected with the human soul; third, I shall treat the spirits which are imported; and last, I shall give details as to the spirits which are mastered by the shamans. When the category of spirits is described, I shall proceed to the other hypotheses which are not directly connected with the hypothesis of spirits.

CHAPTER XI

SUPREME BEING AND MASTER SPIRITS

39. BUGA The term *buya* (*buga, boya, boga*) is known in Nerč. Barg. RTM Khin. Bir. in the sense of greatest, omnipotent, ever-existing, all-knowing being, which is responsible for the existence and regulation of life, who directs the whole world. The same starter is used in the sense of "heaven-sky" not only in the dialects indicated, but also in Nerč.. (Tit.), Ur. (Castr.) and in its modification, *boa* (Oroči) (Goldi, Olča Grube). Its meaning is also extended to "world" in the dialects indicated and in the form *boa* (Oroči) (Goldi, Grube) *buge, boga* (Neg. Sch.). Also in the same dialects it may be used in the sense of "locality" and "earth" which is also met with in Ang. Irk. (Tit.) as well as in the forms *boa* (Goldi, Grube), *boya* (Kum. Iw.) *bogo, buha* (Udsk.), *bug* (Lam.), *boaw* (Enis. Czek.—"Gegend") ; it may be supposed that Manchu *boixon*—the earth, ground-soil, country etc. as well as *pàhhuô* (Nuichen, Grube) ought to be also compared.*

I do not suggest which was the original meaning of *buya* in the Northern Tungus dialects. It might be one of the above indicated meanings,—"heaven", "world", "locality" etc. and it might be "highest being" as well, later on extended over "heaven-sky", "world" ,"earth" and "locality". One thing is evident that in the great majority of cases, in all Tungus dialects including Manchu, we have this stem in one of the meanings of the complex known among the Tungus of Transbaikalia and Manchuria, well established by my investigations.

Thus *buya* amongst these groups may be understood as "highest being", "world", "earth", "heaven-sky" and "locality" (i.e. the world that the speaker knows). In so far as *buya*, a highest being, is concerned, it *is not anthropomorphic* and it *is not one of the spirits* which will be later discussed. The *buya* cannot be introduced by human will into any placing, or human body. The Tungus have no picture, or idea of its appearance. According e.g. to the

Birarčen the *buya* regulates the life of man and animals. The relations between the animals and man are "established" by him. In this form it is rather a "law of nature". For this reason some Tungus say that there is no need for legal regulation of hunting,—the animals will suffice for ever. *Buya* may not be disturbed with the request to send animals; this request ought to be addressed to *bainača* (etc.) (*vide infra* Section 41). The name *buya* is often used in common speech, as it is in the European languages especially before an organized anti-religious movement gained numerous groups in various populations, i.e. when this name was not yet tabooed as a sign of "backwardness." However, in Tungus it is not used in a direct sense when the reference to it is made. Generally speaking *buya* is not of the same every-day-importance as the spirits discussed further which are subject to him on the same footing as human beings and animals, as well as "inanimate" nature.

In enumeration of the dialects (groups) in which this conception and starter are found we do not see some Tungus dialects. This is not due to the lack of this conception "highest being"—"world"—"heaven"—"locality" etc. which may be suspected among the groups which use *buya* in a broad sense of "world" etc. but it may be due to the intrusion of alien terms, and sometimes alien conceptions. In fact, such is the case of the Tungus of Manchuria who begin to introduce a new term, namely *julask'i endur'i* (Bir. Kum.) which may also be used as *julask'i buya*, and simply *julask'i* (and *julask'i*). The latter means "South", and *endur'i* is recently borrowed from the Manchus (*vide infra*). However, since among the Manchus there are many *endur'i*, *julask'i* specification must be made pointing to the location —"clear sunny region of the heavens". Owing to this the term for *buya* is now nearly replaced by *julask'i*. Together with the introduction of the new term—*endur'i*—there have also been introduced some new conceptions borrowed from the Manchus.

It is very interesting that among the Tungus who had fallen under the strong influence of the Orthodox missionaries, this term was perhaps also dropped. * The term for

---

* P.P. Schmidt compared this stem with Mongol bogdo ("holy") and old Persian baga ("god") (cf. Neg. p. 240). This may be still extended for we meet with bugaš—"god" of the Kassites (cf. N.D. Mironov "Aryan Vestiges, etc. pp. 145-6) and naturally Russian and Siavonic bogu ("god"). The Manchu, Japanese, Korean and Northern Tungus ba ～ ba ～ pa—the "place", "locality etc. may be perhaps regarded as a modification of boya—„bova„„boa=bā. As a matter of fact in the above indicated dialects buya has this meaning as well.

* I am not sure of it, for the dictionaries of these dialects were made by the missionaries and travellers who did not go very far in their investigations. In fact, as a rule a Tungus always gives those words and meanings which may be better understood by the ques-

"god" was borrowed by the missionaries from the Tungus term for the spirits or even better to say, for the spirits' placings (vide infra) savak'i. We have, thus, in Enis. dialects xovak'i, xovok'i, šovok'i in Lam. xaŭki (Schiefner), xcuk'i etc, which were perhaps introduced amongst the Tungus by the missionaries. It must thus be expected that the old term will not be found in those records, and yet it may be expected also that the old conception of buγa will be covered by a new one "god" with an old Tungus starter xavak'i. For this reason the term savak'i is not met with amongst the Tungus who were not strongly influenced by the Orthodox missionaries, e.g. in Transbaikalia, in Manchuria and in Amur Region. We meet there with other terms used for Christian God, namely, in Barg. Nerč. also Ur. (Castr.), Nerč. (Tit.) it is burkan, which is borrowed from the Mongol (Buriat) burxan, in Tungus referred to the spirits of alien origin (vide infra). Among the Barguzin Tungus dayačan is also met with in the same sense. In the Amur region we meet with endur'i which was used by the missionaries as the term for Christian "God". All of these terms were used by the Tungus not in the sense of buγa, but in the sense of a new alien conception. However, the introduction of a new conception and new terms, even those borrowed from the Tungus, may be easily followed by the investigator who will also see the loss of the old conception and terms. One of the interesting cases of partial loss and substitution is a new conception of julaik'i of the Kumarčen which approaches very near to the conception of buga, but this may be better understood when we describe the conception of apkaĭ endur'i among the Manchus.

The inference which can be made from these facts is that the conception of "highest being" and the term for it buγa (with modifications), are very old and they are accepted by the Tungus groups who are not at present under a very strong alien influence. Indeed, the Tungus know nothing as to the "origin" of this conception, so in their mind it has existed for ever in their complex. In this form it has already been described by me* and was used by W. Schmidt** for further analysis and comparison.

APKAI ENDURI of Manchu Sp. in Manchu Writ. is transcribed as abkai enduri. It means the "enduri of heavens". It is the principal spirit of the world. All other enduri, spirits of all classes, men and animals are found under his control. According to some Manchus apkaĭ endur'i is a complex spirit, and there is no such individual spirit. However, this point of view is probably a new and modern adaptation, for even during the ceremony of sacrifice, the endur'i are distinguished and apkaĭ endur'i is considered as an individual spirit. In other Tungus languages we meet with only the loan of the term endur'i. It is thus confined to the Southern Tungus groups. This word seems to be borrowed from Indra, for as will be shown, it is not isolated as an element of the original complex in which Indra is found. In some Tungus dialects it is found in the

tioner. Therefore it is very likely that being asked the name for "god" or "highest spirit", he could not oppose any other explanation used by foreigners, e.g. savaki, enduri, etc.

* Cf. Opyt, 1919, p. 14.
** Cf. "Der Ursprung der Gottesidee," Vol. III, 1931.

form andura, ĕndira (Khin.) andur'i (Bir.). As to the origin of the idea "spirit of heaven" it may be connected with the Chinese t'ien 天 and šeŋ 神. According to the Manchus apkaĭ endur'i has seven daughters. Yet he is not indifferent to the female sex: apkaĭ endur'i, is thus a male. This is, of course, the Chinese complex of Yin-Yang. The Manchus, however, believe that the idea of enduri is essentially their own and that the Mongols have no such a conception. More than this apkaĭ endur'i may be responsible for sickness of the people whom he wants to punish or on whom he merely avenges himself. The country, where this spirit is living, is located in heavens. It is ever green, with good water, good fruits, especially good maŋŋa mo,—"oak trees". There are no human beings there. Thus apkaĭ endur'i, as compared with the Tungus conception of buga, is quite different. Although he is very powerful, he is a spirit supplied with all human characters. Therefore he is treated as a human being. The Manchus address their requests to this spirit in many a case, e.g. when the clan would be divided into new exogamic units; at the wedding ceremony when the newly concluded marriage is annouced to him; for taking oath of friendship the friends together pray apkaĭ endur'i and become "like brothers". This last custom is not of Manchu but of Chinese origin. Yet, the spirit is regularly addressed every year, and also in the case of conflicts with the other spirits, for luck in business and life in general, and so on. The spirit accepts the sacrifice, which will be described in a special chapter, and it has its own placing. Such a one is erected in the middle of the inner yard, in front of the principal house between the house and gate, in the form of a wooden screen with a high wooden post. It is called iŋb'e; in Chinese houses it has a different function.

Such is the conception of the Manchus who do not very much depend upon the books in which the same spirit may be again adapted to the Chinese t'ien-šeŋ and to the Chinese complex in general. We have some written documents on this spirit known to the Manchus of the XVIIth and XVIIIth centuries, namely, in Kang Hsi's dictionary of Manchu language (manju gisun i buleku bitxe) and special treaties on the Manchu rites (kesi toktobuxa manjusai večere metere kooli bitxe) with a preface written by Chi'en Lung. In both documents we find indications as to the practice of the cult of heaven (abka) also known to the early Manchus. Chi'en Lung opposed abka to fučixi (Buddha) and enduri. However, in the new rite the first place is occupied by Buddha (in Kun-niŋ-guŋ, a Buddhistic temple) and the second place is occupied by šaŋsi enduri. The latter with a great reason is identified by L. Langlès * as Chinese (Shang di). The latter seemingly is šaŋ ŭi 上帝, which in Chinese is also referred to the Christian God, and in this sense used only in recent time. Such a shifting of importance of the formerly used apkaĭ to the second place, after Buddha and its replacing by the newly discovered

* Ch. de Harlez (op. cit, p.p. 14-15) did not want to accept this connexion but he could not oppose any other explanation to both L. Langlès and C. von der Gabelentz. As a matter of fact, šaŋsi is not a Manchu name and the Manchus had another name for their own spirit,—apkai enduri. The reason why t'i (Chinese)—se'i (Manchu) is probably that in Manchu t+i in which t is palatalized t' is used almost exclusively in the Chinese words; s'i in Manchus linguistical complex is nearer to the Chinese t'i than to the Manchu ti, cf. tiŋeri ‖ siŋeri in Manchu.

Christian šaŋsi was due on the one hand, to the Chinese influence and on the other hand, to the idea of introduction of the Buddhistic complex and some knowledge of Christianity among the Manchus. In fact, at the beginning of the Manchu activity in China the Manchus very often used "heaven" (abka) in the sense approaching that of the apkaĩ endur'i which was usually translated into Chinese as t'ien. After the Manchu settlement in China this conception gradually disappeared from the complex and the Chinese shang-ti replaces it as one of the group enduri (šaŋsi enduri of the ritual), while the first place is occupied by Buddha which might become the "national" or better official, state religion of the Dai Tsing. Thus the old Manchu complex in Peking, at least of the XVIIIth century, greatly changed. However, the new spirit šaŋsi enduri did not reach the Manchus living in the Aigun district and they preserved the old notion and term opka.

As we have seen apkaĩ endur'i is not like the Northern Tungus buŋa,—but is a spirit, anthropomorphic and one of the class endur'i. This fact is perhaps indicative that the old conception apkaĩ—buŋa was replaced or even lost, prior to the Manchu coming into political power, for there may be, as a matter of fact, no cult of buŋa with the sacrifices, regular prayers, and all ritualism necessary for influencing spiritual but anthropomorphic "beings" enduri. It may also be noted that even in Peking the Manchu complex šaŋsi enduri occupied a special position, for the shamans (a special kind of shamans vide infra) were not in charge of serving it, while it was so with Buddha, and amongst the Manchus of Aigun the apkaĩ endur'i may be served by the shamans. Even in this respect an overlapping of the complexes is evident.

When apkaĩ endur'i was introduced among the Tungus populations of Manchuria it received further modifications. First of all, the term apkaĩ endur'i has been modified into julask'i endur'i (Kum. Bir.) or merely julask'i which is a designation of the spirit according to its location in the southern section of the heavens. Further he may be called ejin,—the master, ruler, chief etc. Second, this spirit is now addressed in cases such as the division of clans, success in hunting, declaration as to a new shaman, infectious and other diseases, and on many other occasions which formerly were not of sufficient importance for the disturbance of buŋa, still preserved in the complex of these Tungus. Third, this spirit is served with a sacrifice and importuned with regular prayers. Fourth, this spirit, introduced to some Tungus, introduced the knowledge of making and keeping the fire. It is considered as a guardian of the house, which shows a strict relation between man and spirit. Fifth, this spirit has a permanent placing,—a post with a bunch of straw and the vertebra of either a roe-deer, or of a reindeer (Cervus Elaphus), or of a wild boar; after the sacrifice, two anthropomorphic placings, which are used probably for placings of the "servants" of the spirit, are thrown far away from the place of sacrifice for freeing the spirits-servants. One may now see that this spirit is still nearer to the spirits described below than to the Manchu apkaĩ endur'i. Amongst the Khingan Tungus èndira (or andura) burkan is in the same position, and it may be supposed is of the same origin but curiously, in addition, it has to be explained by burkan (vide infra) and he has horses of different colours,—white, black, red and chestnut. The horses are connected with the rain, lightning etc. which is indica-

tive of the complex character of this spirit. In this form it is still further from apkaĩ-buŋa and even Manchu apkaĩ endur'i.

In the previous lines I have mentioned that endur'i was used by the Orthodox missionaries for translation of the Christian term "God" into Goldi. Among this group the conception of apkaĩ endur'i, buŋa, julask'i etc. has not been recorded. However, I. A. Lopatin gives a note from which it is evident that the Goldi have this conception,[*] in a form perhaps very near that of the Manchus. However, no details are given so that it is difficult to say to which group the Goldi enduri belongs. It should be pointed out that the "sky-heaven" amongst the Goldi is known under the Northern Tungus terms boa (bova, boani—in Samagir, and Samar respectively, cf. P. P. Schmidt, S. S.).

From the above shown facts it is thus evident that among the Northern Tungus the conception of endur'i, as a new and previously unknown spirit, has overlapped buŋa of the old complex, which resulted in a partial loss of the old complex. We may suppose that among the Manchus this process is still more advanced, if it is agreed that Ch'ien Lung's statement is correct. Among the Northern Tungus who happened to be under the Russian influence, the old complex was superseded by the new one (for the Tungus), namely, the Christian God which was given the absolutely misleading names such as "savak'i", "endur'i" etc.

Some facts may be here quoted for showing that the idea of buŋa, as it is shown at the beginning of the present section, is also known amongst the neighbours of the Tungus here discussed. According to L. von Schrenck (op. cit. Vol. 3, pp. 107-108) among the Gilaks, the term yzigy (Grube) is referred to a being absolutely "good", whom they do not represent, to which they do not pray, or offer sacrifices. Amongst the Mongols there is also a being similar to buŋa which they call teŋri, as supreme being, heaven. Amongst the Buriats there are several teŋri having no images and living in the heavens. They correspond to the special enduri (cf. C. Ž. Žamcarano, op. cit. p. 391). I.A. Podgorbunskii gives for "good" (of the Russians) burxan, which is analogous to what we have seen among the Tungus. Near to the Mongol teŋri is perhaps the Yakut conception of taŋara, which is the "sky, category of benevolent spirits", and "god" (E. K. Pekarskii, Dictionary, pp. 2551-2552). However, V. Sieroszewski (cf. Yakuts, pp. 651-652) gives a different definition of Ajy tojön which, according to him, is a manifestation of the supreme power which is not benevolent, nor malevolent, which is not a being, but the "Being" in general. He is located in the seventh heaven (sky) and he does not interfere with human affairs; it is useless to address to him any prayers and sacrifices. As a matter of fact, this description gives us an almost simi-

---

[*] This investigator says (op. cit. p. 211): "The form of enduri is so diffuse and its cult is so simple that the strangeness to the Goldi psyche strikes ones eye. But most surprising is its nonconformity and even hostility to the shamanism. Enduri never patronizes the shamans and the latter never address him in their prayers."

This description corresponds to that of buŋa and enduri amongst other groups. These characteristics of enduri have brought I. A. Lopatin to the idea that enduri is of a Chinese origin, which idea I cannot, naturally, share with him.

lar picture of *buya*. * Together with the above mentioned parallels there may be also compared the Chinese conception which, according to its meaning, is not a spirit but the "principle of nature", is not a being and it is not supposed to be honoured and is not influenced by the sacrifices and prayers.

The above facts show that the Tungus conception of *buya* is not at all an isolated phenomenon and it has its parallels amongst other ethnical groups living among the Tungus and influencing them. At the present time, I think it is impossible to restore the spreading of this conception and to establish its origin. Perhaps this idea belongs to very old conceptions such as, for instance, "soul" and thus its initial starting centre is lost for ever, and even perhaps is not human in the sense of "homo sapiens" as a zoological species.

40. CONSTRUCTION OF THE WORLD   In the previous section we have already touched upon the problem of the location of the spirit *apkaĭ enduri* but then the Tungus idea about heaven, earth, sky etc. was not clear.   In order to facilitate the references to these conceptions in the following sections I must now give a short description of Tungus ideas and hypotheses as to the "world".   This task is not easy at all, if one wants to have the *Tungus idea* and not its interpretation.   First of all, there are several hypotheses which are accepted but in different degrees among the groups and yet with individual preferences for some of them.   Moreover, an extensive "folklore" (so understood by the Tungus themselves) exists which gives, sometimes in a poetic form, description of the world.   Such descriptions are not also uniform amongst the groups.   In which degree the poetic interpretation of the world is accepted by the Tungus depends upon the individuals too.   In fact, the Tungus who are familiar with the hypotheses regarding the construction of the world do not accept a "folkloristic" (in their eyes) interpretation of natural phenomena and regard this interpretation to be mere fancy-stories good for children.   However, since the line of demarcation between the two is not sharp at all.   The Tungus sometimes hesitate as to whether some "facts" or hypotheses are the product of "folklore" or they are the product of critical "scientific" cognition of the world which even without being completely understood still may be accepted when supported by the authority of culturally "superior" people like the Mongols, Chinese, Manchus and Russians, who have their books from which they may learn many facts and "truth."   However, the Tungus who are not versed in the theories, especially children, may very easily accept a "folkloristic" interpretation as a "truth."

* Cf. E. K. Pekarskiĭ (op cit. p. 48) ürüŋ aĭy tojon. S.V. Jastremskiĭ (op. cit. p. 5) describes it as an anthropomorphic and human being, a spirit. However, the situation amongst the Yakuts is very handicapped by two conditions; namely, the introduction of the Christianity which long ago began to penetrate the Yakut complex (the Russians appeared amongst the Yakuts at the beginning of the seventeenth century) and the fact that most of the investigators were not indifferent to what it was possible to discover and in which way their discoveries might help the cause which brought them to Siberia (most of them were political exiles). Yet at that time the ethnographers in gathering their data usually followed questionaires (vide supra Chapter III) and approached the groups investigated basing themselves on their own ethnographical complex. So the adaptation of the facts to the theories was not rare amongst them.

The task is not difficult if we postulate that the Tungus do not make a distinction between the "scientific theories" which they have, and "folklore"—a product of poetic cognition of the world. As stated in the Introduction the investigators used to make the most striking pictures for the readers. I believe that such a representation of the Tungus ideas may become absolutely misleading. However, it is not easy to distinguish these two different approaches, though both of them are Tungus. Therefore, I want to warn my readers that what they find in the present section is only an attempt at giving Tungus ideas which are more or less generally accepted by the adult intelligent persons.

One of the most diffused and accepted conceptions of the world known to the Barguzin and Nerčinsk Tungus is that* the world is a complex which has always existed and was not created.** It is called *turū*. It was and it is divided into three worlds, the upper world *uyidúnda;* the middle world—*dúnda*, which is composed of the land—*jorko*—and the sea—*lamu*—in the middle of which *jorko* is found; and the lower world *orgidunda=örg'idúnda*, or *bunil*. It may be here pointed out that *turu ~ tur* in different dialects has different meanings. So in Borz. Nomad and Barg. it is used in the sense of "world—universe"; however, in Bir. Kum. and Khin. *tur* is used for "earth—soil", *dúnda* seems to be connected with the Mongol term for "middle"*** and is used only in the sense of "middle world"; however, the same word in the form *dunna* (a case of assimilation) (RTM) is used for "earth—soil," "earth" as opposed to the sea, also an "elevated locality" or even an "elevated position of flat land"; *jorko* (Ner. Barg.)—is the "land," "earth—soil"; *uyi* and *orgi=örg'i* mean respectively "upper" and "lower" in the sense of relation; *bunil* is from *buni*—the "dead", from the stem *bu*—to "die"; "*l*" is a suffix of plural, so the whole means,—"the dead men." The upper world is organized as a system of skies, where are located the sun, moon, stars and a series of spirits and *burkan* or *buya*; the souls of some people may also reach this world. The system of skies actually plays no important rôle and many Tungus believe it to be a Buriat conception. The middle world is also a complex system. According to the shamanistic idea, there are two snakes (*kulin*) which being in the sea support the land (*jorko*), but the Tungus would reservedly add: "so the shamans say". This world is peopled by the animals, man and also spirits. The lower world is dark and peopled by the dead people (their souls) and a series of spirits. The life is organised there in a more or less similar manner to that of the middle world. The entrance to this world is located in the north-western sector of the middle world. Amongst the same Tungus groups there is another conception too,—it denies the existence of *uyidúnda*, but recognizes only *dúnda* and *bunil*. With this conception the location of spirits is changed: the spirits supposed to live in the upper world are brought to the earth and placed on high peaks. The question as to the sun, moon, and stars remains unanswered. My informer,—a shaman,—told me

* A brief description given supra pp. 61-62 needs some addition. Instead of sending the reader back, I shall now again reproduce some facts.
** However, it is admitted that at that time which is named merely nonokon ("earlier", "before") there was no land or sea, and these were created by burkan (buya).
*** Cf. my Aspects, p. 144.

that such was his opinion but he pointed out that the opinions differ.

In all probability the "three worlds" conception is not a Tungus conception which becomes evident especially in view of the shifting of the term *tur*, introduction of a Mongol term, and attributes of the upper world which will be later described.

Nearly the same conception of the world is found among the Tungus of Manchuria, Birarčen. The universe is *buɣa* and the worlds are the upper—*uɣillan*, the middle—*ėrgin, orgu bojen* and the lower—*buni; uɣillan* is *uɣil + la* (direction) +*n*, which may be thus understood "the (world)· upwards"; *ėrgin,*—"the living (world)"; *orgu bojen*—the lower people, as opposed to *buni* [from the same stem as *örgi* (Barg. Ner)]. However, the upper world consists of nine heavens; the three first strata· are occupied by the spirits *endur'i*, the fourth—by the sun, the eighth—by all the stars (and planets), and the ninth by the moon. According to some Birarčen, the lower world also consists of at least two strata: *buni* and still further *ėla gurun*. The latter is not a Birarčen term but is borrowed from the Dahurs, who themselves received it from the Manchus (*gurun*). This is connected with the theory concerning the fate of the soul and it will be discussed later. The middle world is located in the ocean and is supported by a snake the movements of which produce earthquakes. However, this hypothesis is not shared by all Tungus. This Tungus group is familiar with the theory of *galbu* [cf. *galabi̇galap‖ ɣalba* (Mong. Rud), cf. *Kalpa*, Sanscrit.]. The world, according to these Tungus, changed several times due to fires, after each of which new people and new spirits appeared. (These catastrophes are explained also by floods which is accepted by the Manchus). After the fire the earth turned upside down. In Birarčen it is called *ɣalbu kallären*—the world changes. It is evident that the conception *ɣalbu* is borrowed.

The other Tungus groups have about the same conceptions of the world with minor variations chiefly depending upon the degree of influence of neighbouring groups. As to the Manchus, they recognize the existence of the universe consisting of three worlds as it is amongst other Tungus groups. However, together with Buddhism some more complex *apka* ("heaven"), *na* ("earth") and *natolorg'i* ("earth outside") [cf. *tulergi* (Man. Writ)] ideas have also penetrated the Manchu complex. The complex structure of the upper world is described in the books known to the Manchus. The lower world is also described in a special book *Nišan Saman* which is regarded by some Manchus rather like a "story" and not "history". Therefore the description of the lower world does not gain the absolute credence of the Manchus. In this section I will omit the folklore.regarding sun, moon, stars etc. which is not accepted by all Tungus as credible hypotheses.

41. **CONCEPTION OF "MASTER SPIRIT" AND SOME PRINCIPAL SPIRITS**   Amongst the spirits known to the Tungus, as well as to other neighbouring ethnical groups there is a great number of spirits which are regarded as masters of regions, localities, groups of animals, as well as individual animals and men. They are called in general

by a term known amongst different groups as *ojan* (RTM. Bir. Kum. Barg.) *ojon* (Nerč.) *ėjan* (Bir.) *od'ėn* (Khin.) *ėjėn* (Manchu)*. This is not a special term for a special class of spirits, but it renders the idea of "master", "khan", "ruler", "husband" etc. A shaman who masters his spirits is also their *ėjėn;* the spirits which have something under their control are also *ėjėn.* So the above discussed *julask'i* is also *ėjėn,* but *buɣa* is not so, for *buɣa* is not personal, not a human like being. The spirits which are formed from the human souls and haunt the taiga are not *ėjėn,* but those of them which happen to become influential and to take the· control of a region or a group of similar errant souls are *ėjėn.* Since the animals have their own souls and organization in many respects similar to that of man, some of them may also become *ėjėn.* Thus any spirit is potential *ėjėn,* just as any man potentially is so. Naturally, the mastership may be acquired by the spirits and lost as well. Yet, not only spirits may become "masters", but also some animals are regarded as "masters" of other animals and even man. For instance, the tiger is regarded by the Barguzin Tungus as the master of all other animals.** In the same position are found some sea-animals in the Gilak complex. Again in this case the human relations are transplanted into the realm of other animals. Owing to the variable character of the spirits which are called *ėjėn,* the shifting of *ėjėn*-ship, . variability of the competence of *ėjėn,* and their non-spiritual functions, the *ėjėn* must be regarded rather as a particular function amongst the spirits and non-spirits and as such the *ėjėn* cannot be separated into a special groups of spirits, as was often done, especially by the Russian ethnographers of the old school. I shall now proceed to this group of spirits.

BAINAČA or BAJAN AM'I.   These two terms have
THE MASTER SPIRIT OF   the same meaning. The
HUNTING AND TAIGA   first one is borrowed from the Dahurs amongst whom *ača* corresponds to *am'i*—the "father"—of the Tungus; *bajiɣ* (Dahur, Poppe), *bajin* (Dahur, Iwan.) [cf. *bajan* (Mongol, Manchu)], *bajan* (almost all Tungus dialects except for a few groups)—"rich". In the first two

* This word is known in a great number of Tungus dialects; cf. W. Grube's parallels *ėjin* (Goldi) (p. 11); also in Buriat—*ezin;* Mongol (Xalxa)—*ezen* (Podgorb.); *ej(e)n ‖ ejen* (Mongol, Rud.). The Tungus varieties are met with even in the form of *ydi* (Udsk. Midd.) The latter is not certain.

** The Tungus conception of the tiger as *ėjėn* of other animals is nearly the same as that of the Europeans who call the lion the king of animals. However, in the European complex it may be a purely folkloristic creation, a product of artistic imagination, while amongst the Tungus this idea is based upon the facts observed which indicate that in some regions the tiger is the most powerful animal which is actually independent on other animals and "rules" them at its will. If we consider "master" as a conception concerning spirits only, the designation of the tiger as "master", as is actually done by the Tungus and other groups, may lead to a misconception of the tiger's position and this animal will be supplied with supernatural "spiritual" qualities not by the groups investigated, but merely by the ethnographer. As a matter of fact, this has often been done and the whole question has been extremely involved and confused. In every case when we meet with the conception of *ėjėn* we have to find out what is the actual nature of the "mastership".

forms the name of the spirits is understood by the Tungus and Dahurs as it may be translated, namely, the "rich father". In the first form it is met with amongst the Khingan, Kumarčen, Birarčen and Dahurs, in the second form only amongst the Birarčen. However, the same spirit is known amongst the Yakuts under the name of *bajanaī* which is derived by E.K. Pekarskiī from Turk *baī*+*änä* [cf. Altaic. *pajana*] and *baī bajanaī* is translated by this author as "rich *bajanaī*". According to V.M. Ionov (cf. his "Spirit-master of the taiga among the Yakuts") *bajanaī* is a master of a group of animals, namely, the elk, fox, hare, ermine, musk-dear, mountain sheep, mustela (*soloyo*), and three birds only; these are generally those animals which are not hunted with bow and arrow. He is dressed in Tungus garment,—apron,—rides the reindeer and, according to some Yakuts, looks like a Tungus (op. cit. p. 5). This investigator supposes that this spirit has been borrowed from other ethnical groups (op. cit. p. 21). There is no doubt as to the meanings in Tungus and Dahur, but at the same time the idea, character and functions of this spirit are similar among the Yakuts and Tungus. Thus, the question as to the etymology of these names remains in obscurity. The Turk *baī*+*änä* might be the source for folk-etymology of Dahurs and Tungus, and Turk *baī*+*änä* might be as well a folk-etymology of *bajan am'i*—*bajanaī*.

Baīnača is met with everywhere in the taiga. He is pictured by the Khingan Tungus as an old man very tall, with white skin, a long gray beard covering his chest, with the eye-lashes about seven centimetres long. He rides a dog which has legs over a metre long.* He has a wife—*on'i* ("mother")—and two children—a girl and a boy. However, the Kumarčen say that the couple has no children. According to the Birarčen, *baīnača* or *bajan am'i* is an old man with long beard and he uses for his riding, the tiger.

Baīnača is the spirit which distributes the animals and sends them to the hunter. He is their "master".** So that if one wants to hunt one must ask *baīnača* to send the animals. Here is the reason why the Birarčen ask the question to the hunter "*aja mahin? baīnača buraje?* i.e. "Is the luck good? Is *baīnača* giving?". He thus gives *mahin* i.e. the hunting luck. *Baīnača* has his own form of placing, namely, the Tungus cut off the bark and partly the wood of a fresh tree in order to make a plane in which with the hunting knife they carve the eyes and mouth. There are very often made two placings, one for the husband and one for the wife *baīnača*. Amongst the Khingan Tungus two large permanent placings are made on the larch tree:

---

* This picture of haīnača was given to me by a Tungus who had seen him personally. He said "Once I hunted the squirrel. During three days I could kill (only) twenty-five squirrels. I could not do more (than this), for the gun well shot and hit the target, but could not kill the squirrel. Then I prepared four flour cakes and put them on the dalkon (platform erected for sacrifice). Soon I saw an old man (as described) came from the west, from the river, and took the cakes in both hands. Then I fell down on my knees and prayed: "Help me to kill!" The baīnača went southwards and I killed before noon forty squirrels and during the following two days altogether, one hundred and twenty (squirrels)". Such an evidence in the Tungus eye is, of course, solid enough. Since the existence of the spirit is presumed by a series of other hypotheses, this type of stories about baīnača is found frequently amongst the Tungus and all of them are more or less alike, so that I will not quote them.

** The Birarčen suppose that he is also looking after the domesticated animals, which seems to be an extension unknown amongst other groups.

one in the mountain pass near the sources of the Tura River (a tributary of the Gan River) and another in the mountain pass near the source of the Nuktukali River (also a tributary of the Gan River). The Mergen Tungus have such a placing on the banks of the Gida River (a tributary of the Byetraia River). These are visited by the Tungus passing by who leave some small sacrifice,—horse hair, some food, small birch-tree branches etc. Small placings, also on the trees, are made before going to the hunting, and after the hunting, usually on the mountain passes, when the animal is killed. The face of the placing is smeared with the blood of the killed animals, an exception made being of only the elk (Cervus Alces). This limitation exists, in so far as I know, only amongst the Birarčen. As a rule the placings must be made in a place rarely visited by people, at certain and rather long distances from the campment, for it is supposed that the spirits stay in places rather wild, and certainly in the forest. Among the Khingan group *baīnača* may have his own horse *oyyun* (*vide infra* Chapter XVI) of white colour. This horse is not used by outsiders, but it can be used by the women of the family. *Baīnača* may also cause sickness or mere nervous tension, so in this case a sacrifice may sometimes suffice, but sometimes a shaman must be invited. In this case baīnača will be treated (amongst the Birarčen) like any other *burkan*. However, such cases are not frequent.*

It may be noted that when the Manchus go to the taiga for hunting they also make placings and perform the complex of rites. According to the Tungus, the Chinese hunters follow this example as well.

During my work amongst the Tungus of Transbaikalia I did not find the name *baīnača*, or *bajan ami*, but the request as to the animals and thanks for sending them are addressed to *dayačan* (*vide infra*) and *burkan*. I have not observed any special placings. Amongst RTM. this spirit is called *mahun ~ mayun ~ mahin* and it is considered as "master" of the animals, especially Cervus Elaphus and master of all rivers, mountains etc. So he must be addressed with prayers. He has a wife *on'i burkan* —the mother—and three sons *uta burkan*. In the evening time they may pay a visit to the wigwams where there are placings for them and where they are honoured. The same spirit is also guardian-spirit of the family. No placings are now made. However, in former days they used to make a special hunting accommodation—*panāgo*—in the form of a plank with thongs for carrying on the back the utensils and hunting booty widely used among various Asiatic groups. The upper part of *panāgo* was curved to represent the face which was used as placing for *mahun* and was regularly "fed" after the hunting. In olden days after the hunting they used (perhaps still use, but I did not see) to make *dèrègdè*. The latter is a wooden piece, 25-30 centimetres long, with roughly cuts out for designation of the eyes and mouth and with long shavings left on as is done amongst the Aino and Gilaks who perhaps borrowed it from the Japanese. The sharpened end of the *dèrègdè* was thrust into the ground. Several placings of this type were made and fixed outside the wigwam. The mouth was

---

* Among the Khirgan Tungus I once observed a young man who was very nervous. Such a state was ascribed to baīnača. A placing was made and the young man was cured. However, the success of my cossacks in hunting was also explained by the fact of making a placing.

smeared with blood of animals and in front of placings some cooked meat was put for the spirits. The members of the family knelt in front of these placings*. Some Birarčen also call *bainača mayin*, but in this case it is done for abbreviation: "to make *mayin*" i.e. "to make placing for *bainača* in order to pray him to give *mayin*".

Indeed, the case of the RTM is not typical for as stated this group has for a long time been under Russian influence. I suppose that the name of the spirit giving "hunting luck" has been forgotten as it is in the process amongst the Birarčen. *Mahin ~ mayun* etc, is "hunting luck". In fact, amongst the Barguzin Tungus who adopted for the spirit master of hunting animals an alien term—*bvrkan*—still use the word *mayin* as *mayun* referred to the lucky guns with which many animals have been killed.

As I have already pointed out (*vide supra* p. 90) apart from the hunter's skill the statistical phenomenon of chance cannot be understood by the Tungus as it is understood by the statisticians, but the hypothesis of a spirit which directs and regulates chance is quite satisfactory for soothing the Tungus mind disturbed with the riddle of statistical occurrence of "killing" and "not killing," "meeting" and "missing" animals. By this remark I do not say what was the first,—the idea of the spirit regulating the life of animals and being in certain relation to man, or the observation of facts of uncertain frequency of meeting and killing animals. I do not even adventure to suppose whether the original meaning of *mahin* (and variations) was the chance ("luck") or the spirit regulating this "luck". One thing is evident that from the functional point of view all groups here discussed have the hypothesis of spirit regulating hunting (sending of animals) and they have the idea of "chance". The diffusion of this complex and diffusion of some terms (*bajanai, bainača, bajan am'i*) (*mayin*), also the loss of the elements and complexes and their substitution do not allow us to form any definite idea as to the original source of the idea of "luck" and "spirit—regulator". Both of them seem to be very old and to have a long history perhaps lost for ever. **

OM'IS'I (UM'IS'I) (OM'I, UM'I) This spirit lives in
SPIRIT REGULATING DIS- the southern section
TRIBUTION OF SOULS of the heaven and its
function is to give souls to the children. Amongst the Khingan Tungus this spirit is supposed to live in south western section and to be a complex one, namely, *om'i*—a male and *um'isma*—a female. If one wants to have children one must ask this couple. They have a wigwam and a tree on which the souls of not-yet-born children are sitting in the form of birds.*** The couple has a horse (perhaps, many of

them) *om'is'i murin* with which the souls are sent down to the earth. The reindeer Tungus of Manchuria suppose that this spirit *om'i* also protects the child. The Kumarčen suppose that this spirit, whom they call *um'i ~ om'i* is a female and has no husband. Among the Birarčen the same spirit is known under the name of *om'is'i* or *um'ism'i* corresponding to *oyos'i mama* of the Manchus, and also has no husband. This system thus is based on supposition that the souls are given by the spirit *um'isma ~ om'isma ~ om'is'i ~ om'i ~ um'i*. These names are connected with the term used for "soul" which as shown is *om'i ~ um'i*. Among the Barguzin Tungus the "soul" is called *om'ijan* and is sent by a spirit of the class *dayačan*. Among the Birarčen there is now introduced a new spirit which has something to do with *um'is'i*, namely, *n'ayn'ay* of Chinese (cf. *infra* Section 42). This spirit is used by the shamans and will be treated later.

According to the Manchu system *oyos'i mama** which is also rarely called *xutur'i mama* ("happiness"), sends souls (*womeyi fojoyo*) to the children and animals on the order of *apka endur'i*. In the house there must be for every male-child a kind of placing for her: an arrow with bunch of pendants, which must not be destroyed nor thrown away for the children may have boils and other troubles. However, the Manchus have also accepted Chinese *n'jayn'jay* as a special protector of children and women, but the shamans have nothing to do with the spirit. Since the introduction of the conception of *n'jayn'jay* the Manchu complex increased with all spirits known to the Chinese. However, they do not play very important part in general, with the exception of special spirits which send to the children diseases like measles, small-pox, chicken-pox, etc. This will be treated later.

Among the Barguzin and Nerčinsk Tungus the spirit *om'ijan* (*jan* is a suffix) is supposed to look after the souls of the people. So the spirit is asked to help in the case if the soul is not stable.

THE SPIRIT OF FIRE Golomta, galayan, toyoljin,
toyoman, toyo on'in.

The spirit of fire is known amongst the Tungus groups. However, their ideas regarding this spirit are not quite alike. Amongst the Barguzin and Nerčinsk Tungus this spirit is supposed to be an old woman *toyo on'in* ("fire mother"), *toyo on'o* ("fire grandmother"). The spirit has no placing for it stays in the fire of the family (wigwam). With this spirit there are connected two more spirits, namely, *toyiljin* and *toyoman* who have a certain function in the shamanism when the shaman goes to the lower world. The people must be very nice to the fire and careful with the fire, i.e. to feed from time to time, not

---

* Similar placings were made also in the case of sickness.

** Indeed, there may be proposed several more or less credible hypotheses, but since they cannot be used for further inferences they are useless for an investigation, and even dangerous when used. For instance, on Tungus—Mongol soil *bajin-majin-mahin-mayin* is possible. Yet, the idea of "wealth" (rich) and "luck" may also be of the same semantic group, but I do not propose it for it may take us so far that we might be lost in an ocean of hypotheses, as is common with many speculators.

*** Among the Goldi the soul is known under the name of *om'ija* and descends into the women which results in her pregnancy.

I suppose that this record of P. Šimkevič (quoted by I. Lopatin, op. cit. p. 199) was not correct for all Tungus groups do not connect pregnancy with receiving *om'i*—the soul—and regard this phenomenon as a natural one. Moreover, the soul (*om'i*) may leave the body (sickness) and yet the child may be born without *om'i* and will survive for a certain time. For this reason one must ask the spirit to give the soul.

* I. Zaxarov gives *omosi mama* as a shamanistic spirit, goddess of happiness, protector of children and posterity. Indeed, this is a wrong interpretation. The shamans have nothing to do with *omosi mama* and she is not a protector.

to spit into the fire, not to touch it with knife, and generally sharp iron, etc. The violation of this prohibition may greatly affect the Tungus. So the Barguzin Tungus have the following story:

"Once a woman with her child was staying in her "wigwam. A spark fell on the child. The mother got angry "and hit the fire with her long knife. Then she moved to "another place. When the wigwam was erected she tried "to make a fire, but the fire did not appear. Then she went "back to the wigwam she had left. She discovered there "an old woman, with her back cut into two parts, lying in "the place where the fire should be. Then woman who had "returned slaughtered a reindeer, covered the old woman "with the fresh meat. The old woman warmed herself and "told to the woman: "Well, never do so like you did: Live "well!" Since that time the Tungus observe the customs of "good treatment of the fire".

I have already in SONT pointed out that the bride when adopted by her new family as wife of one of the male members must make sacrifice to the fire which constitutes an important item in the wedding ceremony.

Amongst the Khingan Tungus this spirit is called *golomta*.* The spirit is an old female, about twenty-five centimetres high, very fat, and red like fire. She must be well treated and every three years she must have a sacrifice of a domesticated buck. Amongst the Kumarčen Tungus it is known as *golumta*. They have a variant of the above given story: the points of difference: the woman was sewing; the spark burned her work; she poked the fire with scissors and then could not make fire in a new place; when she returned she found an old woman with perforated eyes crying; she gave some fat to the old woman.

The Birarčen know the above version of fire spirit but some of them also adopt red faced spirit *kôšin* which is a Chinese spirit (Chinese *xôšèŋ* 火神). They call the spirit *golumta* and sometimes *toyoljin* in the sense "the one living in the fire", also *galayan* (the stem *gal*||*yal* Mong. Rud.—the "fire") and the same stories are known**. This spirit is very important in life and must be carefully honoured by regular sacrifices every morning and every evening. On the new year day every one who comes to the wigwam or house must first bow (or kneel) before the fire, and after this to the old man. This Tungus group has a form of swearing' *golumta ičeran*,—"the fire spirit sees",—analogous to *apka ičeran*, "the heaven sees", borrowed from the Manchus. They relate:

"Once there were two wigwams. One of women went for water and saw two women one of which was very fat and another one very thin. The fat one said out: 'To-day I will set fire to the wigwam'. The thin one said: 'There is in the wigwam our saddle'. The fat one: 'Well, the saddle will not be burnt'. The woman was very astonished and remembered that there was really neighbours' saddle in her wigwam. Then she waited for fire. In fact, during

the same day the wigwam with all her belongings except her neighbours' saddle burnt to ashes".

According to the interpretation two women, fat one and thin one, were the spirits of fire from two wigwams.

Amongst the Manchus we meet with an entirely different complex, namely, *tua enduri* of Manchu Writ. is, of course, Chinese *xôšèŋ* (vide supra). Yet, amongst the Manchus of Aigun district this spirit is not in vogue, but another spirit is of importance, namely, *jun fuě'k'i*, i.e. the "Buddha of the stove" ("mouth of the.... "), which will be discussed in a special chapter.

THE SPIRITS OF THE LOWER WORLD. INMUNKAN, ILMUNXAN, IRLINKAN, ETC.

The spirit of the lower world under these names is known among the Manchus, and the Tungus of Manchuria and Transbaikalia. This spirit is connected with *erlik xan* of the Mongols (Xalxa, Rud.) identified by A. Grünwedel (op. cit. pp. 130, 170) with Yama (Sanscrit) and *gšin-rje* (Tibetan). Amongst the Tungus of Transbaikalia and RTM* it is known under the name of *erlikxan→irlinkan* while amongst the Manchus *ilmunxan* and amongst other Tungus groups either under the same name (Birarčen) or under its modification *inmukan* and *inmunkan* (Khin, Bir. Kum). The Buddhistic spirit *Yama* in Manchu is called by the same term. According to the Khingan Tungus, he had originally been in this world and afterwards he was sent to another world (*bun'i*), where he now remains with his wife. According to the Birarčen, the spirit *um'is'i* is under the orders of *inmunkan* which is also the opinion of some Manchus who say that this spirit (*oyos'i mama*) is living in the lower world. According to the Barguzin Tungus *irlinkan* is anthropomorphic being and he is master of the spirits *ojdu* living in both the middle and the lower worlds. Among the Manchus and Dahurs there are many stories devoted to this spirit whence it would be possible to give more details but the Tungus, who know these stories, regard them as "folklore". It is evident that the idea of the spirit with its functions as master of Hades, judge of dead souls (amongst the Manchus and groups influenced by them), etc. is of non-Tungus origin. The name *inmunkan-ilmunxan* and *irlinkan* seems to originate from the same source, for *ilmun — inmun* in Tungus have no etymological connexions.** Alternation of such type is not rare in the Tungus languages. The images of this spirit are known from the Chinese pictures, bronzes, etc. but there are no placings used amongst the Tungus. The role of the ass in the Manchu complex is evidently one which is indicative of its non-Manchu origin. It is confined to the lower world only. It is absolutely lacking in the system of shamanism. However, all minor spirits, and especially the *ibayan* (vide Section 44.) are afraid of the ass's leg. It may be here

---

* In RTM. Kolomtan=xolumtan (Yakut, Pek. "the place for fire") has no meaning of spirit, but "what is found under the fire" i.e. the fire place. (Cf. also Mongol yolumta, golumta). In the sense of spirit it is known also in Mank. dialect. The parallels are also found in other dialects and groups.

** The woman becomes angry because the fire produces the noise like: s'ip-s'ip-s'ip!

---

* They assert that this name is received from the Yakuts which cannot be confirmed, in so far as I can see.

** Perhaps except Manchu where we find stem ilmu—the submerger, to detach oneself, etc. which may be perhaps connected with the origin and history of Yama who went down, was submerged in the lower world, was detached from the other spirits. However, I do not insist on this etymology.

noted that in the group of six kinds of *wuǰima*, i.e. the "domesticated animals", the ass is not included,—it comprises horse, ox, sheep, dog, pig and fowls (under the name of "chicken" *čoko*). The other spirits connected with the lower world will be discussed later.

42. MANCHU ENDURI AND VARIOUS TUNGUS SPIRITS. Among the Birarčen and Kumarčen under the name of *endur'i* several spirits are known which play the rôle of "masters". Many a spirit may be called by this term which is undoubtedly borrowed from the Manchus, in a recent time. The previously known spirits have been re-named, and the new ones have been adopted. So we have *guskü endur'i*,—the "wolf *endur'i*," which is the old *baïnača; toyo endur'i*,—the "fire *endur'i*", which is the old *golumta; n'ayn'ay endur'i*, which is the old *julask'i endur'i* and still older *buya*. There are new ones, as *ukur* (the "cow") *endur'i, murin* (the "horse") *endur'i* also *tudukan* and *mudurkan endur'i* to which I shall return. Together with the new spirits and new names some new ideas were introduced as well. For instance, *mudurkan endur'i* and *toyo endur'i* are supposed to be opposite spirits which destroy each other, which sounds like a "philosophical" construction of alien (Chinese) origin. The group of *endur'i* is also called *ajelga* which will be discussed later too. However, the group of *endur'i* essentially is a Manchu group, and it is very numerous. Indeed, among the Manchus themselves it is not an original Manchu discovery. The term *endur'i*, as shown, is only a Manchu adaptation of a foreign term and the chief source of information regarding this group of spirits is found in the Chinese system. The Manchus do not accept all Chinese spirits, but make certain selection; e.g. according to the Manchus, they do not accept the spirit of commerce, quite important among the local Chinese merchants, as well as many other spirits. In the Manchu complex the chief distinction of these spirits is that they are not usually malevolent, although sometimes they may be so, and yet through their agents they may cause sickness. However, in such a case they are not influenced by the shamans, but they may be influenced only by prayers and sacrifices. These spirits do not enter the people themselves.[*] The same term is also referred to people of "right life" after their death. The spirits are supposed to live in the upper world in an ever green region, mentioned before (*vide supra* Section 37). Nature of the spirits is such that these spirits violate the women and girls, so a conception from them, coming to the women in sleep, is admitted by the Manchus as possible. I think that the Manchus, who are very naturalistic in this respect, admit such a possibility only as a good explanation of happenings disapproved of by the public opinion. However, sexual dreams amongst the females are common and thus there may be made a theoretical inference as to the possibility of pregnancy in exception of the natural way. The images of these spirits are known from the Chinese pictures which are

usually used as placings for these spirits when sacrifice is served and these spirits addressed. In Manchu books, thirty-four spirits of this class are distinguished. Here I give a list of spirits, in the alphabetic order, which are commonly known.

Ajèn endur'i—The spirit of thunder which depends on *apkaï endur'i* [cf. *akǰan* (Manchu Writ.)]. This spirit is not from the lower world.

Agura endur'i—The spirit of arms (*agura*) and utensils, in the calendar list it occupies twenty-eighth place. There is a festival organized during the summer. It may be noted that besides the arms, utensils in general are included.

Aižin endur'i—The spirit of gold [*aisin→aižin* (Manchu Sp.)] which is supposed to be the spirit of commerce amongst the Chinese; it is the thirty-first spirit of the calendar list; its functions are the regulation of misfortune from the war, epidemics, drought, etc. Evidently *aisin* ("gold") has brought to a new conception of the functions of this spirit.

Alin'i endur'i—The spirit of the mountains (*alin*). This spirit is connected with the regulation of the life in the mountains and forest. So the hunters and travellers have to address themselves to this spirit. This spirit is in use only among the *iči manǰu* (the new Manchus), but it becomes also known among other Manchus. Amongst the Chinese it is called *šansènje* (山神爺). Under its orders are the tiger and wolf which have their own masters *tasxa* and *guska endur'i* who must have a special sacrifice [pig, chicken, bread (Chinese *mantou*)]. This spirit may be very harmful by its interference with the hunting and travelling, and with frightening the people with both tigers and wolves. This spirit is not given in the list of calendar spirits, but it is of great importance, for according to the Manchus, they "formerly lived as a wild people."

B'a endur'i—The spirit of the moon. The sacrifice is made in the evening (full moon) of 15th day of eighth moon. Its importance is not high.

B'iyàn enduri—The same as *alin'i endur'i*—but perhaps it is only a subordinate of *alin'i endur'i*, for the usual association of this spirit is with the tiger. Amongst the Chinese hunters this spirit is associated with any tiger met with which is not characteristic of the Manchu complex. In Manchu Writ. *b'igan*—the "wilderness"; L. Zazarov designates the spirit *bïgan i enduri* as that of desert roads and steppes.

Bušukü endur'i—The complex spirit of this name forms one of elements of the complex *n'ayn'ay* and has at its disposal two subordinate spirits: *bušukü mama* and *bušukü gèxè*. The latter is extremely dangerous if she is not satisfied with the prayers and sacrifices. (*vide* Chapter XIII, description of the diseases). It is not found on the calendar list.

Gèlxun endur'i mama—It is probably one of the group of *opos'i mama*. The functions are not clear. The bow and arrow with pig's bones attached and

---

[*] But the Chinese, according to the Manchus, have a Shantung spirit—*šandungèr*—which speaks through the young boys and girls (11-12 years old). They cover their faces (eyes?) with a tissue and then children must show simultaneously similar number of fingers. The more the coincidences the better the harvest. The spirit enters the man who directs the operation. The Manchus say that this spirit is very little known in other provinces of China.

hung up when a boy was born, was called by this name. It is not found on the calendar list.

jousaŋ—The Chinese spirit connected with *laoje*, vide *laoje*.

Kwayguŋ—The Chinese spirit connected with *laoje* and *jousaŋ*, vide *laoje*.

Laoje—The spirit and its name are of Chinese origin (老爺). On the picture the spirit is shown on horse back and it is considered as "good for horses". In the case of sickness a pig sacrifice must be given to this spirit and his satellites (*vide supra*). During the sacrifice the horses must have long pieces of silk tied on their tails and manes. The horses during certain period must not be used by women and for carts. According to the Manchus, there were three Chinese heroes who, after their prayer to *apkaĭ endur'i*, became brothers. One of them was *laoje* and two others were *jousaŋ* and *kwayguŋ*. Their placing in the form of a picture is put in the kitchen garden at the left of the principal house, in a kind of a small shrine. All three spirits are often called *endur'i* and *mafa*.

Luŋ-waŋ-je—is a spirit borrowed with the name (龍王爺) from the Chinese. Its functions are connected with the small streams and rivers. It is the oldest of the series. Its images (Chinese) are like that of *apkaĭ endur'i*. However, it is also to be asked for protection by the people who navigate. In Manchu it is also called *bĭbă mudur'i endur'i*, which seems to be connected with *mudur'i endur'i* (*bĭbă* is not clear, but seems to be connected with stem *bi*—the "existence."). *Vide infra* Mudurkan of Northern Tungus.

Muĭan voćko—although he is called *voćko* (*vide infra*) some Manchus consider him as a spirit *endur'i* helping, patronizing the carpenters [*muĭan* is in Chinese; in Manchu Writ.—*moi faksi*]. This spirit was not formerly used amongst the Manchus but at the present time he received a certain popularity for protecting e.g. new constructions. As placing, or merely symbol the carpenter's rule made of bone is used.

Na i dalaẋa endur'i [in Chinese *Ty Weŋ* (地翁)]—is a spirit looking after the fields, also the construction of the house (in so far as the land is required). According to the Manchus, this spirit is independent, but it seems to me that it is only a different name (perhaps a different manifestation) of *apkaĭ endur'i*. It is probably borrowed from the Chinese.

N'aŋn'aŋ endur'i—The complex spirit (vide supra *bušukú endur'i*, also *oŋos'i mama*) borrowed from the Chinese (娘娘). The images are known from the Chinese but not used. The placing is made of earth,—with two faces, four eyes, and two noses,—which they put in the temple (*m'ao*.)

Sou-sen-lao-endur'i—That spirit of Chinese name and origin which rides a reindeer. This spirit is addressed with prayer and sacrifices only by the old men. The Manchus evidently have no definite idea about it. It seems to be connected with certain conditions of senile marasmus.

Taḷmen endur'i—The spirit of fog [*talman* (Manchu Writ) —the "fog"] which looks like a function of *apkaĭ endur'i*.

Tarkin endur'i—The spirit of lightning, [cf. *talk'an*—the "lightning" (Manchu Writ.)] which looks like a function of *apkaĭ endur'i*.

Tuɣè endur'i—The spirit of (heavy) clouds which looks like a function of *apkaĭ endur'i* [cf. *tugi* (Manchu Writ.)]

Vèɣè endur'i—The stone spirit; the complex spirit consisting of a *mafa* (old man) and *mama* (old woman). There are two large stones on the way from Aigun to Tsitsihar, which are supposed to grow. The stones are surrounded by a fence; little by little a temple was formed, because of the numerous visitors. Women who wish to have children address their prayers and make sacrifice in form of pieces of red tissue with thanks written upon them, which are hung on the fences. Warriors pray to this spirit for victory.

Wuće endur'i—The spirit of the door (*wuśe*) [in Chinese *mènśènje* (門神爺)], whose function is to protect the entrance against the spirits *ẋutu* (vide infra). Formerly it was used only by the Chinese but gradually it has been introduced among the Manchus.

Wuẋiɣa endur'i—The spirit of stars. It helps in the case of skin diseases, swellings, boils, etc. The greatest part of Manchu clans do not know this spirit, but some of them do, e.g. *wujata, faktu, nimaći, pujamći, wuxe* and some others. The pig sacrifice and prayers are made at night time. The fact of selection of clans is rather significant, but the clans are both *fè* ("old") and *ići* ("new") Manchu.

Xua endur'i—The spirit of the yard, which is the same as *apkaĭ endur'i*.

There are some other spirits *endur'i*, e.g. protectors of smiths, particular forms of *n'aŋn'aŋ*, etc. also a group of spirits connected with the spirits of the lower world *ilmunẋan endur'i*. The important spirits, fourteen in number, are represented, for instance, in the temple which was erected, according to the Chinese practice and style, by a rich villager in Kalunšan, a village near Aigun. The temple is called *toksoĭ alban m'ao*, i.e. of village, public (state, governmental, communal) temple, in which there is a picture of all *endur'i* painted in the Chinese style. At least twice a year, namely, during first five days of the first moon, and on the thirteenth day of the fifth moon, the villagers gather for prayers and sacrifices to all the spirits. The choice of *endur'i* to be managed in the public temples is not alike in different cases observed. There may be fewer or more than fourteen spirits[*]. Perhaps in the same group of *endur'i* there may also be included some other spirits which are not called *endur'i*, but the character of which is near to that of *endur'i*. These spirits have been introduced into the Manchu system after the classification of spirits in the

[*] E.g. I knew a temple of this kind erected for preservation of forest and it was called: alban m'ao enduri, so the Manchus believed that there was a special endur'i for the preservation of trees. However, such a spirit does not individually exist.

calendar list had been made, so that among the Manchus they are known either without any classification or under the group of *mafa*. The spirits known under the name of *endur'i* may be also classified in a different manner, namely, the group of *apkaĭ endur'i*, in which there would be included *taĭmen, tuʒe, tarkin, wuʒin, ajèn* and others. However, these spirits now are more independent then they were originally and in this way *apkaĭ endur'i* has already differentiated and as compared with the Calendar List some spirits of the group *endur'i* have already vanished. On the other hand, it would be also possible to separate another group of spirits headed by *ilmunxan* which I have not even treated under the name of *endur'i*. However, some of these spirits, as will be shown, practically have already become more important than *ilmunxan* himself. A new complex *endur'i* has been introduced under the name of *n'ayn'ay* which is of a recent Chinese origin, but which also plays a more important part than other spirits owing to the discovery (cognition) of certain diseases previously unknown. Among the Manchus who live on hunting or near the people who live on hunting, the complex spirit of mountains and forest has also appropriated more importance than, for instance, the spirits connected with the city life. Yet, we have also seen that there are some *endur'i* which are adopted only by *some* clans and are not recognized by other clans. As a matter of fact, to make a list of these spirits is impossible, for not only in different localities, but also in different professions (agriculturists, hunters, citizens, etc.), in different clans and even in individual families the lists are different. The Calendar List of spirits was only one of the static pictures which might be taken at that time. Indeed, it was reflecting the complex which existed among the authors of the List, so in other Manchu groups and regions the lists might be quite different. At the present time the complex also is different for in addition to the regional and other differences there now exists the difference in time. During the period from the moment of compilation of the List to the present moment many old spirits were excluded, the function of other spirits was changed and new spirits, chiefly from the Chinese complex, incorporated.

In continuation of the present section I shall now give a list of spirits which are found among the Northern Tungus groups observed. These are spirits which according to their character, origin, and present functions are very close to the Manchu *endur'i*. Here it may be pointed out that the list of spirits found in several Tungus groups is shorter than that of Manchu *endur'i*. This fact is interesting and can be easily understood if we remember a rather recent penetration of the Chinese spirits among the Manchus and lack of written records among the Northern Tungus who gradually forget their knowledge of alien spirits, and seemingly do not need to have a very long list of spirits.

Ajelga (ajelgan)—so are called amongst the Birarčen two spirits *ukur endur'i* and *morin endur'i*. However, there are many other *ajelga* which sometimes simply are the souls of dead people and which occupy some rock or mountain and be-

come "masters". Yet, *inmunkan* (Bir.) may also be called *mūyi ajelga**. The etymology of *ajelga* is not clear. Perhaps *ajelga* has the stem *āje—èjen,*—"the master" etc. [cf. *ej'il*(e) || *ejele*—to govern, rule, control. (Mongol, Rud.)] with which supposition the term may be rather recent.

Daval—The spirit is known amongst the Nomad Tungus of Mankova and other Tungus influenced by the Buriats. It is supposed to protect the cattle. Its name is borrowed from the Eastern Buriats. Under the name of *dabaĭ* it is known among the Buriats as *oγgon* [cf. C. Ž. Žamcarano, (op. cit. p. 380) who says that although this spirit had originated from an educated (*bakši*) girl, who was a Buddhist, the spirit has become protector of cattle-breeding.]

D'umnèr'id'ira is known amongst the Barguzin Tungus as spirit of lightning [cf. N. D. Mironov, "Kuchean Studies", p.p. 76-77 (164-165) footnote in which *d'umnè* (the stem, for *r'id'ira* are suffixes) is compared with Sanscrit (chiefly Vedic) dyumna—"splendor, majesty", also "lightning."] The stem *d'umnè*, in so far as I know, has no parallel and on Tungus soil no credible etymology.

japnaja is known amongst the Reindeer Tungus of Manchuria. This spirit is living in the lower world and eating, swallowing (*jap*—to eat, swallow) everything.

jarajarguči is considered by the Tungus of Transbaikalia as master of the sea (*lamū*) which surrounds the earth, also master of all waters and fishes. It is anthropomorphic, but it has no legs. It has no placing. There is no doubt that we have here Mongol *jar* + *jarguči*, i.e. "the order", + "supreme judge" (cf. Kowalewsky, p.p. 2300, 2305), so that the Mongol complex has been adapted by these Tungus and "judge" seems to be quite alien in the Tungus complex.

j'iač'i is known amongst the Mankova Tungus as spirit protecting the tent (family, house). This

----

* Here we have term *mūyi* which may be suspected of being an old term. First of all, it must not be mistaken for *mun'l*, i.e. "ours", —*mū* is not *mun*. Second, we have a series of spirits in the names of which we meet with this term. So amongst the Tungus of Yakutsk gov. (Lam.) there are two spirits *buxo muyani* (the spirit of the earth?—buxo) and *tuγger muyani* (the spirit of the lake), where the stem *muya* is increased with suffix *ni*. There is in Tum. *buyĭlkan*—a kind of spirit. Amongst the Goldi we have spirits called *muxan* (I. Lopatin, op. cit. p.p. 227, 224). In Enissy dialect we have *moxa*—the forest, thickness. Perhaps, the spirits called *mayun* among the Nerčinsk, Barguzin, and Reindeer Tungus of Manchuria are also connected with the same idea (*ajelga*) and stem, *mūyi* undoubtedly is a contraction of some other complex which probably was of type *muCV+ni* contracted as *mūyi*, where *yi* is suffix of "genetivus". On the other hand in Bir. Kum. Khin. we have *bua,*—*bea* (which are contractions of *buya-beya*) in the sense of "wild forest". "thickness". It is very likely that in this case we have *buya,*—*muya* with variations (which is a phenomenon met with in Tungus, e.g. *mu*—*bu* "we") in the original sense of taiga, "primitive forest," etc. In fact, the terms like *buya, inmunkan, bajnača,* and others originally are not Tungus terms, while *muyan, moxo, buya* in the sense of "forest" also *mayun* in the sense of "spirit of forest", in so far as I can see, have no parallels and look like a very old stem.

spirit has been borrowed from the Buriats (also *ĵiači*). However, the affinities of this spirit may be easily established with *ĵ'iači burkan* of the Tungus of Manchuria (*vide infra*).

Jol is known amongst the Khingan Tungus, Kumarčen and Birarčen, as a spirit protector of horses, also cattle. The name of this spirit is probably borrowed from the Mongols who have *ĵol, zol* (Buriat, Podg.), the "happiness, way, fate" [cf. ibid. Yakut *ĵol;* Turk. *ĵol*].* The placing for this spirit is made of a piece of leather about a foot square; in the upper part there are two anthropomorphic images, usually made of lead, one of which is a male and the other is a female—a couple of spirits. The leather may be also ornamented with tissue of various colour and beads. After the birth of new calves and colts there must be attached small bones to the placing and the spirits must be given a sacrifice ("fed") and prayers. Amongst the Tungus Birarčen living in houses of Chinese type, the placing can be made of a piece of wood—a plank of the above indicated size and with the same details. Every family which has horses and cattle usually has one in its tent, or wigwam, or house. These placings cannot be approached by the women. Indeed, the spirit, its name, and the type of placing (like *oygon* of the Buriats) are borrowed. Perhaps we meet with the same spirit among the Goldi. In fact, *ĵuli* (P. Šimkevič, op. cit. p. 56), *ĵulin, ĵuli* (I. A. Lopatin. op. cit. p. 222) is considered as protector of the family and house. Let us point out that the house in Goldi is *ĵo* (*vide supra* footnote).

Garku is met with among the Barguzin Tungus. There is a double spirit called *ĵur* (two) + *garku* + *tal*. It consists of a couple, a male and a female; according to these Tungus, everything has originated from these two spirits. In the text of a shamanistic record I have met with the sky-heaven—*n'ĵan'ĵa* and moon—*b'ega* which also produce everything. The term *n'ĵan'ĵa* (with modification) (Bir. Nerč. RTM.) usually referred to the sky, in this function is met with only in this case. However, the idea of male and female spirits, sky—heaven, and moon, are common. Cf. also the Chinese complex female—male,—Yin-Yang.

Mudurkan (*muduĵe*)—The spirit of water is met with among the Birarčen. He is male and is represented as a dragon (*mudur*). He has under

his control the fishes, regulation of water supply etc. He is also addressed in the case of needs for horses. According to the Tungus conception, he did not fight the *apkai endur'i*, which theory is of Chinese origin known to the Tungus but refuted by them. This spirit has a dragon-like straw placing five or six metres long, put on a heap of pebbles or stones. During summer, and especially droughts, the Tungus have a ceremony borrowed from the Chinese. This spirit is very popular among the Manchus as *mudur'i endur'i*.

Muktukan is known amongst the Kumarčen as a spirit of little importance. Perhaps its existence is due chiefly to the misunderstanding of the Manchu name for "temple"—*abkai muktexen*. Although there is a name of a Tungus hero *Mukteokan*, he cannot be taken as responsible for the existence of the spirit, but his name might be that of a spirit formerly better known.

Nalkán, Om'i nalkán, is met with among the Barguzin and Nerčinsk Tungus. He is considered as "master" of a special group of spirits known under the name of *oĵan* (*vide infra* Chapter XII) which live on the earth. He has only a head; the body and limbs are lacking. The Nerčinsk Tungus suppose it to be the chief spirit of *uyidunda*—the upper world. *Kan* is certainly "khan", so that the name is *nal**. It has no placings. (cf. also *om'is'i*).

n'ón'a is a very malevolent, or better to say dangerous spirit, living in the water, known only among the Khingan Tungus. No details are available.

Tamnidira is known amongst the Barguzin and Nerčinsk Tungus as spirit of fog, rain, clouds etc. which corresponds to *talmen endur'i* of the Manchus. *Tamni* (*dira* is a suffix)—the fog (cf. *tamnaksa, tamna, tamnaya* of various dialects).

Tudukan also *Turkan* and *Tuduĵe* is the spirit of the earth which is also called *turkan* (*tur*,—the "earth"). According to the Khingan Tungus and Birarčen he has a black face (like the Chinese picture). According to the Khingan Tungus, he lives under the earth and uses only a black horse. Therefore as *oygon* (*vide* Chapter XVI) he is given a black horse. The recent origin is especially clear for he is addressed on all matters concerning agriculture and partly horses (the Birarčen). This is a spirit of secondary importance. The spirit is sometimes called by the Birarčen in a Chinese manner *tuduĵe*. Placing of this spirit is usually a Chinese made picture. Amongst the Manchus from whom he is borrowed he is known as *na i dalaxa endur'i*.

---

* Cf. also *ĵeĵĵy* (Dahur, Poppe)—placing for spirits (during shamanizing). However, Poppe's translation is not certain. It would seem perhaps more natural to look for etymology into the Tungus dialects. In fact, we find very good words, namely, the house-family *ĵu~ĵo* but in Tungus *ĵol* cannot be formed from *ĵu~ĵo* in the sense of the name for a spirit. Yet, the functions of this spirit and *oygon*-like appearance point to its being borrowed from the above indicated groups.

---

* Undoubtedly it is borrowed from the Chinese together with the ceremonies. Vide supra *tuyg-way-ĵe*. The drowned people instead of going to *ifmunxan* go to *mudurkan*.

** Perhaps the etymology of this name is naixan (Manchu)—"the khan of earth" with new functions amongst these Tungus groups,

CHAPTER XII

SPIRITS FORMED FROM THE SOULS AND SPIRITS

INCORPORATED INTO THESE GROUPS

43. HUMAN SOUL In Chapter IV, I have given a general description of the soul and its complex organization. We have seen that the soul is not a very stable element of man (and animals), and owing to its complexity it may gradually disintegrate without resulting in a complete extinction of the living organism.

The Tungus need proofs of the existence of soul and its complex organization. The proofs are numerous. In the analysis of the process of proving we shall now find how these complex souls exist and which rôles they play. The first soul of the Manchus or *wuneŋi fojeŋo* and the first soul of the Tungus of Manchuria may be easily observed in the manifestations of exterioration* of the soul, e.g. the loss of consciousness, not followed by death, travelling during dreams, communication at a distance, intrusion of the soul into other people, etc. These facts are so numerous that the Tungus (including the Manchus) do not hesitate as to the reality of the existence of soul.

It is different with the second soul of the Tungus and third soul,—*olorg'i* (external) *fojeŋo*,—of the Manchus. However, its existence may be also proved. Its existence is seen, so to say, indirectly, but the Tungus may sometimes see it directly and experimentally. For instance, among the Birarčen a man once found a piece of broken mirror. When he looked into it he saw instead of his own face a mule's head. Being disgusted, he naturally threw away the mirror. However, competent people explained the case; namely, he saw his own soul which in previous reincarnations might have been that of a mule. In fact, from time to time the Tungus find such mirrors in which they may see their own souls. Indeed, there the question is about the second soul, which is considered by some Tungus to be the principal soul after the loss of which it is impossible to revive. Its traces can also be seen when it leaves the body on the seventh day after death. On this day at night the Tungus put some ashes or sand on the threshold or in the entrance of wigwam and see what kind of foot prints are left by the soul. These may be that of a man, a horse, a roe-deer, a chicken, or other animal. The activity and existence of this soul is also supported by the cases when this soul introduces itself into living people who may tell, after their own experience received in this state, what is the nature of this soul and what it wants. Indeed, the theory of soul in general, for it can be found in the books written by clever, educated people and yet sometimes under the inspiration of the spirits. Among the Manchus this soul may also leave the body during sleep, so that the Manchus as well, form their idea about its existence from the fact of dreams. It ought to be pointed out that sleep is explained by the Manchus as due to the

retardation of the blood circulation and not to the absence of this soul, while the loss of consciousness is explained as due to the departure of the first soul, which may also leave people because of a sudden fear.

The existence of the third soul which for some time remains with the corpse and later stays with the members of the family amongst the Birarčen is proved chiefly by the experience of the people who often see their parents in their dreams, during hallucinations etc. However, the Manchus have no need to explain it for, according to them, this returns to *oŋos'i mama* for being given to other children. Some Manchus suppose that this soul remains with the corpse as it is amongst the Birarčen, but it does not go to stay with the family. In this case the first soul would be supposed to go back to *oŋos'i mama*. So the function of *oŋos'i mama* is production of souls. The question why the Birarčen needed this theory is that they did preserve their own idea that the soul remains with the family (clan) and they adopted the idea of complex soul and the idea of a spirit (*om'is'i, oŋos'i* of the Manchus) which gives the souls to the children. The Tungus (Birarčen) do not stop their observation of facts which may be used for supporting the hypothesis of soul. They suppose that the soul may leave the body without causing direct death which may occur some time later. However, the soul which leaves the body is noticed by some animals who react in a special manner. For instance, the foxes and wolves in seeing a soul, begin to bark which, as known, is not common in these animals. This is also used as one of evidences of the exterioration of the soul.

The nature and organization of the soul may be still better understood if we consider the case of twins discussed by the Birarčen. Since the souls are given by *om'is'i* to one child and since two children are born the soul must be divided into two parts: one part to each child. As long as the twins are alive they may have a single soul in common, but when one of them dies, the other child cannot be unaffected, since the two "partial" souls must go as one to the world of dead people and another to stay with the corpse. Owing to this both children twins usually die within a short period. Naturally the death of twins is used as proof of the existence of soul. Here it ought to be pointed out that the soul is stabilized rather late, so if one of children dies in early childhood another one may survive. Yet, if the twins already are adult the death of one is not so dangerous for the other, as it is in the middle period of childhood. However, I could not find out any explanation of the difference*.

---

* I use here term "exterioration" in the sense of physical removal, displacement of the soul. The same remark refers to "exteriorate".

* Perhaps this is connected with the idea that the threefold souls are received later. The opinions regarding this delicate matter are not fixed. Some Tungus suppose that the twins have two souls and thus the death of one of them will not be followed by death of the other. It may be here pointed out that the recent investigations as to twins have shown that the uniovular twins very often die about

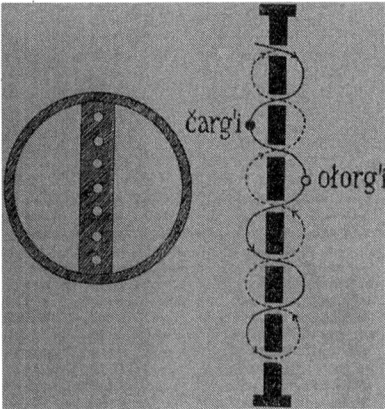

According to the Manchus, the soul may be located in different parts of the body. There is a circle in which is included a plank with seven holes [n'amèn nadan sayga, i.e. circle (also heart) seven holes.]* The wuneyi fojeyo remains stationary, while čarg'i and olorg'i are moving so that the first is always ahead of the second and they are always found separated by the "plank". They must not hinder their respective movements. If this movement is regular, the owner of the soul is well balanced and sleeps well. In case of fear, and similar conditions the movement of souls may be accelerated and thus the distance between them shortened which the person would feel. As result of fear the olorg'i soul may leave the body and the person would be sleepy and dreamy. The case of absence for a long time of one of the souls may also cause not only a feeling of uneasiness and confusion, but also a complete unconsciousness and even death if the period of absence should be extended over a certain time. So that, for instance, the absence of čerg'i and olorg'i will not be followed by death at once but the death will occur within a certain time. The liver also has something to do with the soul; a very brave person is supposed to have a large liver. However, if the liver is taken away the soul is not affected, so that liver has only a certain influence on, but is not the placing of the soul.

Amongst the Tungus of Manchuria (Birarčen and Kumarčen) it is supposed that the absence of the first soul may result in the loss of consciousness, but when the second

at the same period. Seemingly, this fact did not escape the Tungus attention and they explained it by their hypothesis of soul. Yet, since this tendency is not observed in biovular twins the facts also did not escape the Tungus attention whence we have their hesitation as to the possibility of a generalization of their hypothesis.

* It is very likely that the Manchus borrowed their theory from the Chinese. In fact, "Yin Chow (殷紂) (1122 B.C.) killed Pi Kan (比干) and dissected his heart to see whether it had seven openings" cf. E. T. Hsieh "A Review of China anatomy from the period of Huangti". C. Med. Journ., 1920. Anat. Suppl., p. 8.

soul leaves the body there is no great chance to call it back and death is inevitable. It does not mean, however, that the corpse, which is not yet decomposed, cannot be revived. Such cases are known and they will be discussed later.

Among the Barguzin and Nerčinsk Tungus I have not been able to find out the details concerning the organization of the soul. They suppose that the soul has its history of migrations, for it is given to the new-born child by dayačun (which is a general term for master spirits) om'i nalkan at the moment when a soul leaves the middle world caused by the activity of spirits and natural senescence. However, since they recognize om'i, irlinkan, also an'an, etc., it is very likely that their system is a composite one, as that of Birarčen, and thus they also recognize the threefold nature of the soul.

If we describe the history of the soul, as it is understood among the Birarčen, it will run as follows. The child is born with what is received from the parents, namely, èrga —the life-breathing and what is received from omor'i i.e. omi—the soul,—the self-reproduction and growth energy. (This conception is rather new; it is connected with an originally non-Tungus complex). The soul an¡an in small children is not stable at all and at any moment may leave the body (an'an—the "shadow, immaterial substance", is an old conception, as the stem preserved in Manchu fajaya || fojeyo). When it is stabilized (the child becomes conscious) the soul—sus'i—consisting of three parts, settles. However, the first soul may occasionally leave the body without causing any great harm, except loss of consciousness, but it cannot leave for a long time. The second soul may also leave the body, but only for a short time as a long absence would result in death. This soul, after death, goes to the world of the dead and is at the disposal of inmunkan and it may later be returned to this world to some male or female child or to an animal, or it may remain unemployed. The third soul remains with the body as long as the body is not decomposed. When it leaves the body it goes to remain with the family members. The conception of threefold soul is a new one, so that in the Birarčen conception different complexes are included: the old one of an'an, the new one of omi, and at last that of the threefold soul—sus'i.

The Manchu idea of soul essentially differs from that of the Birarčen. The èrgèn is received from the father. The threefold soul is given by the spirit opos'i mama. The first soul is the true soul which cannot leave the body without causing death. The second soul may temporarily leave the body which results in dreams and loss of consciousness. The third soul also may leave temporarily without causing death. The third soul returns to the spirit of the lower world ilmunxan and it may be used again as the Birarčen believe. The first or second soul returns to opos'i mama. The non-Tungus origin of this conception is evident.

The disturbances in the stability of the three elements of the soul and their relation to the life-breath (èrga), also temporary leaving of the body by the soul, explains to the Tungus all cases of individual trouble and at the same time confirms their conviction in the correctness of their hypotheses. The methods of regulation of the life of the soul will be treated in two other parts of this work, but now we shall proceed to the possible activity and continuity of the souls.

44. HUMAN FIRST SOUL AND OLORGI FOJENGO EXTERIORATED. This is the simplest case of independent existence and activity of the soul, which can be produced consciously and unconsciously by the people. The case of unconscious leaving of the soul to escape from its placing, which is the human body (*vide supra* Section 43), is especially frequent during early childhood, so a special effort must be made for keeping the soul within the placing. With the growth of children the soul becomes stabilized. However, it may rather easily leave the body and yet without any cognized desire on the part of the owner (placing) of the body, i.e. the man. Yet, owing to a special effort the soul may be consciously and intentionally exteriorated in order to act (1) at a distance since the placing-body, as physical in its nature, cannot be transferred together with the soul; (2) in hidden form for not being recognized; (3) for dealing openly with the similar souls of other people now living or who were living and now are dead and whose souls have no more their placings; at last (4) for dealing with spirits the nature of which is similar to that of the soul.

Such an exterioration of the soul practically occurs very often during dreams when the people want to communicate with other persons and especially during the shamanistic performances. We shall later see that this operation is neither easy nor absolutely harmless, for sometimes the soul may not return to its placing and thus the person may die. Naturally, with the help of certain methods the soul may also be exteriorated by other persons too. Indeed, death is one of ways of exterioration but there will also be exteriorated the other component souls. The simplest case is when the soul is exteriorated by means of unconsciousness, e.g. a blow on the head etc. Yet, the specialists, like shamans also know how to call out the soul and they may re-introduce it into the placing (body) at their will. This side of the question will be discussed when other practical methods are described.

It should be pointed out that the first soul as well as *olorg'i fojeŋo* possesses a very important peculiarity, namely, it represents in its exteriorated form all parts of the body. When it is placed into another placing and the placing is totally or partially destroyed the soul will be also damaged in corresponding parts. Thus after the return of the soul into the original placing (body) the body will also suffer from the damage of the parts of the body corresponding to the damaged parts of the soul. This is the old conception of soul—shadow (*an'an-fan'a—fojeŋo*) which is the basis of "magic" methods for harming other people, widely used by "bad natured" persons.

—————————

BON (BUN) AND IBAGAN. This is a special case when the first soul (and *olorg'i fojeŋo* of the Manchus) and also the second soul (and *čerŋ'i fojeŋo* of the Manchus) leave the body and the *èrga* (the "life") ceases to show its activity, i.e. when the death occurs. Before the complete destruction of the corpse the dead person may revive, if the corpse is used by some spirit (or exteriorated soul) as a placing. The revived body would not possess the characters proper to the living person, because the second soul would be absent, but even physiological functions to some extent might be restored.

Amongst the Tungus of Manchuria, except the Reindeer Tungus, amongst the Manchus, and also the Dahurs, there are many stories regarding such cases. I shall first quote some of them in order to show the idea as to the phenomenon.

In the Birarčen and Kumarčen dialects such a revived corpse is called *boŋ* (rarely *buŋ*, also very rarely by a Manchu term *buaŋi ibaɣan*) (*vide infra*) which ought to be compared with Mongol, Durbut Belse, *boŋ* (compared by A. D. Rudnev with Mongol *bok* || *buŋ*,—the "devil", in Russian translation *čort* which is a very doubtful translation). By the Tungus this term has been probably received from the Dahurs. The Tungus in explanation of *boŋ* would also say *boŋ* is a "fresh (i.e. newly formed) *s'irkul*". However, *s'irkul* is a generic name for all spirits left after the death of people and even sometimes spread over other spirits which may be malevolent. It is not a class of spirits by themselves but rather a "bad word" in reference to the spirits, which also in an abusing sense, may be referred to "bad people." In Manchu it is called *ibaɣan ~ ibaɣan* (Manchu Writ.) corresponding to *ilbaɣan ~ ibaɣan* (Manchu Sp.). The translation given by I. Zaxarov is not correct. Ch. de Harlez gives meaning of *bigan i ibaɣan*: "ibagan, esprit follet habitant les montagnes, les rives des fleuves, les forêts et les buissons" (op. cit p. 21) which translation is also not correct, [*] for it means merely "*ibaga* of non-peopled region". The Manchus, analogous to the Birarčen, would also call it *xutu* which term corresponds to *s'irkul*.

The *boŋ* may be formed in two ways, namely, at the period when the soul has already left the body, but death has not yet occurred; then a spirit, usually one of spirits of other people who could not reach the world of dead people, introduces itself into the body without soul which continues to live and act, but in an abnormal manner. Another case, which is still more common, is that when a spirit introduces itself into the buried corpse which begins to move and behave and may again have physiological needs. So that some cases of mental troubles following sickness, may be classified as *boŋ* especially if the sick person is used as placing by one of the *burkan* (*vide infra*). The formation of *boŋ* usually occurs during the droughts[**] and as a rule only during the period when the temperature is not low, in spring and summer. *Boŋ* has dark-red blood which is known from the experience of those who *killed* them, for after being shot, *boŋ* may die altogether. The reason why the Tungus shoot them is that when the *boŋ* are encountered by the people, the latter may become mad, so it is recommended that *boŋ* be shot at once. It is the same with the spirits. According to some Tungus who are supposed to have met *boŋ*, the *boŋ* are very short in stature,

[*] Still less is correct the translation of *manggiyan* (i.e. *maŋian*): ibagan-i duwali as "compagnon de l'ibagan" (ibid, footnote 8), for it actually means "of the ibagan clan". However, even the Manchu authors of the dictionary—buleku—probably did not know the difference between ibagan and spirits which may enter the placings, for ibagan means the spirits and the placing together while *maŋian* is a spirit.

[**] The drought is described as a natural but accidental phenomenon: tuksaṇin bulörduk jüran, odinin uröduk jüran, i.e. "the fog (steam, clouds) from the marshes comes out (while) the wind from the mountains comes out", so in this way there is no precipitation, the clouds are brought down to the mouths of the rivers and the region is affected by a drought.

less than a metre tall, and they live on the meat of the badger.* This description is rather referred to the Manchu *ibayan* which are supposed by the Tungus to be somewhat different from *boy*.** *Boy* differ from normal people by long hair; they usually have a very small lower jaw or no jaw at all and some other abnormalities,—e.g. a third eye,—and for this reason they hide themselves from men. The *boy* are living on the meat of badgers which they hunt, while *boy* themselves are hunted by dogs and wolves which devour them. Most of *boy* are females. Here I give some cases.

"A man (Birarčen) was hunting alone. On his return from his daily work he saw a woman sitting in his wigwam and hiding her face. Then he gave her some meat which she accepted by extending her hand behind her. So he repeated the same experiment the next day, but this time instead of boiled meat he gave her a piece of raw meat which she ate. Then he decided,—it is a bad sign, he must kill her. He again returned to his wigwam, gave again some meat, asked her some questions to which she did not reply. Then he shot her; she screamed and ran away. Next, morning he followed the blood traces up to a coffin near which a wounded woman, then dead, was found by the side of her new born baby. The man took the male baby-*boy* and educated him. During the childhood of the boy he once fell down and lost his power of speech; afterwards he spat out a large clot of blood. A few days later he began to speak again. When he was grown to manhood, the man who had educated him found him a wife and he married and had children."

Another case. A man was hunting and met on his way a newly-erected coffin (on piles, *vide infra*, Chapter XVII). He heard screams of babies from the coffin, which he opened and in which he found new-born twin babies which he took with him. One of them died soon; the other was educated and was shown to me in the village Celu in 1916. He was an absolutely normal boy. The Tungus believed that their mother was a *boy* who ran away from the coffin. The boy was given a name indicating his origin.

Third case: "A man was successfully hunting. Coming back to his wigwam he found in it a woman. He asked her where was her home and which was her name. To all these questions she replied that she did not know (*b'i os'im sara*). Then they began to live together: she was cooking and looking after the man. Four or five days later he proposed her to share with him his bed and blanket which she accepted. So they slept together. Then they returned (evidently to the permanent station or even village). Everything was good. She was working. Then they married. Three or four months later he again went for hunting (and took her with him). Once she was searching

on his head for lice; then he did the same to her* and he discovered under the hair (on the head) an eye. He was so terrified (by his discovery) that he immediately went to see his clansmen. They decided that she must be *s'irkul* (*boy*). Then for some time he observed her without being noticed,—she was like a human being. Again a fear took him and he together with other people left her alone and migrated ("nomaded") to a distant region."

I have given here three cases considered by the Tungus as *boy*. However, the last case perhaps is not so, for the woman might have been one of those who from time to time run away from other ethnical groups and thus must hide themselves and their names, at the same time remaining unknown to the groups which they join. The "eye" under the hair is a pure imagination due to the fear of the unknown (origin of the woman). The hypothesis of *boy* is a justification of the fear.

According to the Manchus, *ibayan* is the corpse of a dead person which was entered by a *xutu*.** *Ibayan* is covered with hair and instead of normally walking it jumps. Such an *ibayan* may be produced from the corpses of people who died in a bad hour of the day when *xutu* haunt the place. The same may happen if a cat should jump over the corpse and in case the person died by a bad death (*vide infra* Chapter XVII). *Ibayan* leaves the coffin and tomb during droughts.*** When *ibayan* gets out of the tomb it moves only in straight lines and catches in its arms everything which may happen to be on its way. If it catches a human being the latter dies immediately. When *ibayan* is discovered then the Manchus gather the people from the village and kill it with an axe. The body is burnt to ashes. The bodies of the people who were killed by *ibayan*, also trunks of trees caught by *ibayan*, etc. must be burnt together with the *ibayan*. In the regions occupied by the Dahurs, the *ibayan* or *boy* are very frequent, especially in the region near Mergen, in the valley of the Nonni River.

The shamans sometimes call themselves *ibayan* in sign of self-abasement, for minimizing their own importance, and say that they are similar to *ibayan* for they are possessed by the spirits, and not that the spirits are possessed by the shaman, which is supposed to be amongst the good shamans.**** This might be a source of some misunderstandings with the translators into Chinese from Manchu, and from Manchu and Chinese into the European languages.

From the series of stories regarding *ibayan* and *boy* and from the Tungus idea about them it is evident that there may be distinguished the facts (to be more exact, the Tungus ideas about the facts), the facts misinterpreted under the influence of this hypothesis, and further extension of the original hypothesis and modifications of facts under different stimuli, also their increase with the poetic imaginative

---

* An old man once met a group of *boy* which he frightened by shooting with his gun. They ran away and he found a badger with its legs tied as it is prepared for sacrifice. Another man saw a "short man" at whom he shot; the shot missed so a second was fired hitting the "short man" who screamed and disappeared. Then the man lost his way. He surrounded himself with three big fires that night for protection and when daylight came, his mind became stable but he was ill afterwards for a long time.

** This Tungus inference is based upon the comparison of the evidences given by the Manchus and the Tungus relative to *ibayan* and *boy* respectively.

* As to the lousing it may be noted that it is an expression of personal sympathy, as well as sexual love. Cf. B. Malinowski, "The Sexual Life of Savages" and still in a broader setting of the problem R. Yerkes.

** More exactly, the body is entered by one of the souls which are not admitted by *ilmunxan* or the soul which could not reach him. When the second soul *čerg'i fojeŋo* leaves the body then such an errant soul (*olorg'i fojeŋo*) enters the corpse.

*** It ought to be noted that the Manchu burials are not made very deep in the ground (vide infra).

**** Cf. for instance in Nišan Saman the shaman calls herself by this self-abasing name.

creations. The factual side is rather simple: there are cases when the people, especially women, are buried when death does not actually occur, and the buried people are in a lethargic state or merely in the state of profound and long unconsciousness. Such occurrences amongst the Tungus groups may be more frequent than amongst some other groups for among the Tungus the practice of "exterioration of soul" is very common. The women are more susceptible to it than the men. Naturally, if the burial takes place during a cold season the body insufficiently dressed and not warmed is frozen within a few hours and death takes place because of the freezing. It is thus natural that the cases of boy are not observed during the very cold season. The facts of the women who give birth (I have heard of at least two cases, and the child of one case I personally knew) after their "burial" now are evident. The boy have blood and can be killed, they may be hunting, and hunt badgers. The reason why they hunt it is very simple: this animal runs very slowly and it is the only one which can be killed with a simple stick,—other weapons are lacking. The opinion regarding their physical features, as distinct from that of common people, is not uniform and some Tungus recognize in them no difference and even can marry them, as it is seen from Case three. On the other hand, a woman buried and raised again from her tomb is helpless against wolves, or dogs when the latter are sent by man to hunt her. Yet, she, herself, knows perfectly well that she is a boy and thus she must behave as a boy is expected to do. Moreover, she knows that she may be killed and that nobody will believe that she is not a boy. On the other hand, she cannot stay in the coffin when she is awake for anyhow her hunger and her hope to restore her normal position would force her out of the tomb. It is not difficult, for among the Tungus the planks of the coffin are not strongly fastened and among the Manchus the coffin is only covered with earth. The second case, when the woman was not found in the coffin, is natural for she might have run away to obtain food for herself and naturally she could not follow the foot prints of the man who took her children, for she would know what her fate would be. Indeed, the small size of ibayan and their great number gathered for hunting badger, as well as another case, that of a small man, are cases of hallucination or even simple imagination, sometimes under the influence of alcohol (for which reason, according to the Tungus practice, people leaving for a long journey must not drink at all). The jumping of ibayan may also have a certain background of reality, namely, the legs of the corpse are usually tied with a piece of cloth, so that when the legs cannot be untied the only way of moving is by jumping. Whether this was ever observed or is a theoretical supposition of the Manchus I cannot now say. The attacking of people is also natural in self-defence and hope of possible escape from the fate of ibayan.

Indeed, since the fact of not-identified life is a fact which may heavily oppress the consciousness of the people who decide upon the burial, the cases of boy and ibayan must be represented as cases of an abnormal order, whence the naturalistic facts are supplied with the imaginary details and the number of cases is increased.

The Tungus thus solve two problems: they explain the state of lethargy as an effect of interaction of partial souls and in these cases they have a new proof of the existence of the multiple soul. As shown in the Tungus mind these cases are not spirits, but physical bodies serving as placings for errant souls (spirits). Therefore we cannot include these cases under the heading of spirits.

45. GROUPS OF SPIRITS When an adult Tungus dies there is a problem of importance,—to rid this world of his or her soul. As a matter of fact, this must be done with a certain skill by the people who know practical methods of sending the soul to the world of dead people,—buni. These methods will be described in the Part 3. However, some souls connot be transferred there owing to (1) sudden death without witnesses; (2) accidental death due to various causes, except war; (3) inability of the relatives, shamans, or other people who have to transfer the souls. In such a case the soul remains in this world so to say free and beyond any control, and it may find either a temporary or permanent placing. Yet, some of these souls may become errant souls entering various placings for a short time and always doing harm to the living people. Such souls are called sirkul in Bir. and Kum. and zutu in Manchu. As shown, by the Tungus and Manchus these terms are sometimes wrongly referred to the spirits and even people, also boy and ibayan. But such categories as sirkul and zutu are not at all definite, so it is much better to avoid the use of these terms. Those souls which reach the lower world do not cease to exist. They form a special group of spirits, bunil, which live more or less like the people of this world and they also need some attention, at least periodically, for they may visit this world again. These are relatives, clansmen and ancestors.

The importance of the individual soul-spirits is not the same. Some of these spirits may become very powerful—both malevolent and benevolent—some of them may even be used by the shamans. I shall describe them, systematically going from less important to more important spirits.

———

ARENK'I are spirits produced from the souls which did not reach the lower world. Under this name they are known amongst the Kumarčen, Birarčen and also the Tungus of the Amur Gov.[*] Under the name ar'inkʻi amongst the Tungus of Yakutsk Gov. (Lam. and Tum.) spirits of the same type are also known, but they are identified by P.V. Olenin with the Yakut abasy.[**]

Etymology of this word is that it may be derived from the stem ar—to "revive" (intrans.), e.g. referred to the people [arran (Bir.),—he revives], vegetation (after winter), insects, hibernating animals, etc. Since arenkʻi is nomen agendi from ar it may be translated "reviver", "one who makes to revive", but not "resurrector". The arenkʻi have no body. They are very numerous in the forest and marshes. However, they sometimes penetrate

---

[*] The Tungus of Saxalin Island and Amur Gov. use this term for the souls which have not received special church services,—Requiem of Russians. Indeed, this is a new function.

[**] In the dictionary of the missionaries, e.g. Lamuts, ar'inks is translated as "devil", "tempter". The missionaries in the Enisay Gov. used the same stem or for forming a series of words for "resurrection", "resurrected Jesus Christ," etc.

to the store houses erected even near the wigwams. They place themselves in rotten, hollow trees, also sometimes even in living trees. When the Tungus cut down such a tree they may hear: *onōī!*—i.e. "painful," screamed by these spirits. Such an accident is sufficient for causing a serious illness with a fatal issue,—the people lose their minds and die. When these spirits stay in the rocks, they may be called *kadarn'i s'irkul.*—(of the rock *s'irkul*), or *urȫn'i s'irkul* (of the mountains *s'irkul*). These spirits are numerous on the banks of the Amur River. As a rule they are more numerous near graves. The *areŋk'i* may be seen in the form of light, usually bluish or reddish, also sometimes moving, but when people approach them, they run farther away. They whistle. They produce echo. During great frost the noises produced by ice and trees are ascribed to the activity of *areŋk'i*. Their activity is also seen in the phenomenon of luminosity of soil, rotten wood, etc.,—the wood or soil are "burning" because of the presence of the spirit, but there is no heat. During stormy weather their activity greatly increases. These spirits are not very harmful for the people who have strong will power and self-control, but the fearful people may fall under their influence. So that the echo sometimes may lead the hunter astray and knowing that this is the spirits' activity the man must be very careful in interpreting the significance of the phenomenon, and pay no attention to it. It is evident that when *areŋk'i* introduces itself into a corpse the latter may become *boŋ*. They do harm to people by throwing small stones, branches of trees etc. at them. These spirits are afraid of fire which may protect man against them; even a burning match may protect man. The spirits are described by the Kumarčen as miserable beings: they have only skin and eyes; they have no tobacco or meat and thus they are always hungry for in their food they depend upon the people's generosity. Generally speaking they are mischievous, especially where there are found in great numbers, e.g. near graves and particularly in the locality called *Orodon*, on the banks of the Kumara River, and they always steal meat and make all kinds of trouble for the people; they whistle, make fires etc. The season of their greatest activity is the autumn, but they are badly affected by the snow from which they must protect themselves. When a person is alone he may see them, but when there are many people these spirits do not show themselves. According to the Kumarčen, they are divided into clans which fight between themselves. Their "master" is *inmunkan.*

How the stories regarding these spirits are formed may be shown by two facts recorded among the Birarčen. (1) Two men were hunting. They were surprised by a very severe storm with lightning, thunder and wind. They could not make a fire and they had no dog with them. The whole night they protected themselves under the hunting wigwam (hemispherical made of bark *kūm'i*). The *areŋk'i* were whistling, throwing small stones, and branches against the wigwam; rotten wood was burning. As a matter of fact, to pass a stormy night without fire and a dog (the spirits are afraid of dogs), under a willow wigwam, when at any moment it may be destroyed (e.g. by falling of rotten trees) is not a pleasant experience. (2) "A man who was drunk went on his journey. He saw at night two roe-deer. He shot. The roe-deer did not run (which is indicative that they are not real roe-deer but spirits *areŋk'i*). Then he fell asleep. In the night he saw again four roe-deer. He fired nineteen

times but each time missed and the roe-deer did not run away. It is true, he was lucky to kill a big male roe-deer next morning. The next night he again saw (*areŋk'i* in the form of) fire, as big as a human head which moved towards him. Then he screamed and burnt a match; the spirit began to reduce and become reddish before disappearing altogether." Indeed, a case of delirium is evident.

Thus it may be formulated: various natural phenomena like luminosity of soil and rotten wood, multiple echo, errant fires (ignis fatuus) of marshes, noises produced by some physical bodies with the lowering of temperature, also all noises which cannot be understood, are interpreted as activity of *areŋk'i* and their existence is proved by these facts. The cases of fear and imagination, also of delirious hallucinations increase the number of facts for supporting the hypothesis. The cases of delirious insanity are ascribed to the influence of these spirits which are not dangerous for a strong mind, the Tungus believe.

However, these spirits may become stabilized in some localities and become, so to say permanent in making trouble for the people. Such is, for instance, *kadarn'i* or *urȫn'i s'irkul* which inhabit rocky places and mountains. This spirit is especially dangerous when the man is alone. First it frightens the man, who being already terrified, falls into the spirit's clutches. The people perish especially often during the winter, because of the spirit called *doŋgnotočo s'irkul* (*doŋgnoto*—"to freeze"). The spirit also appears in the form of a man who suggests sitting down before a hillock (in frozen marshes) or in front of a bush as though it were a fire. The man then takes off his clothing (as the Tungus usually do), and spreads his hands before the imaginary fire, to warm himself whereupon he soon falls asleep and is soon frozen and so dies. Naturally, the man's soul becomes a new errant spirit. This spirit may lead the people astray by different methods, but chiefly by influencing the mind. So that all cases of loss of one's way are ascribed to these spirits for the Tungus are sure of their own ability of orientation when they are normal. These spirits sometimes take people and keep them for a long time. For instance, a spirit of this kind caught a man, took him to a cave on the banks of the Amur River (near the village Radde), and kept him there for several years; the man returned to his people but he could not explain what he had done and how he had been living. During the hunting these spirits sometimes go ahead of the hunter and send away the animals; in such a case the only way to stop their activity is to give them some "food" (*vide infra*).

The places where people have perished owing to the drowning, being frozen, killed by the trees etc. are called *galegda* and the people must avoid them. Any man who should happen to be there would be influenced by the spirits to act in the same way as the people who perished: e.g. to commit suicide by hanging, to go into deep water (the Tungus do not swim very much), and to expose himself naked before a shrub, tree, or a hillock as though it were a fire etc. The Tungus say that in the place where there has been a case of drowning, every one or two years there will be some more similar cases.

Some of these spirits may become quite powerful and influential. They may become "masters" of a mountain, small region etc. Such a spirit is called *ajelga*, or *urȫn'i ajelga* (of the mountain *ajelga*). In the Khingan Mountains there is a peak (mountain) known under the name of *borul doksŭkŭ. Ajelga* is living exactly there. It is black and also its horses. During the hunting, it produces noise and in all possible ways makes hunting difficult. This spirit, after a night of troubles (the spirit used to make trouble on the salty soil especially liked by the cervines) was seen by the Tungus, whence its description is so well known. *Ajelga* may cause very serious sickness. The only way to manage *ajelga* is to make a good sacrifice of any animal including the elk (*Cervus alces*) which may happen to have been killed. This spirit may assume the form of an animal. In fact "a Maakagir man (Birarčen) was hunting and saw a deer which he shot, after which the animal changed into a man. The Maakagir man then fell seriously ill. Since that time the people of clan Maakagir make two wooden anthropomorphic placings about 20 centimetres long, or two hillocks, by which they erect a *toro* (a post) and an elevated platform (for sacrifice). From them, other people learnt how to do it."

Among other clans the sacrifice is simplified, but as a placing for this spirit, two small hillocks are used. In former days, according to the Birarčen, they carefully observed preventive methods for avoiding bringing out *ajelga* when they stayed near large mountains and graves. After sunset they did not make any noise, did not cut trees, stopped the children's crying, and so on. If it were attracted it might become like a *sĕvĕy*. Such a case occurred with a shaman of Malakul clan; this spirit was mastered by a shaman who now (1916) lives in *Pŭli* (near the Sun River) and *ajelga* became *sĕvĕy*. Naturally, since that time danger from this spirit is greatly reduced. (cf also *supra*, Chapter XI).

XUTU. I have already pointed out that this term is not applied to a definite group of spirits but it may be used in the same broad sense as *s'irkul.* Yet, perhaps it is still broader for the Manchus admit that even *endur'i* and *mava* can harm the people in which case they also may be called *xutu.* However, the Manchu language possesses no special term for spirits of the class like the above discussed *areyk'i* and others. Perhaps, the term *sula* is one to which reference is made. *Sula* literally meaning "free" "unemployed", produce very great harm when they introduce themselves. However, this term is rarely used and the Manchus usually specify the kind of *sula*, or *xutu.*

The Manchu say that any *fojeyo* which did not reach the world of dead people is a *xutu.* [*] Such a spirit may appear when the clan spirits are temporarily absent or when they do not take care of the people, *voǒko karmaraku taraku,* i.e. "*voǒko* guardian does not catch, stop (—the spirit)."

Xutu may originate from the souls of people who committed suicide in any form or from the people who died through poisoning; but since the soul cannot cross rivers, e.g. the Amur River, the souls of those Manchus who die on the Russian side of the river remain as *xutu* (Here it is presumed that the way to Manchu Hades lies on the Chinese

side of the river!); *balju xutu*[*] are formed from the hairs of corpses[**]; *fažĕmĕ pučĕye xutu* (*fasime bučexe xutu,* Manchu Writ.) are formed from the souls of people who have committed suicide by hanging; *b'ira xutu* (i.e. the river *xutu*) are formed from the souls of drowned people; *moroskun pučĕye xutu* are formed from the souls of people killed (even in case the body is buried) and the most common case is that of *pučĕye xutu* (dead people *xutu*). The number of these spirits may be increased by addition of other spirits, but the Manchus are not sure as to their origin. These are e.g. *mayga mo xutu* ("oak tree"), *jagda mo xutu* ("pine tree"), *bana xutu* ("place") etc. Therefore it is not recommended to bring home trees that have been cut near cemeteries. The Manchus have succeeded in observing these spirits, so they describe them as being very short in stature (less than three feet tall) with flat noses and very small lower jaws, dressed in short coats like those of the Dahurs.

These spirits fear men much more than women, so that when the latter are alone the spirits produce all kinds of noise. Generally, they begin their activity in the dark when the lamp is blown out. For the reason of the existence of these spirits the Manchus never cut off their nails,—the *xutu* may use them. These spirits are more numerous in the villages than in the cities. One of the peculiarities of *xutu*, as well as other Manchu spirits, is that there is no shadow (from light) (the *ibayan* naturally has a shadow.) These spirits may cause strong headache, if one meets them. They frighten the people; even some disturbances of mind may occur which are not, however, very dangerous. These spirits are not usually treated with sacrifices but they are frightened by the human voice and usually run away. Also, they do not like the light. However, they may become very dangerous when they succeed in introducing themselves into a corpse. Then they become *ibayan xutu* (*vide supra* Section 44). Indeed, it is also different when these spirits turn into powerful spirits, as we have seen among the Birarčen. In this form they are called by different names and are treated in an entirely different manner. This will be described in the following part.

ODJAN *Ojan* is a special group of spirits among the groups investigated known under this name only among the Barguzin and Nerčinsk Tungus. *Ojan,* in so far as I can see, means merely "master."; Their history, according to a Barguzin shaman, is as shown. "In olden times the earth was burnt.[***] Nothing was left. The *buga* remained alone, two children,—a boy and a girl,—two do-

---

[*] The Manchus compare it with the Chinese kai. However, xutu may also be called (and it will be a polite form) nai ("of the earth") torg'i ("inner part", "inside") [cf. dorgi (Manchu. Writ.)] n'alma ("people"); but the Manchus would add n'alma akú ("not man"). Let us remark that although the man (n alma) is living on the earth he cannot be called nai n'alma but welyun,—i.e. "living", "alive."

[*] I. Zaxarov's translation does not seem to be correct, at least for the present time.

[**] This xutu is regarded as one of the harmless "home" xutu (the etymology of balju xutu is not clear). During the night, it approaches the people (the Manchus sleep on the heated beds with their heads turned toward the inside of the room and feet toward the outside walls) and pulls out their hair. The head gradually becomes bald. The spirit may be seen as light (compare arenk'i), but one cannot catch the spirit unless one puts on one's shoes backward which the xutu do not like. If one succeeds in catching the light one will find one's own hair.

[***] Cf. the same idea amongst the Tungus of Manchuria and other groups as well.

mesticated reindeer fawns, two (?),* two reindeer (Cervus Elaphus). The boy grew up and the girl grew up. They began to multiply. *Buya* came. So they lived and became about thirty people. Then they were ashamed,—too many people is a shame.** They said, 'Let us hide*** fifteen children without reindeer.' They left fifteen children in a bad place, in a stony region, among the rocks. They (the hidden children) became like *buga;*—we cannot see them. They help us. From those fifteen who left we have originated. So it was."

Since that time the *ojan* live in all three worlds. In the middle world (earth) they choose the places with stones and rocks, useless for the Tungus. For instance, they live on the tops of mountains which surround the lake Baunt (in Northern Transbaikalia). In the valley of the river *Usoi* (a tributary of the Great Amalat) there is a cave with an entrance descending almost vertically to the bottom that cannot be seen,—the Tungus found very often roe-deer's bones left near the entrance, and even once a hunting bag; these were evidence of *ojan's* activity.

The Tungus have many "facts" supporting their hypothesis. So for instance, "A young shaman, twenty eight years old, was not recognized by other people. Once there were many people in the wigwam. An old man, weak and tired, suddenly appeared and said, 'How do you do! There no more place (to sit).' The shaman took one of the men away the seat and invited the old man in. The old man sat down. The shaman ordered the slaughtering of a reindeer and served the old man with meat. The old man ate and wanted to leave (the wigwam). The shaman told the people present: 'Take him out with honour.' They replied: 'But there is nobody here.' Then he, himself escorted the old man out and coming back to the people gathered said 'Why did you not do it?'. The shaman was happy."

Another Barguzin Tungus saw on the top of a treeless mountain near the sources of the *Cina* River (a left tributary of the Vitim) a hollowed place, ashes, a teapot, cups etc. There he saw the *ojan* but was unable to communicate more details for he lost his mind.

A Nerčinsk Tungus was very drunk and after a night of trouble caused by *ojan* at day-break saw a man of unusual size. When the man began to approach, the Tungus fell down and lost consciousness. After that time he lost his mind. The man of unusual size was *ojan*.

Generally, when a person meets *ojan*, the person becomes abnormal,—losing his mind. Therefore one must avoid the *ojan*. The Tungus must not descend into the above mentioned cave for they would be destroyed by the *ojan*. They must not go too far from the camp after sunset, for the *ojan* might steal them. These spirits always attack the shaman during his performances, by shooting arrows which may hit the shaman unless he turns his back protected with iron ("placings") toward the flying arrows or catches the arrows with his hands. In former days there were some cases in which those spirits killed the shamans.

---

* In the copy of my MS. which I have, there is omission of a word,—in so far as I remember, "elka".
** It is not clear why it is "shame". I suppose that the expression was not absolutely correctly used or the translation is wrong. However, I find no other suitable word. It is possible that it merely is: "they became anxious",—having too many people causes anxiety.
*** "Hide" practically means "to leave alone, to let them die."

The *ojan* as other spirits of this group very often lead the people astray and the Tungus lose their way.

The mode of life of these spirits does not differ from that of the Tungus,—they have their wigwams, their reindeer, which cannot be seen by the common people, and they hunt animals. But owing to the original mischief done to them (leaving them among the rocks) they are not friendly to living men. Sometimes they make difficulties in hunting, they frighten the people, they catch the people, they make the people lose their minds. On the other hand, the same spirits may help the man in his undertakings and they are protectors of the reindeer. In fact, if a Tungus does not treat the reindeer kindly the spirit may kill such a man. It is especially strict with the slaughtering of the reindeer in which a gun must not be used.

These spirits have no special placings. When the Tungus want to make these spirits benevolent they give them some "food" (sacrifice) and generally when the Tungus eats or drinks, he throws into the air small pieces of food or a few drops of liquid (tea or spirits) as the usual sacrifice, almost automatically performed. Many troubles which lately have occurred amongst the Tungus are explained as due to the neglect of these spirits. In former days the Tungus very often used to offer sacrifices of reindeer to these spirits, but at the present time (1912-1913) this is rarely done. In case the spirits become too annoying the Tungus address themselves to the other spirits—*irlinkan* and *nalkan* which are supposed to be masters (*dayačan*) of *ojan*. The spirits must not be called *ojan* (It is understood when the Tungus speak to them, especially in the night time when the spirits may respond to their name even without being addressed.) but they must be called *am'i* (father) or *am'itisal* (fathers).

46. ANCESTORS. NORTHERN TUNGUS SYSTEM

The souls which reach the world of dead people do not remain indifferent to the living people. Amongst all Tungus groups they do play an important part. We have just seen that in case the soul cannot reach the other world it becomes a real danger to the people. Therefore, after death one of first aims of the living people is to send the souls to their right place. When the souls are admitted for permanent living in the lower world they do not need so much attention and they do not so much annoy the living people.

In all Tungus languages the terms for "ancestors" are derived from *bū*—to die. So we have *buni* (Barg. Bir. Kum. Khin.), *buno* (RTM.) (Bar. Nerč.), *bunil* (Nerč.) etc. and merely *bučo* ("dead"), etc. in the sense of dead people's souls in the lower world, or even the Lower World. Hades. According to the Tungus conception, the conditions of life in *buni* are about the same as those in this world. The souls need and like some food, they need dress, they need many other things as the living people do and even perhaps somewhat more for the country (world) in which they live is not attractive at all. First of all, it is a realm of darkness and cold. Yet, the souls which are reduced to their immaterial existence are still worrying about the people left in this world. Moreover, many of them, according to some Tungus at least, have to pay for their mistakes made during their life-time.

Buni is located in the north-western section of the

world, the entrance being located at the most northern point reached by the sun during the summer. It may be noted that this point is subject to some variations owing to the latitude, so it may be found in NWW and NNW. However, I have never heard of other directions. The way to *buni* is long and difficult. The way goes across lakes (e.g. amongst the Barguzin Tungus across Lake Baikal), rivers and ranges of mountains, until it reaches the river which is controlled by the spirit *gaĭ* among the Barguzin Tungus and which must be crossed before entering *buni*. The way is haunted by different spirits which want to catch the souls. According to the Barguzin Tungus, the sea (lake) coast and a part of the way is watched by a bear and the souls are located in the wooden houses *gula* (square, with a roof!). According to the Birarčen, on the road there is also a raven which watches the soul and flies to the family of the soul's owner when the soul begins to move towards *buni*. According to the Reindeer Tungus of Manchuria, one has to go NW and cross a layer of earth seven fathoms deep before reaching *buno*, where there is no sun. The Birarčen and Kumarčen, under the Manchu influence have adopted the idea that this world is separated from *buni* by three rivers; the first one is the Red River across which a one-legged man carries the souls in his canoe. This man is called in Manchu *toxolo age*, i.e. the "lame brother." Indeed, he is the same personality as the Greek one and the Red River is the Greek *Stix*. The second river is the Yellow River, after crossing which the soul meets with *Mongoldaĭ Nakču*, i.e. *Mongoldaĭ* "senior of the mother's clan", which examines the case before allowing the soul to cross the Black River beyond which *Inmunkan* reigns. This description corresponds to that given in the Manchu book *Niśan Śaman*. On the way to *buni* the sun becomes more distant and lower, so that the light decreases. Before the entrance the light is like that of twilight; at last there is no light at all and after crossing a high range, there is *buni*.

According to the Birarčen, beyond *buni* there is *èla gurun* from which the souls never return and it is a real death and vanishing of the soul. The souls of very bad people are sentenced to this punishment by *Inmunkan*. In the case of good conduct during life the soul may even remain without being sent to *Inmunkan* and it will become *endur'i*. The soul which has passed several times through people, may also remain as *endur'i*. This is, of course, a new theory adapted to the idea of recompense for high morality. Such people-souls—are called *durōv'i dasača*, i.e. the law (regulations, modus) corrected (improved). In the case of very bad conduct of a person, his soul may be refused admission and thus it would become errant *s'irkul*, already described, or it may be left in *buni* for expiation of sins and also it may be killed. It may also be transferred to an animal of low standing, e.g. the mule, insects, etc. However, in the eyes of the Tungus this is not a degradation but it does not help to attain eternity. The second death is also adopted by the Barguzin and Nerčinsk Tungus as a probable issue. These Tungus and the Reindeer Tungus of Manchuria admit that the souls of people of good conduct may also be admitted to *wyiski*, where there are found some "spirits-masters", instead of to *buni*. Such good people are called *haja* (RTM) and *mayun* (Barg. Nerč.). Together with good people the rich people also are admitted to *wyiski* as *mayun*. I think that in these cases we have partial adoption of the

Russian complex.

The spirits staying in *buni*, according to the Birarčen, are divided into two groups, namely, *ileli buni* whose names are mentioned during the sacrifice and which may be harmful or useful to the people, and which are not further than the fourth generation, and all other *buni* which are called *ajor buni*. The latter are not of importance and they cannot harm nor do any good to the living people.

The aspect of these spirits, when they come to this world, is pitiful: the spirits are hungry, weak, hardly moving along their stony way in the twilight (cf. *infra* Chapter XVII, the text of prayer). However, they are not harmless and the living people may often suffer from their mischief. So, for instance, an old Kumarčen greatly suffered from them,—he had very bad eczema and swelling of the legs, his two horses were killed by them, etc. The chief trouble was that the old man did not exactly know which deceased relative was angry with him and what was wanted, —this might have been his father or his mother or his junior brother. In such a case the only way is to give a good sacrifice. Sometimes, *buni* do not give *mahin* so that the hunter cannot kill the animals. In this case the *buni's* usual way of acting is to make the hunter temporarily blind, or send off the roe-deer, or change the normal refraction of rays (the Tungus say, "like in water") which gives a wrong position of the animal etc. These spirits may sometimes be responsible for a real insanity which requires great effort on the part of the shaman of the clan. The Birarčen admit that a menace of beating the *buni* and a promise to leave them without food may be quite effective and may make the spirits less aggressive. Placings for these spirits are always made in the form of an anthropomorphic straw figure about sixty centimetres long with two arms and two legs supplied with two toes but perhaps there is no particular intention of making only two toes but only the straw material does not permit of giving more details. This placing is sitting on another placing, a dog, made also of straw.

MANCHU SYSTEM   The Manchu system in many a respect is different from that observed among other Tungus groups. As to the structure of the lower world it is in main lines adopted by the Tungus of Manchuria so I will not repeat here what has already been discussed, and for details I shall refer to the Manchu book *Niśan Śaman*. The Manchu lower world is located in the southwestern section and is built up with a still greater similarity to the world in which the Manchus live. This is partly due to the existence of lists of ancestors, well preserved in written form. It is peopled by a great number of spirits, officials keeping gates, writing records (*n'almabè k'arara endur'i*—the spirit keeper of the book), the spirits of mules, horses oxen, pigs etc. but sheep, dogs, monkeys etc. are lacking. These spirits are also called *endur'i* and they are under *Ilmunxan* orders. The Manchu picture is a complex of elements borrowed from Buddhism and Taoism.

If the soul *fajayŋaĭ fojeŋo* is admitted by *Ilmunxàn*, it may be transferred to another man, or animal or it may be left in the lower world. If the man lived as he should his soul may be given to a child, even may become either *endur'i* or *fučʹkʹi* (*mava fučʹkʹi*) and it may become a guardian spirit or *vočko*. But if he was a bad man his soul may be incarnated into the animal used by the people to whom he caused harm during his life. However, this soul may not also be admitted as it happens, for instance, in the case of suicide. Then it also becomes a *xutu*. But even in this case there are some issues which will be discussed later. The third soul leaves the body on the seventh day after death and remains in the other world, unless the soul could not be taken there, especially if the man died before the limit given to him and known from the book of life, kept in the other world. Such souls, as we have seen, become *xutu*.

The essential difference between the Manchu and the Tungus system is that the Manchu ancestors may become spirits-guardians and they would be called *mafa* or *mafari* (Writ.) (plural) *mavarʹi* (Sp.). However, this term referred to the superior classes of relatives (*vide* SOM), is also referred to some spirits which are not at all real ancestors, as a sign of honour and esteem. As a matter of fact, in such a function they do not act like "ancestors", but as any other spirits of importance. Therefore they will be treated in the following Chapter XIII.

All clan-ancestors who are admitted to the lower world are now called *pʹoyxn vočko*, but the same term *vočko* is referred to the shamanistic spirits (*vide infra*). In Manchu Writ. it is *večeku;* the shamans call them *věčin* or *wečin*. In Chinese these terms were rendered in a way which indicates that the Manchu terms cannot be derived from Chinese. * The etymology in Manchu gives no more hints, for the verb *veče* (*mbʹi*),—to "sacrifice to *vočko*", and *věčٔn*,—the "sacrifice", do not help at all, the verb itself might be of secondary origin. ** The same spirits may be also called *sagdasʹi vočko*, i.e. "the old ancestors-spirits", and even too short in Chinese *japu* (家 譜), i.e. the family record,—used in the sense of "clan list."

Besides *vočko*, *věčěku*, *věčin* there are some other terms for this class of spirits. They are sometimes called *beise*— "princes", as it may be seen from the list of *amba wuse* clan spirits (*vide infra*.). Yet, there may be used other honourable addresses. The *vočko* call themselves, i.e. when they are introduced into the shaman, *ěndu*, which ought to be connected with *enduri*, *enduriṇa*, etc. It is difficult to give an English translation of this term,—it is referred to

the high spirits *endurʹi*, to the souls which do not migrate from one animal to another but remain free, to the souls of emperors; yet, it may be referred to the monks, to wise, clever people, and so on. Perhaps it may be translated "saint, immortal, wise". One meets with another term which is an usual term, when the spirit is introduced into the placings for sacrifice, namely, *jukten ~ jukte.* For instance, in Manchu *monʹi vočko* ("our spirits") is equivalent to *monʹi jukten*, so they say in prayers *věčěrě věčěku*, *juktere jukten*, where *věčěmbi* means to "perform the rites", and *juktembi*,—to "sacrifice to the spirits". However, I. Zaxarov and Manchu dictionaries give *jukten*,— "the sacrifice." I do not venture to explain why the meaning of *jukten* has changed. There is one more expression in reference to the spirit, namely, *ělen* by which term the spirits refer to themselves, per the shaman's mouth naturally. So we have exprssion *monʹi ělen de gemu say taifin*, i.e. (solicit) "to our people all good and peaceful", while in the ordinary language and in reference to the human groups one has to say *monʹi pôdě* (Manchu Sp.), or *monʹi pʹoyundě*, i.e. "to our family (clan)".

The Manchu idea about *věčěku* is that this is *a group of ancestors of the given exogamic unit*, which has also its own administrative organization headed by *mokunda*. The Manchu has the following expression: "how many exogamic units and chiefs, so many (complexes of) spirits."* The Manchu borrowed from the Chinese their method of recording the clansmen into a list from which one may find the relations between the members of the clan.** The list is called *věčěku mafai těmgětu* i.e. "spirit ancestor's certificate", which corresponds exactly to Chinese *ja-pu* (*vide supra*) ; the same is also called *sagdasʹi vočko*, i.e. "the old ancestors—spirits", and even in Chinese (*japu*). Every clan has its own list which is in charge of an elected clan chief,—*mokunda*. Every three years on the clan meeting

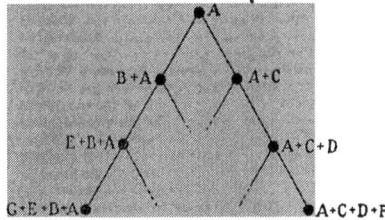

---

* Although the Chinese characters used for rendering *vočko*, *věčeku*, and *věčin*, are selected with hints as to the meaning of these terms, still these expressions are not Chinese. For *večeku* and *večin* there are given the following transcriptions: 我家戶 (or 古) [phonetically *wejʹaxū* (or kŭ)], which in translation gives "my", "family", "house, family, door" (or "ancient") and 我覾 [phonetically *wečin*] which in translation gives "my", "relatives", the latter being a very frequently used character for expression of the idea of closeness, and particularly various classes of relatives.

** The etymology seemed to be very simple to Ch. de Harlez who has connected the stem *veče* with Sanscrit and Avestic *yaj*, *yaz* "honorer d'un culte", "offrir un sacrifice." However, the difficulty is that, the suffix ( ) ku is not one which may make an adjective, as Harlez supposed (ibid p. 14), but the nearest function of this suffix is that forming nomen agendi (cf. I Zaxarov, Gram. p. 72, §42, 6.). Indeed, in this sense *večeku* might have meaning of "placing" with the help of which the spirits were offered their sacrifices. Then, *večeku* was not originally a term for "spirit". However, in Manchu Sp. the verb *večembʹi* is used only when the sacrifice is given, while there are other terms for actions with the shaman's spirits *vočko*. Yet, the ancestors—spirits are not called *večeku* but *pʹoyun vočko*. Thus the etymology of the term *večeku* is not clear.

* Ch. de Harlez's (op. cit. p. 13) translation "les génies domestiques, protecteurs du foyer et de la famille, mais surtout les âmes des ancêtres . . ." is not correct. The Manchu dictionary (the Mirror, XIII, 9 section) is not correct for not only these spirits are honoured at home. A. Rudnev gives *weičeṇ* which corresponds to *večin* and which certainly is a term modified owing to the Chinese phonetic complex. Yet, these spirits as shown are not only shamanistic spirits. I. Zaxarov's translation based on Chinese and Manchu sources is erroneous and misleading, namely, "the spirits of heaven and earth, spirit of the house—penates," compared with Mongol *ەyḡot*, with idol, etc.

** Regarding the clan organization vide my study "Social Organization of the Manchus", which may help in understanding of the problems regarding the spirits.

the list is revised and completed. The persons belonging to other clans are not allowed to see the list.* It is evident that the people recorded in these lists are different in different clans (at the present time,—*mokun*). However, since the clans as new exogamic units always are in the process of formation and re-grouping, many clan lists have common ancestors, for the oldest ancestors recorded are reproduced in the newly formed clans as their own ancestors. This is shown in the scheme above, vide p. 143.

Moreover, since the keeping of the List among the Manchus was introduced rather late, many clans could not go very far into their genealogies. However, with the translation and transcription of the Manchu clan names into Chinese, when the Chinese clan names were often taken for Manchu clans, the Manchus confused the names with their bearers and very soon began to include into their lists the ancestors which were known to the Chinese bearers of the same characters for their own Chinese clans. Therefore, in many Manchu clan-histories we find Chinese traditions as to the Chinese clans. Owing to this, the Manchu clans sometimes have common ancestors which are not truly so, and even which are not Manchus. Yet, since the length of clan-lists becomes excessive and such lists practically impossible to be copied and preserved, the Manchus began to abbreviate them. So that some of the lists about which I could gather information were a mere collection of meaningless names written in certain order but with no connexion between the names (relatives) to be found. Indeed, the periods near to our times are better represented. Owing to the fact that some traditions are connected with the names of some ancestors, their names have more chance for being preserved. In this way there is gradually produced a selection of ancestors worthy of attention while the other ancestors are gradually forgotten. Thus the clanlist actually represents in a detailed manner only a few generations, while the earlier generations become poorer and poorer and at last they are merged into the confusion of traditions. The consequence is evident,—the ancestors regardless of their names and connexions ought to be symbolized. The Manchus did this in the form of "placings" for spirits, which in all clans (nowadays, *mokun*) must be naturally different, and actually they are so. For instance, the placings for *p'oyun vočko* of the *kor'jo xala* consist of two groups of five and nine silk ribbons called *sorgun*, about thirty-five, to forty centimetres long, and four to five centimetres wide. During the sacrifice they are hung up to a stand in front of which there are put some pieces of silk tissue. The number of ribbons and their colour may vary, but as a rule the numbers must be odd. In some clans the placings consist only of either silk pieces or ribbons. As distinct character of the *iči manju* placings they include some wooden placings in the form of three horses. However, one of the *fè manju* clans, namely, *tura xala* has three horses on one of which there is image of a human face. Formerly their complex was similar to that of other *fè manju* clans, but they have lost their *köli* (written rite and enumeration of *vočko*) and since that time they have no more *p'oyun saman*, who used to deal with these spirits. In the case of division of the exogamic clans there must be done also division of the placings for spirits which are identified with the spirits themselves, for beginning from

that very moment the new spirits are not "worshipped" by all members of the clan before its division. The *Moygo* clan has a quite different kind of placing for its clan-spirits, namely, there are five wooden anthropomorphic (with legs, arms, faces, eyes, noses) placings, about fifty or sixty centimetres long, dressed in silk and attached to a piece of silk. The members of the clan *koir'i* can use and pray the spirits of the *moygo* clan. The reason is that the *koir'i* originally were not numerous but they had a *ta saman* (*vide infra*). Then these two clans formed *kapĕ'i* i.e. double (clan). It is quite peculiar to *moygo* clan that they bury, together with the corpses of their clansmen, placings for clan-spirits. However, this custom has been recently given up. Owing to this practice some of *moygo mokun* have less than five placings. In one of the New Manchu (*iči manju*) clans there is a special placing consisting of *muĵuya n'imaya vočko*, i.e. "the carp fish spirit", made of wood, and three *B'iyen vočko*, also anthropomorphic wooden placings. Some New Manchu clans, as e.g. *voufala* clan, have *samdara n'uryan vočko*—i.e. "for shamanizing a picture spirit", which is called also *poi* or *p'oyun vočko* and they usually have a very limited number of Chinese-like pictures of ancestors. *. The ancestors-spirits may have reserved for them a special horse or even several horses which are supposed to be used for riding by the spirits. Such a horse is brought into the house, put in front of the placings for spirits, and silk ribbons are attached to the mane—*sorgun voitaxa mor'in*,—i.e. ribbon attached horse,—and burning incense is brought near to the nostrils of the animal. Such a horse cannot be used by the women and clansmen wearing mourning dress. The horses are chosen among those which have been cured by prayers addressed to the spirits *vočko*. The placings, in a box, are put in their usual place reserved for them—on the *amba nayan*, the heated stove-bed facing the entrance, in the left corner called *tal xos'i* (cf *da xošo*, of Manchu Writ.)—"the principal corner". Only once a year, on the days of yearly sacrifice, they are taken out and placed as shown before. They are kept together with the list of clansmen, so nobody can touch them. Naturally these restrictions are especially rigourous for the women who are not clan-people and who may have menstrual blood.

The character of the spirits also is different, which may be seen in the difference of sacrifices; for instance, some spirits do not accept blood sacrifice. So that e.g. in *vouza* (even *vuza*) clan the spirits do not take it and the placing must be carefully hidden when the bloody sacrifice is given to *apkai endur'i*. In this clan the number of ribbons is very large. Yet, the spirits in some clans require different kinds of blood sacrifice, e.g. mutton, pig, etc. **

Yet, there is a very important division of spirits into two groups, namely, those of the day road (*ineyi ĵoyun vočko*) and those of night road (*jamĵ'i ĵoyun vočko*). The theory of "road" will be discussed later (*vide infra*, Ch. XIII) so that now it may be only noted that *jamĵ'i ĵoyun vočko* very often produce illness among the clansmen and they like blood sacrifice (given in the dark), while *ineyi ĵoyun vočko* are chiefly protectors of the clansmen and they do not need blood. In the group of *jamĵ'i* there are many females, while in the group of *ineyi* the female-spirits are

---

* I once saw a clan list (cf. SOM p. 58 et seq.).

* Cf. the case of *sagda xala*,—SOM p. 63.
** Cf. *moygo xala*, SOM p. 24.

few. The *jamj'i* are known only in the clans of *fè manju*.

The descriptions of the ritual given in some Manchu books are descriptions of rituals characteristic of different clans. Such manuals existed in many clans, but at the present time many of them are lost. The well known book *manjusa i večere metere kooli bitxe* gives a description of spirits known in the clan *ǵ'oro xala*, Golden Branch, which was that of the Imperial Family. Naturally the ceremonies and spirits of this clan are not the same as those of other clans. The ritual and prayers also are different. *

A detailed description of spirits and their placings in the existing clans about which I have information from the ethnographical point of view is not interesting so I shall confine myself to the above remarks.

The spirits may cause sickness e.g. by introducing themselves into the living clansmen. It usually happens during night time (*vide supra*: *jamj i joyun*) when the person begins to tremble and throw himself about. After this the person usually sees in a dream the spirit-ancestor which says what it wants. The women are more subject to these night visits. Once the spirit of a great grandfather introduced himself into a small boy during his meal. So the boy threw away the bowl with food and was seized by convulsions. The ancestor, as it was found out, wanted to have a shrine and a memorial stone erected upon his grave. Yet, sometimes the ancestor-spirit may introduce itself into a clansman during the time when the soul of the clansman is absent. In this case the clansman may become insane, and it would be extremely difficult to cure such a clansman. Moreover, since they all the time are in the house their looking or "breathing" at different parts of the body may suffice for producing a serious sickness at any moment. In case the spirit was promised a shrine with its placing (usually a Chinese made picture of the ancestor), the promise must be fulfilled for otherwise the spirit would call again, and therefore the spirit must not be "cheated". According to the Manchus, these cases are common. Sometimes the ancestors are wrongly suspected of doing harm to the clansmen and when they are seen (by the shaman) they may reject the wrong accusation and even indicate the actual spirit trouble-maker. The cases of introduction of ancestors-spirits into the shamans will be analysed in a special treatment of shamanistic spirits some of which also are ancestors. In order to neutralize the activity of the spirits, the Manchus sometimes have to promise that their children will become *p'oyun saman*.

However, the ancestor-spirits *vočko* may also become protectors. We have already seen (*vide supra* p.) that these spirits may act as protectors against the spirits attacking clansmen,—they protect the house and family against other spirits. But if one does not treat them properly they may allow the spirits to penetrate the house. *Vočko* are very important in protecting women lying-in. Therefore, the prayers and incense are given to them during labour.

During the wedding ceremony the couple must also make a sacrifice to the spirits. The adoption, by the clan, of a new member formerly belonging to another clan may be done only after a participation of the candidate in the clan sacrifice to *vočko*. After the sacrifice all persons present at the ceremony are considered to be "brothers", i.e. members of the clan. However, practically this is not observed, for the foreigners are, though very rarely, admitted to the sacrifice and not all of them become "brothers".*

The relations between *vočko* and other spirits are rather complex. Since these spirits may be dissatisfied with the fact that the man looks for help from the shaman's spirits, they must be informed about it and they must receive some sacrifice. If this is not done a conflict may originate between the shaman's spirits and *vočko* which may still more affect the condition of the sick clansman. These relations become more complex when the clan-spirits *p'oyun vočko* become shamanistic spirits. In this function they come to fight all spirits.

The spirits *p'oyun vočko* of the wife's clan [*in'i* (her) *tan'd'in'i vočko* (*tančin* so the woman calls the relatives of her clan when she is married)], and that of the mother's clan [*mon'i* (my) *xon'd'ix'in vočko* (*xon'd'x'in*,-my mother's clan)] ought to be considered. For instance, during the first visit to the wife's mother's house the newly married man must make sacrifice. Also the mother's clan-spirits must not be disregarded during the visits.

In the Manchu complex we find a series of spirits which have evidently originated from the souls of the ancestors. These spirits are known under the class name of *mafa* (cf. *supra*). However, the term *mafa* may be misleading, although it means "old man," "ancestor" (e.g. *mafar'i* is often used instead of *vočko*), but it is also used in the sense of "honourable person" etc. In this sense this name is sometimes referred to the spirits which are not at all "ancestors," but to spirits of different, even alien, origin with which it is advisable to maintain good terms and for this reason they are called *mafa* as it is, for instance, with the tiger and bear. Owing to the difficulty of defining the actual origin of some spirits called *mafa*,—the Manchus themselves do not know their origin,—I shall include them in the group discussed in the next chapter. In case the origin is known I shall point it out. Moreover, the number of such undefined spirits is not large.

In the foregoing lines I have already mentioned the existence of the shamans in some Manchu clans. Here I had in view the shamans which in Manchu are shamans only by name. The complexity of the theory of spirits, and the existence of elaborated rituals and prayers, also the need of regulating activity of the ancestors-spirits have imposed establishment of specialists who are in charge of looking after and managing these spirits. As a matter of fact, they are nothing else but "clan priests" who are either elected by the clan, or merely appointed by the clan authorities (*mokunda* and clan meetings), or just persons taking those duties on themselves owing to their personal vocation. In Manchu they are called *p'oyun saman*, i.e. home ("family," "clan") shamans. They greatly differ from ordinary *saman*,—"the shaman",—for they do not introduce into themselves the spirits and they do not "master" spirits. However, this distinction cannot be accepted as absolutely

---

* Some more details will be given later. Indeed, the complex of p'oyun večko in this clan was under special conditions for the Imperial Family and the whole clan, on the one hand, were under a very strong Chinese influence (at the period of Ch'ien Lung, the process of sinifying was almost completed), and on the other hand, they wanted to make smooth their relations with both the Chinese subjects and the other Manchu clans. However, the Imperial Family could not evidently influence very much the Manchus living far from the capital.

* I have never been invited to joining clan although I assisted at the ceremonies.

sharp for there is a clan (*nara xala*) in which the *p'oyun saman* do introduce the ancestors-spirits into themselves and act like genuine shamans. I shall return to this problem in Part 3.

47. MANCHU ANCESTRAL CLAN SPIRITS

The Manchu clan spirits comprise not only the ancestors but also spirits-protectors which are of non-ancestral origin. Practically the spirits of ancestral origin play a more important part and therefore they require more attention on the part of the clansmen than the spirits-protectors. Yet, the direct ancestors--spirits remain more or less unknown for they are numerous and only a few of them are remembered by the living generations. However, their names are now written down on the clan lists so they may be "worshipped" all together. Therefore the clans need to register the spirits-protectors which ought to be remembered and cared for by the clansmen. Since these spirits are of non-ancestral origin they might be better treated in the following chapter, but it would be inconvenient for in the Manchu mind the clan--spirits both of ancestral and non-ancestral origin are believed to be of ancestral origin or connected so closely with the ancestors that they cannot be separated. Owing to this consideration I shall give some examples of clan-spirits which are both of non-ancestral and ancestral origin.

Below I give three instances of *p'oyun vočko* (Manchu Sp.) [*boĭgun večěku*, (Manchu Writ.)] of the Old Manchu clans which I have selected from my material for showing degree of similarity and dissimilarity. All of them are taken from the written records as they are kept among the Manchus.

1. *amba wuse xala boĭgun beĭse* (10)
great(1) wuse clan clan princes (spĭrits)
( ) (2) *ineyi večěku n'uğan*(8) *taje*(3) *čuxaĭ jayin*(4)
first section day spirits: Nugan Ancestor, Soldiers' Commander;
j'ai fěn(5) *ineyi večěku an'ču*(6) *fuč'ik'i abkaĭ juse* Children
second section day spirits: Golden Buddha, Heaven's Children
ineyi ičeđě b'ja i ves'ižundě(7)
on the new day at the rise of the moon
jamj'i večěku čolo n'jai ačulǎn suru s'jaru s'imge s'jaru agara keku
evening spirits list: Niai-Achulan, Suru-Siaru, Simge-Siaru, Flying Cuckoo
momoro somoro
Momoro-Somoro
wujun wečěn.
nine spirits.

2. *Sakda xala boĭgun večěku*
Sagda clan clan spirits
ineyi večěku čolo šayg'in taje(3) *šanzu nendu nuneu taje čuxaĭ jayin*
day spirits list: White Pheasant Ancestor, Shanzu Nendu, Nunen Ancestor, Soldiers' Commander
men'i sefu(17)
Our Teacher,
kěję pusa(18) *fuč'ik'i jixa*(12) *nadan beĭse*(13)
Kedje Bodhisattva, Buddha came, Seven Princes
ineyi ičeđě b'ja i ves'ižundě

on the new day at the rise of the moon
jamj'i večěku čolo
evening spirits list
xos'i(14) *đě texě xos'i* (28) *nja-je-i*(29)
in the corner seated corner,
ělěn(15) *đě texě enđur'i*(16) *nja-je-i*
in the house seated spirits,
naren nareiko naĭrgun x'janč016 jarğo junğaĭ jure-jukten(19)
Naren-Nareiko Nairgun-Hianchu, Djargo-Djungal, Couple of Spirits
ineyi ičeđě b'ja i ves'ižundě
on the new day at the rise of the moon

3. *Guwarg'ja xala i boĭ večěku juan ǎun soor'i*(20) *ineyi večěku wujun soor'i*
Guwargia clan clan spirits fourteen places: day spirits nine places,
jamj'i večěku sun'j'a soor'i
evening spirits five places.
ineyi večěku čolo: čuxa jayin n'joxun beĭse(21) *čejǐn taĭze*(22)
day spirits list: Soldiers' Commander, Blue-Sky Prince, Golden Owl Taitse,
iltamu sefu n'iltamu sefu tarčime sefu abkaĭ jusen
Iltamu Teacher, Niltamu Teacher, Tarchime Teacher, Heaven's Children
aĭs'in ančulan(23) *aĭm'i dasatan*
Golden Owl Aimi Rulers(?)
jamj'i večěku čolo abka či vas'ixa amba s'jenčo(24) *sun be šurděrě*
evening spirits list: Heaven from descended Great Siencho the Sun Revolving
sureĭ s'jenčo
Wise Siencho,
naĭ ělěn narxun(25) *s'jenčo šajen mafa*(26) *mudan mama*(27)
Earthen People Thin Siencho, White Old Man, Stooping Old Woman

1. The clan wuse has two subdivisions (*gargan*),— "great" (*amba*) and "little" (*ajige*).
2. There is evidently omitted *wuju fěn*, i.e. the first section, vide infra 5.
3. *taje* is abbreviated form of *ilajeje* (cf. Chinese) "great grand-father" which is referred to the older generations in general, i.e. "the ancestors".
4. cf. infra Chapter XIV, Section 54.
5. *fěn* is a Chinese word *fen* (分) to "divide", which in Manchu is usually pronounced *f'in*. It is rather curious that the Manchus use a Chinese word instead of a Manchu word.
6. *Anču*(n)—"gold" in Nuichen language, corresponds to *aĭs'in* (Manchu Writ.)=*aĭčin* (Manchu Sp.), e.g. *aisin fučixi*. However, *anču* now is not associated with "gold," "golden," but it is like a name of a special Buddha.
7. *Ineyi iče*—the first day of the month (moon).
8. Names of spirits which cannot be translated with certainty are merely transcribed.
9. *Wujun wečěn*—nine spirits (*večen*=*wečěn*; *večěku*=*vočko*); i.e. four spirits of the day road and five spirits of the night road.
10. *beĭse* is used as an unusual politeness. cf. note 21.

11. The white pheasant is a heraldic sign used on the Manchu uniform.

12. Perhaps *jixa* is not "came" but "who responded on call."

13. *nadan beise*, i.e. "seven princes" are seven spirits, which may be seven Tathâgatas— the predecessors of Gautama Buddha quite popular in Mongolia and Tibet.

14. *Xos'i*—is "corner" in the house where placings of spirit are seated; it corresponds to Manchu Writ. *xošo*.

15. *Èlèn* is understood by the Manchus as "family house".

16. Term *endur'i* is used as a polite, "good expression," to please the spirits.

17. *Men'i sefu*—"our teacher" which seems to be referred either to *čuxai jayin*, the founder of shamanism or to *kèjè pusa* and other Buddhistic spirits. *sefu* is a Chinese word *šifu.*

18. *Kèjè* is evidently a Bodhisattva (*pusa*) which, however, could not be identified.

19. *jukten* is also a term referred to *večèku* when they are already invited. I. Zaxarov gives *jukten*,—the "sacrifice" which is perhaps the original meaning of the term.

20. *Soor'i* is called the place occupied by the spirit in the system of clan spirits; cf. *soorin* (Manchu Writ.)— the "seat, throne, position," etc.

21. *n'joxun beise*, the first component can be translated as sky—blue, but it is a name; *beise*—prince—is an honourable title of the spirit, or even that of a class of spirits.

22. *Cejin taizc*, the first component can be translated as "gullet", but it is a name; *taize* is the name of many Chinese emperors and here used in the same sense as *beise* (cf. *supra* notes 10, 21.)

23. *Ais'in ančulan*, I think here there is a repetition of *ais'in* and *ančku*, both of which are "golden", (cf. supra note 6.). However, *ančulan* is "the owl", "golden owl, with large ears." The etymology of *ančulan* is not clear.

24. *s'jenčo* is rather a group of spirits.

25. *narxun*—"thin",—may be used for showing insignificance of the earthly people (*na i èlèn*) as compared with "great" and "wise" *s'jenčo* dealing with the heaven and sun.

26. *šajen mofa*,—gray haired "ancestor", *vide supra*.

27. *mudan mama*,—with round back (due to the old age) female-ancestor.

28. *xos'i* is a repetition required by the rhythm.

29. *Nja-je-i* is a refrain used in singing.

The lists of spirits of the New Manchu clans are much shorter and usually they contain a few spirits of day road only. The above lists may be compared with the list of *ḍ'joro* clan quoted by Ch. de Harlez (cf. op. cit. pp. 17-18.). The translation given by this author is not correct. However, I cannot venture to make all corrections needed. One may see that in *ḍ'joro* list there are seven names which are met with in other clans, e.g. "noihon talji" (corr. *n'joxun beise*), "ancu ajara" (corr. *anču-lan ajara*, *vide* note 23, *ajara* is component of *ajara keku*). Yet, some other names are particular to this clan, e.g. the group of *n'jays'i*.

If we analyse the composition of clan spirits the latter may be grouped into five classes, viz. (1) the spirits which have been borrowed from other groups, as, for instance, *pusa*, *fuč'ik'i*; (2) the spirits which have been incorporated perhaps from various sources including the old Manchu complex, e.g. the groups of *s'jenčo*, cuckoo, owl, etc.; (3) the spirits which are not real clan ancestors but which might be Manchus who actually lived and became spirits e.g. *čuxa jayin* (Soldiers' Commander), the group of *sefu* (teachers); (4) the real ancestors of the clan, whose names are not now preserved; and (5) a large group of clan spirits whose names are recorded in the written clan list.

It may be noted that the clan lists are always supposed to be different and, according to the Manchu ideas, there may be no two clans with similar lists of spirits. Yet the list of clan spirits is a secret from other clans, so that the list, prayers, and significance of spirits cannot be understood by the outsiders. Of course, practically this is not always observed and in the case of *ḍ'joro* Imperial clan, we have even published ritual, but outsiders are not usually versed into the secret and cannot explain all details regarding the spirits. [*] However, the choice of spirits is limited and every clan wants to have "good", famous spirits in its lists. Owing to this we meet with various spirits which are common for several lists. There is no doubt that the Manchus themselves sometimes know very little about the spirits included into their lists for the records are not always detailed enough and oral tradition cannot transmit all details. Another point of interest is that it is very likely that the Manchu clans imitated the list of *ḍ'joro* clan and the *ḍ'joro* published ritual sometimes served them as a pattern in which they must introduce some changes required by the idea that no similar lists nor ritual may exist. I think that a limited number of words and particularly adjectives used are sometimes incidentally combined, as it may be seen e.g. from the cases like *ais'in ančulan*, *anču fuč'ik'i*, *ais'in fuč'ik'i*, etc. (note 23) *n'joxun beise* of *guwarg'ja* clan and *n'joxun taize* of *ḍ'joro* clan; *ajara keku* of *Wuse* clan and *anču ajara* of *ḍ'joro* clan. Such instances may be increased being taken from the comparison of lists of other clans. So that formalistic moment ought to be held to account for the character of clan lists.

As to the beginning of this system of clan spirits I think it is not one of ancient institutions among the Manchus, but is quite recent. As a matter of fact, the eclectic list of spirits of the clan of the Imperial family was made only at the rise of the Manchus as political rulers of China. The ancestral tradition did not play any important part in the old Manchu system, but it was probably confined to a loose idea of ancestors as it is amongst other Tungus groups. The chief reason for this was the lack of practical means to keep the names of ancestors. With the spreading of Chinese complex of "ancestor worship" the Manchus felt an imperative need of some spirits to be worshipped. They have picked them up from various sources and assumed them to have been bound with the clans. As soon as it was formulated in a written form by the clan *ḍ'joro* the other clans followed the example and the matter was settled. Owing to this the difference between the Chinese and Manchu system of clan spirits is quite essential.

* It is so to say in the order of things that Ch. de Harlez could not find explanations which he wanted to have. Cf. op. cit. p. 17.

CHAPTER XIII

BURKAN, FUCHIXI AND OTHER SPIRITS CHIEFLY OF NON-ANCESTRAL ORIGIN

48. PRELIMINARY NOTE: **Classification, Terms, Diseases, Roads, Complexes, and Forms.** The group of spirits discussed in the present chapter differs from the groups which have already been discussed in the previous chapters. First, as a rule these spirits introduce themselves into the people and thus they ought to be managed by special methods; this is the difference between the usual behaviour of the first group (Chapter XI) and that of the present one. Second, these spirits are not of ancestral origin; in this respect they differ from the spirits discussed in the previous Chapter XII. Third, although these spirits are not "benevolent" spirits, practically they may be so. Fourth, these spirits are in majority, spirits of foreign origin.

Although the Tungus realize the existing difference between this group of spirits and other groups they do not often make a very sharp dividing line between them. The chief reasons are that the Tungus opinions are not uniform; the Tungus are not all equally versed into these theories and hypotheses; and the Tungus approach to this problem is mostly practical, i.e. how far the activity of these spirits, regardless of their origin and character, may be turned to serve the Tungus interests; and last, the terminology itself may be responsible for misunderstandings. For instance, the Tungus when angry with the spirits may call all of them s'irkul and xutu, or when the spirits are not particularly malevolent and may be used for helping the people the Tungus of Manchuria may say so in a literary manner: tar burkan—endur'i adali, i.e. that spirit is like an endur'i (chiefly "good", benevolent). So that the last word adali i.e. "similar", "like," may be easily dropped and burkan will become endur'i. I have often observed such discussions when the Tungus wanted to find the place of some spirits in their system. Yet the same terms are very often referred in a "wrong way" by the Tungus themselves, the chief reason for which is the semantic changes. For instance, although the original meaning of burkan was that of Buddhistic spirits, the same term is often referred to the spirits borrowed from the Russians (among the Tungus of Transbaikalia) and newly discovered spirits, e.g. amongst the Tungus of Manchuria. Owing to these conditions the classification which I give here cannot absolutely cover all the spirits, they can not all be included in the units created by me. However, for the time being I do not see any other way of systematizing the spirits for the practical purpose of exposition, and when there are multiple characteristics of the spirits I shall point them out.

A good light is thrown on this group of spirits when we analyse the origin of terms and their present meaning, and when we make clear our idea regarding Tungus theory of diseases and "theory of roads."

The term burkan is known among all Tungus groups here discussed, except the Manchus among whom the idea of these spirits is associated with Buddhism and some spirits of this group are called fuĕ'k'i. Let us point out that futixi of Manchu Writ. is exactly "Buddha", but it is also referred to all Bodhisattvas and to religion as a whole. As to the origin of this term it might be received from two sources, namely, from the Chinese and from some other groups which existed at the time when the Buddhism made its first appearance amongst the ancestors of the Manchus. As a matter of fact, in present Chinese Buddha is fo or in some Chinese dialects but admitted by Bar. A. von Staël Holstein (Bibliotheca Buddhica, Vol. 12, p. 141 et seq.) as possible bur [*] also in some other dialects fut (Fuchow, Sinning) whence P.P. Schmidt (cf. "Grammar" p. 50) compared futixi-fuĕixi. Of course, it is possible, but the question remains about—xi. Indeed, such a suffix might exist in Manchu, and yet such a suffix might exist in the language spoken by the ancestors of the Manchus, but that will be a mere hypothesis. Yet, the final t in the Chinese dialects considered as a stable final consonant also is a hypothesis, for such a t does not exist. [**] Still more, the existence of a Chinese form from which futi derived is hypothetical. On the other hand, the neighbours of the Manchus,—the Koreans and Mongols,—have pul [***] and bur respectively. The latter was received from another source, the Uigurs, among whom Buddha was burqan, burxan, purqan dissected by W. Bang into bur+qan [****]. In the light of the Kuchean language, which is responsible for the migration of many words from India, and where there is found pud [*], N.D. Mironov referring to W. Radloff's table of letters suggests that the Uigur characters for r and t might be confounded and adopted in reading one for another, whence there might originate pud (Kuch.)→but→bur. In this setting of the problem Bar. Staël's supposition as to a Chinese origin of Uigur bur may be shortened, for the Uigurs were in a direct contact with the Central Asiatic groups. In favour of a Central Asiatic origin of Uigur burqan speaks its compound character. In fact, burqan is a simple translation of Kuchean pūdñäkte

---

[*] Originally bur was discussed still earlier (cf W. Bang "Turkologische Briefe", Zweiter Brief, p. 249).

[**] B. Karlgren who is one of prominent partisans of the possibility of restoration of old forms of "Chinese language" and dialects, which naturally turns into a scaffolding of hypotheses, in his "Analytic Dictionary" gives b'įuə t (p. 48) as "Ancient Chinese" form of fa. Fortunately, we do not need all these hypotheses for showing an alien source of Manchu and Tungus terms.

[***] It may be also noted that A. Forke ("Der Chinesische Dialekte") in Fuchow finds an indefinite final sound, something between t, l, and h. Indeed, such "indefinite" sounds do not exist, but seemingly this sound has not been analysed by the investigator. Is it not L (cf. my "Phonetic Notes on a Lolo Dialect", Section IV), whence it may be reduced to l in Korean pul? Or, is it from Uigur-Mongol bur?

[****] Cf. W. Bang, op. cit. pp. 249-250. · The possibility of dissection is illustrated with a series of instructive examples. In reference to the Tungus language the possibility of dissection has been discussed by myself (cf. Sramana-Shaman", pp. 119-120), in Uigur it is admitted by Bar. Staël and P.P. Schmidt (cf. "Der Lautwandel". etc. p. 63). Here I omit other discussions and suggestions dealing with the term burkan, as for instance that of P. Pelliot, B. Laufer and others who did not contribute to the clearing of the problem and thus may have only historic interest.

[*] Cf. N. D. Mironov "Kuchean Studies. I. Indian Loan-Words in Kuchean", in Rocznik Orjentalistyczny, Tom VI, pp. 89-169; vide pp. 162-163 (pp. 74-75 of reprints).

In which the component *n'äkte*, in its turn, corresponds to Sanscrit *deva* (of Buddhadeva), as it has been indicated by N. D. Mironov and confirmed by necessary similar cases.

There is no question that the Mongol term *burkan* [with dialectal variations *borxan*, *burxan*, *boroxan*, *burxyn* (Rudnev), also *p'urgän*, *ŋurxan* (Smedt-Mostaert), etc.] has been received by the Tungus, probably from the Mongols. It is usually found in the form *burkan* (Barg. Nerč. Bir. Kum. Khin. Mank.) (Ur. Castr.) and rarely as *burkän* (Nerč. Khin.). In so far as I know, no such a term is known amongst the groups living beyond the contact with the Mongols (and Buriats). It is unknown amongst the groups living East from the Birarčen, such as groups of Goldi, Udehe, Oroči, and Negidals; yet it is not used amongst the Tungus of Amur Gov., Yakutsk Gov., and Yenissy Basin. Amongst the groups which are in contact with the Manchus and Chinese this term is not needed because of the existence of *fuč'k'i* and *fu* referred to Buddha (and Buddhism).

This term is referred, as we have already seen, to the spirits of different origin (cf. *supra* Chapter XI) and yet as a new word, fashionable and convenient, it may be sometimes referred even to the spirits which formerly used to have different names, e.g. *buya* among the Barguzin Tungus may be called *burkan* together with others, and evidently new *dii minores*. Yet, it may be referred, but very rarely, to the spirits which have originated from the souls of dead people. In this respect a separation of spirits based only upon the term *burkan* is not satisfactory. · At the present time *burkan* is often used in the same indefinite manner as *s'irkul* and *xutu*. Yet the *burkan's* placings are very often called *savak'i* which, as will be shown, is a term of an earlier origin.

However, there are some limitations for using this term, namely, it cannot be referred to the ancestors-spirits and it cannot be referred to the spirits which are mastered by the shamans, although there are shamanistic spirits of similar names. Amongst the groups which have adopted term *endur'i* a large group of spirits being included in this term may also be eliminated.

The existence of these spirits is very closely connected with the ideas regarding origin of diseases and with the idea of managing them for practical use in various daily affairs. So now I will proceed to the Tungus conception of diseases. Another aspect of the spirits is their organization, ways of their activity, and their relation to the people. Therefore, I will give a general description of these spirits before proceeding to the description of particular spirits.

In the previous chapter I have several times referred to the sickness caused by the spirits. It would be erroneous to assume that in the Tungus mind all DISEASES are due to the activity of the spirits. In fact we have always seen that the Tungus recognize not only sickness due to the mechanical causes, but also to the presence of small (microscopic) animals (*kulikan*) which may produce various troubles. In this way a great number of diseases may be excluded from those which are explained by the spirits' activity. Apart from the cases when the abnormal condition of the people is understood as temporary absence of the soul,—a case very common,—it may be perhaps generalized that the Tungus are inclined to see the activity of the

spirits in all cases when the psychic activity is shaken. So for instance, the condition of delirium either complete or partial, is explained as due to the activity of the spirits. The action of spirits may be twofold, namely, when the spirit enters the body and when it affects the body, so to say, from outside, e.g. by spreading special waves through the air, the nature of which is immaterial in the Tungus sense of this conception. However, sometimes the mind may not be affected at all, while the body will be affected by the spirits. Indeed, with the accumulation of experience, the supposed activity of the spirits is either limited or extended, which depends upon the analysis of facts observed,—the finding of causes of diseases which are not ascribed to the activity of the spirits,—and upon the intrusion of new ideas (hypotheses) regarding spirits, produced by other ethnical groups. Therefore among different groups we observe different attitudes towards the same diseases and towards the same spirits. More than this, the opinions of individuals differ too. This may be compared with the similar ideas among the European ethnical groups at different periods, in different social strata, and in different regions. As a matter of fact, the variations are numberless. It is impossible to describe them all, so we must confine ourselves to only a general outline and to finding of common ideas regarding pathogenic spirits and particular cases of special interest.

In the theory of the spirits treated in this chapter there are two points of importance, namely, the spirits act along ROADS and their character is complex.

The Tungus including the Manchus suppose that the activity of spirits is going along the roads called in Tungus *okto* in Manchu Sp. *joyun* (*jugun*, Manchu Writ.) the original meaning of both being "road," "way," "journey along the road," etc. So that every spirit has its own *okto* (*joyun*), lying in the direction from the spirit to the people. The "roads" are called by the name of spirit, e.g. in Bir. *buniln'i okto* (the lower world spirits), *eèvèn'i okto* (the special shamanistic spirits), *sumu burkan'i* (*sumu* spirit) *okto*, etc; in Manchu *mavari* (special group of spirits *mava*) *joyun*, *pučeye saman'i* (dead shaman's) *joyun*, *pušuku* (spirits *bušuku*) *joyun*, etc. These roads are classified according to their general directions and locations, e.g. upper roads, middle roads, lower roads which correspond to the threefold system of the world; also they may be classified according to the time of day,—the day [*ineyi* (both Tungus and Manchus)] roads and night [*dolbor* (Bir. Kum.), *jemj'i* (Manchu Sp.)] roads. The roads may be called "black (*sayale*, Manchu Sp.) road, etc. There are also roads according to the points of orientation, e.g. southern, western, northern and eastern, and roads of directions between N and W, N and E, S and E, S and W. As a matter of fact, the spirits in general may be classified according to the roads, but that would bring us to great difficulties for the spirits may have several roads. Three roads,—upper, middle and lower—may be identified with three worlds, but these roads are not particularly "good" or "bad,"—they merely are different. The day and night roads cannot be identified as that of upper and lower worlds and as "good" and "bad." These are roads the movement along which is easy (and even perhaps possible) only during limited periods of day light and dark. For these reasons I do not classify these spirits according to their roads.

The theory of road is also known amongst the Tungus of Transbaikalia where, however, I was not able to investigate all details. The neighbours of the Tungus of Manchuria and Manchus—the Goldi—evidently have the same theory.[*] Beyond the Tungus area we meet with this idea among the Yakuts described by V. Sieroszewski[**]. He has given a summary on the occasion of a description of a Yakut method of divination. The idea of roads is also known in Lamaism and Buddhism which seem to be the source of Tungus idea.

When the Tungus use a placing for spirits they also use some "placings" for roads. These may be represented in the form of long things, e.g. silk ribbons, ropes, thongs etc. So that the spirits are supposed to descend along the "road" into the placing reserved for them. In the same way, if the Tungus should want to show to the spirits their direction, they would make a "road". The spirit first descends on the antenae, by which it reaches the post and descends, then it follows the road which is attached to the post and at last it reaches the placing. Such a placing may also be human body. For this reason the Tungus are rather careful with posts and possible roads—as for instance, ropes, ribbons, etc.—in order to avoid accidental self-introduction of the spirits.

———

The spirits may be simple and they may form a COMPLEX of manifestations. The instances of simple spirits we have seen before in the group of spirits treated in the Chapter XI. The group of spirits here discussed includes some simple spirits which may have only one road and only one manifestation, but most of them are complex spirits. By this term I shall thus designate related groups of manifestations, the number of which may vary from two to seventy-two, as observed, for instance, in ain'i burkan. The manifestations may have therefore different roads and corresponding placings. The complexity of the spirits must be understood as various possibilities of spirits' activity. The manifestations may have their own names, as in the complex malu burkan, or they may be designated as a certain road of a certain spirit. When the Tungus deal with these complex spirits they address themselves to the whole complex or to a particular manifestation of the spirit. The distinction of different manifestations, as will be shown, has very great popularity among the Manchus in their conception of shamanistic spirits. The same may be seen in the Goldi complex. Amongst the Birarčen and Kumarčen some spirits are extremely complicated and include an always increasing number of manifestations. The idea of manifestations is one characteristic of Buddhism, so it may be supposed that among the Tungus (and Manchus) it has been modelled on this pattern.

———

As to the origin of these spirits they may be of local origin, but most of them are borrowed by the Tungus from other ethnical units and this is the reason why the designations among them are either burkan or fuᵈkⁱi which as shown are Buddhistic spirits. The other spirits of the same group may be also borrowed from the neighbours and although they do not belong to the group of Buddhistic spirits they may be called so, for this term is convenient for all spirits of non-Tungus origin. The discovery of new spirits is made in two ways. First, the Tungus may learn from their neighbours that the latter have some spirits which are unknown amongst the Tungus. Then they would inquire what are the characteristics of these spirits, and then they would decide whether the Tungus themselves have similar spirits or not. In case there is a complete or a partial but essential coincidence of characters, the Tungus would say that they also have these spirits, but they are called by different names. It is likely that the name of the spirit would be changed, if the Tungus group is under a strong linguistical influence from the neighbours. In case the Tungus have no such spirit they would investigate to determine whether similar phenomena are met with in their own group. In case the inquiry reveals these phenomena, the spirit will be adopted usually together with the name. If the inquiry gives negative results there may be two issues, namely, (1) admitting that such a spirit may also be active amongst themselves, they would accept it, which is likely to occur when the group from which they learn about the new spirit is very strong and influential among the Tungus; (2) admitting that such a spirit cannot be active amongst themselves, they would not accept it but they would keep in mind that a certain group has a certain spirit of no importance for the Tungus. Newly discovered diseases are subject, for instance, to such a treatment. For instance, before coming into contact with the Chinese, the Tungus distinguished some diseases like typhoid fever, from influenza. From the Chinese they have learnt that these diseases are different. Therefore they accept the idea that pathogenic spirits are also different, so the new spirits have a great chance of being introduced. The life in villages very often results in essential change of the psychic stability. Therefore, if this phenomenon is explained as due to some particular spirit, the latter has a great chance of being adopted. In this way the complex of spirits is always subject to variations and new spirits are continually introduced, while the old ones are rejected.

The Tungus enter into relations with these spirits the expression of which may take different form. The spirit may remain dōna (Bir. Kum.) or dōn'i (Bir.) (i.e. "foreign, alien") burkan and quite incidental in Tungus dealing with them. But when the character of the spirit is investigated and the Tungus know how to deal with it, they may make the placing and keep it with the family belongings. In this way the spirit would remain near to the family and, when carefully looked after, it may seem even useful to the members of the family. When the spirit receives recognition from many members of a clan, placings for it are made by many families and at the gathering of clan meeting this spirit may receive a regular sacrifice. In such a case the spirit would become a clan spirit or mokun'i burkan.[*]

The number and character of the clan spirits are different when clan complexes are compared. They cannot be

———

* Cf. I. A. Lopatin, op. cit. p. 215. It is evident that this author underestimated this theory so he did not pay due attention to it during his investigations among the Goldi. In so far I can see from the description of the spirits the Goldi have a well developed system and theory of roads.

** Cf. "The Yakuts," vide Scheme, p. 671.

* It may be here noted that mokun in the sense of clan is used by these Tungus only in recent time. cf. SONT.

regarded as real "protectors" of the clan, but they must be better regarded as spirits whose pernicious influence is neutralized by the clever and skillful methods of the clansmen. Naturally, since for the spirits there are permanent placings, which are called *savak'i* or *savak'ičan*, i.e. spirits' small placings, for brevity these placings also may be called *burkan* instead of "*savak'ičan* of a given *burkan*". Yet, reindeer and horses of different colour are reserved to them, for carrying the placings and for use by the spirits.*

Another modification with relation to the clan spirits is that of the spirits brought by the woman from another clan when she marries. They are called *nāfil burkan*. Conflicts between *nāfil* and *mokun burkan* are possible, for in the relation to the clan spirits those brought by the woman are *dōna*. The *nāfil burkan* problem is also complicated by the fact that the woman has her monthly blood discharges to which *mokun'i burkan* are not indifferent. Indeed, as to the manifestations of *mokun'i burkan* they do not differ from that of *mokun'i burkan* of the woman's clan. However, usually the placings include only those of the *malu burkan*, which is only one of *mokun'i burkan*.

A further function and partial modification of the *burkan* happens when they may be mastered by the shaman. As a matter of fact, most of the spirits may be mastered and from that moment they are not only harmless for the members of the clan to which the shaman-master belongs, but they may also be used on different occasions. In this function the spirits are not called *burkan;* they are called *sèvèn*, and so they will be treated in the following chapter.

We can now see that the conceptions of clan spirits among the Manchus and the Tungus are entirely different. While amongst the Manchus these clan spirits are real or supposed ancestors, i.e. as in the Chinese complex, amongst the Tungus they are various spirits adapted to the needs of the clan and by tradition transmitted from one generation to another. Owing to this it has been necessary to include them in different chapters. Another point of difference is seen in the fact that the group of *burkan* and *fuč'k'i* are not alike amongst the Manchus and Tungus of Manchuria. *Fuč'k'i* are not so complex as are the *burkan*. Usually they have very limited manifestations and remain very closely connected with the Buddhistic spirits in general. Yet, the group of *mafa* (*mava*, Manchu Sp.) is lacking in the Tungus complex. This group among the Manchus is a composite one consisting of spirits of various origin, in this respect being similar to the *dōna burkan* of the Tungus. However, with the increase of relations between the Tungus of Manchuria and the Manchus the *mafa* began to penetrate the Tungus complex.

49. CLAN SPIRITS OF THE NORTHERN TUNGUS   In this section I shall give a description of the clan spirits chiefly observed among the Northern Tungus groups. The order in which they are here shown is that of their importance in the Tungus complex.

MALU (BURKAN) (SAVAKI).   This complex spirit is known among the reindeer Tungus of Transbaikalia and Manchuria, also among the Tungus of Manchuria. The term *malu=malu=*(*maro*) amongst all these

* Vide Chapter XVI, Section 62.

groups is referred to the place in the wigwam, as well as in the tent and the house, facing the entrance. When combined with *burkan* among the Khingan, Kumarčen and Birarčen, and with *savak'ičan* amongst the Reindeer Tungus of Manchuria, *savak'i* among the Barguzin and Nerčinsk Tungus, it means the spirit. This *burkan* is a clan spirit among all groups.

According to the Birarčen, this spirit is *ojor*, i.e. "early, old", and it originally existed together with *buga* and *bun'i*, while all other spirits were then unknown. It is very likely that at that time it was called *savak'i*. This term is now referred to the box in which the placings for this spirit are kept. In fact, as we shall see, *savak'i* amongst other groups may be referred to the placings, and to the spirit itself. It is remarkable, that some Birarčen suppose that this spirit was borrowed from the Dahurs, but the spirit itself is of Tungus origin. So the story runs as follows: "Once a Dahur was running (for hunting) and was hungry. He saw a box hanging up near a Tungus (*tèya*—the Tungus who were not enrolled in the Bannermen organization) wigwam which he thought to contain some dried meat. Then he stole the box. The box contained no meat but placings for *malu*. The spirit did not want to leave the Dahurs and settled amongst the Dahurs becoming the most important Dahur (clan) spirit. From the Dahurs *malu* has reached the Tungus of Manchuria." However, according to some Tungus, a half of the spirit was lost,—it went back to the *tèyaèen*. As a matter of fact, the term *burkan* may be of Dahur origin, since the Dahurs did trade with the Tungus of Yakutsk Government and with the Tungus of Manchuria serving as a link between two groups, e.g. in the XVIIth century and later.

Malu burkan consists of several manifestations which may be studied in the placings for this spirit, so here I give a description of a complex placing observed among the Birarčen.

(1)   Two anthropomorphic placings *doldika,—as'i* (female) and *n'irai* (male). This manifestation causes bad sickness in which the articulations are affected. I think those are the rhumatism, gout, etc.

(2)   Two round placings called *čolpon* (star Venus), —*as'i* (female) and *n'irai* (male) (*vide supra* pp. 56-57). This manifestation causes the eye trouble which may badly affect the hunter's ability. I think these are trachoma, and other various infections, particularly gonococcous infection when the spirit is carried by the women from another clan.

(3)   Two anthropomorphic placings *kayatkan* (the etymology is *kayan*(—*t*)+*kan*, *vide supra* p.52f.) *as'i* (female) and *n'irai* (male). This manifestation causes diseases of the internal organs, especially common in females; gynecological cases greatly increase the total number of cases. It is considered as "master" of the whole complex. For this reason the complex may be represented only by this manifestation.

(4)   Two anthropomorphic placings with nine indentations on the head,—*mayi* (a name of mythological beings who lived before the Tungus spreading), *as'i* (female) and *n'irai* (male). *Mayi* is also called *jeyin dilči mayi*, i.e. *mayi* with nine heads, which may be compared with the old Chinese complex. It may also be called *jeyy'ildar mayi.* (cf. *infra* Ch. XV). The functions are not clear but the spirit is considered as a very dangerous one. It is especially common among the Dahurs.

(5) Two long pieces—*tākan* (the bridge), *as'i* (female) and *n'irai* (male). This manifestation causes trouble of the vertebral column. I think the cases of tuberculosis of vertebrae are included.

(6) A round flat piece *dilača* (the sun, which is a male) and a half of a round piece—*b'ega* (the moon, which is a female).

(7) Two lizard-like placings,—*isela* (the lizard), male and female.

(8) Two snake-like placing,—*kulin* (the snake, worm), male and female.

(9) Two turtle-like placings,—*kavila* (the turtle), male and female.

The functions of these manifestations (6,7,8,9) could not be definitely established. Various troubles of internal organs, particularly severe pains in the intestines etc., are ascribed to these manifestations. Yet, according to some Tungus, these manifestations are of those animals the forms of which the clan shamans may take.

(10) Two halves of anthropomorphic placings,—*koltoyde* (also *kaltaydi*) (from *kalta* half), male and female. This manifestation causes partial one-sided paralysis of the limbs.

(11) Two one-legged anthropomorphic placings *čičul*, male and female.

These manifestations may be increased with the following ones: a long fish-like placing *k'iribu* (*k'irbu*), or *ajiratkan*—the sturgeon (and the kaluga);* also a placing like a human face—*dèrègdè* [cf. *supra* and *infra*, also *bada* and *dèrègdè* (RTM)]. This placing is merely another form of the *kayatkan* which may be used instead of the complete complex.** These two placings are found in the *malu* complex of the clan *dunānkān* (vide details in SONT). (Cf. P. V. Šimkevič, op. cit. Addition IV.). There may be also found a special placing; *bojun'i algači malu*, i.e. *malu* with the elk's leg.

In the Birarčen clan *malakul* the *malu* complex is found in a reduced form, but the chief of the group consists of *om'i* (father), *on'i* (mother), *ogdi utèn* (big child) and *utèn* (child).

The placings in different families may differ. In maakagir clan it consists of only *kaltaka*, *čičul*, *doldika* each by one, the sun, moon and two Venuses and also four anthropomorphic placings (*an'akan*) for minor spirits sent for communication with other spirits, but there are two birds lacking in other clans. During the sacrifice they also make eight and nine, altogether seventeen *an'akan* which are distributed as shown in figure below.

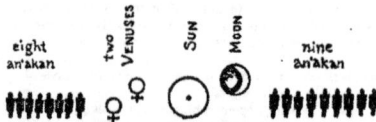

eight an'akan — two VENUSES ♀ — SUN ☉ — MOON ☽ — nine an'akan

The placing for *malu* may also be made in the form of a piece of blue Chinese material with anthropomorphic

---

details, also the sun, moon, Venus and other manifestations. However, the usual material is carved wood. The size may vary from about three to twenty centimetres. However, for convenience of transportation, the Tungus like better to have them in small size. All of the manifestations are usually attached together with a thong to make a bundle. Since they are hung up over smoke during sacrifice and are fed with blood and other kinds of food, they usually become covered with a layer of fat, dirt and smoke, and have a very dark colour and a strong odour. Amongst the Birarčen they must be made of wood of the black birch tree. In explanation of this requirement they have a story relating how the spirit *malu* was introduced amongst them. The essentials of the story are that a small boy left alone was fed by *malu burkan* until he attained the age when he could play. He always played on the bent trunk of a black birch tree. After his continued use of the trunk, the bark gradually fell off. When the trunk was without bark it began one day to speak to the boy about *malu burkan*. Since that time the Tungus make the placing from this wood.

When the placings are made of wood they may be called *mōma* (etym. *mō*—tree-wood; *mōma*—"wooden"), or *mōmate*, which name may be used for designation *malu burkan*. The white horse reserved for this spirit bears two white and blue ribbons, and is called *oygo* or *oygočil*, i.e. one which has *oygo*. The idea is that the spirit uses the soul of the horse for riding.

It may be noted that in this complex the manifestations are represented by males and females. These manifestations correspond respectively to the day and night roads of every manifestation. This complex cannot be identified with the animals, phenomena of nature (sun, moon, and stars) or even ancestors' souls (*kayan*), but these manifestations are a result of syncretic creation by the Tungus who accumulated their knowledge regarding diseases and possibilities of transformations (i.e. the taking of certain forms) for travelling, chiefly along the lower, night roads. At a certain historical moment this knowledge was systematized in the form of the *malu* complex. Various manifestations are not at all natural phenomena expressed in the placings, but are diseases and forms which may be assumed by the clan members for defending themselves against the aggressiveness of the spirits. This especially is evident in the case of *tākan* (the "bridge",) also *jey'in dūlči mayi* (probably of Chinese origin), and others. Yet, the sun and moon are the spirits called so and not the natural phenomena. *

Among the Khingan Tungus and Kumarčen the complex of *malu* is nearly the same as the above described. The number of manifestations is subject to great variations, as among the Birarčen.

Among the Barguzin and Nerčinsk Tungus I have seen chiefly the placing *bada*,—the face made of a piece of iron or brass, or birch bark. The number of *bada* belonging to a family may be rather large; I have seen over ten. The size ranges between two and twenty centimetres. They keep with these placings also wooden placings and placings made from soft material such as skin and tissues. They call

---

* K'irbu seems to be a Tungus adaptation of kirfu (Manchu Writ.) which is not exactly sturgeon; ajiratkan is a Tungus term.

** In form of a "mask" it is used by the shaman who puts the "face" on his face to show that the spirit *malu* is within him. This spirit protects.

* As a matter of fact, the existence of some diseases or troubles might have been originally connected by the Tungus with the activity of the sun and moon. Yet, this may be mere borrowing in a ready made form from e.g. the Mongols Cf. sara-nara complex of the Mongols.

them *mok'il* (cf. SONT, also *infra*). In the same bunches of *savak'i* there are found wooden anthropomorphic placings for the nine headed *mayitkan*, wooden placings for tiger, sun, snakes, bear, also eagle's feathers, hare's leg, and once I have seen a wooden triangle with nine anthropomorphic placings, which probably belonged to another *burkan* (*vide infra, fiaci*). These spirits were clan spirits and they were opposed to the spirits of other clans. A white reindeer was reserved for spirits. Unfortunately my information regarding this group of spirits among the Transbaikalia Tungus is not detailed.

Amongst the Reindeer Tungus of Manchuria, according to what I could find from the old people (they have given up shamanistic practices and their complex of spirits, they formerly used to have *malu*. These spirits were identified with *ojan* of the Barguzin Tungus. In the group of placings called *savak'ičan* there were anthropomorphic images, white swans, and an eagle (*k'iran*) which was the most important manifestation. At the present time these do not exist any more,—"all died out", according to the Tungus expression. After the hunting these spirits were served a sacrifice. A white reindeer was reserved for these spirits, as it is in Transbaikalia. From these fragments it may be seen that the complex was different as compared with that seen amongst the Reindeer Tungus of Transbaikalia and in Manchuria.

Among the Goldi some manifestations of the *malu burkan* are met with in different shamanistic complexes (*seon*). Whether the Goldi also have the spirits of the same type as the Tungus here discussed has not been investigated. Both P. Šimkevič and I. A. Lopatin had paid attention to the shamanistic spirits but they did not communicate regarding the clan non-shamanistic spirits. However, it is almost sure that the Goldi have, besides the shaman's spirits, also the clan spirits. It is very likely that the shamanistic spirits, at least some of them, are at the same time the clan spirits. The Tungus Birarčen told me that it is so among the Goldi of Sungari who have in great part, the same spirits as these Tungus, for instance, *jey'in džlči mayi, čičul, ajiratkan, doldika,* also animal forms,— the snake, lizard, turtle, etc. are also found in Goldi complex. However, the Goldi, in so far as it can be seen from the published material, do not call them *malu*. Still this term is known and it is referred to the place in the house facing the entrance (*malo* cf. I. A. Lopatin op. cit. p. 82. also *malu* W. Grube's Goldi Dictionary p. 117) i.e. just as it is observed amongst all northern Tungus groups, even those not using the conical wigwam, e.g. some settled Birarčen and nomad Tungus of Transbaikalia, and once I. A. Lopatin mentions (op. cit. p. 154.) *malu seon* which receives sacrifice from the bride in her future husband's house during the wedding ceremony. The placing for spirits is a post called *gusi*. In his further treatment of the spirits I. A. Lopatin gives no details. However, one of his complex spirits seems to be *malu*.

NADJIL BURKAN OR KANHAN.   These are the same spirits as *malu burkan* when they are brought by the women from their clan. Among the Birarčen they are called *nāj'il* by which term the relatives of the wife are called by her when she leaves her clan and as a wife belongs to another

clan. The term *nāj'il* is borrowed by the Birarčen from the Dahurs among whom it means "my mother's relatives", so that in the mind of the woman she has in view chiefly her mother, and thus her mother's spirits. [*] Amongst the Kumarčen and occasionally among the Birarčen these spirits are called *kayan—ka'an* which sounds exactly like the spirits which amongst the Birarčen are supposed to protect the child in its early period. Among the Kumarčen, the term *burkan* is referred to the spirits of the husband only. Naturally, the complexes of *nāj'il burkan* or *kayan* are similar to *mokun'i malu burkan*. Here I give a short description of a complex observed in possession of a woman who received these placings when she was four years old, after a very great illness and long shamanizing. She always kept them near herself. All placings are made of wood. (1) A half-moon, two centimetres in diameter; (2) the sun, fifteen millimetres in diameter; (3) a bird with its head turned back, made of a root of a tree; (4) two stars, "evening and morning stars",—two small wooden balls about one centimetre in diameter, with small handles for string; (5) two snakes in the form of two sticks eight centimetres long, with a string wound around them in a spiral; (6) two lizards; (7) two bridges about five centimetres long; (8) a carp (fish) with horns; (9) a half-man about five centimetres long; (10) one-legged man about five centimetres long; (11) two anthropomorphic placings with eyes, mouth, legs, but instead of arms only hints in the form of protruding wood, about six centimetres long. From a comparison of the above described complex of *malu burkan* and present *nāj'il burkan* is evident that they are different only in some respects. The placings are always kept in the wigwam in the place where the woman sleeps. They must not be mixed with the husband's clan spirits and generally other spirits. Other women must not sit on the place under the *nāj'il burkan*. The same is recommended to the men who may catch these spirits although the men are not forbidden to sit on this place. For this reason the hostess must show the place where the guests may sit without any harm for themselves. It is very interesting that these spirits may be transmitted from the mother to the daughter and in this way the woman may carry back to her brother's clan the spirits of her mother, where naturally they will not be harmful for clansmen, for there they are *mokun'i malu burkan*. Such a situation was usual when these Tungus systematically practised cross-cousin marriage and were bound by marital relations only between two clans (cf. SONT). However, at the present time the *nāj'il burkan* are usually destroyed when the woman becomes old and it can be done even when she is young but does not need the spirits with her, i.e. practically when she is not sick. In fact, not all women want to have the placings with them. Usually the women when married have no placings, but with the first trouble, as for instance sickness, or nervous excitability, mental unrest etc. they make the placing through which

---

[*] The term *nāj'il* in Dahur may be perhaps connected with *nayačn* (Mongol). However, the situation is more complex than it appears at first. In fact, this term is used by the Tungus in two forms *nāj'l ~ naja.* Both *na* (in the form *na* and its derivative *ina*) and *j'i ~ ja* are met with as terms for designation of the progeny of my sisters (especially in the dual system) and junior group of "my mother's clansmen"; *naj'l ~ naja* might originate as well in Tungus soil. However, as far as I know, it has not been recorded in this form (cf. SONT and SOM).

from time to time the spirits of the women may be called. When the placing is made, or received from the mother, it is very likely that some troubles are inevitable. This is especially true with the eye troubles (male and female *ɛolpon*) which may result in a complete blindness. Once a woman had sore eyes, and the husband decided to act and burnt with a red-hot iron the eyes of *naĵ'il burkan*. Owing to his mistake in acting so, the next day the woman lost her eye altogether. Once I was said to have caused eye trouble (conjunctivitis) to a woman by examining her *naĵ'il burkan*. In another case one of two Venuses had disappeared from the complex of placings and the effect was that the woman had trouble with her eyes. So that many women and men are inclined to rid themselves of the spirits when it is possible.

Among the Barguzin Tungus the wife's spirits are in the same position and have the same effects as with the Birarčen and Kumarčen. The placings *mok'il* among these Tungus correspond to *kaɲan* as we have already seen in children (cf. SONT. p. 280). It may be thus supposed that the term *naĵ'il burkan* has been received from the Dahurs, while the older term was *kaɲan* still preserved among the Birarčen as a term for the spirit-placing protecting the child, analogous to *mok'i* among the Barguzin Tungus who have this spirit in the clan complex and as protector of the child.

MOKUN DJIACHI BURKAN is one of the clan complex spirits (cf. *supra ĵ'iaɛi* p. 132) which is known among the Birarčen and Kumarčen. It may be dissected as *ĵ'ia+ɛi*, where *ĵ'ia* is "happiness, luck" (Bir.) [borrowed from the Mongols, *ĵ'ian, ĵ'iĵan || jaĵayan* (Rudnev),—the "fate" (cf. *ĵ'iĵā*, Dahur, Pop)], so that *ĵ'iaɛi* is "one who has luck, happiness". It is sometimes called *ĵ'elɛi burkan*. The same spirit seems to be also known among the Barguzin and Nerčinsk Tungus. This spirit is supposed to be very old. It was received from the Mongols together with *matu*. According to a Birarčen version a boy of 6 or 7 years old was playing, on the river bank, with these placings which he had taken from the river; since that time the *burkan* is known.

The placing is made of two pieces of Chinese cloth, white and blue, each about one square foot. The upper part of the blue cloth is covered with a piece of sable or squirrel fur. Two anthropomorphic images made of lead and tin are fixed on it. On the piece, of white cloth, there are fixed two anthropomorphic placings and below them two pieces of "golden" or "silver" Chinese paper, through which the spirit is "fed", i.e. the spirit is offered the blood sacrifice once every three years. During the sacrifice the placing is put facing South and a long string (the "road") is attached to the placing. There are attached to the string anthropomorphic images. The *mudur* (dragon) makes it difficult for the spirit to go along the road. This spirit has a horse *oɣgo*, which must be of very light brown colour with dark mane and tail—*sapil*—with a white ribbon as sign of *oɣgoɛi*. This spirit is useful in the cases of disease, and it looks to, or better to say, helps in the welfare of the clan (and family). In spite of the fact that in the book of destiny everything is foreseen, this spirit may help to improve the life conditions. In fact, "once a young boy was carrying on his shoulders the placings for this spirit. He was tired

and hungry and crying. Then he heard a voice: Your older brother has killed an elk.—Hurry up! When the boy reached the elder brother's campment there really was an elk killed."

In addition to the above placings there are also eight (or four or two) anthropomorphic placings either attached to the cloth, or separate and made of wood,—*an'akan*, two *mudur* (dragons) and two birds. This is *dāril*, or *ĵ'iaɛi dāril*, or *dolbor*,—the female half of the complex, with the night roads. The male half *dayari(l)* with the "noon roads," may have nine, seven, five or three anthropomorphic placings *an'akan* and sometimes a special wooden piece with nine anthropomorphic placings and nine pendants of the form shown in the figure below.

Sometimes they add the sun, moon and two *ɛolpon* (Venuses). Then the Birarčen say that it is a combined *matu* and *ĵ'iaɛi*. So that sometimes one may see the combinations nine males + eight females; or five males + four females, or three males + two females, which is indicative that both halves and both roads are in action.

I have seen the placings with nine *an'akan* and pendants amongst the Barguzin Tungus, so that I suppose that they also have this spirit. However, I know no details regarding it. Among the Goldi a similar placing is seen on plate XXIV No. 61, which is *g'irk'i* of the Goldi. The description given by I. A. Lopatin (op. cit. p. 228) corresponds to the combined (though abbreviated) *matu + ĵ'iaɛi*. Amongst the Goldi it is used by the hunters who carry with them these placings and "feed" them in the case of "bad luck" in hunting.

MOKUN'I KAIDEN is one of the family complex
(KAIDUN) BURKAN spirits known among the Birarčen. Sometimes it is transmitted and in this way it becomes clan spirit. The term *kaidun* is not a Tungus term and it has no meaning. It may be compared, in so far as I know, with *kaidun* (Manchu Writ.),—the "rider going on alone or ahead of a group," also "usual, permanently used" (Zaxarov.) This spirit originated in the mountains. The placings consist of two pieces of red and yellow cloth of about one square foot, with images. The first one is for the half of the night, the lower road (*dolbor orgu okto*), while the second is for the noon half, the upper road (*ineɲdulin uɲu okto*). During the sacrifice the "roads" are attached in the form of strings.

The first male group contains the following manifestations —five men and five birds; two dragons and two trees; while the second female group contains four females and four birds; also two dragons and two trees. When the sacrifice is given a corresponding number of anthropomorphic placings, birds, dragons, and a special an'akan are made. However, this is not a regular practice, for this spirit has its permanent placing above described. A horse for carrying and serving spirits,—oŋgočí,—is selected among the light-bay coloured horses and has two ribbons of red and yellow colour. It is supposed that this burkan always stays (kaiduʔ) at the same place and therefore there is a special construction as shown on figure below, built up for it in a

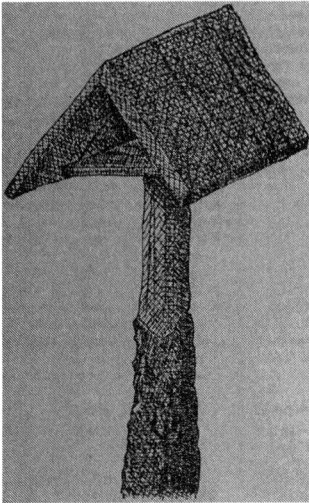

place which would not be frequented by outsiders, for this spirit does not like foreigners.* The importance and significance of this spirit is compared with ǰ'iači dārīl. It is not very common.

This spirit has a third road which is the manifestation consisting of nine anthropomorphic placings, nine birds and two dragons. What is the function of the third road I do not know. This spirit has not been mastered by the shamans.

___

MOKUN'I KAROL BURKAN   is one of the clan complex spirits, identical to kaidun and, according to some Tungus, it is the same as

* The same shelter for placings of kaidun burkan may also be used for keeping other placings. But this is considered as an innovation.

kaidun, only the name is different, they say. However, some Tungus have karol, while some others—kaidun. Karol has been mastered by the shamans. The name is supposed to be of a shaman who then evidently mastered kaidun. The spirit has originated in the mountains. (vide infra, karol sereŋ)

50. DONA (FOREIGN) BURKAN.

ADJELGA BURKAN   is a burkan newly formed from a spirit discussed in Chapter XII. It seems to be of "night road." The manifestations are limited. There are two anthropomorphic placings which may be substituted for two actual hillocks which protrude in the marshes.

AJIN'I BURKAN   (also called aji burkan) of Birarčen and Kumarčen is a complex spirit which contains seventy-two manifestations. The term ajin'i, or aji may be connected with aji—"the taiga, the steppe, and generally the place without dense population." But this is an indication as to origin of the spirit and not as to its activity, for as will be seen the ability of the spirit becomes very intensive in a dense population.* This spirit seems to be located in the south-eastern section of the sky, for the sacrifice (usually a cock) and placings are put in this direction, with relation to the campment.**

The placings for this spirit are usually made by the painters who are specialists. The manifestations are different diseases. Three principal groups may be distinguished, namely, (1) or'ebar'i, which remains with the family and it is impossible to rid oneself or the family of this spirit. In all probability here the Tungus have in view such conditions which are perhaps hereditary and not very serious, or even mere predispositions to certain diseases which are not very infectious. In Tungus this term has no etymology and it does not sound like a Tungus term.*** There is a placing for this group of manifestations: there are upper and lower roads; the manifestations comprise two dragons, two trees, also an'akan of which there are four for the lower road and five for the upper road. The upper part of the picture is filled up with birds, gadflies, flies and other insects. (2) Ţörültan (also töreltan) is a group of manifestations which inhabit villages (and cities) and go from house to house (or wigwam to wigwam in permanent seasonal campments). The people affected by it have headache, fever etc. The etymology as to Birarčen seems to be simple,

* It must not be compared with all,—"the village"—of some Tungus and Mongols. Vide infra, one of the manifestations, called aiin'i (of village); cf. Yakut ajĭkyt (Pek.).

** One of them artistically made, was the creation of a Dahur master who worked under the direction of a Tungus shaman.

*** I have not found it in other Tungus dialects. Perhaps it may be regarded as a Manchu compound term in which ör'i is "the male sexual element", and bar'i is "part, present." from ba+mbi,—"to become inefficient, weak, exhausted." Indeed, I do not insist upon this etymology. Still less I would insist upon a Mongol etymology from or || oro (Rudnev),—"to come in, to blow (wind), to assume, to intrude etc." Both suppositions are good for explaining the Tungus meaning of or'ebar'i. Let us remark that a Dahur origin of this term is the most probable. In fact, we have ör'ē "one's own" and bār'i "to keep, catch etc.", met with e.g. in combination jasbar'i,—"to bury" (Poppe).

namely from *töril* (Bir.),—the "dust". * However, the word *töril*,—the "dust,"—likely may be a new one while at the basis of *törütan* is *tör'i* (Dahur, Poppe), tör || *tögeri* (Mongol) (Rudnev),—"to wander, to go round," etc. also *tör'i* (Dahur) || *toguri* (Mongol, Poppe)—"to walk, to go round." So that it may mean "spreading, infectious". 3) *tulilaṣi buaṣi (aṣi burkan)* is a group of manifestations which affect the people in the taiga, in the places where there are people. The etymology is clear: "of the outside, of the *taiga*." The same manifestations may also be called *aṣin'i suġdun*, when *suġdun* is "steam", "vapour", "immaterial substance" (cf. Manchu *sukdun*). The symptoms of its activity are such that one may suspect cases of pneumonia, typhus, typhoid fever, etc. i.e. the diseases which are more serious than those of the second group.

Here I give some details as to these manifestations as observed in different cases. (1) High fever, pain in the abdomen, no appetite, great weakness, no vomiting; the illness lasts about three weeks; the sick person drinks cold water all the time. The disease is "internal". No shaman can help, so that one of the experienced people must pray and give a sacrifice (a cock is preferable) before the placings. The intervention of a shaman may result in an immediate death. This is *tulilaṣi buaṣi*. (2) Very high fever, followed by hallucinations, loss of consciousness, pain in the abdomen, head and limbs; great weakness; the disease lasts six weeks. (3) Very high fever in a small girl, if there is no change in the condition there must be *tuliliṣi buaṣi*.

The seventy-two diseases are distinguished as symptomised in cough, bad cold, pain in the neck, pain in the throat, eye trouble (not serious), ear trouble, headache, etc.

The classification of these seventy-two manifestations, according to the above indicated three groups, is subject to discussions. The above indicated nine small diseases are supposed to be carried by the spiders, gadflies, ants, butterflies, turtles, frogs, crayfish, ticks, and grasshoppers.

* In fact, töril—the "dust" may be produced from turi (the "earth, soil), whence turikalan—"it became dusty" (Bir.). However, it is more likely that törütan as it is derived by the Tungus from turi is a folk-etymology of a foreign term; vide infra.

This spirit has not yet been mastered by the shamans. The whole complex is supposed to be of a very recent origin chiefly due to the mixing with other groups and living in the "crowded" villages. There are no permanent placings for the second and third groups, but during the sacrifice the Tungus make, depending upon the "road": two of each,— dragons, birds and anthropomorphic placings, and four *an'akan* which represent the manifestations of the lower road (*orgu okto*)* and two dragons, and two birds with five *an'akan* for the upper road (*uṛu okto*). For the sacrifice there is erected a special kind of platform as shown above. This type of platform is also used for some other sacrifices. However, some Tungus think that the above described placing for *or'ebar'i* may also be used for the other two groups of manifestations. So it probably is in their minds, but they do not want to keep the placings for the spirits may remain there for ever and thus may cause new troubles.

___

BAINACHA BURKAN   (cf. *supra* p. 126) is known among the Birarčen In case *baïnoča* causes a disease a permanent placing may be made (in the form of a picture representing an old man and an old woman, sometimes with the children) which will be carried on with other *savak'i*. In this form *baïnoča* would be called *burkan*, but it has, in so far as I know, only one road and only one active manifestation. It has not yet been mastered by the shamans and is met with very rarely as *burkan*.

___

DALKUR BURKAN   is known among the Khingan Tungus. About this spirit it is known only that it is very mischievous and dangerous.

___

GECHAN BURKAN   *vide*: *num'in burkan*.

___

KADAR BURKAN   known among the Kumarčen and Birarčen is rather rare. The name *Kadar* means "rock, cliff," where it made its first appearance. It is very likely that it is one of the forms analogous to *aṣelga*. It has a placing made in the same form as that for other *burkan*.** It is also known among the Dahurs. There has been produced from this spirit a *seven* which may give some additional light as to the character of this spirit.

___

·N'ANN'AN BURKAN   also is a very complex spirit known amongst the Khingan and Birarčen (I am not sure about the Kumarčen). The term

* The existence of the lower night road is denied by some Tungus and as placing they use only three an'akan.
** Unfortunately, the only placing which I could see was in its great part eaten by a cow which succeeded in pulling this placing out of the box. The Tungus say that it was similar to that made for sumu burkan.

as shown is of Chinese origin (*vide supra* p. 131). However, the Tungus language possesses a term of similar phonetic form usually *n'ayn'a*, *n'ayŋna* (Bir. Ner. RTM) (Ang. Tit.) also known in Manchu,[*]—the sky. Thus, in the Tungus etymology the name of the spirit may be connected with "sky." The spirit is located in the south-western section of the sky (heaven). It has great number of manifestations distributed between two large groups, one male and the other female. The latter contains seventy-two manifestations which are various diseases chiefly in children.

Particularly, the manifestation of *n'ayn'a burkan* known as measles is called *n'ičukan on'in,*—"the small mother." One of conditions of helping the child is to please the spirit, and first of all, all requests of the child must be immediately satisfied. This spirit likes fruits and for this reason the child must have, if possible, fresh fruits. The same method is used when the child is affected by the smallpox due to the spirit *ilga on'in.*[**] It may be noted that the wigwam or house are tabooed when the spirit shows its activity. In other words, the infectious character of these diseases is evident to the Tungus. In this group there may be also included chickenpox (sometimes called *ilga* borrowed from Manchu *ilxa mama* of the *oyoś'i* complex), scrofula, and other diseases especially manifested in the skin troubles. The Tungus say that most of the diseases which appear in children in the form of skin trouble are due to this spirit. However, it ought to be pointed out that not all diseases are classified so, and seventy-two manifestations are perhaps formed by analogy with *ajin'i burkan*. The male group has been "born" in the mountains.—It has the same placings as the *sumu burkan* (*vide infra*). The placings are pictures made by the Chinese and representing the complex *n'ayn'ay*. On the Tungus pictures there must be represented a white fox under the feet of *burkan*. The female group for the sacrifice has a placing which consists of three men (perhaps females?) made of wood. The spirit had been mastered by the shamans and became *sèvèy*.

NIKOLA UGODAN BURKAN   a newly acquired spirit with several manifestations, known amongst the Barguzin Tungus. The spirit has originated from the Russians. As a matter of fact, it is merely *Nikolai Ugodn'ik* (Saint Nicolas) of the Orthodox Church much worshipped by the Russian low classes. This spirit has not been mastered by the shamans.

NUMIN BURKAN OR GÈCHAN   is a spirit which shows its activity where there are barracks with soldiers. Among the Tungus it is rarely observed. It comes from the Numin River. It seemingly has several manifestations which may be chiefly connected with the venereal diseases. The meaning of the second name *gèčan* is not clear. I have seen no

---

* E.g. n'ayn'a oxo or n'ayn'a tučixe,—the clear sky has come out (out of clouds).
** Identification of diseases was not always easy, so that not all of them could be connected with definite spirits of this group. Moreover, among the Tungus there is no perfect agreement as to the correlation between the spirits and diseases. Instead of ilga onin, the Tungus also used the term degde, a verb by which there is designated the effect,—"to come out on the surface".

placings. This spirit has not been mastered by the shamans. As to the connexion of *numin* with the name of the river I have some doubt. In fact, as we have seen on several occasions, alien complexes are adapted by the Tungus. It is very likely that here we have the name of honour of *Erlik xan* (already known as *Inmunkan*, etc.), namely, *nomun xan* which is so styled among the Mongols, as well as among the Dahurs, and which has received a new function among the Tungus.

ONKOR BURKAN   is a complex spirit, similar in organization to *sumu burkan*. It is known only among the Tungus, Birarčen and Kumarčen. It has originated in the mountains. As to the name it seems to be of Dahur origin,—*oykor,*—"wild", "wilderness" etc., evidently a Dahur learned translation of the name of a Tungus spirit (cf. *kadar burkan*).

SUMU BURKAN   is a complex spirit which is known among the Kumarčen and Birarčen. It has come from the Dahurs together with the name [cf. *sum* (Dahur) *sum ~ sumu* (Xalxa) *sûme*, (Mong.)—the "temple" (Poppe)]. The Tungus identify it with *java mava* of the Manchus amongst whom it made its first appearance. It has two groups: the night road consisting of a female with several girls, and placings,—two birds and two *an'akan;* and the noon road consisting of a male with several boys and corresponding placings.

This list of spirits which are not a direct consequence of the souls of dead people and which may cause diseases and various other troubles may be increased with some other spirits of less importance. If the investigation is carried out among other Tungus groups and in a more detailed manner among the groups like the Khingan Tungus and some Transbaikalian groups, amongst whom I did not stay for very long time, there may be found some spirits of importance. However, to what has already been described, there will not be added many details which would influence the inferences that we shall later make, so that I shall not enumerate the spirits which I shall not need for my further treatment.

---

51. SPIRITS OF THE MANCHUS   In this section I shall give a list of Manchu spirits which are not of ancestral origin, and which cannot be regarded as "spirits masters". In this group of spirits the first place is undoubtedly occupied by the group of *fuč'k'i*. As I have shown *fuč'k'i* is a Manchu term for Buddha or Buddhism. So we may say that the existence of these spirits is due to the penetration of Buddhism. Indeed, their Manchu form is quite different from the forms of theoretical Buddhism.

FUCHIXI, according to the Manchus, theoretically is an individual guardian spirit. Each one of them must have a permanent place (placing). Yet, in principle, *fuč'k'i* are considered as benevolent spirits. However, in practice they are neither individual guardians nor benevolent spirits. According to the Manchus, these spirits are not so numerous among the Manchus as among the Mongols. These spirits are very numerous in their manifestations and they may be incidentally caught by the people,—this will be *fuč'k'i joyun* (literally—"Buddha road"). However, these spirits may be managed by the people who must make placings. Buddhistic pictures, usually bought in the Chinese shops, serve as placings before which from time to time some sacrifice must be put and prayers recited.* The spirit *fuč'k'i* may sometimes remain with the people during six or seven years and produce various troubles. I saw a man who during the business travelling to the upper Amur River district (*Xumas'an*) caught a *fuč'k'i* and following he went through a period of bad fortune; he had to move from a house to another, where this spirit came into the conflict with other spirits; his son was seriously ill during several months; his business did not go well, etc. Then it was decided to erect a shrine for this spirit in order to neutralize it and to give it a location ("place") for permanent living.** The spirit must now receive periodically sacrifice and prayers.

Formerly there were Buddhist priests and monks who did it very well. The shaman's intervention was not considered desirable because the *fuč'k'i* might come into conflict with the shaman's spirits and in this way the clan spirits also might be involved in the conflict.

MAFA or MAVA   is a group of spirits which is found in a relation with *fuč'k'i*. The term *mafa* (Manchu Writ.) in reference to the spirits is not met with in the Manchu dictionaries and in the Manual of Rituals (*večere medere kooli bitxe, vide supra*, p. 123). In Manchu Sp. it is known as *mava*. This group seems to be of relatively recent origin due to the need of differentiation of a special group of those spirits which have originated from old animals. It is supposed that some animals live a long life, become wiser than man and so their souls attain immortality. Such animals are local mustelidae, amongst the Manchus increased with hares and rats, and among the Dahurs increased with foxes and sheep. This complex has begun its penetration into the Northern Tungus complexes, as well. An animal which has lived one thousand years becomes black and wise, the animal which should live ten thousand years would become white and still wiser than the black one. Generally speaking these spirits are neither malevolent nor benevolent, but they may cause great trouble in the form of diseases, unhappiness, etc. and must be always carefully watched. Permanent placings are kept in

* Cf. a detailed prescription in *Manju medere večere kooli bitxe*. Although the high style of the ritualism of the Imperial family always served as a pattern, among the common people the sacrifices and prayers were greatly simplified.

** Perhaps the spirits *fuč'k'i* have received a certain popularity among the neighbours of the Manchus. So, for instance, among the Goldi, P. Šimkevič has also recorded this spirit (op. cit. p. 52) as *pučiku*, but chiefly connected with hunting. I. A. Lopatin mentioned *pučiku* met with amongst the Goldi of the Tunguska River and rarely met with among other groups (cf. op. cit. p. 216). Whether it is really a shamanistic spirit (*seon* of Goldi) or not is impossible to say for I. A. Lopatin uses *seon* in reference to all spirits, except *enduri* and *buseu*, which he designates as "devils" (*ê'ert'i* of Russian) (op. cit. p. 210).

every Manchu house, and regular prayers and sacrifices offered.

In simple cases, *fuč'k'i* and *mafa* are dealt with by any one, but in complex cases there may be required assistance of specialists called *axa mafa* or *mafar'i*, and sometimes that of experienced shamans. However, the latter must be avoided, for the intervention of shaman's *vočko* may bring new complications. With the decrease of influence of Buddhistic monks, their functions have been taken by *mafa* (*axa mafa, mafar'i*). So gradually the *mafar'i* became familiar with the character of these spirits and began to manage them. However, the spirits sometimes take their own ways and also the *mafar'i* use spirits for their personal ends. Therefore there have been formed new *mafar'i joyun* which formerly might have been called *fuč'k'i joyun*.

Some of the *fuč'k'i* spirits and the newly created group of *mafa* were adopted and later adapted by the Manchus so that they began to play a permanent rôle as guardians. I shall now describe some of these.

DJUN FUCHIXI · is the spirit of fire which consists of a male and female (*mafa* and *mama*) and which is found in almost every house.. Their number corresponds to the number of stove openings (*jun*) belonging to the family-units when they have separate kitchens. The placings are Buddhistic pictures which are put outside of the house, in a small shrine,—"house." Yet, the spirits also use as their placing not only the stoves, but also the earthen accommodation (*xolboko*) put in the middle of the room with burning charcoal for heating. One week before the new year the old picture is burnt and seven days after it is replaced by new one. Before entering a new house one must perform sacrifice and prayers before *jun fuč'k'i*. Newly married people must give sacrifice. When the people do not pay due attention to this spirit it may cause various diseases.

TAKTO MAFA (MAVA)   is a complex spirit mastered for protection of the house *takto*, i.e. the house which is located at the left, usually eastern, side of the Manchu manor (cf. SOM, pp. 93-94). It is represented on the picture as an old man. It has its own "road." A horse may be reserved for this spirit, as it is with *apka endur'i*. Various troubles, in the form of diseases and high nervousness, may result from the activity of this spirit, so that the Manchus must be careful in treating this spirit. Prayers and sacrifices are served on the occasion of the new year, marriage, etc.

JAFAN MAFA OR JAVA MAVA   is a complex spirit mastered for protection of the whole Manchu manor. The term *jafan→java* originally meant the kitchen garden (from Chinese "yuan"), but at the present time the activity of these spirits spreads over the population of the manor. The picture is put in the kitchen garden in a construction similar to that for *jun fuč'k'i*. This spirit is very often responsible for various diseases which require a careful attention of the shaman. The finding which of the above described three spirits is responsible for an illness is not easy, so that there are special methods for recognition of the "roads" of these spirits.

SOLOX'I MAFA or *SOLX'I MAVA (solx'i mava)* is a complex spirit which was formed from a very old mustela (polecat) and it is compared with *takto mava*. It may produce serious sickness. There exists an idea that some animals like the sable, polecat, *fóx* and others may attain great age of one thousand and even ten thousand years after which they change colour to black and even white—and become "like *fuč'k'i.*" Amongst the Northern Tungus they may become *sèvèŋ* of the shamans. I have included these spirits in the present group for they are not of ancestral and human origin.

ILXA MAMA is a complex spirit which produces smallpox, chickenpox, measles, and other diseases described in the previous pages (*vide supra* pp. 131, 157) as spirits known among the Tungus. *Ilxa* means "flower" and *mama*,—"female spirit." This complex is not Manchu origin. It is an imitation of the Chinese *n'aŋn'aŋ.* There are distinguished *ajige ilxa mama* (small flower female spirit) causing measles, and *amba ilxa mama* (great flower female spirit)—causing the smallpox. There seemingly are some other manifestations, but the Manchu refer to the Chinese books, so that the actually known and incorporated manifestations are only two above mentioned.

BUŠKU or *BUSUKU (WRIT.)* is a very dangerous spirit connected with the blood complex. In order to produce such a spirit the woman may take a wooden anthropomorphic placing of small size (from six to ten centimetres long with arms and legs) and wrap it for a certain period in the cloths used during her menstrual period and soaked with blood. If there is no blood available the placing may be wrapped in the woman's trousers. Then the placing is put in the wardrobe or chest of drawers where there are garments of the persons whom the woman intends to harm. If she wants to harm the people living outside of the house, she may make a short invocation keeping in her hands the placing and thus send (*jabumb'e* or *wuŋg'imb'e*) it even into another clan. The next day, the person to which the spirit was directed will fall ill. The disease is manifested in disturbances of articulations, even breaking of the tendons etc. called *buškui jorun,—buška* road. The spirit is more powerful than the *endur'i, voóko,* and all *xutu.* The person affected by this spirit is called to be *buškulèmb'e* (a verbal form, also *buškulèya,* "part. perf"). There is no treatment, and the shamans are afraid of it, too. * If the spirit does

* Indeed, the translation and explanation given by I. Zaxarov are not correct. Details given by Ch. de Harlez, namely, bušuku, "hutu également difforme qui attaque les petits enfants, les bestiaux et les animaux domestiques. Ils ont pour compagnons les Yemji et les Ibagan qui jouent le même rôle" (op. cit. p. 21). Indeed if Ch.

something against the woman's will she will scold it, but she will style it *èjèn,*—the master,—as a form of politeness. Such a woman, who usually behaves very politely with the people, may send the spirit to affect also domestic animals which become lame, blind, etc. without any visible causes of their condition. Such women are not frequent,—according to the Manchus, at most one per thousand. For instance, in the village Kalunšsn there was only one woman of this kind whom I used personally to know.

As a form of bad manners the men would sometimes call an old woman, quick and clever in her activity *bušku mama.* It will not be offensive but simply in fun when referred to an old woman.

The situation becomes more complicated when we proceed further with this inquiry. In fact, there is even *bušku endur'i* which is called *bušku mama* or *bušuku gèyè* (senior women of the clan, and generally an honourable woman, a lady). These are under the control of *n'aŋn'aŋ (vide supra ilxa mama* and others). If the needs of this spirit are not satisfied the spirit will manifest itself in the form of a sickness beginning by swelling of the legs, and followed by death, etc. which may last during several generations.

This spirit under the name of *BUS'EKU* has great popularity among the Birarčen and Kumarčen who have given me some more details. These Tungus say that it may be produced by the women according to the above given practice among the Manchus, with the exception that the chest of drawers and wardrobe which are not used by the Tungus do not figure and that it may be produced by a man as well, if he takes blood from gums between the first incisors on the upper jaw. The spirit little by little, "eats" the people, destroys the blood and bones. This spirit cannot exist beyond man and is always "placed" in man. Usually it comes to young girls and men who are not old and persuades them to accept it. Then if the person is not resistant enough, she or he would prepare a placing, made of straw and covered with cloth. The placing must be regularly served with fresh blood according to the above given prescription. Then the spirit begins to "eat" the people who are living with the spirit-keeper, leaving her or him, up to a certain time, probably intact. This spirit also attacks other spirits and if it succeeds in destroying them, then a general collapse of the clan may occur. However, this spirit was mastered by the shamans and some of them may influence this spirit even in the families where the spirit has already settled for a long time.

Indeed, the activity of this spirit is subject to great variations among different groups. This spirit though known among the Kumarčen, plays no great part in their life. Among the Dahurs this spirit is mastered by the shamans as it is among the Birarčen, but it is not so amongst the Manchus. Yet, the frequency of trouble caused by this spirit also depends upon the variation of local

de Harlez did not misunderstand the information which he had such a confusion of facts and relations might be due only to a loss of the original complex by the Manchus who lived for a long time in Peking and perhaps did not want to show to the Chinese how "barbarous" was their conception of bušuku and other spirits. As a matter of fact, the same confusion is caracteristic of I. Zaxarov's translations and explanatory notes. The practical inference from these facts is evident,—it is impossible to treat ethnographical subjects basing oneself on the written documents only. This case is more than a common one among the specialists who treat similar subjects and naively believe that they know the existing complexes.

conceptions. We have seen that Manchu *buŝku* is a complex in the manifestations of which we may include various diseases, while amongst the Birarčen this spirit produces, in so far as I could see, trouble of bones and blood chiefly. Thus there may be- perhaps included: syphilis, leprosy, tuberculosis, which actually may affect several generations, and are very often manifested at the age of puberty. Yet, the imagination does its work too. Among the Manchu *buŝku* occupies a very important part in the folklore, while it is very rare in Tungus folklore. Among the Goldi this spirit seems to be also known under the name *buseu* (*bus'eku—buseu*). However, I.A. Lopatin and evidently P. Šimkevič did not pay due attention to the character of this spirit and I. A. Lopatin (op. cit., pp. 211-212) identified it with *amba*,

and called these spirits "devils" (*vide supra* p. 158 f.). *Amba* actually is not the name of a spirit or a group of spirits, but merely is "great" used for avoiding the name the calling of which may awaken the activity of the spirits named. It is essential that *buseu* looks for blood when fed by the shaman (?) and "it tortures the people and drinks their blood" (op. cit. p. 212), which gives the same details as *buŝku* and *bus'cku*. Indeed, the change of shamanistic spirits into *buseu*, and the turning of the souls of people who had committed suicide into *buseu* is not very likely. Probably different spirits are confused, and I. A. Lopatin has designated too many spirits under this general term. In fact, the Goldi may use this term in a wide meaning as the Manchus do with *xutu* and Tungus do with *s'irkul*.

CHAPTER XIV

THE SPIRITS MASTERED

52. GENERAL CHARACTERISTICS OF THESE SPIRITS.
TUNGUS TERMS The present chapter is devoted to a detailed description of the Mastered Spirits which I have separated into a special group. It ought to be pointed out that these spirits are not at all "protectors" or "benevolent spirits" of the shamans. These spirits are those which are *mastered by the shamans*. Among all ethnical groups here discussed, the shaman is their *ojan, ėjèn*, etc. i.e. "the master." The relation between the shaman and the spirits will be discussed later, when the nature of shamanism and functions of the shaman are described.

In the Northern Tungus dialects of groups here discussed the spirits mastered by the shamans are called by different terms which may be brought to the common stem *seva*, while amongst the Manchus there is another term, namely, *voĉko*.

Among the Tungus of Transbaikalia, the Barguzin group, the Khingan group and the Reindeer Tungus of Manchuria the term is *seva;* among the Khingan, Kumarčen and Birarčen Tungus it is *sèvèy, sèvèn;* the latter is known among the Reindeer Tungus of Manchuria and Mankova Nomad Tungus. According to I. A. Lopatin (op. cit. p. 219) the Goldi term is *seon*, in an evidently approximate transcription.[*] S. Poniatowski twice gives *sevo* for Goldi spirits. However, among the Goldi C. Maximowicz recorded *sèwa, s'ewwa* (W. Grube, p. 91.) in the sense of "idol," i.e. evidently a "placing" for some spirit. In Olĉa we have seen *sevo* "an idol, god" (P.P. Schmidt). Also, L. von Schrenck mentions "idols" *seva*[**] among the Samagir group of Goldi and among the Olĉa.[***] S. Brailovski (op. cit. p. 184) says that the Udehe divide their spirits into two groups namely, "good" spirits,—*syn*, and "evil" spirits,—*sakxa, ènaĉi*. Indeed, this is not true for "good" and "evil" are not evidently of Udehe complex. Here *syn* undoubtedly is *sèn*, i.e. contracted form of *sèvèn*. As a matter of fact,

the Udehe have inclination for contraction of certain words.[****] Indeed the final *y ~ n* in Tungus may be of a secondary origin, as a suffix which is very common. Thus, the stem is *sVvV*.

We met with this stem when we discussed the name for "God" and the term for "placing", and even the term for the "box" in which the placings are preserved. Since the analysis of these words may help us, I shall proceed to give it. We have *šovok'i, xovok'i, xavaki* (Enis.) and contracted forms *xaŭk'i, xeuk'i* (Lamut, Schiefner) (perhaps, *xŭki*) used in the sense of "God" (introduced probably by the Orthodox missionaries); *sewek'i* (Barguz. Nomad Tungus, Poppe) is "idol made of rugs"; *sèvèk'i* (Mank.), *savak'i, sèvak'i, sèwèk'i* (Bir. Kum. Khin.) is "placing in general"; *sevek'i, seweki, sevoki, sŏk'i* (Bir.) is "spirits of, burkan type"; *savaki, šavak'i, s'avak'i* (Barg. Nerĉ.) is "spirits of burkan type and placings for spirits"; in Goldi, Oroĉi, Olĉa we meet with *sevoki*—"idol, a god (according to P.P. Schmidt); *heūunn'i* (Lamunxinskii, P.V. Olenin's record is not sure) is "placings", which when cleared from suffixes will be *hewu=sevu*. With the above indicated variation *sŏk'i* (Bir.) probably we ought to connect Oroĉi *seka*, and perhaps Goldi *seka*[*], Oroĉi *šaka* (Margaritov), *s'aka* (Leontovič).[**] I. A. Lopatin also gives *sekka*,—"devils", etc. supposed to have been borrowed from the Oroĉi. *Sekka* looks like either emphatic or imperfectly perceived *sèka*.[***]

Let us now classify these data. We have thus *sVvV*, and *sVvV+ki* with their variations and contracted form *sV+ki*. It is evident that the forms with suffix-*ki* are based upon the same stem *sVvV*. Let us remark that the con-

---

[*] He says that the Goldi term is nearer to "seon" than to "sèvèn" of my approximate transcription.

[**] It should be transcribed seva and not zeva as it is figured in the Russian translation of Schrenck's work.

[***] Cf. his work "On Natives, etc.", Vol. 3, pp. 113, 120.

[****] In the transcriptions of Tungus sound *è* by the Russians the sound Y is often encountered since for Russians it is acoustically near to *è*.

[*] Cf. Poniatowski in the compound name seka+ni sela+ni mama,—the wife of enduri, where seka and sela with suffixes are referred to the spirit enduri.

[**] They usually palatalize, e.g. s'ama ~ sama, the shaman.

[***] Perhaps in the same group there ought to be included Manchu *soko ~ noku*,—the "spirits" (the spirits of the earth and heaven, the penates spirits to whom the shamans' pray, according to I. Zaxarov). However, in Manchu Sp. I have never met with this term where it evidently is obsolete.

traction is going on *sewok'i→scok'i→sōk'i;* indeed, if the contracted original form is *seveki*, we have to expect *sěki*, or *seki.* As to the variations of the initial *s~š~h~x* they are quite common in the dialects liable to aspiration and palatalization. Thus, the original stem is *sVvV.* As to the semantic variations it may be noted that, if we leave aside new meanings like "God", "box" and perhaps "placing", there will remain a series with the meaning "spirits with which the shamans are dealing". In this strict meaning we meet with the stem *sVvV* in various dialects, namely, Darg. Nerč. Mank. RTM. Kum. Bir. Khin. and Goldi. Since this conception in Tungus is connected with a special kind of shamanistic spirits, there are found very limited semantic variations, and they have no etymology in Tungus,—I am inclined to look at it as an alien term. Furthermore, since the terms like *burkan, saman, enduri* and many others of the same complex are connected with Central Asiatic languages and with the primary source of Buddhism,—India,—I am inclined to see in it one of the loan-words from India, namely, the name of god Çiva who, as well as his son Kārtikeya, was supposed to be protector of science and who was fought and at last subjugated. A. Grunwedel has identified the Çiva deities with the local Tibetan and Mongol spirits. Might it not be different with the Tungus? As to the question at which epoch it might happen, we have, naturally, to go to the beginning of shamanism (śramanism) when the terms were received by the Tungus. However, before it is shown in the same clear manner as it was with *saman* and *burkan,* there will remain other possibilities as to the origin of this stem and conception. Here it may be pointed out that the colloquial Northern Chinese term *šifu* (師 傅)*—"the teacher"—has been assimilated by the Manchus as *sêfu* and it has undergone a further modification in Birarčen *sebú* (Bir) || *sêfu* (Manchu) referred only to the "shaman-teacher".** In fact, the soul of the deceased shaman often, if not usually, becomes one of the spirits, while the old shamans and their souls are "teachers" of the new generation of shamans. Thus, in Tungus soil *šifu→sêfu* might easily become a general term for "shamanistic, mastered spirit." It is especially true of the Manchu complex in which the principal spirits are souls of the old teachersshamans. In pointing out such a possibility of the origin of *sVvV,* I do not believe it to be a better hypothesis than the first one, from Çiva. For the time being I leave aside some other still less possible suggestions as to the origin of *sVvV.*

As to the Manchu term *vočko* in reference to the shaman's spirits it may be pointed out that the term does not differ from that used for "ancestors" which has already been analysed (*vide supra* p. 143), by which I do not presume to say whether the term for shamanistic spirit was one which later covered the ancestral complex in general or vice versa. The chief characteristic of the Manchu system is that the spirits mastered are confined to the clans and for the greatest part, are ancestors of the living generations so that the

* P. P. Schmidt ("Chinesische Elemente im Mandschu," p. 386) gives for š**i**-fu, sy-fu, the same characters with translation "Lehrer, Meister".

** This term has been introduced into Birarčen quite recently. It may be pointed out that in Manchu Sp. sêfu may change into sevu, sevo, i.e. analogous to efimbi, èvembe, etc. The Tungus form sêve might be thus received as Manchu Sp. modification of Chinese sifu.

same spirits may be included in the ancestral groups of spirits mastered and non-mastered. Thus the term *vočko* has no particular meaning "spirits mastered by the shamans", but merely "ancestors" who may be prominent owing to their potential influences on the living generation.

We meet with some other terms by which the spirits mastered may be called. For instance, the Birarčen, when they are angry with the spirits' activity, call them merely *s'irkul* (*vide supra* p. 138) and the Manchus would call them *xutu adali,*—"*xutu* like." The Reindeer Tungus of Manchuria used the parallel term *haja(n)* as equivalent to *sêvèn* and which seems to be of Yakut origin from *ajy* (*vide* Pekarskii, pp. 47—49). However, this term was referred only to the spirits which were needed for shamanizing *wiski,* i.e. to the upper world complex, while for the lower world there was still used *sêva.* The same is true of the Barguzin Tungus amongst whom the shamans call their spirits *ojan* generally except the shamanizing to the lower world for which they used also the term *seva.* Indeed, the *ojan* are a particular group of spirits (*vide supra* p. 140) which were mastered by these shamans. When the *sêvèn* enters into the shaman it calls itself by the shaman's mouth, *äjön~ ajön~ajen = (*ajon),* while the *sêvèn* belonging to (controlled by) a shaman are called *shaman'i on'ir,* both of which terms are not clear. When two Birarčen shamans introduce spirits they call each other *dorel* and oppose themselves to the common people,—*asarun.*

———

CHARACTER OF SPIRITS. As to the general character of these spirits they are not benevolent at all. When they enter people who cannot master them, these people affected may "lose their minds" altogether and perish. We shall see later some examples of this. These spirits are rather malevolent, and mischievous, even when they are mastered. For instance, in the Birarčen clan *dunänkän,* because of a *seven,* many people perished;—one was burnt, another killed, children were sick, etc. Another case: there was a shaman who had a very mischievous spirit; the shaman was ill and in his dreams he saw that he bit the finger of a child; in fact, the child fell sick after this dream; all this was done by the spirit. Third case: there was a shaman-beginner whom a certain spirit did not like; the shaman-beginner went hunting but he was not successful; then he made a special operation of divination with his gun and found out that a *seven* of another shaman was making trouble for him; then he made a *bami* (placing made of straw) and perforated it with his knife; on his way home he wounded himself with his knife in exactly the region where the *bami* was perforated; he told the story to other people and soon after that died. The case is explained as due to the mischievousness of the shaman's spirit which did not want to have him as its master, took the form of another spirit (belonging to another shaman) and compelled the inexperienced shaman -beginner to carry on the operation by which the spirit was affected and since it was actually the spirit of this shaman the latter had to commit the same act on himself (naturally the spirit as such did not suffer of the injury).

The spirits carry on continuous war and minor quarrels between themselves and with the other spirits, which may greatly affect the people. To regulate these quarrels is very difficult for one must know exactly the "roads" of all spirits which might be affected by *seven*. Such wars sometimes continue during several generations and thus the people live under conditions of uncertainty expecting at any moment to be affected by this war. Owing to the quarrels the spirits sometimes eat the sacrifice prepared for other spirits, so that those which are deprived of their regular sacrifice become angry with the people.

However, the spirits, which belong to the same shaman, may co-operate and sometimes they ask the shaman to bring some more spirits for carrying on their duties. The shaman never refuses and sometimes calls five or six spirits together. The same relations may be established as a permanent system of co-operation of a group of spirits. These spirits are not also liked by other spirits, so that if one wants to call these spirits one must ask the other spirits to leave free passage for them. Such spirits are, e.g. the ancestors, *ṭᶙlask'i, ᶄuᶒ'k'i* and others.

The activity of spirits may be recognized by the "roads" or effects as seen on the people. They usually have several "roads" so the effects on people are different. For instance, the night road of *ṭ'iaᶒi sᶒvᶒn* will be different from the night road of *kadar sᶒvᶒn*, as well as their "noon roads." A mistake in establishing the "road" may lead to further complications for the spirit which should receive the sacrifice, would be envied by another spirit which actually made trouble and the disease would continue and even the condition of the sick person might become aggravated. Experienced people may recognize the "road." The "road" may sometimes be understood as the road along which the souls of sick people are carried out by the spirit.

The spirits possess their own will and character. However, they may change it under the influence of their own experience. So, for instance, once a spirit did not want to be photographed (i.e. the shaman in the state when the spirit was introduced) but although it refused, I was told that when the spirit should have become accustomed to the camera, this would be possible. In fact, it was done later. The spirits do not like, also, certain kinds of food and every one has its taste, but if they accustom themselves to a new food, they may like it. So it was, for instance, with new alcoholic drinks of foreign origin, tobacco, sweets etc. The spirits (manifestations) of certain roads do not like light, some others do not like darkness. They also react on change of weather,—rain, cold, heat, etc.. They are also very sensitive as to their treatment by the people and therefore the people and especially the shaman must be pleasant to these spirits when they are to be attracted or to be used. For instance, the female spirits among the Manchus, want to hear something about beautiful flowers, to be praised for their beauty, etc. The spirits must not be disturbed if they are not urgently needed. *

All of this detailed information regarding desires and roads of the spirits is received from two sources, namely, from the observation of the shaman's behaviour, when he introduces spirits into himself, and from observation of the *sᶒvᶒn* themselves speaking through the shaman when the

* The spirits buni are not so particular about being disturbed. So once a shaman sang for the phonograph and after having finished the prayer to the buni he said: "Do not be disturbed; I was only singing that for this machine." But he categorically refused to disturb (into the phonograph) the spirit sᶒvᶒn.

spirits are introduced into himself. However, once a year, or more rarely when all of the shaman's spirits are "fed," i.e. when they receive their sacrifice, they say about themselves what they were before, how they lived and in general whatever they may wish to say, through the shaman. In case the *sᶒvᶒn* is not a Tungus, the shaman speaks in other languages, e.g. the Yakut, Mongol, Manchu, Chinese and also perhaps unknown languages. In such a case, the shaman or his assistant gives later on an interpretation of what was stated by the spirit.

The methods of attraction of the spirits and dealing with them are different, but what is essential is that every one must have its own placing and this is the reason why the placings are so numerous and varied and there must be something corresponding to the individual inclination of each spirit which would attract it to its placing. For this reason it is in some cases strictly necessary to erect posts with "roads" for dealing with the spirits. When the spirit is in, then it may be served with sacrifice and it may be influenced by the persuasion of those who have attracted it into the placing. When the spirit is attracted into the placing it may also be influenced by the methods of forcing spirits either to stop harmful activity or to direct activity in a desirable way. Also the spirit introduced may be taken far away and left there or even transmitted to other people. The dealing with the spirits in so far as practical ways are concerned will be described in Part 3.

———

ORIGIN OF SPIRITS. The origin of spirits is different too. We may distinguish (1) the spirits which have been transmitted from time immemorial, from one generation to another, (2) the spirits which have been recently borrowed from the neighbouring ethnical groups, (3) the spirits which are incidentally subdued by the shaman, (4) the ancestors-spirits and (5) the spirits formed from animals and men whose souls remain in this world.

The first group ought to be accepted as a matter of tradition. However, this group is not very stable owing to the fact that the spirits, like everything else, are influenced by the current fashions. Since the shamans do not master all of the spirits of the group and sometimes do not use all of them the spirits may gradually fall into oblivion. In this case, the Tungus say that in olden days there were certain spirits but there are no longer strong shamans who know how those spirits may now be mastered. These spirits would not be active.

The group of spirits received from other ethnical groups is very numerous. In fact, at the present time all Tungus groups are living under interethnical pressure always increasing.So that if there are some new spirits which become known to the Tungus and if these spirits produce their effect upon the people it is very likely that sooner or later the spirits will be mastered by one of the shamans, and in this way their harmfulness would be neutralized. However, there are great limitations as to the possibility of spreading of the new spirits. These limitations are due to the difference between the cultural complexes,—the cultural complex in which the new spirit makes its first appearance and that in which the spirit ought to be incorporated. So that if the spirit is "born" in the conditions of an agricultural complex and is closely connected with this complex, it would not be active, although theoretically known, amongst the Tungus until the moment when the complex underlying it is assimilated by the Tungus. However, since the Tungus usually are very easy in respect of their adopting alien cultural elements and complexes, they do adopt new spirits more than other ethnical groups. So the Tungus always complain about themselves: they say that other ethnical groups are not so much attacked by the spirits as are the Tungus. This group of spirits is naturally subject to gradual change due to the conditions that we have already seen in the case of the spirits transmitted by the tradition.

The group of spirits which are incidentally mastered may be of various origin. So, for instance, the shaman may meet during his travelling a new spirit, unknown to himself and to other people. If he should succeed in introducing this spirit into himself and if the spirit should do some useful work for the shaman, the spirit would be adopted and it might become more important than any of the other spirits of the shaman. Naturally this group of spirits is very individualistic and many of them perish with the shaman's death. However, some of them may survive, being transmitted to other shamans of younger generations. For such an issue the principal condition is that the shaman must give full information as to the character and behaviour of the spirit newly acquired.

The fourth group of spirits formed from the souls of dead ancestors and particularly shamans is very elastic. Some Tungus groups incorporate all shamans' souls into the complex, as it is with the Manchus, while some other groups try their best to manage a shaman's soul in such a way that it would stay inactive in the world of dead people. Naturally, this group of spirits always incorporates new members and loses the old ones.

The fifth group is very small and it may be considered as a group of incidental spirits. In fact, the animals which attain great age (*vide infra* p. 168) may become *burkan;* when they become *burkan* they may be mastered. The discovery of a new animal *burkan* depends, of course, on the individual considerations of the shaman. Naturally, the souls of these animals do not go to the lower world. The same is true of the human souls which are not admitted into the lower world and they are not incarnated, but remain free as *burkan.*

From the above remarks it may be seen that the spirits are different as to their origin and naturally they are very numerous. The reason that shamans have so many spirits may be seen from three conditions: (1) the shamans have to adopt the spirits which are transmitted through tradition; (2) the shamans master the spirits which are affecting them personally and those which affect the people; (3) the shamans master the spirits which may be useful for them. The last group now requires our special attention. During the shaman's activity he needs to have the assistance of spirits which possess different manifestations. For instance, the shaman needs to go with the souls of dead people to the lower world; on his way he meets with rivers, mountains, and other obstacles, so he must have such spirits whose manifestations can aid him to go across the rivers, to pass high mountains, etc. During his fighting with other spirits he sometimes needs to assume the form of birds, insects, and various animals in order to be able to follow the spirits; therefore he must have spirits which have these

manifestations. It is natural that if the shaman learns that there are some new spirits which have useful manifestations, he will try to master the new spirit. It is thus natural that shamans are not all alike and there may be very powerful shamans who possess many manifestations and yet there are some other shamans who are very weak and possess but few manifestations, so their activity is very limited. From the description of the spirits this may be still better seen.

ALIEN AND *CLAN SPIRITS.* The spirits mastered by the shamans may be classified in two main groups, namely, the clan spirits and the spirits *dŏna*—"alien, foreign." The spirits preserve this distinction even in case when the clan shaman masters the spirits of the clan which are of an alien origin, —we have already seen that the Tungus distinguish the clan spirits like *malu* and some others. So that when the shaman masters these spirits, or better to say, some of their manifestations, he may become clan shaman, but the same shaman may also master spirits which are not clan spirits. Still, being mastered they will not become clan spirits. However, when the same *dŏna* spirits are transmitted from one generation to another (shamans of the same clan) they may naturally become clan spirits, but they would be used only by the shaman.

Practically, as we have seen, all spirits may be mastered with the exception of *buga* and *inmɨnkan* (*irlinkan,* etc.). Yet, even the latter may be mastered in some of his manifestations, e.g. *moggoldaĭ nakču* has been mastered. All depends on the shaman's art. However, the spirits though mastered preserve some independence and may sometimes act against the shaman's will.

There are two purposes in mastering the spirits: (1) to deal with them when they harm the people, and (2) to assume the manifestations of the spirits when the shaman needs them for his fighting with other spirits, or needs to deal with other spirits, or wants to use them for his own purposes. Owing to this the complex of clan spirits also depends on the inclinations of the shamans who previously existed in the clan.

The Tungus suppose that every clan has its own spirits which never introduce themselves into the people who belong to other clans. Such spirits may be simply *mokun'i burkan* (*vide supra* Section 49) which are as such transmitted from one to another generation of the shamans. This is the case of many Manchu shamans. Since all Tungus clans have *malu burkan,* all clans have also *malu sèvèn* which in this way is clan *sèvèn.* The question now arises since the *burkan* is the same amongst the groups how does the difference exist between the clans in respect to their specific spirits. This difficult question is answered in the following way: the complex (*malu*) is the same, but the origin of the spirit is different. For instance, the *Birarčen* clan *dunänkăn* has received its *malu* from the clan *kargir,* but the clan *kargir* originally (we have seen, after a migration southwards, *vide* SONT) lived near Lake Hanka (South Ussuri Region) and therefore *malu* is of different origin. The *ĭerga sèvèn* is from the Ussuri River and therefore it is different. I need not explain farther, for there are many similar cases in the European complex.

In every clan there are certain variations in the number of manifestations of the same *sèvèn*, and also in the prayers and ritual. The clan *sèvèn* cannot be expelled from the clan but always remains, and must be treated in the most polite manner. The spirits must have regular sacrifice. In case these spirits have no shaman-master they become extremely harmful for the members of the clan.

The number of clan *sèvèn* is subject to variation which depends on the previous shamans and these *sèvèn* may also increase and decrease. So in some clans there is more clan *sèvèn* than clan *burkan*. Naturally it may be vice versa. In the case of the *dunänkän* clan the process of assimilation of *dōna* spirit is now going on: "There was an old shaman "who was a bad natured person. During his life he caused "much misfortune to the people,—some of them lost their "horses, others lost their children. Then four shamans "decided to destroy this shaman. He went for birch-"bark into the forest. As soon as he left his birch-bark "canoe, he saw a tiger and a bear coming to attack him "(These were forms assumed by the other shamans!) but "he defended himself with his axe. He ventured to his canoe "and said: 'Now it is safe. I will extinguish all of them.' "When he reached home he put on his costume and "shamanized three days and three nights. After this he " 'began to die' but before dying he said: 'Never mind. All "of you will follow me.' After his death there remained his "*dōna sèvèn* which went from one family to another (in the "clan) and everybody suffered from it. Nobody could "master this *sèvèn*; if a shaman had taken it he would have "died soon,—the spirit did not want another master, but it "did not want to leave the clan so it will remain there for-"ever." There was an idea of taking the spirit up to the Kumara River where there were no members of this clan. But even this operation would be extremely difficult and it might be good for a period of three to four years only. And yet even for such a temporary alleviation there should be required a very experienced shaman and a copious sacrifice consisting of either a roe-deer or a pig and a great number of wood-cocks. The opinion of the clansmen was that it would be better to find a good man who could master the spirit.

This is an illustration for showing how the *dōna sèvèn* may become clan *sèvèn* and naturally at least for a certain time this *sèvèn* will be one of the most powerful spirits of this clan. However, the clan *sèvèn* when absent for some time will return, but this time perhaps as *dōna* and so it will be again adopted.

However, the distinction of clan spirits (*mokun'i* or *kalan'i sèvèn*) and alien spirits (*dōna sèvèn*) is quite essential, for it is always hoped that the *dōna sèvèn* may be sent off and they will do no harm to the people, if they are not exceptionally powerful spirits, while if the spirit is a clan spirit, the Tungus have to consider them as something of which they cannot rid themselves.

Among the spirits *dōna* there are very many which are connected with certain localities. So, I have met with *Selimdi'i* (a river, tributary of the Zeia River in the Amur Gov.) *dōna sèvèn; Num'in* (a river, tributary of the Nomin River) *dōna sèvèn; Argun* (a river, an important tributary of the Amur River) *dōna sèvèn; Town* (a River, the left tributary of the Sungari River) *dōna sèvèn*. The *dōna sèvèn* may also be from other ethnical groups, so, for instance, amongst the Birarčen there are several *dōna* which

have been received by the shamans from the Reindeer Tungus of the Amur and Yakutsk governments, and even from the Yakuts. Among the Manchus there are as a rule several spirits from the Northern Tungus and Chinese, and also Mongols. When such a foreign spirit comes, the shaman speaks, better to say is supposed to speak, the language of the spirit. However, these spirits may understand the dialects of the assistant shamans and gradually begin to answer in the mother tongue of the shaman and his assistant. Why the shamans have these spirits may be answered when we discuss the question of the shaman.

ANIMAL MANIFESTATIONS. There remains one more important point to be cleared up before we proceed to the description of the spirits, namely, the animal manifestations of the spirits.

From the previous exposition of the facts it might be quite clearly seen that the Tungus idea as to the animals is such a one that the animals cannot be spirits themselves or act by themselves as spirits. There are no animals possessing the power of spirits which may interfere with human life and activity. In the previous treatment of the spirits we met with some cases when the *souls of animals* might become spirits, but the same souls might also be incarnated into the people. * Yet, the animals as such do not act, but the animal forms may be assumed by the spirits. So that if the spirit is "clever" (in Tungus *balbuka*, a term which is referred only to the spirits), it may have different manifestations in which it may be as strong as a tiger, or as swift as a deer; it may fly as well as a bird or it may go into the water like a fish, and so on. However, the spirit will not be the tiger, the deer, the bird, the fish. The spirit will have (to possess and to master) the' immaterial substance of the animals which possess these qualities of strength etc. and it will use these qualities for its own purpose. Yet, it will not be these animals at all, and they will not be material in their nature. However, the people may mistake them for material beings,—the animals. The situation is complicated by the fact, according to the Tungus idea, that the animals, with their bodies, may be entered by the spirits and in such a state spirits will act with the bodies of these animals, "animated" by the spirits, i.e. just as in the case when a man is possessed by the spirits, and as *ibayan* and *boy* is possessed by them,—no Tungus would agree that these are animals or corpses which are acting. Since the Tungus must designate these qualities of spirits by some terms, and they have to show the qualities in their placings they speak of and represent the animals in their physical features. Indeed, to invent new terms is not easy; still to express them in a complex formula, e.g. of the type as "the spirit's manifestation having strength like that of a tiger" is too complex so they say merely "tiger" and they

---

* The animal spirits, i.e. the spirits which might have formerly lived in the animals, are known but the Tungus do not associate them with definite animals,—individuals and even species. The spirit might go from one animal to another and even to man in this way gathering its experience and knowledge. So that if the Tungus are asked from which animals the spirits are, it is very likely that they would answer,—"We do not know it, but according to what the spirit says, it may be supposed that at a certain time it was in certain given animals."

represent the "placing" in the form of a stylized tiger. Here it is timely to say that the placings are never realistic, but are always represented in a stylized form. It is not that the Tungus do not know how to make realistic images of these animals, that they are "primitive", but the Tungus do not need to have realistic images; the spirits (sèvèn) perhaps would not recognize them as their placings.*

The question as to the animals' role in the shamanism of the groups here discussed is absolutely clear,—the animals as such play no part at all. As I have shown, the Tungus do recognize a certain mental power in the animals, sometimes they recognize the superiority of the animals in physical power, sharpness of sight, refinement of sense of smell etc. but all of the Tungus believe in their own mental superiority. They go still further; they do not recognize that there are men who can do more than they do unless these men possess the spirits through and with the help of which they may act. However, this will not be "human" power. In reference to the animals I have never heard that the animals may actually possess the spirits, but the animals as well as men may be *possessed* by the spirits. Therefore everything which was written in reference to the rôle of the animals, their particular supernatural power over man, and generally the relation between men and animals, needs revision and careful critical analysis. Otherwise one may become the victim of one's own imagination regarding the "primitive mentality". Indeed, what is stated in the above lines is referred strictly to the groups investigated. I do not intend to spread my inferences, based upon the groups investigated, over the groups which I have not investigated. I suppose that in some cases there may exist hypotheses regarding other animals which are supposed to possess "supernatural power", but in so far as the neighbouring groups as the Goldi, Oročí, Gilaks and others are concerned, I do doubt the possibility of supplying them with the ideas never possessed by them regarding the animals.**

These remarks are necessary in order to warn the readers against misunderstanding of the facts observed. Indeed, for abbreviation I shall use expressions like "animal manifestations," "birds," "dragons" etc., but it will be always understood that these are not animals which are "worshipped" or accepted by the Tungus as "supernatural" beings.

I shall now enumerate some usual animals manifestations which are: the tiger and bear for their strength; the wolf; the hare because of its tracks which are always intricate and it is difficult for the hostile spirits to follow them in order to find the shaman; the Cervus Elaphus and Cervus Alces which beat with their antlers; the mustela (*soloɣo*), fox, and sable which may penetrate without being

* During my work amongst the Tungus groups I have cleared up this question quite definitely and I gathered some specimens of their realistic pictures of the animals represented sometimes in their stylized form for "placings."

** Most of the records regarding these groups left by the investigators, such as L. von Schrenck, R. Maack, S. Brailovsky, V. Arseniev and especially L. Sternberg and I. A. Lopatin show the great fallacy of having tried to adapt the facts to the existing European conceptions of the "primitive man" and to find among the groups investigated by them everything which was at their time written in the manuals of ethnography. It is not surprising that everything—animism, idelatry, totemism, fetishism etc.—were discovered although they did not actually exist in the forms pictured by the investigators.

noticed; the horse and ox are also used; the eagle (with a white tail), swan, and many other birds are also used for flying and the eagle for attacking; the insects are also used. These manifestations are usually employed by the shamans when they have to go to the lower world or to fight the spirits in this world.

Following the same line of ideas are manifestations of spirits in "natural phenomena," like the thunder, lightning, the whirl wind, the fire, the rainbow, and others. Behind these manifestations there are usually found spirits which are "like" a certain phenomenon. More than this, some of these manifestations were created by the shamans who lived before and were called by these names as shamans who were known as possessing these manifestations. Again it is thus evident that the shaman's soul may be placed in a whirl wind, clouds, and so on. However, there may be no manifestations like the sun, moon, and also stars for these forms cannot be assumed by the shamans, nor spirit. So if they are met with e.g. as in the case of the *malu burkan* and *malu sèvèn*, they are mere symbols (symbolized placings) without any hint as to possibility of mastering these celestial bodies. They are thus rather "names" of some spirits. As all natural phenomena, they are directly controlled by *buɣa* (*vide supra*). There may be also manifestations like a cart, dwellings, etc. used for the same purpose.

53. LIST OF SEVEN   The List of *sèvèn* here given is based upon that recorded among the Birarčen, but I shall make references to other ethnical groups when it is possible and needed.

ADAR cf. ODAR   is a clan *sèvèn* (*Kargir* and *Dunänkän* clans) of minor importance. It has only one group of manifestations of night-female-low road, with two anthropomorphic manifestations, two birds and two fishes *adăr*. It is supposed that this *sèvèn* is now found in a reduced form after the division of the clan (probably *karɣir* clan at the beginning of the last century). This *sèvèn* is supposed to stay in the water (river).

ANGNA   *áɣgna* is a well known *dôna sèvèn* met with among many shamans. When the spirit introduces itself the person becomes insane (*olon, vide infra* Chapter XX). No placing is made. Naturally it is of middle road, called by special name *áɣgna* road. Perhaps it is merely the third group-manifestation of the *kadarn'i sèvèn* (*vide infra*).

AGDI DARIL   is a clan *sèvèn* met with in several clans and considered as a very important spirit. *Agdi* means "thunder," *dărîl* means "the *sèvèn* of night road". If the clan has no such spirit and if a member of this clan should meet on his way in taiga a tree struck by lightning the man may become very sick unless a *kaïdun dărîl* were made which will remain as a clan *sèvèn*. It has manifestations of night road *dărîl us'i dolbor* represented in the form of two *an'akan*. It has also a complex of nine males and nine females (women). One of its manifestations is the brown owl in which form the shaman goes. Yet there are several other animal manifestations,—the tiger, leopard, crane, boa-constrictor and dragon. It may also be noticed that during the performance,' wormwood is used as incense. This *sèvèn* is supposed to have preference for staying in the clouds,

In another clan I have found two groups: (1) Midday road with the manifestations represented as a wigwam put on nine trees, two dragons, nine birds, nine *an'akan* with three rainbows and nine bunches of grass on the right side of the wigwam. The complete sacrifice comprises a reindeer (*Cervus Elaphus*), two roe-deer, and nine of each, wild geese and ducks. (2) Night road with the manifestations represented as two trees, two anthropomorphic placings; the pig is used as sacrifice.

AJA AMTASAL—AM'ISAL (The second term is not correct though it was regularly used by an assistant shaman),—*aja* ("*good*") *amtasal* ("forefathers")* evidently is a *sèvèn* which was formed from the ancestors, perhaps not very old. I have never met such a spirit among other Northern Tungus groups. I think it might be an imitation of the Manchu complex (*vide infra*), particularly the clan *vočko*. With this spirit the shaman may go to the lower world. I suppose there may be no special placing. The spirit must be of lower, midnight, north-western road. A red string is put on the neck of the sacrificial animal.

BUSEKU is a special *sèvèn* which is neither *dōna* nor clan *sèvèn*. Its description is already known from that given in Chapter XIII (*vide supra*). This spirit has been mastered by some shamans,—I knew a shaman amongst the Birarčen and another shaman among the Dahurs (*vide infra*). Owing to the character of this *sèvèn* it is considered as bad and the work with it dangerous. The placing is the same as that used for calling on the spirit. The shamans use this *sèvèn* in order to neutralize disastrous activity of the spirit.

ČUCUN, vide *malu sèvèn*

ČULOGDI, vide *malu sèvèn*

DEγI, vide *malu sèvèn*; indeed, *deγi* (bird) manifestations are common in other *sèvèn*, as well.

DÈRÈGDÈ, vide *malu sèvèn*

DJAGDAR *jägdár* is a special *sèvèn* which is transmitted in the clans by the shamans, though it is not considered as a clan *sèvèn*. Etymologically *jägdár* ought to be connected with *jVgd*, of various dialects [cf. *jekse* (Manchu)],—"burn," "fire," etc. When the people burn any part of the body, the shaman may use this spirit for healing. There are three roads represented by different manifestations:

1. Middle road: two birds (made of straw or dry grass) and nine *an'akan* (wooden).

2. Noon road: five birds and five *an'akan*.

* Ama+ta+sal; ta is a Manchu suffix for plural used in terms of relationship, never used in Northern Tungus, sal is also a composite suffix sa+l both for plural; as is used in Manchu, l in Northern Tungus. Sal is chiefly used in Northern Tungus dialects on special formal occasions chiefly in speeches. Ami (father)+sa+l=am'isal.

3. Night road: four *an'akan*, two birds, and two boa-constrictors.

When the *sèvèn* is introduced into the shaman, the latter may touch red-hot iron, put his hand into the burning charcoal, boiling water etc. When the spirit is introduced the fire, including tobacco pipes, must be covered with something in order to avoid the introduction of the spirit into the pipes, fire place, etc. This spirit is especially common among the Dahurs, and as we shall see, among the Manchus. However, only among the Tungus does it attain such a complexity. No connexion exists between *golumta* and this spirit. The fire in the fire-place connected with *golumta* must also be protected. Indeed, this spirit is borrowed by the Tungus.

DJERGA [DARIL AND *jerga* (*däril* and *s'erä j'erg'i*) *SERA DJERG'I]* according to my information, is a very important clan *sèvèn* which contains three roads, namely,

(1) *jergá* (or *j'erg'i*) middle and neutral road: nine *an'akan*, five birds, two dragons;

(2) *s'erä j'erg'i*, male noon road: five *an'akan*, nine small birds; this manifestation usually comes first, before the third road;

(3) *j'erga däril*, female, night road, which may be also called *dolbór us'i*: four birds, two *an'akan*, two boa-constrictors. The terms are somewhat ambiguous *s'erä* is "rainbow," and *j'erg'i* is "kind, sort" in Mongol [cf. *jirxe* ‖ *jerge*, also Dahur *jérgï* (Poppe)] and Manchu (*jergi*). However, the Tungus have different term for "kind, sort" etc. *j'ergá* is never used in the sense of *j'erg'i*, but in some dialects (e.g. Mank.) it is used instead of Mongol *jegerde* the red colour (for horses), whence *jarda* (Bir. Kum.). Whether *jerga* (Mank.) is the same as *jerga* (Bir.) in the name of the *sèvèn* now is difficult to say. The functions of this *sèvèn* could not be exactly established.

DJEIDJ'I *jeïj'i* is a *dōna sèvèn* (in some clans it may be clan *sèvèn*), very old and very important. It is identified by the Tungus (Birarčen) as *J'iači burkan*. It has two manifestations, two dragons, which are supposed to live in the South and are of the noon road. The spirit, as a complex, lives in the South-West. I have not heard about the night roads.

DJUNGÈN KAIDEN *juŋgèn käidèn* is a *dōna sèvèn*, but it seems to be one of the group *käidèn* (*vide infra*). No details regarding *juŋgèn* are known.

IBAγAN is not a clan *sèvèn*. When it introduces itself into a man, the latter is very likely to become a shaman. It is evident that *ibaγán sèvèn* is a spirit borrowed from the Manchus in so far as the name is concerned (*vide supra*). Perhaps there was a certain change of meaning when the spirit was adopted by the Tungus for they already knew *boy* corresponding to *ibaγán* of the Manchus.

ILAVUN, vide *malu sèvèn*

ISELA, vide *malu sèvèn*

JOKO, vide *malu sèvèn*

KA'AN, vide *malu sèvèn*

KADARN'I (or *KADAR*) may be both clan and *dŏna sèvèn*. The term is only in-dicative of the origin of the spirit,—from the rocks. If this spirit is a *burkan*, when mastered, it may be a clan *sèvèn*. But there are also many spirits which may originate in the rocks and they would be called *kadar*, and they will be *dŏna*. I will give some cases from which the character of this spirit may be better seen.

"A man was hunting in the mountains when he saw "a white roe-deer [in so far as I know 'a white roe-deer "does not exist unless it is a case of albinism]. He shot at "it but failed to kill the animal and lost his mind. He be-"gan to run aimlessly and soon became shaman. This "spirit is the chief spirit of this shaman." The sacrifice consists of a Cervus Elaphus, the placings are two hillocks with the grass bound with a string like hair and put on a platform erected on piles. As a matter of fact, this ritual is very likely to be the same as that for *afelga burkan*.

Another case of the same spirit is: "A man forty years "old began to lose his mind. Once in the evening during "the hunting he was challenged by a *dŏna sèvèn*. After "fighting with the spirit he returned home with a dirty face, "a broken hat, and a broken instrument for holding ever-"burning fire. * Then they made a placing and he shot "with his flint gun. After this he became normal. Soon "after this he again lost his mind and then he had to make a "costume and drum and to become shaman. Then it be-"came evident that this was a *kadar sèvèn*, and a *dŏna* which "wanted to fight the man." This seems to be an incidental *kadar sèvèn* which may be opposed to a regular *kadarn'i sèvèn*. The latter has three groups, with manifestations by three roads, namely,

(1) middle road, with five *an'akan* and four birds;

(2) male, noon road, with four *an'akan*, five birds and two dragons;

(3) female, midnight road, which may also be called *áŋna* (*vide supra*) or *kulüljin* (*vide infra*) with two *an'akan* and two boa-constrictors.

KAIDUN *käidun* is a clan *sèvèn*, mastered *käidèn burkan*. There are very few shamans who may have it. The Tungus interpret *käidun sèvèn*, as a "free, independent" spirit. The night road—*käidun* (*käidèn*) *däril* is held as responsible for mental disturbances (cf. *supra*, *agdi däril sèvèn*).

KAROL At the present time it actually is a clan *sèvèn*, but formerly *dŏna* and it is considered as *dŏna*. No sacrifice is given. This *sèvèn* is very "bad,"—should a person die because of its activity it would make its home in the lower part of the skull, with the apertures for the eyes as windows; from the intestines, it would make the

* When the Tungus go hunting they have a stick on the sharpen-ed end of which they fix a piece of burning agaric. This is an important element in the Tungus complex for they cannot some-times produce fire and without it may easily perish.

bridle; it would make its cup from the skull. There is only one road,—male, noon road with two *an'akan*, two birds with heads turned on one side and called *muréil dèyi*, i.e. "birds having horses." According to one of my informers, *karól* is merely a noon manifestation of a *sèvèn* the midnight manifestation of which is *käidun*. Cf. *mokun'i karól burkan* (*vide supra*).

KOLTONDE *koltoydé* vide *malu sèvèn*.

KULILDJIN (*vide supra Kadarn'i*) is midnight manifestation of *kadarn'i sèvèn*. *Kulüljin* is probably from *kuli*(*n*)—the "snake"; it can be under-stood as "one acting with the snakes" (cf. also *kulin sèvèn*).

KULIN—vide *malu sèvèn*.

LAMALAIČEN *lamalaičen* is a *dŏna sèvèn* in its mani-festations absolutely similar to *n'aŋn'a sèvèn* (*vide infra*) with which it is closely connected. When dealing with it one has to erect two high posts. Its origin is closely connected with Lamaism,—the name is from *lama*,—the priest (lamaist),—and the spirit is considered as being of Mongol origin.

MALU is a clan *sèvèn* which must be mastered by every clan shaman. It is known in different manifes-tations among all Tungus groups here discussed (vide *malu burkan*) which continue shamanistic practices. Among the Birarčen and Kumarčen at the present time there is only a female midnight road; the male, neutral, noon and other manifestations have separated themselves long ago. As es-sential difference from other *sèvèn*, *malu* has permanent placings carried by the shamans. Yet, on the occasion of shamanizing they also make new ones which may differ in size. The placings which I have seen slightly differ from those of *malu burkan*. Each manifestation, separately, is also called a certain *sèvèn*. Here is a list of manifestations.

1. Two *kä'án* (cf. *kayan*) which are two females (women)
2. Two *dèrègdè* (cf. *dèrègdè* in *malu burkan*)
3. Two *koltoydè* (cf. P. Šimkevič, Addition III).
4. Two *maŋi ĵeŋ'in dülči* (cf. *malu burkan*).
5. Nine *joko*, i.e. the Yakut *sèvèn* which have been in-corporated.
7. Two *dèyi*,—"birds",—which are used as manifestations for the shaman's travelling in the air.
8. Two *mudur*—"dragon" (they may be represented as P. Šimkevič *ĵarga*, cf. Addition V).
9. Two *čulôgdi* [they may be called also *čuču*(*n*) (*r* and *l* for "plural")],—i.e. one-legged *sèvèn* which is use-ful for transportation of the souls to the world of death. Cf. *doxolo agè* of the Manchus.
10. Two *ílävyi*,—i.e. one who makes "dry" "thin"; it seems to be a spirit causing and helping the shaman in the case of exhaustion (some diseases).
11. Two *samyäli*, i.e. "the one with a broken chest," for treatment of the tuberculosis.
12. Two *täkan*, i.e. "beam" put e.g. across a small stream (bridge), which is used by the shaman when he needs to cross the river for taking the souls of the dead peo-ple or to reach the world of death with other intentions. One may also see:

13. Two *isela*,—lizards (cf. P. Šimkevič *xafa jarga* of Goldi) which are needed by the shaman for crossing water.
14. Two *kulin*,—snakes; these manifestations are needed for crawling without being noticed by one's enemies.
15. Two *odár*,—fishes with horns (a kind of carp) of very large size, considered very important, almost like dragon (*mudur*). This fish may break the ice in the frozen rivers. It seems to me that it is the kaluga (a fish related to the sturgeon). It is also used as bridge (cf. *tăkan*).

Theoretically, there may be some other manifestations. Usually the shamans have at the beginning of their activity only three or four animal manifestations (especially female-shamans), and not all manifestations are mastered. For shamanizing the Tungus fix in the ground a small stick on which they hang up the placings. The general conception of *malu sèvèn* is that originally it was a man, deformed by various diseases, who now shows how to cure them (different manifestations) and when mastered it helps in various diseases (as described in *malu burkan*), in carrying on the soul of dead clansmen etc. This *sèvèn* is supposed by many Birarčen to have come from the reindeer Tungus of the Amur and Yakutsk governments.

MANI JEɣIN DILČI   vide *malu seven* and *malu burkan.*

MOMATE   so may be called *malu sèvèn*, for the placings are made of "wood" (cf. *supra*).

MUDUR,   vide *malu sèvèn.* Indeed, *mudur* manifestations are met with in many other manifestations, but when the Tungus say *mudur sèvèn* they understand *malu* group.

N'ANN'A   *n'ayn'a* also *n'oyn'a* is a clan (in some) or *dōna* (in some other clans) *sèvèn* which is mastered *n'ayn'ay burkan.* The best known effect of the *sèvèn* naturally is smallpox, a manifestation called *avača n'ayn'á.* The spirit has originated from a female—animal (unknown). This spirit has three groups of manifestations in which, in so far as I know, the sex of the roads is not distinguished, namely,

(1)   Three anthropomorphic manifestations.
(2)   Noon roads with five birds and two *an'akan.*
(3)   Midnight road with two birds and two *an'akan.* The *lamalačen sèvèn* is very closely associated with this spirit.

N'IRGIR   in some clans is a very powerful clan *sèvèn.* It is also called the *sèvèn* of storm. However, *n'irgir* is a name of a clan (*vide* SONT) and it is supposed by some Tungus that it originated in this clan. There are two groups of manifestations, namely,

1.   Noon road with seven or nine trees, two dragons, three rainbows, also *an'akan* and birds, seven of each.
2.   Midnight road with two *an'akan* and two birds.

ODAR   vide *malu sèvèn*

ODIN   vide *sāg'i sèvèn*

SAGI   *Säg'i* (or *odin*) is a *saman'i seven; säg'i* is "the whirl", *odin* is "the wind"; it has only one road which contains nine whirl winds coming from different directions, which have no placings, and five birds made either of straw or grass.

SAMGALI   vide *malu sèvèn*

S'ERA DJERG'I   vide *j'erga sèvèn*

SOLONGO   *soloygo* is an animal (mustela *soloygo*) manifestation which has grown into a complex *sèvèn.* I have no details regarding this *sèvèn.* It may be supposed that it is connected with the Manchu-Chinese complex.

SUNUSUN   is a clan *sèvèn* (in the *dundakän* clan). It formerly was a shaman who died and his soul was not allowed by spirits to go to *buni.* In this complex there are found his own father, mother, wife and children. Therefore when this spirit enters the shaman the latter makes himself hunch-backed (when Sunusun's father enters), or he cries like a child when one of Sunusun's grand children enters.

TAKAN   vide *malu sèvèn*

UKS'I,—the swan,—is one of the animal manifestations which was especially common among the Tungus of Yakutsk and Amur governments, but among the Birarčen it is almost forgotten.

US'I   vide *jerga sèvèn.*

From the above given list of *sèvèn*, and preliminary remarks it may be seen that the list is far from being complete, for as stated there may be created spirits by any new shaman and the alien groups present a rich source of new spirits. Yet the list might be good only for a certain moment, for the spirits are not only incorporated but they are also forgotten. The same is true of the shifting of spirits from the group of *dōna* into the group of clan spirits.

54.   VOČKO of the MANCHUS   As shown, the general Manchu term for this group of spirits is *večko* (*vide supra* Chapter XII). However, the Manchus also distinguish their own clan *večko* and outsiders which correspond to *dōna*, above discussed. In Manchu they are called *tulerg'i večko*, in explanation of which the Manchu say *tulerg'i večko* is *èjèn aku* (i.e. master not), *večko*, or "spirit without master." Such ones may be, for instance, Chinese spirits. "Once a man was sick for a long time; he refused to accept the spirits; the shaman took them away and mastered them. They were of Chinese origin".

The Chinese, Tungus, Mongol, Dahur, and any other spirits may become *tulerg'i večko*, but after certain time they may be included into *čolo večko* and thus they may become Manchu clan spirits.

Amongst the spirits there may be one which after a certain practice becomes the principal spirit of the shaman who acts through this spirit. It is called *talaya* (*dalaxa*, Manchu Writ.) *večko*, i.e. the spirit which headed (the other spirits).

Kojala voćko are called spirits which belong to the clans with which the shamans are connected (*vide* meaning of *kojali* in SOM.)

When the spirits introduce themselves into the shaman on his call, the spirit call other spirits *ǰulen**, while the shaman is called by them *èǰèn*—"the master", and he styles himself *aǰ'iǵe èǰèn*, i.e. "little master".

The Manchu system of spirits mastered in many respects is different from what we have seen among the Tungus of Manchuria. The first important difference is that the group of spirits is closely bound with the clan spirits and actually it is only a group of special spirits of the clan left by the shamans of preceding generations. The second characteristic distinction is that the Manchu spirits are much formalized and since the Manchus possess, at least at the present time, their own writing system although they formerly used Mongol and Chinese systems, it was possible to record spirits in the form of lists of spirits which were copied and recopied by the new generations. Such a list of spirits is called *većeku ćolo bitxe*, i.e. "spirits list book," or *većeku ćolo gebu*, where *gebu* is "the name". It may be noted that *ćolo gebu* is almost a tautology. As a matter of fact, *ćolo* in Manchu is an "honorific name", a special name used as substitute for the actual name, title, etc. being a "loan-word" from Mongol,** while *gebu* is "the name". Such a list may contain a short description of all spirits. However, not all clans used to have them. At last, since the Manchus are accustomed to have pictures,—an evident imitation of other complexes,—they represent their spirits and in this way there are preserved even minor details of the spirits' accessories which may be figured in form of pictures. Such picture is called *n'urγan* (*nirugan*, Manchu Writ.). They are made in water colours in one, two or more large pictures showing all spirits of large size. So I have seen figures about thirty centimetres high.

Indeed, the lists of spirits and pictures of spirits are excellent documents for a detailed study of Manchu spirits. However, it is not enough to have these documents for giving a comprehensive description, for the same formalized symbols may be used in a different "sense". Yet, it is very difficult to have the lists of spirits which, as shown, are secret for outsiders, and one may happen to see pictures only on rare occasions of great performances (*vide infra* Chapter XXVIII) to which the outsiders are admitted only in exceptional cases.

I have at my disposal several *ćolo* of different clans, e.g. *kolg'a, wuǰala, nara, sagda, wuza* and other. Almost a complete list of spirits is given in *Nišan Saman* who belonged to the *ɵ'ǰoro* clan. Yet, I have seen two complete *n'urγan*. From what I know about the *ćolo* and what the Manchus say about *n'urγan* of other clans, it may be supposed that the *n'urγan* of other clans do not differ very much as to their general character,—the uniformity is rather typical of the Manchu complex. I saw one of these *n'urγan* during several days without being disturbed, so I shall now give some details. The *n'urγan* consisted of four water colour pictures on cloth, made by a Chinese

master, with all characteristic manners of Chinese bad village-painters.

The whole system of *voćko* consists of rows,—*wur'i*, which are sometimes also called *faidan*—the line of soldiers, etc.—Each row-line is headed by a principal spirit,—*taʌaγa voćko*. The rows may be called by different names, e.g. *poiγun*,—of earth; *sèlè*,—of iron; *toišun*,—of brass; *vèγè*—of stone, etc. Every *voćko* has its definite place called *soor'i*.

FIRST PICTURE: in the middle of the first row in a pagoda,—*luzā* (a Chinese word 樓子)—where there are "sitting" *maʌfa saman mama saman*, i.e. "honourable shamans, male and female." Beside them under trees there are standing two *k'ilin voćko*, i.e. the Tungus (*k'ilin, vide* SONT) spirits, the characteristic functions of which usually are that they have either a gun or a bow and arrows in their hands.

The second row contains various *voćko* either in *luze* or not; *xele* (speechless) *maʌfa* which is the chief of the row, is found there with a jar of wine; he is surrounded by *batur'i* (heroes) and *maγi* (endowed with great abilities), these *voćko* are represented as masters of their special abilities, e.g. one of them can take coins out of a kettle of melted metal; another one (*fulg'an maγi*) can go barefoot into a heap of burning charcoal; a third would put a red hot iron belt around his waist; a fourth can put on, instead of shoes, red hot iron ploughshares; a fifth can use a ladder made of swords turned with the sharp edges upward; a sixth would be put under the knife of the straw-cutter the handle of which would be pressed by several people, without harm to the *maγi voćko*; a seventh would perforate his sides with two knives, and so on.

The third row contains a dragon, snake, boa constrictor with some human figures.

The fourth row contains a tree with five cuckoos and two other birds under a tree.

SECOND PICTURE.   In the fifth row in a *luzā*,—(?) *mama* and at the right side of her a shaman, the grandmother of the present generation. In the sixth row—a group of *xexe voćko* [which wanted to have a new shaman in the particular case described in Part 4 (*vide* Chapter XXVIII)] one of them receives a *voćko* from another woman shaman and the first one expresses thanks (by a special posture).

In the seventh row headed by *m'oćan mèrgèn* (skilful in gun shooting) on horse back and in Chinese dress, there are eight *k'ilin* (Tungus) *voćko* who surround the head of this row.

THIRD PICTURE.   In the eigth row there are represented *p'oγun voćko* [clan (strictly) spirits] which are headed by *ćuxa ǰaɤg'in* (a military chief) (*vide* Chapter XII; *ǰaγin = ǰaɤg'in*). In the ninth and tenth rows are located various spirits which could not be identified.

FOURTH PICTURE   which consists of three or four rows represents *p'iγau voćko*,—forest spirits, which are found only among the *ićl manǰu*. Their chief is called *onduri* (! !) (i.e. *endur'i*); there may be seen several *k'ilin* (Tungus) *voćko* with several *ǰuran k'jo* (roe-deer); also several males and females near by

---

* The etymology is not clear. I. Zaxarov gives a word *ǰulexen*,—the "evenness, equality,"—which seems to be of the same stem. cf. also *ǰal* (RTM),—the "companions in hunting, comrades."

** Cf. I. Zaxarov, p. 948; cf. Mongol *cola, colo* (Kowalewsky, p. 2204); it has been borrowed by some Turkish dialects (cf. W. Bang "Turkologische Briefe", 1932, p. 99) as *sola ∼ šola*.

which there are several spotted deer with four leaves of a red flower in each, in their mouths; there are two tigers which are being fought by two big birds of prey; there is also a blackfaced spirit with a leopard, *jačin tasza saman* [i.e. dark (black) tiger shaman]; there are many rocks, mountains and swift streams represented as characteristic of the region where these spirits live. *

It may be noted that the above persons are dressed in old fashioned Manchu dresses and some of them have long and short coats characteristic of the present dress among the Northern Tungus of Manchuria. As. another characteristic feature of the above described complex is that there are very few Chinese spirits (*vočko*) and a great number of *k'ilin vočko* (Tungus spirits), while Dahur spirits are absent. The shamans are dressed in their usual costumes with the brass mirrors. In one case the large mirror is surrounded by eight smaller mirrors.

Generally the type of *iči manju* (New Manchu) complex is different from that a *fè manju* (Old Manchu). In the first type there are many Tungus spirits, but the Chinese spirits are not numerous, the special group of *p'izan* (taiga) *vočko* also is present and usually very numerous. Among them *jačin tasza saman* (*vide supra*) is considered as a very important *vočko*. It has even a special sacrifice consisting of a cock and a boar, instead of a hen and a sow. Yet, the "New Manchu" spirits are supposed to be more mischievous and dangerous, e.g. "A man who was drunk declared that he did not believe in the spirits. Soon after that two near relatives and all his children died." Even copious sacrifice of sheep and oxen cannot help to win the spirits' sympathy. If the children should turn the placing with the faces to the wall almost surely there would be some diseases in the family and there will be needed a special sacrifice and prayers.

Every clan has its own complex of spirits, but there are many of the same spirits which are met with in several clans. These spirits are, so to say, ever and everywhere present as it is with the Northern Tungus spirits. The same spirits, e.g. the above mentioned *mafa vočko* and *mama vočko*, are found in most of the clans and still they are different in every particular clan.

. Here I give a translation with notes of the list of spirits of the clan *kolg'a* (or *kora*). This clan is believed to be one of typical clans of the Old Manchus (*fè manju*) which has preserved its ritual and list of spirits. The original list of spirits had been in a good condition, so that it might be copied without great difficulties. I have chosen this list of spirits among several lists which I have because as stated it is typical and very old. The MS. was in better condition as compared with other lists. However, this list is not complete in so far as detailed description of spirits is concerned. I cannot state whether these details are found in other lists which I did not see, or they are transmitted by oral tradition. It is very likely, and it will be later shown, that the Manchus did not record all details, and yet the record of spirits is undoubtedly an innovation.

* It may be also noted that every n'uryan includes a spirit called sakda sèfu saman ("old teacher shaman") which I have failed to locate in the given n'uryan.

"In the southern region there are open, clear mountains. In the middle of the mountains there are three "rocks. In the middle of the rocks there is a beautiful "walled town. In the middle of the town there are eight "pairs of trees.(1) In the middle of the trees there is an "ornamented (many-storied building) pagoda(2). In this "pagoda there were distributed(3) twelve rows (of spirits) "headed; all governed by the leading spirit(4) *Agjulan*(5) "shaman who stays(6) holding a drum "*Erinbuku*(7) assistant shaman who stays holding a javelin. "Next comes a green tree. On the top of this tree there "were cuckooing "five kinds of cuckoos(8). On the first branch there was "cuckooing "*Yellow Cuckoo;* on the second branch there was cuckooing "*Red Cuckoo;* on the third branch there was cuckooing "*Green Cuckoo;* on the fourth branch there was cuckooing "*Black Cuckoo;* on the fifth branch there was cuckooing "*Streaked* Cuckoo. Next come spirits "*Agjana*(9) brother(10) who rides a chestnut horse with a "quiver on the left and on the right(11) attached to "his sides and who stays holding a halberd "*Cagjana*(12) hero(13) who rides a roan horse with a quiver "attached on the left and on the right and stays "holding two swords. "*Arsulan*(14) brother who rides a piebald horse, stays holding a javelin "*Arsulan* strong hero who rides a white horse, stays holding a pair of clubs "*Erdemupa xèlè*(15) valiant hero(16) stays holding a drum "this spirit is gathering all kinds of information; "he investigates cases "*Ajulan* brother(17) stays holding trihedral spear with "three teeth "*Sar'in'ju*(18) sister(19) and "*Ser'in'ju*(20) sister stay both holding kerchieves."

1. It was impossible to find out the kind of tree. In Manchu *zandu* is given by I. Zaxarov as "rice", which is quite correct. However, in the present text the Manchus understand *zandu* as a "tree". From the pictures which I saw I could not identify the kind of tree.
2. In Manchu *tusè* [corr. *tuzà* (Manchu Sp.)] means "many-storied building". In the picture it appears as a pagoda. (Cf. supra)
3. *samdame bixè*, as it is in the text is not from the "verb" *samdambi*,—"to shamanize", but it is "to be in rows with interruption" (cf. I. Zaxarov, *samdame tarimbi*) which I translate as "distributed".
4. The leading spirit of a row has above itself a leading spirit of the whole complex.
5. *Agjulan* is a kind of bird which I could not identify. However, it is not a bird, but a man's name. The man was first a shaman in the clan and he has become a leading spirit of the whole complex.
6. As a special shamanistic expression the Manchus use "verb" *dosimbi* which in reference to the spirits means "to be, to stay in, to come into." In reference to the living men it is equivalent to "to be, to live."
7. *Erinbuku* I leave without translation. He was assistant shaman of *Agjulan*. The name is a composite one,—*erin*+*buku* (cf. for *buku*, infra footnote 13).
8. These five cuckoos are names of persons. . I give

translations of Manchu words for colours by which the cuckoos are distinguished.

9. *Agjana age* is the name of a spirit of minor importance. *agjan* is "the thunder," for *age* vide footnote 10. This spirit, when the man was alive, was brother of next spirit *Cagjana*.

10. The term *age* is common in the names of spirits of a secondary importance. However, it is not a term of relationship.

11. The word for quiver is omitted, but it is understood that "left" and "right" are quivers.

12. *Cagjana* seems to be a parallel formation to match *Agjana* (cf. bootnote 20).

13. In Manchu *buku* referred to "very strong person," "wrestler" etc. I translate as "strong hero." This is a special group of spirits of a third rank.

14. *Arsulan* literally "the lion" here is a man's name.

15. *Erdemuya xèlè*, where the first one is "wise, virtuous" and second is "the stutterer" is the name of a shaman who has become a spirit. In the lists of spirits one meets with "stutterer," "dumb," "speechless" and others. Here the functions of the spirit are given while usually they are lacking.

16. *baturi* are almost equivalent to *buku* (vide footnote 13), but they form a special group of spirits and for this reason I translate it as "valiant hero."

17. This spirit helps in the case of very serious diseases. The meaning of the name is not clear.

18. *Sar'in'ju* literally "gray haired" (cf. I Zararov *sari*, but *sarinjambi*, a "verb," has a different meaning).

19. *gèxè* is analogous to *age* (vide footnote 10).

20. *Ser'in'ju* literally "liar, gossip, etc." It responds to *Sar'in'ju*, analogous to *Agjana—Cagjana;* such doubled spirits probably originate owing to the stylistic requirements of the text of *ćoto*.

1. There may be used in reference to the spirits either *dos'imbi* or *texembi*—"to seat," as it is used in the case of emperors,—"to seat on the throne", and in the case of people staying in a certain locality.

2. *balan* can be translated "fearless". This spirit is the first assistant of the first spirit of the complex *Agjulan saman* (vide supra) and it is the first spirit of the second row.

3. *Agjan* can be translated "thunder", (vide infra footnote 4.)

4. *beise* is a Manchu title, the second rank (the first is *beile*). This spirit *Agjan beise* is used when the soul "falls down" being frightened by the thunder. The spirit is indicated when needed by *Xete Mafa* (*baturi*).

5. *Argudai* brother never comes (to the shaman), if there are sick people in the house; in general it comes also very rarely even in the new year sacrifice.

6. *juru Mèrgèn*—this may be understood as "*juru*—wise", or "a pair of wise (men)". The Manchu hesitated as to the function of this spirit and even whether, there are two or one spirit. These are Tungus (*k'ilin*) spirits

7. *Doxolo age* is "the lame brother" who takes human souls across the river in the world of dead people. This is a spirit which helps the shaman in this operation.

8. *Durgire Dutu* can be translated as "mumbling deaf". This spirit comes only once a year, the day of the yearly sacrifice.

9. I find no meaning of this name.

10. *Sèsèreku* can be translated "dishevelled" (cf. *sèsèrembi*—"to make, to put in disorder"). This spirit is used when the shaman goes to the lower world and must visit dangerous "wild" places.

11. *Er'in'ju* sister helps in the case of sickness of females, both adult and children. The name is associated by the Manchus with *erin* "the time".

12. *Ver'in'ju* sister has the same functions. The name is a doublet of *Er'in'ju* but its meaning is not clear.

13. *jiŋgèl* is a kind of parrot; *iŋgèl* seems to be a doublet. The functions of the spirits are not established.

14. *jiŋju* is a kind of "golden hen"; *Iŋju* is analogous to doublets in other cases, but the meaning is "silver hen".

"The second row; in the northern region there is jagged rock. In the middle of the rock there is ornamented "pagoda. In the pagoda there sat[1]
"*Balan*[2] valiant hero who stays holding a drum
"*Agjan*[3] *Beise*[4] who stays holding a javelin
"*Argudai* brother[5] who stays holding a pair of swords
"*Argudai* strong hero stays holding a toothed spear
"*juru Mèrgèn*[6] who stays holding a gun
"*Doxolo* brother[7] who stays supporting a drum
"*Durgire Dutu*[8] brother who stays holding a javelin
"*Arguśan*[9] brother who rides on the black horse and stays
   "holding a javelin
"*Arguśan*[9] strong hero who rides on the chestnut horse
   "and stays holding a javelin
"*Sèsèreku*[10] brother who rides on a piebald horse and stays
   "holding a pair of clubs
"*Sèsèreku*[10] strong hero who rides on a roan horse and stays
   "holding a large halberd
"*Er'in'ju*[11] sister and
"*Ver'in'ju*[12] sister, stay holding a pair of brass mirrors
"*jiŋgèl*[13] sister and
"*Iŋgèl*[13] sister stay holding ribbons
"*jiŋju*[14] sister and
"*Iŋju*[14] sister stay holding a drum."

"The third row; in the eastern region there are open clear mountains. In the middle of the mountains there are two pairs of trees; there is Veren Namu[1] walled town. In the middle of the town there is a beautiful pagoda. In the pagoda sat
Seimenju[2] shaman who stays holding a drum :
Daifu mama[3]
Ciŋ-śe[4] sister
Bai-śe[5] sister who stay holding a pair of kerchieves
Ais'n Meŋun Mujuźu[6]

1. *Vèrèn Namu* literally is "small sea waves"

2. *Seimenju saman* is the first spirit of this row. It is used during the shaman's going to the lower world. During the sacrifice it sees that the rites (*kooli*) are correctly performed. The meaning of the name is not clear.

3. *Daifu Mama* is a female spirit helping in case of diseases of very small children. The name is from Chinese *tai fu* used for designation of a rank.

4. *Čiŋ-še* is a female spirit which comes only on the new years day. The name is Chinese,—"the gray snake."

5. *Bai-še* the same as *Čiŋše;* from Chinese,—"the white snake."

6. *Ais'in Meŋun mujuxu,*—"golden and silver carp,"—complex spirit fishes.

"The fourth row; southern (midday) direction; there "are open clear mountains. In the middle of the mountains "(there is) a thick pine forest. In this forest, being head "(of the row) there was sitting, covering the sky
"*Amba Daimin*(1) who shades the earth
"*Narxun Daimin*(2)
"*Aḷxa Daimin*(3)
"*Kuri Daimin*(4)
"*Keksere Gasxa*(5)
"*Lebšere Gasxa*(6)
"*Fuḷg'an Gasxa*(7)
"*two G'joxun*(8)
"*five Kiḷxu*(9) all stay holding drums".

1. *Amba Daimin,*—"the great eagle" which is the principal of the row. This spirit as well as other spirits of the group are shamans.

2. *Narxun,*—small.

3. *Aḷxa,*—many coloured, piebald.

4. *Kuri* dark brown.

5. *Keksere Gasxa; gasxa* are called all large birds of prey, as for instance kite, hawks, etc. Whether *kersere* is a classificatory name of a kind of bird, which does not seem to be found in 1. Zaxarov's Dictionary or it means "joyful" I cannot say.

6. *lebšere gasxa; l'ebšere* does not seem to be clear,—whether it is a name or merely "fierce."

7. *fuḷg'an*—"red."

8. *g'joxun*—"falcon."

9. *kiḷxu*—"heron."

"The fifth row; western region; there are high "mountains. In the middle of the mountains there is a "many-coloured(1) walled town. In the middle of the town, "a many-coloured(1) pagoda. There were in rows
"*jatuŋa* shaman(2)
"*Jatuŋa* assistant shaman who stay all holding drum(s)
"*Seletu*(3) brother who rides a black horse right (quiver "and) left (quiver) attached stays holding iron "club
"*Seletu*(3) strong hero who rides a horse with white hoofs "right (quiver and) left (quiver) attached stays "holding iron spear
"*Seletai*(3) brother who rides gray-chestnut horse right "(quiver and) left (quiver) attached stays holding "a large halberd
"*jeryule*(4) brother who rides chestnut horse right (quiver "and) left (quiver) attached stays holding a pair "of swords
"*jeryule*(4) strong hero who rides white horse right "(quiver "and) left (quiver) attached stays holding a pair "of clubs."

1. *bočoŋo* from *bočo,*—"the colour"; it may be also translated "bright".

2. *jatuŋa* shaman is the head of the row, *jatuŋa* is "sharp".

3. *Setetu, Selotai*—man's name from *sèlè*—"iron".

4. Meaning of the name is not clear to the Manchus.

"The sixth row; in North-East-North region; there are "great mountains. In the middle of the mountains there : "is a high mountain. In the middle of the mountain there "are two pairs of trees. In the middle of the trees (there "is) a shiny pagoda. In the pagoda sat
"*Baḷen*(1) valiant hero who stays holding a javelin
"*Aŋfan beise*(2) who stays holding a pole-axe
"*Sergudai*(3) brother who stays holding a narrow spear
"*Aisuḷdai*(3) brother who stays holding a toothed spear
"*Beisuḷdai*(3) strong hero who stays holding a drum
"*Sarxudai*(3) brother
"*Sarxudai*(3) strong hero who stay holding (?)" (4)

1. *Baḷen* is the head of the sixth row.

2. cf. second row, footnotes 3 and 4. The spirit helps to liberate the soul by producing thunder.

3. These are men's names. The functions of the spirits are not established.

4. It is omitted what the holding involves but the Manchus repeat *apkai asu na xošoka* without understanding their meaning. *Asu* may mean "net, coat of mail" but then "heaven" is not clear. Yet, *asu* may also mean "code of laws, regulations." The meaning of *na xošoka* may be understood as "parts of the earth", so the whole expression may mean something like "heaven law for all parts of the world." Although such an interpretation may be accepted, in the text it is stated that the spirit is "holding" something which must be one of usual things, as a drum, a spear, and other shamanistic paraphernalia. There may be made another supposition, namely, this phrase is a remainder of a fuller text which is now forgotten. Something of this kind has happened with the text concerning *Erdemuŋa xèlè* (*vide supra*, footnote 15). I suppose that in the full text there should be an explanation of all functions of all spirits, as I happened to hear at the election of a new shaman (*vide infra* Chapter XXVIII).

"The seventh row; there are the jagged rocks. In the "middle of the rocks there is iron(5) row.
"In this row are staying·with iron helmets on their heads "and holding toothed spears
"*Sèbèžun* shaman(1) and
"*Serxur'i*(2) assistant shaman (each) stay holding drum
"*Sele Sèèè*(3) stays holding a spear
"*Sele* strong hero stays holding a pair of clubs
"*Sele Mèrgèn*(4) stays holding a gun
"*Sele Sertu* stays holding an iron bar
"*Sele Ser'in'ju* stays holding ribbons (descending from the "helmet)
"*Sele Wukun'ju* sister
"*Sele Er'in'ju* sister (each) stay holding a pair of brass "mirrors"

1. *Sèbèžun* shaman is very joyful, gay spirit. When he comes, especially at the new year sacrifice, every body

smiles and laughs. He says to every one something "nice and good".

2. man's name
3. *Sele Sèèè* does not seem to be a complete designation of the spirit. For *sèèè* I have the translation,—"the sock of plough," but this is a man's name. In another text I have another meaning,—"turtle."
4. *Mèrgèn*—"wise" (cf. Second Row, footnote 6).
5. For this reason the spirits have addition *sele*,—"iron".

"The eighth row; in the South there are high moun-"tains. In the middle of the mountains there is *jerg'iŋa* "walled town. There were staying (in row)
"*Ingelji* shaman(1) who stays holding a drum
"*Ingelji* assistant shaman who stays holding a spear
"*Durgide Dutu*(2) who stays holding a drum
"*Bèlin Bèlèe*(3) who stays holding a spear
"*Xorxodai*(4) brother when it comes it steals things(4)
"*Doxolo* brother(5) who stays pressing a drum
"*Imziu Mama*(6) who stays holding a drum

"two *kun'jaŋ* teachers(7) who stay holding drum(s)"

1. This spirit is called when there are sick people. It is the head of the row. *Ingelji* is the man's name.
2. cf. Second Row, footnote 8.
3. *Bèlin bèlèe*,—"dumb-deaf" or "olon" (*vide infra* Ch. XX). This spirit is never called when there are sick people.
4. According to I. Zaxarov "bold". The things are stolen by the spirit during the shamanistic performance (kleptomania?).
5. Cf. Second Row, footnote 7.
6. This female spirit helps in the case of smallpox. She also protects, takes care (*erśembi*) of the child. *Imziŋ* is not a Manchu name.
7. *Kun'jaŋ śifu* "Miss teacher" (姑娘師傅) is certainly Chinese.

"The ninth row; in the West there are even mountains. "In the middle of the mountains there are rows of pine trees. "In the middle of the rows there is a great walled town. In "the middle of the town there is a great pagoda. In this "pagoda sat
"*Wukun'ju mama*(1) who stays holding a drum with two "girl-attendants
"*jinčol*(2) and
"*Inčol*(2) who stay holding kerchieves.
"*Temturè* brother who rides a chestnut horse stays holding "a javelin
"*Temturè* strong hero who rides a black(!!) horse stays "holding a trihedral spear with three (..?..)
"*Sarzudai*(3) brother who rides a grey-chestnut horse stays "holding two swords
"*Narźuśaŋ* brother stays holding a drum
"*Narźuśaŋ* strong hero stays holding an iron spear
"*Serźuśan*(4) brother
"*Serźuśan*(4) strong hero (both) all stay holding drum(s)"

1. *wukunju ~ wukunjo* is "spleen" (cf. I Zaxarov, "the bile, bladder") this spirit is head of the row.
2. These names may be those referred to "beautiful gold-en birds".
3. "gray haired".
4. "intelligent, quick, smart".

"The tenth row; in the South there are high jagged "rocks. On the top of the rocks there are birch tree "avenues. In these avenues were living

"*B'iren Buku Tasxa*(1)"
"*Tar'in Tasxa*(2)"
"*Muxan F'isu*(3)"
"*Aĺxa F'isu*(4)"
"*Icbśere Iefu*(5)"
"*Sajan Sulen*(6)"
"*Sajan Tasxa*(7)"

1. "female strong hero tiger" which is head of the row.
2. "male tiger".
3. "male leopard".
4. "piebald ("spotted") leopard".
5. "fierce (attacking) bear".
6. "white lynx".
7. "white tiger"

"The eleventh row; in the East there are even moun-"tains. In the middle of the mountains there are high "rocks. In the middle of the rocks there is stony row. In this row are ranged
"*Karaya*(1) shaman who stays holding a drum
"*Karaya* assistant shaman who stays holding a javelin
"two *k'ilergi*(2) brothers who stay holding two guns
"*k'ilin*(2) strong hero who rides a white gray(3) horse and "stays holding a gun
"*k'ilerčan*(2) brother who rides a black horse and stays "holding a gun
"*k'ilin*(2) assistant shaman who stays holding a spear."

1. *karaya, kara*,—"black". This is the head of the stony row which is chiefly, if not exclusively, a Tungus row.
2. *k'ilergi, k'ilerčan* are modifications of *k'ilin*,—"the Tungus".
3. "white-gray" colour is used when horse has mane and tail darker than other parts of the body.

"The twelfth row; in the North there are Earth spirits, "the earthy row. In the row there are ranged
"*Naijulan*(1) shaman who stays holding a drum
"*Argudai* brother who stays holding a spear
"*Alire*(2) *Maŋi*(3) who stays holding a toothed club
"*Sujara*(4) *Maŋi* who stays holding an iron club
"*Faykara*(5) *Maŋi* who stay holding two swords
"*Sele Sèèè*(6) who stays holding a spear
"*Mudur'i*(7) nine fathoms long
"*jabjan*(8) eight fathoms long
"*Čečerku Meixe*(9)
"*Aisin Meŋgun Iygali*(10).
"This shaman named *Laju* of *kolg'a* clan lived in *Ajige Iŋ* "(Small *Iŋ* village) seventeen li's(11) southwards from the "town."(12)

1. *Naijulan*=ŋa+i+julen, i.e. of earth spirit(s). It is the head of the row.
2. "supporting, helping".
3. *maŋi, vide infra.*
4. *Sujara*,—"leaning", "pressing against."
5. *Faykara*,—"falling down."
6. cf. *supra* Seventh Row, footnote 3. It has been ex-plained by the Manchus as "turtle."

7. *Mudur'i* is a spirit which helps the shaman with water.
8. *Jabjan* i.e. the boa-constrictor.
9. "mad snake."
10. "golden-silver small bird".
11. One li is about half of a kilometre.
12. From Aigun city.

———————

The above given text of the list of spirits of this clan does differ in many respects from the short review of spirits observed in the previous section in the pictures of *wujala* clan. I have seen several other lists and I find that they are subject to variations. However, all spirits may be classified in the groups of (1) old shamans males and females, the founders of shamanism, who are usually called "shaman" and who are assisted by their "assistants"; (2) the female group which is sometimes separated; (3) the group of *buku, batur'i* and *mayi;* (4) the group associated with the animals; (5) alien spirits; (7) varia.

1. *Cuxa jayg'in* is a spirit which was formed of the soul of a military chief (*vide infra.*); it is included in all groups of *p'oyun voćko* whence among the New Manchus it has been included in the group of *saman'i voćko.* As to the clan spirit called *Čuxa jayg'in*, according to the Manchus, "they adopted this spirit as a real clan spirit". This spirit is also regarded as first founder of shamanism. It may be noted that *Čuxa jayg'in* is included in the group of the shaman's spirits amongst those clans which have no regular *p'oyun* (clan) *saman* i.e. usually amongst this New Manchus*. Amongst the Tungus this spirit is known as *burkan* responsible for the diseases spread over by the soldiers and by the people who stayed in the barracks. Its placing is made as a picture of a *jayg'in* (i.e. the "colonel"), two *jalan jayg'in* and some soldiers (among the Goldi cf. P. Šimkevič, Add. 21 and 22.)

Mafa and *Mama Saman* are very old shamans whose names are sometimes lost. They are found in many clans. When the *Mama voćko* comes the shaman smokes several pipes one by one. These are sometimes equivalent to *sagda éjèn voćko saman*, i.e. "old master spirit shaman."

Naijulan saman is a spirit which was formed of the soul of a shaman of the same name. This spirit helps the shaman to find the cause of disease. The etymology seems to be *nai,*—"of earth", *julan,*—"spirit". The same spirit (*nai voćko* in *Nišan Saman*) helps in finding the soul of dead people.

Neibuntu is a spirit which was also formed of a shaman, but in *Nišan Saman* it is mentioned as spirit giving happiness, (cf. *neibuntu endur'i,*—the eleventh spirit of the series of twelve *endur'i*, I. Zaxarov.) *Agjulan saman* and *Kitan'ju mama* are sometimes used for helping children, so that there are some people who were cured with this spirit and who are called by these names.

2. The female group is sometimes separated by the Manchus themselves into a special row in which they are called *xèxè (gèyè, gège) voćko.* However, they are merely souls of female shamans with no particular functions.

3. The goup of *buku, batur'i* and *mayi* is subject to great variations in clans and in individual shamans.

———

* It may be noted that korg'a clan is one of the New Manchu clans, but they have no such a spirit because in the matter of spirits they formerly fused with korg'i which was an old Manchu clan.

These are spirits of shamans or like-shamans, people of various origin who succeeded in mastering fire, their own bodies etc. *Buku* in Manchu and Tungus means "strong", being near to the well known *bagatur, bātur* etc. of the Mongols and Turks, also known among the Tungus, in Manchu (Writ) *baturu*, also *baturo* and *batur'i; mayi* etymologically may be connected with *maya,*—"strong", "endowed, talented, good" etc. This is a group of heroes also found among the Northern Tungus and Goldi. In this group there are spirits which are good with mastering fire, *jáya* ("fire", cf jaxa, Manchu Writ.), *baturo* or *tua* (fire) *voćko* or *jaya f'ikur voćko* [*jaya f'ikur =jaxa de fekurembi* (Manchu Writ.),—"to jump into the fire"]. *Mafa* and *mama* are also used instead of *baturo.* Amongst the Chinese (*nikan*) shamans this spirit is called *xošen laoje* (*vide supra*) also used by the Manchus who do not speak Chinese. It is supposed that if this spirit enters the shaman the latter may handle the fire, so he may go with bare feet into the burning charcoal, jump on the burning wood put into a cavity made in the earth etc. and he and his dress as well would not be burnt. There is a special group of spirits which use all kinds of arms and instruments. One of them may be skilful with the lance, another with the spear, third with long knives, sabre, etc. During the performance all these instruments must be present, at least in symbols.* Among the group *mayi* there are, for instance, *Maitu, Aljidai, Baitu, Sergudai, Lukšere lefu, Arsulan* ("lion"), *Iygalji. In Nišan Saman* there are also mentioned *Neibuntu* (this spirit is sometimes one of the important spirits, cf. *supra*), *Tuak'antu, Baturo saman* and others. All these names are merely names of spirits which may also be names of persons. The whole group may be called *mayi.* However, it is considered as a group of minor importance. When the shaman acts with the help of these spirits he takes off his head-dress (*vide infra*). They are never separately prayed but only together with other spirits. Generally, they always are ordered as servant-like spirits. This group of spirits is essentially based upon the ritual side. It is especially numerous among the Chinese.

4. The groups of spirits associated at least by names with the animals is very numerous, especially among the New Manchus who have *ü'iyan* group. As amongst the Northern Tungus these are not animals, but manifestations assumed by the spirits. The animals are also found together with different spirits of the first two groups. The animals used are: tiger (*tasxa*) and bear (*lefu*),—all shamans have them; lion (*arsulan*,—an animal which is known only from books including the term); wolf (*n'uxu, n'oxu*),—not all shamans have it**; fox, snake; boa-constrictor (*jabjan*), dragon (*mudur'i*) which is regarded by the Manchus as an animal actually living; deer; the roe-deer (*ġ'jo*) is sometimes considered as a complex spirit, but some Manchu doubt as to its existence. Among the domesticated animals as manifestations there are found only dog and horse*** (*morin voćko*). Generally the Man-

———

* The Manchus formerly used arms made of iron, but at the present time they are usually made of wood.
** There is also a special spirit known under this name which is not mere manifestation but complex by itself—n'uxu voćko. This spirit is very strong and mischievous.
*** Among the New Manchus this spirit plays rather an important part and it is used chiefly in the taiga. As a rare and exceptional

chus admit that there may be formed a special spirit from the animals, very old and wise (cf. *supra*). When the animal manifestations are used the shaman imitates the voice of the animals, but does not sing. Among other animal spirits there is one which is very important, namely, *mujuɣu n'imaɣa ·voĉko*,—"the carp fish spirit,"—a wooden placing for which is made among the New Manchus. When the shaman has this spirit he may go under the ice like a fish. The bird manifestations are not numerous;—there are very many cuckoos, falcons, and hawks; the latter is more important than the others and it has a special sacrifice (the shaman eats raw pig's liver and drinks a half cup of fresh blood). Yet there is one more *voĉko* considered as very important, namely, *amba daimin voĉko*, i.e. "great eagle spirit," which comes into the shaman, as well as the boa-constrictor and the dragon, very rarely and which is a complex by itself. The groups of spirits of natural phenomena are very small among the Manchus. There is only one namely *agjan voĉko* (the shaman produces sparks with flint), which is considered as an important, but very rare spirit.

5. The groups of alien spirits is numerous. It comprises the Tungus (*k'ilin*) spirits and Chinese spirits. The Tungus spirits are met with almost in all clans, while the Chinese spirits are common among the Old Manchus. Under the name of alien spirits I include only those spirits which are so cognized by the Manchus. However, in the Third Group there are many spirits which are of Chinese origin, but they are not separated from the whole group as alien spirits. Perhaps many spirits in the First Group are also of alien origin.

6. The group of ancestor spirits as such is introduced only by the New Manchus into their series of spirits. However, most of the shaman spirits in the list of old Manchu spirits actually are also ancestors, but they function as shamans and not as ancestors.

7. The group here separated comprises the spirits such as, for instance, *mongoldai naĉĉu* which plays its part in the lower world (*vide supra*), also *ðoxolo age*, i.e. "the lame brother," who carries the souls of dead people across the river. This group may also be increased with all other spirits connected with the lower world.

It ought to be also added that the spirits are also surrounded by their assistants who may have various functions. These may be actual assistant shamans (*jar'i*) or they may hold some special position and have particular duties, or even to be mere servants attending the needs of their masters. In such a position are found spirits called *gèĝè* (also *gèɣè ĝèxè*) ("*sister*"), some *mayi*, *buku*, *batur'i* and *k'ilin*. The names of the subordinate spirits sometimes remain unknown to the Manchus, and still more often they are a repetition of the names of principal spirits. The animal manifestations are also increased with the birds which are not used by the shamans. They play chiefly a rôle of a crowd surrounding important spirits, e.g. the distinction of different colours of cuckoo is far from the actuality. Generally, the Manchu complex of spirits is usually built up of elements which are required by aesthetism and convention.

case the Manchus make an anthropomorphic wooden placing without legs and without arms, and put it in the hollowed trunk of a tree. Indeed, it is not an ordinary animal manifestation.

The familiarity of the Manchus with their spirits (they are actually too numerous) is not equal. In fact, the shamans usually have at their disposal very few spirits, and many of them are no more disturbed by the shamans. The lists and pictures which are used are not detailed enough, so that about some spirits the Manchus know no more than we can know from the same documents*.

55. SPIRITS OF OTHER TUNGUS GROUPS   Amongst the Tungus of Transbaikalia who still speak Tungus, I have found two systems in practice, namely, one among the Nomad Tungus and another

* As I have already shown, the Manchu books treated by Ch. de Harlez and L. Langlès actually are books treating the ritual of the clan spirits and some other spirits picked up as important ones, from the point of view of ĝ'jore clan. From this point of view they are of little use for us. The sources regarding Manchu shaman spirits, in so far as I know, are confined to the work of A. D. Rudnev ("New data, etc."). It is absolutely evident that the source of information was not reliable at all, and he did not know very much about shamanism. A professional spy of a low standard, liar, half-sinofied, an individual who spent a long time abroad,—naturally he could not be seriously used as source of delicate information regarding shamanism. Indeed, he knew something about it when living amongst his native people and when he could use his knowledge he did it by supplying A. D. Rudnev with pictures and meaningless songs, as for instance all "Fragments of the" (op. cit. pp. 18-19). In fact, the text of the first fragment is a collection of words which happened to come to his mind for keeping A. D. Rudnev busy, so he sang:

[*ko xo i ke xo—oĭ käi koŭ ko xo i*]
ĝèrènei welĉen mini ɓoje ɓaĭɣa bade
[*oĭ käi koŭ*]
jarði sini bèje dónţi
tetxa ɓi ɓ„ori jambi

What is here placed in brackets consist of meaningless "refrains" with which ignorant people begin to imitate the shamans. Gèrèn is supplied with ei which is not needed; the whole expression gèrèn veĉin means "all spirits"; mini boje is a refined expression used only by the educated Manchus which I do not meet in common shamanistic texts,—it is an imitation of the supposed-to-be known "high Manchu style." baiya bade in a shamanistic text is meaningless, for baiɣa is "I prayed" and bade may be only a compound suffix ba (accus.) + de (dativ—locat.). Since he could not compose another sentence he used again a short "refrain" and continued; ðjarði is not clear sini boie dóndi is again half literary imitation,—"listen"; tetxa is a distorted tere utxai which may mean "after that", instead of mini boje he used this time common bi, forgetting his high style; baori is used in a wrong way for it should be in Manchu Sp. baobairi; baori may be used only by the people who do not know Manchu Sp. ri in this function (direct.) is not used alone but always with ba (accusat.) The whole fragment is very simple: he begins to sing, he does not find what he can sing and says,—"listen to me who prays I will now go home." The other fragments are in the same style. All of them show that the man did not know his own language and was just abusing A. D. Rudnev's confidence. The pictures and their interpretation are the product of ignorance and intentional abuse of confidence combined.

The conceptions of relationship between the shamans and other spirits are interpreted in the most fantastic manner. Indeed, "God" and "devil,"—bog and ĉert of A.D. Rudnev's notes,—have nothing to do with shamanism. As to the spirits, the informer collected various names together and supplied various spirits with the characters and functions not typical of them. Yet, there are mixed up even purely Chinese spirits which the informer happened to remember.

From the above remarks it is evident that this material has a very limited linguistical value and it has no value at all from the point of view of information regarding the spirits. Therefore, I believe that this material as misleading, intentionally wrong, must be rejected *in toto*.

among the Reindeer Tungus. For instance, the Mankova Tungus have adopted the Mongol (Buriat) spirits *oygun* but call them *sèvèn*. Such are for instance, *kètal* which is a very mischievous and dangerous spirit; *kolultu* which has been formed from a girl who ran away into the mountains and died there; *tänäg'ja*, a spirit [from *tänäg*,—'insane, idiot" (Bir. Mank.)] which produces in the shaman an effect of "insanity". There is no doubt that the spirits are only partly the same as amongst other Tungus groups in Manchuria.

Amongst the Reindeer Tungus of Transbaikalia there is a different complex, but my information is not complete, so that in order to avoid misconception of their system, I shall not now present these facts. The complex of mastered spirits amongst the Reindeer Tungus of Manchuria is also different, for it includes a special series of spirits *haja* which may be identified as *ajy* of the Yakuts. However, since shamanism does not exist among them any more these spirits are known only from the traditions. Among the Kumarčen Tungus there are spirits of the same type as amongst the Birarčen, but among the Khingan Tungus there are some spirits recently borrowed from the Mongols and a special group of spirits of minor importance called *ėwvun*.

The system of shamanistic spirits among the Dahurs, as it may be seen from the previous sections, contains several spirits of the same names and type as among the Birarčen. Indeed, since the Dahurs speak a Mongol dialect and since the penetration of Lamaism among them still stronger than among the Tungus, the list of spirits is still richer in purely Buddhistic elements. However, I have no complete list of this group.[*]

I have to abstain from the comparative analysis of the

Goldi complex. The authors who gathered material among the Goldi, namely, P. Šimkevič and I. A. Loptain submitted it to a classification and remodelling and adopted a simplified terminology which does not correspond to the actual groups distinguished by the Goldi themselves and which should not be confounded. Owing to this, with the exception of *anduri*, the group of spirits which are not mastered by the shamans does not figure in the list of I. A. Lopatin. However, it is absolutely evident that some of these spirits are not at all *sèvèn* (*seon*), i.e. the spirits mastered, but belong to some other class of spirits, as for instance, *juli* (*vide supra*),[*] also *dusxu* and *g'irki*. From the description of the Goldi spirits it is evident that they distinguish male and female roads (I. A. Lopatin call them "husband and wife"), also the subordinate manifestations of *bučėu* and *ajexu*, various animals and especially tiger,[**] bear, leopard, snakes, birds, insects, dragons etc.

According to the Birarčen the complex of Goldi spirits is composed of a half of spirits known amongst the Birarčen and they have a great number of Manchu spirits which is quite natural for the Sungari Goldi are one of "New Manchu" (*ići manju*) groups. The Amur Goldi have a large number of pictures *n'urxan* (I. A. Lapatin) (*n'uryan* of the Manchus). According to the Birarčen, the Goldi complex also includes a great number of Dahur elements.[***] Yet, the whole complex called by I. A. Lopatin *dusxu*,[****] according to this author perhaps with a good right, is supposed to be borrowed, through the Manchus from the Chinese.

[*] I. A. Lopatin insists upon the fact that he did not find any other term for spirits except seon. It is very possible for since in the language gradually worked out by the Goldi and the investigator, the Goldi used term "seon" in reference to all spirits as the Tungus do with the Russians when they use "burxan," "bog" of Russians also savak'i. In fact, the terms like burkan and fuk'k'i might also exist amongst the Goldi, for they were connected with the Manchus whence they might have fuk'k'i. Generally speaking many a term although distorted may be analysed and compared with Northern Tungus, Manchu and Dahur terms as we have seen in the case of seon, juli, and others. However, such an analysis without a detailed description of spirits is very risky, so I like better to abstain from it altogether.
[**] Indeed, amban seon (abbr. ambanso) is not "the Tiger" as I. A. Lopatin thought, but is is "great mastered spirit" which may have the tiger as one of its manifestations; doonta is not also "the bear", but a special group of spirits.
[***] It may be supposed from the time when the Dahurs were political masters of the region, i.e. before the settlement of the Manchus on the banks of the Amur River.
[****] This seems to be a technical term for the kind of placing and not the name of spirit.

[*] N. N. Poppe has given "a short sketch of shamanism" among the Dahurs ("Dahur Dialect", pp. 8-14) from which it is rather difficult to form an idea as to the spirits. No list of spirits is given and some confusion of facts may be suspected. In fact, it is not indicated on which occasion the shaman was singing; whether this was the shaman who was speaking, or his spirit introduced into the shaman (ibid. pp. 26-31). Seemingly this was an animal (a fox?) manifestation of a complex,—Otǒš ügiŋ, Gan'e'j lam, Orč'iŋ dǒg, of southern "road". It may be noted that the second component was a lama (Buddhist priest). Indeed, to speak about "spirit-protector" among the Dahurs, as N. N. Poppe does, without giving evidence is impossible for we depend on their neighbours, the Tungus and the Manchus, the shaman is master of spirits. This seems to be so among the Dahurs as seen from the text recorded by N. N. Poppe, e.g. p. 27. However, on p. 28 mentioning of "master" is referred to the chief spirit of the complex borčǒxǒr,—"spotted pea",—a name received by Otǒš ügiŋ after her crying (ibid. p. 12). Thus, borčǒxǒr probably is only one of oŋgǒr—corr. sèvèn—which is a complex spirit headed by Otǒš Ügiŋ, alias borčǒxǒr.

CHAPTER XV

VARIOUS HYPOTHESES

56. HYPOTHESES. In this chapter I shall give a description of and mention various hypotheses some of which are intimately connected with the theory of spirits while the others are independent of this theory. Thus there will be no uniformity in the exposition of the facts which are grouped here arbitrarily.

1. BLOOD Regarding blood among both Northern Tungus groups and Southern Tungus groups there are several theories which may be grouped together. At the basis of these theories there is a common supposition that *the blood possesses certain properties which may be pernicious to people and which may produce strong reactions on* *the part of spirits.* First of all let us point out that the blood is regarded as a form of sacrifice easily assimilated by the spirits for it is liquid and when it is still hot it evaporates, even with visible steam, so that the spirits may assimilate it easier than any other kind of "food." Yet, blood is considered as delicious food by the people,—the Tungus and Manchus are very fond of the sausage made of blood, so it is supposed that the spirit would like it, too. But there are other aspects too. As a matter of observation, the Tungus have some correct conceptions particularly in reference to the menstrual blood which may be infectious and they do have conception that the blood may contain some properties transmitted by the mechanism of inheritance. According to the Birarčen, some spirits, as for instance, *malu* and *dayar'in jiači,* follow the road of blood when the woman marries to anther clan. Owing to this a series of precautions must be taken in order to avoid the mixing up of other spirits on this road. The spirit which comes by this road must be sent back by this road and it cannot be sent to another clan. It is thus evident that here we have conception of latent diseases on the one hand, and hereditary diseases on the other hand. In the theory of spirit *bušku* we have already seen the idea of infection transmitted by and through the blood, both from females and males.

The idea of danger from the menstrual blood has grown into a complex increased with a great number of secondary hypotheses. According to all Tungus, the spirits do not like blood, and consequently the women who have menstruations. Naturally, the clan spirits are excepted. As I have already shown, the woman is avoided and restricted during the life period when she *may have* menstruations and especially during the days of discharge. The restriction covers not only the period of discharge of blood, but the whole period of life for the menstruation is "woman's business" about which she does not speak and therefore there is no guarantee that she may have blood at any moment. Moreover, it is supposed that perhaps the women sometimes are careless in the observation of purification. The woman must not step across the man lying, his hat, and all parts of dress, etc. which naturally may commonly occur for the Tungus have no furniture and usually sit or lie down on the ground. If she does so, especially with the hat, the owner -man will have no luck in hunting and in general. Owing to this the men are careful in keeping their hats in hands or by hanging them up, and they do not leave their clothes on the ground where the women may accidentally pass. Indeed, from the psychological point of view it is clear that if something of this kind should occur, the men, who believe as to bad effects of the blood, would act in agreement with the supposed to be effects. If an *endur'i* should happen to be touched by menstrual blood, according to the Tungus of Manchuria, it would become "man", i.e. common spirit which has no "immortality." The other spirits are also destroyed by the blood. The Manchus in this respect are particularly strict, the women are not even allowed to be present at the ceremony of sacrifice to the husband's clan spirits. It is believed advisable to keep old women and young girls who have no menstrual discharges far away from the placings for spirits. It is a different question how far all these restrictions and fears practically influence Tungus life. Indeed, there are individuals, among both males and females, who violate regulations and have no strong fear,

but this is a general question of acceptation, partial and total, of the existing complex.

In order to alleviate the great burden, as these restrictions and fears are, the Tungus try to find out various methods of neutralizing blood effects. I speak of "alleviation" which is not always cognized, but which actually is reached by the continuous re-adaptation of the individuals and complexes. The simpliest method of neutralizing the spirits' activity on man is to carry with oneself woman's bones, from a female skeleton as it is rarely done among the Birarčen. Here I mention the bones which are connected with blood. In fact, the blood and bones are connected in some way. The Tungus (of Manchuria, at least) believe that the father's bones absorb children's blood, while it is not so with the bones of other people.* Yet, the blood destroys bones, as it is shown in the case of *bušku* spirit. However, the influence of the blood may go still further which is seen from the fact already mentioned, namely, an avoidance of curative hot spring after a pregnant woman's bathing in it. The same idea is spread over the period of the child delivery, during which the woman is particularly dangerous in the respect to spirits. However, the last regulation, in so far as the husband is concerned, may have another reason, namely, to protect the mother from too early sexual intercourse. As to the influence of menstrual blood on man the question is complicated by the fact that men may occasionally have sexual intercourse with the women when they begin to have discharges and nothing particular happens to them, which is well known among the Manchus. However, the latter suppose that the sexual intercourse during the menstruation is dangerous for the women who may be affected by illness. Owing to this the Manchus sometimes extend the period of abstaining up to seven days after the menstruation. The Manchus practise no other purification but simple washing. Among both Northern Tungus and Manchus the woman-shaman cannot carry out shamanistic performances. Yet, during the menstrual discharges and postnatal period the woman must not go on a boat on the river, to cross the river etc. for the spirit of water may be offended. The same holds good for fishing.**

If we summarize the above quoted facts it may be thus formulated that the Tungus (and Manchu) attitude regarding blood forms a complex based upon the facts observed (infection through blood and special condition of menstruating women), theory of inheritance and supposition that the spirits do not like blood which is confirmed by the facts observed and misinterpreted.

---

2. FOUR EYED ANIMALS   The hypothesis of one additional pair of eyes in some animals is wide spread among the Tungus. The inference is made from the observation of skin fold under the eyes in the Cervus Elaphus, with corresponding cavity in the bone, and bone cavities formed above the eyes in the horse. The case of Cervus Elaphus cannot be explained by the Tungus who do not know the function of the fold and its strong smelling secretion. In the horse there is no secretion

* Here there may be suspected an influence of some Chinese ideas.

** Vide SOM,—two special methods of fishing.

from the cavity which is formed owing to the form of the skull bones and position of muscles with a rather loose skin cover. This case probably is a further extension of the case of Cervus Elaphus. The Tungus explanation, in its character, supposes that the Tungus admit possibility of physical changes in animals, as we have already seen in their ideas regarding loss of hair in man (vide supra). The explanation as to why the lower pair of eyes has disappeared is that the Cervus Elaphus has lost it owing to the continuous crying with tears. On this occasion a story is told (explanatory myth). The spirit (it could not be established which one) has taken away the additional eyes of the horse. When the deer and horse lost their eyes it became possible to kill the deer and to ride the horse.

3. EXTINCTION OF STRONG HUMAN RACE This hypothesis is very common among the ethnical units for which there are special psychological reasons. Among the Tungus of Manchuria this extinct race is called bukuljin [buku,—"strong" (Barg. Nerč. Mank. Khin. Kum. Bir.) (Manchu) (cf. Turk būk, Mong. bözö, etc.)]. They were men who lived in olden days. They were so strong that they could pull trees out of the ground. With a general weakening of the human kind the bukuljin have become extinct. According to the Birarčen, the bukuljin became extinct when they no longer needed to use their strength for carrying on the trees after having been taught by endur'i to cut trees and make fire. Still earlier there existed another kind of strong people who were even stronger than bukljin. They are called mayi (Kum. Bir. RTM.) and their former activity is seen in the irregularities of the nature, e.g. the rocks in the middle of the river bed (the Amur River), rocks rolled into the valleys from the mountains etc. These beings were much larger than the bukuljin and men of nowadays. According to the folklore, mayi went to the sky, so that the constellation of Orion is called mayi (vide supra Chapter V).* Mayi with nine heads is also figured in the complex malu burkan (and sèvèn).** Amongst the Manchus under this name, as shown (vide supra Section 52), is known a special kind of shamanistic mastered spirits whose chief characteristic is their art and ability of manipulation with various weapons and implements, and naturally physical power. The etymology of this name is not absolutely sure, namely, from mayga (Bir, Nerč) (Manchu) [manga (Neg. Goldi, Oroči) (Sch.), cf. also Gilak manga—maga], also maya (Ur. Castr.), mayya (Nerč.),—"the strong (hero), wrestler, etc." and mayyu (Tum.),—"hard, atrocious"; yet there is another series mandi (Bir. Khin) with the assimilated and simplified forms: manni (RTM.), man'i, mani (Bir. Kum.)***—"hard, difficult, strongly, etc." To the last form is probably related

* The same term is used for heroes of Tungus stories. It is also met with in Goldi (marga) and Gilak folklore (usually, maga). It is referred to the folk-stories' hero man-eater. In Transbaikalia in the form man'i (Nerč), mayi(?) (Ang. Tit.) it is referred to the bear. Owing to this the Orion is sometimes associated with bear. Indeed, E. I. Titov's translation "čort" (Russian "devil") is a mere misunderstanding.
** Among the Barguzin Tungus it is called manitkan, where t and kan are suffixes.
▨▨▨ cf. Yakut stem mūyi, particularly in mūyiljit—"to make effort"(?)

mändäg'i of Yakuts found in ūs mändäg'i· (the star mändäg'i),—"the Orion's belt", which remained unexplained by E. K. Pekarskii.* From the above facts it may be seen that amongst a great number of groups there is a certain association between "strong," "hero," "special kind of spirit," "Orion," etc. and thus the strong people gradually left the earth.

4. ARCHAEOLOGICAL AND PALAEON- The Tungus, as
   TOLOGICAL REMAINS   many other groups, explain the large stone implements found in their territory as being the effect of thunder. This explanation probably is not of Tungus origin, but it is borrowed from other ethnical groups. In fact the Tungus do remember arrow heads made of stone, and they recognize them as such when they find them. Most of the archaeological remains in the form of walls, fortresses and pit dwellings abundant in the valley of the Amur River are ascribed to the Dahurs and to the Russians (of the XVIIth century). The palaeontological remains attract attention of the Tungus as well. I have already pointed out that the Tungus interpret the shells as an indication that formerly there was sea-bottom in the places where now mountains are found. The bones of large animal are sometimes understood as bones of dragons (mudur). However, I once discussed this matter with the Tungus when I happened to find a skull of a quaternary rhinoceros and a skull of a quaternary large bos in Transbaikalia. They were carefully examined by the Tungus and were recognized the first one as a skull of a very large horse and the second one as that of a large ox, which do not any more exist in the locality.

5. SPIDER-LIKE BEINGS Amongst the Birarčen there is a hypothesis that each "species" of the animals, has one large spider-like animal which makes a large net. These nets are made of thick rope-like loops. Man is caught in such nets. I could not find the origin of this idea of net, but considering its limited distribution at the present time I hesitate as to placing it.** It is possible that this idea was formerly wide-spread. Yet, it may now be of a secondary origin, of a metaphoric origin.

6. THEORY OF JIN AND JAN I have already shown that this Chinese theory of female and male principle has penetrated amongst the Tungus and Manchus. This theory finds its expression chiefly in the philosophical conception of life and only partly in that of existing phenomena classified. The sun is con-

* The parallelism is really remarkable; cf. Manchu maygi and Yakut mūndji,—"during"; i.e. analogous to Tungus mayga-mandi,—"hard, strong," and mayi (Tungus), mändäg'i (Yakut),—"the Orion". which facts seem to indicate that the stem is maa, and mayi, mayga, mandi etc. are new formations with the help of suffixes.
** The idea of net with which spirits catch the human souls is known in Chukchi complex (cf. W. Bogoras summarized in "Einstein and Religion" 1925, p. 4. in Amer. Anthrop.)

sidered by some Tungus as male, while by the others as female. Thus there may be combinations of two sisters, husband and wife with reverse rôles of the sun and moon. Incidentally the Chinese ideas make their appearance, but they do not seem to be stabilized. However, the distinction of male and female manifestations correlated with southern-noon and northern-midnight roads may be due to the assimilation of this conception. I do not mean to say that the Chinese idea of *jin* and *jaŋ* is the primary source. Perhaps, it would be safer to regard it in its philosophical form as an adaptation of an older conception. Yet, the discrimination of sex roads in its application to the spirits (*burkan*) seems to be rather recent, the spirits themselves being recent.

7. HYPOTHESIS OF MICRO-ORGANISMS (*Kulikan*). This hypothesis has already been mentioned on different occasions, e.g. in the case of explanation of diseases, also of the human and animal male-cell. It may now be also indicated that the Tungus (Birarčen) in this case evidently group not only facts actually depending upon the micro-organisms, but also other phenomena, for instance, many diseases which are not due to the pathogenic micro-organism, but to the dis-equilibrium of the tissues. In this case the Tungus merely extend the hypothesis over unknown but symptomatically similar phenomena. It may be also pointed out that the Tungus admit possibility of growth of micro-organisms, as it is in the case of worms observed in wounds, intestines, flesh (meat) etc. and embryological growth. However, they also admit that some of these micro-organisms never attain large size and thus cannot be seen. They act accordingly with this hypothesis. For instance, it is supposed that during the warm season the micro-organisms may multiply in any kind of food exposed and for this reason any food which is not especially preserved by drying or reducing to powder (e.g. meat) must be consumed within three days. Such food after three days may cause serious illness, because of the *kulikan* (micro-organisms).

8. PREGNANCY BY UNUSUAL WAYS   I have shown that the Tungus and Manchus have a very clear idea as to the cause of pregnancy in man and other animals. However, some ideas of unusual ways of pregnancy circulate among them. So, for instance, among the Manchus there are circulating Chinese books, e.g. 西 遊 記 in which they find stories regarding women's state when women become pregnant by looking in the water and seeing their own reflexions. This possibility of pregnancy does not seem to be likely to the critically be-having Manchu minds. The same critical mind prevents the Manchus from believing into the possibility of pregnancy from the spirits *endhr'i*, and even *xutu* or in dreams from the dogs, horses, asses. Such dreams are frequent with the girls. Then they cry and must be immediately awakened by other people. In the case of a story of a girl's pregnancy through the spirits there is very little chance that the Tungus or Manchus would really believe it,—there will be immediately taken up special measures in order to

find out the man responsible for it. However, sometimes family secrets cannot be exposed and the honour of the girl must be defended. Therefore, although nobody believes in the theory, it is formally admitted that such a pregnancy might occur exactly in the given case. Indeed, in folklore, both Northern Tungus and Manchu, there are many stories regarding capture and violation of women by the animals, especially bears and tigers. However, these stories are regarded as "untrue", or the bears and tigers are regarded as people who assumed these animals' bodies, thus they are not real and common animals. Considering the Tungus theory of pregnancy and inheritance of physical and other features it is not likely that they would admit the possibility of pregnancy from these animals. The Tungus and Manchus are not ignorant as to the impossibility of impregnation of the females of other animals by man[*].

9. ANIMALS IN THEIR RELA-   In the previous sections
      TION TO THE SPIRITS   we have seen on several
                              occasions that the North-ern Tungus and Manchus admit that the spirits do behave differently in reference to the animals. Some spirits are afraid of certain animals, and particularly of their claws, skins, bones, teeth. The idea itself seems to be very old while the discoveries of the Tungus along this line are always renewed.

The Manchu clan spirits are very particular about the dog,—the dog's blood may make the spirits run away from their placings and from the clan. However, it is not so amongst the Chinese (*n'ikan*) and in a much lesser degree among the New Manchu. The skin of this animal, even its fur, cannot be brought to the house where there are placings for the clan spirits. An exception is made only for very influential people, and the Manchus have a special very typical expression (cf. SOM. p. 91). Naturally, the meat of dog is tabooed for these Manchus. The dog is supposed to play a special part in the operations with the spirits when the latter are brought to the lower world. Yet, as previously shown, the dog may be used as a placing for some spirits and is buried under the threshold, for fighting the spirits. The latter are afraid even of dogs' barking. Amongst the Northern Tungus the dog does not play such a part as it does among the Manchus, but the dog is also used for carrying the souls of dead people. However, the dog in this case is sometimes called "black fox."

The spirits are afraid of the bear's paw which is used for protection of children, also for protection of the house. The udder of reindeer and cows is scratched with the bear's paw when the milk is poor or there is any trouble with this organ. The bear's paw is used by all Tungus groups and Manchus. With the same purpose of keeping away the spirits, the hedge-hog skin or the bones of sable, claws of lynx, etc. are hung up above the cradle, in the doorway, etc. In these cases it is supposed that the spirits may attach themselves to them and thus they would be stopped on their way.

On the other hand there are animals which are liked by the spirits. These are all animals which are given as sacri-

* Occurrence of intercourse with animals is known more or less among all groups as practised if not among themselves, then among the neighbouring or other ethnical groups.

fice. It is very common that the animals are kept for a long time for serving as sacrifice. A suckling pig is sometimes taken by the Birarčen, raised on special food,—the acorn of quercus dauricus,—and later "sacrificed." In the meantime the spirit becomes accustomed to the animal and "likes it." One cannot give the animal away without causing some misfortune to the members of the family.* The roe-deer, Cervus Elaphus, as well as chickens are preferred by the spirits.

It should be also mentioned that among a Tungus group, namely, the Reindeer Tungus of Manchuria, I have found a tradition according to which the Tungus have originated from a bitch dog which was impregnated by a man,—spirit-like man, about seventy years old who descended from the heavens. From this union the *evenk'i* have originated. However, among neither the Tungus nor the Manchus did the dog become an ancestor-like animal. Evidently among the Tungus this complex either is dying out or it did not exist in a well-developed form. The first supposition is more likely for the dog still plays very important part in the carrying on the souls of dead people.**

---

10. CORRELATION BETWEEN PHYSICAL FEATURES AND CHARACTER All groups here discussed have a quite definite idea as to the possibility and even certainty of a correlation between the physical features and character of the people and animals, which are naturally transmitted through the mechanism of inheritance. These observations are so common that it is understood as evident that from the observation of physical features one may make practical inferences as to attitude towards other people. As compared with other ethnical groups there is nothing unusual in the Tungus ideas about it. However, the Tungus in this respect do not confine themselves to the impressions, but they summarize various observations. For instance, among the Khingan Tungus it is supposed that the person is not good if the fat of the elk (Cervus alces) sticks to the lips, which is not observed in all people, the explanation being that such people have not enough "heat" inside (*budiyadu*) and such people have also bad "heart"; the red ridges on the forehead are also considered as sign of bad nature; physical weakness which is not due to the disease is also

considered as sign of bad character. Indeed, the behaviour is a great source for warning Tungus as to the character of the people. For instance, the people who do not look straight into the eyes, or look with fixed ("impertinent") eyes; the people who titter and giggle when speaking; those who refuse to accept tobacco and food from other people, etc. are considered as bad-natured people. The attitude in the state of drunkenness is also considered as indication of the character. In the same way the Tungus believe they can know the character of the animals with which they are familiar, e.g. dogs, reindeer (amongst the reindeer breeders), and horses (much less than the reindeer even among the horse breeders).

57. SYSTEM OF HYPOTHESES. Among the Tungus **1. AMULETS** groups and Manchus there is a belief that there are various things which may bring luck in different branches of human activity. Such things are usually incidentally found in the form of natural abnormalities, monstrosities, rare unknown things, etc. If the Tungus happen to learn something new along this line they include it into their complex without any hesitation. Owing to this there now is in vogue a belief into the possibility of finding treasures, ever-lasting food, etc., borrowed from the Chinese, Mongols and even Russians. The function of the amulets in Tungus life is not great, but they never refuse to collect them and keep, for nobody exactly knows what is true and what is not, but to keep these things is not difficult. Yet one likes to have a hope of finding a fortune, or luck. The coincidence of "luck" with finding or using amulets often brings confirmation of the supposedly existing correlation between amulets and luck. Owing to the character of this hypothesis of the amulets and particular hypotheses regarding relationship between particular amulets and particular forms (cases) of luck are subject to great variations, not only among the ethnical groups but also in the life of generations and individuals. I will here give a list of amulets which, as a matter of fact, may be extended by more detailed investigation of the groups and even individuals. Naturally the amulets are much more fashionable among the Tungus who are in close contact with the other ethnical groups, and especially among those who are under the Chinese influence.

The amulets are called among the Manchus and Tungus groups influenced by them,—*bôbai*, [cf. Dahur *ðaobai* (Poppe),—"precious", "precious thing"; Manchu *baobai* (Zaxarov),—id. from Chinese 寶 貝 bao-bei] while among the reindeer Tungus of Manchuria and those of the Amur Government it is called *ajeya*. Amulets may be carried on the cradles, with the tobacco bag, attached to the spirits. Many amulets have been formed from the placings for spirits and special things used for protection. Therefore to establish the line of demarcation between an amulet and former placing for spirits or protector against them, is impossible. Such is also the Tungus attitude in this matter. If such an amulet is found and if it is followed by luck in hunting there must be given sacrifice to the local spirits or to the spirit which is held responsible for the success. Once I met with the hypothesis that all amulets are produced by the spirits and therefore one must consider any amulet as indicative of future luck to be produced by the spirits,—

---

* In Čelu village there was a man who decided to raise a pig for sacrifice. This is not easy for the Tungus dogs very often destroy the suckling pigs. The pig had grown up and the spirit dżulask'i endur'i was accustomed to it. When the Tungus was prepared to sell the pig, the children did not want to give it up, and they soon became very sick. The man made a special divination with the gun and found out that the spirit did not want the pig to be given away. The pig was kept for several months more. When it was fat enough, it was killed and the spirit received the pig's ears and blood while the meat was sold for Mex. $56 (about 65 kilograms). The illness of children ended.

** It is remarkable that many ethnical groups have the idea of their origin from the dog, e.g. the "aboriginal" groups of China, Ainos, etc. [This question has been lately discussed by W. Koppers, "Der Hund in der Mythologie der Zirkumpazifischen Völker." In reference to the Tungus vide p. 387. Cf. C. H. Liu "The Dog-Ancestor, etc." where some bibliography is given.] It may be noted that amongst the Tungus there is a bitch which is impregnated and not a human female which is common in the folklore of other ethnical groups discussed by W. Koppers.

the spirits therefore must have regular sacrifices from those who carry the amulets, and if the sacrifice is not given it will be very bad for those who carry the amulets. Indeed, this idea puts a certain limitation upon the collecting of amulets. However, this is not a general belief.

Here are a few examples of articles used for amulets:

Double nuts, and other double seeds, are supposed to bring good growth to the child and therefore are attached to the cradle (Manchu and Birarčen). The Tungus are not sure whether it may bring luck or not, but since there must be something for making noise for lulling the child, they attach them to the clothes, cradle etc.

A small black stone with a hole through which a thin thong passes for being attached to the clothes, cradle, etc., the meaning and influence of which is not clear (various groups). It is used for increasing milk in mares among the Khingan Tungus who drink this milk and also make of it a kind of brandy (arak'i).

A small piece of metal found in natural state with a hole (RTM).

A black pebble in the form of human foot (Birarčen).

The roe-deer heart covered with hair (I have not seen it) (Tungus of the Amur Gov.).

The antlers of roe-deer females which is, of course, a rare occurrence (Kumarčen).

A transparent stone incidentally embedded in the shell of a fresh water mollusk (Birarčen).

The black fox which has become very rare (Birarčen).

The white mustelidae, e.g. sable, solongo, [amongst all groups perhaps because of the great value given to it by the Chinese (Manchu) emperors].

The Chinese small silver images (sculptured) of unknown meaning, together with a lynx claw attached to the tobacco bag (Manchus).

A red transparent stone (bought from the Chinese) which contains "water" inside; if one "oints" (rubs) the eyes with it one may see through stone, iron, wood, the human body, etc. (Birarčen).

A hard tumor from the stomach of a Cervus Elaphus was carried during the entire lifetime of my informer's father. The tumor was discovered by my informer, fastened with a bunch of wooden placings for spirits, and his mother explained its significance; he usually carried it with him but had recently lost it (Birarčen).

A flower with leaves, carved in bone, was discovered in the internal organs of a carp; it had been preserved for a very long time but was later lost (Birarčen).

From the Chinese, the Birarčen Tungus have learnt that in the cave located near the village Radde there must be very important amulet for during the winter hot gases are permanently escaping from the cave which is indicative that there must be an amulet guarded by a boa-constrictor which is breathing.

There are some amulets which produce light with the help of which one may move with great speed, even in the air, one may produce horses and carts for travelling, one may find unlimited number of hunting animals, etc. but it is very difficult to find such an amulet, and it is known only from stories.

Generally, every thing which is rare, new for the Tungus, exceptional and beyond their understanding may be regarded as an amulet which may bring luck. What the amulet may bring depends on what the Tungus know about

it from the alien folklore and their own imagination. Yet, the psychological condition, condition of confidence in success, is also an important factor in the consolidation of this hypothesis.

It may be thus formulated that there are two kinds of amulets, namely, the amulets which are sent by the spirits as indication of luck in hunting and in general, which are essentially Tungus in their origin, the effectiveness of which is confirmed by observations as to the frequency of coincidence; and the amulets and their effects found in the ideas of neighbouring groups the effectiveness of which has never been checked up and is admitted as true only owing to the credit given to the information received from the ethnical groups whish possess a certain power. However, it may be pointed out, the second group of amulets plays its part chiefly in the folklore and not in Tungus life, for the Tungus do not absolutely rely upon the hear-say of other people.

2. SIMILIA SIMILIBUS Among all Tungus groups there are many cases which may be understood as due to the hypothesis that when a certain action or state is produced by man it may be reproduced again and in a different form even without man's acting. However, the situation is not as simple as that, for there are at least two different conditions of the possibility of inference of similia similibus. The simplest case is that when the action is used as a method of communicating the idea or request to the spirits regulating or responsible for certain phenomena. Second, there may be a case of influence on the immaterial substance introduced into the placing. Third, the pure case of similia similibus the mechanism of which remains hidden from the people. As a matter of fact, I might confine myself to the third group only, but some examples may be useful for giving a more exact idea and showing the difference between the three cases only seemingly similar.

When the Khingan Tungus and Manchus whistle for producing wind the idea is not that the whistling will do it, but the idea is to call the attention of the spirit and to communicate to it the idea: "we want you to produce wind". Yet, the whistling and hissing constitute a method of calling spirits. Some of them easily respond to this call. Owing to this whistling cannot be used without thinking of possible consequences. The Khingan Tungus make straw images (not placing!) of animals which they want to kill, and they shoot these images; they do so for showing the spirits what they want. Indeed, the same can be done by telling the spirits. However, this case may be still more complex.

When the Tungus make a placing, call into it the soul of people whom they want to harm and then shoot or partially destroy the placing, the idea is that the exteriorated soul is placed in the placing and when the placing is partially destroyed the soul would be also destroyed and thus as a consequence the body of the owner of the soul will suffer too. This method is widely practised by all Tungus and on different occasions.[*] However, if we do not hurry with the

---

[*] The Manchus told me that in the village ofoꞏo tokso (Kalunšan, Chinese) there was a Japanese "doctor" who used to make effigies of his possible patients. So he would take a piece of paper and write upon it the name of the patient and then fix it upon the wall with nails after which he would perforate the written name. Many

solution of the problem whether the telepathic action and transmission of ideas is possible or not, if we remember what has already been stated in reference to it, (and still more will be stated), perhaps in the case of similar actions there is more than a simply groundless hypothesis of the possibility of influencing the people "on distance." Indeed, the case of a Tungus who burnt the eyes of his wife's placings for spirits (najil, cf. supra) and next morning the wife lost her eye, is different, for here is typical case of post hoc—propter hoc. No doubt the eye had been infected for a long time, the process was advanced, and at the last moment before the perforation of the eye ball the husband happened to carry out his operation with his wife's spirits. In every case, thus, we must know exactly how the Tungus understand the action.

Let us now take, for instance, the case of the power supposed to exist in different organs. If a Kumarčen Tungus should eat tiger's eyes he might become absolutely fearless. In order to have good teeth one must clean the interdental spaces, and naturally the gums, with the hair from tiger's moustaches. These cases are, as a matter of fact, different. In fact, in the first case the fearlessness is supposed to reside in the eyes for the tiger fixes the enemy with its eyes but there seems to be very little probability as to the physiological effect of the tissues of the eye, while in the second case, a light massage with the hard hair may have its beneficial effect on the gums. One instance more. Among many ethnical groups the liver is supposed to be the place where the soul resides*. Yet, since the correlation between certain psychic conditions and that of the liver is a well known fact, it cannot be supposed that it is absolutely unknown to the people like the Tungus and Manchus,—the troubles of the liver followed by pain and change of behaviour are too evident. A further generalization is easily made. The Manchus say about the fearless people that they have amba fayun—"great liver", and the people with such a large liver are not afraid of spirits. Why not try to eat liver in order to get fearlessness? In fact they do eat it always raw.** All these groups are quite expert as to the difference of the reaction of the organism to different kinds of food, and they do it quite consciously when they select it for different purposes. For instance, bear's fat during the winter is used for keeping the body warm, and different kinds of meat are classified from the point of view of heat produced and strength given to the organism. These are facts learnt from the experience of generations. They know also the effects of embryological tissues and that of the growing reindeer antlers. Thus in their attitude in this question, they do not ascribe to the liver and different organs a super-natural power, but they suppose that these organs may contain something which may have specific influence on the organism. The question whether they are wrong or right in their supposition is not what we are now interested in. As a matter of fact, the basis of the idea is observation of difference in the physiological effect of different tissues and supposition that psychic condition may depend on the selected food. Both propositions are now practically and theoretically admitted by the medical science and biology. How-

ever, it is very likely that a "skeptical ethnographer" of the last century when seeing the organo-therapeutic modern preparations, without knowing the mechanism of their effectiveness, would also classify them as "magic"; the fact of females eating their placenta after the delivery he would use for showing superiority of human being as compared with the animals; the fact of "popular belief" that the twins very often die simultaneously would be also explained as a "superstition", while the facts now gathered place before our eyes a new and still "mysterious" fact of common occurrence of the almost simultaneous death of uniovular twins.

Indeed, it is very possible that the Tungus in the case of the tiger's eyes, roe-deer liver and other similar cases commit the error of over-imposing various hypotheses which cannot be regarded as correct ones, and yet it is very possible that the confirmation of the effects is wrongly interpreted, but it is absolutely evident that their reasoning is naturalistic and does not very muih differ from any other reasoning based upon insufficiently studied facts and postulated hypotheses which are not yet checked up. In this respect their reasoning does not differ, in principle, from that of medicine and psychology of the last century, and perhaps in the eyes of future generations their point of view will not differ very much from that of medicine and psychology of our days.

The Tungus Birarčen as shown use the snake for making poisonous bullets (cf. supra). Indeed, to what degree they are "magicians" in this case may be solved only by a careful chemical analysis.

The Tungus avoid coming in contact with the families which produce twins and triplets, for a similar case may occur with other people. Is it an observation of the facts that infection (e.g. syphilis) is responsible for twins, triplets and other abnormalities or is it a simple case of similia-similibus?

In the families where children die, the Birarčen (also Manchus) use preventive methods. On the living children they put rings on ear, bracelets on the ankles and wrists, and head (fontanel). These are methods borrowed from the Chinese and probably partly preserved from the earlier times,—the tatooing. The idea is that the spirit will not attack persons who are taking such measures. The Birarčen also put on the wrist of the child a narrow piece of hedgehog skin in order to keep away the spirits. Among the Manchus similar methods are used and yet they also put on child's neck a white string for protecting child until he has gray (white) hair. Indeed, the Chinese methods described by H. Doré, among the Manchus and Tungus are mere imitation. When the child has eye trouble the Manchus cut eye-glasses from brown paper and put them on the child. The case of marks and eye-glasses are cases of correspondence with the spirits. It is different with the treatment of abdomen in children when the Manchus put "red paper" on it instead of Chinese "red plaster on paper." Experimentally is known that the Chinese red plaster is very effective, but medical side of the plaster escapes the Manchus' attention and they use only "colour".

The Tungus Birarčen in order to prevent the spirit of thunder from killing them by mistake, must whistle and make noise in order to show their presence. Also, the axe must be put with the sharp edge up for the same purpose,

---

of the people became sick and had to go for medical assistance. Naturally, the Manchus were greatly indignant about this dangerous activity and denounced this "doctor."

* The Manchus and Tungus do not assert it.

** The Manchus eat roe-deer raw liver for preserving good sight.

i.e. for showing that there are people, and probably that the spirit may cut itself with the sharp edge of the axe.

The Tungus in general, as well as Manchus, are very careful with their nails and hair cut. These cannot be thrown away. The reason is that the parts of human being may be collected by other people and used as a good placing for the soul of the man to whom the hair and nails belong. Moreover, they may be also used directly by the spirits.

In order to exhaust the typical cases I will quote a case which is a good illustration of the Tungus idea similia similibus. I have measured a Nerčinsk Tungus. I recorded his name, clan, age, etc. which is needed in such a case. I took his photo. At last I asked him to sing me something for phonograph record,—he was a good singer. Then his akʼi ("senior clansman") energetically protested and told me: "You have taken his measure, his name and his picture. Now you want to take his voice. What will be left him?". According to his ideas if I should be in possession of all his personality which as his double would be carried by me to St. Petersburg, there bad-natured people might use it for their manipulations. Indeed, in this case there was no "complex of individuality", the possessors of which as far as possible want to preserve the personality mysterious and independent, owing to the fear of being easily read by the outsiders who may also use their knowledge in personal interest. The last case is also met with amongst Tungus but it would naturally take a different form as compared for instance with the Europeans,—it will be "animistic" and "magic".

Amongst the Manchus it is strictly observed that a foreigner arriving at the house at the moment when dust is swept out of the house must not stop on it or go across it. By doing so the man may influence the small particles of dust and dirt which were produced by the members of the family and in this way produce harm to the people. In case somebody in the house should fall ill, it is very likely that the visitors breaking this regulation, would be accused of producing the misfortune. Naturally, nobody would risk breaking friendship.

I might increase the number of instances which may look at first as "magic", but which are not so actually, i.e. in so far as their function and "origin" are concerned. However, not everything may be treated in the way above shown. Indeed, among the Manchus and Tungus there are some methods the meaning of which cannot be clearly understood at least by myself while these people cannot give good reasons. Such is, for instance, the case of the selection of "happy people" among the Manchus for accompanying and performing the ceremony of wedding. These people must have no dead members in their families, i.e. man's wife and woman's husband, also all their children must be alive. Here it is supposed that if they are "happy" the new married couple will be also happy.

Amongst the Barguzin Tungus when a man is about to die, they slaughter a reindeer, take the heart out of the still warm reindeer and put it on the breast of the dying person. This is also practised among other groups when they may have a fresh heart. In order to activize the growth of teeth in children, the parents must throw away the milk teeth. Among the Manchus these must be left on the roof of the house. Such instances are not very common amongst the groups here discussed and I cannot

classify them as cases of pure and simple similia similibus "magic".

---

3. DIVINATION OF THE FUTURE The Tungus, as well as Manchus and most of other existing ethnical groups accept the idea that by means of special methods one can predict the future. This complex usually is of great psychological importance and among the Tungus it is not ignored. Although it is recognized that the common people are not endowed with this power in the same degree as the shamans who may know the future with the help of spirits, it is also recognized that there is some connexion between the facts of future and some facts of present moment, so that by knowing certain facts of the present one may foresee the future. In this general description there is nothing particularly characteristic of the Tungus. But the question is about the facts which are considered, as sufficient for prevision of future, and thus, pre diction. As a matter of fact, some facts as indicative of future are not at all without foundation, as for instance the case of sign of successful hunting when the raven goes ahead of the hunter, although the Tungus do not understand the mechanism of this peculiar form of co-operation between the raven and man, and ascribe this fact to the same "mysterious" connexions as, for instance, itching of palm as sign of success, etc. We may distinguish two cases, namely, (1) divination based upon various methods, and (2) prevision of future based upon observation of special signs.

The reading of future and divination naturally are beloved occupation of the Tungus and Manchus, but are almost monopolized by the shamans. Besides this most liked form of shamanistic fortune-telling which is based upon the shaman's mastering of spirits and which will be discussed later, there are some methods used by the common people, but most of them are recent imitation of Chinese, Mongol, and Russian practices. The divination by means of the cracks of the burned shoulder blade (scapula of sheep, reindeer, and other animals) is known, but this art among the Tungus does not go as far as with the Mongols,—the whole operation looks like an unskilful attempt, as it is true of other methods of divination. There has been introduced, especially among the Birarčen, a new method of divination with the rifle, but it is not of a Tungus origin. Among the Manchus the Chinese fortune-tellers enjoy great appreciation and in some cases they may be responsible for an enormous increase of this item of family expenditure. Yet, some Manchus versed in the Chinese methods try to use them too. There are two methods especially popular, namely, tossing up of five coins and burning of incense sticks,—three sticks are put together and according to the speed of their burning there may be received different combinations indicative of future.

It is different with various signs observed. As stated some of them are not at all senseless, but a great number of them are cases of mere post hoc propter hoc; and yet still a greater number are responsible for the future because of their influence on the Tungus activity. I shall now give some examples; an exhaustive presentation of all facts gathered cannot be done here.

The dreams occupy a very important part in the complex of signs indicative of future. This question is extremely delicate, for it is now known that dreams may reflect "unconscious" complex, while the actions in reality may be conditioned by the same complex. Thus the coincidence of both may not be absolutely incidental. Second, the dreams may condition the dreamers' attitude in his daily life, by the mechanism of self-suggestion. Third, as shown before, the case of telepathic communication in dreams must not be dismissed, and so the dreams may result from an actual perception of facts at a distance, whence they may be factual prevision of events. At last, the incidental coincidence of dreams and real events may be mixed with the above shown cases of casual connexion between the dreams and reality. Yet, the question is still much complicated by the fact of symbolization of forms and situations, as well as by emotional complexes, for the symbols loaned from other ethnographical complexes may change their "function" in a new complex, i.e. become to some degree independent of the original function, and to remain even "functionless symbols" transmitted by tradition. In the complex of dream divination there were thus included observations and inferences of various origin, so that their analysis might form by itself an interesting psychological essay. Here I shall give a few facts without attempting to give their analysis. According to a Birarčen informer, the dreams appropriate their meaning individually (i.e. the symbolization is an individual matter). In this case the canoe means the arrival of guests, some misfortune, especially death; various animals mean shamans, who according to the Tungus, may assume the form of birds, snakes, dogs, etc.; during pregnancy of one's wife to see a snake means to have a son, to see a bird means to have a daughter. A Khingan informer told me that dreaming of shooting his own horse and skinning it means a success the next morning in hunting Cervus Elaphus with good antlers.

The birds as messengers of "luck" are known among all groups. For instance, among the Khingan groups the taw (in Khingan Tungus, taw) foretells success in hunting, and brings news from home and back; for this reason the youngs of this bird are caught and kept, especially by children, near the house. If it cries joyfully it means that some of family members have killed an animal; if somebody must fall ill this bird produces an interrupted (staccato) cry; if the bird cries irregularly it means some misfortune. The partridge is also a sign of hunting "luck", but not always, —if two partidges should suddenly fly away in front of hunter, the latter must quickly say: "One branch! Two branches!" and so on, where "branch" means the forks of the antlers of the Cervus Elaphus and it is supposed that the birds would descend on the antlers of an animal with the indicated number of branches (the greater the number of branches of the antlers the dearer are the animals), but if the partridges fly away before the hunter can say anything or if they descend in view of the hunter, there will be no luck in hunting. In previous pages I have already related the cases observed amongst the Birarčen of "luck" brought by the raven (vide supra).

In the same way the snakes may indicate "luck" in hunting. For instance, among the Khingan Tungus it is supposed that if a snake would crawl into the wigwam without biting the people it would mean a success in hunting*.

* My informer had a visit of two snakes; the next morning he killed two Cervus Elaphus with good antlers. Another day during

A snake once slipped into the baby's cradle and coiled itself around the baby's neck; this was considered as a sign of good "luck" for the child who from that time always was very healthy. Naturally, snakes must not be killed.* The human body is also a source for producing various signs. For instance, the Birarčen suppose that if the muscles contract themselves without control it means good "luck" in hunting and the Khingan Tungus think that if the hand is itching it means the "luck" in hunting,—there will be "blood" and "skin",—spirit bainača would give an animal.

A great and certain source of good information as to the future for the Birarčen is the fire,—the various types of noise produced by it. All abnormal phenomena produce a great impression on the Tungus and they are often interpreted as warning. For instance, among the Birarčen a mare produced twins and died; soon after this the father of my informer died too; then the neighbours were greatly frightened by these two facts and believed that all of the people and the horses would die in a near future. Indeed, twins in horses is not a frequent occurrence, but how the inference as to the future has been made I could not find out.

The natural phenomena also receive their special meaning. For instance, among the Khingan Tungus it is supposed that if the wind turns back the flags of a company going out for war, the company will be badly defeated. Therefore, it is safer to return home immediately.

_____

4. BAD AND GOOD PLACES,   The Tungus and especially
   DAYS AND PERIODS   Manchus have the idea that
                           there are "bad" and "good"
places, days, hours and periods. The theory is partly based on the above mentioned theory of roads, also that of jin and jaŋ, according to which the places may be dangerous neutral and good. This theory also finds good support from the Chinese books for divination and definition of "lucky" and "unlucky" conditions. It is thus natural that the directions by which dangerous spirits are going are not good, while the directions free of the malevolent spirits are good. Let us take some instances. The directions North and West, and all the directions lying between, are considered as "bad", while directions of South are not so. The day roads are better than night roads. The odd days of the month which are jin are considered unlucky. The hours of the day among the Manchus are named by the animals and spirits e.g. endur'i èr'in, mor'in èr'in, etc. and there is ʑutu èr'in too; the people who die at ʑutu èr'in may became ibaŋan. However, this opinion is not adopted by all Manchus. The same is true of the hours when one wants to undertake some important business, particularly wedding ceremony, burial etc. Among the Birarčen the twenty-fourth day of the month is considered as a good day for hunting while the twenty-fifth is bad.

his rest at midday, a snake crawled near to him and slipped under his trousers; this was considered as a very good sign of success. It must be pointed out that in some regions of the Khingan Tungus territory, snakes are very abundant. They penetrated our tent, that of our cossacks, and even once a snake spent its night under the sadle cushion used by the cossack as his pillow. In this particular place thousands of snakes are sheltered in a hot cave during the winter and they come out in spring.

* Our killing of snakes found in our tents produced the most strong impression on these Tungus, but the misfortune, according to their ideas, might affect us, not them.

Generally among the Tungus these ideas are not so important as they are among the Manchus. Among the latter the knowledge of this matter is still not sufficient, so the Chinese specialists must be consulted in every case. These ideas only gradually penetrate amongst the Northern Tungus. Therefore the Tungus who are in contact with the Manchus, Dahurs, and Mongols know much more about these things, and the Tungus who are living far away, know very little, if anything. Indeed, the distinction of days and hours is possible only on the condition of observing the calendar, and divisions of the day.

In the case of choice of the place for burial, the Tungus prefer those which are "gay", i.e. attractive, from the Tungus point of view. These places would be "good". In the case of choice of a "good" place for wigwam they would avoid the places traversed by the path because of the spirits which may follow it.

The situation is greatly complicated owing to the fact that there are some places "bad", because of the spirits which are there settled. So the case of the removal of the families from one to another house are frequent, if there are several subsequent misfortunes in the family. Indeed, in all cases which I knew the decision was conditioned by considerations of a practical order too. For instance, the house might be too old, or too big for a reduced family, not convenient for winter season, etc.* It is very common that the misfortunes

occurred in the families are explained by the fact of bad place chosen for the burial of ancestors, but the Manchus very rarely transfer bones to another place. This fashion did not develop into such a hyperthrophy as it happened with the Koreans who are kept busy throughout whole of their life by transferring ancestral bones from one to another place.

The analysis of cases of "bad" and "good" places and periods requires great caution, for the choice of place and period very often depend on the consideration of a practical order, but since the reasons are forgotten they may be as "bad" and "good" with reference to the "luck" etc. which, as shown, in many a case has nothing to do with the groundless hypotheses.

It may be also pointed out that in the Manchu and Tungus ceremonies there are also several prescriptions of avoidance, which may also be called "bad" and "good" but which actually are merely of the code of politeness, as a complex by itself needed for regulation of social relations. There are, for instance, customs of descending the horse when passing a house of honourable persons, to avoid stepping or sitting on the threshold in the house, for threshold is called "neck of the houselord", and many others of the same type.

---

* For illustration I shall now give an instance. In Kalunšan a Manchu petty official built up a large, well ornamented house in 1908. The construction cost $1500. Three years later (the down fall of the Manchu Dynasty) the family began to suffer from various misfortunes: the children were often sick, the head of family lost his position, and lost money in several undertakings; also, he got a

spirit during his travelling. Therefore the family was reduced and the house was occupied only about a third as compared with the formerly occupied space. The house required a large quantity of fuel which could not be bought. So the man decided to sell the house. Nobody wanted to buy it for the house was built on a "bad" place, although he wanted to have for his house only $150. At last, a man decided to buy it for $400 in order to transport it to another place. The house was sold and the family went to live in a small house.

PART THREE

PRACTICAL CONSEQUENCES OF HYPOTHESES

CHAPTER XVI

METHODS OF INFLUENCING SPIRITS

58. PRELIMINARY REMARKS The present part is chiefly devoted to the practical ways of regulation of various relations which originate between the human beings and spirits. Before proceeding to the description of the methods in particular cases I shall now give the present introductory chapter for showing the methods and their practical general application.

In the present and following chapters I shall give some instances of managing souls and spirits without shaman's and other specialists' assistance. Indeed, the occasions on which the Tungus and Manchus are acting according to their own knowledge of methods are much more numerous than those when they appeal to the specialists' art. Yet we shall see later on that there are very serious reasons for avoiding specialists, particularly shamans.

As a matter of fact, the spirits are so numerous and so frequently met with along the way of the Tungus, and they keep themselves so near to the Tungus families, that every one must know at least the simplest methods of managing spirits and methods of avoiding their harmful activity. There may be distinguished various signs which are considered as indicative of the spirits' activity. In fact, from the description of the spirits we have seen that these hypotheses explain many facts which without these hypotheses would remain unexplained and, on the other hand, the hypotheses themselves sometimes may bring some superfluous consciousness and produce unnecessary fear, and consequently, result in a reduction of adaptive functioning, in individuals and groups.

Spirits' activity is very often supposed to take place in all cases when the situation does not correspond to the expectation. For instance, if the hunter has a good rifle to which he is accustomed and which he knows, provided the cartridges or charge of powder are good and correct, the missing of hitting an animal is ascribed to the influence of spirits. The spirits can make gun too heavy or too light, they can turn it aside, and so forth. This will not be, perhaps, noticed by the hunter. Indeed, in most cases of this type we have a simple case of self-suggestion or an explanation of the chance of hitting. In the same way the hunter would explain the chance of missing animals in spite of a great probability of meeting them, provided the footprints are found and the hunter takes all necessary precautions for preventing himself being seen, smelled or heard by the animals. The spirit does not want to give "luck",—to send the animal in the direction of the hunter. Yet, the incidental coincidence of "bad" events in the life of a family sometimes remains unexplained as a case of chance, but it might be explained as result of an intentional and malevolent influence of spirits[*]. Still more common is this attitude in case of diseases which sometimes affect indiscriminately both weak and strong, healthy, members of the community. A great number of cases of psychomental troubles which remain beyond the Tungus understanding such as effects of parasites, partial destruction of the organs, or as cases of adaptive disfunction, is often explained as result of spirits' activity. Indeed, the cases of slight deviations from the average behaviour, especially those resulting in the phenomena of loss of adaptiveness to the situation, which are felt by the persons affected by them, are also explained as due to the spirits' activity. In the same groups of phenomena is found the case of "loss of soul",—total and partial,—which is due to the same spiritual nature of the soul as that of some spirits.

There are cases in which the Tungus always has an occasion of seeing activity of the spiritual world, for which he must find a suitable opposition when the situation affects his interests. Since, as shown in previous chapters, there may be found different explanations of the same phenomenon, the Tungus must make a correct diagnosis of the case in order to find an effective remedy to it. Not in all cases it can be done without a competent assistance of specialists, which will be treated in other chapters, but there are cases when it can be done and there are different preventive measures, which I shall treat first.

It is well known to the Tungus that some spirits are permanently menacing him, or they may come at any moment and there is no other means, but to satisfy them with prayers and sacrifices, for these spirits cannot be avoided. His own observations and those of other people carried out during a long time, have convinced him of this truth. Therefore, the Tungus is prepared to deal with these spirits throughout his whole life, but he will do everything possible for reducing the burden of constant anxiety about them. He would make his prayers and sacrifices no more than required by his own self-confidence in security, and he would spend possible minimum energy on it. These are first of all his own soul, those of his family's members and souls of ancestors; in second place, the spirits of his own clan, spirits of his wife's clan, spirits of taiga, spirits of heaven, and some other spirits, with which he has nolens volens to deal, such as *māfa* and *fuĕ'k'i* of the Manchus.

On the other hand there are spirits which may be easily

* It must be pointed out that in many a case the Tungus look for explanation of these phenomena into the inherited psychomental condition as some above shown instances of inheritance already discussed in Part One.

187

avoided. Since there are localities where the spirits are present and may become harmful when approached, particularly at night time or in a state of intoxication, therefore if possible to avoid it he would not go there at all, and he would not go there at night or being drunken. There are rivers haunted by spirits which may take hold of people, —those rivers will be avoided. There are women who may be carriers of their clan's spirits,—these women will be avoided in so far as their sexual attraction may be fought. There are hundreds of spirits which may attack man when he is not protected by his own spirits, or if he loses self-control. Here we have a long list of places and persons to be avoided. Some of these may be justified from the point of view of hygiene or from the point of view of physical safety, as, for instance, contagious diseases such as small-pox, measles, venereal diseases, infected regions, rapids in the rivers, etc., but among these there are many which exist only because of the theories and hypotheses. In the group of these spirits we may include a great number of spirits which inhabit the taiga, mountains and marshes, and spirits which belong to other clans and to other ethnical groups. Incidentally these spirits may have their share in sacrifice and prayers.

Yet, there are spirits which are not yet well known,— they are not yet carefully investigated,—but their presence is suspected and they cannot be avoided. In order to neutralize their activity the Tungus would take great precautions for avoiding their anger and for avoiding them in general. On this ground, the Tungus would give a short sacrifice of tea, wine, meat, and generally of everything which he, himself, eats or drinks, in the form of throwing of pieces of his food and sprinkling of some of his drink into the air or into the fire. In many a case, the Tungus cannot say to which particular spirit the sacrifice is served, and he would do this almost automatically. Indeed, this is an important preventive measure.

In Tungus practice there is also a great number of prohibitions, taboos, which are strictly observed, but they are not connected with any of known spirits. In this case the Tungus attitude is simple: "Since these practices were established by our forefathers and they were not established by the caprice of people, but after a long experience, why should we abolish them. They might be created for protection against the spirits which were known to our forefathers, which do now exist, but remain unknown of our young, ignorant generation." Indeed to break with these prohibitions is always possible, but the experiment may sometimes become more costly than a faithful imitation of the older generations, and the taboos survive without even being explained. However, since an accumulation of taboos may arrest normal run of life and may become absolutely unbearable, some taboos are gradually dismissed and new ones, still unexplained and usually removed from the neighbours, occupy their place. The complex of taboos, many of which often have nothing to do with the hypotheses of spirits, is almost always explained as a practical method of preventing malevolent activity of the spirits. So in this case, the explanation of taboos with the help of pre-existing hypotheses is of secondary origin, as many taboos themselves. Indeed, there are some taboos, for instance, those regulating social relations, which do not need to be explained, but even in this case the practice of taboo may often be supported by fear of entering into troubles with the spirits, sometimes of an unknown origin and description.

At last, there are some spirits which may be sent away by frightening or destroying them. These may be spirits which originate from the souls of dead people, chiefly those who perished without receiving a ritual burial, also souls of shamans who have a "bad heart" and other people's souls which may do harm to the people. Destruction or merely injuring of spirits (also souls and consequently bodies which are carriers of souls) is usually done by means of destruction of a placing into which the spirit or soul has been called. Neutralization of shamans' souls constitutes an important group of cases of this type. Again, without a shaman's help this is not an easy undertaking, and common people are rather reluctant to undertake it.

The diagnosis of the diseases and special psychomental conditions, especially in women and children, forms one of the constant occupations of the Tungus. First of all it ought to be pointed out that amongst the Tungus certain diseases and conditions producing subjective effect of uneasiness are perhaps even more frequent than amongst other groups and for which, on the one hand, the conditions of life are greatly responsible, and, on the other hand, it may be supposed, the existing psychomental complex, in which the special psychomental conditions are created and resolved, is a favourable ground. Owing to the fact that the shamans and other specialists are not competent to treat certain cases, and even their interference may result in complications, every Tungus must possess a certain knowledge in diagnostics. As shown, the Tungus recognize existence of infectious diseases which may be treated with medicines and even preferably by the foreign doctors; they also recognize some other contagious diseases which, for theoretical reasons, must not be treated by the outsiders and especially with medicines; and yet they also recognize conditions which are due to the activity of spirits and which must be treated either by the Tungus themselves or by the specialists, particularly shamans. So that every Tungus must recognize whether the case requires assistance of specialists,—they may be foreign (Chinese, Mongol, Russian) doctors, or merely experienced man, or specialists dealing with certain spirits, at last the shamans,—or the case can be treated by himself with the help of other near relatives. Success greatly depends on the diagnosis. Indeed, in a great number of cases the error in diagnosis, committed by the Tungus, may be responsible for his own condition; for his error he will feel remorse and it is very likely that in such a case he will feel he must take special care of the soul after the death.

By giving the above picture of the Tungus activity respectively as to his own soul, those of other people, spirits, and at last diseases, I do not want to produce impression such as that which is made on readers by the great writers on the "primitive peoples",—the Tungus does not remain in a continuous struggle with the spirits and he is not at all oppressed by them. The troubles caused by souls, spirits and diseases are common, so the Tungus must be ready to find a good solution and to take necessary precautions. These conditions put on him great obligations, but in his theories and hypotheses he finds sufficient explanation and practical means for neutralizing effects of his own psychomental complex upon himself, in order to be functionally adapted for continuity of the species and maintaining its welfare. In the description which will now follow

I shall give methods used by the Tungus without very much touching the problem of functional significance of these practices. This will be discussed in the conclusive chapters of the present work.

59. CLASSIFICATION OF METHODS From the description of the nature of spirits and souls we have seen that they possess such characters that man can communicate with the spirits and influence them, when necessary. For man the most important thing is to know how to do it, and, thus, to know the character of spirits.

We may distinguish two cases, namely, first,—the spirits appear according to their own will and ought to be dealt with by man; second,—the spirits are called upon by man with a definite purpose of dealing with them. In the first case the man has nothing to do except to cope with the situation. The man must take special steps in order either (a) to use their presence in his own interests, or (b) to neutralize their malevolent influence on man. In both cases man has to take special steps which will be similar to those used in the case when spirits are intentionally called. In the case when the spirits are approached intentionally the practical steps consist in establishing a contact with the spirits and in influencing them.

In establishing contact with the spirits we may distinguish a case when the contact is established for a very short time by means of an appeal to the spirit, or by means of a complex prayer in which cases the attention of the spirits would be attracted and the desired contact established. In another case, namely, the establishment of a long contact may be achieved by means of a short appeal, or a complex prayer by which the spirit may be detained near by the man. This may be achieved by keeping the spirit by a long prayer and constant repetition of the address to the spirit and by location of spirit in a "placing" or loculus known to the spirit. The placing may be temporary or permanent. Temporary placings are used for particular cases of need of a contact, while permanent placings theoretically are supposed to be used for ever. Both temporary and permanent placings (loculi) may be different, namely, (a) natural placings, e.g. rocks, wooden trunks, trees, streams, mountains, also houses, stones, fire-places, etc. and all other placings which are not purposely made by men; (b) especially made placings, which may be of wood, iron, brass, straw, and also paper and other materials, as pictures etc. which in their further "growth" may attain the size of shrines and temples; (c) animals which are supposed to be used by the spirits as permanent placings or just for riding; (d) man. Here we may distinguish two cases functionally quite distinct, namely, the shamans who intentionally introduce the spirits into themselves (*vide infra*) and the people into whom the spirits are introduced, which is common, for instance, in the case of some diseases.

When the spirits are attracted by man, they may be influenced in the interests of the people. The methods of influencing are subject to great variations, which depends on character of spirits, ability of the peoples and particular aims in influencing spirits. Since the character of spirits partly corresponds to that of living people methods used are similar to those used amongst men in their relations.

The Tungus use conviction of spirits as a means of bringing them to accept man's views. In this case they would use typical reasons which may be expressed in an address to the spirits in a form of a prayer, more or less fixed and formalized, or in a form of free creation adapted to the particular need of the case. The spirits which are considered protectors of man, and those which are very powerful are usually informed of the facts which must be brought to their knowledge, and possible signs of obedience and submission must be shown, again either in a form of fixed prayer or in a form of a free creation, which usually is also a glorification of the spirit. However, with some spirits the Tungus apply different methods, namely, they would use the characters of spirits for managing them,—the spirits may be frightened or threatened by man; they may be deceived by man as when the spirit is called on to take a placing and afterwards these placings are destroyed, and there are other methods of the same kind. The spirits may be praised and by "nice words" attracted by man and afterwards treacherously captured by man or given up for destruction to other spirits. Yet, the most common method is dislocation of a spirit and its confinement to another placing from which it cannot go out; the expelling of spirits is the most frequent occurrence, and on the other hand, the method of keeping spirits near by is also used. There is also a policy of gaining sympathy with the spirits by appealing to their personal interests. Sacrifice ought to be included in this class of methods. However, a sacrifice may sometimes be promised and the promise will not be fulfilled, i.e. the

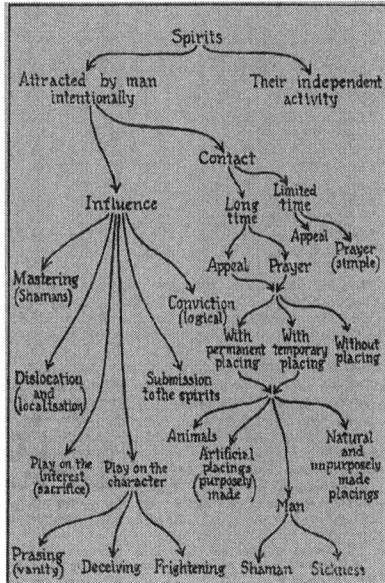

Spirits

Attracted by man intentionally — Their independent activity

Contact

Influence — Long time — Limited time

Mastering (Shamans) — Appeal — Prayer — Appeal — Prayer (simple)

Conviction (logical)

Dislocation and (localisation) — Submission to the spirits — With permanent placing — With temporary placing — Without placing

Play on the interest (sacrifice) — Play on the character — Artificial placings (purposely made) — Natural and unpurposely made placings

Animals

Man

Prasing (vanity) — Deceiving — Frightening — Shaman — Sickness

spirit may be deceived. Another way of gaining the sympathy of the spirits is an exaggerated praising of the spirits,—their glorification, which is not always sincere. At last, at the present time a very important and common case of managing spirits is to obtain their submission by shamanistic methods and similar methods of mastering spirits, or making of them servants of man.

The above described methods of dealing with the spirits may be summarized in the scheme here shown.

It may be seen, thus, there are three aspects, namely, placings for spirits, sacrifice and prayers which ought to be treated in a more detailed manner before we proceed to the description of particular cases.

60. PLACINGS FOR SPIRITS I use the term "placing for spirits" for the following reasons. The Tungus idea of spirit is that the latter possesses such properties that it may be located, embodied in a certain physical body. The spirit must be "placed" and when it is placed the Tungus may deal with it. As a matter of fact, the idea has been received by me from a Tungus-Birarčen—who explained to me the function of "placings" in the following words. When I asked him what the reason was of making wooden and other placings for spirits, he replied to me by a question: "How may the spirit know where is its place (oron)?" and he continued by another question: "If you invite somebody would not you show your guest place where he might sit?" Therefore there must be made for the spirit a special place-seat which would be recognized by the spirit, and which would not be used by other spirits. So that, the idea of place-seat for spirits is quite clear and simple for the Tungus mind. In my earlier work in Russian* I used the term vmest'ilišče, which may be translated in English "receptacle", "depository". However, these terms are not good, so that in other works in English I used alternatively "placing" and "loculus". Since the Tungus "place" their spirits, I now prefer the technical term "placing" which in my eyes gives a better starter. I abstain from using the term "idol", "fetish" etc. frequently met with in ethnographical publications, for these terms have quite different meanings. The Tungus placings as such have nothing "supernatural", nor "sacred"; even they are not symbols of spirits, nor their images. Moreover, usually they are not considered as a product of art.** They may be destroyed, substituted by other placings; even jokes about them are allowed. However, it is possible and admissible only on the condition if there is no spirit located, "placed" at that moment. This term is better than any other, for as previously shown, animals, people, and all natural phenomena, such as rocks, trees, etc. may become placings as well. From the Tungus point of view there will be no difference as to the function of these placings and those made purposely. Although the conception of "placing" is quite clear in the Tungus mind, the Tungus dialects and Manchu possess no special generic terms for all "placings", but they possess different terms covering different groups of placings.

Amongst the Tungus of Transbaikalia the placings carried on by the people together with other belongings are usually called burkan (cf. supra Section 48). Amongst the

Tungus of Manchuria and Mankova they are usually called savak'i (phonetic and semantic variations vide p. 160)* and special placings for shamanizing to the lower world amongst the Transbaikalian Tungus and RTM are called sēva (cf. supra p. 160). Placings which are made of wood may be called mōma, i.e. wooden, or wood, e.g. mōma (Nerč. Khin.) momate (Bir. Kum.); placings made of metals may be called according to the material used. However, this practice is not common.** Yet, there is a special term for placings made of straw for calling in and sending off the souls of dead people and generally when dealing with the lower world: bām'i (Bir. Kum.) bōm'i (Mank.).*** There is one more general term for placings, namely, an'ikan (also an'akan) (RTM, Bir. Kum.)**** used for shamanizing, particularly to the upper world, or for dealing on the upper roads. Other terms may be those referred to the particular spirits, e.g. malu, kaɲan. jol, etc. or the general manifestations as bojo ("man"), dēɲi ("bird") etc. or to the form of placing, as bāda (Nerč. Barg.) ("the face") corresponding to dērēgdē (Bir. Kum.), etc.

From these facts it is evident that we cannot put as the basis of classification of placings for spirits their terms in Tungus dialects. Indeed, the placings may be classified according to the spirits for which they are reserved, but, as seen, such a classification will be good for the classification of spirits and not their placings for the same placing may sometimes be used for different spirits and vice versa,—different placings may be used for the same spirit.

The size greatly depends on the mode of life and individuality of possessors of placings. Generally, amongst the groups which live in a settled manner the size of placings may be larger, and temporary placings, which are thrown away after the performance, are usually larger than permanent ones. The shape is closely connected with the kind of spirits, but at the same time the same shape of placing may be used for different spirits. The material is also subject to great variations,—placings for the same spirits may be made of wood, brass or straw and yet reduced to a picture. Such a variety of form, size, shape, material, etc. depends on the fact that the placings for spirits are not "idols", nor "icons". The process of selecting form etc. may depend on individual association or it may be received through tradition. In fact, we have seen that placings for ajelga amongst the Birarčen are usually made of two dried hillocks. It is so because for the first time the spirit happened to be placed in a hillock. However, if there is no hillock, the Birarčen make a wooden anthropomorphic placing. Since the spirit is once called and enters the placing, it may always know that the particular form of placing is reserved to it and it will not refuse to enter it when called again. The

---

* Vide "Essay, etc." 1919.

** Exception must be made in reference to some Manchu "placings" (vide supra).

* In Negidal P.P. Schmidt gives the same word for "cross" used by the Orthodox Christians.

** In Nerčinsk dialect golden placing are called golema [cf. gaoli (Bir.), gauli (Khin.), gōli (Mank), goli (Ur. Castr.),—the "brass"; cf. gulli(n) ‖ γaoli, Mong. Rud,—Korea, brass (cf. Chinese 金,金 Korea]; cf. golima. (Tit. Ang.)—"of brass". It is evident that "golden—brass" is according to the colour. Indeed, golden placings are rarely met with. I have not seen them,—they are mentioned in folklore.

*** No etymology in Tungus is found. Perhaps it is connected with Mongol stem bum met with in "earth", "place", "mound", "burial", etc. In fact, the vowel of the first syllable is not certain in Tungus, while Tungus bVm is always connected with "death complex."

**** Etymology vide supra p.52 f.

difficult moment is to call and "place" a spirit for the first time. The spirits, for a long time known amongst the Tungus, may have nearly the same form of placing amongst all Tungus groups to whom the spirits are known. The Tungus also know that the spirits would come when called into a placing of a definite form. Instead of carrying out doubtful experiments with calling these spirits into a placing of a new form, they would prefer to follow the experience of previous generations and that of other ethnical groups. On the other hand, there are conditions which are responsible for the change of form of placings. Here I want especially to mention forgetfulness, adaptation to the existing complex, adaption to the material and individual creation, also fashions.

Under the present conditions of life the Tungus are often separated for long months from their clansmen. Not all of them are familiar with all details concerning spirits, and they do not always perfectly remember the form of placings,—which I know from direct observation of facts,— but it may always happen that they would need to call the spirits. In such a case they would make the placing according to perhaps imperfect remembrance. Should they succeed in calling in the spirit which would "place" itself, the new variety of placing might be adopted by the family and thus transmitted to the succeeding generations. If the new form happens to be "better" from the practical point of view, it may be easily imitated by other groups (families, and later clans, ethnical groups, etc.). Some placings, as for instance *kayan* of the *najil burkan* (women's *malu burkan*), are sometimes thrown away or sent off with the river's current. Between the destruction and restoration of the placings *kayan*, there may sometimes elapse more than a generation, which period is sufficient for forgetting some details, as to the form, shape and material. Amongst the Khingan Tungus after the owner's death all placings may be thrown away, and they would be restored only when urgently needed.

The adaptation to the existing complex is a very important condition. In fact, the number of spirits, as shown, is subject to variation, therefore the placings must be also adapted. If a Tungus meets with a placing used, for instance, amongst the Goldi who are living in settled villages he would not be able to reproduce an exact copy of this placing for they often are too heavy for carrying on reindeer back, on horse back, or on his own back. Therefore they are reduced and some details may disappear altogether. In fact, some placings, which are similar as to their *form* and which are reserved for the same spirits, amongst the Goldi attain the size of several feet, while they are found reduced to a few centimetres amongst the Tungus who have adopted nomadism. In the same group the size also is subject to variations. For instance, amongst the Birarčen the size of the placing of the *malu* complex varies within a range in which the smallest placing would be ten times smaller than the largest one. A Birarčen woman might not sometimes want to have them of large size and so her husband would make them very small. The largest placings for spirits are observed the Udehe and Oroči of the Maritime Gov. who live in a half-settled manner, the smallest being observed among the Tungus of Manchuria, and especially among the Birarčen. However, it ought to be pointed out that temporary placings, as for instance, for *aſelga* may attain very large size. Yet, the temporary placings amongst

the Reindeer Tungus of Transbaikalia (e.g. the Barguzin) sometimes are large. Once I observed an anthropomorphic placing over forty centimetres high.

The material may be greatly responsible for the form and size. In Transbaikalia the placing for *malu*—the manifestation *bāda* ("face")—is made of iron and rarely brass. The form naturally is flat, the design consists of the perforations and points made with a sharp stamp. The general appearance of this placing is quite different from the wooden "face"—*dèrègdè*—of the same complex observed amongst the Birarčen. When the placing for *Baìnača* is cut on a trunk of a standing tree it is naturally large, but when this cannot be done, a piece of wood with a few cuts may suffice as placing. Amongst the Manchus and Tungus the placings made of straw or dry grass are common for spirits of lower world,—ancestors,—and for carrying the souls of dead people. The size of these placings,—usually man-like and dog-like figurines,—is larger than that of those made of wood and they are much heavier. The Tungus of Manchuria call them "fat man". The placings made of metals like silver and gold,—such ones are very rare,—would be, of course, very small.

The pictures are usually made by the specialists of non-Tungus origin. They are usually made on paper pasted on a piece of silk or other tissues. They are mere reproduction of Buddhistic and Taoistic pictures amongst the Tungus who are in contact with the Manchus, Mongols and Chinese. Naturally they are made according to the existing patterns. However, I have seen some pictures, e.g. amongst the Birarčen, which were made on special order and represented spirits, at least their number and sex, required by the Tungus complex; the images were usually stylized in Chinese way. Amongst the Manchus there is a special form of pictures,—*n'uryan* (Manchu Sp.) (corr. *niruγan*, Manchu Writ.),—which represent shamanistic spirits in a typical manner of Chinese iconography. However, these pictures cannot be regarded as typical placings for spirits.

Introduction of pictures as placings for spirits has produced great changes; namely, the placings have lost their plasticity and form, and they have been formalized to become almost mere symbols of placing. In the same way the introduction of tissues,—borrowed from the Mongols, an imitation of Mongol *oγgon* with zoomorphic and anthropomorphic applications made of tissues, leather, and metals with some ornamentation,—is responsible for reduction of size of placings, loss of expressiveness and plasticity. Still more simplifications were introduced amongst the Manchus, who began to use ribbons of different size and colour as placings for their spirits. Naturally, they become much like simple "symbols".

The individual tastes in the matter of choice of form and material play their important role in the final appearance of placings. Indeed, a good wood-carver who pays attention to details would make a placing accurately reproducing the original type; but he may also add some particular traits unknown in other specimens, e.g. more details or some ornamental elements. This may also influence the size of placings.[*] In fact, I have often observed that some Tungus are inclined to make large placings, while the

[*] It is a well known fact that the preference for very small size or very large size of all things is intimately connected with the psychomental complex of individuals, even in so far as it is conditioned by the system of the glands of internal secretion.

others would prefer small placings. If they should make unusually large or small placings they would point out it by saying: "Look how large (or small) are these placings!" One can see that they would like to have approval of their deviation from the idea of the usual size of placings.

When placings of different periods are compared one may notice that they may differ as to the form and size. For instance, the great grandmothers of the present Tungus women of Barguzin group preferred small size of *báda* made of brass, while at the present time much larger size is preferred, the maximum length being four and even five times larger. Amongst the Birarčen, as I have already pointed out, the size of *kayan* at the present time is much smaller than it was three or four generations ago. If these people are asked why the size is different, they give the explanation, e.g. referring to the convenience of carrying placings, or they would say: "The large size is better" or "The small size is better". The same is true of the form and ornamentation which are subject to the variations in time. There is no doubt that the variations of this type are due to the fashions which spread among Tungus groups like any other fashions in dress, language, etc. They may be due either to the alien influences or to the local spontaneous variations.

From the above remarks it is evident that the form, size and details in placings for the same spirits are subject to great variations, and for these reasons their identification presents great difficulties, it even sometimes becomes absolutely impossible. Yet, one cannot sometimes say: which spirit is supposed to be introduced into a placing: a certain form and shape for the same type of placing may be used for different spirits, even within the same ethnical unit.

ATTITUDE TOWARDS THE PLACINGS. Generally the placings are considered by the Tungus for their material value, also as remembrance of former possessors, and whether they may be used by the spirits or not also whether the spirits are found there, or not. The metals being rare among the Tungus, the metallic placings, as such, are of a certain value, to the Tungus. The same is true of pictures which are brought from the Chinese and Dahurs. In a lesser degree it may be referred to the silk placings. Yet if the Tungus must spend a long time for carving wooden placings, they may also have value as such. Still more will be valued costumes used by the shamans, shrines (among the Manchus), skins of rare or large animals, etc. Therefore the Tungus attitude in preserving placings is conditioned at first hand by the consideration of their value, as goods.

The second condition,—the remembrance of former possessors,—is of importance, too. The placings are sometimes transmitted from one generation to another and the owners connect with them the former possessors, as a kind of reliquiae. Therefore, one rather often meets with the placings transmitted for generations and the Tungus would remember various details as to the former owners.

It is different when the placings may be occupied by the spirits. The Tungus would be very careful with these placings, fearing to disturb them, sometimes even to approach them. It ought to be pointed out that in this case they behave in such a manner not towards the placings but towards the spirits. Let us now consider the case of a malevolent spirit which may temporarily have introduced itself into the placing. The attitude of the Tungus may be different; namely, if the spirit may be sent off with the expectation of its final leaving, the Tungus would introduce the spirit in the placing and throw it away, and the spirit together with it. If the spirit from time to time should want to have food, the placing would be kept ready, in order, by means of sacrifice, to neutralize the spirit's activity. Yet, if the placing itself might be attractive for the malevolent spirits and if the Tungus suppose that other spirits would not introduce themselves into the placings, and if at the same time the malevolent spirits may harm the people by introducing themselves into the placings (including men), it is very likely that the placings would be thrown away. Let us now picture a case when the spirits are benevolent and neutral, but occasionally useful. There may be different solutions as to the keeping of placings. First of all, if there are placings for the benevolent spirits the latter being left without regular food may become harmful, therefore they must be "fed", which would result in constant care of spirits and placings. Since the Tungus can sometimes rely upon themselves, they do not need any special assistance on the part of spirits, so the placings will be very likely thrown away. I do not need to enumerate many other combinations all of which would result in three attitudes: special care of placings, which may be due both to the fear and to the desire to have spirits near by; indifferent attitude; and desire to throw away the placing again for different reasons,—to rid themselves of spirits, to eliminate the possibility of spirits' coming back etc.

The attitude also greatly depends upon the prevailing ideas amongst the groups. For instance, the spirits are not uncritically accepted by the Tungus into their complexes, therefore among the Birarčen no attention will be paid to the icons already known amongst the Tungus being under the Russian influence, if they do not recognize "spirits which have come from the Russians" as powerful and sometimes dangerous. The Birarčen, and other Tungus groups as well, very often deny the foreign spirits' power over themselves, whence they do not at all consider foreign spirits and placings for these spirits.

Amongst the Tungus groups the females, especially during sexually active period, recognized by menstruation, are not allowed to touch placings for spirits and even to approach them, the chief reason being that the women themselves are bearers of their own clan spirits which may mix up with those of other clans, and that most of spirits do not like women's blood. However, the same is true of the men who do not belong to the family and who must not come into the contact with the women, especially when they have their clan spirits' placing*. In all cases when the Tungus do not know the purpose for which the placings have been made, they will not touch them for fear of disturbing and attracting to themselves spirits whom they do

---

* However, the fear of spirits does not keep away men from approaching women with sex intentions, which as I have shown (vide SONT, pp. 209 et seq.) is a common practice amongst the Tungus. In similar cases the Tungus males know the ways of neutralizing the danger coming from alien spirits. Yet, there is no doubt that in some cases at least the fear of spirits may act as a mechanism which restricts men in their sexual activity.

not know. It is not recommended to lose placings for *burkan* (amongst the Tungus of Manchuria), for if there is no place to come in, the spirit may settle in one of the clansmen. Since it is not always easy to know which of burkans may have introduced itself into the clansman, it will be necessary to shamanize which is, of course, a difficult and expensive undertaking. And then, after shamanizing it will be necessary again to make a new placing, and by a special sacrifice invite the spirit to leave the body of clansman and come into the placing. Thus, it is better to preserve placings and not to lose them. On the other hand, the women when growing old throw away their placings *kapan*, for their presence in old age is more harmful than beneficial and after the menopause the women do not so much suffer of their clan spirits. I know several cases of sending off placings in a small boat put in the current of the rivers.

From the above analysis it is evident that the placings as such have nothing to do with the Tungus attitude, but material and work spent on them, memories associated with them and especially spirits' activity connected with the placings are considered. A valueless placing may be of great importance for the Tungus, while a very expensive one may be thrown away if a malevolent spirit may be introduced there and sent off together with the placing. It is thus evident that in every particular case the observer of the Tungus must know exactly the function of the particular and individual placing, its value as goods, and the relationship which exists between the people, spirit and placing, before making up any judgment as to the Tungus attitude towards the placings.

61. TYPES OF PLACINGS   I shall now describe some typical placings. WOODEN PERMANENT PLACINGS. Among all Tungus groups wooden placings are used for the complex spirit (*burkan*) *malu* (*vide supra* Chapter XIII). The shape of the manifestations is more or less alike among all groups. One may find, stars, snakes, lizards, sun and moon, the form of which is more or less alike. In case of the placings for spirits which have animal manifestations—e.g. tiger or bear,—or manifestations using those animals for locomotion, the animals would have the necessary characters sufficient for showing what kind of animal was understood by the makers. The groups which use colours, as for instance the Goldi, supply tiger and leopard with stripes or with spots. The size of these placings, even in the same complex, will not be a sure indication of the kind of animal, for the size is also indicative of the power of the manfestation. These animals may be supplied with wings and bird tails etc. which are not indicative that these are compound animal manifestations, or still less "mythical animals", like licorn, griffon, Egyptian ox, etc. but these marks of distinction will be indicative that the given animal manifestation may move in the air "like a bird". In the same way, the fish fins added to zoomorphic and anthropomorphic placings are indicative that these manifestations may go under the water "like a fish". Therefore, in every particular case one must exactly know whether the manifestation is an animal or the animal is used itself as a placing for the soul (particularly that of the shaman). At least it is indicative of the spirits' ability to move or behave "like the particular animals". Let us

remark that the accuracy in the understanding of functions of placings and their meaning is very useful for avoiding unnecessary "scaffolding" of hypotheses as to the "primitive conceptions"[1] of spirits.

One of typical placings is a "face" which is used for the principal spirit of the group *malu*. It is called *báda* (Barg. Nerč.) *dèrègdè* (Bir. Kum. Khin. RTM.)[*] which merely means "face". It may be made from various materials but it is usually made of wood.[**] Among the Tungus of Manchuria it is not of a large size,—I have seen it varying between three and six centimetres. There may be two "faces",—one representing a female and another a male which is marked by symbolized hair on the chin and upper lip, also cheeks. Amongst the Transbaikalian Tungus it is usually made of birch bark, and is very large. Amongst these groups the group of *malu* may be confined only to these placings. That is the reason why this form of placing is met with so frequently amongst different Tungus groups. Yet, I have met with large wooden placings of mask-like appearance, embellished with hair, beads, etc. Amongst the shamans it may be still more elaborated and of large size. It may be attached to the shaman's costume. However, amongst the shamans of Manchuria it is lacking, as well as other placings for spirits of the *malu* group. It ought to be pointed out that this placing must not be taken for "symbol of the sun," etc. which was guessed by some authors. Amongst the Tungus it has nothing to do with the sun, except the round-form of the face.[***] The manifestations of tuberculosis with special sign of exhaustion as thinness of the body, broken chest etc. also are more or less similar. The manifestations of rheumatism with broken legs, or with a half-leg cut at the height of knee are not so uniform. The half-legged manifestation is met with in another function, namely, as placing for "Lame Brother" who carries the souls of dead people across the river. The form of this placing may greatly vary. Here[****] I give a picture of this placing which has been found on the place of a burial in Saxalin Island, left probably by the Oroki. It may be noted, that it is a combination of fish (sturgeon?) and man. Amongst other groups "Lame Brother" may be perfectly anthropomorphic. Amongst these placings there is one with nine indentations symbolizing nine heads of a manifestation *malu*,—*mayi*. Owing to the presence of indentations the placing may be identified without error.

As stated, the size and details are subject to great variation. As regards the material amongst the Tungus of Manchuria, with the exception of RTM, the placings *lege artis* must be made of black birch wood, or if one cannot have it, of poplar wood. However, in North Transbaikalia these trees are not frequent, at least in some regions, and the placings can be made of any available but strong wood. As

---

[*] Among the Mankova Tungus this term is referred to the placing for taiga spirit, made on the tree.

[**] I think it may be supposed that the iron, brass, tin, etc. are materials which were not used formerly. They are undoubtedly an innovation.

[***] By this remark I do not want to say that it is so in general, and that my remark holds good for among other ethnical groups. We have already seen the same form of placings may be used for different spirits and even "symbols".

[****] Vide p. 194. No meaning of another placing here represented could be established. In all probability that it is another manifestation (bear+bird) of one of spirits accompanying souls to the lower world.

to the names given to the placings of this type by the Tungus groups, they are subject to great variations.

One of characteristic features of the Tungus placings is that the distinction of sex usually is not marked by the details of sexual organs. However, once or twice I have seen among the Khingan Tungus these details in placings, for a female spirit. The reason why they do not show these details is that the placings are supposed to represent spirits dressed according to the Tungus fashion. In fact, among the Barguzin and Nerčinsk Tungus the wooden placings are covered with chamois. The chamois may be cut to symbolize the hair, form of clothes, and other details. Yet, it may be ornamented with coloured small beads, even painted, also ornamented with reindeer neck hair. In these dialects the placings are called savak'i (Nerč.), šavak'i (Barg.). Most of these placings are "faces",—bāda,—in which the presence of ear-rings and beards and moustaches is indicative of the sex of manifestations.

It ought to be pointed out that amongst the Kumarčen and Birarčen malu burkan under the name of kayan are possessed only by the females. Amongst the Khingan Tungus, according to one of my informers, any man may also have the placings for malu burkan. The placings after the owner's death are always destroyed. Amongst this group there are some placings of larger size and with sharpened end for fixing it into the ground during the performances of sacrifice. Amongst the Tungus of Transbaikalia the men have them too. After death of the owner the placings may be preserved being transmitted to the daughters among the Tungus of Manchuria, while amongst the Transbaikalian groups, the placings are taken out of the family bunch of placings and hung up to a birch tree. Amongst the Reindeer Tungus of Manchuria as well as that of the Amur Government, and according to these Tungus amongst their people living in the Yakutsk Government, the great part in permanent placings is occupied by the anthropomorphic placings (bojol) and those representing swans. The swans are typical of these Tungus groups while other placings of the group malu are not very elaborate. In Transbaikalia I once saw a permanent wooden placing made in the form of triangle fixed on a shaft and with nine anthropomorphic small placings. This was a special placing for spirits connected with the hunting. Such placings seem to be also used by the Goldi* and by the Birarčen. Among the Manchus permanent wooden placings are very rarely met with. Bows and arrows are made when boys are born. They are connected with the spirit xutur'i mama and they cannot be regarded as placings in the above given sense. The same is true of wooden "shrines", of very small size, in which the Manchus keep pictures of various spirits. Amongst the Khingan Tungus the shamans sometimes have "placings" which represent various local animals hunted by these Tungus. Although cut in a very rough manner, they represent very realistically morphological peculiarities of the animals and sometimes their characteristic movements. These are not placings for spirits but symbols for communication with the spirits about the animals symbolized. Here I point out once more how it sometimes is difficult to make up the idea of functions of some placings and symbols**.

WOODEN TEMPORARY PLACINGS. Such placings are used during the shamanistic performances, also during sacrifices to certain spirits, or in special cases of some spirits, which may occasionally harm the people and at the same time may be managed without the shaman's assistance. Amongst the Transbalkalian Tungus there are anthropomorphic placings for spirits called toyoljin and toyoman made from the larch tree wood. They usually are about thirty centimetres long; the legs are not marked and the head is symbolized by pyramidal form on which they make cuts representing two eyes and a mouth. The placing reserved for the spirits sêva is much larger,—about fifty centimetres long,—and it is supplied with legs and "hints" as to arms. Usually it is made of rotten, soft wood. The fishes and bears, needed as animal manifestations for shamanizing, are made of a hard wood and the form, in spite of great conventionalism and roughness of work, may be easily recognized. As in other cases of "primitive art" it suffices to give an idea of the animals by putting emphasis on some particular characteristic. There is also quite typical placing of toli or joli,—the "salmo taimen", —in the form of a fish with horns, much larger in size (about sixty centimetres) than other "fishes". This is one of the "manifestations" of shaman's spirits. It may also be pointed out that they make a raft consisting of four wooden pieces with fish-like heads, one hundred forty to one hundred sixty centimetres long, and a special instrument for "cleaning" etc. all of which are thrown away after the performance. However, the equipment used for shamanizing to the upper world are made from birch-bark: birds (diyi) and anthropomorphic placings (an'akan) which in double number are attached to the trees especially prepared for shamanizing. The placings are small, from ten to fifteen centimetres long.

Amongst the Tungus of Manchuria temporary placings for shamanizing are made of soft wood and thrown away or just left on the spot. There are two groups of placings called an'akan and bâm'i, both of which are anthropomorphic. The first (small size) are usually made to represent manifestations of various complex spirits of day roads. They can be made either with or without arms and legs, as shown in the above picture, the size greatly varying according to the case and personal choice. They may be made in numbers of two, five, seven and nine with a corresponding number of birds made also of wood. Their number depends, as shown, upon the spirits. The an'akan may be accompanied by mudur, i.e. "dragon", the number of which also depends upon the spirits. An'akan without arms and legs are made for sacrifice to julask'i. In this case they represent placings for spirits-envoys and not julask'i itself. Bâm'i can be made of dry grass, straw, when it is available, also rotten wood and fresh wood. It is usually in single or double number of much larger size than

---

* Oral communication of L. Sternberg. Cf. also I. A. Lopatin, Table XXIV, 61.

** These may be easily classed in the group of facts pointing

to zoolatry, totemism, etc. although they have nothing to do with them. Yet, from the above instance we may see that the wooden pieces which represent animals may be mere symbols, understood by the spirits.

an'akan and, as a rule, with legs and arms roughly cut. *Bâm'i* is used for night roads of spirits. The same placing is made for the spirits coming from the lower world, i.e. ancestors, but in this case it is always accompanied by a placing representing dog. The presence of a dog is a distinct character of complex placings. The *bâm'i* made of wood, birch bark and rotten wood, are used for calling all spirits and souls of other people, as well as they are made for action similia similibus (*vide supra* Section 55). In the first cases they are real placings and after the operation— admonition, sacrifice, threatening and even shooting down, —they are thrown away, while in the case of action similia similibus,—e.g. shooting or cutting of *bâm'i* which is supposed to represent a person which is found at certain distance,—it is not so. However, it is impossible to distinguish for which purpose the *bâm'i* has been originally made.

Perhaps to the same group of temporary placings there may be related the placing made for *bainača*. Although it is merely cut on a trunk of living tree, the Tungus do not always return to the same placing for making their sacrifice, but they cut a new one if they want to have a placing for sacrifice.

The Reindeer Tungus of Manchuria make four anthropomorphic placings without arms and legs called *homoko* or *homokokan* (RTM), also *toyoljin*. Although there formerly also was *toyoman* its forms could not be established. *Sêva* used to be made of rotten wood with arms and legs, as amongst the Tungus of Transbaikalia. The placings are thrown away after the rite.

In order to avoid repetition there may also be mentioned temporary paraphernalia of shamanism which are not placings, but which are also often left after the shamanizing. Amongst the Tungus of Transbaikalia,—the Barguzin and Nerčinsk groups,—there is a pair of wooden freshly cut staves called either *morin* ("horse") or *oron* ("reindeer") and which are used by the shaman during his travelling (*vide infra* Chapter XXV). After the performance they are left at the spot together with other placings. Yet, sometimes, there are also made *gula* ("house") which is supposed to be located in the other world. It consists of four wooden planks about thirty centimetres long, fixed together to form a square construction. Among the Tungus of Manchuria, also among the Goldi, Gilaks and neighbouring groups, one also sees "houses" of different type,—a house with a sloping roof which in vertical, frontal cross section gives a triangle,—in which they put *an'akan*. At last, amongst the Tungus of Transbaikalia there is made a special apparatus for purification, consisting of four narrow wooden pieces fastened together in form of a square. The inside of each piece is cut to form teeth. The square is sufficiently large for an adult man to go through. This apparatus is used after shamanizing and is called *s'ipkan* and *čipkânin* (Barg. Nerč.). Among the Kumarčen some placings after shamanizing are put into a bird's skin.

PLACINGS MADE OF SOFT TISSUES AND SKINS. There is a series of placings used for children made of old tissues and skins. They have already been described (SONT pp. 280 et seq.), so that I shall now only point out that the anthropomorphic placings are reserved for the spirits which are supposed to look after the child, and there is a special placing, usually made of skin coloured black, which is placing for child's soul.

Under the Mongol (Buriat) influence amongst the Tungus of Manchuria (except RTM) and amongst the Mankova Tungus the *oygon* have become very common. They are made of a piece of skin or tissue,—cotton, silk and others,—with applicated anthropomorphic placings, also horses and various symbols, as the sun, moon, stars etc. also small bones of some animals. The placings differ as to the colour of the tissue, form and number of small placings. They may be ornamented with tissues of different colours, some sewing, hair, and painting. Amongst the placings of this type the most common is *jol* (*vide supra* p. 133) which is found in almost every family. Amongst the Tungus of Manchuria there are placings of this type used for other spirits, e.g. *kaldun burkan, jlači burkan,* and others (*vide* Chapter XIII).

Quite a special position is occupied by the Manchu placings for clan spirits, as stated (*vide supra* p. 144), of various colours and slightly varying shape.

PLACINGS-PICTURES. This is an innovation introduced amongst the Tungus of Manchuria (except RTM), Manchus, Goldi, and some other Tungus groups of Maritime Gov., chiefly under the Chinese influence. Their patterns are that known in Chinese iconography. The Chinese printed pictures appear beside those made by hand work of Chinese, Dahur and Mongol craftsmen. However, it ought to be pointed out that the personages shown in these pictures do not always correspond to those understood by the Tungus,—some Chinese "gods" may be understood as Tungus spirits. The same is true of the Buddhistic pictures. Therefore, if one sees such pictures amongst the Tungus it does not yet mean that the alien complex is already accepted, and yet, let us remark, the Tungus placings sometimes may be used for the spirits received from the alien groups, including Taoistic and Buddhistic spirits. Among the Tungus influenced by the Russians there have been lately introduced Russian icons which however have not yet been assimilated[*]. It ought to be pointed out that among the Manchus one must distinguish placings from the pictures. The Manchus have pictures of shamanistic spirits (*nirvgan* ‖ *n'uryan*), but they are not "placings" in the above given definition. As to the technique they are made by the Chinese craftsmen, and thus in so far as the style is concerned, they are Chinese. However, there is a tendency to represent spirits, according to the Manchu conceptions.

PLACINGS MADE OF DRY GRASS AND STRAW are used exclusively for spirits of night roads and ancestors who come from the lower world (also a night road) on their visits to the middle world and for receiving "food" from living people. The placings may consist of one anthropomorphic placing made of twisted dry grass or straw, and one or several dog-like placings. When there are no "dogs" the anthropomorphic placing is used for spirits. The size may vary, but it is usually between forty and fifty centimetres high. The Tungus of Manchuria call it *bâm'i*

---

[*] I have some indications that under the pressure of communistic authorities the old icons of Christian complex are now replaced by the pictures of prominent communistic leaders put together with pictures of the late Emperor, Grand Duke Nicolas, and generals. If the Tungus groups in Siberia survive it is very likely that a few generations later the above indicated pictures may become new iconographic patterns of new spirits or even old spirits adapted to a new complex, as it has already happened with the alien iconography amongst the Tungus groups of Manchuria.

(Kum. Bir.) or merely "fat man" (*burga bojo*), while the Manchus make it of straw and call it *orxo n'aḷma* (Manchu Writ.) [corr. *oryo n'ama* (Manchu Sp.)],—the straw man. The dogs are called *n'inak'in* (Kum. Bir.),—the dog; and *orxo indaxun* (Manchu Writ.) [corr. *oryo indayún* (Manchu Sp.)],—the straw dog. After the sacrifice they are thrown away toward the North or North-West. Instead of a "dog" there may also appear a "reindeer", even among the groups which at present have no more reindeer breeding.

SPECIAL TEMPORARY PLACINGS. Two hillocks, dried and a little shaped, are used among the Birarčen as a placing for the spirit *ajelga* (*vide supra*, p. 132) which permits to recognize the spirit. Among the Reindeer Tungus of Manchuria there are used wooden chips left uncut on a wooden stick. Such placings are known among the Goldi, Gilaks, Ainu, also among Tungus groups living near the above mentioned groups, as the Oroki of Saxalin Island, Oroči and Udehe of Maritime Government. It may be pointed out that this type of placing is well known in Japan, where they are very elaborate. It is likely that the above mentioned groups through the intermediary Ainus have received them from Japan.

PLACINGS MADE OF METALS. I have already stated, that the use of metals for placings is rather limited, —the Tungus do not work metals. It also holds good of the Manchus who have their metallic implements and weapons usually made by the Chinese. However, the Tungus know a little of the art of smithing and they can make what they want of iron, brass, and silver, also, but rarely gold. The usual way is cold smithing. Lately the *bāda*,—i.e. "face",—amongst the Tungus of Transbaikalia are made of brass, tin, and rarely, iron. The size is subject to variations,—from three to twenty centimetres; the usual form is an oval, imperfect imitation of the face. The placings are usually flat, the nose, mouth and eyes as well as the hair being symbolized in some way, suitable for the material. Small metallic images may be also found on the placings of *oygon* type (*vide supra*). Placings made of soft tissues). Together with the penetration of Christianity, the cross, usually made of silver, has made also its penetration amongst the Tungus of Transbaikalia. The métallic placings are very numerous on the shaman's coat, hat, etc. But these special placings will be discussed later.

PLACINGS MADE OF ANIMAL SKINS. Such placings are met with amongst all Tungus groups, except the Manchus. The skins together with the head and legs may be used as placings for animal manifestations of spirits, e.g. in the case of sending sacrifice to the spirits. The souls of animals killed may be also used for the same purpose and their skins would be needed. However, in this case skins will not be placings, but the animals will be envoys of men or used directly by the people. However, to distinguish in which function the skins are used is not always possible. To this question I shall also return later. So I shall now confine myself to an enumeration of the animals used. The skins of the following animals are used: hare, especially amongst the Tungus of Transbaikalia; pole-cat; sable; sheep (Tungus of Transbaikalia); reindeer amongst the reindeer breeders (for transferring the souls of dead people and for certain kinds of sacrifice); horse (for the same purpose amongst the Tungus of Manchuria); hedge-hog (amongst the Manchus and recently other groups); snakes; some

fishes; turtle and toad usually dried (amongst the Tungus of Manchuria). Amongst the Tungus of Manchuria the skins of ducks and geese are largely used too. The Tungus also use parts of animals, e.g. the bear's paw, the teeth of reindeer, sable, tiger; bones of various animals (especially on the cradle); rarely antlers and horns of various animals. Here again they may have various functions,—as well as for "magics" and as "amulets".

ANIMALS AND HUMAN BEINGS ARE USED AS PLACINGS among all Tungus groups, but since they are not intentionally made for this purpose I will now leave them without discussion.

62. RESERVED ANIMALS: Among all groups here discussed the practice is maintained of reserving domesticated draught animals,—the reindeer and the horse,—for the spirits. The animals may be reserved for two different purposes, namely, for carrying placings for spirits and for the use of the spirits which are supposed to ride on the backs of the animals.[*] The spirits are also supposed to hung up to the tail, mane, and ribbons attached to the animals, as well as to the hair on the neck of the reindeer. Whence several precautions and prohibitions result. Amongst the Reindeer Tungus of Transbaikalia there are two kinds of reserved reindeer *oygun* and *jasil*. Since the analogy with the horse reserved is almost complete the term may be treated as common. *Oygun ~ onyun* (Barg. Nerč. Kum. Bir, Khin. Mank.) ought to be connected with the Mongol term for spirits *oygon* still used by the shamans amongst the Buriats,[**] where reserved horses are also known. Since in Tungus this term has a very narrow use and it is confined to a limited group of dialects of groups living in a close vicinity from the Mongol speaking populations[***] it may be suspected of being of Mongol "origin".

Amongst the Reindeer Tungus any reindeer may be selected and the animal is marked with a small ribbon attached to the ear, passed through a perforation. The rib-

---

[*] Once I heard from the Barguzin Tungus that the reindeer reserved is also used for communication with the spirits, as a special envoy. However, I am not inclined to accept such an explanation. It is more probable that the animals are supposed to be used by the spirits as a kind of moving placing and thus the communication with the spirit becomes easy. This Tungus group, being influenced by new ideas, might have changed the original meaning of this practice or even they might give an explanation which in their eyes seemed clearer than their own conception, for a foreigner as I was. Indeed, the soul of the reindeer may be used as an envoy but in this case it should be exteriorated, consciously as the shamans do it, or unconsciously, or through liberation of the soul by slaughtering of the animal.

[**] In Mongol, according to Kowalewsky, "génies tutélaires, mânes, mets offerts aux mânes", connected with "pur, saint", etc. and *oyyon morin*—the horse *oygon* (reserved). At the present time the *oygon* complex is competing with Lamaism (cf. C. Ž. Żamcarano, op. cit. p. 380) in Transbaikalia and gradually substituted in Mongolia (Grünwedel, op. cit. pp. 84 and 180) by the Buddhistic complex. I think it would be perhaps dangerous to identify this complex with "shamanism", for in the Mongol complex the *oygon* occupy a larger position than the simple shamanistic spirits, and they have evident connexion with the dead ancestors.

[***] The Barguzin Buriats in Transbaikalia are neighbours of the Barguzin Tungus, the Uldurga Buriats are neighbours of the Nerčinsk Tungus, the Dahurs (cf. N. N. Poppe's dictionary *oygon delbur*,—the *oygon* mane in horse, also Xalxa dial.) and the Barguts are neighbours of the Tungus of Manchuria.

bon is called *sekan*,—the "ear-ring". These reindeer have to carry placings for spirits, shaman's costume, etc. The animal may be slaughtered, mounted by man and children of both sexes, and also it may be loaded. Usually, the *oygun* is established after some sickness* or after any other misfortune in the family. Amongst the Nerčinsk Tungus, who have no reindeer, the functions of the reindeer is reserved to the horse, i.e. just as it is among the Buriats. Amongst the Birarčen group the horses are reserved for different spirits. Their colour must be black, white, red, and dark brown, while piebald horses and those of other colours are not used. The exception is made of *kaidun burkan* the horse for which must be of light-bay (isabel) colour. Every family which has placings for spirits must have a horse *oygun*. However, horses are also reserved for the spirits for their own use. This is done when there is some sickness amongst the family members or horses, or if there is some calamity to be prevented. Sickness and repeated accidents with the horses are usually interpreted in the sense that the spirits want to have *oygun*. The same colour of *oygun* horse would be preserved in the family for the same spirit. The *oygun* must not be used by the people who do not belong to the family and the women, nor for all things *ak'ipču*. It may be used by the male chief of the family. However, sometimes men outsiders may be permitted to ride, if a saddle-cloth belonging to the *oygun*-horse is put on its back before the saddle is put on. Amongst the Khingan Tungus there is an evident fashion of reserving horses to various spirits. So, for instance, white stallions are often reserved to the spirit *bainača*, and a black horse is reserved to *tudukan*,—so that all horses which are used by men and children are sometimes reserved to the spirits. This is especially true of these Tungus for they have very few horses. The horses *oygun* amongst all groups have special marks: ribbon in the mane or tail.

Amongst the Tungus of Transbalkalia there is another kind of reserved reindeer called *jasil* (Barg. Nerč.), which seems to be similar to *itik* (RTM.), of white colour male or female. *Jasil* is distinguished by "ear-rings" and a kind of "amulet" hung up under the neck. The animals cannot be slaughtered and must be left to die by natural death. After death the corpse must be put on an elevated place,— usually a special platform,—so that the bones might not be disturbed by wild animals. According to the Tungus, during the period from May to the end of August, when there are wild ducks and thunder storms, and when lightnings are possible, nobody except very young boys can ride on the backs of these animals and they may not be loaded. Yet, before riding a special purification must be done. It consists in exposing the penis to the smoke produced by burning *laedum palustrum* (the same purification is used before mounting *oygun*). In general, the attitude towards this reindeer must be very kind and polite,—no harm, pain, suffering, even simple displeasure must be caused to it. Even words, when talking to it, or about it, must be carefully selected. During the travelling the *jasil* must go ahead of the caravan. Owing to a privilleged position, according to

the Tungus, the *jasil* sometimes reach the age of forty years.

However, the functions of *jasil* were not absolutely clear to myself during the investigation; they are not better now. First of all, there must be only one *jasil* to a clan. After the death of the predecessor, a new *jasil* is indicated by the clan shaman, who knows it from the spirits (*ojan*). The *jasil* is handed over to one of clansmen for his care and responsibility. If he fails the *jasil* can be given to another clansman. Its connexion with the clan, even, perhaps including its name* is peafectly evident. Yet, the *jasil* is considered as an "envoy" of the clan for communication with certain spirits. In the case of sickness amongst the clansmen there must be made sacrifice of smoking *laedum palustrum* before *jasil*.

Amongst the Manchus we also meet with horses reserved to the *p'oyun večko*. As will be described, such a horse is marked with ribbons. However, among the Manchus this complex is rather poorly represented. I could find no special term for such a horse.

The above given description reveals some interesting points, namely, the domesticated animals are used as carriers of placings for spirits and as placings for the spirits, as well as special envoys. This practice seems to be of non-Tungus origin, and yet of not very old one, in so far as it may be seen from the terms and geographical distribution of this practice. The animals at any rate cannot be considered as "sacred" ones, or as possessing some exceptional properties of a supernatural order.

63. SACRIFICE   As stated the sacrifice, in various forms, is one of the most important methods of influencing spirits. The idea of sacrifice is to satisfy a spirit (or a group of spirits) with something which is believed to be useful, interesting, and generally attractive to the spirit. The Tungus dialects possess no special term as

---

* The sickness or misfortune of members of the family is not directly connected with the establishment of oŋgun, but its establishment depends upon the placings for spirits to be carried with. Yet, although a shaman may be connected with it, this is not shaman's function,—the oŋgun may be established without shaman's interference.

* In Tungus dialects and Manchu we find no satisfactory etymology of the term jasil. However, in Mongol we find a series of words connected with jas || jasuŋ,—the bone, branch of clan, clan, etc.—a recent loanword in Tungus of Mankova (SONT, p. 121). It is almost sure that at a certain moment in the past the Barguzin Tungus used this Mongol term in the sense of "clan", now replaced by another Mongol term omo—omok (Barg. Nerč. Mank.). It may be also noted that in "religious" texts of the Birarčen I have found jaso used in the sense of "kind", "mankind", "human species".

Or, perhaps the term jasil may be connected with the stem jase—"the law, administrative regulation". etc., but I doubt it. Amongst the Manchurian groups, this term is unknown. All other groups use oŋgun, and in somewhat different functions. The RTM use a term jtik which, in so far as I can see, may be connected only with Yakut (Pekarskij, p. 3847) ytyk (of Turkic origin,—"the animal consecrated", etc.). However, the term jasil in its modification jašîǁ is also recorded by E. I. Titov amongst the Angara and Irkutsk Gov. Tungus, i.e. neighbours of the same Buriat groups. E. I. Titov indicates that the white reindeer is reserved to the "master" of the taiga. I have some doubt as to the reservation of jasil to this "master". The same interpretation is given by this author to oŋgun and tyngor (doubtful transcription). In this case the reindeer is reserved to lesnómu (Russian) which is indicative that this author wanted to say "to the spirit of the forest". In fact, such a reservation is practised, but as shown amongst other groups jasil is reserved and functioning for a different purpose. Tyngor looks like tengri of the Mongols. There is always conflicting information from this author (E. I. Titov), when he treats various "superstitions" about which he is "sceptical".

"sacrifice" or "to sacrifice"—they use either a general term "to pray", or they specify: "to feed" (the spirit). The Manchu language possesses such terms. e.g. *jukten*, but it is used also in the sense of "spirits", which is also true in reference to *večen*. The Manchus usually call the act of sacrifice by a verb *solimb'e* (Sp.) which is "to invite" and "to invite to take the food".

There is a technical question as to the ways how the sacrifice is accepted by the spirits, which may make clearer the Tungus conception of sacrifices and their practice. One must not think that the spirits consume it as it is, the spirits take only the "immaterial substance" of the sacrifice. Yet, "immaterial" ought to be understood in the Tungus sense. As shown, the smells produced by things and animals, the vapour to which they are reduced, the smoke produced by burning, are "immaterial"; at last the reduction of things and animals by the process of putrefaction and decay also liberates the "immaterial substance" and breaking of some things may result in the same effect. Since the spirits are "immaterial", they assimilate the things in their "immaterial" substance, and thus the spirits prefer the forms of sacrifices in which the latter may be easily assimilated by them. For this reason fresh, hot blood which produces a visible evaporation is better than cold blood; the hot meat is better than cold; a sacrifice with odour is better than one which cannot be smelled; the visible odoriferous smoke is the best form for assimilation by the spirits. Owing to these conceptions, the sacrifice may be given in various forms regardless its kind, —it may be boiled, given fresh, reduced by burning, putrefaction and decay, and even merely broken*. As to the preferences of spirits for different kinds of sacrifice, the Tungus must know them beforehand. In this case their reasoning is based upon: (1) their knowledge received from the previous generations; (2) the information received from other ethnical groups which are already familiar with the spirit; (3) their own experiments; (4) theoretical considerations; and (5) special methods.

The first two do not need to be explained, but the Tungus experiments and theoretical considerations require some additional remarks. If there should be a new, unknown spirit, the Tungus would try to call it and feed (give sacrifice) with something available. If the spirit accepts the sacrifice, which is seen from the fact of fulfilment of human desiderata, then the form of sacrifice is considered as corresponding to the character and taste of the spirit. If there is no effect of sacrifice the Tungus suppose that either the sacrifice was not served in a proper way, and they would try to change the ritual and wording of prayer, or the kind of sacrifice must be changed, e.g. they would give instead of reindeer blood, that of sheep. It is typical of the Tungus that they would begin their experiment with simpliest form of sacrifice and they would further proceed to the more costly sacrifices. Indeed, the guess-work has great importance in the choice of the form of sacrifice to the new spirits.

Theoretical considerations are not of less importance. Let us suppose that a new unknown spirit (for instance, the spirit causing a disease which was previously unknown, e.g. the effect of alcoholism) in some respects is similar to another spirit, already known (e.g. hysteria), the inference

will be that the spirit is of a given road-direction. Then, since other spirits of the same road and direction are supposed to accept blood sacrifice, the newly discovered spirit will have the same sacrifice.

Here I give another example. As shown, certain diseases observed in infants are supposed to be controlled by a complex spirit which, according to the Tungus ideas, consists of several spirits some of which are still unknown. Let us suppose that the child has a new, unknown trouble. It will be decided that this is a new spirit connected with the complex spirit known before and as such it will be satisfied with the sacrifice of the type common for the spirits of this group. In this case there will be a sacrifice of a cock, or simply burning of incense.

All spirits connected with the lower world accept blood sacrifice, therefore any new spirit of this group will have blood sacrifice. All spirits of the upper world amongst the Tungus of Transbaikalia accept the sheep, therefore any new spirit of the upper world will have a sacrifice consisting of sheep.

At last, what is understood here as special methods consists of shaman's ability of seeing and knowing with the help of his own spirits which would tell him what kind of sacrifice may be accepted by a new spirit. After an experiment the form recommended may be accepted as a usual practice.

It must be kept in mind that for sacrifice the Tungus use only those things which practically are available. Therefore it is likely that with the change of the domesticated animal, the one formerly used for sacrifice will be replaced by another one. The extermination of some wild animals may result in the substitution by other animals. The loss of animals, like reindeer, horse, sheep, swine, etc. may be followed by introduction of some new sacrificial animals, e.g. hens and cocks. Indeed, the change of the animal and suppressing of blood sacrifice must be preceded by a series of experiments which must give satisfactory results. In such a state I have found, for instance, the Nerčinsk Tungus who had partially lost their reindeer and for sending souls of their dead people they had adopted another animal, namely, the horse. Still many of them were hesitating as to the possibility of such a substitution. Among the Birarčen there was no more question about such a substitution, but the question was about a complete suppression of horse sacrifice, for many of them had no more horses. For special forms of shamanizing the Reindeer Tungus of Transbaikalia must have sheep. However, sometimes they cannot get them from their neighbours,—the Buriats,—and they substitute a very young reindeer fawn. Still, they would like better to buy a sheep in order to be sure as to the effectiveness of the sacrifice. The Tungus of Manchuria very well know that they must have for sacrifice to the spirits of Chinese origin, e.g. *n'ayn'ay*, some special nuts, Chinese dates, etc. as is always offered by the Manchus, but since the Tungus cannot always buy them they substitute what is available. They say that it is much better to have what is required, but since they cannot get it, they have to use a different kind of sacrifice. The same is true in reference to the pigs, chickens etc. which are used by the Tungus who deal with the same spirits as the Manchus. Owing to this the pigs and chickens are sometimes substituted for other animals too, but even wild animals may replace pigs and chickens. These conditions must be kept

* *Vide supra* Part I, Chapter IV.

in mind when the forms of sacrifice are discussed and compared amongst different Tungus and other groups. As a matter of fact, the same spirit may have a different form of sacrifice only because of the difference in the economic conditions of groups. On the other hand, the same form of sacrifice may be used for different spirits because of the fact that the animals required are not available. For instance, some Manchu clans, namely, *moygo xala* must have sheep as sacrifice to the ancestors, while the Reindeer Tungus of Barguzin taiga use the same animal for their sacrifice to the spirits of the upper world. Yet, both of these groups are not sheep breeders, but they have received this sacrificial animal from the Mongols, who use it much more widely than any other group of this part of Asia. Still, the sheep as a sacrificial animal is not used amongst the Tungus of Manchuria who are neighbours of the Mongols and Manchus.

There may be distinguished the following forms of sacrifice 1. Blood sacrifice, when fresh blood is required; 2. Animal sacrifice cooked; 3. Plants and candies, also cooked cakes; 4. Symbolic substitutes, including written characters; 5. Incense; 6. Varia, e.g. silk kerchief, hair, silk and other tissues, flowers.

1. Blood sacrifice is used among all Tungus groups and Manchus. It is used for the spirits of night roads for the spirits of the lower world and ancestors, for the spirits of shamans (*sèvèn, seva, voèko*), and in some cases for the highest spirit of the world. REINDEER are used amongst the reindeer breeding groups; the SHEEP amongst the Tungus of Transbaikalia, as a substitute for reindeer, and amongst some Manchu clans (e.g. *Moygo xala*); the PIG is very largely used amongst the Manchus and rarely amongst the Tungus of Manchuria, who borrowed it from the Manchus; the HORSE is used only for carrying away the souls of dead people, and blood as a last sacrifice for the deceased person, amongst the Tungus of Manchuria and those Tungus of Transbaikalia who have already lost their reindeer; the OX is used as a sacrifice amongst the Manchus and Tungus of Manchuria,— the Kumarčen and Birarčen,—on occasion of great sacrifice to the highest spirit when two clans divide (amongst the Tungus), and during the great shamanizing (details of which will be given later) ; amongst the Mankova Tungus a BLACK COW and a BLACK HE-GOAT are used for a special form of shamanizing; amongst the Manchus, Tungus of Manchuria and Mankova Tungus WILD ANIMALS and especially the roe-deer, are used for spirits of the taiga, and as a substitute for other animals; the BEAR is used only amongst the Birarčen for a special *sèvèn;* the *BADGER* (*mayn'i*) [cf. *maygigu, dorgan* (?) (Manchu Writ.)] is used as a regular sacrifice amongst some old Manchu clans (*fè manju xala*)*; the DOG was used as sacrifice to the *p'oyun voèko*, e.g. in the clan *tokur xala* [*tokoro, toyoro* (Manchu Sp.) corr. *tokoro* (Manchu Writ.), *tāu* (Chinese)], where lately the dog was substituted by the sheep**; the fol-

* At the present time badger is replaced by a pig. However, in difficult and serious cases the Manchus try to find a badger. which is not easy because of the relative rarity of this animal.

** Although the remembrance of this practice is quite fresh the Manchus of this clan are somewhat ashamed of this old practice,

lowing birds are used: CHICKEN (amongst the Manchus and Tungus of Manchuria when they can get them); DUCKS and GEESE (amongst the Kumarčen); SWANS (amongst the Birarčen whose *sèvèn* consider swan—*uksi*— as the best sacrifice-food).

The ritual consists of a ritual slaughtering of the live animal which will be described later; the collecting of its blood into a receptacle, which may be of a definite form; and smearing with it the mouth of the placings, usually especially made on this occasion, or drinking of blood by the shaman who is supposed to have the spirit in his body, or at last by spilling blood into the space (to the spirit of heaven.).

Instead of blood, also together with the blood, there may be given other parts of the animal, for instance, liver, also pieces of meat, at last even the whole animal or its skeleton and skin. In case the animal should be used for transporting the soul, the skin is taken off and hung up on the place of burial. The skins of other animals are also used for sending spirit-messengers, e.g. the reindeer amongst the Barguzin Tungus, the duck and geese amongst the Kumarčen. The bones, as a rule, must not be broken.

The above indicated animals are used in cooked form for the spirits of upper, day roads. However, since the meat is eaten by the people who are present at the rite, the cooked meat is also given to the spirits of night roads, as well as to the spirit of heaven and to the deceased people. In certain cases some parts are considered especially preferred by the spirits, as a mark of sacrifice, as for instance, vertebrae of sacrificed animals fixed to a post erected on the spot; skulls of sheep, bears or horses mounted on a special platform; antlers of reindeer and of roe-deer; lower jaws of sheep and of other animals. Choice of particular parts of animals depends on the same conditions as that of kinds of animals. It may be noted that in almost all cases the Tungus and Manchus make blood sausages which are also given to the spirits. Amongst the Manchus, owing to the borrowing of cooking art from the Chinese, the ritual is still more complicated. However, in this case the elaborated dishes have no particular meaning. For instance, there are served "eight cups and nine plates" (*vide* SOM, p. 85) or less complicated meal consisting of "six cups and six plates" which are also used during ceremonies of a wedding. Amongst all Tungus the use of salt in preparing cooked sacrifice is strictly prohibited. Generally, the Tungus and Manchus give the spirits those kinds and forms of food which they themselves appreciate unless there are special kinds and forms preferred by the spirits. However, the last group is always in the process of decrease, being gradually replaced by the kinds common in the given ethnographical complex.

The plants, candies, cakes and other similar sacrifice-food stuffs are used in a very limited scale by the Tungus who have no access to the market and who themselves do not use those products in their usual activities; but amongst the Manchus these products occupy the most important place in the rites. Various kinds of nuts and dates, also various fruits are common in sacrifices to *fuc'k'i* and *mafa*, also some *endur'i*, but they are not usually given to

for the dog is not a "good animal" for the spirits of day-roads,—if a dog is given to the p'oyun voèko it would mean that all these spirits are of "bad roads." The name of voèko which prefers this animal is xèrèn buku.

the *p'oɣun* and *saman voĉko*. It is perfectly clear that these kinds of sacrifice have been borrowed, together with the spirits, from the Chinese*. However, under the stress of poverty and sometimes impossibility of buying these products from the Chinese shops, the Manchus replace them by other products. The cakes may be of different origin and make, namely, bought from the Chinese and made at home. The cakes made at home are of special interest and they are used in sacrifice to the *p'oɣun voĉko*. Their description will be given later (*vide infra* Section 74). Candies, bought from the Chinese, may be used without special ritualistic regulations. The Tungus who may buy them from the Chinese and Russians would also use them as sacrifice, especially for the souls of recently dead people, above all for a dead child. In the coffin they would put everything which might be liked by the child, e.g. candies, cakes and also milk. The same is true of the adult people who may receive also tea, tobacco etc. Classifying of these donations as sacrifice may be rejected on the ground that the food etc. with which the dead people are supplied are not "sacrifice", but it will not be correct, for these things are given to the souls, and in principle and idea, they do not differ from the sacrifice to the ancestors, whose names are lost, and to other spirits.

Wine is an essential component of sacrifices amongst all Tungus and Manchus. However, it is not always possible to get wine. There are used: Chinese wine made of gaolan (a kind of millet); Manchu wine (*nura*) made of millet, used especially for sacrifice to *p'oɣun voĉko;* Mongol wine made of milk used by the Tungus living in the neighbourhood of the Mongols; Russian vodka used by those Tungus who are living near the Russians. The grape wine is not used in a common practice, although some Tungus groups have access to it. Amongst the Manchus some sacrifices, e.g. *fuĉk'i* and *mafa* may require special kind of wine of Chinese production. The wine may be poured into the fire, and on the placings for spirits; put in a receptacle into the coffin; sprinkled into the air, especially for the spirits not called but which may be present; drunk by the shaman when the spirit is introduced into him. For some performances the wine is absolutely necessary, e.g. when the spirit is particularly inclined to drinking wine. The sprinkling of wine into the air has become so common among the Tungus and Manchus that they do it almost automatically, even when drinking for their own pleasure. Other drinks, such as tea and milk, are also used, and in the same manner, as sacrifices. However, the use of tea is much more limited and the use of milk is confined only to the Tungus who have reindeer or cattle. Amongst the Nomad Tungus of Transbaikalia the products of milk, e.g. sour cream, white cheese, butter etc. are also used for regular sacrifices.

Various kinds of *incense* are an almost inseparable part of the sacrifice amongst the Tungus groups. Smoke of plants and of special Chinese incense is considered as a pleasant and easily assimilated sacrifice. It is pleasant because of a "good smell" and it is in form of gas.** As incense

the Tungus use what is found to be handy. Amongst the Tungus of the taiga regions there are used heather, *leadum palustrum* [*saɣk'ɨra* (Bir. Nerč. Khin.) *saɣkɨra* (Nerč.) *saɣk'ɨrɨ x'jan* (Manchu)], juniper [*ârĉa* (Bir.) *arĉi* (RTM.), *arca* (Mank.); cf. *arĉa* (Dahur) *arca* (Buriat) *arĉa* (Mong. Rud.)], also some resinous shrubs which could not be identified. All of them are also used for purification. Amongst the Manchus there were formerly used twigs of wild rose.* Amongst the Manchus and Tungus living in Manchuria near the Manchus, the Chinese incense *âjen-x'jen* (香 of Chinese; the same term is preserved but slightly modified by the Manchus and Tungus) has lately received great recognition, especially for the spirits received from the Chinese. Amongst the Manchu clan *nara* in the sacrifice to the *p'oɣun voĉko* instead of *âjen-x'jen* there is used burning of oil (in a lamp). However, in this case the function of burning may be "fire" and not smoke produced by the oil. With the introduction of *âjen-x'jen* the number of bunches of stick began to play some function in the rituals. The importance of the incense is so great that the whole sacrifice may be confined to it.

Under a separate heading of "various sacrifices" mention may be made of sacrifices of various things, such as pieces of silk; ribbons; silk blue kerchieves bought from the Mongols [*xadak, xûdûk* ∥ *kaday* (Mong. Rud.)] by the Nomad Tungus and rarely by the Reindeer Tungus of Transbaikalia, also by the Khingan Tungus; hair of horses attached to the trees reserved as placings for local spirits, especially amongst the Tungus influenced by the Mongols; e.g. the Nomad Tungus of Urulga and Mankova, partly the Khingan Tungus, who practise the erecting of *obon* [cf. *owo* ∥ *oboɣa* (Mong. Rud.)] in the mountain passes and on top of mountains; pieces of various tissues attached by the Tungus of Manchuria to the placings for *burkan;* natural flowers and artificial flowers used as sacrifices by the Manchus; skins of animals, e.g. mustelidae, foxes, hares etc., especially albinos and unusually dark coloured specimens, also their bones, horns, claws and hoofs. Among these there may be found the most unexpected things, such as empty bottles and tins, dolls etc. which may be regarded as interesting enough for the spirits. However, this class of sacrifices is not very common amongst the Reindeer Tungus. Many of these sacrifices may be regarded as mere symbols and *pars pro toto*. The last group of symbolic sacrifices covers all forms of sacrifice in which the sacrifice is symbolized by something, e.g. hoofs, antlers or bones of the animals would symbolize the animals (*pars pro toto*). In the same group there ought to be included images of animals, particularly domesticated animals, and of men. These are not placings but symbols of sacrifice. Under the Chinese influence, there have been introduced images made of paper, including silver shoes (bars), and "paper money", etc. widely used by the Chinese in their managing of the spirits and souls of dead people. These practices are known only amongst the Manchus and those Tungus who have already fallen under the strong Manchu-Chinese influence. The Manchus are going still further in their imitation of the Chinese symbolism when they write on a piece of paper the

---

* Necessary data regarding the Chinese may be found in special works on Chinese complexes, e.g. in H. Doré's work and in the description of Manchu rites by Ch. de Harlez.

** When the sacrifice is burnt in the wigwam or in the house it does not at all mean that the sacrifice is given to the spirit of fire,—

the fire may be used as a method of reducing the sacrifice to a gaseous state.

* bola seɲk'i is now no more used, but still mentioned in the shamanistic texts; cf. bula i ilxa (Manchu Writ.),

names of things to be given as sacrifice and burn the paper as it would be a sacrifice of things. Indeed, the paper and written words on it in the Manchu mind are not the physical sacrifice to be received by the spirit, but only its immaterial substance reduced to a symbol. Of course, such a conception might be reached by the Manchus only after a long process of reduction of the sacrifices to their symbols, and the Chinese influence here seems to be stronger than the Manchu imagination. Again, this form may be easily accepted by any Tungus as soon as it is practically shown that the sacrifice in this symbolic form may be accepted by the spirits.

The Tungus attitude towards the sacrifice has been demonstrated, but there remains to be shown how the practice of sacrificing may vary under the conditions of Tungus life. I have always pointed out that the fact of lacking of some animals or other sacrificial things, needed according to the tradition or experience of other groups, may change the rituals. No less important is the limitation imposed by the relative scarcity of material for sacrifice. In fact, amongst the Tungus living on reindeer breeding the sacrifice of this animal cannot be very frequently practised for as I have shown the average number of reindeer per family is very small among all groups investigated.* Therefore the Tungus may now sometimes combine several spirits for a sacrifice of a reindeer. Amongst the Tungus of Manchuria who have no domesticated animals, except horses and dogs, the limitations go still further, for in order to have "fresh blood" they have to buy pigs and other animals from their neighbours. However, the pigs are not cheap and they must be brought from distant Manchu and Dahur villages. The same is true of sheep bought by the Tungus of Transbaikalia from the Buriats.

If the Tungus and Manchus are frightened by the spirits' attack, they must make sacrifices all of the time, which practically is impossible. Owing to this, some spirits do not now receive any sacrifice except some incense and a part of the sacrifice shared with the other spirits of greater importance. Here it may be pointed out that the influence of such a fierce and troublesome spirit may gradually decrease just owing to the fact that this spirit will not too often receive its too big sacrifices and the people would be convinced that the spirit is not as dangerous as it was originally believed. So, an over-estimation of spirits' power, which would require too many sacrifices, may become a hindrance for maintaining this spirit and later on the spirit is liable to fall into a complete oblivion, while modest spirits may survive for a very long time. As a matter of fact, this is true of many other ethnographical phenomena which become a burden for the ethnical unit.

From my observations amongst the Tungus I may say that every family may have possibility of making a sacrifice hardly more than two or three times a year. Amongst the rich Manchus, and Nomad Tungus who possess numerous flocks of sheep and herds of cattle, it may be quite frequent, but still they cannot satisfy all the spirits. Amongst the Manchus the sacrifices are usually confined to a few nuts, dates, to fruit, to cakes or even merely to paper symbols

* Vide SONT, pp. 31-32.

and burning of incense, while the sacrifice of pigs and oxen is a rare occurrence,—three or four times a year. However, besides these considerations the Manchus and all Tungus groups have serious impulses from time to time to make sacrifices, i.e. an imperative desire to have fresh meat of particular animals,—the pig and reindeer,—and an interesting performance, especially if it is connected with the shamanism. This impulse very often underlies the initiative in sacrificial activity. So from my experience I knew very well that should the Tungus be for a long time without fresh meat from hunting, they would find a decent pretext for slaughtering a reindeer as sacrifice to some ancestors or spirits which were supposed to disturb peaceful running of their life. On this occasion the family performing the sacrifice would invite all neighbours to have their part of the pleasure of eating the fresh meat. Next time, another neighbour would do the same, and so the whole group from time to time and rather often may enjoy good meals. Indeed, the spirits do not receive very much,—small pieces of cooked meat, a little of the fresh blood, sometimes the skin which at certain seasons is not good for industrial purposes, or the antlers and hoofs. Therefore, although the requirements of the spirits are very great, the material losses of the Tungus are not as great as that.

Amongst the Manchus I have observed nearly the same picture. The Manchu diet is not as rich in meat, as that of the Tungus living on hunting. As a rule, the Manchus do not slaughter their animals unless there is a good pretext,—a wedding or funeral, or shamanism, or merely a sacrifice to the spirits. If there were sufficient justification for slaughtering nobody would disapprove, especially on the condition that the neighbours are invited to have their part of the fresh meat. Practically, as many people are invited as can be satisfied with a full and good meal. Besides regular sacrifices, e.g. on spring and autumn festivals, when the meals are taken by clans, there are occasions such as sudden diseases of the people or merely psychic and nervous instability which may require a blood sacrifice of a pig.

However, there are some cases when the people are really persecuted by the spirits and the Manchus begin to slaughter on the right and left,—chickens, pigs, oxen,—till the animals are destroyed. The neighbours and clansmen enjoy the food, and also, they often offer assistance by supplying animals, but still oftener by opening credit to the unfortunate family. I knew a family which during half a year destroyed all their animals and became greatly indebted. So that the chief of the family saw himself obliged to liquidate his household and to go as a simple servant to work in another family, while other members were taken in by other clansmen's families. The clansmen and neighbours very much regretted this and even expressed their doubts as to the rationality of such extreme measures. As a matter of fact, the family was ruined. But whether it was so because of overeating, or because of psychosis, I do not venture to say. Still the opinion of the neighbours and clansmen was inclined to accept the hypothesis that the family in question was badly attacked by the spirits which must be fought at any price.

Certain abuse of rites and sacrifices is observed amongst the Manchus when they produce great expenditure on buying and burning paper symbols, such as silver bars, houses, carts with horses, furniture etc. sometimes amounting to several hundred dollars. In this case the Manchus are the prey of vanity developed and cultivated amongst them with great art by and through the alien channels,—the Chinese complex. In this case the clansmen and neighbours have only moral satisfaction of being kinsmen and co-villagers of a rich man, without any other benefit of ritual zeal, such as good food, social gatherings, shamanizing and endless discussions as to the spirits*.

64. COMMUNICATION WITH THE SPIRITS BY MEANS OF LANGUAGE Under this heading I understand various methods of coming into contact with the spirits by means of language. As the basis of these relations with the spirit, the Tungus and Manchus have several hypotheses, cf which the principal are: the spirits understand human speech; the spirits react on speech nearly in the same manner as it is with the human beings; some spirits do not understand common speech and must be addressed in a special language.

When the Tungus and Manchus want to communicate with the spirits they call the spirit by its common name or by a special, honorific name, or merely in any other form of calling its attention. If the spirit is already placed in a placing the task is simplified, for the spirit is supposed to see and hear the man speaking and to understand that the words are addressed to it. The list of terms with which the spirits are impersonally addressed comprises terms used for senior relatives, such as "father", "mother", "grandfather", "grandmother", "ancestor" etc. which express the idea of submission; the Manchus use a richer vocabulary comprising also flattering adjectives and titles. There would follow an expression of the essential of request. Amongst the Tungus, a short address usually is a free expression of desire but it is formalized into rigid formulae

* It may be here pointed out that the above described conditions of functioning of ethnographical complexes observed among the Manchus and Tungus are not characteristic of them alone. Justification of enjoying unusual food with good drinks is common amongst other ethnical groups as well. The cases of vanity are too well known to be illustrated here with the examples observed among other ethnical groups, so I shall now give one of the instances, in fact quite a striking because of its complexity, which I have before my eyes in certain places of the Far East where diplomatic and consular representatives of different powers spend their time by inviting one another for dinner and luncheon parties under the pretext that there must be created and maintained good relations between the countries which they are supposed to represent. When there are no international gatherings they do the same under the pretext of maintaining good relations within their national group. Even third and fourth secretaries are very active on the level of their rank, although no diplomatic consequences would follow from their gastronomic activity. Indeed, for the young generation these gathering have another additional function too, namely, practising in conversation and manners, but it is not always realized. At last, professional justification of these gatherings, i.e. as means to receive mutual information also is quite a naive justification. However, the same results such as to create no open discontentment, to practise in social life, and to gather information, might be achieved by other means, less ruinous for the health and treasuries of respective governments when the complex "parties" overgrows its initial function. Indeed, I am very far away from the idea that such an activity is useless or that it may be abolished, for if everything is rationalized, there will be perhaps so little left of the ethnographic complexes that the ethnical units would not be able to exist. By this example I am intending to show how the ethnographic complexes are maintained and how psychic and physiological needs are satisfied without even being understood by the performers.

amongst the Manchus who use, e.g. èļxe talfin ("the peace"), xuturʻi ("the happiness"), etc. just preceded by the name of the spirit, and repeat them almost automatically. A little more extensive formulae but not less rigid are found to be numerous in the material of rites practised by the Imperial Family of Tai-Tsing*. Every Manchu clan has such formulae which, it may be supposed, have been made in imitation of the Imperial court.

It is different with the long addresses on various occasions which cannot be foreseen by the people, but even in this case there may be again distinguished formalized addresses and free improvizations, the latter being more and more substituted by the formulae.

When a Tungus of Transbaikalia addresses himself to the spirits he would mention the spirit to which he turns his words and then he would proceed to the exposition of the matter. All of his address will be a free improvization in the section dealing with the exposition of the matter, but the enumeration and naming of spirits would be formal, for all Tungus more or less have the same complexes of spirits, and they must naturally remember them in definite words. The Tungus of Manchuria will do the same if they are not too strongly influenced by the Dahurs and Manchus. Every Tungus can easily make an address which is not formalized. However, lately amongst the Tungus of Manchuria there appeared a new type of prayers called buač'in and borrowed, in so far as method is concerned, from their neighbours,—the Dahurs and Manchus. It consists of a formal address to the spirits and their enumeration, formal exposition of the request with the substitution of the names of the persons or clans which address their request, and a formalistic conclusion. According to the present ideas, accepted by far all Tungus, the spirits would be more attentive, if the formulae are exactly reproduced. Thus, the form as such has great influence on the issue of the address. It is not surprising that the buač'in contain a certain number of Dahur terms and expressions rather difficult for understanding even by those Tungus who carry out the performance. It may be here noted that amongst these Tungus the form of formalized prayer—buač'in—has made its appearance as result of reaction against the shamanism which, as will be shown, may sometimes become a real burden for those who practise it. Since the Dahurs were successful in managing their spirits with this method, the Tungus have adopted the same practice. Nearly in the same position are now found the shamans who memorize expressions and titling of the spirits and thus formalize at least the first address to the spirits and their first address to the people gathered in the name of spirits. However, such a formalism is possible only within the limits of well known facts, while when the shaman has to deal with special cases of troubles, which imply his being called by the people, he must become improvisator, and so the shamans are.

The Manchus went still further in the matter of formalizing their addresses to the spirits. Every clan has its own formulae when the prayer is addressed to the clan spirits, to the spirits of heaven (abka enduri); every shaman has his own formulae when dealing with the spirits (vočko), and especially when making to them a general sacrifice; every Manchu addresses himself in a similar man-

* Vide Ch. de Harlez, op. cit. and especially "La religion et les cérémonies impériales".

ner to the spirits *fuĕ'k'i* and *mafa* which do not differ in clans. In imitation of the Imperial Family the Manchus have recorded names of spirits and rituals called in Manchu *ĕolo b'itxe* and *kŏli b'itxe*,—i.e. "the book of the list of names" and "the book of rites",—so that no change of the established rites and words is formally allowed, for a spirit cannot respond to the appeal and request, if there should be a change of names and rites. It is very interesting that the fact of written records of the ritualistic side of dealing with the spirit in many a clan has resulted in the loss of means of communication with the spirits when the written documents were lost during the Boxer troubles in Aigun District.* No restoration from memory of the old written records could be immediately done and owing to this many a clan has now no longer possibility of communicating with their spirits. So the whole performance consists only of repeated bowings, kneelings, and a few words such as *ĕl,xe taif in* and *xntur'i.* However, the Manchus are rather sceptical as to the effectiveness of such incomplete performances and if they continue them they do it only by fear: The spirits may become very harmful if there is even no ritualism, though imperfect. On the other hand, the idea that the rites must be in conformity with the old formulae detains them from trying to create a new rite. This is an interesting instance of how written language may be responsible for the loss of the complex. The shamans following the good example of the clan priests (*p'oyun saman*) have also recorded their *ĕvlo* and *kŏli,* which has also resulted in the further formalization of performances possible. According to the Manchu idea of this function, there are specialists who can deal, by means of prayers and rites strictly formalized, with the spirits of non-clannish origin and at the same time of non-shamanistic origin, such as *fuĕ'k'i* and *mafa* which can be managed without shaman's assistance. Although I have seen no written records of their "prayers" and "rites", I have heard that they do exist as a professional secret amongst the *mafari* (*vide infra* Section 80) which is only natural.

An important source of formalization of rites was Emperor Chi'en-Lung's idea to preserve the old practices which by his time already began to have been lost by the Manchus who fell under a strong Chinese influence in Peking. In the preface he pointed out that in his clan (*ġ'ĵoro*) there was practised strictness in reference to the wording of prayers (*jōn'i forobure g'isun be jojonggo obumb'i*) and that formerly the shamans (evidently, *p'oyun saman*) used to know the language from childhood and thus proper ways of dealing with the spirits. It is evident, that at Chi'en-Lung's time (enthronement 1736, death 1799) the rites needed both corrections and artificial preservation because of loss of language. So that the formalization of Manchu ritual did not occur on the genuine Manchu soil, but it was implied by the disintegration of the old Manchu complex. In fact, by his time the Imperial Family was already under a strong Chinese influence and what is found in the book of rites (*manjusai veĕere medere kooli bitxe*) is not an exact picture of the original Manchu complex. Yet, the Manchus who were not yet so far sinized followed the authority of

their Emperor and as a pattern adopted his above mentioned manual of rites, other similar books as well, while the great shamans at least partly preserved the original complex. As a whole the complex of clan rites amongst the Manchus does not look a genuine Manchu institution. This Manchu influence was supported by the Chinese influence which was not also in favour of free improvisation.

Other groups of Manchuria, such as the Dahurs, in this respect were under a double influence,—the Manchu-Chinese formalism and Mongol Lamaistic complex. The latter is also inclined to a stubborn formalization, so amongst the lamas of Mongolia the formulae occupy an important place in the complex. The Dahurs and Manchus, especially the first ones, in their turn influenced the Tungus of Manchuria who at present although preserve the original type of ritualism, have also included many formalistic elements into their complex of dealing with the spirits.

The language understood by the spirits naturally corresponds to the ideas of the Tungus as to the spirits. We have already seen that many spirits are not of a Tungus origin and as such they are not likely to understand Tungus language. In such a case the Tungus would rather use a foreign language known to the spirit. Such one may be Mongol, Manchu, Chinese, Russian, Dahur, Yakut, which depends on the source of borrowing and Tungus ideas about it. If the language of the spirit is unknown, the Tungus may use just a few words which are supposed to be understood by the spirits and which actually may not be words of the language of the ethnical group from which the spirit is supposed to be received. Such words may become absolutely "meaningless" and in the eyes of observers who are not familiar with the mechanism of ethnographical variations they may be interpreted as "magic". In such a position are found those Manchus who have received some spirits (e.g. *k'ilin voĕko,* cf. *supra* p. 175) from the Tungus and instead of speaking to them in Manchu they try to utter some Tungus (*eveŋk'i*) words which in fact are mere refrains of Tungus songs and prayers, such as, *jaga-ja,* etc. On the other hand the Tungus, who do not know the Manchu language but who at the same time must deal with the Manchu spirits, sometimes use isolated Manchu words. The same is done by the Manchus and Tungus when they have to deal with the Chinese spirits, and the Chinese shamans also use isolated Tungus and Manchu words for the same purpose.

Although speaking in a foreign language to the spirits of foreign origin is always preferable, the Tungus, the Manchus as well, who have often to deal with these spirits, gradually begin to use their own language. So that it may be formulated that together with the increase of Tungus familiarity with the alien spirits, the latter begin to understand Tungus language. This is not understood by the Tungus, but they silently recognize that the Tungus spirits understand the Tungus language and since a spirit would remain with the Tungus for a long time it would become Tungus spirit (e.g. *malu burkan, vide supra* p. 151) and thus it can understand Tungus. It may be pointed out that *buga* (*vide supra* p. 122), according to the Tungus, is common to all peoples and it can understand all human beings which ever language they would use in praying it. On the other hand, in reference to some spirits the Tungus are positively convinced that a special language is needed. In

---

* According to the communication of the Manchus, in the same position were found the Manchus of Tsitsihar district and even in Peking and other localities, where the Manchus suffered loss of their houses,

such a position are all spirits which have been recently introduced amongst the Tungus and all those which have not yet spread their influence over the Tungus.

Yet, when the Tungus and Manchus do not know how to address a spirit they may use the language of gestures, as they would do when speaking to foreigners who cannot understand them, but who can understand gestures. This language of gestures may grow into a special complex of ceremonial bowing, kneeling, hand gestures, face gestures, —e.g. opening and closing of the mouth, eyes etc.—in the Tungus eyes sufficient for communicating with the spirits. Such are forms of language used when dealing with many foreign spirits, as well as in the case when the prayer is always the same, e.g. in the case of prayer to *buya*, and in the case when the wording of a formalized prayer is forgotten. So that there are different causes for the existence of gesture language used instead of word language (sounding starters). Therefore, the fact of lacking of prayers and oral address to the spirits does not mean that the spirit is of an alien origin.

It is very commonly observed that the prayer begins with some foreign wording and further continues in the spoken dialect of the speaker. In such a case it is supposed that the spirit better responds to the foreign call, but it can understand the language. Yet, sometimes the prayer is pronounced without being believed to be understood. In this case the Tungus would act as the mother would do with her baby, or a Tungus would do when speaking to the animals which are not always supposed to understand man's speech word by word but only a general attitude of the speaker. At last, the speaking to the spirit may be a form of actual monologuing, so to a listener it may appear incoherent in its construction and choice of expressions.

In the above lines I have shown that the prayers sometimes cannot be understood at all even by those who make them and still much less by the investigators, without being at the same time conventional "magics".

It may be pointed out that the language (spoken) of prayers therefore includes on the one hand, a certain number of petrified expressions and words no more used in the current language,—for the fear that spirits cannot understand new words,—and on the other hand, a great number of alien words and expressions, sometimes even formulae, which have been borrowed as a special language good for foreign spirits. Owing to this the language of prayers must be looked at as a special language containing both very old elements and very recent loan-elements which again make an analysis of the text rather difficult. In addition to this it may be also indicated that in prayers the Tungus use a certain number of suffixes, sometimes even doublets with the same function, which are used for making prayers more rhythmic and "nice", also at the same time different from the common speech.

As to the structure of addresses, the address may be made in the form of ordinary speech and in a rhythmic and rhymed forms. The problem of rhythms and rhymes will be discussed elsewhere,—in the work devoted to the folklore and language. The address made in prosaic form, which is simply pronounced and not sung, as a rule has no definite structure except that required by logic, while the addresses rhythmed and especially rhymed have quite a definite form. Usually they would begin with a refrain twice repeated; then the strophes consisting of a limited number of syllables are separated by the same or abbreviated refrain. In the pathetic parts of the address the strophes may become very short.

The musical contents of the addresses is of importance, too. There are quite definite motives used for particular kinds of addresses, as for instance that of Birarčen address to the ancestors *Gojamel;* while there are also motives which may be used for prayers and addresses to different spirits. Let us remark that the motives after an analysis appear to be of various origin, as it is also with the spirits and rituals. So we meet with the Chinese elements, by side of Mongol motives. However, there have been recorded no Russian motives. Naturally when prayers are connected with definite motives they are more stabilized than in the case when the motives, rhythms and rhymes are not used for making definite forms to the prayers.

The CONTENTS of addresses to the spirits are naturally different. Here it ought to be pointed out that there must be distinguished ordinary prayers and shamanistic performances which besides the ordinary prayers addressed to the spirits at the beginning and at the end of performance, include the improvisation, sometimes conventionalized, of the shaman who is supposed to be speaking and singing, during the extasy, on the part of the spirit. Naturally, the subject of his speech and songs greatly depends on the case to be dealt with by the shaman. However, even in these cases of improvisation quite conventionalized forms are met with which are characteristic of some spirits. Such is the instance of the Manchu shaman when he recites for the first time the list of spirits and is supposed to possess the spirits speaking through him. Since the lists of spirits are more or less alike and since, as shown, they are sometimes recorded in a written form, they become accessible for the people and naturally formalized. The fact of recording lists of spirits has also another aspect, namely, the lists of spirits are becoming more alike, as the addresses to these spirits.

There may be distinguished different types of addresses to the spirits, which may be classified as follows.

1. Thanks expressed to the spirits for successful hunting and addressed to the spirit which sends (direct) the animals, e.g. *bainača, b'iran endur'i,* also spirits which may be held responsible for it as *ojan, malu,* and others. The short address usually consists of a short enumeration of the hunting spoil and conventional expression of thanks. The thanks are also expressed to the corresponding spirits for giving health to the people and domesticated animals. Such are included into the ceremonies of annual sacrifice amongst the Manchus and Tungus influenced by the Manchus and Mongols, also when diseases are over, particularly the smallpox, measles, etc. The expression of thanks is usually followed by a special prayer as to the continuing of favours.

2. Requests for sending animals, for good weather,—dry or rainy, in dependence on what is needed,—for good harvest, for increase of domesticated animals, for health of men and animals, for protection of life against malevolent spirits, for mercy from the male

volent spirits, for continuation of life, for fecundity and fertility of men and cattle, for wealth in general and happiness as it is found by the individuals or groups of individuals, the clan, village. The length of a prayer is variable: the formalized Manchu prayers are long, while those of the Tungus are much shorter, but at the same time they leave some room for improvisation.

3. Requests for help in the case of diseases, threatening of death, hostility of spirits, etc. in which there may be also included prayers—intrigues—directed for raising hostilities between the spirits.

4. Prayers to various spirits in view of neutralizing their malevolent activity or for gaining their sympathy. The addresses followed by sacrifice to the ancestors may be included into this group when there is no request or expression of thanks. This form of address is very common as a preventive measure. Their form is subject to variations, but usually they are formalized only in the case of address to the ancestors, for other spirits are influenced by these prayers only on specified occasions of troubles and therefore are composed ad hoc. Naturally, amongst all groups prayers to the ancestors are more or less formalized, but the greatest stabilization has been reached amongst the Manchus.

5. Invitation to accept a sacrifice which is addressed to all spirits and has more or less conventional form, for the address usually includes the name of the spirit, specification of the sacrifice and its purpose.

Indeed, the types of prayers and addresses are not rigid at all. A prayer may include all five types of address. So it is, for instance, in the addresses to the spirits at the annual sacrifice among the Manchus, when the spirits are thanked for the past favours, are prayed for assistance in professional works, and maintaining health, at the same time they may be neutralized by various methods and asked to accept the sacrifice.

65. INFLUENCE ON SPIRITS THROUGH THEIR CHARACTERS In the previous sections we have seen the important part of the placings for spirits, sacrifices and various forms of address. These are based upon the knowledge of the nature of the spirits but these methods cannot suffice when the Tungus have to manage spirits, especially in complex cases. We have also seen that the characters of spirits are very different and they reflect, with a greater or lesser fidelity, behaviour of human beings in the given ethnical unit and amongst the neighbours.

As shown, the spirits may possess intelligence in different degrees. Therefore, the Tungus in dealing with the spirits of high intelligence very often use the ordinary method of logical convincing. In this case they state reasons why, for instance, the spirit must leave the body of people attacked by it. These may be, for instance, that the spirit has mistaken the person, that the spirit has misinterpreted human attitude and wrongly wants to revenge itself, that the spirit will not gain from its hostility, and so forth. Some spirits are considered so stupid, as for instance *areyki*, that no logical convincing of them is possible. On

the other hand the spirit *buya* and some *endur'i* are supposed to be so intelligent that they do not need to be convinced, —they know themselves everything much better than man does. In dealing with them a simple declaration may be considered as quite sufficient. The group of spirits which may be convinced by logical method may be smaller and larger. The clan spirits amongst the Tungus of Manchuria are the spirits which may be convinced by such reasons and therefore the sacrifice and other methods of influencing are not commonly used.

The spirits who are not believed to be very intelligent may be influenced by deceiving them. For instance, in this case, the Tungus would call them with very sweet words, then they would introduce them into the placing for spirits and when the spirits are there, the latter may be thrown away together with the placings, and so dismissed. The spirit may be also promised a certain sacrifice in the future without actually being satisfied with it. Indeed, the variations of methods of deceiving are numberless, for these methods are invented ad hoc. Their choice is not stabilized. However, there are some common tricks largely used by the Tungus. These are, for instance, promise of sacrifice, sending off by introducing spirits into special placings, etc. In some cases the Tungus do it quite ritually: they know beforehand how they must deceive the spirits.

The spirits which are fearful may be also frightened by shooting at them, crying, beating them when they are introduced into the placings, threatening them with revenge, and so forth. The ancestor-spirits are sometimes managed in these ways, for they are often quite fearful. Such methods are not used for dealing with *buya, endur'i* and many clan spirits.

Since the spirits are sometimes inclined to vanity the Tungus also may use this behaviour as means to manage the spirits. So that, the Tungus would exaggeratly praise the spirits for their power, wisdom, etc. without believing themselves in what they say. The spirit may accept the praise and would become benevolent or just neutral.

The spirits' greediness for food in general, and especially kinds of food liked by them, is the most common method of influencing them. So the Tungus would make sacrifice and yet sometimes they would only promise it, postponing the performance of sacrifice sometimes for years if the spirit would not be dangerous. Such a policy is especially common amongst the Manchus and Tungus of Manchuria who make the spirits wait for sacrifice until the spirits would manifest their discontent. Indebtedness of the Tungus and Manchus to the spirits very often passes over their power ever to pay the spirits. Indeed, the promises are very often forgotten and the spirits may be deceived. Besides food, the spirits may have special interests, e.g. in having beautiful flowers (amongst the Manchus), incense, beautiful placings, at last in the satisfaction of being regularly looked after and honoured. So the Tungus use these particular inclinations of the spirits for managing them.

There must especially be pointed out two ways of managing the spirits, namely, the submission to the spirits and mastering of them. In the first case the man shows a complete submission to the will and activity of the spirit and, with the postulate of a benevolent character of the spirit, he may hope to get the maximum of benefit from the situation. Yet, the conscious and complete submission may also take place in the case when the spirits are far superior to man in their power and thus they cannot be managed by the above enumerated means. The person may be controlled by the spirits, but it does not mean that this person may not be rid of spirits,—competent people can accomplish this by various means. Yet, in the case of complete submission there always is some chance that the submission may favourably be accepted by the spirit and the latter, even a malevolent one, may become harmless by taking upon itself protection of a weak man.

It is different with the control, or mastering of spirits. This constitutes the art and method of the shamans and will be treated later. Here it may be only pointed out that the mastering makes of them "servants" of the shaman who is their real master and who directs their activity at his own will, as long as he is strong and healthy. Naturally, the man or woman who feel themselves stronger than the spirits can master them, while those who feel themselves weaker than the spirit, cannot do it.

The attitude of the people towards the spirits also defines the methods of speaking and generally communicating with the spirit. The address may be very polite, composed of selected expressions which are used by juniors when speaking to seniors. For these reasons the spirits are addressed as seniors, e.g. *ama, am'i, on'o, on'i* (in Tungus), i.e. grandfather, grandmother, mother; also in Manchu e.g. *belse,* ("prince"), *sagdas'i* ("old generation"), and

various terms for designation of the ranks of high officials. In agreement with this, the speaker call himself by various humiliating terms indicative of his social and personal inferiority, e.g. "your child", "stupid child", "dumb-deaf" and the like. However, the spirits which are not very powerful and whom the speaker wants to frighten, would be addressed by their names or even humiliating names and the expressions may be very rude. Yet, there may be used bad jokes, jeerings, and mockery offending the spirits. In addressing the spirits of no great importance the speaker would abstain from using high style, too. Owing to this the dealing with the spirits whom the Tungus want to expel may begin with very polite and selected expressions and when the spirit is introduced and sent off, the way of speaking may change into a rough form. It may be here noted that in shaman's speech there are met with sometimes humiliating expressions which, however, sometimes are that referred to the shaman himself and sometimes referred by the spirits to themselves, which depends on the situation: whether the spirit is already introduced into the shaman or not. Since the shamans during their performance introduce several spirits one after another, but with interruptions, their speech may change in style so that very experienced assistant-shamans cannot sometimes understand whether it is the shaman speaking for himself or it is the spirit speaking through the shaman. Therefore, the analysis of shamanistic texts sometimes cannot be sufficient for defining the style appropriated to definite spirits.

CHAPTER XVII

SOULS AND THEIR MANAGING

66. SOULS The first occasion to deal with the human soul occurs, as a matter of fact, before the appearance of its bearer,—the child. We have seen that amongst all groups here discussed the souls are distributed by the spirits. In fact, although it has not been definitely cleared up by me how the souls are distributed amongst the Reindeer Tungus of Transbaikalia but we have seen that, according to these groups, the death of a man results in the birth of a new soul in the other (upper) world and the soul may be sent to a new-born human being. The Tungus of Manchuria recognize that souls are distributed by a special spirit. The same opinion is shared by most of the groups influenced by the Manchus who accept this idea which is perhaps one of Chinese origin. Thus, it is natural that the Tungus and Manchus, when they want to have children, must address themselves to the spirits which distribute souls to the children. Nevertheless, it does not mean at all that this is the only way to get children with a normal soul, they are born without any prayers, or sacrifices to the spirits, and yet sometimes against the will of the parents, as, for instance, in the case of illicit children. The Tungus and Manchus address their prayers and sacrifices only in the cases in which no children are born and when the lack of children as well as their premature deaths, are explained as spirits' hostility or the lack of their attention to the children. Here it ought to be pointed out once more

that the Tungus regard pregnancy and process of embryo growth as natural phenomena which require no interference on the part of the special spirit-distributor of souls, but which may be influenced by these spirits and the latter must be also asked for fertility, if it be lacking. The spirits distributing souls,—amongst the Tungus *um'iama, om'is'i,* etc., among the Manchus *oggos i mama,*—may be asked to give children (more exactly: souls) and this performance may be carried out either by the persons directly concerned or rarely by the shamans. I know no text of prayers addressed. As to the sacrifice, it may consist of incense, commonly used in the group, fruits and flowers amongst the Manchus and some wine, and generally light, not-bloody, sacrifice amongst the Tungus. Sometimes there is hung up on a tree a small model-cradle, which is not a placing, but a symbol understood by the spirit.

As soon as the child is born there appears the need of special care of the soul, for as we have seen (*vide supra* pp. 52, 135) when the child is born the soul is not yet stabilized. Therefore various precautions must be taken for keeping the soul in the child's body or at least near the child, in special placings,—*kayan, an'an,* etc. Another very important precaution is that the child must not be frightened by anything, for the soul may leave the body. An arsenal of special placings for spirits and souls, birds, trinkets, etc. are used for attracting the child's soul to the child or at least to its cradle in the case the soul should evade.* A great number of these things cannot be explained by the people who use them, for many of them are simply transmitted from mothers to daughters, from fathers to sons without being explained and "rationalized". Gradually the soul stabilizes itself in the body, but since the possibility of its leaving the body still remains great, other methods are added in order to keep it in the right place, and to call it back when it is needed.

In connexion with this there may be described an important (among the Manchus) method of finding a child's soul, which defines some practical steps to be undertaken. In Manchu the method is called *fojeyo wulamb'e*, i.e. "the soul to search (look for)", or *fojeyo orun wulamb'e*, i.e. "to look for the place of the soul." For this purpose two porcelain cups are used, one of them containing water and another one empty but covered with a piece of paper. A woman, usually the mother, with her finger sprinkles the water on the paper. Naturally the water gradually soak through the paper and may accumulate in a drop, "like an eye" on the other side of the paper. In this case it would mean that the soul of the child has really "fallen" (*tuxexe*). Then the cup with water is emptied on the floor and in the form of the spots one may see whether it was a man or a dog which had frightened the child. The drop containing the soul, naturally together with the paper, is put, for four or five days, near the placing for the spirit *jun fuĕk'i*. This method is effective only in case the soul should be somewhere near, in the house or in the yard. But if the soul were far away, the mother would strike nine times on the lintel of the entrance-door with the spoon used for millet. The soul must return for this is "the mother who is calling it back." If a child less than twenty years old should be frightened in a place outside the house, the mother must take the clothes of her child and go to the place, where she would put them down on the ground and then dragging them back home, she would all of the time call back the soul, which may return. At last, in very bad cases the soul may go as far as the world of dead people. Then the mother must put some incense on the drum and call back the soul. However, the mother cannot always be successful in this method and a shaman's assistance is usually required.

Amongst other Tungus groups the methods of bringing back the soul are simpler than that described above. The essential of it is calling back by the name of the bearer of the soul, attraction of attention by various means etc. but the principal methods are known to the shamans only. This will be treated in special chapters. The methods of keeping the soul in the body are numerous, but the chief of them are the same as in childhood, namely, avoiding sudden frightening when the soul "falls down", avoiding sudden awakening, for during the sleep the soul may be absent;** carefulness in dealing with the spirits which may enter the body during the absence of the soul

or may enter it and gradually push out the soul; recovery and reinstallation of the soul in the body. The chief worry is thus first, to avoid everything which may produce an emotion of "fear" and for this reason the Tungus try to avoid situations in which such a "fear" is possible; second is that they would avoid spirits which may take hold of the soul and for this reason the Tungus do their best to avoid the spirits and to eliminate their malevolent activity. This is a policy which may be followed by any one if one is familiar with the environment, and if one is not over-oppressed by one's own complex of spirits. Naturally, the adult people, and especially men, take care to protect the young generation and women against such accidents. Practically it results in a very kind and careful treatment of the people.

67. DEATH I shall now proceed to the last moment, namely, death when the soul is irreversibly removed from the body, while the methods of managing souls during the life, I shall reserve as matter to be treated in other chapters.

In the Chapter VII I have shown that the Tungus, as well as the Manchus, regard death as a natural phenomenon if it occurs in old age, but they do not regard it so if it occurs at the age when the people are still strong and efficient. The Tungus attitude towards death of children is not like that towards the death of full-grown people. It is silently admitted that the children may much more easily die than adult people for their souls are not yet stabilized and they are not so much regretted by the relatives. The death of adult people is usually regarded as an abnormal phenomenon due either to an accident, or disease in which the responsibility is usually put on the activity of the spirits. In this respect the Tungus do not differ from the Europeans who usually regard death as due to the factors which by human art may be eliminated, e.g. infectious diseases, social conditions etc.

Death is recognized by the loss of consciousness which is due to the fact that the soul leaves the body; by the arrest of the heart action which may sometimes be temporarily suspended, but must be resumed within a certain short period;* and by the arrest of breathing as an important sign of life, although it may stop (as it is supposed to be observed in hibernating animals who do not breathe), but it must also be resumed soon. During this uncertain period between "life" and "death" there may be undertaken special steps in order to revive the heart and breathing,—the life—*erga*,—and to turn back the soul if it be absent. The Reindeer Tungus of Manchuria observe that when the soul (and "life") leaves the body, the latter becomes heavier than it is during the life.**

As a matter of fact, the Tungus would accept any method of saving life if it should be possible. Methods which they have at their disposal are not numerous. In order to continue breathing and heart action the heart of the reindeer (observed amongst the Barguzin Tungus) may

---

* Vide description of cradle SONT, pp. 278 et seq.; and SOM, p. 117.

** According to the Reindeer Tungus of Manchuria with whom all Tungus could agree on this point, "fear" is due to the fact that the soul (om'l) sleeps when the man sleeps and when the man is suddenly awakened the soul being frightened flies away. The same is with the "fear" in an awaken condition,—the absence of the soul is perceived as "fear".

* The heart work is recognized by the Birarčen and Kumarčen by the pulse at the wrist,—majin-sudala or erga-sudala,—or a direct observation of the heart beating.

** The same they say about heavily drunken people. The same idea is shared by the Russian population of the Argun River. Indeed, they did not weigh with the weighing instruments, so this is an impression which may be well understood.

be put on the chest and the body must be covered with several clothes in order to keep it warm. Yet, the number of clothes put on perhaps may also play some rôle for nine are always used. If the person "is dying because of lack of breathing", the reindeer may be brought in, put on the dying person with the mouth to mouth.

When the soul (consciousness) is absent they call it back, and ask the spirits to bring it back, if it has left the body owing to the intrigues of other spirits or bad people. The soul may be called by the people whom the person (soul) knows. The spirits may be addressed by any one who knows how to do it*. When a child is dying the mother would sit with it, call the soul back with all possible tenderness which a mother may have. They would put some food, for instance, milk near the child, placing for soul etc.

In case the sickness were caused by a well established spirit, the struggle for life would be taken up by the shaman who would do his utmost in respect to the spirit. If the soul had left the body and was already on its way to the lower world, he would proceed there for catching the soul and putting it back into the body. The shaman may greatly help in such a case if the soul is not yet far. They also try to influence the spirits in the sense of compelling them by prayers and menaces to leave the ill person alone. Among the Barguzin Tungus it is supposed that if the death should occur during a thunder storm it is easier for the shaman to call the soul back for his spirit ("thunder") is near. Yet, if there are many people present, it is also good, for amongst the present people there may be some "happy persons" and the soul would return. It is supposed that the soul of a child is much easier to call back than that of an adult person.

When the consciousness is not lost the dying person usually knows and is prepared to die; an elderly person would be surrounded with the near relatives to whom the person would give last orders, if any were needed. I have observed once a Manchu, a young boy of twelve years old who was very sick. The "doctor" 's diagnosis was that the mother was responsible for it because she had scolded her boy who being badly offended, took some water and fell ill. Indeed, the mother was very sad about it. The boy was recollecting his short life: he remembered all members of the family who had taken care of him, pointed out that his school work was useless, since he had to die. He expressed his regrets that his death would produce a bad impression on his parents. The people did not deny

that he must die,—in their ideas they will live in another world, if their souls are safely brought there.

However, it does not at all mean that these people would not struggle for life even when the situation is considered hopeless. Yet also, it does not mean that they do object their departure to the lower world. They would strugggle for life as long as possible, which is especially evident in the case of accidents with animals and other "natural phenomena". So that the Tungus attitude towards death is that of submission to the inevitable for a premature death sometimes may be avoided. Most of cases of suicide which I know,—and according to the Tungus and Manchus all cases,—are committed in a state of psychic depression, unusual amongst these groups, or as a result of an effect or temporary excitement due to the influence of spirits or feeling of vengeance, as it is in the case of daughters-in-law amongst the Manchus and children, who by their death want to make suffer the people whom they should like to have persecuted by their own souls. The old people are prepared to die and yet sometimes the shamans predict death (cf. SONT. p. 321). Under the Chinese influence the Manchus also prepare a coffin and women prepare for themselves special shoes with lotus flower ornamentation. Yet, the Tungus must also have some special shoes prepared for this occasion. Voluntary death after the age of sixty or self-isolation is known amongst the Manchus, but according to them, they do not practise it.

68. PREPARATION OF THE CORPSE FOR BURIAL AND MANAGING OF THE FIRST SOUL When death is established, the attention of the people is turned to the problem of the soul and its transportation to the lower world. Various steps must be undertaken at once. So after the death of adult people the Manchus hang up on the gate a piece of blue tissue—*targa*, or of different colours in the case of taboo, if there is smallpox or a new-born child, or serious shamanism.

When an adult person passes away and death is recognized, the Barguzin Tungus smear the breast and abdomen of the corpse with reindeer blood, if a reindeer can be secured and cover the face with a piece of material or skin; the Birarčen cover the face with paper* which must not be taken away. The body is put on the ground covered either with the skin, or rugs, or simply fresh cut branches of trees, or with the wooden planks. The head is turned westward and thus the feet eastward. However, amongst the Tungus of Manchuria, the head is turned to *malu*, and the feet to the entrance regardless of the orientation of the dwelling. The corpse is dressed in the best available clothes and covered with some cloth or chamois. Amongst the Tungus of Manchuria, the clothes are made similar to those of the Chinese in material and shape when possible, but the only footwear which may be used is *gočun***. Amongst the old people these clothes are prepared long before they are needed. The Reindeer Tungus of Manchuria and Transbaikalia use only the ordinary style

---

* I have witnessed a few cases of death. In a case amongst the Barguzin Tungus after several attempts at reviving the body by pushing it and especially the head, calling back the soul, the Tungus asked me to help them by calling spirits, too. A group of men rushed to the near standing trees,—northwest from the wigwam, —hung up on a tree a small bell, made four marks with the axe on the tree and beating another tree with an axe, they called with tears burkan omokol! (burkan come!), nikola-ugodaŋ omokol! [Saint-Nicolas (vide supra p. 157) come!]. They asked me to join my voice. I knew that I must produce something new, unusual. Since I had in mind nothing rhythmic except Latin exceptions and propositions I rhythmically and with all possible expression recited them: caro, arbor, linter, cos, merces, quies, seges, dos, etc.; and later: ante, apud, ad, adversus...and so on! The impression was such as I never expected,—they stopped their prayers and were listening to me as a marvelous man who knew how one can influence spirits. I do not need to add that the corpse of the woman dying under nine overcoats did not revive.

* Owing to this the faces of living people cannot be covered with paper, even for protection against the flies.
** These are long, well-ornamented moccasins which are commonly used during dry, but cool weather.

of dress although the best, and according to the season. The thongs are left free and the clothes are not buttoned. The arms are put straight along the body and the legs are fastened with a thong or with a kerchief. A child's corpse is dressed in corresponding clothes, but the body is put with the head turned eastward (amongst the Tungus using wigwams); some food preferred by the children is put near the head. Various food and drinks,—meat, milk, tea, are put near the head of the corpse of the Tungus. On the breast, there are put a pipe and tobacco bag. A group of people sit around the corpse. From time to time the people present must change the food throwing into the air small portions of solid food and a few drops of liquid food. The rest of this food and tobacco are either thrown into the fire or eaten by the people present. The people must be present all of the time for watching the corpse and keeping away animals. It is still supposed that the soul may return and the death did not yet occur. The people who are not near the corpse talk as usual, and do their current work.

Amongst the Manchus the death is recognized by the absence of breathing, movement of the breast, and lifelessness of the eyes. The body is left for losing temperature. Then the relatives close the eyes,—the children to the parents, husband to his wife and vice versa, junior relatives to senior relatives, and parents to the children. The mother would say: "Don't worry, go on peacefully". If the eyes are left open it means that the deceased person, i.e. the soul, is "worrying". The people then gather around and begin to cry. No conversation about usual things is allowed. The corpse is dressed in several dresses one put on over another. There may be 3,6 or 9 and somtimes 5 or 7. The old men prepare for themselves their dresses to be put on them after death. The usual colour is gray. The pattern as well as the quality, is slightly different. The hat is made of the same form as that used by the officials, but it should be black without marks of distinction of grades. The shoes for the men must be black and with paper soles. All these things can be bought in the Chinese shops. However, the young people are usually dressed in the dresses they liked during life. In the case of the men, the head is shaven, according to the custom, i.e. leaving a plait. The face is covered only with paper.

The body is deposited on the planks put on the floor with the head turned to the *amba nayan*, i.e. usually westward and with the legs to the entrance. A pig's head and a burning oil lamp* are put near the head. Candles and kerosene lamps are prohibited. The incense is kept burning all of the time. The silver bars and coins, made of golden and silver paper, are put into paper bags,—nine "bars" in each, —with an inscription, e.g. "to the father for burning golden and silver paper coins one bag,"—and followed by an exact date: the day, month, and year. Let us remark that the Manchus generally like all kinds of formalistic inscriptions on different occasions, in which they imitate the Chinese. However, if the person is young and there is nobody younger in the clan system, no paper money is burnt. Naturally, the inscriptions vary only in the first word,—to whom the money is given. Since the money is needed by the deceased person, paper money in great quantity is burnt at the feet of the corpse. It must be burnt because only in immaterial

form can it be used by the souls (spirits).

When the corpse is in the wigwam or in the house one must be very careful with the soul of the deceased person. It is especially dangerous to produce wind or to raise dust in the air when the floor or ground are swept. Animals,—dogs, cats and chickens,—must be carefully kept away. There are two reasons, namely, (1) the dogs are used for carrying the soul into the lower world, so that the soul may use a dog before the shaman can accompany it with all necessary precautions and it might run when it liked or it might stay in this world and harm the people, as *zutu* (Manchu) *s'irkul* (Tungus of Manchuria); (2) the animals may accidentally jump across the corpse and take off the soul; besides they may produce wind, so the paper covering the face may slip off and the corpse may revive. According to the Birarčen's conviction such cases have occurred. However, not all of them believe in such a possibility. Amongst the Reindeer Tungus the reindeer cannot harm the soul and corpse. The same is true of the horse and other domesticated animals, but the dogs must be kept far away.* Amongst the Tungus one is allowed to speak in a loud voice, and there is no obligation to cry, as amongst the Manchus. I have noticed that the children had fear of their mother's corpse and did not want to approach it. Generally, the Tungus and Manchus fear corpses** for, as a matter of fact, there may be various complications with the soul which may remain in this world, and with the spirits which may enter the corpse. From the psychological point of view it is interesting that the Tungus usually find some consolation for themselves. So they say that the person was very sick and perhaps it was better to leave this world; or they might say that the death of an adult person was not so disastrous, for just recently there had been a marriage and thus new members will be born. They express their regret to the people who remain, e.g. small children, the husband and others; in this way the attention of the people is attracted to something else other than the bold fact of death as such.

The corpse remains for a certain time unburied. This period is subject to great variations amongst the groups here described. So, during the cold period the corpse may be preserved for a long time, but during the hot season it decomposes too fast and thus must be buried sooner. However, amongst the Tungus, the corpse usually remains unburied for one or two days. The shortest period which has been recorded is that given by V. P. Margaritov amongst the Oroči who bury as soon as possible, and the longest among the Manchus who sometimes keep the body, put in a coffin, for a very long time. The reason is, on the one hand, imitation of the Chinese and on the other hand, in some cases need for calling junior relatives who may be absent and who must perform certain rites.***

---

* Oil lamps are made of various materials. At the present time they are usually made of iron. Their form is that of a bowl, slightly elongated.

* It is quite possible that the original fear of the dogs was due to the possibility that they would devour the corpse which might, as will be later seen, produce great complications for a peaceful liquidation of earthly life. Cf. the case of destruction of the corpse by dogs (V. P. Margaritov, op. cit. p. 29).

** Cf. V. P. Margaritov. op, cit. pp. 29-30. However, amongst the Goldi (cf. P. Šimkevič, op. cit., and I. A. Lopatin, op. cit.) the attitude is somewhat different,—the husband or wife of the deceased spouse spends the night with the corpse before the corpse is put into the coffin (I. A. Lopatin, p. 286).

*** This is also the reason of delay of burial amongst the Goldi (I. A. Lopatin, op. cit.).

69. LIQUIDATION OF THE CORPSE The next important step is putting the corpse into the coffin. This moment may coincide with that of burial amongst the Tungus, and they may be separated by months, as amongst the Manchus.

In former days amongst the Northern Tungus the usual way of burying was to put the corpse into a wooden box erected on piles. Such a construction is shown in a water-colour illustration in SONT (facing p. 14).[*] This form of burial was described by Th. von Middendorf amongst the Tungus of Yakutsk Gov., by R. Maack in the Wilui district, also by W. Sieroszewski amongst the Yakuts who, under the influence of their neighbours, the Tungus and Yukagirs, used this form of burial (op. cit. pp. 619-621). However, the Yakut shamans were not buried but were put in coffins. Amongst all Tungus, small children are even now buried only by hanging the corpse covered with birch-bark, on a tree or putting it into a hollow tree trunk. The Manchus also practise this form of burial for the children below the age of three years. The body is covered with oat-straw and laid on the tree branches,—*pučeye n'aļma tědurě čuaŋ* (Manchu Sp.), i.e. "dead people for lying bed" (*čuaŋ*,—Chinese 床). The shamans are sometimes also buried in this way.

For erecting a burial place the Tungus usually find two trees not very large, located át a distance of about two metres. The trees are cut about two metres above the ground. Instead of trees there may be used especially erected posts on which there are fixed cross-beams about six or seven centimetres thick serving for supporting planks, on which the body is deposited. Then the body is protected with planks, on which the body is deposited, as well as with planks from all sides and fastened with cross-beam and a system of wooden nails and fasteners. Such a con-struction is very solid and cannot be destroyed by the animals. Any trees or wood can be used for this purpose.

At the present time this is the usual way of burying amongst the Kumarčen, and the Khingan Tungus. I have been told by them that sometimes they simply put the corpse on the erected platform without wooden protection, but I could not find out in which cases they practise this and I observed no such burials. The Reindeer Tungus of Manchuria, within the memory of old people used to bury in the same manner, and their predecessors in the region (*ŋuyal, vide* SONT, p.64 and others) did the same. Instead of coffins they also used a hollow tree which was naturally a mere simplification of practice. Even now, al-though formally Christians, they sometimes bury in hollow trees which they put straight on the ground. At the end of the last century the Birarčen generally practised burial in erected coffins. The shamans are still buried in this manner. Amongst the Tungus of Barguzin and Nerčinsk this form of burial is still practised when the Tungus can do it, i.e. at a certain distance from the Russians.

The children are buried in a simplified manner, name-ly, when the child is very small it is put into the cradle which is erected on the branches of a tree and there left; when the child is above the cradle age the corpse is put in a hollow tree, cut into two halves, and put either on a tree or erected on piles.

L. von. Schrenk has left[*] a description of Oroči tombs which differ only in details from the above given description and the fact that the coffin was made first and put on the erected piles (trunks of trees). The description of V. P. Margaritov[**] does not differ from that given by L. von Schrenk. It may be pointed out that at the time of L. von Schrenck the Olča used to bury persons who were murder-ed in the coffins lifted,—i.e. exactly as described by him amongst the Oroči. Yet we find mentioning of the elevated coffins among the Kidans and perhaps the Sien-pi in South Manchuria, true without indication whether this practice was general or exceptional one[***].

The burial in coffins on erected piles is called in Tungus, Barguzin and Nerčinsk,—*gula*—which means any wooden angular construction, e.g. storehouse for grain amongst the Russians, dwellings in the lower world etc.[****] The Nerčinsk Tungus also use a special term *bilo*. The Re-indeer Tungus of Manchuria, as well as other groups of Manchuria, call it *g'iramk'ivun* which is from *gira*(n),—"bone".

If we summarize the above facts it would be clear that this method of burying is connected chiefly with the Tungus, and formerly it was evidently practised amongst the Man-chus (preserved for young children and shamans), Olča (preserved for murdered people), Goldi (preserved for children). In the Yakutsk Gov. this form is known amongst the Yukagirs and Yakuts influenced by the Tungus. Out-side of the present Tungus area, but in their vicinity, it is known, in historical time, amongst the Sien-pi who might include some Tungus elements. Indeed, many other par-allels may be found in more remote regions.

Under the influence of other ethnical groups some new and different methods are also introduced and old ones simplified. Instead of coffin described above the Birarčen very rarely use a canoe in which they put the corpse and leave the current of the river (the Amur) to carry the canoe together with the corpse. Amongst the Oroči the burial in a canoe is also known, but the canoe is used as a coffin and is not left to be carried by the rivers.[*****]

Amongst the Manchus the coffin must be made of pine tree with a roof with a double slope, by which the Manchu coffin differs from those used amongst the Chinese and Dahurs,—the Dahur coffin is a flat and long box. The coffin is usually put straight on the ground and protected with wooden planks; afterwards it is covered with earth, so that the burial looks thus like a small mound. The size of the ear-then mound depends on the importance of the person. This way of burying now is nearly general amongst the Birarčen, who, however, sometimes also put the corpse into the earth, but not very deep. Amongst the Goldi, Oroči, also Yakuts the coffins are left open on the ground and sometimes pro-tected only with a fence. As a matter of fact, the putting on ground may also have place amongst the Tungus who

---

[*] Another illustration is reproduced from my photograph by M. A. Czaplicka (op. cit., Plate 15).

[*] L. von Schrenck, op. cit. Vol. III, p. 144 (which are his notes from diary).

[**] V. P. Margaritov, op. cit. p. 30.

[***] cf. E. Parker "One Thousand Years, etc." p. 297.

[****] Lately among the Khingan Tungus it was extended to the wigwam. However, this term is associated chiefly with the idea of elevated square dwellings. [cf. guli (Ang. Tit.),—to hung up on elevated platform, storehouse, also on trees etc. Indeed, the Buriat uļgoxu, has nothing to do with guli; a derivative gulimačin cannot be translated as E. I. Titov does.]

[*****] cf. V. P. Margaritov, op. cit., p. 30.

usually bury in erected coffins. Amongst the same groups, as result of recent Chinese influence the Chinese coffins begin to penetrate as a common practice. So, for instance, amongst the Manchus Chinese coffins are now bought and kept for a long time, as just is practised amongst the Chinese. The Tungus of Manchuria, when they can afford to have Chinese coffins, do the same, but amongst them it occurs rather rarely. The ornamentation of Chinese style with paintings is now gradually introduced too. It is likely that the sumptuous coffins, met with amongst the Goldi and Oroči, are of the same origin.

Although amongst the Manchus influenced by the Chinese the grave *lege artis* must be digged in depth between nine and twelve feet and not less than seven feet, also the place and direction are defined by the specialists (Chinese fortune-tellers) and the time (hour and day) are also fixed, but practically it is not so. I have seen graves so shallow that the coffin could not be covered, so that required being protected by additional planks and covered with stones and earth to form a low tumulus. The usual Manchu direction of the head is south-west.

Amongst the Tungus living in Russian territory the practice of burial in earth has been gradually introduced under the Russian influence. In fact, Russian authorities and the Church attempted to convince the Tungus of the necessity of burying in the earth,—the first chiefly for hygienic considerations and the second owing to the existing Christian tradition. However, it is far from becoming a general practice. The Tungus who live near the Russians do practise this form of burial, but the Tungus who live at a long distance preserve the old method. In fact, there are serious difficulties for digging frozen earth, even in summer remaining so in most of territories occupied by the Tungus. Yet, since the Tungus are not numerous and have no iron spades, sometimes the digging cannot be done at all. Indeed, the graves are very narrow and never deep,—at most one metre. No special coffin is made, but the bottom and walls of the grave are protected with wooden planks between which the corpse is deposited and covered with one or two planks. Again, under the Russian influence the Tungus have begun to make regular coffins.

Amongst the Birarčen the burial of Manchu or Chinese type was recently practised only as a temporary disposal. After a certain number of years they used to take out the bones and, after their careful cleaning, to transport them to the clan cemeteries some of which were located in the Russian territory, in the basin of the Zeia River. If carrying of bones is too difficult the bones may be collected and burnt, so that only ashes will be transported to the cemetery.[*] This practice is not typical of the Tungus and ought to be regarded either as due to the foreign influence or as result of breaking of the old practice of burial in the erected coffins. The removal of bones and their cleaning are known, e.g. in Kwantung amongst the natives (local Chinese), also amongst other far distant groups. However, the idea of removal of the bones is very common amongst the Koreans and is not quite hostile to the Manchus who ascribe some psychomental troubles amongst the clansmen to the badly chosen place for burial, and in which case the place may be changed. The Birarčen explanation why the bones are carried to the cemetery is that it is im-

possible to carry the corpse while the bones can be so carried, therefore the corpse must be left to decay and bones must be cleaned, for when uncleaned they smell bad. The idea of a clan cemetery may be also of a recent origin for amongst most groups no practice of cemeteries is known. When the Tungus of Manchuria were organized by the Manchus the latter might give them the idea that they must have definite places for burial of clansmen. By these remarks I do not want to solve the problem whether the Birarčen have received their practice from other ethnical groups or follow some very old practice, or even have themselves created a new practice. All three suppositions are admissible.

Amongst the Manchus the place for burial *lege artis* must be chosen according to the Chinese book already mentioned. In spite of it, cemeteries are gradually formed if several clansmen are buried in the same place which would show itself to be "good". The Tungus of Manchuria when familiar with this practice do the same, but usually have no specialists for finding the place and therefore they act according to the old practice. The practice amongst all Tungus living in a state of continuous migration is the same,—they bury at a short distance from the place where death occurred,—for transportation of the corpse at a long distance is extremely difficult and very often absolutely impossible. The place is usually chosen, if possible, on the slopes of mountains, and preferentially on the northern slopes. The place is usually covered with forest and thick shrubs. An important condition of choice is that the place of burial must not be near any path, which incidentally may be haunted by other spirits and thus the way to the burial can be shown to the spirits by the path.

There is a definite orientation of the burial amongst all Northern Tungus groups; namely, the head is orientated to North-West, or West-North-West, the reason of which is that the souls are going to the other world in North-(West-North-) West direction. The children are orientated with the head to South-East or South-East-South, for the souls of children may return to the spirit which distributes the souls. However, I meet with a contrary fact amongst the Reindeer Tungus of Manchuria who assert that they bury children in the same orientation to North-West as the adult people. Here the question is, however, how big are the children meant by these Tungus. Amongst the Khingan Tungus I have seen a small child buried in its cradle on a tree, so that the face (in a semi-sitting position as it is always in the cradle) was turned to North-West, in which position the head was turned to the South-East.

70. SPECIAL CONDITIONS OF BURIAL We have already seen that the children are not buried in the same way as the adult people. Amongst the Manchus the children below the age of three years are buried on the trees. The corpse is covered with wooden clips and straw also birch bark. The Manchus say that this burial is practised for children for facilitating the return of all three souls to *oyos'i mama*. The children from three to ten years are usually buried in the grave, but without any coffin,—the corpse is put on the planks on which the corpse was deposited after death. The male children above this age are buried in simply-made coffins.

Shamans are buried on trees like children, in the case

---

[*] Burning of bones has a curious parallel among the Kidans who as I have shown (SONT) incorporated some Northern Tungus.

if the shaman—it is supposed his spirit—asks them to do so. This form of burial for the shamans was general in former days. This old practice is rationalized as follows: the spirits cannot protect the corpse when it is buried in the earth. A shaman cannot naturally be buried on trees,—e.g. in the steppe regions,—and therefore the shamans are often put into an ordinary coffin which is left unburied on a hill. A small aperture is left in the coffin in order to give shaman's spirits a possibility of free circulation. According to my informers, burial of shaman-women on trees is not practised.

In former days about in the middle of the last century, the corpse of girls of less than twenty years old were burnt together with the coffins. The reason was that there was nobody, after their death, to take care of soul and body. In fact, even a young man of fifteen years may have younger brothers in the clan, while the girls, according to the exogamic practice, have to leave the clan and there will be nobody left in the clan for taking care of them. However, since the soul is the soul, so it may produce great harm to the people, and the corpse may be used by other spirits in which way the girls corpse may become *ibayan*, the safest way is to destroy the body. Indeed, the Buddhistic practice of cremation came to help the Manchus.

Cremation is also used in the case of partial destruction of the body by wounds and especially by the loss of members. However, sometimes a dismembered corpse may also be put together and buried in this form, but it would mean that the people do not want the soul to be restored. Thus the cremation helps to restore the soul which is damaged by the dismembering of the body.

In the case of death punishment through decapitation the head ought to be put in its place and fixed by sewing it to the corpse. This operation is done by hired people. As in other similar cases, the chief difficulty is that the soul is also damaged by the decapitation. Let us point out that in the case of decapitation of a shaman the spirits take care by taking out the soul before the act and in this way the soul is not damaged.

In case of destruction of the body by wild animals or its partial destruction and dismembering the Manchus would do as in the case of damage in war, i.e. the remains as well as the clothes would be put together and the burial would be simplified for the "soul is broken"*; the corpses of persons killed by lightning are buried in a simplified manner, namely, without coffin for lightning strikes liars, squabblers, those who abuse with bad words especially in reference to the parents, those who like chicanery, etc. whence the Manchu swearing: *ājen targ'imb'e*—"thunder strike (you)!" used in reference to the persons worthy of this particular end.

In the case of drowned people, when the corpse is not found, a burial *in effigia* is carried out with the clothes found at the bank of the river or those taken from the wardrobe. The trouble here is that the second soul is merely drowned together with the body. For this reason, evidently, L. von Schrenck has observed a burial of a drowned Goldi, from whose tomb a string was extended to the water (cf. op. cit. Plate LXVII); the string was a "road" along

* However, it must be pointed out that the opinions of the Manchus as to the fate of men mutilated and dead at the war are not uniform. In fact, there is an opinion that all warriors' souls are freely admitted in the lower world, so that the living people must not worry about them.

which the soul might return to the body. The souls of drowned people instead of going to *Ilmunxan* go to *Mudurxan* who live in the Amur River. On the seventh day of the seventh month there used to be organized regular performance: there was made a canoe with lanterns and people made of paper (the Chinese complex); when the canoe was far from the bank it was set on fire; fire crackers were burnt, too. These are souls of drowned people who complain to *Mudurxan* as to their fate.

The vagabonds,—people whose origin and names are unknown,—are either thrown away or buried without coffin. The same is done with the people who have no relatives and are very poor. If any care is taken, it is done only because of possible complications with their souls.

The corpses of persons who commit suicide by hanging are buried in coffins, but separately from other clan members, and with no complex ceremonies.

Husband and wife must be buried side by side, because they will live together in the other world.

In former days the old men, over sixty years of age, according to the tradition, were buried alive in the earth, but without any coffin. The Manchus say that, according to the Chinese books, this practice was abolished after a case: "There were so many rats that the people greatly suffered; then an old man who was over sixty told that there existed cats, which might destroy the rats. So they got the cats and people were saved from rats. The Khan then ordered to honour old men and leave them to live up to death and bury them in coffins". In connexion with this it may be also pointed out that, according to the Manchus, in former days they used to build special houses of light construction in which the old men over sixty years ended their days by starvation.

Amongst the Birarčen special forms of burial are practised for the shamans, who are buried in the open,—the coffin having a special aperture for the spirits and left open as it is among the Manchus. The children up to the age of ten years are usually covered with Chinese cloth and put in the grave without coffin. We have already seen that infants are buried in coffins, according to the old custom, i.e. on piles for the reason that if the corpse is buried in the earth, the mother would have no more children. Adult people who have old mothers may be, therefore, buried in graves. The persons who commit suicide are buried as usual. I have recorded no facts regarding differences in the burial amongst other Tungus groups.

71. LAST CEREMONY Amongst the MANCHUS the corpse, put on planks, remains in the house three days. In these days all relatives assemble. In the meantime the coffin is prepared. For covering the walls and bottom of the coffin they put cotton wrapped in some cotton material; incense sticks, which are supposed to preserve the corpse from decay, are also put into the coffin. The corpse itself is covered with several blankets. The hat of deceased person and personal things, especially those liked by the defunct, are put in the coffin and then the corpse. The son's duty is to nail on the cover of the coffin which he does, saying: *amal xadayamb'e jala,*—"father, be careful of nails"; for it is supposed that accidentally the soul may be damaged by the nails. The coffin is taken out of the house through a window. In the yard there is a previously prepared temporary, very light construction, made of mats (*linpay*, Chinese) and covered with white cloth, called *zoboł maikan*,—"coffin tent",—in which the coffin is put, so that the feet of corpse are turned towards the gate.

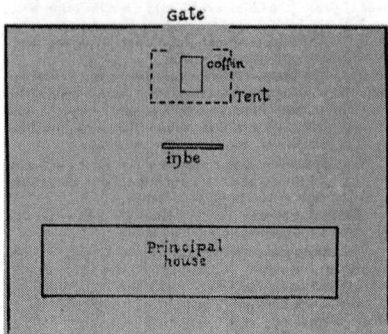

Gate

coffin

Tent

iŋbe

Principal house

Near by the head there is put a table with a sacrifice which consists of the pig, rice, etc. altogether "six dishes". The people who must cry and remain in a kneeling position occupy certain places: the son takes the right side of the coffin with all other male relatives in order of their respective positions; the females go to the left side of the coffin, the first being the wife of the deceased person. The effigies made of paper, according to the Chinese complex, are also prepared in the tent: *lor'in* (asses), horse with saddle, carriage, several boxes with paper clothes and paper servants, all of which are afterwards burnt. However, the Manchus like still better things made of iron, such as kettles, utensils etc. which are put in the grave. These things, which are smaller than the usual size, are made by the Chinese in Algun. After the first ceremony the people present go to the house and have their ritual dinner which in rich families consists, usually of "nine cups and eight dishes" (*vide* SOM p. 85) with the difference that there is no "red vegetable"; in poor families there may be "six cups and six dishes" and in very poor families only four dishes. The dishes are served by the son or nearest junior relative (of the deceased) who makes a deep genuflexion, as in the wedding celebration. The meals are never taken by those who wear mourning dress, on the *nayan* (Chinese *k'an*,—stove beds, the usual place · for meals), but on the ground. The "paper money" is burnt and the wine is poured three times.

Near the construction, where the coffin remains, the Manchus erect a post, similar to that seen near the temples. To the post there is attached a piece of red cloth over three metres long and ending in five separated strips, "like five fingers", called *fan* (Chinese). Later on, when the coffin is taken out to be conducted to the grave, the people present rush to the red cloth and tear it to pieces, so that every one present may have a piece of it "for happiness". According to some Manchus, this is a Chinese custom but in former days the Manchus used to prepare a piece of cloth with a head, legs, arms and body which was also destroyed by the

people present at the funeral.[*] According to some other Manchus, the Chinese practice is to make a "man" from white material.

Junior members of the clan of the deceased person must wear mourning dress of Chinese type or at least some white marks distinguishing it. The women take off their ear-rings.

The coffin remains in the special construction for different periods,—seven days in summer, when possible three weeks, and up to seven weeks in winter. The ceremony of removal of the coffin to the grave is called in Manchu *fojeŋo faryun*,—"the carrying forward of the soul",— which points to an older and different complex, for at the present time the liquidation of the soul does not take place at this ceremony. The performance is now carried on according to the Chinese complex—the son, or a junior goes ahead preceded by the bearers of lanterns and when possible, musicians, also bearers of paper horses and other things; male clansmen follow; then comes the coffin carried by either relatives or hired people, but an end of the cloth covering the coffin is held by the principal mourner; less important relatives and carts with the females follow the coffin; no woman can go ahead of it. Indeed, the pomposity of the procession depends on the wealth of the family. Practically, a rich family may use all kinds of expensive details invented by the Chinese undertakers.

The coffin is hurriedly lowered into the grave which is immediately filled up with earth[**]. All relatives must cry in a high-pitched and loud voice, and the juniors must recite prayers. The chief mourner burns the paper money as well as all other paper things and pours nine cups of wine on the fresh tomb. The relatives *zon'ᴇx'in* make a show of throwing their mourning dress into the fire, but they keep it. Afterwards, everyone returns home.

The next action takes place on the ninety-ninth day when relatives go again to the tombs, make sacrifice, burn paper money and make a show of throwing their mourning dress into the fire. However, ·the principal mourner is supposed to wear his mourning dress for three years, and his wife must not put on gold rings, ear-rings or brooches, but only silver ones.

———————

Amongst the REINDEER TUNGUS · OF TRANS-BAIKALIA the corpse must remain unburied for at least twenty four hours, sometimes it may remain so up to three days. Before moving the corpse, the wigwam is transferred to another place and thus the corpse is left under the sky. The Tungus fasten two long wooden pieces together to make a kind of litter upon which they put the corpse. On the way, they stop several times (I have observed three times), make a fire and offer a small sacrifice by burning *laedum palustrum*, perhaps also tobacco and by pouring tea with milk into the fire and face of the corpse. Behind the

———————

[*] I do not venture to compare this custom with that formerly observed amongst the Dayaks who ate their old men. They were on this occasion lifted up, to catch with their hands a branch of a tree where they hung as long as they could maintain themselves and when they were exhausted and fell, were eaten.

[**] As shown in winter the coffin may be only slightly covered with earth. If it is impossible to dig out a deep grave, the coffin may be left unburied and buried later. · The same is done when the coffin must be transported elsewhere.

corpse, a reindeer loaded with belongings of the deceased person is brought by one of the clansmen,—two travelling bags, a winter coat etc. but not all of the belongings. Then the procession stops at the place of burial and one more sacrifice is made. The reindeer is killed, according to the common method. The coffin inside is smeared with blood. There are put in it *laedum palustrum*, the bags with some flour, clothes, a palma (a long knife), some kettles, several vessels made of birch-bark with cakes and various things, also a tobacco bag, pipe and matches. On the breast they put some tea leaves. When a man is buried, they put with him a bow and arrow, skins, etc.; with a woman they put the *tijavın*, a special staff used by the women to balance themselves when they ride on the reindeer.

The reindeer is skinned and the skin is left together with the antlers and hoofs. The skin is fastened upon a bar horizontally fixed to two trees and left hanging there. This is the reindeer which will be used by the spirit (soul) of the deceased person for going to the lower world. Over the skin is put a piece of roe-deer skin, over this a saddle and last, a winter coat. The head of the reindeer is turned toward the North-West.

The meat is cooked at that place and eaten by the people present; a small part of it is left as food for the deceased (soul) and put at the head of the tomb.

If there is no reindeer, the Tungus may also use, in the same function and manner, a horse. In male burial, instead of normal bows and arrows, small models are very often used. All implements and weapons which are sharp must not be left in condition good for use,—so the string of the bow is detached, the knives are made blunt, etc. The reason given is that the soul may use these weapons and implements against the living people. However, this explanation is doubtful, for not only are the weapons broken but the kettles also and some of the clothing is torn. The basis of this practice is the idea of a liberation of "immaterial" substance, while blunting the knives etc. is of a secondary origin.

Amongst other Tungus groups the differences regarding things put into the coffin, the sacrifice and arrangement of the burial consist of the details. Among the BIRARČEN in former days all things put into the coffin were broken. At the present time they are usually only damaged, e.g. the sharp implements and weapons blunted. Instead of usual weapons they also put wooden models of the spear, hunting knife, etc.; instead of matches the Birarčen put flint. The body is put into the coffin in the yard and is taken from the house (if it is a house of Chinese type) through the door, if the deceased person is a member of the family, if not, through the window. This preventive measure is taken with a view not to show the way back to an outsider. When the coffin is nailed, the Birarčen begin to feel some safety as to possibility of appearance of a *boy* formed as shown of the corpse. The burial itself is rather simple, as compared with an elaborate Manchu-Chinese complex, on the pattern of which it is made. It is accompanied by a ritual crying of the relatives and sometimes, but not always, by a rite of burning some paper-money, also an insignificant sacrifice.

Among the KUMARČEN everything must be broken. but the Manchu-Chinese elements are very rarely and poorly represented.

Among the Tungus who have horses this animal plays the part reserved to the reindeer amongst the reindeer breeders. Yet, with a decrease of number of horses the

latter may be substituted in the ritualism of burial by other animals, and even merely by new symbols.

72. FURTHER OPERATIONS WITH THE SOUL Various things are put into the corpse because if the soul is lacking something it might become angry with the people who remain in this world. More than this, the soul may avenge itself for such negligence. According to the Reindeer Tungus of Manchuria, if they fail to satisfy the needs of the deceased people some other (clansmen) relatives will soon die. Indeed the chief anxiety here is the management of the soul and here we come in touch with theories regarding the soul. We have seen the soul consists of three elements, amongst the Manchus and some other Tungus groups. The question as to when the soul actually leaves the corpse determines the Tungus behaviour in respect to practical ways of getting rid of the soul.

We have seen that the soul for a certain time remains near the body; so the soul must receive everything as if it were a living person. This period may last a rather long time. Then at last the soul must be taken to the other world. Amongst the Reindeer Tungus of Transbaikalia it is supposed that the departure of the soul follows the burial immediately and therefore the reindeer is slaughtered at the tomb. Indeed the soul may meet with obstacles on its way and it ought to be helped by competent people, sometimes even by a shaman, but these measures may usually suffice to end earthly activity of the soul. It is different with the Manchus who believe that the soul remains ninety-nine days with the living people. However, according to the common opinion, the *olorg'i fojeyo* departs on the seventh day.

On the seventh day the Manchus make a placing for the soul which is made of clothes put on the bed-stove (*nayan*) as though it were deceased person. It receives food, tobacco and wine, and an oil lamp is put at the head of the placing. The participants burn paper-money, and have a ritual feast of "six cups and six dishes." The Manchus call it *fojeyo tučimb'e*,—"the soul goes away." Up to that time the soul remains in the place, where the person died, in a form "like steam." The operation is usually carried out without the shaman's help[*]. The people present cry and pray the soul to leave the place. The soul is supposed to depart before midnight leaving some footprints on the ashes put on the threshold. The reason why the soul leaves before midnight is that cocks crow and dogs bark at midnight and the soul would be frightened.

In spite of the fact that the soul is away, three weeks later the Manchus organize a new sacrifice which consists chiefly in burning paper-money etc. on the grave, if the burial is already accomplished. The same is done on the thirty-fifth day and at last on the hundredth day. However, here is the management of the soul already settled in the other world. On the hundredth day the operation actually occupies three days. Two days in advance, the Manchus begin to prepare all necessary food, cakes etc. They buy paper-money, human figures, animals, boxes etc. all made of paper. If the family has no money to buy them, they make everything at home. The night before this day, the near relatives,—the wife or husband.

---

[*] The soul sometimes does not reach the other world and in this case it would require special measures on the part of the shaman.

children and others,—gather together near the place where the person died and burn some paper-money and other articles made of paper, in front of an altar. The things prepared for the next day are put on the place formerly occupied by the deceased person. Then the people present take a ritual meal and write down in Manchu (or in Chinese) a detailed list of everything which had been prepared for burning, with the names of the contributors. The people assembled cry with loud voices when it is required, then suddenly stop, when the rite is performed, and continue their usual conversations and laughter as is usual with all Manchu rites. The next morning all bearers of mourning dress gather together and go by foot or on carts or sledges to the tomb. The things and people present are located as shown in accompanying figure.

All of them cry loudly, while the paper things are burning. Then they throw food into the fire and make show of throwing in the mourning dresses, but instead they

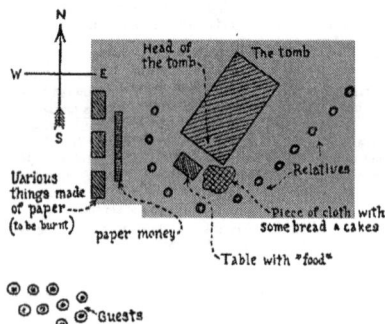

take these along and in a great hurry, in crowd return, almost run, to their homes. Such a performance may cost several hundreds of dollars when there are many people and many things are prepared for burning.

Under the influence of the "poverty factor" the ceremony may be reduced to a few pieces of paper-money and a small sacrifice consisting of a cock or a hen.

The sacrifice ought to be repeated during the life of the near junior relatives. Sometimes on the tomb or near to it the Manchus erect memorial stones with the usual inscriptions. However, it is done rarely for stones are very expensive and one has to pay something to the government when one wants to erect the memorial on the roads or near the roads. The practice of the hundredth day sacrifice is in conflict with the idea of sending off of the soul on the seventh day. In fact, some Manchus express their doubt as to the need of this performance. They would say that since the soul has already been settled (about which they are sure for on the seventh day the soul goes away) there is nothing left on the hundredth day to be dealt with. This point of view is not accepted by other people who say that if there were anything left in the grave, there would be no reason to keep the tombs, and yet the Chinese do observe

these practices. For safety's sake, the Manchus maintain this practice, too.

———

Amongst the Birarčen the seventh day is supposed to be a very important day—*nadan ineŋi eus'i fūran*—"the seventh day the soul comes out." On that day the old men put some ashes, on the threshold, sit down quietly and wait for the moment when the soul goes away. During this time they ask the soul: *ajakan'ji genèkäi, orūja ôj'i taana*—"peacefully (good) go, bad don't do (produce)", also all kinds of "good words" which sometimes last for several hours. At midnight the soul goes away leaving footprints on the ashes in the form of footprints of a chicken, roedeer, horse, and other animals, for it is supposed that the souls go to the animals. On the hundredth day a performance takes place, in imitation of the Manchus: when possible paper-money, figures, etc. are burnt. "Everything must be written down" (but it is not done!) and burnt together. In former days they used to kill a horse which was supposed to be used by the soul. At the present time the horse is not killed, but it is attached for the whole night near the tomb on a very long bridle. Instead of a horse the Birarčen now kill a pig and even sometimes an ox, but these are not killed for travelling of the soul, but as sacrifice-food. If everything is regularly arranged, the soul happily will reach the other world, very rarely does the soul return. In the last case the shaman's intervention is necessary. The performance on the hundredth day is called *g'iramna javoran, s'ena luktän*, i.e. "the bones (one) takes, the mourning dress (one) throws away." However, this expression does not correspond to the present practice, for the bones are now left untouched, and the practice of mourning dress is mere convention which is not actually observed.

The Birarčen assert that slaughtering of a horse was borrowed by them from the Dahurs who are horse-meateaters and under whose control the Tungus were a long time before the spreading of Manchu influence and later Chinese influence. Generally the Tungus do not like horsemeat, so that at the present time less than a third of the Birarčen would eat it.

Amongst the other Tungus groups the seventh day and hundredth day performances can be carried out earlier. So, for instance, amongst the Khingan Tungus the slaughtering of the horse and, thus, transportation of the soul takes place on the third day after death. Besides the horse skin with hoofs they leave at the spot also some wine, paper-money and figures, as already described, and sacrifice a sheep, sometimes a pig, and even an ox. It is very important to have rice, also millet, as food liked by the souls. Amongst the Kumarčen the whole performance is made during the night time and besides a horse they also kill several pigs, which they have to buy from the Manchus.

Indeed, the influence of the Russian Church among the Tungus of Transbaikalia and Reindeer Tungus of Manchuria has also produced its effect upon the practices regarding liquidation of the body and soul. The help of the priests is of importance in this matter, for the Tungus are relieved of their anxiety. Accordingly with the Church regulations the Tungus customs were also partly modified. From the ethnographical point of view these new practices are not interesting for they reflect a new combined complex of the original system and elements borrowed from the Russian system, the old idea of complex soul being preserved and new methods of managing it being borrowed.

It may be here noted that as a whole the death-burial-soul complex amongst the Tungus is subject to great variations, according to the sources of cultural influence. Some moments of the complex may receive greater emphasis than the others, while some elements may be rejected altogether and the others may be forgotten. From this point of view the Goldi complex is very interesting.

Among the Goldi it is supposed that the soul on the seventh day after the burial, must be brought by the shaman to a special placing reserved for it, *fan'a*. I. A. Lopatin gives the term for the act: *n'imgan*. This term as will be seen is met with in other dialects in the sense of —"to shamanize" and particularly when the shaman goes to the lower world, so that it is not a special term. The Goldi on this day make the *fan'a* which is a placing for the soul made in the form of an ornamented pillow which is also covered with the clothes of the deceased person, including his hunting hat. If the deceased person was a female, the Goldi attach the ear-rings to the pillow. Near the pillow they put a specially made wooden placing *ajam'i fan'alko* with a hole in which they thrust a tobacco pipe which is changed from time to time. The widow of a deceased man goes to sleep near the *fan'a*. Etymologically *fan'a* ought to be connected with *an'an*,—"the shadow", whence, "the soul" (*vide supra* p. 52). Amongst the Goldi this placing for soul may be preserved for years and it would regularly or irregularly receive some sacrifices. With good reason, I. A. Lopatin has connected this practice with that known amongst the Chinese prior to the XIIth century, since which time the tablet with the inscribed name on it, began to play the rôle of the placing. Amongst the Goldi the operation with *fan'a* has received great emphasis, naturally, together with the idea that it is very difficult to send the soul to the world of dead people. Evidently this was a particular case of growth of a complex which is found in a very rudimentary form amongst the other Northern groups and also little developed amongst the Manchus. The Goldi shamanistic performance is very complex and it includes several actions which are not particularly interesting to be treated. The bringing of the soul to the world of dead people takes place much later, sometimes several years later. This performance lasts several (three) days and consists in verifying whether the soul is really placed in *fan'a*, and bringing it to the other world. The complex is called by I. A. Lopatin *kaza taor'i*, which is, of course, Manchu *ǧɵsa dorɵ*,—"the sorrow law (custom)", whence there has originated a complex shamanistic performance of going to the lower world, etc. known under the verb *ǧɵsa→kaza*.* Therefore the souls may remain in this world for a long time and become a source of trouble for the living people,—sometimes the Goldi cannot organize the performance immediately, while their theory of soul includes no alleviating issues. I doubt the assertion of I. A. Lopatin who says that with this performance there is destroyed the last connexion between the dead and living

people,—to be sure the souls of dead people even when they are in the lower world need some care and sacrifices.*

As an interesting peculiarity of the Goldi, it may be also noted that they use a dog instead of a reindeer or horse. The dog's skin is put in front of the tomb and the soul of dead person travels on it, i.e. dog's soul. However, we have already seen that the dog in its connexion with the souls is not met with only amongst the Goldi.

We may now summarize the practices met with amongst the Tungus:

1. The soul is a complex, the elements of which at different times leave the body.
2. These elements have different fate in their existence after the destruction of the body.
3. The elements need a certain intervention on the part of living people for making them harmless.
4. The moments of departure of souls are different amongst the Tungus groups, owing to which the performances connected with departure may take place at different times.
5. The liquidation of the corpse and sending off of the soul may take from two days to several years.

There are at least three complexes intermingling amongst some Tungus groups, namely, (a) the old Tungus complex in which the part of the shaman is reduced to the participation as that of any other member of the clan; burial in open coffins, erected on piles, travelling of the soul on some domesticated animal;** (b) the Chinese complex with its system of managing the soul with paper symbols, mourning dress, etc. which is well represented amongst the Manchus; (c) the Goldi complex in which the old Tungus elements, are combined with the Chinese elements and a particularly important place is given to the shamans. Other complexes, such as Russian, Mongol and others, have only secondary importance.

As we have seen from Part Two the activity of the souls, either in the form of newly formed spirits or in the form of souls, continues and living people must watch and take care of them.

73. CLAN PRIEST—P'O₁UN SAMAN. The greatest growth of the complex managing souls of dead people, as we have seen, is found amongst the Manchus. There is no doubt that the idea of a regular managing of souls of dead people has been received by them from the Chinese, but it has also received

---

* W. Grube gives kasaté-, kasaterá,—"schamanieren, jedoch nur von den Todenschamanen gesagt." However, it cannot be compared with Gilak kas'a'—"Schamanentrommel,"—which is almost certainly 'gis or g'isarun of the Tungus and Manchu gisun—"specially made sticks for bringing out sounds from the shaman's drum." Vide infra Ch. XXIV.

* Between two performances some other minor sacrifices are made which are called by I. A. Lopatin *j'azj'i*; those are some food and wine offered to the *fan'a* and other placings. The term itself is merely from *j* ag,—to "burn". These performances are also much more complex amongst the Goldi than amongst other Tungus groups and they seem to have grown much later, as a secondary phenomenon.

** What is called here "old Tungus complex" actually consists of various elements some of which may be compared with those known among other ethnical groups. For instance, "cleaning of bones" and erected coffins were used among the Sien-pi (the first millenium A.D. in Southern regions of Manchuria and Mongolia); the "horse" was used among many groups of the steppe area, from the Scythians in Europe to the Hiun-nu in the Far East; the complex of "utensils put in the coffin" was still more widely practised. However, at the present time no reliable restoration of those complexes is possible.

its particular forms owing to the original Manchu conceptions.

Amongst the Manchus the clan system and "ancestor worship" are so intimately connected that one cannot be understood without another. Yet, the Manchus used the institution of shamans for creation of a special kind of clan officials dealing with the souls of dead clansmen. These are p'oyun sāman, poixun saman (Manchu Sp.), boigon saman (Manchu Writ.), who are not usually the shamans, as they will be later treated, but who may be better regarded as clan officials whose function is that of THE CLAN PRIESTS. I have already shown that tho "shamans" described in the medere večēre kooli bitxe and other official documents are not shamans but "priests". In the Imperial Family, where no factor of poverty might arrest the growth of this institution, but the factor of almost limitless wealth did influence the overgrowth of this institution, there was little by little created a special social group whose function was to carry on sacrifices. Indeed, it was neither typical nor historically justified in the Manchu complex as a whole, but it has grown because of the need to create something original, different from what was known amongst the Chinese, and to support the governmental organization from the point of view of its connexion with the world of spirits.

The Manchu clan population, as shown in my work on social organization, was not numerous, so the clans did not need to have a special social group of priests, and owing to the same condition they could not afford to have such a group.

The souls of dead people used to reach the other world without any special intervention on the part of the shamans, yet the p'oyun saman had very little to do with it. The intervention of the shamans was needed only in the case of a reappearance of the souls in the form of spirits, and in the case when the souls of ancestors were already settled in the other world, but needed some attention on the part of living people.

Every clan (mokun) must have a p'oyun saman. The p'oyun saman is appointed by the clan meeting, the candidate being selected amongst the clansmen familiar with the ritual and traditions of the clan. When the Manchus say saman they understand it as "real shaman"; therefore they always use the compound term p'oyun saman. However, there may be several p'oyun saman, even ten and twelve of them, but only one of them would perform functions of clan priest; he would be called ta saman (Manchu Sp.) [da saman (Manchu Writ.)]. Ta saman is elected at the time of the autumnal sacrifice (bolori amsun, —vide infra Section 74), if the old ta saman should refuse to serve his clan or should have died.

Ritualistic tradition is transmitted by ta saman, for young p'oyun saman learn from the experienced ones and under the direction of ta saman. Usually the ta saman opens and concludes the performance. He is always present in all clan sacrifices and he observes that all clan rites be correctly performed. In this function he is like ţunga mafa who is defined wuxer'i baltabè alif i antxožib'e tagilara n'aļma e.i. "the man who is attending to all business and guests", in social functions such as, for instance, a wedding ceremony. The functions of ta saman are considered a great honour. One may become p'oyun saman by devotion, as it is common with the women, also in the case of sickness. Here I give an instance which is rather typical. In spite of the fact that the last pig was eaten as a sacrifice to the p'oyun vočko, a young boy died. The father decided to become p'oyun saman and for this purpose he had to spend about fifty dollars for buying pigs, etc. since he had no money (he had no work for a long time!), he borrowed money from other people.

Amongst the New-Manchus the functions of ta saman are performed by the čao ejen, i.e. "the chief of the house-family". Amongst the Chinese (Nikan) there is no p'oyun saman. On the other hand in some old Manchu clans the p'oyun saman introduce into themselves spirits and act like the "real shamans" do. Such is, for instance, the case of nara xula (Nara clan), where the p'oyun saman is even assisted by regular assistant-shamans. The women may also become p'oyun saman. The dress of p'oyun saman consists of a skirt, s'iša, a special head-dress, and drum, in the clans where the spirit may be introduced into p'oyun saman, but the costume may be reduced to a small drum about thirty-five centimetres in diameter, as is usually seen in New-Manchu clans. Details regarding shaman's costume will be discussed later. The p'oyun saman never interferes with diseases and other cases where the "real shaman" is acting. The chief and continuous function of the p'oyun saman is to look after the regularity of sacrifices and prayers to the ancestors, and to preserve purity of rites and prayers. With spreading of written language they began to make books of rites and prayers. However, most of these were imitations of the books of the Imperial clan. After the boxer movement many Manchu clans lost their books and owing to the decrease of knowledge of the Manchu language no restoration was undertaken. In my time, I have seen some books (in manuscripts) of prayers, but found none on detailed description of rites. So that at the present time these are transmitted only through the oral tradition. The rites of clans present great variations as well as the placings for spirits (vide supra pp. 142 et seq.). The functions of ta saman and that of p'oyun saman may be reduced to a silent genuflexion and kneeling in front of the placings for spirits, also burning of incense, and the performance may develop into a complex of rites and acts covering days. Some rites will be described later. Naturally the p'oyun saman must keep in secret the number of spirits and rites, for the people belonging to other clans may use their knowledge against the interests of the clan, e.g. by calling spirits and influencing them, "bribing" by sacrifices, etc. This makes of p'oyun saman more than a clan official, but indirectly protector from the clan enemies.

The functions of p'oyun saman naturally extend farther than the simple problem of clan spirits. In fact, they do decide upon the question of division of the clan, for before exogamy can be restricted there must be performed a division of clan spirits, p'oyun vočko. So the usual way of division of the clan is the division of spirits. As shown, when the clan is numerous, division may begin from the division of the placings for spirits, after which there will be a division of spirits and later on a complete division of two clans and permission of intermarriage. This is an interesting case of a social function which must take "religious form" before being effective. Therefore the division of clan may be called merely sorgun fačaxa xala—"the silk placing split clan", i.e. the clan which has already split the spirits. In this case the p'oyun saman have to decide whether the splitting of the clan is possible or not, whether the marriage between two clans is admitted or not.

Another complex problem faced by the *p'oyun saman* is regulation of relations between the clan spirits *p'oyun vočko* and other spirits, particularly shamanistic spirits. We have already seen that sometimes spirits' activity of the shaman may be resented by the clan spirits. Yet, the spirits of outsiders may sometimes mix with the clan spirits when benevolent activity of the clan spirits may be entirely neutralized. It also happens that the spirits of outsiders consume sacrifices given to the clan spirits. Thus the *p'oyun saman* and especially *ta saman* must carefully look after the interests of the clan spirits. In the clans where the clan spirits may introduce themselves into the clansmen the functions of the *p'oyun saman* extend still more for they must help the shaman to bring out the spirit without offending other clan spirits. All these questions being extremely complex, require a great knowledge as to the manifestations of the clan and outside spirits. In case the clan spirits should become very harmful the *p'oyun saman* cannot help and the "real shaman" is invited to help. However, the *p'oyun saman* would take on himself great responsibility when the clansmen invite a "real shaman". This aspect of the clan spirits activity will be discussed later.

74. AUTUMNAL SACRIFICE. The functions of *p'oyun saman*, as a clan priest who serves the interests of his clansmen and clan ancestors and spirits, may be better seen from a description of ceremonies. The principal ceremony of the year is the autumnal sacrifice to the clan spirits. According to the

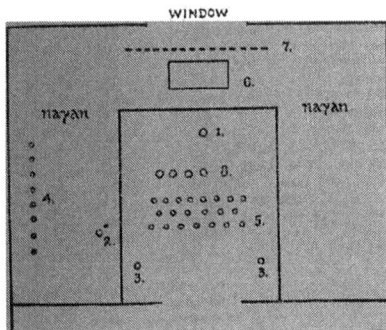

WINDOW

1. *Ta saman*
2. a man beating drum
3. two men with castanets (*čark'i*)
4. small children sitting on the stove bed
5. adult people standing in the middle of the room
6. a table with sacrifice
7. placings for spirits
8. *p'oyun saman* (four)

prescription of Manchu rites, every clan (*mokun*) must carry it out once a year, but if the clan cannot do it, other people may help it, and if such help does not come, the sacrifice may be postponed. However, it ought to be carried out at least once in every three years.

The autumnal sacrifice,—*polor'i amzun* (Manchu Sp.), *bolori amsun* (Manchu Writ) may be organized in the tenth, eleventh or twelfth moon, roughly corresponding to November—January. It must be carried out in the house where the placings for the clan spirits are preserved. The clan organizes but the responsibility for the expenses may be taken by a rich man or a family (*bao*), or even a group of families of the same clan (*mokun*). At this sacrifice the clan spirits (*p'oyun vočko*), i.e. the ancestors, receive thanks from the living clansmen for successful harvest and general welfare of the clan. The sacrifice may be and usually is followed by a special sacrifice to the spirit of heaven, *apka endūr'i*. Several days before the sacrifice one must inform *ta saman* who may give permission for carrying on the sacrifice. If he consents, he promises to attend the meeting. Two days before the sacrifice the organizers send horses with carts to bring the women born in the clan but married to other people. They may be invited together with the members of "my mother's clan". On the next day the women put on *večun*,—the aprons,—and perform the preparative work. Anyhow they must keep themselves far away from the placings. They begin to prepare *čaruya èfen*, i.e. cakes fried in oil, made of millet flour (*fus'ixe wufa*) and in the form of a laurel leaf*. The cakes are made with special chopsticks *èfen čarure mosapka* (short wooden chopsticks) which are kept under the stove and which must not be touched without need. The second day about 4 p.m., the placings for spirits are put on the bed-stove on the left side of the room or on the great *nayan* in front of the door. In front of them a table is put, with a sacrifice which consists of several cups of wine**, according to the number of placings. *Ta saman* and *p'oyun saman* temporarily occupy their places on the bed-stove. When this arrangement is made the *ta saman* and the *p'oyun saman* descend to the ground. If a "real shaman" is present, he must not sit; but he must be standing to show

---

* **Fixixe—ūsiku** (Manchu Writ.) is a kind of small gelatinous millet. In Manchu Sp. it is either fiške or fus'ixe. Here is a description of the method of preparing čaruya èfen:

The ta saman who was also the master of the house, brought about 50 kgs. of flour which was put into a wooden tub. The mistress of the house poured some hot water into it and made the paste. The paste was put on the wooden trays and one after another these were taken by the men, to the kitchen. In the meantime, the women, standing by the kettle with boiling oil, were very skilfully making the paste into small cakes which were immediately put into the kettle with boiling oil. A few minutes later, the cakes were taken out by the men using colanders, and were put to cool in the air. The cakes in a mass were put for a time in front of the great bed-stove (amba nayan) which served as a place for setting the sacrifice. Afterwards the men began to pat the dough made of the half-cooked cakes. Several people took places on the bed-stoves at the small tables set in front of them. A group of men continued their patting of dough, another group rolled the paste to make it thin and flat, and a third group sitting at tables were making small cakes in form of a laurel leaf, about seven centimetres long, three centimetres broad and six or seven mm. thick. There were fourteen people busy with this work.

** The ritual wine is nūra made of millet, which is something like a very light alcoholic drink, a little sour, produced at home. At present this wine may be replaced by the ordinary Chinese wine made of gaolan. This drink was known among the Nuichen (cf. E. Chavannes, op. cit. p. 404).

how inferior he is as compared with the clan spirits. The first p'oɣʉn saman to act is either ta saman, or the youngest one of p'oɣʉn saman for whom this performance may be his first experience. The acting saman puts on a s'iša and special skirt, if it is required by the ritual practised in the clan, takes in his hands the drum, and recites the first prayer. Two or three men beat a small drum and castanets (čark'i), while other p'oɣʉn saman repeat, after the first saman, words of the prayer. At last, ta saman comes out and begins to make special movements with his body and rhythmic sounds with the trinkets of the s'iša. Then he recites a prayer addressed to the spirits of the evening road (jamj'i počko). This prayer is repeated three times and each person present at the performance takes a cup of wine, which marks the end of the performance. In the afternoon of the third day the same performance is repeated and cakes are put on the table as sacrifice to the spirits. Since in the evening a blood sacrifice, accepted only by the spirits of the evening road, must be offered, the placings for the spirits of the day road are put back into the boxes. With nightfall young clansmen bring a pig into the room and put it on the table, which is taken from the bed-stove and put on the ground, in front of the placing for spirits. All the time drumming, the ta saman makes a round about the table. Then the breast of the pig is opened and the heart is pulled out first. Blood is collected to be later used for sausage. The pig is carefully washed, the internal organs are taken out, and the body is dissected, according to a special rite. From section (7) the testes and penis are cut out and thrown away; two sections (8) are reserved for the ta saman; by two long cuttings the back is prepared for separation of the ribs from the vertebral column. The meat with bones is boiled and put together, as if the pig were alive, in front of the placings for spirits on the table for sacrifice together with the cakes. The pig can be only boiled, for the spirits assimilate sacrifice only in the form sugdun ("steam") which corresponds to the "immaterial nature" of spirits.

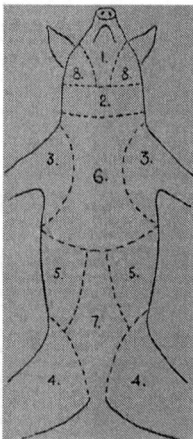

The whole performance must be made only by the light of an oil lamp of a very "primitive" form*. There are some spirits of the night road which cannot come and accept

* The lamp is made, at least now, of iron in the form of a rather low cup about six centimetres high and about fourteen centimetres in diameter, supplied with a short handle; the wick is made of flax and the lamp is half-filled with bean oil. In former time; these lamps were made of stone. I had a chance to excavate some such lamps (in 1916) on the banks of the Amur River. These lamps still known in

sacrifice even with such a light, so when they are called to come, the light is blown out and the clansmen for some time remain in the dark, weeping and calling to their ancestors in the most expressive and pitiful manner. However, this performance observed was rather short after which the rite of x'jenč'i tebumb'e (stick incense put) was performed and the clansmen went to eat the pig.

In some other clans this performance may be very long which depends on the number and power of spirits which have "night roads" (jamj'i počko). In another case observed by me, the performance with the "night road spirits", without any light lasted for several hours. Ta saman was very active and when the lamp was again lighted, he looked exhausted and was covered with perspiration in spite of the fact that the temperature in the room was about 0° C. The people present were crying with very harsh and loud voices and with tears, and beating the ground energetically, with their foreheads. (One could hear the noise of the impact.)

During the performance in the clans which have well developed rituals, as in most of the old (fè) Manchu clans, the highest tension of emotional condition may be attained, in which the extasy of the performers and especially of the ta saman, may turn into what is characteristic of shamanistic performances, i.e. when the spirit enters the shaman's body. Such is the case of the nara clan where the ta saman uses a special head-dress (helmet) with brass birds used only by the amba saman (real shamans). The shaman and musicians* may bring the audience up to a high pitch of excitement, by the changes of rhythms, musical and verbal expressiveness of songs, combined with growing excitement of the shaman himself, who makes special movements with his s'iša for producing rhythmic sounds varying from pianissimo to fortissimo. Such a performance may produce a complete illusion of the reality of spirits present at the rite. The reaction of the people present at the performance becomes much stronger when they begin to feel the presence of the spirits in the person of the saman or when they feel the spirits near,—in their mind there is always some chance that the spirit may enter one of them. Such occurrences, as shown, are possible, naturally in dream.**

As I have pointed out, this performance is not, in all clans, as rich as that described above. In some clans it may be confined to a silent kneeling and sacrifice of a few incense sticks. The women are not allowed to attend this performance, because of their menstrual blood which is not admitted by the spirits. The persons who do not belong to the clan are admitted as a rare exception. Those who are admitted to pray the clan

North-Eastern Asia and America constitute one of the elements of the palaeolithic complex in Europe, and in neolithic stations of Japan.

* The art of these amateur musicians consists in giving rhythm, varied with forte and piano, crescendo and diminuendo. In spite of the simplicity of musical elements to be combined, as a whole this music may become very effective, in so far as the process of excitation of the saman and the audience is concerned. It did not take a very long time for me to learn these methods and to perform in these orchestras. A specimen of this music is given infra, p. 223.

** I have never heard of the nervous fits occurring in such performances and ascribed to the entry of the spirits. There are two reasons for it, namely, the ta saman is supposed to receive into his own body the spirit if it should wish to come and second, such performances are rather rare while the occasions for introducing spirits are quite frequent.

spirits· with the· clansmen are usually considered like brethren, clansmen (*axundo adali*). The day following the night sacrifice the guests and women who are married to the men of other clans are taken back to their homes. In the morning of this day another important performance, —the sacrifice to the *apkai endür'i*,—is carried out. It will·be described in the next chapter.

The prayers amongst different clans, as stated, differ as to their contents and wording. There may be no prayers at all, as is observed amongst the New Manchu clans. Yet, there·is also a certain similarity as to the contents, choice of expressions, etc. which may be seen from two examples given below.

Here I give translation of two prayers which are typical of the clans where the rituals have not been forgotten. Translation has been made from texts written by the *p'cyun saman*. In the first reading of these manuscripts I met with some difficulties especially in using special terms and expressions the meaning of which I established at the spot with the help of the same *saman*. However, even after this, no perfect translation can be given, because of difference between the Manchu complex and that of European groups. I did not wish to go far from the original text and therefore my translation is awkward, without being at the same time a word-for-word translation, as I usually give in this work since such a translation of a text might make it impossible to understand the meaning of the prayers. So I have permitted myself a slight stylistic polishing. Footnotes given below will explain some special expressions and they will show at the same time some ethnographically interesting details.

1. PRAYER ADDRESSED TO THE SPIRITS OF *GUIVARG'JA* CLAN. After an enumeration of the spirits (*vide supra*) there follows:

"All· equal(1) fourteen clan spirits(2) at so-and-so "year, for so-and-so business, so-and-so sacrifice is pre-"pared. Brandy and light millet wine(2) put(32) together, "two bunches of incense put in front(33) I respectfully "offer· and insistently pray: Take the sacrifice purposely "made, deign to accept sacrifice purely(4) and cleanly "prepared. Prolong the grandchildren's life(5) as well "spread roots; make· the grandchildren numerous as well· "grown leaves. If there be headache amongst the senior "and junior clansmen(6) make it light; if there be burning "fit(7) in the forehead wait during the night; if there be "any kind (of spirit)(8) take it away; if there be any "vapour (spirits' activity)(9), disperse it. Don't let "(them) come in contact(10), don't let them approach near "by(11). If the roots widely spread(12), I will offer liberally "counted sacrifice; if the leaves are numerous(13), I will "much pray every one(14). Make the riding horses hand-"some looking(15); make the oxen working in the fields "healthy looking(16). Make them fat by feeding on tender "kind of grass(17); let·them live up to an old age by feed-"ing·on thick and· tall kind of grass(18); look after the "pigs(19) and· make·them plentiful. Don't make us to be· "deceived(20) by the bad; don't· let us to be ruined·by "pernicious things(21). Important matters being ex-"hausted small matters remain. If there is anything which "might produce opposition, push them(22) southwards(23);

"if there is anything which might make spirits angry(24), "throw them(25) northwards (26). Keep away the wars(27) "(carried on) by the. world of the dead people; keep away "the mischief of *bušüku* to the living people; keep the "happy days(28) in order; defend the clan people(29) during "the bad days. Between the seasons give peace(30) to the "clansmen, from the seniors down and from the juniors "up(31). If you provide peace, without missing time I will "offer sacrifice to the spirits, without missing periods I will "pray spirits for happiness and that they give strength."

2. PRAYER ADDRESSED TO THE SPIRITS OF EVENING ROAD OF SAGDA CLAN. After an enumeration of the spirits (*vide supra*) there follows:

"On the first day of the new moon (*month*) the "incense put(32) together; two bunches of incense put in "front(32); brandy and light millet wine(2) in front put "in a row; the great sacrifice prepared and put on the "table,— (all) be given to the spirits. When *endür'i*(33) "descend that they will accept the sacrifice(34); when the "spirits (*roćko*) come down that they will seize the "vapour (of the sacrifice). In the year of sheep there was "small sickness(35) amongst the poor people of the family; "there was infected air(36) amongst the suffering people of "the clan. In the year of sheep in the fear of death the "ignorant(37) men by the mouth(38) producing promised(39). "Ever resurrecting(40) spirits, merciful spirits take "away death-causing sharp sickness(41), keep away long "illness. Slaves(42) are greatly missing their work; chil-"dren much disobey. Important (matter) finished, small "(matter) remains. The principal exhausted, the re-"mainders(43) are left. Give that leaves well numerous "grow, that roots well spread. I pray very much that every "one increases, I pray by giving sacrifice that every one(45) "spreads. Alleviate the head from the fever, (amongst "all) from seniors down(44) from juniors(46) up. Put end "(cease)(47) to the burning fit(7) in the forehead by "stroking on the head and massageing the neck. Make ."(use) ride on handsome looking(15) riding horses; send "for work the working oxen well healthy looking(16). "Make (them) eat thin kind of grass(17) up to their fill; "make (them) eat thick and high kind of grass(18) up to "the old age. Don't leave fall down good hair; don't make "split·the ends of the tail hair(48). Fill up full stable(49); "fill up full yard(50). If there should be amongst our "family people *bušüku*, don't let it approach near by(11); "don't let come into contact(10). Bring out the spirit "Ten "thousand years",(51) turn back the spirit "A thousand "years"(52), which crack the skull and break the vertebral "column. During good days(28) keep the seats(53); during "bad days sit at home(54). The bad take away, the good "make (us) to meet. Look after the home (people), "protect the yard. (animals). Take away bad spirits "(*xutu*), give (us) happiness."

---

1. Wuxer'i-texer'i—"all equal",—is a shamanistic expression; cf. texeren (Manchu Writ.) (Zax.)—the similarity, comparison.

2. "light millet wine"—*nurè*—stronger than beer, a little sour; in the style of well known Chinese rice wine of Chekiang used by the Manchus. It is possible that the expression *ark'i nurè* be should be understood merely as "light millet wine", *ark'i* being here a generic term for all alcoholic drinks. I translate "brandy and" for in some clans the Manchus use both the Chinese wine-brandy and Manchu *nurè*.

3. In the text there is *elen i endu ĵo'iĝun i jukten*. In Manchu

Sp. eꞔen is referred to the people, the house people, also to the clansmen; ꞓolꬶun is referred to the same; endu, cf. enduri and ꬶukten (vide supra. ibid.). In so far as I know, it is impossible to give any other translation but "clan spirits", for actually they are mokun i voꞔko of ordinary speech. All four terms are chiefly used in prayers, and, I guess, chiefly for rhythm.

4. gꞮyun,—"pure",—a shamanistic expression in reference to the sacrifice; cf. gꞮygun (Manchu. Writ.),—the attention.

5. subēya,—the blood vessels: arteries and veins; fig. expression for "life".

6. The expression: amba ꞔi vèsꞮixun, oskun ꞔi fosꞮixun is understood by the Manchus as "senior and junior groups of the clan". However, amba is great and oskun [corr. osokon. (Manchu Writ.)] is "small"; oskunꞔi is interpreted and identified by the Manchus as eskunꬶi (vide SOM pp. 45 et seq.).

7. ꞓerꞮ,—"high fever", corr. ꞵero (Manchus Writ.),—"to become hot red, white face, etc."

8. ꬶergꞮi,—"the kind", in shamanistic language ꬶergꞮi is used instead of "ꬶergꞮi of so- and-so spirits causing sickness".

9. sugdun,—"the vapour", is understood as immaterial activity of spirits, vide supra.

10. and 11. xanēl (still oftener xanꞮꬶe in shamanistic prayers) and ꬶanꞮꬶe in function of "adverbs",—"near by"; ꬶan is nearer than xan.

12. This expression means: "if the generation spreads like roots"; cf. supra full expression.

13. This expression means: "if the generation becomes numerous like leaves".

14. tome,—"every one"; perhaps it is a contracted form of tolome of the previous sentence tolome fulu ꬶꞮiynekꞮi—"I will liberally offer sacrifice", corresponding to tome ambula baꬶkꞮi, cf. infra, note 45.

15. jaꬿsè and jaꬿseya,—"handsome", in reference to the horse when it has even and glossy hair.

16. taꞮmꞮin (cf. tamin, Manchu Writ.),—"erected hair", when the hair is standing up which in oxen is considered as a sign of health.

17. taꞮmen is a kind of short, tender grass, good at certain seasons.

18. suꞮxa is translated by I. Zaxarov as "wormwood"; however, the Manchus use this term in reference to other kinds of high grass.

19. literally wugdun i wuꬶima, i.e. "domesticated animals of sty" (six kinds,—horse, pig, chicken, etc); wugdun,—"half underground construction" also referred to the human dwellings. Such sties are now used only for pigs, therefore I give in translation "pigs".

20. aꞮtere corr. eꞮtere (Manchu Writ.)

21. ganꞮuya, literally "marvelous, unknown, strange, ominous, etc." (cf. I. Zaxarov). However, here it is understood as "unknown, marvelous things which are pernicious".

22. gꞮldame can be also understood "press on, turn to".

23. "South" is a sector where "good" spirits are found.

24. aꞮꬶambꞮi in this sense is referred only to the spirits.

25. vaꞮꬶambꞮi,—"to throw (ritually) a small sacrifice".

26. "North" is a sector where "bad spirits" are located.

27. bulun of the text is translated as "heap, crowd" etc. of the saman's interpretation. However, this cannot be understood so, I suppose. According to I. Zaxarov's translation of bulun it corresponds to bulꞮn-buloy of Tungus (e.g. Bir. Kum.),—"the war carried on by spirits". This may be supported by an analogy of the further sentence buꞵuku de kꞮimun be tèmè, where kimun is "mischief, hostility", etc.

28. SoꬿꞔꞮoxo,—"odd"; the odd days are "happy days".

29. ꞓoiꬶun,—"the house"; i.e. the people who are living in the house, whence "the clan people".

30. èꞮxe taꞮꞮin,—both terms mean "peace", èꞮxe—"peace" in the sense of moral peace and safety from the illness; taꞮꞮin (from Chinese taꞮ pꞮiy 太 平 ,—"a condition of peace") peace in the sense of safety from the spirits.

31. In this case the expression, discussed in the note 6, is differently constructed,—fosꞮixun is referred to amba ꞔi, while vèsꞮixun to oskun ꞔi, which may permit to give a new interpretation as shown in the present translation. This may be

supported by other notes (vide infra—notes 37, 44, 46).

32. Verb tabumbꞮi,—"to Ɪyut"; in the prayers it means "to put as sacrifice, to sacrifice".

33. endurꞮi is used as a "polite" address to the clan spirits, who are not endurꞮi.

34. Ojo,—"the sacrifice", or better to say "the immaterial substance of the sacrifice", the material part of which may be eaten by the people present. Cf. I. Zaxarov, ojo, oꞝo gaimbi. The etymology of ojo in the sense of sacrifice is not clear, but it can be hardly connected with ojo—"the top", etc.

35. jaꬿsꞮi,—"a small sickness", is rather "smell of sickness", "agent of sickness"; the Manchu say sꞮinꞮi ꞓodè nꞮimeku jaꬿsꞮi ꞓꞮi, i.e. "in thine body sickness jaꬿsi is"; cf. I. Zaxarov jaꬿsan—jaꬿšan,—"the sickness".

36. SuksꞮi is nearly sugdun,—"the vapour"; according to the Manchu conception sickness is going on through the air which when "saturated" with sickness becomes suksꞮi.

37. Oskun, cf. osoxon (Manchu Writ.), vide note 6. Here this term used in the sense "small, stupid, ignorant like children". The shamans use it referring to themselves and opposing themselves to the spirits.

38. ayga ꬶanꞮꬶimbꞮi,—"to speak", literally, "to beget with mouth".

39. It is supposed: "the sacrifice", i.e. promised the sacrifice.

40. veꞮxumbꞮi, corr. veꞮꬶumbi (Manchu Writ.).

41. ꬶaskan,—"a short sickness"; cf. gasxan (Manchu Writ.) translated by I. Zaxarov as "epidemic diseases".

42. axasꞮi gurun,—"the kind of slaves"; gurun,—"kind or species, power, nation, etc.".

43. ꬶaꬿsꞮi is a shamanistic expression,—"the charcoal, remainders, what is left", etc. cf. danšan (Manchu Writ.).

44. fosꞮixun, corr. fusixun (Manchu Writ.) cf. also note 31.

45. donꞮime is understood by the Manchus as "every one"; however, cf. note 14, where in an analogous case we have toleme, →tome also understood in the first case "every one". I am not sure as to the translation.

46. esuken (cf. notes 6 and 31) is understood by the Manchus as a derivative from esexen (Manchu Writ.). However, its use is parallel to that of oskun.

47. duꬶxèrꞮi; no exact meaning could be established. It seems to be a form from duxembi, u→uꬶ is possible.

48. This is one of symptoms of bad health of animals.

49. guan [cf. I. Zaxarov, guanse which P. Schmidt (Chinesische Elemente, p. 254) derives from 圈 栓 (guan-sie) of Chinese, —"hölzerne und eiserne Fesseln"] is opposed to the open yard,—xuꬶ. In both of them different kinds of domesticated animals are kept, as it is also amongst the Mongols; guꬶa is a part of the yard (xuꬶ) separated by heavy wooden fences.

50. cf. note 49.

51. "Ten thousand years" is a technical term for a special class of spirits (cf. supra).

52. "A thousand years" is a term, cf. note 51.

53. i.e. "do not disturb yourself".

54. i.e. "come to the home of people to help them".

The prayers here shown are in many respects similar, although the clans are different. The prayers of other clans which I have usually are shorter. It may be noted that they differ in many respects from those adopted by the Imperial clan of ꬶꞮꞝoro. But it may be supposed that the published rituals served in many a case as a pattern for other prayers. In fact, one meets with the repetition of the same phrases and ideas. On the other hand, it is also probable that the pꞮoyun saman of the clan ꬶꞮꞝoro used some old forms which may have been later somewhat "ennobled" by the learned Manchus.

Indeed, the formalization of the ritual has resulted in a loss of the emotional element in the performances of pꞮoyun saman who have become especially formalistic in the performances of the Imperial clan rites, repeated too often for remaining emotionally effective.

It ought to be also pointed out that the complex of ancestral spirits amongst the Manchus has been completed with the spirits of non-clannish origin. Formally they are regarded as clan spirits, but their connexion is not clear nor convincing for the Manchus themselves. Those spirits whose names are not sometimes known are now treated in a formal manner. If an ancestor, whom the living people remember, manifests activity it practically becomes more important than any ancestor of formalized complexes.

The rituals of sacrifice are subject to variations in different clans not only in reference to the length of performance, but also in reference to its character. For illustration I shall now give an instance. In *Moŋgo* clan (*vide* SOM, p. 24) two sacrifices are made: one is carried out in the house and another one is carried out in the "mountains". In the first case the sacrificial animal is a pig and there are two cups of *fus'ixe* with bean oil in which two holes are made for fixing two wicks soaked in bean oil and burning during the ceremony. In the second case, an ox is used. After the first sacrifice the clan people go to the near lying mountains and erect there a temporary shelter of large size with a sloping roof on two sides. The placings for spirits are transported from the house and put as at home. An ox is slaughtered in the same manner as the pig. No drum is used during the performance. For *apkai endûr'i* this clan uses a sheep as some other clans do. Amongst other peculiarities of ritual there may be pointed out, for instance, the use of oil lamps instead of incense during the performance. In *sagda* clan the sacrifice to *apkai endûr'i* consists of a pig. The *šaɣin* (white) *moŋgo* clan has no *p'oɣun saman*, so his functions are performed by the great shaman; the sacrifice consists of a pig at home and a sheep in the "mountains." The *wuri* (gray) *moŋgo* has *p'oɣun samon* and therefore it is regarded as *fè manju*, while the first one as *iči manju*. In *wujala* clan, also in some other clans of the *iči manju* group, there are made *toxoli èfen*,—small flat cakes, about two centimetres in diameter, made of *fus'ike wufa* (cf. supra), but boiled in water; and *taišima èfen*, made of the same flour, but larger in size and covered with some beans*. However, some old Manchu (*fè manju*) clans also have *talšima èfen*. In some Old Manchu clans the badger was used as sacrificial animal, but this practice has been recently given up and the pig is now used. The reason of giving up the badger was relative rarity of this animal greatly destroyed by the ever growing population of Manchuria. The music,—from drum, castanets, and small drum for keeping rhythm —is also subject to variations in some clans being shorter or longer as to the thematic contents. In some clans only a part of the theme is used, or it may be combined with another end. Indeed, the rhythmic variations are not numerous, so that similarity of rhythms is quite common, and combinations are also limited. Here I give for illustration some examples. *Kor'i* clan for day road spirits use the rhythm:

Fuča clan rhythm is confined to the first two bars

* As an ordinary food for every day, taišima èfen are covered with red sugar which is not allowed for sacrificial purposes,—the clan spirits dislike sugar.

Here above I give an example of music performed by the Guwarg'ia clan orchestra during the annual sacrifice to the clan spirits. The shaman produces different pitches of sounds from the drum by beating drum at different sections.

repeated during the first half of the performance and two other bars repeated during the second part of the performance.

The above given instances of variations of sacrificial rites in different clans are sufficient for making up a general idea of the character of rites and their components. It may be pointed out that the complexes are different in clans, but consist of the same elements, e.g. even the rhythmic theme may be cut into its components or exist independently, as we have seen in the case of *kor'i* and *fuča* clans; the same sacrificial animals,—pig, sheep, oxen—are figured in different combinations. The elements may be of different origin, e.g. the five-stone fire-place preserved from prehistoric times; Chinese incense recently borrowed, by the side of the surviving oil lamp required by the rite; splitting of sacrifice: in the house and in the "mountains", etc. What is characteristic of all rites is that they must be fixed, transmitted by tradition (we have seen the state of mental confusion in the clans where rites are partially lost), and regularly performed, for alleviation of the clan consciousness from the fear of dissatisfying ancestors—spirits, which is also only a form of explanatory formulation of the psychomental state characteristic of the Manchus. After the sacrifice one can feel this mood (behaviour) of self-confidence and satisfaction amongst the performers of rites and even all clan members which is typical of similar psychological conditions. Indeed, whether these are home-made "ancestors" or spirits borrowed from other groups or some other form of formulation of the psychomental state in which alleviation comes from the supposed-to-be-effective removal of disturbing factors and from a collective action.

75. SACRIFICES AND PRAYERS TO THE ANCESTORS AMONG THE TUNGUS . We have seen that the spirits of the lower world, — *buni*, who are not spirits which accidentally remain from the dead people, but who are near relatives and ancestors of the people now living,—from time to time make their appearance in this world and constantly preserve their connexion with it. They may cause sickness and may interfere with the hunting (economical activity) of the living people. When the Tungus observe some evidence of the activity of *buni*, sacrifices if possible and requests are made to the *buni* in order to persuade them to leave the people alone and even to help living people in their activities.

The sacrifice consists of some animal freshly killed on hunting or slaughtered for this purpose, the blood and meat of which are given to the spirits-ancestors. Amongst the Reindeer Tungus the animal is reindeer, while amongst the groups which have no reindeer, the place may be taken by the animals hunted, preferentially roe-deer; and amongst those living in contact with other groups, by sheep bought, e.g. from the Mongols, (Buriats), by pigs amongst the groups living in contact with the swine breeders, as, for instance, some Tungus of Manchuria.

The animal is slaughtered according to a different method than that described in the previous sections and works. The blood, collected in a special receptacle, may be given in its fresh form or sausages may be prepared. Amongst the Tungus of Manchuria the blood is given in a special plate of canoe-like form called *moyoro*, also used

for meat and liver, and the latter are given without being cooked at all; however, the blood and meat must not be salted nor generally spiced. The meat must be boiled and never roasted.

Also placing must be made for the ancestors, as shown in Chapter XVI, which are "fed" with the sacrifice; and after the ceremony, the remains of the sacrifice are thrown in a north-western direction. Practically the greatest part of the animal slaughtered is eaten by the people present.

Here I give, as an example, two prayers recorded amongst the Tungus of Manchuria, the Birarčen of *Dunänkän* and *Malakul* clans (vide SONT, Index, p. 407). The translation given is not a free translation and at the same time it is not made word by word. The prayer of this type is called *bunildu*,—"to the dead-people world" and "to pray" is rendered by a derivative from *bunildu*.

1. PRAYER OF *DUNANKAN* CLAN

"Shadow-people, climbing
"On the edges of mountain ridges,
"Trotting along the rugged stony way,
"Soundlessly talking along the shadowy way of ancient grandfathers',
"Looking forward at the dusky way,
"Droning in the nine tombs,—
"There will be no lie.
"Sit down with the legs under yourselves on the side places in the wigwam,
"Listen, elders from the world of dead,
"Carefully listen to your man from the lower world who is speaking and who has made the fat straw placing (for you).
"Do you understand who is speaking?
"Whatever accept from your stupid child (who is) from the place covered with wormwood(1).
"Who is soiling himself in the ashes, mentally weak, stupid like wood, who understands nothing.
"Take nicely the trip which is exposed, take without hostility, accept (it) (through) the fat straw placing;
"Eat the blood, eat the soup, take up the liver.
"I lift up the meat on the sacrificial plate (in the form of a canoe) on which I have put (meat) like a mountain and heaped it like a faggot.
"Give hunting luck (both ill and good).
"Anything ready being taken, your stupid children, believe (me), will be thankful.
"Look for the black dog, trot along the rugged stony way,
"Cover with the net-bag(2) (and)
"Go ahead!
"The stupid people will wonder: so much you expect from their neighbour.
"You will badly meet (shoot) stupid people;
"You will beat stupid people."(3)

2. PRAYER OF *MALAKUL* CLAN

"I will offer sacrifice to the people from the world of dead.
"Who are sitting with their legs under themselves on the side places in the wigwam(4).
"In the twilight of evening
"Fat placing I plaited of straw, put on the black dog led by the rein in hand.
"In the evening twilight I erected a post for spirits.
"Climb on all four along the dry grass covering the tent.
"Sit with the leg under yourselves with the family people,

"Gather together with your children.

"Go back! Don't turn back again

"Trot along the rugged stony way; go along the way of dead people, don't turn back.

"I prayed old grandfathers, I offered sacrifice to the ancient early ancestors."

1. Mentioning of "wormwood" as place, where the living people are found, means that they live in the places left by the previous generations; in Manchuria the old sites of settlements and even that of Tungus camps, when deserted, are often covered with wormwood.

2. Mentioning of "net-bag" is not clear. A net-bag made of thongs is an important accommodation for travelling,—the kettle is put in it. The Tungus do not start their travelling without verifying whether the net-bag with implements is at the due place. However, no net-bag is now figured among the things used for performance of sacrifice, but only during the burial.

3. The meaning of last passage is that neighbours of the man who gives sacrifice may try to intrigue against him, saying that the sacrifice was insufficient.

4. "Side places" in the wigwam are reserved for ordinary guests.

In so far as I could find out, amongst the Tungus of Manchuria prayers are not of the same contents in different groups, clans, and even individuals. Among the Tungus of Transbaikalia I found no prayers of this type, and I was told that the prayers as a ritualistically established method of dealing with the spirits did not exist. In so far as I observed, this sacrifice is given by the shaman during a special performance. Essential differences exist between the Tungus and Manchu prayers. First of all, the Manchu spirits are individually distinct spirits, while amongst the Tungus they are treated *en bloc* which depends on the conception of ancestral spirits. Second, the Manchu prayers are deprived of vivid picture colours, while in Tungus prayers they occupy an important place in the text which depends on the general type of Manchu formalistic attitude in the matter of spirits. Third, the Tungus prayers do not include enumeration of details regarding health of clansmen and others, while the Manchu prayers are free from the request of "hunting luck". Yet in the whole ritual there are also great differences. For instance, the autumnal sacrifice amongst the Manchus is always correlated with the sacrifice to the spirit of heaven, while amongst the Tungus it is not so; the placings for spirits are entirely different,—the ribbons amongst the Manchus, and anthropomorphic placing with a dog amongst the Tungus; the sacrificial process is very short amongst the Tungus and very long amongst the Manchus; the Tungus spirits are all of night-lower road, while those of the Manchus include both evening and day roads. The above shown differences may suffice for showing that there are no essential similarities between the two complexes, except one, namely, both the Tungus and the Manchus have a complex of ancestors. Some elements found in the Birarčen complex as essential ones are not unknown amongst the Manchus, but they are not included in the complex of ancestral ceremonies. Here I have particularly in view the complex of returning Manchu spirits from the *pučeye gwrun* ("dead world") and sent back with the help of straw placings on the dog's back, commonly used amongst the Manchu when *pučeye joyun* (dead road) is held

responsible for the troubles. This element remains common amongst the Birarčen and Manchus, but amongst the Manchus it has a different function.

There is no regular periodical sacrifice amongst the Birarčen, but they offer sacrifice as soon as there are signs of harmful activity of the spirits. However, the sacrifices are not very frequent. A Birarčen family would not offer sacrifice more than once a year, but usually less often than this. The harmful signs are, for instance, the lack of luck in hunting. In this case the Birarčen suppose that the *s'irkul* is proceeding ahead of the hunter and frighten the animals which run away. These may be either remote ancestors or very recently deceased clansmen. A sacrifice may be sufficient for neutralizing harmful activity of the deceased people of the clan. In one case, for instance, a man being a good hunter, could not get any animal during two months, while his associates in hunting were successful; the man made two anthropomorphic placings and a dog, and gave some roe-deer meat; after this he was very successful in hunting.

These spirits may also cause sickness which, according to the Birarčen, happens very rarely. The same method,—a sacrifice,—may help in this case, as well. The prayers used on this occasion are the same as shown above. Amongst the Kumarčen I have observed a bad case of their activity. An old man was affected by them with eczema from which he suffered for several years. Also, they destroyed two horses. He could not say which of the relatives was responsible for all these misfortunes, whether father, mother, or some of brothers. Then he decided to make a sacrifice of a young roe-deer, just killed. The *bâm'i* was about sixty centimetres high made of rotten wood with a flat face on which with charcoal there were marked the eyes, mouth, nose, and eyebrows. The body was covered with twisted dry grass, as well as were arms and the legs with two toes feet. The *bâm'i* with a small stick in its hand was put near a birch-tree, and a fire made near by. The mouth and hands of the *bâm'i* were smeared with the fresh blood, the bowels of the animal were hung upon the arms. Then, boiled meat and some tobacco were put on the burning charcoal and the smoke produced thereby was directed to the placing, for the spirits would easier assimilate a sacrifice in the form of smoke. A short address in which various known relatives were mentioned was followed by singing *gajamei*. When this was over, the old man put his own hat on the *bâm'i's* head and extinguished the fire.* It may be pointed out that the boiled meat was burnt in smoke, which is not allowed amongst the Birarčen. Nearly the same methods are used amongst the Khingan Tungus. However, there may be incidental including of locally borrowed elements. In so far as I know amongst the Reindeer Tungus of Transbaikalia and Manchuria there is no regular sacrifice to the ancestors, as it has been just described. Perhaps it is due to a recent influence of the Orthodox Church which had taken the duty of looking after the dead peoples' souls. However, in the past it was perhaps not so. In fact, the shamans are now dealing with these spirits during their performances (*vide infra*) and the placings for souls (spirits) of dead people are

* The fire was extinguished because the ancestors do not like it. Actually it was done because of the dry weather of the season when the fire may easily spread by burning dry grass and afterwards the forest.

carefully looked after by the family members. It is very likely that from time to time they are "fed" as it is observed amongst the Tungus of Manchuria. Yet, the spirits known under the name of *ojan* are seemingly connected with the spirits produced from the souls of dead people (cf. *supra* pp. 140-141).

Under the Manchu influence and in a direct imitation of the Manchus, the Tungus groups of Manchuria were on their way to introduce the Manchu complex. In my work SONT I have shown that the clan organization amongst them had also been influenced by the Manchus, so that lately there was used a new practice of keeping records of clan members in the form of a written list, the new term for "clan"—*mokun*—and there were regular meetings and election of the chief *mokunda*. Together with the introduction of these new institutions there was also introduced an animal sacrifice. Instead of ribbons and other similar placings used amongst the Manchus, the Birarčen used the list of clan members in front of which the sacrifice was exposed. The sacrifice consisted of pigs, from which it may be supposed that the Tungus considered these spirits (ancestors) as having night road and thus the Manchu complex was significantly modified and adapted to the Tungus conceptions. After the downfall of the Manchu Dynasty in China, the animal sacrifice was given up together with the Manchu clan (*mokun*) organization.

CHAPTER XVIII

SPIRITS MANAGED WITHOUT SHAMAN'S AND

OTHER SPECIALISTS' ASSISTANCE

From the list of spirits given in previous chapters it might be seen that some of them can be managed without assistance on the part of specialists, while some other cannot be dealt with by the persons who do not know special methods, at last those spirits which may be managed only by the shamans. Since in the present part I am dealing with the practical methods of managing spirits I shall follow this distinction as a method of classification of the facts to be presented and analysed. Indeed, there are some objections as to such a distinction of spirits, but I do not see any other and better way to present facts. Although in the last chapter we have been confined to the operations with the soul, still we had to touch upon the participation of specialists, like *p'oyun* and *ta saman*. As a matter of fact, some spirits may be dealt by both the common unskilful people and specialists, so that even in the present chapter we shall include some performances which are participated by the specialists and sometimes even shamans. The managing of the spirits described in this chapter can be done by individuals as well as groups of them, like families and clans.

76. SPIRIT OF HEAVEN   I shall now give my description of methods beginning from those connected with the Spirit of Heaven, the best developed and formalized amongst the Manchus. There is no doubt that this complex has been received by the Tungus from the Manchus, quite recently, and the Manchus of Aigun district were evidently influenced by the example of the Imperial family in which this complex had assumed a special importance, as a distinct character of the Emperor's family. Indeed, the ritual practised in the Imperial Palace by a whole corporation of specialists (*saman*) greatly differs from that used amongst the Manchu villagers of Aigun. While in the first case we have a system artificially cultivated under the conditions of practically unlimited financial means and stimulated by the vanity, natural for the Imperial court, which had nothing in common with the popular practices.

From the point of view of Manchu ethnography, the popular practices are of greater importance as demonstrative of the existing psychomental complex, while the Imperial Ritual ought to be considered only as a potential source for borrowings. To picture Manchu complex with the facts picked up from the written records of this ritual would mean to commit an elementary methodological error,[*] so I shall leave it aside.

As to the question how long ago the practice of sacrifice to the spirit of heaven was established we may reply only with a supposition,—this practice seems to be very old amongst the populations of Manchuria. In fact, in the history of the Nuichen[**] we find several indications as to their "religion", the "religion" practised by the ancestors of the emperors. Although Buddhism was already introduced amongst these populations, still the chief complex comprised the old practice of sacrifices to heaven and earth which was believed to have been originally practised by the Nuichen.[***] It may be thus inferred that the spirit of heaven was an old practice, but whether it was an original practice of the ancestors of the Manchus or it was borrowed in its turn from the Chinese or Turks and Mongols must be left open for discussion. One thing is clear; the practice of sacrifice to the spirit of heaven has not been recently introduced amongst the Manchus. As to the ritual it reveals no contrary evidence.

---

[*] Although a ritual such as that of the Manchu Imperial Family might grow only in the Manchu-Chinese complex, it was not typical of the Manchus. I point out this case as one where we can still see how the error may be committed by an historian and ethnographer when they wish to identify practices of political chiefs, emperors, kings, very rich people worthy of attention of their contemporaries with the "popular practices of the epoch". Unfortunately a great number of pseudo-historic descriptions of past civilizations are based upon the facts of this class. What documental value they may have is evident.

[**] Cf. "Histoire de l'Empire de Kin ou Empire d' or", translated from Manchu Aisin gurun i suduri bitxe, by Ch. de Harlez, Louvain, 1887.

[***] Ibid, p. 126. As to the state of Nuichen vide infra.

APKA ENDUR'I (*vide supra*). The ritual described below forms one of the parts of the *Bolor'i amzun*, treated in the previous chapter, and it is performed on the fourth day of the sacrifice, i.e. when the sacrifice to the clan spirits is over. It does not attract as many people as the sacrifice

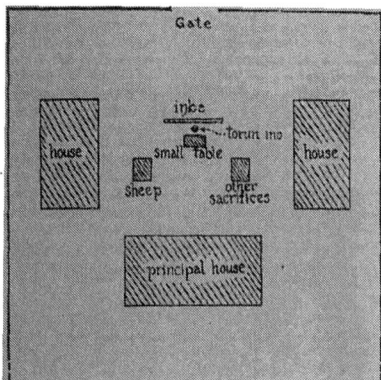

to the ancestors and many guest-clansmen leave the host, in whose house the sacrifice is organized, on the morning of the fourth day, the day of sacrifice to *apkaī endūr'ī*. Relative shortness of the ritual and relative poverty of prayers are also indicative of a secondary importance of this complex.

The whole ceremony is carried out in the yard, which in the climatic conditions of Manchuria cannot be regarded at all as a circumstance favourable for growth of the complex. In fact, the ceremony ought to be carried sometimes in the temperature below 30°C., while the spring sacrifice at the present time is practically out of practice.

In front of *iyb'e* (*vide* SOM, fig. pp. 94, 95, also above figure) a special fire-place is made. It consists of five stones of pyramidal form weighing each about from ten to fifteen kilograms or even more.* A big kettle is put on it for cooking sacrificial meat. Amongst the *fè manju* prior to the ritual the pig must be prepared by burning the bristles, which is called *f'iča'alaya jali*, i.e. "burnt meat", while amongst *āči manju* the bristles are taken off by softening of the skin with boiling water. The pig is slaughtered and prepared as it has been described in the previous chapter (*vide supra* p. 220). When the pig is cooked small pieces of meat are taken from all of the

sections of the dissected animal, and fixed on the top of the post (*toydo mo*),* always erected in the middle of *iyb'e*. For this rite five clansmen are selected (*sun'ja xala n'aīma*) who lower the post while the *ta saman* attaches the sacrifice. No drum, no music and no singing are used during the performance. The *ta saman* recites a prayer, in a very fast tempo, and puts some stick incense in front of the post. After having eaten there is performed rite of collecting all bones and water used for cleaning vessels,— *xala mokun k'irayi moro ofoyo muke tučimbum'e*,—"clan bone cups washed water make to come out." The three ribs taken and broken with a hammer or with an axe and all bones and water are thrown in front of the *iyb'e*.** The dogs are waiting for this moment,—they rush immediately to finish bones and water, while the men hasten to enter the warmed houses.

Amongst some clans instead of a pig there may be sacrificed a sheep the ritual being somewhat different. The sacrificial animal is brought and put on the ground in front of the post (*torun mo*), so that the forelegs are crossed on the head and bound together, the hind legs are held by the clansmen. The breast is opened with a knife and the heart is stopped by pressing the aorta with a hand introduced through the aperture in the breast. The lower fractions of the legs are cut off and the body is dissected in the same way as it has been described in the case of pig preparation. The breast part (*tungan bokton*, or *čejen*) is reserved as sacrifice and put in front of the *iyb'e*.*** A vertebra with a bunch of straw is smeared with the fresh blood of the sheep then attached to the top of *torun mo* which is re-erected. The sections of the sacrificial animal are cooked in the kettle also put on the five-stone fire-place. When they are boiled small pieces are cut off from all sections of the animal and put on the small table in front of *iyb'e*, together with two small cups of wine and a big cup with millet. All sections of the animal are put together as if the animal were alive and exposed on a table standing in the centre of the circle formed by the clansmen sitting on the ground and using no tables, which are not allowed to be used in this ritual feast, for, as the Manchus say, tables were not originally used by them and are an innovation. Neither drum nor music, nor singing is used during the ceremony. The *ta saman* briefly recites a prayer, the clansmen kneel in front of the *iyb'e* and beat the ground with their foreheads. The women are not allowed to be present at this sacrifice.

Insead of a pig or a sheep, an ox may be also sacrificed. Indeed, the preparation of an ox for sacrifice and its eating requires more time and people, but the rites do not very much differ from that with the pig or sheep.****

---

* The five stones of fire-place is an interesting fact for during the excavation made by us on the banks of the Amur River in 1915 in many dwelling sites there were found five stones exactly in the centre of dwellings and with evident signs of fire effect. Near the stones there were usually found broken earthware, ashes, charcoal. The exact dating of dwellings, usually pit-dwellings of under-ground type, sometimes presented certain difficulties. However, all of them may be connected with the dwellings which are mentioned in the Chinese chronicles as typical of early population of Manchuria. It may be also noted that amongst the *iči manju* the five stone fire-place is made for sacrifice to *mafa* (*vide infra* p. 232).

* In former days the Manchus used to have only torun (cf. Tungus turu, toro; vide infra) or toydo mo (toydo,—"straight, erected"), as it is widely used amongst the Tungus and some Mongol groups. The iyb'e is an innovation and according to the Manchus it is erected for making "very nice" and it is borrowed from the Chinese.

** The same performance can be carried out without any participation of p'oyun saman and ta saman.

*** The breast rection of a sheep in the Mongol complex is an important element in the ritualistic performances. It is also a part of honour. Together with the animal it seems to be an element of a non-Manchu origin.

**** The ox sacrifice was more practised in former days than at the present time. The chief cause of change in practice is probably "poverty factor" and numerical decrease of clans. I had no chance

During the days of sacrifice to the ancestors and clan spirits, as well as the day of the sacrifice to *apkaĭ endŭr'i* also a few days after the last sacrifice the house is tabooed for the people who do not belong to the clan. It is especially strict in regard to people who belong to the "families" where either a death, or child delivery, or illness due to a spirit have recently occurred. For keeping away such "dirty people",—the clan spirits and *apkaĭ endŭr'i* do not like "dirt,"—the Manchus hang up on the side of the gate a piece of wood with a bunch of straw,—the sign of taboo,—*targa*.

The sacrifice to *apkaĭ endŭr'i* is also organized on other various occasions, e.g. for declaration to this spirit about important events such as election of a new shaman which will be later discussed, and separation of the clans. In dependence upon the purpose of sacrifice the text of the prayer is changed.

———

The complex of *apkaĭ endŭr'i*, as I have shown (*vide supra* p. 124) has made its intrusion into the complex of the Tungus of Manchuria amongst whom it is better represented in the groups which are influenced by the Manchus, so it is better represented amongst the groups living near to the Manchus, in villages, and very little known amongst the groups living in the mountains.

Amongst the Tungus of Manchuria it is known under the name of *apka endŭr'i* (or *andur*) which is a direct borrowing from the Manchus, yet it is also known under the name of *julask'i endur'i*, and simply *julask'i*, *i.e.* "southwards". As shown this spirit may consist of two elements: a male and a female, which have their envoys, so that the spirit may be considered as a complex. In some respects this spirit is comparable to the Manchu *apkaĭ endŭr'i*. Amongst the Tungus the sacrifice is made on different but very important occasions, e.g. the separation of the unit into two new exogamic units,—clans; announcement of a new shaman; rarely for regulation of the natural phenomena, such as weather, droughts, etc. when human interests are affected; at last, for helping against other spirits when the latter cannot be fought by men. In some respects this complex spirit, as shown, is a new substitute for *buya*, which cannot be influenced, in the Tungus mind, by the sacrifice.

Amongst the Birarčen a post five or six metres long is fixed into the ground. To the top of the post, after the sacrifice a vertebra of the animal sacrificed and a bunch of straw are attached. Two anthropomorphic wooden placings, without arms but with two legs, are put on the ground, near the post; these are placings for envoys* and after the sacrifice they are thrown away in a southern direction. Sacrificial animals may be either a pig, or a reindeer (Cervus Elaphus); no other animal can be used.** Sacrifice is not often practised,—no more than once a year, and usually rarer, especially when the whole clan is involved into the action. The sacrifice may be given by an individual when he imagines that this spirit may help him

to observe it myself, but the description given by the Manchus reveals no new elements in the complex.
  * These placings are called omute, literally "hook", but the etymology is not certain.
  ** Amongst the Kumarčen the roe-deer can also be used. The same is true of the Khingan Tungus.

and in this case the question is solved individually; the sacrifice may be given by the clan on great occasions when a new shaman is produced, when the whole clan is affected by some misfortune; at last, it may be given by a group of families of different clans, e.g. those living together in a village. The chief difficulty consists in the requirement of reciting a prayer which must be known, naturally, by heart, and in preserving for a while the sacrificial animal,—the pigs are brought from the other people,—the Manchus and Chinese, for the reindeer now being rare is not always available.

The prayer is recited by a man, while two others fix the vertebra and straw and put placings to the post. The prayers are subject to some variation which is evident from the examples given below.

Here I give two examples of prayers, called *buačin*, from which it is evident what is the character of spirits and for what purpose they receive sacrifice. These prayers may be addressed on the occasion of a sacrifice made by the individuals or families, or clans. If there should be some concrete aim of sacrifice, it would be indicated in the prayer.

1. PRAYER (*buačin*) ADDRESSED TO JULASK'I; the Birarčen, Malakul clan.

"Male Southern Enduri who seated himself at the "gate, Father who seated himself at the door, Mother who "seated herself at the corner (of the house), listen to this. "Meeting is sure, there is no aimlessness (for coming): a "sacrificial pig, boar-pig, is to be given to you, the post "inclined (for sacrifice), the ritual sacrifice pushed forward "with straight eyes (honestly). Speaking reasonlessly, "insisting honestly do not neglect to listen to one who is "below you praying, one who is bowing in front of you. To all this listen."

2. PRAYER (*buačin*) ADDRESSED TO JULASK'I; the Birarčen, Dunänkän clan.[6]

"An orphan is babbling nonsense, but stretch your "ears for anything which he is saying. Anduri's envoy "protecting gate and warming house[1], South-Father from "Southern Region who protects from misfortune[2] and "defends from bad[3], Anduri-Father listen. To-day sick-"ness affects family people. When passing along defend "from sickness your people from the Lower World. One "who is worshipping in front of you, one who is praying in "front of you has burnt pure incense. Purify with hot "spring water, protect against misfortune. Cure the "people of the family of that who is bowing in front of you. "Father, send off children's diseases[4] from the one who "is praying. Mother, defend from bad the one who is "praying. Wash with cold spring water, raise from the "pillow (head of the sick people), improve from day to "day, make freely to breathe (taking) from the bed. Cure "old diseases quickly, clean intestines. Restore eight "generations[5]. So at midnight I have in good heart and "with good words everything prayed."

  1. It means "keeping alive".
  2. Sickness in man and animals, lack of hunting luck, etc.
  3. "Bad" which is produced by the spirits.
  4. It is meant here smallpox, chicken-pox, measles etc.
  5. "Eight generations" means "all people of the clan".
  6. In this translation I have attempted to keep as near as possible to the text.

The first prayer is an invitation of the spirit for sacrifice. It is followed by exposition of needs and requests which do not differ from those addressed to the clan spirits. The second prayer is a special prayer containing exposition of needs and requests addressed to *juɫask'i*.

3. PRAYER (*bnačin*) ADDRESSED TO JUɫASK'I; the Birarčen, Maakagir clan.

A. [A sacrifice is given]

"Southern God(1) who is moving and ever thinking, I "bring forward a blood sacrifice. I erect two posts and "bring forward a blood sacrifice. Take up the blood "sausages; drink blood; eat soup. Listen to one who is "reciting (his) prayer, who is bringing forward blood "sacrifice, and who is erecting posts to the Southern "Enduri(2). Listen carefully to your kneeling man from "the lower world. As I am worshipping you they (people) "are praying from the time when the ancient ancestors "lived, from the very beginning and ending with this "(time). Make clean from spirits the wigwam in taiga "and house here (in the village), constantly love, and think "of everything outside and inside(3). Protect from mis-"fortune, do not allow infections to enter, and so on to the "end"(4).

B. [Continuation; a request to give hunting luck]

"Push forward, send good luck. Add some more "benefit to one who is running along the edges of mountain "ridges. Send forward in front, do not protect any-"thing(5); on the top of mountains—the male roe-deer, in "the small passes—the female roe-deer, on the northern "slopes of the mountains—the Cervus Elaphus, on the "rocks bordering rivers—the roe-deer fawns. In this way "send. That the other people do not see, do not send "them anything(6). Wherever I should go do not protect "anything. Carefully listen: me, an orphan, I pray [??] "go to the place *jakso*, and remain in the place *birg'e*(7). "When in the heights(8), listen and continue as usual. God "has gone".

1. Buya of the text I translate as God. However, "Southern buya" is a combination of an old idea and of a new idea.
2. Here instead of usual andur'i, the Manchu term enduri is used. The reason is that a prayer to this spirit is a very important matter, so that to use a Manchu term is "good"; the Manchus are a source of ritualistic innovations.
3. "Outside and inside" there are meant two groups of diseases.
4. "On to the end", i.e. "for ever".
5. This spirit may send animals if he does not protect them; if he protects them, the hunter cannot kill them.
6. In the Tungus complex this request is somewhat unusual. In fact, the idea is to eliminate other Tungus-competitors which is in conflict with the Tungus social ideas and their idea about regulation of hunting. The man from whom I have recorded this prayer was not a man of average Tungus behaviour. Some of his acts were decidedly disapproved by other Tungus.
7. jakso, jaso, joso is a special place where the spirits are living; birg'e is a place where buya remains. No details could be found. Seemingly these terms are not of Tungus origin.

77. CLAN SPIRITS The methods of influencing these spirits are: a. their localization in the placings especially made; b. regular sacrifices with a more or less stabilized ritual and prayers; c. various methods for comforting spirits.

Every Tungus of Manchuria, except the Reindeer Tungus, has to deal with the clan spirits, which as shown

are not particularly benevolent nor malevolent so long as they are properly managed. For being so they must have permanent placings which have already been described. The placings are taken out when the Tungus believe the spirits of being malevolent or when they want to receive from them some assistance, e.g. in going through family difficulties, in carrying on hunting, and the like.

Not every family of a clan must have placings for clan spirits. As shown they are made when the malevolent activity of the spirits is suspected, or to prevent it, so that some families may have no placings at all. The care of spirits in the form of sacrifices and prayers is usually taken by the oldest representatives of the branch of a clan, but when the placings are handed over to junior members the latter take care and responsibility of managing them. In this way functions of clan-prayer are transmitted to juniors.

The possessing of placings for clan spirits presents some troubles too, for there must be reserved a special horse—*oygun*—for carrying placings (cf. *supra*) and yet the presence of placings may be also responsible for frequent visits of the spirits. As a matter of fact, many Tungus prefer to have no placings at all, and those of them, who have placings, are always busy with the problem of managing spirits.

The rituals of sacrifice differ in clans and in spirits, as well as in spirits' roads, even as practised by individuals, which depends on the particular cases. From time to time, usually not less than once a year, the spirits receive their sacrifice and are formally offered prayers. For this purpose special placings may be made of wood, usually of somewhat larger size, for the *malu burkan* and others, as it has been shown in Chapter XVI. Permanent placings are taken out from boxes or covers, hung up and the ritual arranged. However, in all cases some "food" or incense must be given, and there must be expressed in words the purpose and qualification of the sacrifice. Usually the Birarčen and Kumarčen use one of the wild animals killed in hunting, but there are no regulations as to the kind of sacrificial animal.

The *malu burkan* always requires fresh blood, with which the placings, purposely made, are smeared. The placings are located as has been shown (cf. *supra*) by pairs of males and females. For *jiači burkan* placings are located in a different manner; in the middle there are put the sun, the moon and two venuses on the left eight *an'akan* and on the right nine *an'akan*. The contents of prayers depend on the immediate impulse of making sacrifice, and more or less stabilized text of prayer. As to the first, there may be sickness of clansmen, or members of the family carrying placings, lack of "hunting luck", economic depres-standing, selection and establishment of an *oygun* and the sion due to various causes which remain beyond the under-like.

The following specimen is a short prayer (*bnačin*) used in the Malakul clan of Birarčen, when a new *oygun* is given.

"I attach a horse-messenger (for so-and-so spirit), I "bring forth the colour (i.e. the horse). I fasten the bridle "to the post erected for the spirit (of so-and-so colour). I "was thinking to tell the spirit of the hair (i.e. the horse), "to accept the hair which I have brought. I now obligingly "give a messenger-horse to be accepted, of a pure colour, "for riding on the long tail, for going on the mane, for "sitting like birds on the ribbons attached to the horse, for "being accepted, for matching the colour. Having smoked "with incense, I sacrifice (the horse) to you (so-and-so spirit)."

Amongst the Kumarčen and Khingan Tungus the managing of clan spirits in main lines does not differ from that observed amongst the Birarčen. There are minor variations which are due to the fact that the Birarčen keep themselves busier than other groups with the clan *burkan*, while amongst the Kumarčen the ancestors are a more harmful group, and amongst the Khingan Tungus more attention is attracted by the spirits like *Bainača, Tudukan* and others which are not clan spirits. Yet, among the Reindeer Tungus of Manchuria with the loss of the old complex and its partial substitution with that of Christianity, the clan spirits,—*malu*,—do not now receive any special attention. In so far as I could gather from inquiring of old people, the rites and prayer were different as compared with those of the Tungus of Manchuria. The practices amongst the Reindeer Tungus of Transbaikalia are again different. The chief difference consists in the fact that the care of spirits belonging to the clan is not that of the common people, but that of the shamans. The common people when suspecting a malevolent activity of the clan spirits, especially those of ancestral type, usually make a small sacrifice without any complex rites nor prayers. The placings consisting chiefly of *bada* are lifted and shaken, a few words are uttered expressing the cause of the attention to them, and the blood is again and again smeared. The shaking of placings is a very typical method which I do not know amongst other groups.

Amongst the Tungus of Manchuria the spirits of the wife's clan are not, at least in some cases, of lesser importance than that of the clan. We have already seen that these spirits may be extremely harmful both for the women, who bring them to the foreign clan, and for the outsiders as well, who may be easily affected by them through the women, e.g. in the case of contact with the things *ak'ipču*. In most cases eye troubles are ascribed to these spirits; yet they may mix up with other spirits and in this way produce great confusion of all relations between the spirits and men. This imposes, first of all, a very good knowledge of the spirits' character and methods of managing peculiar to the clans. The precautions taken in dealing with the women, who do not belong to the family, in many a case may be justified by the fact of common infectious diseases.* Indeed, in many a case these spirits cannot be held responsible but the attention is turned to them. In so far as psychic stability of women is concerned these spirits are of special importance for in many cases a prayer and sacrifice may bring an essential alleviation to the women suffering from an instability. As to the art of managing them, it is the husband's duty. Regularly or according to the needs he would perform sacrifices and prayers, and take some special measures, as shown in the case of the man who burned the eyes of the placing, with a hot iron which was done because these spirits were not of his own clan. We have seen that the placings are made almost exclusively in the cases when there is suspicion as to

* Trachoma and gonorrhoea of eyes may be supposed to be of common occurrence amongst the Tungus who are in contact with other groups. Etiology of some cases of eye trouble ascribed to najil burkan čolpon ("Venus") manifestations are undoubtedly of this order.

the spirits' activity. Signs of activity are, for instance, sickness of the wife, and children, "nervousness" of the wife, nostalgia, irritability, or merely uneasiness. As soon as the spirits have their placing they may be satisfied with sacrifice and prayer, and the psychic condition of the woman may improve. When the sickness is over and the woman is not liable to troubles, then the placing may remain untouched for a long time. At last, they may be dismissed altogether by sending them down the river with the current. The reason why the Tungus practise this is that the presence of placings itself is not reassuring at all, the spirits are attracted by the placings and when attracted they may harm the people. So the issue of a complete dismissal of spirits is common, especially when the woman is getting old, i.e. when the occurrence of "psychic" instability, after menopause, is rarer than during the sexually active period.

In the performance of sacrifice the Tungus of Manchuria use the same placings which are handed down by the woman. Naturally since they are, during the sacrifice, smeared with blood, and are not particularly protected against dust, smoke and moisture, they become "old," i.e. dirty and covered with grease, dried blood, smoke and dust. This is especially true when the placings are transmitted from the woman to her daughter and later to the grand-daughters.

Address-prayers to the *najil burkan* are subject to great variations. They may be confined to a short mentioning of the kind of sacrifice and name of the *burkan*, or may attain the dimensions of a prayer as shown in the example here given.

Here is a prayer addressed to the spirits of *Čakčir* clan by a man of clan *Maakagir* (*mǎkagir*).

"I pray *najil burkan*. Foreign[1] people, you have "come to foreigners. Čakčir people have come to the "Maakagir people and I worship you as I worship God. "Worshipping you, I periodically give sacrifice (and "prayers). Married couple *mayi*, married couple *mǒma*, "married couple *koltonde*, married couple *čičul*, married "couple *doldi*, I pray all of you together. Having made a "birch-bark box for spirits, I am worshipping every month. "Look after[2] the side-places of yours.[3] *Najil burkan* "continue to be as usual towards one who is kneeling (and "worshipping). Since you have come to the foreigners, "continue to improve (everything). I knew some of your "children, and living people. Me, fool and stupid one, I "speak being mixed with grass and wood. Stupid like "wood (branches of a tree) I ask beloved (spirits) to main-"tain the peace, to clean, to protect from : misfortune, "oppose infectious maladies. Listen as I am going to ask. "Continue as before. We put forward everything which "is prepared. We gently approach what is prepared. So, "listen, understand as I am going to ask. I am constantly "asking to love (us?), to go to[4] and to remain in law. "[Then the spirit has gone]."

1. Angnaki of the text is referred to the people of other clans with whom marriage is not prohibited. Cf. SONT.
2. More exactly: "do not leave to be occupied by other spirits".
3. The side place in the wigwam is occupied by the wife and her husband.
4. Jaksor is a special place where the spirits remain. Cf. supra p. 229, Note 7.

Among the Reindeer Tungus of Transbaikalia and Manchuria I have found no such a complex system of managing the wife's clan spirits. As shown, the complex *naȷ̌il burkan* is not perhaps of a purely Tungus origin, but it might be borrowed by the Birarčen from the Dahurs. In fact, the Kumarčen in reference to the same complex of spirits use another term,—*kaɣan*,—as it seems to be also true of the Reindeer Tungus of Transbaikalia who use *mok'it*. In so far as I know, the rites and prayers are much less complex amongst the Reindeer Tungus than amongst the Birarčen.

78. **VARIOUS SPIRITS** Spirits the managing of which does not require specialists amongst the Tungus of Manchuria are various spirits of taiga, e.g. *balnača, aȷelga, kadar,* etc. If these spirits are suspected to be malevolently active, a sacrifice and a short admonition are advisable. The same is sometimes done in view of preventing them from doing harm to the people. Indeed, the people who are inclined to see the spirits' activity would see it more frequently than other people. There are some formulae for calling spirits to enter the placing before giving the sacrifice; there are also some forms for specification of the sacrifice and purpose on which it is given. However, apart from a few conventional phrases these prayers-addresses usually are improvisations which may sometimes go further than a few words uttered by the man giving sacrifice.

BAINAČA The addresses to *baȷnača* are common amongst the Tungus of Manchuria and to *maɣin* amongst the Tungus of Transbaikalia. They are made before the hunting, during the hunting, when there is no "luck", and after the hunting, when there is some spoil. Yet, they may be made during the migrations when the permanent placings are met with,—trees with carved faces of a male and of a female, sometimes (amongst the Khingan Tungus) made on the important mountain passes and important places for hunting. The address or some mark of attention must be produced by the travellers.

The address has no fixed form and usually contains only a short request to send animals or protect during travelling. If there is some sacrifice to be given, it must be specified, too. However, since every one must do it, and since not every one possesses the power of imagination in order to make an improvization and knows formulae, the address may be confined to a silent kneeling, or even a profound bow, and silent presentation of a sacrifice, for the Tungus usually try to behave in a friendly way with the spirit.

Amongst the Tungus of Khingan group the complex was greatly influenced by the Mongols. The placings for *baȷnača* are found in the passes* and as sacrifice there are given hairs from the mane and tail of horses, branches of trees, ribbons, etc. which are usually found on the Mongol *obon*. Yet, there may be also accumulated some stones. In case of great need of assistance of this spirit there can be made a regular sacrifice. The sacrificial animal is the

sheep, which is once more indicative as to the Mongol influence, for the sheep must be bought from the Mongols.

Amongst the Birarčen, I have found no placings for *baȷnača* in the passes. Placings are made on the trees. The sacrifice for receiving luck (*maɣin*) in hunting,—is made by the oldest man of the hunting association and consists of some boiled millet in small portions burnt in the fire put near the tree. It may be noted that the fact of sacrifice of millet is an indication of a strong alien influence on the complex. As shown, this spirit may also bring sickness. In this case, a special placing would be made,—a piece of cloth with some applications,—which is preserved and regularly "fed" together with the other *burkan.*

Amongst the Reindeer Tungus of Transbaikalia the sacrifice consisting of hunting animals is given to various spirits of the taiga for receiving "luck." The spirits, as shown, may be called "luck" (*maɣin, maɣun,* etc.) as it is also amongst the Reindeer Tungus of Manchuria. There are many *maɣun.* Together with these spirits there may be classed the spirits called amongst the Tungus of Transbaikalia *daɣačan* which are "masters" of various kinds of animals. Therefore these Tungus when giving sacrifice as expression of thanks for successful hunting or as a prayer to give (send) animals address themselves to the particular spirits of the animal species or locality. In so far as I know, there is no fixed address.*

In all cases the Tungus idea is that the spirit would be benevolent and willing to send the animals to be killed, or it would protect the people in travelling and will not do any harm to them, if it receives some mark of attention or food. No threatening is used against this spirit.

———

Among the Manchus the group of spirits which may be managed without assistance of specialists is rather numerous. In this group we may include *ȷun fuč'k'i, takto mafa, ȷaȷan mafa, apka endūr'i (wuȷin endūr'i)* and others to which a sacrifice may be given by any one. The need of managing these spirits is so common that no specialists can be called. The sacrifice usually is very small,—it would consist of some fruits, cakes, etc.,—and prayers are very short.

The spring sacrifice,—*n'iɳg'ar'i amzun,*—in April-May must be included in the same group of performances. The reason is that this sacrifice amongst the Manchus has gradually lost its former importance, so it is usually carried out without great formality. However, even in recent time the spring sacrifice was quite an important event, and consisted of a sacrifice to the ancestors and clan spirits, as we have seen in the autumn sacrifice, and a special sacrifice to the spirit of Heaven—*apka endūr'i.* At the present time the sacrifice to the clan spirits is made only in the case when there would be sickness amongst the clansmen, while in an ordinary case, it would consist of a short performance in the fields, at the moment of the first ploughing.

———

* Such placings of permanent character are found e.g. in the Khingan passes reached from the valley of the rivers Tura, Nuktukali and Murel, (all tributaries of the Gan River) and Sivaȷa (tributary of the Derbul River). The isolated placings, made on various occasions and individually, are frequently found in the places of hunting. However, no sacrifice is left.

* It may be noted that these Tungus are extremely sceptical about the Buriat practice of erecting obon in the mountain passes. Looking at them the Tungus laugh at the naïvety of the Buriats who believe that the spirits may be satisfied with silk ribbons and similar sacrifices. Such a negative attitude may be understood if we remember rather hostile relations between these Tungus and Buriats who are pushing away the Tungus from their territory.

The sacrifice is addressed to *wužin endür'i*, which is a manifestation of *apkai endür'i*. The Manchus put on a small table some steamed bread, of Chinese type (*mantóu*), eggs and burning incense and the following words are pronounced: *ère an'a apka endür'i kèè'ida wužin jaka fulofulo labdu sän bon'jibu*—"This year Heaven spirit favour field things plenty much good make grow." Then they make several bows touching the earth with the forehead.* Together with this spirit another spirit of the same type ought to be mentioned, namely *nai dalaxa endür'i* (*vide supra* p. 131) which receives in the fields a sacrifice consisting of bread and incense, and which belongs to the same complex of *apka endur'i*.

Takto mafa and *jun fuĕk'i* which are important spirits quite often receive sacrifices in Manchu manner, but without any special performances, on New year's Day, on the fifth day of the sixth lunar month and the fifteenth day of the eighth lunar month. The great sacrifice consists of fifteen rolls of bread (*mantóu*) and five kinds (*sun'ja jerg'i xaĕin*) of "fruit" (*tub'ixe jerg'i jaka*), i.e. red sugar, nuts, apples, dates (*ziphus joujoubi*) and small Chinese apples. The same sacrifice is given by the bride after the marriage ceremony. When the spirit affects the children in the form of diseases it receives a sacrifice consisting of a cock or a hen. No doubt there are some more or less fixed forms of prayers, but usually the Manchus confine themselves to a silent kneeling, and touching of the ground with their foreheads. The prayer consists of an indication of the spirit, specification of the sacrifice and immediate reason for offering the sacrifice. It may be performed by any one, but for getting a better effect the *p'oɣṇ saman* may be asked to perform it. The complex cases of diseases are treated by the mafa and shamans which will be discussed later.

Jafan mafa (also *java mava*) is very often responsible for the troubles in the family, e.g. sickness, nervousness, etc. So it should receive sacrifice of the same objects and on the same days as *takto mafa* and *jun fuĕk'i*. Such occurrences are common when the spirit is deceived by the people and does not receive sacrifice on the days established. Usually these are shamans who must help in finding out the cause but there is also a method of finding it without the shaman's intervention. The method is known as *šoforo g'idamb'e*, which ought to be understood as "pushing out of a sickness." *Šoforo* is "sickness," "contagiousness" compared with the claws or feet of an animal which penetrate into the flesh (or wound) and cannot be easily pulled out. It is always performed by the women. They take a wooden oval plate (forty or fifty centimetres long) called *funske* and fill it up with a kind of millet. Uttering some words, the woman pours a cup of millet, fills it up to the edges and covers it with a piece of silk. The cup is passed around the sick person during about twenty minutes

* Formerly, the sacrifice was performed by the district chief who according to the calendar on a certain day used to come out into the fields and open, with ploughing, the beginning of field work. This corresponded to the well known ceremony of ploughing formerly performed by the Manchu emperors in the temple of agriculture at Peking. At the present time the custom is given up. However, this ceremony as well as the whole complex of spring sacrifice was not considered by the Manchus as an important event. This ceremony as practised by emperors was of very old Chinese origin. It is mentioned by Confucius and it attained great importance during the Sung Dynasty.

and then the cover is removed to see if the millet has diminished or not. If the millet has diminished to half of the quantity taken, it is indicative of the spirit's presence, —the *jafa mafa* has eaten it. In case of positive answer, they make a sacrifice consisting of a pig prepared according to a rite as it has already been described. There are various methods for finding out whether there was a malevolent activity of the spirits *xutu* or not. This may be found by the method of exception and verified, for instance, by the experiment with water and chopsticks carried out at night-time. They take a cup with some water and put it on the bed-stove in the corner of the house. Then three chopsticks are carefully cleaned and put into the cup. If they keep erect it means that the *xutu* is responsible for the trouble.* When the cause of trouble is found special steps may be taken in order to prevent the spirit from making trouble. These methods are sacrifice, prayer, protection with the skin of a hedge-hog, bear's paw, etc. However, when the activity of *xutu* is discovered the shaman's assistance is necessary for neutralizing it. The sacrifice may consist of various things and there is no fixed ritual.

OɣGOSI MAMA is addressed with a sacrifice and prayer by the women in the cases of child delivery, sterility, also smallpox, chicken-pox, measles and other similar diseases of children. The husband can perform the ritual only in case the woman is very sick and cannot do it herself. The sacrifice consists of bread and incense. However, in the case of children's diseases the specialist *axa-mafa* must be called and he performs the ritual and defines whatever is in order or not. The shamans do not usually interfere with this spirit's activity. However, the women-shamans may sometimes be useful in dealing with children's trouble, and they may also deal with *oɣgos'i mama*.

From the point of view of child-welfare, close to this complex is that of spirits responsible for the diseases common in children: measles, smallpox, chicken-pox, and others. As shown they are included into the complex of Chinese origin and are represented by several spirits: *ajiɣo ilxa mama* ("small flower spirit"), held responsible for measles, *ilxa mama* ("flower spirit"), held responsible for smallpox, etc. As a matter of observation, the Manchus have come to believe that children must be isolated,—the house is tabooed for foreigners; the children must be put into a quiet place and fed with delicate things; noise must be avoided. All these requirements are supposed to satisfy not the child, but the spirit. The intervention of Chinese doctors and shamans in the course of sickness is considered as undesirable. However, some sacrifice chiefly consisting of incense, and some prayers addressed to the particular manifestation of the complex spirit are advisable, in the difficult cases of diseases. After the recovery, sacrifice and prayers are required. I have not recorded any prayers of this type. In so far as I know, they are rather short, and many people do not know them, so the ceremony is silent. The non-Manchu origin of the complex, namely, Chinese origin, is evident. Generally the Manchus, as well as the Tungus, do not regard the above mentioned infections as real diseases. It is supposed that they are not at all harm-

* I could not verify the statement of the Manchus that the chopsticks may stand in the cup, and I could not find out how and by which psychological process the Manchus arrive to such an observation.

ful for children, who may live better when marked by the attention of this complex spirit. When children fall sick the Manchus seem to be happy. According to the Manchus, there is no mortality, due to these diseases. However, as shown, preventive methods for a further propagation of infection are taken. When children succumb owing to the complication, this is explained as malevolent influence of various spirits, e.g. *jafan mafa, jun fuč'k'i, takto mafa* and even other spirits, so that the Manchus have to deal in these cases with a conflict between the spirits and their mutual relations. Naturally these are treated by the competent specialists. When it is found that there is a real "disease", the Chinese doctor will come; when there are Manchu spirits, they are dealt with by the shamans, or at least *axa mafa* and *p'oyun saman*.

———

In some Manchu clans there used to be practised a special ritual sacrifice served to *b'iran endŭr'i*. Such was, for instance, the case of *nara* clan in which there was given a special sacrifice of nine pigs for expression of thanks on the occasion of good hunting. However, this practice is now given up and the ritual is forgotten. It is quite possible that the sacrifice "in the mountains," still per-

formed in some clans, originally was connected with this complex and its loss may be explained as due chiefly to poverty,—the Manchus cannot now afford such a rich sacrifice. But without denying the possibility of influence of the "poverty factor" the giving up of this practice may also be understood as due to a further disintegration of the hunting complex amongst the Manchus, which process is seen in many other manifestations.

In the above description of the cases and methods of dealing with various spirits we have made reference chiefly to the cases of sickness. However, the spirits *takto mafa, jun fuč'k'i* and *jafan mafa* are also kept responsible in the case of troubles with vegetable-garden plants and with cattle. Owing to this, a great number of cases of this type requires sacrifices to these spirits, which may be also benevolent and useful for assuring family prosperity. A great number of methods may be used in connexion with the regulation of the activity of these spirits; some of these methods may appear to be "magic," while actually they are methods of communication with the spirits by means of "gesture" language. Some of these methods have already been indicated in the previous chapters, but their detailed description in particular cases will not reveal any new aspects of the psychomental complex. In the ritual practised they may also occupy an important place and yet the whole operation may be confined to the ritualism only.

CHAPTER XIX

SPIRITS AND VARIOUS CASES DEALT WITH BY THE SPECIALISTS

79. SPECIALISTS In the previous chapters I have already mentioned, besides the *p'oyun saman,* the existence of specialists who may and sometimes must deal with some cases of spirits' activity and generally with the defence of men against sickness, death and various forms of misfortune affecting individual life and that of groups. In these groups I do not now include the shamans for the following considerations. First of all, the shamanism forms a complex by itself which must be treated separately; second, other forms of dealing with the spirits have been partly created under the influence of a reaction against the shamanism for which, as will be shown, there are very serious reasons; third, other forms are not so elaborate as the shamanism, and they are subject to great variations, in the degree of specialization and differentiation among different ethnical groups. I do not now need to bring evidence for supporting my approach to shamanism as a special complex,—this can be seen from the description of special shamanistic spirits and a brief characterization of methods to deal with these spirits. But conditions which are responsible for a negative reaction on the shamanism, and consequently, for creation of a new form and new methods for dealing with the spirits ought to be pointed out.

It is believed that the shamans in dealing with the spirits sometimes become instruments of the spirits and as instruments they may be used against the people by the malevolent spirits. Yet, as will be shown, the shamans fight between themselves causing by this a great harm to the

people, and if shamans have bad personal character, they may be very dangerous for the people, even of the same clan or group. Owing to these conditions, many Tungus and Manchus are inclined to avoid shamans' intervention and generally prefer to keep themselves away from the shamans. Since such a *negative reaction* on shamanism has appeared amongst the groups, especially Manchus and Tungus of Manchuria, new hypotheses have also made their appearance. These hypotheses are of two orders, namely, (1) there are spirits which cannot be mastered by the shamans and who are responsible for various troubles which had been formerly dealt by the shamans; and (2) there are other methods of neutralizing spirits and even of turning them to be benevolent towards the individuals and groups. As soon as these two hypotheses had been recognized, it was not difficult to elaborate a new system of spirits and methods in compensation of a great decrease of shamans' protective activity. Indeed, it ought to be pointed out that an increase of spirits' activity, even with a maintaining of the former limits of shamans' activity, might also happen but, as a matter of observation confirmed by the Tungus, it may be said that the shamanism has somewhat decreased. To this question I shall return again, but what is now stated will suffice for demonstration of the conditions under which the introduction of new forms was possible. In connexion with this it will be timely to point out that the interethnic pressure in the form of cultural borrowings regarding spirits did act along the same line. In fact, the introduction of Christianity and Buddhism, as well as other systems, greatly contributed to an appearance of alien cultural complexes as whole.

Indeed, even in the earlier period there were people who might deal with the spirits or who might influence them, at least people who might predict the future, decipher dreams, and treat certain diseases, but in so far as facts are available, in the Tungus soil there were created no specialists and in the Tungus conditions no such profession could be created, which is quite evident from the description of the Tungus social organization and history of Tungus groups. It was different among the ancestors of the Manchus, as for instance Nuichen, who were under a strong Chinese influence and whose social organization might permit having a great variety of professional groups. The same is true of their neighbours, the Dahurs who were connected with the political organization known as Great Liao Dynasty, and at present they have and earlier they used to have, a social and economic organization which permitted some specialization. In fact, ethnically these are the sources of influence, over the Tungus groups here treated, which are responsible for appearance of some new forms of specialization among the Northern Tungus.

After these remarks I shall proceed to a description of kinds of specialists found among the Northern Tungus groups and Manchus.

Existence of wizards and medicine men, in the conditions of Tungus life was possible but these specialists were not differentiated into a professional group. Among all Tungus groups it is now recognized that there are persons endowed with a special ability to know the future, to interpret strange dreams etc. They are called iǒan (RTM) derived from the stem iǒ,—"to see,"—met with in other dialects in a sense close to this. Such persons are consulted as competent people whose opinion may be useful. In their deciphering of dreams they use their own experience and that of previous generations. Actually they are keepers of the common tradition. As shown, in some cases, their interpretation of dreams may correspond to the future expectations (vide supra). On the other hand, keepers of tradition regarding medical art applied at least to surgical cases and simple cases of therapeutic treatment with medicines, —mineral and non-mineral,—always existed. Such people are not styled by any special term except "wise", "old", etc. in the sense of personal wisdom and experience. They are met with among all groups and they are not considered a group apart. But in so far as simple dealing with the spirits is concerned, as we have seen, it required no creation nor differentiation of a special group of professional or semi-professional priests with exception of the Manchus, among whom this group has made its appearance probably at a late time as may be seen from the recent source of borrowing,—the Ritualism of the Imperial Court in Peking.

Among the Tungus of Manchuria, especially the Birarčen, there are specialists* who pray to the spirits and carry out complex rites of sacrifice to various spirits of the group burkan, particularly dǒna burkan. The dialects of these groups have no special term for these specialists. When the Tungus are asked what kind of people are these

specialists, they answer: mafa adali, i.e. "like mafa", of the Dahurs described below. In fact, the Birarčen and Kumarčen frequently observed Dahur performers-mafa, whose art of praying and giving ritual sacrifice did impress these Tungus by the novelty of methods, their complexity and in some cases their evident effectiveness. It was quite natural on the part of the Tungus to have observed them, to have learnt the methods which, shall I add, are rather simple, and to have applied them in analogous cases. It was not only natural, but it was advisable to have used the Dahur methods for the spirits were dǒna, and particularly of Dahur origin. However, the Tungus were not blindly imitating the Dahurs,—they composed their own prayers in Tungus and adapted the ritual to their own complex. Both prayers and ritual as compared with the Dahur pattern, are now somewhat simplified. The simplification has especially affected that aspect of mafa performance in which the Dahurs use powers unknown to the Tungus. Observation of the Dahurs has been supported by that of the Manchu practice of axa mafa methods and of Chinese specialists occasionally met with in the Tungus territory. Then in Tungus eyes these methods have received especial importance. However, the new practice has called into life a new group of people who might thus enjoy a special position amongst their own people, quite honourable and equalling that of the former "wise elders" and that of foreign,— Dahur, Manchu and Chinese,—specialists. It may be here noted that in spite of a special position the Tungus specialists receive no reward, nor remuneration for their trouble in carrying out complex rites and they do it for the pleasure of serving the people and for the honour bestowed upon them by their co-villagers in the form of some extra drink, invitations to eat together, etc. But drink and food motives are not essential. The specialists of the foreign groups are in a different position, for their profession may support them in their simple mode of life making them quite free of troubles and hard work and at the same time giving them sufficient security in the sense of permanent source of income.

80. MAFARISM Amongst the Dahurs and Manchus the mafa are frequently met with. The Dahurs for their designation use the term mafa, which is a loan-word, I suppose, from Manchu. In Manchu they are termed axa mafa, or simply mafa→mava in plural mavar'i, where the original meaning of mafa is "grandfather", and axa—"slave", "servant", etc. However, mafa—mava is also applied to a class of spirits already described (vide supra) and dealt with by mafar'i, so that the term for this class of specialists is perhaps connected with this class of spirits. By this term there are designated persons who can deal with some spirits and who possess a special art of divination and partial mastering of spirits by threatening, neutralizing and even destroying them. As methods of influence they use sacrifice, prayers, and transportation of spirits; yet, in some cases they introduce into themselves spirits mafa, and owing to this they are called by the name of spirits, and distinguished from the shamans. The mafa have no shamanistic paraphernalia for their work, no special dress. However, amongst the Manchus they sometimes use drums borrowed from the p'oyun saman or other shamans, if the performance happens to take place in a house where there are drums. On the other hand, they

* I have not seen them amongst the Khingan Tungus, but I have been told that these specialists exist amongst the Kumarčen and Mergen groups.

have some professional paraphernalia, of Chinese origin,—from the Chinese doctors, monks and jugglers.

Amongst the Manchus the *mafa* are supposed to be in intimate relations with the mustela *soloyo*, and perhaps with the hare. These animals after living a very long time, "one thousand years," or "ten thousand years" become "spirit like" and help the *mafa*. However, the spirits *vočko* never help the *mafa*, so that they are usually competent only in what they have practised and learnt from other *mafa*. At the present time the Manchus very often use the *mafa's* talents for a modest remuneration. At the request of the public, at the meeting, they may produce any kind of wine, bread, fruit, by special "supernatural means" which are mere juggler's tricks; they may perform expelling of *xutu* by a very complex method; they may satisfy with a sacrifice some spirits, e.g. *ilxa mama* amongst the Manchus; they may deal with various spirits unknown amongst the common people; they may speak, with the help of *mafa* spirits, any language they wish which gives a particular power in dealing with foreign spirits; they may produce various kinds of tricks which cannot be done by the common people, but which are known to the Chinese travelling jugglers.

From the psychological point of view there is a great difference between the *mafa* and the shamans; namely, the *mafa* have any kind of exstasy, they do not bring up the audience or themselves to the state of a passionate contact with the spirits. The *mafa* are not believers in their own art,—they are professionals who live on their profession without any sign of sincerity.

Among the Dahurs the *mafa* are supposed to be connected with the spirits formed from very old foxes, "one" or "ten thousand years." Here it may be remembered that mustelidae, foxes, perhaps hare also rats alternate among the groups here discussed. Some mafas have also spirits of sheep, also very old individuals, so ,that when the mafa wants to predict the future he calls this spirit and imitates the sheep's bleat. The mafas use the same methods both among the Manchus and Dahurs.

We have some hints as to the history of this profession. First of all, it ought to be pointed out that the spirits *mafa* ~*mava* are a new group introduced into the Manchu complex, whence it reached the Dahurs and furthermore some of the Northern Tungus. It may be supposed that the spirits of this group did not yet exist at the moment when the above discussed Ritual of the Imperial family was composed, i.e. in the eighteenth century. The spirits *fučixi* were originally dealt with by the Buddhist monks, but later on the managing of *fuč'k'i* was undertaken by the mafas. Some elements of the *mafa* complex definitely point to the Chinese influence, if not even origin. Yet, the Buddhistic and other Chinese monks,—half-medicine men, half-"sorcerers", and generally a professional group,—might originally have no place in the genuine Manchu organization based upon the strictly outlined clan system. There is no little doubt that they were introduced among the Manchus at a very recent time. This new complex has gradually become an indispensable element of the Manchu complex, but it has also been adapted and modified by the Manchus. In the meantime the Buddhistic monks' influence has decreased among the Manchus and these monks have ceased to frequent the Manchus as much as they used to do,—the Manchus have learnt themselves the art of managing *fuč'k'i* and *mafa*, as well as other spirits

introduced amongst them by the monks and foreigners. It may be supposed that the Manchu specialists had begun by learning methods of dealing with *mafa* spirit,—whence their designations originated,—afterwards they mastered the art of dealing with Buddhistic spirits. When this art was assimilated, the Manchus began to propagate it amongst their neighbours. It may be thus said that the system in question has resulted from the introduction, adoption and adaptation of a foreign complex within at most the last two centuries, or safer to say, within the last two or three generations. The analysis of the process of assimilation of this system by the Tungus makes still clearer the mechanism of its formation among the Manchus and Dahurs, to which question I shall return a few pages later. Owing to a special character of this complex it ought decidedly to be distinguished from shamanism and the complex used by the common people. Indeed, the persons possessing this art may be called *sorcerers*, but at the same time, the complex outlined has some characteristic elements of distinction which incline to call the whole system by a special term, namely, *mafarism*. In fact, *mafarism* is an evident opposition to shamanism, even a by-product of a negative reaction on shamanism, but at the same time it is based upon the fundamental principle of animism and even voluntary introduction of a spirit (*mafa*) into the performer which is typical of shamanism. Thus, in *mafarism* there may be distinguished elements of alien origin such as the jugglers' methods and the professional character of the specialists; the Manchu-Dahur elements, such as prayers, needs, etc.; and on the whole,—shamanistic pattern,—the introduction of spirits.

For illustration I shall now give some cases of *mafarism* which I have observed.*

1. In the Birarčen village *Čelu* a Dahur speaking his own language, Mongol, Manchu, local Tungus dialect, Chinese, and a little Russian appeared for some performances of mafarism. The meeting was held at night in a Tungus house of Chinese type. The purpose was finding of the cause of sickness of one of members of the family. The mafa was sitting in the middle of the room in complete darkness, by the side of the sick man. Three men were holding the door closed with a rope. Then suddenly fox-mafa spirit arrived and through the performer, who took the pulse of the sick man, began to speak in a low voice. The spirit gave some insignificant advice and the séance was over. After the performance the mafa told stories in different languages.

2. Another case in the same place. ·An old blind Dahur,—who was styled *mafa* and even s'*en'šan* (Chinese!) arrived with the purpose of attending several sick people. The people gathered in a house. The mafa ordered the door closed and held so with a rope. Then he put on the table several bottles of "red wine" (coloured Chinese ǥaolan wine), some nuts, dates, etc. and began to call the *mafa* spirit. *Mafa* came with a great noise, suddenly

* It is interesting to note that the mafas did not like my presence at their performances. In all cases I could attend the meetings only because of the Manchus and Tungus who wanted me to be present. So on their insistance I could attend them, even in spite of a certain opposition of mafas.

opened the door so that the people who held the door with the rope fell down, and it began to roar and scream. Then the spirit was invited to have a drink, but it produced noises indicating anger and taking possession of a bottle by an experienced movement of slapping the bottom of the bottle with the palm, got the cork out and could be heard to empty the bottle into its mouth. This operation was going on in absolute darkness. Then the blind Dahur began to wrestle with *mafa*-spirit until the latter became silent. Then another *mafa* arrived by the same way, from the region of *Luydur kadar* (Lundur rock in the neighbourhood of the town Mergen); he began drinking "red wine" and roaring and screaming and repeating in "pidgin-Russian": "vódka daí, vódka daí, vyp'ju xóču!" ("Give wine, I want to drink!"). He also repeated some words in Mongol and Tungus. After this appearance the mafa-performer introduced into the abdomen of the sick man several needles ten centimetres long, one of which was red-hot. When the performance was over the mafa told several stories in different languages.*

The second performance was not running in a smooth way. Before the performance a Tungus by the name of Daurko wanted to verify whether *mafa*-spirit would be really present or not, so he promised to light a match during the performance. However, when the time came for the *mafa*-spirit to arrive the mafa-performer asked:

"Who did want to light a match?"

Nobody answered, so the mafa continued:

"Daurko, come here!"

Daurko had to obey; he approached the Dahur who struck him with a stick three times and ordered him to kneel and to knock his forehead on the ground. Daurko again obeyed and the next morning he had on his head a mark, an evidence of the experience of the disobedience and inquisitiveness of the previous night. I do not need to say that Daurko's intention was communicated to the Dahur mafa before the performance.

It may be here noted that both performances are of the same type: the closed door kept with a rope, required darkness, and speaking different languages. It may be also noted that the performance was carried out with an evident naïvety of impressing the Tungus with very simple tricks of cooperation with the assistants who performed spirits' part in the setting of the program. Yet, some Tungus seemingly remained sceptical up to the end. Such a character of *mafarism* is rather typical, in so far as I could find out from the inquiry of the Tungus.

Among the Manchus I have seen several performances of the same, or nearly the same, type, also praying and sacrifices which are not interesting enough to be related here in detail. However, there is one of some importance which I shall now give in detail.

XUAŠEN FUDERE MAFAR'I ("flowery tree bringing out specialist") is a night performance which aims to send away the spirits producing trouble. It consists of several parts, of which the first one is called: *ajen n'imeku ăomb'e*,—"which sickness descends", or "the finding of cause of sickness." For finding it, the *mafar'i*, provided he consents to the performance, takes three incense sticks and a cup of wine. Holding in his hand the incense sticks the mafa looks through them into the wine for finding out whether it is a *xutu*, or *mafa*, or *endūr'i* who are responsible for sickness. For sending away a *xutu*, the method *xuašén fudèmb'e* is used. *Xuašén* is a willow branch with leaves taken off. Instead of leaves there are attached artificial flowers made of paper (white, red, yellow, black and blue) and artificial branches of the tree with leaves all made of paper. Such "beautiful trees" exist in the other (lower) world and they are attractive for *xutu*. This "tree" is put into a special receptacle *x'jaza*, wooden and of large size* filled up with black or red beans. A model of a shrine, made of birch bark, and a certain number of anthropomorphic "placings",—about ten or thirteen centimetres high,—made of straw are put under the "tree." The number of placings depends on the number of *xutu* responsible and discovered by *mafa*. In addition to them there may be made straw-horses on which the *xutu* is supposed to go away. Behind the "tree" a low table for sacrifice is put on the ground. The sacrifice consists of a boiled cock, "five kinds of fruits" (*sun'ja xačin tubixe jaka*) (cf. *supra*) one of which may be Chinese candles, from fifteen to twenty-five rolls of Chinese bread (*mantóu*) and pieces (about seventy-five centimetres long) of red, white and black cotton tissue. Mafa sitting on an ordinary seat occupies his position behind the table with the sacrifice. He may hold a drum, if such one can be found in the house or in that of neighbours. His aim is to call the *xutu* and to compel it to accept the sacrifice. When *xutu* arrives, it takes a place in the anthropomorphic placing made of straw. After a long admonition of *xutu*, the "tree" and placings are brought out and thrown on a public road. During the transportation of *xutu*, the mafa and people following him must not look back at the house just left. The *xutu* is supposed to take the road and leave again for another world. Since the cock and the pieces of cotton tissue are remuneration for the mafa's work, they are handed over to him after the performance. Sometimes mafa may be assisted by the voluntary assistants, as it is with the shamans.

It is different when the troubles come from an *endūr'i*, which cannot be "expelled." In this case *endūr'i* must receive a sacrifice (after the performance handed over to the mafa) offered in day time and *endūr'i* must be admonished to leave the person affected. It ought to be remembered that the only *endūr'i* which produces sickness is *apka endūr'i*, which is also the principal one. The prayers are very elaborate and constitute a special art and individual achievement of mafa, but they are not mere improvisation made ad hoc. However, the ethnographic contents of these prayers' is not very rich:—they are compositions of conventional, formalistic expressions. Experienced assistant shamans can carry out some of methods used by *axa-mafa*, as well. The same can be done by any one who is sure of

---

* He told an interesting story about the first shaman. It may be pointed out that this story was considered as genuine and of good source for the Dahurs are versed in these questions, while the Tungus are not. The story was not textually recorded by me so I do not reproduce it here.

* *x'jaza* corresp. to *xijase* of Manchu Writ. loaned from Chinese 匣子, sia-džy, according to P.P. Schmidt. However, it is not merely "Kiste, Kasten", as P.P. Schmidt translates, but it used to be a unit of measure for grain and beans, an important element of the Manchu complex.

the sequence of rites to be performed and addresses to be recited.

In addition to the art of dealing with these spirits the mafas are familiar with some methods of Chinese medical art. Indeed, how extensive is the knowledge of the *mafa* in this vast field, it is not of my competence to say, but I suppose their knowledge cannot be very deep, for the mafas are not good scholars and they receive no special preparation through a direct contact with the Chinese good doctors. What they assimilate is chiefly some tricks, manners, and fragments of knowledge carried by adventurers to the remote regions of the Aigun district. Yet, the mafas have also assimilated many tricks practised by the travelling Chinese jugglers who from time to time visit Manchu villages and pretend to possess their art through the intermediary of spirits. The Buddhist and Taoist monks also are not free from methods of deception for impressing their professional influence over "barbarians" of Manchuria, including the Manchu villagers,—for by means of various tricks, known to the jugglers in China, they may be more impressive than by reciting of Chinese philosophers. Some of these tricks were assimilated as real tricks, and conventional performances, but in some cases they were assimilated as quite effective methods of managing spirits,—the point which could not be entirely destroyed by the foreign (Chinese) influence. The Manchu mafa when using various methods, evidently borrowed, did sincerely believe in the possibility of controlling spirits' activity. It may be also noted that in the process of adaptation of this complex the Manchus have introduced their own idea of "mastering" *mafa-*spirits by the specialists. Therefore from the Manchu point of view the difference between mafa-performers and shamans is that of difference of the mastered spirits,—*mafa* and *roéko.* One meets with this as a formulation of the difference, amongst the Manchus. We have seen that amongst the Dahurs these functions have been still increased with telling of stories in different languages which now forms a distinct character of this profession. So the entertainment of idle people has become one of the functions of mafa.

Since mafa-performers were quite successful in dealing with some spirits and in some special cases, the field of their potential activity has greatly increased. At the present time, they are called by the people in cases of need of fortune-telling, medical treatment, expelling of some spirits, praying to the spirits which are controlling children diseases, and many other occasions including the festivals when one wants to have a good entertainer to tell stories and to sing. It is also interesting at which historic moment, namely, the moment of an intensive contact with a foreign group, —with the Chinese,—it appeared amongst the Manchus; and in which social surrounding and organization its appearance was possible,—namely under the conditions of a further disintegration of the clan and social differentiation of the Manchu population. Yet, there is one more interesting point; namely, the psychological type (including individual complex and ethnographical complex in which they are formed) which supplies the candidates for this profession. I have many a time observed amongst the Manchus, and it has also been confirmed by my observations amongst the Dahurs and Tungus, that the mafas are usually quite normal

persons, somewhat lazy, in so far as regular and common work is concerned, very quick in the orientation in a new situation, self-confident, greedy of personal gain (profit), inclined to disregard the choice of means for reaching their aims, on some occasion impertinent, on the other— cowardly,—i.e. what, in common language of city low class populations is called "clever," "smart," and "leaders." Indeed, a social type could grow only in the conditions in which the Manchus were already shaken in their interethnical and internal ethnical position. The same is true of the Dahurs and, as will be shown, of the Tungus. Such a monopolizing of various functions by the mafa and selection of individuals for this function is a very interesting phenomenon from the ethnological point of view, i.e. particularly the process of variations of ethnographical phenomena. Indeed, the existence of mafarism is quite ephemeral. It may be predicted that on the condition of preservation of the same course of the process, it will very soon disappear.*

81. MAFARISM AMONG THE TUNGUS The fate of mafarism amongst the Northern Tungus is very interesting. It has just begun its penetration and its forms are quite adapted to the Tungus complex. As amongst the Manchus, it has originated chiefly as a result of an alien influence,—in the particular case of the Birarčen, that of the Dahurs. Amongst the Birarčen, the Dahur mafas enjoy the good fame of being great masters of their art who may compete with the native shamans. From time to time they are invited by the Tungus for dealing with the cases analogous to those observed amongst the Manchus. However, since the Tungus are not in the same economic position as the Manchus, they cannot have them as frequently as the Manchus do. At the same time, some Tungus try to learn this art by imitation of the alien pattern. I have met a few Tungus Birarčen who had already mastered a part of this art. All of them knew a great number of prayers composed for neutralizing various spirits of the group *dōna burkan.* They also knew clan prayers of different clans, generally they were better equipped for praying in their own clan and for outsiders. Yet, some of them knew details of various sacrifices to the spirits. They were sometimes called in difficult cases of sickness by the people who did not belong to their own clan, but as to remuneration for this work none was paid, but there were rewards in different forms, namely, "service for service among friends" or just by recognition of their great talent and growing personal influence. Some of these Tungus have learnt various methods of divination which they had gathered from various sources,—from the Dahurs, Chinese, Russians,—as for instance divination with omoplate, rifle, burning incense sticks, coins, chopsticks, and many other methods which could be gathered locally from competent people. Some of these people already knew a great number of methods of calling spirits into special placings and expelling them

* Amongst the so-called civilized groups, especially those which do not possess great internal stability such a temporary monopolizing of various functions and very general success, amongst low classes of populations, are common, too. It may be seen, for instance, in an exceptional monopolizing for popular treatment of all branches of theatrical art and music, by the music-halls, movies and talkies.

afterwards; manipulations with *bām'i* and other methods were usually repudiated by the Tungus on the ground of their immorality and possible harm to the people. However, in so far as I know, perhaps with one exception, none of them applied methods of pure and simple deception and juggling. Still although they were familiar with the Tungus medical art, none of them could treat with Chinese medicines and "pulse". So that the specialists who existed at my time were not yet specialized and equipped with all of the mafa's art and were what may be called "amateurs and beginners." As a psychological condition it may be pointed out that they did not believe in the shaman's power; they actually criticized the shamans and called them "backward people" as opposed to the people with a "modern trend of ideas" expressed in mafarism. Most of them were decidedly reluctant to speak seriously about the shamans and shamanism, and they pretended not to know how one can manage the spirits without the shaman's assistance. Another trait of interest is that most of them were not absolutely certain of the efficiency of mafarism alone, and they gave it more potential value than the professional mafas, i.e. they were more sincere in this matter than the real mafas. I was very persistently asked by many of them about the effectiveness of mafarism and the sincerity of Manchu *mafar'i;* they frequently confided in me their suspicions as to deceptions generally practised by the mafas. On the other hand, the same people wanted to believe in mafarism and they repudiated shamanism.

For giving a concrete instance of a mafa beginner, I shall describe a Birarčen whom I knew intimately and whom I saw in different situations. This man was over thirty-five years old, constitutionally rather strong, married and the father of several children. All his life he had stayed in the village (Čelu), where he had a piece of land worked by Chinese hired labour, a house of Chinese type, some cows, horses and from time to time some pigs, most of which were kept for sacrifices. He did not practise hunting, postponing under various pretexts the hunting trip in the mountains. But he was rather keen on various incidental sources of income, e.g. incidental transportation of goods and people, restoration of a Chinese woman who had run away from her husband,* and so on. In his habits, he was rather sober, he was not addicted to drinking, gambling with cards and running after women. He distinguished himself under the Manchus and was appointed *boško* (one of two amongst this group) to assist the Manchu chief of the group. Under the "republican system" he did not lose his position (a paid position).** He was on friendly terms with the local Chinese shopkeepers, also incidental visitors from Dahur villages where he had several personal friends, being connected with all of these people by some business about which he avoided speaking. He spoke the Dahur language fluently, and knew some Chinese and a little Russian. As a personality, he was not like other Tungus, even from a physical point of view as well as to manners. One could not feel very sure of him and the Tungus were always complaining about him

*   The husband of this woman asked the Tungus to find his wife for which a remuneration was to be given. No one wanted to accept this proposition which according to the Tungus code would be regarded as shameful, but the person in question accepted it.

**   Description of conditions of this administrative system, vide SONT pp. 112-115.

pointing out instances of his non-Tungus behaviour, e.g. the case with the Chinese woman produced a very bad impression on all Tungus. Seemingly he was involved in a case of bad character in connexion with money belonging to other people. As to his mental power I could not say that he differed very much from other Tungus, but the trend of his ideas was quite different. While in the average case the Tungus like to face various "philosophical problems" concerning spirits, world, etc. his attention was directed to practical problems of increasing his prosperity, and at the time he was deeply interested in mafarism and largely practised it when occasions were met with. I had some suspicion as to his direct assistance of a blind Dahur mafa who fooled the Tungus with the *mafa*-spirits, and various tricks. He did not believe in shamans, but did not dare to come into conflict with them because of fearing their revenge by their powerful, in his opinion, means.

Such a man was one of influential promoters of new ideas of mafarism and he was quite successful in his propaganda.* Since there was no Dahur mafa and he himself was already familiar with the methods of *mafarism,* he was often invited by his Tungus friends to interfere with the spirits' activity. He received no direct remuneration for it.

From the general characteristics of this man, who was fatally going to become a mafa, it may be seen that he was already in conflict with the Tungus complex; he was not very honest from the Tungus point of view, his stimulus in life was personal success in the sense of increase of his own wealth and weight of his social position; and he was not as laborious as other members of his community.

Other candidates for mafarism amongst this group were not so definitely hostile to the Tungus complex, but all of them were slightly in conflict with it, although they did enjoy a certain esteem and they inspired a certain fear to their co-villagers.

Amongst these Tungus, as well as amongst the Kumarčen, for the specialists of this type no special term exists. They are described as people who "know prayers" (*buačin sären*), so that the emphasis is put on their knowledge to manage only certain spirits.

Important spirits with which these specialists are dealing are *dōna burkan,* i.e. the spirits which remain beyond the clan competence and which at present are only incidentally mastered by the shamans; the souls of various origin, from living people, especially shamans' souls and dead people, especially those who were not buried; and various other spirits of little importance.

Amongst the spirits, the first place is occupied by *ain'i burkan (vide supra)* which is now held responsible for a great number of diseases and is connected with the conditions which are new for the Tungus, of living in villages. After finding out which manifestation of this spirit causes the trouble special steps for neutralizing the spirit are made. The first step is always the same,—making of three pictures (they may be bought) corresponding to three groups of manifestations and "roads," and putting in front of them of Chinese stick incense,—three sticks in front of every picture. If after three days there is no change in the condition of the sick person, a sacrifice of a cock must

*   One of reasons in favour of mafarism was that the shamanism began at that time to be persecuted by the Chinese new republican authorities which, however, did not oppose mafarism.

be given according to a complex ritual. For some manifestations it may be a boiled cock, collected fresh blood; a great number of sticks of incense which are put in a southeastern direction from the suffering person. Some others require different sacrifices shown in the prayers below. Wooden placings are made on this occasion: there may be three combinations according to the roads and there may be special placings for particular manifestations of the spirit. The performer sings a prayer, usually consisting of two parts, namely, invitation to the spirit to come into the placings and invitation to accept the sacrifice accompanied by a formal ritual pointing to the sacrifice. The last part is concluded by an invitation to leave the person affected and to go back to a "nice place."

I. PRAYER (buačin) TO THE SPIRIT Ai; manifestation or¹ebar'i which consists of nine girls and nine boys(1). Anthropomorphic placings are made of wood.

A. Invitation.

"Ai spirit, I pray southwards, I kneel and bow down "to you. Having lit pure incense, I pray to the lower(2) "(manifestations): listen to this. Having erected a post "I worshipped good(3) spirit and the pure spirit's place in "South. Listen to this: me, poor one, I insistently pray. "Listen to me, speaking poor man. I insistently pray: "don't. dress your ears neglectfully: don't listen to "gossips(4); listen just as (I pray). Love us as beloved "children. Children have no money(5), no luck: add money "and luck. Listen to what I sing, me, stupid like wood, "stupid as this: raise up (sick people) from the bed, raise "up the head from the pillow. Take back the vapour(6); "carry on your back; clean as you clean hemp(7); help to "get better your stupid children".

B. Sacrifice is given.

"Meeting for a blood sacrifice is fixed. Smear yourself "with blood; take the blood sausages; eat soup; taste lungs; "take kidneys; taste liver. Protect against the vapour(6). "The long sacrificial vessel (?(8)), the round sacrificial "vessel put in a row, I serve sacrifice which consists of in"ternal organs. I have erected a post for sacrifice and a "platform. I leave the sacrificial blood to flow out. "Listen: accept as it is. Listen in the heights(9). Go to "joso place, go to b'irg'e place".(10)

II. PRAYER (buačin) TO THE SPIRIT AI, manifestation tuliaɲi (boɲi, torg'etan, tor'eltan(11)).

"I pray the spirit Ai. I attract attention without any "'news; I talk nonsense; I pray without any business(12). "Still listen, Ai spirit. I have erected a post for talking

1. Details concerning manifestations of this complex spirit vide supra. Here I use term Ai because it is so found in the text. However, the Tungua usually call this spirit Ain'i.
2. In the text the term "manifestations" is omitted. "Lower" is understood as "lower manifestation", i.e. manifestation of low roads.
3. "Good spirit" is a flattery.
4. Mentioning of "gossips" is rather unusual in the Tungus complex. Cf. supra Ch. XVI, Section 73, the second prayer, footnote.
5. Mentioning of "money" is an innovation, indeed.
6. "Vapour" is "immaterial substance" of diseases.
7. This comparison with "hemp" is, of course, of a non-Northern Tungus origin.
8. A word following "vessel" could not be understood.
9. "Heights" in which the spirits remain.
10. Joso, etc. and b'irg'e are those places where spirits live.
11. Details concerning this group of manifestations vide supra.
12. All this passage is a self-humiliation.

"nonsense. Such as I am, I am asking for luck.' Ai spirit "comes out. Such as I am, I see you exactly as you are. "A meeting is fixed to meet this (sacrifice). Having made "a messenger I have asked, so that listen (to me). Give "what I am requesting. Having dressed up your ears be "indulgent to one who is bowing. Raise up from pillow; "raise up from the sleeping rug, raise up from the bed. "To this I have made (you) to listen. Come surely, "without failure, to meet. What living people do know? "Direct yourself, govern yourself. Go to the place b'irg'e, "fly to the heights."

──────────

Here I give a case of specialists' intervention in absence of shaman. A small boy of five or six years old fell sick: he had headache, vomiting and apparently, high fever. The father hesitated and undecided whether to use some medicines or not. An old man—specialist in this matter and husband of the old blind female shaman—proposed to find out the cause of sickness and treat it. First, he carried out divination with the rifle method; he then declared the trouble was produced by the greatest clan sèvèn (vide supra) which was dissatisfied at being without a master (at that time the clan dunänkän had no shaman!) and was going from one clansman to another clansman producing sickness of the children. Therefore the spirits must have a sacrifice which should consist of a pig and a goose, given to the night road manifestations and midday road manifestations respectively. During three days prior to the sacrifice, the family must pray to the spirit. Then there were made two dragons of wood and two bäm'i of straw for night road and nine an'akan and nine birds of wood for midday road. All of them were put together about one hundred metres South-West from the house, were prayed over and given sacrifice. The child recovered, and everybody was convinced that the old man was right in his diagnosis.

This case is interesting for it shows how the specialists may take functions of shamans in their absence, and how the shamanistic methods are incorporated into a new competing complex.

One of the common and important operations practised by these specialists is that with bäm'i. Bäm'i is a placing made of straw or of birch-bark and it may be used for different kinds of spirits and souls. The operations described below can be carried out by anyone who believes in the effectiveness of the proceedings, and who knows the ritual. The essential of this operation consists in preparing a bäm'i, calling into it the spirit or soul and shooting it with a rifle. That the spirit is really placed in the bäm'i is confirmed, for instance, by the fact (observed amongst the Goldi) that bäm'i is moving when it is put into the paper lantern lighted with the stick-incense, for the shadow made by bäm'i on the paper screen is moving.* When the bäm'i begins to move then it may be shot. Another confirmation is found in observation of facts; namely, after shooting bäm'i the people are often relieved of their trouble, and if it were a soul of living people, the latter may have injuries, exactly in the places as the bäm'i was damaged by the shot (details vide supra). One of the cases is that the hunter cannot hit the animals with his

* Principle of Chinese "moving shadows".

rifle,—it becomes too heavy. Then the specialist may arrange the following operation: the rifle is kept in hand and man must try to lift it up with one hand. In the meantime there are recited the names of all spirits one by one,—all *s'irkul*, all *burkan*, all *sèvèn*. When one arrives at the name of the spirit making rifle heavy, the latter suddenly becomes light and it can be easily lifted up by one hand. In this way the spirit is discovered. Indeed, the psychological mechanism of this operation is evident. Then *bām'i* and a dog are made of straw (dry grass). The man who promises a good sacrifice prays the spirit to come in. In the meantime some shooting powder is put under the *bām'i* and when the spirit is supposed to have entered the placing the man sets fire to the powder and *bām'i* is exploded. In the case the trouble-maker is 'a shaman, they put *bām'i* under a heavy stone, and the shaman would be sick until the *bām'i* is rotten. However, the shaman may be relieved of his sickness, if the man who performs the operation with *bām'i* gives sacrifice to the shaman's *sèvèn*. As a matter of fact there are hundreds of methods for manipulation with *bām'i*;—personal imagination and invention play very important part in the creation of new forms.* Pictures

* I have made several suggestions to the Tungus as to the new methods of dealing with bām'i, e.g. to influence them with strong chemicals, such as sulphuric acid, and for attracting souls by using combination of photographic pictures, phonographic records, and written down words pronounced by the person whose soul ought to be called. They were recognized by the Birarčen as probably quite effective and worthy of experiments. Here it may be pointed out that my second suggestion resulted from the objection made to me by a Nerčinsk Tungus when I was carrying amongst them my investigations. In prevision of this obstacle I had to clear up my way by explaining my real intentions which were not to use "voice," "images" and other records against the people. When the Tungus had be-

and photographs, may be also used instead of *bām'i*. These are still better for the soul may easily recognize its placing.

However, in some cases the Tungus recognize that none of the above described methods may be effective, so they abstain from calling man *buačin sāren*—specialist who knows prayers—and they make no *bām'i*. These are chiefly cases of hopeless diseases and situations in which the existing hypotheses of spirits are not needed. For instance, if a man should cut his hand sinews, he would know that nobody can help him; if the rifle is worn out, they would not use any "magics", for it is clear,—the rifle is too old; if a disease is too far advanced, the specialists may refuse to attend, even if the disease were caused by a spirit.*

I shall now leave the methods of managing, neutralizing and fighting spirits for the facts here brought forth may suffice as illustration of a general description of conditions which called to existence the mafarism and its Tungus modification and which underlie the propagation of new methods and together with them, alien influence. I should consider it useless furthermore to overload the present chapter with more facts which will be a simple repetition of the facts here already presented.

come more familiar with me and found that I was not "bad hearted" man they had no fear of giving themselves up to me.

* A child nine years old was sick because of ain'i burkan and it was treated as usual. When the child became very weak the parents called a shaman, who although he carried out his work did not succeed. Then a specialist was called, but he refused to go and explained to me that it was too late,—"here even a shaman cannot help". On this occasion I had enumeration of cases which he would not attend.

PART FOUR

SHAMANISM

INTRODUCTION

When I was planning a scheme of the present study into the psychomental complex I had in view to include the present part as a series of chapters in the previous PART THREE dealing with various methods of practical solution of problems resulting from the recognition of a series of hypotheses expounded in PART TWO. In fact, it would much better correspond to the factual position of the shamanism in the Tungus and Manchu complexes. However, the complex of shamanism covers such a vast field of phenomena and facts observed that their description would require more space than that of all other "practical ways" discussed in the previous part. On the other hand, shamanism is a complex by itself which may exist independent of other practical ways and thus it may be treated separately as I myself have treated it in one of my previous publications (cf. "Essay", etc. 1919). An abstraction of this complex is neither possible nor desirable for this complex forms only *a complex* within a larger complex, so that the chief hypotheses put as the theoretical basis of shamanism, are not characteristic of

the shamanism alone and they cannot be artificially extracted from the complex in order to satisfy minds which want to approach shamanism in its abstraction. In fact in my publication just mentioned, I expounded some fundamental principles underlying shamanism. To understand the functioning of shamanism one must start from the general theoretical and factual equipment of the Tungus. Yet I have a serious objection to giving this part the title "shamanism"; such a title may give a wrong impression that I have the idea of considering shamanism as an abstraction or giving an independent existence to shamanism parallel to Buddhism, Taoism, Mohammedism, Lamaism and other systems, as is commonly done when shamanism is given an abstracted form covering phenomena which actually have nothing to do with shamanism. This will be better seen when the question as to nature and contents of shamanism are discussed, but at present I wish only to point out that by giving this title I had in view only technical convenience of treatment and presentation of the complex of shamanism.

CHAPTER XX

PSYCHOLOGICAL CONDITIONS OF GROUPS INVESTIGATED

82. PRELIMINARY REMARKS Every good observer of alien ethnical units is usually first impressed by the differences in the behaviour of the observed unit as compared with his own. The analysis of an alien behaviour and comparison with other groups soon brings the investigator to a quite opposite conclusion, —a seeming similarity between all groups. However, still a deeper penetration of investigation into the details reveals aspects which appear to be peculiar to the individual ethnical groups and which require special technical conditions of investigation. These special conditions are a continuous observation of individuals and groups during a certain, and rather long, period of time in what may be called laboratory and clinical conditions. Indeed, the last condition for the field investigators is out of question. There remains only possible extension of the period of investigation and a great number of cases superficially observed, on which the observer may check up his tentative suggestions. Unfortunately, in field work one sometimes comes in touch with rare cases which perhaps will be no more met and the observer's guess may remain unconfirmed.* Such are conditions of observers and such are

* At the present time possibility of field observations is much wider than it was before which is due to an elaboration of special

conclusions which may be formed at the spot. However, a great deal of correctness of observation depends on the observers themselves. So, according to the above formulated attitude of the observers, some of them cannot go further than the first impression of diversity of a new unknown complex, as compared with the known one, while in some observers the pre-existing theories may serve as a sieve through which only selected facts will be allowed to pass.

Yet, the scope of observations during the work does. not remain the same. In fact, at the beginning of the investigation, there are recorded chiefly facts striking for the observer while the familiarization with the group and individuals observed shows other facts worthy of being recorded because of their special importance in the system

methods of observation Cf. for instance, tentative programme for this kind of observations compiled by F. H. G. van Loon and R. Thurnwald ("Un questionnaire psycho-physio-morphologique pour l'étude de la psychologie des races", in Revue Anthropologique, 1930, rp. 262-277) which may be very useful for observers. However, further extension and elaboration of detailization are needed, as well as special adaptation of the methods for the field-observers. Yet I should like to point out that what I have told in reference to the programmes and questions for the field observers holds good for this particular case.

of equilibrium of the given unit and not only because of striking features. For instance, a man's abstaining from drinking wine amongst some Tungus is a fact to be immediately recorded, for it leads to other special psychological conditions of the subject, while the same phenomenon amongst other Tungus groups has no interest at all. Another instance; a woman's great tenderness to children, as a common phenomenon, would not attract any special attention, while in the case of some groups, when it occurs, may bring to discovery of some peculiar complex. Generally methods of judgment as to the psychic abnormality of individuals from their attitude towards the society becomes useless, if we do not know the fundamental mechanism of the given society and a great number of details which condition its "normal" functioning. This is the second serious excuse for certain omissions in my observations, for the familiarity with the complex was not equal in groups and was not equal at different periods of investigation.

There is one more serious condition in the observation and in the treatment of the psychopathological cases in different ethnical groups, namely, their relativity. "Abnormal cases" ought to be referred to the existing psychomental complexes as they are observed in the ethnical units. To take for illustration a rough example,—behaviour characteristic of an average Italian in the milieu of Finns would be considered as sufficient for suspecting a certain abnormality, perhaps psychic instability of the Italian individual transplanted, while a Finn transplanted to the Italian milieu would raise the same suspicions as to an abnormality pointing to the lack of psychic response. One more example: an "extravagance" in dress in males, e.g. especially marked inclination to the care and particular attention to the attractiveness in dress, in an ethnical milieu in which dress complex does not occupy an important place and the forms are conventionalized and stabilized, would be sufficient for turning psychiatrist's attention to the sexual complex of the individual, while the same behaviour in the milieu of ethnical unit in which dress complex is not suppressed the extravagance in dress will leave observer indifferent, for it is a common phenomenon.

Indeed, in these cases I have in view only those cases which cannot be identified as *pathological* conditions etiologically and diagnostically easily traced to the classical cases of psychiatry, i.e. the cases dealt with by the psychiatrist and not by the ethnographer. Within the same ethnical unit even the psychiatrists meet with the cases known in legal medicine as cases found on the line of demarcation between "normal" and "abnormal".

When a series of ethnical units possessing different cultural and psychomental complexes are considered together, the line of demarcation is subject to a shifting in dependence on the existing different psychophysiological complexes and different psychomental cultural complexes. Therefore, when we extend our investigation, both in covering various units, and in going deeper into the details within the same ethnical unit, simplification of diagnosis ought to be rejected and the "standards" previously found ought to be put aside till the investigation is completed. If the observer would take as a starting point of comparison the standards of "normality" and "abnormality" found in his own ethnical milieu it is very likely that he would find many more abnormalities in an alien group than in his own group. As a matter of fact, the impressions produced by the ethnical units one on another—little familiarity with the complexes supposing—usually tend to the conclusion as to the psychomental abnormalities of the neighbour either in the sense of psychic instability, or that of lowered psychic reactions, or that of mental deficiency. These facts are very interesting for the analysis of internal ethnical relations and interethnical reactions which sometimes may lead to the discovery of the characteristics of the psychomental complex of the observers themselves. I now point out these conditions in order to show how difficult is a successful and an absolutely reliable investigation into the psychological conditions of ethnical units. But in spite of all the difficulties, the facts must be recorded and so they are even against the will of observer, sometimes unconsciously, for he must adapt himself to the unit in which he is doing his work, especially concerning delicate matter of "religion and beliefs".[*] When the process of observation is cognized by the investigator, it is still better from the point of view of final outcome of investigation. On the other hand, by pointing out to the character of observations I want to explain the paucity of my observations in some respects, and their abundance, which sometimes even cannot be used, in some other respects. Indeed, the relative utility of facts to be observed may be realized only after the analysis of the whole material is over, but lege artis all facts must be recorded, so that the abundance of some facts in some degree does not depend on the investigator, if he does not abstract, quite artificially and methodologically unjustified, a certain group of phenomena.

Naturally, in the present exposition I shall not give all the facts recorded, but in so far as possible I shall try to give picture as a ground for discussion of a particular subject,—shamanism in its function of self-regulating mechanism of the psychomental complex,—so I shall leave aside those cases—perhaps quite interesting from the point of view of psychopathology—which have no direct bearing on the subject. On the other hand, I shall dwell on some other aspects which would attract no attention, when found in the European complex, but which have great weight in the Tungus complex.

83. PSYCHIC AND MENTAL TROUBLES It is impossible definitely to say how frequent are cases of insanity amongst the Tungus. The reason is not only that no statistical observations have been carried out, but also that the number of Tungus population is very small. In fact, the Tungus groups

---

* Some ethnographers are so sceptical as to their own ability of observation and preparedness for this kind of work that they avoid these investigations and do their best not to see the facts, although they know them, e.g. from their own reactions and ways of adaptation to the people under investigation. As a matter of fact, the investigator who is absolutely lacking tact will be unable to remain even a short time in contact with the people. Practically he must leave the people because of uselessness of his staying even for record of "material culture and social organization" preferred subjects of investigators. The history of ethnography gives us some instances of tactless investigators who were refused permission to stay with the people; only absolutely tactless "explorers" lost their lives during the work amongst the "savages". In this respect the investigation of "civilized" nations is in a somewhat different condition and the "methods of tact" prove sometimes to be useless. To this question I shall return in another work, but now I shall conclude my remarks by pointing out that in an average case, the record of all facts is not only possible but it is very desirable.

here discussed, as shown in SONT, rarely exceed two thousands of individuals. True, the Manchus of Aigun district are more numerous, but still they are not more than some twenty thousand people. In these conditions statistical observations confined to such a limited population cannot be convincing. There is one more condition to be pointed out, namely, in the conditions of Tungus life the insane individuals are not isolated nor especially protected and thus they perish soon after loss of their ability of taking care of themselves. The destruction of such individuals occurs even probably much earlier than the evident signs of insanity make their appearance which would imply isolation of the individual affected. The life of the Tungus, threatened at every moment by the natural agents and wild animals, requires a special vigilance which may be within power of absolutely normal persons only. Accidents which may eliminate the insane individuals are frequent, but it is very risky to diagnose causes of accidents if one bases oneself on the Tungus statements. In fact, the same accident may be due (1) to the coincidence of circumstances independent on the individual; (2) to the self-suggestion, as will be shown, very common amongst the Tungus and which cannot be regarded as a condition of insanity; and (3) to a real insanity. It is very likely that in all three cases the Tungus explanation of the accident will be the same,— the interference of the spirits. However, in some cases the Tungus and Manchus distinguish three classes of accidents. In the first class the accident would be ascribed to the carelessness of the man who did not foresee the possibility of an accident; in the second class it would be ascribed to the influence of spirits and in the third class to the abnormal condition of the man. So we now approach the Tungus and Manchu ideas as to the insanity.

I have found various theories in circulation. For instance, some forms of insanity by the Manchus are ascribed to the penetration of water (after drinking) into the liver, whence a great excitability of the individual, and "shadowing" of the heart may occur.

The conception of insanity may be also understood from the "gnoseological" theories professed by some Manchus. As shown, according to the general opinion amongst the Manchus, the Manchus *ɣun'imb'i*—"think"—with their heart (*ɣun'in*), which is a physical organ and at the same time its function is emotionally perceived as "thought", "idea", "emotion", etc. The head has nothing to do with the "mind". The cases of insanity, according to the Manchus, are more frequent amongst the intelligent but hot-tempered individuals. It is explained as "shadowing of the heart",—*ɣun'in bur'imb'i*,—while normal man has a "clear heart". Occurrence of a sudden insanity preceded by a condition of excitement and "psychic instability" is explained as due to the "shadowing of the heart" (which is a quite realistic and so to say materialistic shadowing) with something, the nature of which is not clear. From this conception it is evident that the Manchus, at least some of them, have a quite realistic theory as to some cases of insanity, although the part of heart and its "shadowing" cannot be accepted as corresponding to the reality. It may be here noted that the emotional perception of "shadowing" is quite admissible and that the conception of heart as an organ of thinking process is quite positivistic for the thought in its emotional manifestation is per-

ceived by the heart.* In some cases this shadowing functionally is thus connected with the liver, but the occurrence of "shadowing," in so far as I could find, may be due to other conditions as well. The Manchus admit possibility of medical treatment of these cases. This may be classified as a physiological theory of insanity. This theory does not include all possible cases of insanity. A group of cases is explained by the theory which postulates the soul to be a complex of three balanced elements (*vide supra* pp. 134 et seq.).

Insanity may occur in case a spirit (*xutu, vide supra* p. 140) introduces itself in the absence of one of components of the soul (*fojeyo*). The treatment is very difficult because the shaman must call out the spirit, send it off, and to call back the soul.

However, the spirits may use the human body as "placing" and introduce themselves even in the presence of all components of the soul. So the individual would be "possessed" by these spirits. This is a very common occurrence: when the individual was sick, the spirits were promised to have a special shrine (*m'ao*), and the promise was not fulfilled. Since the Manchus widely practise cheating of spirits, as the spirits do with the Manchus, these occurrences are common. The spirit, usually one of *fuč'k'i* or *māfa*, enters the body which begins to tremble and scream. Then the spirit through the mouth of the individual expresses its desire of having a special, and promised, shrine. The treatment is not difficult,—to build up the shrine.**

Amongst the Tungus I have recorded no theories regarding insanity, except that of the spirits which produce trouble. Again the basis of this theory is the idea of the triple structure of the soul and possibility of using human body as "placing" by the spirits.

The violent insane people in Bir. and Kum. are called *xōdu—kōdu* [*cf.* Dahur (Poppe) *xōdōl*,—"a fool" (? S. Sh.)] and *gêrèn*, corresponding to *gara* (Nerč.) which are equivalent to *xōdu—kōdu*; also *gani* (Nerč. Barg.) [*cf.* Buriat Podg.) *gani,—ibid; gân* (Dahur, Poppe),—"mad", *gani* (Mong. Kow.) "être en fureur, s'emporter", etc.] However, in Bir. we have a verb "to become insane"—*gêrèn*, which, in spite of similarity with the above *gêrèn*, seems to

* "Positivistic" point of view amongst the Europeans tries to locate "thought" in special and particular sections of the brain, which is one of naive positivistic conceptions based upon various hypotheses the chief of which is abstraction of the brain. In this aspect the "positivistic" point of view is not far from that of the Manchus, who with a full right may speak of localization of the thinking process in the heart for they feel it.

** A difficult case was reported to me by the Manchus: "There is a Chinese young girl in Shantung. She went into the "kitchen garden to collect some vegetables (so-called Chinese cabbage "—n'oɲg'in sog'i in Manchu). Then she suddenly lost her conscious-"ness and fell on the ground. When she recovered she returned "home, looking like not-human being. She sits like a Buddha, refuses "food. Her mother asks her to eat, she replies: ɛI am endür'iɜ. "In this position she remained for six years. The people put in front "of her some sacrifices: mantōu (bread), and stick incense. She "does not move, does not comb her hair, does not wash herself, but "remains clean and well combed. By sitting so, she is now covered "with dust (like Buddha). Twelve shamans shamanized, but nothing "could do. They fear themselves. She speaks only once a year— "on the new year day, when she asks for a m'ao for herself. The "shamans proposed to bury her, but the local authorities did not allow "it. It is not certain whether this phenomenon is due to an endür'i, "xutu or even večko. Therefore, the girl is not considered as insane".

be a metathesic form of the Mongol *ganirana;* and in Mank. *koira,* a loan-word from the Buriat *k'eirā.* These terms are usually referred to people who are violently insane. The insanity may be explained or not. In case it is not explained by spirits, it is accepted as a matter of fact.

The Tungus also distinguish forms of insanity which may be classified as idiocy, also some forms of harmless and not violent insane behaviour. The persons so affected are called *bālin, bēlēi* borrowed from the Manchu *beli, belen,*[*] which is equivalent to *oloŋ* (Bir.).[**]

In order to complete the picture of gradations of mental conditions I want to point out that the Tungus have other terms for mentally inferior people who are not abnormal. These terms are *tānā* (Bir.), *tānāy* (Mank.) *tānāk* (Ur. Castr.) [cf. *tenek* (Buriat, Podg. Castr.) *tènèg* (Dahur, Poppe); *teneg* (Mong. Kow.)] commonly used in the sense of "weak-minded," as opposed e.g. to "wisdom of spirits"; *nantkun* (Bir.) [cf. *mentuxun* (Manchu Writ.)] *xulg'in* [cf. *xulx'i* (Manchu Writ.)] both of which are rarely used; *modumoĉo* (Bir.),—"stupid like wood" [cf. *moĉo* (Manchu)—mentally dull, blunt (by birth)]. I omit some other terms of which it is not clear whether they mean "stupid". or "abnormal".[***]

The above enumerated terms demonstrate that the Tungus possess several terms for distinction of "violent insanity", "idiocy and harmless insanity", "special condition-*oloŋ*" (*vide infra* p. 245) and "mental inferiority". It must be pointed out that the Tungus may use a combination of these terms, as for instance, *bēlēi kōdu* (Bir. Kum.) which designates a violent condition of *oloŋ.* It is interesting to note that a great number of these terms used among the Northern Tungus are rather recently borrowed from powerful neighbours of the Tungus: the Mongol speaking groups and Manchus, quite analogous to the Greek-Latin terminology of a great number of European groups.

In accordance with the Tungus classification I shall now give a description of the conditions. According to the Tungus, the causes of violent insanity are not the same. It may be due to various causes symbolized in different spirits, and different forms of their activity. This has to be found out by the shaman and he may recognize whether the case is curable or hopeless. In fact the diagnosis can be wrong and there may be made several attempts at curing without any essential effect. It would be then inferred that the shaman failed to find out the actual cause, or he was not skilful in treating, or lastly that this was beyond the possibilities of the shaman. For instance, the violent insanity caused by the *s'irkul,* the local spirits *ajelga* and the like, can be cured, while that produced by a thunder stroke, and a whirl wind (these are spirits too) are usually regarded as incurable. During my travelling and living amongst the Tungus I have never observed cases of violent insanity.

The condition of *bālin—bēlēi* not associated with *kōdu,* i.e. harmless insanity, idiocy, etc. are not curable and they may be caused (according to the Birarĉen) by some spirits.

Some forms of *kōdu* (violent insanity) may gradually change into that of *bālin.* Yet, a great number of cases are considered as inborn condition. In this case the Tungus would say: the person was born in such a state. Inborn and acquired speechlessness are separated into a group called *jaba* (Kum. Bir.) [cf. Manchu Sp. *jaba;*[*] Mongol *jawā;* Chinese (啞 吧) *jaba*], *imtoi* (Nerĉ.).[**] However, the Tungus also use a general term for "idiocy", when it is an inborn condition, and they may say: "the subject is sick", when it is acquired. Speechlessness may be ascribed to the spirits' activity and to a physical defect, e.g. after a contusion. The Tungus would not use this term when speechlessness is associated with idiocy, unless the speechlessness as such is needed to be indicated.

The terms *tānā, uantkun, modumoĉo,* etc. are not referred to persons psychically affected but only to those who are mentally inferior, unintelligent by birth. Yet, as we have seen, they are freely used for self-humiliation in prayers to the spirits.

I have separated the cases which are designated by the Tungus as *oloŋ.* This is a condition frequently met with,—it is described below under the name of "oloniem", —of which the Tungus are quite conscious. However. the Tungus designate by this term only those cases in which they see "uncontrolled imitation", while other cases of "hysteria arctica" are explained as due to the spirits' activity. When a person *oloŋ* becomes violent the Tungus call the affected person *kōdu oloŋ.* As stated above, the Birarĉen sometimes use *bālin—bēlēi,* borrowed from the Manchus, instead of *oloŋ.* The etymology of *oloŋ* does not leave any doubt: cf. "verbs" *olo* (Bir.)—"to be suddenly frightened", *olomb'i* (Manchu Writ)—"to tremble from fear ;"[***] *olo (l)* (Mank.)—"to jump aside" referred to a frightened horse; *olo* (Nerĉ.),—"to fall into misfortune",[****] etc. In all these translations we can see a common element, namely, "useless acts or effects produced under the influence of a sudden fear." Thence there are derivative verbs of the type of e.g. *olondokon,*—"to be affected by this condition *oloŋ*" (Bir.). The Tungus idea of this condition is thus quite clear in the sense that the spirits are not considered responsible for it. I have been frequently told by the Tungus how the person may become *oloŋ* without any interference on the part of spirits, but this will be discussed later. However, it is different when *oloŋ* become violent, as it is, for instance, in the case of *aŋŋa sēvēn's* activity.

I shall now give two examples of condition which are not considered by the Tungus as "abnormal" ones, but which would not be so regarded in an European milieu. Some other examples will be shown in the chapter dealing with the shamans.

1. A man about forty years old among the Barguzin Tungus being drunk was struck by thunder when sitting under a tree. He was ill during a certain time. Since that time he abstains from drinking wine, for, according to

---

[*] The etymology of this word is interesting, for it points to the character of condition. Vide infra the same page.

[**] I. Zaxarov translates: "stupid, fool, senseless, etc." which is not quite correct, for it is referred to a special condition.

[***] In most of the existing collections of these terms, the authors did not pay attention to the particular characters of the psychomental condition designated by various terms.

---

[*] In Manchu Writ. another term is used; namely, *xeĉe. xeĉen aku* which can be compared with *xeĵegeĵ, keĵekeĵ* [xeĵe + ugeĵ] of the Mongols and Buriats. The term is referred to the defect of speech only, including even minor defects. However, in Manchu Sp. this term is now superseded by *jaba.*

[**] The etymology is not clear.

[***] *olomb'i* seems to be incompletely translated by I. Zaxarov, the trembling is only one of external manifestations.

[****] In fact this is a particular meaning of *olo,* which in this dialect must be wider.

him, a certain connexion existed between his being intoxicated and the thunder stroke. He can no more hunt. He lives on occasional work, e.g. guiding Russians, small transport business, etc. He is usually silent, avoiding to look in the speaker's eyes, his voice is unusually weak, but he is very fond of telling stories and greatly interested in shamanism. Sometimes his speech is inconsistent, as well as his stories. He was under my observation during four or five weeks every day. He is an invalid in the conditions of Tungus life. The Tungus avoid to provoke in him the condition further described as "olonism", but he is not *olog*, and generally is not considered as "insane", but just "a man who was struck by thunder" and now possesses a certain queerness. In the European milieu he would be considered "abnormal", and most likely placed into an asylum.

2. Among the Nerčinsk Tungus a man over forty years old, being intoxicated with wine in the state of uncontrolled excitement killed a Russian. He was put into jail for eighteen months. Since that time he is afraid of drinking wine. He is seemingly "normal", but he does not hunt. Instead of that he has some cattle and horses on which he lives. From time to time he remains silent and absent-minded, so that he does not react on stimuli. He avoids Russians and Buriats, but he has a definite inclination to Buddhism.

The above given facts as to the Tungus conception of psychomental abnormalities may be summarized as follows. The Tungus and Manchus explain certain conditions as inborn ones which, as such, have nothing to do with the spirits; such are some cases of idiocy, speechlessness, feeble-mindedness etc. Another class of cases are those which are due to the "hysteria arctica" which, as will be shown, are explained by the Tungus usually as "bad habit" by which not only men, but also animals (horses) may be affected. The Manchus explain some cases of insanity as due to a physiological trouble of the heart and liver. The Manchus and Tungus explain the greatest part of serious psychomental troubles as due to the activity of spirits, and these troubles are classified and treated in accordance with the characters of the spirits and with the diagnosis. Yet, the last groups of cases may be dissected into two subgroups: namely, cases when the abnormal condition is due to the fact of an external influence of the spirits, which may take violent and harmless forms, and cases when the abnormal condition is due to the fact that spirits are using the human body as a placing, which may also produce violent and harmless forms.

It must be kept in mind that even in the cases when insanity is explained as due to the spirits, this explanation must not be taken as too much simplified,—a spirit is very often nothing but the specification of a pathological condition and some spirits do not take any concrete form, except that of observed pathological manifestations. These spirits can never be approached by men, but may be influenced through other spirits.

84. "OLONISM," SO-CALLED "IMITATIVE MANIA." On the perfectly reasonable supposition that we can operate with the generalization "hysteria" M. Czaplicka ("The Aboriginal Siberia," p.

320) has pointed out that most of the symptoms of arctic hysteria are met with in Europe, except that of imitative mania* which distinguishes "hysteria arctica" from other forms. But the first question is what can we call hysteria in general, and whether this generalization really covers more than mere symptoms? Therefore, I am rather reluctant to use this very broad designation, but I will keep it as the title of a further section in which I shall treat undoubtedly different forms of psychomental troubles in various degrees affecting the social behaviour of the individuals, and which cannot be classed as "insanity", "idiocy", etc. However, imitative mania ought to be excluded as a "symptom" of hysteria, and as a special condition, which will be shown in the present section.

The "imitative mania" (*chorea imitatoria*) has been described by a great number of authors amongst the populations of Siberia and even amongst the Malays.** As to the geographic distribution of this condition we can now include Manchuria, where "imitative mania" is common amongst the Tungus and Manchus and is also known amongst the Dahurs.

There are two hypotheses as to the "imitative mania", namely, (1) it was ascribed as due to the arctic conditions in which the newcomers cannot adapt themselves and fall into a state of psychic instability; (2) it was connected with the "psycho-physiological nature of the Mongols". The first hypothesis was proposed by a great number of investigators in Siberia for whom the conditions of arctic regions seemed to be "abnormal". They were themselves persons born in different climatic conditions, the reaction on which could also have been "abnormal", and occurring especially during the dark season and during the periods of change of seasons, etc.*** As to the last condition I have some doubt as to the statistical reliability of the observation, especially considering the fact that the troubles appear at any season when they may interest the people. I leave without explanation the last condition which will receive its full significance after my further description. M. Czaplicka has pointed out that in the presence of imitative mania among the Malays it is safer to define this condition as due to the extremes of the climate: "hysteria of climatic extremes" (op. cit. p. 323). This author is inclined to connect this condition with the "psycho-physiological nature of Mongols" (p. 324). However, it may naturally be remarked that "Mongol" is a hypothesis which has never been proved to be a fact; and it is now not permitted to speak of the "Aryan stock" as not being subject to this condition. I point out that in both hypotheses there may be some truth, viz. psychic instability in an unusual milieu and hereditary predispositions for certain physio-

---

* Chorea imitatoria, of Dr. Kashin, cf. M. Czaplicka, op. cit. p. 324.

** Beginning from the eighteenth century up to our days the travellers and medical doctors reported various cases in their modifications. Instead of repeating once more I make reference to M. Czaplicka's work (op. cit. pp. 309, et seq.).

*** The reaction on different conditions is summarized: "dark winter days, light summer nights, severe cold, the silence, the general monotony of the landscape, scarcity of food, etc." (M. Czaplicka, op. cit. p. 321) which reflects rather reaction of observers than that of natives of these regions. Most of these observers are accustomed to sunshine, dark nights, moderate temperature (especially in the well built houses), city noise, variety of scenery in streets and theatres, rich food in restaurants and in families of well-to-do class (in old Russia).

logical conditions, but actually both are different aspects of the same situation, and for the time being we cannot make a choice between the two hypotheses. We even cannot say whether we really need them for the understanding of the actual functioning of the psychomental complex.

I shall not describe here all cases which I have observed, for a great number of them are a mere repetition of known patterns, and a great number of other cases are mere varieties, truly curious, owing to their unusual forms, but not interesting from the point of view of their analysis.

———

I begin with the most common case, namely, the repeating of the last word, the so-called "echolalia". It is commonly observed amongst the populations here discussed. It consists in the repetition of the last word, phrase, sentence. Evidently the affected person does not grasp the "meaning" of the complex of the starters, i.e. the person does not correctly respond to the conventional function of the starters, or this function is inhibited.* The "causes" of this condition may be different: (1) the authoritative requirement of the teacher or parents to repeat the question before giving an answer** which may turn into a habit; (2) the requirement of repetition of the last word in "religious" (e.g. shamanistic) performances, when the whole audience repeats after the shaman his last word which is needed, as will be shown, for bringing the shaman and the audience into the state of extasy, and which may also turn into a habit; (3) the repetition of "words" prohibited by social customs, but constituting an important element in the psychomental complex under the pretext that these words were already pronounced, e.g. in Tungus such ones are starters for genitalia, and sexual act; (4) the disfunction of the system of conditioned reflexes.

I now want to point out the difference between the two conditions; namely, unconscious repetition,—real echolalia —and violation of existing customs under the pretext that they have been already violated by other people, which permits expression of inhibited complex. This may lead us to the next step, namely, the occurrence of using "bad words",—coprolalia of Sir William Osler,—which may be started by a pronounced word. The reaction may be short or long, it may consist of a repeated word or a whole series of "bad words". In this case a good deal of growth of complexes depends on the individual imagination and the stock of prohibited "words". Since a great number of prohibited words are those concerning the sexual sphere, the coprolalism may take a sexual form, but actually it is not confined only to the sexual sphere. In fact, in complex cases we meet with the combination of sexual and "religious" elements the common use of which is prohibited. A further complication may be seen when aesthetic terms are mixed with "vulgar" ones, and still more complex are the cases when sexual and religious prohibitions are violated by their association with aesthetic and even "scientific" complexes. Indeed, these are very complex forms of

"coprolalism" in which the subjects are operating not only with "words" but also with conceptions, which does not make their nature and function different. The change of "coprolalism" depends on the change of the cultural complex, and on the amount of prohibited words and prohibited associations. These prohibitions and violations are often not understood at all. For these reasons I rather prefer to avoid such a term as "coprolalia", for the first component is nothing but the expression of a reaction.*

From the above shown approach to the problem it may be seen that the essential condition is not the sexual element, but the fact of social prohibition which may be violated either by using words or by using prohibited association of conceptions and starters. It may be regarded as a social violation and thus meet with opposition on the part of the society, i.e. be considered as a form of "coprolalism", or it may be approved by the society as a "bright idea" which produces an unusual reaction. When the reaction becomes common the new association loses its effect of a starter of an unusual reaction and thus it loses its "coprolalic" function. A few instances may help us. The language of some professions, e.g. sailors, is very rich in prohibited terms and associations. Among the sailors these expressions and associations become a kind of seasoning to their language : without which the language is no more a real "sailor's language", but that of common people of other professions. Gradually the coprolalic character of these words and associations in this way loses its acuteness. W.W. Radlov once told me that when a Kirgiz child is taking his mother's breast he repeats expressions which would make a sailor blush, but the Kirgiz mother only approvingly smiles, for she is not allowed to use the same words, while in the language of the Kirgiz men they are not at all prohibited. Some professional groups amongst the Russians (before the Great War) possessed a rather elaborate system of expressions in which there might be mentioned and associated e.g. genitalia, bread, God, etc. Within these professions this "coprolalism" has degenerated into a complete loss of "meaning",—some expressions have become a simple "seasoning" without which the speech could no more function,** even used merely for filling up rhythmic omissions, while in other social groups they preserved their "coprolalic" character. "Coprolalism" of prohibited associations, more rarely words, is frequently met with in the writing of those authors who disagree with the existing complexes, by which they want to attract attention to themselves, or to abolish one of existing "superstitions", or to satisfy a desire of the self-expression of inhibited complexes. It should be noted that during the periods of social disequilibrium and ethnical disequilibrium these public manifestations are especially common.*** My point is that coprolalism is a

———

* My approach to the language as a system of conditioned reflexes is of a special importance for the understanding of the condition of "echolalia", as well as that of "coprolalia" discussed below. Vide my work "Ethnological and Linguistical Aspects, etc.", Chapter 2.

** I have frequently observed it amongst the students of foreign languages who studied them with bad teachers.

———

* By this remark I do not intend to discredit the symptomatic value of this condition for practical needs of psychiatrists, who are supposed to be familiar with the complexes of their own ethnical units and rarely meet with extra-ethnical cases. However, for the needs of ethnography it can be used only with reserves.

** In dealing with different social groups I have found that such a seasoning was necessary when one needed to be fully understood. Therefore the "coprolalic" expressions were indispensable when one dealt with the group that used them, or when one needed to show one's own belonging to a definite social group (which might also be "psychological"). There are very numerous stories (statement of facts) which are usually figuring as "anecdotes", but actually they are not so.

*** The Russian literature of the post-revolution period was very broad phenomenon which is conditioned by the existing social systems, and it is relative, for it functions as such only when socially disapproved: the social disapproval affects either a social group, or a sexual group, or even an age group. The group of phenomena (words, conceptions, ideas, feelings, etc.) may be different. "Coprolalism" can be understood, cognized, and it may be taken for something else: e.g. originality, brightness of mind, will power, strong character, sexuality, etc.*

I deemed these remarks necessary before going into the analysis of the Tungus complex, for the Tungus and Manchu "coprolalia" is more complex than it appears at first. "Words" prohibited among young women, are not so among men who would use them without any shade of "bad" meaning,—they would be used as latin terms are used in a European hospital.** Children are not allowed to use these terms for they do not need them so much as adult people. Young women are also not allowed to pronounce them because of the association of these terms with sexual relations about which, owing to complex psycho-social conditions, the young woman must not "speak". However, the old women do use these words, even with a sexual allusion for they are not restricted in sexual respects and there is no power to check them up, for junior generations cannot interfere. Such bravery of old women and teasing of young women is quite common, not only amongst the Tungus,—to talk about sex may become for an old woman sufficient compensation of central nervous habits, even when physiologically she can no more function as a woman or she has no more suitable partners. Since amongst the Tungus the old women are not actually restricted from using these words, a great number of them seize any occasion for repeating them after another person. Their attitude in this case may be understood (1) as a manifestation of their own sexual complex,—a desire to revive in their minds their previous experience; (2) as an occasion for showing their superior social position, when they are not restricted; (3) to challenge the young women in order to see the reaction and to amuse themselves; and (4) a real case of echolalia. The case of an old woman reacting on a starter by producing a series of "indecent" words is more complex, but it is in the same line of phenomena in which the last case (4) is found and it ought to be interpreted as a responding chain of conditioned reflexes.

Indeed, from the observation of old women I could see, or at least suspect, all four conditions of reactions which with the help of supplementary conversations and "deepening" could be often established, and sometimes understood,

saturated not only with coprolalism of associations, but a serious attempt was made there to introduce expressions (sometimes self-understood under the symbols of initial letters, as it is met with in other Western literatures), which were coprolalic for all social groups except some professionals. "Coprolalism" of associations and even of expressions is known among the fashionable writers of all epochs and peoples. I do not mean here "pornography" the function of which is different and very specialized being chiefly connected with the sexual complex. The "anarchistic", "socialistic" and other generally unrecognized writers who sometimes preserve anti-coprolalic outer forms, are particularly inclined to the "coprolalism" of associations.

* Theoretically it may be supposed that with a further change of the European complex there will appear some new forms of coprolalism. They do appear but they are not recognized.

** In connexion with this it can be noted that the Tungus accept as substitutes terms borrowed from other ethnical groups, e.g. the Manchus, Mongols, etc.

at least perceived, by the women. In the first case they would turn their conversation to their previous experience (not all Tungus are "hypocritic!") ; in the second case they would point out that nobody can interfere with them; in the third case they would frankly say that they wanted to tease the young women. Perhaps in the last case they would not recognize an automatic reaction, but these are usually associated with other conditions of "imitative mania" and can thus be checked up in the last complex. When taken separately they may be brought about by the above outlined conditions, which may not always be established with due certainty.

It is different when we have a case of a young woman who is socially restricted from using these words. No doubt, in a great number of cases coprolalia in young women is a mere expression of their sexuality, as a revival of experience or its future possibility. That such an attitude is possible,—I do not want to say: "a fact",—is proved by the fact of women's interest in sexual problems, especially in so far as the women themselves may experience in this field. In fact, the women talk about it. When they respond in a mixed society, when the latter consist of males and females (usually there must be several females together), the sexual response becomes especially evident, for a good deal of the success of the reaction depends on the men who are present. In this case we touch on a new side of the problem, namely, sexual exhibitionism to which we shall proceed later. But, it will now be sufficient to point out that the presence of an audience greatly helps reaction. It is more likely that the woman would show no reaction if she is certain that other women will repeat the same prohibited word, or a series of words. However, in young women there is a great inhibitory condition; namely, they are not allowed to pronounce these words, and if there are present elderly men (much less if there are elderly women) the inhibition will be sometimes sufficient to prevent the production of a reaction. This is one of reasons why women are so free in their language in the presence of members of the Tungus clans, the marital relations with which are not restricted, as also with a foreigner whom they do not fear.

The ease of breaking of these social restrictions is possible only if the woman is very "impertinent" and "does not care" about public opinion, when she manifests her "independence" (such cases do occur among the Tungus), or in the case when she cannot control herself because of pressing need of sexual satisfaction. Such cases may occur when the woman is left alone for a long time or when she is in disagreement with her husband. The question now is: how many cases of real echolalia and coprolalia, as phenomena which are not conditioned by the normal state of young women, may be found in thousands of similar reactions observed in a great majority of Tungus young women? And another question arises: why do some ethnical groups consider all these cases as excusable ones under the justification of a "pathological condition", typical of the Tungus oloŋ? After a continuous observation and hundreds of experiments in various circumstances, I have come to the conclusion that in exceptionally rare cases there is really "pathological" condition of oloŋ, "imitative mania", while the rest of the cases are all due to the possibility of a manifestation either of sexual complex or of a social "rebellion" under the cover of images of "olonism".

It is thus evident that this symptom of imitative mania is quite misleading in most of cases, and it may be considered as a real symptom only in the presence of a complex of other symptoms.

Here it is necessary to point out that not only sexual complex may be found under the prohibition, but also some other phenomena. Unfortunately, my observations in this respect are not very numerous. However, I may indicate that the words like *s'irkul* amongst the Tungus of Manchuria, and *xutu* amongst the Manchus may produce the same reaction not only amongst the females, but also among the males. When they were pronounced (e.g. by myself) they always produced an "echolalic" effect: *s'irkul*, *s'irkul*, *s'irkul*, etc., or even a "coprolalic" effect,—a long enumeration of various spirits. One of the conditions is that the people must not name them because they may really come, and the second condition is that some Tungus are not reluctant to challenge these spirits. Side by side with these "words", the observer may obtain a positive result with foreign words echolalically repeated, but the nature of the phenomenon is still more complex and after my experiments its simplified explanation does not satisfy me.

The inference which may be made from the above given facts is that at the basis of these phenomena we have not only inhibited sexual complex, but also other inhibited complexes, and therefore these reactions should be generalized over all socially prohibited phenomena, both in males and females, and only in rare cases we have a real psychopathological condition which is used by the Tungus as a justification of their violation of existing social prohibitions. Therefore, the investigator must not overestimate the significance of this "symptom". As to the real Tungus reaction I shall speak about it later.

85. IMITATION OF MOVEMENTS Imitation of movement is not observed as frequently as imitation of "words". It consists in the imitation of movements produced by persons, animals, and things. The initial imitated movement may be produced by other persons with the definite purpose of obtaining an imitative reaction. One of the important conditions of success of the reaction is that the person susceptible to it must be unprepared for the movement.

For illustration I will now give some instances.

Case I. A young man (Birarčen), about 22 years old, anthropologically type beta,[*] healthy, well fed, stout, showing perfect normality of reflexes (knee-reaction, eye-reaction, equilibrium); medium intelligence; a good, steady worker. When he was eating his millet, the other men would suddenly attract his attention and begin doing as if they would fill up their mouths with millet with a speed that would not permit the swallowing of the food. He would immediately imitate stuffing millet into his mouth, till no more place would be left in the mouth and the breathing would become impossible. Then he would leave his laughing companions and run away to empty his mouth. After which he would return to the table in order normally to continue his meal. The performance is not very often done. This was his "number". No other forms of

[*] For reference to the anthropological types vide my publications "Anthropology of Eastern China" and "Anthropologische und gynäkologische Beobachtungen an Chinesinnen" etc. where characteristics of males and females are given respectively.

imitation were observed in this case. I do not venture to assert that the man was, in my presence at least, ashamed of the happening, but he did not protest. The performance was observed by myself several times,—the Tungus wanted to show me his talent.

Case II. A man (Khingan), about 42 years old, type gamma; rather weak, not attractive, shy; usually quiet and normal; self-sustaining by hunting; no observations as to the reactions and mentality. He performed *erectio penis* in public. One of the men present would do as if he was masturbating. The man would take out his penis and in a few seconds produce erectio, to the great satisfaction of all present men and especially women. A burst of general laughter would bring the man to his "normal condition" and he would run away. I have seen several times this performance. In so far as I could find out, it was done especially for the amusement of the women present.

Case III. A Manchu middle aged man, apparently normal. When there was a gathering of people, one of them would suddenly but slightly strike the man. Then he would do the same to his neighbour. The chief attraction was to surprise the persons who did not know the "number" and would react on *oloy* by anger or indignation; or transgress the social customs, e.g. when the *oloy* would touch a woman or a senior who became an object of general joke and laughter. In this case the *oloy* is used as a means to see the reactions of other persons. The man in his movements was really "very funny", and it was still funnier to see those who reacted.

Case IV. A man, Birarčen, of about middle age, from a family where many abnormal cases, and "bad temper" are observed. He used to imitate movements of other people, but showed a definite inclination for the knife (long hunting and table knives), axe, etc., which was dangerous for other people. One day he was sitting alone, with his small son, in the wigwam. A knife fell down in front of him (evidently, the knife had been in the hanging hunting belt). He seized it and thrust it into his son's body. The man soon afterwards died.

In the first case, as well as in the second, the subjects were encouraged and even provoked by the audience to produce their "number". In the first case the interest was confined to seeing the unusual sight of a man, who does not know how to eat, to fill up his mouth with millet and to watching his very fast movements which produced an unusual and queer impression. In the second and third cases the main interest was in the psycho-sexual and social sides respectively: showing erectio penis to the women present and observing their surprise and violation of social conventions. In all cases the subjects attract attention of their communities and become for a while a centre,—they are actors, sometimes envied actors, such as in the case II. The case IV is different, because of its dangerous nature for the community, which is evident from the final result: the murder of the son, and the subsequent death of the subject.

I have pointed out that in the three first cases the performers are "actors". This is rather an important condition at the beginning of "imitative mania". The Tungus observers told me that usually "they began by showing something", after which they assumed this practice as a habit. Many children would try to imitate, but the parents would stop this habit and it receives no further development. Indeed, the eating of millet is just a minor, harmless distraction, which introduces a joyful element of variety into the life of the Tungus confined to small groups. Yet the man is of importance as an actor, for he has something distinct and individual,—his own invention. Still more interesting is the second case in which a new complex is added, namely, sexual exhibitionism. So the motivation of "imitative mania" receives a new support, individually from the side of inhibited sexual complex, and publicly a possible (potential) sexual excitement of the women in the presence of men, and an exhibition of what is suppressed by the social conventionalism.

That such an exhibitionism as a psychological phenomenon exists among the Tungus, may be seen from the fact that among all Tungus groups a certain attention is paid to the sexual organs of children. The children, under the pretext that they are children and do not understand what they do, are asked to exhibit their genitalia in the presence of adult persons, who enjoy in seeing children—performers. However, among the Tungus groups this practice is not equally in vogue. Its greatest development is observed among the Khingan group,—i.e. exactly in the group where erectio penis was performed,—the children, especially girls sometimes of the age of ten and even twelve years, are requested to show their genitalia. They willingly do it, for the adult people do approve it (I cannot now assert that the parents always are present and frankly approve their children). As to whether the children are absolutely conscious of what they do—personally I think that a Tungus child of ten or twelve years may be so—is not of importance, for we are interested in the social side of the exhibitionism. However, no adult person may be allowed to do it, unless such a person is supposed to be affected by "olonism" or "imitative mania". I do not think that such an effect as erectio penis can be performed without involving any sexual complex of the individual, especially in an individual of forty two years, and in a few seconds. So that on the part of the subject there is a strongly manifested condition of sexual exhibitionism, which has been developed by exercise and general social approval. Indeed, such a public manifestation of exhibitionism approved socially is not yet a "pathological" condition. In other cultural complexes it may assume only a different form,—it may be "sublimated".* Thus the fact

* Indeed, the whole theory of "sublimation" is particularly ethmographic in its foundation and principle. But we do not need to discuss it here. As to the forms of exhibitionism they are sometimes really camouflaged under such symbols, as showing of shoes, special ornamentation of stockings (which is sometimes even not understood), etc. that the initial form cannot be realized. However, public exhibitionism of parts of the naked body is not banished altogether. Music halls and theatres allow quite frank demonstrations of front and back views by means of abrupt movements of very short skirts. This method is supposed to be a simple and artistic form of classical choreography which is also a mere justification. Still further this public exhibitionism is carried in particular cases in theatres and even cafes, where naked women, even a waitress, may appear for a moment with a certain justification or without any justification. Exhibitionism may be rationalized, as it is with the modern movement of nudism, and it may be socially conventionalized as it is with the bath-costumes on the sea-beaches in all parts of the world, and so forth.

Indeed, for hot tempered puritans these forms of exhibitionism are not admissible, for they use other symbolization. However, the multiformity of exhibitionism does not suppress still older forms, such as for example the denudation of the posterior as a sign of disdain in disputes among the Scandinavian farm women, still practised in recent years, a gesture which was not unknown in other parts of

itself is not yet indicative of a pathological condition of subjects who practise it. Some forms of European exhibitionism—direct and symbolized—may be regarded as mass psychosis by the Tungus who practice different forms. Even among the Tungus the forms of exhibitionism, as observed for example, among the Khingan group, may be regarded as an "abnormal" phenomenon, as it would be regarded by a foreign observer thinking and acting according to his own ethnical complex.

It should also be added that in the Case II, the subject is not only an exhibitionist among those who want him to be so, but he is also an artist, as in the Case I. The artistic stimulus ought not to be overlooked when we analyse the situation. No doubt that he was stimulated in his first steps by approval, as a particularly endowed actor.

Such cases are not considered by the Tungus as abnormal ones, but they are appreciated as a social distraction. In observing various cases of this kind and that of Case I, I have come to the conclusion that the performer is not always unconscious of what he is doing; yet he is not in a state of perfect consciousness of what he is doing, but he cannot stop it. In a great number of similar cases the performers could stop it, but they did not actually need to do so, and they were ready to pay something for the privilege of being social performers of the groups. To this question we shall come still nearer, when other forms are discussed. For the time being it may be only pointed out that in some cases "olonism" was merely "performed".

It is different with the Case IV. First of all, the act committed by the man was not socially approved, and he was not willing to commit it. It was against his will. However, even in this case not everything was beyond the ethnographic complex. I mean an interesting detail, namely, the operation with the knife. It is a fact of importance that among all Tungus groups the knife occupies the chief place in the complex "killing in the state of an imitative mania". The knife figures in a great number of "stories-facts" recorded by the Tungus. However, among the Yakuts [according to Sieroszewski, quoted by M. Czaplicka, op. cit. p. 310] another implement is added—the axe. While among some other groups the spear may also be used. This fact is interesting, for all those who are affected by "imitative mania" know the implement or weapon which ought to be used when an occasion of its being used appears. This is a condition well known in other cases which are not at all regarded as abnormal ones. So, in the "imitative mania" an element of consciousness does appear, even in the heaviest cases when the subjects act as "abnormal" at their own peril and that of people near to them.

Besides the knife which can be used as a weapon, any other thing may be used, even a piece of wood, water, or fire, or, in general, that may be at hand for throwing against the person who actually harms the subject or is

Europe. Indeed, cases of active and passive exhibitionism, must be distinguished, for in the case of passive exhibitionism the hired naked women may remain professionally indifferent,—the chief stimulus of their exhibitionism is a new form of social adaptation. Yet, the public "indecency" of the type of my Khingan Tungus, and rare practices of copulatio modo bestiarum, as it is done e.g. among the Chukchi in some important performances, are not absolutely unknown phenomena among the "civilized mankind", among whom they may appear in secluded but still public institutions and under disguise of new symbols, even on the theatrical stages and especially in "movies and talkies",—a real source of ethnographic information.

supposed to do so. Since the above indicated means of self-defence and the performance are rather inoffensive, the cases of "imitative mania" in which they are practised are not considered as harmful and merely serve as a source of amusement. From this point of view, as to the mechanism of imitative mania described in Case IV and others, when weapons are used, it remains the same, for the subject knows what kind of weapon may be used. However, between Case IV and all the other cases of the same group there is a difference, namely, in all cases, except IV, the subjects know that their action is harmless, while in the Case IV they know that it is harmful.

The question is how far and how long the subjects preserve consciousness? And whether they are conscious at the first moment of committing an act? From the observation of a great number of facts and evidences published by other observers it may be supposed that at the first moment, immediately after the loss of psychomental equilibrium due to the unexpectedness of some change in the situation, e.g. when a person of the milieu in which the subject finds himself, makes a sudden movement or produces an unexpected sound or complex act,—there is a moment of shaken consciousness when the act of "imitation" is committed. It is difficult to say how long this lasts, but it may be supposed that it is not a very long time, for at the next moment the subject may take measures for stopping his state of uncontrolled imitation. There are evidently different means for reaching this aim: (1) the subject may direct his fury against the cause of his state, whence an aggression may sometimes result in the murder of the actual producer of trouble, or who is wrongly supposed to be so (Case IV); or an aggression may be connected with the complex "weapon", when it may be directed against the ground, wood, utensils found at hand; (2) imploration of the producer of trouble to cease his influence by giving a contrary order, which is a conscious act (a great number of cases already published; vide M. Czaplicka, op. cit.); (3) avoiding of a direct influence of the producer of trouble by running away (e.g. Cases I and II). From these facts it is evident that the subject restores, at least partially, his equilibrium almost immediately after committing an act implied by a momentaneous disequilibrium. However, the restoration of self-control may be complete, as in the case of running away, or it may be partial, as in the case of imploration, which supposes that the subject must receive a contrary order. The last case is rather complex, for it presumes a subjugated ("mastered") will of the subject. It is a remarkable fact that "imploration" is observed chiefly in females. It is evident that there again is an element of consciousness in the continuing state of imitation, and it is only supposed by the subject to be an uncontrollable state. We may thus point out that the initial condition of the act—the use of a weapon, form of the "number", etc.—are consciously perceived, and the following state is also consciously perceived, so that there remains only a short period, perhaps covering a fraction of a second, when the subject is "unconscious". This may be proved by the method usually practised, namely, when one wants to maintain a state of "imitation" one must produce subsequently a series of sudden acts for connecting the states of "imitation" into a chain. Indeed, if there is presumption that the subject loses his will (theoretically it may be so), the chain may be formed with long intervals; when there is no such presumption, the chain

must be continuously renewed without leaving the time for taking a rest. If it is presumed (a conscious act) that the aggression is allowed, an act of aggression may be committed at the moment of completion of the period of "unconsciousness". For avoiding it, new acts must be produced for connecting the state of imitation with the physical exhaustion of the subject. The Tungus experimentally know of all these particular cases which they describe, as far as it is possible, in their language. I am certain that for them, at least for the more intelligent individuals, the carrying of experiments on olon is not a simple amusement, but a large field of observation of this peculiar manifestation of human psychology. In a great number of cases I did not fail to observe the fact that many Tungus were observing and wanted to find an explanation of this phenomenon.

Considering the above given analysis of the phenomenon and its complexity I am rather reluctant to use various terms introduced in ethnography and psychiatry, such as "imitative mania", "chorea imitatoria", echokinesis, etc., for they represent pathological conditions, while the condition here described cannot actually be so generalized. Putting aside social effects of this condition and individual variations, I am rather inclined to accept the Tungus approach of the problem in which they designate by the term olon the initial condition of a sudden disequilibrium produced by a sudden change of the situation, voluntary or unvoluntary. In the further treatment I shall therefore use the term "olonism".*

Some new light on "olonism" is thrown in the analysis of the "origin" of this condition in individual cases. I have already pointed out that, according to the Tungus, it is a habit. Let us see how far this statement can be accepted. In the instances of cases I and II we have already seen that they presume a pre-existing practice in this direction, before reaching the necessary technical perfection in the performance. In the Case IV such a preliminary training is not needed. However, as in the other two cases, there is a preliminary condition: such an act as the using of a knife is known from a previous experience of other olon. I need not point out that in the case of very simple forms of "olonism", as seen in the echolalia and coprolalia analysed before, the examples for imitation are handy. Thus, the olon has predecessors—the knowledge of previous experience and training in a definite direction. However, there may be some individual invention—based upon an imaginative process, or upon the trial-error method, which is not important—which may be confined to one or several numbers dependent on the individual ability. Such inventors and well trained olon are particularly appreciated.

First of all, the children are not affected by "olonism"; they are not permitted by the adult people. The olonism may originate gradually, beginning with a joke approved by the audience, and it may originate suddenly after some

* I want to point out once more that I am introducing this term with a certain reluctance (vide supra p. 235 where I make the remark regarding a new term mafarism). But the old term gives a misleading idea as to the discussed phenomenon. The fundamental character—"imitation"—is not observed in all cases of "olonism". On the other hand, in cases of chorea, echokinesis etc. the initial condition of a sudden frightening (i.e. change of situation) may also be absent. It is clear, we have a special condition in which socially and psychologically a pathological condition may be altogether absent, but the phenomenon will be present.

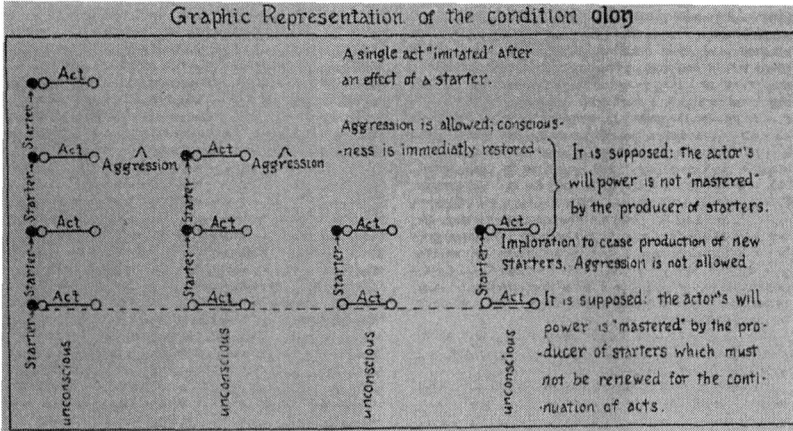

Graphic Representation of the condition olon

1. It is supposed that any act must be repeated.
2. Inhibition of certain acts is introduced.
3. It is supposed that certain acts ought to be committed.
4. Possibility of doing them may require preliminary practising.
5. It is supposed that the will power of the actor may not be "mastered" by the producer of starters.
6. Arrest of a further "acting" is made by the producer of starters, if he would "master" the actor's will power.

striking event, as in the case related by R. Maack (cf. his "Viluisk District of the province of Yakutsk" p. 28), when a woman, being terrified by a bear, threw herself between his paws. However, olonism can soon become a condition harmful for the group in which the subject is living. We have already seen that in this case the Tungus would not call it *oloŋ*, but *kŏdu oloŋ;* and if the subject does not perish, owing to an accident, he will be taken under the care of the clan and his neighbours, who would try to create around him a milieu of quietness and avoidance of sudden changes. Yet, in so far as he would be affected by the condition *xŏdu*, he would be, very likely, treated by an experienced shaman. In the further description I shall revert to this condition, which is "etiologically" quite different from olonism. In all cases of olonism the element of social approval and disapproval plays the most important part—society may stop or develop it. In case the subject causes too much harm to himself, it is very likely that he will be surrounded by conditions of control and will have no chance to manifest any signs of olonism.* Yet, as shown, without a social stimulus, i.e. the recognition of subjects as "performers" and their feeling of being so, olonism is not likely to develop as a phenomenon.

Anyone among the Tungus may become *olog*, and some foreigners are also subject to this condition, whence there are two important conclusions: olonism, as a phenomenon, does not presume a special individual predisposition, and this state may be assumed by individuals belonging to different ethnical groups and possessing different complexes.

For illustration, I shall now quote a case of mass olonism related by Dr. Kashin to Priklonskiĭ ("Three Years, etc.," 1890, pp. 49-50). "One day, during a parade of the 3rd Batallion of the Transbaikal Cossacks, a regiment composed entirely of natives, the soldiers began to repeat the words of command. The colonel grew angry and swore volubly at the men; but the more he swore, the livelier was the chorus of the soldiers repeating the curses after him" (quoted by M. Czaplicka, op. cit. p. 313). There is not the least doubt as to the condition of nervousness and general state of health of the men (probably Buriats and Tungus) who had been carefully selected by the Russian military authorities. The whole situation is clear: the colonel, who was a Russian, produced an unusual impression on the men, for at a parade the form of command might be more expressive, than in everyday life, and the situation was dif-

* Many of the reports regarding olonism are made by travellers who were sometimes accompanied by cossacks and other Russians. Before such an interesting audience the Yakuts and Tungus would wish to make a show and produce necessary acts for inspiring a "number". The local Russians like these "numbers" and provoke them. The impressions of such travellers may be quite erroneous

as regards the frequency of real olonism. In my practice I have observed many cases, but some individuals did not show their "numbers" for weeks, not to say for months, while the cases of "echolalic" and "coprolalic" «olonism» were observed every day, their symptomology being the same, but the etiology being of quite different order, e.g. individual sexual repression, social conditions, etc.

ferent with respect to the strain: the Buriats and Tungus wanted to show, before the gathering of the public, the promptness of their reaction. Instead of the required automatism in response to the command, they repeated it. Being frightened, they repeated also the swearing. If the colonel had wounded himself with his weapon, they would have reproduced the action as well, and if he had led them to an attack against a superior enemy, they would have followed him and perhaps would all have perished automatically, in performing what had been done by their leader. Such a state may be interrupted only by the suppression of the source of subsequent reactions; or by a still stronger source of new reaction. I do not want to carry further this discussion which may bring us to the most interesting problem of automatism caused by a certain starter of reflexes, well known in the phenomena of the unorganized crowd and especially in the organized units which possess more or less similar psychomental complexes and well-established systems of reflexes.*

The phenomena of mass olonism may also be observed in some conditions of shamanistic performances, but I shall revert later to this particular case.

Another interesting aspect, already mentioned, is that olonism is easily assimilated by foreigners. These facts can be observed among the Russians settled in Siberia near the groups practising "olonism". By mere imitation of olon, which at the beginning may seem quite amusing, the practice may become a habit. In simple cases it may be seen in the form of "echolalia" and "coprolalia",—their nature being varied,—which may become a habit beyond the possibility of subduing it. When movements (conventionalized and even symbolized) are produced by a sudden change of situation, then a classical form of olonism appears. Its technique (in so far as psychological and training conditions are concerned) is so simple and so generally applied that the subject does not need to be familiar with the ethnical group whose pattern is imitated for the first time.

As to the social character of the phenomenon we have some evidences in the facts regarding frequency in different groups and sexes. Among the Manchus "olonism" is much more frequent with the males,—the women are disapproved if they practise it. It is particularly true of "coprolalism", —the Manchu woman is much more "decent" than the Tungus women. If we include "coprolalism" in the complex of "olonism", the frequency of this condition will be found higher among the women than among the men in Northern Tungus groups. One more fact of interest is that the forms of "olonism" threatening the well-being of persons affected are more frequent among the males than among the females. Naturally in all groups and in all individual cases there are great variations of forms and these evidently depend on the existing cultural complexes.

* Although the psychological nature of these phenomena is not always clear, the benefit of their use is known to all those who professionally deal with masses of human beings. In such cases there is no question about "conviction," "hypnotic influence," "leadership" etc. These conditions may sometimes facilitate the working of the "olonistic" mechanism, but they are not its primary condition at all. These methods are practically known, but not every one knows how to use them practically. In this connexion it may be pointed out that certain conditions which are ascribed to the "psychology of the crowd" are not typical of the crowd alone. Reflexal automatism is not characteristic only of the crowd; in a great many cases the key is the inducer of reaction and the individual reactions.

From the analysis of this phenomenon we can also see that it may easily spread among neighbours, as well as among any other ethnographical complex. In fact, olonism has been recorded in all parts of Siberia, arctic and subarctic; in Manchuria which cannot be characterized even as "sub-arctic"; it has been observed in North America as well. The most different groups are familiar with it, e.g. the cattle-breeders, Yakuts, the hunters, Eskimos, the "civilized" agriculturists Manchus, and so forth. However, I do not presume that this was due to the diffusion alone,* for although the mechanism of spreading is clear in the instance of Russian settlers, still the historic evidences are lacking, and for the time being linguistical** facts give us no reliable hint for suggesting a history of this phenomenon. Owing to its simplicity and potential universality it may originate in distinct ethnographical conditions as well. In fact, similarity of this phenomenon among the Malays and the above indicated groups is such that one cannot distinguish them. As it has been shown, it is also known in other complexes, but in other forms, and is not so frequently observed. The form may become misleading, but the phenomenon remains the same. The form may result in primary adaptation, and yet, it may result from secondary adaptation. Finally, in one complex it may have some social function, while in another complex it may appropriate a different function, the psychological condition being everywhere the same. Functional difference may camouflage, to the eyes of observers, similarity of psychological conditions too.

In conclusion I want to point out once more that in so far as pure and simple olonism is concerned, i.e. when no other "pathological" conditions are intermixed, it is not an abnormal phenomenon in the Tungus complex; as it is regarded by the Tungus, it has a certain social function,—as a performance and instructive observation,—without which the Tungus life would be empoverished; it is liable to diffusion, fashions, and variations, both individual and ethnical, is rooted in the normal psychomental complex and, as such, it must be separated from the facts gathered under the name of hysteria.***

86. HYSTERIA   Among all Tungus groups and Manchus I had a great number of occasions to observe what may be called classical forms of hysteria,**** as they

* In studying the geographical expansion and the statistics of the frequency of this phenomenon one confronts the impossibility of comparing published data. Some investigators of the Yakuts assert that almost all Yakut women are liable to this condition. The same cannot be stated with respect to the Tungus. It may be thus inferred that the present real centre is among the Yakuts. However, such an inference may be erroneous, for the observers do not agree as to the symptoms sufficient for the authentication of this condition. It is something like two opposite opinions with regard to the European women, e.g. "almost all women are hysterical" and "hysteria is a relatively rare occurrence". I may say that almost all Tungus may become olon, but not all of them are so. Perhaps it is also true of Yakut women. Therefore, for the present, our information as to the geographical and statistical diffusion of this condition does not permit to make a statement as to the present centre of the phenomenon. Still less can we speak of the meaning of the present diffusion and frequency.

** For this reason I omit the linguistical analysis of the parallels from other languages.

*** I shall revert to the question as to why such a great number of investigators collected all facts under this heading.

**** Since I have mentioned "classical hysteria" I deem it useful to

are described among the Europeans. During the period of quietness a woman (I speak of women, for I observed them much oftener than men) shows no physical signs of her condition,—she is as any other woman of the group. Her behaviour does not essentially differ from that of other women. However, one can bring the woman out of her condition by various forms of inducing excitement or laying stress on the special points which constitute the complex of individual cases, e.g. sex complex, "religious" matters, personal pride, etc., lastly even by producing visual, auditory and other physical irritation. The woman may become liable to the change of her behaviour, e.g. she would become irritable, reacting too strongly on every external source of change of the situation; she would avoid looking at one directly, her eyes would be aimlessly fixed for an unusually long time at things or persons, or simply lost in the space. Such a state may gradually increase to the state when the woman would lose her usual ability of daily work. The period may be crowned by a fit associated with laughter, weeping, and later on "arch", closed eyes, localized insensitiveness, "difficulty" of breathing, physical (alleged) pain in the chest and heart, etc.; she would look for a dark place. Fits are more frequent in the evening and at night, than in day-light. They seem to be more frequent during the summer than during the

make some reserves. After the rejection of Charcot's hysteria by his own disciples and after the introduction of new interpretations (e.g. psychoanalytical, physiological, "mental", etc.) of this condition, the fact of its existence was not dismissed. It is interesting that the number of "classical" cases has greatly diminished in some countries (e.g. in France among the female patients), while during the great war it markedly increased among the soldiers. In Russia I have also observed a decrease of frequency of fits among the hysterical females, even an entire "recovery", after the downfall of the national government, when a great number of women had to face the hardships of civil war with all its consequences. Numerous facts may also be added gathered by the ethnographers, including myself among the Tungus populations, which definitely point to a periodicity of fits affecting very numerous persons who are quite "normal" and who afterwards "recover". Undoubtedly, these facts point to a process analogous to the spreading of a cultural complex which may be accepted or rejected, as well as to a formal analogy with contagious diseases. In fact, the hysterical fits are remarkably similar among quite different ethnical groups and at different historical periods, the traits of difference being those implied by the difference of cultural complexes. The part of imitation and adaptation in the spreading of hysteria is as great as in other cultural phenomena. Even in individual cases one may observe how hysteria is imitated, especially by daughters from their mothers' pattern (whence the idea of hereditary hysteria, should the hypothesis of heredity be postulated, is only natural even without presuming a physical predisposition for it) which naturally may be repeated by the descending generations. Without presuming whether individuals suffering from various physical defects (functional and organical, particularly glands of internal secretion and cerebral lesions) form an especially favourable ground, or practising of hysteria leads to a disfunction of some functional systems, we may now say that any essential changes of milieu (such as anti-hysteria propaganda, military clash, economic "depression", civil wars, etc.) may influence frequency of cases. Indeed, there are some individuals who are not at all susceptible to hysteria, while others are particularly liable to it. On the other hand, the form of hysteria is liable to variations and the degree of intensity of hysteria is defined by a symptomatic analysis, the latter being an ethnographical phenomenon itself. Thus, should the symptoms change under the pressure of a new ethnographical complex, the degree would not be perceptible until new symptoms are established. Should the form change, the hysteria would not be noticed at all. Therefore, the "classical hysteria", which is well known, may disappear and instead of it a new form with new "symptoms" may appear which will not be at once noticed by the contemporaries.

cold season, in the encampments (I never observed them during travelling, but usually in conditions of relative comfort) than during migrations.

One of the characteristic features of this form of hysteria is that the women do not hurt themselves during the fits. If they should fall to the ground, the head would not be hurt and it would happen in the dark place of the wigwam (or house, among the Manchus), which is not typical of fits such as in epilepsy. A fit may occur owing to a sudden fear, as well as in the case of olonism. The fit may be gradually "prepared" by the woman, evidently through a process of self-excitement, during which she imagines herself "miserable"—to be without her clansmen or mother, not loved by her husband, haunted by the spirits, etc. Naturally during this period the normal appetite is absent, the woman is evidently depressed, but she can sleep; she would be sexually indifferent in most cases observed, but not always. I shall now give a description of a case which will be later needed for another purpose.

A Manchu woman of about thirty-six years, physically strong, of a muscular type with a moderate fat deposit, as usual; anthropologically, she was near to the type Alpha I, although some characters pointed to the type Delta; she was tall, had a moderately long rhomboid face with developed cheek bones, very dark eyes of moderate size with narrow brows on a receding forehead; a mouth of large or perhaps medium size with medium lips; a narrow nose of aquiline form which together with a sharp chin and the receding forehead formed a sharp profile; the skin was rather darker than usual among the Manchus; the jet-black hair was straight. She was not usually talkative, but solemn, concentrated, "intraverted", for which special social reasons existed. Married at the age of twenty to a boy of eleven or twelve years, she became the mistress of her husband's father who was a handsome man, an official and a shaman at the same time. A son was born after one year of marriage. Evidently the husband was not the father of her son, for the sexual relations between them began much later and were interrupted soon. The father-lover-shaman was executed for a "political crime" (vide Chapter XXVIII). The husband on reaching the age of sixteen years, after the discovery of his situation, deserted his wife. Several attempts were made by the wife, directly and through a special go-between, to restore marital life (sexual relations), but the husband refused referring to his wife's stupidity, saying that she was uncivilized, and that she did not appeal to his sex feelings. The woman was desperate, but as far as I could find out, owing to the peculiar conditions of the family, she had no more lovers, nor "younger brothers" (cf. SOM p. 100 et seq.) who might have been substitutes for her husband. During a year or so she suffered from fits which are typical of hysteria. If it happened in the house, she might produce an "arch" etc.; if she ran away prior to the culmination, she might be found in the near forest, sitting (cramped) on a tree or just thrust between two trees growing close together. The observation showed that the fits were correlated with the introduction of the spirit of her first lover. She wanted to get rid of this condition, but the means tried were not successful. Further details will be given later.

The cases of classical hysteria are not very frequent, i.e. only a few, perhaps one case in every Tungus group, but the cases of potential classical hysteria in which the period does not culminate in a fit, and cases which may be only suspected of being of this type, are very frequent. It is impossible to say whether we have here a real hysteria or something else which in some respects and symptomatically looks like hysteria. Indeed, in the complex of symptoms of "hysteria" some symptoms are not at all characteristic of hysteria alone. Thus *when they are not numerous* it is sometimes impossible to diagnose hysteria.

As an example of a complex case, which cannot be easily defined, I may refer to one related by me in SONT, pp. 268-269. The woman was subject to cycloid states of excitement and depression, in which she would be alternately very gay and cheerful, and very morose, silent and shedding tears without any reasonable cause.

The above described condition of the Manchu woman I have compared with the "classical hysteria", but the latter is not always observed alone. It may be associated with other conditions as well. It may be rarely observed that it is definitely associated with the cyclic psychoses and with the state of paranoia, when the woman is permanently affected by various fears, maniacal ideas, sometimes caused by her physiological disturbances or definitely pathological condition.* Such a state may be associated with restlessness, insomnia, etc. which ruins health. It would be quite erroneous to include every case of this complex type in the group of hysteria, but their separation from the "classical form of hysteria" is also not easy, especially in the conditions of field work. However, in some cases this is possible, and it ought to be done in order better to understand the nature of hysteria.

On the other hand a great number of cases which may have a certain symptomatic similarity with hysteria are not so. In fact, a great number of cases symptomatically pointing to hysteria are found in connexion with the spirits' activity, especially before the election of a new shaman which will be discussed later on, so I shall now give a description of some special conditions which, not always reasonably, were taken as pure and simple hysteria ; namely, the possession by spirits and incomplete sleep.

87. SELF-INTRODUCTION OF SPIRITS Self-introduction of spirits into the persons awake or asleep is a common phenomenon among the Tungus. Indeed, in both cases the self-introduction of spirits is based upon the firm conviction of the Tungus that (1) the spirits exist; (2) the spirit may enter the body; (3) the spirit may act when introduced. If this complex prerequisite does not exist no introduction of spirit is possible. It is clear that the theory of spirits, as has been shown, is not created by insane persons, but is discovered after a minute observation of facts, verified and experimentally proved. It may be erroneous from our point of view, but it is perfectly logical and sound, if the fundamental postulate is admitted. With the further deepening of the same idea and its adaptation to any individual situation, it may easily become not only an explanation of the phenomena of psychic life, but also a justification of certain psychic conditions. Since the theory is adopted, since it may justify individual behaviour, it may

* The condition of "paranoia" finding its expression in mania persecutiva observed among very young girls at the period of puberty and among young women giving birth to the first child, has been recently emphasized by R. D. Jameson, op. cit.

assume a new function, i.e. the introducing of certain psychic conditions which may be pleasant to those who have them.

The maintaining of internal functional tension needed for the adaptation to the changing milieu,—either varying primary milieu or varying secondary milieu,—is not easy and it requires a permanent effort of the will power. When the individual loses his ability of self-control this must be justified by something, for the social milieu accepts no breaking, without any reason, of the "functioning order". The theory of spirits gives both an explanation of this condition and its justification: such a breaking of acting order is possible, for there are spirits and it occurs because the spirits want it. Such an explanation and justification are accepted by the society, and the self-introduction of spirits comes into the ethnographical complex as one of its important components. Like any other complex, it is gradually created in the ethnical unit. The hysterical person knows from the observation of similar cases and hearsay that the person must perform certain acts. These acts are, for instance, singing of certain tunes (*rhythmed*), uttering of certain words (in a known language), sitting on the ground or bed, covering of the face with one's own hair, etc. In such a state the person may completely relax, weep and loudly express himself (within a certain limit), either directly or as *porte parole* of the spirit. As a matter of fact the spirits usually express things which cannot be expressed before the seniors, or before the children, and the most secret desires may be expressed without any personal consequence, e.g. a young person holding a spirit may require personal attention to herself or himself in the form of a sacrifice, prayer, etc.; he or she may express sexual desire with indication of the person desired, which can be done directly or in symbols, without being blamed for it etc. After such a relaxation calmness and satisfaction are restored for a while. Yet, physically it is not tiresome,—no physical effort being made nor is any harm done to the organism.

It should be noted that such a condition usually occurs at the hours of darkness when the self-concentration is easier and the external world does not disturb the actor. This is one of reasons why the subjects in day light usually close eyes or cover them with dishevelled hair. However, they are usually very attentive to what is going on around them and occasionally they may slightly open an eye to see the effect of their behaviour. Such a fact is not likely to occur, when the person is alone, or when there is nobody to observe, e.g. only small children or only very old people and no neighbours are near by. Still less is the chance of this occurrence during travelling or in any other responsible and difficult situation. However, it may occur even in these conditions, but other favourable conditions must be present, such as a gathering of people, or as a form of conscious or unconscious protest against the hardship caused by other persons. In all this situation the spirits will be held responsible by the person affected and by the witnesses.

Unfavourable conditions for such an occurrence are serious illness, advanced pregnancy, various other conditions that keep the mind busy with other worries, or some other distractions, e.g. social gatherings, etc. which require particular attention.

These comparatively simple forms of relaxation from self-control, and from that of the society, may attain great complexity. For instance, the most common form is "running away into the forest". The person may run comparatively far and remain in a "wild state", sitting among rocks. It happens commonly that they climb up a tree, or thrust themselves between the near-standing trees or branches of a tree, assuring themselves and other people that they cannot liberate themselves, but they often return home without the help but somewhat ashamed. If they do not return they are discovered (as has been shown, a Tungus may easily be found by his foot prints and other signs!), which sometimes takes several days in unfavourable conditions of weather, e.g. running away before a heavy rain, or a snow-fall. The "running away" usually occurs during the seasons when there is no great danger for the person to remain even several days without food and fire. I have not heard of very dangerous occurrences, although they were admitted as possible by the Tungus. Indeed, the "bringing home" consists in admonition, promise to fulfil the request, etc. finally by taking home by force. Such occurrences are more common with females than with males. In very rare cases the people may be left to their fate.

The "running away" and "bringing home" may assume still more complex forms when several elements are combined, but this does not change the essential character of the condition. It may also be pointed out that the "arch" is not usually observed, as well as other typical features of classical hysteria.

The most interesting point is that the forms are not very varied. I have mentioned (1) hiding from light; (2) crying and singing; (3) sitting on the ground or bed; (4) running away; (5) hiding in rocks; (6) climbing on trees; (7) thrusting oneself between the trees and branches. These forms are repeated by hundreds of people affected in the same sequence of performances. Indeed, there are minor individual variations, e.g. if there are no trees, no rocks to be hidden in, if the person is too fat for climbing up, etc. some substitutes for completing the situation may be introduced.* These methods are repeated from generation to generation, transmitted by tradition, and there can be little change in the performance, for the person might be suspected of not being affected by such and such a spirit.

The question is this: are the persons fully conscious or not of what they do? I think this question can be answered by saying in a sense that they are conscious, but they do not want to be so, and after and before the performance they do not act "logically", i.e. going from fact to fact, making slow inferences, acting step by step, etc. but they act quasi-unconsciously. In this condition, if they wish, they can forget everything, but their forgetfulness is not "sincere" for the next time they may introduce corrections into the performance if the latter was not "correct", and they do remember, when necessary, all 'details, even in a "normal" state.

Another aspect of the same practice is the social side. Society does not disapprove the persons affected, but special attention is paid to them, for such persons are *remarkable,* they are marked by a trait of distinction. When the person is affected, members of the community are in-

* Among the groups living in villages, such as Manchus, the person affected is very likely to climb up to the beams of the grain house, etc. Among the Europeans faute de mieux store rooms, cold attics, even toilet rooms, etc. are used, the public places being watched by the police. Among the steppe dwellers, the persons affected run about in the open, till day-break.

terested in the person, speak about the person, ask for information, etc. In this case the situation is still more favourable for maintenance of this practice than in the case of olonism,—the person is connected with the spirits, and is not only a "performer". Yet, these persons may become important members of the community, as persons through whom spirits may speak; at last, as will be shown, the shamans come out of this group. This fact is important, for the persons who may be affected are attracted by the special social position which results from the fact of their being visited by spirits.

However, if "the running away fits" become too frequent, they may create a condition of social invalidity,— the person affected cannot work and cannot be relied upon when travelling and in daily routine work. The situation becomes especially serious when the subject is a young mother with several children, or an important man (working man) of the economic unit (family). The Tungus would regard such a person as normal, but as one affected by the spirits, and special measures would be taken in order to liberate the person from the spirits' visits. The shamans are playing an important part in this matter. Practical methods will be discussed later.

From the observation of facts it may be inferred that the greatest part of all men and women may be affected by this condition, perhaps women more than men. However, there are some special conditions too. Firstly, children are never and old persons are rarely affected. The most favourable age is the one soon after puberty. This fact can be used for an etiological observation. It ought to be pointed out that not only these ages are favourable, but persons of older ages may also be affected. Secondly, the persons who have no heavy responsibility in carrying out daily routine work are more free, and therefore, in the case of such an occurrence, they may be left to be affected by the spirits, as persons of secondary importance while in the case of important members of the family serious measures to expel the spirits are taken as soon as possible. Third, there exists a theory that the spirits would look for young persons among whom they may find a "master",—the shaman. So that the frequency of occurrences of these conditions in young persons is greater because of the social position of these persons and because of the existing theory. In some cases a great majority of the young people may be affected and so this condition may become a mass phenomenon. Such occurrences happen usually, if there is no shaman (*vide infra* Chapter XXI). In this aspect the phenomenon is such that it cannot be treated as a condition particularly due to the individual predisposition of "abnormal" order, for the observation of the Tungus does not reveal that the majority of them are "abnormal". I am also reluctant to look for an explanation of these cases in the psychological conditions characteristic of the ages when an essential change in the system of the glands of internal secretion, particularly sexual glands, may become a disturbing factor, for the period of life during which the persons may be affected does not correspond to the ages when such changes occur. Lastly, this condition can be easily cured either by social pressure—disapproval!—or by the individual treatment by the shaman.

Description above given points to the fact that this condition is imposed by two fundamental characters; namely, the ethnographic nature of the complex in its elements and theoretical presumption of the spirits' activity,

On the other hand, it cannot be correlated with an "abnormal" psychic state of the persons affected, but as has been shown, it may be regarded as a recognized form of relaxation, at least for a time, both individual-psychic and social. However, if the affected person begins to practise "fits" too often, he or she may become invalid as a member of the community. In this aspect there is no other possibility as that of regarding this phenomenon as a socially "abnormal" and due to the lack of psychic adaptation. As to the mass phenomenon, it has another function; namely, the selection of capable persons for a certain social function (shaman) which may have an "abnormal" appearance without being so socially and individually—psychically. It is true that it is very "clumsy" and may appear "abnormal" in the eyes of those observers who are accustomed to a different ethnographical complex, e.g. such as the European complex. Owing to the above described character of this condition and within the limits when it does not disturb the functioning of the society, it is absolutely "normal".*

Indeed, when it is combined with other conditions, such as "olonism" (which is not frequent, because the majority of persons are affected prior to the time when olonism occurs) and the classical form of hysteria, it may become harmful, as a "syndrome" of conditions, quite inoffensive when observed alone, but badly disabling the affected persons when combined.

88. VARIOUS CONDITIONS DURING SLEEP Various cases of "abnormalities" occurring during the sleep are often observed among the Tungus. I have already shown that, according to the Tungus hypothesis, during the sleep the soul may be absent. Only one of the components of the soul may be absent, for the total absence of the soul would put the person in a condition of definite danger. On the other hand, it is supposed that the spirits may enter the body during the sleep. Whence we have three cases, namely, (1) the soul is absent and travels elsewhere; the experience of the soul may affect the body which speaks ("body"-"mind"-"life") even while the person remains asleep; (2) the soul is absent and the spirit enters the body, which speaks being induced by the spirit; (3) the soul is present and spirit enters the body, which speaks for the spirits, while the body is asleep, and the soul is "mastered" by the spirit. In all these cases there would be the phenomenon of speaking, singing, even moving in the sleep,—now generally regarded as an "incomplete sleep". The latter cannot be regarded as an abnormality, until it becomes harmful for the health.

Among the Tungus one can frequently observe these cases. About the same ages and sexes are affected, as in the case of possession by the spirits.

The subject affected by this condition may sing during the sleep, or speak for himself or on behalf of the spirit. The Tungus sometimes speak foreign languages, e.g. Buriat, Russian, Manchu, Chinese. In some cases they speak these languages only in the sleeping state, while

* I am prepared for the possibility that my point of view will not be easily accepted by some ethnographers, but I cannot avoid pointing out that these cases cannot be covered by "hysteria" which is very often only the reaction of the observer to an alien complex, when other ethnical groups are observed.

they cannot speak them being awake. This constitutes one of the great puzzles for the Tungus who have only one possible explanation; namely, the spirits are speaking. This phenomenon is very interesting, and thus I have used all possible occasions of observing it in sleeping persons and especially in shamans during the performance, which, as will be shown, is not very far in its nature from the condition here discussed.

First of all, it must be kept in mind that the spirits, at least some of them, are believed to speak only certain languages (vide supra p. 204). Secondly, the knowledge of alien languages is very common among almost all Tungus groups. Thirdly, the perception of what the persons asleep say is not always perfect, and the imagination of the listeners makes the necessary completion. But it is a fact that some persons, who do not speak foreign languages, do speak them in their sleep and sometimes not very badly. The only possible explanation is that the study of a language does not follow the only way which may be easily seen by the observers from the outer manifestations of the progress made by the person.

I shall now permit myself hypothetically to discuss this question with all possible reserves as to the further application of my reconstruction. There is one remarkable fact, namely, the children of pre-school age, and those of low school ages may learn a foreign language in a few months, after which they can speak quite correctly and with a correct "accent". Some adult persons may learn to speak a foreign language in a few years, while for others this is absolutely impossible. Lastly, there are adult persons who cannot learn them at all.* I cannot go into the details of all variations and possible psychological conditions which have nothing to do with the relative ability for studying a language.

Children learn a language by the simple method of imitation, in which they do not reason, but try to speak as clearly as possible for making themselves understood. If the process of imitation is not hindered by inhibition, the learning does not take a long time.** Then in schools study comes from books; unconscious imitation is nearly banished and instead of it a new method is introduced, a foreign logical method, implying study by memory and practice in words, "rules" of grammar,*** etc., where everything is expressed in a rough and deeply conventional form of an imperfect graphism. The process is thus artificially made very slow. The student is prevented from working "unconsciously". More than this, he always keeps in his

* Hindrance for study of a new language apparently is also found in the fixed chains of conditioned reflexes.
** Here I have in view a frequent occurrence, when adult people restrain children from quick, unconscious imitation and learning, e.g. by producing the feeling of superiority of the parents' language and of hate for an alien language, etc., which in most cases is not a conscious act on the part of the parents.
*** I do not need to point out that there is nothing more artificial and unnatural than the present grammar composed in imitation of the Latin grammar, nearly two thousands years old. It is a rare case of blind imitation and ethnographical conservatism which may be understood only from the peculiar psychomental complex of those who "specialize" themselves in philology and from the very beginning accept a series of postulates. This is a well known fact to all those, even among philologists, who critically approached the problem.
Let me add that the failure of creation of new grammars is another complex phenomenon of an ethnographic order. But this question will lead us too far from "well established truths", so I may run the risk of being misunderstood.

mind: the longer he studies, the better he may know.* In addition thereto, if there is a conventionalized "school language", then it is practically impossible to learn a language.

With those who do not go through this "schooling", as it is with the Tungus, who marvelously quickly learn languages, there are other inhibitory conditions, namely, the interethnical relations and the relative shyness of the Tungus—they do not want to offend the hearer's ear by speaking badly, and they believe that they cannot learn a foreign language, just as foreigners cannot (superiority complex) learn the Tungus language. However, since the Tungus meet with the foreigners and listen to them, they unconsciously learn their language, but very often believe that they cannot speak. In the state when the *logical thinking is in force*, they cannot speak, but as soon as the "logical" (adopted and approved by the ethnical group or unit) way of thinking is eliminated, they can speak. Such an elimination occurs at the time of sleep, when the existing ethnographical complex does not hinder practical application of what the persons actually know by the process of unconscious assimilation of facts (and foreign languages too). Indeed, if the person knows no language at all, he or she cannot speak.** Moreover, I want to emphasize that the well known phenomena like "the speaking of various languages", as known among some Russian sectarians, also "twelve languages of twelve disciples", and so on, are not in the line of the phenomena discussed above. In the case of the Tungus speaking alien languages we have a real knowledge of languages. The situation is sometimes complicated by the fact that these are not persons who speak them, but spirits without the introduction of whom the persons cannot speak.*** Howsoever, this is the Tungus solution of the complex puzzle produced by the conflict between the ethnological control of a logical control of the psychomental complex and a successful solution of the problem of studying foreign languages, while European observers consider it as "hysteria." The difference between

the two is not very great.

I have dwelt so long on the phenomenon of "speaking languages", because the above analysis permits us to understand many other similar phenomena in which the mind of the subject is left free to express itself without being bound (within certain limits) by a restraint of free self-expression with inhibitory conditions of the ethnical milieu, of the given ethnographical complex and especially of the social group of juniors and generally of clan members. From this point of view there is a great similarity between the condition described in the previous section and that described in the present section. In both cases we have a situation in which the person permits himself to speak more freely than it is allowed, i.e. the subject obtains a special occasion of relaxation, in both cases the subject attracts, consciously or unconsciously, attention to its personality. Namely, in the first case the whole performance may occur—and I suppose it is so in most cases—under the control, at least partial, of the consciousness, while in the second case the subject is in a state of incomplete sleep, and may actually forget everything which happened in the "dreams", the control being confined to that of the ethnographical milieu unconsciously accepted.

The occurrence of speaking and generally, of expressing one's self in the sleep is likely to take place in the case, when introduction of spirits, as described in the previous section, is disapproved, and when the subject knows that such an act is impossible, as well as in the case when the subject is too shy for figuring half-consciously as "possessed" by the spirit. In these and similar cases, the inhibition will be so strong that only with half-dormant consciousness, as in sleep, the subject can find a way of self-expression. Indeed, in the matter of sexual relations, especially when the subjects are bound by their social position, such occurrences are very likely to happen, and they cannot be regarded as hysterical manifestations, as it has already been done by some authors.* These are as much natural as sexual dreams symbolized or not, "sublimated" or not. The difference is that the Tungus are liable to an incomplete sleep which, as such, cannot be regarded as an "abnormal" and "pathological" condition. In so far as incomplete sleep is concerned, it is likely that the subject will speak (or sing) of such things, facts and feelings which are inhibited in a "normal" state. Since the Tungus young unmarried persons are not restricted in their sexual life, where tragedies rarely occur, the sexual element is rarely represented, while "social oppression"

---

* An interesting instance of how the study of a simple alphabet may be retarded is given us by the Manchus. Their alphabet contains 38 "letters", but the Manchu teachers succeeded in creating about fifteen hundred syllabic combinations which were studied in the schools not less than three years, for the Manchus did not guess that they could read sound after sound. The learning to read Manchu actually takes no more than, for instance, to read German for Germans.

** This is not typical of the Tungus alone. I have observed cases when the Europeans were surprised that in their dreams they can speak foreign languages much better than when they are awake, —speech runs fluently and it is correct. When they are awake their "tongue" makes false movements, they cannot remember "words" and rules of grammar. In the Freudian system this is explained, as many other things, by a desire of speaking well, etc., while actually in the dreams these persons simply have no inhibitions of a "logical ethnographical order". In this way Freudianism maintains many other "prejudices" and gives them a quite scientific appearance, at the same time by justifying the existing ethnographical complex retarding necessary changes of the complex. Leaving aside the practical (logal, medical, educational, etc.) importance of Freudianism, I must say that its retarding influence on the deepening and progress of science will be still stronger felt in the future.

*** Some travellers in Siberia have noted the fact of speaking foreign languages in the sleeping state or in that when spirits are introduced. These facts produced a great impression on the travellers who were inclined to explain them as phenomena of hysteria. Of course, many of them did not know that foreign spirits do speak foreign languages, when these languages are known to the affected persons (and to the shamans).

* Among others I have here in view the case related by W. Jochelson ("The Yukaghir and Yukaghirized Tungus", Vol. I p. 32) when a Yakut woman fell in love with an occasional visitor and expressed herself in a sleep too frankly. The situation was simple: the healthy, strong woman is sexually excited by a stranger, wants to think and even perhaps to tell the stranger in her incomplete sleep the fact which certainly is not a secret for her. The stranger may know her feelings; the husband regrets her being attacked by the spirits (abassy), and our observer refers to the case as hysteria. Every one, who makes observation, both among his own people and other ethnical groups, comes from time to time in touch with similar occurrences, the only difference being the form. We are unable to notice the forms to which we are accustomed as sharply as those to which we are not accustomed. Since I have the occasion of mentioning this investigator's observation, I want also to point out that he, as well as many others of his time, were inclined to see too much "sexual" complex, so that more "sexual" than other cases were recorded. However, "arctic hysteria" has nothing to do with most of these cases, both sexual and asexual.

(seniors versus juniors), spirits, and other similar matters are more frequently the themes. By this I do not want to say that the sexual complex does not appear at all. It does manifest itself in words and even in quite frank movements of the body, but the sexual complex cannot be generally considered as causa prima of this condition, being in other cases manifested in "sublimated" and "symbolized" forms.

It is evident that such a condition, rarely occurring, is not harmful at all, but if it does not leave the subject to have complete rest during the sleep, the condition may become harmful, as it is with self-introducing spirits, "classical hysteria", etc. In this case the Tungus usually decide to have recourse to home means, and to the help of the shaman, for in all similar cases the spirits are held responsible for the conditions, and treatment is not very difficult.

89. SELF-SUGGESTION AND SUGGESTION The chief characteristic is this: a person performs a series of acts which are not fully conscious or completely unconscious, but which can easily be so. Such an automatism in acting is possible only on the condition that the consciousness is intentionally or unintentionally eliminated. It may cover a greater or lesser series of acts. It is used when the person is certain about the ability of successfully reaching the end of the act without the interference of consciousness in the process. It may be practically applied when the person is able to give such an "order". The latter presumes the ability of a temporary suppression of consciousness. The benefits of such a method are great, e.g. the act can be carried out leaving the mind free of the worry of thinking over minor details and to be used for other purposes; in the case of repugnant work it may be done without causing harm; in the case of a compulsory act the latter is easily performed; and so on. It is done in everyday life for the practical purpose of carrying on daily routine.

There may be two methods of elimination of consciousness of acting (1) the person does it either by conscious decision, namely, "I must accomplish such-and-such an act", or by unconscious performance of a series of acts; (2) the person may be influenced in the same sense by another person with special methods and owing to a series of preexisting conditions, e.g. the acceptance of the theory of spirits. In all these cases the characteristic feature is the same: the consciousness is eliminated. Naturally, all cases of suggestion and self-suggestion can be included into the group of these phenomena.

It is an absolutely arbitrary procedure when a category of cases of self-suggestion is introduced as an "abnormal condition" into the treatment of ethnographic phenomena. In fact, what can be included into this group and when are we allowed to speak of self-suggestion? The analysis of cases, when self-suggestion is advanced, shows that there are included cases which cannot be "rationally" framed in the observer's complex and cases which result in harmful effects upon the persons themselves or upon their surroundings. Yet the cases of harmless self-suggestion are excluded from the observer's field. However, the last group of cases is immeasurably more frequent than the first and the second groups.

A great number of acts, even very complex ones, in so far as the sequence of elements is concerned, are done in a psychological state, when details are not cognized and when they succeed in a way that every next one is a consequence of the preceding one. Here I have not in view simple cases of well stabilized complexes of conditioned reflexes, but a *series of acts which may be cognized* at any moment, but are not, of which the persons may be conscious.

If they are not cognized and if they are not interrupted, the aim is attained without being noticed by the actors, and this process is then similar to that of self-suggestion. However, a new element is introduced into the conception of self-suggestion, namely, a temporary elimination of cognition and a person's will, which are substituted either by the acting person himself and unconsciously, or by some other persons. Indeed, the introduction of this element only artificially isolates some cases from a group of functionally absolutely similar phenomena. This becomes especially evident when cognized cases are selected from among the above mentioned cases, which have already been selected, viz. those cases which may appear either very strange, unusual, to the observer, or which are harmful to the person. After these limitations and eliminations the number of cases dealt with becomes very small, which gives them an appearance of abnormality, especially when very strange and striking instances are selected.

A seeming disfunction (so considered from the point of view of the persons and units) appears when this form of abbreviation of the psychomental mechanism does not serve to the interest of the acting person and to that of the group. Such an occurrence is likely to happen, when the premises are wrong, or when a special stimulus appears and as such is beyond the condition of suggestion and self suggestion. Therefore in all these cases we have to go to the source—the premises and special stimuli. Their effect on the "disfunction" is variable. It depends on the character of the persons and on the stimuli, in both their quantitative and qualitative expressions. When they are numerous, the "disfunction" will be greater than usual. In so setting this problem, we can easily distinguish actual "causes" from "effects", when a group is greatly affected by cases of suggestion and self-suggestion. It is also clear why, during the period of changes, the Tungus units are more liable to this form of disfunction.

Now there is a need of some cases for demonstration. The most common occurrence among the Tungus is that the hunter cannot hit animals with his rifle, although he may be a good hunter, good shot may have a good rifle. Such a case may occur if he violates some of the hunting prohibitions, or if there are spirits that interfere with his hunting. The condition is this: the hunter commits a violation; he *knows* from the existing theories, also confirmed by the observation of other similar facts, that he can no more hit the animals; he misses them when shooting, which still more increases his conviction of the impossibility of hitting. Practically his error is in the theory of relation between the violation and the spirits, and then the interference of the spirits into hunting. The treatment is simple and practical: he must give satisfaction to the offended spirits. If he does it, the spirits will leave him alone and he will hit the animals as before. Since he *knows* that there is a way out, he applies it. In this way the theory of spirits, with reference to this particular case, is neutralized in respect to its harmful effect. Indeed, this is a common and very simple case, it is also well adapted, for it is too frequent and too important in daily life; but there are some cases when no means to remedy the fallacy of the theory is found effective and the case must be treated by an experienced man—the shaman. But in some cases even a shaman cannot help and all harmful effects result from the situation.

Another common occurrence, already discussed, is that of the entering of sprits into the human body. The person knows that if the spirits should enter, the eyes must be covered with hair, the person must take a sitting position, and sing. Therefore, when the person is sufficiently healthy and the spirit enters, the person does everything according to the existing complex. The acting may be both unconscious or conscious. Since this condition requires some physical effort and the person gets tired and cannot perform what is required, the spirit is supposed to leave the body. The "normal" condition is restored. It is evident that in this case we have again a pre-existing theory, and in addition to it a complex of "spirits' visit" which conditions the whole process of self-suggestion. The remedy for the restoration of normal condition is also included in the complex.

There are rare persons whose ability of control of physiological functions attains a very high degree. In such cases some facts may be observed which produce a very deep impression on the observers. Bleeding from the skin, swelling "like in pregnancy" of the abdomen, insensibility to pain and heat, and other similar phenomena are frequently observed, especially among the shamans during their performances. However, the cases, like the above described *erectio penis*, sudden vomiting, enormous sudden power of the muscular system, and the like, are also observed, not only in the shamans. Indeed, in all these cases "self-suggestion" plays a very important part; it produces these effects, and at its basis suppositions as to the effect of spirits are easily found.

Such physiological effects may attain a still higher degree in the case of "voluntary death." In the description of shamans' performances we shall meet with the observed conditions, the maintaining of which might and does result in death. Deaths occurring at dates defined beforehand are known among the Tungus. However, I have not observed them myself. Suicide by self-suggestion, when the physiological system ceases to function, as well as other similar cases, have as basis also pre-existing ideas. In fact, when a Tungus is certain that he or she must die, everything possible would be done for stopping the physiological function of the organism. It may be guessed that this operation is done through the disfunction of the central nervous system. However, even such an effect of self-suggestion cannot be considered as an abnormal phenomenon, as well as suicide in general, which is regarded as a "pathological" phenomenon only by those who postulate a series of hypotheses. Of course, I exclude all cases of suicide which are conditioned by a morbid state of the whole organism, as, for instance, glandular disfunction, lesion of the central nervous system, etc. Suggestion, which does not differ from the auto-suggestion, except in that some person influences the subject, has its specific technique. The effect of a successful suggestion is reached by different methods, the first step being a partial or total elimination of consciousness of the subject. This may be reached (1) by convincing the subject of the superiority of will of the acting person; (2) by hypnotic technique; (3) by convincing the subject that

spirits are acting on him or her. Most of these cases will be discussed later in the chapter dealing with the shamanistic technique and performances.

Cases when auto-suggestion gradually becomes a constant and harmful condition of persons liable to it, are observed among all Tungus groups. Since the nature of this phenomenon remains hidden from the Tungus and they work out only a system of counterbalancing elements that give only a partial remedy and for each case separately, no practical methods, except shamanistic ones, are used. How far these conditions may affect populations will be better seen from the next chapter; but for the present I shall only point out that the individual may be affected so far that "voluntary death" and a complete invalidity may result from uncontrolled auto-suggestion. Even in such heavy cases the cause may lie not in the morbid condition of the subject, but in the state of the psychomental complex remaining quite "normal".

90. CONCLUSION In this chapter I have reviewed various cases of psychomental conditions disabling the Tungus from acting as "normal" persons, i.e. persons who may develop a maximum of their social (ethnical) adaptive activity. We have seen that the Tungus distinguish different forms of incurable and curable disability, as well as of temporary acute and chronic disability. They distinguish conditions due to physical sickness and to spirits and, also those due to "bad habits".

Owing to the fact that the cases of pathological insanity among the Tungus are exceedingly rare, I have not treated them in detail, for they have no great weight in the psychomental complex of the Tungus. In fact, these cases form no special problem among the Tungus, for their mode of life is not of the nature to protect "wild insane persons", even for a short time, and harmlessly "insane" persons they will protect for only a little longer period. However, the Tungus have to deal in their daily life with very numerous cases superficially considered by the observers as "pathological" and as real insanity, while they are not so. A great number of these cases are nothing but a different ethnographical phenomenon unknown among the observers' ethnical group. No fewer groups of other phenomena are due either to the spreading of a certain ethnographical complex, as we have seen in the case of "olonism", or to the acceptance of the possibility of "relaxation", at least for a while, or to the pre-existing theories and ideas, the acceptance of which results in various conditions. All these cases are not at all due to "pathological conditions", but to a temporary disfunction of the psychomental complex, as a complex that regulates the relations between the individual and milieu, and within the individual himself regulates reactions, which are called into existence by the milieu or the internal equilibrium of the complex itself. Owing to the fact that these conditions are not of yesterday, the Tungus had time to create various methods the regulation of the complex in such a way that the equilibrium is restored almost automatically, or by the affected person very soon after the disabling, or, lastly, by the ethnical unit through the special mechanism of shamanism. However, this mechanism of self-regulation cannot always follow the tempo of variation of the secondary milieu, whence a great number of cases of individual disequilibrium originates. The latter cannot be immediately restored, whence a seeming susceptibility of the Tungus to the psychopathological conditions may be suspected. In conclusion of the present work I shall show that this situation is not characteristic of the Tungus alone, but the need of a correct diagnosis usually escapes attention of the "pathologists".

Individual cases treated in the present chapter cannot give a picture of the actual importance of these phenomena.

in the Tungus ethnographical system. Neither do they suffice to explain the anxiety of the Tungus which prevails among them, when they meet with these phenomena. Finally, these phenomena are not sufficient to explain how the Tungus have come to create their clumsy mechanism for the regulation of the psychomental complex under the varying conditions of the milieu. These aspects will be clearer, when we discuss the conditions which are created by the spreading en masse of these phenomena.

CHAPTER XXI

MASS AND INDIVIDUAL PSYCHOSIS AND ITS REGULATION

91. MASS PSYCHOSIS IN GENERAL Various conditions, discussed in the preceding chapter,—i.e. in heavy cases when these conditions disable the affected person too often, or affect his or her physical health,—attract the attention of the Tungus, as abnormal conditions which require intervention. However, in this case, it would not become a social matter, for only the family, or at most near relatives, would be interested in the case. But the above described conditions may affect a very great number of persons who belong to the same unit —usually a clan, or a village, and even an ethnical unit. In this form the condition can be considered as mass psychosis, which may take two forms: an "epidemic" form that suddenly affects the unit and soon passes away, and an "endemic" form that from time to time affects groups of persons, even the same persons who belong to the same unit. The condition may also become acute, assuming extremely dangerous forms, and it may be long lasting, but not very harmful,—a chronic type. In using these terms "epidemic" and "endemic", "acute" and "chronic" I wish not to be misunderstood,—these are mere metaphoric expressions, which now do not presume any idea of "infection", although the analogy with an infection is rather great, and goes so far as to make application of "prophylaxis", "disinfection", and "antiseptic treatment" possible. However, this will be a mere metaphor, for the essential for these conditions is imitation and functional disturbance, chiefly due to the disequilibrium of the complexes.

In the description of spirits known among the Tungus we had occasion to see how the groups may be affected by the spirits. We are now interested in the problem of the effects produced by them. On the other hand, we have seen that the number of spirits among all Tungus groups is great, and is gradually increasing. However, at the same time some of these spirits are also gradually forgotten, so that spirits of different age, origin and effectiveness are mixed up in the complexes. The renewing of the list of spirits is a very interesting phenomenon, for the introduction of a new spirit practically means an individual or a mass psychosis for a short or a long time. Indeed, not all spirits produce such an effect, for some new spirits leave the psychic complex of the Tungus well equilibred, and some other spirits are invented (guessed) for the alleviation of the psychomental tension, sometimes caused by other conditions of Tungus life.

When the Tungus learn about the existence of spirits,

for instance, among the Chinese, there may be two results; namely, the spirit may appear as an active one among the Tungus, or it may appear as a powerless one among them. The spirit may become influential in two different ways. Let us take the case of *ain'i burkan* which, as has been shown, is not of a Tungus origin. There was a time when the Tungus did not know about the existence of this spirit with its various manifestations. However, the infectious diseases ascribed to this spirit, at least some of them, were not unknown among the Tungus. It is very likely that some new diseases, formerly unknown among the Tungus, were also brought by the Chinese. The theory of this complex spirit perfectly explains all kinds of diseases of this group. So the Tungus now include in the list of these spirits' activity not only diseases produced by the contact with the Chinese, but also all other diseases which were known before.

In this case it is not likely that the acquaintance with the new spirit would bring mass psychosis, for the whole series of diseases are infectious; but the spirits of a foreign origin, in the Tungus eyes, will still be active. Indeed, among the Tungus, when they become acquainted with a new spirit symbolizing infectious diseases, there may be some cases of an imaginative sickness ascribed to the newly discovered spirits. But it will not last very long. Such an imaginative sickness is known among the students, beginners in medicine, when, with the progress of their studies, they suspect themselves of being affected by various diseases they are studying. As a matter of fact, the study of psychomental troubles, which are not conditioned by the physiological disfunctions, may have quite a bad effect on the students who have no well balanced and resistant minds.

Another case will be that, when a new spirit symbolizes not infectious diseases, but a certain psychomental condition which disables the affected persons. In such a case the spirit may become active immediately after the Tungus learn about its existence. In fact, when it is known that there are spirits which may produce upon girls an effect similar to that of a spirit in Shantung (cf. *supra* p. 243 f.), some Tungus girls who are susceptible may also become affected, imitating the Shantung girl, if they know how to do it, or creating a new form adapted to the Tungus complex.

However, not all spirits can become active among the Tungus, and the Tungus are conscious of it. Such cases will be those caused by the spirits symbolizing infectious diseases which do not affect the Tungus, and by spirits which symbolize psychomental disfunctions that are unknown to the Tungus, or cannot be introduced among them. In this case the conviction that such-and-such a spirit has no power among the Tungus is a perfect guarantee for the elimination of the new spirit's activity.

As to the psychomental nature of this conviction, I think that we have two distinct groups of cases, namely, a conscious and unconscious opposition, and a lack of psychomental susceptibility. In fact, some alien psychomental conditions disable the affected persons so much that their introduction among the Tungus would be equivalent to a destruction of the affected individuals. Therefore, these conditions, symbolized in spirits, will not be introduced at all. Into the group of cases of non-susceptibility of the Tungus we may include, for example, most of the cases connected with the sexual complex. In other ethnical groups, especially those which practise late marriage and which disable their members from normal sexual functions, a sexual maladjustment may be responsible for some psychomental troubles, while the Tungus in this respect are found in a somewhat better position (cf. SONT). Indeed, in these cases the Tungus conviction is a simple statement of facts,—the Tungus are not susceptible,—while in other cases the Tungus usually are, I think, unconscious of their methods of self-preservation, when they accept the idea of their inviolability by some spirits. This is merely one of the curious mechanisms of a self-regulation of the psychomental complex.

One may frequently hear from the Tungus complaints of the spirits that harm them. So I have several times heard them saying: "We are in a very bad position, for we have too many spirits. Our neighbours, the Russians, are happier, for the spirits do not harm them". On the other hand, one may also frequently hear their statement that such-and-such spirits of the Chinese, Manchus, Mongols and other neighbouring groups are powerless among the Tungus. These are facts of great interest, for the Russian spirits (so from the Tungus point of view), in so far as they are "named" spirits (e.g. Jesus Christ, Saint Mary and various saints), do not produce such harm as the spirits adopted by the Tungus. Naturally, if these Russian "spirits" become known among the Tungus, they do not produce effects similar to those described in the previous chapter. By this remark I do not want to say that the Russian complex is free from the attempts at a theoretical justification of "hysteria" and other "hysteria-like" conditions, and that no other forms of producing these conditions are known among the Russians. However, there is an essential difference, namely, theoretical justification and other forms producing psychosis are not identified with the spirits of Tungus conception. Yet, their functioning presumes a social system quite different from that of the Tungus, and a different psychomental complex which for the Tungus is out of reach. Owing to this, the conditions which produce instability of the Russian psychomental complex remain unknown to the Tungus, and the Russian "spirits" as stimuli and justification of psychoses are absolutely harmless for the Tungus.[*] However,

theoretically these harmless spirits may be assimilated and adapted by the Tungus for the same function as their own harmful spirits. Such one seems to be the case of some *mafa* which among the Dahurs (cf. *supra*, p. 236) "speak Russian".

As to the other statement concerning powerless spirits, it is also a fact of importance as a condition eliminating certain cases of mass psychosis, owing to the conviction that the spirits are not powerful among the Tungus and as an indication that certain psychoses cannot affect the Tungus.

———

These are special conditions of the formation and existence (functioning) of the complex of mass psychoses. Doubtless the Tungus mass psychoses are based upon certain psychomental conditions which are "human" and are observed among other ethnical groups as well. However, this point of view gives us access to the problem of how the complex of mass psychosis is formed and how some elements are found in a complex, while other elements are absent. In particular cases of psychoses we have seen that they are gradually formed of the elements either borrowed from the neighbours or invented by the units themselves. Indeed, in these conditions the interethnical milieu is a permanent source of new elements. So we may say: the stronger the interethnical pressure, the richer the complex, i.e. the higher the chance to stimulate and to justify the mass psychosis. On the other hand, we have also seen that another favourable condition for the formation of this complex, an intensification of its function, is the condition of changing milieu which requires readaptation of the individuals and groups. Here I do not specify the kind of milieu. It may be a primary milieu, a secondary milieu in its various forms or a tertiary milieu.

In the case of primary milieu its change takes place because of the migration of the ethnical units, and because of the periodicity of short cycles. I now speak only of the periodicity of short cycles, for the periodicity of longer cycles affords the necessary time for a reaction, and readaptation, while in the case of short cycles immediate individual adaptation and that of groups of individuals is required.[*] This fluctuation of environmental conditions

———

[*] I must point out that such a broad comparison of the Tungus and Russian complexes is good only in general lines. As a matter of fact, among the Russians from time to time there appear "movements" which have "pseudo-religious" stimuli and justification of psychoses usually known under the technical term of sectarianism (s'ektantstvo). In its multifarious forms it may attain dimensions of

mass psychosis affecting normal reproductive functions, etc. The "spirits" do play the same rôle as among the Tungus, though the forms are different. Here I also want to point out that the stimuli and justification of psychoses, both individual and mass, among the so-called civilized groups assume such forms that they are not at once recognized even by the psychiatrists. Moreover, the psychiatrists themselves may play the rôle of stimulators and justificators of some psychomental disfunctions, as has been suspected by some French specialists in hysteria (after Charcot). However, cf. *supra* p. 252. To this question I shall briefly return in the conclusive part of this work.

[*] I leave aside the problem of how the individuals may react on the energy, chiefly electrical, as it seems emitted by the sun during the periods of spots, for the investigations known to me (cf. Sviatskiĭ, op. cit.) do not show how far other ethnical groups may be affected by this condition. The investigation has been carried out among the Russians, so that we cannot say whether the same reaction can be postulated as effective among the Tungus. I admit that some ethnical units may acquire great elasticity in this respect and may not react at all directly on the special condition of the sun. However, here the question is confined to the direct influence, while indirect influence, as produced on the plants-animals-ethnical units' equilibria may greatly affect the individuals and especially ethnical units.

requires immediate reaction in the sense of adaptation to the periodical changes of the conditions of life, particularly of the supply of food. The point of importance is the change, as such, and not the more or less "favourable" conditions created by them for survival of the groups. It should be noted that there may be different effects of cyclic influence which depend on two conditions, namely, the local intensity (some regions are more and other regions are less affected) and elasticity of the psychomental complex of individuals, just as a form of cultural adaptation, and physiological adaptation which possesses lesser or greater elasticity and which, in the case of great elasticity, permits the unit harmlessly to change milieus; while in the case of very limited elasticity, the unit may survive only in the conditions to which it is accustomed. The seasonal and daily periodicities do affect the system of equilibrium, but they are of such a short duration that every individual can easily adapt himself to them. However, the seasonal periodicity undoubtedly has a great importance, both direct and indirect, which is evident from various reports of travellers who observed intensification of psychoses during some seasons, e.g. in the winter. However, in so far as Tungus are concerned, I cannot say whether there is any seasonal variation. I did not observe it. Yet, I have some doubt as to this phenomenon among other groups; namely, the question remains to be answered how far the factor of forced inactivity, need of distraction and forced gathering of many people under one roof are responsible for the intensification of phenomena regarded as "pathological" conditions. The daily variations have a great importance on behaviour;—individual fits during the morning hours are almost unconceivable among the Tungus, the most favourable hours being those after sunset. However, several aspects of the above described conditions are involved, namely, relative leisure in the evenings, possibility of hiding one self in the dark, also natural weariness of the nerves after the daily work, etc. These are factors which have very little to do with the change of environmental conditions, as directly influencing individuals, i.e. the influence of light and temperature as well as, perhaps, special rays, more active in the dark. Seasonal and especially daily variations are of such a short duration that the individual elasticity may easily be created.

From the above considerations as to the influences of a changing milieu, we may suppose that the psychoses may occur in especially favourable conditions during the periods of changes, especially cyclic changes of medium length (eleven-twelve years periodicity) connected with the sunspots and after the change of territories which differ in respect to climate.

The change of secondary milieu is also a factor favourable for the psychoses. In fact, any important change, e.g. in the methods of food supply, in the system of social organization, etc. requires a readaptation of the psychomental complex. Instability during the period of readaptation is, of course, a well known fact, which does not require any special comments. The question is as to the intensity of the readaptation of the psychomental complex. In fact, if the process of readaptation occupies a very long period, it may proceed at a slow pace without affecting the functional equilibrium, but if it requires a short period, a special effort must be made which in individual cases and in groups, may easily result in a temporary disequilibrium which may facilitate manifestations of

phychoses. In this way we introduce the idea of relativity of the process of changes referred to the unit of time. So that if the change proceeds at a certain speed the psychomental complex must change constantly and must adapt itself, in order to preserve its functional effectiveness in the newly created systems of adaptive equilibria. Naturally, when the tempo of variations is very high and the psychomental complex cannot be adapted with the same speed, the internal conflict is inevitable. In such conditions individual and mass psychoses are very likely to occur.*

Another condition of relativity is that of inborn ability of psychomental changes, the elasticity of individual and therefore also of mass psychomental complex.** For the present we have to leave this remark without any further development, for we do not actually know whether there are any special *inborn conditions* in the ethnical units, i.e. different degrees of "conservatism", i.e. the sticking to the existing complex, or "reformism", i.e. the indifference as to the existing complex and readiness to change it at any moment. One thing is evident, namely, within certain limits variations of the ability of elastic adaptation of the paychomental complex depend not on the inborn conditions, but on the previous *tempo of variations*, to which tempo the ethnical unit is already adapted. Therefore, the chief condition seems to be the evenness or smoothness of the tempo of variations, the tempo itself depending on what may be compared with "full capitalization and amortization" of the produced change. In such a setting of the problem we arrive at another problem, namely, that of impulses of variations and their variable intensity during periods of utilization, and thus of the process of increase of population. This problem may be set only in so far as the processes are concerned in well adapted and not declining units; but with the declining units the situation is complicated by the conditions of inverse movement—the loss of adaptation and adaptiveness, and the lack of necessary response to the interethnical pressure. These questions may be left aside for the time being.

Finally, the change of psychomental complex may occur without being caused by the need of readaptation to the changing secondary milieu. Here I have in view the simplest case of changes which occur in the psychomental complex owing to the interethnical pressure, and to the increase or loss of the elements of the pre-existing psychomental complexes which we have already seen and which we shall discuss later.

The interethnical milieu in its direct and indirect manifestations produces the greatest influence on the conditions of the psychomental complex. An indirect influence consists in the changes of the complexes of material, technical adaptation and social organization, which have to be made,

---

* Vide supra pp. 17 et seq.
** In a pseudo-scientific justification of heterethnical reactions a tendency to explain ethnical differences from the "hereditary" (racial) condition was lately prevailing. Naturally, it was immediately opposed by a contrary tendency, namely, that of explaining them from the "cultural" differences, also the "environment". The "truth" is not always found in between two opposite opinions. As shown, both forms of adaptation actually are the same. However, certain functional phenomena are undoubtedly conditioned by the morphological and physiological characters of the organism, so within these limits "inborn conditions" may be held responsible. Unfortunately, no adequate investigations have been carried out,—we cannot now seriously use all gathered "facts".

owing to the interethnical pressure. The direct influence is the pressure of alien ideas (theories, conceptions) and behaviour as a source of imitation. In the previous pages of this chapter, I began my discussion precisely by showing a picture of this influence, for it is very evident and it is subject to a simple distinction among other elements. We have seen that a new spirit, discovered by the Tungus among their neighbours, may in certain conditions be easily introduced, and this fact alone may suffice for shaking the psychomental equilibrium of the individuals and groups and thus produce a mass psychosis. In this way the pressure of interethnical milieu is a permanent and direct source of ethnical psychomental disequilibrium, or, better to say, a permanent source of impulses of variations which require re-adaptation of the complex.

The above given picture of conditions responsible for the mass psychoses among the Tungus,—and it may be generalized for other ethnical units which are in quite similar conditions,—shows that there may be two theoretically fixed extremities (1) the condition of a perfect stability which theoretically (and only theoretically!) may be of two forms: a static stability and a dynamic stability; and (2) the condition of a perfect instability, which may be also of two forms. In fact, with an unvariable primary milieu, an unvariable secondary milieu (perfect adaptation in the given conditions), and an unvariable interethnical pressure, a perfect static stability may be created. The individual cases of psychoses, chiefly brought about by the physiological disfunction, and as "normal" variations of "normal" condition (its extremities), will have no further spreading. On the other hand, the well balanced milieus and correct adjustment of the tempo of their variations and that of the psychomental complex will produce a dynamic stability as a system of moving equilibrium maintained by an adaptation of impulses of variations and responses. From the diagnostic point of view these cases are not difficult, and practically no static stability is observed.

The condition of complete instability, as a theoretical proposition, may be suspected to be static in the case when the physiological condition of the ethnical unit is a permanent source of psychoses. Such a case is not of common occurrence, for in the history of ethnical units it may occur only in the case of a complete biological decline which brings the unit very near to complete extinction. It is very unlikely that such a unit may survive for a full generation. Under the present condition of interethnical pressure such a unit would disappear within a few years. The case of a complete dynamic instability may occur in the condition of lacking adaptation as to the changes which proceed and as to the tempo of variations. This occurrence is also not frequent, and it is a theoretical one, for the unit has no time to maintain it and perishes early.

The groups, practically observed with respect to the conditions of mass psychoses, are usually found in the conditions ranging between the above indicated limits. The state of a perfect dynamic stability is not observed, as well as the state of a complete dynamic instability, for both may occur only for a short time in rare cases, as a mass phenomenon lasting no more than a few weeks or a few months, in the conditions of a shaken ethnical equilibrium.

In the first case the equilibrium is restored, or the unit perishes; in the second case the centrifugal and centripetal movements rearrange the ethnical unit and the former equilibrium is restored.

In order to avoid here a possible misunderstanding I want to point out that, when in some ethnical units the mass psychoses take new ethnographical forms, they cannot be easily recognized and are often left unnoticed. This is very frequently the case in ethnical groups which are undergoing a process of positive impulsive variation, when mass psychoses usually remain unnoticed. On the other hand, if the ethnical unit is under the condition of negative impulsive variation, manifestations of mass psychoses can be easily seen, for they usually repeat one of the forms already experienced in the past. Indeed, in the observation of alien groups the situation is enormously complicated by the fact that the observers, as a rule, reflect their own complex,—they react on an alien complex,—so that normal phenomena may be taken for "mass psychosis", while real psychoses may be left unnoticed.

It happens often that the observer avoids inevitable errors only by limiting the scope of his work, confining himself to a selected group of facts (e.g. "behaviour" is one of the ways of selection) and by giving up the idea of operating with the psychomental complex as a whole. Indeed, such a justified avoidance of attacking the problem does not leave a great chance for reaching the goal of the investigation, i.e. the finding of a mechanism regulating psychomental complex in groups.

Undoubtedly any one who is interested in the problem would ask: how far the new spirits may produce mass psychosis, and how far the general psychomental-physiological conditions of ethnical units are responsible for the appearance of the new spirits? This question would be answered in accordance with the psychomental complex of the questioner himself, but it seems to me that if we have no direct indications as to the psychomental-physiological conditions, this question cannot even be put. A psychophysiological condition, an existing cognition of it,—both in physico-chemical forms and in symbolization,—and a complex of its stimulation and justification form a system which does not allow us to solve the equation by an abstraction of various aspects. Even a successful analysis of a great number of cases does not permit us to generalize, for there will remain a certain group of facts which do exist, but are not yet analysed and described, and they may conceal the great secret. In other words, our present knowledge is not yet sufficiently advanced for such generalizations, and even for an adequate description of the system.

As far as possible the cases, like those observed among the Tungus, ought to be analysed and described, while the answer to the above indicated question must be left to the future.

As has already been shown, in some cases we may speak of spirits more or less definitely in the sense of their being the cause, and of psychosis as of an effect, while in some other cases we may speak more or less definitely of psychosis as a cause, and of spirits as of an effect, not only in terms of time, but also in terms of analysis. Yet a great number of cases will still remain, about which nothing definite can be said. In order to show how difficult the analysis can be I shall now point out that the alien origin of spirits and their history are not always certain, in the sense of showing the precedence of spirits to the psychosis, for the spirits may be only a new formulation ("cognition") of a pre-existing psychosis. And still more difficult is the case when two aspects of the system,—the psychosis, its cognition and explanation (spirits),—are occurring simultaneously, e.g. under interethnical pressure.

92. **FORMS OF PSYCHOSIS AND UNITS AFFECTED** I shall now give a description of how a psychosis may spread and affect units. The best case for such demonstration is the case when the spirits of a clan lose their master, the shaman.

We have seen that it is believed that there are spirits which introduce themselves into the persons. It is also believed that these spirits can be mastered by one of the men of the clan. When the spirits have no master, they begin to harm the people by introducing themselves into the clansmen. From the experience of former generations the effects of the self-introduction of spirits, as described in the preceding chapter, are known. If there is an active shaman-master who is governing the spirits that introduce themselves into the clansmen, they may easily be revoked by him; but if he is no more active, e.g. because of physical disability, sickness, etc., or if he dies, the spirits cannot be expelled. In such a case we have a quite definite idea of the conditions in which the spirits may become harmful, of what happens when they are harmful, and how they may be controlled. In this way the whole operation with the spirits and mass psychosis is an elaborate ethnographical complex, gradually worked out and well balanced.

In case the spirits are free, either because of the shaman's death or because of his abstaining from actual control of the spirits, they begin to enter the clansmen and to produce various harmful acts. So, for instance, a man who is an excellent hunter would not be able to kill animals, because the spirits would lift up, or turn down or aside the gun at the moment of shooting. His family and other people, depending on his hunting, would have no more food supply from this source. As soon as other clansmen learn of the case, the same may happen with other members and so all of them would be convinced that the spirits want something and that by impeding the hunting they wish to attract the attention of the clansmen to themselves. Other manifestations of the same complex spirit, or some other spirit may enter the young people of the clan.

Some of the young men would lose normal sleep, would sit on their beds, speak and sing in a half asleep state and thus would not have the necessary rest; their thoughts would be concentrated upon the spirits that haunt them; they would be distracted, and absent-minded; they would neglect or miss their duties in the family work and would gradually be disabled altogether. Some other clansmen might "run away into the rocks or forests" where they would remain for days without food and even some of them would perish. Others, who are inclined to "olonism", might become dangerous during momentary uncontrolled states; they might throw various utensils, burning wood or hot water, on those supposed to induce reflexes; they might even use weapons, like knives, axes and rifles and so the most harmless and amusing *oloy* may become *kōdu*. Other clansmen would have "nervous attacks" at the moments of great responsibility, e.g. during the crossing of rivers, keeping in their arms children, handling hot water and fire. Accident after accident would follow and

several persons might perish altogether. This would be a case of a real mass psychosis which might put the clan into a state of complete social and economic paralysis threatening the very existence of the clan.

As a matter of fact, in such cases there will be no disturbing factors, but the idea that the spirits are "free" and the whole condition of the unit will be merely a complex ethnographical phenomenon following a certain pattern. It may be stopped at any moment, if there is a man or a woman who can "take control of the spirits." This may be done at the very beginning of the mass psychosis, or when the psychosis attains great dimensions.

I have been told that sometimes a clan may be affected for a long period, when it is impossible to find a "master" for the spirits and the latter cannot be expelled. In such a case a clan may gradually lose its ability to control psychic life and the members, one after another, may perish. Indeed, the perishing will not be caused by accidents only, but the members, being exhausted by a certain kind of spirits, would perish of infectious diseases (other kinds of spirits), undernourishment, etc. Other clans of the unit may interfere with the case, but they may not be always successful in their attempt.

The above described case is not characteristic of the clans alone. In fact, if the spirits, which produce harm, are clan spirits, only clansmen will be affected, but if the spirits are not clan spirits, the whole ethnical or regional unit may be affected by a condition analogous to that of the clan psychosis.

Such occurrences, according to the Tungus description, are frequent when the spirits come from outside, i.e. from other ethnical units and are not yet mastered. Personally I have not observed such cases, but theoretically they are possible. Let us suppose that the Tungus should discover a new spirit, such as for example *ajelga*. This spirit may harm the people who are living or visiting this locality, regardless of their belonging to other clans. However, some clans may master this spirit, as has happened in one of the Birarčen clans (*vide supra* pp. 155, 167), and the spirit will no more harm those clansmen, so long as there is a "master". But, the people who belong to other clans are liable to suffer from *ajelga*. In a great number of cases of appearance of such a new spirit, the condition does not become known at once, but only gradually, and when it is mastered in a clan, its activity is eliminated. So the function of self-protection of the ethnical unit is performed by the hypothesis that almost all spirits which produce psychoses can be mastered in the clan. However, there are some spirits, especially alien spirits, which cannot be mastered at all and therefore other methods of fighting them are elaborated; e.g. neutralization of the spirits' activity with the help of clan spirits, and particularly with the help of shamans. In such a case the "treatment" will not be an automatic one, but will be carried out in all individual cases. The situation is greatly complicated by the fact that some spirits, according to the Tungus theories, can by no means be expelled and neutralized. Still more the situation is complicated by the fact that not all spirits are known. In fact, there are some infectious diseases, such as influenza, perhaps typhus. paratyphus. etc., which are symbolized as spirits, which cannot be fought by the ordinary methods,—i.e. mastering and expelling. On the other hand, the psychic condition of mass psychosis, in some cases, may be wrongly understood as one caused by the same spirits, or more exactly, as un-known manifestations of these spirits, so that the shamans may abstain from intervention, and the psychosis may produce the most harmful effects. This is especially common with the new alien spirits which are not yet carefully studied, and which may be supplied with powers lacking in the original alien complex. Such was the case with some Russian and Chinese spirits, when they became first known among the Tungus and the Tungus did not know from direct sources all peculiarities of these spirits. How-ever, with the course of time, and with a familiarization with the spirits, additional theories are usually elaborated and the potential mass psychoses are eliminated.

Indeed, the cases when spirits affect small territorial units, especially villages, are much more frequent, owing to the fact that the villagers are living in close contact and new spirits easily penetrate. In principle it does not differ from the effect upon ethnical units, and this is also true in reference to the practical methods of fighting new spirits.

I have just pointed out that in fighting new spirits great help comes from the idea that most of the spirits are confined to the clans and that they may be mastered within the clans. Indeed, this attitude is not without foundation, in so far as the facts support it. In the description of spirits we have seen that the psychomental peculiarities of the clans do exist and they may be symbolized in special spirits. The nature of these peculiarities is twofold; namely, to some extent they may be "inherited" conditions and may be formed as a functional cultural complex,—"a social character". The Tungus themselves are conscious of the fact of heredity, which I have demonstrated in the case of peculiar sexual behaviour continued during several generations (SONT, p. 323), inherited sexual peculiarities and in the case of affective behaviour apparently typical of some lines in a clan, e.g. in the *Dundankün* clan of the Birarčen, a line which was affected by various troubles of psychic order. Perhaps the difference in clan characters partly inherited, may also be seen in the case of the *Bajagír* and *Kaltagír* clans of the Khingan Tungus (SONT, pp. 343-344). If we add clan tradition to the inherited characters, it will be clear that the Tungus may form the idea that some spirits are confined to the clans. We can now also support this idea by the fact that, as soon as the clans exist and the members of a clan are more familiar with their own complex and they freely communicate with one another, there is formed a special milieu,—a clan (group of families) milieu,—in which the members are psy-chomentally connected to a much greater extent than the same persons may be connected with other members of the same ethnical unit. If now we remember that the Tungus social system, in a great number of cases, is still based upon the dual clan organization, bound by cross-cousin marriage, the idea of specific clan spirits, very often similar in the two matrimonially connected clans, may be as correct as the idea of special psychomental com-plexes preserved and transmitted from generation to gen-eration in the ethnical units. This idea is natural for the Tungus psychomental complex and the Tungus accept it: we have seen that some spirits cannot affect the Tungus.

It is thus evident that the clan organization in the matter of mass psychosis is of the greatest importance, not only because the Tungus believe that the spirits may affect a clan as a whole, but also because the clan is the

carrier of inherited psychomental predispositions, for certain psychoses, and is the place where the cultural com-plex is preserved. From this point of view the conditions of Tungus groups among which the clan organization is in a state of decline are more susceptible of being affected by alien spirits. This does not exclude the smaller groups with-in the unit, in which the mass psychosis may easily be fought. Therefore one of the phenomena of ethnical decline is not only disintegration of the social organization, but also general liability to the mass psychoses. In such a state those Tungus groups are found which are encountered in the process of the reorganization of their social system, especially in Siberia, and partly in Manchuria. As a matter of fact, all these phenomena of disintegration are correlat-ed to such a degree that one cannot see where the cause is and where the effect. On the other hand, if there is a gen-eral loss of belief in the harmful spirits, the dispersion of the clan organization may facilitate the process of losing harmful beliefs, for the clan is the unit where these beliefs are preserved and practised. It should be noted that from this description of the units in which mass psychoses may occur it is also evident how erroneous an introduction of the conception of special "religious" units can be, as it is done by some authors.

The mass psychosis confined to the clans, to the ter-ritorial and ethnical units, may originate and be fought within the same units. Among the Tungus the most im-portant place in this respect belongs to the clans. An ex-ceptional condition, when the spirits and psychoses are be-yond the clans, is found chiefly, if not exclusively, among groups which are found in a state of cultural and social disintegration.

93. SYMBOLIZATION OF PSYCHOSES We have seen from
    AND METHODS OF TREATMENT the previous section
                                that the mass psy-
chosis may affect clans and other units to such a degree that the unit can perish altogether. On the other hand, we have also seen that the Tungus are very susceptible to the individual condition which may be favourable for mass psychosis. But, we have also seen that the source of the psychosis may be pre-existing in the form of hypotheses and theories and alien influences, on the one hand, and pro-bably physiological conditions due to physical causes, on the other hand. Since all these phenomena can be under-stood by the Tungus only in terms of spirits' activities, and since these Tungus explanations are sufficient, the sym-bolization of psychoses, and their classification, assume a great importance. This analysis of psychic phenomena and their classification constitutes one of the current needs of the Tungus, as without them they may easily become a prey of psychoses. Whether their hypotheses as to the spirits are correct from the point of view supposed to re-present a scientifically established truth or not, is not im-portant, if we want to make clear the mechanism of regula-tion of the psychomental complex and of fighting harmful phenomena. If the Tungus, with the help of their hypo-theses, can classify psychoses, that occur among them and can fight for a restoration of psychic equilibrium, it shows that the Tungus solution of the problem is practically effec-tive, and thus correct. One of the conditions of their suc-cess in this respect is that they regard these phenomena not as "pathological" cases, but as phenomena being in the order

of "normal" things which ought to be regulated. When in the European complex we abstract a series of psychic phenomena, the regulation of which escapes medical art, and we separate a series of "pathological" phenomena which may be either treated or left as hopeless cases, there still remain a greater number of cases which have all the necessary symptoms of non-pathological conditions and on this ground are even not analysed and no "treatment" takes place, although the nature of these phenomena of mass psychoses is not less dangerous than that observed among the Tungus. I shall revert once more to this problem, because a comparison of the groups of the European complex with those of the Tungus may help us to understand that a "pathological" character of "mass psychosis" observed among the Tungus appears to be so only in the eyes of European observers, while analogous phenomena among the Europeans, assuming a new, previously unknown form, remain unnoticed, and the mechanism of self-regulation of the psychomental complex also remains little cognized, if at all. The substitution of "ideas", "movements", "philosophical systems", "fashionable psychological theories" and other phenomena for the Tungus spirits, and the substitution of conditions, in which no normal function of ethnical units becomes possible, for the mass psychosis, as described; as well as the substitution of other methods, hardly better understood than the shamanism— do not change the nature of the phenomenon. Forms are different, ethnographical contents are different; but the essentials remain the same. The complexity of the same phenomena among European groups is natural, for the groups are numerous and therefore the ethnographical complexes are naturally not as simple as among the Tungus.

It should be noted that, when the Tungus try to analyse and classify (symbolize) cases of mass psychosis, they do not realize that they are acting by the system of a self-regulating mechanism, but their activity must be explained by something less abstract. They try to find practical methods of ridding themselves from the influence of spirits or from the harmful psychological conditions symbolized in spirits. Still, the action will not be directed against the spirits in general, but, in every individual case, for helping the affected persons. There may be fighting against the complexes of spirits and against the individual spirits; the practical solutions will depend upon the character of the problem of the psychosis.

As to the process by which the Tungus reach this aim it is not simple, for there are many variations; but I shall now give only a rough idea of the process.

Case I. The spirits are known. The person is affected by a certain harmful complex manifested by symptoms: partial loss of consciousness, involuntary movements, "arch", pronouncing of known words and sentences, etc. Another spirit must be called in with the help of which the harmful spirit may be expelled, or the harmful spirit may be asked to leave the person alone, etc. If the result of influencing the spirit is positive, the diagnosis is correct, and then, without mistake, it can be used in other symptomatically similar cases.

Gradually a list of spirits with their peculiarities and the practical methods of their ejection is created.

Case II. The spirits are unknown. The person is affected by a certain condition with a combination of symptoms never observed before. The words pronounced are not clear (they may be, e.g., foreign words), etc.

The possibility of a foreign spirit (a foreign language is used) suggests itself. If such a spirit is known among other ethnical groups, which must be found out through a direct inquiry, the case is treated either according to the practices known in other ethnical groups, or by methods of convincing the spirit, or of its expulsion with the help of some other, but well known spirits. If the operation is successful the method is used in other analogous cases. If it does not work, new variations of the known methods are made, or a new hypothesis as to the character of a new, unknown spirit is proposed. Its characters are defined, and various methods are applied. If one of them succeeds, it is incorporated into the complex. If none is effective, the case may be declared hopeless, until a successful solution is found, usually by the method of trial and error. However, some cases of psychomental troubles shown will be ascribed not to the spirits, but to the physical causes.

Undoubtedly, one of the greatest Tungus discoveries along this line was that of the mastering of spirits. How it was made, is difficult to say. Perhaps it was not a Tungus discovery at all, but a Tungus interpretation of some other complex, which could be used among the Tungus as "mastering". In fact, since a spirit may be mastered and must obey a human being, a case of mass psychosis caused by a spirit or a group of them may be easily treated by "mastering". If this is so, the persons affected by it may become liberated from their psychosis. This is a method of mass treatment. However, not all spirits may be mastered at once, for first of all, a good understanding of the character of the spirit and its ways is needed. Some of them may remain for a long time independent. Yet, the Tungus do not need to master all spirits, for not all of them are harmful and not all of them can be really useful , and at least a certain number of them, e. g. those symbolizing certain infectious diseases, are not mastered, but only summoned when needed. It may also be added that some spirits remain for a long time on the list of mastered spirits, but they usually manifest no activity. They remain almost inactive in the complex. The analysis of spirits shows that some of them have in all respects absolutely similar effects, and not all of them are used. Being already replaced by new spirits, sometimes borrowed from other ethnical groups, they remain on the list partly because of inertia, and partly because of theoretical presumption: the more numerous the spirits the more powerful the man who masters them. Whence, the Tungus usually gather a great number of them.

Of no less importance is another Tungus discovery, namely, a spirit can be used against other spirits, or a group of them against another group, as individual spirits. Therefore, mastered spirits may be used as a weapon against other spirits.

I need not repeat that most spirits are believed—and this is a hypothesis of great practical value—to possess human characters, and interests. Indeed, it greatly helps the operation with them. This is a very interesting fact, for, indeed, human beings may create spirits only reflecting their own psychomental complex. In this respect the Tungus analysis and knowledge of spirits, as seen from the spirits met with among the Tungus, are very near to the realities if we admit the fundamental proposition, namely, that of independent existence of spirits.

The question is now as to how the spirits can be practically fought. Extensive knowledge of the existing spirits within the clan and ethnical units, and even among the neighbouring groups, and the knowledge of symptoms indicative of the spirits' presence are required. On the other hand, a knowledge of the methods by which the spirits' activity can be neutralized is indispensable. It is thus evident that the Tungus are in great need of specialists who must be acquainted with spirits and methods of fighting them, and who must be good diagnosticians at the same time, not to speak of their possession of personal character which must be authoritative. Such a specialization is one of the conditions for success in fighting psychoses. The specialists dealing with these phenomena among the Tungus are shamans who perform a distinct social function in the regulation of the psychomental complex. In reality, such specialists are not at all recognized as such, but they do exist for this function, created, as a result of a long adaptation, chiefly by the methods of trial and error, but sometimes with a deep insight and foresight, which becomes evident, when the complex of the shamans is analysed and when the investigator becomes familiar with them as personalities.

However, as will be shown later on, and as it has already been pointed out in the section dealing with mafarism, the shamans meet with opposition and have to face hostility and "competition" on the part of other methods. These are the conditions of "normal" existence of social phenomena formed as a result of a certain system of equilibria. For an observer who would not penetrate into the functional mechanism of shamanism, the mafarism, the simple prayers and sacrifices, and other methods which partially compete with the functions of the shamans, may appear to have greater importance than they actually have in the complex, and they may cast a shadow on the actual functions of shamanism.

A quite distinct character of the shamans is that they "master" the spirits, they introduce them into themselves, by which operation they liberate the clansmen, or their co-villagers, and generally members of the unit to which they belong, from the influence of spirits. The shamans perform the whole operation of introduction of the harmful spirits without being possessed by them. Such a function may be compared with that of a safety valve,* which will be clearer when we proceed to the details of the psychomental complex of the shamans themselves and persons who practise shamanism; but for the present I omit these details.

It would be erroneous to suppose that the shamans and shamanism are a cognized complex, although their functioning as *safety valves* is understood by the Tungus. In fact, shamanism has assumed, for its functioning, forms which conceal its function altogether. First of all, the assistance of shamans in the case of individuals affected by the spirits is an individual service; secondly, the mastering of spirits is done in the form of special psychic conditions of individual candidates; thirdly, the liberation of the units from the mass psychosis is not noticed; fourthly, most shamanistic performances are made in such a manner that the aesthetic side is always attractive, both for the performer and the audience. As a matter of fact, such

* I have introduced this conception in my first publication on shamanism (1919, "Essay," etc.), the conclusion of which in English was given in J. R.A.S. N.C. Br. 1923. vol. LIV pp. 246-249, and reproduced (1929) in SONT, pp. 364-366.

a form of self-regulating mechanism of the psychomental complex is not' a phenomenon exceptional in its forms and absolutely unknown among other groups. Usually, the self-regulating mechanism does exist without being cognized by those who need it. Moreover, it may be supposed that its cognition would perhaps destroy its functional value for the regulation of a mass psychosis.

Instead of giving a conclusion of the present chapter, I want to touch upon a practical problem of policy towards the observed individual and mass psychoses. This side does not concern us, in so far as it is a practical problem, but it has its ethnological aspect too. As such, it deserves to be analysed. After a brief discussion of the psychomental conditions in the individuals and masses of populations, those who quite sincerely intend to interfere with the life of ethnical groups, such as the Tungus and Manchus, to their interest, would be inclined to accept the attitude which may be summarized as follows. Since the psychoses may be produced by the existing theories concerning the spirits, these theories must, first of all, be abolished, together with the complex of shamanism, which creates and maintains them. Such is the attitude of ethnical groups who have different complexes and, according to their conviction, have themselves reached a higher stage of "culture". The can be observed in both Russians and Chinese, and even partly among the Mongols, who wanted to liberate the Tungus and Manchus from their fear of spirits and "barbarous" practices of shamanism. In this respect, the communists who rule the populations of Siberia, and who believe themselves to be free of "superstitions", are still more naïve in their manifestations of interethnical pressure and its "scientific", "materialistic" and "marxian" justification. I shall revert to this question later on. Indeed, with the help of all modern methods of education, it is not difficult to destroy Tungus belief in the spirits. The substitution of a religion, like Christianity, for the Tungus beliefs is also practically possible, as well as the substitution of faith in the coming paradise of socialism. It is especially simple if the change of ideas can have some practical benefit for the Tungus (individuals). It is still easier to fight the shamans as carriers of functions, and shamanism as a complex. A series of "regulations" and governmental orders can do it within two generations. But the question is this: can the fundamental hypothesis—the influence of spirits on the psychoses—be accepted as a postulate, or not? If the belief in spirits is destroyed, as well as shamanism as a *safety valve*, will the psychoses disappear or will they take new forms, perhaps now unforeseen ones, and even forms which will not be recognized at once? These questions as has been shown, cannot now be answered. Therefore, there seem to be other reasons, why these ideas of enlightenment of "savages" and "barbarians" are so common among the "civilized" mankind. Certainly, other ethnical groups are not very much concerned, if under conditions of uncontrolled psychomental complex smaller groups should perish altogether. That such a possibility exists may be seen from the observed facts, viz. small ethnical units affected and left without assistance perish very quickly. Under these conditions a large group may pass much more easily through the period of psychomental disequilibrium, even when a self-regulating mechanism is not yet worked out. In fact, a partial loss of resistance and a partial loss of population do not mean that the unit perishes; the unit with its internal differentiation may work out such a mechanism during the state of disequilibrium, and with the remaining resistance and remaining population it has a certain chance of restoring its interethnical position. However, a small unit, once shaken by the loss of power of resistance and population, cannot survive, and usually individuals who remain after the catastrophe are dispersed and join other ethnical units. This is one of the interesting aspects of the ethnical variation under always growing interethnical pressure, under which only large ethnical units and numerous ethnical colonies may create higher forms of adaptation and thus survive. Owing to this condition, the experiments with small groups are much more dangerous in the sense of threatening their existence, than the experiments with large, numerous groups. At tne same time it is much easier for the large units to carry out an experiment on small ones, because the small units may be harder pressed than the large ones.

Actually this worry about the establishment of safety from mass psychoses by the abolition of beliefs in the spirits and shamanism (and other similar forms of self-regulating mechanism) is nothing else but a justification of interethnical pressure. Therefore, the question whether the spirits produce psychoses or psychoses produce spirits must first be cleared up from the ethnographical features, i. e. the influence of a justification of interethnical pressure.

One thing is evident: since ethnical units possess a system of spirits (beliefs) and an organized self-regulating mechanism of the psychomental complex, and since with the help of this mechanism the psychoses—which are not at all a privilege of those who have beliefs in spirits and shamanism—may be regulated, the units seem to be well adapted for survival in the given conditions. Indeed, the psychoses, beliefs in the spirits, and the safety valve mechanism cannot be separated, for they are only different aspects of the same functioning psychomental complex. In the forms, as described, can we really regard the psychoses as a "pathological" phenomenon, or is it safer to consider them as normal ones, in so far as they may be regulated by shamanism? This question is quite timely, for other phenomena of mass psychosis observed among the Europeans are not considered at all as "pathological" ones, but very often they even receive the name of "progressive movements". I am inclined to add that the greater number of European observations on "shamanism" and "psychoses" and the especial attention to the outer forms of these phenomena, which are sometimes exaggerated, are mere ethnographic reactions of Europeans on alien complexes. In the greater number of cases these reactions are badly affected by the "superiority complex" and the justification of interethnical pressure on weak ethnical groups, sooner or later liable to be destroyed by large ones. Within these limits ethnography, until now, did not go much further than other "humanities".

CHAPTER XXII

SHAMANISM IN GENERAL

94. ORIGIN OF THE TERM "SHAMANISM" The term "shamanism", as a scientific term, is a derivative of "shaman", so that first we have to go to the original source. The term "shaman" was introduced into the western complex by the Russians who first met with the Tungus in the seventeenth century. During the following century several travellers, for instance, Gmelin, Georgi and Pallas, also the historian Miller gave descriptions of practices performed by the specialists known among some Tungus groups under the names *saman—šaman—haman.* Into the western complex this term penetrated in the form of "shaman", doubtless borrowed from the Tungus of the western regions of their territory, who use the word *s'aman* which was perceived by the Russians as *šaman.* In Europe it made its appearance a little later than in Russia. Although it was introduced by E. Ysbrants Ides, it became familiar only at the end of the eighteenth century, through the works of Russian travellers. Indeed, the shamans were first understood as a kind of "pagan sorcerers", which meaning has persisted up to our days among laymen [*] and partly was responsible

for hampering the understanding of the phenomenon itself.

The fact that the term *saman* which in the Manchu language, in observed original facts, referred to the entirely different phenomenon "*p'oyun saman*" (vide supra p. 217) contributed to the acceptance and maintenance of the term "shaman" as a generic one designating specialists in dealing with spirits.[**] In this respect an analogy between the history of the term "shaman" and "Tungus" is interesting, for it reveals the presence of three facts, namely, "western tendency" to generalize with an inadequate knowledge of facts; a strong influence of "symbolism"; an incidental origin of terms. However, the difference between the history of these two terms is of some interest too. While a term of an alien origin *saman*, as will be shown, was assimilated by the Tungus before meeting European investigators, the terms "Tungus" and "tung-hu" were not introduced into the Tungus languages, both being of different origin and referring to different ethnical groups. The extension of the observation over other ethnical groups of Siberia, among whom the term *saman* was even unknown, brought the

---

[*] P. Pelliot (cf. šaman, J. A. 1913, Mars—Avril, p. 466) literally gives the following definition: "le terme de chamanisme, dérivé de celui de «chamane» ou sorcier sibérien, est aujourd'hui passé dans la langue courante de l'ethnographie religieuse. Le "chamane" est le même sorcier......etc.". Evidently this definition is given for the use of rather ignorant people, and it may be supposed as a result of

P. Pelliot's desire of being better understood by his readers unfamiliar with ethnography.

[*] It must be pointed out that the Manchu complex of dealing with the spirits, in so far as it could be seen from the rites, was not interpreted as "sorcery" but as an adaptation of Buddhism (cf. L. Langlès, op. cit. pp. 14 et seq.).

ethnographers to a generalized conception of a certain complex opposed to Christianity and other "religions", whence there was only one step to make from this generalization to a new religion, styled "shamanism". The ethnographical elements, of which the complexes styled shamanism consisted, were also found in ethnical groups living in different parts of the world, and on this ground "shamanism" received a still broader application, in reference to the complexes which could not be styled by one of the terms already in use, as Christianity, Buddhism, Taoism, Lamaism, etc. and various complexes known as ancient "religions" of the Egyptians, Assyrio-Babylonians Romans, Greeks and other historically known groups. On the ground that there are practices of medical art, known beyond the groups familiar with the above indicated "religious" complexes, various facts of medical art, even badly understood and sometimes interpreted in terms of "magic", were included under the same title of shamanism and thus the famous "medicine-man" was also included under the same general heading, which since that time has lost even its little scientific value and began to function as a collection of various strange and "primitive" practices, and *horribile dictu*, methods of thinking, serving as a screen on which the greatness of European civilization might be better demonstrated and ingenuity of authors' genius exercised. The result of such a trend of ideas was most disastrous for their authors—they were merely acting as formulators of the psychomental complex of large masses of the population, of ethnical groups among which they were living and working; but the scientific investigation into the nature of the phenomena styled "shamanism" did not go any further. On the other hand, gathering of facts, which were not so much in vogue as fabrication of explanatory hypotheses of a few of them known and their analysis, was steadily progressing. One by one these theories were proposed and rejected, so that we still are far from facing an accomplished construction, but have only fragments of facts and some rare extensive descriptions which do not allow us to make generalizations of an old type. "Shamanism" as a European creation has collapsed and we have to revert to the initial point of investigation—to the Tungus shamanism.[*]

SHAMAN ETYMOLOGY Tungus terms are met with a great number of modifications which may be easily brought to *samaŋ*. In fact, we have (1) *saman* (Nerč. Bir. Khin. Mank.) (Ur. Castr. Neg. Sch., Barguz. Nom. Poppe) (Manchu Sp. Manchu Writ.); (2) *haman* (Lam) (Kirensk Tungus, Czek.;

* In the present description of shamanism the reader will find no references to a great number of publications dealing, both directly and indirectly, with the Tungus "shamanism". I shall refer only to those works which bear some originality of scientific thought, even though erroneous, and those which contain original and reliable facts. The reasons for my abstaining from quoting other publications (with the exception of those which may not have come to my knowledge, —certainly, not numerous) will not all be the same. Some of these publications were premature attempts at generalization; others reveal a striking lack of competence in the treatment of this complex phenomenon; still others are an incomplete digest of literature; fourthly, there are pretentious compilations on great subjects; fifthly, there are journalistic speculations; sixthly, there are plagiarisms. To give a review of all these works is quite useless, for together with other similar productions, in other scientific fields, these works will soon be regarded as a useless wasting of paper, ink, and human energy.

Vilui, M.); (3) *raman* (Tum); (4) *s'aman~s''aman* (Barg. RTM. Amur); (5) *s'ama~šama~sama* (Goldi groups, Schrenk, Schmidt) (Oroči, Sch.), i.e. all the known Tungus groups have one of the modifications of *saman*. In some records we meet with a distinction of the *a* which in the second group may be distinguished by an accent (Ivanovskii in Dahur, the character of which is not indicated) and length (Poppe in Barguzin Nom.). In most of my own records I did distinguish a musical accent due to the higher tone of the second *a*. However, the Manchu *sama* (Manchu Sp.) is accentuated on the first syllable *sáma*, which accent may be effected both by a protraction of—*á*, and by enhancing its tone (higher in tonality). The final *n* may change into *ŋ* (in Manchu Sp. Rudnev and in Dahur) commonly observed, and it may also disappear altogether (Goldi-Oroči groups). In fact, the final *n* in many Tungus dialects in this word seems to appear as a suffix, for it is subject to alteration and omission, e. g. the Barguzin dialect produces the plural in the form of *s'amas'al*; some other dialects may also produce it from the stem *sama*, i.e. *n* being considered as a suffix; while other groups give *samanal, samaŋsa*, etc. These facts are interesting, for they show a considerable oldness of the word and its assimilation seen from the fact of suffix formation by analogy. This is supported by the derivatives of the type of *samas'ik* (Bir. Nerč.), *hamaŋik* (Lam),—"the shaman's costume"; *sama* (RTM), *samdo* (Bir) (a derivative from the Manchu *samadambi→samda*), —"to perform shamanism"; by the side of *hamanda* (Lam), —ibid,—produced from the stem *xaman*. In all Tungus languages this term refers to *persons of both sexes who have mastered spirits, who at their will can introduce these spirits into themselves and use their power over the spirits in their own interests, particularly helping other people, who suffer from the spirits; in such a capacity they may possess a complex of special methods for dealing with the spirits*. Such a meaning is correlated in all Tungus dialects and languages and no other meaning is given, except in the Manchu language, in which, with the increase of the word *p'oyun*, it now refers to the specialists who perform prayers and sacrifices chiefly to the clan spirits, as well as to the specialists of the Imperial Court for the performance of rites required by the cult of the spirits in general. In the Tungus languages a great number of words are derivatives of *sama* (*n*), but besides these derivatives no word may be connected with *saman*, which remains an isolated technical term,[*] so that one must apply to other possible sources of borrowing of this term, always keeping in mind the possibility of further semantic variations of the original.

As to other ethnical groups among whom *saman* is now known, they are confined only to the Dahurs who use *samán* (Ivanovskii), *samaŋ* (Poppe). Historically this word is met with in the Nuichen language, as recorded in the Chinese transcription of the twelfth century read by P. Pelliot[**] *šan-man* and identified by him with *saman*. In fact, his translation of the Chinese text is as follows: "*chan-*

* All etymologies,—and they are numerous,—proposed by W. Banzarov, Ch. de Harlez, J. Nemeth and maintained by their followers (e. g. B. Laufer, P. P. Schmidt) are mere misunderstandings. In my part of "šramana-Shaman" (cf. p. 116, footnote 36) I give two Tungus stems which might be further misleading in setting forth premature etymological comparisons.

** op. cit. p. 468.

man, en langue *jućen*, cela signifie une sorcière". It is thus likely that the word did exist in the twelfth century in Manchuria, and referred to the specialists who might have been called in Chinese "sorcière".* In the Tungus meaning the word *saman* is unknown in other languages, where there are other terms for it [Kowalewsky gives the Mongol *šaman*, as a Manchu word (*saman*)]. Among the groups now living near the Tungus such terms are (1) *bügä*, *bögä*, *buge*, *bū* of the Mongols, used to express the same phenomenon as the Tungus shamans; it has been compared with Turkish terms for "sorcerer", "sorcery", etc.** (2) *udagan* (Mongol); *odogoy*, *udayay* (Buriat); *udoyay* (Yakut),—"the female shaman" which has been adapted by some Tungus groups, e.g. *idakon* (Mank) (Ur. Castr.), *odakon* (Nerč), *odoyan* (RTM), *idokon* (Barguz. Nom., Poppe) in the Mongol sense and evidently by the groups directly influenced by the Mongols (Buriats) and Yakuts; it should be noted that this term is not used by most of the Tungus groups of Manchuria (except RTM), also by those of the Amur and Maritime prov.*** (3) the terms based upon the stem *kam* are found among the Turk speaking groups, but they did not enter into the Tungus dialects. The Tungus dialects possess some other terms which will be discussed later on, but they have no such importance as *saman*, though they are technical ones.

B. Laufer connected the series *buga* with the Tibetan *aba* and the Chinese *bu* (*wu* "shaman?" S. Sh.), which, for the time being, I naturally leave as it is, for it does not concern us. The series *udagan* seems to remain with the Mongol speaking groups and Yakuts, for its borrowing by the Northern Tungus is evident, and so it is recognized by the Tungus themselves.

Several comparisons have been made of the Tungus word "shaman" with words of other languages, of which the first, namely, the indirect derivation of *saman* from the Sanscrit *šramana*, is correct. Putting aside the criticism of this parallel which can now have only a historic and ethnographic interest,**** we face only one difficulty, namely,

---

* As regards the limitation of the sex, it has no importance, for the Manchus, and hypothetically their ancestors, might have used both sexes.

** Etymological analysis of terms of this type, in so far as semantic variations are concerned, presents sometimes unsurmountable difficulties due to the translations of terms and their expression in terms familiar to the authors. Some of the authors do not distinguish the important difference which exists between "shaman", "sorcerer", "wizard", "diviner", "fortune teller", "juggler", "clan priest", "medicine-man" ets., all of which in the translations of incompetent recorders and writers may occasionally be "generalized" as "sorcerers", and among the more learned of them as "shamans". However, not all of these terms may refer to the "shamans" in the sense used among the groups whose terms are compared and "translated". Indeed, these phenomena are "generalized" as a group of phenomena little known to the authors who oppose them to their own complex of "civilized scholars".

▨▨▨ Udagan served to V. F. Troščanskiĭ (op. cit., p. 116) to show universality of the term udagan—"the female shaman", and hence to prove that originally the shamans were women, and male-shamans were established after the separation (hypothetic, of course,) of the Siberian groups.

**** The idea of such a parallel first occurred in the eighteenth century, in the writings of La Croze and Georgi (cf. B. Laufer, op cit. p. 362). L. Langlès definitely wrote, in 1804, "quoique le Chamanisme ne soit réellement qu'une corruption du Samanéisme, il a déjà été prodigieusement altéré et défiguré par ces Tatârs grossiers et vagabonds" (op. cit. p. 18). P. Abel Remusat, J. Klaproth, P. V. Vasiliev, Max Müller and A. H. Sayce maintained this parallel. Naturally,

---

that to show how a term can migrate from Central Asia to Eastern Asia.* As a matter of fact, we have no direct evidence for showing exactly at which historic moment and who could have carried it so far away and how its other function was substituted to its original one. However, the analysis of facts makes this difficulty not so great as it was usually pictured by the opponents,—such a migration of terms and ethnographic elements, even of complexes, is a common occurrence, and the facts concerning shamanism and shamans give us many instances of this kind. As a form of my final conclusion—it will be clearer when we go through all details of shamanism and the history of the spreading of Buddhism in Northern Asia—I may now state

in many cases this etymology was a mere guess, for there are important differences between saman and šramana, as well as between shamanism as a complex and the Buddhist sect as a complex. Indeed, no direct connexion is possible, but until recent times it was impossible even to connect the terms by means of diffused links and to establish an ethnographic causal connexion between these phenomena, which might be clearly demonstrated to those who could not grasp this idea by intuition or to those who, owing to different motives, did not wish to understand it. It was strongly opposed by W. Schott who in three papers criticized this parallel on the ground, which is now out of date and etymologically wrong, that sam was the Turk kam, connecting saman with sambi (Manchu Writ.) "to know" (recently this etymology was again maintained by P. P. Schmidt in "The Language of the Negidals," p. 31). It was L. Langlès who pointed out that "leur (shamans) nom général et primitif, je crois, est chaman"......"Les Mantchoux écrivent Saman, et Sama, enchanteur. Les Téléoutes les nomment kam, kammeâ, ou Gham" etc. (op. cit. p. 18); D. Banzarov proposed a phantastic etymology (1846). Ch. de Harlez who accepted W. Schott's criticism, especially for the reason that there were no connexions between India and China, on the one hand, and the Tungus, on the other hand, that the Chinese "sha-man" is distinct from saman, which is quite correct, but in a different sense, and he proposed his own phantastic etymology: saman is "drum" whence samdambi, etc. (cf. op. cit. p. 28 et seq.). J. Németh accepted W. Schott's hint sam.—kam and went further in the formulation of a new "phonetic law" s—k etc. B. Laufer did not add to the positive contributions of the opponents' thesis, but hastened to adhere to J. Németh's view, introducing a journalistic style into the discussion, and reviewing the literature (cf. my part of "šramana-Shaman, Etymology" etc.). What may be noted in this opposition is that all the opponents rejected the original parallel for various reasons, and all of them gave various etymologies, none of which can be considered as satisfactory from the point of view of the Tungus philology. This opposition did not help, but it greatly increased the literature regarding this etymology, making of it a kind of "great problem" in which the greatest impediment was what may be called learned obscurantism.

* The fact of lack of parallels from Central Asia and the lack of facts regarding the nature and history of the spreading of Buddhism and Shamanism, served as a strong point for the seemingly reasonable discarding of this parallel. However, with the discovery of dead languages of Central Asia the situation greatly changed. A. Meillet was the first to point out the similarity of Tokharian samäne and the Tungus word (cf. "Le Tokharien," in Indogermanisches Jahrbuch, 1914, Vol. 1, p. 19). F. Rosenberg (Public. M. A. E. RAS. Vol. V, pp. 378-379, "On Wine and Feasts in a Persian National Epic Poem") quite independently pointed out a possible parallelism of the Sogdian and Tungus saman. N. D. Mironov on two occasions (cf. his part of "šramana-Shaman"; also his "Kuchean Studies," R. O. Vol. VI, pp. 164-165) compared with Central Asiatic samäne, sâman, ssamana, which have originated from the Sanskrit šramana, whence the Chinese term šan-men, was also transcribed (沙門) a fact known for a long time. In all these languages the indicated terms are used for the designation of a Buddhist monk identified with a certain sect introduced from India to Central Asia. Thus, we now know how šramana penetrated into Central Asia. During the first millenium it also spread to China, Western Asia and even Europe, where in variants it was known and associated with Buddhism among the ancient Greeks and Persians.

that the connexion between Central and Eastern Asia through the Kidans (Western Liao) and later through other Eastern Asiatic groups was maintained; the ancestors of the Manchus and Dahurs, who both now have the term *saman*, were also familiar with Buddhism; the shamanism is not a very old complex and it is saturated with elements borrowed from Buddhism (and Lamaism) which, in so far as the complex of spirits is concerned, has already been shown; it may be supposed that the term *saman* was introduced through these ethnical groups and it might have escaped its incorporation into the Mongol complex; the Chinese šan-men, is not responsible for *saman*.

As has been shown, we find among non-Tungus groups and even among the Tungus groups some different terms for the phenomenon we call here "shaman". The absence of the term *saman* will not prevent us from including the bearers of different terms into the group of shamans. Thus the term "shaman" will be used as a technical scientific term. From this point of view it would perhaps be better to exclude it altogether, in order to avoid a conscious or unconscious confounding of the complex here described with that already created in the minds. In other words, —the symbol (starter) "shaman" must perhaps not be given a new function corresponding to my interpretation of shamanism, based upon its study among the Tungus.

In discussions of this kind, a "symbol" may lead astray the whole discussion. However, I do not introduce a new term, because I hope that it will be possible to save the term "shaman" to be applied to the phenomenon here discussed. Without wearing out this term by the use in reference to very broad generalizations, and at the same time clearing it from various malignant tumors—theories which associated shamanism with sorcery, witchcraft, medicine-man, etc.[*]— the term "shaman" may still be preserved.

I shall call *shamanism* the Tungus complex which is connected with the shamans. This term may naturally be extended over other groups possessing complexes which, without a confusing generalization, may be considered as similar ones, regardless of whether their similarity is due to the diffusion of a complex from a certain ethnical group, or might come to the same forms, as it is observed in the cases of parallelism. Naturally, we must first of all have an exact idea as to the methods of defining whether we are dealing with "shamanism" or not. Therefore, I shall now proceed to the chief characteristics of shamanism, as it is observed among the Tungus.

95. FORMAL CHARACTERS OF SHAMANISM

A. *MASTERING OF SPIRITS* The most important and characteristic condition which makes of an ordinary man a shaman is that he is a *master of spirits*, at least of a group of spirits. This relation is rendered by the terms *èjen* (Manchu Sp.), *èjan* (Bir.), *ojan* (Bir. Kum. RTM.), *ojon* (Nerč.) *od'in*

[*] I might, perhaps, introduce such a new term, but I know two facts: firstly, that new terms generally meet with opposition when they are not yet adopted by "public opinion", and secondly, that, in professional circles, indulging in the creation of new terms, instead of new ideas, is a common phenomenon, sometimes producing a new confusion of phenomena already known. I believe that the old terms must, as far as possible, be preserved, by assigning them new functions when they fall into disuse.

(Khin.). So the spirits call their master—shaman, naturally through the shaman's mouth. We have seen that the mastered spirits may be particularly malevolent and benevolent, and at any rate are not spirits-guardians, and the shaman is not "elected" by them. This aspect of shamanism will be clearly seen when details and "election" of the shaman are discussed. As to the treatment of "mastered" spirits, it naturally depends on the existing complex of ideas concerning relations between "master" and his "servants". According to the Tungus and Manchu complex, the master must take care of the spirits, feed them and handle them, when he wants to introduce them into himself. The difference between a shaman and a *mafa* is thus essential. The latter knows how to bring the spirit into contact with the people, but he must fight him, and he is not a "master" of the spirits. On the other hand, the difference between a person who is possessed by spirits (e. g. manifested in some nervous and psychic troubles) and a shaman is also essential, for the shaman introduces spirits into himself at his own will, and when he wants it, i.e. the shaman uses his own body as a placing for spirits. A voluntary introduction of a spirit is also a characteristic of shamanism, but the spirits may also be called in and introduced into other people at their invitation. The same is true about the next step, namely, the expulsion of the spirits, which is beyond the power of ordinary people. Thus among the shamans a voluntary introduction and expulsion of the spirits are only particular cases of "mastering". Let me stress the importance of this difference which is great, when the election of the shaman is carried out, and which is realized by the Tungus who are always very careful as to the diagnosis, whether the person is possessed by the spirits or the spirits are possessed by the person. No Tungus or Manchu would recognize anyone as being a shaman, if the person could not *possess spirits* in the above indicated sense.

B. *LIST OF SPIRITS* In connexion with the above indicated element of the complex it may be pointed out, that the shaman must have several spirits possessing various qualities, the latter being used by the shaman when the spirits are introduced. Indeed, the number of spirits possessed is subject to variations. The shaman is supposed to have, at the beginning of his career, at least one spirit (usually, a complex one), with the help of which he may master other spirits, or at least know them. As a matter of fact, the shaman at the beginning of his career usually does not have very many spirits, but he masters them gradually. However, if the shaman should fail to master many spirits, which he needs for assuming their special power and using it as a means to fight other spirits, he would not be recognized as a real shaman by his clansmen and outsiders (*agnak'i*), and it is very likely that he would give up his practice of shamanism without any pressure of "public opinion". It may thus be stated that a candidate, before being recognized as a shaman, must have a certain minimum of mastered spirits. Therefore, cases when shamans were recognized and lost their recognition, because of their limited number of spirits, are met with among all Tungus groups. The Tungus and Manchu would say: So—and—so is a "small shaman"; he or she is not a "real shaman". When the practice of shamanism is given up, because of the lack of new spirits, the person is said to be no more a shaman. The number of spirits that should be mastered depends, firstly, on the ideas current among the ethnical groups, e.g. among the Manchus the number of spirits is very great, as shown in the list of spirits (*vide supra* pp. 168-174), while among the Northern Tungus it is much smaller; secondly, on the number of years during which the shaman has practised, for it is supposed that the number of spirits must increase. From observed facts I have inferred that among the Tungus of Manchuria the number of spirits with the beginners is five or six, while by the end of a good career all spirits are mastered directly or with the assistance of other spirits. As has been shown, the number of spirits is also a measure of the shaman's power:—the more powerful the shaman, the more spirits he has, and vice versa; the more there are spirits, the more powerful is the shaman. In conclusion it may be thus formulated: the shaman must have a list of spirits.

C. RECOGNIZED METHODS Among all groups various methods of dealing with the spirits are known. In the opinion of the Tungus, the knowledge of these methods is indicated by two facts: firstly, the shaman knows the spirits from which he may learn the methods of dealing with them, or he knows with which spirits he has to deal, because these spirits are mastered; and secondly, the shaman must know, from learning them, a series of methods of attracting spirits, of offering them sacrifice, and, generally, of dealing with them, when they are not attracted into himself. Since the complex of spirits (their characters and needs) is a complex created through the accumulation of elements by the previous generations of shamans, it is transmitted through the mechanism of tradition, consciously or unconsciously assimilated by the new shamans. Since a complex of methods, used when the shaman is free of spirits, is considered as obligatory for shamans, because of their effectiveness already verified by previous generations, this complex of methods is transmitted through the mechanism of tradition and must be known to the new shaman. Naturally, candidates who wish to become shamans, but do not know these methods, cannot be recognized as such, because it would be supposed that spirits known to the Tungus by their habits are unknown to such candidates. So among all groups there are elaborated complexes of methods which must be known to the shaman. This does not mean that the Tungus would not recognize shamans of other groups who do not know spirits of the given ethnical unit, just because of the difference in methods used. The Manchus recognize the power of Tungus shamans, although the latter know nothing about Manchu "rites" and methods, and the Tungus would not deny to the Manchu shamans their quality, but they would say that these shamans cannot deal with Manchu or Tungus spirits respectively. Yet, the requirement of knowledge of methods does not presume that these methods cannot be reinforced by means of new ones. As a matter of fact, the methods are changing, for newly mastered spirits may have their own ways and requirements. The common attitude is that the Manchu and Tungus like to see something new along the line of introduction of new methods brought forth with the new spirits. Shamans who introduce these methods are considered as "great shamans". Another source of changes in the complex of methods used by the shamans, when they have no spirits introduced into themselves, is the alien influence. The Manchus and

Tungus do not object to the introduction of a new method known among their neighbours, if the method is really effective and practicable. Thus the complex of methods for dealing with the spirits is gradually changing, but a part of it is always transmitted and serves as a condition for the recognition of the shaman's ability. It should be noted that in some cases the complex of methods may turn into a rigid system of ritual which is not a typical aspect of shamanism, but one of the visible signs of decline,[*] while a free imagination of the shaman and his ingenuity in the invention of new methods is also limited and, when unlimited, may turn into an individual phenomenon beyond the ethnical recognition. It may thus be formulated: shamanism in its functioning in ethnical groups presumes at least partial acceptance of a certain complex of methods for dealing with the spirits, rites of sacrifice and prayers, also methods of introduction of spirits, with all complexity of this operation.

D. PARAPHERNALIA RECOGNIZED Among all groups here described and other ethnical groups, where shamanism may be suspected or its existence may be proved, various paraphernalia are found used by the shamans during the performances. It is supposed that without these paraphernalia shamanizing is impossible, and therefore the persons who have no such paraphernalia cannot function as shamans. In this way paraphernalia become an absolutely indispensable component of the shamanistic complex. However, the composition of this complex is very variable. In fact, the minimum which I could observe among the Tungus was a *toli*, a Chinese brass mirror with pendants, and a drum. The *toli* is necessary as a placing for spirits, while the drum is needed for the shamans' self-excitation, without which they cannot bring themselves into the state of extasy. Yet, the complex may attain great dimensions, when the shamans possess several costumes, e.g. for shamanizing with the help of the spirits of the lower world and of those of the upper world. These costumes consist of a complete attire: headdress, coat, trousers, apron, shoes, all with accessories; a great number of placings for spirits, such as, among the Manchus, pictures of large size, as described in preceding chapters, several drums, etc. Indeed, when the shaman is supplied with all attributes of the performance, he may more easily attain his aim of mastering some spirits and fighting others. When the paraphernalia are limited, the shamans' power is greatly reduced, e.g. they cannot go into the lower world without a special costume, and such an expedition may sometimes be required by the situation, as we have seen in the case of spirits and methods. The importance of the costume and its composition depends on the character of this complex in the ethnical units. Among the Manchus the costume itself is rather simple, while among the Barguzin Tungus and Nerčinsk Tungus of Transbaikalia it is very complicated; among the latter a shaman cannot go into the lower world without a complete "harness", as they say, while among the Manchus a shaman may have only a special headdress; occasionally he can even do without the special headdress. So that from the point of view of richness of the costume there is no fixed measure, but all depends on the locally or ethnically

---

[*] It will be shown that among the Manchus the tendency of purification of the shamanistic methods is one of the conditions of the change of shamanism into a conventionalism of priesthood.

assimilated complex. As to temporary paraphernalia made for the occasion, and their variations with the ethnical groups, they depend on the character of shamanizing i. e. the kind of spirits and the individual character of the shaman, the kind of spirits to be mastered by the shaman, the degree of wealth of the unit and even that of the shaman personally. Some of them may afford to spend money and energy on making up rich costumes, while others cannot do it. It should also be pointed out that the forms of costumes are variable among the ethnical groups and within a group. Their variations depend on the same conditions as those of the methods, i. e. some elements and complexes are transmitted through the mechanism of tradition and compulsorily adopted by the individual shamans; innovations are introduced by the shamans either as a result of borrowing from the neighbours, or as a result of their own invention, always on the condition that the new elements do not come into a conflict with the pre-existing complexes. This process of increase of the old complexes may go parallel with the substitution of new elements for old ones. Thus, from the point of view of contents and variations the paraphernalia complex is not a stable, petrified complex, but its reduction to zero may be responsible for the disintegration of shamanism. As will be shown, such cases are actually observed among the groups which are not allowed by the local authorities to shamanize and among whom the paraphernalia are sometimes destroyed by the same authorities. Here it may be added that besides the permanent paraphernalia there are others made on every special occasion of shamanizing and used only once. Indeed, even without permanent paraphernalia the shamanizing may be carried out with a temporary equipment and costume ad hoc. Thus, the absence of permanent paraphernalia is not yet indicative of the absence of the complex of shamanism, but this condition is typical of the complex in the state of decline. I may then formulate that the shamanistic paraphernalia, in the form of a special dress, musical and other instruments, and placing for spirits, are indispensable elements of shamanism.

E. THEORETICAL BASIS

It can be stated that the practising of shamanism presumes that the shamans accept some theoretical basis of shamanism, i. e. a general theory of spirits, their particular characters, and the practical possibilities of dealing with spirits. However, this does not mean that every shaman is a theoretician who can explain everything that he or she is doing. Far from that: most of the shamans cannot explain many operations of shamanizing, and in many cases they are quite unaware of their performing a shamanism which is actually based upon a strictly elaborated theory of spirits and their mastering;—shamanism is a functioning of the ethnical units, the shamans are its organs. However, there are some theories and hypotheses which the shamans must know; they are: recognition of the existence of spirits; the possibility of their removal from one placing to another, including man; the possibility of mastering them in the above given sense. Naturally, every shaman must know what to do. The shamans must know the character of the mastered spirits and of those with which they have to deal. Indeed, some shamans are real theoreticians of shamanism, while some others have a rather limited knowledge of theory. The same refers to the knowledge of facts. It would not be

exaggerated to say that among the shamans there are great encyclopaedists who are familiar with the spirits of other ethnical groups, while there are others who may know a very limited number of spirits with which they personally come into contact. Variations of theoretical interest in the problem of shamanism and variations of knowledge of facts depend on the individual character of the shamans, but the above indicated minimum of knowledge of theory and facts is absolutely indispensable for becoming a shaman. Therefore I may formulate as follows: the theoretical basis of shamanism, as understood by the shaman, is one of the formal conditions for the recognition of shamanism.

F. SOCIAL POSITION OF SHAMANS RECOGNIZED

As far as I can see, this is the last formal character of shamanism. We shall later on see how a person becomes a shaman, but at present it will be sufficient to point out only some of the required conditions. When there is no shaman in the clan or in a settlement (or territory), a quest for shamanism appears. In fact, there may be many candidates for the position of shaman, but among them not all may become "shamans". As has been shown, the candidates must know certain methods, must have a certain number of spirits, must "master" them and must have a necessary minimum of theoretical and factual knowledge of shamanism. When the candidates have satisfied these conditions, they may be recognized as possible candidates. However, such a recognition is not sufficient for becoming a shaman. The candidates are required practically to show what use they can make of the spirits, and shamanistic methods; how deep their general knowledge is; whether they satisfy the moral requirements of the community or not. This may be shown in a series of performances for helping people in distress and confirmed by the general opinion as to the moral character of the candidate. When the shaman successfully passes through this period of his career, he may be assisted in making paraphernalia and in offering a regular sacrifice to the spirits. After these preliminary steps he may be recognized as shaman and the people may seek his assistance. Then he would function as a shaman. Among all Tungus groups there are many persons who pretend to be shamans, but they are not recognized as such by the other members of the unit to which they belong and do not become actually shamans, i.e. the people will not seek their assistance. In the greatest number of cases, in general, and in all cases among the Manchus, the shamans are connected with the clan organization. However, the shaman's belonging to a definite clan is not an absolute character of shamanism, for the clan system may be destroyed altogether, but shamanism may survive in the social units of different formation, e.g. in territorial units, villages, and even in groups of professional character. The chief condition is the existence of a group which distinguishes one of its members by bestowing upon him their confidence. Such a recognition is usually marked by giving the shaman a certain name of distinction which, at the same time, designates his functions, i. e. "the shaman". The term itself, as has been shown, is of secondary importance, but what is really important is the "meaning" which is connected with this term (symbol, still more restricted "starter"). Of secondary importance is the question as to whether the shaman's position is paid or not; is it a profitable occupation or an occupation involving personal loss. It may be formulated thus: an assumption of a special social position by any member of the community who takes upon himself the shaman's functions is one of the formal characters of shamanism.

The present section may be concluded by an enumeration of the essential formal characters indispensable for shamanism in full function: (1) the shaman is a master of spirits; (2) he has a group of mastered spirits; (3) there is a complex of methods and paraphernalia recognized and transmitted; (4) there is a theoretical justification of the practice; (5) the shamans assume a special social position. These characters of shamanism are met, with the exception of first two characters, in many other complexes which cannot be called "shamanism". For instance, in the phenomena of *p'oyun* and *mafari* of the Manchus we meet with all other characters, viz. special methods, paraphernalia, theoretical justification, and special position. The lamaistic priest also possesses all the above indicated characters. Therefore I shall call shamanism only those complexes which cover all above indicated characters.

96. PSYCHOMENTAL CONDITIONS OF SHAMANISM

Indeed, the primary condition of shamanism is a recognition of the existence of spirits as they were described in Part Two. From this point of view a *special system of animism* lies at the basis of shamanism, for not every animistic system can serve this purpose; e.g. Lamaism in its practice dealing with the spirits cannot be used for this purpose. The same is true of other systems which practically, in the understanding of the laymen, deal with the spirits. Here it must be pointed out that whether the theory recognizes such spirits or not is of secondary importance for the ethnical groups, for what may actually concern them are the spirits with whom they are familiar and whom they represent in their minds according to their own ideas, and not according to the formal theories of these systems. The reason why Lamaism cannot be used is that the spirits are not mastered by the lamas and it distinguishes benevolent and malevolent spirits, while the Tungus are rather sceptical as to the potential benevolence of spirits and at the same time they believe that the most malevolent of them can be mastered, and in this way they solve the problem of the "good-evil" complex. This attitude reveals quite a different psychomental behaviour of the Tungus complex. Yet, the complexity of the moral teaching of Buddhism, which intrudes into the system of spirits dealt with by Lamaism, remains beyond the Tungus interest, and at the same time it confuses the rather simple problem of playing on the equilibrium between the benevolent and malevolent spirits, according to the Tungus, practically treated by the lamas. The same is true of other systems based upon the recognition of two forces in the play and their moral formulation. The methods used by the Chinese Taoists also do not cover the Tungus requirements. The Tungus would say: the Chinese have different spirits and the Chinese do not know how to deal with Tungus spirits. The popular representatives of this complex, who incidentally appear among the Tungus, are unable to solve psychological problems faced by the Tungus. The latter accept these monks, and those who pretend to be monks, as imposters, as mere and simple *mafa* or even jugglers, and often treat them as dishonest persons who try to fool "the poor ignorant Tungus". To the problem of Tungus reaction on alien complexes I shall revert in other places.

Possibility of mastering spirits is the second important condition of shamanism, without which shamanism can not exist. The Tungus and Manchus are conscious of these two conditions when they say that only Tungus and Manchus themselves can manage their own spirits and these are numerous.

It is safe to suppose that the state of extasy, observed among the shamans and among the candidates, who may be very numerous, cannot be created without a certain individual instability. In fact, among the candidates extasy usually turns into a half-delirious hysterical condition; among the shamans it remains on the very dividing line between the two: normal stable state and abnormal unstable state. A candidate who would not know how to bring himself into a state of extasy, would never be credited by the people to have shamanistic power, and could not become a shaman. It may thus be stated that, in so far as the beginning of shamanistic practice is concerned, it presumes that the people who choose this function are subject to the intentional or unintentional psychomental conditions which, when observed in the European complex, cannot be regarded as absolutely "normal". This is an important psychic condition of shamanism. As we have already seen, a great number of spirits are supposed to be responsible for conditions which may be generalized under the heading of *adaptive instability of individuals and groups* which may be expressed in a lack of "correct" (i.e. usual in the given ethnical milieu) response to the milieu and the situations, in a lack of self-protective behaviour, etc. They are also held responsible for pathological conditions due to infections and for cases of serious disturbances of mental and nervous complexes taking forms of violent insanity. As will be shown, the psychomental instability among the Tungus and Manchus is subject to variations. The latter may be more and less intensive and they may affect smaller or larger groups of people. Of course, I have here in view chiefly those disturbances which are not due to organic troubles, as the effect of diseases affecting the brain, which are not subject to periodical variations, as well as cases of senile marasmus understood by these groups as a "normal condition of senescence". As a matter of fact, this psychomental instability sometimes becomes so intensive and such a large group of people is affected by it that the existence of the whole group may be seriously threatened. Indeed, these conditions are greatly due to self-suggestion, they may be treated by the same psychological method. Such methods are: firstly, a treatment by the shamans with the help of special spirits and in view of expelling the spirits that produce the trouble; secondly, a concentration of all spirits in one place and their mastering, which is achieved by the election of a shaman from among the candidates. As soon as the shaman exists, the spirits are not free to do what they like, and consequently they leave the people alone,—the people *cannot be sick, for there is no more cause for it.* As a matter of fact, the troubles which affect a great number of people disappear and peace is restored. Such a mechanism may reasonably be understood only in one possible way, namely, we may suppose that it has been created, absolutely unconsciously, as a result of the adaptation of the ethnical units, where the individuals had to adapt themselves to their own psychomental condition and to regulate it. In this sense shamanism is a result of the functioning of the self-regulating psychomental complex, and the shamans are a kind of safety valve.

In so far as I could see from the fragmentary description of shamanism among the groups which had not been known to me personally, both Tungus and others, this aspect and the function of shamans and shamanism are not confined to the limited group of Tungus and Manchus investigated. They may of course be veiled with the complexity of conventionalistic forms of performances and the theoretical side may be less developed than among the Tungus,* but the essential of the complex in most cases is the same.

I do not consider the phenomenon in question as an "abnormal" one which may occur only in the conditions of ethnical disintegration and decline. The facts which we possess would not agree with this supposition. Ethnical units which were not declining at all, e.g. the Manchus in the seventeenth century, and perhaps some Buriat groups, were greatly inclined to the shamanistic practices. The Tungus groups, which might successfully resist interethnical pressure, as most of the groups here described, and which, in spite of unfavourable conditions, might keep their population on the old level, also practised shamanism. Having before our eyes these facts, we cannot say that shamanism has resulted from the condition of ethnical decline. On the other hand, there is no little doubt that psychomental instability may be one of the aspects of the decline of ethnical units, and instability is a favourable ground for shamanism. Another question is how and with what effects shamanism functions among the groups in decline and whether it may be organized as an accomplished system or not. Thus, the existence of shamanism does not directly depend upon particular and specific conditions of intensive growth and intensive decline of ethnical units, but it depends upon the above described psychomental conditions of units and the existence of shamanism as an ethnographical complex, already known in its final, accomplished form, or in the forms which might hint at the creation of this complex. It should be noted here that among the Tungus and other groups which show a decline of their population and loss of culture, and which in general are visibly declining units, shamanism usually appears in its declining aspect, while the individual psychomental complex may be quite stable and thus there will even be no ground for shamanism, in so far as the appearance of candidates is concerned.

The above mentioned internal conditions of units are also essential, and for completing the picture of the complex of shamanism it will be safe to add that there must be units in which this complex may exist, for it is essentially a result of group-adaptation and, moreover, there must be groups organized and possessing some traditional mechanism. This condition, as will be later shown, is of great importance for the understanding of shamanism, which cannot be treated as an abstraction.

Thus, the psychomental conditions of shamanism can be characterized, as formulated above, in four aspects: (1)

the shamanistic practices, which presume the existence of shamans, may originate only on the susceptibility of falling into the state of extasy; (2) shamanism may exist only in ethnical units among which there is a need of treatment of harmful psychomental conditions in a particular form affecting a great number of people; (3) shamanism is the mechanism of a self-regulating psychomental complex; (4) it is essentially a group phenomenon; yet, still more narrowly, it is an ethnical phenomenon on which depends both the variable psychic conditions and the theoretical background which exists in the given units.

97. SHAMANISM When we combine together the formal and psychological characters outlined in the previous two sections, we may form an idea of shamanism as a complex. In this definition, and only in this one, I shall treat shamanism as an ethnographical phenomenon observed among the Tungus and Manchus. It will now be clear why I wish not to extend it over the groups in which some of the above enumerated characters are not found at all, or are found in different functions of the different psychomental conditions. In fact, if we include under the same heading the complexes, like mafarism, observed among the Manchus and Dahurs in its mature forms, and if we cover with this term complexes of the Chinese elaborate system of fen-šui, with gooa reason treated as one of the fundamental conditions of Chinese rural complex, and if we mix up with it professional "magicians", "medicine-men", European witches, etc. none of these would gain in clearness, and no light would be thrown on these phenomena. Such a pseudo-scientific generalization, even though supported by the abstraction of common elements, would not differ very much from the old-fashioned descriptions of "popular superstitions", "pagan customs and usages", "animism", "primitive mentality" and so forth.

I do not indulge in the hope that this point of view will be accepted by all readers and I expect that there will be suggestions as to treating shamanism as a particular case of a more general phenomenon. As a matter of fact, it may be easily identified with a complexly built-up art of fighting psychomental troubles and even many diseases treated by medical art. Hundreds of facts may be brought forth for the support of this identification, the logical conclusion of which would be that shamanism is a "primitive form of medical art". This would only partly be true, for shamanism has other functions as well, e.g. a general regulation of the psychic stability of the units, which is not a function of medical art, but of "good government". Shamanism, as a complex, also includes many facts which form the primary milieu, and in its theoretical setting of the problems of milieu it explains a great number of phenomena of milieu in general. It might thus be styled a system of "philosophy". In fact it has been done. However, such an identification of shamanism would not be formally correct, for as has been shown, shamanism is a further complication and a consequence of "philosophy" in which it cannot be included as a component. Moreover, the practical side of shamanism cannot be included in shamanism treated as "philosophy". Finally, by a number of authors and perhaps by the majority of ethnographers shamanism is treated as a "primitive religion" and shamanistic practices are regarded as a "religious phenomenon". If so,

---

* Regarding the degree of development of the theoretical part of shamanism in ethnical groups I must point out that the finding of it is not easy at all, for this presumes great familiarity with the people and language and such relations between the people and the investigators which would not hinder a friendly attitude of both sides.

either "religion" is understood in a sense including medical art, regulation of psychic conditions, "Naturphilosophie", etc., because these elements are found in shamanism, which would evidently be inconsistent, or shamanism is treated narrowly in the sense of a complex of spirits, including the theory regarding their nature. But in this case "religion" would be deprived of the ethical element which is perhaps its most important and sometimes its only element. As a matter of fact, as a complex, shamanism has nothing to do with ethics, its most essential element is a regulation of the psychomental equilibrium by the above described methods, as well as the medical art. Indeed, some of the functions of shamanism in other ethnical groups may be taken up by entirely different elements which are never considered as "religion". An approach to shamanism as to a "religion" among religions finds expression in the opposition of shamanism to other religions. However, such an opposition cannot be made, because shamanism may perfectly well survive side by side with the religions, such as Buddhism and Christianity, as they are understood by the ethnical groups recently converted. In fact any religion which does not oppose the idea of spirits and the possibility of their independent existence is not in conflict with shamanism.*

* For the Tungus, many of whom were baptized, the refutation of shamanism seems to be an inconsistent requirement. The most curious symbiosis of Christianity and shamanism might be observed among the Nomad Tungus of Transbaikalia who were admitted into

By emphasizing the impossibility of a complete identification of shamanism with "medical art", "philosophy" and "religion", and by pointing put that shamanism includes some elements characteristic of these complexes, I do not want to say that shamanism is an undifferentiated complex, a kind of primeval and primitive complex, which was the point of departure for differentiated complexes of "medical art," "philosophy", and "religion". In fact, such an approach is employed by many writers on "primitive" people, but it is a mere hypothesis which does not serve to clarify the phenomenon, merely allaying one's mind with some explanation of the "unknown". Indeed, shamanism is not an initial complex in a chain of an "evolving" process, but a complex of secondary formation. Such an inference is drawn from the analysis of this complex, element by element, and as a whole, from the standpoint of its actual functions, and from that of the cognition of the owners of this complex. Indeed, the inferences made from such an analysis might be erroneous, but historic evidences relating to shamanism in general and its elements fully support the result of our analysis, pointing to a secondary character of shamanism.

the Cossack military organization (groups living near the Mongolian frontier, in East Transbaikalia, particularly on the banks of the Argun River). Since these Tungus were formerly Orthodox Christians, shamanism was not allowed to be practised, but they did use shamans for the needs of cattle breeding; they pointed out that "the shamans are better than the Orthodox priests in so far as the care of cattle is concerned."

CHAPTER XXIII

NOTES ON THE HISTORY OF SHAMANISM AND HYPOTHESIS

AS TO ITS INITIAL FORM

98. FACTS OBSERVED The evidences for showing the secondary origin of shamanism are the testimony of the Tungus and the Manchus; the historic tracing of elements constituting shamanism; the indirect indications found in the present distribution of the elements and in the complex of shamanism; and the terminology. After this analysis I shall have to show the possible ways of the formation of shamanism and possible impulses for its appearance.

According to the Manchus, the beginning of shamanism ought to be referred to the beginning of the eleventh century, namely 1033 A.D., when one named čuxa ĵaɲin (ĵaɲ'in), literally "soldiers' commander", appeared, who left his spirits vočko to spread over three provinces—those of Mukden, Kirin, and Saxalan (Heilungkiang). The Manchus assert that this datum is found in the "Chinese books". However, they could not show me the passages. There is no doubt that the Manchus' association of the inauguration of shamanism with a definite person and at a definite historical moment, confirmed by reference to the Chinese source, evidently known to the Chinese annalists, must not be accepted as the date at which shamanism made its appearance.

The first shaman, čuxa ĵaɲin, is at present a vočko, and a spirit recognized by all Manchus. The Manchus say: "during the Kin Dynasty there was a war between the Manchus (ancestors!) and Chinese. The Chinese Emperor took hold of čuxa ĵaɲin and ordered him to be beheaded. So he was. But even beheaded the shaman did not fall down, and the Chinese Emperor called him vočko". He has also been incorporated into the list of dōna' burkan by the Birarčen (vide supra, p. 174) as a special Birarčen spirit. However, some Manchus assert that shamanism actually came into vogue still later, namely, together with the establishment of the Manchu Dynasty, while prior to that the Manchus had only p'oɣun vočko, and shamanism appeared only during the Ming Dynasty.

At the beginning of the twelfth century, as has been shown, (vide supra, p. 269) the term "shaman" is mentioned by the Chinese as a Nuichen term for "sorcerer", which they did not recognize as their own term ša-men, both of which have originated from the common source śramana. However, it is not certain from the Chinese text what kind of "sorcerer" was meant.

According to the Birarčen, the first shaman among them was a Dahur and, according to most of them, he lived at a recent time. However, scme Birarčen suppose that the first shaman was a Goldi (žèĵèn), from whom shamanism was adopted by the Dahurs and later by the Birarčen. Another opinion is that they had no shamans at all until the sèvèn (spirits which may be mastered and introduced) appeared from the Mongols, and the first shaman was either a Dahur or a Manchu.

The most categoric statement is made by the Reindeer Tungus of Manchuria who assert that they received shamanism before their coming to Manchuria (first half of the last century, cf. SONT. pp. 67-71) from the subjects of the *bogdo kan*—i.e. the Emperor of China—who might have been either the Dahurs and Solons or the Manchus. As a matter of fact, the shamanism of Tungus neighbours—the Kumarčen and Khingan groups—is quite different.

The Reindeer Tungus of Transbaikalia were not able to tell me anything about the "origin" of their shamanism, but they did indicate that there are shamans among their neighbours. The lack of a definite statement regarding the beginning of shamanism is not sufficient for asserting that these groups have no notion as to the beginning of shamanism. I admit that during my investigations among these groups I perhaps did not meet with Tungus who were interested in the historic back-ground of shamanism. Individual interest differs even among the Tungus,—some of them may be interested in history (establishment of facts), others in literature (folk-tales). This remark holds good for the groups of Kumarčen and Khingan Tungus. I was able to record only a remark among the Khingan Tungus pointing to the similarity of their own shamans with lamas, but whether it was meant in the sense of functional similarity or of common origin, I cannot say; an informer of the Mankova Tungus pointed to the similarity between the Buriat shamans and Tungus shamans.

In reply to the question: how far folk-lore, as defined by me, can be used as an evidence of the origin and character of shamanism, I should say that, in general, this kind of evidence is rather unreliable, but it may be used as a corroborative argument. The stories concerning the "first shaman", which at the same time may be stories of the origin of shamanism, usually rich in imaginative elements showing the great power of shamans, are of no interest for the present discussion. However, among the Goldi and Oroči, there are several variants of a story, apparently of local origin, which explains the institution of shamans for the release of souls, i.e. their transportation to the other, lower world. The same story usually includes the myth of three suns which burned Earth, and that of a brother and a sister from whom men originated.* Indeed, in the Tungus and Manchu complexes the release of the souls of dead people is a very important function; but only among the Goldi and groups influenced by them the shaman plays such an important part in this process. We have seen that burial and expediting of the soul may be done, among the described Tungus and Manchus, without the assistance of a shaman. The latter is required only in the cases when the soul cannot reach the other world, i.e. in "abnormal" cases. As evidence of the origin of shamanism the above quoted stories offer no historic light. However, it does not mean that the groups,

---

* Cf. P.P. Šimkevič, "Materials, etc." and I.A. Lopatin, "Goldi", pp. 237-238 in reference to the Goldi; cf. P. Margaritov, "Oroči", p. 29. Among the Oroči it is presumed that the shaman existed before the first death of a man—that of his son—occurred.

---

which have the above indicated stories that refer the origin of shamans to the period when immortality of man existed, have no other ideas as to the origin of shamanism. As will be shown later on, the folk-tales are usually mere fictions to the Tungus groups, as novels are to the Europeans.*

The opinions of the Manchus, Birarčen and Reindeer Tungus of Manchuria are not based on "folk-lore"; these groups themselves consider their statements as historical facts, and so they may be further considered. No contradiction is seen in the Birarčen indication of two sources—the Goldi and Dahurs, as I have shown, the Birarčen have been composed of two groups—one which lived side by side with the Goldi on the lower course of the Amur, and another one which undoubtedly was long ago in contact with the Dahurs. The Birarčen's indication of spirits appropriated from the Mongols is interesting, for it chiefly means the group *burkan*, doubtless of Mongol origin.

In the description of spirits we have already met with the fact that a great number of them may be very easily connected with those of other ethnical groups; many of them are considered by the Tungus as spirits received, at different historical moments, from their neighbours. In fact, the term *burkan*, referred to a great number of spirits, is a Mongol term, being only a modification of "Buddha," and when among the Tungus Buddha is mastered, the term applied is that which is used for shaman's spirits in general, i.e. *sVvV*, which does not seem to be of a Tungus origin. The complex *malu*, which according to some Tungus of Manchuria was received from various neighbours, contains some manifestations which are certainly not Tungus, e.g. *maŋi* with nine heads. Such complexes as *ĵiači, n'aŋn'aŋ, lamalalčen,* have preserved their non-Tungus names. In the Goldi shamanistic complex we meet with *seon pučiku,*** which is the Manchu *fučixi,*** i.e. Buddha;*** the nine-headed

---

* Indeed, the lack of historic data in the works of the authors here quoted may be due to the fact that these authors did not carefully inquire into the "actual" origin, but were seeking in the folk-lore for an explanation which would better agree with tne conception of shamanism as of a primitive religion—a conception prevailing among the ethnographers of the old school. In fact, the answers that I received as to the origin of shamanism would seem to many investigators as an evident error on the part of the informers, because they are accustomed to the idea of the primeval character of shamanism. Most probably such answers would even not be recorded, as it is done with numerous absurd answers which every investigator obtains during his work, especially when his knowledge of the language is defective. In fact, the questions as to the "first shaman" figured in all written and unwritten instructions. The more the "origin" was fantastic the more authentic it was believed to have been. By pointing out the conditions under which investigators are working, I do not wish to say that all groups possess historical data concerning their shamanism. Since the historical facts which may interest us are not always cognised by the ethnical groups, and since the groups in question usually have no written records, the chance to get "historical facts" about shamanism is not very great, especially if the introduction of shamanism took place several centuries ago, was gradual, and was not marked by any particularly striking facts to be easily memorized and associated. Yet, we also meet with secondary explanations of the origin of shamanism, such as that, for instance, which asserts that the first shaman was the "devil". Indeed, this association is that of the Russian complex.

** Cf. I. A. Lopatin, op. cit. p. 212, and P. P. Šimkevič op. cit. p. 53 (?).

*** I do not mention the Goldi verb pud (V) (W. Grube—Maksimovič "shamanieren"), which comes from the Manchu fudešembi referred to a definite action of "bringing out" [cf. Manchu fudembi] the spirits (very uncertainly translated by I. Zaxarov), and which is not connected with Buddha, whence the Manchus produced their fuč'k'i.

mayi plays a very important role; the whole group *dusxu* is borrowed from the Chinese.[*] The Manchu spirits *vočko* include a great number of non-Manchu spirits, but the chief spirits among them are souls of the shamans, in which respect the Manchu system differs from that of the Tungus of Manchuria and the Goldi. The Oročì have the same nine-headed *mayi*, and according to I. Nadarov, the Oročì of the region of the Iman and Bikin rivers (tributaries of the Ussuri) simply call the shamans "lama".[**] Indeed, the facts which connect Buddhism with the system of spirits used by the shamans among the Tungus may be multiplied, but I believe that the above given are sufficient to show that, in so far as the spirits are concerned, a great number of them are Buddhistic spirits, or those which were recently borrowed from their neighbours directly or through the intermediary groups, such as the Manchus and the Dahurs.[***]

The analysis of shamanistic paraphernalia gives us a new series of facts pointing to an intimate connexion between Buddhism and shamanism. However, for the present I shall not treat this question in detail, for it will be treated in a special chapter. I shall now only indicate some elements. Among all groups the brass mirror, widely used in Lamaism as one of the indispensable components of the altar, is an element without which shamanizing is impossible. So that when there is no costume, the shaman can perform with the mirror alone, while when there is no mirror or its substitute,[****] no performance is possible. In all Tungus dialects and in Manchu it is designated by the same term, namely, *tŏlí* (Bir. Kum. Khin.), *tăl* (Nerč.), *tolo* (Nerč. Barg.), *toli* (Goldi, Olča) (Manchu Writ. Sp.) which is connected with the Mongol *tŏl* [] *toli*, also the Buriat *toli* (Podg.) and the Dahur *tol* (Poppe), *toli* (Ivan.). Mirrors can be either "found in the earth" or received from the shamans-predecessors, or bought from the Mongols, who receive them from China and Tibet. The animals represented on the back of the mirror are interpreted by all groups according to their own imagination and knowledge. Among the Tungus of Manchuria the shamans use a head-dress on the front side of which there are five images of Buddha. Buddha's images are sometimes replaced by ornaments (flowers of Chinese style). The swastica and Christian cross are widely used by all shamans. The boa-constrictor and various snakes are symbolized in the shaman's costume, although unknown (boa-constrictor), or are of no importance (snakes) in this region. These sym-

bols are evidently not a local invention and yet they are neither a Mongol one. The Manchu shamans have a series of weapons and instruments familiar to Buddhism, as it is practised, and the pictures of some spirits show a correct reproduction of the costumes of Buddhist priests.

I shall not give evidence of common elements found in the performances and ideas, as for instance, the change of the world, the organization of the world, the way to the lower world and the various spirits which are borrowed by the Tungus and Manchus from the Buddhists and Lamaists, for these elements might be borrowed independently of Buddhism. I shall even leave without discussion the fundamental psychological conditions and the behaviour, for these may still be contested.

Beginning with the term "shaman", and following the analysis of spirits and other elements, we always discover the same situation, namely, that Buddhism has some intimate connexion with shamanism. However, the difference between Buddhism and Lamaism, on the one hand, and the variations of shamanism, on the other hand, are so essential, that the latter cannot be regarded as direct modifications of the former, or even as their "caricature", according to the expression of Vasiliev.[*] The prevailing ideas of the last century tended to discover a direct "relationship" and "kinship" between cultural phenomena. Diffusion of cultural phenomena was usually understood as a simple transplantation of complexes. In addition to this, subsequent ethnographical complexes were supposed to be intimately related by the connexion of evolution of primary forms. These methodological premises necessarily produced their effect upon the solution of the problem Buddhism-Shamanism, although in the works of the earliest writers on the subject, as Hyacinth, Palladius, Vasiliev, who possessed a great insight into many observed phenomena, Buddhism was suspected to be at least partly responsible for the existence of shamanism. In the works of a great number of writers who followed them elements of distinction tending to prove theoretical presumptions regarding primitivity and evolution were chiefly emphasized and accepted as postulates, and no attention was paid to Buddhism as a possible source of influence. True, in the writings of some authors there was the tendency to show that shamanism was not so "barbarous" as it was pictured, and that it was identified with "priesthood". Ch. de Harlez wrote "c'est un ministre du culte, au caractère grave, au maintien solennel, etc." (op. cit., p. 26). This author, as well as all others who shared his opinion, rejected "disgusting features of shamanism" and concentrated their attention on the *saman* of the Imperial Court who was not "shaman" at all, but a real priest and minister of a new religion recently created by the Manchus from pieces of their own old complex, Buddhism, and the Chinese complex, and perhaps, if not probably, for political use—to impress the Chinese, and at the same time to cement the Manchus together as an ethnical unit. Generally speaking, this attitude was common among those authors who wanted to make alien complexes "decently looking", to bring them nearer to their own, to bridge the gulf between the existing complexes, but who at the same time formally preserved the idea of such a gulf. It should be noted that in the attempts to solve the problem of the "origin" of shamanism, as well as to find the etymology of the word "shaman", the failure of the investigators

---

[*] I. A. Lopatin, op. cit. pp. 228. He points out that it was received through the Manchus. One of his illustrations represents a n'urxan, a picture of spirits evidently made on paper or silk. Such pictures are called in Manchu n'urgan. In I. A. Lopatin's work an interesting statement is found; namely, Saint Mary and Jesus Christ are also called by the Goldi seon, but it is not clear whether we have here a specific term or a generalized one.

[**] In making this quotation from I. Nadarov, S. Brailovskij (cf. op. cit. p. 191) says that he could not verify this statement.

[***] The presence of alien spirits has sometimes been interpreted as due to the disintegration of shamanism under the influence of Lamaism and Christianity. Such was the opinion of the old evolutionistic school which postulated great age and primitivity of shamanism. However, an analysis of the spirits shows clearly that in the Tungus and Manchu complexes the spirits, being borrowed from left and right, are still undergoing a process of assimilation and adaptation, and of integration into the existing complex which is still a living shamanism.

[****] This may happen, if the Tungus cannot find one. However, the substitutes are not considered as good as the original.

[*] Quoted by B. Laufer, "Shaman".

chiefly depended on their being impressed by general conceptions and theories and guided by their desire to prove or disprove some propositions which were actually needed for the strengthening and supporting of the stability of their own complex. To this question in its general setting I shall revert at another place, where the "science" will be treated as an ethnographical phenomenon. However, at present it is much easier to treat the problem of shamanism than it was before. First of all, we do not need to presume that the complex of shamanism "evolved" from a more "primitive" complex; secondly, we do not need to suppose that it is "more primitive", on the ground that its philosophical contents are not so much elaborated as those of the theoretical Buddhism of philosophers; thirdly, we know that the complex of shamanism may appear without Buddhism being wholly transplanted; fourthly, we know that the similarity of complexes may be created owing to a continuous diffusion of elements and their partial or complete integration in a new ethnical milieu; fifthly, we know that similarity of some elements may be due to a similarity of conditions underlying the complexes; sixthly, we know that in different ethnical milieus the same complex may have different adaptive functions; seventhly, we know the limits of possible inferences which can be made from the historic sequence of complexes and elements which form complexes; eighthly, we know that an old complex may be readapted to the new elements; ninthly, we know that the tempo of diffusion, adaptation, and adoption of elements and complexes is not the same for all elements and in all ethnical milieus. Although the above indicated methodological propositions are now well known, they are very often omitted in practical problems of analysis of ethnographical complexes. So, before proceeding to a further step in the treatment of the problem of shamanism, I want to recall these propositions to the mind of my readers.

99. BUDDHISM For the moment we need not discuss shamanism among all ethnical groups where it has been discovered. We shall therefore confine ourselves to the groups herein discussed. In connexion with this one more fact is needed; namely, whether at the moment of the first records of *saman* in Manchuria Buddhism was known to the local populations or not?

In spite of a quite artificial denial of Buddhism in the Far East among the Tungus and the Manchus, for the first time advanced by W. Schott, the latter was categorically supported by B. Laufer[*] who pretended that no missionaries had ever penetrated into the regions inhabited by the Tungus, which, by the way, was not at all necessary for the spreading of Buddhism, and which, moreover, was historically not true. Since this question has special importance for a correct solution of the problem of shamanism, I shall now give a short review of the diffusion of Buddhism in the Far East, a topic that may be better treated together with that on the penetration of alien elements into the Tungus complex in general, which will be discussed in one of the further chapters.

[*] In a special paper devoted to the "problem" of burkan. As in the case of "shaman" his aim was to disprove a connexion between "burkhan" and "Buddha", and in this was to support the idea of a great antiquity of the shamanistic form of "religion". The ideas of W. Schott were directed to prove the reality of what may be called "altaic complex".

We need not point out that Buddhism made its first appearance in China[*] nearly a millennium before the time to which the beginning of shamanism is referred by the Manchus. In Korea, Buddhism appeared in the fourth century A. D.,[**] and it was introduced by missionaries who, as it may be supposed, had generally a rather strong influence on the Koreans. The Buddhistic missions, which visited very remote regions, were quite familiar with Central Asiatic groups and converted the greater part of Asia to Buddhism, or at least had a great influence during the first millennium.[***] The Uigurs, who could be supposed to have been neighbours of some Northern Tungus groups, were already strongly affected by Buddhism in the second half of the same millennium. In fact, the Uigur Khagan, who in 762 A.D. attacked China, stated in his proclamation: "Cette religion (Manicheism) est subtile et merveilleuse; il est difficile de la recevoir et de l'observer. Par deux et par trois fois, avec sincérité (je l'ai étudiée). Autrefois j'étais ignorant et j'appelais «Buddha» des démons", etc.[****] In this translation "des demons" are given in the plural, which is not clear from the text (ibid, footnote 2). The translators introduced the plural, because they presumed that the Uigurs were not Buddhists before they became manicheists; so they say: "par «Buddha», ils doit donc s'agir ici de divinités chamaniques "......" Schlegel également s'était refusé à admettre qu'il s'agit ici du buddhisme".

I dare say that speaking of "divinités chamaniques" is not a sign of being familiar with shamanism. One can only wonder why E. Chavannes and P. Pelliot did not wish to accept the clear statement of Khagan and introduced their own interpretation. As for Schlegel, he may have had particular reasons to reject Buddhism. At his time hypotheses were more appreciated than facts. I have pointed out this case to show, by the way, how a theoretical presumption in a delicate ethnographic problem may affect even translators' work. With the publication of new facts concerning an early spreading of Buddhism in Central Asia, in a close neighbourhood of the Uigurs, and in the Far East, with which the Uigurs were familiar, it becomes improbable that the Uigurs could avoid their acquaintance with Buddhism. An abundance of new Uigur texts,[*****] true, of a later period, confirms this supposition.

[*] Sir Charles Eliot ("Hinduism and Buddhism. A Historical sketch", in three volumes, 1921, London) points out that in 65 A.D. one of the princes (of Chu) was Buddhist and that there were sramanas and upâsokas, but Buddhism had actually penetrated still earlier (op. cit., Vol. 3, p. 245).

[**] Buddhism was formally introduced in 372 A.D. It should be noted that it was greatly altered as compared with the original form, the moral teaching did not play so great a part as in other ethnical complexes; some new elements were introduced into the architecture; seven stars were joined to the complex (it should be noted that the same seven stars figure in the Manchu compound complex of Imperial rituals); the practice of Buddhism mostly reflected political events, e.g. the alteration of Chinese, Mongol and Japanese influences and the internal strifes were very often connected with subsequent changes in "religious fashions". (cf. Sir Charles Eliot, op. cit. Vol. 3, 386 et seq.).

[***] Apparently Buddhism made its first appearance in Mongolia still earlier. Sir Charles Eliot says (op. cit. Vol. 3 p. 245) "in 121 B.C. the annales relate that «a golden man» was captured from the Hsiung-nu". The "golden man", according to this author, might have been Buddha's image.

[****] E. Chavannes et P. Pelliot "Un traité manichéen retrouvé en Chine", J. As., 1913 Jan.—Febr. p. 193.

[*****] Cf. e.g. W. Bang's series of "Türkische Turfantexte", in Sitzungsberichten der Preussischen Akademie der Wissenschaften, 1929-1930, Berlin.

Moreover, the Uigurs were in regular relations with the Chinese who by that time were familiar with Buddhism. Another question is how far the complex (Buddhism) was assimilated and modified in the process of its adaptation. The Kidans, who were the political heirs of the Uigurs, were versed in the Buddhistic practices, which may be seen from brief indications of a Chinese witness who remained seven years among the Kidans and in the tenth century returned to China. He gives a summary description of the Kidan capital, Si-leou (西樓) located in the basin of Sira Muren (now Čagan Suburɣan) in which he found a great number of Chinese professionals: "on y trouve des artisans pour les manufactures de tissus de soie, des fonctionnaires, des lettrés, des docteurs en sciences occultes, des religieux et des religieuses bouddhistes, des taoistes; ce sont tous des gens du Royaume du Milieu."[*] This is not surprising, for their kinsmen, prior to that time, were not only in contact with the old Buddhists of Central Asia, but were, at least for some time, the political masters, when Western Leao was established. Perhaps it is not incidental that in the language of the modern Dahurs we find both *samǎŋ* (Poppe), *samǎn* (Ivan.) and *burxan*, since the Dahur tradition connects the Dahurs with the Kidans as offsprings of the same ancestors.[**]

The political heirs of the Kidans, the Nuichens, who are direct ancestors of the Manchus, were from the beginning of their political career familiar with Buddhism. In the history of Kin Dynasty we have several explanatory passages by Ch. de Harlez.[***] The founders of the Kin Dynasty, who lived in Korea, were not unacquainted with Buddhism. One of them, Agunai, was an adept of Buddha. This fact ought to be referred back to the fifth generation from 1070 A.D., i.e. hardly less than one century and a half earlier, or, roughly speaking, to the beginning of the tenth century. With the establishment of the dynasty Buddhism spread so far that the Emperor Si-Tsong had to moderate the enthusiasm, e.g. in 1174 he spoke of the uselessness of erecting too many Buddhist temples for getting wealthy, and in 1179 A.D. he spoke of the delusion of people who sought the assistance of monks. In fact, the monasteries became so numerous that the government had to impose on them some restrictions. In spite of several attempts to approach the emperors, made by the Buddhistic professionals, the government was not inclined to bestow its favours upon them. The emperor Si-Tsong opposed the old Nuichen complex to that of Buddhism, and the former showed nothing which would permit us to infer an existence of shamanism. However, a Chinese traveller in the Nuichen country in 1125 A.D.

[*] Cf. Ed. Chavannes, "Voysgeurs chinois" etc., in J.A., 1897, Mai-Juin, pp. 377-442, (p. 399).
[**] Cf. SONT, p. 84 et seq. It should be noted that the Great Leao state was a composite one, consisting of the direct ancestors of the Dahurs, Kidans, Hi, and a Northern Tungus group. Later on some other groups were also incorporated. At the time of the Chinese witness, the Kidans were not yet completely unified with their western neighbour Leao, although they resembled it (Cf. E. Chavannes, op. cit. p. 405)—"plus à l'Est est le Royaume de Leao," and E. Chavannes remarks: "il est assez singulier de voir mentionné ici un royaume de Leao distinct de l'empire Khitan" (ibid. footnote). Thus, the Kidans conquered their neighbours—the Hi, and the Dahurs conquered the small Northern Tungus state, after which they joined to form the Great Leao, associated by some writers with the name of Kidans. We may say that incidentally it might be associated with the Hi and the Dahurs as well.
[***] Cf. op cit. "Histoire de Kin," also "La Religion".

observed a certain spreading of an alien complex. I shall give here some quotations from an account left by Hsin K'ang-tsong (許亢宗) who visited the Nuichen in 1125.[*] He mentioned Hai Yun (海鑑), a temple with monks, near the sea, outside of the Great wall (ibid. p. 407). The music was the same as that of the Chinese (ibid, p. 413)[**] and "le royaume du Milieu a imposé les rites et les règles de ses anciens rois et .. les barbares eux-mêmes se servent de la langue chinoise pour faire foi" (ibid, p. 431). In the reception hall of the Kin emperor (probably, Tai-Tsong), who was one of the predecessors of Si-tsong—an antagonist of Buddhistic influence—there were images of Buddhas (ibid, p. 431). The emperor's head-dress was like that of the Buddhist monks.[***] Thus the Nuichen seem to have received their Buddhistic elements from various sources; namely, as indicated, from the Koreans and from the Chinese, directly and through the intermediary of the Kidans. The cultural influence of the Kidans was very great, which is evident from various facts that point to the source of the cultural elements, and of course from the fact that the Kidans were still earlier in contact with Buddhists —the Chinese and Central Asiatic groups.

From these facts it is evident that some elements of Buddhism, as an ethnographical complex, might have been assimilated by the populations of Manchuria not only through the process of the diffusion of elements, but even by a direct imitation of the complex represented by the professionals. Since the government did not favour them, but the complex had already made its appearance among the population, is it not natural to suppose that this population itself began to practice the tricks of the bonzes which proved to be successful? The same phenomenon may now be observed in the establishment of the new complex of mafarism, called into existence owing to the persecution of shamanism, a reaction against it, and an imitation of the Chinese, "s'enšan"—half-bonzes, half-doctors, half-literati, and especially half-impostors, and professionals. Yet, such phenomena of imitation and readaptation are of frequent occurrence among all people of the Earth.[****]

[*] Cf. E. Chavannes, "Voyageurs chinois ... etc.", in J. As., 1898 mai-juin, pp. 361-489.
[**] The music was received through the intermediary of the Kidans, four orchestras of whom were used at that time at the Imperial Court.
[***] "(Le souverain) avait la tête enveloppée d'un bonnet de couleur noire, dont les attaches pendaient par derière, comme sont aujourd'hui les bonnets des religieux bouddhistes" (ibid p. 432).
[****] I.I. Gapanovich, who spent a long time among the Russian and native populations of Kamchatka and the Oxotak region, told me a very interesting fact of the same kind. The local people in a small settlement was for a long time no chance to hear a holy service in the local church because of the lack of a priest (orthodox). A travelling merchant, who happened to pass there, was asked to perform the holy service and he did it, although it was against the precepts of the Church, and it may be supposed, he was not in agreement with the established practices of the Church, in so far as the service is concerned. One fact more: a political exile on the Saxalin island, a Jew by religion and conviction, was asked to do the same, on the day of the Orthodox Easter, but instead of that he read some passages from the New Testament and by a choice of passages and the expressiveness of his reading he produced a mass emotion manifested in a general weeping (cf. V. Bogoras-Tan, in Ethnografia, pp. 270, Year 2, Vol. IV, 1927, Moscow). The above given instances show how a function, usually performed by the ministers of a special religious body may be taken up by laymen. The formation of new sects is very often due to the same conditions. In fact, the Mormonism in America, the Christian Science and other similar movements are of the same order—readaptation of a complex in the absence of com-

Among the Mongols, who were neighbours of the Nuichen, a similar process was going on. In the thirteenth century there was a competition between the shamans, Lamas, and Christians. In this matter Chengiz Khan occupied a neutral position and adopted a policy of laissez-faire which soon resulted in the firm establishment of Lamaism. Shamanism could be preserved only among the Buriats and perhaps the Dahurs who practised it in the seventeenth century.* An overwhelming spreading of Lamaism in Mongolia took place only after the political collapse of the Mongols, especially under the Manchus, who politically did not see anything harmful to themselves in the absorption of the Mongol energy by religious matters.

During the Ming Dynasty in China Manchuria was under the cultural influence of the Mongols who were already Lamaists. The Chinese also continued their cultural pressure. Buddhism penetrated into the remotest regions such as, for example, that of the mouth of the Amur River, where in the fifteenth century a Buddhistic temple was erected.** Buddhism in Manchuria spread further under the Manchus. In the territory occupied by the Manchus we meet everywhere with Buddhistic temples, shrines and single evidences of Buddhism.*** Under the Manchu rule the cult of Buddha with *pusa* (Bodhisattva), generalized by the Manchus as *fuč'k'i*, and Buddhism as a complex, were assimilated by the Manchus to such a degree that some of Buddhistic elements cannot be recognized at once. The Manchu emperors composed, or perhaps only recorded and enriched practices borrowed from Buddhism, and increased them with the Manchu original elements, making of the acquired Buddhistic elements an important instrument for their own use. A great number of Buddhistic books were translated into Manchu, and Emperor Kang Hsi was the author of an original work on this subject.**** As to practices, the Manchus at the time of Hyacinth* used to have for funerals all three kinds of monks, as it was with some Chinese funerals.** Among the Manchus of remote

region, such as, for instance, Aigun, there appeared *fuč'k'i mafa* and *fuč'k'i mama*, i.e. specialists in dealing with Buddhistic spirits, or perhaps even monks of local origin. However, during my stay among the Manchus (1915-1917) I met not a single *fuč'k'i mama* nor *fuč'k'i mafa*. According to the Manchus, this practice disappeared some time before my visit. It may be supposed that to the Manchus, who needed a great number of people for official functions, it was practically impossible to sacrifice a part of their population to the monasteries. For this reason, there were more *fuč'k'i mama*, than *fuč'k'i mafa*, and none of them were widows. Together with a loss of former prosperity—which happened during the Boxer movement and owing to its consequences—the last *fuč'k'i mama* disappeared. We have seen that mafarism appeared as a substitute for special, in their secondary nature, functions of the Buddhistic monks and clergy among the shamanistic populations of Manchuria. Thus Buddhistic monastic movement made only a short appearance, without producing on the Manchus any important effect.* An essential difference between the hostile attitude of the Kin Dynasty and the favourable attitude of the Manchu Dynasty towards Buddhism may be noted. Moreover, as has been shown, the Manchu emperors assimilated Buddhism and formed a new complex in which Buddhism received a place of special honour. This fact is indicative of a great change in the complex of the Manchu populations, who by that time adopted Buddhism, assimilated it and incorporated it into their own complex. It lost thus its dangerous character as an alien cultural complex, as it had been under the Kin emperors who with good reason objected to its penetration among their subjects, since it was acting as a factor destroying imperial power.

Naturally this special, even privileged, position of Buddhistic elements in the Manchu complex has greatly simplified the process of penetration of Buddhism amongst the non-Manchu groups of the Far East. In fact, temples of syncretic character were erected even beyond the area occupied by the Manchus, especially in those occupied by the Mongol and Buriat groups, e.g. in Hulun-Buir and Transbaikalia, also in the Dahur territories in Manchuria. However, it must be pointed out that Mongol Lamaism is perhaps of a different origin, namely, directly from the West.

The question is now how far and how deep this complex penetrated the non-Manchu population? The testimony

petent specialists. The adaptation of the theory of evolution by the non-biologists to cultural phenomena is in many respects a process similar to those of the above given instances.

* Cf. E. Ysebrants Ides. op. cit., where in Manchuria Dahur lamaists near the present city of Čičikar (Tsitsihar) are mentioned.

** Cf. P. V. Vasiliev, "Zapiska o Nadp'is'ax", in Izv. Imp. Ak. N., Vol. IV, No 1; St. Petersburg, 1892. The excavations carried out in different places in Manchuria reveal a great number of elements which may be connected with Buddhism. But as we have no direct statements of contemporary travellers, and historic records, we need not rummage in archaeological evidences.

*** R. Maack gives a description of temples on the banks of the Amur River. It should be noted that this traveller also observed a Confucian temple near Aigun.

**** It was entitled enduringe tačix'an be neǯǯeme badarambuxa bitxe, a well known work. Cf. P. G. Möllendorff "Essay on Manchu Literature", and other publications on Manchu literature.

* Cf. his "China in her civil and moral conditions" Vol. IV, p. 27 (Second edition, 1912, Peking). Hyacinth made the same error as L. Langlès and Ch. de Harlez when he identified shamanism with the rituals of the Manchu Imperial family. Yet, he supposed that this complex, when brought to the "nomad Siberian shaman", had been distorted because of the "ignorance of shamans".

** The Chinese syncretism was known for a long time, but it was usually interpreted as a kind of aberration of people who were not versed in the true religious systems. B. M. Alexeiev [cf. "Notes from the domain of Chinese temple syncretism" (in Russian) in "Oriental Memoirs" (Vostočnye Zapiski) (publ. by the Inst. of Liv. Oriental Languages), Vol. I, 1927 p. 283-296 Leningrad] had published a well documented paper on this subject. He has shown that practically all three systems, i.e. Confucianism, Taoism and

Buddhism have concurred to satisfy the practical needs of the population. But a great number of local deities were also included in these complexes, slightly differing in the regions of China. These are real ethnographical living complexes, while the philosophers remain confined to their study and nobody considers them. Yet, this is not characteristic of the Chinese alone. The fate of Buddhism in Mongolia, where Lamaism incorporated local spirits (cf. A. Grünwedel, op. cit.) and adapted them to the complex of the Mongols, differs from that of China only in respect to the number of incorporated elements. The condition may be observed in Christian practices among different ethnical groups of Europe, many of which have incorporated into their complexes the local saints and even sometimes pagan spirits.

* The Manchu government did not favour such a movement among the Manchus, but it did so in Mongolia, where a great number of people were thereby excluded from marriage and reproduction, i.e. an effect was produced which corresponded to the aim of the Manchus, who strove to reduce the possible danger from a numerous and semi-independent population. Sir Charles Eliot also notes: "still, on the whole, Manchu dynasty showed less favour to Buddhism than any which preceded it" (i.e. the Mings and Yuans) (op. cit. Vol. 3, p. 280.).

cf travellers of the seventeenth and eighteenth centuries is not very rich, nor always reliable. In J. B. du Halde's "Description" (Vol. IV, p. 13) we find a mention of the Yu-pi ta-tse of the Ussuri River (evidently the Goldi) who, according to the French Jesuits, had no "idols": "les idoles même de la Chine n'ont point encore pénétré jusque chez eux. Apparement les bonzes ne s'accomodent pas d'un pays si pauvre, et si incommode. ...." etc. However, it does not mean that the ideas did not penetrate there. It is not surprising that in 1869 Th. Busse, who was very familiar with the local groups, wrote* that Buddhism had very deeply penetrated into the same groups. A decade earlier M. V'en'ukov** visited them and saw several small shrines and images of Chinese origin. It may thus be inferred that Buddhism made its appearance among this Goldi group not later than in the first half of the last century. The Oroči of the Ussuri River went still further, for there was found a shaman who had his shrine, which is quite unusual for the shamans, with pictures painted à la chinoise.*** The southern group of the Oroči of the Maritime prov., who are called Udehe, also Tazy, are "Buddhists",**** while their neighbours investigated by S. Brailovskiï were only influenced by Buddhism. It should be noted that the southern group adopted "Buddhism" under the influence of the Chinese who had long ago penetrated into this region and who were "Buddhists". A part of the Goldi of the Maritime prov. in 1916 were also Buddhists.*****

In Manchuria the Birarčen used from time to time to meet lamas and visited Buddhist temples in the regions occupied by the Manchus and Chinese. However, among these groups no formal adhesion to Buddhism was observed. The Khingan Tungus were required to attend at least once a year a religious Buddhistic ceremony near Hailar (in Hulun-Buir). The Mergen Tungus had occasions to meet lamas, and visited temples in Mergen. Their near neighbours, the Solons, have adopted the Dahur complex which includes Buddhistic elements. The nomad Tungus of Transbaikalia, in Mankova and Urulga, use both shamanism and Lamaism which in their complex form together a solid symbiosis. No competition between the two could be observed. The Barguzin Nomad Tungus are in a similar position. The Buriats are responsible for the penetration of Buddhism, which was especially easy with the Tungus groups, such as the Nomad Tungus of Urulga, who gave up their own language and now speak a Buriat dialect. Finally, the groups of Reindeer Tungus of Transbaikalia were in contact with the Buriat Lamaists and were ordinary patients of lamas, particularly in the regions of the Tungus area. These occasions are used for lamaistic propaganda. However, at least apparently in some instances, the lamas may be responsible for a direct encouragement of shamanism. This has been recently observed in Mongolia. The most interesting facts are communicated by G. D. Sanžeev who visited, in 1927, a Mongol

group, the Darxats, who live in the northern confines of Mongolia near the Lake Baikal. He reports* that the lamas sometimes advise people affected by certain psychomental conditions to become shamans and that the lamas are in contact with these spirits. Further, even a lama may become a shaman, as in the case reported on p. 56. From these instances it follows that Lamaism, as it is now practised in Mongolia, may stimulate and maintain shamanism, as a complex. However, these cases may be rejected under the pretext that shamanism is not "pure" among the Darxats; but still these facts are interesting for they point to such a possibiltiy at present, and we must admit that in former days it may have been even greater than now.

We can now conclude this section by formulating that Buddhism began its penetration among the populations of the regions herein treated during the first millennium A.D. Ethnical groups were influenced by it in different degrees, the first place in this respect being occupied by the Koreans, the second by the Mongols (the Buriats being excluded), the third by the Manchus and Dahurs, the fourth by the Buriats, the fifth by the Goldi and Oroči and some Nomad Tungus (including the Solons) ; the remainder of the Tungus groups, such as the Olča, Birarčen, Kumarčen, Mergen, Khingan, Barguzin and Nerčinsk and the former Šemagir of the Lake Baikal (now extinct) were either incidentally visited by Buddhists, or would come themselves into contact with them. I have no direct information regarding the Angara Tungus and the Kalar group, also the Tungus of the Amur prov. except that these groups are in contact with the above indicated Tungus groups, and that formerly the Dahurs, and perhaps the Manchus, used to go as far as the northern slopes of the Yablonov mountain range for their regular trade in the confines of the Yakut area, while, as far as I know, the Buriats penetrated into the region of the upper Angara Tungus. Such relations between these groups were maintained since their settlement in the regions of their present habitation, i.e. for some groups for centuries. It is not surprising that the Tungus complexes are saturated with elements borrowed from Buddhism and Lamaism which are revealed in the analysis of spirits and other elements of shamanism.

100. HYPOTHESIS: SHAMANISM STIMULATED BY BUDDHISM We have seen that the complex of shamanism, as observed among the Manchus and Northern Tungus, is a relatively recent one. We have also seen that this complex consists of a great number of elements which may be entirely brought back to the original source of borrowing—Buddhism. Yet, we have also just seen that Buddhism made its appearance among the populations of Manchuria and of neighbouring regions many centuries ago and apparently prior to the epoch when saman was for the first time mentioned in Nuichen and prior to the moment at which the Manchus recognized the existence of shamanism (1033 A. D.), while it spread among various ethnical groups— the Southern and Northern Tungus, the Mongols, and some Palaeasiatics—as a complex, or in its elements, as far

* Cf. "Sketch of the land tenure in the Amur", in "Bibliotéka dla čtenija", 1860, Aug.-Dec. (in Russian).
** Cf. "Travels along the frontiers of Russian Asia" (in Russian), St. Petersburg, 1868; pp. 89-90.
*** V. Gluzdovskiï "Catalogue du Musée de la Société pour l'étude de la Région de l'Amour" (in Russian), Vladivostok ("Zaplaki", Vol. XI, 1907 p. 97.).
**** Ibid, p. 86.
***** Cf. V.V. Solarskiï, "Present legal. etc." p. 149.

* Cf. G.D. Sanžeev, "The Daraxats. Ethnographical Report of a Visit to Mongolia in 1927", Leningrad, 1930.

as the southern regions of the Yakuts' area. The first inference which may be made is that there is evidently an intimate connexion between shamanism and Buddhism. The question is now as to the character of this connexion.

This question may be put in two ways, namely, (1) is it a connexion which is due to the common elements borrowed by the creators of shamanism, or (2) is Buddhism responsible for the existence of shamanism as a powerful stimulus. If the answer to the first question is in the affirmative, another question will arise, namely: what was the complex of shamanism before the influence of Buddhism brought it to its present state, and what sorts of shamanism existed among the different groups before the penetration of Buddhism? True, we have but a few facts, but all of them lead to the conclusion that at that time no shamanism, in the above defined sense, existed. In fact, the Nuichen Emperor Si-Tsong, in his opposition to the penetration of Chinese influence, pointed out that the sacrifice to the Heaven and Earth was the original practice of the early Nuichen.* It is remarkable among all Northern Tungus here described that only the "spirit of heaven", buga, has no direct signs of alien influence and is recognized by all Tungus as a fundamental Tungus element. Another element, common to all Tungus, and which cannot be directly connected with Buddhism, is that of the managing of souls of dead people. All Tungus groups recognize it as an old practice. The Birarčen say: "Before the Tungus (evenki) had only buga and buni". However, this element is not particularly a Tungus one, and it may be supposed that the Nuichen, who practised burial, also possessed the complex of the soul. So that there were at least two complexes—the spirit of heaven, a single God, and the souls of dead people to be cared for. All other spirits which are not mastered by the shamans, like bainača, nolumta, inmvnkan, irlinkan, f'iači, and others, are so foreign that their names can be easily brought to the original sources of borrowing. The Tungus themselves indicate an alien origin of such a "fundamental" Tungus spirit as malu. In so far as the analysis of these facts goes, we cannot give any satisfactory evidences for including some other spirits into the original Tungus complex. However, I hasten to point out that this negative indication cannot suffice for asserting that originally there were only the two above indicated complexes, and the belief of the Tungus that there were only these two complexes may be discredited by saying that other complexes may have been lost, e.g. replaced by the now existing ones, and that the Tungus have not preserved any remembrance of them. Perhaps such a scepticism will be too great. We also find no early evidences as to another important condition of shamanism, namely, the idea of mastering of spirits and their introduction at will. It is not mentioned by Si-Tsong, and the Tungus are unanimous in asserting that originally the art of mastering the spirits did not exist among them, but was practised among their neighbours, e.g. the Manchus, Dahurs, Buriats and Yakuts, and especially by lamas.** The

* Cf. Ch. de. Harlez, Histoire de l' empire de Kin, p. 136. I now omit the enumeration of social practices pointed out by him.
** The Tungus of Manchuria suppose that the Dalai Lama is the real master of all burkan and rēvēn and can send them off at will. Many Tungus do not like lamas as a permanent and original source of dissemination of spirits. The ordinary lamas can do this, but only with a great effort and when being in a great number. A case was quoted for proving this. In the valley of the Nonni River there was

absence of shamans in the earlier Tungus complex does not imply that there were no vizards, old experienced medicinemen (even without any attributes conventional among the ethnographers who generalize strange phenomena under the names of "shaman" and "medicine-man"), and specialists who knew methods of sacrifices to buga and buni. However, in the conditions of life of hunters-wanderers the existence of professional priests is almost out of question. In fact, every Tungus knows how to pray to buga and how to make a sacrifice, and every Tungus knows how to manage souls of dead people. Moreover, among all Tungus groups the shamans have nothing to do with buga, and among most of them they interfere with the dead souls only in case of trouble, i.e. when the soul does not go straight to the world of the dead, usually in consequence of the interference of other spirits. Moreover, the lack of shamans does not imply that there existed no other spirits, like those formed from the souls of dead people whose bodies were not buried in a proper manner. So that an exclusion of the shamans from the present Tungus complex would not mean that nothing would be left of the spiritual complex and various methods of fighting diseases and human miseries. It is very likely that some of those functions were taken over by the shamans, just as at present some shamanistic functions are taken up by mafarism and various religions.

There is a very interesting fact, namely, the formation of p'oyun saman in the Manchu complex which offers some new light too. In fact, these specialists for the rites of the Imperial family were known under the name of mere saman. Their functions were exactly the same as those of the Manchu p'oyun saman, but it was also their duty to take care of temples and to perform much more ceremonies than those observed among the common Manchus. Indeed, such an elaborated system of ceremonies, with a large number of saman employed for this purpose, was needed by the Imperial family, because the Manchus had to have their own complex and such one was the Imperial Family. On the other hand, a new institution could have been established only after the Nuichen downfall, for as has been shown the Nuichen Imperial family did not accept an open intrusion of Buddhism. The last emperors of the Kin, Chang Tsong (in 1194 and 1204) and Hsiuen Tsong (in 1215), under the pressure of an influential group, had formally to introduce the Chinese cult of the Sun, Moon, Wind, Rain, and Thunder, i.e. that of the earlier Chinese Emperors and that of Confucius, but Buddhism was again left aside. (Ch. de Harlez, Religion. pp. 59-60). Thus the shamans are mentioned as Nuichen "sorcerers" prior to the collapse of the Kin Dynasty. Thus the shamans existed prior to the elaboration of the Imperial ritualism of the Manchu Emperors. What was then the nature of this new complex? We have no evidence, except that of Ch'ien Lung who pointed out that the rites of veneration of Heaven, Buddha and the spirits večeku, which existed from the time of the foundation of the dynasty in Mukden (beginning of the seventeenth century), were altered at his time so much that it was necessary to secure the assistance of old men who might help in its restoration (Ch. de Harlez, o. c., pp. 61-63). To what extent these rites

a Dahur who fell very seriously ill. He could not recover, in spite of the efforts of all shamans. Then the lamas insisted that he must drown in the Nonni River the placings for the spirit. The man did so and nine lamas "lamaized" (a Tungus verb produced from lama) nine days. The man recovered. The spirits were expelled "for ever",

were altered we do not know, but one thing is evident, namely, that the complex of the Imperial family in Peking could not be the same as that of villagers, for the Imperial family could not have many elements characteristic of what the Chinese literati used to style as simple "sorcery". The Imperial ritual had to be made similar to that of the high Chinese class which accepted a worship of ancestors and Buddha. The *saman* were ennobled and turned into priests. When the worshiping was regulated and legalized, it began to spread among villagers, who again with their spirit characteristic of clan organization introduced their own variations in the form of a simplification of the ritual and a change of the list of spirits, which, according to their ideas, "must be different in every clan". The priest received the name of *p'oyun saman*, a group of which was headed by *ila saman* and definitely opposed to the ordinary *saman* of olden days, who may now be also called *amba saman* i.e. "great shaman". Why did the Manchus need to make a specification: *p'oyun*? It is clear: *saman*, as a starter ("symbol"), was already occupied by the shaman and there was no other special term for the clan priest proposed by the Imperial decree, except *saman*. If Ch'ien Lung expected to abolish the practice of real "shamanism", in the eyes of "civilized Chinese" quite a barbarous complex, by the introduction of priests named *saman*, he completely failed, for the Manchus assimilated both complexes. Moreover, some clans, as we have seen in the case of the *nara* clan, practised the introduction of ancestral spirits, as it is done by real shamans.

It may thus be concluded: the early Manchus were already half-Buddhists, which is more than natural, for their masters, the Mongols, being themselves Buddhists during almost four centuries, culturally influenced the Manchus. In its Mongol and Chinese forms Buddhism, officially admitted, was not the same as that which had already penetrated into Manchuria under the Great Leao Dynasty (Kidans); and wandering *śramaṇa*, changed into *samana*, had no more access to Manchuria and thus were transformed into Nuichen-Manchu *saman*, as we know them, e.g. from the epic poem "Nišan Saman" referred to the Ming period in China. Such a transformation might take place as early as the time when the *saman* was mentioned as Nuichen "sorcerer" and perhaps near the year indicated by the Manchus, 1033 A.D., as the moment when first *vočko* spread over the Manchuria populations.

It now remains to represent the psychological conditions of the process of adaptation to this *new* complex by the ancestors of the Manchus, and its sweeping extension over an enormous territory. First of all, we see from the history of Buddhism that the new religion was gradually adopted by various ethnical groups, but this process took several centuries before reaching the remote regions of the Amurland. In the same way Christianity spread over the populations of Siberia and finally was totally or partially adopted, even by the groups now living beyond the limits of the former Russian Empire. These facts show us that alien ethnographic complexes may spread and that the process does not take a very long time. Now, what could have been the reaction of the Manchu ancestors when they met with the first propagandists of Buddhism who might have been "missionaries" or merely "adventurers", or at least "clever people" who discovered a new way to earn their living, as it is commonly seen in wandering Chinese monks and lamas. It is very likely that these first in-

troducers of a new complex were *samana* connected with the declining groups of Central Asia and the Kidans. When they appeared among the population of Manchuria with their teaching about a new and particular kind of spirits—the whole range of bodhisattvas, spirits of the upper and lower world, the Sivaistic complex—whom they could dominate and with whose help they could relieve human miseries; when they showed new methods of curing diseases and new tricks with which most professionals impress the laymen, these populations could neither reject the new complex, nor resist the temptation of learning something new and effective. This attitude we now observe among all peoples, but at that time it was quite easy among the population of Manchuria which was found under a great and varying interethnical pressure. In fact, one after another strong political units were formed which revolutionized the life of the half-hunters, half-fishermen, half-agriculturists of Manchuria. After the introduction of the high Chinese civilization in Bohai, when many students were sent to China, this newly formed unit collapsed under the pressure of a Mongol group of Kidans. The latter pushed their influence to North China, Mongolia and Central Asia and dealt the last blow to the Turks. As soon as they had established themselves in Barin, they were attacked by the Nuichen, who, following the path of their political predecessors, within a short period adopted an alien complex—chiefly Chinese—and fell under the pressure of the Mongols.[*] The archaeology of Manchuria and of the Amurland shows a picture of these alterations, the rise and collapse of ethnical groups, their sudden increase and sudden decrease, the shifting of political centres and populations, and the extinction of peoples and the complete destruction of their settlements. There was no stability even for a short period of a few centuries, and the rôle of leading ethnos was handed from one group to another. I cannot go here into details concerning the psychological conditions of the leading ethnical units in states of rise and decline, which, as has been shown in the Introduction, are quite distinct, especially as regards the psychomental stability of the units. But even without such an ethnological discussion, it seems clear that peoples who were undergoing sudden changes and who were so much inclined to learn from their neighbours anything new which might serve for their survival, were less stable than any other peoples and formed the best soil for the growth of various complexes built up of elements borrowed from different sources. Were they not looking for explanations of their individual and ethnical misfortunes, which might be so easily connected with the appearance of new spirits, as it is now with the Manchus and Tungus? Being people of strong biological resistance—the proof of which is that most of them survived a series of collapses—could they not try to master and fight these spirits by all means? And was not the new theory of mastering spirits by means known to the ecstatic shamans a natural issue of the conflict between different complexes which already possessed the most essential elements for forming a new complex of shamanism, as it is now observed and was already known during the Mings? Naturally in these conditions a thin social layer of learned Buddhists, who beyond any doubt existed among the upper class of the Kidans, Nuichen,

---

[*] Analogy between the ethnical decline of the Nuichen and Manchus is remarkable, especially in so far as it is manifested in the loss of language.

Mongols and Manchus, were reduced to dust and disappeared gradually with every new collapse, and the large masses of the population kept only those elements which could be easily understood and incorporated into the preexisting complexes. It was just the same as that which happened with the Manchus before our eyes, and it could not be different because of the special conditions of a shaken interethnical equilibrium.

As soon as shamanism was formed into a complex, it began spreading among the neighbouring peoples, who in their turn were pressed to accept a new enlightenment in the matter of the newly discovered world of spirits and to learn new methods of fighting their own psychomental instability, chiefly produced by a high interethnical pressure and a high tempo of variations. However, in the process of adaptation of shamanism each group introduced its own corrections needed for the adaptation of both the former complex and the newly acquired elements. Together with this process, the original elements were gradually disappearing and the newly acquired ones were modified. With the coming of the new world of spirits the Tungus appeared to be richer in alien spirits than other groups, so they have already begun to reject some of them. "The Russians",—they used to say,—"are happy, because they have very few spirits, while we have to fight all kinds of spirits—*s'irkul, burkan, sèvèn*—which come to us from all sides—from the Mongols, Dahurs, Manchus, Chinese and Russians". I did not try to disprove it, for they probably could not understand the new forms of manifestations of the instability of psychomental complex among the so-called civilized nations and the new forms of its self-regulation. However, the Tungus understand the nature of their spirits no more than the "civilized nations" understand manifestations of their own psychomental complex, especially those units which are undergoing, at a high tempo, variations under strong interethnical pressure.

Such were the psychological conditions of the peoples of Manchuria which greatly facilitated the spreading of shamanism, evidently northward and eastward from Manchuria.

In our further exposition of facts concerning shamanism we shall meet with another wave which overflowed the Tungus. This wave seems to be directly connected with the Yakuts, but many facts seem to indicate to its more southern initial stimulus. This stimulus may be suggested to have been located in the northern confines of the present Mongolia; but historically it must probably be referred to an earlier date than that established by us for Manchuria, for the complex which may be supposed to have been "shamanism" (perhaps, for the time being, it will be better to call it "*boism*" from *bo* of Mongols?) was defeated by Buddhism in the thirteenth century, while the Uigur phenomenon, in some respects similar to shamanism, perished still earlier. However, the Mongols, and especially the Uigurs had both become familiar with Buddhism much earlier than the eastern group. They were nearer to the centre of Buddhism in Central Asia, and Buddhist missionaries were quite a common phenomenon among them. Perhaps Lamaism had to fight the first shamanistic by-product of the early spread of Buddhism.

I am not personally familiar with the groups of Central Asia and Western Siberia, where "shamanism" is still practised, and we have no complete analysis of the psychomental complexes of these groups. I shall therefore leave

to the specialists—Turkologists and Mongolists—the solution of the question as to the second centre of shamanism affecting the Northern Tungus.*

Although the above expounded hypothesis of the formation of shamanism under the stimulus of an early Buddhism, with a great number of evidences on which it is based, is in my own eyes almost certain, I cannot consider it as an established fact, as is often done when the inventors wish to be convincing. Whether it be called a fact or not, it does not make a difference, for there are at least two points in my construction which are hypothetic and which I wish to emphasize before leaving this subject. Firstly, I do not know whether there was any ethnical group connected with Manchuria which incorporated Buddhistic monks of Central Asia, who called themselves *samane*, which I accept as possible, if not probable; and secondly, I do not know at which historic moment the transformation of Central Asiatic "šamanaism" into "shamanism" occurred. Everything points to the Kidans as the responsible ethnical units, but we have no facts. I set some hopes on the deciphering of Kidan written documents and perhaps on archaeology. But even these documents may not clear up the question, for the process of transformation might have been left unnoticed at all and thus not recorded; and the archaeological evidences may be lacking, as they will be lacking after the extinction of the Tungus who now do not use unperishable materials. The interpretation of these documents is also not always reliable, as has already happened with the famous discovery of shamanism in quaternary Europe. The evidences of this order, without a thorough knowledge of the psychomental complex, may be quite misleading.

Thus, the origin of shamanism stimulated by Buddhism, as formulated here, will perhaps remain forever a hypothesis, the belief in the correctness of which may increase with the analogies; but its hypothetic character will perhaps not change.

101. CONCLUSIONS AS INTRODUCTION   From the facts
              TO THE FOLLOWING CHAPTERS   expounded in the
                                                            previous sections
it may thus be inferred that shamanism among the groups

* F. A. Rosenberg (op. cit. pp. 378-379) called attention to the fact that in a Christian Sogdian dialect and in Pehlevi used in Turfan, * smn was used for the designation of the Christian "devil", while in Mongol and Uigur šmnu, šimnu, šumnu, according to F. W. K. Müller (cf. "Uigurica", 1908 p. 58) and Salemann (cf. "Manichaica", V, 1913, p. 1129), were used in the sense of "evil spirits". [cf. Kowalewsky's dictionary; however, in Mongol the situation is complicated by the fact that there are two sources for the complexes originally issued from šramana, i.e. a Central Asiatic, in which saman, as stated above, might at least at a certain moment, turn into "evil spirit", and šramana received from the written original documents on Buddhism; the remoteness of borrowing from the Central Asiatic complex greatly hinders the linguistic analysis of existing terms]. The same author draws attention to the relations which existed between Buddhism and shamanism (what kind of shamanism? S. Sh.) as it appears from the order of the Uigur Khagan. In fact, in connexion therewith it may be pointed out that the shamans' activity among the Yakuts and some Turk (in a mild form reflected in the shamanism of the Reindeer Tungus of Transbaikalia) is sometimes connected with "par excellence" evil spirits ("black shamans"), as opposed to good ones ("white shamans"), and the Yakut opinion above quoted as to the first shaman and devil receives a different meaning, which points to a connexion between the Central Asiatic "evil variety" of "sramanism".

here studied cannot be regarded as a very old cultural complex. The Tungus themselves consider it as a complex which originated, according to the Manchus, in the eleventh century, and according to other groups—the Birarčen and Reindeer Tungus of Manchuria—still later, and through the influence of other ethnical groups—the Manchus, Dahurs and Goldi. On the other hand, many Buddhistic elements are found in the complexes of shamanism which can sometimes be traced to the original sources, i.e. the ethnical groups from which the elements have been borrowed. It may be also noted that, in so far as components are concerned, shamanism shows great differences, when observed in the ethnical units, and these differences may be understood as due to the differences of the imitated original patterns, also, to a certain amount, of the inventiveness manifested in different degrees by the ethnical units. However, among all groups here discussed shamanism reveals the same fundamental characters outlined in six formal and four psychomental characteristics (*vide supra*, Section 95). These characteristics are thus generalized: shamanism as a complex does not migrate, is not borrowed, even does not exist. Concrete phenomena actually exist, e.g. the belief in the possibility of such and such a spirit being mastered, a definite form of head-dress, a concerete method of self-excitation by a rhythmic movement of the head, and so forth. Therefore the ethnical groups sometimes refuse to recognize the "shamanism" of their neighbours and cannot be influenced by it. Moreover, shamanism may remain without being recognized at all and without being "symbolized" by a special term, while *it will function* as a complex of elements borrowed from the neighbours and invented by the groups. Shamanism, as a component of the psychomental complex, has its various functions, the principal of which, from the biological (ethnological) point of view, is the self-regulation of the psychomental complex of the ethnical units, so that it belongs to the group of delicate mechanisms of equilibria of the psychomental complex, created in the concrete conditions of ethnical units, as aggregates of physical individuals, with the concrete ethnographical elements both borrowed and invented. Finally hypothetically, but with a great amount of certainty, I have traced its beginning to the influence of Buddhism, which as a new and alien complex did produce its stimulating effect, both in the sense of creation of a kind of psychomental unrest and in the sense of creation of a new method of regulation of this unrest. Therefore, shamanism may be approached from three points of view, namely, (1) the descriptive ethnographical, the aim of which is to show how the ethnical units understand the elements of which the shamanism consists, and how they understand the whole complex, when its existence is recognized; (2) the functional-ethnographical, the aim of which is to find out the rôle of shamanism in the systems of the given units; (3) the historico-ethnographical, the aim of which is to restore, as far as possible, the formation of the existing complexes and, as far as possible, to trace the history of the elements.

An analytical distinction of these three points of view is practically useful, for meeting with a new complex we may say how far advanced and exhaustive our investigation is, and in which respects it ought to be completed. Naturally, it will also put certain limitations to the methodological possibility of premature inferences of a theoretical character, which will also save time, and the energy of

students of shamanism who will not need to go into the details of theoretical constructions of those authors who did not actually know shamanism, but who wrote about it. In this way ethnologists and ethnographers will receive a long list of documents, left by these authors, for an analysis, as documents reflecting varieties of the European psychomental complex and reactions on the non-European complexes. Indeed, the review of existing descriptions of shamanism among the Tungus groups does not leave us great hope, even in so far as facts are concerned—they are extremely fragmentary. Unfortunately, the best of these publications, such as that of P. P. Šimkevič and I. A. Lopatin, who have given descriptions of some aspects of shamanism among the Goldi, do not even give a complete list of spirits, and their descriptions of the shamans' psychomental state in general and during the performance are reflecting more the observers' reactions on the performance than the object of observation. The other authors, such as L. Sternberg (cf. "Divine Election, etc."), have quoted a few facts, but in their selection, inspired by the pre-existing theories, they appear as being still less interesting than other observers who confined themselves to giving partial descriptions of paraphernalia and performances, even though in the light of their own "authors' complexes". Such are the descriptions of S. Brailovskiĭ (Udehe), I. Nadarov (Oroči). Beyond and within the limits of the groups here discussed, the descriptions relate in the same fragmentary manner to the groups of Transbaikalia, the Enissy prov. and the Yakutsk prov. Earlier travellers, beginning from the eigteenth century, also R. Maack, A. von Middendorf and others of the last century, contributed only very general remarks and very brief descriptions. Special investigations, like those of K. M. Ryčkov did not give even an incomplete picture, as that which we have of the Goldi shamanism. Such a state of the investigations into shamanism cannot be said to be at its beginning; this field is not a maiden one, but at the same time there has not yet been given a complete description of the formal characteristics of shamanism. Chiefly, description of some strange paraphernalia, special shaman's dresses, and some parts of performances were given. The principal cause of such failure is the complexity and strangeness of shamanism as a phenomenon, and the lack of knowledge of the language, not to speak of the investigators' failure to assume an "objective" approach to the problem and to free themselves of theories jeopardizing the issue of the investigation. In fact, such a situation is not characteristic of the investigators of the Tungus alone. Of all investigators N. A. Vitaševskiĭ best realized this situation and made a new approach to the problem of the description of shamanizing, as observed by him among the Yakuts. This investigator recorded in 1894 a case of shamanizing, as a "behaviourist" would have recorded it, and he demonstrated it in 1917[*], seemingly as a reaction against a habit of writing about shamanism in too much generalized forms. Indeed, a great number of recorded details are needed for every newly described form, but when they are observed in mass, some details, being invariably repeated, become mere model and need not be recorded every time. However, a great number of observers used to begin by passing their observations through their own complexes, chiefly leaving records of only those

[*] In "Publications du Musée d'Anthr. et d'Ethn." Vol. V, 1917-1925, pp. 165-188.

facts which impressed them. Moreover, all investigators among the Tungus used the mediation of translators insufficiently trained for this kind of work, or the conversation was carried on in broken Russian little known to the shamans in general and not at all to some of them. In addition the defective methodology of inquiries must be pointed out. In fact, the questions asked by the investigator very often contained answers consciously or unconsciously desired by the investigators; the inquisitive behaviour of the investigators, who usually did not conceal their attitude of "superiority", tended to make the shamans suspicious and hostile towards the investigators; to "interest" the subject of their investigation, the investigators very often used to give them, during the inquiry, gifts in cash and other things, which created absolutely unfavourable conditions for the investigators who, instead of the truth, were served with tales they were looking for. In a much better condition were those investigators who by their origin were connected with the people, such as D. Banzarov, M. N. Xangalov, Agapitov, Ž. Žamcarano, who, being Buriats themselves, were not handicapped by anything, except their theorization and the adaptation of the Buriat complex to the Russian scholars' mentality. The case of a group of political exiles who in the second half of the last century were settled among the Yakuts, such as E. Pekarskiĭ, N. A. Vitaševskiĭ, V. M. Ionov, V. L. Seroševskiĭ (Sieroszewski) and others, is also different, for many of

them did become familiar with the Yakuts, but one obstacle ought to have been overcome by them, namely, the idea of immeasurable superiority of "civilized men", which in its new variety was unfortunately, preserved by many of this new group of observers.

The exposition of the facts concerning the Tungus shamanism is different, owing to the lack of good Tungus comparative material. The facts at my disposal are also not sufficient for answering all questions that arise, when the material is analysed. Indeed, there are numerous variations of some of these facts, as they have been observed at various times and among different groups, while other aspects are represented by a very limited number of facts and sometimes even by a single one. Wherever it is particularly important, it will be specified, whether the facts are common or only occasionally observed ones. In shamanism, as in other aspects of the psychomental complex, it is practically almost impossible to give an exhaustive outline; the colours used for the picture are also in reality not as vivid as they appear in a special work in which the facts are condensed. After all, shamanism is only one of the aspects of the psychomental complex which in the systems of ethnical and individual equilibria occupies a modest place. To have a correct picture of the functional importance of shamanism, the colours must be attenuated; shamanism cannot be studied apart from the existing general psychomental and cultural complexes.

CHAPTER XXIV

SHAMANISTIC PARAPHERNALIA

102. PRELIMINARY REMARK Among all Tungus groups and Manchus, as well as their neighbours, shamanistic performances require a certain number of special things used only for this purpose. These things may be called by the general term "shamanistic paraphernalia". Their number and forms vary greatly among the Tungus and the other groups. Since they are easily accessible for observation and since they may be collected for museums, the investigators of various groups have left rather rich documentation of this side of shamanism, both in descriptions, with or without illustrations, and in museum specimens. In the present work I shall give only a summary description of the observed paraphernalia, for I am now unable to illustrate my description with photos and specimens which are at present beyond my reach. But as without any illustrations my description may become incomprehensible, I shall give, when necessary, some reproductions of my own drawings from the diary, which must consequently be regarded not as a documentation, but as mere illustrations to the text. In some cases I shall also refer to the publications of other investigators who have given reproductions of photos and good drawings.

In the paraphernalia a great number of elements can be distinguished, the principal of which are (1) the costume which may consist of several elements: coat, apron, trousers, shoes, etc., or may be reduced to a single element, e.g.

the coat, skirt, apron; (2) the head-dress; (3) the staffs; (4) the brass mirror-*toli;* (5) the drum with the drumming stick; (6) other musical instruments; (7) various placings for spirits, independent of other placings; and (8) various other implements. The complex of the paraphernalia may be rich or poor, for which there may be different reasons which will be discussed later. Although theoretically a case might be imagined where there would be no paraphernalia needed for a shaman's activity, such an occurrence has not been observed. So, as a statement of fact, we must say that there is no shamanism without paraphernalia. It can be supposed, and it will be shown when the performances are described, that the paraphernalia are needed for the performances and that without them the effectiveness of shamanism would decrease to such an extent that it would lose its functional "value" and would naturally be given up as a complex. In fact, the costumes and other paraphernalia are needed by most of the shamans for the production of self-excitement, self-hypnosis, and hypnotic influence over the audience. It should also be noted that, together with the increase of the curative power of a shaman, there is usually an increase of paraphernalia. If a shaman has no paraphernalia, he or she is not a good shaman in the eyes of the people. The richer the paraphernalia, the more influential the shaman.

In looking at the geographical distribution of the elements it can be quite clearly seen that some coincidences are revealed with the ethnical group here discussed, and also with the geographical grouping of elements in the complexes. Both within the complexes abstracted, and within the ethnical units the combination of elements presents such a great variety that sometimes it is impossible to trace the lines of demarcation between two complexes connected with ethnical groups. However, there are no two absolutely similar complexes of paraphernalia observed in the individual cases of shamans, even within the same ethnical unit and within the limits of the same (our theoretical construction) cultural type. The chief reason is that, as a rule, every shaman has his or her own complex of spirits, and with the change of fashions a great freedom in the choice of elements and their variations is left to the individual shaman. The choice of shamanistic paraphernalia is not a rigidly fixed, ceremonial complex. In this respect no comparison can be made with the Buddhistic paraphernalia, or with any other uniform complex ceremonial attributes. However, there is also an interesting exception, namely, the Manchus, among whom a tendency to uniformity is well expressed; but there are special reasons for this, which will be discussed later on.

With a greater or lesser probability of representing reality I shall try to trace the boundaries of complexes and their possible formation, but my chief aim is to give facts needed for the analysis and demonstration of the functioning of the complexes.

103. COSTUME (DESCRIPTION) Under this heading I shall give the description of various forms of costumes which may consist either of one or of several pieces which by themselves form a complex. Among the Tungus groups we meet with the following terms: *samás'ik—ŝamáŝik* (Bir Kum. Khin. Nerč. Barg. Mank), *hamayik* (Lam), by the side of *idägä* (Ur. Castr.), evidently a Buriat term; also *naim'i* (Tum. I have some doubt as to this record—it is only the skin of a female reindeer). In Manchu it is *saman'i ètku*, i.e. "shaman's dress". In Goldi it is simply "dress, cloth"—*tetu*, [cf. *tet'i* (Tun.),—"the dress"; cf. *tet* the stem of "to dress", in a great number of Tungus dialects]. Most Tungus groups have a special term derived from *saman*, with the exception of the Manchus and groups influenced by them, also of groups like Ur. (Castr.) and Tum., where it has been replaced by other terms or perhaps even not been recorded.

Among the *Reindeer Tungus of Trasbaikalia*—the Barguzin and Nerchinsk groups—one can distinguish two types recognized by the Tungus themselves. These are the costume-duck, and the costume-deer (Cervus Elaphus) which will be described separately, and which are used in different forms of shamanistic performance.

THE COSTUME-DUCK consists of a coat, an apron, trousers, knee-protectors, and shoes (moccasins). The material used for the coat may be chamois, made either of deer (Cervus Elaphus) skin or of elk (Alces Alces skin. The cut does differ from that of an ordinary coat, i.e. a coat resembling the modern European morning coat. The difference is that the back part is much shorter and ends in a tail symbolizing the duck's tail.[*] The sleeves are supplied with a fringed strip of

chamois symbolizing the wings. The borders are also trimmed with a chamois fringe and hanging strips of chamois, all of them symbolizing feathers. The coat is usually ornamented with white reindeer hair from the neck, widely used by the Tungus as a material for ornamentation. Ornamental motives are various combinations of lines, strips and circles, much like those observed in the bone-carvings of the Chukchis, Eskimos, Samoyeds and other inhabitants of North Siberia and America. However, I have seen also a coat which was ornamented along the borders with applied coloured crosses of about 5 or 6 centimetres. According to the Tungus, the "cross" greatly helps in shamanizing—it may "have power".[*] The ornamented parts may also be coloured with the usual colours —black, red, brown, yellow, and blue. The coat may also have applied ornamentation symbolizing the bones of a duck. Instead of an ornamental symbolization of the skeleton, corresponding symbols of all bones made of iron may be used. Their number may be confined to only two bones of the wings, or all bones of the skeleton may be reproduced—it depends on the material facilities for procuring iron, which is not common among the Tungus. Usually the iron parts are not made by the Tungus, but are received in exchange from the Buriats and Yakuts.

In addition to the ornamentation of borders with the common "geometric" figures there exist ornaments made of white hair—stylized images of domesticated reindeer, Cervus Elaphus, Alces Alces, bear, wild boar, musk-deer, roe-deer, heath-cock, also ducks, and anthropomorphic images. However, these images are not an indispensable element of the "duck-costume".

Besides these, so to say permanent, elements there is a variable number of pendants made of iron and brass which, however, are not typical of the duck-costume.

The coat is usually supplied with two series of eight bells of two forms: conical and spherical. The bells are real series for they form two definite musical accords in the frontal and back parts of the coat needed for the shamanistic performance and used by the shamans quite intentionally. The complex of bells and trinkets is called *arkalan* (cf. *infra*).

THE COSTUME-REINDEER consists of the same elements, and is made of the same material. The cut of the coat does not differ from that of an ordinary coat. The ornaments may be lacking, but the coat must have a set of iron bones symbolizing a complete skeleton of Cervus Elaphus. As compared with the "bones" of the duck-costume those of the reindeer-costume can easily be distinguished, e.g. in representing sternum, ribs, and limbs. Animals and bells are attached to the coat as it is with the duck-costume, but they are in a greater number and there are special conical trinkets attached to other parts of the costume. In addition to the zoomorphic and anthropomorphic figures several other symbols are attached: e.g. a boat, a raft, a bow and an arrow, a semicircle ("moon"), a circle ("sun"), a ring ("rain-bow"), a square hole ("heaven," the hole being the entrance into the

---

[*] However, the "tail" may even lack, as I have observed in some costumes.

[*] I am not sure as to the origin of this cross-ornament, which might be a simple imitation of the Orthodox priests' chasuble. · It is not in contradiction with the Tungus idea: since priests use this "ornament", it may be useful for the shamans, too.

upper world used by the shaman) ; there may also be found: "stars", "thunder", "harpoons", as well as placings *bādo*. These are symbols of phenomena with which the shaman has to deal during his performance, when travelling into the lower and upper worlds. The animals are manifestations of spirits which can be assumed by the shaman during the performance.

"SNAKE". Both the duck and reindeer costumes have a certain number, not less than one, of chamois strips, about ten centimetres wide and over a metre long. These represent *kulin*—the "snake", but they are supplied with two heads, a tail, split into several parts, and four fringes symbolizing the legs; the eyes are made of small glass beads. If there are several "snakes", the largest "snake" is attached to the back, while two small "snakes" are attached to the two sides. The big "snake" was styled by the shamans as "the most important spirit who gives advice to the shaman".

MOKIL. On the back there are also attached images, known as *mokil*, made of chamois dyed black. There may be only two pairs, but there may also be four, as well as nine, or even 9×4, 9×8, 18×4 and so forth. These combinations of two and nine are frequently met with in shamanistic paraphernalia and performances. Many series of nine are met with chiefly in the duck-costume, while that of two is found in the reindeer-costume.

The two types here distinguished are not always strictly followed. I have seen some costumes in which the elements of duck and reindeer were mixed up. The number of pendants and ornaments also greatly varies, depending on whether the shaman can afford to have two special costumes and how much they can be ornamented. *Lege artis*, the duck-costume, is supposed to be good for shamanizing in connexion with operations with the spirits of the upper world, while the reindeer-costume is supposed to be good for dealing with those of the lower world. I was even told that the reindeer-costume is "too heavy for going to the upper world". In fact, a good costume with all pendants, bells, etc. may weigh about forty kilograms, while an ordinary duck-costume will not be much heavier than a usual Tungus garment. It should be noted that the duck-costume *lege artis* possesses *mokil* in many series of nine, and has no symbols for boat, raft, etc. needed for travelling across the water for reaching the lower world. It must also be remembered that the travelling in the lower world, as will be described later, is much more difficult than the travelling in the upper world, so that the shaman-beginners usually have only the duck-costume. When they begin to go to the lower world, they attach more and more iron pieces so that by increasing the number a new, second costume, the reindeer-costume may be "constructed". When this is done all of the metallic pieces are taken off the duck-costume and transferred on to the reindeer-costume. From that moment the shaman would alternatively use his two costumes for special forms of shamanizing.

From the above description of the two types of costumes it is evident that they are connected with two forms of shamanizing, which with the ethnical parallels will be discussed later on.

THE APRON ·(*uruptun*) (Bar. Nerč) is the most important part of the costume, for the shaman can perform, at least some acts, with the apron alone, but not the great shamanizing to the upper and lower worlds. In shape, the apron does not differ from the ordinary Tungus one, which is a piece of chamois with thongs for tying it around the neck and others for attaching it around the waist, about seventy or eighty centimetres long and from twenty-five to forty centimetres wide, just enough for covering the chest and the abdomen,[*] used by all Tungus as a supplement necessary to their open morning-coat-like dress in the Siberian and Manchurian climatic conditions. The apron is ornamented with strips of coloured chamois, or it is painted with the usual colours and ornamented with white reindeer hair. The whole apron is covered with a design symbolizing the world-universe—*turú*. In the middle there is a line, from which, at the height of two thirds, two other lines go up at a certain angle. This is the larch tree—*irakta*—above which the upper world—*ugidunda*—is situated. Two anthropomorphic symbols, representing "two great shamans who died long ago" and to whom the acting shaman must pray for helping him to shamanize, are found in the upper part. There may be more than two symbols—four or eight. "If these shamans should fall down to the earth, the whole universe would collapse." The middle part of the design represents the Earth—*jorko*—(the middle world without the ocean). The lower part represents the lower world. The apron may be trimmed with a fringe and eight iron birds—*dèyil,*—apparently "ducks".

A brass mirror *tōlō,* (*vide supra* p. 278) is attached to the apron. This is the most important element of the apron and of the whole costume. According to the shamans, such a mirror cannot be bought, but it must be found in the earth—it is sent by the *burkan.*[**] On the unpolished side the shamans distinguish in the centre a snake—*kulin*—which is naturally a dragon, and animals: a wolf, a cow, a roe-deer, a cow's head, a cock, a sheep, a horse. etc. which actually represent twelve. cyclic animals. When the shaman looks at the polished side "he can see everything", i.e. it helps the shaman to hypnotize himself.

These Tungus find it often very difficult to get a mirror like this, but among the Tungus of other regions they can be easily found and their number is sometimes very great, e.g. over twenty. The size of the mirrors is subject to variation, e.g. I observed mirrors of from about twelve centimetres up to thirty centimetres in diameter. (*vide infra*, pp. 291-294; and *supra* p. 278).

THE HEAD-DRESS (*oroptun*) (Barg. Nerč.) (cf. *oro*-"the top of the head") presents many varieties. However, there can be distinguished at least two forms, namely, a form without iron reindeer antlers used for the duck-costume, and another form with iron antlers for the reindeer-costume. The shape of the head-dress is variable. I have observed, for instance, one made of *five* strips: four chamois strips sym-

---

[*] Cf. SONT p. 142. It is used throughout China, especially by children, also among the Miaotse (cf. W. Koppers "Miaotse etc.).

[**] This is only a theory, for when the Tungus want one, they can have it from old costumes of deceased shamans. They get them from the Buriats as well. The Buriats can tell the Tungus that the mirror was found in the earth, although actually it came from China or Tibet with other Buddhistic paraphernalia.

bolizing "snakes", with glass beads for the eyes, joined together on the top, and a fifth strip making a band around the head, so that four sections were open leaving the head uncovered. The old type of the Tungus head-dress was like this. Now this kind of head-dress, with a visor attached to the band, so that eyes are protected, is used for the summer hunting. The shaman's head-dress of this type had three ermine skins attached and also three polecat skins which "will defend the shaman with their teeth, like dogs". The four "snakes" of which the head-drees is made, look behind the shaman to warn him of any danger from the rear. However, ordinary Mongol (Buriat) hats and also skull caps, as other forms which perhaps are not typical, are frequently met with.

The reindeer-costume's head-dress is an iron band supplied with four strips of iron and surmounted with iron antlers (Cervus Elaphus) with five or six branches. The iron has an underlying skull cap made of chamois. Strips of chamois representing "snakes" hang from the tips of the antlers and a fringe falls from the frontal part covering the shaman's face. The strips and fringe may be made of silk or other available material.

The head-dress occupies the second place in importance for the performance. Very often a shaman may have only his apron and head-dress. In certain cases, during the performance, the head-dress is taken off.

THE MOCCASINS are of the usual form, light, with a long upper part, ornamented with material (*torgomó*) and usually called *jús'ik*. If the costume represents the reindeer, the moccasins are supplied with iron parts symbolizing bones of reindeer, and have trinkets of a conical form.

THE TROUSERS and *KNEE-PROTECTORS* are found in very complete costumes but are not indispensable components of the costume. They are made of chamois in the usual form, but several pendants and symbols are added, such as "bones", either of iron, or as a design of coloured chamois, white reindeer hair, etc.

THE SATFFS made in pairs, called "horses" and "reindeer", used for dealing with the upper world, may be considered as a part of the costume. Wooden staffs representing "horses" have hook-handles symbolizing the head of the horse. Iron rings and conical trinkets, as well as various addition, such as "snakes", kerchieves and fringe, may be attached. The "horses" are used by the shaman during his travelling. Such articles are sometimes altogether lacking in the shamanistic paraphernalia used among the Reindeer Tungus, but special staffs representing the "reindeer" (domesticated), called *oron* (*oror* plural—the reindeer), and made new for every performance, together with other temporary paraphernalia, are used.

VARIA. Besides the above described elements of the costume there are other permanent parts which are either put on by the shaman during the performance or kept near him. Several "snakes" made of chamois, sometimes twisted, also made of other various material, are attached to the sides of the costume. There is also a long lasso made of twisted chamois, supplied, like a snake, with two eyes (beads). With this lasso—*ušitó* (Barg)—the shamans capture any soul of the people, should it leave the body. The

lasso used for going to the lower world, (*buni ušitó*), is very thick and long, and is attached to the costume. A ring-like piece made of leather or chamois, richly ornamented with beads, hangs at the shaman's breast; another piece of rectangular form, called *olon*, is attached at the shaman's side. I could not find out the significance of these two things.

NOMAD TUNGUS OF TRANSBAIKALIA I have not observed very many costumes among the Nomad Tungus, but all of them were "reindeer-costumes". The difference between the costumes observed among the Reindeer Tungus and those of the Nomad Tungus was as follows: (1) a great number of "snakes" made of cloth and strips also twisted pieces of cloth, sometimes very like the "snakes" of the Buriat costume, and (2) a great display of "horses", used for almost all occasions, including visits of the shamans to the lower world. These Tungus say that their costume does not differ very much from that used by the Buriats and well known from several descriptions.

As it can be seen from the above description, the reindeer-costume, in many of its characters, is met with among the Tungus, Buriats, Yakuts and Turk-speaking groups of South Siberia and Mongolia. The Tungus costume is particularly near to that of the Buriats and Yakuts. A borrowing of elements is evident. I may point out an abundance of iron parts which are not usually made by the Tungus, but are received from their neighbours: the moon, sun, rain-bow, stars, etc. as well as the boats, rafts, bows, and arrows are especially conspicuous with the Yakuts; a great number of snakes which acquire a special importance among the groups speaking Buriat and Turk; "horses" which are evidently a Buriat element. Among the Tungus these elements are naturally adapted to their conditions of life, so that some elements will be better represented than the others and some of them are substituted by Tungus elements. As a whole the Tungus connect their costume with that of their neighbours and do not pretend to be inventors. Moreover, the reindeer-costume is sometimes connected by them with the "black faith" of the Buriat and Yakut complex, which has very little to do with the Tungus complex and in their own language sounds almost like a meaningless translation. In the Russian translation *ď'ornaja v'era* the Tungus associate it with Russian *čort*—the devil. In fact, in the Tungus complex, as has been shown, there is no notion of special "evil" spirits, as opposed to "good" ones, and the term —"black"—itself is quite a foreign conception. In the Tungus complex it is correlated with the "lower world".

It should be pointed out that the reindeer-costumes are much rarer among the Reindeer Tungus than among the Nomad Tungus who live side by side with the Buriats, while the duck-costume has not been observed by me among the Nomad Tungus. Contrarily to the reindeer-costume of the "black faith", the duck-costume is sometimes connected with the "white faith". The latter is supposed to be connected with the upper world. However, we have seen that, even in the costume, elements of "black faith" and "white faith" may be mixed up, which points to the fact that for the Tungus this distinction is an alien element. As has been shown, the shamans-beginners cannot deal with the lower world, but when they become ex-

perienced *they can deal with both, and in the same costume,* which may represent a mixture of two complexes.

'All of the indicated facts point to a foreign origin,
probably chiefly Buriat, of the reindeer-costume, while the
question as to the origin of duck-costume I leave open, for
the time-being, for further discussion.

REINDEER TUNGUS OF MANCHURIA   I have seen
no costumes
used among them, for during my visit to this group in the
Bystraja River region there was only one shaman who lived
near the Amur River. Another shaman, the senior
"brother" (*aki*) of my informer (a man nearly sixty years
old), died in 1912 and his "harness"—the costume—was
put on a platform near the grave in the valley of one of the
upper tributaries of the Kumara River. According to my
informer, it might also have been hung up on a tree. In so
far as I could find out, there were two kinds of shamans:
those going to the lower world ("earthly") and those going
to the upper world. The first ones were very rare. However, the costume was the same. It was "like the Yakut
shaman's costume", supplied with a great number of iron
trinkets and pendants. The head-dress was supplied with
iron antlers of Cervus Elaphus with a different number of
branches: from three to six,—the "stronger" the shaman,
the more branches.

TUNGUS OF MANCHURIA   Among the Khingan group
the shaman costume is
comparatively much poorer than that of the Tungus of
Transbaikalia. There is not the least doubt that it is a

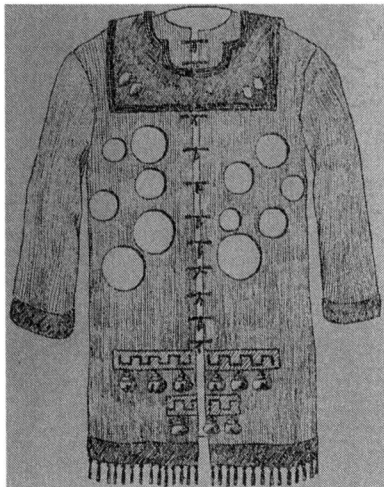

different complex. All the costumes (I have seen four or
five of them) are of the same type, but they show some in-

dividual variations. The costume consists of a coat, made
of common Mongol cloth and rarely of some skins
(chamois), usually of single thickness. The front fasten-
ing is by means of an indefinite number of thongs which
are tied. There is no collar and no slash is made on the
sides, which is usual in the Tungus coats. The borders may
be ornamented with fancy Dahur silk cloth. At the front
there are two strips of different cloths (or chamois) bearing small ball-bells. Above the row of bells, several *tōlā*
(brass-mirrors), the number of which varies, are attached.
In one case I observed twelve mirrors. The lower
board may also be supplied with iron trinkets of an indefinite form. Once I observed a piece of an iron ring-
armour. On the back there happen to be, but not always,
several strips of cloth ornamented according to the Dahur
style,—i.e. the mixed sino-mongol-manchu ornamental complex, and silk ribbons. There is a rather important component of the costume, namely, a kind of short stole made
of cloth with little ornamentation and some (I have
observed eight) univalve shells commonly used by the
Tungus and undoubtedly received through the intermediary
of some merchants (Chinese and Dahurs). The function
of this component is not known to me, but in a more
developed form it is known among the Birarčen.

The head-dress consists of a calotte made of any
material ornamented and supplied with small iron antlers
of Cervus Elaphus. In one case I observed only one half
of the antlers. There may be some ribbons and chamois
strips attached to the top of the calotte and hanging at the
back.

The same type of costume is observed in its well
developed form among the Birarčen and Kumarčen.
Among these groups I have seen many costumes, some of
which were most elaborated.* I shall now give a summary
description of one of them observed among the Birarčen.

The costume consists of three components: the coat,
the "stole", which may be also simply called "collar", and
the head-dress. The material used among the Birarčen is
chamois made of the skins of Cervus Elaphus and Alces
Alces. Skins of other animals cannot be used. The preferred material is Alces Alces skin; but if it is made of
Cervus Elaphus, a part of it, namely the upper back must be
made of Alces Alces.** The long coat is cut in the same
manner as with the Khingan Tungus, i.e. without the usual
slits on the sides and without a collar.*** Under the sleeves
two apertures, about ten centimetres long, are made, called
oon'i, through which the spirits enter the shaman. Near
to them rings with ribbons may be attached, on which
bunches of kerchieves (*vide infra*, p. 292) are fastened.
These rings with ribbons are called "wings". In the front
there are three *ayaptun* (Bir.)—wide strips with ball-bells,
altogether 9 × 3 bells on each side. On the right side, in
the upper part, there is the *asaran*, a big bell with silk and
other kinds of kerchieves collected after successful shamanizing and attached to the coat. The sleeves have two
ornamental bands—*ičáptun*—at the height of the elbow

* Unfortunately a good specimen which I bought and included
in my collection is now in the Museum of Anthropology and Ethnography of the Russian Academy of Sciences and thus, for the time
being, is not accessible to me. The same refers to the pnotos.
** It should be noted that the material used among other groups
is different. However, in the Birarčen territory it is not easy to get
skins of Alces Alces.
*** According to my informers, shamanizing in a dress with a
collar would be impossible.

(*iča*) and *uksáptun* on the cuff (*uksa,*—"the sleeve"). The lower border may be supplied with a fringe made of chamois, dyed black. On the back there are four brass mirrors, the upper ones being slightly smaller (*vide* the figure below). Below the waist there is the *irg'ivlán* (*irg'i,*—"the tail"),— a large piece of chamois, with chamois applications, but without ornaments, attached to three ball-bells and supplied with nine hanging ribbons.

is put on the costume. There may be two *ukoptun,* namely, one with mixed coloured beads for the night road spirit *jerga sèvèn dolbor,* and another one, with light blue beads, for the day road spirit *jerga sèvèn inepi.* The shaman may have some other *ukoptun* for clients, but they would be slightly different. The third important piece is two bunches of kerchieves received by the shaman for his shamanizing. In each of the two bunches, there is an ermine skin. The bunches of kerchieves are hung up at the sides of the coat.

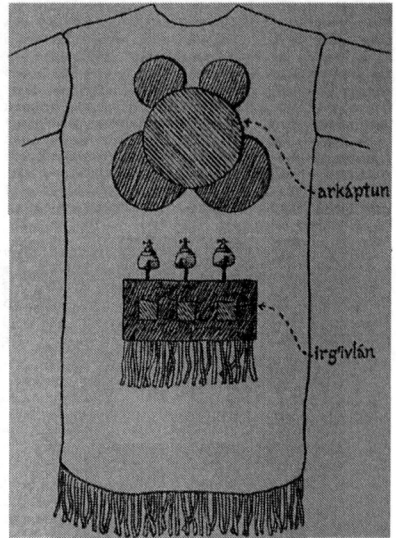

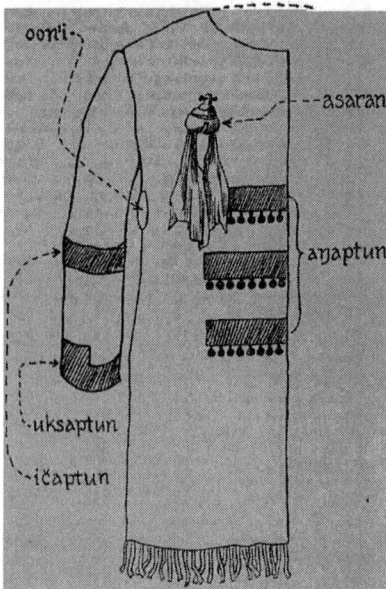

The frontal part may be supplied with brass-mirrors— twelve mirrors on each hem. The mirrors I observed were not real mirrors, but especially made disks with an ear. Additional mirrors also may be attached to the frontal part and along the lower border.

Three pieces are added to the costume, when the latter is put on for shamanizing. The principal is *arkáptun,* which is a large brass mirror, about twenty-five centimetres in diameter, with kerchieves attached to it. On the *arkáptun* the symbol of a special shamanistic bird—*solbar dèyi*—the so called "Chinese phenix", may be found. The *arkáptun* is attached to the back, above the four smaller mirrors; it is usually kept separate and can even be left in the house where a shamanizing had taken place, for the spirits of the shaman may remain in it for a long time (especially for children). If the principal spirit of the shaman is the *jerga sèvèn,* nine brass rings will be attached to the *arkáptun.* Another piece is called *ukóptun.* It consists of three strings of glass beads, at the ends of which small brass mirrors are attached. During the performance *ukoptun*

The collar *jakáptun* is a very elaborate piece, as shown in the figure below. It consists of a piece of chamois with two pieces attached to its ends, so that, when the

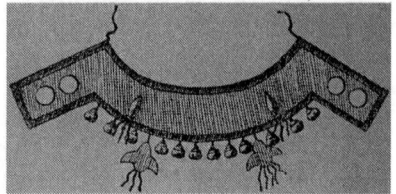

collar is put on, these two pieces form a square piece, like that of the dress of Catholic priests. Each of them has a pair of small brass mirrors and five strings with glass beads and a ball-bell, at their ends, i.e. altogether ten bells, which are not shown in the figure above. Two wooden "cuckoos" *kukkú*, each supplied with a tail, symbolized by three ribbons, the middle one of which has a small bell, are attached to the collar.* When the collar is put on, the cuckoos are on the shoulders. Two more "bird-like" pieces made of cloth and ornamented—*jajaŋku*—are attached to the collar. They are supplied with three or five ribbons symbolizing "roots" — *kalbaŋkan'i, tikaṇin.***** Moreover, twelve ball-bells are attached to the collar.

The third component of the costume is the head-dress, *g'ēva* (Bir.). It consists of a strip of chamois about nine centimetres wide supplied with small hooks and eyes for keeping it around the head. In the middle of it there is a brass mirror (sometimes an iron or brass piece of an oblong form). On the upper part seven ornamented pieces are attached and each of them is supplied with a bell and five ribbons (*kolboŋku*). They are maintained in an erect position by a wire framework. The ornament is a mixture of Chinese, Manchu and Tungus elements. Under the brass mirror, i.e. in the part corresponding to the face of

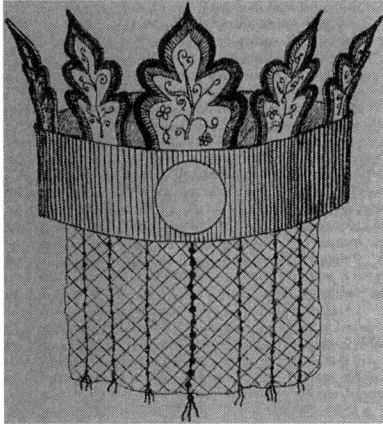

* The cuckoos may sometimes be in symbolized nests (ujin). Usually they are simply attached to the collar.
** I could not find out the meaning of jajaŋku. The nearest meaning of it may be jaja,—"the placing for ancestors' spirits". But I am not certain. The "roots" are not clear, too. Cf. kaibu (Neg. Sch.) (also T. Sch.)—"the belt". Indeed, a transfer of the belt to the neck and shoulders as "collar" is a quite possible occurrence. Tikan is "root". Indeed, the whole collar may represent a tree with birds on it. The explanation of the collar as a tree, is confirmed by the Tungus who say that maŋi (spirit, vide supra pp. 151, 167) keeps in "a half-arm" a tree on which a cuckoo is sitting. From the head of maŋi, who has nine heads, something is coming out which is considered by the Tungus as a simple ornament (ilga); but this is not so. On the other hand, when the collar is on, the "bird-like" pieces are exactly on the scapulae, which in Manchu are called xalba, whence Bir. kalbaŋku for the pieces (ŋku is a suffix, cf. jajaŋku.) It is very likely that we have here some foreign (Manchu) terms which now are not used in these languages. There is no doubt that the whole collar is not of a Tungus origin.

the shaman, there is the *čurakta*, a piece which, because of its function, may be called a mask; it consists of black lace with seven strings of beads (*ē'ikta*). When the head-dress is put on, the mask covers the shaman's face, but the shaman can see through it. It corresponds to similar fringes used for the same purpose in other types of head-dress. It should be noted that this form is an imitation of the head-dress used by the Mongol and Tibetan lamas, and met with on the heads of some Buddhistic deities*. In fact, when the Tungus can find them ready-made, with Buddha images, they use them and particularly appreciate them as a very powerful shaman's garment.

It should also be noted that this form of head-dress is not the only form met with among the Birarčen and Kumarčen—the calotte with antlers, as described among the Khingan Tungus, and of more elaborate forms, such as those observed among the Reindeer Tungus of Transbaikalia, are also met with.

Formerly among the Birarčen a staff was used, called *tijavun*, but it is no more used nowadays. *Tijavun* is a term for the staffs used by the Tungus for mounting reindeer (SONT) (Nerč. Barg. RTM; all reindeer breeders), also when using ski (Nerč. Bir.), and by old men in general [cf. *teifun* (Manchu Writ)—a staff, cane for old men]. The staffs are still used by the Goldi shamans. But their form corresponds to that of the sticks used for driving the dog-sledge.**

The total weight of the above described costume, which belonged to a young female shaman, exceeded thirty kilograms. It was so heavy that old shamans could not put it on and stand, when there was no spirit in them. However, the weight of the costume usually does not decrease with the shaman's age,—new brass mirrors being always added. I shall revert once more to this question.

These Tungus groups are not the original inventors of this form of costume. In fact, the complex is lacking an essential part of the common Tungus dress, namely, an apron. The Tungus ornaments are superseded by the alien ornaments, recently introduced among these groups. The form of the coat is not Tungus, the "collar" is not a Tungus element, as well as the head-dress. The brass mirrors are imported, as well as the laces, ribbons, and beads. The shaman's costume of the Reindeer Tungus is different, as well as that observed among the Manchus, Goldi and other groups (*vide infra* p. 294). I could not myself see the Dahur costume, but I was told by the Tungus, and the Dahurs did support their statement, that the Dahur costume is like the above described costume of the Birarčen. This statement should be kept in mind, and since the Dahurs are the source of a great number of cultural elements among these Tungus, it may be supposed that the Dahurs supplied the Tungus not only with the spirits, but also with the costume.

In the territory occupied by the Tungus a further complication of the same costume is met with, namely, over the coat there is a skirt used by the Manchu shamans, and over this skirt there is another one consisting of long ribbons. Indeed, this is a mere addition borrowed from the Manchu shamans. Such a form is met with among the Tungus of the Jalu River—the *jalčen* (cf. SONT), who are under both Dahur and Manchu influence. The Mergen Tungus, as

* Cf. e.g. A. Grünwedel, op. cit., Figs. 90,100,107.
** Cf. I. A. Lopatin, op. cit. p. 282.

well as the *jalčon*, and the Khingan Tungus, like to use shells for the ornamentation of the costume, so that the borders, hems, collar and head-dress may be richly covered with shells. The Buddhistic origin of "eyes" and swastika is evident. I have also been told, but never saw it myself, that some shamans have a certain number of iron pendants similar to those observed in the costume of the Reindeer Tungus.

MANCHUS The Manchu shaman's costume is entirely different. In Manchu it is called *samaní ètku*—"the shaman's clothes" or *ʃ'un ètku*, but together with the other paraphernalia it can be called *ayura* (*agura*, Manchus Writ)—"the implements and utensils in general". It consists of the following parts: coat, skirt, special belt, and head-dress.

As a whole it is known as *vočkoì ètku*, i.e. the spirit's dress, not that of the shaman.

The coat is cut of red Chinese cloth as a common short coat—*kurume*—the upper part of which is ornamented with an application of four black designs covering the chest, the back and the two shoulders. This is an ornament which is commonly met with in the Manchu complex, and which is called "hook ornament" (cf. *supra* pp. 111-112). There is no doubt that it is an ornament formerly widely used in China and Mongolia, and it cannot be considered as a very old Manchu ornament. On the back there is a square piece of scarlet cloth, about twenty centimetres wide. This is partly covered by a large brass mirror, as in the Birarčen costume. The frontal part may be covered with

a great number of small brass mirrors, but there must be at least two large mirrors and two smaller ones in the places corresponding to the breast. The coat was formerly covered with a great number of bones, carved and ornamented. According to some Manchus, there were also symbolized "wings", made of iron and brass. However, at present they can no more be seen, even though I have looked over several costumes. Besides, they are not found on the pictures of spirits (former shamans), a great number of which I could see on the *n'urgan*, i.e. "the spirits' pictures". Perhaps the "wings" were not wings at all.

The skirt descends a little below the knees; it consists of a piece of blue Chinese cloth plaited at the belt. It is called *xoškan* (Man. Sp.) [cf. *xüsixan* (Man. Writ.)]. It is sometimes cut into two halves for making the movements easier. Such skirts are used also by the *p'oʃun saman*, and it was used by the shamans of the Imperial family.[*] The question as to the "origin" of the shaman skirt is interesting; so I shall now give some details. It is not a specific shaman's garment. Such skirts were formerly and are still used by some professionals in China, e.g. in Kiangsu and other provinces. It is also a common winter dress of the Gilaks and of shamans.[**] The skirt is also used by the shamans among the Goldi who ornament it with various designs,[***] among the Oroči, and Udehe,[****] not to speak of the Goldi groups, such as the Olča and others. It would be erroneous to consider it, as L. von Schrenk did, as an old primitive Gilak garment, for it is met with among the Manchus and Chinese. The Japanese woman's skirt, that of the Malays and even that of the Polynesians and ancient Egyptians are also the same garment. In this part of Asia it is found chiefly along the coast and on the islands, and for this reason I have connected it with the early palaeasiatics in general. L. von Schrenck gives the Gilaks' term for skirt *kos'ka*, which is certainly the above mentioned Manchu *xüsixan* applied to the shaman's skirt and to that used by women.[*] However, it should be noted that the skirt in the Chinese complex, as well as in the Gilak complex, is not at all a woman's garment, so that in shamanism it cannot be connected with the sexual complex. Thus we see that such a form of garment is very common, but the Gilaks received it perhaps from the Manchus, and the shaman's skirt is quite a recent phenomenon pointing to its coming from the Manchus, for the Northern Tungus, as the Oroči, Udehe, and Goldi do not know this garment beyond its special use for shamanism.

Some Manchu shamans, especially powerful ones, use another *xoškan* put over the first one. The second one is a belt with very long fringes, usually fixed on strips of cloth.[**]

The belt with trinkets,—*s'iša—s'iša* (Manchu Sp.) and

[*] Cf. L. Langlès, op. cit. pl. VII, No. 39; Ch. de Harlez, op. cit. pl. VIII. No. 8.

[**] Cf. L. von Schrenck, pl. XVIII and LXII indicating a common dress; plate LXI representing an acting shaman. Among the Gilaks they are made of seal skins; cf. description, p. 82 Vol. II.

[***] Cf. I. A. Lopatin, op. cit., pp. 259-260.

Cf. P. Margaritov, Plate VI Fig. 79 among the Oroči. Cf. S. Brailovskiĭ, op. cit., p. 185 among the Udehe.

[*] The term xusixan in Manchu is connected with a series of words of the stem xusi—to wrap, to cover; cf. also the Goldi xoz'a— the shaman's skirt.

[**] In Chinese Sp. both of them are called č'ūnxa.

even *šiža*, which are common but very curious variations of Manchu dialects,* is a large, usually leather strip to which conical iron trinkets about fifteen and more centimetres long are attached. The belt is attached in front, so that the trinkets are on the back. The number of conical trinkets is variable. Altogether it makes a rather great weight, I suppose over ten kilograms. The function of the trinkets is purely musical. They are usually tuned in a definite manner. The shaman rythmically moves his or her back and the trinkets produce a characteristic sound. Such belts are used by the *p'oyun saman*, and by the *saman* of the Imperial family.** It is known among the Goldi groups, the Oroči, Udehe, also the Gilaks. Among these groups this belt may have some other trinkets added, as, for instance, among the Goldi, brass mirrors, ball-bell etc., but it may also be very much simplified, as among the Oroči. Among the Gilaks it is in some respects simplified, for the trinkets are attached to a string, but the trinkets are more varied.*** The geographical (ethnical) distribution of the trinket-belt coincides with that of the shaman's skirt. It seems to belong to the Manchu complex.

The head-dress,—*iksè*,—among the Manchus is of the greatest importance and there are different forms. The head-dress with birds is made of a calotte with a brass framework, as in the Northern Tungus groups, on the top of which brass birds are fixed; there may be one, three or more birds. The birds suggest the peacock, have small heads, heavy bodies, small wings and very long rich tails. The head-dress is decorated with a "hook ornament". In the front of the head-dress there is a brass mirror and a fringe hanging down to cover the face of the shaman. However, the birds may also be different. I have seen a big bird—a symbolized falcon—and two smaller birds symbolizing pigeons. The birds, when fixed to the top, may also revolve. During the performance this is used by the *p'oyun saman* of the clan *nara*.**** The birds are dismounted or the head-dress is taken off if the shaman introduces into himself some spirits, such as *buku*, *mayi*, all animal manifestations and others. There is a special head-dress when the shaman is going to the lower world and introduces into himself the *naïjulan saman vočko*. These are called *naï iksè* (i.e. "of earth head-dress"). This head-dress is made of iron and is supplied with iron antlers of Cervus Elaphus, similar to those of the Northern Tungus and called in Manchu *s'uk'a naï iksè*. I have also been told that there is a different kind of head-dress *guran'i iksè*, i.e. "roe-deer head-dress", which is put on when the shaman introduces into himself the roe-deer spirit during the autumnal sacrifice. I do not know the details of this head-dress, except that natural antlers of a roe-deer are fixed to it.*****

104. CLASSIFICATION OF COSTUMES — The above given descriptions of shaman's costumes permit us to distinguish four types used among the ethnical groups here discussed.

1. The *reindeer-costume* in the most complicated and fully symbolized form was formerly found among the Buriats and is at present preserved among the Nomad Tungus and, a little less, among the Reindeer Tungus of Transbaikalia. Going eastward we continue to meet only with hints at the reindeer-costume, namely, with iron antlers on the head-dress of the Khingan Tungus and the Goldi, sometimes the Birarčen, and on special occasions among the Manchus. Among these groups no other elements of the reindeer complex exist. The reindeer-costume is met with among the Tungus of the Yakutsk prov. and the Enisei prov., also among the Enisei Ostiaks who are Palaeasiatics. Beyond this area only hints at the reindeer complex are met with. As far as it can be seen, the facts seem to point to the region about the Lake Baïkal as a centre of diffusion of this complex.

The reindeer-costume is the one in which the shaman may go to the lower world, particularly for searching for or for settling souls of living and dead people respectively. The reindeer is the most convenient "manifestation" (of some spirits) for going to the lower world, and therefore the costume is a symbolized reindeer—a placing for this manifestation—in which the shaman feels himself swift, vigilant, watchful, the best animal the Tungus know. However, the shaman may also assume other manifestations for reaching his aim, and even, being dressed in this costume, he may assume still other manifestations, which have nothing to do with the reindeer, e.g. a series of spirits of the complex *malu* which may be helpful in his travelling. It may be pointed out that among the Buriats the idea of a reindeer, as a manifestation, has gradually given place to the idea of the shaman's riding on horseback, symbolized in horse staffs, while among the Tungus the staffs still represent the reindeer. This fact raises the problem of the former complex of the ancestors of the Buriats, which I do not want to discuss in this place, owing to its complexity. In so far as I know, there is a very essential difference between the Buriat and Tungus forms, namely, the Tungus form contains an apron, a component of great importance in the Tungus shamanism. The apron is known to be used only by the Tungus groups. Indeed, the loss of the apron by other groups is not entirely out of question. The second distinction is that among the Buriats the horse-staffs are of primary importance, even now when the costume is nearly given up, while the Reindeer Tungus shamans use them rather seldom and they are replaced by the temporary reindeer staffs. Finally the "snakes" are

---

* I have an interesting Manchu transcription in these forms in a text. So the Manchus would say that there are *šiža* and *s'iša*, two different things; but they cannot explain the difference.

** Cf. L. Langlès, op. cit., Plate VI, fig 29; Ch. de Harlez, op. cit,. Plate VIII, fig. 5.

*** Cf. L. von Schrenck, op. cit.; Plate LXI gives a specimen. The increase of the belt with various trinkets may be due to the "poverty factor".

**** The head-dress with birds is also known among the Dahurs, who have only one bird which revolves on the head-dress.

***** In this connexion I must point out that natural antlers were sometimes used by the people living on the banks of the Amur River. In 1916 I saw an iron framework with natural antlers of Cervus

Elaphus excavated on the banks of the Amur River (middle course) and preserved in the city museum of Blagoveščensk. It was impossible to identify to which ethnical group it might belong—the Manchus, Dahurs, or some of the Northern Tungus groups. Indeed, the antlers are known in the Buddhistic performances of mask dances called Tsam. Antlers are used for the mask *šaba* (Tib.), *buga* (Mong.), i.g. "Cervus Elaphus", which is also known in the Buriat shamanism. When I asked the Tungus and Manchus why they do not use natural antlers, the reply was the same, namely, they are too heavy for the head and clumsy, especially during the performances, while iron antlers are as effective as natural ones. It should be noted that the roe-deer antlers are very small and light.

not so numerous in the Tungus form as in the Buriat form.*

2. The *bird-costume* in its most complicated form is found among the Yakuts who have a complete iron skeleton of a bird; it is also common among the Reindeer Tungus of Transbaikalia. Among them this form must have no iron parts, if there are two costumes,—a reindeer and bird-costume. The bird-costume has a still smaller area of extension. However, with a certain imagination, the Manchu costume, more exactly, the Manchu head-dress, may be regarded as a symbolization of the bird; but this point of view will be erroneous—at least now the birds are only special placings for special manifestations of spirits, needed for certain forms of shamanism.** I have shown that the bird-costume is used by the shamans when they go to the upper world, and when they need a light flying body, like that of birds. They say that it is easier to go, when the costume is light. However, if the shaman happens to have no bird-costume, he may go to the upper world in the reindeer-costume, which actually happens during the shamanistic performances, when the shaman does not change his costume. Considering the geographical extension of the bird-costume, it may be supposed that its centre of diffusion is the territory now occupied by the Yakuts.

Here it should be noted that a co-existence of the two forms of this costume among the Tungus is not at all indicative of a "dualism" in the European sense, but these forms exist because of two technically different forms of performance used for dealing with different groups of spirits. Theoretically there may be more than two forms of costume, as it is observed e.g. among the Manchus who use more than two forms of head-dress on different occasions. These head-dresses might also be completed with different coats and other paraphernalia.

It is interesting that among the Reindeer Tungus of Transbaikalia the bird-costume is much more common than the reindeer-costume, the chief reason of which is not a greater or a smaller influence of neighbouring groups or ideas, but the fact that the dealing with the lower world is much more difficult for the shaman—from a technical, psychological point of view—than the dealing with the spirits of the upper world.

The Yakut form has seemingly penetrated as far as Manchuria, where it was used among the local Reindeer Tungus. It may be pointed out that the Yakut form contains an apron which is not used in the common Yakut dress complex. The apron is also met with in the shaman's costume of the Enisei-Ostiaks, a group greatly influenced by the Tungus. By these remarks I do not want to say

that the Yakut form is based upon the Tungus model with an apron, for the latter might have been introduced among the Yakuts from a different source.

It must be added that the Goldi also seem to have a kind of costume which symbolizes a bird. I. A. Lopatin (op. cit, p. 264) does not say whether the cut of the costume is different from that of the costume used by the shamans when they go to the lower world (on the occasion of bringing souls of dead people); but he distinguishes two kinds of costume, namely, those used by "great shamans" who have a regular head-dress and shamanize for dealing with the world of the dead, and those of "small shamans" who have no regular head-dress and do not deal with the world of the dead. The costume of the second group of the shamans is supplied with eagle feathers attached to the shoulders and the back of the coat; once twenty-seven pieces were observed. The conical trinkets must also have the form of bird feathers, and the coat is supplied with a fringe which symbolizes "feathers". The hat (apparently a calotte) is also supplied with a small iron bird (the cuckoo). I. A. Lopatin points out that, according to the shamans, this kind of costume is used by them when they have to fly. Thus it is evident that the idea is the same as in other cases, but the type of costume is different and cannot be connected with the complex of "upper world".

3. The *Manchurian form*,* as it is described among the Khingan Tungus, and Birarčen, and as it is known among other Northern Tungus groups of Manchuria, by these groups is related to the Dahur form which I could not verify. This form, at least at present, does not symbolize any animal manifestation of spirits, its most striking character being the prevailing importance of the brass mirrors. The head-dress is variable, an imitation of the Buddhistic form, being one of them. Whether the "Manchurian form" of costume can be brought back to the initial Dahur form which, in its turn, was an imitation of another model, cannot be stated with certainty. However, a collar put on separately, an evident imitation of some Buddhistic models, the head-dress, the brass mirrors, etc. point to the initial form—a Buddhistic garment perhaps first imitated by the Dahurs and later increased with other elements.

4. The *Manchu form* does not symbolize anything, with the exception of the head-dress which, as has been shown, may be different for different purposes of shamanizing. The best expressed form of this costume is found among the Manchus in a simplified form, used by the *p'oyun saman*—the clan priests and shamans of the Imperial family who are also clan priests. It is met in modifications among the groups which occupy the regions situated in the basin of the Sungari River and the lower course of the Amur River and the adjacent eastward regions, with the addition of those of the middle course of the Amur and the Nonni River, occupied by the Manchus, who have that form, but with the exception of the regions occupied by the Northern Tungus and Dahurs who have no Manchu form.

It can be noticed that this type of costume changes the further it is from its geographical and ethnical centre of diffusion. In fact, the elaborated forms of the head

---

* It should be noted that "snakes" show an evident decrease of their importance in the shaman's costume when we leave the regions near the lake Baikal. In fact, the greatest number of "snakes" is observed in the costumes used by the Mongol and Turkic speaking groups of Mongolia and the southern regions of Siberia. Among the Nomad Tungus of Transbaikalia they are much less important, and still less in the costume of the Reindeer Tungus; and they are of minor importance in the costume of the Tungus of Manchuria and entirely disappear in the costume of the Manchus. The centre of the "snake" element seems to lie South-West from the Lake Baikal.

** The Manchu statement about the "wings" of the costume cannot be accepted as a matter of fact. Vide supra p. 294. "Birds" are met with in the costume of the Tungus of Manchuria as "placings" for spirits. As shown, the costume may have a "tail" (irg'ivian). However, as a whole, the costumes of the Manchus and Tungus of Manchuria do not symbolize a "bird".

* I give this name to this form, because there is no other adequate term. As has been shown, it cannot be identified with the Dahur form. On the other hand, it cannot be called by the term of its symbolization, for the latter is lacking. My chief objection to this term is that it can easily be mistaken for the Manchu form discussed below.

dress with brass birds are replaced by wooden shavings; the brass mirrors by iron trinkets; the heavy belt with iron conical trinkets by a belt with various trinkets; the elaborated ornamentation by local ornamental motives or entirely omitted. On the other hand, the form is increased with new elements, such as various placings for spirits attached to the coat in the Goldi costume, a more elaborate form of head-dress for the performance, when the shaman goes to the lower world, as it is in the Goldi head-dress. Thus we may see, on the one hand, an impoverishing of the original complex and, on the other hand, its enrichment with local elements, which result in the formation of distinct local forms, as that of the Gilaks and Goldi. It was doubtless the Manchu costume that penetrated into these groups. In fact, even the terms for the different parts of the costume and, in general, the paraphernalia preserve their Manchu forms. The terms used by the Gilaks* are partly Manchu terms or those received through the intermediary of the Northern Tungus—probably Goldi modifications and Goldi Northern Tungus terms.** L. von Schrenck suspected that the centre from which shamanism had penetrated into the lower Amur was somewhere on the continent.*** The Goldi costume is still more convincing in this respect. In fact, the elements and terms they use clearly show their "origin" from two sources, namely, the Manchu complex, partly modified, and the Northern Tungus additions. Since the history of the formation of this group of ethnical units is now clear,**** the formation of a "mixed" complex of the shaman costume is also clear.

The above outlined four costume complexes can be traced in other shamanistic paraphernalia. I shall duly indicate it. In main lines we have already seen that the complex of spirits gives us the same kind of evidence.

105. DRUM Among the shamanistic paraphernalia, independent of the costume, the most important is the drum. Drums, regardless of their form and details, are used for shamanistic performances as a musical instrument for keeping the rhythm, for self-excitement of the shaman, and for influencing and regulating the psychic state of the audience. As to the musical character of this instrument, I shall leave it for a further treatment, and shall now confine myself to a description of the form of drums.

Among the Transbaikalian Reindeer Tungus the drum is called nimyaŋk'i [which is nomen agendi from nimɣa (Bir. Nerč. RTM), nimɣana (Ur. Castr.),—"to shamanize, to perform", (vide infra, p. 309)]. Among the Angara Tungus (Titov) it is n'amnánki (this transcription raises some doubts as well as nĭmnganki given by the same author for Nerč). But this term is unknown in the Tungus dialects of Manchuria, where the following words are used: uŋtuvun (Bir. Kum), uŋtuɣun (Khin), and untũvun (Ur. Castr.), untun (Lam. Tum.) which should be connected with untun (Manchu Writ)—"the drum", never used in Manchu Sp. for "shaman's drum". The Birarčen also use

* Cf. L. von Schrenck op. cit. Vol. III.
** Miss Czaplicka (op. cit., p. 210) with good reason has pointed out the Manchu and Tungus influence on the Gilak shamanistic complex.
*** Ibid. p. 121.
**** Cf. SONT and especially my "Northern Tungus Migrations. Goldi and their ethnical affinities".

another term—tuŋkä, which is the Manchu tuŋken—"a drum in general". The Manchu Sp. term is jimčin—jemčin, corresp. Manchu Writ. imči, imčin [cf. Goldi umčufu (Lopatin)]. Such a distribution of terms is very interesting for many a reason, both ethnographically and linguistically, especially when we compare the uniform distribution of the term for "drum-stick".

Among the Transbaikalian Tungus the drum is found to be of two forms, namely, a regular oval and an egglike, the greatest length being between sixty-five and seventy centimetres. The rim, from six to eight centimetres wide, made of larch or birch wood, is covered on one side either with the skin of Cervus Elaphus, or with that of Alces Alces, so that the edges of the skin cover the rim and are fixed to its inside. The inside of the drum has a large ring placed approximately in the centre and held by thongs attached to the small rings fixed at the rim, so that they form a cross with a large ring in the middle. The thongs may be partly or totally replaced by the movable iron pieces with the thongs attached to the small rings of the rim and with the large iron ring. This construction is used for holding the drum in the left hand (for right-handed persons). Instead of a ring, a cross about fifteen centimetres long can be used.

At the internal side of the rim there are two iron braces with eight flat iron disks, with a hole in the centre as trinkets. They are called sekan,—"the ear-ring". A variable number of conical trinkets may also be attached to the rim. Once, I saw four pairs, but there may be only two or eight pairs as well, but always by pairs. Other various placings and trinkets may be attached in the upper part of the drum on a special brace, e.g. I have observed a combination of a quadruped animal, a human face (báda), a bell and a conical trinket.

The external part, used for drumming, is covered with various designs, some of which I shall now describe as an illustration.

I. As a whole, the design represents dunda, the earth, as a firm part of the world; the shaman may use his drum as a canoe for crossing the sea. The design executed with double lines reproduces that found on the apron (vide supra p. 289). At a certain distance two lines corresponding to the actual form of the drum make a frame for the design, so that the internal lines are connected with the central design, while a double line runs near the border of the drum. Between the lower four pairs of lines eight lines connect the outer double lines. Two pairs of anthropomorphic images are placed on the left and right sides of the group of eight lines near to them. The part of the drum outside of the lines had in the upper section eight and at the lower part six pairs of anthropomorphic images. Between these two groups, on each side, the following animals are represented: the Alces Alces, the Cervus Elaphus, the roe-deer, the musk-deer, the cow, and the domesticated reindeer.

II. No design is placed in the middle of the drum. Between two lines there are two pairs of anthropomorphic images in the upper part and the same number in the lower part, and on both sides four animal images: Alces Alces, Cervus Elaphus, and two domesticated reindeer—a male and a female.

III. From a double lined circle in the middle eight double lines are brought to the border of the drum, representing eight legs on which the Earth is standing in the sea.

In other drums I could see no definite designs, for they were worn out by the use of the instrument.

The usual colours used for the designs are graphite, oxide of iron, colouring matter of the bark of some shrubs etc., which are common among these groups.

The drum-stick is *giss* (Barg. Nerč.). The term is interesting. We find in the same sense: *g'iš* (Ang. Tit.), *g'isavun* (Bir.), *g'is'ivun* (Khin. Kum.) (Neg. Sch.), *gisivun* (Mank.), *g'es'il* (Goldi, Lop.), *gehun* (Lam), *jehun* (Tum) *g'izun* (Manchu Sp.), which, I think, should be connected with *gisun* (Manchu Writ.)—"the word, speech" [in Manchu Writ. *gisun k'exe*—"the drum stick"]. All Tungus say that the drum "is speaking."* Among the Transbaikalian Tungus it represents a slightly bent wooden piece from three to four centimetres wide and from thirty to forty centimetres long, with a handle somewhat smoothed and rounded. The side used for drumming is covered with a piece of reindeer skin (with the hair). The opposite side is sometimes supplied with two or eight iron rings which act as trinkets.

Among the Nomad Tungus (Urulga, Barguzin and Mankova) the drum and stick are similar to the above described.

My information regarding the drum and drum stick among the Reindeer Tungus of Manchuria is confined to the statements of the old people. I have already pointed out that the costume was like that of the Yakuts. The same is true of the drum. The drum stick was always of wood and represented the head of an eagle, evidently borrowed from the Yakuts.**

Among the Khingan Tungus the drum has a regular round form or slightly oval and egg-like. It is not so deep as that of the Transbaikalian Tungus, three or four centimetres only, and it is smaller in diameter. There may be no design, nor ornaments. The internal side is supplied with a large iron cross, every branch of which is attached to the rim with two thongs. In the upper part of the drum, on the left side, there is a small hole,—it is "the drum's ear". The skin used for the drum must be only that of a male roe-deer; skins of other animals are not used. There may be also designs about which I shall now give some details.

I. A special construction—*turu*—is painted; it consists of two poles standing upright and connected by a cross beam (there may be two cross beams), used in some important performances of a personal character; (instead of poles there may be two trees with branches); around the *turu* there can be different animals, as shown in the case II.

II. In the centre of the drum stands the shaman with his drum turned westward (the top of the drum is the north) and surrounded by a circle; the body of the shaman is symbolized by a circle; another circle, that passes near the border, leaves on both sides, at the top and foot, a space for four pine trees, between which images of the following animals are extending from West to North: Cervus Elaphus, domesticated reindeer, roe-deer, bear, tiger, dragon ("thunder" with legs, it is neither an animal nor a man), bustard, swan, hare, goose, and at least two cuckoos and *urokono*, which can swallow a man (evidently some big sea animal).* The stick is a simple piece of wood slightly worked out. Nothing particular can be noticed on it. The drums have sometimes an iron ring, instead of a cross, for holding them.

Among the Birarčen the form of the drum is similar to the above described. All drums which I have seen had neither ornaments, nor designs. However, the Birarčen told me that perhaps there had been formerly some designs. Some trinkets (*g'irg'iwlan*), like those described before, are usually attached to the rim (*uŋ*); the latter is made of larch tree (species growing in a twisted form; very strong wood used for carving utensils), and the drum is covered with the summer skin (rather thin) of Cervus Elaphus. The drum-stick is usually made as among the Khingan Tungus; but once I saw a drum-stick made of tendons of Cervus Elaphus covered with roe-deer skin (with hair). Such a stick is very elastic, but it requires a special skill in drumming.

Among the Kumarčen I have seen details of only one drum which did not differ from that just described.

Among the Manchus the drum, being always of a round shape, very shallow and of small size, is made of common wood covered with roe-deer skin, with a handle of the same type as that above described among the Khingan Tungus, and supplied with "ear-rings" and trinkets. It is sometimes covered with painted flowers, butterflies and small birds of an ornamental meaning. The drums are made by craftsmen, sometimes Chinese. The drum-stick is an ordinary wooden stick covered with the fur skin of pole-cat (*soloŋgo*). The drum used by the *p'oyun saman* is exactly the same as that used by the *amba saman*. The shamans usually have two drums, one of which is drummed during the performance, while the other is dried on the open fire to make it better sounding, and so they are used alternatively. This holds good for all Tungus shamans, but not all of them can afford to have two drums.

In so far as I know, the drum of this type is also met with among the Dahurs and Chinese (*n'ikan*) shamans; several drums which I saw were similar.

It is worth mentioning that during the sacrifice performed by the Manchu *p'oyun saman*, besides the shaman's drum the following instruments are used:

---

* For comparative purposes, Ur. Castr. is *toibur* borrowed from the Buriat (Castr.) *toibur*. Other terms exist among the Turkic and Mongol groups. However, the Dahur term *g'asūr* seems to be connected with the Manchu term. P. Šimkevič gives the Goldi term *ges's'el s'con'i*, which is still more curious, for it means "drum-stick of the shaman's spirit", i.e. "word, speech of the spirit". It should also be noted that Manchu Writ. *gisun*, according to P. P. Schmidt (Chin. Elem. p. 246), is a loan-word from the Chinese gü-dzy [句子] which is not met with in Nuichen. No other possible etymology is seen in Tungus.

** In this connexion I must point out that the eagle does not play any important part in the Manchu-Tungus shamanism. True, among the Tungus eagle feathers are sometimes used, as well as skins and feathers of other birds (cf. supra, among the Goldi), but there is nothing specific in it which would permit to building up theories such as that of L. Sternberg ("The Cult of Eagle", Vol. V, Mesc. of Mus. of Anthr. and Ethn. 1925).

* During our stay among this group the Tungus saw me doing some water colour "painting" and, knowing my experience in shamanism, asked me to paint the above indicated figures. I did it naturally by restoring what could be seen on the drum and what was indicated to me by the shaman. As this production was one of a "foreign master", I decided to put a mark of distinction for warning further collectors of ethnographic specimens (I knew at that time of some regrettable occurrences of such kind!). I did not sign my name, but wrote down the following (textually): "sic transit gloria mundi! made by N. N. 1915 VI 27". I wonder if this drum has been collected and is in some Museum, and some studious ethnographer is puzzled by it.

(1) A small barrel shaped drum called *tuŋken*, with both sides covered with roe-deer skin, the sound being produced with two wooden sticks. The drum is put on a wooden stand. This is a common Chinese instrument, borrowed by the Manchus together with the term.

(2) Wooden castanets, several or only a pair, of common Chinese type. Both instruments are indicated as ritual instruments used in the Imperial family (cf. figures in L. Langlès', and Ch. Harlez' works).

The Manchu type of the drum is met with among other groups, where the Manchu costume is found. Among the Gilaks, Udehe, Oroči, and Goldi the drum is a little larger, —but not always—very shallow and usually without any pictures. Among the Goldi (cf. I. Lopatin, op. cit. p. 262) the form is ellipsoid (?, I think egg-like), and it is a little larger than the Manchu drum. No iron cross is mentioned, but a system of thongs is used for holding the drum.

The geographical distribution of this form overlaps that of the Manchu costume and spreads further over the Tungus of Manchuria. It differs from that used by the Tungus of Transbaikalia. The latter seems to be connected with the still more complicated form of drum used by the Yakuts. The Yakut drum is even supplied with resonators, and is much deeper.[*] This form in its full complex shape is found among the Central Asiatic groups, such as the Soyots, Altaians, and others. The last form, instead of having a cross or a ring used for holding the drum, is supplied with a wooden heavy handle diametrically fixed to the rim. Lastly, mention should be made of the Chukchi drum with a wooden handle to which it is fixed, as it is in the Tibetan big round drum, both sides of which are covered with skin. Thus the Chukchi drum is a half of the Tibetan one. It was connected by H. Balfour with the Eskimo form, but I do not think that it could be pretended that the Eskimo form is the initial one. With a still greater probability it may be supposed that the Tibetan round form with a wooden handle was the first to spread in Asia, including the Eskimos, and was preserved among the Chukchi and Eskimos, but modified and complicated, especially by the Central Asiatic groups.[**] As a matter of fact, on the periphery of the drum-territory we meet chiefly with small round unornamented drums, with and without a wooden handle, while the nearer we come to the regions of Central Asia, the more the drum becomes complex, with local variations of shape and details. Various hypotheses can be built up as to the original inventors of the various forms, also of their sequence, but in my eyes such hypotheses are very risky, for a complexity of Central Asiatic forms may be of a secondary origin, while the relative simplicity of the Reindeer Tungus drum may be a result of the reduction of the original complex form, as well as a local variation of a still simpler form. Moreover, the question as to the Manchu drum may be solved not as a variation of Central Asiatic form, but as a continuity of some earlier "drum", and even of a non-Tungus origin somewhere in present China.

The most interesting fact is that the geographical distribution of the drum-forms does not correspond at all to that of the forms of the costumes. This fact goes parallel with other similar facts, all of which point to the need of a careful approach to the problem of "migration" and formation of complexes.

The methods of holding the drum are different. In the Manchu-Goldi method the upper part of the drum is kept very near the head of the drummer, while in the Northern Tungus method the shaman holds the drum at a certain, rather great distance. The change of the position of the drum influences partly the character of the sound (*vide infra* Section 119).

106. BRASS MIRRORS I shall not repeat now what has been written as a statement of facts and mostly as a guess, for this may carry our discussion too far. From the facts expounded in connexion with the description of costumes we can see that the brass mirrors, formerly widely used in China and still preserved in the Buddhistic complex, evidently have their own principal centre of diffusion and two rather interesting centres of a seemingly secondary growth. We have seen that brass mirrors are called among all ethnical groups here discussed by the same term of the steam *tVt* (*vide supra* p. 278). Among the Reindeer Tungus it is believed to have a mysterious origin from the earth, and it is so rare that not all shamans can afford to have one. It should be noted that among the Yakuts and their western and northern neighbours, it is lacking. When we move southwards and eastwards it becomes more frequent. In the Manchu costume it is a piece of great importance, but there are already several brass-mirrors which still have a certain significance. However, in imitation of the Manchus, the Tungus of Manchuria have come to use the mirrors not only as objects with a certain meaning, but also as mere rattles and ornaments. Besides, as there is no possibility of getting so many genuine mirrors, the Tungus use modern imitations. In the Birarčen complex all iron parts may be replaced by the brass mirrors, and thus to manifest a secondary growth of the phenomenon. It would not be very hazardous to suppose that the Manchus are responsible for this abuse of brass mirrors, while the original idea of using them is not a Manchu one. In fact, in other ethnical groups, such as the Chinese, Mongols, and Tibetans, these mirrors were known much earlier.

The "meaning" of the mirror is not the same among the ethnical groups here discussed. For instance, the Transbaikalian Tungus usually regard it as a means to see the world, i.e. it is used for the concentration of the mind and bringing one's self into a state of a light extasy, as will be shown later. The Birarčen consider it as an important placing for the principal spirits of the shaman, and use it in this function. The Goldi consider it as a mirror in which human deeds are reflected; but they also use it for self-protection against the spirits' arrows (cf. I. Lopatin, op. cit. p. 231 also P. Šimkevič, "Material, etc."). The last function is also that of the Manchu mirror. It was also said to function, among some western Tungus groups, as the "sun",[*] which theoretically is also possible.

---

[*] The drums with resonators may also be met with, but occasionally, among the Northern Tungus groups who are in contact with the Yakuts.

[**] Cf. W. Schmidt, op. cit. p. 338, where he makes the suggestion of connecting the Eskimo form with the Buddhistic complex. Indeed, the transmitting links might be the continental groups, as well as the early coastal migrations.

[*] The identification of the mirror with the "sun" is as doubtful as the identification of all round pieces with the "sun" or "moon". Such was the case with the wooden and metallic face-like placings bäda, interpreted, according to the European complex, as a "symbol"

The enumeration of various functions of the brass mirrors shows that a brass mirror is one thing and its interpretation another thing. Moreover, the variable use of brass mirrors shows another aspect. As an element of cultural complex it may perform various "functions" and have a different "weight" in the complex, which partly depends on the possibility of getting brass-mirrors and partly on their "meaning". Naturally, their complete lack may produce one of the following three different effects, namely: (1) the loss of its use; (2) the substitution of some other material for the old symbol; (3) the manufacture of false mirrors. All three cases have been observed. However, I must point out that the substitution is sometimes difficult to be detected. For instance "round pieces" of iron symbolizing in some case the "sun", e.g. in the Yakut costume, may have a quite independent "origin". Thus the "sun" exists in the Birarčen complex of malu, without being connected with the brass-mirror; in another case an iron disk may temporarily symbolize the brass-mirror, which is rarely observed among the Tungus; however, it will not symbolize the "sun".[*]

107. PLACINGS FOR SPIRITS AND VARIA   Among all groups the shamans have special placings for the spirits. These can be divided into permanent and temporary ones. Here I shall confine myself only to a short description of the permanent placings, the temporary ones being reserved for treatment at the corresponding places in the description of performances.

Among the permanent placings we can distinguish those which are common to all people of the given group and those which are particular to the shamans. The first group has already been described, so that it can now be

pointed out that the shamans usually have placings for their clan spirits, which may be large in size and carefully made.

Among the Reindeer Tungus of Transbaikalia, in addition to a great number of bāda, there are special wooden placings for various dayačan ("master", vide Section 41), such as that of the bear and others. Without their help the shaman "may perish". During performances the placings are hung up at a post or at one of the poles of the wigwam. Apparently some of these placings (sevak'i) are transmitted from one shaman to another. I have seen some of them which were over one hundred years old.

Among the Khingan Tungus I have carefully examined the contents of a box with placings of a female shaman and I have found out that, besides the ordinary malu (kayan) of a larger size than usual, there were Chinese pictures of the Taoistic complex, pictures of various Bodhisattvas, etc., as well as several placings for burkan (apparently jerga and others) and a wooden "tiger".

Almost all shamans among the Tungus of Manchuria have a wooden face deregde (cf. bāda) ornamented with glass beads, hair and moustaches. The "face" is attached to the costume only during the shamanizing, when the spirit malu is called in. When the shaman wants the spirit to come in he may also put deregde over his face, and all manifestations of malu (there are at least twelve) may then come into the shaman, for they know that the principal one is in.[*]

Together with the placings for spirits tallies must be mentioned, which are used by all shamans of Manchuria. A tally is a wooden stick, sometimes three-angular in cross section, with marks made with a knife, for keeping records of the number of times every spirit has come. One day I

---

[*] of the sun, whence a theory, of "sun-worship" and other scaffoldings originated. The sun may be one of the elements, and actually it is found very commonly; but it is very far from the "solar mythology" of Europeans. Cf. J. G. Georgi's "Bemerkungen", interpreted by C. Hikisch "Die Tungusen", Dorpat, 1882 and maintained by other authors. J. G. Georgi could not enter into details, and G. Hikisch had a very confused idea about the Tungus, such as they are. However, since the mirrors have cyclic animals, the Tungus may know that this is a representation of one of the solar cycles, in short—the Sun.

[*] I also want to point out that it is very undesirable to classify elements of the shamanistic complex in general according to their importance, as does U. Holmberg ("The Shaman-Costume", 12) who, when speaking of "secondary objects", mentions "a kind of metal mirror". Indeed, as has been shown, brass-mirrors are in some Tungus complexes a central element of the paraphernalia complex and they may be a sufficient substitute for the whole costume. So they are of "primary importance" (vide infra, p. 289). There is another instance: the "horses" in the Tungus complex are of a secondary importance and may be made at the spot and thrown away, while in the Buriat costume, now used, they are the only a preserved element and thus function as an element of primary importance. In fact, anything in a complex may become of "primary importance", while an element formerly of "primary importance" may become one of "secondary importance" and even get lost altogether. However, it does not give us the right to speak of "degeneration"—a common opinion in works of the old school—as does the same author, for there may be cases of substitution, and, besides, this point of view presumes that formerly there was a costume composed of a great number of elements, which was not always the case, but may be an occurrence of a secondary character. The change of this complex does not mean "degeneration" of the complex of shamanism, but only its re-arrangement in the ethnical complex as a whole.

[*] It seems to have been identified as the "sun" by the early travellers, which is wrong. The greatest popularity of masks in Asia is observed among the Koriaks (cf. W. Jochelson, "The Koriaks"). Still more numerous are masks among the groups of North America, e.g. the Tlinghites (cf. S. A. Sternberg "Matériaux du Musée concernant le chamanisme des Tlinghites" in Publ. M. A. E. Vol. VI, 1927 pp. 79-115 in Russian). Since S. A. Sternberg points out some characters of distinction between the American and Siberian costumes, I want to make some remarks. She points out that the Tlinghit costume has no iron parts, while they abound in the Siberian costumes. But we have seen that the Manchu costume, the Birarčen costume, and even the Reindeer Tungus bird-costume may have not a single iron piece. Moreover the iron was only recently introduced in America. S. A. Sternberg says "the iron is here substituted by bone and only partly by brass" (p. 113). She points out the presence of trinkets and says that the drumming is done by the shaman's relatives and guests, which is not typical of Asia. This is also not correct. We have seen that castanets are used in the Manchu complex; at some moment the drumming must be done by other people among all Tungus. As has been stated "masks" are also met with in Siberia. The otter is met with in the Tungus shamanism (Birarčen). True, the neck-lace is lacking in most of the Asiatic costumes, but this is the only distinction of importance. In fact, the style of ornament and an evident fusion of "shamanism" with the "totemistic complex" are an original and local phenomenon. However, it is most evident that in different complexes of shamanism we always meet with "local" phenomena; so to meet with some "local" phenomena in America is still more natural. It should be noted that masks are used in shamanism only in particular cases. It is very likely that in the shamanism of the Manchu and that of some other groups masks were formerly used much more than now. But, the masks in the Tlinghit complex may have another "origin", i.e. an adaptation of an American complex to the needs of shamanism, and the masks of lamaistic performances (Tsam) must not be overlooked, when some masks and peculiar costumes of the Asiatic shamans are found.

saw twenty-six marks of the principal spirit (a female manifestation) which had come to a female-shaman (Khingan Tungus) ; in other cases the number was smaller. There may be several tallies, if the record is kept of several spirits. The tally may sometimes be supplied with a carved anthropomorphic image. It is kept with the placings.

Among the Tungus of Transbaikalia there is a special symbol of the earth (*dunda*), made of chamois, between ten and twelve centimetres wide and from ten to fifteen metres long, so that it may be fixed in the interior of the wigwam on the walls, the tail and the head being connected. There are really a head and a tail. It is called *javdar* (*javdar* is the plural of *javdan*). This term in Tungus may be connected with *jabdan* (Neg. Sch.),—"the snake", *tavjan~jabjan* (Bir. Kum.) [*jabjan* (Manchu, Writ. Sp)—"the boa constrictor" (*vide supra*, p. 73)].* Images of human beings, various animals and reindeer, usually painted or affixed, may be seen on the *javdar*. Together with the latter there are two *kulin* ("snakes") which maintain the Earth in the ocean and which are symbolized in the form of long (the same as *javdar*) twisted thongs, covered either with cloth or with chamois and supplied with eyes and mouths made of glass beads, and with tails of chamois split into two or three strips. The "snakes" are put round the wigwam together with the *javdar*.

Among the Khingan Tungus the *javdar* is made of cloth and to the same purpose. They are much poorer than those among the Reindeer Tungus, and they may even be reduced to a narrow strip without any design. Among the Birarčen *tabjan*—"the boa constrictor"—plays a part in the shamanism.

Various instruments are used by the Manchu shamans. Such ones are e.g. halberds, swords, tridents, war-axes, arrows, etc. When the shaman introduces into himself one of the spirits of the groups *mayi, baturi*, and others, he uses weapons and instruments characteristic of these manifestations. This group of paraphernalia is an imitation of the Chinese actors performing theatrical pieces and of Chinese pictures of various spirits. Some of them are even not met with in the Manchu complex. They do not exist in the complex of the Northern Tungus paraphernalia, and in the Manchu complex they are looked upon by the Manchus themselves as elements of a secondary importance. In fact, shamans sometimes use these paraphernalia when they wish to produce an impression on the audience; but, at least at present, most of the shamans do not use them at all.

Besides the above described musical instruments used by *p'oyen saman*, as well as some special utensils used by the Manchus and Tungus, described in the sections dealing with the sacrifices, the Tungus and Manchus have no more special shamanistic paraphernalia.**

108. ATTITUDE TOWARDS THE PARAPHERNALIA Our description of the shaman costume would not be complete, if we do not give details as to the Tungus attitude regarding the costume. Un-

---

* This term seems to be met with among the Nomad Tungus of Urulga, as *jabdar* referred to the strips attached to the shaman's head-dress.

** In different publications on this subject some other musical instruments were mentioned among other groups, e.g. the so-called Jews' harp, balalaika (Russian) and others. However, admitting

---

fortunately the early authors sometimes give quite a wrong picture. Remaining within the Tungus groups I have again to quote I. A. Lopatin who, by the way, reflects rather well the common attitude of ethnographers. In reference to the Goldi he speaks of the sacredness of the costume (op. cit. p. 259). His predecessors, such as L. von Schrenck, P. Šimkevič, S. Brailovskiĭ, P. Margaritov and others, did the same, when they considered the objects here discussed as "religious", "sacred", etc. Such an approach is entirely erroneous as a formulation of facts and as a method. This is a simple transplanting of the European religious complex into a distinctly different one. I do not deny that in some cases there may be a complex approaching "sacredness", as opposed to the complex of profane things and persons,* but no such facts are observed among the Tungus groups.

The Tungus attitude towards the costume is defined by the following conditions: the costume is a placing for the shaman's spirits; the costume may gather other spirits, and the latter may come into a conflict with the shaman's spirits; the women who have menstruations may frighten the spirits, for they have special spirits, or the other spirits are afraid of blood.

Since the making (sewing) of clothes is generally carried out by women, there is no exception for the shaman's costume. It is desirable that the costume be made by women who have no menstruations, i.e. by very young girls and old women, but if there is no such women, the sewing may be done by any other woman. However, when the work is finished, the costume must be "purified" with smoke of plants used for this purpose. Among the Manchus the work is done by girls and widows. The iron and brass parts are made by common smiths, usually Chinese.

The shaman's costume in the Manchu complex is considered as *vočkoĭ ètku*, i.e. "a dress of spirits". Therefore one must not use bad expressions when speaking about the costume, one must not do anything which might offend the spirits, e.g. spit, etc. Thus, the costume must be treated in absolutely the same manner as the other placings for spirits, e.g. the ribbons etc.

Since the shamans are acting on behalf of their clans, the making of a costume is a clan business, and the clansmen contribute to it. When the costume is worn out, or burnt,** a new one is made; but parts of a costume may also be

---

that they may be used by the shamans in general and not during the performance, they are not elements which must be included into shamanism as a complex.

* e.g. A. V. Anoxin (op. cit.) gives a description of the process of receiving a new costume by the shaman who is inspired by his chief spirit. The costume must be altered, if it is required by the spirit, and after this it may be used. I do not understand why this author says that the costume becomes a "sacred garment" after the corrections are made. He points out that the female cannot put on a male-costume and vice versa, but this has nothing to do with the sacredness, for e.g. the woman cannot wear or touch a dress belonging to a male, and a stranger would not risk to touch the things worn by a female. We have seen that among the Tungus such an attitude is inspired by the idea of special properties of woman's blood. The same is known of other groups in Asia. Such an "impurity" of the woman has nothing to do with their "non-sacredness". A. V. Anoxin points out that the costume must be isolated from other things (i.e. clothes), which is not a sign of sacredness, but a means of avoidance of bringing the costume in contact with the things which may be placings for other spirits and which may receive the spirits from the shaman's costume. Indeed, no idea of sacredness may here be involved.

** A great number of costumes were burnt during the Boxer rebellion in Manchuria.

renewed, or repaired. The costume can be given up on various occasions.

1. If a clan cannot afford to have a shaman (e.g. when the clan is too small), the costume is brought to the forest, on a mountain, and hung up on a tree. After a certain time the spirits may leave the costume, and then it becomes simply an old, useless thing. If a new shaman appears, it will be necessary to make a new costume, and the spirits will enter into it.

2. If a clan wants to make a new costume, the old one is brought away as in the first case, but the spirits are asked to move to a new costume. Their entering is recognized by the fact that the shaman feels them and is able to shamanize in the new costume.

3. Somebody makes a present of a new garment to the shaman, and the old costume can be taken away.

No renewing of costumes is at present practised, the chief reason of which is the prohibition of shamanism by the Chinese authorities. Under this pretext the clansmen very often refuse to contribute their money. Such a condition could be created only in the present relative decline of shamanism and in the ethnical disintegration of the Manchus in general.

It is believed that when the shaman introduces into himself the spirit of fire (cf. *supra* p. 128), the costume would not burn, even though the shaman should jump into a heap of burning charcoal; however, if there is no spirit, the costume would burn as any other thing, in spite of the fact that it was being used as a placing for other spirits. Generally it is believed that if there is no costume, the spirit (*vočko*) would not come, and the shamanizing without costume is not regarded as a real shamanizing. There must be at least a *s'iša* and *toli*.

After the shaman's death, the costume may be handed over to *jarumbo*, i.e. to the house which used the shaman's assistance (details will be given later), where it will be preserved until a new shaman appears. Only some of the paraphernalia used for the secondary spirits, e.g. the trident, swords, axes, etc. are buried together with the shaman. If one of the children of the deceased shaman has been inclined, during his father's life, to become a shaman, the costume would remain in the shaman's family. However, the question as to whether the candidate would become a shaman or not, is decided by the clan.

The drum and other instruments have nothing sacred in them, but there is a strict recommendation to avoid the production of sound, when the shaman does not act, the reason being that the spirits may respond on the drumming by coming and entering the people who cannot master them. On the same ground the shaman's costume cannot be put on by people who are not certain of being able to master the spirits. It is clearly shown by the fact that the Manchus did not oppose my looking for details and handling the costume as much as I wanted: in their opinion, my attitude would not be offensive to the spirits. In this way the Manchus, who are experienced and "strong in spirits", do touch the costume without harm to themselves and to the spirits. Some who are not afraid may even put on the costume. Playing with the drum, when there is no danger of attracting the spirits, is very common. So one may see before and after shamanizing "fearless" persons who touch the paraphernalia and beat the drum.* During the performance many people also touch the shaman's paraphernalia, especially the drums and special instruments.

Certain precautions are used when the costume is carried from one place to another, but these precautions are of the same character as those of avoiding contact with other spirits, particularly the hostile spirits, keeping off woman's blood, and abstaining from useless disturbance of the spirits.

The same attitude is characteristic of other Tungus groups. As among the Manchus, the costume is a clan affair. The clan has to decide about it and usually helps in making it. Among all Tungus groups the costume is made by the women. It is desirable that they be of the age when there is no menstruation. If there is no such woman, any one can do it, but the costume, when ready, must be purified with the smoke of certain plants. The metallic parts are made by specialists—rarely by Tungus, but more commonly by Buriats, Yakuts, and other neighbouring groups,—while the wooden parts are made by the Tungus themselves. The costume is a placing for the shaman's spirits, so that when he or she puts it on, the spirit will come into the shaman almost without fail. The costume must therefore not be put on by people who cannot master the spirits. The people's fear of touching it is the fear of introducing the spirit into themselves. As among the Manchus, the idea of avoiding women's blood inspires certain precautions in the women's coming into a contact with the costume. However, there are some parts, as for instance *toli* in *arkaptun*, which may be left near a woman, when she is attended by a shaman, and there is no danger for the spirits or the shaman. Thus, there are spirits which are not afraid of woman's spirits, and in this case the woman may touch some paraphernalia of a shaman. Such ones are spirits of her own clan and those of her husband's with which she has become familiar and which are familiar with her. In fact, it must be so in principle, for female-shamans are common among both Manchus and Tungus. There is, however, a limitation, namely, when the female-shaman is menstruating, she does not touch the spirits' placing. Thus it is generally recommended to be careful with the shaman's costume. When the costume is carried on reindeer back or on horse back, it is put separately and is supplied with special thongs for packing.

The shaman's costume, among the Birarčen, remains for six days in the wigwam (or house) where the shamanizing was performed. Some parts of the costume may remain still longer. For instance, the *toli* is sometimes left for years in the home of a child, when the child's soul was saved by the shaman. In this case the spirit "placed" in the *toli* would watch over the child's soul.

After the shaman's death the costume is put on a special scaffold, near his or her tomb. Among the Tungus who are settled in villages the costume is kept in the house. There are still some spirits which place themselves in the costume, so that the Tungus say: the costume may show signs of life—it trembles and makes a noise with its iron and brass parts. A candidate for shamanship would know exactly in his dreams where the costume is and would come

---

* Every assistant shaman must practise drumming before he can assist the shaman; I did it myself quite commonly without producing any negative reaction in the Manchus, even when I was not performing my duty as an assistant-shaman.

to that spot. Then the costume might be bought (among the Birarčen), for a horse or so, from the relatives of the deceased shaman. However, the costume cannot leave the clan, and it will not be taken by a new shaman, if the spirits of the deceased shaman are hostile to him, or vice versa. The perishable parts may be renewed, so only the metallic parts are taken. In this way the costume may be transmitted from one to another generation, but always within the same clan.

However, the costume, even though carefully kept in the house or near the tomb, is a source of worry, for the spirits are in it. The costume cannot be thrown away, for there are spirits in it, and if they get free, they may bother the people. Therefore the Tungus always face the following problem: whether it is better to send off the spirits together with the costume, or to leave a permanent placing for them and thereby to avoid the creation of a new shaman. In case the spirits do not bother the people, it is very likely that the people who keep the costume would try to get rid of it without destroying it, i.e. to send the spirits off together with their placings. As a matter of fact, the spirits may leave the costume at any moment* and again make trouble to the clansmen; it is therefore safer to send off the costume and the spirits. Naturally, in the taiga there are many costumes which are left untouched and finally are altogether forgotten.

Among the Tungus groups the shaman may gradually renew his or her costume, so that during the life-time all parts may gradually be replaced. We have already seen that there may even be made two costumes for different forms of shamanizing.

The same attitude is characteristic of the Tungus with reference to the drum. The Tungus attach to it no idea of sacredness. The drum is merely an instrument. I have seen among the Khingan Tungus a man who, wanting to shamanize, used an ordinary enamel basin ("made in Japan") as a drum (cf. infra. Section 128). What the shamans need is an *instrument*. However, some ideas ensuing from the complex "instrument" are also connected with drum. As with the Manchus, the drumming without the intention of calling out the spirits is not practised, especially in the dark, for the spirits may arrive. For this reason the Tungus dislike idle drumming and use to stop it. However, when such a danger is out of question, one is allowed to joke and to beat the drum, provided that the drum is not damaged, e.g. by drunken people.

The drum may also be used in the treatment of certain diseases, but then it is used only as an instrument, e.g. for gathering swallowed things, as in the case of a swallowed and rejected needle, of the kidney of a sacrificial animal eaten by one of the persons who attended a sacrifice, etc.

109. CONCLUSION From the above given description of the shaman's costumes and other paraphernalia the following general inference can be made: *the complex of paraphernalia is formed of elements of various "origins"; the elements may assume different functions in the given complex; in different complexes the same elements may have different importance (weight).*

Naturally a general question arises as to the reason of the existence of the costume. In fact, such a question has been several times put by several authors and answered by them in various ways in accordance with their own complexes.* V. M. Mixaĭlovskiĭ,** who made forty years ago an attempt to deal with shamanism, put special emphasis on three conditions, namely, the costume is needed for making an impression upon the audience; the sounding parts are needed for impressing the sense of hearing; the components of the costume have a symbolic meaning connected with shamanism. Such an interpretation does not help much and is not correct. First of all, shamanism cannot be explained as "an intentional production of impression", for, as has been shown, such is not the nature of shamanism. This was the point of view of early travellers and missionaries who believed that the shamans are knaves and impostors who want to produce an impression on ignorant people.*** It is quite true that the costume, as such, is a musical instrument as well, and we shall later discuss this subject, when the performance is described. We shall then also show what influence the same musical instrument may have

* Owing to this, the acquisition of old costumes does not present great difficulties among the Tungus—the costume has nothing sacred, nor any memorial value for the living people. The only question is whether it is possible to hope that the spirits may be carried away by the new owner or not. The second question is, that if the shamans have already left the costume they may introduce themselves into one of the clansmen and a new costume will be needed which is a costly thing. Therefore, in a case of a shaman who was drowned together with two other women, by accident during the drifting of ice in the Amur River, it was possible for me to buy her costume, which remained in the family for several years, for a price below that of the brass alone. Moreover, after having bought the costume, I received gratis other things, e.g. an ukoptun, etc. which belonged to her, but were kept in other families. I was told: "We are glad you are taking away the costume and all paraphernalia, for perhaps you will carry away to St. Petersburg not only them but also all the spirits". The costume in question is supposed to be in my collections of Tungus of Manchuria in the Museum of the Academy of Sciences of St. Petersburg.

* It would be futile to discuss all kinds of guesses, e.g. regarding the animal form of the costumes. For instance, Karjalainen conjectured that the shaman must "hide his everyday appearance in order to remain untroubled at other times from the side of the spirits which he must raise for the performance of his duties" (I quote U. Holmberg, op. cit. pp. 20-21.), while Kai Donner remarks, by the way, that the shaman bore a cap embellished with the sign of his "totem-animal" (quoted by U. Holmberg, ibid.). E. K. Pekarskiĭ and V. Vasilev ["Coat and Drum of the Yakut shaman" in "Mater. conc. Ethnography of Russia" (Russian Museum of Emperor Alexander III) St. Petersburg, 1910, vol. I], who gave a description of the Yakut costume, and A. V. Anoxin, ("Materials concerning shamanism among the Altaians" in Publ. of Mus. of Anthrop. and Ethn. of RAS. vol. IV, 1924, pp. 1-148), who gave a description of the Altaian costume, are much more sound in this respect.
** V. M. Mixaĭlovskiĭ, "The Shamanism" (in Russian), Moskow 1892. Soc. of Friends of A. and Eth. I. U. M. This work is now out of date and, in so far as "theory" is concerned, is not to be considered as a reliable source.
*** In the same manner speaks I. A. Lopatin (op. cit. p. 259), when he asserts that the costume of the Goldi shaman shows a tendency to produce on the spectator an impression of "something supernatural and divine" and in this way to dispose the spectator to "prayer and reverence". As a matter of fact, the spectators have nothing to do with prayers and reverence. I. A. Lopatin is wrong when he asserts that the shaman produces a very strong impression on the Goldi, when he is dressed in a costume. We shall later see that the Tungus and Goldi do not react in this way on the costumes, but if they really are afraid of something, they fear only spirits which may be introduced into the placings of the costumes. In the descriptions of ethnographers of all sorts of nations the shaman's costumes and the shamans themselves produce a greater impression upon the reader, than they do upon the natives, whose reaction is usually quite different and is brought about by other motives.

on the shaman himself. It is also perfectly true that the costume has a symbolic meaning, as has been shown in the analysis of the costume. But the question is: what is the purpose of having such symbols and various instruments which are not symbolic? This cannot be answered before we analyse the psychological conditions of the audience and the shaman during the performances, I shall therefore leave this question unanswered for the time being.

CHAPTER XXV

SHAMANISTIC PERFORMANCES (DESCRIPTION)

The present chapter is devoted to a description of various forms of shamanistic performances and to special cases which we shall need later. Indeed, I bring first these facts which perhaps will not be fully understood without reading the following chapters; but as I have no other means to expound the facts, I have to follow the chosen way, namely, to proceed from facts to their analysis. Thus the present chapter will deal only with the statement of facts. It should be noted that I shall not give all cases observed, for a great number of facts are subject to a classification, and it will be sufficient to give only some typical cases, and some special cases which cannot easily be classified. In exposing the facts I shall not give all details in every case, but shall give only schemes, for the details are repeated and recombined, according to single cases of shamanizing and to the shaman's personal choice.

The verbal forms for "to shamanize" may be derived in the various dialects from *saman*. Thus we have in RTM *sama* (+suff.), in Mank. *sama+da*, in Bir. *samda*, in Tum. *xamal*, in Lam. *xamandal*, and in Manchu *samdamb'i* all of which may be translated—"to shamanize". However, this term is lacking in several dialects, e.g. in Barg. Nerč. Khin, apparently also in Kum. In Bir. *samda* is certainly a loan-word from the Manchu *samda*, which is a contracted form of *sama+(n)+da*, where *da* is a common suffix, *n* and *a* of the stem have been contracted. It should be noted that the final *n* is subject to omission in all cases except Lam., where the stem *saman* is increased by two suffixes (+*da*+l). It is also curious that in Mank. the stem *samal* is a plural form of *saman*. These facts complete my discussion of the etymology of *saman* in Tungus. Besides these terms there are other various terms used by the Tungus and Manchus for "to carry out such and such a shamanistic performance". As far as I know, there is no special and general term. These terms will be analysed in due course.

110. SHAMANIZING TO THE SPIRITS OF THE LOWER WORLD Among the Bargu-zin and Nerčinsk Tungus a special form of shamanizing is distinguished in which the shaman enters into contact with the spirits of the lower world. The occasions for this form of shamanizing are usually troubles among the clansmen, which may assume greater or smaller dimensions according to the number of people affected and the intensity of individual sufferings. The troubles may differ in character and consist in psychomental disequilibrium, psychomental unrest affecting hunting ability, various sicknesses, and even "lack of luck" in everyday's life. A shaman may be asked to find out the cause. In a special performance, when the shaman calls into himself a spirit, he would find out, with the help of the spirit, the nature of troublesome spirits and ways to neutralize them. In this "small shamanizing" he finds out what has to be done. Thus it may be found out that the spirits of the lower world are responsible, and the only way to neutralize them is to offer them a sacrifice in the lower world and to speak to them "nicely".

As shown, besides various spirits the lower world —*orgi dunda*—is also peopled by the ancestors' and recently deceased people's souls. The latter have an especially great importance, for these persons may be known personally to the living people, and it is very likely that they may raise particularly strong emotions, especially in children, widows and widowers.

This form of shamanizing is defined by the term *örgisk'i*, which is used as a "noun", although the literal meaning is "in the direction of *örgi*" or "lower, western (side)" (cf. my "N. T. Terms of orientation", p. 179). The chief action is a sacrifice. The only sacrificial animal which can be used is an adult reindeer. Special preparations for a sacrifice must be made, including temporary placings and the shaman's instruments. During the day or early evening the following things are prepared of larch tree wood:

1. Four narrow planks, about 140—160 centimetres long with a symbolized head; these are four "fishes" (*oldól*) which form a raft on which the shaman crosses the sea (Lake Baikal) for taking the sacrificial animal to the lower world.

2. A piece, 60 centimetres long and 8 or 10 centimetres in diameter, with an end sharpened like a tail and another one supplied with two horns; it symbolizes *tóli~jóli*,—"the taimen" (Lenok Taimen of salmo), which breaks through the rocks, clears up the road from stones and also helps in the sea-voyage; it is put between *oldól*—fishes.

3. Two stylized bears which go ahead of the shaman, and two stylized boars which keep the raft afloat, if it sinks on the way; and on the land they clear the road through the thick forest.

4. Four small fishes which go ahead of the raft in the sea.

5. Four elks (Alces Alces)—in the form of a piece of a young thin larch tree, about 60 centimetres long—which show the way when the shaman is coming back and which help to row on the raft.

6. Four pieces, wooden planks about 30 centimetres long and 10 centimetres wide, put together to form *gula*—the house in which the people live in the lower world (It should be noted that in the lower world people are living in houses instead of wigwams!).

7. Four anthropomorphic small pieces called *toyoljin* (plur, *toyoljir*) which symbolize spirits watching the four corners of *gula*; the legs and arms are lacking, the pyramidal upper part, with symbols for eyes and mouth, symbolizes the head.

8. Four anthropomorphic pieces called *toyoman* (plur. *toyomar*) which symbolize spirits which help the shaman to take the sacrifice to the lower world; the form is about the same as (7).

9. An anthropomorphic placing made of rotten larch tree, with arms, legs, a carved head, with eyes and mouth, called *séva* (or *sévaja*), which is the shaman's spirit helping him to carry the sacrifice; a symbolized knife with a "belt" is attached to the *séva*.

10. Two wooden staffs with an end split, to symbolize the reindeer foot, called *oror* ("the reindeer") on which the shaman travels on the land.

11. Two special "purifying instruments" called *s'ipkan* or *ŏ'ipkanin* each made of four or eight narrow wooden pieces with notches on one side, put together to form a quadrangle with the notches inside; they are used for purifying the persons present at the performance in order to remove the spirits which might come into the people during the performance and later enter into conflict with the other spirits.

Direction in which things are thrown

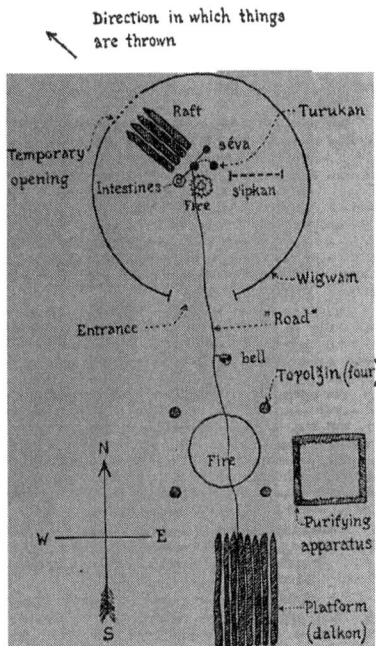

It should be noted that all these paraphernalia, with the exception of taimen and *séva*, are made in numbers 2,4, and 8, which is typical of this form of shamanizing. The symbols of various animals and things, which form a complex of paraphernalia, will be used by the shaman during his difficult travelling. If they are properly made, the shaman may go easily, while their absence does not mean that the shaman cannot go to the lower world.

First part. When everything is ready and there is no longer light in the western sky, where the sun sets; the clansmen come to the wigwam. Outsiders are not allowed to be present. Together with the other people the shaman arrives, and his permanent paraphernalia are also brought into the wigwam. After taking some tea, the shaman puts on his head-dress and apron. In the meantime the drum is dried on the fire. Then it is handed over to the shaman who begins, slowly and not loudly, to drum. Soon after this he begins to sing. He mentions *dunda, ŏrgidúnda, toyo* ("fire") *sevak'i, on'o toyo* ("mother fire"), *on'o dunda,* ("mother earth"), *fur garkutal* (cf. *supra* p. 133) the name of the clan to the "ancestor" (dead) of which the sacrifice is offered, etc. In this song-declaration the statement is made of the reason of the sacrifice, to which spirit it is made, and what kind of sacrifice is offered.[*] The tempo and rhythms greatly vary. One of the women continuously produced smoke of a certain resinous plant, not identified, and brought the plant near the shaman, that she could breathe the smoke. (Such a smoking is used in all forms of shamanizing). This part of the performance is concluded by a divination with the drum stick or a cup: the shaman, with closed eyes, throws it into the air with such a calculation that it must turn over several times; if it falls down with the back (convex) up, all present people say *čok!*[**], which means "good", if it falls down with its concave side up, the people remain silent. The drum-stick is handed over to the shaman being held by the end opposite to the handle. After the divination some people continue to take tea, remaining in the wigwam, while the other people prepare outside the second part of the performance.

Second part. The placing for *séva* (9) is put on the back of the reindeer which is to be sacrificed. The reindeer is led four times around the wigwam, in which the shamanizing takes place, in such a way that the animal must step over the log (*turukan*, vide infra), which is put on the ground near the fire at a distance of four metres from the wigwam. After this operation, the reindeer is stopped near the fire and killed according to a special ritual. The brain is destroyed by introducing a pointed stick through the aperture in the skull (from the neck). The blood is collected into a birch bark bucket. The skin is taken off together with a part of the skull, the antlers and hoofs. The animal is cut into small pieces to be cooked later. All wooden paraphernalia are sprinkled with blood. Outside of the wigwam a four legged, or two legged platform, about one and a half metre high is erected on which the sacrifice will be

---

[*] As during the shamanizing, the shaman (a female) was evidently improvising, owing to the circumstances, it was impossible to record the text of the declaration.

[**] The expression čok! is not used only by the Tungus; e.g. the Eniseians have suuk! ("Let it be so!") (cf. Anučin, "An outline of Shamanism among Enisay Ostiaks" in Publ. of Mus. A. and E., Vol. II. cf. also čôkô=čoko (Yakut, Pek.)—"the same, in good time, exactly", etc.

put later on. This is the *dalkon* used in all great sacrifices. Two high posts of young larch tree without branches and leaves, called *turukan*, are brought into the wigwam vertically and put near the fire-place, so that the tops of the posts protrude from the wigwam. A bunch of white hair from the neck of sacrificed reindeer is attached to the top of the post. One of the posts is connected with the platform by a thong, which is the "road" for spirits. A bell is attached to the thong-road, outside of the wigwam. Four *toyoljin* and "purifying apparatus" are put outside near the fire. In the wigwam, *séva* with a knife is attached to the same post.

The raft consisting of four fishes (1) fastened together and the taimen (2) is brought into the wigwam. They are put in the north-western sector of the wigwam, and the skin of the reindeer, with the head directed North-West, is put on. The bucket with blood is put near the *séva* and the reindeer intestines, wound on a small wooden stick, are hung up to the *turukan*. The *javdar* are put on the wall of the wigwam, the placings for spirits of the shaman are hung up near the raft.

The whole preparation takes about an hour. Then the people again gather in the wigwam and the second part of performance begins.

During this part the shaman must exteriorate his soul and take the immaterial substance of the sacrifice to the lower world. In this operation he has help from various manifestations of his spirits—bear, fishes, boar, anthropomorphic, etc. On his way he meets with various difficulties of the road and attacks of other, unmastered spirits and sometimes of those which are sent by other shamans against him. The spirit *séva* is carrying the sacrifice, the intestines and the blood (used for sausage!), and is helping the shaman.

The performance runs as shown below. The shaman sits, drumming and singing. He rises, hands the drum to the assistant and takes up the reindeer staffs. He begins to sing, to move rhythmically and from time to time makes short leaps, while his assistant is drumming. On every strophe the assistant and other people reply by repeating either the last words or special words—the refrains. The tempo gradually increases and the replies become more and more persistent and louder. The shaman takes a big cup (about 100 cc.) of vodka, about forty per cent strong, and smokes several pipes of tobacco. Singing, jumping, and general excitement increase. Gradually, the shaman brings himself into extasy. When this happens, the shaman falls down on the raft and remains without moving. Now the drumming is slow and the singing stops. If the shaman remains motionless for too long a time, he is sprinkled with blood, three times. If there is no effect, the shaman is recalled by singing. Then the shaman begins to reply in a weak voice to questions asked (in singing) by two or three persons sitting by his side. Then the shaman rises. This evolution is repeated *four times* in the same order; the falling down on the raft means that the shaman (naturally his soul) takes a rest.

When the shamanizing is over, they bring a purifying apparatus *s'ipkan* and put it near the *turukan*, that the people may go through it. *Séva* is brought nearer to the raft and is attached to another *turukan*. The clansmen begin to move from West to East around the fire-place and every one hands over to the shaman a portion of the intestines.

The shaman hangs them on the head and shoulder of *séva*. When the clansmen pass in front of the shaman, he lies down and they step over his body, and passing through the purifying apparatus make two full rounds. After this performance the shaman sings, rather a long time, and at last jumps to the reindeer skin, cuts off two legs and throws them together with *séva* in a northwestward direction, making a hole in the wigwam cover, if he cannot succeed in opening it without damage. At the same time the raft is quickly dismembered and thrown in the same direction. In the meantime the drumming assumes a very fast tempo and the singing becomes very loud. Finally, the shaman throws himself on the reindeer skin and for a long time remains motionless and silent. Light drumming with singing continues. Then the people begin to call back the shaman. If he does not reply, they sprinkle some blood on him and direct sparks of fire (produced by flint and steel) at him. If there is no effect, the people who are present become very nervous, for the shaman may not return at all and thus die (*vide infra*).

When the shaman's consciousness returns, the people lift him up, pass around him, produce sparks with flint and steel, ring the bell and beat the drum. They express their joy that the shaman has returned from *buni*, the world of the dead. Then the shaman sits down, seemingly exhausted and lightly drumming, sings. A divination with the drum-stick is once more performed. Yet, the old part of performance is over. The people and the shaman drink tea and eat meat which is already boiled. This part of the performance takes about two hours and may last still longer.

After an interruption lasting two or three hours, i.e. already at daybreak, the third and last part is performed, which is carried on in the same way as the first part. The shaman gives a short address to his spirits, expresses his thanks. In the case here described the intestines were handed over to the mother of one of the oldest clansmen. The reindeer did not belong to this clansman, but to another man who had an extra reindeer. Yet, the old woman's soul being satisfied, the whole clan's ancestors are pleased. The whole performance is naturally a clan business.

According to the Tungus, this performance would not differ very much from other similar performances *örgisk'i*. I have been told that in main lines the same form of shamanizing is practised among the Tungus of the Nerčinsk taiga; however, I did not observe this.

One cannot have very often occasion to see this form of shamanizing, for reasons the principal of which is that the travelling to the lower world is considered as a very difficult and dangerous operation for the shaman. There are very few shamans who do it; the same shaman would not do it more than a few times a year. The shaman must also have all necessary paraphernalia, and it is desirable that he should have a reindeer-costume.

It should be noted that most of the actions and paraphernalia are figured in the numbers two four and eight, which distinguishes *örgisk'i* from the form of shamanizing discussed below.

Shamanizing to the lower world is practised among all Tungus groups. However, many varieties of ritual and purpose exist. As shown in the case of the Reindeer Tungus of Transbaikalia, the aim was to neutralize a malevolent activity of the clansmen's ancestors. The paraphernalia and sacrifice are also quite elaborate, such as are not met with among other groups.

The aim of shamanizing may be: (1) a sacrifice to the souls of dead people, personally and known by their names, and to ancestors in general; (2) the bringing back of the soul captured by the spirits, but which can be brought back; (3) the transfer to the lower world of the souls which do not leave this world, without the shaman's interference.

We have already seen that in the case of the Tungus of Manchuria sacrifices can be carried out by specialists without the special assistance of the shaman. However, if the spirits are not well known, it must be found out by the shaman, and so their assistance is also required for carrying out the sacrifice. If spirits are known and the sacrifice must be taken to a definite spirit (soul), the shamans are asked to carry out this operation. In fact, only shamans can go into the lower world for bringing back the souls of living people. The transfer of the souls to the lower world requires the assistance of a shaman only if there is a reason to suspect that the souls may remain in this world and would thus disturb living people. This is the case of all shamans' souls which want to remain in this world and may become new harmful spirits, especially souls of those shamans who were evil-minded persons, as will be shown later.

In Bir. and Kum. the form of shamanizing is defined by a special term (verb) g'elěu.* It is very rarely practised by the shamans, for not all of them can stand the difficulties of travelling and dealing with the spirits of the lower world, i.e. not all of the shamans have special sêvèn to help them in this work. Among those groups I have never observed such performances, so that my information regarding this form of shamanizing is gathered from the Tungus. This form of shamanizing can be done only in the dark.

If, according to the shaman's declaration, it is found in a shamanizing (little shamanizing) that a soul is really captured, a sacrifice would be made to the sêvèn in order that he may "help" to go to the lower world, buni. The nature of the sacrifice depends on that of the particular spirits which "help" the shaman. The performance is confined to the calling into the shaman the spirit which accepts the sacrifice during the extasy (the shaman eats meat and drinks blood). This constitutes the first part of the performance. The second part is the shaman's travel to the lower world. During this journey the shaman must go down a mountain range (in a northwestern direction), where he may meet with difficulties caused by the spirits of other shamans and other spirits which are in conflict with his own spirits.** On his way he has to go through a small hole, near which the spirits and other shamans may capture his soul. The journey is reported by the shaman, who sings all "les péripéties" of his travelling. Sometimes he uses his special implements for self-protection: he covers himself with the tōli or the drum to avoid the arrows shot by the spirits; he may fight, shoot the spirits

* I do not know the etymology of this term. The Tungus "translate" it as "to go to buni", and in Manchu it is xan'aǯamb'i.

** Therefore the shaman must be very careful when he selects the spirits to be used for this operation.

and, lastly, some sacrifice may be offered. At his arrival to the entrance to the lower world the shaman has to cross three rivers, where he meets with the spirits of the lower world. Finally he enters the world of darkness, and the assistants must produce with steel and flint sparks to light his way "like lightening."* He must find there the soul, and after a fighting or after diplomatic negotiations, he brings it back, meeting again on his way all kinds of difficulties. When the soul is brought back, it is reintroduced into the affected person and with this, the second part is finished.

The last part, which consists of thanksgiving to the shaman's spirits for their assistance, is usually carried out on the following day, or even several days later. This is a simple sacrifice performed during the extasy.

Among the Reindeer Tungus of Manchuria in "olden days" (the last shaman who did this had died previous to my visit) used to shamanize to the "earth", but there are now no more shamans who can do it.

Among the Nomad Tungus of Mankova the form of shamanizing to the lower world is quite different. I had no chance to see this performance myself, but I have detailed information of it from the Tungus. The operation is called samalda ("shamanize") èrgeli (the same stem as ōrgi) and it is carried out in the dark (tarildula osi dolbo ōe'a èrgeli, I was told). As sacrifice they use a black

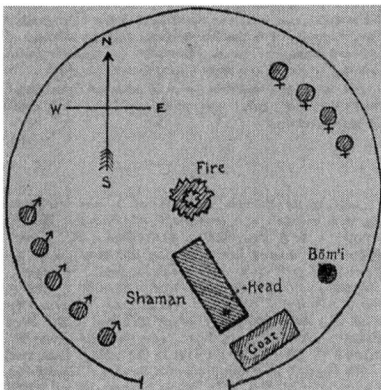

domesticated goat. There is made a bōm'i (vide supra p. 190) with a face of a piece of birch bark, the eyes, nose, mouth and cheeks being designated with charcoal, and with a body of dry grass. If there is a sick man or woman for whom the shamanizing is needed, a dress for bōm'i is made of the dress belonging to the sick person. A black cow is attached outside the tent (it can as well be supposed that

* A functional difference should be noted in the using of flint among the Reindeer Tungus of Transkaikalia (vide supra p. 306) and the Tungus of Manchuria.

the cow was previously killed). The goat is slaughtered and the mouth of *bŏm'i* is smeared with the blood. The bones and meat are boiled.

During the extasy, when the shaman reaches the lower world, he lies down and all people who are present, including women, turn three times around the fire-place and jump over the shaman (as among the Reindeer Tungus). The shaman remains on the ground for about half an hour. Experienced men hold his ankles and count the movements of the articulation or pulsation (I could not find out which). After nine "movements" it is supposed that the shaman has done his business in the lower world, and with the smoke of burning laedum palustrum he is brought back to consciousness. Three wooden sticks (*ark'ivun*), with seven pieces of goat meat fixed on each of them, are attached to the belt of *bŏm'i*. The spirit *buni* (a spirit of the lower world) is introduced into *bŏm'i* by the shaman. Then the *bŏm'i* is put on the black cow and taken in a south-eastern direction, where, at a certain distance from the tent, it is thrown away. However, the cow is not killed, but is handed over alive to the shaman. The meat of the goat is not eaten by the people. It is thrown away together with the *bŏm'i*.

The following should be noted: (1) the use of the cow as the animal preferred by the *buni* spirits (cf. the dog among the Manchus, the reindeer among the Tungus; in fact, some populations of Manchuria as well as of other neighbouring regions still use the cow as draught animal, cf. SONT); (2) the use of a *black* cow and a *black* goat, of which the latter is not eaten by the people; (3) the direction in which the sacrifice is sent is the South-East, while among other Tungus groups it is the North-West; (4) the numbers of acts are three and seven. However, the shaman works through his *sèvèn* and *sevek'i* (spirits and placings).

It is evident that this form is different from other forms described, and it can be supposed that it is not a Tungus invention.

———————

Among the Manchus this form of shamanizing is designated by the verb *xan'atamb'i*, which in the Manchu complex is "to go (the shaman) to the dead world" (*buĉeye ğurun*). What may happen during the travelling to the lower world is described in the Manchu poem *Nišan saman*. This poem or record of shamanizing, is in so far as I know, the only document written on shamanism.* It relates the story of a case that happened at the time of the Ming Dynasty. A young man, the son of a rich man, Yuan Wei (*juan wei*), who lived in a village by the name of Lolo, went to the Hsi-ling Shan mountains for hunting. During this hunting trip he died. The female shaman, named Nišan, took on herself the task of bringing back the soul of the young man, and she shamanized accordingly. Her shamanizing-visit to the lower world, meeting with the various spirits, including her own husband and other people, her

———————

* In 1915 I found a copy of this poem near Aigun and it was translated and analysed. This document is rather long. My copy contains between nine and ten thousand Manchu words which, in printed form with translation and notes, would form a work four times larger than the original text. Owing to this, that work cannot be included in the present publication. Also for the present main topic, not all of the details are interesting.

finding of the young man's soul and restoring it were recorded.

Of course all shamans know this book. However, as shown, they do not imitate each other to an absolute degree, but every shaman does something of his own. Therefore *Nišan saman* is not an exhaustive document for giving a description of the spirits used by the shamans and the methods employed by them. Furthermore, the ritual side is only partly represented.

The shamanizing to the lower world is also rare among the Manchus. However, I have observed it three times, which, together with *Nišan saman* and various oral communications of the Manchus, both shamans and common people, give altogether a rather complete picture of this performance. One of the performances on which I base the present description was carried out by a Chinese (*n'ikan*) shaman.

The existence of Chinese shamans will be discussed later, but now I want to point out that the difference between the Manchus and Chinese shamans in the routine of performance is confined only to the language.

The case which required a shamanizing was under my observation for nearly eighteen months with interruptions. In a family of a former petty official, who with the downfall of the Manchu Dynasty lost his position, a small boy eight years old fell sick. In so far as I could guess, he had first pleuritis and afterwards various troubles of kidneys and water metabolism. He was attended by thirteen Chinese local doctors and several shamans. I saw three complete and very elaborate performances, one of which was to deal with the lower world. None of them could find out the cause of the sickness and the means of curing it. Generally people were inclined to think that spirits were the real cause of the sickness. This time, after a preliminary shamanizing, it was found out that the cause of the trouble might be a shaman, a relative of the boy's father, who had died long ago. The shaman wanted therefore to see him personally and to ask him what he wanted. The shaman, a huge heavy and muscular Chinese (*n'ikan*), was considered as a very able man. He worked chiefly only with ten *voĉko*—which is quite sufficient for a shaman —of which five *voĉko* were Chinese spirits, *n'ikan voĉko*, namely:

1. *ĉ'aĉin saman*—"the earth-worm shaman"
2. *ar wei kun'ay šifu* (*saman*)—"two girls teachers (shamans)"
3. *xŏšan laoje*—"the fire spirit" (which is not afraid of fire)
4. *taošin laoje*—"the sharp implements and arms spirit" (which is not afraid of sharp implements and arms)
5. *cunpi kudu civel j'ayj'un*—"the hedge-hog spirit" (very small and rolling)
6. the wolf spirit
7. the chief (*talaxa*, in Manchu) Tungus spirit
8. the second Tungus spirit
9. the third Tungus spirit
10. this last spirit was not identified

This shaman was quite popular and quite busy, being invited to visit some villages situated in remote regions. He naturally was an *amba saman*, and could attend people belonging to different clans. In observing this shaman, I came to the conclusion that he was a professional, i.e. that he lived on this profession.

Since the case here described was difficult, he was assisted by another shaman, a Manchu, who performed the duties of the chief-assistant, and there were two other assistants.

The performance began after sunset. An ordinary table was put on the *amba naγan* (the principal bed-stove, facing the entrance) with the following sacrifice: two cups with millet, with three sticks of burning incense in each; fifteen (three times five) rolls of Chinese bread (*māntóu*); seven small cups of Chinese wine (two bottles left on the table); two bank-notes of one rouble each; and in the middle of the table a boiled chicken, the blood of which had been taken away before the cooking.

The shaman took off his clean coat and put on a rather worn one, for he might soil it when falling down to the floor. First he refused to put on a belt with trinkets, for fear of attracting the attention of the policeman (the Chinese government, as stated, prohibited shamanism and persecuted shamans, so that they had to consider this when shamanizing). However, he decided to put it on, for the police station was far away, and the policemen did not leave the station; and the house was standing far from the main road (on the bank of the river).

The boy's father, who himself was *p'oγun saman* of his clan, after burning some incense, prayed his clan spirits to excuse him that he went to the help of a stranger shaman who was not of their clan. It was necessary to do this for avoiding a conflict between the spirits of the shaman and those of the clan, which may result in further complications of the disease. The shaman who failed to cure the boy, did the same, begging his own spirits to abstain from any hostility against the spirits of the acting shaman.

The acting shaman made an appeal to all his spirits: Chinese, Manchu and Tungus. He explained the case and asked for assistance. Then he called his principal spirit (*voćko*). He took up the drum, beat rythmically and sang. Extasy approached; the rhythm changed and the tempo increased. The assistants were ready with a rug on which the shaman might fall when the spirit came. Then the spirit arrived, the shaman trembled, jumped, still producing a rhythmical noise with *s'iśa;* then suddenly he handed over to the assistant the drum and fell down upon the rug. The assistant asked him questions and from the dialogue one could understand that the shaman was to go to the lower world.

Two *ilxa mo,*—"the blooming trees"—were now prepared. These were two branches of willow tree with smaller branches, the ends of which were broken off. The branches were adorned with paper of five different colours: white, red, blue, yellow and green (perhaps black?). This is the tree which attracts the spirits of the lower world; souls are living on beautiful trees. The "trees" must be put in a "beautiful" (gay and joyful) place (however, this could not be done, I think for two reasons: the season was not favourable, for the middle of April is too cold; and the shamanizing might have attracted the attention of the policemen), or inside of the house, near the door. On a table placed under the "trees" there were put four cups with Chinese wine (*zānśin*), 5 × 3 fifteen rolls of Chinese bread, five plates with nuts, dates (*zyziphus jujubii*), candles etc. i.e. "five kinds of fruits", two cups with millet in which burning stick-incense was put and a cup with fresh chicken blood. This sacrifice must be exposed at the moment when the shaman reaches the lower world.

The shaman introduced into himself (drumming, singing, "extasy") the spirit "wolf". The physical effect of the extasy is that the shaman's body is very rigid, the legs are stretched, the arms are bent and the elbows are pressed against the body. The shaman was brought into the room, and put on the rug in front of the table with the sacrifice. The assistants tried to bend his legs and straighten his arms: the articulations produced a noise, but the assistants could not make the body relax. After several movements the limbs relaxed and the shaman lay with his abdomen and face down. The shaman kept in his arms a cushion covered with a blanket. Then the light was blown out and the action continued in the dark. The shaman was singing, making a noise with *s'iśa,* scratched the earth of the floor (the earthen floor of the house) "like a wolf". The assistants tried to find out what the shaman saw and what he said. As a matter of fact, his speech was rather confused. The result obtained was that the old shaman-ancestor did not do harm, but the sickness was due to a spirit of the group *māfa*. The spirit some six or seven years previously was brought by the father from the upper course of the Amur River (in fact he used to deal with another Manchu in smuggling alcohol). In order to make this *māfa* benevolent, it was necessary to erect a temple (*m'co*), where a placing (a picture) of this spirit was to be put and regular sacrifices offered. However, the father was not certain about it and asked for confirmation once more. It was again confirmed that the spirit *māfa* wanted to have a special *m'ao*. After this the blooming tree, together with the sacrifice, was thrown away, far from the house, and some paper money was burnt as sacrifice to the dead people (the ancestors). Then the shaman returned to his normal state. He now sat as usual on the stove-bed, tired, and sweating.

With this operation the shamanizing to the lower world was finished. However, the shaman continued the performance by dealing with other methods to restore the soul, which will be described in another section.

———————

Among the Goldi the form of going to the lower world is of great importance, for the shaman must take the souls of dead people to that world, while this is done only in rare cases among the other groups here described. The first operation with the soul in Goldi, according to I. A. Lopatin, is called *n'imgan*, which in other languages is merely "to shamanize", [*n'imya* (RTM, Bir. Nerč)—"to shamanize"] while the last operation is the actual settling of the soul in the lower world. It is called *kaza taor'i* [I. A. Lopatin, —p. 309, which, I think, is merely *ģaza dōr'i;* cf. *ģasambi* (Manchu—"to sorrow, to cry, etc"; and *ģasa* (Goldi, Grube),—"traurig werden",—*dōro~dōr'i—*"the custom, practice, law, etc."]. This operation is sometimes postponed till the time when the people have money enough (*vide* I. A. Lopatin op. cit. pp. 310) and also until there is a shaman who can do it, for there are only a few shamans who can perform it (cf. L. Sternberg, "Divine Election", p. 478).[*] This fact is very interesting as a peculiar

———————

[*] L. Sternberg (op. cit.) asserts that the shaman whom he happened to meet "was the greatest" for "he was the only one who performed the last office of commemoration, i.e. he conveyed the souls of all dead Golds to the buni". But L. Sternberg somewhat exaggerates the importance of his chief informer. As shown, actually

specialization of shamanism for the purpose of taking human souls to the lower world. Two descriptions of the shaman's travelling are given by P. P. Šimkevič and I. A. Lopatin. Therefore I shall not reproduce it here. There are some differences of the details, partly due to the manner of observation and recording.

In one or another form shamanizing to the lower world is known among the neighbouring groups of the Goldi, such as the Oroči, and Udehe. However, no detailed accounts are known.

III. SHAMANIZING TO This form of shamanizing can
THE UPPER WORLD be practised only by those groups which have a definite conception of the "upper world" and the shamans who want to deal with the spirits of the upper world. However, some groups, although dealing with the spirits of the upper world, have no specific performances. Some of them I shall now describe.

IN BARGUZIN TUNGUS "shamanizing to the spirits of upper world" is called *uyisk'i* or *n'jan'ja*. *Uyisk'i* is the direction upwards, *n'jan'ja* is a complex of spirits analysed before. This form of shamanizing is rather short and much more frequent than that previously described. This form is practised among both the Barguzin and the Nerčinsk groups. The following things are prepared:

1. $9 \times 3 = 27$ young larch trees, which are called *čolbot* "the birch trees"; the larch tree is used in loco of birch tree which is not very common in the region. There must be at least one young birch tree, which is somewhat larger than the larch tree and the crown of which is preserved. The latter is called *čarg'i*.* The trees are ornamented with coloured pieces of cloth, i.e. just as it is practised among the Buriats.

2. A young larch tree with branches and leaves cut off, *turukan* (i.e. the small *turu*) with two cross beams—steps of a ladder—*uyikón*—which may be symbolized by two bindings made of bark or other material. This "ladder" is used by the shaman for climbing to the *uyisk'i*.

3. 9 times 3 times 2, or fifty-four, birds—*díyit*, which are supposed to be "ducks"—are made of birch bark and attached by pairs to every *čolbo*. The ducks help the shaman to go upwards.

4. Two long narrow planks with nine holes in which *an'ján* are fixed; *an'ján* are anthropomorphic placings cut out of wood, the planks are attached to the *čolbot*.

5. A platform of usual form on which the sacrifice is put after the performance.

6. There may be some *s'ipkan*, of a very small size, The *čolbot* (supposed to be birch trees) are put in but they are not always used.

three groups, being supported by a cross beam in such a

such shamans are not as rare as that, and the question actually is about the shamanizing to the lower world in general—not all shamans can do it, but usually (among the Manchus and Tungus) this operation is done for the benefit of clansmen. Thus, every clan usually has a shaman who can go to the lower world, but does not do it very frequently.

* The term čarg'i is perhaps of a Buriat origin; cf. čarga || čirya (Mong. Rud.) "the rod used for pulling the cart". However, in Tungus we have čar (RTM)—a long wooden plank used as framework of a canoe. The etymology is not clear.

manner that 2×9 with *čarg'i* are directed with their crowns eastward and nine "birches" are turned in an opposite direction.

The sacrificial animal lege artis must be a sheep, bought from the Buriats and sometimes brought from a long distance. In a case which I know the animal was brought on reindeer back by a female shaman from the Buriats who lived at a distance of about 200 miles from the Tungus. However, a young reindeer fawn may also be used, if it is impossible to have a sheep. The reindeer or sheep sacrifice is carried out by the shaman's soul with the help of *an'ján* who would bring it to *dayačan*. The ducks help the shaman to fly up.

The purpose of shamanizing is to take the animal to the spirits of the upper world. This may be necessary for various reasons. In two cases, which I knew rather in detail, the reasons were sickness of children. The *dayačan* was asked to return the soul of the child affected by sickness. The method and kind of sacrifice are defined in a special shamanistic performance, sometimes several days and weeks, even months before the operation.

The first part of performance is similar to the first part of the shamanizing *örgisk'i*, so I shall now omit the details, except the last section, when by the divination with the drum-stick it is found out exactly and at the last moment, whether the spirit *dayačan* would accept the animal—a young fawn or sheep. When the answer is positive, the animal is brought to a place cleaned and prepared beforehand, where a big fire is lit. The animal is forced to lie down, and four or five strong and experienced adult men hold it. A man performs a ritual slaughtering: he opens with an ordinary knife the chest and pulls out the heart which naturally requires great strength and skill. Not one drop of blood is allowed to fall on the ground. The blood is collected into a special receptacle. Then the skin, together with the hoofs, antlers and eyes, are taken off and hung up to *čarg'i*. This skin is called *dóri*.* The head is separated and cooked together with the meat. The bones are separated, cleaned free from (boiled) meat and put on the platform together with the stomach, liver, bowels and other internal organs. The hair from the neck is cut off and with the lower jaw is hung up to *turukan*. The latter is brought to the wigwam, where the shamanizing takes place, and put in the middle in an erected position. It is connected with *čarg'i* by a thong with a bell outside of the wigwam. This is the "road" already seen in the shamanizing *örgisk'i*. In the part of the road which is in the wigwam a small (like a toy) cradle (a child was sick) and some anthropomorphic placings made of chamois are hung up. The *javdar* and permanent placings for spirits are hung up in the same way as in *örgisk'i*.

The second part opens with the shaman's drumming and singing. He does not mention *bunil*, *séva* and other spirits used in the shamanizing *örgisk'i*. A little while later he rises to his feet and begins, always drumming, to jump and dance. He approaches the child** and waving his drum he takes an anthropomorphic placing, sprinkles it with fresh blood, and hands it over to the child. This is the placing for the spirit which will take the sacrifice. Then the shaman hands over to his assistant his drum and takes

* The etymology is not certain. Perhaps the Manchu *ǰóro* whence *dör'i*.

** I have seen this performance twice, both for the treatment of children.

two horses-staffs which are a permanent component of his equipment. He smokes four or five pipes of tobacco, takes a big cup of vodka and reaches a state of extasy. A part of the wigwam cover in the south-western corner is raised and the shaman, always jumping and dancing, while the assistant is drumming, takes the small toy-cradle in his hands and falls into the arms of the people surrounding him. At this moment he has reached *uɣisk'i*—the upper world. The shaman is turned round by the people, sparks are produced with steel and flint, as it is done in the shamanizing *örgisk'i*. This part ends in the same manner too.

The people and the shaman have some boiled meat and tea. A few hours later the last part is performed. It does not differ from that of *örgisk'i*. The kettle in which the meat was boiled is hung up on the *čarg'i* and left there for ever.

The shamanizing *uɣisk'i* can be carried out at night or in the day as well. A very heavy costume must not be used for this shamanizing. For this reason the shaman must have two costumes, using the one which has no iron parts.

Before the shamanizing is carried out the shaman may insist upon moving the wigwam to another place; but after the shamanizing the wigwam must remain for three days at the same spot.

It should be noted that paraphernalia are used in multiples of nine; certain actions are repeated three times; staffs-horses are used; the sacrificial animal is a sheep (when possible); the whole performance, as far as I could find out, is not connected with the clan, but it is rather a family business; *čarg'i* and *turukan* are used, which is quite common in the Buriat-Mongol and generally in the Central Asiatic complexes.

A brief comparison of these two forms of shamanizing will be sufficient for seeing the great difference between the two complexes. The above indicated requirements for the shamanizing *uɣisk'i* rather point to their having been borrowed from the Buriats.

112. VARIOUS FORMS OF SHAMANIZING Among the Reindeer Tungus of Transbaikalia small performances may be given a great number of times. No sacrifice is offered. The performance always consists of one part and may be carried out at any time of the day, with the exception of a special form *tuksav'i*, which is always done at night, after sunset. The term *tuksav'i* is a derivative of the stem *tuksa*—"to run", perhaps the stem of *tuksak'i*—"the hare"—is the same.* The skin of a hare is used in this form of shamanizing for carrying the request of the shaman to *uɣidunda*. During the extasy the skin is thrown out through the smoke aperture in the top of the wigwam. The divination with the drum stick is carried out three times —at the beginning, in the middle and at the end of the

performance. It may be pointed out that the sending of the hare as a messenger is especially common among the Buriats. This form of shamanizing requires a full costume, while other forms of little shamanizing can be carried out only with some parts of the costume, such as the head-dress, the apron, and always the drum.

In the performances of small shamanizing the extasy does not always occur, but the whole performance may be confined to a "prayer" followed by some drumming and singing, when the shaman may do, as the Tungus say, only "shaking" of his own *savak'i*. Indeed, such performances are very common. However, the shaman may also act without any dress and even without the drum, but there will be no proper "performance". Such is, for instance, the case when the shaman "performs" in a half-asleep state, also when he is at home and desires to perform quite aimlessly, or for finding out something (this will be seen later).

Among the Nomad Tungus of Mankova there is a special form of shamanizing—*uɣila*—upwards, which is also called shamanizing *baron julaski*—"right southern" (east south). The shaman offers a sacrifice to the spirits of the upper world and goes there himself. Sheep (cf. the above of the Reindeer Tungus) and a white horse are used as sacrificial animals. However, the horse is not slaughtered (cf. the above case of Mankova Tungus with the black cow).

Among other Tungus groups and Manchus there is no shamanizing to the spirits of the upper world. As shown (*vide supra* Section 76), these spirits are satisfied with a sacrifice offered by ordinary people (Northern Tungus) and the *p'oɣun saman* (among the Manchus).

Among all Tungus groups various forms of shamanizing are known which are not connected with the lower or upper world, but which are needed for managing and mastering spirits living in this world. The occasions on which the shamanizing is carried out are numerous. Some of which may be indicated here as instances are: (1) the liberation of a person from the spirits, which may be (a) those of a shaman, (b) clan spirits, (c) foreign (*dōna*) spirits; (2) the liberation of a group of persons (usually clansmen or rarely co-villagers) from the spirits, as in the first case; (3) the expulsion of malevolent spirits and their mastering, if possible; (4) the sacrifice to the spirits who may be benevolent or malevolent par excellence; (5) the divination of causes of troubles with the help of the shaman's spirits; and other various occasions which cannot be even foreseen, for the combination of the spirits' activity and the character of spirits and methods of managing them depend on the shaman's ability, the existing theories and the ever increasing Tungus knowledge as to the alien spirits and methods used by the neighbours. In the forthcoming pages I shall describe some shamanistic performances.

Case 1. The Khingan Tungus. A man over forty is affected by an unknown spirit (cf. Section 128, Case 4). He himself has made several attempts at shamanizing, but it was supposed that he cannot master the spirits, while the latter master him. The performing female shaman is a young, but experienced shaman. The aim is to find out what kind of spirit is doing harm. For this purpose she introduces into herself her spirits (*sèvèɳkan*). By the above indicat-

---

* Cf. tuksa (Bir. Khin. Nerč. Mank.) (Ur. Castr.), cf. tuks'i (Bir.) tuɣa (RTM) tuč (Tum.) [suʝu (Manchu Writ)]. In spite of the fact that tuksá may be the stem of tuksav'i (the form of shamanizing) [tuksak'i "the hare", and tuksá, etc.—"to run"], I am not absolutely certain as to the connexion of tuksav'i and tuksak'i, although the hare is used as a messenger. As a matter of fact, tuksav'i may be one of the forms derived from the stem tuk (V)— "to bring up, to erect, to lift up, to send up" used in Barg. Nerč. Bir. Kum. Khin. as a term designating the act of communicating with the "upper world" spirits.

ed method—increase of tempo of drumming and singing—she brings herself into the state of extasy and the spirit enters her. Through the spirit the shaman wants to find the road of the spirit which affects the client. She goes (in her extasy) to the wigwam of the family (the man was travelling with me, so that the family was left some fifty or sixty miles behind) and she reported how the members of the family were doing. Then she dealt with the *burkan* of the family and found out that the trouble came from the family (clan) *burkan*. A sacrifice of two sheep must be offered to him on the twenty-fifth day of the next moon (month). During the performance the shaman fell down several times, at the moment when the spirit entered into her. The people who were near her supported her and lifted her up "just like a piece of wood", the body and limbs were rigid. Before the entry of the spirit she increased the intensity of the singing and drumming and began to tremble; when she was travelling (her spirit), she jumped and beat the drum with great force. During the shamanizing there was *kokuneĭ sèvèn* when *kèku-kèku* is used as a refrain. The shamanizing began at 10:25 p. m. (in July) and ended at 11:25 p. m. There were two male-assistants, while a large number of women present at the performance repeated the refrain. The reaction of the audience was positive, i.e. the people who were present did not disturb the performance—the shamanizing was not interrupted by jokes and various tricks, which is rather common, especially if there are foreigners and foreign influence is strong in the group.

Case 2. The Khingan Tungus. An old woman of over sixty years who herself used to be a shaman, had a year previously been disabled and could not walk. She was lying half-naked under the *jampan* (mosquito-net covering her bed). Her placings for spirits, as well as the greater part of her belongings were burnt the previous year in an accidental fire. The wigwam (in July) was partly covered with a winter cover, partly with a summer cover, a sign of great poverty. Her daughter-shaman visited her and wanted to find out the source of her mother's trouble. The daughter put on herself the shaman costume of the old woman and called to herself her *sèvèn*. During the extasy another spirit (*dalkur*) visited her, but she could not recognize this spirit. However, this spirit entered the old sick shaman and through the old woman declared that it wanted a sacrifice—a wild boar. This revelation was communicated as follows: in front of the old woman there was put the end of a long thong which was put on the shoulder of the acting shaman, the latter reported in singing that the old woman would give a sheep instead of a wild boar. At the same time the shaman insisted that the spirit must immediately leave the old woman. The shaman tried to push away the spirit by smoking *laedum palustrum* and by frightening the spirit with drumming and singing and even simply threatening it. The shaman was assisted by a great number of women who were making a great noise.

Case 3. The Khingan Tungus. The purpose of shamanizing was to find out how I would travel with my expedition. The performer was the same as in Case 1. The shaman made a general call for all spirits *čuvun*, whereupon a *sèrèy* arrived. This is a spirit which is dangerous for children. All children were therefore sent out of the wigwam. This spirit also "eats" buttons and all people present had therefore to button their coats to protect the buttons. Be-

fore its coming a *javdar* was put round the wigwam.* The shaman "made stick"—the body and limbs were rigid—and "arch". She fell down to the ground before a young man had time to support her. (This occurrence produced general laughter). The spirit wanted to have some boiled millet. A cup of millet was brought in and was passed round to the people present, and a portion of the millet was thrown into the air. The people shout *pè*! (in approval). After the departure of this spirit the children were allowed to come in. For the sake of safety the spirits were sent off by a movement of the drum in front of the children. A dog was brought into the wigwam and waved over the head of Madame Shirokogoroff who was also concerned in the shamanizing for she was "travelling with the party". Another *sèvèy* arrived. In order to help the introduction of the spirits, the people present at the performance produced excitement in the shaman by their yelping and cries, always increasing in tempo. She did the same by means of turning faster and faster. After the spirits left her, a purification with smoke was made—a bunch of burning grass was waved between her legs. The result of the shamanizing was that the travelling would be successful and three deer (Cervus Elaphus) with antlers would be killed.

Case 4. The Birarčen. The purpose of shamanizing was to ask for the help of a *sèvèn* for curing a boy. There had been two shamanizings three days previously—one in the day time and the other at night—but no definite result had been obtained. The boy was brought from the school where he was living** to the house of his relative who was performing (rather poorly) the function of the assistant. After the shamanizing the *arkaptun* (with a brass mirror, *vide supra* p. 292) was left above the boy's bed.

When the spirit was introduced, the shaman (a female) was helped by the assistant. The spirit declared that the child would perhaps die. This produced a reaction on the part of the assistant (he was a relative of the boy) who protested against the coming of the spirit if it could not help the boy. The spirits required a pig as sacrifice. The assistant replied that he was a poor man and could not afford it. However, after a long bargaining, it was decided that the sacrifice would be offered two weeks later, on the first day of the next month. After the shamanizing, a piece of yellow colth was given to the spirit and hung up together with the *arkaptun*. The operation lasted until over one o'clock a.m.

About ten days later, i.e. before the term fixed at the shamanizing, another shamanizing was performed. In the meantime the boy had been cured and a pig had been bought. The shamanizing consisted of two parts performed at night, and on the next morning. As far as I could find out; the sacrifice was offered to the spirit of the shaman which had been helpful in the sickness of the boy.

This time the shamanizing was performed outside of the house. The shaman put on the costume and prepared herself for the extasy. The boy was sitting in the middle, while the shaman went round him with her drum. This time the shamanizing was not easy, for there was no assistant to help her. There were also present some people who interfered with her performance. The Chinese teacher,

---

* *javdar* was simply a rope covering only a part of the wigwam.

** The school established by the Chinese government. Some of the children lived in the school.

who was present, was a man of "modern style": he did not believe in shamanism and tried to disturb the shaman. Every time when she passed near him, he pushed or kicked her with his heavy leather shoes of European style. The shaman became nervous and could not concentrate. During the performance a spirit arrived who had nine female and nine male manifestations. Eighteen people were thus required to go rhythmically dancing around the boy, the shaman being in the centre. However, there were only seven women to perform and they were shy in the presence of the sceptically behaving Chinese teacher and the indifferent Tungus men who did not dare to join them in the presence of the teacher. The shaman became still more nervous, so that, when the women did not follow the increase of tempo in her movement, she slightly beat them with the drum stick. No effect was produced. Her spirits became angry and the shaman beat vigorously the women who ran away. Thus the performance failed. The second part was performed in a very simple manner, as an ordinary sacrifice, with the usual incantations and prayers.

' Case 5. The Manchus. The purpose of shamanizing was to cure five members of the family who were sick for several days (seemingly of some usual infection in the winter season). There was a large gathering of people who occupied the bed-stoves and stood up near the entrance. The sick members of the family were lying and sitting on the parts of the stove-bed near a small table put on the principal bed in front of the entrance. The sacrifice consisted of two cups of ģaolan brandy, 3 × 5 = fifteen rolls of Chinese bread, a boiled chicken (it was brought later) and of burning incense sticks fixed in a big cup with sand.

· The shamanizing began after eight o'clock in the evening. The shaman put on his full dress. As usual he was supposed to bring himself into extasy. The assistants, as well as other people present at the shamanizing, repeated the refrains. The spirit entered the shaman, he trembled; his forehead was covered with perspiration. The shaman then fell asleep. This is a somewhat theoretical sleep, not "sincere". The people who are present at a performance evidently realize the conventional character of the performance, and thus they act according to the requirement of the ritual. While the shaman "slept", being surrounded with burning incense, the people chatted by way of pastime.

The next day the shaman came again (to the village from another village). In the evening he lay down on the stove-bed and, being surrounded by burning incense, fell "asleep". A man was sitting near him and watching him. During the sleep (evidently concentration of power) the shaman began to tremble and to roll about violently on the bed. He cried out the name of the spirit which did harm to the child. As quickly as possible an instrument, consisting of a wooden plank, about sixty centimetres long, was brought, at one end of which four sticks, about twelve centimetres long, were fastened with a piece of paper around them to form a lantern. A bunch of burning incense sticks was placed inside this lantern. The spirits were supposed to come into the lantern. All lights were blown out. The incense was kept by the shaman and put in front of the usual place for placings. The shaman called the spirit, the people present at the performance replied with refrains. This continued for two hours and a half. The shaman looked into the lantern from time to time, but the spirit did not wish to come in. Everybody was tired. The shaman

drank tea several times and was evidently very tired. It was decided to stop the shamanizing—the spirit would not consent to enter. The shamanizing, carried out during two days, practically failed.

Case 6. The Manchus. (This case is a continuation of a shamanizing to the lower world described above, vide supra p. 308 et seq.). Another attempt was made at bringing back the soul. The cup with the papers was put on the head of the child, and the head with the cup was covered with a heavy fur hat. This operation apparently failed—the soul did not return. After a short extasy the shaman decided to find out what kind of maја was making the trouble. The way chosen was to allow the spirit to talk through the child. Burning incense was put near the child in such quantity that the child was half-asphyxiated—he was evidently suffering from both his physical condition (very severe oedema: the abdomen was swollen as well as the face) and the smoke; he was screaming the whole time.

The shaman was sitting by his side drumming and exciting the child with his harsh voice, calling the spirit to come and speak. However, the child did not move and did not tremble, which would be considered as a sign of spirit's presence. The spirit—so it was decided—did not want to come in. The shaman suggested an immediate sacrifice of blood (of a pig) to the spirit maја. The people rushed out of the house and tried to catch a pig.* The only pig which they possessed ran away. The sacrifice could not be offered. I had a suspicion as to the sincere desire of the family members to slaughter the last pig. Then the shaman made a new attempt at helping the child with a spirit from the group baturi, namely jaya vočko—"the fire spirit". The spirit was introduced by means of ordinary methods. The assistant handed over to the shaman a bunch of sticks of burning incense. The shaman put the burning ends into his mouth for a second, and then blew immediately against various parts of the child's naked body. Then the incense was dipped in oil, lighted again and the ends thrust into the mouth of the shaman for a moment after which he again blew on the child. The shaman did this with evident effort: he was heavily breathing and spitting out oil. Afterwards, when the whole bunch of incense was burnt, the shaman began to massage the entire body—the abdomen, chest, back, arms and legs with burning alcohol. A big cup of Chinese wine (xanšin, made of ģaolan, from sixty to sixty-five per cent alcoholic) which was burning, was brought in by the assistant, and the shaman took the burning wine with his hands and smeared it on the body rubbing it in. Then, from a distance the shaman sprang upon the child and sucked the body at different parts of the abdomen (especially the naval region, that of the liver, stomach, bladder, appendix and spleen) so that blood appeared; the shaman spit the blood and seemed to be nauseated. After every sucking he cleaned his mouth with wine, but did not vomit.** During the presence of the spirit of fire, which is considered as a very important and dangerous spirit, one of the assistants produced very intensive drumming and all people present sang (refrains) and screamed the whole time. The excitement was general. The performance was concluded by a declaration of the shaman, in the state of

---

* The pigs are sometimes living in a half wild state. Cf. SOM. pp. 131 et seq.

** It was suggested to carry out another operation with four red-hot irons (for pressing), but there were no irons in the house.

extasy, that the spirit *mafa* wants to have a sacrifice consisting of "ten kinds of food". The whole performance lasted five hours and thirty minutes. It was finished at 2:30 a.m. The child was very tired, as well as the shaman, his assistants and the people present at the performance.

Case 7. The Manchus. A man of thirty years old was sick and lying in bed for two months. This was a complex case in which the cause of the trouble was not definitely established, but from the previous shamanizing it was found out that the source of the trouble might be either a *mafar'i*, or a *saman-xutu* (soul of a dead shaman), or even a group of various spirits. The shamanizing lasted three days. In the first night it was found out that the cause of the sickness were combined (put together) roads—*kamčibuye joyun*. On the second day an attempt was made at curing with the help of the shaman's spirit. There was a treatment with the brass-mirror; the shaman massaged the abdomen and the back of the patient; the same was done with ten Chinese rolls of bread (*mantõu*). After being used the breads were thrown through a closed window. If they go through, breaking the paper (paper is used instead of European glass), it is considered as a good sign, if the breads fall back, it is considered as a bad sign. The treatment was not successful, and it was decided to carry out a big shamanizing in order to send off all spirits of the three roads.

Prior to the beginning of the shamanizing various placings were made, needed for all three groups. A part of the placings would be used for the introduction of harmful spirits, another part for indicating to the spirits the way out and a third one to bar the passage back. After the shamanizing the first and second groups would be thrown away, the third group would be brought outside and buried about one metre deep in the ground at a place where three roads (ordinary men's roads) would meet.

The shamanizing of the third day began (night time) by the preparation of the performance. Two tables were put (a small table on short legs) covered with red, white, and black cloth, so that every colour covered a third of the tables. On one of them (the left table) placings were put for *mafar'i*—a male (*mafa*) and a female (*mama*)—and a corresponding sacrifice—a boiled chicken—and 5×3 or fifteen rolls of Chinese bread. By the side of this table *sula mafar'i xutu* (*vide infra* p. 316) was fixed—an anthropomorphic placing which was later thrown away. The "blooming tree" *ilgar'i* or *ilxa fodoxun*—"the blooming willow tree"—was fixed on the table (it could also have stood behind the table). It was supposed that the spirit would be attracted to the tree by "pleasant words" and a net (*sugdun dĕgdĕrĕbure asu*, "vapour-lifting net", where "vapour" is identified with the immaterial substance of the spirit or the disease). Near the tree Chinese "paper money", as used in funeral ceremonies, was put. The performance was opened by a prayer *baire g'izun*—"praying words." The shaman put on himself a special head-dress used for going to the lower world. After the introduction

of the spirit, the shaman went to the lower world. The spirit asked the dead shaman, who, according to the acting shaman, was the cause of the trouble, what was the reason for disturbing the man. The reason was that the sick man was *jarun* of the dead shaman, i.e. he belonged to the family which had used the dead shaman. When the shaman died, all his spirits remained without a master and made trouble to *jarun*. The dead shaman was asked to leave the man alone and was promised a sacrifice. What was needed for this operation had been already prepared on the right table. The placings: the shaman, the assistant, an animal (*gurgu*—"a quadruped wild animal covered with hair") and a bird (*gasxa*,—"wild bird in general"), paper money, and the net were taken outside, partly burnt (paper money) and partly thrown away, together with a "blooming tree". The operation with the *mafar'i* was much simpler: after a prayer inviting *mafar'i* to come in, the placing were taken out and thrown away. This operation was done in ordinary head-dress, after an interval lasting about half an hour. When this operation with the *saman xutu* and *sulu mafar'i xutu* was over, a special bunch of other small things was used. These were to take away the small, sometimes unknown, spirits called *nadan xači saxalin xutu*, i.e. "seven kinds of black (road) spirits". Since these spirits were those of the lower world, the shaman again put on a special kind of head-dress *nai iksĕ* (*vide supra* p. 295). A string connected with the bunch was attached to the index of the shaman's left hand. (The string is taken off the finger when the shaman falls down, i.e. when he reaches the lower world). Thereafter the shaman and the assistants took a bunch of objects, including a small bow and arrow, and various sharp things (called *joyun meltĕrü jaka*, i.e. "road cutting things"), took them out and buried them at the spot indicated by the shaman. In this way the road of the spirit was barred, the spirits (for they are afraid of sharp things) could not return. The chicken and cloths as well as other things which were used on the table were handed over to the shaman. As they had been used in the performance, they could not be taken back to the house, for the spirits might find their way back.

The place for the burial of the above indicated things was found at the distance of five hundred metres from the house, at the crossing of three roads (used for carts). A pit eighty centimetres deep was dug. All "sharp" things were put in and covered with earth. The shaman drummed and rhythmically pressed the earth with his feet to make the spot even. Then the shaman returned to the house, where the people were waiting for him. Near the entrance a fire had been made in order to prevent the return of the spirits together with the shaman. The shaman stopped at the door and continued drumming, while all the people who had gone with him to bury the "sharp things" passed under his arm, as he held the drum. This operation was for purification.

After this the guests, the shaman and the masters of the house ate a supper consisting of a pig slaughtered on this occasion, but not as a sacrifice to the spirits.

CHAPTER XXVI

CLASSIFICATION OF SHAMANISTIC PERFORMANCES

AIMS OF SHAMANISTIC PERFORMANCES From the instances of shamanizing shown in the previous chapter it can be seen that the aims of shamanizing may be different, but not all cases are seen in the above instances. When summarized, the aims of shamanizing may be classified into six groups, namely; (1) divination (discovery) of the causes of various troubles and of the future; (2) curing of persons; (3) transportation of the souls of dead people to the world of the dead and the governing of souls; (4) sacrifice to the spirits; (5) management of spirits and souls (including "mastering"); (6) various (e.g. new shaman). One and the same performance may have several aims, and it may have only one of the above indicated aims.

113. DIVINATION AND DISCOVERY DIAGNOSIS AND TREATMENT The discovery of causes of troubles and the divination of the future are the commonest aims of shamanizing. The shamans perform this very often, as a preliminary step, in order to find out what step should next be taken. Therefore, this almost always precedes the great shamanizing. In the latter it may constitute one of the parts or it may be carried out some time before the great shamanizing, i.e. in some cases even several months prior to the shamanizing. Among the Reindeer Tungus of Transbaikalia the divination, as a rule, is included in the shamanistic performance, as a conclusive part of the performance, or it is inserted into other parts. Finally, the shamans themselves are interested in getting acquainted with the spirits' activity, or with other people, and especially with the future, so that they very often perform "divination and discovery" even when they are alone.

The frequency of these practices and the methods of divination and discovery are variable in individual cases of the shamans and in ethnical groups. In fact, the shamans, among the Reindeer Tungus of Transbaikalia, are more inclined to these practices, than those among the Tungus of Manchuria and the Manchus. Some shamans devote to them more time than others, and I have met with some shamans who did this only when it was necessary for the performance. Those of them who are interested in finding new methods of divination and discovery practise this much more than those who follow the known practices.

In so far as the methods are concerned, divination and discovery may be distinguished (1) in the state of extasy; (2) in the state of sleep; (3) with the help of various technical and often mechanical means; and (4) by simple logical reasoning. In the first case the shamans believe that they can see the causes of troubles or the future with the help of the spirits which must be introduced into themselves. In order to introduce a spirit the shaman must first bring himself into a state of extasy. The question as to the nature of extasy, and the possibility of "divination and discovery" in this state, I leave for further discussion. The second method—in the state of sleep—is based on the

same idea of spirits' help during the shaman's sleep, when the shamans sometimes find the solution of problems set before them when they were awake. In the third method, technical and mechanical means are numerous. Such as, for instance, divination by means of the throwing down of a stick (*vide supra* p. 305), the burning of incense (*vide supra* p. 183), the throwing of cups, etc. all of which are based upon chance. Throwing of rolls of Chinese bread (*vide supra* p. 314) through a window paper is more than a simple game of chance, for the paper may be stronger or weaker, and the strength of the shaman may vary, as well as the hardness of the breads. Still more place for personal interpretation is found in the divination on the cracks of the omoplates of animals subject to the effect of fire. This method is known in Asia from time immemorial* and is widely practised, especially by the Tibetans and Mongols of our days. In this method a great accumulation of the previous experience constitutes the whole art, in different degrees assimilated by the shamans, some of whom do not practise it at all. I need not explain the last case of divination and discovery based upon reasoning. It is done without the help of spirits, e.g. the shaman considers all symptoms of the disease, supposed to be produced by a certain spirit, and makes his inference as to the cause; the shaman may also consider all available facts and make his inference as to "luck" in the hunting, or travelling, or weather. In the same group we may include all cases in which a shaman influences himself or other people who act according to his prediction. Lastly, some shamans may foretell the future without a direct help of spirits, e.g. as to the arrival of other people, the change of weather, the movement of fishes, etc., and they sometimes believe themselves to be acting independently of spirits. Individual shamans use the above indicated methods in different proportions, which depends on the character of the shaman, his experience, and his belief in the effectiveness of these methods. A young inexperienced shaman will surely not rely very much on his or her simple reasoning. The choice of methods also depends on the knowledge of various methods (especially of the group of mechanical methods) within the ethnical groups. Since it is so, the methods may become fashionable and they may be easily forgotten. Naturally these must be known to the groups practising them as good and reliable methods. They become so either being borrowed from other ethnical groups which are considered to be superior to the Tungus, e.g. the Chinese with their numberless methods of divination or the Russians, with their fortune-telling with cards, or when the new methods are introduced by the influential shamans, whose credit is great among the given unit. Owing to these conditions, the complex of mechanical methods among the Tungus groups and individual shamans is variable. In some cases these methods may become of great importance, even for testing the shamans themselves by the audience, or for making the shamans themselves sure of their solving of some problems. Such a "hyper-

* Cf. for instance, divination bones found in prehistoric sites, also in historic sites, in China.

trophy" of the divination complex does occur among some Tungus groups.*

It should also be noted that all these forms, with the exception of cases when the spirits are helping, are practised by some Tungus and especially by the *mafaⁱi* among the Manchus. Naturally in the groups, among whom divination is widely practised by the common people, the shamans confine themselves only to the forms where spirits are needed. Here there may be a case of shifting of function.

Indeed, on the formal ground, that shamanizing is considered as a complex requiring extasy, the "divination and discovery" carried out without extasy could not be regarded as "shamanizing". However, this point of view cannot be accepted, if we regard shamanizing as a complex operation consisting of various elements, in other words, as shamanizing actually is. "Divination and discovery" carried out by the non-shamans and without extasy cannot be regarded as "shamanizing". From the above given facts it thus appears that shamanizing for divination and discovery of the causes of trouble, or for foretelling the future may be lacking in the performance, and it may by itself constitute a performance (e.g. Case 3, the Khingan Tungus). It may be also a very complex operation, or a combination of various methods, and it may be confined to a simple "reasoning" and a conclusion not differing from those practised by the common people.

DIAGNOSIS AND TREATMENT which may be accomplished in different ways are thus an important moment in the shamanizing. I shall now give, in addition, some more details.

When a shaman is called in among the Manchus, the case is as follows. He takes note of all symptoms and decides whether the assistance of a professional doctor or a treatment with medicines, hot or cold mineral springs etc. is needed. He may find out that a pure and simple psychological state of the patient, such as fear, anger and, in general, strong emotions, not involving any spirits could be suspected. A special treatment may then be used to call back the soul, which does not always require the assistance of spirits and which can be carried out without extasy. Finally, there may be cases of interference of various spirits. The Manchus distinguish nine cases, in which different causes are suspected.

1. *saman joʏɯn* (shaman's road) may be suspected if there is a wicked shaman who sends various spirits in order to harm the people. This is recognized by the behaviour of the patient—he or she may repeat the name of a spirit, or of the shaman, or imitate the attitude of a spirit, as it is believed to be, or that of the shaman. Extasy and nervous attacks or fits are likely to occur. In order to neutralize this harmful activity, either a simple introduction of the spirit (the shaman) into a special placing or its sending off is effected, or a very complex performance takes place. The usual placing on such occasions is one made of straw, dressed in a shaman's costume made of paper and supplied with all shamanistic paraphernalia also made of paper and exactly imitating those of a shaman.

2. *sula joʏɯn* (*sula* road) = *xutu joʏɯn* [*sula* is a spirit

* Cf. for instance, the case of divination with small stones, and others, among the Goldi during the identification of the soul to be brought to the lower world (cf. I. A. Lopatin, op. cit. p. 307, where P. Simkević's observations are quoted).

of unknown origin, much weaker than *xutu*; it is a loan—cf. *sula* (Mong. Kow.)—"faible, lache, vide, libre, sans charge, qui n'a aucun emploi", etc. cf. *soal* (Dahur, Poppe) *sulù* (Xalxa, Poppe)—"free".] is recognized in minor troubles of the patient. One, two or three anthropomorphic placings and a dog are made of straw. The *sula* may be introduced and sent off.

3. *pučèye xutu joʏɯn* ("dead people's spirit road") is recognized if the patient sees one of the dead persons in his hallucinations and dreams. Anthropomorphic placings according to the number of spirits (*xutu*) seen are made of straw.

4. *sayale joʏɯn* ("black road") usually occurs in the case when the people remain without regular burial. Such spirits require regular food, clothing, etc. They may remain for a long time among the people; e.g. the clan *sagda* (*sakga xutu*) has such a spirit, and it is very difficult to send it off. Its presence is recognized by the same signs: extasy, fits, attacks, dreams, etc. A dog and up to twenty anthropomorphic placings—all of black paper—are made. The sacrifice consists of a black chicken. A complex shamanizing is usually required.

5. *mafaⁱi (mavarⁱi) joʏɯn* ("mafa road") is recognized, if the patient performs acts which are known as a speciality of *mafa* spirit. *Fodoyon mô*,—"blooming tree", is made by which the spirit is called in and sent off.

6. *sula mavarⁱi joʏɯn* ("free mafa road") (*sula*, cf. No. 2; there are some "free *mafa*"). *Fodoyon mô* ("blooming tree"), three kinds of coloured cloth, each about sixty-five centimetres long, and a small shrine of birch wood are made.

7. *pušuku joʏɯn* ("pušuku road") (cf. *supra* p. 159) is recognized by a pathological condition of the blood. The shamans usually refuse to interfere.

8. *pučèye saman joʏɯn* ("dead shaman's road") is recognized by the activity of spirits left by the deceased shaman. Straw placings for the shaman and his assistant are made. The best way to cure is to take up these spirits.

9. *pučèye jarɯn saman joʏɯn* ("dead helping shaman's road", i.e. the shaman who assisted the people now affected)—the same as in No. 8.

In all these cases an ordinary hen is given as a sacrifice; only in Case 4, the hen must be black.

Another group of cases are those of various *xutu, fuč̣kⁱi* and other spirits, not mentioned in the above cases, which may take hold of the soul. The diagnosis is made according to the character of the spirits.

The methods of diagnosis among the various Tungus groups are in the main the same; the behaviour of the patient, his own indications, his dreams, nervous attacks, fits and an occasional state of extasy are indicative of the presence (self-introduction or introduction by a shaman) of specified spirits. The condition of the patient may also be indicative of diseases caused by "spirits" of certain diseases. The treatment of such cases would depend on the character of the spirits, and thus the shaman may decide, whether a simple treatment with medicines is needed, or a prayer and sacrifice, or whether shamanizing ought to be performed with the assistance of the shaman's spirits. It should be noted that the diagnosis can be made by any competent person without the shaman's interference, and the shaman can be asked to act, in order to send off or fight a definitely indicated spirit.

In case the shaman cannot make a diagnosis without extasy, a performance with the introduction of spirits into himself takes place and with the help of those spirits the cause of the trouble is found out.

114. TREATMENT OF PERSONS When the cause of the trouble has been found, the shaman may refuse to take up the case (e.g. *pušuku joγun*), if it is considered as hopeless, or he may recommend treating the patient with medicines, dealing with the spirits by means of prayers and sacrifices, sometimes carried out without his own assistance, or he may take on himself the task of dealing with the spirits. When the shaman abstains from interference or when he recommends treatment without his assistance, the function of shamanizing is not involved; these occurrences will not be discussed here, as I confine myself to cases when the shaman performs.

From the Tungus point of view, "troubles" may be classed in three groups, namely, (1) disfunction of the soul, (2) interference of the spirits without their entering into the person, and (3) interference of spirits with their introduction into the person.

The simple disfunction of the soul is a common occurrence. There may be cases such as, for instance, sudden fear, when the patient is not affected by the spirits. In such cases there is disfunction of the soul, which, as shown, according to the theories, is a complex system. The threefold organization of the soul of the Manchu in this respect went very far in defining the conditions in which there is no smooth correlated movement of souls (*vide supra* p. 135), the true soul, the outer soul etc. The Birarčen, by accepting the theories of the slight stability of the souls, are inclined to see the source of trouble in a temporary or permanent instability of these souls. The situation is still more complicated when lack of correlation between "soul" and "life" (*èrga*) is suspected. The treatment of both "soul" and "life" would naturally require special combined methods. It is thus evident that we have the same naturalistic theory of the complex of soul and life as the basis of explanation of this group of troubles.

The spirits may produce harmful effects without introducing themselves into persons and remaining outside. This happens often with spirits which frighten the people, particularly the children. The existing theories may help to find out which spirit did interfere. The effect of the spirits's activity is a lasting disfunction of the soul. Therefore, attention must be paid to the source of the continuance of such disfunction. However, attention will also be paid to the necessary restoration of the normal function of the soul. Naturally the character of the trouble depends on the character of the spirits. This group of psychomental phenomena, which result in the disability of persons in their social functions, is explained by the theory of spirits.

The spirits may introduce themselves into the person with either a continuous or a periodic disfunction of the souls, or the spirit may act only in the presence of an undisturbed soul. The explanation of these phenomena is based upon the hypothesis of the spirits' self-introduction into the human body.

As I have already shown, on several occasions, the analysis and classification of all these cases from the point of view of psychiatry brings us to the conclusion that we actually have here different kinds of "troubles". The greater part of the cases cannot be classified as real psychomental "diseases", but only as conditions of instability; while some of them can be labelled neurasthenia, hysteria, paranoia, and various mania, etiologically due to various causes. The Tungus system actually deals with the symptoms, some of which may be common for different conditions due to different causes. As shown, cases of real insanity among the Tungus are not frequent, while psychomental maladjustment and instability, very often produced by self-suggestion, are common, and their treatment is quite possible.

There are three principal groups of methods used by the shaman, namely, (1) without introduction of the shaman's spirits; (2) with the help of the shaman's spirits but without introduction of the spirits into the shaman; and (3) with introduction of the spirits into the shaman.

From the results of the diagnosis and from the knowledge of various methods of curing the shaman may come to different decisions as to the particular cases of interference. Some of them I shall now describe.

CASE 1. Disfunction of the soul by itself, without spirits' interference, in which the shaman does not seek the help of his spirits. This is the most common occurrence in the shaman's practice. The shaman finds out the kind of disfunction of the soul, e.g. temporary absence of one of the souls, or lack of balancing of the souls, or a combination of both. In case of absence of one of the souls he will find which is absent; in case of lack of balance (unequal movement of the three souls through the seven holes—a Manchu theory), he will determine which of them is running too fast. Since, the function of the three souls are different, the characters of disfunction are also different. In fact, the "true" soul, identified by the Manchu with the "individual consciousness", may be overshadowed by the "reproductive" soul (is it not perhaps connected with sexual complex too?) and by the general physiological-psychological soul; the "reproductive" soul can be overshadowed by the other two souls, or also one of them may be weakened. The system of the Tungus of Manchuria, although slightly different, explains the same cases of disfunction by the temporal absence of one of the souls.* As pointed out (*vide supra*, Ch. IV, p. 51) there may be some additional interpretations of the system of the soul, e.g. when the conception of *dô* (Bir.) is introduced. However, this new element does not change the idea of disfunction. How near the Tungus and Manchus come to the actual condition of slight disturbances of psychomental functions is a different question, but one thing is clear, namely, they recognize as a normal condition that, when the psychomental complex is functionally well balanced making a person "normal", i.e. like the majority. Lack of balance is seen in the behaviour of the affected person, and the disequilibrium may come from two causes: an increase or a decrease of functional activity of the threefold soul, and even the fourfold and fivefold complex of the human psychomental function. It should be kept in mind that the people believe in the possibility of the regulation of the equilibrium of the components. The shaman also believes in this. In case of disturbance, the shaman may

---

* Unfortunately my understanding of the system of the Reindeer Tungus of Transbaikalia was not so complete as it was in the case of the Tungus of Manchuria and the Manchus, so I cannot tell how they conceive the condition of disfunction. That they have this idea is evident from the treatment of such cases.

find that the "true" soul ("individual consciousness") moves too rapidly and would take various steps for retarding this movement, e.g. the spirits of the clan might be asked to bring quietness, or a sacrifice to these spirits might be offered, or he might talk about the matter, saying that "now everything will be well". These actions produce an effect upon the affected person. Among the Tungus and Manchus, who believe in the instability of the souls of children, the cases of absent soul are cured by means of various methods: special placings are made for the souls of children, sometimes crying and restless (anthropomorphic placings of blackened skin), which are put in front of the child. The attention of the child would be attracted by the movement and so the child would no longer cry. Groups of placings, made of wood and metals, and amulets which, when shaken, produce rhythmic noises, would have the same effect on the hearing as the blackened placing on the sight, and the child would become quiet. If there were no effect, it would be supposed that there were other causes for the discomfort of the child.

When adult people are supposed to have lost one of their souls, the shaman calls it back by ordinary words or by singing and makes rhythmic movements to re-introduce the soul. Instances have already been given of the ritual of finding and re-introducing of souls. If a person affected by disequilibrium is not actually sick, all of these methods may be quite effective, as would be any other forms of suggestion and hypnosis. However, if the person is left without the shaman's help, the condition may gradually lead to that of complete social disability.

Thus, in these cases, the shaman may give the patient an analysis of his psychomental condition, which may suffice to correct "the balance"; he may recommend some mechanical method of various complexity having effect on the sight and the hearing to lull or to concentrate the attention of the child; he may carry out a hypnotic operation, or make a strong suggestion. In all of these cases which, let us emphasize, are frequent, the shaman could stop the further increase of the psychomental instability.

CASE 2. Disfunction of the soul by itself, in which the shaman brings forth some of his spirits without introducing them into himself. These are cases which in the eyes of the shaman are more serious, involving the affected persons and their relatives and in which the shaman would decide that he himself could not succeed in curing. He would then call one of his spirits, and with a prayer, or even a sacrifice, would ask the spirit to help him. In this case one or several placings for the shaman's spirits would be left with the affected person. Such a placing may even be the brass mirror used as one of the important components of the costume. There may be made a placing for the spirit and it will always be carried on his person. Periodical small sacrifices may also be prescribed. Naturally, the shaman would assure the patient or his parents (particularly the *mother* of the small child who is still suckled by her) that there will be no more trouble. The effect is evident: all these measures would act as a continuous hypnosis and suggestion, while in the case of the suckling child the mother would become quieter and the child too. Such occurrences are also very frequent* and the effec-

* This is not the shaman's privilege: the existence of special woman's spirits (placings kayan, najil burkan, etc.) is of the same order.

tiveness of the treatment is more common than failure. In the case of a wrong diagnosis other means can be used.

CASE 3. Disfunction of the soul by itself, in which the shaman introduces into himself one or several of his spirits. These cases are much rarer, even comparatively very rare, and they are very serious in the eyes of everybody. In this case shamanizing would be performed, the shaman would introduce into himself spirits and would act with their special power. After the shamanizing, the shaman would leave one of his spirits to remain with the affected person. If improvement of the condition results and the person is young, his name would be changed and that of the spirit would be adopted. This measure would be explained by saying that the person was being "protected" by the spirit. From the psychological point of view, during impressive performances and with the presence of a powerful spirit in the shaman, the patient is, at least for a while, deprived of his will power and becomes more susceptible to the suggestion. If the remembrance of the performance is renewed by periodical sacrifices, prayers and even by a new name, the suggestion may become continuous. The person, formerly affected, may be restored to social life. The variety of forms of performance is indeed great, for it depends on the choice by the shaman of a spirit which may help, and the spirits are very numerous.

CASE 4. Disfunction of the soul caused by the spirits without their self-introduction into the affected person, in which the shaman does not use spirits in his treatment. These cases are frequent, although in some groups they are rarer than those of Case 1. It may be so when the patient shows signs of being disturbed by the spirits and cannot accept the idea that the condition of disfunction depends upon himself or herself. In the diagnosis some hints are found as to the kind of spirits: the person may see or hear them, or may behave as though he or she can see or hear them. Apparently, there ought to be included all cases in which the shaman guesses (he may be unconscious of it) that the person cannot understand his trouble without supposing the presence of a spirit. The shaman may use a prayer to the spirit-disturber, a sacrifice to this spirit, a strong intimidation of the spirit and its introduction into a placing which, together with the spirit, is thrown away. When the spirit is neutralized, the shaman may restore the equilibrium of the soul, if it is found to be in disequilibrium. Thus the performance may consist of two actions: the elimination of the spirit's activity and the restoration of the soul's normal function. After the performance some paraphernalia may be left for maintaining the belief in the disappearance of the spirit. A still more complex case is that in which the disturbing spirits must be localized (women's spirits, etc.), or when the spirits which cause the trouble must be transferred to the lower world, etc. In such cases a very complex operation is needed, which requires the introduction of spirits into the shaman. But there are special aims of regulation of the relations between the spirits and the people, and these cases will be treated later.

CASE 5. Disfunction of the soul caused by the spirits without their self-introduction, in which the shaman uses his spirits. These cases are rarer than those of Case 4. The essential difference is that the shaman must use one of his spirits, in order to fight the spirit-disturber, or simply to protect the person. The actions of the shaman may consist in a prayer to his spirits and in charging them with a duty. If the spirit is left with the person (in a plac-ing, including the brass mirror), periodical sacrifices and prayers may be offered by the affected persons or their re-latives and there may also be a change of the name. The performance may become quite elaborate and long, but it will not become a great shamanizing. In such a case a more powerful influence on the person is used during the action (the spirits), and the effect may be made continuous.

CASE 6. Disfunction of the soul caused by the spirits without their self-introduction, in which the shaman uses introduction of the spirits into himself. These cases are rather rare. The shaman would act as in Case 3 and Case 5 combined. A performance of great shamanizing is rather complex, even in the simplest case, but if special methods of dealing with the spirits are needed, shamanizing may assume new aims concerning the fate of the spirits.

CASE 7. Troubles produced by the self-introduction of the spirits (to which disfunction of the souls may be associated), the shaman acts without the assistance of his spirits. These cases are not frequent but usually the sha-man does not at once succeed in curing. They are more serious than the cases described in Case 4. The aim of the shaman is to suppress the activity of the spirit and, if possi-ble, to send it off by the same means as in Case 4; but the spirit must be first dislodged.

CASE 8. Troubles produced by the self-introduction of the spirits; the shaman uses his spirits. These cases are not frequent and usually they form a preliminary step. The shaman acts as in Case 5, but more skill is required, for the need of dislodging the spirit is impending.

CASE 9. Troubles produced by the self-introduction of spirits, in which case the shaman introduces into himself one or several spirits. These cases are very rare and usual-ly occur when the procedures of Case 7 and Case 8 do not produce the necessary effect. Such a great shamanizing usually comprises an act of dislodging the spirit and send-ing it off, or even its mastering by the shaman, in case of a new, unknown spirit. Therefore other aims usually ap-pear in the shamanizing.

From the description of these nine cases it is evident that the shamanizing may be quite effective, if there is no deep pathological condition underlying the trouble. Prac-tically, the greater number of cases treated by the shamans are of such a nature that the various forms of suggestion and even hypnosis are quite sufficient for relieving persons of their disability. It can also be seen that there is a great variety of methods employed by the shamans in conformity with the diagnosis. In the simplest cases an explanation of the disfunction to the patients, who afterwards influ-ence themselves by self-suggestion, may be used; hypnosis is produced by simple drumming and singing, and after-wards suggestion of prompt or continuous action may be employed; a permanently influencing remembrance of the suggestion may be left; when the case is difficult the person may be impressed by a sudden action of spirits, which may restore the usual behaviour, and at that moment the shaman may make his suggestion.

There is no doubt that all these methods have been em-pirically worked out and established as practices well adapted to the needs of the ethnical units, where they are preserved by the mechanism of tradition. Naturally, when the shamans are performing their treatment, they are not conscious, in the same way as are European neurologists and psychiatrists, of what they are doing. Neither are the patients, who give credit to the shamans conscious of their actual condition. All of them follow certain practices adopt-ed by the ethnical units in which they live. The full credit given to the shamans extremely facilitates their work. The whole system of treatment, as shown, is based upon the theory of the complex nature of the soul and the hypo-theses as to the spirits. Whether these theories and hypo-theses are accepted or not, is a different question, but as a form of Tungus (and Manchu) adaptation they are, in some instances, a more effective approach to the practical goal of curing and enabling patients to restore their social ef-ficiency, than are some very learned modern theories and methods of treatment of psychomental disequilibria. These theories and hypotheses have resulted, on the one hand, from a penetrating analysis of the facts and, on the other hand, from their practical empirical application, correction, and verification. Let us also remember that the shamans, as stated, do not always take the trouble of treating, not always can they correctly diagnose whether a treatment is possible or not; also not all shamans possess equal ability in diagnosis and they are not equal in their art of treatment. In all the above indicated cases there may be failure due to an error, either in the diagnosis, or in the practical applica-tion of methods.

115.   SETTLING OF SOULS AND THEIR MANAGEMENT   Finding of errant souls after death, their mana-gement and transporta-tion to the place of settled life in the lower world are im-portant aims of shamanizing. As shown, the souls of dead people may produce various troubles: the souls of persons who are not buried according to the rites will re-main in this world and will, in some cases at least, introduce themselves into the living people, or they may annoy living people with their continuous requests for attention, food, etc. The shaman has to find the souls and to satisfy them, until they are settled in the lower world. Indeed, this is sometimes done by the common people too, but not all know the methods of finding souls and localizing them in tempor-ary or permanent placings, so that the shamans are usually called to do this, especially if the death occurred far away. When the soul is transferred to the lower world—which operation requires the shaman's art in some cases—the souls may again disturb the people by their requests and needs. The management of souls in the lower world, their return to this world, and their reinstallation into the lower world are operations which are usually carried out by the shamans. These operations are different, because the common people, without the help of special spirits, cannot go to the lower world without running a great risk of re-maining there, i.e. of dying. When pressed by need, common people may call the souls from the lower world; but there is again a great risk that these souls will not re-turn and will continuously disturb the peace of living people. Owing to these conditions, the common people prefer to leave these operations to the shamans.

From the character of the souls of dead people at least four aims of shamanizing result: (1) finding the souls and managing them in this world; (2) sending them to the lower world; (3) managing them in the lower world; (4) bringing them into this world from the lower world.

Just as in the cases of treatment, the shamans may per-form with or without the help of the spirits, whence different forms of shamanizing originate. In fact, when the shaman and the people are certain that the shaman may see the souls, call them, and manage them with his prayers, sacrifices, and "nice words", he would do this without disturbing his spirits. If he is certain that the soul would directly and without difficulties go to the lower world, i.e. when all customs are observed, the deceased person was not particularly attached to the living persons, the deceased person was old, and the living persons have accepted the fact of the death— then he might not call his own spirits. However, when he has to deal with the lower world, or to bring souls back, he must have the assistance of his spirits.

It should be noticed that among different Tungus groups all dealings with the souls are not of equal importance. This depends on two conditions: firstly, on the idea of how far the souls are active in the lower world and of how far their influence may spread in this world; and secondly, on the idea of how difficult their installation is in the lower world. From the psychological point of view souls may occupy the place of other spirits as the cause of psychomental disequilibria, which may be produced by conditions independent of the existing theory, but may depend on the physiological condition. The groups which hold the souls responsible for various troubles would pay much less attention to the activity of other spirits, and vice versa. The "ancestor worship", "filial piety", etc., when transferred into the Tungus complexes, may strenghten the idea of the souls' influence on living people. Among the Manchus the cases when people are disturbed by the souls are therefore much more frequent than among other Tungus groups, and particularly the Tungus of Manchuria, who are disturbed chiefly by the souls of unburied people and *burkan*. The souls of unburied people disturb the living people among the Tungus of Transbaikalia still less. The second theory, namely, the degree of difficulty of sending souls off to the lower world, is much stronger among the Goldi, than among the Tungus of Manchuria. As shown, a great part of the shaman's energy (great shamans!) is used in sending off of souls. In this operation the Manchus use no shamans, while the Tungus of Transbaikalia only occasionally use them. So, we have some instances when the shamans are almost free of the trouble of going to the lower world, as it has been observed among the Birarčen.

GROUP 1. Finding the souls of dead people and managing them in this world can be done by the shaman without the introduction into himself of the spirits, i.e. the performance may be confined to the discovery, without extasy, of the whereabouts of the souls and to the calling them by various means—e.g. drumming, calling by their names, "feeding" (sacrifice), etc. The Goldi have much more trouble in this respect, for it is presumed that *it is difficult to find the souls*—they escape, they want to remain free—and a special art is needed for finding them with the help of the shaman's spirits. When they are found, they must be temporarily located in a special placing (*fan'a*). Whence there has been created a complex performance of neutralization of souls of dead people before their settlement in the lower world. This is done to prevent the self-introduction of souls into the living people and the disturbance of their calm psychomental functioning.

GROUP 2. Sending off of the souls to the lower world is carried out among some groups by shamans without the introduction of spirits, e.g. the Tungus of Transbaikalia (I think all of them), and those of Manchuria. However,

in a great number of cases there is no need to ask the shaman for assistance—the souls proceed to the lower world by themselves, if they are provided with the necessary equipment. Among the Manchus the Chinese complex of sending off of souls does not require any special assistance of the shaman. It is different with the Goldi—the souls (I do not think that it is true of all souls, but only of those which belong to adults, and middle-aged people) are not easily carried into the lower world. The shaman must therefore introduce his spirits into himself and go through all the hardships of visiting the lower world.

GROUP 3. Managing of the souls in the lower world may be carried out in the form of prayers and sacrifices, even without the shaman's assistance. However, when the souls become very troublesome, the shaman may interfere and carry out prayers and sacrifices without introducing his spirits into himself. This is done when the desire of the souls is well known to the shaman. However, there are cases when a personal meeting with the souls by the shaman is needed. In this case the shaman must himself go into the lower world: he introduces certain spirits, after great preparations, as described in the preceding chapter. In individual cases among the shamans and among different ethnical groups the forms of shamanizing and of direct impulses for performing it are subject to numberless variations.

GROUP 4. Bringing souls back into this world is always carried out with the assistance of shaman's spirits. This is a most complicated and difficult task. Two cases may be distinguished, namely: (1) the case when the soul is needed for its re-installation in the body, i.e. the revival of the corpse, when the other souls are still near to it (it is supposed that the corpse is not yet decomposed, i.e. the "matter", "animus", and some souls are present); and (2) the case when the soul is needed for being placed in this world. The first case is rather simple: the soul is found and brought back by the shaman; it is re-installed in the corpse and the person, supposed to be dead, is revived. Moreover, bad cases may also occur, namely, the other two souls may become loose, or they may lose their equally regular movement (Manchu theory), so that even after the reinstallation of the soul the person may suffer from psychomental trouble. In case of failure (e.g. when death has really occurred), the shaman makes no more efforts, for it may occur because of the actual decomposition of the corpse or the holding of the soul by the spirits of the lower world. Naturally, the performance is the most elaborate and difficult. The second case is much more complex for there may occur different situations, e.g. the soul may be brought back for its permanent location in a special placing and for further care, or the soul may be mastered by the shaman.

The shamanizing may be directed toward one of the aims, or it may be included in a more complex shamanizing. This would depend, as in other cases, on the given conditions, on the individuality of the shaman, and on the practices which exist in the given ethnical units (or group).

116. FIGHTING OF SPIRITS   comprises definite aims of
          AND SOULS   forced neutralizing of spirits
                            and souls of other people,
particularly of shamans. I have included into this group all cases whose aim is not "curing" and also cases of "curing"

which cannot be regarded as cases of simple "curing", but which use fighting of spirits as a method of "curing". The cases of fighting souls of living people and especially those of shamans ought to be included in the same group. As a matter of fact, as shown, no essential difference exists between "souls" and "spirits". Their properties are the same, and they can be fought with the same methods. However, the souls must be separated into a special group, for the effects which may be produced on souls and spirits are different.

An open fighting of spirits and souls is usually carried out by the shaman, when their activity becomes harmful for a great number of people, and sometimes for the shaman himself, so that the only radical solution is to do away with the spirit or soul for ever, or at least to secure a permanent protection. Therefore shamanizing may be performed independently of the current necessity, e.g. in case of direct attack on the people.

The methods used by the shamans are like those used in other cases, namely, with or without the assistance of other spirits, the former being carried out with or without the introduction of the shaman's spirit into the shaman. A new method is now also used, namely, the introduction of the harmful spirit into the shaman and its complete "mastering". I shall now analyse some cases.

CASE 1. The shaman does not use his spirits and has to fight a spirit or a soul. It is done when other means e.g. sacrifice, prayers, etc. are inefficient. The harmful activity of the spirit can be established from the observation of the condition of the affected persons: there may be recurring nervous attacks, inefficiency in hunting, hallucinations, etc. The shaman would then decide to fight the spirit (or several spirits). By nice words and even by a sacrifice, or merely by the promise of a sacrifice the shaman may invite it or them into a special placing. When the spirit is introduced, the shaman takes the placing and throws it far away in a certain direction (road). In order to prevent the spirit from coming back, the "road" may be cut by means of digging a ditch, or burying sharp cutting things, rarely skins of animals, such as hog or bear's paws, etc. These methods are especially common among the Manchus. The spirit may also be sent off with the river current, as it is often done with the women's spirits *kayan* (Birarčen). Such are the most common methods, but the shamans may invent some new methods or some variations of the old ones. It should be noted that the shooting of spirits may theoretically be effective, but the shamans avoid it (e.g. among the Birarčen) for the reasons which will be shown later.

Fighting of souls of common people and especially those of shamans is considered necessary when a continuous harm is noticed, produced by other persons to the people, who ask the shaman's assistance, or to the shaman himself. A supposition as to the nature of the harm and the persons doing it is reached in the same way, as it is with the spirits. The diagnosis is facilitated by the fact that the personal attitude of the "enemies" is known. The soul is called into the placing and can be managed just like the spirits. Another method is shooting, as already described (*vide supra*, Part Three). In both cases the effect is that the persons may die or become temporarily sick, or at least may feel uneasy and will be afraid to renew their harmful activity. From the formal point of view the performance may be very long, lasting several days, with the shaman singing

and drumming, but his spirits will not be involved.

CASE 2. The shaman asks for the assistance of his spirits for fighting other spirits and souls. The difference with the previous case consists in a greater complexity of the operation and a greater security for the success. However, there are also negative sides of this method, namely, the shaman's spirit may disobey him and he would come into a conflict with his own mastered spirits. Another negative side is the danger that the spirits or souls which are fought may, in the process of fighting, mix up with the shaman's spirits and may harm the spirits and the shaman himself. The performance consists of two preliminary acts, namely, the calling in of a shaman spirit for assistance and for the placing of the spirit that is to be fought, and the act of deporting of the enemy spirit, while the shaman's spirit is left to protect the person or the shaman himself. In this case the shaman's spirit will be left in a special placing or in the brass-mirror. Here there may be another way out, namely, the spirit that is to be fought is left alone by the shaman, but the shaman's spirit receives the order from his master-shaman to fight the enemies when necessary. In this way the fighting is carried out between the spirits.

The same is done when the shaman has to fight souls. The effect on the souls is still more complex than in Case 1, for the shaman's spirit may produce continuous trouble to the persons that are to be fought, (cf. "treatment", also *supra* p. 316, *saman joyun*, of the Manchus). If the shaman leaves his spirits by the side of persons that are to be fought, the spirit may enter them. The spirit may also become "mixed" with the enemy of the shaman's spirit and produce disturbances among the spirits themselves; e.g. the spirit may "eat" other spirits, destroy them; the spirit may "eat" the sacrifice destined for other spirits and consequently produce dissatisfaction of these spirits with the shaman, who will be suspected of neglecting them (no sacrifice).

CASE 3. The shaman uses his own spirits in order to fight other spirits and souls. The difference between Case 3 and Case 2 consists in the introduction of the spirit into the shaman to give him more power for fighting. Sometimes the shaman has to find the spirit whom he cannot see or reach without the help of special spirits. In fact, some spirits are so clever, that they would avoid approaching the woman, so the shaman must assume the form of one of his spirits in order to approach the spirit that is to be fought. The performance would be most difficult and complicated, the aim being to fight the spirit and to send it off, even to destroy it, if possible—to "eat" it with the help of the shaman's spirit.

In the case of fighting souls, the shaman, with the spirits introduced into himself, can do this easier, because the souls (of a shaman or other people) can be approached, the shaman's activity being left unnoticed. However, in spite of its relative easiness for the shaman (he is in a state of extasy), shamans do not like to apply this method, for it actually means an open war with other people and shamans who naturally belong to other clans. Thus, such a method means inter-clan war carried on for destruction of the psychomental equilibrium of the enemies (i.e. what used to be called during the great war in Europe the "moral"). Such wars between the shamans will be discussed later.

CASE 4. In order to fight spirits the shaman "masters" them. Such an occurrence is common when a new spirit appears among the population, or some of the old spirits, previously comparatively harmless, become harmful, but can be "mastered". The diagnosis is made after an observation of a great number of cases of the spirit's activity, and the conclusion as to the impossibility of dealing with all cases separately. Then the shaman decides upon the necessity of "mastering". The operation itself consists in the voluntary introduction of this spirit into the shaman. During the first extasy of the shaman the assistants make an enquiry as to the character of the new spirit, its desires, intentions, etc. When this is done, the spirit may be re-introduced, when needed, and in this way the people are liberated from the danger of being disturbed. If the new spirit is not very important, it is "mastered" independently, or it may be submitted to a control by other spirits (usually, the first spirit of the shaman). This practice is very common among the Tungus of Manchuria. Naturally most of these spirits are *dōna*, i.e. foreign (not clan!) spirits. However, the shamans do not like to have recourse to the mastering of spirits, for they must be absolutely certain that they can do it. If a shaman cannot "master" a spirit and introduces it into himself, he may be "mastered" himself by this spirit, i.e. he would become "crazy", might "lose his mind", etc. It is very unlikely that a young, little-experienced shaman would try such an introduction;—it is more likely that he would choose one of the other methods, e.g. the sending off of the spirit (as in the above cases), or the treatment of individual cases ("treatment"). Such a performance is very complicated and it may be carried out in different ways—with or without the help of the spirits. It is more likely that it will be carried out with the help of all spirits of the shaman, for they have to agree as to the adoption of "a new servant of their master". Thus there will be a continuous change of spirits introduced into the shaman one after another, and the whole performance will have a quite special form. The introduction of a new spirit—its mastering—may also take place at the annual „feeding" of spirit. In such a case the performance will be still more complex. The "mastering" of the spirit (soul) of a deceased shaman is of course a special case.

CASE 5. *VARIA*

117. SACRIFICE, VARIA AND CONCLUSIONS   Sacrifice to the spirits, as a special aim of shamanizing, is commonly observed, and it can be segregated into a special group. A sacrifice may by itself constitute a performance. In fact, the yearly sacrifice to the spirits of a shaman is a great event in the clan. Among some groups, such as, for instance, the Manchus, it lasts several days and is carried out with great solemnity. However, it may also be reduced to a very simple performance, as it is among the Reindeer Tungus of Transbaikalia. As in other cases of shamanizing, different methods may be used by the shaman, i.e. without and with the help of shaman's spirit, with and without their introduction into the shaman. Thus, in so far as forms of performance are concerned, the methods greatly vary.

In a simple case the shaman may call the spirits by a prayer, by drumming, and by inviting them to a sacrifice. The occasions for a sacrifice may be different, e.g. sickness of the people, thanksgivings for recovery, as well as for remaining on good terms with the spirits. When the matter concerns sickness or recovery, the sacrifice is only a part and merely a means of a greater shamanizing; so it ought not

to be regarded as a special form. However, there are also cases when sacrifice constitutes the only purpose of shamanizing. These are cases: (1) when the shaman offers annual sacrifice to his spirits; (2) when the shaman, after assuming his functions as a clan-shaman, must offer a sacrifice to all his spirits. As a rule, both acts are very solemn and important, and since they are connected with the person of the shaman, they will be described in a special chapter dealing with the shaman.

Under the heading "varia" I include all cases of performances which cannot be grouped with the preceding types of performances. Some of them I shall now indicate. One of the rare purposes of a performance is that connected with the formal recognition of a new shaman. It is exceptional as to its complexity and frequency. In fact, among some groups, e.g. among the Manchus, it may last nine days, and usually not less than three days. The new shaman is usually created only after the death or the disability of the old shaman, and it may happen only once in a shaman's life. This performance will be further discussed.

More frequent are the performances connected with the regulation of cattle breeding, hunting and fishing, when the shaman intends to eliminate a harmful activity of spirits and to attract the attention of the spirits which regulate the life of animals. The analysis of these cases is not always easy. In fact, in the case of sickness of cattle, or horses, or reindeer, the shaman may actually deal with the problem of neutralization of harmful spirits. The performance will then not differ from the case of "treatment". However, there may be another case, namely, a request, addressed to the corresponding spirits, to increase the number of the domestic animals. As shown in the preceding chapters, this is usually done among the Manchus by the *p'oyun saman*, i.e. the clan "priests", and by experienced persons among the Tungus, and even merely by persons who know the prayers. I have never heard of great shamans performing this function. Moreover, an interference of shaman's spirits with the activity of other spirits is usually considered undesirable.

Interference of the shaman with hunting and fishing is also not an interference in a direct sense. Indeed, as in the case of domestic animals, the shaman as a good singer and person familiar with prayers, may influence the spirits controlling animals, but the shaman would not act with his spirits, whose interference can bring a new complication of relations between men and spirits-masters. However, as shown, the shaman may interfere in case a person cannot hunt or fish, being disturbed by the spirits. In this case the shaman would act not on the spirits-masters, but on the spirits which affect the hunters and fishermen. Lastly, the shaman may be interested in hunting and fishing, as a divination of the future, as fortune-telling. In this case, as shown, it will be a simple case of "divination and discovery", which has nothing to do with the influencing of spirits-masters which control animals. I could find no cases when the shaman would directly interfere with the activity of these spirits; in the Tungus complex it is impossible. When one is not familiar with the essential functions and aims of performances, one may easily make this misinterpretation of the shaman's performance.

For the same reasons the shaman very rarely figures in the matter of child delivery, for the spirits which are held responsible for the success are beyond the shaman's control, and the interference of his spirit may only be harmful (cf. SONT, p. 275, SOM, p. 113). His assistance is required only in exceptional cases. The shaman does not act, as a shaman in the wedding ceremony (cf. SONT, p. 234), but he may act as a simple singer. These instances show that in every case when the shaman is acting, the aim must be definitely established, and particularly it must be found out, whether he uses his spirits or not. As will be shown, the shaman's personal character has also to do with his functioning in cases relating to this group "varia", and this should be taken into consideration, when the cases are analysed. For instance, a bad-natured person (shaman) will not be allowed to do many occasional varia performances, while a good-natured shaman will often be called upon. The errors on the part of observers are very likely in all such cases.

_____

From the description and analysis of various cases of shamanizing it can be seen that the aims of performances may be very numerous, and that new ones may appear at any moment. However, not all of them are frequent, and in most of the cases there are several aims of shamanizing, combined in one performance. Since in different cases different aims of shamanizing may be combined, their classification into a rigid system is practically impossible. The Tungus and Manchu systems as to the classification of performances may be of little help to us, for all of them distinguish, on a formal ground, only three forms, namely, (1) when the shaman goes to the lower world, which implies a rather long shamanizing; (2) when the shaman performs a long shamanizing without going into the lower world, which is usually designated by the adjective "great"; (3) all forms of short shamanizing without discrimination of whether the shaman calls into himself his spirits or not. It is evident that this classification can be absolutely misleading, for in the subdivision (3) one has to include a great variety of shamanizing carried out with various aims and in different forms. A classification based upon a distinction of two fundamental forms, in their turn based upon the fact of introduction (extasy) and non-introduction of spirits into the shaman, also cannot be considered as satisfactory, for in some very important cases of shamanizing the spirits are not introduced, e.g. when a new shaman is created, or when a spirit is mastered for the first time; while there are cases of shamanizing on minor occasions, such as "divination and discovery" when spirits are introduced. Owing to the complexity of shamanistic performances, it seems to be safer to classify them simultaneously, according to the aims, the place of acting (one of three worlds), and the participation of the shaman's spirits. Only such a threefold classification may give an exact definition of the particular forms of shamanizing, but in some cases it will be rather complex, for one and the same performance may include several types of shamanizing.

Another approach may also be made from the point of view of psychological effect and psychological condition of the shaman; but this principle cannot be made the basis of classification, for it presumes a detailed analysis impossible in the great majority of cases. However, this side of the problem is most important in the functional system of shamanism, and will require supplementary analysis of performances in general and in particular cases.

CHAPTER XXVII

ANALYSIS OF SHAMANISTIC PERFORMANCES

118. PRELIMINARY REMARKS From the above given descriptions of shamanizing it can be seen that the forms of shamanizing should be regarded as any other ethnographical complexes—they consist of variable elements and it may be supposed that each of them has a certain function in the complex. Therefore, our analysis, in order to be complete, must enter into further details.

First of all, it should be pointed out that the basis of all performances consists in theories concerning the characteristics of the spirits and the possibility of the regulation of their activity. In order to understand the fact that, for instance, among the Transbaikalian Reindeer Tungus the shamans, in great performances, are usually dealing with the spirits of the upper world, and that the Manchu shamans have very little, even almost nothing to do with the spirits of the upper world, we have not only to refer to their respective conceptions of the spirits, but also to find out how the functions of the shamans are distributed among these two different groups. Here it should be noted that the principal spirit of the shamans' spirits—*s'aman'i dayačan*—in the complex of the Reindeer Tungus of Trans-baikalia is transferred to the group of spirits inhabiting the upper world, while the Manchus have no such principal spirit, and all shamanistic spirits are located in this world—chiefly on the tops of mountains. Among these Tungus the shaman's spirit is only one of their great spirits of the upper world, and this spirit is naturally closely connected with the other spirits of that world. It is not a simply "mastered spirit", but is almost a protector, while other spirits are "mastered". Thus the Tungus shaman has nothing to do with it. In fact, the function of dealing with the spirits of the upper world, such as all classes of *endur'i* has been taken up by the *p'oyun saman* (who, as shown, is not at all a shaman, but a priest), by common experienced people and by representatives of religions, such as Buddhism and Taoism. Moreover, among the Manchus, a great number of diseases, such as, for instance, smallpox, chicken-pox, measles, and others, which especially affect children, are considered as a special group of infectious diseases controlled by the group of spirits of the upper world (Chinese complex of *n'apn'aŋ*). A great number of other pathological conditions are considered by the Manchus as diseases, which sometimes ought to be treated by specialists—Chinese doctors. Naturally, all of them are exempted from the potential scope of shaman's interference. Among the Reindeer Tungus of Transbaikalia the same cases are ascribed to the activity of the spirits which may be managed by the shamans. Since the existing hypotheses and theories as to the regulation of diseases are different, the competence of the shamans is also different, and consequently there is a difference in the cases attended by the shamans of these two ethnical groups.

There is one more condition which produces difference, namely, the great number of methods of producing extasy and carrying out the performance. The Manchu shamans borrowed their methods from the Chinese and the great Buddhistic priests, while the shamans of the Reindeer Tungus of Transbaikalia have these elements from a different source—the Buriats, Yakuts, and other neighbours who possess distinct complexes.

We have already seen that the paraphernalia used by the Manchus and Tungus of Transbaikalia are also different, being received and adapted for different purposes. For instance, an elaborated complex of iron implements is found only among the Manchus. Practically these paraphernalia have an influence on the process of shamanizing. It is thus evident that in these two instances we have two distinct complexes of shamanistic performance, which are conditioned by the existing complexes of spirits, theories concerning the treatment, technical methods of shamanizing, and different paraphernalia.

When we take two very distinct complexes, we can easily see how their structures can be understood as a result of the historic formation and readaptation of elements into a complex with a definite function; but when the complexes are more or less alike, it is more difficult to see the functional mechanism and the internal equilibrium of the complexes, which is necessary in order to understand both the functional mechanism and the equilibrium of the complex.

The difficulties of this case can be seen, for instance, in the complex of the Manchus and that of the Tungus of Manchuria, the latter being much nearer to the Manchu complex than the complex of the Reindeer Tungus of Manchuria, but at the same time distinct enough for revealing some characteristics of functional mechanism and an original system of the equilibrium of the complex.

Among the Birarčen the theory of spirits accepts the class of *endur⁺i* which cannot be dealt with by the shamans, almost in the same way as among the Manchus. It is therefore natural that the shamanizing to the upper world is not practised. This function, however, is not performed by a *p'oyun saman*, but merely by experienced people. Among the Birarčen the complex of spirits of the upper world, as active factors in human life, are of a lesser importance as compared with the same spirits of the Manchu complex. The complex of spirits responsible for diseases of children, or, better to say, regulating these diseases—smallpox, chicken-pox, measles, etc.—are regarded in the same way as among the Manchus, but the group is increased with another series of complex spirits *ain'i burkan* which produces a great number of diseases (apparently typhus, paratyphus, influenza, etc.) which cannot be treated by the shamans. Hence, we have still a greater number of diseases, (as compared with the Reindeer Tungus of Transbaikalia) which are exempted from the shaman's competence. Some

methods of shamanizing are similar in the Manchu and Birarčen complexes, as for instance, the properties of the shaman when he introduces a fire-spirit. It is very likely that the source is the same—the Chinese complex. On the other hand, the shamanistic paraphernalia in general are quite different, and this fact implies certain differences in the technique of performance, e.g. the absence of the belt with iron conical trinkets in the Birarčen costume excludes the necessity of making rhythmic movements with the back during the performance, the sounding effects being produced by the brass mirrors chiefly fixed on the frontal part of the coat. Thus, the Birarčen costume differs from the Manchu costume, whence there are differences in the technique of performance.

Here we have again two complexes which are different and which, at the same time, possess a great number of common elements. When we compare two pairs, namely, the Manchu—Reindeer Tungus, and the Manchu—Birarčen, we can see that the difference in the theory of spirits in the first pair shows a difference of the performance-complexes, but in the second pair this is not so, for in both cases the spirits of the upper world are exempted. It must be also noted that the exclusion of the spirits of the upper world in the Manchu and Birarčen complexes may historically be due to two different conditions, namely, the shamans may have been gradually eliminated from the interference with the upper world, or the spirits of the upper world may have been introduced much earlier than the shamans, and thus were not included in the groups of spirits dealt with by the shamans; or it may have happened later, as it would be, if these groups should now adopt, for instance, Christianity.

The difference of the trinkets on the shaman's costume in all three instances is such, that the performance themselves differ: in the Manchu complex there is an intensive side-movement with the back, in the Reindeer Tungus costume—a play of differently selected bells in the back and front parts of the coat, in the Birarčen complex—a slight jumping to produce a rhythmic noise of all brass-mirrors. These are facts of great interest, for, in spite of the difference, the same aesthetic and hypnotic effect of the performance is reached. One can clearly see what the function is of the trinkets, brass-mirrors and bells, although all of them may be differently "explained", and justified by different theories.

When we analyse element by element, and complex by complex, the facts concerning performances, we will obtain the same picture of geographical and ethnical distribution of types of performance and definite complexes observed in different ethnical groups, as we did in the case of the analysis of the shamanistic paraphernalia. However, there will not be a perfect correlation. I shall give here some instances.

(1) The performance of great shamanizing, when the shaman goes to the lower world, is carried out among the Goldi chiefly for bringing souls of dead people to the place of settled life, while among the Manchus it is done chiefly for finding out the cause of a sickness which has been ascribed to some deceased person, and among the Reindeer Tungus of Transbaikalia it is usually carried out merely to maintain relations with the dead clansmen and to assist them if they need something. Among the Manchus the care of souls of clansmen is a duty of the *p'oyun saman;* the carrying of souls, among both Manchus and Reindeer Tungus of Transbaikalia, is not a duty of the shaman. A

special use of this form of shamanizing among the Goldi seems to be a local phenomenon, also practised by their neighbours—the Udehe and the Oroči—but unknown among the Tungus of Manchuria. I do not mean to say that this performance has never been practised by the Tungus of Manchuria, but it is not practised now. The caring for the souls is much more typical of the Goldi complex—perhaps it is one of the manifestations of Chinese influence—than of any other complex, including the Manchu one. Therefore, it may be supposed that the shamanizing to the lower world among the Goldi is of secondary origin. However, there is no other direct evidence to support this supposition.

(2) The performance of shamanizing to the upper world spirits, as found among the Reindeer Tungus of Transbaikalia, the Nomad Tungus (a slightly different complex!), and the Reindeer Tungus of Manchuria (also a different complex in so far as this statement is based on oral communication), but it is unknown among the Manchus and Northern Tungus groups of Manchuria. As stated, this form of performance might not exist at all among these groups. Considering the fact that the complex of the upper world is especially well represented and shamanizing according to this complex is practised among the Buriats and Yakuts, and that there are some elements (wooden staff-horse, counting by nines, terms, etc.), which cannot be suspected of being Tungus inventions, but are used especially by Buriats, we may suppose that this complex of performance was borrowed by the Tungus from the Buriats, or was inspired by the Buriat complex. If borrowed, it was greatly modified, and perfectly adapted to the Barguzin and Nerčinsk Tungus complexes. The complex of the upper world performance is almost a direct imitation of the Buriat complex, and that of the Reindeer Tungus of Manchuria seems to be either an imitation of the Yakut form, or was strongly inspired by the Yakut complex. The above shown three forms of the performance that exist today may thus be of different origin, but in all cases are well adapted to the existing conception of triple spirit-world and to the possibility of influencing the spirits.

It will be useless to proceed further with the analysis of the various forms of performances which, as a matter of fact, reveal no new aspects as to the character of ethnical and geographical distribution of complexes. As shown by the above demonstrated cases, the analysis of performances is more difficult than that of the paraphernalia, for the chance of parallelism in shamanizing is greater, than in the imitation of forms. The same theories and the same methods, which as such may be independent of the performance as a whole, may be responsible for the creation of similar forms of performance. Thus, although we may carefully mark down all data and reconstruct the complexes, these methods of dealing with the problem will throw no new light on the general character of shamanism, or on the spreading of particular complexes and elements. Our hypothetic complexes might become quite artificial, and as an instrument for further dealing be quite dangerous constructions. However, there are some aspects in the performances of all types and in all groups which can be further analysed and generalized: (1) the technique of performance; (2) the ritual; (3) psychological conditions of the performance; and (4) the social aspects of the performance.

119. TECHNIQUE OF PERFORMANCE The technique of performance among different groups and individual shamans is subject to great variations. However, there are many common elements and methods. A certain number of these elements and methods depend upon the paraphernalia and the general conditions of shamanizing, e.g. the dwellings, conditions of weather, etc.. The sex of the shaman also has a certain influence. In fact, the female shamans are physically weaker, shorter in stature, and their movements are not exactly like those of the males. Therefore, in discovering common elements, the differences in paraphernalia and other "material" conditions, as well as the sex of the performer must be kept in mind.

Shamanistic performances are usually carried out in the dark. However, some forms of shamanizing, e.g. among the Reindeer Tungus of Transbaikalia, the shamanizing—at least a part of it—to the spirits of the upper world, may be carried out both by day and at night, which depends on the shaman. According to all Tungus groups, the spirits come down to the shaman much easier during the dark period of the day, and some spirits cannot be brought and dealt with in the day time. This is true not only of the shamans, but also of other people. The first idea that comes to one's mind is that during the day time the people are busy, and this is the reason why the shamanizing is carried out at night. However, this supposition must be excluded, for e.g. the Tungus in the day time, during almost the whole summer, are free, because hunting and nomadizing are carried out during the dark hours of the day. In most cases the dealing with the clan spirits among the Manchus takes place during the day, while the shamanizing is performed during the night hours. The inference to be made is that the darkness is a favourable technical condition of shamanizing—the spirits come more readily in the dark, as the Tungus assert.

In almost all forms of shamanistic performances, when the extasy of the shaman and the excitation of the audience are needed, i.e. with the exception of some cases when the shaman is alone, several technical methods for bringing up a necessary psychic condition of the shaman and the audience are used. These are rhythmic effects, music of the performance, particularly rhythmic movements, dancing, drumming and production of various noises with the costume, also singing or reciting, and the contents of the text of the performance, i.e. description in words of the relations between the shaman and the spirits, the people and the spirits.

The performance is usually opened by the shamans with a soft almost monotonous drumming at a slow tempo, in 2/2 and 4/4 time. This moment corresponds to the drawing of the attention of the spirits. No singing is used. The shamanizing in rare cases begins with a very passionate introduction. In these cases spirits have already entered the shaman during his actual or supposed sleep. This would mean that the shaman and the audience are psychologically prepared for the performance. This may take place also when the shaman is certain of the sudden effect of his passionate introduction, or it may also happen with beginners, when they must overcome their own shyness by a sudden start, and at the same time produce a favourable impression on the audience. In fact, it is often believed that a candidate-shaman is "suddenly entered by the spirit", wherefore the performance must begin suddenly.

The sounds of the same drum are not alike. First of all, the pitch and clearness of the sound depend on the dryness of the skin. In fact, before the drumming, the instrument is usually prepared by drying it on an open fire—this is done even during dry nights. When the drum is not prepared, it does not produce a good clear high pitched sound, and the shaman is unable to obtain the effect of the rhythmic influence. Many shamans have two drums which are alternately dried and used. When the shaman does not meet with the sympathy of his audience and assistants, his or her drum is left without drying and it may lose the needed quality. The shaman can have his drum tuned lower or higher, like a kettle drum, and can thereby produce these effects. For instance, in some parts of the performances the drum is only slightly dried in order to produce a low tone, while in other cases it must be high pitched. Secondly, the drum produces different sounds depending upon the part which is being beaten—the centre, or the periphery. As a matter of fact the drums, especially those with resonators, do not produce a simple sound, but a complex one, consisting of a principal one and some supplementary sounds. The principal drum may be made forte or piano, which essentially changes the musical effect of the drumming. Furthermore, the way of applying the drum stick (especially the elastic ones) has a great influence on the character of the sound—e.g. the strong sharp strokes which are rarely used; strokes followed by a pause, which stops the vibration of the skin; the sharp frequent strokes which increase the vibration (coincidence of subsequent vibrations); the sharp frequent strokes which stop the vibration (interference of subsequent vibrations) (the shaman must know his drum!); forte and piano, crescendo and diminuendo give a great variety of sound, which may in some cases be a very low, even, almost uninterrupted monotonous sound; in other cases a high, sharp, also almost uninterrupted sound, but exciting; the sound may also be deep-low, sharp-low, and so on. Still more varieties are produced if the shaman uses double sounds, obtained from the centre and the peripheral sections of the drum, especially combined with stopping and repetition. Furthermore, the sounds of the drum can be increased by means of trinkets and even bells. Their rhythmic shaking may produce new additional sounds—noises of a definite musical quality. From the above remarks it is evident that the shamans can produce a great variety of sounds with distinct effects upon themselves and the audience.[*]

This slow and soft drumming of the beginning of the performance produces its effects: the attention of the shaman is concentrated, as well as that of the audience. The spirits may now arrive at any moment. Since the arrival of a spirit means extasy, the drumming shows gradual increase of tempo and gradually changes from piano into forte. There may be a change of the rhythm too. At the moment of culmination of extasy the shaman usually makes the last fortissimo stroke and throws away the drum. The drum can fall down, but it is usually taken away from the shaman's hands at the due moment.

The dressing of the shaman in his costume, even partly,

e.g. only apron and head-dress, or belt with conical trinkets (Manchus), can take place prior to the first drumming, or at the arrival of the spirit. When the shaman is dressed, he has at his disposal new means of producing sounds—various trinkets of the costume. As I have already pointed out, in the Tungus costume they can be arranged in such a way, that different parts of the costume could produce distinct complexes of sounds, e.g. to the upper part (on the back and chest) thin pieces can be attached which would produce a high pitched rustling; to the middle part heavy iron rattles can be attached which would produce moderately pitched sounds and to the lower part conical trinkets can be attached which would produce a low pitched "clinging" sound. The costume may also be supplied, e.g. in the front and back parts of the coat, with assorted bells to produce different musical accords. The sounds of the iron trinkets and of the brass mirrors (especially when they are different in size and thickness) are naturally contrasting. The art of the shaman consists in knowing how to use this source of sounds. An inexperienced or non-musical shaman will produce merely a rhythmic noise, and he will not be appreciated by the audience; while a good shaman-artist uses all possible varieties of sounds and, when needed, an impressive tutti. Indeed, a good shaman knows how to arrange his costume. A shaman who does not know how to use these effects will simply be considered as a bad shaman.

The use of the musical attributes of a costume is possible only when the shaman is moving. The movements may begin at the moment of the first calling of the spirits, but the maximum can be reached only when the shaman stands up and begins his "dancing". It may consist of rhythmic movements of the whole body, which produce variable tutti: piano and forte, short (staccato) and continuous (tremolo); or rhythmic movements of different parts of the body, affecting different sounding groups of trinkets; or alternation of movements of the whole body and its parts, e.g. only the front or back sections of the waist with the bells, and the upper or middle part of the trunk. These movements, correlated with the production of simple and combined sounds, entail various "steps", rhythmed in 4/4, 2/4, 3/4, time, all with variable accents. The shaman makes, for instance, two soft movements forward, alternatively producing sounds with the front and back parts of the coat, and one sharp movement back producing sounds of all of the trinkets. They may be increased with the additional movements of the shoulders producing a continuous high pitched rustling. A long phrase may be concluded by a tutti—forte, produced by a short strong leap on the spot. So the "dancing" is partly called forth by the necessity of producing rhythmic sounds. But there is also another reason, namely, the association of the visual rhythm to the sounding rhythm, and the shaman's reaction on it. In fact, the shaman's rotations, e.g. round the fire place, and on his own axis may attain such a tempo that the shaman may at least temporarily lose consciousness.

During the dance the shaman may or may not use his drum himself. In the latter case the drumming is produced by the assistants, sometimes even with two instruments at the same time. The drumming must exactly follow the movements of the shaman, so that the rhythmic noise produced by the costume is increased by that of the drum. It is thus evident that the assistants must know the art of drumming and must understand the shaman's movements.

[*] The art of playing the drum, as good shamans do, is not easy. I had to spend some time before I could reproduce some varieties of sounds. As a condition of the performance it is much more than a simple "drumming". Some interesting remarks as to a Yakut shaman have been made by N. A. Vitaševskiĭ (op. cit. pp. 174-175).

The changes of movements, and the ensuing musical effects, correspond to the spirits' activity, when they are introduced into the shaman, and to what the shaman (his soul) does during his travellings. For instance, when the shaman needs additional increase of extasy, the movements become faster and the music becomes louder; when the shaman is already in his trance, this condition must be maintained by keeping the same tempo and rhythm; when the shaman falls down, the drumming must be stopped at once, at least for a while, if he is in a deep trance, or it must be reduced to a pianissimo tremolo. The individual character of the shaman is of great importance, and the assistants must know it.

There are two effects more produced by the shamans by the musical content of their singing and the sense of their words. First let us consider the musical character of the singing. It should be noted that most of the shamans possess rather good voices, from the European point of view. The majority of them are male—baritones, and female—contraltos. I do not remember having met tenors and mezzo sopranos, and only in a few cases I met with rather high bassos. The Tungus, as well as Manchu shamans sing in two manners, namely, with full voice in European manner, and with gutturalized voice (the falsetto of Chinese singers is not used, perhaps with the exception of Chinese shamans). The shamans first practise singing, and they must be rather careful with their voices, for the performance sometimes lasts several hours.

The shamans do not sing the whole time during the performance. They begin by drumming without singing, the latter being gradually introduced into the performance. Since the introductory part usually consists of the invitation of the spirits, the explanation of the cause of shamanizing, etc., the singing is rather quiet and monotonous. When the spirits are approached by the soul of the shaman, the singing becomes passionate and it culminates in a scream of extasy when the spirit enters the shaman. After the spirit has entered into the shaman, the singing changes in melody, in rhythm, tempo and character (there may be even a change of the voice!) and it turns into a dialogue—almost a recitative—between the shaman and his assistant. Thus, the music becomes usually poorer, than before, and the sounds of the drum and of the attributes of the costume grow fainter. The shaman is then usually sitting on the ground. However, the shaman's travelling and the further increase of his extasy may be accompanied by a singing of a richer musical production.

When the shaman sings he is always "helped" (according to the Tungus expression) by the assistants and even by other people, who usually repeat the same refrain, first given by the shaman. The refrains may be shorter or longer, as seen from the examples given here, and they are always connected with certain spirits. However, there are also some refrains which are used only for special types of shamanizing, e.g. when the shaman goes to the lower world. The refrains have a great importance in the performance, for they intensify the emotion of the shaman and the audience in different directions: depression, sadness, joy, excitement. They also act as an intensified hypnotic method on the shaman, the audience and sometimes on the sick person that is being treated, especially when the singing is well executed. On the other hand, when the shaman is not "helped", the performance may fail altogether.

The shaman's singing and the "helping" of the audience, together with the drumming and the music of the costume, performed by an experienced shaman, the assistants, and the "helpers", may thus form a very complex and varied musical performance of the greatest emotional effect upon the performers and the audience. A musical analysis of this complex manifestation is out of question, for, first of all, it was impossible to record even a small part of the actually produced sounds. In fact, the performances, carried out at night time in wigwams or badly lighted houses (among the Manchus), cannot be directly recorded. Secondly, most of the music cannot be rendered at all with the European notation and thirdly, the complexity of the sounds is so great that only a poor idea of it could be given. A small part of the actual musical side of the performance might be memorized and later reproduced, but only a very small part of them might be put in the form of European notation. Phonographic recording is also technically impossible, for the shaman and the audience are in extasy and the use of the phonograph would disturb their finely balanced emotional state.[*]

These remarks may serve as an explanation of the fact that the present description of the shamanistic performance cannot show the exceptional psychological power of the musical part of shamanistic performances. Persons without defective musical ability feel the emotional effect which is aesthetically perceived; those who cannot notice it, cannot understand and cannot penetrate the essentials of shamanism.

I refer below to a few examples of shamanistic "songs" which have been published, but I must note that, as single songs reproduced by the shaman, they give a poor idea of shamanistic music as a whole. If a comparison is permitted, I should say that they are like the segregation of the score of one instrument of a great orchestra. Nevertheless they are interesting.

Madame Shirokogoroff has published some shamanistic songs[**] and J. Yasser has analysed some of them.[***]

---

[*] The musical side of shamanism was one of the aspects which attracted special attention of Madame Shirokogoroff; we tried to record what was possible. Several dozens of phonographic records now preserved in the Museum of Anthropology and Ethnography of the Russian Academy of Sciences, contain samples of various groups, but they were only partly deciphered. However, the shamanistic "songs" were not taken during the performance, but on special request, so that they cannot be considered as an exact reproduction of shamanistic "songs" during the performance. The deciphering of the records and their notation represented unsurmountable difficulties. This was true not only in our case. The experienced analyst of folk-music, S. Maslov (of Moscow), could render in European musical notation only four of the twelve records of Yakut songs, and they were but approximate ones (quoted from J. Yasser's paper, vide infra) (cf. also remarks to H. H. Roberts and D. Hemmes, "Eskimo Songs", by the first author who analysed phonographic records, p. 17 et seq.). Indeed, a great number of needed signs are lacking in the European notation. The only way of obtaining a reproduction of a shamanistic performance is a record with the most recent recording instruments, and there will still remain the problem of analysis and description which are, at least at present, beyond reach. In fact, it is impossible to give in words an exact description of musical and painting creations—one must see and hear and understand them.

[**] Cf. Elizabeth N. Shirokogoroff, "Folk Music in China", in The China Journal of Science and Arts, March, 1924, pp. 6, with 51 examples of various songs, including ten songs of the Manchus and Tungus.

[***] Cf. Joseph Yasser, "Musical Moments in the Shamanistic Rites of the Siberian Pagan Tribes", in Pro-Musica Quarterly, March-June, 1926 pp. 4-15. As I show below, no supposition as to the

From the analysis of these songs we see that some of them are composed in a pentatonic scale, which fact points to a Chinese influence, if we agree that the pentatonic scale is a Chinese one. However, such an assumption cannot · be made, for the Chinese pentatonic scale itself is only one of the variations of a still wider ethnographical element— "the pentatonic scale".* By this remark I do not want to say that the shamanistic songs used among the Northern Tungus and Manchus did not come from China. Their Chinese origin is quite possible, but they might have been borrowed quite independently of "shamanism", while a pentatonic scale might have been used among the Tungus before shamanism had originated in its present form. However, the fact of musical connexion between the shamanistic songs and the Chinese cultural complex is of importance, when we group together other facts concerning shamanism. The Tungus have employed what they had at hand for building up this complex.

It remains now to discuss the question of the contents of shamanism expressed in words. First of all, it must be pointed out that in almost every shamanizing there is something new, for the occasions of shamanizing are not alike and the relations which originate between the spirits and the shaman, in connexion with the shamanizing, are not the same. On the other hand, some moments in shamanizing are essentially similar, e.g. the calling of definite spirits will be more or less similar in all cases; in a sacrifice frequently offered to the spirits, the wording of the address will be more or less the same; if the shaman uses the same spirits, for instance, for treating persons, sick of the same diseases, by sending off the spirits, the wording will be nearly the same. Here it should be noted that some forms of shamanizing are extremely rare, as for instance, the shaman's going to the lower world, which, among the Reindeer Tungus of Transbaikalia, takes place once in several years and under variable conditions. Owing to this we find in shamanizing: (1) some well fixed elements, as for instance, prayers to the spirits on the occasion of a ritual sacrifice, and calling of spirits, frequently used by the shamans; (2) some other elements very rarely used and therefore leaving a certain liberty to the shaman in the choice of wording; and (3) some elements which are always renewed, for the spirits are new and the conditions requiring shamanizing are variable, demanding almost spontaneous creation on the part of the shaman. In a great shamanizing the fixed elements form only an insignificant part of the shaman's songs (wording), while the greater part of them are the product of his direct and spontaneous creation.

When the shaman begins a performance he usually pronounces in a more or less distinct manner—it depends on the individual ability of diction—the words for calling spirits which are usually known to the audience, or at least to some of the listeners. As we have seen in the examples of prayers (cf. supra Part Three),** the expressions and construction, as a whole, are products of poetic creation. They prepare the audience and the shaman, and they transfer them into the world of images. At the next step, the shaman in a rhythmic and sometimes rhymed form may expound before the spirits the concrete cause of the shamanizing, which is understood by the audience. The audience takes it emotionally, for the cause concerns them personally, as, for instance, the sickness of senior relatives, beloved little children, etc. In this way the world of images is connected emotionally and personally with the living people, and tho shaman, as an intermediary between the two, establishes a close contact with the audience—he becomes the link. If the spirit which is called in is one with whom the shaman and the audience are familiar, the words sung by the shaman are known and sometimes quite clear. The spirit is present in person and the emotion of the audience, directly produced by the words, becomes more intense. The dialogue between the spirit, especially a spirit which is not known, and the shaman's assistant is always very exciting, for the solution of the problem can be found in what the spirit says through the shaman, helped by the assistant. In this part of shamanizing a great part of what is said (sung) may be misunderstood or unintelligible altogether, for with the approach of the extasy at that moment the words pronounced by the shaman may not be clear. If the spirit is a foreign one whose language cannot be understood (the shaman himself sometimes does not know it, and confines himself to a repetition of a few words quite confused), the assistant and the audience try to understand the spirit's words from the gestures of the shaman. This augments the intensity of the emotional state of the audience. Lastly, when the shaman attains the extasy, his words may become still less understandable than during the period when the shaman maintains (responds to) a dialogue with the assistant. However, every word pronounced by the shaman is interpreted or misinterpreted by the audience, every one understands it in accordance with the produced situation as the result of a series of reactions in each personal complex, due to the stimulus of the shaman's words and to his whole performance in public. Finally, there may arise a situation when nobody would understand the shaman and the audience and even the experienced assistants could only guess the meaning of the shaman's behaviour. However, in such cases the psychic tension of the audience does not decrease, for the audience · is in the presence of and in contact with the spirits: the imagination responds in one direction, if these spirits are dangerous and in another direction, if the spirits are benevolent.

From the words pronounced by the shaman the audience may follow the shaman's progress in his interference in the world of spirits; by means of the pronounced words the shaman leads the audience towards the desired state, i.e., in most cases, a state in which suggestion and hypnosis become possible. Herein lies the importance of the contents of the words pronounced in a performance.

If the shaman fails to attain his aim, in so far as the wording is concerned, he is not considered to be a good shaman, although perhaps the audience and the critics cannot formulate the actual defects of the shaman. In fact, the audience is very often unable to understand the shaman; but if he cannot be understood at all, he is not good in the public opinion. If the period when his wording is very confused lasts too long, the audience becomes also tired, and the shaman is not considered to be a good one. Thus

Chinese source of shamanism is needed for understanding the fact of "Chinese" scale in shamanistic songs of the Tungus.

* A very instructive, for an ethnographer, analysis of the history and geographic distribution of the pentatonic scale, also of the infradiatonic scale, is found in J. Yasser's work "A Theory of Evolving Tonality", N. Y. 1932, American Library of Musicology, Contemporary Series: Volume One.

** Here I give no specimens of shamanistic "songs" and "prayers" (I shall give them in another publication, dealing with Folklore) because as far as style, language and construction are concerned, they do not differ very much from the above cited examples.

the relation which is observed between the shaman and the "master" the spirits, but when they are in the shaman, they audience is very delicate. The shaman is supposed to may act according to their own will; the latter point is admitted. Furthermore, the audience is supposed to be influenced by the spirits, which is actually the shaman's influence. If the audience cannot understand the spirits, the psychic tension is relaxed and the audience becomes dissatisfied with the shaman, for the latter cannot sufficiently "master" the spirits.

While a complete record of the text of a shaman's performance is technically possible, with the help of modern instruments, a great part of it cannot be understood, and would be only an incoherent, inconsistent string of phrases, even of words, some of which may be even words of a foreign language, or merely meaningless combinations of sounds supposed to be the spirit's language. This is especially true of the moments when the shaman changes the spirits, or when he is in a state of unconsciousness, complete or partial. A part of the shamanizing, also important, is when the shaman is silent and the audience can only guess what is going on with him.

Most of the records of the shaman's songs which I myself have made, and also which have been made by other observers, are only prayers of the shamans, quite stabilized and known by heart by the shamans, by their assistants, and also by those who frequent performances. "Callings" of the spirits can also have a fixed form. It should be noted that the Manchu poem, or rather a record of shamanizing, the Nišan Saman, here often mentioned, is either a pure artistic production or a simplified record, which the authors might have modified with additions, interpretations and omissions. So it cannot be considered as an authentic record. However, the assistants of shaman, as will be shown, after long practice with the same shaman, may have a more or less correct idea of the performance and may represent the process in the shaman's words. A certain fixation of the process of shamanizing is theoretically possible, and it does exist, even in sections of shamanizing, when the shaman is half-conscious, but it would naturally be subject to great individual variations; when the shaman acts alone, the individual variations may be still greater.

In the above description of the technique of shamanizing I have not referred to definite ethnical groups here described. However, in the matter of technique, the ethnical differences are of great importance. In fact, first of all, the musical means of drums and costumes are not alike. The Manchu costume may produce only rhythmic noises with the belt, and movements with the back. Owing to this, the "dancing" of the Manchu shaman does not include complex movements with different parts of the body and is relatively simple. The Manchus live in houses, where the space for the shaman's moving round is very limited, so the "dancing" does not assume very complex forms and there may be no such movement as that round the fire-place. There are also essential differences between the technique of the Reindeer Tungus shamans and that of the Tungus of Manchuria. In fact, the musical possibilities of costumes, as shown, are quite different. When we proceed to the description of the shaman's state during the extasy, the difference will be still better seen. There is one more factor which has a great influence in the technique, namely, the degree of fixation of rituals, especially stabilized owing to the existence of writing among the Manchus. This aspect will be discussed in the section dealing with the ritualism.

120. ASSISTANT OF THE SHAMAN In the above given descriptions of particular cases of shamanizing and in the analysis of the technique we have already several times met with the active rôle of the assistants. In the matter of technique, a great part of the success of a performance depends upon the assistant. From a description of the assistant's functions the actual rôle of the assistant will be clear. As far as I know, there are two terms for the "assistant", namely, eróɯ (Bir. Kum.) and jär'i (Bir. Kum. RTM. Manchu Sp.). The first one is perhaps connected with the verb er(u) (Tum. Mank.),— "to pull, to draw, to carry", etc.; in fact the eróɯ is "pulling" the shaman, "helping" him. The second one is perhaps connected with jär, jära (RTM),—"the shaman's song"; jar'imbi (Manchu Writ.),—"to sing prayers", etc. when the services are performed (Zax.) [Buddhistic and "shamanistic" (p'oɲun saman, evidently)].* The assistance of eróɯ or jär'i consists in helping the shaman to maintain his extasy and to find out what the spirit says and wants, when it is introduced into the shaman. Thus, the assistant, at the beginning of the performance, prepares the drum and helps the shaman to dress himself. During the performance he changes and dries the drum, if necessary, but this may be done by any one of the audience. When the shaman sings, the assistant must "help" him with the repetition of the refrains, and usually other people follow the assistant. When the shaman can no longer do himself the drumming, the assistant carries on the drumming and in this way "helps" the shaman to maintain his extasy. So the assistant may also maintain and enforce the state of extasy by rhythmically screaming and by exciting the shaman. When the spirit enters the shaman, the assistant asks various questions and even bargains and quarrels with the spirit, if necessary. When the shaman falls down unconscious, the assistant watches him to know the moment when the shaman must be brought back to consciousness. When the shaman is in a state of extasy, the assistant takes the drum and continues the drumming, both for maintaining the shaman's state of extasy and for controlling the behaviour of the audience. These functions are very important for a successful carrying out of the whole performance as regards the result, the assurance of the smoothness of the performance and the shaman's personal safety. A good assistant, who is familiar with the shaman's character, his

---

* The above given Tungus etymology of eróɯ is perhaps not correct. In fact, the Mongol language may be the source of this word; cf. eriku—to "investigate" ["demander, s'informer, puier" (Kow.)], erii—"demande, prière", etc. which render the meaning of eróɯ as one who is investigating what the shaman says. The Tungus term has no great importance and the possibility of the omission of this term in other groups must be admitted. In fact, the Tungus use it very rarely, as will be clear from the description. Another term jär'i, ought perhaps to be also connected with a Mongol stem. In Manchu Writ. it has not been recorded, the verb jar'imbi is isolated, the jär'i ("assistant") does not sing or pray. In Mongol we have the stem jar used in words expressing of the idea of "to serve, to send", etc. which corresponds to the function of jär'i. In Manchu Writ. jar'imbi may be of a secondary origin. Cf. Yakut stem jары in jarɪɡɪɪ,— "to busy one's self with the same, to attend, to investigate (e.g. a sickness)", etc. (Pek. p. 795) which may be carried further to the stems met with in other languages, such as jar (V), d'ar (V), etc. For these reasons I do not insist on the Tungus "origin" of these terms.

ways of performing, his language and complex of spirits etc., may make the performance easy and smooth, and would get out of it a much greater result, than an assistant who lacks the qualities and fitness. An assistant, who is not experienced in general and who does not know the shaman whom he is assisting, may turn the performance into a torture for the shaman and will lessen the results of the shamanizing. Thus there are good and bad assistants, and good assistants are rare. The quality of an assistant depends upon his familiarity with the shamanizing, his acquaintance with the shaman, and his general intelligence. No assistants are met with among some Tungus groups that have been investigated. For instance, among the Reindeer Tungus of Transbaikalia I have not heard of assistants, although there were some persons who usually helped the shamans by keeping time, singing refrains, etc. The Tungus of Manchuria told me that the institution of *erów* (*jär'i*) is a recent one, and that originally there were no assistants. I admit that this statement is correct. According to the Manchus, the assistants were established by the first shaman. In fact *Nišan Saman* had a 'regular assistant *ta jär'i*, i.e. the chief assistant; so there were even several assistants.

During the performance of the annual sacrifice, when the spirits come one after another into the shaman, the latter asks the question: *takam'i takaraku?*—"do you recognize?"—which greatly abbreviates the performance, if the assistant can guess at once. When the assistant · cannot guess, the shaman gives a hint by naming the row (*jaídan*), and the assistant usually enumerates, one after another, the spirits, till he reaches the introduced spirit. Therefore, the shamans like to have assistants experienced in the work. Usually *ta jär'i* knows by heart all the ritualistic recitals of spirits and the whole ritual. Some forms of shamanizing, as will be shown, may require several assistants, so that "leading assistants", as opposed to ordinary ones, are distinguished.

Any one may become assistant to a shaman: a man, a woman, a young or elderly person. However, among the Manchus, a woman does not perform the functions of an assistant. The shaman may have one and the same assistant, or he may have several assistants, or no assistant at all. The function of the assistant may as well be carried out by persons incidentally present.[*] Generally speaking assistants are not persons of fixed and definite social standing, but at the same time if there are several assistants, one of them may be preferred by the shaman. Such an assistant may thus assume a special social function, whence a special social position will distinguish him, or her. As a special characteristic of the assistants it should be noted that, almost as a rule, they are not inclined to become themselves shamans. One of the reasons is perhaps that the assistant

[*] During my work among the Tungus and Manchus, when I was acquainted with the technique of shamanizing and especially the language, I sometimes performed the duties of an assistant. The first time when I ventured to do it, was an exceptional case among the Birarčen. The shaman had no assistant and was in a rather difficult position, the reason being that some Chinese were present who were very hostile to the shaman, so that the usual assistants did not do their duty, under the pressure of "public opinion". Since the case seemed to me exceptional, I began assisting, and as I did not disturb the shaman in shamanizing, it was very encouraging for me and did open new possibilities for my investigations, and especially for the penetration into the psychology of the shamans and into the technique of the performance.

must not allow himself to be overcome by extasy, but must carefully follow the shaman, to observe and, when needed, to come to his assistance. There· is a special selection of persons who are not susceptible to extasy, but who understand the essentials of the performance. If besides the performing shaman, there were another shaman, the latter might perform the duties of an assistant. As will be shown, the old shaman who is "teaching" a young one, may perform the duties of assistant too. As a · matter of fact, in his first performances the new shaman is usually assisted by experienced shamans.

When a shaman is performing, helping is not confined to his assistant alone. When a shamanizing is difficult, the people present at the performance may assist the shaman, as well. Besides drying the drum, and especially in forming a sympathetic audience, help is, first of all, lent by the singing of refrains. In observing shamanizing, I have found out that the functions of assistants are usually performed by men, while a great number of females make up the chorus. Among the Manchus the females are less active than males, and in some performances of clan shamanizing they are even not present. The institution of assistants in the complex of *p'oyun saman* is different. The assistants are clan officers and the females are not allowed to "help". The function of assistants is carried out by the *saman*, while the chief priest is *ta samcn*.

121. PSYCHOLOGICAL TECHNIQUE Important elements of the shamanistic performance are those psychological conditions which can be generalized under the name of EXTASY. It affects not only the shaman, but also the audience and the persons who need this condition for their treatment. Extasy is reached by means of a gradual increase of emotion through the rhythmic music, the "dancing", and the contents of the text of the shaman's songs and the self-excitement. Emotion is needed for three purposes, namely: (1) as a means of producing a sympathetic audience for the shaman, who must not be discouraged by a lack of response or a negative reaction on the part of the audience, when he is bringing himself into extasy; (2) for inspiring faith in the performance on the part of the persons who need shamanizing for their treatment; and (3) for the audience itself which likes the state of extasy produced by the performance. As to the creation of a sympathetic audience, this question will be fully discussed in the chapter dealing with the shaman. Since in the greater part of all cases of shamanizing the essential of the performance is the influence on individuals, the audience is brought into a state of extasy which also ·influences and prepares the respective person for the conclusive act of the shaman's suggestion. For this reason the audience must be as numerous as possible, to form a *crowd*. Practically this aim is achieved by various means, some of which I shall now point out.

First of all, the aims of the performance, as for instance, the treatment of a sick member of the community, the driving off of a harmful spirit, etc. are by themselves of a nature to attract and concentrate the attention of the participants in the performance. · It should be noted that in small Tungus communities the relations between the members are usually very friendly, so that a misfortune affecting one of them is likely to produce among all a sentiment of sorrow and a desire to help.* This feeling will be still stronger, when the members of the community are bound by blood relationship through the father or mother—the clan connexion. If it is a case of managing spirits, for which the shaman is often called, the members of the community are also emotionally touched by the fact of being near to a harmful spirit, or even several spirits. Among the Tungus and Manchus these spirits are realities, so that emotive reactions are quite easy and natural. Therefore the persons who attend a performance are not psychologically indifferent, but are emotionally prepared to be influenced. The beginning of a performance, when the shaman prepares himself for introducing a spirit, brings the audience at once in a state of expectation of further increase of emotion. The rhythmic music and singing and later the "dancing" of the shaman gradually involve every participant more and more in a collective action. When the audience begins to repeat refrains together with the assistants, only those who are defective fail to join the chorus. The tempo of action increases, the shaman with a spirit is no more an ordinary man or relative, but is a "placing" for the spirit; the spirit acts together with the audience, and this is felt by every one of the audience. The state of many participants is now near to that of the shaman himself, and only a strong belief in that in the presence of the shaman the spirit may enter only into the shaman, detains the participants from being "possessed" in mass by the spirit. This is a very important condition of shamanizing, which, however, does not reduce the mass susceptibility to the suggestion, hallucinations and un conscious acts produced in a state of mass extasy. The shaman, both consciously and unconsciously, may maintain this state of the audience. When he feels that the audience is with him and follows him, he becomes still more active, which effect is, in its turn, transmitted to the audience.

After the shamanizing, when the members of the audience recollect the various moments of the performance, their great psychophysiological emotion and the hallucinations of sight and hearing, they have a deep satisfaction, incomparably greater than that from the emotions produced by theatrical and musical performances, literature and general artistic phenomena of the European complex, because in shamanizing the audience consists at the same time of actors and participants. This is a very important condition of shamanizing and this component of the complex is one of the reasons justifying the maintaining of shamanistic practices. I shall revert to this question.

The person to be treated by shamanizing is greatly influenced when the audience begins to feel the extasy, for he or she is the object of the shamanizing. In the technique of the performance, the role of the audience in preparing the sick person is great, and there is also the direct influence of the shaman on the sick person. Besides the

* This is, of course, a very important condition which may be understood only with a great effort by those who are living in large communities, in which the sickness and death of members do not produce any emotion, unless the persons may be personally affected by the sickness or death. There may exist only a hypocritical attitude, or an artificially created, almost hysterical sensitiveness as to the misfortune of the "neighbour". I point it out because the Tungus attitude may be erroneously explained as one typical of "primitive society", while actually it appears as a function of density of population and of centripetal movement.

methods equally effective on the audience and the sick person, the shaman uses a series of special methods. These are, for instance, drumming and singing at only a short distance from the patient, continuous massaging of different parts of the body, stupefaction with smoke (*laedum palustrum*, twigs of coniferous trees, Chinese incense, etc.), direct suggestion—an order given by the spirit who must not be disobeyed—and lastly, various forms of hypnotizing of the person who is being treated, in his or her half-asleep state, the effect of both, suggestion and hypnosis, being possible only when the sick person's will is no more active. In order to reach this state to convince the person that he or she must submit to the spirit (not to the shaman!), the shaman would use various methods, the principal of which is a demonstration of his personal power and that of his spirit during the performance.

In the descriptions of shamanistic performances met with in the ethnographical records those demonstrations are very often portrayed in a distorted form—as imposture and tricking of the audience. Such an approach (with the exception of cases when the shamans have become professionals, e.g. Chinese) is absolutely erroneous, both from the point of view of the motives of the shamans and from that of technique.

As shown, the shamans, especially among the Manchus (under the Chinese influence, I suppose), use a great number of tricks for proving the presence of spirits. Such are e.g. all operations with fire. As a matter of fact, an inexperienced ordinary man cannot take into his mouth burning incense, as shown above, or step on a heap of burning charcoal, etc. without hurting himself. The shamans do it, sustaining sometimes only slight injuries which do not prevent them from going ahead with the performance. These facts are interpreted as due to the power of mastered spirits, and not to the shaman personally. If he succeeds in these tricks, the audience and himself believe that the spirit is actually present. Since it is so, the patient is convinced of the shaman's power. In almost all performances the shamans make divinations in some form. The aim is the same—to convince the audience and the sick person of the spirit's and the shaman's power. I shall now give some instance. The shamans (though not all of them) may often say what the persons present at the performance are thinking or doing. In many cases this is very simple, the thoughts of persons who have been for a long time under the shaman's influence and with whom he has been since long acquainted being easily guessed by him, and when the audience is in extasy, the shaman's guess may be simply explained as the result of a suggestion on his part. But there are cases which are not as simple as that. For instance, a shaman accused a young man present at the performance of having eaten a kidney of a sacrificial animal. Nobody could suspect that the shaman would know who had done it. (I think in this particular case he could not have seen it, for he had been busy with other things.) However, it may be supposed that he was able to know who of the young men present could have committed such an act and thus to formulate his accusation accordingly. The shaman ordered the man to give back the kidney, which was immediately vomited into the drum. The shaman's suggestion to vomit was perfectly convincing for the audience, for no other of them could have done it.

Here is another instance. At a performance two

men were present who did not believe in the shaman's power. The shaman took a coin from one of them and continued his performance. After a while he asked one of the sceptical men to open his hand and the man, to his great surprise, discovered the coin in his hand. Naturally, he, as well as the audience, were convinced of the great power of the shaman. The technique of the trick was probably as follows: the coin was handed to the man when he was unconscious of what he was doing and could not remember the fact of his taking the coin. As I shall later show, it is questionable, whether the shaman himself was absolutely conscious of his act.

The number of facts of this class is very great in different publications on shamanism among various ethnical groups. In a great number of cases observed by myself I did not find that the shamans were conscious of tricking their audience. However, such cases do occur, as will be shown in the next chapter.

SELF-SUGGESTION, SUGGES- must be considered as
   TION AND HYPNOTISM the fundamental me-
      thods of shamanistic technique in the performances. In fact, a real extasy of the shaman, which may influence the audience, can occur only when the shaman himself is convinced of his possessing spirits. I do not minimize the effectiveness of the shaman's art and ritualism, but alone they are not sufficient for permitting the shaman to act as he does, and he must have a certain sincerity in influencing other people. Therefore, as a rule, the performance comprises several acts of a self-suggestive character. On the other hand, the aim of the shaman, e.g. in the treatment of a person or in sending off of a spirit that affects a numerous group of people (the clan), is to make the patient and the audience believe that he can do it.

It is achieved in the only possible way, namely, by convincing the patient and the audience, by means of demonstration in a series of proofs, as shown in the preceding lines, followed by an effective suggestion. The latter can be done in form of a direct order to the spirits, or to the sick person, or to the audience; or in the form of a hint understood by the persons present at the performance, or finally, perhaps, in the form of a telepathic action. The principal condition of success is the *mastering of the will* of the patient and the audience by various means (the latter, as will be shown, can be supposed to be practised by the shamans) and especially by the performance itself. Therefore, bringing the patient and the audience into the state of extasy is not the aim, but a means for making a suggestion when needed. In such a state the audience becomes susceptible in the highest degree to hallucinations. I give here some facts in addition to those which were recorded by other travellers, especially V. S'eroševskiĭ, W. Jochelson and W. Bogoras.[*]

Among all groups the great shamans are believed to possess power of flying away (physically, with their bodies), remaining suspended in the air, and walking in the air. When the audience is in a state of extasy, it may clearly hear the spirits' voices, the spirits' steps, etc.; it may see the spirits (some of them) and perceive peculiar smells produced by some spirits. In reality theoretically this is a physical impossibility; it cannot be proved experimentally, nor by the evidence of travellers who, being normal, will not confirm these "facts". However, there is no need of it, because even in a mass hallucination the voices of non-believers would always be outweighed by those of the believers; for such a belief is needed by the ethnical units which practise shamanism.

I have been frequently told by the Tungus that they cannot see, hear or smell many things which are perceived by the shamans and by a great number of the participants (crowd) during the performances; but often the lack of perception of these phenomena was ascribed to personal defects: "I cannot see (hear or smell), because I am not physically fit for doing it (just as with people having defective eyes, ears and noses)". Thus, the theory adopted by the Tungus, namely, that these phenomena exist, is more influential on the Tungus mind and behaviour than a direct observation of facts, and the facts are rejected with the help of another hypothesis—physical defectiveness of those who do not perceive the phenomena.

Hypnotism is also widely used. We have seen from the description of performances that the persons who are being treated are sometimes brought into the state in which they are partially disabled in certain functions, during which state suggestion is much easier for the shaman. The technical methods of producing a hypnotic state have been already indicated.. Indeed, as far as I could find out, the shamans do not realize that they are using hypnotic methods, for these methods have been gradually and empirically worked out and are concealed in the complex of the performance. According to the Tungus, these methods are due to the character of the spirits. Naturally, the same is true of all forms of self-suggestion and suggestion; the shamans do not act as do European medical doctors, practitioners, who, when using these methods, are perfectly conscious of their nature and effect.[*] Generally speaking, unconscious but effective methods used by the shamans is one of the distinct characters of shamanism. In a great number of cases, from the point of view of modern medicine, they cannot be understood, because European medicine itself is an ethnographical phenomenon. In fact, to treat a certain complex in terms of another complex does not always lead to the understanding of the actual functions of the former complex.

122. NEGATIVE REACTIONS The observation of a great
    AND PERFORMANCES number of cases of perform-
      ances shows that the reaction of the participants differs. There are individuals who blindly accept the shaman's influence and that of the audience, and they may even do everything in their power to maintain it; there are individuals who indifferently follow the current behaviour of their milieu and passively submit to the shaman's influence; further, there are individuals who remain sceptical and require "proofs". In-

---

[*] It should be noted that some of the facts recorded as hallucinations were actually not such. Their pseudo-positivism did not permit them to distinguish some "strange cases" of acting in extasy from cases of simple hallucination.

[*] Indeed, in the modern European medical art there are methods of this order, but they are not so understood by the patients and the doctors themselves. The assumed form is that of treatment with medicines which are not effective in the curative sense and may even be physiologically harmful, but when applied may empirically prove to be effective.

cluded in the latter group are those individuals who show militant negative reaction.

The influence of negative reactions on the performance is great. We have seen in Case 4 (*Vide* Chapter XXV, Section 112) that a performance could not succeed, because of the circumstances. We have also seen that potential negative reactions do occur, but may be neutralized by a conviction that the persons who remain beyond the shaman's and audience's influence are not fit. In consequence of foreign influence—the influence of Christianity and Buddhism, and of the Chinese. Russians and Mongols who assume a sceptical attitude towards shamanism—there are strong currents of scepticism towards shamanism among the Tungus and Manchus. In a further chapter we shall discuss this question and its effect upon the variations of shamanism, but for the time being we need only point out that a sceptical attitude does exist, and probably, in one or another form, has ever existed, and that shamanism is a result of all these conditions.

The attitude of individuals showing negative reactions may assume various degrees of intensiveness. In the above mentioned case the teacher kicked the shaman, so that the latter had physical difficulty in carrying on a performance. Foreigners, especially Russian visitors—the local cossacks, workmen, and traders—and the Chinese as well, often disturb the shamans, who are acting, by pulling at the dress, by placing obstacles in the way of the shaman etc. during the rhythmic moving, by causing confusion in singing, by making critical remarks etc. Such forms of active negative reactions are rarely observed among the Tungus and Manchus themselves, partly owing to the fact that they are socially disciplined people, partly because they cannot propose anything better than shamanizing and also partly because they are not quite sure in that there are no spirits. Their sceptical attitude is chiefly due to the critical attitude towards the shamans as persons and performers. Such an attitude can originate from the fact · that the shamans may not exactly follow the usual common forms, while the individual may be of a militant conservative character. A slightly negative reaction is commonly observed among the Tungus and Manchus who cannot be influenced at all by the shaman and the audience. They remain beyond the complex of collective extasy and collective activity. Such individuals, even without any intention, may produce confusion in a smoothly running performance. Their presence alone may suffice for disturbing the audience in its attempt to reach extasy.* Moreover, if the audience includes too many individuals who are not susceptible to extasy, it may react too slowly to the shaman's suggestions, and the performance may therefore fail. It may proceed, but only as a series of well known actions, so that, while the performance would be carried out form-

ally, it would not attain its aim.* Such failures can be actually observed, and very often the public opinion is inclined to see the cause in the shaman, instead of in the audience. As shown, this is one of the reasons why the shamans sometimes produce various tricks, in order to gain an influence over the indifferent group of the audience.

Here it may be generally remarked that since an indifferent attitude of the audience towards the shamans and their performances is especially created, when an alien influence becomes strong, it may be necessary to have recourse to some method of gaining over an indifferent audience, such as the introduction of various tricks (psychological, as well as mechanical and physical), some of which may have been learned from the professionals and shamans of alien groups (e.g. as in the case of the Manchu *mafarism*. *Vide supra* 234 *et seq.*). In this way shamanism may become saturated with elements which originally were merely means of controlling the audience, and the performance, as a whole, may be turned into a theatrical performance, as it is sometimes observed in the shamanism of ethnical units which have fallen under a strong alien influence. Therefore, one of the sources of essential changes in shamanism is the loss of an active sympathetic attitude on the part of

---

* A tactless persistence of an investigator, supplied with his fountain pen, camera, phonographic apparatus and other devices of a scientific investigation, may alone create around him an atmosphere of hostility. Interference by inquiries may disturb a performance to such a degree that it may turn into a simple ritualistic sequence of acts. This would be especially troublesome if the investigator were a representative of a politically superior group. Demonstrative behaviour of the "investigators-observers" may have quite the same effect, although the observers themselves might be quite benevolent and good-natured persons. A great number of such observers seem not to understand that they must be inobtrusive, attracting the least possible notice of the audience and the shaman, when a performance is going on.

---

* The shaman finds himself in about the same difficult position when he undertakes a performance in a foreign milieu which cannot reach extasy. Indeed, such a "staging" of shamanism gives not only a distorted picture of the actual performance, for there is no audience which cooperates with the shaman, but it is psychologically impossible for the shaman to succeed, for there is no purpose of shamanizing. The stage is not the usual milieu in which shamans perform, while the milieu is an essential component of the complex. Lastly, several elements, as for instance, smoking of incense, drinking of wine, incidental indecency etc., must be also omitted. Indeed, anybody who is familiar with the shamanistic texts (prayers) as well as tunes and "dancing" can reproduce them, but it will not be shamanizing, but rather a most vulgar farce. I once observed the staging of such a shamanistic performance in a very learned society, even in a special ethnographical section of this society. The meeting was attended by prominent ethnographers, dressed as for theatrical performances and learned discussions. They were seated along the walls of the hall, the middle part of which was reserved for the performer. The performer was a native student of the local university. He was making his way; he was inclined to drinking and his supporters were not always satisfied with him; he did not miss the opportunity to create a sympathetic attitude on the part of his superiors, teachers and supporters. Since this performance might raise him in his social standing, he performed. He pretended to be a shaman, which was not true. I do not know who was the initiator of this theatrical performance, the actor himself or one of the ethnographers. The man could produce no extasy, only jumping and uttering some words incoherently (I believe there was no specialist who could understand him), making a noise with his staffs (which had been taken from a museum), singing something without the necessary assistance, while the ethnographers sat by, assuming an air of deep observers who would penetrate into the "psychology of shamanism" and draw very important conclusions. This performance was a mere farce in which the role of the native impostor was the smallest one, for the whole of the learned meeting was itself a staging of "ethnographical observation of a staged performance". On my part, I am certain that the native was laughing at seeing the serious, almost tragic, faces of the ethnographers. In so far as I know, similar performances were several times carried out in various societies. They are worse than the staging of the "life of savages" in exhibitions, zoological gardens, reserved territories (for the attraction of tourists), and "fêtes foraines", for in all these cases there is no pretension of scientific observation. I have related here this case, for it is a good demonstration of an erroneous idea as to the methods of investigation, admission of a possibility of observing ethnographical phenomena of so great a complexity as the shaman's performance, taken out of its sphere.

the audience towards the acting shaman. This can be produced not only by a strong alien influence, but also by other causes to which I shall revert in further chapters.

123. PSYCHOLOGICAL BASIS OF PERFORMANCE

From the instances given in the previous description and analysis of performances we can see that the shamanistic performances, with their aims and methods, have a purely psychological basis with its theoretical justification. Indeed, the cases attended by the shamans, as well as performances carried out by them for themselves, are not always successful, the main reason thereof being that the psychological moment does not always help and the shamans may make mistakes in their diagnosis, whence in answering the practical question: whether they may help or not. We have already seen that some shamans may refuse to attend cases which are known to be absolutely hopeless. Still the shamans may come to this conclusion only after the accumulation of some diagnostic experience and general knowledge, and when they possess that peculiar ability which is called "intuition". The problem is complicated by the fact that in a great number of cases attended by the shamans a shamanizing may fail to help the respective person, but may help to restore the psychic equilibrium of the clansmen. In cases of the "liquidation" of the souls of deceased relatives, the mastering of spirits, etc. this appears most clearly, for no individual patients are involved. Thus the shaman's performance produces psychic stability among the clansmen or villagers.

Let us now take a hopeless case in which the psychological condition of the patient cannot help, as for instance, typhus with high fever, loss of consciousness, etc. Indeed, no psychological effect on the patient is possible, and the "success" of the shaman's intervention will be due to a mere chance of recovery from typhus. We have seen that the Tungus of Manchuria would regard this case as one caused by a special spirit *ain'i burkan*, so the shamans would not interfere with it. However, for the relatives of the individual affected by this disease the question is to help in any way, and they would pray the spirit to leave the body, or to be merciful to the affected person. Among the Tungus groups which do not know this disease, because of its relative rarity, the shaman may attend the case as any other in which psychological influence may have its positive effect on the issue of the sickness. In case of failure, he would not be blamed. So, the Tungus do with many other diseases which they have contracted from the contact with other ethnical groups, e.g. small-pox, which in some instances of epidemics has swept up to fifty percent of the clan population; measles which can be harmful, even causing death; various forms of "influenza" which sometimes ravage the native populations of Siberia and Manchuria. However, these cases were gradually excluded from those attended by the shamans, who themselves would take preventive measures such as vaccination, isolation, etc. However, such an attitude would be adopted by the shamans when the theoretical side of a new disease is worked out in such a way that the shaman would be forsaken, and his place taken either by the priests, or by experienced people who know prayers, or by professional medical specialists. The shamans take a part in the creation of new theories, but they are not alone to do it. Before the practical ways are found,

or before the hopelessness of shamanizing is realized, the shamans must perform their shamanizing, the chief aim of which would be to maintain the "moral strength", the psychological resistance, in case of a calamity. Thus, the shaman would act chiefly on psychological grounds of the persons who are not sick, but who are "emotionally" and socially affected by the hopeless sickness of one of the members of their community.

Besides these cases, there is a great number of diseases of various infectious character in which the psychological condition may have a decisive influence upon the issue of sickness. We cannot discuss here the question how far the psychological moment can be hold responsible for the issue of a great number of diseases, but it is empirically known that the psychic condition does influence the issue. and this reason is sufficient for taking the necessary measures for the creation of psychic equilibrium, for avoiding disturbances, etc. The question is only about the choice of methods for reaching this goal. Whether it is kalium bromatum, silence, soft shoes and rugs, attitude assumed by the doctor and the nurses who attend the sick person, and hundreds of other methods—is of no importance, provided the aim is achieved. The choice depends on the imagination, the empiric finding of the best conditions, the theoretical calculation, etc.; and among the groups practising shamanism the method is a regulation of the relations between men and spirits. The shamans will do their best to apply this method in all cases in which they are not certain that their interference would be absolutely useless and would only compromise shamanism. So the shamans will carry out a necessary performance, the effect of which will be that the patient will become more certain of a good issue of his sickness, and thus his psychological condition will be more favourable. Naturally the shamans will not refuse to attend a sick person, even though this person be in a hopeless state, e.g. in the last stage of long tuberculosis (*malu burkan* complex). The shaman's sacrifice and prayer may alleviate the psychological condition of the person who is conscious of his approaching end, and the moribund would thus not be left to his own self. In this form the shaman would function in the same way as a Christian priest who for the reconciliation of a dying person with his fate would give him the hope of a better life in the future, or as a positivistically disposed philosopher who would convince a dying person of the inevitability of death, of its beneficial effect upon "evolution", even upon the formation of new forms of chemical combinations, etc. The shaman, priest and philosopher are needed for facilitating the parting with life, and in all these varieties of methods the essential is the same, while the methods are only correlated with the existing cultural complexes. Even in such cases the shaman's assistance is required, the community being in need of help to one of its members, and the success of the shamanizing should be estimated not only as the practical relief to the sufferer, but also as an assistance lent to the community, which suffers because of the suffering of its member. This becomes still clearer in hopeless cases when the moribunds are very small children who do not ask for the shaman's assistance.

However, the above enumerated cases do not form the majority of those dealt with by the shamans. The greater part of them are cases of regulation of purely psychological conditions which may be harmful for individuals and for the communities, such as clans, villages and ethnical units. As shown, the performance itself is a psychological operation, aiming at the community and working through it. There is no need to insist upon the fact that the interference of the shaman with psychomental disturbances, as shown before, is very effective in the majority of cases. When the matter concerns individuals, the community is not indifferent as to the final effect of the performance; firstly, because the individual is a member of the community; secondly, because usually it is the community which takes the initiative in calling a shaman; thirdly, because the community itself is acting in the performance. When the shaman "masters" a new spirit, or when he enforces obedience to one of the clan spirits which would attack clansmen, or when he sends off a spirit—an operation which must be made with the help of the whole community—the effect of the performance extends to the whole community and is an act of social importance. Naturally, in these cases the only aim of shamanizing is a regulation of the psychomental complex of the community.

A positive effect of the performance is achieved, if the community believes that the spirit is neutralized by being mastered or expelled; the effect of the performance will be doubtful, if the opinions of the members of the community differ, and there will be no effect if the community does not accept the shaman's solution. Thus, the essential point is the psychological readiness of the community to accept or to reject the shaman's solution, and action.

Since in all these cases the acting agent is the community itself, the shaman can only be regarded as a special organ of the community. The issue of a performance depends on the personal ability of the shaman, in so far as his performing corresponds to the expectations of the community, and in so far as it is accepted and thus becomes effective. His individuality in the performance is thus greatly limited by the existing ethnographical and ethnical complexes. *The performance must therefore have a form which would correspond to the ideas of the community about the performance and be in accordance with its susceptibility to the influence of suggestion, to hypnosis, and to extasy.* This aspect of the shamanistic performances leads us to an important problem of ritualism—its variations and the degree of stabilization.

124. RITUALISM IN SHAMANISTIC PERFORMANCES I shall call *shamanistic ritual* any action of the shaman and participants in a performance which is invariably repeated in various performances. I shall not distinguish the rituals according to the reasons for which they exist, for that may lead to an error due to the rejection of some elements and the preservation of some others and to the confusion of rituals of distinct types in our groups. However, in order to reach an understanding of the nature of ritualism in shamanism, we must classify the rituals. The fact that ritualism exists in shamanism becomes quite clear, when one observes a great number of performances. In fact, it can be noticed that the shamanistic performances include a great number of elements which are perfectly identical in different performances. A comparison of these common elements shows that certain elements are imposed by: (1) the conditions of the milieu; (2) the instruments, implements and, in general, by the paraphernalia used; (3) the

theories forming the basis of shamanism; and (4) the need of influencing a person, an audience and the shaman himself. When these conditions are the same, the elements of the performance may also be the same. For illustration, I give here some instances.

The movement of the shaman around the fire-place will not be met with among the groups living in houses; the slaughtering of the sacrificial animal will not be carried out in a house, as well as a performance among the Reindeer Tungus and Tungus of Manchuria whose wigwam is not roomy enough for this operation; while when a pig or a chicken is used, the slaughtering can be done in the house, among the Manchus; "complete darkness" in the room, where the performance of going to the lower world is carried out, is required among the Manchus; while among the Tungus who live in wigwams it is not required, for the fire cannot be extinguished and relighted in the wigwam, and the nights are seldom very dark.

The Manchus and the Tungus of Manchuria use the same type of instrument for drumming—a shallow drum—whence there is no difference in using a drum for calling the spirits, and the music is nearly the same; the Manchus have a special drum, borrowed from the Chinese, and castanets, which permit the increase of musical effects, while these instruments are lacking among the Tungus; the Manchu shamans have belts with trinkets which impose special movements with the back, while the Tungus (e.g. of Transbaikalia) have bells on the coat, which require another kind of movement, backward and forward, for producing rhythmic music.

All groups believe in the existence of a spirit which may be "placed"; whence among all groups there is a special operation of calling spirits to enter the "placing". The Manchus have a theory that in the lower world there are trees attractive for the spirits; so the Manchus have a special performance with a tree, while the Tungus, who have no such a theory, have no "tree" performance. The Manchu theory does not recognize that there are spirits of the upper world which can be influenced by the shamans' spirits, so there is no performance of this type; while the Reindeer Tungus of Transbaikalia have this theory, and so their shamans deal with the spirits of the upper world.

The number of instances can be increased ad libitum for proving that the elements of performance are sometimes imposed by the above indicated four conditions. A similarity between these elements of performance, observed in ethnical groups, clans, and individual shamans, may be due to the similarity of conditions, and a dissimilarity may be due to the dissimilarity of the underlying conditions.

As soon as the conditions are changed, the elements of performance must also be changed. This can be observed among the Tungus of Manchuria who sometimes live in houses of a Manchu (Chinese) type.

However, there are some ritualistic elements which cannot be understood as a direct effect of the conditions of the milieu and the paraphernalia, and even as a result of adopted theories, the latter being needed as a justification of certain ritual elements and easily taken as an explanation of the existence of rituals. Thus, there are some elements which are imposed by the reasons residing in the nature of shamanism, in its theoretical setting and practical methods, and there are entire rituals which are justified by the theory and practice. I shall confine myself now to the ritualism which depends upon the nature of shamanism, and also to that which depends neither upon it, nor upon the above indicated conditions.

First of all, it must be pointed out that the shamanistic ritualism has nothing "sacred" in it. Any ritual may be changed, if such a change should be useful for the practical aims of shamanizing. So it is in principle, but there is one exception, namely, that of the Manchus, when they deal with clan spirits (p'oyun saman). Since this exception is very important from the ethnographical point of view, I shall revert to it. On the one hand, we have seen that the aims of shamanizing are very definite and clear; on the other hand, the methods of achieving these aims are subject to variations which depend on the shaman's ability and general knowledge as to the nature of particular spirits. In these conditions, if we have a more or less definite group of aims of shamanizing (subject to some variations, chiefly under the influence of the penetration of new cultural complexes), and if no strong alien influence is found in the work, the choice of methods for dealing with the spirits is not great. So the methods—elements forming a complex of performance—are fixed in conformity with the aims of shamanizing. In this way, methods become ritualistic—they are performed, for they are known to be effective. No stimuli to change them would appear, so long as they are believed to be effective. However, since the complex of rituals may consist of various elements and the reason for the existence of these elements may be forgotten, the shamans would not risk altering them, and they will be repeated, for fear of failing in dealing with the spirits. In the shamanistic performances we often meet with such elements as, for instance, the repetition of certain acts (elements) a definite number of times, e.g. three times, four times etc. No shaman can explain why the same act must be repeated three or four times. At most, he would refer to the practice of his predecessors. In such cases there is no need to see in these numbers a hidden sense, a "mystic influence", etc.—they may have been mere accidents in the performances of the predecessors.*

In fact, an able shaman, owing to an accident, may omit a certain detail of the ritual, and if the result of the shamanizing is satisfactory, he will not be very careful as to the observation of this particular detail, which may disappear altogether. The loss of elements may also be imposed by the change of the cultural complex or the change of paraphernalia and milieu. It may also be replaced by another element, either created by the shaman himself, or borrowed from other ethnical groups. However, there is a limit to the simplification of the ritual, namely, *something must be performed, for otherwise there will be no sign that the shaman was dealing with the spirit.* There is also a certain limit to the change of elements, namely, if the shaman would change them at every shamanizing, the audience would not be able to understand with which spirit the shaman was dealing and how successful this new method (not

yet verified) might be; so the *introduction of a new element requires a certain time.* It should be noted that some performances are not repeated by the shamans every year, and practically it would require the whole life of a shaman to introduce a new element. He would be in a better position, if the new element is known to the audience from their contact with other ethnical groups; but still a negative reaction against an alien complex is always a great impediment to innovation. Anyhow, as shown, in case of a dissension between the shaman and the audience, the performance, in so far as it is based upon the assistance of the audience, may fail altogether, for even permanent assistants will not be able to follow the shaman, and thus the psychological effect of the shamanizing will be missed. It is thus evident that two mechanisms independent of the shaman's will are at work, namely, an accidental loss of elements and an intervention of circumstances, which usually requires a restoration of the complex by means of an invention and by the borrowing of new elements—the mechanism of changes; and the preservation of the complex imposed by the necessity of having *some* complex and by the need of being understood and accepted by the audience—the mechanism of preservation.* As a matter of fact, the mechanism of preservation, in order to be understood, needs no deep psychological speculations as to the character of the primitive mentality, nor of the inherited conditions of "human races". If there is no general change of the ethnographical complex, no strong interethnical pressure, and if the shamanistic art is carefully transmitted, the ritualism will persist without any essential change for a very long time, the only source of changes being some accidental loss of elements.

———

I shall now give some examples of a ritualism resulting from the pre-existing theories and that of a rationalized ritualism of various origin (invention and borrowing).

The ritualism of "posts" and "roads", on and along which the spirits are descending, going away and generally moving, is widely practised by all Tungus groups here discussed. This use is conditioned by the theory concerning the nature of spirits which must know where they can descend (on the post) and by which "road" (a string, a thong) they may reach the placing, or the sacrifice, or the shaman, and how they can return. However, among the Reindeer Tungus of Transbaikalia, the ritual itself seems to have been borrowed from some other ethnical groups (I think the Buriat-Mongols) and applied to the spirits which do not follow the upper roads. Among the Manchus the post is used only for the spirit of heaven, while among the Tungus of Manchuria posts are used only for the shaman's spirits. Among the Manchus the ritualism of "post-road" for the shaman's spirits, as shown before, uses special placings. The Tungus of Manchuria and the Manchus are certain that the spirits will come, even without "roads"; however, the Tungus groups would use "roads" and "posts", even when they are dealing with some spirits of the *burkan* group without the shaman's assistance. If the "post-road" ritual were excluded from the complex of

———

* The search for and guesses as to a hidden sense and mysticism have become so common in ethnographical writings that mere imagination of the authors sometimes form the bulk of investigations. The above given instance of "mystic numbers" clearly shows that since there must be some ritual repeated several times, and since there is a rhythm in the performance and since the numbers are limited (practically from two to ten), there must be coincidence without any "mystic reason". By this remark I do not altogether deny the possibility of the existence of mystic numbers. However, their function would be different.

———

* I do not mention now the written records of ritualism, which are a powerful means of preservation, for I shall revert to this question later on.

the Birarčen sacrifice to the *burkan* group, doubtless almost nothing would remain. In all of these cases the idea is to create the best conditions for calling in the spirits and for managing them.

The theory teaches that the spirits of the dark lower world are fond of fresh meat and blood. This theory may be explained by the ethnographers in various manners.[*] The Tungus explanation is that these spirits (souls) *like meat and blood*, and in this form the sacrifice is easily assimilated, especially after sunset. Owing to this, all operations with the souls of the dark lower world are carried out in the dark, and they form quite a special ritualism. It should be noted that this ritualism includes the element of supplying souls with travelling facilities, e.g. dogs (Manchus), reindeer (Reindeer Tungus), horses, etc. In fact, these are needed and maintained for the practical purpose of dealing with such spirits. The introduction of a new element—e.g. the canoe among the groups which do not use dogs and reindeers as draught animals—is quite possible, but not necessary. However, the latter may be retained, because the souls prefer dogs or reindeer. New elements may be introduced, if the ethnical group learns of them from another group, which is considered to be clever in managing souls. Among the Birarčen the ritualism is rather strict as regards the sacrificial animals: the day road spirits (or rather some spirits and particular manifestations) may use any kind of animals, with the exception of the pig, while the night road spirits must have a pig. Since the pig is not an animal domesticated by the Tungus (they buy them from the Manchus and Chinese), it would be easy to suppose that the complex of night road spirits ritualism is borrowed from the Manchus (and Chinese?). However, the lower world spirits (the night roads) among the Reindeer Tungus require a reindeer (as opposed to the upper world, the day roads). Therefore it is more likely that the reindeer was replaced by the pig, owing to the fact that the Birarčen ancestors were even until recent times reindeer breeders and they were in all probability familiar with the shamanism and the theory of roads (spirits) prior to their loss of the reindeer.

The theory teaches that in the lower world the shaman is in the dark. To help him to find his way out he needs the road to be lighted. The light cannot be produced, for the shaman is in the lower world; therefore sparks are produced with steel and flint—they are "like lightning for the shaman"—whence the ritualism of producing sparks, e.g. among the Reindeer Tungus of Transbaikalia and among the Tungus of Manchuria (I cannot assert this in reference to the Nomad Tungus).[**]

[*] E.g. the ethnographers may suppose that uncooked meat and fresh blood are early forms of food of the time when fire was not used. But such a supposition presumes a series of hypotheses: creation of the managing of souls prior to the use of fire for cooking, late discovery of cooking and maintaining of fire; hypothesis as to the "conservatism" of "primitive mind", etc. all of which are elements of the European ethnographical complex, from which the ethnographers can hardly desist.

[**] The Manchus now do not use the production of sparks. There is no doubt that the flint-and-steel fire production is a new method received by the Tungus from or through the intermediary of the Mongols and Chinese in very recent times. Nowadays this method of fire production is gradually disappearing, being partly replaced by matches and partly rendered useless by the practice of carrying a piece of burning touchwood (especially among the Tungus of Manchuria); so the flint-and-steel have been included in the complex

The character of spirits sometimes requires a definite ritualism. For instance, among the Manchus the spirits (*voč̌ko*)

(1) wolf (*n'uxu*), bear (*iefu*), snake (*meize*), dragon (*mudur'i*) and other "animals"—the shaman roars and scratches the earth (wolf, bear); the head-dress is taken off;

(2) deaf—the shaman cleans his ears, does not correctly answer questions, as if being deaf, until some brandy is sprinkled on him;

(3) group of "heroes" (*buku* and *mayi*)—the shaman takes off his head-dress and uses special instruments, such as a spear, a glaive, a trident, etc.; *buku* and *mayi* in ritualism are distinguished by their movements.

(4) *naifulan*—the shaman puts on a special head-dress (with iron antlers) and follows a strictly elaborated ritual when going to the lower world;

(5) group of Tungus (*kilin*) spirits—the shaman does not speak Manchu, nor Chinese, but he uses a few Tungus words;

(6) various spirits—when the shaman has his hands occupied by weapons and instruments, he hands over his drum to the assistant.

Such a ritualism, connected with different spirits, has been elaborated among the Manchus to such a degree, that an assistant, familiar with the spirits, may guess which spirit is introduced by the shaman. During the performance, when several spirits are changed, with every new spirit the shaman asks his assistant (it is supposed that the spirit asks) : *takam'i takaraku?*—"Do you recognize (me) ?", and the assistant must tell the name of the spirit. If the assistant cannot do it (usually when many spirits are called, which rarely appear, so that the assistant cannot know them —e.g. on the day when all spirits are "fed"), the shaman gives a hint as to the row, and the assistant enumerating one after another arrives at the right spirit's name.

The ritualism required by the character of the spirits may greatly differ in different clans, although the names of the spirits would be the same. For instance, in the *nara* clan the sacrifice to five *māfa* consists of a domesticated goose, duck, chicken, hen and cock, while in other clans birds are not sacrificed.

We have seen that new spirits are always introduced because of discoveries and because of the increase of the number of souls of dead shamans. New spirits may also have a distinct ritualism in which some distinct characters may be introduced. Thus the ritualism would be increased. However, the ritualism imposed by the spirits is still more stabilized in the performance of the *p'oyun* saman. Almost every clan has its fixed nearly "petrified" ritualism.

Among the Northern Tungus groups the ritualism resulting from the character of the spirits is also widely practised. For instance, among the Birarčen some spirits of the group *malu* have their own rituals by which the assistants and the audience may know which of the mani-

of shamanistic paraphernalia. When they are lost and cannot be got from the neighbours, the use of sparks must be discontinued, or the momentaneous lighting must be produced by something else. I should not be surprised, if in place of flint-and-steel, an electric torch light would be used, made in U.S.A. or Japan.

festations is introduced; e.g. (1) one legged—the shaman would become a "lamb"; (2) with a broken chest (*samɣäli*) —the shaman would cough and touch his chest; (3) when the spirit *sunusun* is introduced—the shaman would speak in different voices imitating all three generations of *sunusun;* (4) once I observed a female shaman who produced swelling of the abdomen, when she introduced one of her female *dōna* spirits, as though she had become pregnant; (5) there are spirits which destroy buttons (the Khingan Tungus), which take away and break pipes, etc.; therefore buttons and pipes must be hidden.*

Among the above instances the fourth is especially interesting, for the spirit was an individual shaman's spirit and the ritualism was created by the shaman. Naturally it can be practised only by female shamans.

"Dancing" and singing in the shamanistic performance is also closely connected with the character of the spirits, and still more with the other conditions of shamanizing which will be discussed later. Here I give a list of refrains connected with some spirits, as these refrains are used among the Birarčen.

I. *INTRODUCTIONS* (sung by the shaman) *AND REFRAINS* (sung either by the shaman or by the assistant shaman), corresponding to the spirits:

1. *Adar,—adar-odin-jor, adar-odin-jor, odin-jor;*
2. *aɣgna,—ɣuaɣ-go-gu-su-daī,ɣuaɣ-go-gu-su-daī, gosudaī;*
3. *dāril,—ogdi-rajā, ogdi-xajā;*
4. *dāril (us'i dolbor),—dolbor-kojó, dolbor kōjo;*
5. *j'erg'i,—ja-jaī, ja-jae;*
6. *kadar,—kadaī-xaja, kadaī-xèja;*
    —*kadar-kaŋg'er, dèvar-dauser;*
    —*kadar-kaŋg'er, daīsar-dauser;*
7. *kadar (dolbor),—dolbor'jo-dolbor, dolbor'jo-dolbor;*
8. *karol,—kau-kau-kaoī, kau-kau-kaoī;*
9. *lamalaīčen,—lamaī-xajā, lamaī-xāja;*
10. *malu,—sayk'iraveī-saraveī;*
11. *n'aɣn'aɣ,—n'aɣn'aī-xajā, n'aɣn'aī-xāja*
    —*bajukeī, bajukeī, bajukejuja* (it is used when the child soul is handed over to the shaman);
12. *n'irgir,—k'iy-k'iŋg'ir-uja, k'iy-k'iŋg'ir-uja*
13. *s'erū j'erg'i,—sērū-sērū-sērū, sērū-sērū-sērū* (the last *sērū* is very long);
14. *sunusun,—suī-du-suja, suī-du-suja, suīdu, suīdu;*
    —*suīlasun, suīlasun, suīla, suīla;*

II. *ORDINARY INTRODUCTIONS AND REFRAINS* (for various spirits on various occasions)

1. *bajukeī-bajukeī-bajukejuja* (cf. *n'aɣn'aɣ* spirit)
2. *dafsak'i-dafsak'i;*
3. *dav'i-dav'i-dav'idaī;*
4. *davīsa-kandaveī, davīsa-kandaveī;*
5. *jajakuīla, jajakuīla, jakuīla;*
6. *gaja-gaja-* (especially used when there are sick people)
7. *gawk'iraji-ga-ga;*
8. *gijeī-gijeī-gaja;*
9. *ir'i-uīdja, ir'i-ulaja;*
10. *(ja-ga, ja-g'i, jaga-jaī)* recited three times, and *(ja-ga-heja, ja-ga-jaī)* recited twice, (used when a

spirit tells its history, also at the conclusion of the periodical shamanizing, at the end of a sacrifice offered to the spirits.)

11. *ja-g'i, ja-g'i, ja-g'i jaī; ja-g'i, ja-g'i, ja-g'i, jaī;*
12. *jo-go-jo, jo-go-joī; jo-go-jo, jo-go-joī*

A special refrain known under the name *kokuneī* (*kadar*-complex), — *kāu-kāu-kāu, kāu-jān'i-kāu* — is used indiscriminately. When shamanizing is carried out for illness, etc., the refrains are used:
ja-ga, ja-ga, ja-ga-joī;
ja-ja-g'i (simplified, *vide supra,* 10).

The following refrains are used for prayers (*buaðin*):
1. *julask'i,—ja-gu-ja-ga, ja-ja-gu, ja-ja-ja-ga, jeī;*
    (ja-gu-ja-g'i, ja-ja-ɣaī) twice
    (ja-ga-ja-gaī, ja-ge-jeī)—twice
2. *bunildu,—(gajdmeī-gajdmēī)* twice
3. *najiī burkan,—(kéku-kéku-kékujā)* twice

Specialization of refrains is also practised among the Manchus. For instance, the Tungus (*K'ilin*) spirits require either *jagd-jagd,* or *negd-negd,* but other Tungus refrains are not used; the female spirits usually require *kéku-kéku,* etc. However, some refrains are used for several spirits.* The rhythm of these refrains (and naturally of the texts) are not alike, and the tunes are different too. Together with the rhythm and the music there is also "dancing", which is also different. For instance, in the Manchu clan *n'imači,* the shaman makes a step crossing his feet, as it is often done by the Tungus shamans; but this is not done in other Manchu clans. Among the Manchus the shamans (great shamans, but never the *p'oɣun saman*) introduce additional movements (e.g. the drum is thrown up in the air and caught), which produce special musical rhythmic effects and which are connected with the introduction of the particularly skilful spirits.

As soon as the refrains are stabilized, the stabilization of the tunes and the dancing is also likely to occur, thereafter, one step more, and the texts may also be stabilized. Under these conditions the ritual may be established which will be invariably performed during the shamanizing.

The influencing of the sick person, the audience, and the shaman himself by the latter may also become a source for the creation of a ritualistic complex. In the description of performances we have seen that the shaman's aim is to influence those who have come for treatment, chiefly adults, by means of suggestion and hypnotism. These methods are gradually worked out by particular experiments of the shamans through the trial-error method. The shaman may also apply some new method which may be purposely invented by him. Those of the methods which have proved to be effective are adopted and used, in the cases of various spirits, by the generations of shamans. The Tungus and Manchus do not hesitate to use methods practised among other ethnical groups. If these methods are effective, they would be adopted as well. All the methods, at a certain moment, may become stabilized and repeated on identical occasions (spirits) as a ritual. In a great number of cases it is even impossible to distinguish where a ritualistic act is performed or more or less unconsciously reproduced, and where an act is consciously performed by the shaman who understands its "meaning" and effect. This becomes very clear when we analyse performances carried out by shamans-beginners, and by ex-

---

* It should be noted that in the Tungus complex both the buttons and tobacco pipes are innovations.

* Cf. for instance, refrains used in Nišan Saman.

perienced shamans. But first I want to give some instances of "ritualism" of these three groups.

I. First I shall give some cases with patients:

(1) The shaman approaches the drum to the mouth of the patient and orders the sick person to vomit the contents of the stomach, or the spirit. This is being done in all cases when it is supposed that the curing by vomiting is possible. Indeed, the same performance takes place as a simple ritual, even when the sick child is too small to respond, or when healing is not the direct aim of the performance, but rather an effect on the audience. (All groups).*

(2) The increase of the tempo of drumming and the singing and dancing become a ritual when the shaman does it for influencing the patient, but does not feel himself to be in extasy. This method may become one of the formal components of a performance, as an element of the latter without any direct aim—it would be done because it is always done under the given circumstances. (All groups).

(3) The shaman passes over and touches the chest of the patient with the brass mirror, which is a suggestive movement, quite effective when the patient believes that the spirit that attacks him may be removed into the brass mirror and neutralized by the shaman. The latter and the audience may have the same idea. However, this operation becomes a mere formality, when there is no belief, and it is merely done, because it had been done before. (Tungus of Manchuria, Manchus).

(4) The shaman sucks blood from different parts of the patient's body; the patient, the shaman and the audience may believe in the sucking of the spirits together with the blood. However, this operation, even without a sincere belief in its effectiveness, may be maintained in similar circumstances, the chief active element of the performance being some new method somehow connected with the sucking, but not yet ritualized (Manchus).

(5) For sending off a spirit located in the abdomen the shaman puts across the patient's back or abdomen a sword and hammers it with an axe. No harm to the patient's abdomen is supposed to be produced by this blow. However, since such an operation is physically impossible, the performance includes this "number" as a mere ritual, (at present seldom used). It is most likely that this method was used by one of the shamans who knew some trick unnoticed by the audience and the patients. The operation was repeated, but since it was not artistically performed, the patients and the audience do no more believe in it, although it is repeated as a part of the formal ritual connected with a certain spirit. (Manchus).

---

* Manipulations with the drum are especially used. Among the Khingan Tungus the shaman, when going to the upper world, strikes the drum vigorously three times, and lifts it up; when going to the lower world, he makes movements downward, also three times. When a patient has a pain in the back, or the chest, the shaman makes movements with the drum as near as possible to the painful spot. If there is pain in the arms, the shaman blows into the drum in which a hole is supposed to be through which the spirit leaves the affected part of the limb. If the shaman wishes to harm people, he may do so with his drum: first the drum is passed up and down the chest, then twice put on the rim, to symbolize a cross. For sending off the spirits, a series of quick movements are made with the drum, as though the spirits were being thrown away. Among the Birarčen the bad blood from the affected internal organs is supposed to be collected in the drum.

II. Cases with the audience.

(1) For the creation of a mass extasy the audience repeats refrains with gradually increasing emotion chiefly produced by an increase of the tempo, intensity, and expression. This is a technical method for producing an extasy, usually connected with important moments of the performance. Since it is required so, the audience responds according to the pattern—ritual; but there may occur no extasy if, for instance, the audience does not consider the moment to be of a real importance. This is a common occurrence, for the important and real key of performance may be shifted to another part of the performance and extasy must be postponed. So the whole operation with the supposed extasy may become merely a formal ritual. (All groups).

(2) The participants of the shamanizing feel themselves touched by the spirits which are called by the shaman during the performance; so they carry out purification which consists in going through a special apparatus supplied with hooks or indentations on which spirits are supposed to remain. This is usually done when the shaman deals with the dangerous spirits of the lower world. However, I have observed a case when the shaman was not dealing with the dangerous spirits, but was talking with one of the ancestors, and still the purification was performed, for "the shaman was dealing with the spirits of the lower world". The purification has become a ritual, and its original meaning has been forgotten. (Barguzin Tungus).

(3) Nine participants in a performance in a state of extasy imagine themselves to be placings of nine manifestations of the spirit, and they follow the shaman in rhythmic "dancing". This forms a very complex performance in which the shaman is in a complete psychological fusion with the participants. However, I have seen a case when there were only seven participants who were not at all in extasy and some of whom laughed and made jokes. It was thus merely a formal ritual. (Birarčen).

III. Cases with the shaman.

(1) The aim of the shaman is to bring himself into a state of extasy, which is achieved by various means—rhythmic drumming with an increase of tempo, singing, "dancing" and even drinking wine. When all this is done, it is supposed that the shaman is in extasy and then possesses a particular power of seeing and hearing spirits. However, as the observation shows, the shamans do not always attain a complete extasy, but perform everything which is required, including the peculiar trembling of the body, etc. When the shaman is disturbed by the audience, this cannot be reached at all. This is a fact well known to the shamans and the audience. In spite of this, every important shamanizing includes performances of calling in and introducing of the spirits. So this operation has turned, at least in some cases, into a ritual. (All groups).

(2) It is supposed that when the shaman introduces into himself the spirit of fire he loses the sensitiveness to the greatest heat, which is quite possible if the shaman reaches a state of extasy. However, as stated, this is not a very common occurrence, but the spirit of fire is often needed for treatment. The shaman produces evidences that the spirit is introduced, and he manipulates with fire, hot irons, etc. However, all his operations are made in such conditions that he does not burn himself. These operations are by no means believed by the audience, but

they are carried out, because they were used by other shamans and have already become a ritualistic formality.
(Manchus, Chinese).

(3) The introduction of spirits, as will be shown later
(*vide* Chapter XXIX), followed by an extasy, is an extremely
tiresome operation, so that the shaman, during the evening,
can produce a very limited number of extasies. In imitation of the clan "priests", the Manchu shamans established
a new practice of revision of all spirits once a year (on the
second day of the year). It was supposed that the shaman
must introduce all his spirits one by one. No one believes
it to be possible, for there may be over sixty spirits in the
list of a shaman, but the shamans perform as though the
spirits were actually introduced. So here the ritual of introduction of spirits has grown into a secondary complex
of pure and simple ritualism. (Manchus, Chinese).

(4) The shaman naturally knows all spirits which
come to him. Among the Manchus the number of spirits
attained a very large number, which is partly due to the
writing (*vide infra*, Section 125). It is supposed (a theory!)
that the new shaman must know all clan spirits, and thus
during the performance of initiation he must name them
and introduce them into himself. The elders and former
assistants of the shaman are not supposed to tell the new
shaman about the spirits. When the performance of initiation is carried out, the new shaman cannot name all the
spirits. However, since a new shaman is needed, the elders
and former assistants make hints to the candidate, so that
he can perform this formality. So this important moment
in the initiation has turned into a ritual. (Manchus).

(5) When the soul of the shaman is absent from the
body for a long time, and the shaman remains unconscious
(even the temperature of the body may decrease and the
pulse diminish in frequency and strength!), he cannot
stand, and falls. However, such a state cannot be attained
in all cases of such performances, but the shaman falls
down and gives the appearance of being unconscious, and
he will not respond for some time, sufficient to show that
it is difficult to call him back. So the unconsciousness of
the shaman has become, at least sometimes, a mere ritual.
(All groups, especially Manchus).

(6) Before carrying out his performance the shaman
lies down and sleeps during a few hours. There may be
two purposes, namely, that of taking a rest before a difficult performance, and that of having revelational dreams.
However, very often the shaman does not sleep at all, but
merely pretends sleeping. When the time needed (it may
actually last only less than half of an hour!) is over, he
jumps up as though he had introduced into himself a spirit
during the sleep. This is performed even when the shaman
cannot fall asleep and when the shamanizing is not difficult.
So the preparation for a serious shamanizing has turned
into a ritual (Manchus).

I do not think that other illustrations are needed to
show that the most important methods of regulation of the
psychology of the person to be treated, the audience and the
shaman himself may change into a rigid ritual. However,
in a great number of cases the same "rituals" remain effective methods, and may become a simple formality gradually dying away. This depends on the ethnical groups and
individual shamans—in one group the method will not be
a ritual, while in another group it may become a ritual, and
in a third one it may change into a dying formality.

The answer to the question as to how these methods
turn into a ritual seems to be as follows. First of all, a
general critical attitude toward shamanism destroys the
necessary psychological conditions for maintaining certain
methods; secondly, some methods may turn into a ritual,
when they cannot function as they did before, e.g. in the
hands of the inventors of those methods; thirdly, when new
methods are introduced which lead to the same end, but are
not noticed, while the old methods are preserved as rituals;
fourthly, when these methods are intentionally turned into
rigid rituals and fixed. In fact, although we may observe
all these cases in the shamanism of the Tungus, the Manchu
ritualism is especially interesting, for it demonstrates all
cases in the most striking form, owing to a very strong
alien influence, which leads to a critical attitude, and a
continuous introduction of new methods, as well as to the
fixation of the methods in a written form.

It should be noted that sometimes a new method of
reaching the aim does not at all consist of a great number
of new rituals, but finds expression in a few phrases uttered
and acts performed by the shaman at some moment of the
performance. Still, a shamanizing consisting only of rituals may be effective in its totality; it would influence the
audience and the sick person as it is, for instance, with the
famous ceremonial and ritualism of Lamaism. On the
other hand, an important condition of functional efficiency
of shamanism is its continuous remodelling, by the mechanism of the loss, already discussed in a detailed manner, in
which the shaman's initiative and invention may save the
complex from the reduction to a ceremonialism. Quite a
contrary effect is produced by the mechanism of preservation which, as I shall now show, in the case of some Manchu shamans, may turn shamanism into an inefficient ritualism. Here I have in view the fixation of methods and
theories by means of written records and pictures.

125. INFLUENCE OF   The formation and maintenance
     MANCHU WRITING   of the performance complex, as
                      a combination of methods aim-
ing at the regulation of psychology and rituals, which may
become a rather neutral background on which the shaman
acts, is a mechanism of adaptation which possesses great
elasticity, as long as it is not disturbed by too strong interethnical pressure and as long as it is not fixed. The fixation may be of two forms, namely, a good oral tradition or
an imitation, maintained by a theoretical justification, and
a mechanical transmission, i.e. in a written form. The idea
of fixation is stimulated by the practical consideration of
preservation of the known methods of regulation of the relations between the spirits and the shamans. In fact,
should there be such a simple way of fixation or keeping the
methods in mind, it would be used at once. However, the
effects of such fixation come much later and they are not
understood.

The Manchus began to use their present method of
writing by the end of the sixteenth century. However,
prior to the present writing there existed other methods
of writing, such as the Mongol alphabet and orthography,
Chinese characters, used directly, as well as in their phonetic function, as with the Nuichen system, and perhaps other
systems too; but these were available only to a very limited
number of people—the highly educated social group. The
introduction of the Manchu alphabet and its spreading

among the Manchus occurred during the seventeenth century. It may be supposed that from that time began the fixation of the ritual—its petrification.

In the instance of variations of the terms for "clan" we can observe the effects of this method of fixation: new terms for "clan" were created, while the phenomenon itself continued to exist; however, as soon as the clan was fixed (*xala*), the phenomenon itself gradually lost its functional importance (cf. SOM. and SONT). This was the first important practical application of fixation of a variable social phenomenon, imposed by the consideration of practical need of administration. A little later, namely, in the eighteenth century, the idea of fixation of clan rituals appeared and the Emperor Chien Lung had it done. This fixation was "rationalized" by him, saying that the Manchus might forget their methods of managing clan spirits. Actually there might have been two distinct motives, namely: (1) the preservation of the Manchu cultural complex, in order to prevent the loss by the Manchus of their ethnical consciousness, and to fortify their opposition to the Chinese, which I suppose, was the chief reason for the Emperor's order; and (2) the fear of losing the proved methods of controlling spirits—a special consideration which in the Emperor's mind was perhaps not a reason, but a "rationalization", a justification of this measure in the eyes of the Manchus. However, as I have already pointed out, there might be some other reasons too, namely, the creation of impressive performances that might impress the Chinese. This fixation, as I have pointed out, found imitators in all Manchu clans which recorded the names of the spirits and the rituals in the clan books of "*čolo* and *kooli*", since this measure was concerning only clan spirits, spirits of ancestors and some other spirits, which may be common to a great number of clans, e.g. *čuxa japin*, i.e. the spirits which were known at that time. However, we cannot be absolutely certain whether all spirits, used at that time, were enlisted, or whether they were somewhat selected, in order to be nearer to the model of the Imperial Family (clan). Though perhaps in an incomplete form, the spirits were fixed, as well as the rituals. Since the spirits and rituals were not identical in all clans and they were certainly not recorded with an equal carefulness, some essential differences between the clans appeared. As we have seen, some clans went so far that they preserved the introduction of spirits into the *p'oyun saman*, which was contrary to the Imperial Family model; some other clans distinguished night and day roads' spirits, and most of them did not include Sakyamuni, as it was in the Imperial Family rituals. It is not incidental that the clan shamans are not called *xala saman*, but are called *p'oyun saman*, which is indicative of an interesting fact, namely, that the institute of *p'oyun saman*, which functionally is a "clan shaman", originated at the period when *xala* (the old term for "clan") was no more referred to the actual "clan" (an exogamous unit, etc.). Thus it may now be supposed that *p'oyun saman* appeared at a rather late period, I think, only during the eighteenth century. A complex ritualism which required a *ta saman*, a certain number of *saman* and their numerous assistants (all of them *p'oyun*), could not be performed, for the performers were clan officers, but the clan (now called *mokun*) was not a sufficiently numerous unit to be able to afford the maintaining or a great ceremonial. So the *p'oyun saman* complex was always functioning in a greatly reduced form, even before the Manchu disintegration. We have also seen that a great number of clans have lost their written *čolo* and *kooli* (ritual) and in many a clan the performances turned into a silent sacrifice. This form of "shamanism", fixed and "ennobled" under the Chinese influence, is now dying out, especially under the influence of the political downfall in China of the initiators—the Imperial Family of the *ǧ'joro clan*.

In spite of the existence of a clan ritualism, shamanism continued as it was started at an earlier time. In fact, since the introduction of clan "priesthood", the psychological need of shamanism, as well as its social function and the general theoretical conceptions of the Manchus have not essentially changed. In order to distinguish this unregulated shamanism, the Manchus called the real shamans *amba saman*—"great shaman"—and the further variations of this complex continued; the latter did not die out, but has been enriched, owing to some special conditions. One of these special conditions was a new possibility of fixation. Doubtless shamanism has made great acquisitions of new spirits during the time when a fixation of the clans' spirits and rituals had been made. In fact, the lists of shamanistic spirits show a great number of shamans who lived, died and became spirits. New foreign spirits were also included. On the other hand, ritualism and practical methods of psychological influence have also been enriched from various sources of interethnical milieu—chiefly Chinese, and partly Mongol and Northern Tungus. Therefore it is questionable, whether there are very many old spirits and old methods (those implied by the constant factors being excluded) in the existing shamanistic complex. The record of everything in a new written form was always attractive to the Manchus, as it always was for a great many ethnical groups, including European groups. So the Manchus began it. However, the great variety of individual shamans and always occuring changes did not permit to record everything. One of the cases is the record of *Nišan saman's* performance which evidently produced a deep impression upon the contemporaries and the younger generation. That such a fact as an unconsciousness, perhaps a lethargy, which lasted several days, the intervention of *Nišan* and the recovery of the patient could really happen is quite possible. The text of shamanizing could be memorized by the permanent assistants of the *Nišan*, whose name was also preserved and transmitted, first orally and later recorded. If such a record could be done, then other records could have followed, using the first one as a model. The recording of rituals and spirits of the clan has also stimulated similar work with *amba-saman's* spirits and rituals.

Moreover, another source of fixation existed; namely, the production of pictures—*n'urgan*. When the spirits were not numerous there was no need of having many placings; but when their number attained several dozens, and as the spirits of deceased shamans might not have placings of a special form, it became necessary to simplify the placings. It was natural that images of Buddhistic and Taoistic deities should be represented in pictures. This was done by the Manchus, and thus the spirits were preserved in pictures and their number began to increase. As the pictures could not suffice, additional lists of spirits were made, supposed to be recited at the initiation of shamans. At first they were kept in memory, afterwards they were written down. At present a great number of clans possess

such lists of spirits and prayers. It remained only to record the rituals, which has also been done in some clans.

The effect of the fixation of spirits, prayers, and rituals was that the shamans who wanted to introduce innovations required by the change of psychological conditions
and implied by the existing and ever-changing theories
concerning the spirits, or who wished to drop some of the
elements which might become a simple burden in the complex, could not do it. The specialists in shamanism, referring to the written records, required a particular strictness: since the old shamans did so, the new ones must do
the same, if they want to be efficient in dealing with the
spirits. So in some clans the complex has grown far beyond the limits practically needed for the effectiveness of
shamanism, and gradually it began to turn into an elaborated ritualism. In fact, the number of spirits has increased to
such an extent, that no shaman can introduce them. The
prayers are repeated quite automatically, as it is done in
the lamaistic service. The methods of psychological effects
upon the patients, the audience and the shamans themselves
turned into almost professional tricks of jugglers. Such
a state of shamanism in some clans is not due solely to the
fact of fixation; other causes exist, as well, but the fixation
of rituals was one of the important factors which led to the
loss of the functional efficiency of shamanism among the
Manchus.

However, not everything could be recorded, and formalized: the shamans, when dealing with the spirits, may preserve a certain freedom in the choice of means to produce
the necessary psychological condition. Some of them put
more stress on the methods which could not be bound by
ritualism, and so maintained some direct effectiveness of
shamanism by the side of a complex ritualism. One of the
effects of this situation was that the shamanistic performances, sometimes lasted several days and again became tiresome for everybody, and thus lost their effectiveness. However, the shamans continued exercising their art of regulation of the psychic equilibrium of the clans with new
methods, which thus existed in addition to the written ritualism. It may be supposed that perhaps the same situation was with the shamans, soon after the introduction of
written ritualism of p'oyun saman, for the clan spirits.
Under the new name of amba saman shamanism survived.
Perhaps they will further survive under a third name,
even after the last formalization of the present shamanism.
To this question I shall revert later on.

Owing to the existence of writing, the formalizing of
shamanistic performances went much further among the
Manchus than among the Northern Tungus. Therefore
the impression produced by the Manchu performances is
generally different from that produced by the Northern
Tungus performances, the latter being more "emotive"
and "sincere".

126. VARIOUS MECHANISMS   The complex function
MAINTAINING SHAMANISM   of shamanism, as a
                          self-regulating mechan-
ism of the psychomental equilibrium, is not realized by the
Manchus and Tungus. Through a long process of adaptation the complex has been formed without its principal
function being understood. Since it is perceived by the
ethnical groups from the performances, we may now ask

question as to the conditions, which might assure the existence of shamanism as a complex, in so far as they depend
on the psychology of groups. I now leave aside the problem of the conditions which influence the existence of
shamanism in a contrary sense, to which question I shall
revert in the conclusive sections of the present part.

There are four conditions maintaining the existence
of shamanism: (1) the practical effects upon the patient
and clansmen, in so far as psychic instability is cured; (2)
the social side of shamanism; (3) the "emotional" and
particularly the aesthetic side of the performance; and (4)
the learning of new things.

The curative power of shamanism has already been
discussed, so I need not go into details. A great number
of observations made by the Manchus and Tungus is quite
convincing—the interference of the shamans is effective,
both in cases of individual troubles and in those of mass
troubles. When the shamans fail to cure, this is not always
ascribed to the deficiency of shamanism and the shamans,
but to special spirits, which cannot be fought by the shamans. So the positive effects of shamanism and the
practical utility of the performances is the first, and perhaps the most important, condition for the preservation of
shamanism.

There is also a social side in shamanism which becomes
a condition for its preservation. In fact, the performances
present excellent occasions for gatherings of clansmen and
other people. I have shown that the Tungus, as well as
the Manchus, are sociable in their habits—they like to meet
and to eat in groups. However, there is an important difference between the clan interest in the performances and
that of outsiders. We have seen that psychic instability
may easily occur among the clansmen, many of whom may
be affected. The clan must decide either to influence the
shaman, in case the shaman is able to master the new
spirits, or subdue the clan spirits, should these become
obedient. A performance carried out on behalf of the
whole clan naturally becomes a social act which requires
the assistance and presence, when possible, of all members
of the clan. Thus, a performance of this kind would be
one of the important factors for the maintaining of the
unity of the clan, and since the groups here described are
sociable, they would appreciate performances as a good
way to satisfy their social feelings and to maintain the
unity of the clan, for as we have seen, a great number of
spirits are regarded as clan spirits. A shaman who can
guess his clansmen's desire to have a gathering and who
would propose it in due time would be much more appreciated, than a shaman who needs guiding on the part of
the clan. An able shaman, i.e. one who can grasp the
frame of mind of his clansmen, may become a very influential member and may be even loved by his clansmen,
as a centre of the social life of the clan.

However, even when the shaman does not deal with
the clan spirits in the gatherings for performance, outsiders and clansmen have a good occasion for satisfying
their feeling of sociability. As we have seen from the
description of performances, every individual becomes an
actor, a participant, in this collective act; during the performance, he or she will have and will preserve afterwards the feeling that he or she is a member of a group
of similar people who may act in mass, who may receive
new moral support in their struggle for life and may consider other participants of the performance as people who

may come to their help as members of the same community. Practically, the Tungus life does not offer many occasions for such gatherings—the wedding ceremonies, which are relatively rare, owing to the scantiness of the population of the Tungus groups, or which are still rarer—the commercial gatherings for the annual fairs, so that shamanizing is perhaps the only social performance which is rather frequent. When there is a gathering, almost every one goes to the performance, as to the weddings and yearly fairs. Indeed, the performances being liked as a pretext for social gatherings, shamanism is, in general, socially approved.

From the description of performances we have also seen that the audience is so affected in its emotions that a real mass-extasy may easily occur. Apparently this emotional condition leaves a certain pleasant remembrance; those who had this experience usually want to repeat it again and again. From the emotional point of view the feeling of nearness of the spirits, although mastered and artfully managed by the shaman, also produces an effect of great attractiveness on the participants. Indeed, this emotion is stronger than that produced by a simple theatrical performance or the reading of novels, for the spirits, in the eyes of participants, are realities, and sometimes very dangerous realities. Fearlessness of the shaman who is handling the spirits also produces its emotional effect. It is evident that the shamans who can produce such effects are considered as good shamans and the shamanism, as the source of such emotions, is accepted, approved and supported.

The aesthetic emotions produced by the shamanistic performances are also great. From the description of the technique of performances we have seen that they contain very varied music, as well as some "dancing". The musical side especially has reached a great development in the combination of various sources of sounds, including singing by the shaman and the chorus, with various tempos, rhythms, and even rich tunes. Sometimes, the performance sounds like an orchestral symphony of great complexity. Indeed, this music responds to the musical understanding of the Tungus, and it seems to be attractive only to those who have a certain ability of musical perception. The shamanistic performances include no arias, ariosos, or cavatinas of Italian complex; they include no romance and other forms, of which the European musical complexes (I mean here the musical complex for the general public!) consist. In fact, when the tunes and forms are too different, the music cannot produce an aesthetic effect, it cannot be understood.[*] We cannot now say how the music is understood when perceived. If it is understood, it is appreciated, if it is not understood, it is not appreciated and is rejected under any handy pretext. How such an understanding may be reached is a different question, but for a great number of people understanding of music, especially of alien music, is out of question.[**] The Tungus, when listening to shamanistic music, are accustomed to the musical instruments used, which they

understand, together with their own tunes, all of which, during the performance, produce in them the greatest emotional tension. The emotion here is still greater than that of simple listeners, for many of those present are not only audience but also performers. Only those who have themselves tried to produce collective music can understand how the emotion of a listener differs from that of a performer. The Tungus, at least most of them, know it, and they like to be performers. In a lesser degree the same can be stated in reference to the "dancing" performed by the shamans and the participants (rarely), the "dancing" being much poorer than the music, owing to technical difficulties. However, the rhythm of the movements, the change of the steps, etc. also produce a certain effect.

All Tungus greatly appreciate good artists-shamans. Those of them who possess good voices may be asked to sing, even without shamanizing, e.g. at a wedding ceremony among the Barguzin Tungus. A good artist-shaman would be more successful in reaching the aim of the performance, and he would be considered greater than a shaman whose aestheticism is inferior. Indeed, in a great number of cases the Tungus are not conscious of the fact, that aestheticism which produces emotions makes the audience and the patient more susceptible to the shaman's suggestion. However, apart from the practical effects of aesthetic emotion, the latter is attractive for the participants. The Tungus and Manchus who appreciate music do not miss shamanistic performances. The attractiveness of performances is still greater when the Tungus and Manchus have their part in the performance. Such persons may be found among all groups. I have observed some fervent shamanists, both males and females, who used to participate in all performances, all seemingly chiefly for aesthetic reasons. Thus the shamanistic performances are the only public and collective manifestations of musical and choreographic aesthetism, e.g. among the Manchus who have given up singing and dancing in a ring, still practised among some Tungus. This is the third important condition of maintaining shamanism as a complex.

The fourth reason for maintaining shamanism is that the audience receives very important information about the spirits' nature and activity, as well as about the methods by which the spirits may be fought. The performances, especially when there is a treatment of a difficult case, provide a rich source of new facts as to the phenomena of psychic order. Thus, the performances satisfy a natural inclination toward inquisitiveness, which, as I have shown, (vide SONT, Chapter VIII) is one of the essential traits of the Tungus character. The number of persons who may be interested in performances is still increased by those who, without being interested in learning and observing, are attracted as all those who may be called homines avidi rerum novarum, a mischievous modification of "gossipers".

It can be thus seen that different individual psychomental complexes are satisfied with the existence of shamanism: persons with utilitarian inclinations, in so far as the performance gives an alleviation in the case of psychomental disequilibrium; persons with strong feelings of sociability, in so far as performances cement the clans and

---

[*] Cf. e.g. in "The Oxford History of Music" it is said that Moussorgsky's "style impresses the Western ear as barbarously ugly" (p. 321, Vol. VI, 1905). The fate of composers, such as van Beethoven, who dared introduce innovations and for long time was despised, till he was "understood", is the most interesting one from the ethnographical point of view.

[**] The "ear" of a foreigner, before being accustomed to the Tungus music, cannot perceive more than a part of it, a few melodies

of the whole complex. Cf. supra p. 223. There is even no technical possibility of recording. I think that only great composers, perfect analysts and skilful instrumentators could master this music.

other aggregations; persons with strong aesthetic feelings, in so far as the performances give them opportunity of experiencing these emotions; lastly, persons with strong inclination to inquisitiveness, in so far as every performance may give new facts. As a matter of fact, only a very small group of individuals are indifferent or give negative reactions on the performances. As will be shown, such persons can be found, but their influence could never be strong among the Tungus and even among the Manchus, before an intensive process of ethnical disintegration had begun to shake the whole cultural complex of the Tungus groups.

Perhaps a more detailed analysis of shamanism may disclose some other conditions, which act as a mechanism for the maintenance of shamanism. But what has been discussed in this section is sufficient for showing that there are special conditions which are in a greater or smaller degree responsible for the maintenance of a continuous practice of shamanism. I regard them as a mechanism maintaining shamanism, and thus as a component of shamanism. They cannot be abstracted. These conditions were gradually created and have modified shamanism to make of it what it is. If the comparison may be allowed, these conditions may be compared to the complex of secondary phenomena preceding the act of fusion of the male and female cells for giving life to a new human being. The secondary phenomena, such as the feeling of "love",

the external forms of courtship, the social institution of marriage, the wedding ceremony, etc. are mechanisms of the complex of self-reproduction in definite conditions of human groups which possess certain forms of cultural and physical adaptation. Secondary elements cannot be abstracted, if we treat the problem within the human group. From the point of view of the selective process and adaptation of the Tungus groups shamanism is "acting" as a self-regulating function of the psychomental complex. This final function might remain unnoticed, and would still be possible, for there are secondary conditions which make it attractive for various reasons. These secondary conditions are responsible for maintaining the existence of shamanism, and at the same time they also constitute the complex function of shamanism. However, if there was no adaptive outcome from shamanism, it could not be maintained, for the simple reason that in the long run either a system of elements would be elaborated which would annihilate shamanism, or the ethnical units would be weakened and assimilated, and thus there would be no more bearers of this complex. However, before the last strong aggression of the Chinese and Russians, shamanism was evidently flourishing among the groups here discussed, and, as will be shown, the present disintegration of the Tungus (and Manchu) groups is conditioned by the interethnical pressure and evidently not by a lack of internal functional adaptation.

CHAPTER XXVIII

THE SHAMAN'S ELECTION

127. TRANSMISSION OF SHAMANSHIP On different occasions I have already shown that, apart from the clan priests—*p'oyun saman* —of the Manchus, there are *two different kinds of shamans*, namely, the shamans depending on the clans and shamans independent of clans. Both groups are called *saman~šaman*, but among some groups they are specified. So among the Manchus they are opposed to the *p'oyun saman* and both clan and independent shamans are called *omba* ("great") *saman*. However, among the Manchus themselves, all shamans are connected with clans, but the people apply to the Chinese and Dahur shamans, if a shaman is needed, the former being disconnected with the Manchu clans. As to the Dahur shamans, I cannot say whether they are connected or not. In Manchu the term *amba saman* may be intensified by an addition *xala mokun'i* (the clan)—*xala-mokun saman* or *xala-mokun'i amba saman*— the clan great shaman.*

* This terminology might produce the impression of a certain confusion but there is none. In fact, we have seen that the complex of p'oyun *vočko* is that of exogamic units-clans now acting. These spirits are dealt with by the "priests" and they are not outside of the clan, and even the house (hao═bǒ═ьbǒĺyun→p'oyun), while the clan spirits mastered by the great shamans may leave their clans and go to the other world and may disappear altogether. However, during the shaman's life these spirits remain with him, and they are clan spirits as long as they are recognized as such. Therefore, they are styled *xala mokun'i vočko*, both p'oyun *vočko* and *xala*

Among the Tungus of Transbaikalia the term "shaman" is applied to all shamans, but there can not be several shamans in the same clan. Some of the shamans may be considered more or less powerful. These Tungus know shamans of neighbouring groups and naturally shamans of other clans. Among the Tungus of Manchuria there is a sharp distinction between the clan shamans, called *mokun saman* (Bir. Kum.)—"the clan shaman"—and independent shamans, called *dōca saman*—"the foreign (alien) shaman". Their power does not depend on whether they are clan or independent shamans, but on their personal qualities. In reality, when the shaman is connected with a clan, the conditions of assuming these functions are not similar to those of an independent shaman. The difference will be clearer when the process of formation of new shamans is discussed.

The shamanistic functions in a clan are naturally transmitted within the clan, so that the transmission may assume a form of inheritance. However, it may not always be so, as I shall now show.

Although among the Reindeer Tungus of Transbaikalia no formal prohibition of having two shamans exists, a coexistence of two shamans never occurs. If there were two shamans, these Tungus say, one of them, and more

mokun'i vočko being spirits of exogamic units-clans, in which the Manchus distinguish unmastered and mastered, permanent or shifting spirits.

likely the older one, would die.* The shamanship is transmitted from a grandfather or his brothers to the grandchildren—males and females—from the grandmother (father's mother) to the grandchildren. However, the shamanship may also be transmitted to other young members of the clan, usually missing one generation.** The same practice exists among the Khingan Tungus and other groups, but I have not observed it among the Manchus. However, the missing of one generation may not have the character of a regulation. In fact, the Tungus clans are not numerous, but one of the members must become shaman; the shaman's activity usually lasts more than a generation, for they become shamans rather early and continue this function to their death or loss of efficiency, i.e. on an average of more than thirty years; so by this time the son of the shaman would be too old to become shaman. Moreover, there is another reason, namely, the son is usually looking after his father-shaman, because, as will be shown, the shaman cannot do two things—the hunting and a regular carrying out of the shamanistic performances—so the shaman usually needs support of the junior groups, and therefore both the father and the son cannot be shamans. It is thus evident that the existing practice is not of a legitimate form of inheritance.

Among the Manchus, who live in large families, the son may live in the same way as his father, i.e. devoting his time and energy to the shaman's function. The most common case is the transmission of shamanship from father to son. If there is no son, the shamanship may be transmitted to the son of a brother ("nephew"). A definite tendency to transmit shamanship to the males is observed. The son of a female shaman has therefore more chance to become a shaman, although the daughter may also become a shaman, if she has been sick because of spirits. Cases when a daughter inherits her father's shamanship are even rarer. Moreover, among the Manchus, inheritance of shamanship by people from other clans may occur, if during the shaman's life a connexion between the spirits was formed and if the spirits consent to leave the clan.

The transmission of shamanship consists in a mastering of the spirits left by the deceased shaman. Therefore the spirits are also interested in the question as to who would be their master. In Manchu it is called: *baɣg'jaxa voĉko,*—"collected (gathered) spirits". If nobody in the clan were willing to master the spirits, or there were no person who could do it, the spirits might be "collected" by an outsider. The Manchus say: *en'gu xala voĉkobe baɣg'jaxan'iŋga*—"of another clan spirit (he or she) collects". Such persons may be either members of two clans *kapĉi* ("connected") which have the same shamanistic spirits, or by the family which often enjoyed the shaman's assistance during his life. Such a family (house) is called *jurumbō* (=jarŭm ƀao), and the shaman's spirits are supposed to be acquainted with the members of the family. If there is nobody who can master the spirits and if they cause harm, a shaman, familiar with the case, may accept them too. If the spirits can be carried away by an out-

sider—a new shaman—this may only satisfy the Manchus (and generally the Tungus), for in the mind of the people these spirits are a real burden.* However, it is not always so—the spirits may return. If such is the case, the clansmen would call the shaman who "collected" the spirits, and he would perform the duties which are usually performed by the native shamans of the given clan. In such a case it would be likely that the next shaman would be again one of the clansmen. More precisely the candidate will be either the person who was affected by the. spirits, or another member of the family that was attended by the shaman-outsider, this family in relation to this shaman being *jarumbō.* The spirits may gradually become common in both clans. In this way the shamanship may be shifted from clan to clan, because *the spirits of these clans are not fixed.*

The fact, observed in all groups, of the transmission of shamanship to females who are sooner or later married to members of other clans, might give the idea that the mastering and general dealing with the spirits is going on independently in the clans. This would not be exact. In fact, a female, being married, remains connected with her native clan—she has her own spirits, etc., she is protected by her native clan in case of necessity (*vide* SOM and SONT). If she becomes a shaman, she attends all cases, when it is necessary to deal with the activity of spirits of her native clan; after her death her spirits (clan spirits mastered by her and other newly mastered spirits) will be "collected" by one of the members of her clan (let us remember that in the Manchu complex her clan, and particularly the families attended by her *jarumbō,*) and more likely by one of the grandsons of her father. However, there are some cases when a woman becomes shaman after being married, and yet she may master her native clan's spirits and those of her husband's clan, as an "outsider".

Owing to the fact that the females, when there is no opposition, have more personal chance of becoming shamans (this will be shown later), female shamans are very common; but since the spirits mastered by her are likely to remain with her native clan (psychomental condition), a peculiar form, though not quite regular, can be observed of the transmission of shamanship by omitting one generation. As a matter of fact there are several combinations due to these practices, namely; (1) whether the spirits in the two clans are the same (*kapĉi* clans) or not; (2) whether the mother is succeeded by her son or not; (3) whether there is a dual organization of clans connexion (*vide* SONT particularly p. 370) or not. I shall not describe all possible and observed combinations, for they are evident. I give here an instance.

There are cases of transmission of shamanship from *nakĉu* (or *gusin*), i.e. from the senior males of the mother's native clan, to the candidate. In this case, if there is opposition to the female-shamanship, the transmission of shamanship would proceed as "sex-linked inheritance". The Tungus of Manchuria say that "it is good, because the shamans are good". Generally it is believed that if there are ancestors-shamans on both sides of the father's and

---

* One day I heard that an acting shaman was greatly disturbed by the news that his nephew (brother's son) wished to become a shaman.

** Once I observed an old shaman who was teaching his niece. However, I cannot say whether he was "teaching", as any other experienced shaman would do it, or was handing over to her his spirits, which seems to me doubtful.

* If the spirits show no activity (there is no more any mass psychic disequilibrium or any individual troubles) it will be believed that the clan spirits have left for ever, and no new shaman will be made.

mother's clans, the shaman will be good. In fact, there are clan lines of shamans which satisfy this desideratum, but this is by no means a rule or a regulation.

The above indicated facts show the tendency of keeping shamanship in lines, where there already were some shamans, but practical considerations (no need of having two shamans), the system of organization (e.g. a dual clan organization), the clan specification of spirits, and the intrusion of new spirits do not leave much place for the elaboration of a rigid system of transmission of shamanship.

In case of shamanship, independent of the clan, its transmission is not regulated at all. Those who used to know the shaman personally and those who are familiar with his spirits have more chance to become shamans. However, the transmission has also a tendency to confine itself to the clan of the shaman.

Besides a formal side of the transmission of shamanship, so to say, there is another side, namely, a transmission of the shaman's knowledge to the candidate, which may take place prior to the formal installation of the new shaman or after it. In the first case the old shaman may elect a successor and work with him, in order to prepare him for further functions, to make of him a shaman. Such a "teaching" may last for years. However, in the second case, the old shaman may happen to be forced to teach a person who was not chosen by him. So if the candidate shows inclination to become a shaman during the life of the old shaman and proves himself to be an able man, he may become a shaman during the life of the old shaman, and the latter would "teach" him. The "teaching", as will be shown, may grow into a special complex with which I shall deal further on. The transmission of knowledge may happen independently, when the potential candidate is a clever person, a good observer, who accumulates facts and forms of them a more or less accomplished system of theory and practice. Such occurrences are common.

128. INDIVIDUAL CONDITIONS FOR BECOMING SHAMAN

The formal conditions of transmission of shamanship and "teaching" have minor importance as compared with the individual characteristics of the candidate—the potential ability to master spirits, the condition of health, and the desire to become a shaman. From the description of the psychomental condition of the shaman, in general and during the performances, which will be given later, and

from the previous description of the systems of spirits and performances it is evident that not every one may become shaman. Some observed cases follow:

CASE 1. In 1915, in one of the Manchu villages near Aigun, a case, which may be regarded as typical, was observed. (I give a translation) "A woman's grandfather "and father were shamans. Both of them died and left "spirits (vočko). The spirits entered the woman and she "began "to tremble" (as the shamans do). A new shaman "must be made (people said). However, the clansmen "did not want it. Then they invited a shaman who inves- "tigated the case, interviewed the spirits and declared that "a trial must be made, perhaps somebody else of her clan— "a man or a woman—may become a shaman too. The clans- "men agreed to wait. In the meantime the spirit again "entered the woman and carried her into the forest, into "the mountains. The clansmen rushed after her, but she "quickly climbed up a tree, and sat there on the very top of "it. The men could not get her down and returned home. "Then she disappeared altogether, and only after eight days "of absence she returned home, and said: ‹I was all the "time at home›, while actually she had been absent. Then "she refused to eat and drink. Now she must become a "shaman. In the course of a year all which is needed— "the costume, the wooden instruments, and a spear—will be "made for her. Then there will be a sacrifice to her spirits "—a pig and some Chinese bread. During this year she "will be attended by an old shaman who will teach her".

This case is very simple. The spirits persecuted the woman. She wanted to become a shaman and acted according to the candidates' model—she trembled, ran away, climbed up a tree, refused food, "forgot" everything. It looks much like a case of hysteria, in a heavy form. There were no other candidates and so she had to become shaman, after a special training. That served as a treatment for herself and relieved the clan of the spirits which might have done the same with other clansmen.

CASE 2. This includes several instances of candidates. I shall give here the history of the shamans in the clan sakda (also sādā in Manchu Sp.) recorded by me and given here in translation.

"The great grandfather had been chief of a regiment "(gusaida, written as gusa'i'da). He had a red-haired "horse. The chief spirit juay feŋ laoje (of Manchu pro- "nunciation, which apparently is Chinese 元聖老爺) want- "ed this horse (as a spirit carrier, or perhaps as a sacrifice "for the liberation of the horse's soul needed by the spirit) "which the chief knew from his dreams. The chief refused "to give it. The horse immediately fell dead. The chief "went out of his mind; he assailed people and screamed. "The shaman said that the chief must become (literally: "learn) a shaman. The chief refused. He began to jump "up to the ceiling of the room and to stand legs up and "head down. (Then) he agreed to become a shaman. "The shaman and four assistants (jār'i) initiated him, as "they used to do it in the yamen (i.e. with deference to the "chief's rank.) In this clan no shaman outsider can "initiate, and generally the clansmen are not allowed to "seek assistance of foreign shamans.—During the initia- "tion the spirit (vočko) said that they (the clansmen) "must not go to the shamans who belong to other clans. "The spirit insisted upon giving him a red-hair horse which "was actually bought for the high sum of one hundred taels.

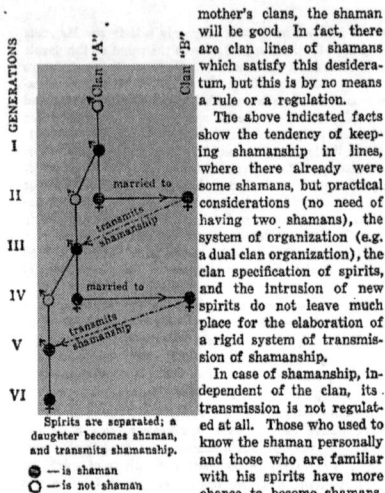

Spirits are separated; a daughter becomes shaman, and transmits shamanship.

● — is shaman
○ — is not shaman

"(Thus the chief became a shaman.) The spirit was very "strict and mischievous, and it did not like other shamans. "The latter fought against this spirit for a long time and "owing to their (the shamans') intrigues the new shaman-"chief, died. Before dying he asked that incense (ajen "x'jen) be burned during three nights and days and that "he should not be buried before three days had elapsed. His "lame younger brother did not comply with this request "and ordered the burial to be effected on the first day after "the death. This was done. The next day five clansmen "suddenly died. The second day two more men died. On "the third day the lame younger brother went to the tomb "of his senior brother. One could hear sounds of trinkets "(of the shaman's belt) and of the drum. When the tomb "was opened, the dead chief was lying as if he was alive, "with a red face. The lame younger brother cut the throat "of the chief with a spade. The chief was again buried. "Every year (since that time) the clansmen were sick, the "people ran mad. A clansman recommended to create a "new shaman. The clansmen gathered and slaughtered "three oxen. The spirit came into a clansman and he "drank (naturally, the man) a bucket of (fresh) blood. "This was k'joγun vočko ("the kite spirit", which can eat "the whole liver of an ox; after eating, the shaman must "leave his assistant, and if he falls down without being able "to keep on his legs, the sacrifice is considered as rejected "by the spirit). When the grandfather (who succeeded "the great grandfather) died, many people again fell ill. "Another shaman declared that a new shaman must be "initiated. Many people gathered, and a man from every "class (jalen) put on a shaman's head-dress. They went "out and, carrying on the initiation a long time, remained "(in the temperature far below zero F°) in the frost. Many "of them could not stand it and ran away. The spirit "descended into one of them and declared: ‹don't initiate "new shamans, during the winter season, do it in spring›. "(However, they missed doing it in due time and) now the "Chinese authorities don't allow them to do it."

The cases are different. The first shaman, probably after or during the division of the clan (vide infra, also SOM), had become insane, which condition was connected with nightmares (the spirits requiring a good horse) and fits (attacking the people, standing on the head). Temporarily he was relieved by becoming a shaman, but the mania of persecution obsessed him (he fights other shamans) and falls into a continuous coma. It is likely that he was buried alive and later killed by his brother. This act produced periodical mass psychosis until the clan established a new shaman—a member of the junior generation. After his death mass psychosis again appeared, but they did not know whom they might select and left it to the spirits on a trial in the cold. Since that time winter psychosis ceased.

Now I shall give some details as to the splitting of this clan and the formation of complexes of spirits, also other details which will be needed later.

"In this xala (clan) two big subdivisions are dis-"tinguished: amba (great) sakda xala and ajige (small), "sakda xala. The complexes of spirits are different. The "amba sakda has also three mokun (i.e. the present exogamic "units, actual clans). The spirits are the same, but the ".'rites and "words" are different. The great shaman is "allowed to perform the ancestral rite (sakda xala amba "sâman večem'i p'oγun vočko) and there are seven bunches "of day-road spirits (ineγi nadan sorgon) and six bunches

"of night-road spirits (jamj'i niγgun sorgon). The sha-"mans are allowed to act only within their own mokun, and "the other shamans are not allowed to assist the sakda-"clansmen".

CASE 3. I observed the case here given in all details during nearly two years. The Manchu clan xujala was in the Aigun district. The great grandmother had been a sha-man. The "grandmother" had been a great and good shaman. She transmitted the shamanship to her son who died soon. Then her nephew became shaman. He held also the posi-tion of an official in the Manchu Bannermen organization. However, soon after becoming shaman, he was executed by order of the Governor General (in Tsitsihar), being accused of spying in favour of the Russians. According to my in-formers this accusation was groundless and was due to in-trigues of the Chinese (not Bannermen!). The spirits were thus left without a master for twelve years. The error of the late shaman's son, whom I knew very intimate-ly and whom I shall designate as A, was that in due time he did not burn the image of his father and did not make a sacrifice, so that his soul could not regularly proceed to the lower world, while it could not become vočko (spirit), for the shaman had been decapitated. In addition to the troubles done by the spirits, the soul of the shaman was also disturbing the clansmen. The shaman's wife, an old wo-man of over sixty years, and his two sons, A and B, both married, were worrying about the soul of their husband and father. The situation was complicated by the fact that the elder son's wife had been in intimate relations with the unfortunate shaman and had a son by him, while her hus-band was married to her, at the age of 11 or 12 years, when she had already been about twenty years old. For a long time no sexual intercourse between the young boy and the adult woman existed. The details as to the hysterical condition of this woman were already given (vide p. 197). Indeed, she not only lost the man whom she loved, but she could not settle her relations with her legal husband, and she was also a transgressor of social customs (vide e.g. SOM, p. 152). Her psychomental condition was thus exceptionally favour-able for an extreme tension in this situation. Moreover, her grandfather and her father had also been shamans. The woman, whom I shall designate here and in the following description (Section 131) by the letter C, had already quite suspicious fits in which she was visited (entered) by the soul of her lover, the deceased shaman, the father of her legal husband. She did everything which happens to the candidates; she ran away into the forest, climbed on trees, refused food, "trembled" etc. Being put in exceptionally favourable conditions (which will be later explained) to observe her without being disturbed by the presence of other persons, I was witness of several fits, during which the most typical picture of hysterical character, with strong sexual excitement, was beyond any doubt: she was lying on the stove-bed in a condition varying between great rigid-ity ("arch") and relaxation; she was hiding herself from light (the experiments were repeated); there was tempora-rily loss of sensitiveness to a needle (several experiments in different parts of the body at different moments); at times continuous movements with the legs and basin were indica-tive of a strong sexual excitement. Her cognition of reality was rather doubtful, for during her fits she did not recog-nize persons being around her. However, from time to time, or at least at the end of her fits, she was quite consci-ous of her surroundings and before a fit she looked for isolation and for a certain comfort for herself during the fit (choice of a stove bed).

The husband of this woman and a great number of influential clansmen 'were against her becoming a shaman. The chief reason was evidently her social position (her relations with the deceased shaman were naturally known) and the character of her fits, in the decipherings of which the clansmen were not mistaken—she was not visited by the spirits (*vočko*) but by the shaman's soul. Her husband was very angry, when she pretended to have a spirit, and he even proposed to take it up himself. But she (the spirit) insisted A could not be a shaman. A's formal objection was that if she becomes a shaman, she would trouble the people, she would not stay at home, and it would be very costly to support her (which, by the way, he did not do!). But she wanted to become a shaman and the spirit—not only the shaman's soul—insisted upon a settlement of the situation; she had already experienced visits of the spirits for more than a year. The other clansmen rejected her, because they considered it shameful for the clan to have a woman-shaman, believing the male-shamans to be cleverer and to "know" more than women-shamans.

There was another candidate, the younger brother B. The clansmen planned first to make him shaman. After a long sickness of B, about a year before the spirits (*vočko*) had entered him, about the same time as they entered the woman C. Several times B visited an old grandfather (a senior of the shaman's clan) who knew *čolo* and *kooli* (list and ritual) of the spirits. After the execution of the shaman, there was nobody who saw performances, and many old men had already died. In fact, as will be shown, the grandfather knew everything about the clan shamanism. The candidate B was, seemingly, in all respects a normal person, but he was neither a worker, nor an honest man, according to some Manchus. In spite of this, the clansmen evidently wanted him to become shaman. Perhaps the entering of the spirit into him was a ritualistic performance.

Since the situation presented difficulties for a simple solution, it was decided to organize a trial of the two candidates, one of whom should be elected and the other rejected and cured.

This case shows candidate C with her disturbed sexual complex, perhaps justified by hysteria, and candidate B who seemingly was an impostor, urged on chiefly by "public opinion". This picture will be clearer when the performance of the election is described.

CASE 4. The Khingan Tungus. In the clan *bajagir* there had been some shamans, but all of them had died. The nearest candidates now were from the youngest generation. However, there were several persons who felt an inclination to become shaman. The son of the late shaman, who had died long before, was a man of fifty-two years. He was not an average Khingan Tungus, but an exceptional person—he lived chiefly on theft of horses from the Russians and Mongols. He had been caught and badly beaten by the Russians several times. Practically, he had given up hunting. In spite of this he had been appointed by the local (Mongol) authorities to be one of the three official chiefs of these Tungus. He was very proud of his official position and he wanted to produce an impression on foreigners by his standing. If this produced no impression, he wanted to impress with something else, including the fact that he might become a shaman. He was much inclined to drink, and when he could get alcoholic drinks, he con-

sumed them immediately to a complete intoxication, after which he became extremely arrogant. When he was sober, he was rather restless. He was not honest (although robbery might be a profession without affecting other elements of the "moral" Tungus complex), inclined to lie and to terrorize his clansmen and other people. At the time of the observation he suffered from parasites (and big worms) which affected his digestive tract, gums and lips. The attitude of the other Tungus towards him was not favourable, so he lived apart with, only the members of his own family, which consisted of children from two wives and some other relatives; altogether there were more people than a Tungus wigwam can shelter, so they lived in two tents, all these people on his income chiefly from robbery; the other members of the "family" did not work. As compared with other people of this group, they were rather poorly dressed and badly fed.

The man could not become a shaman, for he was too old—apparently he had missed the favourable time—and because of the negative attitude of all clansmen; but he had a definite inclination for shamanship. I observed him several times in his attempts to carry out performances. The mood came in the evening, after a day in a depressed psychic state. He had no drum (he had owned one, but in the state of intoxication he had broken it), so he used an enamelled basin; instead of "horses" he used a whip; instead of the head-dress, he used an ordinary kerchief to cover his eyes. He ordered his wife and the other women to assist him, which they did reluctantly; they repeated the refrains unrhythmically, talked among themselves about various things and generally were indifferent to the performer's efforts. He wanted to find out who would kill animals and when (at that time there was an important period in hunting Cervus Elaphus with fresh antlers, but he himself did not hunt); he asked the spirits to send animals. During these performances, he fell on the ground three times, his body rigid, grinding his teeth. Then he was asked several questions, but his replies were incoherent. No extasy could be produced, not even after heavy smoking of tobacco and drinking of alcohol diluted with water. The performance failed: he felt miserable and tried to avoid speaking about himself or his performance. Members of his family, including his son, had the same feeling.

The son, a young man of over twenty years, was also a potential candidate for shamanship, for he was a grandson of the deceased shaman. He was proud of his father's position and mode of life. He had some income from Russian settlers who gave him some money and food (to be left alone by the father who was a local representative of the authority). He was a liar, inclined to sexual pleasure, an impostor, altogether an impertinent youth. His position in the clan was still worse than that of his father. He was not a hunter. From time to time he had sudden changes in his mood: he would become oppressed, very submissive and haunted by all kinds of visions. He complained of a feeling of heaviness in his heart, when the spirits of his grandfather entered him; but no extasy could be produced. At other times, he lost his head, became arrogant, unreasonably aggressive, restless and even ready to commit some foolishness, e.g. once, being dissatisfied with me, he asked me to kill him immediately. No attempts at shamanizing had been made. The father was against having his son to become a shaman; he wanted him to take up the position of a chief, for which purpose it was planned to present him soon to the governor general to be appointed *kavan* (petty official rank). The father planned to make a shaman of one of his brother's sons, a child of about ten years at that time. For this reason, and in imitation of Buddhist monks, the boy's head was shaven. (This was not usually done with candidates, but the father was looking for something very distinguished and marked in all of the boy's activities). For the time being there was no other candidate in the clan and outsiders might take up the spirits.

This case was interesting as a failure to become shaman, in spite of a great inclination. The causes were different: in the father—the personal deficiency and the advanced age, so that the attempts at shamanizing turned into a simulation of the classical hysteria and it was an imposture; in the son—the attempts were checked by the father who would not allow any contradiction to his will. Furthermore, both men were in an unfavourable position in the clan to be recognized as shamans. However, under some conditions both of them might have become shamans.

From the above given facts it is evident that there are certain psychomental individual conditions which are favourable for the candidates who would assume the functions of a shaman. There may be a general disposition in the clan, when many members affected by the spirits and several young men and girls "run away" and perform what is required as signs of the presence of spirits, and there may be individual cases in anticipation of a mass psychosis. Since there are free spirits, these may be taken by any one of the young clansmen, but there must be some indications or motives. I shall now quote some of such cases.

A man may become a candidate to shamanship if for example, he had been hurt by a whirl-wind. However, in some cases the candidate may be rejected on the ground that he cannot "master" the spirits (among the Reindeer Tungus of Manchuria). A girl of fifteen was entered by a clan spirit, so it was decided to teach her how to distinguish questions asked by the assistants; this was done by an old shaman and she became a shaman (now she is forty); if she had not become a shaman, her arms or legs or neck, or back would have been crooked for life (among the Khingan Tungus). A girl was in love with a married man; their relations were interrupted by the interference of the mother and wife of the lover, and the girl suffered greatly; then she was entered by a spirit and became a shaman (among the Birarčen). A young man, while hunting, was frightened and entered by a spirit of an unknown origin; he was sick for a long time but the spirit always returned; then he became a *dōna* shaman and gradually took in several spirits (among the Birarčen).

In a great number of cases, when the spirits are free and there is no shaman, the Tungus and Manchus look for a candidate. A child who has dreams, different from ordinary ones, who is subject to strong emotions, change of mood, and in general, when his behaviour is not like that of other children, is supposed to be a candidate, especially if there had been some shaman in the direct lines of ancestors. Such a child may be told of the possibility of becoming shaman and is gradually prepared. At the age from sixteen to twenty the first entering of the spirit occurs. Prior to this the youth refuses food, walks and wanders about aimlessly and without purpose; he or she may have changes of mood—sometimes being very gay and joyful, sometimes silent and depressed, sometimes sleeping too long, sometimes unable to sleep. After two weeks or more, during the sleep, usually at night, the youth jumps up on the bed and begins to sing like shamans do. If a real extasy occurs, the youth is considered as a future shaman. In all similar cases the individual is gradually prepared and the first extasy is especially announced by irregularity of sleep and of the required food. Such is the most common case among the Reindeer Tungus of Transbaikalia, but it is also practised among other groups, as we have seen in Case 4 and Case 3.

In examining the cases of successful shamans and failures, as well as a great number of cases which are not described here, we may now point out that the age, sex and psychomental conditions of the candidates reveal some tendencies to be noted. First of all, the greater number of cases of becoming shaman falls on the age of maturity. I have never heard of people becoming shamans prior to the age of fifteen years.[*] On the other hand, the candidates are exceptionally rare after the age of complete maturity (physical and social). These cases are usually connected with individual psychomental troubles produced by various causes and, as will be shown, most of such people, after becoming shamans, continue to manifest psychomental troubles.

It is difficult to define the principal condition of age for the selection in becoming shamans. In fact, there may be different causes. Doubtless the learning of shamanistic methods requires a long time, so that the shaman must spend several years, before he can treat people and be a good shaman. But the theories may have a great influence also: for instance, the idea that the candidate can appear only among every second generation. Moreover, the individuals, at the early years of sexual maturity, are more susceptible to the psychomental disequilibrium, which is also true of cases of adult persons who live in physiologically abnormal conditions (Case 3). The social position of candidates is also a factor of importance, because a man or woman who must look after the family ("the principal worker"), has a feeling of responsibility, and there is no leisure for concentration in matters beyond the daily work. It seems to me that the early age of candidates may be conditioned by various causes, some of which may be mere adaptations, while others may be fundamental conditions. Perhaps such fundamental conditions are the psychomental susceptibility during the period of sexual development and the social position, of such kind that individuals who do not carry responsibilities as members of families (as economic units). No general preference as to the sex of candidates can be statistically established, for there are tendencies among some groups in favour of one of the sexes. A preference for males is natural in all groups, based on agnatic relationship in clans, for the women go away. However, if there are clans bound by dual organization and if the clans have the same complex of spirits, this consideration has no importance. However, a preference for males may originate from another consideration, namely, as will be shown, that the female-shamans do not perform at all during pregnancy and the first weeks after the delivery, also during the few days of menstruation every month, so that the

---

[*] Sexual maturity sometimes occurs among the Tungus at a rather late age. (cf. SONT, p. 259; also SOM, p. 110).

female-shaman cannot help her clansmen at any moment, when she might be needed. One more consideration exists; according to the Tungus assertion, females are physically less resistant than males and therefore they cannot carry out very long and difficult performances. In accordance with these conditions it may be noted that among the old (*fè*) Manchu female-shamans are few. However, they existed and the famous *Nišan Saman* was a native of an old Manchu clan. Among the New Manchus, female-shamans are more common. Among the Tungus of Manchuria the number of female-shamans is greater than that of male-shamans, but the greatest shamans, according to the Tungus, are males. The female-shamans and male-shamans, among the Tungus of Transbaikalia, are met with in perhaps equal numbers. In so far as I could see, among the Chinese no female-shamans were known nowadays.

Indeed, the frequency of males and females among the shamans is not yet indicative of the condition of sex in defining candidature. I had the impression that in the case of mass psychosis the females are more affected than the males, and thus there are more potential female-candidates.

The conditions of general health of the candidates has a great importance too; this question will be discussed in the next section, dealing with the "election" of shamans.

129. RECOGNITION AND ELECTION OF A NEW SHAMAN Along with the treatment of various elements which constitute shamanism as a complex, and along with the treatment of various conditions which underlie or result from shamanism, we have seen that the part of a community in defining whether the person, willing to be a shaman, may actually become one or not, and the part of a community in maintaining this complex are always fundamental conditons of shamanism. Without such a social approval, or consent, shamans cannot function. In fact, we have seen that the shaman's chief function is a social function of regulating the psychomental complex of the social unit, which may be a clan where the clan organization is well established, a village where the settled life has resulted in a strong territorial connexion, finally, even a whole ethnical or regional unit, chiefly in the case when the clan organization is not fixed as a permanent system. Therefore the social unit which forms a milieu for a shaman is not only a clan, as it is observed in the greater part of instances, but there may be other units as well. So in case the clan organization is destroyed, the social milieu for a shaman may be shifted to any other existing unit. We have such instances even among the Tungus and Manchus who settle in villages, in groups composed of a few families of different clans. There are some shamans among the Manchus who serve villages, and not clans, whence a new complex of clients' families connected with a shaman has already originated. There is another very important condition which may bring into life a new grouping around an individual-shaman. This is the theory of spirits which may remain outside of a clan. Since *dōna* (Birarčen and Kumarčen) spirits exist, the *dōna* shamans may also exist. This is actually observed among the Birarčen and Kumarčen who are badly attacked by the foreign spirits which, however, are not all included in the complexes of clan spirits. The Khingan Tungus and Tungus of Transbaikalia have no *dōna* shamans; all of them are

clan shamans, as it is also, at least formally, among the Manchus. So long as the *dōna* spirits are not incorporated into the clan lists, the shamans mastering them are "foreign" shamans, but, as stated, the *dōna* spirits may also be mastered by the clan shamans, while *dōna* shamans do not master clan spirits. However, when the *dōna* spirits are entered into the list of clan spirits, the *dōna* shamans cannot exist. It is thus evident that an influx of new spirits may produce shamans independent of the clan. Still, these shamans will not remain without a social milieu. The latter will be formed around them after a series of successful cases of performances. Such shamans may easily become interclan shamans in settlements which consist of mixed clans. Finally, there are shamans who are not clan shamans and who may exist in a special social milieu. There are cases of shamans who belong to distinct ethnical units; for instance, several Chinese shamans practising among the Manchus; there are Dahur shamans practising among the Birarčen; Buriat, Goldi, Manchu and Chinese shamans are occasionally invited by the Northern Tungus. Around them a group of clients will be formed who will function as their social milieu. Such cases may also occur without the interference of foreign ethnical groups, and even without *dōna* spirits, namely, when there are different currents of centrifugal movement in a clan, which result in a loss of social unity in the clan. Since there are dissidents in the matter of treatment of spirits, shamans may appear approved by a part of the clan. Such an approval—a recognition—may lead even to the splitting of a clan. So that from time to time shamans may appear who are not recognized by a community as a whole, but only by a part of it. Anyhow these shamans will have their social milieu.

However, in exceptional cases, a person who has no social milieu, is not recognized as a shaman, still tries to perform, either under a stimulus of practical calculation, or in consequence of a special psychomental condition. I have met a few cases of such persons among the Tungus and Manchus. Here, however, two different situations must be distinguished, namely, (1) when a person who pretends to be a shaman *is not yet formally recognized*, but is awaiting such a recognition, from time to time practises shamanizing without a milieu, and (2) when a person *is not and will not be recognized*, as it was in Case 4, where the performer was not recognized even by his own son, and in the case of a Manchu to which I shall revert later (*vide infra*, p. 365). These are not shamans, because they cannot produce a real extasy, especially without an audience, and they have no social functions, usually no paraphernalia, but they are either dishonest impostors or psychomentally affected people. By this I do not intend to say that they cannot become shamans, but I want only to indicate that they do not function as shamans, have no milieu and probably cannot assume the functions of shamans, because they are not recognized; this may be dependent, at least sometimes, on personal considerations.

Generally there are very few shamans who act outside of the clan and are recognized shamans. Their recognition by the social groups may take a shorter or longer time. If the shaman-outsider is successful, he will soon be recognized; if he is not successful, the recognition may be delayed. A great number of such shamans drop the practising of performances, when the recognition does not come soon. Indeed, such a recognition does not and cannot require any special formal acts. However, from time to time, usually once a year, the Manchu shamans undertake a great review of their spirits, on which occasion admirers of these shamans may produce a demonstration of their recognition.

It is different with the clan shamans whose recognition is usually connected with a complex ritualism, proving of candidates, "teaching", sacrifices, etc. The outcome of this act is a social recognition of the shaman. Actually it is an act of "election" of the shaman, either from the number of candidates designated by the clan, or candidates who present themselves and who are allowed to be tried.

The most important condition for being allowed to carry out a performance of election and recognition is the candidate's will and his ability to "master spirits", which must be proved by at least one successful performance. The second condition is, whether the clansmen want to have the candidate or not. The new shaman may be needed (a case of free spirits which harm the clansmen), and the candidate may prove his or her ability in mastering, but there may be objections of a social order or that of personal character, e.g. the bad character of the candidate (mischievousness, bad temper, etc.; criminality e.g. as in Case 3, the candidate B, etc.); so the candidate may be rejected even before his final trial, or he may be put in such a position that it will be impossible for him to perform, even after the election. In any case, the clan has to decide it, and by this the clan takes upon itself a further obligation as to the equipment of the new shaman with the paraphernalia.

If we consider what has been stated as to the function of shamanism, the shaman, when recognized and elected, becomes a real *safety valve* of the clan. The shaman "collects" all spirits and bears all responsibility for the further psychomental equilibrium of the clan, in so far as it is reflected in the spirits and in so far as they may be fought. Therefore the act of recognition acquires an especially great importance in the Tungus complex.

In the ethnographical literature it has received different names. It was called "consecration", "initiation", etc., which terms are not good, for in the acts here discussed there is nothing "sacred", is no "initiation". In fact, we have seen in the Tungus and Manchu complex that the shaman and shamanism cannot be treated in the meaning of "sacred" phenomena of the European complex. There is also no initiation, for the candidate is already "initiated" before attending the act. Therefore I do not use these terms but I prefer to use a neutral term "Formal Recognition", which is a social act of making of a person a clan shaman. This act may take various forms which I shall now describe and illustrate.

130. CASES OF FORMAL RECOGNITION

I. The Reindeer Tungus of Transbaikalia give us a *CASE OF A CANDIDATE DESIGNATED BY THE CLAN.* A child is selected and educated, i.e. influenced in the required direction by the clansmen and sometimes even by an old shaman; the child shows, in one or several performances, as well as in its general attitude, a certain ability which is required from a candidate before becoming a shaman; the clan informally decides to make of the candidate a shaman and gives him an opportunity of dealing with the spirits. This is a period of trial. So the candidate must help some sick clansmen, practise divination, interpret dreams, etc., which would show that he can be-

come a shaman. The most important moment is that when the candidate, being in an extasy, points out particular marks of the animals which will be sent by the spirits *dayačan* for making the costume from their skins. The candidate is assisted by an old shaman; all clansmen pray to the clan spirits and offer a rich sacrifice. Such animals must have some mark such as, for instance, a white spot on one of the legs, white hoofs, a white head, a mutilated ear, etc. One of the clansmen starts hunting the designated animals and sooner or later finds them. The search for such animals may take several months. In case the indicated animals cannot be found, the spirit may be asked (the candidate introduces it) to send another animal. As stated, the skins used are those of Cervus Elaphus and Alces Alces which are now not common. Anyhow, the needed animals are always found.

When the costume is ready, there is again a great gathering of clansmen. A rich sacrifice, which consists of an adult reindeer, is given to the soul of the last deceased clan shaman. Then the candidate puts on the new costume and performs a great shamanizing as described before. So the candidate becomes clan shaman. The great shamanizing is performed as usual, e.g. with the erecting of *turu*, placings for the spirits, etc. Unfortunately I did not observe such a performance, but the statement of several shamans coincided with that of the old experienced persons. In reality the last performance is a mere formality, for at the moment of the performance the candidate is already an acting shaman. However, the period of trial is of importance, for the candidate must show his ability in treatment etc. I have heard of no other forms of this act. In case the child assigned for this function dies or fails to produce extasy, a candidate is selected among those young clansmen who would be able to introduce spirits, and the whole act proceeds as has been shown.

II. Among the Tungus of Manchuria the procedure is different. The child may be selected and educated, but the first extasy is especially important, for the first spirit *sĕvĕn* conditions further steps of the clan. It is difficult to find it out, for the candidate is usually unconscious and the spirit does not "speak". Sometimes the candidates run away to the mountains and remain there for seven days or more, eating there animals "caught by them, directly with their teeth", and usually they return home dirty with blood, torn clothes, and dishevelled hair, "like wild people". About ten days later, the candidate begins incoherently to speak a few words. An old experienced shaman asks with great precautions various questions. The candidate (the spirit) "becomes angry", but finally designates the shaman who should perform the act. The act is designated by the verb *nmua* (they (*nmnattan*) (Bir.), which may be referred to the act of general sacrifice to the spirits, their periodical review and to the first performance of the new shaman. The old shaman and the new shaman call each other *dovei* (Bir.), when the spirits are introduced into them, while other people are called by them *asaran* (Bir.) and the old shaman is called *sebŭ* (Bir.) [cf. *Sifu→sefu* (Chinese→Manchu)] which is merely "teacher". A certain day, sometimes rather soon after the first extasy, is fixed for the trial. However, the trial may be refused by the clan, if the candidate is considered "undesirable".

Two turŏ are erected in front of a wigwam (theoretically the same may be done in a spacious house) facing south. The turŏ are trees with big branches cut off, but surmounted by crowns. These two turŏ are connected by cross beams, about 90 or 100 centimetres long, in an odd number, namely 5, 7, or 9. A third turŏ is erected in a southern direction at the distance of several metres and connected with the eastern turŏ by a string, or narow thong—s'if'im~s'id'im [which is a "rope"; cf. sit'im (RTM), s'it'im (Yak. Pek.), also sifi (Man. Writ.)] supplied at a distance of about thirty centimetres with bunches of ribbons and feathers of various birds. It may be made of Chinese red silk or of sinews coloured red. This is the "road" along which the spirits will move. On the string a wooden ring is put that moves freely from one turŏ to another. When sent by the "teacher" the spirit is located in the plane of the ring (fŭldu). Three wooden anthropomorphic placings —an'akan, of an unusually large size, about 30 centimetres long, are put near each turŏ.

The candidate sits down between two turŏ, and drums. The old shaman calls one by one the spirits down the southern turŏ, and with the ring sends them to the candidate. Each time the teacher takes back the ring and sends off a spirit. If this were not done, the spirits would enter the candidate and would not leave him. A special man makes marks on a wooden device (a tally, quadrangular in cross section) called kirči jaŋg'i in the shamans' terminology.[*]

During the entering of the spirits the elders examine the candidate who (the spirit) must tell the whole history ("biography") of the spirit, with all details, such as who it had been before, where it had lived (in which "rivers" it had been), what it had done, with which shamans it had been and when the shamans had died, how many times this spirit had been called for the performance of umnā. and many other questions, in order to convince the audience that the spirit is really in the candidate. If the candidate is tired and cannot answer, there is no escape, because the teacher will not allow the spirits to go away. After every night of performance the shaman climbs up to the upper beam and remains there for some time. The costume is hung up on the beams of the turŏ. Since the biographies of great sèvèn are rather long,

and since these spirits do not easily come, and as shown, are numerous, the performance may last several days, no less than three and sometimes 5, 7 and even 9 days.

If the candidate passes through the trial successfully, a great sacrifice to all clan spirits is ordered, for which cows and other big animals are slaughtered.[*]. The turŏ and an'akan are taken away and blood is smeared on the faces of the placings. On the drum and arkaptun cross signs are made with blood.

Such a performance requires a rather long technical training of the candidate, which is done by the "teacher" who explains everything concerning the spirits and ritualism. The costume may either be made, or "found", or it may be borrowed from another shaman. However, a number of brass mirrors must be added to the costume.

I have not heard whether the candidate is rejected after his failure to give satisfactory answers to the elders, but I think that in case of failure, if the candidate is not hopeless, the ritual can be repeated within a few years so that this single performance need not be the only trial to decide the issue of the candidate's attempt at becoming a shaman. Perhaps, it is simply regarded as a formal examination. I was told that the methods used by the Dahurs are the same, and in so far as I can see, it is not a Tungus invention.

———————

III. Among the Manchus the recognition is decided by the clan meeting. There may be three cases. Firstly, the candidate who already has been entered by the spirits and has mastered them, does not raise any doubt and is immediately recognized. The next step would be a solemn form of "recognition", the main part of which is the sacrifice to all spirits of the new (iči) shaman, during which the spirits would be called in. This performance is not long and not all spirits are called by the shaman; the chief performers are the seniors of the clan, who pray and perform the main part of the sacrifice. The second case is that when some doubt arises as to the candidate's ability and a trial must be organized. The third case is that when two or more candidates, who want to become shaman, compete. A long operation with the trial of all candidates is then carried out. However, the candidates may be rejected by the clan, usually on the ground that the candidate is possessed by spirits, i.e., in European terminology, is sick, and therefore needs treatment. When the candidate is admitted, he learns from old men of the clan, or even from the shaman, if the latter is alive, all the names and characters of the spirits which, as shown, may be recorded in the book of spirits. The candidates learn also, as far as possible, the ritual, which is rarely recorded in a written form.

The trial may last several days. In most of the clans the trial and the act of recognition must last nine days, but this is not always observed. In some clans (e.g. the wuza clan), owing to a special character of the spirits, the performers abstain from eating meat during eight days—the spirits do not like it, it is explained—but on the ninth day this fasting is compensated by an unusually rich feast. This fact shows that the clans differ as to the order of acts and

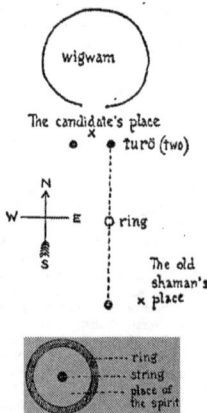

wigwam

The candidate's place
x
● ● turŏ (two)

N

W—E ○ ring

S

The old shaman's
● x place

ring
string
place of
the spirit

———————

* In common language it is called sanyur or saŋgnan. In shamanistic texts there is the following expression of the spirit: kirče jang'edu komnajak'iw,—"on the tally I was wriggling".

* At one of the performances, among the Manchus, eleven pigs were slaughtered which had been bought. Together with drinks the performance cost over five hundred dollars,

rituals, conditioned by the character of the clan spirits, and these, as shown, greatly depend on the former shamans, who may not only discover new spirits, but also become spirits which preserve at least some characters. For the trial the Manchus, chiefly the clansmen, come together in a large house which is put at their disposal by one of the rich clansmen. Outsiders may assist at the performance, but the women of other clans must keep away, when the clan spirits come. A special jury consisting of experienced people may be elected. The number of the jurymen, as far as I know, is not fixed; there may be three members and more, but all of them are naturally members of the clan, or well known experts. A special shaman, who may be one of another clan, is invited for helping the candidate. The keepers of traditions are also invited.

There are two important parts, namely, the reciting of *čolo* (list of spirits) by heart, followed by the answering of questions on the details of the spirits, and the trial. The recital must be done correctly. However, some deviations are admitted—the candidate is a young person and may make mistake, the Manchus say. From the description of lists of Manchu spirits we have seen that there are spirits which can handle "hot" and "cold", which can go into the water, and many others which use swords, spears, etc. If the candidate pretends that he has one of the spirits of this type, he would be required to perform an operation with "hot", "cold", etc. Here it should be noted that these spirits are much more common among the Chinese shamans than among the Manchu shamans whose ritual is simpler and does not include so many tricks. The situation is complicated by the fact that the spirits are distributed according to rows, so that if the candidate pretends to possess the head of a row, he must "master" all manifestations of this row. However, it is also supposed that even a beginner must know the chiefs of the principal rows, whence the candidate may be tried on all manifestations of these rows/ As a matter of fact, so it is in the clans which have included a great number of manifestations with tricks, while the Manchus, little influenced by the Chinese are not very strict in requiring difficult trials. This may be so, if the candidate cannot be formally rejected, but is considered undesirable.

I have already given an instance (*vide supra*, p. 174) of *jaya baturʻi* spirits. To prove that the candidate really has this manifestation he must several times jump into a heap of burning charcoal. There were cases, the Manchus assert, in which candidates were burnt, for they had no spirit, but only pretended having one. This method is now not often used, because, the Manchus say, the shamans have become weak. Here is an interesting instance of what may happen with a candidate who is not desirable to his clan, and at the same time the same instance can be used as an example of the method of treatment practised by the shamans. Among the Manchus of the Algun district a man pretended having a spirit (*vočko*). The clansmen opposed his desire to become a shaman, but he continued to insist. Then an old experienced shaman decided to try the candidate. He ordered a heap of wood (about two tons!), to be set on fire, and when the wood was reduced to burning charcoal, he lifted up his trousers and went (so the record says, but I think it would be better to say "moved towards") into the fire, pulling with him the candidate. It was done on the supposition that if there is real *vočko*, the candidate would go without fear of being burnt. The candidate refused to follow the shaman and declared that he had no *vočko*. He gave up his idea of becoming a shaman and at the same time was cured of the idea of possessing a spirit, if that had been his idea.

Another method of trial is that of one of the *baturʻi* manifestations, which can dive. If the trial is carried out in winter, when the river is covered with ice, they make several holes at a certain distance from one another and the candidate is required to dive through one hole, pass under the ice and come up at the next hole, come out, dive again and come out through the third hole; and so on, altogether nine times. The same is done, if it is a *mujuγu n'imaγa vočko*.

These two instances show to which degree the imagination may go in inventing methods for verifying the candidate's ability and the genuine character of his spirits.

If the candidate survives (there were cases in the past when candidates did not survive) and the trial is considered satisfactory, the candidate is recognized by the jury and thus by the whole clan, as being a shaman. The trial, as stated, may last several days, so the candidate usually becomes exhausted before the expiration of nine days. Therefore the jury may shorten the trial. A good deal of the success depends on the character of the spirits. In some clans some spirits are very slow to come, so the calling of the spirits may sometimes take several hours. Naturally it cannot be changed by the candidate who by the change would show his lack of knowledge of the ritual (*kooli*). Still greater is the importance of the assistance of the old shaman who may do his work in different ways—shorter or longer.

The last day is spent on a sacrifice to the spirits of the new (*iči*) shaman.

I was told by the Manchus that the complexity of the trial, as shown above, and its "atrocity" has been introduced chiefly under the Chinese influence. The knowledge of *čolo* (list of spirits) and *kooli* (rituals) is also an innovation, which could not appear prior to the introduction of written records. If we exclude the above indicated innovations, and omit some details implied by the complications of the milieu and the peculiarities of the Northern Tungus complex, the Manchu performance of recognition and trial is near to that of the Tungus of Manchuria. The latter seem to have borrowed their complex from the Dahurs, who had it perhaps in forms similar to the Manchu complex. However, it should be noted that, although the ritualism was the same, the spirits may have been different, and even, in olden days, there might have been some special elements in the ritualism.

131. A CASE OF ELECTION AMONG THE MANCHUS I give in this section the description of a case which may bring some light as to the actual and present mechanism of shamanism. I give almost totally, only slightly retouched, my record from the diary, preceded by preliminary information relating to the history of the case and the participants, as well as to my own part in it.

The candidates, as well as the actor A, have already been described in the previous section under Case 3. The other important participants were: (1) the old shaman whom I knew rather well, and whom I observed many times in performances; (2) the member of the jury, *Čuntin*, who

was not of the clan *wujata*, but who was one of the greatest
authorities on shamanism (he was a *p'oyun saman*) and
for this quality was asked to assist the case; (3) another
member of the same jury called "an old man of *wujata*"
whose opinion counted; (4) a third member of the jury,
whose opinion was not of importance,—the man was too
old; (5) an influential member of the community, E. The
operation took place in January 1917, in the village
Kalunšan (*Oforo Tokso* in Manchu). As shown before, the
case was extremely difficult because of the hidden conditions of the female candidate C. The case was still more
difficult, because the Chinese authorities did not permit
the carrying out of the performance—shamanism being
formally forbidden. Being on very friendly terms with
most of the above indicated participants, A, *Čuntin*, the
old shaman, E and D, and having had under my observation, for a period over a year, both candidates, I was not
considered as a stranger. All these people were convinced
of my competence as to the conditions, ritual and spirits of
shamanism and the individuality of the candidates. In
fact, on various occasions I could give good advice concerning the persons who suffered from the spirits, or who
needed ordinary medical treatment (I used to send them
with my note to a professional physician). Moreover,
being on "friendly relations" with the local authorities, I
was fortunate to obtain the permission for carrying out
this prohibited performance, which in its turn created still
closer relations with the people and even the clans involved,
and at last I was asked to join the jury as its fourth member. This permitted me to be in close contact with all participants and at the same time left me a certain freedom
of action making me one of those who did not disturb the
actors. It should also be noted that, by that time, I had
already learnt the art of assistant shaman and, when
necessary, I did perform such duties.

A few days before the beginning, a complete set of
pictures (*n'urgan*), which represented all shamanistic
spirits of the clan, was brought from a village situated on
the *sumbira* (the Sun River). Two shaman costumes
were needed for the candidates, one of them for the female
candidate was supplied from my ethnographical collection,
and another was found elsewhere. After spending a few
days talking over the matter, I found out that the participants, and generally the "public opinion", were in
favour of creating a new shaman. However, I found that
some of these people wished most to have an interesting
performance and the concomitant feasts, and some were
joking about the event. Continuous discussions as to the
nature of the spirits and their wishes were going on the whole
time. Then a day for the performance was fixed and the
people assembled. A, who was the husband of one of the
candidates and the brother of another, was especially
nervous about the coming event, so he always returned to
discuss the matter with me, in general and in detail. The
communications of A, who was supposed to be familiar with
the spirits of his clan, were immediately communicated to
the participants. The distribution of the participants is
shown in Fig. below. The shaman and the candidate were
moving. Four pictures were hung up on birch branches in
front of them (*vide supra* p. 169) and two tables were put
on the bed-stove. On the table of the *wujata* clan the following things could be seen: a sacrifice of 3 times 5, i.e. fifteen,
rolls of Chinese bread and a chicken (with all parts uncut),
a model of a Buddhistic shrine, with a Buddha inside, and

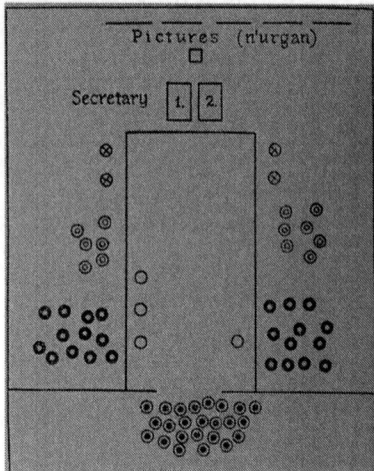

1. Table of wuʒata clan
2. Table of the old shaman
○ - four assistants
⊗ - members of jury
◉ - elders & very honourable persons
○ - clansmen
◉ - young clansmen & guests

four sticks of burning incense on top of it. This Buddha
was employed by the old shaman as a mastered spirit
fuě'k'i.[*] One of the four sticks of incense was especially
assigned to Buddha. On the table of the old shaman there
were 3 times 5, i.e. fifteen, rolls of Chinese bread and a large
brass mirror in front of which three sticks of incense were
burning.

By eight o'clock the jury and the old shaman had
finished a copious dinner which consisted of a big dish—
the *xogŏza* (a kind of low samovar in which, at the choice
of the guests, all kinds of meat and vegetables are cooked
in an excellent chicken soup)—with a moderate libation,
so that the mood of these people was rather good. About
one hundred, or perhaps more, were attending the performance and gradually occupied their places. The secretary took his place at the table of the *wujala* clan to keep
the record; the members of the jury occupied places near
the tables and the ground for action, in order to be ready
to come to the aid of candidates, if needed. A dozen, or
thereabouts, of old men, very honourable persons, were
sitting next to the jury. Nearer to the entrance, the places
were occupied by the clansmen of a certain age in a number
limited only by the size of the big room, perhaps twenty or

* Among the Manchu shamans the mastering of Buddha is a
rare occurrence.

thirty persons. Near to the entrance the ground was occupied by four permanent assistants. However, at critical moments of the performance, even members of the jury acted as assistants.

1. The old shaman, this time assisted by *Čuntin*, drummed and prayed to his spirits. The important spirit *xele mava* arrived and, through the shaman and in the interpretation of *Čuntin*, declared that it was necessary to produce a new shaman. The old shaman continued his praying to the spirits, asking them not to mingle with the spirits of *wujala* clan.

2. One man brought the news that a spirit had come into the candidate C. The old shaman and some other people went to her. Before the performance she had been in a state of great excitement. Now she was in the adjacent house, lying on the stove-bed and making "arch" from time to time; her pulse was 92, her breathing irregular and her eyes closed. Before our coming she had told her mother-in-law that the deceased shaman [who had been her lover (*vide supra* Section 128, Case 3), the husband of the old woman (mother-in-law) and the father of her husband] had come to her. The old woman, a sister of the candidate and the second candidate's wife, sat near her crying. The old shaman spoke to the candidate and wished first to establish friendly relations between the spirits, because the spirits of her native clan and those of his own clan used always to be friendly and were of common origin. Then he invited C to go to the other house and very carefully lead her forward repeating something rapidly and in a low voice. Candidate C was trembling violently all over. She was taken (to the upper left-hand corner) and put on the stove-bed under the pictures, as shown in Fig. above. The "arch" continued and the eyes were closed showing distinct photophobia. The shaman sat by her side, calling the spirits and speaking to them. In the meantime I noticed among the persons present one who fell into exstasy. Fiercely howling in rhythm with the assistants (he was almost speechless) he cried out incoherently (he had also some other physical defects). Suddenly the candidate C sat up on the stove-bed and firmly declared that the performance must be quickly carried out, that everything must be finished on the morrow, instead of in five days, as it was intended. Then a meeting of the jury and the old shaman was held. After a long deliberation, it was decided to ask *čolo* and, if she could tell it, to make of her a shaman. While the preparations were made, it was possible to inquire as to the attitude of the audience.

The opinion was in favour of candidate C. Even a great friend, *Čuntin*, whose daughter had a love-affair with A (the latter usually slept in *Čuntin's* house, especially when the daughter was visiting her mother) showed a favourable attitude towards C, in spite of the fact that A himself did not wish his legal wife to become a shaman. However, how sincere *Čuntin* was I do not know; he had occupied a small official position with the Manchu government for a long time, so he must have been familiar with cunning tricks. He now advanced the idea that it is easy to find out, whether a candidate really has a spirit, or is simply feigning; it is sufficient to prick the candidate with a needle, if a spirit is present, the candidate will not feel any pain; if she refuses to be pricked, it will be indicative that, either there is a "sickness", or the candidate is trying to fool the people. On this occasion *Čuntin* related a case from his own experience. A shaman pretended to have a spirit;

however, *Čuntin* asked him various questions, as to the details and especially the implements used by the spirit, which the impostor failed to answer; then *Čuntin* took from the shaman a written obligation to attend to *Čuntin's* needs during ten years without any remuneration, even if assistance to a dying chicken or pig should be needed.

The authoritative man E, as well as the member of the jury D, were in favour of the candidate C. I naturally joined the opinion of these authorities, although A seemed to be discouraged and the candidate B looked gloomy. The hidden reason seemed to be that the brothers did not wish their father to become a *voǒko*, which would happen if the candidate C became a shaman (and this possibility is even denied on theoretical grounds: the soul of a man, whose head was cut off, cannot become *voǒko*), for the new spirit will not be favourable to the brothers who did not fulfil their duties of filial piety (Chinese complex!).

3. Since it had been decided by the jury to proceed with the trial of candidate C, she was prepared for the performance. The old shaman prayed to his spirits and to those of the *wujala* clan. The *wujala* clansmen fell on their knees in front of the picture, beat the ground with their foreheads, set up burning incence and prayed to the spirits. The same was done by the candidate C. She was evidently afraid of the coming trial and was trembling, although no signs of a hysterical fit were seen. The women arranged her hair, as it is done for girls, in two long plaits*; the skirt and belt with long conical trinkets (s'iša) were put on. When she was dressed, she was almost unable to go out of the house to the spot where a kind of long table with a great number of burning sticks of incense had been prepared. She was helped by many people, including the old shaman, and was almost carried out on the arms of these people. Held up in a standing position by two men, her mouth wide open, she breathed the smoke of incense. The old shaman called the spirits. Then the spirit *mama saman* (*vide supra*, p. 174) came. However, the man who was holding her asserted that there was no spirit, the candidate was not trembling as much as she should be in the presence of a spirit like *mama saman*. The old shaman was furiously jumping and dancing around her, urging her by his movements to come into the house. Hesitating and artlessly drumming, she entered. The old shaman, always in a rhythmic "dancing", began to push her from all sides with his sides and back. The impact was so strong that sometimes both of them fell back in opposite directions. The old shaman took the candidate in his arms and turned her about in the middle of the room. One man held her by the belt. Still no extasy came and she could not fall down on the ground (which is required by the ritual); several times she tried to do it, but she could not fall, and at last dropped down on the rug in a semi-sitting position instead of falling backward "like a stick", being supported by a man. I surmised that perhaps the man who was helping her was not of those who wished to make her a shaman and intentionally did not give her his assistance to prevent her being hurt in falling. Therefore, I pushed away the man and

---

* It should be noted that the reason for dressing the hair in girls' fashion cannot be theoretically explained. The woman with her high hair-dress cannot put on the shaman's head-dress (crown), and when she is performing, her hair would become disordered. By this remark, I do not mean to say that perhaps in some other ethnical groups she must be "girl-like". It is not so among the Manchus and Tungus.

occupied his place holding the candidate by the belt from behind. From this position I could much better follow her and could observe her reactions in the performance.

4. The old shaman asked her to start the *čolo* (list of spirits) during which the spirits are supposed to come, one by one. The candidate was trembling slightly, but in all parts of the body. However, for a very long time she could not start her reciting. As a matter of fact, the drum was wet (not dry enough and barely dried), the husband A was continually interfering with his remarks and other persons were laughing at her. I noticed a man who was even pushing her and evidently provoking acts which are unforeseen by the ritual. I did my best to protect her and asked for a fresh drum. *Čuntin* was furious—he insulted and threatened her. Finally, after three hours from the beginning of her fit, she began to introduce into herself, one by one, manifestations of the *mama saman* row. One after another the series of female *vočko* came. She could describe them; they declared that they had no master; the old shaman (her lover) had not used them for performances; they felt themselves offended by this attitude of the late shaman. Instead of going ahead with the other spirits, the deceased shaman was allowed to come again. He declared that his image must be made, that various inscriptions and "money" (in paper as used in the Chinese complex) must be burned on his tomb, for he was executed without being guilty; his soul could not find peace, but might attain it, if everything was done which he had required. In spite of this valuable information and steps later undertaken accordingly, the audience became furious that the candidate C could not go ahead with *čolo*. She was immediately accused of making a joke out of a serious matter. *Čuntin* said that when a man is treated, some minor cheating is allowed, but if the question concerns clan spirits, one must be strict and careful, and perfectly honest and sincere, for the matter of clan spirits is the greatest matter which exists. A was desperate. He said that he had organized everything on his own responsibility, without formally consulting his clansmen (actually the clansmen had been privately consulted before the performance)[*] therefore such a scandalous issue would not affect the clan, but only A alone and personally. The jury was called again, as well as the old shaman and other seniors. From the discussions it was clear that the general desire of the influential persons was that candidate C should not become a shaman. They said that the female spirits had refused to have a female shaman and that the male spirits did not want to have a male shaman, and furthermore, since the chief spirit *xele mafa* was a male, there must be a male shaman. However, there were voices in favour of candidate C. So the influential man E said that the candidate C was a sincere and good person, and that she had a spirit. In order to clear up some more details I maintained his opinion by bringing evidences of her having had spirits, of the unreliability of the *čolo* test, the fact that the drum had been bad etc. This discussion helped to clear up some uncertain points. After the discussion, the husband A took me aside and told me all the details of his family tragedy which, in fact, I knew only in part and

from other persons. The situation was clear; the candidate C was rejected and by her husband's frank declaration, in a state of great excitement, I could no longer maintain my position. The influential man E, being informed of the family affairs still maintained his former opinion.

At the beginning of the discussion the spirit was "called back" and she was left alone in another room, which permitted me to continue my observation: the nervous fit was not over. After one hour of rest she again dressed her hair, and returned to the room, where the performance was going on. She was exhausted, very sad and depressed, but she was memorizing every word of *čolo*, at that moment already started by her competitor, candidate B. But it was too late to learn the *čolo*, as had been done by the candidate B before the decisive day of trial.

5. During the discussion which continued a long time, while the old shaman was resting, it was decided that the candidate B should shamanize. I asked the candidate B, whether this time he would be successful or not, and he replied with a firm assurance: "there are spirits, and there is *čolo*". This reply made me understand that he knew the list of spirits. However, I was informed by many persons, that the "grandfather" (which means one of the superior to the father's generation-clan) who was a keeper of tradition and who, according to my information, had been visited for the purpose of *čolo*, did not tell him the *čolo*. Of course, one can learn *colo* not only from the "grandfather", and the candidate B could do the same from other people who had attended the periodical sacrifices of the late shamans. From all these doubtful statements and the general behaviour of the participants it was evident that the clan leaders wanted candidate B to become shaman and they admitted as truth, perhaps sincerely believing in what they wished to be the truth. The candidate B with the air of an experienced man, smiling and behaving rather arrogantly, put on the skirt and belt (*s'iša*) and was ready for action. The old shaman prayed to his own spirits and the spirits of the *wujala* clan. The *wujala* clansmen knelt in front of the picture, put up burning incense and heartily prayed to the spirits, as had been done with the candidate C. The old shaman and candidate B both remained standing in front of the tables. The old shaman called his spirits and *xele mafa* entered him. Then there was repeated, in the same order and without variations what has been described above in section 3. The only difference was that the candidate B behaved as an experienced performer: he drummed well. (The drum was always prepared by A and other assiduous assistants and when needed changed). He made strong movements with his back (to produce *s'iša* noise), he danced well, strongly pushed the old shaman and, when he "fell down like a stick" (actually he sat down!), he was trembling much more intensively than the candidate C had trembled and the trembling occurred exactly when it was required by the ritual, while this was not so with the candidate C who had been trembling the whole time. According to the man who was holding the belt, "he was trembling but not very intensively; anyhow the spirit was there". Then the old shaman proceeded with the *čolo*. The candidate B successfully went on with nine spirits and suddenly stopped. Then it was found out that the *p'oyun vočko* had interfered with the performance. It was necessary to call them and pray them to allow the performance to continue.

---

[*] In fact, A could not act in loco of his clan, for there were seniors who lege artis had to assemble and to decide what to do. But evidently they had refused to take the initiative and had allowed A to go ahead, without refusing to attend the meeting and consult as a clan body, and were now facing a fait accompli.

As soon as this difficulty was removed, the performance continued. Slowly and not without difficulties, the candidate recited, though in a very much abbreviated manner, all of the spirits. The participants greatly enjoyed this achievement. I was told that the detailed enquiry would be made later. · The spirit was allowed to leave and the candidate, half-unconscious, very tired, with limp limbs, and wet with perspiration was carried to the k'ang. A kind of deep satisfaction filled the participants. Everything was good—the new shaman knew čolo; he could introduce spirits; he could drum and sing. The old shaman was proud. Then a ritual was carried out: thanksgiving to the spirits by the old shaman, while the new shaman was soundly sleeping under the pictures. It was already 5 a.m. The performance had lasted nine hours. After a meal (a very late supper) the audience dispersed, in order to take a rest.

SECOND DAY A visited the tomb of his father (shaman), in a village situated a few kilometres away, where he burnt the image, etc., i.e. did all that had been required, as revealed through the candidate C the night before. A asked the "grandfather" mentioned before, an old man of seventy-eight, to come and participate in the performance. The old man was brought at nine p.m., when the performance was already going on, and occupied a place by the side of the old shaman's table.

The performance began at 8 p.m. in the same disposition of the performers and audience. The same sacrifices were put on the tables and the same pictures were hung up. The performance began with a prayer to the spirits. The old shaman called the *zèlè mava* spirit which arrived. The old shaman was furiously drumming, while the candidate B, after having put on the skirt and *s'isa*, danced in front of the pictures. Little by little he reached a great excitement and rushed out. Standing in front of the table with the incense, he breathed the smoke until the spirit *zèlè mava* (of the *wufala* clan) entered him. The old shaman tried to lead the candidate into the house, loudly drumming all the time, making a great noise with the belt and rhythmically stamping the ground with his feet. The candidate came into the hall and showed signs of his intention to go back into the yard. The old shaman barred the entrance with his body and sometimes beating the candidate with the heavy trinkets of *s'isa*, compelled him to enter the room of the performance. Then the dancing of the two shamans was performed, so that after changing their respective positions they bumped each other with their backs with great force, which produced a loud noise from the *sisa*. The dancing is supposed to go on until the candidate attains the state of extasy and "falls down like a stick", aided by a man who supported him. (However, apparently this did not occur, for one leg was not "like a stick"; the candidate supported himself with the leg which was not rigid at all). This produced an impression, and the audience began to bring the performer to his senses, because he might have died, the soul being absent for too long a time.

Finally the candidate B sat down trembling. He made an attempt to run away, but a strong man caught him by the belt and kept him. The old shaman started his enquiry. At first the candidate replied inconsistently, but afterwards he began the enumeration of the spirits. The "grandfather" and jury were listening carefully to every word and the secretary was writing down what was said.

An exchange of drinks was done; the spirit *zèlè mava* gave, on the drum, two small cups of Chinese wine to the grandfather who passed them to the candidate, who drank the wine without taking the cup into his hands. The candidate again made a mistake with the row of spirits. The spirit was sent off. Another spirit was introduced outside of the house and the candidate was brought back on the arms of several people who put him on the stove-bed. He "slept".

A meeting of the jury was convoked. This time, with the participation of the "grandfather", a difficult problem was discussed, namely, what was to be done, since the candidate did not know the row of spirits just recited. The "grandfather" was very gloomy. Still more gloomy was A, who with a wry face and the corners of his mouth gone, was walking up and down the room. The "grandfather" was interviewed as to the points in which the candidate had failed. The old man explained that he thought the candidate could hear what was being talked about. The candidate was awakened and a new spirit was introduced. The candidate named, almost without an error, the spirits of the new row and went again to "sleep". In the meantime the "grandfather" was again interviewed as to other rows of spirits; some points were especially emphasized by A and his mother who was in the room, when no spirits were acting. Once more the candidate arose; this time the spirit *zèlè mava* came again and the candidate, glancing at the pictures, went on rather smoothly with the enumeration of the spirits, although he omitted the biographical details which were required. Once more the spirit was changed and *mama saman*, on which candidate C had failed, arrived. It was not easy to call in *mama saman*, which like all other great spirits, will not come at once. She was called in for three quarters of an hour. This time *Čuntin* was helping by correcting the names, and the candidate turned his eyes hopefully in *Čuntin's* direction.

I used this opportunity for making my inquiry as to the "public opinion". There were persons who said that such a hopeless performance was entirely A's fault. He and his mother did not want candidate C to become shaman, but A wanted someone else to remove the spirits for ever. *Čuntin* thought that candidate B was a lazy and dishonest ("he does not pay his debts," he said) man who wanted to be shaman. It was clear that the candidate was helped by other people and he would never be a good shaman, the other people said. Others said that one of the causes of such a situation was that the methods with the trial by fire (a pit with charcoal), or with a stick covered with oxen intestines (the candidate must be able to hold the stick which is pulled by several strong men) and other good methods, implied by introducing group *buku* and *mayi*, had been given up in the *wufala* clan. Some people were much dissatisfied and left the performance before its conclusion. However, A said that "although he (the candidate B) does not know all spirits, he still knows something". Some persons supposed that A's idea was to make his brother shaman and then to rid himself of the trouble of looking after his wife who was sick from spirits and needed a treatment by the new *amba saman* of their clan. A was greatly criticized for this attitude. The influential man E supported his own point of view by criticizing the method of the trial with *čolo*. He himself and *Čuntin* knew *čolo* by heart and they were practising assistant's functions, so that they might easily have become shamans, if tried on *čolo;* as to the trembling, it can be produced after a short training, so it is not convincing, therefore there must be something else. He said that A's wife had a "straight heart" and she might be a good shaman. There was, however, another point of view, namely, since the performance was carried out and the spirits had been named, though with the help of other persons, and since there was trembling, the candidate could be admitted, for everything required by *čolo* and *koolī* had been fulfilled. Such a formalization of shamanism is supported by the instances taken from the Mongol and Chinese complexes. In a somewhat depressed mood this day was finished with the usual thanksgivings to the spirits and the late supper after 5 a.m.

And so the performance continued for six nights. I shall not repeat the occurrences, but shall now point out some facts of interest. The spirit of the unfortunate father of the candidate B once entered him and expressed his great dissatisfaction with A, who did not show him any mark of esteem ("piety complex"), and declared that he had become a spirit (*vočko*) of the clan (even though as shown above this possibility was at first rejected). The wrong was left with A. The latter promised to give a good sacrifice of a large pig to the spirits of the new shaman;

naturally his intention was to build up a bridge for the restoration of relations between himself and his father's soul which was now a spirit. Indeed, he had already spent much money (two pigs—$39.00, incense and straw for the stoves $15.00 altogether more than $55.00), but he hoped that other clangmen, even those of his wife, would help him. Although the new shaman did not know all of the spirits and could name only a part of them, he seemed to have reached extasy on the last day of the performance and fell down unconscious, "as white as paper, so that it was distressing to look at him", and the public opinion turned in his favour; he had "power" and for a long time there had not been such a good shaman. On the sixth night, a sacrifice was offered to the spirits of the old shaman—a cock and Chinese bread, and two pigs were eaten by the participants, as a sacrifice to the spirits of the new shaman.

In my diary I find my conclusive impression from this performance: "It is the crépuscule du chamanisme". But that was only my *impression*, perhaps formed after very tiresome observations. This opinion I am inclined not to repeat, but to modify as follows; an interesting case of readaptation of shamanism to the new cultural complex, in consequence of a partial disintegration of the clan and of the ethnical disintegration of the Manchus.

CHAPTER XXIX

THE SHAMAN

132. METHODS OF THE COMMON THINKING PROCESS From the description of shamanism as a function and from the analysis of performances we can see that the shaman in his function of a clan safety valve (as well as the safety valve for any other community), uses different methods in his investigation and his influence upon the community and individuals. An average shaman does not blindly proceed with a practical application of his art, as summarized in the above indicated (*vide* Chapter XXVI) directions, but he always considers the character of the case with which he must deal and, according to its character, he chooses particular methods. Therefore the first thing to be done is to analyse the case and to diagnose afterwards. The shaman's diagnosis does not differ from any other diagnosis based upon an analysis and recognized methods of inference. He makes an inquiry as to the history of the trouble: whether there are other similar cases or not, i.e. whether this is a single case or a mass phenomenon; he considers all symptoms—fever, pain in various parts of the body, character of the attacks, their frequency and the time of the day when they occur; he talks, if possible, with the person who needs his assistance. Lastly, he comes to a conclusion which may be reached immediately on the spot, or some time later. In simple cases he would do this immediately; in complex cases he would postpone his decision; and in some other cases he would not come to any definite decision, a series of solutions being equally possible. His diagnosis may be formulated in the form of various *causes* which produce the trouble. As has been shown, such ones can be: (1) infectious diseases symbolized either in terms

of spirits or even directly in a hypothetical external physical agent (e.g. "worms" and "micro-organisms" cf. *supra* p. 179); (2) individual physical trouble, due e.g. to traumatic disfunction, old age, individual affection from causes expressed in terms of symbols or in terms of external physical agents; (3) individual troubles of a psychomental character, according to the conceptions of these troubles, expounded in the previous chapters, which may be classified into several groups and may be due either to an individual disfunction of the elements of the soul or to the causes only symbolized or directly understood as hypothetical spirits, which are regarded as realities only to some extent and accepted by ethnical groups and individual shamans with a certainty of various degrees.

This process of the discovery of causes of trouble from the observation of the supposed effects does not differ from that of the common European diagnostics based upon a symptomatic analysis of the condition and upon direct information, as well as direct evidences. The form of declaration of the result, as well as the outer forms of the *performance of diagnosis*, are also essential and they are conditioned by the "customs", which do not affect the diagnosis and the theories that underlie diagnostics. Indeed, when the shaman gives out his conclusion he cannot do it without considering the habits of the people. There may be thus created special performances in connexion with the diagnosis. This is quite clear, if we remember that a European medical practitioner must also "perform" certain acts before pronouncing his conclusion. For instance, he must not do it too quickly, he must show that he is thinking about the case, even though the latter may at the first glance be perfectly clear; he must do it seriously; he must sometimes examine the patient more than he needs for his conclusion. Another way to win the patient's confidence is to give quickly, in recomforting words, after a very brief examination, a conclusion in order to show that the doctor *knows* what should be done. Various methods may be worked out into real "performances", the importance of which will often be greater than that of inoffensive medicines. Among some ethnical (European) groups paraphernalia have also a great psychological influence and therefore are increased in number, not for the gathering of new facts, but solely for producing an "impression". Of course, I have in view perfectly honest doctors who must "perform" for making their diagnosis psychologically acceptable to the patient. Dishonest physicians are not considered here.* The shamans, when they are good, also have their methods, for it is especially important to them to make their diagnoses acceptable, since the greater part of their cases are cases of a psychomental complex.

In the choice of methods the shaman is greatly handicapped by the theoretical considerations concerning the spirits and methods of diagnosis, so he must perform what is required. In fact, in most cases he does not need to have recourse to a complex performance with calling into himself his spirits, but he declares that the patient has such and such a "spirit", or simply "disease", and that he must have either a medical treatment or be assisted by the shaman himself. However, sometimes the shaman must perform the introduction of spirits which are supposed to help him in finding out the cause (to diagnose) of the trouble. Thus a performance, usually purely conventional and ritualistic, is carried out and the shaman declares the result of his investigation, or it is understood by the assistant of the shaman from the shaman's words pronounced during the supposed presence of spirits in him, and communicated to the audience. This is especially done in case the trouble is of a psychomental character, because the shaman, from the beginning of his intervention, must gain the patient's confidence. This ritualism may incidentally grow into a complex—the divination and discovery—treated in Section 113.

The shaman's diagnosis may be made only in special terms and according to the conceptions as to the nature of the troubles which exist among the ethnical groups. A great number of conditions which require the shaman's interference are not covered by the theories and hypotheses accepted by the Tungus, so they are grouped under the symbols of spirits in the same way as, for instance, modern European symbols "influenza", "meningitis", and still earlier ones—"fever", and others. Of course, the shamanistic diagnostics did not reach a very detailed specification of troublesome agents (I omit all cases in which diagnosis may be done without recourse to hypotheses), but, on the other hand, the shaman is not a "medicine man" who must treat everything—he attends only cases in which suggestion, hypnotism and persuasion may be effective. Theories and hypotheses in a great number of instances explain the troubles as due to the spirits, which

* With the growth of the knowledge concerning chemical methods and microscopical analyses, new requirements as to these "performances" have arisen. Whether or not such analyses are needed, the patients require them and they must be carried out. Even when they are of no use to the doctor, he is bound to make them, because "theoretical" medicine insists upon such analyses.

actually cannot be treated in this way, and naturally the shamans fail in their diagnosis. Thus, the possibility of making a correct diagnosis also depends upon the degree of advancement of the classification of troubles. Here the question as to the personal ability of the shamans in diagnosis naturally arises, but to this question I shall revert later on, because now I am speaking of shamanistic diagnoses in general.

In the preceding lines I have thus shown that the methods of diagnosis used by the shamans do not differ in principle from those of the European medical doctors. However, the difference of the result is great. The shamans cover by their symbols a great number of troubles without classifying them in detail, while the advanced medicine may specify them as far as possible, and with a relatively good effect, in so far as the aim of medicine is a treatment. It must be pointed out once more that the shaman's aim is not the same as that of a medicine man, and he is perhaps not interested in the further differentiation and classification of troubles with which he cannot interfere. On the other hand, being perfectly familiar with the psychomental complex of the clansmen, and also with individual complexes, the shaman may perhaps find out the conditions (always expressed in used symbols—the complex soul, spirits etc.) of the patients much easier than the European physicians, apart from the rare clinicists-psychiatrists, who usually know very roughly the psychomental complex of their patients. In fact the chief function of the physicians is not the regulation of individual and mass psychomental complexes, but the treatment of diseases, while a regulation of the individual and mass psychosis is the chief function of the shamans and the aim of their diagnosis is the finding out of the details of psychomental disfunctions.

In observing daily the practice of shamans I have found that in the greater number of cases the shamans confine themselves to the above described simple methods of diagnosis. If they used only these methods, they would not differ very much from common people. However, in difficult cases the shamans use methods of cognition which cannot be framed in the complex of simple logical methods used by ordinary people. Although not all of these special methods are a special privilege of the shamans, they are characteristic as a complex, and this constitutes the special character of the shamans and shamanism as a complex.

Under "simple logical process" I mean here the process which is commonly used in the given ethnical unit. However, the process may be greatly abbreviated after a long use of the same system of links. In fact, a sequence of inferences (based upon facts or established "truths") may be linked in a system without interruptions—from fact to fact, from inference to inference. Such a system will be clear to any one in the given unit. But owing to a long use of these systems they may be greatly abbreviated in the process of thinking. Every ethnical unit has its own ethnographical sequence, and it is subject to some extent to the variations in individuals. When it can be demonstrated in a common sequence, it is considered as *logical* and thus accepted. However, the process of thinking cannot always go along a rigid system of the existing ethnographical "logic", for it would be too slow; so it is abbreviated. The more one thinks, the more abbreviations occur, the wider the spacing between the links marked in the consciousness. Since apparently the whole thinking process is a system of conditioned reflexes of a higher order, the omission of links becomes not a simple "abbreviation", but a new system of established reflexes which function as such.* The shamans who spend their lives on meditation as to the phenomena of psychomental complex, naturally work out an abbreviated system of quick thinking, which may appear in the eyes of laymen as a spirits' gift, while in respect to other branches of activity laymen use the same method without noticing it.

It is different when there are elements of a new situation which must be linked with a system already known. If an ethnographic complex does not know a new element or a new system of linked elements, there appears a necessity of linking them with the old system by a bridge which, at the first attempt, is an imaginative system of links. After the experiment of checking and repetition, the process of linking may change into a system of usual (for individuals, for ethnical units and even for the most mentally slow individuals) linking which will be accepted as such. However, such a bridging cannot be done without breaking the usual requirement of the ethnical group as to the spacing of links. The process may go with large spacings in the known directions, from the known to the unknown, which will be discovered and perhaps later on linked, if necessary. In this case it would be also necessary to eliminate the ethnographic limits of logic, before the result is presented to and accepted by the ethnical unit. However, the process of thinking and checking is not confined to the linking of inferences based upon facts, but it is also conditioned by the complex of already existing systems of linking (a pre-existing system of abbreviated thinking) and emotive and even physiological conditions which may produce new imaginative elements not yet linked and which may imply the choice of the lacking links. This is empirically checked up, and when it cannot be rejected, owing to the new experience (observation of facts, inferences, or systems of linking), it may persist as long as the emotive and physiological conditions are responsible for their existence. The linking of a system of abbreviated thinking may be checked up by the existing (adopted) ethnographical sequences of inferences without interruptions (which are ethnographic in their nature) e.g. mathematically, or with a linked system of "truth". The shamans widely use abbreviated thinking, for they are "meditating" all the time on the same matter. The risk for the shamans in using intuition, imagination with the help of an abbreviated thinking, is not great. Since their process of thinking is always empirically checked up, they gradually correct their systems and give them up, for otherwise the shamanism could not and cannot function— it is, first of all, a system of empirical adaptation. Moreover, the shamans' credit is great, they have time for proving empirically the correctness of their "bridging", and they need not show immediately all links of their thinking process.

First of all, the shamans, chiefly owing to the character of the treated cases, rely very much upon their intuition, which cannot always be put into the frame of a common way of solution of problems. An absolutely correct solution of a problem may sometimes remain little convincing and mysterious, for the links of logical process of inference may be lacking. In fact, discoveries made by the shamans,

being in their nature merely a successful guess, very often require the support of the authority of the shamans as persons who possess spirits, which are held responsible for the success. The shaman's power of intuition, "talent" and "genius", are often explained as the spirits' ability. Moreover, discoveries made by the shamans are very often due to the fact that the shamans use as technique the breaking of the existing ethnical models of logical thinking, based upon an existing limited knowledge and fixed in rigid forms of accepted analogies, syllogisms, etc. The shamans have at their disposal a powerful means of correcting and perfecting the existing methods of making conclusions, namely, the introduction of lacking links, symbolized in the form of new properties of the spirits. And new spirits, as a possibility allowed to the shamans, is accepted by the Tungus, as much as among the Europeans the building up of working hypotheses, sometimes quite unusual, is allowed to the recognized scientists, although these hypotheses —for being convincing and declared to be "truth"—may be as much erroneous as the system of new spirits of the Tungus shamans. In reality not all shamans follow it. To make their conclusions (and new hypotheses) acceptable the shamans have to put them into the form of a "performance" used in the given ethnical unit, i.e. just as it is required from the European "breakers" of the existing ethnographical complexes (introduction of a new conclusion, hypothesis, etc.) who must show their new idea in a seemingly convincing form of formulae, experiment, system of "logical" constructions, etc. In the accumulation of knowledge about the milieu and the "psychic" life reduced to a form of fixed "truths" and "hypotheses" and usually achieved through the breaking of other previously established "truths and hypotheses", the performance is of primary importance. In a great number of cases the form decides the fate of new "truths and hypotheses". In this sense the work and success of scientists depend on the psychomental ethnographical complexes of the existing ethnical units, and perhaps more effort is made for the "performal" side than for the discovery itself. So in the ethnical units, in which the adherence to the complex is strong, the performance may grow into an aim by itself. Moreover, when the science is professionalized, even the performance may lose altogether its functional power. This refers to the search for new truths in general, but the Tungus instances give us a whole scale of variations as to the weight of the performance in the bridging of "old" and "new" truths, all of them being naturally ethnographical phenomena, i.e. elements of psychomental complexes of concrete ethnical units.*

In so far as the shaman uses his intuition in the "finding of causes" he does not differ from any other man who is using the method of breaking of the existing ethnographic complex as a means for proceeding from the known to the unknown. Indeed, the shaman can use this method only on the condition of his familiarity with and his possession of the existing ethnographical complex, for otherwise his mode of "breaking" of the complex may turn into a mere incoherent guess-work, practically quite fruitless and unnecessary for keeping afloat his ethnical

---

* The same may be represented in terms of "channels and strata".

* It must not be forgotten that different ethnical units may have the same ethnographical complex, which may produce an impression of an independent existence of "culture", "civilization", "science" and other abstractions, when they are treated independently of the ethnical units.

unit. This may be compared with the "thinkers and philosophers" of our time (in the European complex) who cannot master the present knowledge and use their power of intuition and guess-work, even in cases in which the knowledge might save them from the most elementary blunders and save their "teaching" from being an incoherent babbling. Indeed, these "thinkers and philosophers" have their function in the existing ethnical complexes; namely, they give a satisfaction to the ignorant (relatively, in the ethnical units) part of the population with a simulation of penetration into the conditions of milieu. This is reached without a great loss of time and strain of the brain on learning facts and generally without achievements of knowledge; it leaves to this part of the population the hope, that such a penetration can be achieved by any one who has leisure and desire; finally, it leads the thought into a stream of dreams (an emotionally pleasant condition) and tickles this population with an "opening" of a special world of "mysterious power of gnosis". This type of "thinkers and philosophers" is only rarely met with among the Tungus shamans, for their function is different, although to the superficial observer the shaman's intuition, thinking and guess-work may appear to be similar to that of the above indicated, so to say, inferior kind of thinkers. By saying "inferior" I introduce the idea of relativity—the practical outcome of an intuition of the shaman's type may be equal to that of the above mentioned "thinkers"; but considering the amount of knowledge among the Tungus and other groups, the "thinkers" would occupy an inferior position in their ethnical and ethnographical complex. Thus the shaman's intuition, as a method of reaching "truth", would be much superior to that of the "thinkers", when it relates to the existing Tungus knowledge.

133. SPECIAL METHODS Besides the common methods—simple logical method and intuition—the shamans use special methods for an intensification of the perception and imaginative thinking, and for an intensification of the intuition. These methods are: reading of thoughts, communication at a distance, auto-suggestive regulation of dreams, and extasy. All these methods in a lesser or greater degree are used by common people as well, but among the shamans these methods have become an essential condition of their art.

In preceding chapters I have already given some facts observed among the Tungus and Manchu, which point to the existence of reading of thoughts. I have admitted the possibility of such a reading which is not based upon a system of inferences made from facts, but seemingly is a direct communication, probably by means of a special kind of physical waves. For the time being the existence of these "waves" is a mere hypothesis, but this may be, at least temporarily, admitted, for the phenomena of "reading of thoughts" in a great number of cases cannot be understood as the result of mere "intuition" or coincidence—a parallelism of thought in two individuals. This peculiarity is not characteristic of all shamans, some of whom may use it in a lesser degree, others in a greater one; but all of them make this attempt. Communication at a distance is apparently based upon the same physical condition. The shamans attain it by different methods, namely, they may do it in their dreams, during the extasy, or in a "normal"

state of concentration on a "desire" in which they "think strongly". In all these cases the shamans say that they "send the soul" with a communication. It must be pointed out that this can be better done during the night, i.e. exactly during the period good for transmission of waves, undisturbed by sun rays. Another condition must not be forgotten, namely, the shamans attain extasy much more easily in the dark. On the other hand, the perception of communication made at a distance is often symbolized in the form of animals which make the communication to those who perceive. The animals—e.g. bear, dog, snake—appear either in dreams (in a sleeping state) or in hallucinations (among the Birarčen). However, these communications may be perceived also in the form of voices heard, or may remain undescribed: "I want to do it, for the shaman wants it; I feel so", the Tungus say. Finally, there may be no perception at all, but the communication may be received unconsciously and will be followed by the acts implied by the communication. The shamans assert that they communicate at a distance with each other, when they are friendly, and they communicate and fight, when they are hostile. The analysis of some of these cases is extremely difficult, for it is not easy to determine whether the communication at a distance was a real one or not. Indeed, parallelism of thought and emotion is a common occurrence. Moreover, there are cases when two individuals (one of them a shaother, nor the occasion on which the communication is made, man or both of them shamans) do not know about each e.g. in the urgent cases when a shaman wants to have the assistance of another shaman and calls him. The nature of these phenomena is not clear, but I do not venture to deny them and to reject them under the pretext of lack of "rationalization".

The communication at a distance and the reading of thoughts are powerful means of abbreviation of the process of cognition which is widely used by the shamans.

The methods of dreams and extasy are of a special character, but they serve the same purpose and are a perfection of means of cognition.

As a rule, the shamans have recourse to dreams, when they have difficult cases or when they have to perform shamanizing. However, the shamans sleep with different purposes. As has been shown, some of them, especially the Manchu shamans, also Goldi ones, according to the description of I. A. Lopatin, go to sleep before the performance, and the spirits are supposed to come into them during the sleep. The Northern Tungus shamans also sleep, but extasy comes later. From the last fact, it is evident that sleep is generally needed for a certain purpose which is, as far as I can see, a rest needed before a performance. However, the awakening in a state of extasy is also not a pure and simple ritualism (though it may be included in the ritualism, as well), but the reaching of extasy in a half-conscious state is easier, and therefore the shamans sleep before the performance. It is different with the cases when the shamans want to cognize, to solve various problems in the state of sleep. The mechanism of this method, as far as I can see it, is described below.

As is known, sleep is not a definite unvariable physiological condition, but it shows different degrees of interruption of psychic functions, beginning with a complete elimination of all physiological functions of perception and a complete arrest of the complex of mental work, up to a partial elimination of a few elements. Indeed, in so far as "mental work" is concerned, there may be also different degrees of its arrest. However, by the side of illogical dream-constructions there may be and, as an observed fact, there are dreams which are free of an illogical character; they are perfectly logical, but with the introduction of imaginative elements, sometimes conditioned by the physiological complex. Thus they may appear illogical not in their construction, but in their final result. One of the important conditions of dreams is that the usual, "ethnographical", complex of thinking, because of a partial elimination of this sphere of the psychomental complex in sleep, may leave the thinking machine to go ahead with the solution of problems presented by a new situation, some elements of which are not included in the ethnographical complex of thinking and therefore cannot be solved within the limits of this complex. When the thinking machine is free from the influence of the acting complex, it may do its work still better, especially if several links are lacking. This is a commonly used method of leaving the solution of difficult problems to the time after a sleep, either at night or in the day-time. Indeed, this may be interpreted as the necessity of a rest for successfully carrying out a mental work, but every one who does this, intentionally or unintentionally, knows that in dreams one may have a continuation of his daily mental work and sometimes finds solutions of difficult problems, which come suddenly, either in dreams or in the first moments of awakening. Yet, if one faces a difficult problem which cannot be solved, the latter is often set aside, so to say banished, from the consciousness, and it may be solved—the process of solution remaining unnoticed—in the "strata of subconsciousness". In all these cases the aim is the same, namely, to suppress for a time the influence of the acting ethnographical complex of thinking. When checking is needed and when presentation of the result of the act of such a thinking is required, the lacking links must be introduced. Thus this method does not essentially differ from the "subconscious thinking", and the question is only about the creation of favourable conditions for such thinking. The shamans have adopted this method as an established and recognized one, regularly used when needed, and they explain it by means of the existing hypotheses and theories concerning the spirits. So that this method is not only non-inhibited, but its use is justified and rationalized. It should be noted here that the shamans may receive a "revelation" in a direct form of a definite statement, or as in the case of communication at a distance, it may be expressed by some special symbolization. The shamans are therefore very careful with the analysis of "dreams", some of which they consider as a "revelation", while the others consider them as mere "dreaming" and have different terms for these two different kinds of dreams. The Manchu shamans sometimes go to sleep only for half an hour and they receive a revelation from the spirits. The Manchu expression is *vočko solimb'e* i.e. to "invite spirits".

The extasy, in so far as the creation of special favourable conditions of the thinking process is concerned, is only a means. The mechanism is that there occurs a partial elimination of perception and a total or partial elimination of the influence of the existing ethnographical complex of thinking, so that the intuition and imaginative thinking meet with no hindrance, or this hindrance is reduced to the possible minimum. However, since the extasy in shamanism plays quite a distinct role and its aim does not consist only

in the creation of favourable conditions for thinking I shall treat it in a special section.

134. EXTASY In the shamanistic performances I have observed different forms or degrees of extasy, so that it is not a phenomenon which may be defined in a rigid simple formula. In some cases it comes near to a condition which may be regarded as a simple hysterical fit, and in another extremity of variations it is a conventionalized ritualism in which the shaman's psychomental complex does not differ from that of his common behaviour—he is only a "performer".

First I shall give a description of the condition of the shaman during the performance, where there is no hysterical fit and when he is not simply a "performer".

In the description of performances we have seen that the shaman may start the performance after a sleep, during which the spirit comes into him, evidently as a continuation of his state during the sleep, when elements which constitute his "normal" state were, at least partially, eliminated. In his condition the *shaman believes that the spirit is in him* and he acts and thinks as though the spirits were acting. Such a state is known to all those who can assimilate a different complex to such a degree that they may be able to describe it (this complex) in all details, and to act as persons who have this complex. Great dramatic and operatic artists, as well as great musicians, assume the complexes as they are known or as they are understood by them. "Talented" writers-psychologists, e.g. of the type of Dostoevsky, assume the complexes created by them (they may be stimulated by the realities, as well) and when they write and go into details, they only record their own states. A writer-photographer can also give a picture, but such a picture would not be "alive" and in the majority of cases would appear to be an "artificial creation". From psychiatry we know of cases of doubling personalities, and "splitting of a personality" into several personalities. Such a state may assume so heavy forms that the person affected by these conditions may become unable to act as a "normal" member of the community. The condition of abnormality consists in the fact that they do not assume other complexes at their will and do not change them at will, but the complexes "come" by themselves. There are also different degrees of eclipsing other complexes: when a talented writer assumes a complex to be described, he does not lose his power of recording, as if he were an observer from the outside. In the case of "doubling" one of the personalities may carry out an observation on the other personality, and even "fight" it. A good reason for the existence of "good" and "evil" spirits is conditioned by such a doubling of personalities, for which state the spirits serve as a mere justification and at the same time also as a means to neutralize harmful effects. The behaviour of persons affected by hysteria is of the same nature: it is supposed that, when there is a fit, the person must act according to a certain scheme, and the person, unconsciously and sometimes consciously, acts in the direction of bringing himself into a psychomental and physiological state in which such an acting would be possible; as known, this is neither easy, nor always physically pleasant. Moreover, a hysterical fit can socially disable the person, temporarily or permanently, and hysterical persons, in normal conditions of their lives, are also unable to control themselves. However, there is no absolute elimination of all elements of consciousness and perception; some of them function well during the fit.*

In the shaman's extasy the degree of doubling and elimination of elements of consciousness, as well as the breaking of the existing ethnographical complex, are variable. However, there are limits on both sides, namely, the shaman's state must not turn into an uncontrolled hysterical fit and he must not suppress extasy; in fact, hysterical fits and suppressing of extasy do not permit to produce an involuntary self-expression of the doubles (spirits) and to render a freedom to the intuitive thinking. Within these limits various degrees of intensity and effectiveness of extasy, may be distinguished. For producing such a state the shaman must possess special psychomental conditions. First of all, he must have the ability of doubling, perhaps even splitting personality, he must have a certain power of controlling his thinking mechanism, he must know methods of bringing himself into this state, and methods of maintaining and regulating this state as long as it is required for practical purposes of the performance, and always considering the presence of an audience and the aims of the performance.

A shaman who cannot produce the needed effects of extasy is considered as a bad shaman; persons in whom an extasy turns into a fit (who cannot control themselves) are considered as possessed by the spirits and therefore cannot become shamans—they must be treated; while those who cannot produce a real extasy cannot become shamans, but may become "clan priests", i.e. performers of sacrifices and prayers.

Physiological and psychic conditions of the shaman during the extasy reveal some interesting phenomena connected with the state, but it will be necessary first to give details as to the methods of producing a state of extasy.

We have seen that this may happen during the sleep,

so that evidently we have here a case of strong self-suggestion, bringing about an action during the state of partial unconsciousness. However, a great number of shamans, even if they perform a "sleeping" before the extasy, practise preliminary acts for bringing themselves into extasy. At the beginning the shaman drums, continually increasing and decreasing the tempo and the intensity, with a definite rhythm empirically discovered, in order to produce a physiological and psychic state in which a suggestion—the coming of a spirit—made by the shaman himself, may have an immediate effect of "doubling". As soon as the spirit is introduced, the shaman must only maintain his state.

This is achieved by the continuous drumming, performed by the shaman himself or by the assistants, and the influence of the audience, which is "helping" the shaman by keeping the rhythm and intensifying the shaman's extasy by impressing him with their singing. Several shamans told me that they cannot perform, if there is no audience. One of them has clearly formulated: "all people present helped me to go to the lower world" (the Barguzin Tungus). We have seen that the audience is also continuously influenced by the shaman, so that a permanent current of influences, radiated by the shaman, is formed, accepted and intensified by a great number of individuals and sent back to the shaman for his further excitement. Whether we understand this state of the shaman—his relations with the audience, mutual hypnosis, suggestion, or even, in a physical form, as peculiar waves, the direct mutual influence of a continuous excitement is such, that the shaman and the audience become a complex—the shaman's extasy is maintained. For this reason the shamans do not like the presence of "spectators" who do not participate in this action. However, they do not object to the presence of persons who do not belong to the shaman's clan, even to such as belong to other ethnical groups, provided they do not destroy the harmony, of the shaman's audience.*

---

* Among the Tungus, as well as among other groups which play with the complex of "doubling personality", the latter may assume quite dangerous dimensions of a mass psychosis. As a matter of fact, examples taken "from life" are not always equally understood and therefore they are not equally convincing. In spite of this I shall now give a parallel widely observed among very distinct ethnical units of our days. After the discovery of the "pathological condition of doubling personality", professionally known to the psychiatrists, this "theme" has gradually penetrated among the laymen, first through the professional novelists and journalists, who used it with success as a "modern and interesting problem", and later through the vulgarizations of "talkies and movies". The effect of this "movement" is twofold. A part of youth finds a good justification for their acting contrarily to the existing "patterns" of social behaviour, but they remain "normal", while another part is actually disabled, being affected almost in the same manner as it was with the "classical hysteria". Perhaps, I should mention a third group, probably the most numerous, which is composed of youth who imagine themselves "doubled", but who are actually following a mere fashion, in order "to be up-to-date". Of course, by keeping their minds busy with useless things and pernicious experiments, they naturally make harm to themselves and thereby to the society where they live. The effects are still heavier when adult members of the society are affected by the same "movement". Ethnologically speaking, more parasites are living on this fashion, than on the hysteria of olden days. As the latter was passively regarded, the new fashion is now commonly regarded as a mere "literary movement", "modern psychology", etc. "due to the complexity of modern life", while actually it is one of the effects of the half-disintegrated organization of social control and a consequence of successful propaganda of mass-psychosis. Of course, this is only one of many other harmful instances, lately produced by "civilised mankind" and taken for granted as a "normal phenomenon".

* The state of the shaman, in so far as the audience may influence him, may be compared, but in a very rough manner, with that of a speaker who may establish a connexion with the audience, i.e. the audience may follow him and he can see it in the changing expression of faces. With every new thought thrown to the audience he gets new stimuli for the continuation of his connexion—he penetrates into the psychomental complex of the audience, and the audience penetrates into his complex. However, if there are too many dull persons who cannot follow the speaker, who cannot understand him, who remain either indifferent or manifest their scepticism, they cannot penetrate the speaker's complex and they deprive the speaker of stimuli. Indeed this is well known to all "speakers" and to the audience, as a means of "putting the speaker down". It should be noted here, that in a great number of cases such listeners quite consciously, because of various reasons which have nothing to do with the aim of the "speaker" to be understood, obstruct the formation of connexion; but there is a still greater number of sceptics who do this because of their fear of the speaker, whose complex they do not want to understand, for fear it may eclipse their own one. The scepticism is rather characteristic of the mentally weak individuals who use obstinacy as a self-protective armour and refuse to understand other people. In shamanistic performances, particularly in the extasy, the connexion between the shaman and the audience is still greater, and a hostile (sceptical) attitude is especially dangerous. In shamanistic performances this element is also represented by foreigners, e.g. Russian gold-mine workmen in Transbaikalia, and "modernized" Chinese in Manchuria, who do not understand the essentials of the shamanistic performance, who fear being influenced by it and who assume a hostile attitude of irony, supposed to be superior. (As a matter of fact in the descriptions of ethnographers we also meet, rather often, with this attitude). Indeed, such individuals are a disturbing factor in the performance and they are not welcome.

The rhythmic dancing has the same effect, both for calling in the spirits and for maintaining them. The costume producing a complex noise is also used with the same aim. I have observed cases among the Manchus and other Tungus, when without the costume the shaman could not produce extasy. The shamans sometimes create in themselves a state, in which they want to perform (produce extasy), and thus can maintain extasy. Two methods are widely used, namely, smoking tobacco and drinking wine. However, the shamans usually neither smoke nor drink before the performance; but it is done when they change spirits and additional excitability is required, or when the shaman is tired. Usually these are supposed to be spirits which want to smoke or drink, but sometimes the shaman may do it in between two spirits. The smoking may be made either with an ordinary tobacco pipe, several of which the shaman may smoke quickly and without interruption—I have seen five and even six pipes smoked one after another. The shaman may also breathe the smoke of laedum palustrum or any other plant with a pleasant smell (all conifers are used), or even Chinese incense (among the groups which can get them, e.g. the Manchus, the Dahurs, and rarely the Tungus of Manchuria). The same effect is produced by the taking of alcoholic drinks, such as Russian vodka and Chinese wine. A strong person may drink more than a bottle of vodka during his performance. In some cases the shamans abstain from drinking, for they say that drinking does not help but makes them weaker.* As a matter of fact, when the shaman oversteps the limit of drinking needed for maintaining extasy, or as a stimulant, when he is tired, he may become intoxicated to such a degree that no extasy can be maintained. The audience would laugh seeing a drunken shaman.

During the extasy the shamans (I have observed several female-shamans) very often weep, so that the face is covered with pouring tears (Barguzin Tungus, Birarčen). The pulse is very fast, but at the moment of deep extasy, when the shaman's soul is supposed to be in the other world, the pulse slows down and becomes weaker and sometimes can be felt with difficulty (I have a great number of observations among all groups). However, when the shamans merely ritualize, there is no such effect on the pulse.

According to the shamans, they feel an extreme lightness of the body during the extasy. This feeling is seemingly also communicated to the sick persons, for the Manchus assert that when during the performance the shaman steps on the person lying on the ground, the shaman is felt to be very light. In fact the feeling of lightness, or in other words, the increase of strength, is a common phenomenon. As stated, the costume may weigh over thirty kilograms. Such a weight is not easy to wear, though it be evenly distributed on the body. An old woman, I saw one day among the Birarčen, could not lift it up and was literally unable to move, when the costume was put on her. However, when the spirit entered her, she moved with ease and at a tremendous speed. In another case I observed a shaman of eighty-six years who was half deaf and half blind (he could not walk alone and, being blind, shamanized at daylight) ; he was so weak that he could not move with-

out being supported and was usually helped to mount his reindeer. The costume was extremely heavy (the old shaman gradually gathered a great number of iron parts)— weighing about forty kilograms by my estimation—and the old man, when dressed, lay on the ground until the spirits came in. Then there was a sudden transformation: he jumped and danced like a youth, his voice was as strong as that of his niece who was shamanizing with him.

In a great number of performances I saw shamans leap without a running start, or from the spot where they were standing (the wigwams being too small), which cannot be performed by the most able Tungus sportsmen, even without the additional weight of the costume. The Tungus assert that the shamans sometimes touch with their heads the upper smoke aperture of the wigwam, at a height of over three metres. I have not seen this (and this may be mere hallucination on the part of the Tungus!), but I have seen them jump to the height of about one metre. Indeed, for doing so there must be an enormous tension of muscles. The weight of shaman's costume is also an interesting fact which throws a special light. In fact, the weight of the costume must hinder the shaman in producing his extasy, so the shaman must make a special additional effort for neutralizing the inhibitive influence of the extra-weight. If the shaman cannot reach an extasy he cannot perform—the costume is too heavy; a heavy costume requires a further increase of extasy. In fact the shaman-beginners usually have light costumes, while the old experienced shamans have very heavy costumes. The Tungus say that a young shaman cannot wear a heavy costume. Among the Manchus, whose forms of shamanizing have been, especially lately, established, as well as among the Dahurs, the costume is not very heavy.

One of the shamans (the Birarčen) told me that each time when the spirit enters he feels very hot and there is a loud noise in the ears, he is unable to understand himself and cannot remember what the spirit says. This feeling of heat is seemingly a general phenomenon, for I myself felt the shamans to be much hotter during the performance (before their swift moving dance).

Among other curious phenomena the case of "sudden pregnancy" already discussed (vide supra p. 338) is to be noted. The assistant shaman is asked to "examine" the abdomen of the shaman; when the spirit leaves the female shaman, the abdomen assumes its former shape. The shamans also produce various experiments, e.g. by wounding themselves, bleeding, burning etc. without any harmful effects. The Tungus say that the shaman may cut his chest with a knife and the next day there will be only a red mark.* The shaman sits and after long concentration blood begins to drop from his forehead. The operation with hot iron, charcoal, etc. produces only a slight effect—on the next morning the hands are red, but not burnt. I have not observed myself these cases, but the Tungus assert that "good shamans" do it quite often.

---

* Among the Birarčen I once observed a female shaman who consumed a great quantity of Chinese wine, and the performance was a failure.

* In this connexion I wish to quote Gmelin's account (cf. Reise, etc. Vol. II pp. 493-497) of his and Miller's experiment with a shaman (Yakut, female) who was compelled by them to perforate her abdomen with a knife. These naïve travellers wanted to convince the Yakuts, that the shamans are cheating them. However, the wound which was so large that the omentum protruded (it was cut off, cooked and eaten by the shaman who was perfectly certain of a good end of her experiment), after two dressings, with resin and birch bark, was healed on the sixth day.

Spirits, the introduction of which may permit shamans to do this, are called by the special term *balbuka* (Bir.).

If we leave aside doubtful facts, there will remain my own observations which clearly show that the physical power of a shaman increases enormously, that his physiological state is not like that of normal people. Extasy requires enormous energy, so that all shamans, whom I observed and who really had been in extasy, were unable to move after the performance and were covered with perspiration; the pulse was weak and slow, the breathing was rare and shallow. Some of them were in a state of half-consciousness, while at certain moments they might have been unconscious.

The Tungus say that during the shamanizing, especially when the shaman goes to the lower world, the death of the shaman may suddenly occur. Such cases, sometimes with details, were related to me on various occasions among all groups, except the Manchus. The Tungus explain that the shaman dies because his soul cannot return (the sign of its coming back is restoration of consciousness), being stopped on the way by other spirits and even by other shamans. Therefore special measures must be taken for calling back his soul, by all possible means. For this reason the shamanizing to the lower world is very rarely performed. The fact itself is not incredible, for if the shaman's heart is not strong enough and if he has, for instance, arteriosclerosis or other similar troubles, which require a quiet behaviour, death may occur because of the effort made during the performance. On the other hand, if cases of voluntary death are known among other ethnical groups (e.g. Australians violating taboo), the shaman's condition may be of the same type: he is convinced that his soul is captured and cannot return and he arrests the normal functioning of the heart and the breathing, the lowering of which is actually observed during certain moments of the performance. Among the Reindeer Tungus of Transbaikalia this form of shamanizing is believed to be so dangerous that there are very few shamans who perform it, and only once in three years or so.

The analysis of the shaman's psychology during the extasy and in ordinary time shows that, in so far as the shaman is concerned, the performance is only a special means to create a special condition which liberates the shaman's "thinking machine" from the influence of the existing mode of thinking. However, the shaman must remain on the dividing line between the state of "nervous" fit and perfect consciousness. The function of the assistant may now be better understood. The assistant really helps and directs the shaman's mental process by asking him questions, only partially perceived by the shaman who must not be brought back to complete consciousness. The assistant must also interpret, for the shaman usually does not remember what he has said, when the extasy is over and the persons who are not experienced cannot understand him.

The state of extasy is probably very pleasant, for as a rule the shamans like to shamanize with extasy, and sometimes they look for an occasion. Indeed, it should be kept in mind that the shamans, being socially needed, may have a social impulse to perform, as is actually rather often observed; but the cases when the shaman, being alone, brings himself into a state of extasy are very frequent, although not with all shamans. It seems to me that the shamans need extasy on the same ground as the hysterically behaving persons from time to time want to have a fit, and the persons liable to the state of creative extasy, e.g.

poets, good musicians and others, want to have a "creative mood". The shamans say that before a performance, when none had been carried out for a long time, they feel "heaviness in the heart and head" which may grow into a feeling of discomfort and even pain. Yet, on the next day, after the performance, they feel themselves "light and pleasant" i.e. exactly as may be observed in the above compared states.*

It should also be pointed out that sometimes the shamans prepare themselves for shamanizing (extasy) by fasting during a certain period (given hours and days). This practice is known among the Manchus. Into the same group of phenomena may be included the limitation of sexual intercourse among the Manchus. However, these limitations may be a result of further application of the theory of spirits, as well as having some connexion with the physiological and psychological state of the shaman. Indeed, the fasting and abstaining from sexual intercourse are only rarely observed, and they are rather individual methods. In some individual cases the fasting and the refusal of certain kinds of food was explained to me as a method of making the extasy easier. I should say, in these cases we have merely an alleviation of the stomach from undigested food. In fact, some kinds of food can be more or less easily assimilated. But some shamans explain this as a result of a special revelation of the spirits, which is a mere "rationalization".**

There are also special conditions when the shamans do not want to shamanize. As a matter of fact, they refuse rather often, especially great shamanizing. As shown, at least among some groups, a shamanizing to the lower world may be performed only once in three years. The shamans may refuse, in case they do not like the people personally, when they are too tired, or if a performance had been recently carried out. In all such cases the shaman would give as a reason that the spirits would not work. In the same line comes the abstaining from performance during

---

* I give here a case which I observed in minute details. A Manchu (details of some interest regarding his activity vide SONT pp. 113 et seq.) pretended to be a shaman of his clan (sakda), but he was not recognized. A man, rather healthy, inclined to good food and drinking, of a muscular complex, as a rule rather quiet, without being indifferent towards the milieu, was under observation several months, practically every day. From time to time he had a desire to shamanize, and then was not as in his usual mood; he became self-concentrated, excitable, of changing mood. On one of such occasions we advised him to go ahead, since he wanted to know through the spirits what was going on in his family (though his connexion with his family was very loose). Then we procured a drum and bought some Chinese incense sticks. When everything was ready, he himself objected: "All this is useless, the spirit will not come". After a moral support on our part he decided to make a trial. At first he trembled and drummed, then the spirit came. He gnashed his teeth, took in his mouth burning incense (supposed to be the "spirit of fire") furiously crying out "kékʉ, kékʉ". Before the spirit left, the man had a second "fit" (trembling etc.) and heavily breathing remained for a while lying on the stove-bed. After taking a rest he was very joyful and happy and declared that he had found what he wanted to know. This case is interesting, for the man was not a shaman, but he performed an extasy which, as far as I could see, was merely a nervous fit, but performed according to a certain model.

** The analysis of the rare cases when shamans of different groups abstain from food is subject to great variations as to the reasons and kinds. No generalization is possible, except that probably the shamans with a poor digestion like to have their stomachs empty. The same is true in reference to the quantity of narcotics, alcoholics and smoking.

the menstrual period, pregnancy and during a certain period after the delivery. In such cases an explanation is given: the spirits do not like *jatka* (Manchu) or *ak'ipču* (Tungus) women. However, the Tungus and Manchu theories as to the spirits can be easily reconciled with this state of women—and it is done in other cases—while the real cause seems to be the impossibility for the shaman to bring herself into extasy and carry out a performance, when she is in a particular physiological condition, or when she is not yet strong enough after childbirth. It seems to me that the theory of spirits is mere rationalization on the part of the shamans, while actually during such a state the female shaman may be physically tired and, as known, may be more liable than usually to nervous fits, so that the extasy might turn into fit.

Another psychologically interesting condition is that the shamanizing (including real or supposed extasy) must be justified, i.e. there must be some "reasons" for shamanizing. As shown before, such "reasons" are help to the people, chiefly clansmen, so that for bringing himself into the state of extasy, when the shaman himself does not want to shamanize, there must be some reason, a stimulus.

I shall now give the description of a case which is interesting from various points of view. A Birarčen female shaman was asked by us to perform her shamanizing for making a phonographic record.* After a rather insistent request on our part, the shaman consented and was willing to do it. The chief objection on her part was that there were no sick people and there was no other reason for shamanizing. Then it was decided to make a sacrifice to the spirit of nine cups of millet and a bottle of "red wine" (a solution of alcohol coloured red and sweetened with sugar). The shaman was dressed as for a regular shamanizing. She tried to call a spirit, which did arrive, but protested against being disturbed without any serious reason—for jest. The angry spirit even used "bad words". In spite of that she was able to bring herself into the state of extasy, during which she wept and sang in a most doleful manner. After this there was a sudden change of mood which manifested itself in a violent forte presto. In fact, it was very difficult for her to bring herself into a genuine extasy, although she wanted it.

To complete the picture of this phenomenon it must be noted that, when the shaman becomes more experienced he does not always use his ability of bringing himself into extasy; he uses this method, so to say, economically. However, since the ceremonial of the performance is carefully observed by the shaman for influencing the listeners and people who need his attendance, the latter do not notice that there is no real extasy. Naturally young shamans cannot do this without a long practice and the penetration into the psychology of the audience. This may be compared with the performance of an artist who does not "feel" the part he is performing, but knowing all details of psychological effect of his performance, acts with perfect deliberation. The same is being done by experienced speakers who control the audience by a series of witticisms etc.**

135. SHAMAN AND SPIRITS We have already seen that the relations between the shaman and the spirits may be defined as those between "master" and "servants". However, such are the relations only when the shaman is really a good and strong person, while a weak person may easily become the prey and an instrument of the spirits.

There is no doubt that from the point of view of the shaman's psychology there are two main types of spirits. There are spirits which actually are various mental and psychological conditions which the shaman needs for his performance of social functions and for his own use, when ordinary methods of thinking are not sufficient for solving various problems. There are also spirits which symbolize conditions of psychic disfunction, and which ought to be "mastered" by the shaman, if he is not to become susceptible to the harmful conditions of various psychoses.

In the description of the history of shamans we have seen that the shaman may begin his life career with a psychosis, but he cannot carry on his functions, if he does not master spirits, or, as has been shown, does not master himself.

By such an approach to shamanism, in so far as the psychology of the shaman is concerned, I leave aside all earlier explanations as to the shamans' psychic condition, which were mostly the result of aprioristic reasoning based on the principle of analogy. These are theories of no interest, except that they depict the European complex. However, there is a new theory which deserves special attention, because of its recent and scientific, in appearance, form. Here I have in view L. Sternberg's theory of the sexual character of the shamanistic complex, generalized up to covering shamanism as a whole and disclosing similarity between ethnographically most remote phenomena. L. Sternberg's "Divine Election in Primitive Religion" was first promoted by the observation of a Goldi shaman who confessed about his sexual dreams to L. Sternberg who says: "the sexual motive of Election in shamanism, a matter so simple and natural to the mind of primitive man, never occurred to me before having met the Goldi Shamans" (p. 481). So we can start from the original point, i.e. the Goldi.

According to L. Sternberg there are assistant spirits and supreme spirit who elect the shaman, whence another question arises as to the 'intimate relation between the elected person and the electing spirit, the problem of the motives, why a certain spirit fixes his choice upon a certain individual and becomes his patron and helper" (op. cit. p. 475). It is evident that a distinction between assistant spirit and supreme spirit is introduced, a distinction which contains an answer—the character of the spirit—"supreme" is presumed, and thence another conclusion as to "choice" is made, further modified and identified with "election", where the conception of "patron and helper" is only natural. All these elements, as "election", "supreme", and "patron", are absolutely alien to the Tungus conception, and the actual key of the theory resides in the first quotation,

---

* At those days I used an ordinary Edison phonograph which was not a very convenient apparatus for recording. It should be noted that our relations with this shaman were very good, sincere and friendly. She was always willing to give me all possible details as to herself and as to her art of shamanism, which permitted me to approach her with such a request.

** Some old professors in their lectures repeat from year to year the same "witticism and tricks"—sometimes even published

ones!—so that the students who are not deprived of humour sometimes begin to laugh before the regular "wits and tricks" are performed. This may be regarded as an artless imitation of real artists turning it into a simple performance, which produces no effect upon the audience. Shamans lacking talent and imagination, as well as ability to control an audience are met with among the Tungus. However, the Tungus regard them as bad performers, and, of course, as poor shamans.

when a whole construction is built up. A guess and a scaffolding of facts supposed to support it!

The fact recorded is a case of a young male shaman who becomes lover of one of the spirits, which also becomes the principal spirit of the shaman. L. Sternberg especially stresses that the spirit is called *ájami*, while other spirits are called *syven* (I have some doubt as to the transcription; cf. *supra* p. 160). However, there is nothing particular in this fact. What is designated by *ajami* has been shown by P. Šimkevič and I. A. Lopatin as the chief spirit which is the head of groups of spirits, i.e. exactly what we have seen in the Manchu complex. Naturally, in every particular case of individual shamans, all depends on which group of spirits is mastered by the shaman. The investigators of Goldi have shown that any group may be so mastered and there will be at the head of a group—usually a series of shaman manifestations—an *ajami* (cf. P. Šimkevič, op. cit. "Materials"). Therefore there may be different *ajami*. Moreover, the Goldi term *ajami* is not applied only to these spirits (cf. e.g. I. A. Lopatin, op. cit. p. 314 and many others)—*ajami fon'alko* figures as a placing for the spirit of a deceased person. Exactly the same situation is observed among the Manchus and Tungus. The first mastered spirit, which helps to master the other spirits, naturally holds a special position in the group of mastered spirits. The term *ajami*, in which *m'i* is a suffix, is perhaps not unknown in northern Tungus dialects in which it appears as *aja(n)~haja*. However, I do not insist upon the parallels. In Manchu such a spirit would be called *dalaxa vočko*, and it is not a "supreme spirit" and "patron".

Now the question is: whether the first spirit is always of an opposite sex or not? L. Sternberg wants it to be so and he gathers facts from various sources, and even from different groups. In the first place he quotes my earlier publication in Russian ("Essay", etc.) in which I have given a brief account of the "election" of a new shaman, already related in the preceding chapter (*vide supra* Section 131). As a matter of fact, the female candidate was rejected exactly on the ground that *she was possessed by the spirit of her lover*, but did not master it, and she was considered as an abnormal person who cannot become shaman. L. Sternberg has omitted this important condition, but he puts emphasis on sexual symptoms of the hysterical fit described. Then, puting stress on the statement of a shaman (p. 478), who was a beginner and did not speak good Russian* and who was evidently affected by some sexual trouble, L. Sternberg asserts that another shaman had a female spirit too, and proceeds to another generalization: the movements of a shaman have a sexual character when he is dancing (p. 481). Really such an enquiry is not easy when it is carried out in a foreign language and during a short stay with the people.** L. Sternberg, being

carried away by his imagination, could not see the simple fact that without moving the lower part of the trunk to and fro one cannot produce sounds of the trinkets, but these movements can have a sexual meaning only in a mind affected by an idée fixe. Practically all of these evidences were gathered among the Manchus, and the Goldi. As to other facts gathered among the Yakuts and Buriats, they need very careful scrutinizing before being used as evidence* and naturally, first of all, a detailed investigation on the spot is needed. I leave aside other evidences brought forth by L. Sternberg, for they are selected as regards their nature and thus a strictly scientific generalization is not possible.** However, I am far from the idea of denying a possibility of such occurrences in some ethnical groups, as a general phenomenon, and as exceptional cases among the Manchus and Tungus. For instance, in the case related

man who fooled him, refusing to sing into the phonograph, saying that "the ajami may kill me for doing it", which was absurd, since the spirit was mastered. L. Sternberg accepted this as bona fide (L. Sternberg, op. cit. p. 479). Probably the greater part of the time this shaman was drunk, for L. Sternberg says "he is always drunk" (ibid). Indeed, an inquiry lasting several hours and carried out by an official (such was in the eyes of the shaman L. Sternberg's position) is not a sure method, even if the investigator does not suggest the answers in his questions. Still less reliable is this method of getting information from a drunken man who in such a state may tell anything which is required of him. Indeed, it was "required", for L. Sternberg by that time already possessed his discovery of sexual motives conceived after the inquiry of the first shaman.

* However, apparently, after an insistent inquiry, L. Sternberg obtained some information from an old Yakut woman who decades ago had left her own people, had married a Russian political exile and investigator of the Yakuts, and had been living over twenty years in St. Petersburg with her husband. This woman was used as a source of information about things she had known in her youth. She was, doubtless, influenced by the eminent colleagues of her husband and might unintentionally have given a description, as she had been desired to give. First of all, it is necessary to examine carefully the question whether, in the Yakut complex, the spirits are "mastered" by the shaman, or the latter is "mastered" by them. Secondly, the kinds of spirits must be distinguished and they must not be mixed up. The spirits abasy, which can be both male and female ones, are by no means shamanistic spirits, while münärik means only "psychically abnormal" people (as well as their souls). The only spirits of shamanistic complex are the ämägät, which can be of different sexes or of no sex, and which may even belong to distinct ethnical groups (cf. E. Pekarskiĭ, Dictionary, "ämägät", e.g. Tungus). It is really impossible to rely upon the statement of an old, half "disethnicized" woman. Still more it is dangerous to rely upon a statement of a Buriat informer who, for winning the sympathy of his eminent protectors, pretended to be a shaman, and, being a real "arriviste", knew perfectly well what his protectors expected from him—the confirmation of their theories. G. D. Sanžeev (cf. "Darxaty". Ethnographical Report on a Journey in Mongolia in 1927", Ac. S., 1930 St. Petersburg; also "Weltanschauung und Schamanismus der Alaren-Burjaten", in Anthropos, Vol. XIII, pp. 538-560) gives some facts showing that the sexual moment may and may not play a rôle in the fate of a candidate to shamanship. Sometimes candidates are also simply "elected" by the lamas (Darxats, p. 457), who use the shaman's art for themselves.

** I want to point out that W. G. Bogoras has found among the Chukchis that the shamans are called enenelit, which exactly means "those possessing a shaman spirit", which presumes no election. After quoting W. Jochelson as to the love relations with the spirits, L. Sternberg remarks, "unfortunately Jochelson does not give us any information, as to whether this spirit is identical with the shaman's beloved spirit of the female sex" (op. cit., p. 489), by which he leaves an impression in the reader's mind that there is such a "beloved spirit". The fact itself is not yet demonstrative of "election" on a sexual ground, but it only points to the liability of the shamans to sexual dreams.

* A great number of shamanistic conceptions cannot be translated into Russian, even by myself, while L. Sternberg did not know the Goldi language, which I know to be the fact, and which is moreover clear from his questions.

** Cf. J. P. Alkor (Koškin) [L. J. Sternberg as Tungusologist, in "At the memory of L. J. Sternberg 1861-1927" published by the Academy of Sciences, Sketches on history of knowledge. Fasc. VII, 1930] who has used the diary of L. Sternberg, relates that this investigator saw the first shaman only once and "pressed with questions (in Russian it is still stronger: don'imal—"vexed", "pressed"!!) during long hours, in the result of which he succeeded in clearing up the problem of the relations of the shaman with his spirits" (p. 141). Not longer were his meetings with another shaby me, the female candidate *might have become shaman*, and thus she would be possessed by a male spirit (not mastering him) on a perfectly sexual ground. However, in so far as the Tungus and Manchus are concerned, no generalization of this kind is possible and no condition of "election by the spirits" is observed among these shamans. So the new theory ought not to be extended to the groups here discussed.

———————

In the previous description (*vide* Section 128) we have seen which are the preliminary conditions for becoming shaman. Such ones may be a mass psychoses which affect a great number of clansmen, or a limited number of them. As a matter of fact, if there is a delay in the "election" of a new shaman, the psychosis may affect a very great number of clansmen. Yet, the extent of psychosis depends also upon the character of the group connected with the spirit. There are cases when the spirit is not recognized by all clansmen but only by a group, even a family (i.g. the case of the *wujala* clan; *vide supra* Section 131), so that only a very limited number of persons may be affected by a psychosis. Moreover, there may be individual cases of psychosis in which a person is usually affected by a newly discovered spirit, very often of a foreign origin (*dōna* among the Tungus of Manchuria). Indeed, such a foreign and individual spirit may become effective on other clansmen as well, and, as shown, it may even become a clan spirit. Lastly, there may be no psychosis sharply manifested, but a fear of its occurrence, which may stimulate "election" of a new shaman; moreover, there may be the need of a new shaman, as a regulator of the psychic life of the group (clan or territorial unit), and this will be sufficient to begin the "teaching" of a candidate for shamanship.

It is thus evident that from the very beginning different initial relations may be established between the spirits and the candidate to shamanship. There is no uniformity.

In case of mass psychosis, the candidates will, at least for a while, be mastered by the spirits and all of them, except one, will not be able to master the spirits, which is brought about by the idea of the existance of the clan shaman and by the idea that, being mastered by a person, the spirit will not harm other people.

In case of individual psychosis, according to the theory, the person is possessed by a spirit, and thus the mastering of the latter is one of the means of curing the candidate.

In case of mastering spirits for preventing them from doing harm to the candidate and other people, also for curing the person affected by a spirit, the candidate becomes at once a master of spirits.

One thing is evident: in all these cases, when the candidate becomes shaman he functions as "master" of spirits, which is expressed by the term *ejin~ějěn* of the Tungus dialects and in Manchu, and which can only be interpreted as "master". These relations are expressed in Manchu as *ějimbe k'iśalemb'e* (*ejen be kiĉelembi,* Manchu Writ.) i.e. the spirits are working for, their master.*

Indeed, in case of psychic troubles, due to unmastered spirits, the shaman actually masters himself, regulates his own psychomental complex, after which he is no more affected by the condition which was the initial cause of his becoming a shaman. The more he practises his art of self-control, the more spirits he masters; the more skill he acquires in the process of his practising, the more spirits (psychic conditions, or imaginary dangers) he masters.

Among the Tungus groups, at the beginning of a shaman's career, the shaman may have a very limited number of mastered spirits. Among them the first spirit, which comes into the candidate and which later on is used for taking control over other spirits, comes sometimes very rarely during the shaman's life and perhaps even only once in his life. For instance, among the Khingan Tungus a female shaman became shaman at the age of fifteen years when a female spirit introduced itself into her.* After that time, for twenty years, this spirit did not come, and perhaps, I was told, it would never come again. However, this is the greatest spirit of the shaman and it receives from time to time regular sacrifices.** Among the Kumarčen such a spirit is usually called *ogdiya sevey,* i.e. the greatest shamanistic spirit. However, *ogdiya* may also be referred to "good", "strong" spirits in general; the shaman will thus be called *ogdiya saman.* The same refers to the Birarčen. Among them I observed that the greater part of the shamans begin by possessing a complex *malu* which, as shown, is sexless. The female shamans in the beginning usually have only animal manifestations of this complex, namely, a lizard, a snake and a turtle which are simple manifestations used for hiding and travelling to distant places (an exteriorization of soul, i.e. "sublimation of the spirit", liberation etc.). The other manifestations of *malu* come later. For instance, as I have shown, a shaman beginner had only three spirits: a *malu,* a *kadarn'* and a *dōna* Manchu spirit. With the age and practice the number of spirits may increase up to more than thirty and, besides the clan spirits, there may be various *dōna* spirits. Among the latter, as a rule, there are Yakut (*joko*) spirits (the shaman is then supposed to speak the Yakut language), Tungus (*tēya*), and seldom Manchu, Dahur, and even Chinese spirits. There may also be individual spirits which may easily leave the shaman (the clan spirits cannot do it).

Among the Manchus the situation is slightly different. Since the list of spirits, owing to the existence of writing, is known and cannot be very much altered, the shamans believe that they must master first two spirits, namely *mafa saman* and *mama saman* (whose names I could not find out) who are supposed to be the most important spirits and who undoubtedly originated among the shamans. Naturally there are "ancestors" in every clan, and they come, at the same time, as chief helpers of the shaman.*** However, they do not become *dalaza vočko* (leading spirits); such a spirit may be gradually formed out of existing spirits, or as one of the new spirits individually incorporat-

———————

* The theory of a guardian spirit, proposed by R. F. Benedict ("The concept of the Guardian Spirit in North America", Memoirs of the Amer. Anthr. Assoc., No 29) and generalized with respect to Siberian groups, naturally cannot be applied to the Tungus and Manchus.

* I knew all the circumstances of this case, for the shaman approached me for making a picture of this spirit, and she had to produce all possible details, before I could apply my "iconographic art" in shamanism.

** It should be noted that the female shaman had a female spirit. Her device with twenty-six marks of spirits' visits was supplied with carved female genitalia and breast.

*** It should be noted that no sexual relations are possible.

ed by the shaman. This is the spirit with which the shaman works more than with other spirits and which takes
charge of all spirits. Among the shamans the choice is
subject to great variations. There are usually present
some Tungus (*kilin*), Chinese (both *n'ikan* and *jergin*),
Mongol and Dahur spirits which incidentally may become
dalaxa. The number of spirits mastered at the beginning
of the career is small, but gradually it may increase. The
shamans usually have at their disposal from twenty to sixty spirits, but not all of them are used. However, theoretically all of the spirits of the list are supposed to be mastered. Therefore the individual lists of spirits actually
used in different clans are not alike. Together with this
the ritualism connected with the spirits is also different.

It may be generalized as follows: the shaman is the
master of spirits; the first spirit mastered may have, but
not always necessarily, a special position; it may be one of
the clan spirits and it may be a foreign spirit; there is no
definite tendency as to the sex of the shaman and that of.
the first spirit, and of the spirits of importance (*dalaxa* in
Manchu, *ogdïya* in Tungus); in general the number of
spirits is subject to variations conditioned by the personal
ability of the shaman, his experience, and thus by the period
of shamanistic activity, as well as by a gradual decrease
of the number of spirits, owing to the changes which occur
in the shaman's activity.

Although the mastering of spirits is a characteristic
feature of shamanism, the relations between the shaman
and the spirits are not like those of a master and his slaves,
deprived of their will and rights. The shamans, to a certain
degree, transfer human relations to those between themselves and the spirits. Since the Tungus and Manchu complex recognizes the necessity of considering the character
of persons whom they master, e.g. junior relatives, slaves
(Manchus), workmen, subordinate soldiers and officials etc.,
they also consider the character of the spirits. The shaman
knows that these spirits may have various desires in accordance with their particular character; he knows that there
are bad-natured, wicked spirits, spirits which are not to be
trusted, even for a moment: spirits which may be trusted;
there are spirits anxious to have benefits from their work
for the shaman, and spirits which are not very greedy. To
be brief—the characters of spirits are the reproduction of
those of human beings, but in addition some spirits are
more powerful than men, so the managing of them presents great difficulties. The shaman must be ready for all
sorts of eventualities and he must carry on quite a complicated policy, for he may sometimes greatly suffer from the
spirits. The question is: what kind of policy should be
adopted? If the shaman shows a "weak heart" by serving
sacrifices too frequently, the spirits may form the idea that
the shaman is afraid of them and they will not work for
him, but will require more and more sacrifices. So he must
not abuse this method. There are spirits which must be
kept in strong hands and even they must be "badly treated" by the shaman; as long as the shaman manifests no
fear, he is safe, but if the spirits see him weakening they
may attack him immediately or may leave him alone and

so he will be attacked by other spirits.* If at any moment
the shaman loses his control, they may lead him to death. I
have already quoted a case of a young shaman who committed suicide. Although rare, such cases do occur from
time to time. Psychologically this case is clear: the shaman
loses control of himself and the idea of persecution and
self-suggestion may bring him to a fatal issue. In order
to neutralize dangerous spirits he may create a kind of conflict among the spirits, so that, for a time at least, he will
not be harmed. Thus, even the methods of controlling the
spirits are a reproduction of the methods used among living people.

It is remarkable that in a great number of cases the
spirits may require of the shaman the performance of a shamanizing and that the shaman cannot refuse to do it—this
is the moment when *the shaman wants to shamanize*. Conflicts among the spirits, created by the shaman, are a remarkable reflexion of the psychic life of the shaman, in
which there are conflicts of contradictory elements of the
shaman's complex, the balancing of which requires additional spirits for fighting other spirits. This method is not
considered (by Birarčen) as a harmless one, for since the
shaman comes into a conflict with his own servants, the
spirits, he may lose his control altogether. When the shaman is involved in such a fight, he usually finishes his life
by an accident, by disease, exhaustion, and, as far as I
know, by insanity caused, according to the Tungus, either
by his own spirits or by other unmastered spirits.

The shaman's tragedy is that he cannot dismiss clan
spirits himself, he can dismiss only those spirits which are
foreign, or his personal spirits. But even this task is
sometimes beyond the shaman's art, and the spirits may
return again and again. Generally speaking, the dismissal
of spirits is not a very frequent practice at the beginning
of the shaman's career; but an experienced shaman, after
a perfect mastering of spirits, can do it. An experienced
shaman may only keep his eye on the clan spirits and they
will not bother him; they would even require of him no
shamanizing or sacrifices. In rare cases the spirits may
leave the shaman alone, even before a very advanced age,
or even before he becomes very experienced in handling
spirits. However, in this case, he will not be able to carry
on his function of a *safety valve*—some other person may
be affected by the spirits, and the latter may be mastered
by a new shaman. These cases exactly correspond to the
changes in the psychic condition of the shamans when with
the advance of age conflicting conditions of the psychomental complex are eliminated by balancing or by dropping of
some elements (e.g. the sexual complex etc.). However, in
case the shaman loses the confidence of the clansmen, the
spirits will affect other members of the clan, and the shaman
would cease to function as a shaman. When the shaman
himself is affected by the spirits, another, but always a
stronger and more experienced, shaman may come to his
assistance. However, such an interference of another shaman is not liked by the shamans, for there is a danger for
the shaman who is helping another shaman that the spirits
of the affected shaman may mix up with the spirits of the
helping shaman.

---

* It should be noted that this is not a function of a "guardian"
spirit. It would be quite fallacious if one should take this attitude
in respect to the Tungus and, I should say, in respect to other
"savages".

Such complex relations, greatly "anthropomorphized" by the Tungus, may look like a very naive and artificial construction of an imaginary world of spirits. However, if we carefully analyse the character of various spirits and all hypotheses connected with them, we shall find that these spirits are merely a symbolization of various psychomental elements and complexes. I have also pointed out that the Tungus do not represent these spirits as anthropomorphic beings, but they are figured, in the Tungus mind, as immaterial (in Tungus sense) "beings", which are satisfied with an immateriality of sacrifice, human actions etc. To describe the Tungus attitude towards these spirits, as it may be inferred from the sacrifice, picturing "ugly looking horrible idols", "queer shaman's costumes", "frightening spirits" and spirits protecting the shaman from other spirits, is but to show a perfect ignorance of this complex problem.* These spirits are hypotheses, some of which are admitted by the European complex as well, hypotheses which formulate observations of psychic life of the people and particularly that of the shaman, and which are quite helpful in the regulation of the psychomental complex to which the Tungus have come after a long period of adaptation.

Let us consider some situations. The shaman must offer from time to time a sacrifice to his spirits; if he does it too frequently, they may disobey; if he neglects them, they may harm him, avenge themselves. If we replace "spirit" by a "certain psychomental element", the regular sacrifice will be understood as a practical means to have a constant check on the shaman's complex by the shaman himself. After the sacrifice the shaman feels sure that he is in control of the spirits. If the shaman is afraid of the spirits, it merely means that there is some essential change in his complex, which he cannot master, and he tries (according to the Tungus conception) to satisfy the spirits with a pleasant sacrifice—he is no more in control of the spirits and they may affect other people who will no longer have confidence in the shaman. Therefore, it is recommended to the shaman not allow himself to be influenced by elements of his own complex. Lastly, a neglect of the spirits may put the shaman under the condition of an accidental growth of one of the psychic elements, which may result in the mastering of the shaman by this spirit, or in disabling him for acting as a safety valve of the group. In all these situations we have a mere symbolization of the complex conditions of psychic life of the shaman and a perfectly adapted system of regulating mechanism created after long observations and experiments. In reality these symbols are based upon hypotheses, but their functioning does not suffer from it. The phenomenon of psychic life is not understood in the same form as the modern science would understand it, but *it is regulated*, and its components are perhaps better analysed (in spirit-symbols) than it is done by psychologists who operate with such conceptions as "instincts" and "complexes".

Let us take another example. In order to neutralize a harmful activity of the spirits, the shaman may make spirits fight among themselves, but this is not a recommendable method. In substituting the elements of the shaman's psychomental complex for the spirits, we obtain a picture of a badly balanced psychic condition, in which

some elements may attain a dominant character, overshadowing other elements. On the whole the shaman would be psychomentally altogether disabled. It is stated that the shaman may even perish, which, in our terminology, would be styled as a maniacal state. According to the Tungus, the shaman must not allow himself to be tempted by experiments with spirits, and the other shaman may come to his assistance. Perhaps herein the Tungus are more right than the European psychiatrists who often underestimate purely psychic and mental conditions in the regulation of psychomental troubles. In reality, hysteria can be easily regulated. If some better methods are found there will perhaps be no need to look for a justification of failures, having recourse to hypothetical patholozo-anatomical and physiologico-chemical explanations of some psychomental conditions now supposed to be incurable. The internal conflict of the shaman with himself puts him out of practical use as a safety valve. The Tungus came to those conclusions after covering with their keen ability of observation a great number of facts. The Tungus hypothesis is wrong, from our point of view, but as a practical solution of the problem it works perfectly well.

Forms of repression of spirits ("bad treatment"), for their wickedness, greediness etc. are mere symbolizations. They may much better be understood in their functioning than as pictures of "idols" and quotations of prayers or addresses.

Such are the "relations" between the spirits and the shamans. I shall now give some instances of practical managing of spirits with the help of sacrifices, but first I want to emphasize that the forms in which sacrifices are made are of no great importance for understanding the actual nature of shamanism. They are interesting as any other ethnographical phenomena which offer some material for ethnology.

SACRIFICES BY THE SHAMAN TO HIS SPIRITS are not offered among all groups with the same regularity. Among the Reindeer Tungus of Transbaikalia a sacrifice is offered, when the shaman feels that it should be done. So it may be delayed for several years. Among the Tungus of Manchuria the sacrifice, consisting of various animals (the more, the better), is given periodically, no less than once every three years. In main lines it is the same as the first shamanizing of the shaman who calls in, one after another, all spirits mastered by him, to show that he possesses them. The shaman addresses to the spirits his request that they remain near him. After the performance the shaman climbs up to the *turu*, where he remains for a while. The shaman assisting the performer carefully checks up all moments of the performance and a competent person makes special marks on the wooden device. During a shaman's life he may offer up to six periodical sacrifices. There is no difference between the sacrifice carried out by the clan shaman (*mokun'i*) and a free shaman.*

Among the Manchus this operation is greatly complicated as compared with the Tungus.** The ritual is carried out on the second day of the first moon of the Chinese calendar. All families that were assisted by the sha-

---

* I need not quote a multitude of names of authors who have taken this attitude in reference to the Tungus and, I should say, in reference to other "savages".

* I myself, had no occasion to observe a periodical sacrifice. The above remarks are the result of my numerous inquiries.
** I have twice observed the ceremony.

man [as has been shown, they are called *jarumbo* (*jarun ðao*)] bring with them various sacrifices which are put in front of the placings for spirits exhibited on the large stove bed (in front of the entrance once I observed the whole adult pig!). The *ta jar'i* (chief assistant) sits on this stove-bed, on the right of a small table with sacrifices and placings; the shaman is in front of the sacrifice; elderly persons occupy places of honour, other people stand behind the shaman, while the women with children sit on the stove beds behind the seniors. The performance begins at eight o'clock in the evening. The shaman puts on what is required by the ritual—conforming to which of the spirits is to come. For calling in the spirits the shaman goes out into the yard and returns. The assistant must recognize which spirit is introduced. If he fails, the shaman once more returns to the yard and comes back again.* The spirits are recognized by the ritual, including "words". After four or five spirits are introduced, the shaman is asked to introduce some more. If he is tired, being old or psychically weak, he may decline it; but if he is a strong man, he will shamanize throughout the whole night. During the performance I once observed, besides *ta jar'i* three more assistants who were "helping" with drumming. Lastly, *ta jar'i* recited by heart all spirits (*ðolo*), while the shaman was only confirming by his monotonous *kēku!* (widely used in shamanism as refrain and "symbol" of confirmation.)

136. WARS BETWEEN THE SHAMANS One of the interesting aspects of the shaman's psychology is the waging of wars among the shamans. It should be noted that not all shamans do it, but only those who are regarded by the Tungus as "bad-natured persons". This personal condition will be discussed later, but I shall now give details regarding the "wars", for they may help us in the understanding of the psychology of the shamans and their relations with the spirits.

The essential of the "war" consists in the mental influence of the shaman who wishes to harm directly another shaman, or his spirits. In the Tungus dialects they are called *buloy*** (Ner. Barg.), *bulen* (Bir. Kum),—the "war" in general; and *k'imun* (Bir.) which literally means,— "hostility, wickedness" etc. [*k'imun* (Manchu Writ.)] with a series of derivatives.

According to the Reindeer Tungus of Transbaikalia and the Tungus of Manchuria, the "wars" among the shamans are very common, but I have not been told so by the Manchus who entirely deny the existence of "wars". The Tungus are inclined to ascribe the wars to the hostility of the shamans of alien ethnical units, which is a very interesting fact as reflecting ethnical psychology.

The battles in a form of competition in art and murder usually take place at night—in dreams—but battles and murder may also occur in a wakening state. I give here some descriptions, in translation, made by the Barguzin Tungus.

* Once a shaman assisted by a man of little experience, had to repeat this operation four times.
** Cf. *buläa* (Ur. Castr.), *bulon* etc. should be considered as a loan word, perhaps from the Mongol *bulija*—"to rob, to take by force" etc.

"One night, the shaman was hunting on the salt-marsh (1); "sitting there, he saw in the night some glittering fire. "As soon as he noticed it, he pulled out his knife. "The fire descended lower. Then he remained sitting "quietly. Thereafter he returned home, reported the "happening and said: «So *Saŋyuni* (2) has come! Keep "quiet and let me fall asleep.» Then he fell asleep and be-"came a shaman (3); while he was sleeping, he began to "follow the aggressor-shaman and reached *Saŋyuni*'s wig-"wam. *Saŋyuni* was sitting at the entrance. He sat down "and began to scold *Saŋyuni*: «You see, I nearly caught "you when you were asleep. You are a bad man. Why did "you go in the form of fire?» *Saŋyuni* was sitting silent "with his head hang down. When the shaman ceased to "speak, *Saŋyuni* told him: «From now on I shall never "do so»."

1. A special form of hunting on salt-marshes grounds which are visited by the cervines at night time. The hunter sits sometimes for hours, and waits for the animals.
2. Sanyuni is the name of another Tungus shaman.
3. "has become a shaman" means that the shaman assumed one of the spirits' forms which permitted him to travel a long way.

Here is another story picturing the war between the Barguzin Tungus and the Yakut shamans.

"There was a great shaman. He had a junior brother. "The shaman saw a great Yakut shaman who, in the form "of a cloud, was coming straight towards them. Then he "said to his brother:"

"Well, what shall we do?"

"I do not know. Do what you want!"

"Then I shall go!"

"He went on in the form of a cloud, rose up above the "Yakut shaman, thrice shot him "with thunder" and killed "him. He returned. Some time later the Yakut shaman "arrived again in the form of a still larger cloud...." and so on.

Among the Birarčen the wars between the shamans may originate on the ground of competition, also on the ground of hostility between the clans. These Tungus have a great fear of the fighting shamans, for reasons which will be clear later on, and they recognize them by the following signs: a fighting shaman never lifts up his arms which he keeps near his body, protecting with the arms the holes, made on the sides of the costume, through which the common shaman's spirit may enter into the shaman. The reasons of the competition may arise, for instance, in case a shaman fails to treat a sick person, while another shaman is successful; the first one may try to avenge himself. He may assume the form [*oboleran* (Bir. Kum.), cf. *ubalambi* (Manchu Writ.)] of different animals and things, in order to approach the second shaman and in this form to attack him. A story was told me of two shamans who changed themselves into a bear and a tiger, fighting in the presence of people, while they were physically separated by a great distance from each other. One of these great fighters might turn into "a cart with horses", which was considered as an especially powerful means of hiding one's self. In fighting, all means are considered to be good, as long as they can be effective.

In the clan *dunänkän* there was a bad-natured man. One day he put in a small cup of brandy of another shaman, of the clan *čakčir*, a spirit (*sèvèŋ*) in the form of a very small fish. The *čakčir* shaman noticed it and, without showing it, he began to sip the brandy very carefully. However, being drunk, he swallowed the fish. Then he became "like mad" and very soon died. The same shaman made many other shamans of other clans perish. The man of *dunānkān* who reported these cases to me was always very careful with his own clan shaman and did not invite him for shamanizing.

Another shaman, whom I knew rather well, during a long time, was carrying on a continuous "war" with a Kumarčen shaman. During this war she lost all her family, all horses as well, so she had to leave for another region (the *Sumbira* River), where, after having become blind, she gave up her shamanizing.

Among the Reindeer Tungus of Manchuria, who came in the beginning of the last century to Manchuria, the shamans were continuously fighting among themselves and with the Kumarčen shamans. Such shamans were called *hulaŋtka*. The last shaman (whose brother and sister-in-law were alive and told me all details of the case and the glorious life of their relative), who died in 1912, was mutilated (always from a distance) by his Kumarčen enemy who "turned aside his head", and he lived so the greater part of his life.

The fighting shamans are especially dangerous for other shamans whom (their souls) they catch on their way back from the lower world. Nobody likes them, for they always produce various tricks for hiding themselves (their souls) from other shamans. Once a Birarčen was going together with a shaman. A bear approached them, and the man wanted to kill it immediately. However, the shaman stopped him from doing it, for he said the bear was himself, i.e. his soul was inside the bear. As stated before, the shamans may assume various forms, so that it is impossible to recognize them, one may involuntarily harm them and thus create hostility, both among the shamans and the spirits. When the shamans are fighting, they establish a real system of spies—various animals—to look after the enemy shaman who cannot guess in which animal the other shaman enters. The most inoffensive bird or insect may be used as a placing by such a shaman. The shamans who know how to assume various forms may well be informed as to all movements of their enemies without themselves being noticed.

The people, even clansmen, are afraid to call on such fighting shamans for assistance. The chief reason is this: these shamans have a great number of enemies, and when they come to a family for shamanizing they leave a *road* (*vide supra* p. 149) which will be used by the spirits; the latter may mix up with the clan (not shamanistic) spirits, being acquainted with them; if the spirit (shaman) fights, then the spirits of his more artful enemy may take over his road and attack the clan spirits and the people visited by the unfortunate shaman.

The fighting shamans among the Birarčen are usually using their *dōna sèvèŋ*—the foreign spirits. Therefore the shamans who use too many *dōna* spirits are likely to be fighting shamans. It should here be noted that they are not elected by the clan. The fighting between the shamans is especially dangerous for children of whose souls the shamans are taking care. Among the Birarčen in one case a shaman, who had taken a child's soul, began to fight. He was defeated and the child fell badly ill. This was discovered by another shaman who reported it to the child's father. The latter decided to beat the shaman who caused

the trouble. The case was discussed by the clansmen who decided to leave the case without interference, for the shaman himself suffered from the spirits,—"this was spirits' business". The origin of *lamalaičen sèvèŋ* is also connected with the shamanistic wars. A shaman sent his spirit which turned over the canoe in which another shaman was sitting. The latter was drowned. The spirit of this shaman remained among the people, became *sèvèŋ* and since that time is known as *lamalaičen sèvèn*.

The hostile shamans (spirits) use bows and arrows (immaterial). When a man or an animal is struck by an arrow, the latter leaves a wound looking like that produced by a bullet. The animals usually perish immediately; human beings are sick during three or four days and may die. There is no possibility of curing these wounds. Sometimes all (domesticated) animals are killed in this way, then members of the family are killed and finally all members of the same clan are killed. The unfortunate shaman, instead of defending his clansmen and being shot himself, is not hit but turns aside the arrow and immediately shoots his own arrow at the first person seen, as it would be in a case of olonism (cf. *supra* pp. 245 et seq). The chief trouble is that the shamans usually do not confess that they are fighting so that only by observing them and by seeing the effects of their fighting, one can arrive at this conclusion.

It may here be remarked that this habit of some shamans has created among some Tungus, e.g. some Tungus of the Birarčen and Kumarčen groups, a rather negative attitude towards the shamans in general. As far as possible the people like to avoid them. However, in many cases of fighting the cause resides in the shamans themselves, namely, good natured persons (shamans) do not fight and they will tell immediately if they are attacked by the shamans, so that measures may be taken against the fighting shamans.

———

The above given description of the wars among the shamans is in reality a description of disturbed psychomental conditions of the shamans. Undoubtedly, they suffer from the mania of persecution which may attain very extreme forms with a fatal issue for the shamans, who very often perish, according to the Tungus. The question as to the nature of the mass sickness of animals and human beings, with the symptom of small ulcers, like those produced by a bullet, and death occurring a few days after the ulceration I do not venture to answer. No suggestion as to the etiology of this disease, evidently infectious, is possible, for I myself have not observed these cases.[*]

Another point of interest is that communication at a distance, the possibility of which we cannot deny, may be used by the shamans (bad natured persons) for a suggestive influence on other shamans, which gives them a strong weapon for the annihilation of other shamans.

In this condition of a shaman a progressive form of mania is very typical. It may also be stated, that one of the methods of getting rid of a persecuting shaman is to give up shamanizing altogether, which, according to the Tungus, is a good means to satisfy the ambition of the fighting shaman. Indeed, when the shaman cannot more con-

[*] Perhaps, it is anthrax, which is not very common in Manchuria, and an epidemic infectious character of which is not noticed by these Tungus.

trol himself, which is an essential condition of extasy, he must avoid such a psychomental state in which the mania of persecution is liable to re-appear. It is stated, that some shamans cannot do it, so they continue to shamanize till they perish because of continuous intrigues of the persecuting shaman.

The small detail of the case of the Birarčen shaman, who being drunk, swallowed a fish, is interesting, for it is indicative of the well known condition by which drunkards are affected—the čakčir shaman was surely the prey of alcoholism. I could not find out very much about him, but I have been told that during his life he rather often indulged in drinking large quantities of strong alcoholic liquors. But in this connexion it should be noted that not all shamans suffer from alcoholism—the majority of them have shown themselves to be more moderate consumers of alcoholic drinks and some of them are entirely abstemious.

From the above given series of cases we may also see that the Tungus are sometimes inclined to ascribe to the influence of the fighting shamans much more than they are able to do. For instance, the malady of the Reindeer Tungus shaman who suffered from disordered nerves ("turned") was perhaps not due to his psychomental condition, but it was attributed to the Kumarčen shaman, as an explanation of an unknown disease. The same may be said of the case of epidemics.

The above said may be summarized as follows. The fighting of the shamans may have a realistic basis in the form of suggestion perhaps produced once, when the shamans meet, and later maintained by suggestion at a distance; the persecuted shaman may be affected by a mania which, to a certain extent, may be treated by means of self-control, i.e. by avoiding extasy; alcoholism is probably a favourable condition for this maniacal state, and other pathological conditions may also be suspected, at least in some cases, e.g. blindness after the fighting, "turned head" etc.; a great number of cases are quite undeservedly attributed to the fighting shamans (infectious diseases etc.), as an explanation of little known diseases. It must particularly be noted that the Tungus do their best to eliminate the possibility of this condition in the shaman, as it appears from the requirement of "good nature" (no symptom of schyzophrenia), from the avoiding and isolating of fighting shamans who may influence other people etc.

As to the frequency of these cases, I have no exact data, but in my investigations I have met only with a few shamans who waged "wars", e.g. the blind shaman (Birarčen) and a Dahur shaman. As to other cases, they were uncertain. Considering the number of shamans observed, it may be thus supposed that this is a relatively rare occurrence among the shamans, but it does exist and, as it is suggested by other shamans, it may threaten the shaman's life. However, I must warn the reader that these facts do not present a general phenomenon of such psychoses among the shamans, but are rather exceptional and rare cases which confirm the idea of the functional side of shamanism, as I understand it.

137. CHARACTER AND ABILITY OF THE SHAMAN   I have already pointed out, on different occasions, that the personal character and the individual ability of the shaman are of great importance. From among the candidates the more

intelligent and skilful would be elected. The character of the candidate is also taken into consideration. If the candidate has a "good heart", he may be allowed to become shaman, but if he manifests bad inclinations, he will be rejected. However, sometimes a "bad heart" shows itself only after the election. In fact, the Tungus recognize that there are good and bad-natured acting shamans. However, the situation is complicated by the fact that the shaman may act under the influence of the spirits, some of which may be very bad. So personally some shamans may be very good, but as shamans not sufficiently powerful, they are unable to prevent the spirits from doing harm to the people. The same is true with reference to the personal ability of the shaman, which may be attributed to the spirits [skilful spirits are in this respect called balbuka (Bir. vide supra, p. 164)] and not to the shaman personally. Thus, in this respect, there is no definite idea as to the relation between the shaman and the spirit. I had sometimes the impression that in the Tungus mind both the shaman and the spirit are the same. This ought to be understood in the following sense: there is no question as to the personal ability of the shaman, but the question is about the spirits which have been mastered by him; thus the spirits are nothing else but an alter ego of the shaman himself. Another point of view is that the shaman and the spirits exist independently. In the latter stating of the problem the individual moral and intellectual character of the shaman ought to be taken into consideration. An intelligent person may better manage the spirits and direct their activity as desired.

The idea of bad natured shamans is especially in vogue among the Birarčen. They believe that almost all dōna shamans are harmful and bad persons, while an exception is made for the clan shamans. However, even the clan shamans may be bad persons, but they can harm only alien people, i.e. outside of the clan, for the clan spirits would not harm the clan people. The shamans of other groups are considered as dangerous and usually bad natured persons. I shall revert to this question later when the Tungus attitude towards the shamans is discussed.

What is symbolized by the Tungus as the possession of good spirits is the shaman's personal talent in dealing with the situations which confront him. We have seen that he must be a good observer and psychologist when he makes his diagnosis. A good shaman may better define whether his interference can help or not, while a poor shaman will act according to the ritual, trying different methods. The art of diagnostics is attributed to the spirits. However, some shamans whom I have seen and known rather intimately were considered as good, while I was unable to notice any special manifestations of their intelligence. On the other hand, I have met with some shamans who were rather superior in their intelligence, in a common sense of the word, but they were not good shamans. To come to a correct definition of the intellectual ability of a Tungus is not an easy task, and in the shaman's practice the chief method is perhaps not that which results from the intelligence as it is manifested in dealing with common phenomena.

Those shamans who were considered as having a "bad heart", as far as I could find out from the concrete cases described and from shamans whom I knew personally, were affected by some psychoses, in which state they might commit acts of hostility towards other people. Such shamans are accused of plotting against the people and domesticated animals, in the same way as it was described in the preceding section.

Here I will give some facts gathered among the Birarčen.

A young man, a good hunter, failed to kill animals. He went a second time. His father, an old and rather rich man (he had some savings and twenty horses) reasoned so: there must be some malicious shamans who interfere by means of their spirits, for the son is an excellent hunter. The old man even knows a shaman who is jealous of his son's success in hunting, so the old man said to me in joke: "It would be good if you would take with you all spirits".

Here I give a typical story, recorded among the Birarčen, about a bad-hearted shaman. «In the clan *dunänkän* there was an old shaman who had a very "bad heart". He used to play bad tricks on people, some of whom lost their horses, others their children. Then four shamans decided to exterminate him. Once he went out to collect birch bark. He left his canoe and went to the outskirts of the forest. When he approached the first trees he saw a bear and a tiger which immediately attacked him (the bear and the tiger were spirits sent by the four shamans). With his axe he could defend himself and even fight these two animals, and he retreated to his canoe. When he was near it, he said: "Well, now I shall exterminate all of them (the people)". When he reached his wigwam, he put on himself his shamanistic costume and shamanized three days and three nights, after which he suddenly died. However, before his death he said to the people who were near him: "All the same! All of you will follow me!" Indeed, such a death was very bad, for the spirit had remained after the shaman and was travelling from one family to another, and all clansmen suffered. The spirit could not be taken in by other people, for it did not want to have any other master besides the deceased shaman».

When I was among this group, the question of sending off this spirit was discussed. It was said that a good (strong) shaman might send it off in three or at most five years, but only with difficulty. Indeed, they discussed, it would be good to send the spirit to a region, where there are no *dunänkän* clansmen. But even for a temporary exile of the spirit a copious sacrifice of a pig, a roe-deer and wood-cocks, besides the services of a good shaman, would be required. A year before my visit one of the sons of one of the clansmen, in spite of a copious sacrifice, had died, because of this spirit. However, this time the wrong was with the father who did not fulfil the prescription: instead of two roe-deer and three wood-cocks, he gave only one roe-deer and two wood-cocks. The father did feel somewhat wrong in having reduced this required sacrifice.

The bad-natured shamans do harm without any reason. Their power is sometimes so strong that they kill animals, even domesticated animals, merely by pointing at them with a finger. The trace of this is a dark spot on the skin.

Among the Manchus "bad-natured" shamans are also found. A great number of the above-mentioned cases (*vide supra*, p. 316) *saman'i joyun* are troubles produced by the shamans. However, it is not likely that within the clan any trouble would be produced by the shaman who belongs to this clan.*

The shamans who have good voices, who dance well,

---

*' The method of sending off the spirits sent by the shaman, is to make a "tree", and a "shaman" dressed in a paper costume, armed with a paper drum etc. The operation is similar to that for sending off mafa.

and drum with variations and in an expressive manner, are considered as good shamans in so far as the performance is concerned. From the description of performances we have seen how important their technique is. It is thus natural that the good technicians are appreciated, although it would perhaps not be realized *what* is appreciated, namely, the art of keeping up extasy and a definite behaviour of the audience.

From the observation of a great number of cases, I have come to the conclusion that sincerity of the shaman and his disinterested carrying out of his function may also be a good compensation for a lack of experience. When the shamans are sincere and disinterested persons, their influence on the audience is much greater, and thus their activity is more effective. However, an artful use of various methods learnt from others is also noticed by the Tungus who would say: "The shaman has actually no spirit, but he knows how to perform". Therefore his influence upon those who understand the shaman's technique cannot be very great. A disinterested performing of a shamanistic function may be affected by two conditions, namely, (1) some shamans possess too great a feeling of their dependence upon the other people, for whose approval they look and thus unwillingly adapt themselves to the public opinion—so they lose their function as "leaders"; (2) some shamans try to have material profit from their functions. The first case is rather characteristic of some Tungus groups in which some freedom, in the sense of personal advancement among the clansmen, is allowed. Naturally, young shamans are more susceptible to this influence, and thus some of them may become a mere source of distraction of the audience. In spite of a temporary success, such shamans gradually lose their power of influencing people, and then they are not considered as good shamans. I have observed among the Northern Tungus no cases of material interest in the shamans.

It is different with the Manchus. The element of personal interest is very strong, either in the form of an increase of influence, which results in demagogic methods of dealing with the clansmen and outsiders, and thus in the subsequent loss of personal influence, or in the form of material benefits resulting from this function. This is especially true of the *amba saman* who are not clan shamans. The actual stimulus of their activity is a profit which may be produced by these functions. Such shamans use all kinds of tricks in order to attract clients who would support them, and they naturally lose their sincerity and real devotion to their clients. They become pure and simple professionals, living on shamanism and they seldom enjoy real influence among the Manchus. Such shamans even find themselves in a difficult position when they come in contact with the groups like the Northern Tungus who do not believe them able to do any good to people looking for their help.

Apparently among the Dahurs this type of almost professional shamans has reached a further stage, namely, they sometimes travel from one place to another competing with the local shamans, Chinese doctors, and Manchu *mafari*. Among the Chinese the shamans are nothing but professionals who compete with other professionals and who live solely upon their trade. As a matter of fact, all of them, whom I saw, were of this type, and the Manchus and Tungus say the same. In the eyes of the Tungus and Manchus these Chinese shamans do not differ much from *"mafar'i"* and "doctors", and their specific shamanistic power is denied.

In the Tungus mind these different types of shamans seem to be classified according to the "quality of their heart", i.e. honesty. Since this condition may greatly affect the practical effect of shamanism on the clansmen, the personal honesty of the candidate is always considered, before he is allowed to become an acting shaman. The candidate may even be entirely rejected on this ground. A really good shaman must be a honest person, serving his clansmen and other people without any idea of making any personal profit from his functions.

138. ACCUMULATION OF KNOW-   In order to complete
     LEDGE BY THE SHAMANS   the picture of the sha-
                              man's activity it must
be added that the shamans are promotors of, or better to say, contributors to the Tungus knowledge.

In the description of the psychic state of the shaman during the performances and extasy I have shown that the shamans must go very deep into the study of the psychology and mentality of the sick persons and the audience. The shamans are observers, collectors of facts which they analyse—the new spirits, or the new manifestations of the old spirits. As shown, in their practical work in treating clients, chiefly in psychomental troublesome conditions, they find various new methods. All this knowledge must be adjusted to the existing theories concerning spirits and methods of treatment, which may keep the shamans very busy, especially when there are too many things to be discovered or when the Tungus come into close contact with other ethnical groups. The adjustment of new cultural elements to the existing complex is a real creative work continuously carried out by "good" shamans. Let me emphasize that when I speak of the analysis and elaboration of new methods this should be understood in the sense of an adaptive creation. A great part of phenomena, as we may understand them, are merely symbolized in simple or elaborated complexes of spirits and special relations existing among them. Indeed, if a person, behaving like a European, were to listen to the shamanistic theories and look at the methods elaborated by the shamans, all efforts of the shamans would appear as a maniacal delirium, deceit of naïve people, "superstitions", sexuality etc., i.e. exactly as shamanism has usually been pictured. This side of shamanism must first be "translated" into the terms of the "European complex" and then analysed, after which it will not appear more delirious than some great philosophical systems of great European philosophers, although the latter sometimes bear all attributes of a delirious complex (sometimes being actually so), especially when abstracted from the cultural complex, of which they were only elements.

There is besides another worry, namely, the transmission of the acquired knowledge to the younger generation of the shamans, to the candidates, and the selection of shamans. The teaching of the younger generation—the mechanism of preservation of knowledge and tradition—is naturally one of the conditions of accumulation of knowledge, as the publishing of scientific works is a means of accumulation of knowledge. However, in this way only a part of knowledge may be transmitted, for the shamans very often refuse to transmit their knowledge to the candidates whom they do not believe to be sufficiently prepared.

The shamans very often refuse to talk about things of their competence with people who cannot understand them. They have even a special term for such people which may be translated "simple", "common" people. However, in shamanism there is nothing "sacred" or "prohibited", and still less "tabooed". The only matter is that not every one can understand shamanism and therefore it is useless for a shaman to talk with ignorant persons. It is not surprising that a great number of investigators find themselves thwarted by the mutism of the shamans, their hostile attitude and their treatment of investigators as ignorant persons, who can be satisfied with any reply. It is especially true of those who travel with various "questionaires" which consist of the most inconsistent questions resulting from the European theories concerning "primitive man" and other imaginary constructions. I am certain that no European scholar would permit an ignorant outsider to come into his laboratory to poke a thick finger into delicate instruments, and to ask with an ironical smile questions concerning the influence of the scholar's sexual complex on his laboratory experiments. Only an extreme politeness and the recognition of the necessity of submitting to the overbearance of powerful representatives of "civilization" keep the shamans from sending off such investigators.

In my experience with the shamans I have come to the conclusion that, as soon as one shows them a bit of understanding, they become desirous to explain more and more, especially if one does not bother them with "fountain pen and note book" and other devices of the alien cultural complex. When one wants to *learn* from the shamans, they are easier in this respect than some European professionals who are anxious to show their authoritativeness in their professions, who very often are jealous and afraid of disclosing professional secrets on which they are making their living, who still oftener are concealing their ideas—provided there are such ideas—from other people, in their fear of being robbed of their poor mental equipment. There were some shamans with whom I could not establish a close connexion. At the beginning this might have been due chiefly to my lack of experience, and later to the fact that some shamans can only learn and have ideas of their function, but do not know how to express them in words—they are not eloquent. This is especially true of female shamans whose shyness can only increase the difficulty of communication.

The acquiring and transmitting of knowledge is a function of "good" shamans who naturally must have broader knowledge, in general, than the average Tungus, especially in so far as the psychomental functioning is concerned. In fact, most of the shamans are always interested in acquiring new knowledge; they pay much attention to conversations concerning problems of their speciality, and they can spend hours in discussing these problems with competent people.

However, it would be superfluous to point out that not all shamans are alike in this respect. Not all of them are equally interested in "theoretical work", and not all of them are interested in acquiring new knowledge. From the description of how a candidate becomes shaman and from the description of the functions of the shaman it is evident that among the shamans there may be different types with different inclinations. A shaman may be a very good performer without being a good diagnostician; he may be a good diagnostician without being a good performer; he may be neither a performer nor a diagnostician, and he may be interested in the above mentioned theoretical work. Since these types are a result of adaptation—they result from the complex conditions sometimes not cognized—the gradation of the creative power among them is not less than that observed, for instance, in the European universities where one may see many types—from professors, who are merely mechanical reproducers of ideas which remain ununderstood, up to creative geniuses. This simple fact has been very often overlooked by investigators.

The function of the shamans as accumulators of knowledge should not be taken as a professional function. Every Tungus may do this, and every Tungus may be interested in shamanism, and thus may be in close contact with the shamans. But since the shamans specialize in this field, meeting in their practice with various cases, they are put in better positions with respect to this aspect of the cultural complex, and naturally may know more and may become more theoretical in this field than the "common" people.

CHAPTER XXX

THE SHAMAN

(CONTINUATION)

139. SHAMAN'S SOCIAL RELATIONS The social relations of a shaman are of two natures: firstly, relations established because of the spirits mastered by the shaman; and secondly, relations established by the shaman with his clients. As we have seen, the spirits are also of two natures—clan spirits and foreign spirits, according to which there may be two kinds of shamans: clan shamans and "out clan" shamans. However, both kinds of shamans need recognition, which may be either obtained by a complicated ceremony of election, with a real trial and a real discussion of the candidates, or by the shaman himself owing to his successful practising of the shamanistic art.

There is a great difference between the formally recognized clan shamans and those recognized because of their personal ability; the shamans of the first group become an essential component of the clan functional organization, while the shamans of the second group are out-clan shamans, whose influence extends over a limited group of "foreign" spirits and a very limited group of personal clients.

In fact, the shaman, after having mastered the clan spirits, relieves thereby all members of his clan from the worry of being badly affected by the clan spirits, and is ready to lend at once his assistance to any clansman. His assistance will be effective and not difficult, for the *spirits are mastered by him*—a small sacrifice, a prayer, and a conversation with a spirit will relieve the patient of his trouble. By this means a great number of cases of psychomental disturbances are almost automatically cured. Moreover, when the clan spirits, which are usually very powerful and well acquainted with the clansmen, are well looked after, they may assist the shaman in his fighting with the out-clan spirits, not to speak of the complex cases when the clansmen's souls cannot normally reach the world of the dead ("lower world") and when the shaman's assistance is simple and helpful, while that of an out-clan shaman may be even harmful, because of the mixing up of his spirits with those of the clan, which should always be avoided.

Thus from the functional point of view, the clan shaman acts as a *safety valve* and as a special clan officer in charge of the regulation of the psychic equilibrium among the clan members.

How close the connexion is between a clan and its shaman, can be seen from the fact of the formation of new clans, as it is observed among the Tungus of Manchuria. I have treated this problem in SONT, where I have shown that the division of a clan is conditioned by the need of a smoothly functioning marriage complex. If there is an unfavourable sex-ratio in the two clans, or there is an important increase or a decrease of one of the clans (especially in a dual orgnization), a splitting of a populous clan is very likely. There are certain regulations as to the time required, but even after a declaration about the division to the spirit *buga* (SONT p. 204), the conclusion of marriages is not assured, until the two clan shamans divide their spirits. So a new clan must be formed and the shaman for the "junior" (*nokun*) clan must be separated from the old one. It is done in view of avoiding the mixing up of the clan spirits which, *according to the theory, must be different*. When this operation is carried out the women may be interchanged. It is interesting that the division of spirits and the appearance of candidates, powerful enough for mastering them, which may occur before the formal declaration to *buga*, is interpreted in the sense that the division can be carried out even before the expiration of the term previously fixed, i.e. usually four or five generations. I have observed several combinations of different types of relations. This fact is very interesting, because here the social organization is reflected in the relations between spirits and shamans. But the division of clans must not be regarded as an act of division of the spirits, and as a reflexion of the relations created by the shamans—the clan division is much older than shamanism.

The obligation to assist the clansmen in need results from the special position of the shaman recognized by the clan. As a matter of fact, this requirement may cause the change of the shamanistic art into a simple formalistic performance. This does occur among the clans which are very populous, and the shaman must attend too many persons. Since the shamanizing *lege artis* requires extasy and thus a great effort on the part of the shaman and since the latter cannot do it very often, the shamanizing changes into a ritualistic formality and as such does not satisfy the people. Among the Manchus a great number of shamans are tending to become mere performers of rituals. L. Sternberg (op. cit.) relates that among the Goldi a shaman, very skilful in bringing souls to the lower world, was busy all the time with these performances, while all the Goldi were waiting for him for years before he could attend the people. Owing to this the clan shamans are sometimes superseded in their art by the *dōna* (out-clan) shamans. There is moreover another condition in favour of the out-clan shamans, namely, in a great number of cases candidates for the clanshamanship, who sometimes are not inclined to shamanship, are forcibly prepared by the senior clansmen, while all outclan shamans assume their functions, because that is their vocation, and they usually have spent much energy before obtaining the position of a "recognized" shaman.

On the other hand, the attitude of the Tungus, and of the Manchus as well, towards the clan-shamans is always somewhat partial, the reason of which is the belief that such a person is needed for the clan (as I understand it, as a safety valve), and partiality of the clan is only one of the effects of a centripetal movement within the clan. The clansmen would always find an excuse if the shaman is not successful; so for instance, he might be said to be young, or too old, or the spirits might be suspected of being too lazy to work for their master, or some new unknown spirits might be suspected to be active. However, if the shaman shows no efficiency in his activity, which may be found out by the experienced elders, he may meet with the general disapproval of his clan and in some cases may arouse all clansmen against himself, as a dangerous and pernicious person for the clan. This is the case when the shaman manifests his "bad heart". The clan may come to the decision to destroy him with the help of other shamans, or at least to cast him out, which practically means nearly the same as capital punishment (cf. SONT p. 198). If the shaman is not appreciated by his clansmen, he also may give up his functions, but, as will be shown, this is not easy and almost impossible.

The Tungus (all groups, the Manchus included) recognize that the shamans are needed for the neutralization and the fighting of the clan spirits (other spirits as well!), and they believe that it would be much better to have no spirits, and consequently no shamans. So that if something were proposed which would eliminate the spirits, they would be ready to accept it. Together with it, the shamans would not be needed either. This attitude is not in favour of the shamans in general, but still it is far from creating a generally negative attitude towards the shamans. However, among all Tungus groups one may also meet with individuals who are hostile to the shamans in general, and according to them, the wrong emanates from the shamans themselves. Their voices become very strong, when the shaman is not supported by other clansmen. Such a movement greatly depends upon the penetration of distinct ethnographical complexes, which will be discussed with more details in the next chapter.

The shaman must face these neutral and hostile attitudes. The young shamans, are moreover bound by the social complex of junior-senior relations. In a great number of cases these relations put them in a difficult position for maintaining their own opinions which may not always be shared by the seniors. These difficulties are not so great when the shaman attains a certain age and the group of seniors becomes small. In this respect the shaman must adapt himself during all his life, for even being a senior he is bound by the will of the clan.

From the above remarks it is clear that the shaman does not become an authority, as magicians and priests do, but throughout his life he remains a clansman whose steps are checked up by the opinion of critically behaving clansmen, the whole clan organization, and, as will later be shown, alien ethnical groups which spread their influence over the Tungus.

A great role in the stabilization of the shaman's position is played by his personal success. If the shaman successfully attends some clansmen, he is invited again, so his position is strengthened. As we have seen, after the performances the shaman leaves his "roads" which are all the time used by his spirits. So that between the shaman and his clients a peculiar connexion, with the help of his spirits and a system of "roads", is firmly established. The influence of an out-clan shaman totally depends upon his personal connexions, while in the case of a clan shaman the same roads of clan spirits, though indirectly, connect the shaman with all other clansmen. A "road" left directly by a shaman greatly reinforces the personal connexion between the shaman and his clansmen.

In Manchu such connexion is expressed by a special term: the family (*bō*, *bao*, cf. SOM and SONT) attended by the shaman is *jarun*; so it is called *jarumbō*, and the shaman is called *jarun saman*. These relations are usually established from the childhood of the shaman's clients, especially in the families which do not belong to the clan. If the shaman successfully treats a child of an age below ten years he leaves *targa*. The latter is a narrow strip of cloth (ribbons) attached to the shaman's head-dress. The usual colour for all shamans is red. In addition to a red strip, two more strips of different colours are given, e.g. yellow, blue, green, white, black etc. These strips are supplied with two round *zoggo* (brass bells) and some fringes from the shamans head-dress. These are conventional placings for the shaman's spirits which are supposed to distinguish them according to the combination of colours, as it is with the *p'oyun vočko* (*vide supra*, p. 144). Such a placing is attached to the back of the child's coat (not always, for the parents become neglectful if the child is in good health) and worn so up to the age of ten years. Naturally the carrier of *targa* must not visit tabooed houses, *jatka bō* (after a childbirth) and *targa bō* (during the diseases produced by *ilxa mama*: smallpox, chicken-pox, measles etc.), also those where people had recently died, for the shaman's spirit may "mix up" with these spirits. Besides *targa* the attended child may receive a brass mirror (*tōli*), which must be preserved on *sēmde* (Manchu Sp.) [cf. *sendexen* (Manchu Writ.), according to I. Zaxarov, *šen* (Chinese "spirit") *undexen* (Manchu—"plank")]—a shelf used for keeping placings for spirits—where the *targa* is also put after the age of ten years. It is called *jarun saman'i sēmde*, and is considered of as great an importance as *p'oyun vočko*. The person attended by a shaman must not seek assistance from other shamans, unless the shaman recommends it himself.* So that the shaman gradually

---

* The girls usually do not receive *targa* and *tōli*.

forms around himself a group of permanent clients.
Every first day and every fifteenth day of a new moon
(month) the client must perform a ritual praying to the
spirits of the shaman. Every year on the second day of
the first moon (month) the client must attend (theoretically the client must come, even being at a distance of "one
thousand li") the shaman's great annual sacrifice, as described before, and bring with him some wine, Chinese
bread, candy and incense (meat is not required!) for the
sacrifice.

In November or December, after the harvest, the shaman during his visit to all houses in the village receives
from every *jarumbō* some supply of grain (millet, wheat, and
others). Rich families give him up to a ton of grain, the
poor ones less. All other houses which are not *jarumbō*
give him not less than about fifteen kilograms. The collected grain may suffice to support the shaman during a year.
It should be noted that different shamans usually do not
meet in the same houses, and a shaman would not go into
a house where there is another *jarun saman*. If a shaman
enters the house in which a *jarun saman* is acting, the latter
would know it immediately and would tell it through his
assistant (*jar'i*). The performance consists in a short
prayer to the spirits and especially *apka endur'i*.

The connexion which is formed between the shaman
and his clients among the Tungus of Manchuria is still
stronger when the attended person is a child. In a great
number of cases, as shown, the shaman takes the soul of
the child (male or female) and keeps it up to a certain age,
sometimes up to thirteen or fourteen years. The shaman
takes under his protection that component of the threefold
soul which returns into other people and animals. If he
would take all three components the child would die. The shaman leaves with the child a bell and brass mirror, or something else from his costume. These are placings for the shaman's spirits while the soul is kept by the shaman. The
placings are always kept in a special birch-bark box near
the sleeping place of the child, and they must not be lost.
If loss should occur, it must be immediately reported to the
shaman who will take special measures for recovering the
control of the absent spirits, together with the placings.
In this function the shaman's spirit is actually a guardian
spirit of the child. After the above indicated age the soul
is revoked by the shaman, and the above mentioned things
are returned to the shaman. Some complications may
arise when the shaman dies before the time of the restoration of the soul. However, it is supposed that all spirits,
and naturally souls, become free after the shaman's death.
If the soul of the shaman and his spirits, also the souls of
children, are not captured by other spirits at the moment
of the shaman's death, the child will not suffer any trouble.
Therefore the Tungus abstain from having recourse to
very old shamans, and naturally they do not ask for any
help from "bad-hearted" shamans who during their fight-
ings with other shamans may be destroyed at any moment.
When the shaman collects the souls of children he makes
them greatly dependent upon himself, and thus a very
strong connexion between the shaman and his clients is
formed. All of them want to preserve the shaman and to
be on good terms with him. In case of trouble they form
his own group of sympathizers, sometimes perhaps even
against their own will.

Naturally the more numerous are his permanent clients

from their childhood, the more influential is the shaman.

Besides this special service rendered by the shaman to
the children, he accumulates a great number of adult clients
who were relieved by him of their troubles and thus became natural friends of the shaman. The adult clients
who are known to a shaman usually address themselves to
the same shaman, so that the latter, after getting more
acquainted with the psychology of the client, becomes indispensable to the client. In fact, in all cases when a renewing of suggestion is needed, the client hardly can peacefully live without his shaman's assistance.

Indeed, if the shaman is at the same time a popular
shaman and a clan-shaman, and if he does not "fight", his
influence upon the clan may become very great. However,
owing to the strictness of the system of social organization, he will not become "chief", or "head" of the clan. As
a matter of fact, a quite special psychomental condition of
the shaman, as was shown in the preceding chapter, would
not permit him to become such a "leader", although he may
be very influential, even with the military leader of the
Tungus, as it was e.g. with Mukteokan and other shamans
who defended with their art their people against foreign
aggression.

From these instances we may see that the personal influence of a shaman may extend far beyond his own clan,
and it will be a case of individual success.

Whether the shaman is liked or not, whether he is
"bad-hearted" or "good-hearted", he always assumes, with
his art and individuality, a special social position, which
imposes a certain ceremonialism in dealing with him. The
shamans are not called by their personal names, even by
the seniors; joking and teasing, which are common amongst
the Tungus, cannot be used with the shamans; the shaman
is usually treated as a "senior". Among some groups the
term "shaman" is not used in addressing the shamans.
Among the Reindeer Tungus of Transbaikalia they are called *nordojar'if'k'i*, which may mean "he who is praying"
(*nordojar'i*,—"to sing" etc.), or even *oyōvun* (Ner. Barg.)
—"the singer". Among the Manchus and Tungus of Manchuria the shaman may be called by the honourable term,
—*aka, ak'i.* or even *èjèn*,—"the master". Among the Reindeer Tungus of Transbaikalia the female shaman may
be called by an alien term *odakón* (cf. *supra*, p. 270).

**140.   ECONOMIC POSITION AND   In the discussion
DIFFICULTIES OF THE SHAMAN   of the transmission of shamanism**
it has already been pointed out that the problem of maintaining shamans is of importance and may have an influence upon the election of a new shaman. Owing to the
psychomental character of shamanism, most of the shamans are put in an exceptional position in reference to the
chief industrial activity of the Tungus—the hunting. In
fact, in Transbaikalia I have met with a shaman who could
not kill big animals such as the elk, Cervus Elaphus, Cervus
Tarandus—and therefore was chiefly hunting roe-deer. On
his part it was a case of self-suggestion. Some shamans
cannot hunt tigers and bears, for these are animals whose
forms may be assumed (they become placings) by other
shamans. A great number of shamans have no assurance
in handling fire-arms. Dealing with the spirits and sometimes being attacked by them, as well as by other sha-

mans, the shaman is usually not certain, when remaining alone, that this will not be used as a good opportunity for attacking him. It must be added that the shamans are sometimes kept busy with their duties of assisting clansmen and outsiders, so that they have no time for regular hunting. Owing to this, among the Northern Tungus, the shamans usually live together with other people who do the hunting for them, look after the domesticated animals, and, in general, take care of them. However, this care never takes the form of a complete control of the shaman's life, but is done within the limits of the usual Tungus relations, when a person partly invalid is assisted by other persons of the same clan.

The female shamans, whose economic activity is different from that of male shamans, may do their work better than the males. The only difference is that a female shaman, being busy with her duties, has no time for various handwork, such as sewing or ornamentation of costumes, reindeer harness, various boxes, etc., so that the equipment of her family is not as much ornamented as that of other females who have more leisure. Since the female shaman is often called from her home, she must also have somebody to look after her children during her absence. Should she have a suckling babe, she would take it with her; but if the children could do without her, they would be looked after by other people. In the Tungus conditions of life this is not difficult—the Tungus usually stay in groups of no less than two wigwams and very often more than two. Being an honoured person, the female shaman may also expect that other females would do some indispensable work for her, such as the curing of skins, etc. The husbands of female shamans commonly do a part of the work usually done by the wives, which, generally speaking, is not rare among the Tungus: men very often help their wives in curing skins, particularly thick, heavy skins, e.g. elk skins, bear-skins, etc. are often worked only by men.

Among the Reindeer Tungus of Transbaikalia the shaman receives for his service no remuneration, with the exception of some food taken after the sacrifice; but he may receive some fresh meat as a present, like any other guest. The shamans also receive kerchieves and sometimes additions to their paraphernalia, but neither have any importance in the material support of the shaman. The shaman never receives money. Thus the shamanship cannot become a profession which may permit the shamans to live only on what they may earn for this service to the clansmen and outsiders.

Among the Tungus of Manchuria the shamans never receive any remuneration, save fresh blood from the sacrificial animal, some drink, wine either bought from the foreigners (Chinese, Russians) or made by the Tungus themselves (berry wine produced by some Tungus groups), and some presents like kerchieves attached to the shaman's coat. The shamans cannot refuse to shamanize, even when there is no wine or kerchieves. They never accept money. All Tungus assert that a shaman cannot become rich. As a matter of fact, all shamans whom I knew personally were poorer than the average Tungus. Among the Birarčen there was a female-shaman with her husband who were so poor that they lived in a corner of a house belonging to other people. The husband was not a good hunter and had to stay with his wife to look after her and their babe. They had even no clothes in sufficient quantity for going to the mountains, and the child was usually half-naked. Another

shaman, among the Reindeer Tungus of Barguzin, was the poorest man in reindeer, and when I knew him he had to go on foot, two reindeer being loaded with his belongings and children. After an accident in hunting he did not believe himself able to carry on hunting as he had done before.

It may thus be said that candidates to shamanship are not stimulated by any material interest, from the point of view of which they are in an inferior position that sometimes makes their lives a continuous suffering from poverty. But it should be noted that among the Northern Tungus the shaman, if he is not a "bad-hearted" person, will not be left to starve to death and will be supported by his clansmen and "clients". But it would be the same with any other Tungus.

The position of shamans is different among the Manchus. Among them, a shaman must shamanize without remuneration only for his clansmen, but clients outside of the clan must pay him. In the description of the sacrifice were mentioned a chicken, a dollar (rouble), a piece of cloth sufficient for a small dress, etc. taken by the shaman after the shamanizing. Small as it is, this remuneration alone may support the shaman, for he can carry out at least one shamanizing a day. With the custom of prayers after the harvest, when the shaman receives presents in grain from all houses of the village and in rather large quantities from *jarumbő*, the position of the shaman may become even better than that of an average Manchu. In fact, it is quite common that a shaman has twenty or thirty *jarumbő*, some of which may be rich, and every year each of them supplies him with a ton of grain. The presents gathered by the shaman on the second day of the new year are also of importance. Presents of wine, incense, candies, bread etc. from a large number of *jarun* may be numerous enough for being used during a long time, and even being sold.

However, the clan shamans, as I have shown, may be kept quite busy by their functions within the clan, so that they cannot make of shamanship a profitable profession. But the *amba saman*, who are not bound by their clans, may reach a relative prosperity.

Among the Manchus I did not observe well-to-do shamans—most of whom were clan shamans—but among the Chinese shamanship has definitely changed into a profitable profession. During my work on the spot I knew several shamans, two of whom lived quite opulently, even in the city (*Saxalan*, in Manchu; *Xeixe*, in Chinese), and all of which were not tilling their fields, nor carrying on any other profession than shamanizing. It seems to me that among the Dahurs there was nearly the same situation, for I have met with shamans who lived by their profession.

The rather difficult economic situation of the shamans is not alone in making their life a kind of martyrdom: the hardships of shamanizing, the responsibility and hostility are associated with poverty; moreover, his movements are bound by a great number of restrictions; the future of his soul is not certain, and above all he cannot give up his shamanship. First of all, the functions, as shown before, keep the shamans in a state of great nervous and mental tension. The latter may personally be perceived as a pleasant condition; but since after every serious shamanizing the performers feel physically tired—it is a tiresome work—the shamans, after a few years of work, sometimes become half-exhausted. This exhaustion may be due to an uneconomical use of energy in the performances, which only sometimes may be based on pure ritualism and tricks, not requiring a special tension of the psychomental complex, and which usually are based upon a real extasy. If the shaman performs too often—I have observed among the Reindeer Tungus of Transbaikalia some cases when three performances of little shamanizing were carried out in a day; a big shamanizing was carried out every night during great gatherings for weddings, etc.—he naturally becomes tired. We have seen that the shamans themselves sometimes want to perform, which may be understood as a sign of the shaman's personal psychic instability. In case the shaman himself should be susceptible to psychomental instability, he might become the prey of his own spirits, if he does not restrict himself in practising performances. So a shaman may gradually bring himself into a state when he would even be unable to carry out his work. If there is no other, very strong, shaman, there would be nobody to help him.

The shaman, being the safety valve of the clan and a clan officer, cannot refuse to assist his clansmen. Therefore, whether he feels himself strong or not, tired or not, he must attend. However, the shaman's psychic condition is not often noticed, perhaps it is not understood, and only when he becomes psychomentally "abnormal", his state is noticed, and then it is usually regarded as an evidence of new intrigues of spirits. Thus the shaman must not neglect his duties. He may be excused only when he is very old and physically weak, or if the shaman is a female, when she is pregnant and generally ak'ipču (tabooed). If there is no such an excuse, the shaman may lose his position; however this happens very seldom. But since in a great number of cases a person becomes a shaman because of his own psychomental condition, which requires the "mastering of spirits", he, being deprived of his right of being a shaman, may lose his recognized ability of self-control and thus become the prey of his spirits. If after giving up this social functioning and after losing his right of shamanizing he should make an attempt to restore his position, he would come into conflict with his clan and a new shaman. So he may become a "bad-hearted" man, with all the resultant consequences. The pressure of the clan is here much stronger than in the case of a common clansman—the shaman is connected with the spirits.

Since the shaman functions as a safety valve and as a regulator of the psychic life of the clan, he lives under the permanent feeling of bearing a great responsibility. In some cases it would not be cognized at all and would not be formulated, as I do it here, but this condition is a serious factor for the shaman, for it takes the form of a complex regulation of the relations existing between the spirits and the shaman himself. However, it is possible that in some rare cases old experienced shamans may come to a formulation of the situation in terms of psychic phenomena and to their regulation, which in turn would increase both the functions and the responsibility. The feeling of responsibility is probably a condition which implies the shaman's readiness to function when needed.

The shaman meets with another difficulty in his activity, namely—hostility. A hostile attitude may come from a smaller or greater number of clansmen and outsiders. The shaman's failure to gain a general sympathy, as I have already shown, may easily grow into a general hostility. In fact, if the shaman makes mistakes in his relations with the clansmen, he cannot be successful in at-

tending them—he will be distrusted. If any trouble should occur, it would be attributed to the shaman; he might be reproached for causing the harm. Naturally, in defending himself, he might create a new hostility, to the extent of being regarded as a "bad-hearted" man who must be thrust out of the community. Such cases become especially frequent, when the shaman does not belong to the clan. As I have shown, among all groups there are always individuals hostile to shamanism in general, so the shaman, even a little known and little experienced beginner, must gain, if not their sympathy, then at least their neutrality.

From the analysis of the relations between the shaman and the spirits, his own spirits and those of other shamans, also his spirits and the complex of other spirits, we can see a great number of various prohibitions, avoidances, tabooes, binding every step of the shaman. Even in his family the shaman must be careful not to harm his wife, if he is a male shaman, or her husband, if she is a female, not to speak of the children. The shaman must avoid harming other people as well, e.g. at the time of childbirth and menstruation, in hunting, fishing and other forms of responsible activity. The shaman's spirits, which he carries with him, may always become involved with other spirits and a continuous trouble may originate from their conflict. Owing to this the shaman is always careful when finding himself among other people, travelling, and carrying on his industrial activity. This implies a special attention of the shaman to his surroundings and allows him still less freedom than that which is usually enjoyed by the Tungus. The reaction of other people on the shaman responds to his cautious behaviour, so that very often the shaman becomes more or less isolated.

Finally there is a special condition more, which deprives the shaman of the usual cheerfulness of the Tungus, viz. the worry about the soul. As a matter of fact, for the shamans departing this life is not as easy as for other people. The soul may remain in this world, may be captured by spirits and afterwards mastered, so that the shaman's soul instead of a settled existence in the lower world will continue to stay in the middle world. This becomes a new source of trouble during his life, and every shaman is constantly worried by this idea. I shall treat this question in a special section and I shall now only point out this aspect of the difficulties experienced by the shaman.

Being put in an unfavourable economic position, performing a difficult work carried on step by step with a lack of certainty, burdened with responsibility, and continuously fighting the hostility of his own clansmen and outsiders, the shaman faces the impossibility of giving up his functions. This can be done only in very rare, exceptional cases discussed in the next section. The shaman cannot give up his function because by giving up his control over the spirits he might involve his clansmen in psychic instability caused by the "dis-mastered" spirits. According to the Tungus conviction, in the presence of the old master the spirits will not easily submit to a new one and they will naturally harm the clansmen. The second reason is that, as shown above, the shaman, by giving up his function, may again be affected by the condition which had compelled him to become a shaman. The third reason is the general opinion of the Tungus that *the shaman must not give up his functions*, i.e. the pressure on the part of the clan, the breaking with which may put the shaman into still greater trouble. Thus, when a man or a woman once becomes a shaman he or she must go on up to death or to psychic invalidity.

It seems to me that without exaggeration it can be said that a shaman's life is a difficult one, it is a continuous self-sacrifice.

———————

In reviewing the hard conditions of the individual existence of the shamans, it would be natural to ask oneself: why do they not give up their functions and why, in view of the further difficulties do the candidates accept such a fate? This question is answered, first of all, by a reference to what has been formulated as to the formation of new shamans from the candidates, and the latter from the mass of the Tungus population. The shaman does not appear by his own will; a new shaman results from the complex system of all pre-existing theories, from the mass psychoses, from individual and perhaps inherited susceptibility for the psychomental state that is needed for shamanistic functions. The shaman is needed by the Tungus. The shaman can help to cure people affected by the spirits (psychomental instability) ; he may relieve sick people, even with diseases of non-psychic order, when this is needed for a successful "self-defence" of the affected organism; he may also, by his presence, give assurance to the people that they will not suffer. This is the result of an empiric experimentation of the Tungus on themselves, which has been reached through a long adaptation. Moreover, the shaman is not rejected, for his public activity is attractive. The Tungus find pleasure in seeing shamanizing and enjoy the emotional participation in it. This is a very important condition, for it is very unlikely that shamanism could be stabilized without this stimulus. Every candidate is conscious of the fact that the community wants a shaman and that he may serve the community. We need not analyse the psychic mechanism underlying this "social service" complex, to some extent even this self-sacrifice, which for us seems to be a fact; but, from the individual point of view, the negative side of this activity is perhaps not so impressive as the positive side, if we permit ourselves to speak of conscious choice and the formation of a decision in such situations. The choice of one's fate and the formation of a decision may not be involved at all, for the appearance of a new shaman is presumed by the existence of the whole complex which is not confined to individuals, but relates to a group, and which usually remains unperceived.

Another question is as to how the individual shamans may use their position for their own pleasure and the compensation for the work they do, and why they do not run away.

In this respect, the individuality of the shaman is of primary importance. First of all, a great number of shamans cannot give up their functions because they themselves may again become sick; secondly, they may be forced by their clans to go on with their work; thirdly, they may find it interesting for themselves, being influential members of the community; fourthly, they may find pleasure in performing, in experiencing the emotional state of extasy, and so on; and fifthly, they may find pleasure of carrying on

this work, because they get an intellectual satisfaction in studying and handling—consciously or unconsciously—the most delicate mechanism of the human psychomental complex.* According to these personal attitudes towards shamanizing, the individual cases of shamans may be classified, and the fact that in this respect the shamans are not alike may be better understood. Indeed, several elements of the accepting of hardship of shamanism may form different combinations and perhaps, in some cases, the hardship will be smaller than the pleasure received from this function.

I leave aside the first four motives for the acceptance of shaman's functions, but I wish to dwell upon the last one, namely, the intellectual satisfaction. In reality, not all shamans are much affected by the spirit of inquisitiveness, but I have met with such ones in some cases. In the preceding chapters, dealing with the Tungus as observers and naturalists, we have seen that they possess, and in a great degree, the ability of observation, even without a practical issue other than the extension of knowledge. The shamans who come into very close contact with the people who must avow to them the truth about themselves—and we have seen that the Tungus do so—have an exceptionally vast field of observation. It is not surprising at all that some shamans continually think about their observations, solve various psychological riddles (in terms of spirits), gather more and more new material, always being greedy of rerum novarum in their field, and in this work find intellectual satisfaction, as any other people who are interested in mental creative work. We have seen that the shamans may become contributors to the Tungus "science"—to the Tungus knowledge. However, to identify shamanism with the search for a theoretical outcome would be an artificial justification of shamanism—this result is achieved only because of individual adaptation by the most talented persons among the shamans, who may find a positive side in their difficult functioning as a "safety valve" and a psychic regulator of the Tungus clans. Such a result is only a by-product of the practice of shamanism by an endowed people as the Tungus are; in some other ethnical group there might be no such an outcome. For instance, among the Manchus I did not find it. Perhaps this is due to the fact that the Manchu complex had previously adopted elements of the Chinese complex, which stopped the further penetration into psychic phenomena, that occupied a selected group of intellectually inclined individuals, and reduced shamanism to that which has been described above. By fixing a difference between the Tungus and Manchus, I give an explanation only in the most hypothetical form; but as a matter of fact, I have not met with thinkers among the Manchu shamans as I did among the Northern Tungus.

141. GIVING UP OF SHAMANSHIP AND SHAMAN'S DEATH I have observed a few cases, when clan shamanship had been given up. It may occur in the case when the shaman becomes very old, loses his sight, becomes physically very weak, and so forth, i.e. because of his physical unfitness. However, as shown in the case of succession to shamanism among the Reindeer Tungus of Transbaikalia, there cannot be two shamans at the same time without a risk that the

———————

* I omit the case of those shamans who make a living on their profession.

old shaman will die. However, if the shaman is not unwilling to die, he may transmit his functions to a young shaman. As I have shown, a similar case of a very old shaman and his niece has been observed. But the old shaman did not shamanize regularly, and thus two shamans lived simultaneously at least for several years. In such cases the clan, seeing the inefficiency of an old shaman, may support a candidate, perhaps without worrying much about the old man. The prohibition, or perhaps only the undesirability of having two shamans at one time, can be better understood, when we consider the existence of a limitation of the appearance of a new shaman which must not be disapproved by the old shaman. However, practically there is no need for a clan to have two shamans at the same time; when the clans are getting too populous, they split, and each of the new unit will have its own shaman.

I have observed a similar case among the Khingan Tungus, where an old shaman did not carry on his duties, while a young shaman was acting.

A shaman may give up shamanizing, e.g. because of blindness. I have observed such a case among the Birarčen. The female shaman was about forty years old. She explained her blindness as due to the fighting with another shaman. However, the Birarčen assured me that blindness cannot hinder shamanizing at all. This opinion cannot be justified, because of the reasons given in the preceding chapters; the shaman must see the audience, but the shamanistic ritual may be performed even by a blind shaman. In this case the female shaman, after her having become blind, was simply discharged by the clan.

It is different with the dōna (outside-clan) shamans who are not bound to remain shamans all their life long. Therefore, when the psychic condition of the shaman does not impose shamanizing, the latter can be given up, and the spirits will not disturb the shaman. The only question is how to transmit the spirits to some other candidate, should the spirits dōna disturb other people. Since these spirits are often supposed to leave the people alone and since they may also be chased, their transmission is not always necessary. Among the Birarčen these occurrences are frequent and the Birarčen explain it thus: the shaman becomes lazy, so the spirits may leave their master. There may occur another case of discontinuation of a shaman's activity, namely, the pressure of the clan. Should the shaman show himself inefficient, even though being young, he would lose his position as a clan shaman by the fact of being avoided. If he is not invited by the clansmen, the reason of his existence disappears, especially if he is not needed for the treatment of sick people, or the carrying away of souls of unfortunate people who by accident remain in this world, etc. It is certain that sooner or later a new shaman will appear and he will be recognized by the clan, and the former shaman will be allowed to give up his position, as he wants; but he will probably not be permitted to resume his functions as a clan shaman. Since the shaman's inability is also connected with his deficiency in the art of mastering spirits, producing extasy, etc., it is very likely that the shaman will not oppose the change of his position. He may also simply become "lazy" and, with the silent consent of the clan, give up the shamanship. Such cases occur, but very seldom, as I was told.

Among the Manchus I did not observe cases of giving up shamanism, perhaps because of the relative rarity of shamans independent of clans. Most of independent shamans belonged to other ethnical groups (Chinese and Dahura). If a shaman becomes less active, it is also a sign of a relative quietness among the clansmen. Among the Manchus the function of the shaman may be partly taken up by the p'oyun saman, who may pray to the spirits, and by mafur'i who are independent of the clans.

The death of a clan shaman is a very serious event in the clan life. Two problems are then faced, namely, the discharge of the shaman's soul and the remastering of the spirits left by the deceased shaman. Among the Manchus it is supposed that the third soul, which must go for a final judgment to Ilmunzan, is not left to descend to the lower world by the spirits vočko. This soul becomes a spirit vočko, and thus all shamans become vočko. However, some special conditions exist too. For instance, in the case of the shaman decapitated by the authorities (vide supra, p. 347) it was supposed that the soul was captured by the spirits early in the morning of the day of the execution, and it was immediately incorporated into a new born child. The second soul together with vočko was busy with guarding the olorg'i soul. However, the soul may not become vočko at once, but only after a period of fifteen years.[*]

If no care of the shaman's soul is taken, after becoming vočko it introduces itself into the clansmen and makes them suffer, until a new shaman appears. The same is true of all spirits left behind. A series of individual psychoses and even a mass-psychosis may occur.

The burial of the shaman does not differ now from that of ordinary people, except that some of the shamanistic paraphernalia, especially a trident spear is put into the coffin, while the costume, the drum and other things are carefully packed into a box and put on the shelf, together with the placings for spirits. However, it was not so in the past, when as shown (vide supra p. 213), a special form of burying was practised.

Thus, among the Manchus the problem as to the shaman's soul is solved in a simple manner and there is no special worry about it. It is not so among the Northern Tungus groups.

When a shaman dies, his soul must go to the lower world, but it must be taken there by another shaman who must be "stronger" than the deceased one. If there is no such a shaman, the soul cannot reach the world of the dead —bunil. Remaining in this world it will have no rest and other clansmen will all the time be disturbed by it.

Among the Tungus of Transbaikalia the shaman's body is deposited in the same kind of coffin, erected on the posts (vide supra, p. 221) as used for ordinary people. All the paraphernalia, with the exception of savak'i, are put together with the shaman, or hung up to a nearby standing tree. Several posts may be erected with carved wooden "birds", which will help to carry away the shaman's soul. The ritual of the burial does not differ from that used for ordinary people. It is not recommended to touch the paraphernalia left at the burial place. Those who touch them may get "mental diseases", they may "lose their minds", i.e. become abnormal.

The new shaman who gathers the spirits left free must appear not later than nine years after the shaman's death;

_____

[*] This was one of the theoretical reasons why the shaman could not be produced earlier, with the shaman's soul-vočko.

otherwise there will be many people suffering from the spirits.

Among the Tungus of Manchuria there are still greater difficulties, for the soul of the shaman may become a new spirit, *sêvèŋ*. As shown, these Tungus are not very inclined to increase the number of spirits and every new spirit is met without pleasure. They are admitted as an inevitable evil. With the shamans who die by a "bad death", as in the cases quoted (e.g. the spirit *lamalačéen*, the old shaman of the Dunänkän clan, and others), the soul cannot be taken to the lower world, and thus becomes a spirit. Fortunately, the Tungus are saved by the lack of written records. Some important spirits are preserved by tradition, while a great number of spirits, formed from the souls of dead shamans and the like, are soon forgotten. Only in this way we may explain the rather limited number of shamanistic spirits of this origin.

To carry away the soul of a shaman to the world of the dead is not easy, even for a good shaman. The chief difficulty is the mixing up of the spirits of the two shamans. If the shaman, who performs the operation of the last transportation, is not certain of being able to master the spirits of the deceased shaman, he must not undertake this operation. The spirits left by the shaman very often want "to keep him in their company", as the Tungus say, so that the shaman must first fight these spirits.

The Tungus like much better to rid themselves of these spirits for ever. With this aim a delicate procedure of sending them off, may be undertaken even by taking them into a new region, or by placing them in special placings and sending these off with the current of a big river, such as the Amur. This can be done only with the spirits *dōna* which are possessed even by the clan shaman; but this cannot be done with the clan spirits which are supposed to stay for ever with a clan. Sooner or later they will find a new master, but in the interval they will try perhaps several persons, making them abnormal, sometimes for rather a long time. I had an occasion to observe every day, during a period of nearly two months, a young man among the Khingan Tungus who suffered from such spirits left by a shaman. The young man had frequent nervous fits, continuously shouting *sêvèn èmèrèn, sêvèn èmèrèn!* (the spirit is coming!) ; he beat his forehead with his fist and made "stick and arch". Until some able candidate masters the spirits, which sometimes requires several years, the people are suffering as described above.

Naturally the shamans know of the approach of their end and are prepared for it, but during their lives there can be no relief for them, for their souls will perhaps not share the fate of those of other clansmen in the monotonous and half-starving existence in the twilight of the lower world. Yet it is better to be settled in the little attractive lower world than to be a "workman", a "servant" of all future generations of shamans.

142. SHAMAN'S PERSONALITY Dealing with the shaman in the preceding sections we have seen the almost tragic figure of this important member of the Tungus society. However, we have also seen that there may be "positive" sides of shamanistic practices in so far as they are perceived and understood by the shamans, However, grouped facts and generalizations do not give a vivid picture of individual cases of the shamans. Together with the description of the election (*vide supra*, p. 347 and Section 131) I have pictured two candidates, but they are not typical at all. Naturally, to give a series of portraits of the shamans would be the best way to fill up this omission in my description, but this is a task which risks to degenerate into a work of too much imagination, for, first of all, I cannot assert that my knowledge of the individuality of the Tungus shamans is so perfect, that I can give facts which by themselves may produce portraits—facts are not sufficient for it. I have observed some shamans during, for instance, nearly two years, but still some sides of their personality have easily escaped my attention. In this respect too one cannot carry out a mechanical registration of facts according to a scheme—one must "penetrate" into the individuality. Such a task is indeed beyond the possibility of a field investigator.

In spite of the impossibility to give a gallery of portraits, I still feel it useful to demonstrate some individual characteristics of some shamans observed by me. Without giving them the great importance of a scientific documentation, I shall relate my impressions:

1. A Barguzin Reindeer Tungus shaman. He was rather tall with a thin, straight nose, blue-black hair, a long head and rather long legs; he was near to the asthenic type, although physically strong and healthy. He lived with his wife and two children in a wigwam very poorly furnished with the usual Tungus equipment. They had only two reindeer. His wife was unusually quiet and silent. The children were normal. No signs of psychomental abnormality could be observed in any member of this family. At the moment of meeting with them the family lived alone, in the middle of a marshy valley; no neighbours were around. The shaman was about thirty-five years old, having practised shamanizing for ten years or even more. He was a clan shaman. He did not like to work, nor to hunt, but preferred to remain for hours in meditation. He was addicted, somewhat more than an average Tungus of this group, to drinking. One of the really distinct elements, very opposite to the average Tungus character, was his vanity and attention to his own person, well pronounced egocentrism. His most interesting pastime was conversation concerning shamanism, spirits, and, in general, natural phenomena, cosmogony, etc. However, when he was not sure, and this was a common case with him, he used to say: "So people say, but I do not know it myself", and "I do not know, whether it is true or not". He did not easily accept a belief, but wished to find the logical connexion of everything, the principal theory as to the spirits being dominant in his reasoning. Indeed, the problems of cosmogony and in general natural phenomena were not affected by this theory. His reason why he did not hunt was chiefly that formerly he had by mistake killed a domesticated reindeer, and since that time he had no "luck". Perhaps, on his part, it was mere justification of his hunting inefficiency, perhaps it was a real psychological condition of fear of doing something wrong. He did not much shamanize and he was not considered as a good shaman, but he was continually communicating, in his dreams, with other shamans, especially with an old shaman of the Nerchinsk Tungus. Owing to his inclination to discussion and his sincere interest in various general problems, it was possible for me to establish with him very

close relations. When he was acquainted with me, he became very frank and communicative. In his speech the expression "common people", i.e. those who are not versed in shamanism, was constantly used. Moreover, in his performances he was quite "artistic" and produced genuine extasy. I had the good fortune to be in contact with him for at least five or six weeks.

2. A Barguzin Reindeer Tungus female clan shaman. She was a heavily built, tall, muscular, seemingly healthy woman of over thirty years; meditative and deliberative in her somewhat slow movements in the everyday life. I saw her daily for a relatively long period and saw her perform a great number of times. The first time I saw her, she arrived with her small babe, being urgently invited to shamanize to the lower world, which, as shown, is a difficult task and a rare occurrence. Her attitude at the first meeting was that of avoiding me, but after I had tactfully left her alone for a time and had given her my support in the discussion of various questions with the seniors, I could discern her attitude of approval of my interest in shamanism and my sympathy with her functions. After I had been able to render her some minor assistance during the shamanizing, she allowed me to observe her as much as I wanted. She did not protest when I asked her questions, took her pulse at different moments of the performance, examined the rigidity of muscles, etc., but even helped me and seemed to take an interest in my findings, which I did not fail to communicate her, and she confirmed what, in her opinion, was correct. Her attitude showed that she was a thinking, self-analysing person, discussing the problem of her own psychic condition. Since these discussions were usually carried out in the presence of old men, she did not hesitate to speak. I did not hear her mention "common people". She seemed not to be much attached to her babe. Her relations with her husband, who was a good hunter, were apparently good. The material position of the family was not bad—she was well dressed, although without pretention. She was considered as one of the best shamans and did not refuse to shamanize, which she did with a perfect art, with extasy, and with evident success, in so far as the audience was concerned. No signs of abnormality could be observed in her. As compared with the other women, she was definitely more silent, she usually avoided looking directly into the eyes of the interlocutor, looking down, and sometimes looking aside. She was not inclined to laughing, joking and idle talk, which is usual with the Tungus, when they are free. She did not participate in night dancing (cf. SONT), nor in gatherings for "five o'clock tea"; she did not mix with the "common women". However, this was done in a simple manner, without any attempt at snubbing people. She merely disliked this kind of distraction, as some other women do.

3. A Khingan Tungus female clan shaman, married, under thirty years. She looked like a great number of other women among this group; she was fleshy and moderately fat, and was quick in her movements. Perhaps her face was somewhat more alive than that of an average Khingan woman. In all respects she seemed quite normal. Her interest in shamanism did not go beyond her performances, although she seemingly liked these very much and looked for any occasion to perform. Her performances were not "artistic" and a certain degree of conventionalism was quite evident; however, I observed genuine extasy during one or two performances. She was not considered a good shaman, and was only called for performances of small importance, such as finding out of the cause of a sickness, divination, predictions etc. Anyhow, I have not seen her perform any shamanizing of great importance, such as the recovery of souls, and the travelling to the lower world. Although I succeeded in coming into friendly relations with her, because of my painting for her some designs on her drum, no "serious talk" (as I understand it) about shamanism was possible—she was willing to talk mostly about the formulas and ritualism of performances. She used to spend her time with other women, doing some work, gossiping, laughing and joking with them. She also manifested a certain inclination to sexual indecency, e.g. when asking me, together with other women, to show my painting along the line of representation of human genitalia on the placings for spirits and on paper; in maintaining conversations on similar subjects and, together with other women, repeating prohibited words, although with some moderation, as compared with the other women of her clan. She was not yet a very experienced shaman and her character with her age may have changed.

4. A Birarčen female shaman. She was twenty nine years old, slender, very nervous, which was especially conspicuous in her behaviour towards her child, the only one who had survived out of four. She used to press the child against her face and breast, kiss it and look at it with great tenderness, which although observed among the Tungus, is but seldom expressed in such a passionate form. Her husband was a poor hunter and even had no horse for his hunting trips. They were very poor. Since I performed the duties of her assistant several times and once took measures for protecting her against her aggressors, I succeeded in disposing her in my favour. She was not willing to talk about shamanism, but she wanted to help me in understanding the details, and even consented to sing into the phonograph. I suppose that her dislike of this kind of conversation depended chiefly on the fact that she did not know very much about shamanism in general, but she "felt" it and had learnt it, so to say, empirically, perhaps without forming any clear idea as to what she was actually doing. She was very shy, and when she did not want to shamanize, she used to refuse in the most categorical manner to do it. She was not a first class performer. In drumming she was not always good, in rhythmic dancing she might change her step, her singing was not clear, and it was difficult to understand her in the state of extasy. Perhaps this was due to the fact, that she was still young and had not yet developed the necessary technique. However, another explanation is possible, namely, she could not master herself and, as stated, she was very shy. It was difficult for her to bring herself into a genuine extasy. When the extasy was reached, she could be nigh loosing her self-control. Moreover, it should be noted that several times she performed under very unfavourable conditions of a definitely negative reaction on the part of at least a numerous group of participants in the audience, and she was living, as shown, in rather difficult conditions, even for a Tungus woman. So that she was "struggling". I have also noticed a certain persistence and even obstinacy in her behaviour, which, together with other facts, made me inclined to believe her to be a case of partial control of an intense state of suppressed "hysteria". However, observing her during several months, I never heard of any nervous fits with her.

5. A Manchu clan shaman. A man about forty-five years old, strong and healthy, in all respects normal. He had a Chinese (n'ükan) wife, and of his several children two had survived. He read Manchu and some Chinese. He had performed his functions for twenty years or so. In looking at him one could not see that he was a shaman. He was not austere in his habits, nor moderate as regards food and drink, which he greatly appreciated. He was considered as a good shaman, very experienced and successful in his treatment. In every case he attended he made a detailed preliminary inquiry and then, if needed, he usually took a decision in a state of sleep. Sometimes he decided questions without sleeping. He was a good performer, sometimes allowing himself to be overtaken by a strong extasy. He was not much interested in general problems and avoided them in conversation, but seemed to be a good analyst of human psychology, in which he was always interested. This may be seen from his special attention to the cases he treated, to the troubles with the people, and so forth. He was invited by the clan, when there was the question of the election of a new shaman to be decided, on which occasion I was particularly able to come into very close contact with him. He was inclined to look at the complex relations of spirits as the chief source of troubles. In his analyses of similar situations he used all his erudition (knowledge of spirits and experience) and was willing to go into minute details in order to understand and explain complex cases. However, since he was living on shamanism and wanted to maintain friendly relations with the people, he was not always sincere in his reasoning and in the advices which he knew would be agreeable to them. He did not oppose inviting the assistance of another shaman in difficult cases, nor did he object to calling Chinese doctors. In one case he himself gave such an advice. With myself and his friend, a Manchu with whom I was also on very good terms, he was usually rather frank,

admitting that in some cases he did not understand the situation. In the above described case of an election he was sincerely interested in finding out the truth, in spite of the fluctuations of public opinion, and he discussed minor details in the behaviour of both candidates.

These five distinct types of shamans, with the other cases described before, including those of candidates, are only some of the existing types. The more shamans I knew the more I saw that every shaman is an individuality. Only with an effort to let aside characteristic differences generalizations might be made. Such generalizations may serve different ends and may be more conditioned by the ends, than by the true and natural grouping of facts. In fact, from the point of view of individual psychomental complex we meet with variations: (1) from a perfect "normality" to typical insanity; (2) from a perfect faith to conventional and conscious acceptance of the shamanistic complex; (3) from a very limited knowledge to complete possession of available facts (in the existing complexes); (4) from individualistic, egocentric cases to a perfect fusion of the shaman's individuality with the social milieu; (5) from a very poor knowledge and poor possession of shamanistic technique to real erudition and an artistic ability of a performer in this art. It is thus evident that two perfectly identical cases are not found, so a theoretically made classification may perhaps appear quite useless, especially since every ethnical group gives its own "colour" to its complex, also variable at different historical moments. For fear of distorting living phenomena by distributing them into the rigid system of a preexisting classification, which may be quite artificial and thus misleading, I leave the question of the personality of Tungus shamans where it stands. Personalities of shamans are strikingly varied and individualistic and they cannot be arranged into a rigid system.

CHAPTER XXXI

PRESENT STATE AND FUTURE OF SHAMANISM

143. LIST OF SHAMANS AMONG THE GROUPS INVESTIGATED In the present section I shall give an enumeration of the shamans personally met with, also heard of from the Tungus. Such a list cannot be complete, for I did not myself meet with all of the shamans and some of them may easily have been forgotten by the Tungus. I made no detailed inquiry about it; but when I had an occasion to speak about the shamans whom I did not know personally, I asked about them. However, only a very limited number of them might escape my recording. In spite of the incompleteness of my material concerning the number of shamans, I give a list of them, for it may give an idea as to how numerous they are, and this alone may be indicative of the actual importance of shamanism in the Tungus complex.

It should be kept in mind that shamanism among the Tungus is essentially a phenomenon connected with the clan organization. As can be seen from the preceding

chapters, the shamans outside of the clan are in a more difficult position than the clan shamans. However, sometimes the clans have no shamans, for years, so that the calculation of the number of clans (given in my SONT) will not give an exact number of acting shamans. There are also shamans who act outside of the clan. Moreover, a disorganization of the clan does not mean the disappearance of shamans, as observed among the Reindeer Tungus of Manchuria, but sometimes, on the contrary, the shamans multiply and become "family-shamans" or simply free shamans, as it is common e.g. among the Manchus. Naturally, it depends upon the general condition of the psychomental complex, particularly on the extent of the psychoses and whether the complex of shamanism is abolished together with the clan organization, or whether it is replaced by some new complex.

* Perhaps the presence of a great number of "shamans" among the Chukchis is due to the disintegration of the clan organization.

TUNGUS OF TRANSBAIKALIA During my work among these groups not all clans had shamans. I have personally seen five acting shamans, all of whom were connected with the clan activity. Among the Barguzin Tungus there were: (1) a very old shaman, of 86 years, who did not regularly shamanize and who transmitted his functions to his niece; this shaman was considered as a very strong, good shaman, although at the time of my seeing him he was undoubtedly affected by his age; (2) the female shaman mentioned in the preceding case, who was a beginner, but who could already perform a great shamanizing going to the upper world; (3) the female shaman described in the preceding section (Section 142) under Case 2, who could go to the lower world (as far as I know, she was the only one who could do it); (4) the male shaman described in the previous section under the Case 1; (5) a male shaman of middle age, not very talented, but who could help the souls of dead people to go to the lower world. I was told that there were some two or three shamans more.

Among the Nerčinsk Tungus several shamans were known: (1) an old, very good male shaman mentioned in Case 1 of the preceding section, who could go to the lower world, whom I had no chance to meet personally; (2) a young female shaman whom I saw only once and about whose ability I was not informed; (3) a female shaman, middle aged, who emigrated from among the Nomad Tungus of Urulga and settled down among the Nerčinsk Tungus in Utesina, near Tèksèr on the Akima River (*vide* SONT); she shamanized and her paraphernalia were the same as those now observed among the Nomad Tungus; I knew her personally. It is very likely, that there were two or three other shamans. However, the Nerčinsk Tungus asserted that the shamans were not as numerous as among the Barguzin Tungus.

Among the Nomad Tungus of Urulga (they now speak a dialect related to the Buriat language) I saw only a male shaman in Narin Talača (a Nomad Tungus summer settlement to the north of the railway station Urulga). I did not see him shamanize, although we lived with him nearly two weeks. There was another male shaman in Delun (a summer settlement near to Nerčinsk), but I have no details about him. The third was the female-shaman, mentioned above, settled among the Nerčinsk Tungus.

In these three groups with a population of slightly over two thousand there were at least fourteen or more shamans of whom less than a half were females.

I have no information regarding the Angara and now extinct Samagir groups. From the Tungus I know that the Barguzin Nomad Tungus had some shamans, but they were not numerous. Some shamans existed among the Mankova Tungus, and among the Borz'a Tungus. I saw one of these. All of them were of the type of the shaman observed among the Nomad Tungus of Urulga.

TUNGUS OF MANCHURIA As stated, there were no more shamans among the Reindeer Tungus, the last one having died in 1912. He lived on the upper course of the Kumara River.[*] However, this does not mean that shamans have not appeared since,

for the memory of shamanism was still vivid.[*] One of the causes of loss of shamanism was the abolition of the clan organization, and another one was the strong Russian influence.

Among the Khingan Tungus not all clans had shamans. I have seen: (1) a female shaman living at the *jodu* River (a tributary of the Gan River) described as "Case 3" of the preceding section; (2) an old male shaman, not active, who was living on the upper course of the Gan River; (3) a very old half-paralysed female shaman who was living on the Derbukan River, who did not often shamanize (cf. *supra* p. 312). I was told that there were probably one or two shamans more, whom I did not see. During my stay among this group the question had arisen as to the creation of a new shaman (*bajagir* clan).

Among the Kumarčen there was at least one shaman in every clan. Since this group had six clans, it might be supposed that there have been six shamans. However, not all clans were then entirely separated, so that there might have been fewer. I have seen: (1) an old male shaman who lived on the middle course of the Kumara River, who seldom shamanized; (2) a male shaman, very good and very active, who lived on the Warakan River (a tributary of the Kumara); (3) an old male shaman, little active, who lived during the winter season in the locality of Orodon.[**]

Among the Birarčen the shamans were more numerous than among the Kumarčen: (1) a female shaman described under Case 4 of the preceding section; (2) a male shaman who lived on the *jumbira*, a tributary of the Sun River, whom I had no chance to see; (3) a female-shaman who gave up shamanizing (cf. *supra*, p. 382); (4) a female-shaman about twenty-eight years old who lived a few kilometres from *Cetu*, who did not very often shamanize, and who had become shaman after a love drama; (5) a male shaman, a beginner who had only a few spirits and who was *dôna* shaman;[***] (6) a female shaman whose shamanism was greatly influenced by the Goldi shamanism. In the Malakul clan after its division there were three clan-shamans. In addition to the above mentioned shamans there were some Dahur and Manchu shamans who lived for longer or shorter periods among the Birarčen.

In so far as I could gather, there were some shamans among the Mergen group and Solons. But I did not see them and I got no details about them.

As can be seen from the above mentioned facts, the total number of shamans among the Tungus of Manchuria was no less than seventeen and, including the Solons, probably far over twenty, for a population of over five thousand souls.

MANCHUS P'oyun saman and amba saman must be distinguished. Every clan of old Manchus has a *p'oyun saman*, so that the number of *p'oyun saman* is very large, according to the number of *mokun*.[****] The *amba*

---

[*] He was buried in the ground and his paraphernalia were put in a store house having a platform. The house was probably burnt during a severe forest fire. He had been a very good shaman, according to his relatives.

[*] In fact, there were some shamans who lived in the Amur Prov., but there was no close connexion between the group living in Manchuria and that living in the Russian territory.

[**] I was told about another male shaman who lived on the Kamala River, but I could gather no detailed information about him.

[***] From this shaman I gathered a good collection of folklore in which he was also versed.

[****] Vide SOM pp. 20-28. As shown, the old Manchus—*fè manju*—have p'oyun saman, while the New Manchus—*ičè manju*—do not have them, as it is among the Chinese (n'îkan) and Tungus groups.

saman are not numerous for the reasons shown before, so that in all villages of the Aigun district, at my time, there were only ten or eleven shamans. However, the majority of them did not carry on their duties because of lack of paraphernalia which had been burnt in 1900, and the clans had not consented to bear the great expense of their restoration. I saw most of the shamans, and all those who were acting, namely, four shamans, one of whom was a female, besides the newly created male shaman (*vide supra* Section 131). In addition to the Manchu shamans there were two Chinese (*n'ikan*) shamans, whom I frequently saw, who performed among the Manchus. One of the Manchu shamans usually performed in Chinese. The Dahur shamans, the number of which I cannot now establish, were also known to act among the Manchus. However, the Manchus decidedly preferred Chinese shamans.

From the above review of the number of shamans among the various Tungus groups it can be seen that the shamans are numerous, and as a phenomenon shamanism, during my living among the investigated groups, was not in a state of decline, but only in a state of continuous readaptation. I shall revert to this subject in one of the following sections.

144. SHAMANISM AMONG THE DAHURS AND CHINESE OF THE AIGUN DISTRICT   As shown before, the Tungus of Manchuria were influenced in their shamanism by the Dahurs. I did not investigate the Dahur shamans, but I have gathered from the Tungus some information and I had an occasion to see a few Dahur shamans. Since the Dahur shamanism is of importance and since the information about it, given by the Tungus, is interesting as reflecting, if not the reality, then the Tungus ideas, I shall now give some recorded details, without pretending to give a genuine picture of Dahur shamanism.*

The Birarčen assert that among the Dahurs the method of shamanizing, the costume of the shaman, and the spirits are the same as their own.** However, the Dahur shamans have some special spirits unknown among these Tungus, but known among the Goldi. The most important spirit among them is a nine-headed spirit (*jeyin dĕlči mayi*) of the group *malu*. The Dahur shamans also operate with *buseku sĕvĕŋ*, which is carefully avoided by the Tungus (*vide supra*, p. 166). The Dahur shamans make wooden figures of the animals (manifestations) which will be assumed by the shaman during the shamanizing. They also like the Fire Spirit, as it is used among the Manchus (manipulations with red-hot iron, burning incense etc.) According to a Birarčen who was familiar with the Goldi

* N. N. Poppe ("Dahur") has published, as specimens of the Dahur language, some texts dealing with shamanism. However, I shall not use this material, for it was gathered from a Dahur group (Xailar) only little known to myself. In the Aigun District the shamans are numerous; I have no information how numerous they are among the Dahurs of the Butxa region, but I was told that there were shamans.

** L. von Schrenck (op. cit. Vol. III, p. 128) observed in a Dahur village (Xoǂmolǂin) a common Dahur shaman's costume. According to his description, the head-dress was evidently like that of the Buddhistic priests, an imitation of which I have observed among the Birarčen (vide supra p. 293), while the coat, of red colour, was supplied with a great number of metallic (brass and iron) pieces. Apparently among the Dahurs there was more than one type of shaman's costume.

shamanism, the Dahur shamans have almost all placings which are used by the Goldi.

When the spirits are left without a master (*èjan*, Dahur) after the shaman's death, no sacrifice is offered to them. The ritual of election of a new shaman is similar to that practised by the Birarčen. The Dahurs have no *p'oyun saman*. Among the Dahurs, a long time ago, much earlier than among the Tungus and the Manchus, a strong movement against shamanism began; so very few *acting shamans* remain there.

Among the Dahurs, the complex of actions, known as *nāra sarú* ("moon—sun"), for curing and protecting the eyes is very widely practised. We have seen that a confused idea of this complex has penetrated among the Tungus. It seems to be greatly developed among the Mongols and Buriats.

Among the Tungus the Dahur spirits are believed to be very powerful and mischievous. The kind corresponding to *xutu* of the Manchus is pictured with a long nose and horns (Buddhistic iconography?). This is one of the reasons why the Tungus are afraid of the Dahur shamans. According to the Birarčen, a great number of Dahur shamans are also "bad-hearted" people, and they may harm the Birarčen and their domesticated animals.

In *Čebu*, during my stay there, an elderly Dahur shaman was living with whom the Tungus did not maintain any relations. He was living by the cultivation of a small piece of his own land. As he was a very skilful shaman, he could have been able to bring diseases upon the people and animals, even without shamanizing, only by means of his thoughts. Having discovered this, the Tungus requested the Chinese authorities to remove the shaman. The authorities categorically refused to do so, on the ground that the Dahur shaman was not shamanizing and therefore should be left alone. However, the Tungus did not share this opinion and they resented the Chinese inactivity.

Such a very negative attitude of the Tungus toward the Dahur shamans began long ago. They relate as follows: A Dahur shaman had a very mischievous spirit (*buseku*). This spirit used to gnaw the Birarčen spirits. So during this shaman's stay among the Tungus many of them fell badly ill. The illness was not very dangerous, but rather a chronic indisposition. This spirit mingled with the Tungus spirits and harmed the people, until a Tungus shaman discovered the spirit and expelled him.

In order to show how the Tungus behave, I shall now give a record from my diary: ‹W. brought the news that a Dahur shaman had arrived. He can shamanize, he said, and has with him an assistant, a Dahur, who had visited us before on several occasions. The Birarčen who were present at the moment of this communication began to discuss: who might be the shaman who had arrived? They knew an old shaman who possessed only very mischievous spirits, which were "biting", and therefore they did not want him to shamanize. Should it be another, a young one, he would be good. Then it was decided to send C.—a young man—to find out where the shaman was staying; if he had put up at a Birarčen family's, he might be allowed to shamanize; if he were in the Chinese shopkeeper's house no contact must be maintained with him. C. returned with the result of his investigation: the shaman who had arrived was the one who had not been expected, namely, a workman of M. (Birarčen). He was known before and was considered as a poor shaman—"he has no spirits", he explained. In spite of this, the Birarčen were interested in seeing him acting and decided to get for him a drum and to find a house for a performance. Since the Birarčen refused to let a *Dahur shaman* shamanize in their house, it was decided to hire for fifty cents a house for one night from the Chinese shopkeeper. "No Birarčen would consent to it, but the Chinese shopkeeper, when he sees cash, will consent to do anything we want"—they said. The shamanizing took place on the next night». The actual cause of their worry was that this shaman was not powerful enough and perhaps himself did not know how to manage his own spirits, and perhaps could not master them, so that they might spread over the Birarčen.

The Tungus also fight Dahur shamans. For instance, a Tungus was ill in his childhood, and a Dahur shaman helped him. But one day the Tungus, who was now grown up, met the shaman and the horse of the Tungus fell ill. The Tungus inferred that the shaman wanted to do harm to him by bringing a sickness upon his horse, the reason being that this Tungus did not supply the shaman with meat. Then the Tungus decided to make an end with the shaman's spirit. He made a straw placing, put before it some meat, and with tender words called the shaman's spirit in. When the spirit was in, he discharged his rifle (with a blank shot, as usual in similar cases) into the placing. Nevertheless the horse died, but the shaman became sick for some time and exactly at the part of his body which corresponded to the spot of the placing that had been damaged by the shot.

The Birarčen believe that the first shaman was a Dahur,* and for this reason they even now do not object to learning from Dahur shamans.

It is thus evident that the Tungus consider Dahur shamanism to be powerful and dangerous for themselves, but at the same time worthy of being imitated.

———

Shamanism among the Chinese is different. I have already shown, that during my visit to this region there were several Chinese (*n'ikan*) shamans, some of whom were professionally living on their shamanistic trade. I knew two shamans, whom I saw rather often, but since they were shamanizing in Chinese, I could only partly understand them and recorded no texts. My chief information about them was received from the Manchus.

According to the Manchus, the Chinese generally are not much addicted to shamanism. The "shantungese" (which is equivalent to "Chinese from China proper", *jergin*) know very little about it, but the local Chinese, formerly incorporated into the military organization, are very familiar with shamanism. The shamans use a red coat, belt and skirt, also a drum and other paraphernalia, as the Manchu shamans do.**

However, the number of their spirits is, as a rule, much smaller, and the shamans are not connected with the clans, which have no *p'oyun saman*, but which, once every

three years perform their rites in ancestral halls (*m'ao*) where tablets and lists of dead and living clansmen (*japu*) are preserved. Outsiders are not allowed to go in.

I have given before (*vide supra*, p. 308) a list of five spirits of one of the Chinese shamans; however, Manchu and Tungus spirits may be used as well. The Chinese shamans commonly use *fuč'k'i*—i.e. Buddha—as one of the shamanistic spirits, while it is not usually so among the Manchus. They meet with a great difficulty, when they have to master Manchu spirits. As they do not know the Manchu language, they cannot read *čolo kooli bitxe* ("books of names and ritual") and have to learn them from their seniors. Usually it is the father shaman who teaches his son who becomes a shaman. I was told that some of these books had been translated into Chinese.

The methods of shamanizing, in main lines, do not differ from those used among the Manchus. However, from my numerous observations of their shamanizing I have found that the Chinese shamans are still more formalistic than the Manchu shamans, the chief reason being probably that they are professionals.

The influence of Chinese shamans on the Manchus and especially on the Tungus is not great. Without denying that in China something formally approaching shamanism, perhaps a form of "mafarism" may exist, I have got the impression that the Chinese in Manchuria had borrowed their shamanism from the Manchus.

———

The Goldi shamanism had a great influence on the shamanism of the Birarčen in Manchuria, and the shamanism of the Buriats on that of the Tungus of Transbaikalia, especially on that of the Nomad Tungus. I have already pointed out that some Birarčen shamans were directly influenced by the Goldi.* In so far as I know, the shamanism of the Goldi of the Sungari River differs from the shamanism of the Goldi of the Ussuri and the Amur. According to the Birarčen, who are familiar with the Sungari Goldi, this shamanism is very near to that of the Manchus. This is quite natural, for this Goldi group is still considered as one of the Manchu groups—*ičе manju*.** However, the complex of placings for the spirits of the Amur Goldi, demonstrated to the Birarčen, reminded them of the placings used by the Dahurs. This too would be only natural, for the Dahurs, in former days, lived near these Goldi and undoubtedly ruled over them. Even now the Amur Goldi have a clan which is called the *daxsur* clan, which, according to the Tungus and Dahurs of whom I inquired about it, is merely *daxur*, i.e. Dahur clan. It should be noted that the Birarčen are not hostile to the Goldi shamanism.***

———

* Some Tungus of the same group suppose that the shamanistic practices came from the Goldi, or even from the Manchus.

** I was told by the Manchus that the shamans of Jergin use a kind of special head-dress made of cloth. However, I could gather no details. The Chinese of Mukden, also those of the Shansi province, have also a drum and a short skirt. But they must shamanize secretly.

* Within the memory of old men now living, the Goldi shamans were met near the present Čelu settlement, namely, about one hundred red kilometres down the Amur River.

** Vide details in my SOM and SONT, also "Northern Tungus Migrations".

*** I had a very detailed discussion of the problem of Goldi shamanism with a shaman who for a long time had been connected with the Goldi. She told me that the Sungari Goldi have in the main lines the same complex of spirits as the Manchus, but they have also a special complex severy headed by a tiger manifestation. In this complex a group of the bear is of the "night road", the group of the leopard (jarga) is one of the "midday road", the complex čani is *odin okto*, i.e. the "wind road". Such a complex does not exist in the Birarčen system, but its elements are seen in the Amur Goldi system.

The influence of the Buriats on the Nomad Tungus is, of course, very great. The Nomad Tungus have imitated the cattle breeding complex, the wedding complex, a great number of social institutions, and some of these groups have even appropriated the Buriat language. As soon as the language is appropriated the influence of the psychomental complex becomes overwhelming. It is thus much more convenient to treat it in terms of the Buriat complex. Naturally shamanism, in its earlier Tungus form, could be preserved only in rare cases. The influence of the Buriat shamanism upon that of the Reindeer Tungus of Transbaikalia is also strong, but it is not direct, while the Yakut influence, at least formerly, was direct.

Among the Nomad Tungus, as well as the Reindeer Tungus of Manchuria, I have not recorded any facts pointing to a negative reaction on the Buriat shamanism. However, the Tungus shamans fought with the Yakut shamans, which shows that the reaction might formerly have been quite negative.

The relations between the complexes of shamanism observed among different investigated ethnical groups are represented in the scheme shown below.

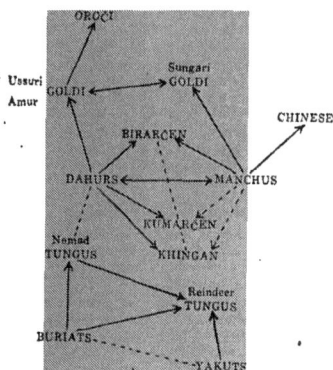

**145. DIFFICULTIES MET   There are three kinds of
WITH BY SHAMANISM   difficulties met with by sha-
                     manism, namely: (1) the
opposition to shamanism met with among the Tungus
groups themselves; (2) the disintegration of shamanism
under the pressure of a conflict with other complexes; (3)
pressure produced by other ethnical groups.** It should be
noted that these difficulties have always existed, so that we
must not look at them as at a new condition of the existence
of shamanism. However, our knowledge of the facts of
earlier periods is either lacking altogether or quite insufficient. So, in order to study the mechanism of the
maintaining of shamanism, we must go into the details
observed at the present time.

This shaman has adopted some of the Goldi elements and she used them in her shamanizing.

*TUNGUS OPPOSITION   It would be erroneous to believe
TO SHAMANISM   that the Tungus, and the Man-
                     chus as well, blindly accept sha-
manism.* On different occasions I have already shown that
the Tungus, before accepting a new hypothesis or theory,
submit it to an analysis, and it cannot be adopted if it is in
direct conflict with the existing complex. The same may
be stated in reference to shamanism as a whole—it can be
accepted only on certain conditions. In this respect the
individual character of a Tungus is of the greatest importance.

In one of the former sections I have given a (Birarčen) case of a criticism undermining the foundations of shamanism by the analysis of the problem of the soul (*vide supra*, p. 119). Such a theoretical approach to the problem is not frequent, but it is met with. In such a case every detail will be scrutinized and nothing will be accepted without a criticism. The chief objection as to the practice of shamanism among the Birarčen is that the spirits produce harm to the people. Therefore, it is better, if possible, to send all the spirits away for ever. The question is only as to how to do it? As shown in a great number of instances, it is done by various means, some of which are quite effective, as e.g. the methods of suggestion and inspiring assurance to the affected people that they will no more be harmed. If the theory of spirits is accepted, it is also noticed by the Tungus, the appearance of a new spirit may have an effect upon the whole population, i.e. partly through imitation and partly because of a similar psychic state of a great number of individuals. The way to remedy such a state is to send the spirit off, and even to deny its existence. This is also frequently done. Since it is supposed that the *dōna* spirits are in general harmful, the Tungus oppose the shamans-masters of *dōna* spirits and they oppose shamans of other ethnical groups practising among the Tungus. From this attitude to a denying of the necessity of having clan shamanism is only one step. Owing to this, among the Birarčen the use of prayers instead of shamanizing is becoming more and more common. If the prayers are effective—and they may be so in all cases when suggestion may help and naturally when the prayers are granted—they can quite successfully compete with shamanism.

Doubtless, in some instances the "bad-hearted" shamans do great harm to the people and to themselves. However, such a condition of the shaman may only partly be due to his psychomental character; but in some cases it is merely auto-suggestion, which is not controlled by the shaman, nor by the other people. In the Tungus mind it is represented as a spirits' activity which may be checked, if the spirits are not disturbed by the shaman himself. For this reason, the Birarčen may assume a quite hostile attitude towards shamanism in general.

Although shamanism, as shown, is quite interesting and sometimes attractive, its negative sides in the eyes of the Tungus may become more prominent, than the pleasure and real help produced by it, and they may give up shamanism or may oppose its spreading. The limitation of the shamans' competence may also be due to the analysis of cases in which the shamans fail to help suffering people, in consequence of which the importance of shamanism may also decrease.

There are cases of opposition to shamanism which arise without any pressure from outside and without any conflict within the existing Tungus complex. However, the analysis of a great number of cases shows that conflicts of complexes and alien influence are more frequently the cause of negative reactions than the "internal" conditions of shamanism.

Since the Reindeer Tungus are greatly influenced by the Russians and Buriats, the negative reactions may be due to these influences, and to an evident disintegration of the Tungus complex.

Among the Manchus internal causes are also found. The chief of them is a gradual formalization of shamanism because of the existence of written records of spirits and of the ritualistic complex. In fact, as shown, shamanism loses its effectiveness, and it cannot compete with other methods of regulation of the psychomental complex.* I have met with Manchus who asserted that if there were a shaman in the clan, there would be more trouble with the people. Owing to this, a great number of clans have given up the "great shamans", and have preserved only the *p'oyun saman*. This negative attitude is greatly encouraged by the necessity of economy—shamanism requires great expense for sacrifices etc.

However, the factor of disintegration of shamanism, as seen in the conflict of the Tungus complexes, seems to be stronger than the internal causes. In fact, the case of the Reindeer Tungus of Manchuria who have already lost their clan organization is a good illustration—the shamans have no milieu, no clans with which they would be connected. If the process of disintegration of the clan organization proceeds at a high rate of speed, the ethnical unit has no time to readapt shamanism as a function in the regional units, and it may perish together with the clan organization. Another case is that of assimilation of new theories, as, for instance, that of a special *burkan* which cannot be managed by the shamans (e.g. *ain'i burkan* with its seventy-two manifestations); in this case a new theory comes into a conflict with the theory of *sèvèŋ*, and the competence of shamanism decreases. Among the Birarčen many people decidedly avoid the shamans and prefer prayers (*buačin*), by analogy with successful experiments with *burkan*. The same situation is created owing to the spreading of mafarism, as it is observed among the Manchus; so the shaman's competence is more and more curtailed. In the last two cases there is a substitution for shamanism, because of remodelling of the whole complex.

Among the Manchus there are persons who are so critical that they say: "Shamanism is a complete nonsense; it is only a great expenditure with no effect". There is another movement, quite marked, which regards shamanism as a sign of backwardness. Such people say: "Shamanism is an old, backward faith". The penetration of the Chinese complex is greatly responsible for this. A Manchu, for instance, was inclined to adopt Confucianism, which he understood as the worship of ancestors, and he asserted that his Confucianism may help in everything, for, in his opinion, all troubles come from the ancestors. There are even persons who absolutely deny shamanism, but still they take their part in the performances, if not as actors, then as spectators. Some Manchus say that they have nothing against the real old shamanism and shamans like *Nišan Saman;* but they are against the new shamans who are dishonest people. However, cases of coming back to

* Cf. the criticism concerning the list of spirits etc. made by one of the opponents of a new shaman (vide supra, p. 357).

shamanism are also observed. For instance, I knew a man who used to have a good position under the Manchu Dynasty and who did not practise shamanism; after having lost his position and after having been befallen by all kinds of misfortunes, he became a very prominent adept of shamanism. When I knew him, he and his wife, who was a Chinese (*n'ikan*), had already sacrificed almost all their chickens and all their pigs, except one which survived. Such delayed revival of shamanistic feelings and practices was occasionally observed.

A great factor in the decrease of shamanism among the Manchus was also the loss of written records and of shamanistic paraphernalia during the Boxer troubles. In fact, since shamanism had already been formalized, the Manchus were not certain whether the lists of spirits and the ritualism restored from memory might be actually effective, or not. Since the shamans were not immediately restored and nothing particularly bad had happened (the Manchus were busy with the restoration of their farming and houses, and later they were deeply affected by the loss of their political position), a great number of shamans were not restored. The same happened with the paraphernalia. As shown in the Manchu complex, these were not cheap and had to be made by specialists. They required a great expenditure. After their destruction they could not be immediately restored, because of the general poverty. When the economic position of the Manchus was a little stabilized and they could afford a restoration of the paraphernalia, the need of them was not as great as it had been before, for a great number of clans had no shamans at all and some other clans, who had shamans, could not yet afford a great expenditure. With their great esteem for the ritualism, the wooden substitutes for iron paraphernalia and the poorly ornamented costumes produced on the Manchus the impression of a decline of shamanism and of the importance of the shamans under the new conditions of life.

———

An important source of difficulties encountered by shamanism is the pressure produced by other ethnical groups. This pressure takes two forms, namely, sharp criticism in its various forms, usually connected with an introduction of new complexes and a direct prohibition of shamanism. The first form, in so far as it is accepted by the Tungus, is a particular case of conflict of complexes; while the second form is possible only under the condition of loss of ethnical independence, total or partial. These two forms are usually combined.

Among the Tungus of Transbaikalia two periods of persecution of the shamans can be distinguished. During the early period of forced Christianization of the Tungus, the missionaries persecuted the shamans—themselves, or with the assistance of the local authorities; sometimes they seized the shamans and their paraphernalia and had the latter destroyed. The second period was that when the missionaries abstained from the forcible conversion of the Tungus to Christianity, but continued their propaganda against the shamans. The first period, in so far as I could gather from various sources, lasted up to the beginning of the last century. Finally the Tungus were left alone, and during my investigations among them (1912-1913) they were free to perform shamanism—the authorities and official representatives did not interfere with the shamanistic practices. The change of policy towards shamanism took place in the middle of the last century.

From the first period the Tungus preserved the remembrance of violence on the part of the missionaries. There is a story which was intended to show the real power of the shamans:

"In olden days—it runs—the Russian priests captured a shaman. They began to burn him. They made a fire and threw the shaman's coat into it. The fire died out immediately. Then they did this a second time and the fire died out again. The coat itself became like water. Then the priests left the shaman alone and did no more harm". But even after the refusal of the Tungus to submit to the influence of the missionaries by these means, shamanism was only tolerated and it was required from the baptized Tungus to abstain from using shamans.

In the territory of Manchuria the situation was not very favourable for maintaining shamanism. Even during the Manchu political control the Manchu authorities supported the clan organization and tolerated p'oyun saman, but were not in favour of amba saman. The situation became very unfavourable after the Manchus had lost their power. Since the establishment of the new Chinese control, shamanism has been formally prohibited, as the Manchus told me, because of the harmful effect of shamanism on the population, according to the opinion of the enlightened new authorities. In reality the local authorities could not make these new regulations effective and in a great number of cases they were simply turned into a new source of income for the local policemen who used to make all sorts of objections, even when the shamanizing was permitted by the local high authorities. For instance, such was the case, when the local governor, on my request, permitted the election of a new shaman to be carried out, but the local policemen wanted some compensation from the Manchus, and this was at last settled. For every shamanistic performance special permission must be obtained from the local police. The Manchus told me that sometimes the administrative zeal went very far, and the shamans, even p'oyun saman, were sometimes arrested. (1) A petty district official (in the Aigun region), with a group of soldiers, "attacked" the p'oyun saman of the nara clan, destroyed all paraphernalia (placings for spirits and clan list, as well as the costume) by fire, and badly beat the performers. (2) Another petty official in a village (Kalunŝan) forced a shaman to go from house to house to shamanize; when the shaman was shamanizing the official beat him and asked: "Where is the spirit?" His paraphernalia as well as that of other shamans were seized and thrown into the Amur River. However, I could not verify these statements. Moreover, the shamans were faced, though rarely, with opposition on the part of private persons.

Among the Tungus of Manchuria in the places where there are officials, shamanizing is admitted only by special request and with the permission of the local yamen. However, during my stay in Ĉelu, the absent chief was replaced by his relative—a Manchu—who was a shaman or, better to say, pretended to be one. One day he shamanized himself in the office of this important place. The local Chinese merchants were rather indifferent to the shamanistic performances; but as I have shown, the local Chinese teacher was quite active in the extermination of shamanism, and it may be assumed, with the best of motives.

As a matter of fact, from time to time there are accidents with Manchu shamans, especially those inclined to use various tricks with fire, sharp weapons etc. According to the Manchus, shamanism was prohibited after the following accident: a Chinese was seriously ill, a shaman was invited to attend him, but he failed, one after another four more shamans were invited, but they could not help. The sixth one, being invited, decided to apply a drastic measure —the operation with the straw-cutter. [The latter is a heavy knife, over eighty centimetres long, one end of which has a handle and the other moves over a block of wood with a groove in which the blade of the knife enters, the straw is put on the wooden block under the lifted knife. The implement is very strong and formidable.] The sixth shaman decided to put the man in the place of the straw and to frighten the spirit with the knife, threatening to cut the body. [The psychological effect of such an operation is evident.] However, the other five shamans, being afraid of losing their influence [more exactly their spirits], surrounded the sick man who was lying on the straw-cutter under the knife and influenced the acting sixth shaman in such a way that he vigorously pressed the knife down and cut the man into two halves. Since that time shamanism has been prohibited". The fact itself is not incredible, but if ever it took place, it might have been the last drop which caused the overflow of the accumulated dissatisfaction of the authorities with shamanism.

Besides the direct prohibition of shamanism, the Tungus and Manchus are very sensitive to the jokes that are made, e.g. by the Russians and Chinese, about their adhesion to the "old faith". Owing to this, the shamanists, who live by the side of these ethnical groups, usually carry out their shamanistic performances in secret, which greatly restricts the practising of shamanism in general and diverts the Tungus and Manchus to new complexes.

146. PAST AND PRESENT STATE OF SHAMANISM Among the Tungus groups and the Manchus the prevailing idea about shamanism is that under the present conditions shamanism is in a state of decline. However, this statement must not be accepted without a critical analysis of the facts.

The opinion of the Tungus and Manchus is based upon the supposed-to-be-historic fact of the earlier flourishing of shamanism and the present signs of changes in the existing psychomental complex. Let us consider first the "historic" facts.

The Reindeer Tungus of Transbaikalia believe that the shaman in olden days—"two thousand years ago"—used to be much stronger than nowadays. For instance: "A shaman who took part in the war with the Mamugir (evidently one of the Northern Tungus clans, vide SONT) used to assemble all his people (i.e. those belonging to his ethnical unit, which at present cannot be identified, but may have been connected with the clans now incorporated into the groups of Barguzin, Nerĉinsk and Reindeer Tungus of Manchuria) and to hide them from the enemies. He would wave his hand, and the trees and rocks would fall down. This shaman died long ago. When his help was needed one must pray to him".

According to the same Tungus, the shamans were formerly great fighters and gradually destroyed each other. At last there remained only one very strong old shaman.

In this way the supposed decline of shamanism is explained. These Tungus have a great many stories of this kind. The Nomad Tungus of Transbaikalia have the same ideas about their old shamans.

The Khingan Tungus share the same opinion. There was a strong shaman, *Mukteokan* of the *Dulugir* clan, who alone could keep off the Reindeer Tungus who came from the present Yakutsk prov. He used to produce thunder and lightning, and even in the summer he could produce a lot of snow which did not melt for three days. Another powerful shaman was *Gantimur*. This is the name of a Dahur leader who in the seventeenth century brought a Tungus group (probably *Solon*) from Manchuria to Transbaikalia, which led to a long diplomatic controversy between the Chinese and Russian governments. A third, very strong shaman was that of the *Kaltagir* clan, but his name is forgotten. *Mukteokan*, with whose name we shall meet again, and Gantimur had very short bodies—twice the distance between the outstretched thumb and index long, i.e. from 35 to 40 centimetres, very long arms and legs, and very small heads. Both shamans *Mukteokan* and *Kaltagir*, died at the time when Gantimur left Manchuria.

The Reindeer Tungus of Manchuria also remember that great time when they had very strong shamans, the last of whom perished recently. These strong shamans with the help of their art could kill people. This group has now no more shamans, except those who are living in the territory of the Amur province.

The Birarčen have many tales about the above mentioned *Mukteokan*.[*] It is generally believed that the shamans were so good, that even the Russians (cossacks living on the opposite side of the Amur River), used to appeal to the shamans in cases when doctors could not help. In evidence thereof they have stories like the following. "One day a general, from Blagoveščensk, called a Manchu shaman to help his little daughter who had swallowed a needle, which the doctors could not extract. The shaman influenced the girl with his shamanizing and after he had three times beaten her neck with his drum she spit the needle out into the drum". The Birarčen assert that in former days, the shamans were not numerous, but they were very powerful, while at present there are many of them, but they are "bad shamans".

The Manchus quote a long list of prominent shamans of the past, such as *Nišan Saman*, the founder of shamanism *Čuza jaqin*, who was decapitated, and many others who are now included into the clan lists of *vočko*; they also complain of the present lack of "good shamans".

In all these groups there is a strong belief, that formerly the shamans were much more skilful than at present. Of course, we have no means to decide which shamans were more powerful, the old ones, or the present ones. But, as a matter of fact, the idea of the deterioration of the human species is a natural phenomenon functioning as one of the elements of the mechanism for preservation of the existing ethnographical complex, on the one hand, and as an explanation of the natural dissatisfaction of the people with the existing state of the groups, on the other hand. So that the idea of good shamans in the past may be understood as due to these psychological conditions. There is one more condition favourable for the formation and preservation of this idea, namely, the growth of criticism, due to the con-

* The stories concerning Mukteokan will be published in the Tungus Folklore which is in preparation.

flict of different ethnographical complexes. The Tungus groups, which now exist, cannot easily admit miraculous acts of the shamans. The possibility of producing thunder and lightning, snow, falling down of trees and rocks etc. is admitted, but nowadays is never observed.

Indeed, at the present time some ethnical groups, e.g. the Reindeer Tungus of Manchuria, partly also the Dahurs and Manchus, may lose their complexes. However, these facts cannot be used as evidence of a general decline of shamanism. First of all, the case of the Reindeer Tungus of Manchuria, as they are found now, is not indicative of anything, for they are in a typical state of general ethnical disintegration, as we have seen from other evidences and particularly from the fact of the disintegration of the clan organization, the loss of folklore and the substitution of the Yakut and Russian complexes for the Northern Tungus complex. The Manchus, as they were observed in 1915-1917, were also in the state of ethnical disintegration, which may be seen from the loss of their language, their ethnical consciousness etc. I do not know in which condition the Dahurs were, for I carried out no extensive investigation of this group; but since the Dahurs were closely connected with the Manchus, it can naturally be supposed that their complex may have greatly been affected by the loss of their former privileged position as rulers. In these cases the loss of shamanism is not due to internal causes of the cultural complex, as such, but rather to a general ethnical disintegration of the Reindeer Tungus of Manchuria, the Manchus and probably the Dahurs, followed by an absorption of these disintegrated populations by other ethnical groups and, finally, by physical extinction. Sometimes not only shamanism is declining but also all other cultural elements.

In spite of the fact of penetration of alien complexes, such as the Russian and Chinese, the other Tungus groups, here discussed, were not found to be losing shamanism. We have seen that almost all of these clans did have shamans, and among some groups, as for instance the Birarčen, shamanism was in a flourishing state. In so far as the factual side is concerned, the idea of a decline of shamanism, asserted by a great number of investigators, cannot be supported. However, I must make a few preliminary remarks as to how this idea was formed.

First of all shamanism has never been thoroughly investigated, as we have seen from the short review of the existing literature concerning this aspect of the Tungus psychomental complex. Secondly, one can form an idea of the state of the phenomenon in two different ways, namely, historically by carrying out a series, or at least two investigations for the time sufficient for observing non-incidental changes in the complex, which, as known, has not been done; and ethnologically, by means of the establishment of characteristic features of growing and declining cultural elements and complexes, which method till recent years has not yet been sufficiently perfected to be relied upon. Thirdly, the inference as to the decline of shamanism, as stated, having been formed without an adequate investigation, was implied by the whole complex of European ethnography of the last century and particularly by the theory of evolution. On the third proposition we must dwell longer than on the first two, which are mere statements of facts.

The essential conditions which imply the idea of the decline of shamanism are: (1) shamanism is a very old complex among the so-called "primitive" groups. As shown, for proving this proposition, facts of formal similarity are gathered from functionally and "genetically" different complexes; this naturally gives an artificial mosaic picture; however, in the eyes of a reader, who possesses no critical mind, this construction appears to be quite realistic and sufficiently reliable for serving as the basis of further investigations; (2) shamanism, as it is theoretically built up, appears to be very "primitive", a phenomenon of "animism", and as such, according to the idea of evolution, it must give place to more "advanced" complexes; this proposition is naturally a mere theoretical extrapolation of a hypothesis on an unknown phenomenon, as shamanism was, which cannot be accepted by a critically behaving mind, both in methodology and in facts dealt with; (3) shamanism has grown on the soil of various psychopathogical conditions characteristic of "primitive" groups; this is taken for granted, but is not shared by all theoreticians. Here I omit more or less ingenious constructions playing a subordinate rôle.

The next step is to show how shamanism gives place to other complexes, for it is always understood that shamanism is "acting". In this respect facts of a quite different importance and function are grouped together: cases of ethnical decline in which shamanism perishes as one of the elements; cases of strong interethnical pressure under which shamanism may be replaced by new complexes, or may disappear altogether, leaving an empty place; cases of reduction of elements of shamanism which are taken for a decline etc. Such facts are always abundant, so that one has only to select them—a merely mechanical, automatic work. When this is done, the construction is ready for functioning.

I have not yet mentioned, perhaps the most important, condition of the existence of such a general attitude among the scholars, which is an ethnico-psychological one, i.e. with the cultural and political conquest of the world (characteristic of the leading ethnoses) the Europeans are convinced that the other cultural complexes are doomed to perish and that the non-European groups must submit themselves to the European groups. Therefore shamanism cannot be in any other position as that of a complete decline, as soon as the groups in which it is found are in contact with Europeans. The theory of progress helps to justify this attitude of the militant leading ethnical groups and to frame it in various attractive aspects, according to current fashions and existing ethnographic complexes. This psychological condition is responsible for the existence of the theoretical scaffolding found sometimes even with critically behaving minds, but ignorant of other ethnographical complexes.

The ethnical groups, which are supplying the material for the above indicated theoretical scaffoldings, also give "evidences" as to the decline of shamanism; the latter is accepted as bona fide. However, as shown above, the attitude of ethnical groups towards the past is subject to the influence of a special mechanism, as has been described, so that it must not be accepted without adequate criticism. Let us first take the facts referred to at the beginning of this section and let us clear them of imaginative elements, then we can agree with the Tungus and Manchus that there were great shamans in the past. However, at present, as well, there are good shamans who, supplied with the same

accessories as the shamans of the past, will grow into "great shamans". The same mechanism will be found at work; the groups which have no written records and which are now losing their shamanism will lose it for ever, and there will be no remembrance of their declining shamanism.

It would be absolutely unreasonable to suppose, that shamanism did not suffer from the conditions of adaptation in the past. First of all, we have seen that shamanism had its difficulties in the past, e.g. under the Nuichen Emperors who pressed upon the Nuichens with their "religious" and political ideology of a "cultured government". Although we have no direct evidences as to the persecution of shamans, we have evidences as to the persecution of Buddhists and we have the interesting fact of the decapitation of the first shaman who gave his spirits to the ancestors of the Manchus. There was thus a time when shamanism was not favoured. We know from historical records that the Siberian Tungus were also pressed by the Russian Christians who wanted them to give up shamanism. Later the Russians did not molest them, but shamanism did pass a difficult period of persecution. We have another instance, namely, that of the Mongols who seemingly practised shamanism, but under the pressure of Buddhism have now given it up. In spite of this, the Darxats, recently described by D. Sanžeev, still have it in a flourishing state and in a peculiar form of symbiosis with Lamaism. At least from the time of great Manchu emperor Kanghsi, who was already influenced by the Chinese philosophical ideas, the Manchu emperors did not favour shamanistic practices and used only p'oyun saman.

So shamanism itself has resulted from a conflict of various complexes. It has come out as a complex of adaptation, which we may see from the analysis of the hypotheses on which shamanism is based, from the analysis of the paraphernalia, from the forms of the performances, borrowed by one group from another, as well as from the analysis of the psychic conditions of the units and of the shamans themselves. At all moments of the history of shamanism it has been under the pressure of changing equilibria, and it could not be a fixed complex: some elements were declining, others remained, and still others were growing in their functional importance. So that at every moment, especially in the presence of almost disintegrating groups, which were losing this complex, the conclusion could be drawn that shamanism was declining. Perhaps a remark made by Ch'ien-lung as to the loss of ritualism of the p'oyun "shamanism", might also be applied to the "great" shamanism, but that was more than a century and a half ago, and p'oyun "shamanism" was not yet declining at the time of my investigations among the Manchus.

If we do not postulate that shamanism was an universal monolithic "religion" which existed by itself as an organic phenomenon, if we do not postulate its "primitiveness", and if we critically analyse facts—we ought to infer that shamanism, as it was investigated by me, was still a "living" phenomenon, showing quite clearly its complex origin as the result of adaptation of ethnical units. These ethnical units were always under interethnical pressure, losing their cultural complexes (in elements), adapting it at every moment, and sometimes perishing, as bearers of these complexes. The relative complexity of the problem of shamanism is due to (1) the observers' reactions on an alien complex, (2) the bearers' reaction on the variations of shamanism, (3) a series of postulates, and (4) an operation with the abstraction—"shamanism"—identified as an evolving organic entity.

After these remarks we can now proceed to the details regarding factors which cause the disintegration of shamanism, which will also serve us as a general explanation of the disintegration and the integration of the Tungus cultural complex.

147. SPECIAL CONDITIONS OF THE
TUNGUS CULTURAL COMPLEX
UNDER ALIEN INFLUENCE

First of all we must have in sight, that the cultural complex and particular elements perish, when the bearers perish, either owing to their extinction, or because of their ethnical disintegration. This condition of loss of the cultural complex is very often forgotten. Among the Tungus ethnical units, as I have shown, there are some in this state of disintegration, and these facts are neither demonstrative of the condition of cultural complexes, nor convincing as regards the restoration of the history of the complex, particularly of shamanism. What we must deal with are the alien complexes and interethnical pressure produced upon the Tungus groups, for the internal conditions of variations of shamanism have been already shown.

There were three important complexes which in the history of shamanism appeared as special conditions. These were the Mongol, Chinese and Russian complexes which produced their pressure upon the Tungus shamanism. I might schematize these conditions as Buddhism, Chinese syncretism and Christianity, but it would be an artificial approach to the problem, an operation with abstractions, for these religions influenced not only the Tungus shamanism, but also the whole of the above indicated ethnographical and ethnical complexes. In fact, the medical art as used by the Chinese doctors, lamas, and Russian doctors produced its effect upon shamanism; the philosophical ideas and the positive knowledge of these great ethnical groups produced their effect in a not lesser degree.

Unfortunately, the investigations into the ethnographical complexes of these groups, with the exception of religions,* are so poorly advanced that we cannot form an idea as to the actual weight of the influence not connected with the religions. However, in studying the present realities, we may suppose that other influences, such as medical art, philosophical ideas, positive knowledge etc., may have been as much effective in the past as they are now. Owing to the paucity of facts which we possess, the influence of religious conditions will be our chief field of references. It should here be noted, that these religious systems are also connected with other aspects of psychomental complexes of the ethnical groups, who are bearers, so that the religions may be, at least indirectly, indicative of a general influence which must be kept in mind as a possibility if not a certainty.

The Buddhistic influence, as stated, has reached the Tungus by two ways, namely, from China and from the Mongols. As I have shown, shamanism itself seems to be a "digested" result of a Tungus (and Manchu) reaction on Buddhism. However, I do not base my investigation on this hypothesis, for Buddhistic influence continued after the formation of shamanism as a complex, and was again deposited as a secondary layer. In fact, we have seen that fučk'i was recently mastered by some shamans among the Manchus, as Buddha (burkan) was also mastered by the Tungus shamans after a long operation with sèvèn. There is no doubt that Buddhism made great progress during the later historic time. So, for instance, at the end of the seventeenth century the greater part of the population in Transbaikalia—the Buriats and Tungus—were shamanists and the Mongol groups, who had newly arrived in 1689, were headed by superior lamas. In 1712, the arrival was noted of fifty Tibetan lamas who were distributed among the Buriat clans. It was noted by Bishop Nil that the Buriats showed opposition to Buddhism, and that the success of the lamas was due to the Tibetan medical art. This is an interesting fact. Since that time the Buriats send their children to the famous centres of Buddhism. In 1741 only 150 lamas and eleven dacan (temples) were recorded, while in 1774 there were 617 lamas and 16 temples.* The Tungus neighbours of the Buriats fell under lamaistic influence much later. In spite of this, according to the official sources of 1897, the Tungus, called here Nomad Tungus, (with the exception of the Mankova group) were lamaists. However, as shown, it was not so, even later, in 1912-1913. These Tungus groups had shamans as well. One of the shamans in Narin Talača mentioned in Section 143, was both shaman and lama. The groups of Mankova and Borz'a practised both Lamaism and Christianity and used to have shamans. Lamaism penetrated together with the Buriats into the Barguzin Tungus territory where lamas performed duties of doctors among these Tungus, for Russian medical assistance could not be given to this remote group i.e. the same as was seen in the Buriat regions in the eighteenth century.**

This second spreading of Buddhism, this time well organized and systematic (it was assimilated by the Mongols), was considered as the first appearance of Buddhistic influence. The number of 9258 Tungus lamaists, given by S. K. Patkanov (op. cit., p. 232), or 26.9 per cent of the whole Tungus population of Transbaikalia, is a great over-estimation of the actual position of Buddhism among the Tungus of Transbaikalia.

Nearly the same can be said of the situation in Manchuria, where the first Buddhistic influence, manifested in shamanism, was overcovered by a rather late spreading of Buddhism, partly under Mongol, and chiefly under Chinese influence, direct and through the Manchus, who soon after their settling in China became fervent Buddhists. In this way Buddhism has penetrated into the remote regions of the Amur River, where rare lamas and bonzes practised religious propaganda and medical art, and have founded several temples. However, their direct influence could not affect very much the Northern Tungus who received this second wave of "true Buddhism" through the

---

* There are deep ethnographic reasons why Europeans were always interested in Buddhism and other alien religions—they went so far as becoming "iconographists"—remaining quite indifferent to other aspects of psychomental complexes. One of the unfavourable conditions was the fact of an inadequate preliminary education, chiefly philological, of the greater part of students of alien religions.

* S. K. Patkanov, Opyt, Vol. I, Fasc. 2, pp. 222-224.
** This was repeated by the American protestant missionaries in China, although with much more moderate success.

hands of the Manchus and Dahurs, who themselves partly re-adapted it by fusing shamanism with Buddhism. In fact, this wave of Buddhism reached the Tungus only after the restoration of the Manchu control over their territories, after the treaty of Nerčinsk of 1689, when these populations settled down in a more or less permanent manner in their present area. However, in the territories occupied exclusively by the Tungus in Manchuria and Mongolia no temples, no monasteries, even no lamas living there permanently were found.

In summarizing the importance of the Buddhistic influence on shamanism, it may be stated that its gradual substitution for shamanism still continues. We have seen that some Tungus groups adapt and completely remodel it by incorporating into the complex of shamanism, as it is done by the Tungus of Manchuria, while among the Nomad Tungus of Transbaikalia it exists side by side with shamanism, as a complement of the latter in the "acting" psychomental complex. The most effective influence of Lamaism on the Tungus complex was, on the one hand, the medical art of the lamas, which was quite successful in the treatment of a great number of diseases and on the other hand, an introduction of a great number of new hypotheses, concerning the structure of the universe, the interpretation of astronomy, the existence of upper and lower worlds with corresponding subdivisions, new spirits of two types, definitely malevolent and benevolent etc. All these hypotheses were interesting to the Tungus and with their help many phenomena remaining obscure could be better explained. Apart from Lamaism, the influence of the Mongol complex on the Tungus, who were in direct contact with the Mongols and Buriats, was still stronger, for, as shown, the Tungus living in the steppe region and in the transitory belt have partly adopted the cattle-breeding complex and partly the social organization, in some cases even a new language. Through the medium of language the new psychomental complex was introduced. Indeed, since the hunting complex with all characteristically Tungus elements was given up, it could be replaced only by the Buriat (and Mongol) complexes, so that these Tungus have given up their old complex and have become cattle-breeders of an "inferior" quality as compared with the Mongols. The ideas, art, folklore etc. have been altered, and the Tungus complex is now only faintly preserved. Moreover, intermarriage with the Buriats has already resulted in a marked physical change of the population and in their psychology, in so far as it is conditioned by the inherited physical conditions.

The Chinese complex, as a factor disturbing shamanism, was no less important than the second spreading of Buddhism of Mongol origin. In the instance of the Manchu complex we have seen that the latter has absorbed Chinese elements. Living side by side with the Chinese in Manchuria into which the Chinese had penetrated before the Manchus became an ethnical body, the Manchus gradually adopted the Chinese complex, only slightly modifying it, as an adaptation to their own complex. However, since the flow of the Chinese influence is practically permanent, the assimilation of new elements (their adaptation to the Manchu complex) becomes easier and easier. At the moment of the investigation of the Manchus, they were in the pro-

cess of losing that thin layer of the Manchu complex which was preserved, owing to the privileged position of the Manchus in China. The language was about to be lost, even in the Aigun district, the last region where it had been preserved. With the loss of the language and with the political isolation the total disappearance of the remains of the old original psychomental complex could soon be expected.

The positive knowledge, especially that connected with agriculture, was for a long time borrowed from the Chinese. Together with the spreading of Chinese books, and particularly with their translation into Manchu, the Chinese complex was adopted first by the educated groups and later it penetrated into the most remote Manchu populations. However, the Manchus have preserved shamanism, and they have passed it on to some Chinese groups in Manchuria. In reality it was from the beginning built up of a great number of purely Chinese elements or received from the Chinese. We have seen that the Chinese spirits, both directly borrowed or adapted, were long ago incorporated into the Manchu lists of spirits. The Chinese prestidigitators' tricks introduced by the Manchus, were adapted and incorporated into shamanism. Of course, after a dissection of the Manchu shamanism to its elements, very little of the original Manchu elements will be found; the only original features that remained were: the functioning of this complex as a safety valve, as a self-regulating mechanism, and a few elements created in the process of adaptation, e.g. some *vočko*, first shamans, prayers and performances in Manchu, as long as the language was preserved, which was also saturated with Chinese elements. Finally, the Chinese ritualism and formalism, closely connected with the existence of a written language, and the gradual penetration of the Chinese language have taken away the means of readaptation of the shamanistic complex. This meant a general paralysis of the mechanism of the psychomental complex.

Although the Chinese influence on the Northern Tungus was much lesser, some of the Tungus groups have been entirely sinofied. Such is the case of some Udehe, namely, their southern branch known under the name of Taze (investigated by S. Brailovskiĭ). This was the only group which for a long time was under the Chinese influence.* Some other Tungus groups, e.g. all Tungus of Manchuria, have received Chinese elements through the Manchus and partly through the Dahurs. i.e. already modified and adapted, in which form they sometimes do not look like Chinese elements.

The direct influence of the Chinese in recent years has become much stronger than it was before, even among the Manchus during their rule over China. In fact, schools are now established where teaching is done in Chinese, and the Tungus have come into a direct contact with the Chinese whom they imitate consciously and unconsciously. This influence can be arrested or merely delayed, only owing to the preservation of ethnical consciousness among the Tungus. We have seen that the Chinese "laugh" at the Tungus "backwardness", when they see shamanistic manifestations. On the other hand, the Chinese bring with them new knowledge, new hypotheses concerning this world, which the Tungus cannot reject because these theories are relatively

* According to V. V. Solarskiĭ (op. cit.) a certain part of the Tungus groups of the Maritime Prov. and a part of the Goldi were converted, under the Chinese influence, to Buddhism of the Chinese type.

simple and soothing the mind. The Tungus have now begun to assimilate the Chinese complex directly from the Chinese themselves. Shamanism can hardly resist this pressure. Again, as in the case of Lamaism, the chief factor destroying shamanism is not the theory, which may be assimilated by shamanism, but the medical assistance given sometimes quite successfully by the Chinese doctors. This assistance proves that in some cases, when the shamans fail to cure, the Chinese medical art may help, which shows that the Tungus cannot rely only upon the shamans in a most important matter such as the curing of diseases.

The Russian-Christian influence is much younger than the Buddhistic-Mongol and syncretic-Chinese influences. Some elements might have penetrated to the Tungus even before the first appearance of the Russians on the Tungus territory, but these elements might have been received as a new form of adaptation by the neighbours. They were certainly not very numerous. However, the Russian advance in Siberia brought the Tungus into direct contact with the Russians, who soon became their political masters.

At least two periods of the Russian influence can be distinguished. The early period, when Russian settlers and adventurers acted as pioneers, and made an impression not of "possessors of a superior cultural complex", but only of a unit strongly organized from the military point of view; and the second period, when the Tungus gradually became familiar with the Russian language. The Russians became then acquainted with the Tungus and could communicate them the principles of Christianity, medical art, positive knowledge and various hypotheses of their own. Although all Tungus did not become Christians, a great part of them adopted Christianity and gave up shamanism.

Christianity was at first introduced among the Tungus by compulsory baptism; but some of them accepted the new religion spontaneously, perhaps moved by political considerations. Such was probably the case of the *Gantimur* family which was baptized in the seventeenth century, apparently soon after their flight from Manchuria. The Nomad Tungus who were ruled by *Gantimur* gradually adopted Christianity together with the agricultural complex, while another part, as shown, adopted shamanism and nomadism of the cattle breeders of the Buriat type. Some of the Nomad Tungus have combined three complexes: shamanism, Lamaism and Christianity. In the northern regions of the Yakutsk and Enissei provinces the efforts made by the missionaries till the middle of the eighteenth century were not yet sufficient even for a formal adhesion of the Tungus to Christianity. However, with the change of policy, which consisted in giving various privileges to the christened Tungus, there was a great increase in the formal adhesion. In 1897, according to the official census, there were no more shamanists in the Maritime, Amur, and Yakutsk provinces and in the Irkutsk province there were 6 per cent, in Transbaikalia 45 per cent and in the Enissei province 12 per cent of "pagans", i.e. shamanists. However, a formal adhesion to the Orthodox Church did not mean much. A great part of the Tungus who lived on hunting and reindeer breeding practised shamanism.*

* According to V. V. Solarskij (op. cit., p. 151) the first mission was sent to the populations of Eastern Siberia in 1711 and it

Among the Reindeer Tungus of Transbaikalia I have gathered some data as to the spreading of Christianity, which I shall now give as an illustration of the situation. In the eighteenth century these Tungus did not speak Russian at all, while the missionaries apparently did not know Tungus. The Tungus regarded baptism as a form of submission to the "White Khan", i.e. the Russian Emperor. In their eyes baptism had no religious significance. However, as shown, the missionaries began at first to fight the shamans, which undoubtedly produced a great confusion of ideas among the Tungus. I happened to find in the Archives of the Bauntovskaja Uprava (*vide* SONT, i.e. the office of the lake Baunt Tungus Administration) a report of a local petty official who in 1840 stated that among 906 souls of the Barguzin Tungus (Lake Baunt group) only one hundred were baptized. The latter did not differ from those who were not baptized. The petty official made an interesting remark about the Tungus: "they keep their word, although being very rough in manners and extremely savage and timid. They do not know Russian. Their own language, very incomplete, is composed of a mixture of the Manchu, Mongol and Tartar languages". However, documents dated 1839 pretend that there were baptized adult people and children in an unlimited number. Still, in 1842 only one family was baptized. After that time the Christian activity became intensive. On November 22, 1852, the church warden of the Barguzin (city) Church of Transfiguration of our Lord, Mixail Černyx wrote a letter (numbered 12) to the Tungus clan chief (one of the administrative units) that he was ready to cancel the debts of the Tungus to the amount of 1050 roubles on the condition that his debtors accept baptism. Soon after this letter there was an official communication about the baptizing of thirty Tungus of various ages, between newly born up to 73 years. The increase of proselytes became quite important when it was announced that those who accepted baptism would not pay taxes during three years. After this there were produced several lists of newly baptized thus dispensed with taxation, followed by a document to the Uprava in which it was pointed out that the same persons must not be baptized a second time. Evidently, the Tungus interpreted baptism as a condition for being dispensed with paying the tax. In 1869, according to an official communication, there were 256 males and 162 females baptized, and 177 males and 25? females unbaptized, i.e. 59 per cent were not yet baptized. Under 1870 I found a new list of baptized Tungus, and in addition to it a document signed by the Bishop, in which a list of names of the baptized Tungus, who must not be baptized a second time, was given, and the order contained that each baptized should have a certificate of baptism. I have seen some of these certificates in the Uprava. However, at my time the Tungus did not read Russian. In the years 1860-1870 a missionary stationed at Irgen, near Chita, was very active, but since that time the adhesion of Tungus to Christianity was confined to a formal visit of a priest, once a year, to a chapel built up on the banks of the Lake Baunt, when all baptisms, wedding ceremonies, and

founded a permanent residence in Kamchatka. In 1742 an expedition consisting of an archimandrite, two ieromonachs (regular priest monks), an isrodeacon (regular deacon monk) and several students of the Moskow Orthodox Academy began its activity in Kamchatka, which continued for seven years. In the first quarter of the nineteenth century there were five or six missionaries in all of the Irkutsk diocese administering the Yakutsk province and Kamchatka.

a requiem for all those who died during the year were performed.

The penetration of Russian gold miners into the Barguzin taiga brought the Tungus into contact with the Russians, from whom they learnt Russian, at least those who entered into business relations, and so they could be easier influenced by the Church. The discussion and the discrediting of shamanism were common. The missionaries made also several attempts at educating some Tungus in their schools. These attempts failed. One of these young men, after his graduation from the lower ecclesiastical school abducted some reindeer and left for a little accessible region of the Maja River, breaking off his relations with the Church. Another, after his graduation, became a clerk in a gold mine and, being proud of his superior position, did not maintain any relations with the Tungus. A third one, who lived in Chita, did not want to return to the taiga.

At the present time (1912-1913) the great majority of these Tungus are Christians. However, their knowledge in this field is rather poor. I have met with the greatest authority among them, a man who could hardly read Russian; but he was chiefly interested in geography and biology. He gave me his interpretation of Christianity: the upper world is paradise, the lower world is the hell, but there are no sinners there; the "master of man" is *ann'el* (i.e. the angel), while the "master of bear" is a certain saint, and that of the shamans is *Nikola ugodaŋ* (i.e. Nikolaĭ Ugodnik of the Russians, Saint Nicolas), and so forth. A Nerčinsk Tungus who was employed as a workman by a Russian merchant and was supposed to be quite versed in Christianity, on my question about Jesus Christ asked me: "Does he live in *julja*"? (a Russianized Tungus village, near Nerčinsk). This provoked a series of questions on my part, but it was evident that he never had heard about Jesus Christ. The Nomad Tungus, a part of whom settled in the Urulga village and became agriculturists, and who were for more than a century Christians wanted to convince me that the sacrifices to the spirits practised by them were like the sacrifice given by Jacob to the prophet Elias.

The holy service, which the Tungus had occasions to see in the chapel of Baunt and in other places incidentally visited by them, was not understood as it should be, but it produced a great impression on the Tungus. They now use some Orthodox-Christian symbolism, as for instance a cross on the shaman's coat; some small ikons may be found among the *savak'i* too; the brass cross may be used as an amulet; they also are making the sign of the cross, in imitation of the priests, but it means only an expression of high esteem.*

Such a relatively poor result of Christianization of the Tungus was due to two conditions, namely, the inefficiency of the forms of propaganda and the difficulty of destroying the Tungus psychomental complex in so far as it is expressed in shamanism. As regards the inefficiency, it was so when the first Russians wanted to convert the Tungus by force and the Tungus resisted it; it did not change much, when the Russians wanted to attract them; it did not improve when the Tungus were left relatively free—they were formally recognized to be

* In 1913 we were visited in our tent by a group of Tungus just arrived from a remote region. They entered the tent, knelt in front of us, made most fervently the sign of the cross, as if we were ikons, and presented us with a half-bottle of vodka. (Russian brandy). I have often observed the same way of addressing the particularly respected clan seniors.

Christians, but the priests could not maintain a connexion with them.

The most negative impression was produced on the Tungus by the zealous missionaries, some of whom destroyed placings for spirits, shamanistic paraphernalia, etc. for proving that the spirits had no power, which, as I have shown, could not be convincing for the Tungus. S.K. Patkanov (op. cit., p. 219) relates that at the early period some missionaries among the Enissei Tungus used to pass their time in drinking, selling wine to the Tungus, and even entering into illicit relations with the local women. Such a behaviour produced a strong negative reaction on the part of the Tungus who attempted to kill some of these missionaries.

However, the Russian policy in the propagation of Christianity did not remain the same. While at the beginning of Christianization the latter was enforced and later, even during the eighteenth century, the method of Christianization was rather formalistic, the idea of baptizing every one was given up as early as 1822, when (on July 22) the "Code of Siberian Natives" was promulgated and made the basis of all further regulations. In fact, the Siberian natives were granted the right to perform any rites and to have any religion they wished, which was later on incorporated into the general Code (article 67). Moreover, the articles 1700 and 1701 of the "Code of non-Orthodox Religions" emphasized that the conversion to Christianity could be made only by means of conviction and not by force; the civil authorities were charged with the duty of protecting the natives against any attempt at limiting their religious liberty. This policy implied a change of attitude towards the missionaries, whose activity had never found a great support from the government. After formal conversions to Christianity a great number of missionaries' institutions ceased their activity altogether. For instance, the Turuxansk mission was officially closed in 1873* and the Tungus were served by ordinary parish-priests, who usually did not know the Tungus language.

After the formal adhesion of the Tungus to Christianity there were appointed priests who, according to the Russian practice, in a great number of cases received no fixed salary, or a very small one, but had to be supported by the remunerations received for baptism, weddings etc. and paid by those who needed the priest's assistance. This practice was also introduced among the Tungus who were formally recognized as Christians. But, as shown, in a great number of cases the Tungus did not understand the significance of these acts and the form of the remuneration, and the latter sometimes turned into a "tribute". In more recent times, the mores became milder, but still the visit of a priest, who in the name of the Church used to collect his own "tribute" in furs, was not always agreeable to the Tungus. In 1912 I observed a priest who arrived in a settlement of the Nomad Tungus for collecting *in natura* the remuneration for his past services, in form of milk products, such as cream, cheese etc. He was going in his cart from family to family, collecting these products. Under Russian conditions this could be made without lowering the moral and religious influence of the priest; but on the Tungus it produced an impression of a new form of official "tribute".

* According to a note by a special missionary of the Turuxansk region, Ieromonax Makariĭ, who certified the authorship of a Tungus dictionary recorded in this region (MS.).

However, some of the priests and bishops merited a great esteem on the part of the Tungus for what had been done for them. Such was, for instance, a bishop who lived in Chita in the nineties of the last century, and who, according to the Tungus, "did much good, like a shaman". I have also heard good opinions as to the priests living at the present time.

The Russian penetration into the regions of the Far East, namely, the Amur and Maritime provinces, was delayed by two centuries, so that Christianization of the local Tungus groups was also delayed. However, as shown, a great number of Tungus of the Amur region came from the Yakutsk province, where they had already been baptized. The Reindeer Tungus of Manchuria, who had also come from the Yakutsk province, and even a part of Birarčen, mostly of the clan Igačagir, were Christians before their coming to Manchuria. On the other hand, special efforts were made for converting the Goldi of the Amur and Ussuri regions and their neighbours—the Oroči—so that within a few decades these groups formally became Christians, with the exception of the small group which adopted Buddhism (vide supra p. 282). According to I. A. Lopatin (op. cit. pp. 56-58) the christianization of the Goldi went on under the rather favourable conditions of a positive reaction of the Goldi on the Russian control of the Amur region. However, as this investigator asserts, the Goldi did not much assimilate Christianity, although they used to attend holy services, to baptize their children etc. This fact is interesting, because great efforts were made for their christianization and a certain number of sacred books and prayerbooks, as shown, were translated into the Goldi language. Naturally, the language was undoubtedly a real impediment in introducing Christianity. This was realized and special efforts were made by the missionaries and priests. As an evidence of this period we have some collections of Tungus words gathered among the Enissei Tungus, among the Tungus of the Yakutsk province and among the Oroči, and even some translations of the New Testament, etc. into Tungus and Goldi.[*] However, these efforts were in vain, for the activity of the missionaries was stopped after the collapse of the Imperial Government.

The spreading of Christianity did not affect very much the existence of shamanism, with the exception of cases when the Tungus were ethnically disintegrated, as for instance the Russianized Tungus of Transbaikalia who live on agriculture and such groups as the Reindeer Tungus of Manchuria and the Reindeer Tungus of the Saxalin Island (the latter emigrated at the beginning of this century from the Amur prov.)

Perhaps more effective was the medical assistance given to the Tungus by the Russians, though in a very limited area. The possibility of medical treatment of some diseases, which formerly were treated by the shamans, has had an unfavourable effect upon the shamanistic tendencies of the Tungus, I mean those of them who can have medical assistance, e.g. those living near the Russian settlements in the gold mining regions, in villages etc. A few schools attended by the Tungus produced the same effect. Those who passed through the schools lost their absolute confidence in shamanism. The spreading of school education among the Tungus groups in the Russian territory was not uniform. In fact, it was practically impossible to concentrate in

schools Tungus children of groups which lived on hunting, for their parents were "wandering", so that only single children could be taken away from parents. In fact, this was done in different groups. On the other hand, the Tungus who lived in a more or less settled manner could be educated in schools. The Tungus of Transbaikalia who adopted agriculture and a settled life began to receive their education in schools as early as in the middle of the last century. The children could be admitted into the Russian schools as well. Among the Goldi[*] the first schools were started in 1867 (perhaps earlier) and in 1903 among the Goldi groups there were already eleven schools. In the years 1913-1914, 129 children were registered in Goldi schools (in 1915-1916 only 103 boys and girls); some schools had boarders. A great part of these schools had been organized by the educational department of the Holy Synod, and thus were controlled by the Orthodox Church. The teaching was first made in the native language and later in Russian.

Besides the above mentioned schools some private schools were scattered in the regions inhabited by the Tungus. Such was, for instance, a school on the banks of the Bureja River (the Amur province). The Tungus children were also admitted into the schools kept in the gold-mining regions, where the Tungus were educated together with the children of other ethnical groups (the Russians, Yakuts, and others).

Thus, Russian influence as a factor of disintegration of shamanism began its strong penetration among the Tungus through the school education as well.

The effect of all these influences was that shamanism began to weaken, which was realized by the Tungus. Their attitude was: "Shamanism is an old faith, so we must preserve it, for without shamanism the Tungus will perish!" as I was more than once told by the Barguzin Tungus. Some epidemics, like smallpox, reindeer epizooties etc. these Tungus explain by the decline of shamanism, which, as I have shown, cannot be justified.

Since I have touched upon the influence of Christianity, I must also mention an effort made by the French Jesuits who translated the New Testament and some other works into Manchu during the period when the fathers were on good terms with the Manchu Emperors. However, this effort was sterile. Among the Aigun Manchus I have seen some of these books but they were not such as to attract the attention of the Manchus, and no influence produced by them could be seen. If it had any influence, it was confined to the Manchus of Peking who thereafter were soon "sinicized", and thus could have no influence upon the shamanists of Manchuria.

A real and perhaps the strongest blow to shamanism came from another side, as we shall see a little later.

The use of foreign personal names may also be taken for measuring the degree of the loss of the Tungus complex.

---

[*] For details cf. "Aspects".

[*] In subsequent years this number fell to eight because of strong epidemics and it was found undesirable to have mixed schools which accepted both Russian and Goldi children. Some schools were also closed because of lack of pupils. V. V. Solarskij (op. cit. 133-148) gives a great number of details and his criticism of the practised system. Cf. also I. A. Lopatin (op. cit. pp. 58-59) who has given a short description and his criticism as to the education. This author points out a special ability of Goldi children for calligraphy and drawing, in which they are superior to the Russian children. This investigator asserts in general that the Goldi are capable pupils and are strong in arithmetic.

Among the Reindeer Tungus of Transbaikalia I found a list of names which were used parallel to the Christian names, like John, Paul, Nicolas, etc, given at the baptism. However, among the Nomad Tungus of Urulga the names of Buriat origin were adopted and no Tungus names were used. Among the Reindeer Tungus of Manchuria no Tungus names were preserved, they used only Russian names. Among the Tungus of Manchuria Tungus names and seldom Dahur names are used, but among the Manchus Chinese names are used parallel to the Manchu names and sometimes the Manchu names are no longer used.*

148. **PRESENT STATE AND FUTURE OF SHAMANISM** From the preceding sections of the present chapter and from earlier chapters it can be seen that shamanism, as a complex which has resulted from peculiar conditions and various influences, reactions on them, and adaptation of complexes for the maintenance of the psychomental equilibrium, was an always changing, varying complex. In spite of a very strong pressure and even prohibitions, shamanism has been able to survive up to the present time. Among the Tungus groups which preserved their ethnical integrity it is not in a state of decline, but in a state of elastic adaptation and therefore is subject to variations.

It may be reasonable to ask oneself: how long will shamanism survive? This question might be left unanswered, as it concerns the future; however, such a question would be natural on the part of the reader, and I feel myself sufficiently prepared to answer it, at least hypothetically.

I have already shown that the chief factors of the disintegration of shamanism are the strong penetration of alien complexes and particularly the elimination of a great number of cases formerly of the competence of shamans. From this point of view the Tungus and Manchus are now found in a quite different position than before. They are now surrounded by groups more numerous than they are themselves, and these groups possess cultural complexes with which shamanism cannot compete. As a matter of fact, this is a new era in the history of the Tungus. In Siberia there is the strong influence of the Russians who are opposed to shamanism and may destroy its old theoretical foundations by the introduction of medical art, school education, and a new complex of religion, based upon a certain ethical teaching. The Tungus come more and more in contact with the Russians who during the nineteenth century have gradually involved the Tungus in their economic system. In my SONT I have shown the

degree of the dependence of the Tungus on the Russian economic system and the new interethnical relations to which the Tungus were subjected. The situation in Manchuria did not differ much. With the millions of Chinese immigrants from China, Manchuria ceased to be a Tungus territory even in its remote regions—the Chinese penetrated everywhere and gradually bound the Tungus with new economic relations. In a lesser degree than in Siberia the Tungus began to use the assistance of Chinese medical professionals and to absorb Chinese theories. These Tungus had no other issue but to submit to the strong pressure.

One of important conditions of this situation is that all territories around the Tungus are peopled more densely than their own territory and they have no more place to escape from the pressure of these new, powerful groups. In recent years a new ethnical factor has appeared, namely, the Japanese who will perhaps produce a still stronger cultural pressure upon these populations.

However, the chief condition of the present situation is not the pressure, as such, but the fact that the Tungus, as well as the Manchus, cannot withstand this pressure having already lost their former power of resistance in the given interethnical milieu. Owing to the new forms of adaptation, new ethnical groups being very numerous will undoubtedly, sooner or later, absorb the Tungus, as dispersed ethnical groups. However, the blow has come even earlier than it might have been expected, and from a side unforeseen before, namely, a very intensive disintegration of all Tungus groups living in Siberia and the regrouping in the ethnical equilibrium in Manchuria.

I have shown in SONT that, owing to the collapse of the former economic relations which had been established between the Russians and the Tungus groups, the Tungus found themselves in a more difficult position than other ethnical groups, so that some of the Tungus groups *physically* perished soon after the collapse. This position of the Tungus may be better understood, if we remember that a great number of them could not live any more without food supply, without a regular supply of fire-arms and powder, without a supply of cloth for clothing etc., for animal food was not sufficient for maintaining the Tungus population. Moreover, their organization and knowledge were already adapted to the new conditions of ethnical existence on the principle of close co-operation* with another ethnical group—the Russians. When the latter fell into a state of disorganization, the Tungus could not readapt themselves to the new condition—their organization was not elastic enough—and they began to die out. Such was the fate of two groups in Transbaikalia, namely, the Samagir who lived on the Lake Baikal and the Reindeer Barguzin Tungus, which is evident from the report of E. I. Titov's introduction to his Tungus Dictionary (cf. SONT). A large group of the Nomad Tungus of Mankova and Borz'a migrated to Mongolia, where, being surrounded by other ethnical groups, they will soon be assimilated, and thus will ethnically perish. V. N. Vasiliev (op. cit.) gives a picture of the physical extinction of the Tungus in the Aldan-Maja region and the Ajan-Oxotsk region. So, for instance, he says that only 12 families remain (about 50-60 souls) from the third *Ežan rod* (administrative unit) which in 1897

---

* I give here some names which may have some meaning, while others have no meaning at all. Transbaikalian Reindeer Tungus: Katowul, Dašševul, Gačevul, Sogdavul, Ošawul, Čutavul, Čutavul in which wul—vul is a suffix for male names; Kirig, Mardon, Matuk, Saygun'ï, Siyirkon, Duvunča, Nokondun, Murčetkan, Irbon, Galdi, Nirba, Čufsaai are used without a suffix as male-names. Ganfur, Dono, Čanik, Sundža, Kiromak, Saždak, Umužak, Kirožak, Saikak, Kurulbik in which lak, mak, dak, bik etc. are suffixes, used for female names.

Here are some names used among the Tungus of Manchuria Katadu, Ufigan, Tuyuldin, Katasin, Infabu, Indačan, Jandačan, Urpa, Čemuyga, Moido as names used for males. I have a series of personal names from the stories, but I do not give them here. Some of them are old Tungus names (e.g. Tibfavul), while other names are Tungus, but of a seemingly recent origin; lastly there are many Manchu and Mongol names. As to the Manchu customs vide SOM.

* I do not discuss here the question who was favoured by this co-operation which very often turned into a merciless "parasitism" of small groups of "merchants" on the Tungus.

(according to S. K. Patkanov, op. cit. pp. 123) consisted of 512 members (a great part of them lived then in the Amur prov. and other regions). Some of these groups took part in the civil war on the White-Russian (anti-communist) side that resulted in a great loss of lives, which, considering the small number of Tungus, is very important. They also took part in the migration to other regions, where naturally they may survive only on one condition, namely, that other Tungus units would become extinct, as it was observed in Transbaikalia, when it was occupied by the groups coming from the North. It is thus evident that a great number of Tungus physically perished during this period. However, the destruction of the Tungus attracted the attention of the Soviet Government which realized the economic effect of the Tungus decline, i.e. the impossibility of producing furs for the world market without Tungus work. But this plain fact was perhaps not sufficient for a fruitful attention of the government absorbed in still greater problems of a planetary revolution. However, the sentimentalism of the revolutionaries was greatly affected by the perishing of the Tungus groups, as well as of other non-Russian natives of Siberia. Thus, two movements combined in one, quite sympathetic with the Tungus, namely, in the decision to support them economically and to reorganize them according to a new system which, according to the ideas of the inventors, must save these units from a complete destruction and at the same time which would not allow them to fall under an anti-communistic influence.

In the firm belief that one day mankind will not be differentiated into ethnical and racial groups, but will form a homogeneous mass of population equally enjoying the advantages of a new economic and social system, the communistic theoreticians do their best to approach this ideal condition by the unification and the cultural levelling of all groups, on the one hand, and by supporting small ethnical groups against the populous and culturally superior groups, on the other hand. Practically the first aim is achieved by the creation of a uniform administrative organization and by the propaganda of marxism; the second—by giving autonomy to the small units. An ethnological analysis of the situation shows that these two seemingly contradictory positions merely reflect new ethnical relations which were created after the collapse of the Russians, chiefly the Great Russians, who as an ethnical group used to play the part of the consolidator of the greater unit—the Empire, on the one hand, and a strong centrifugal movement in general resulting in the consolidation of the territorial and ethnical groups, brought about by the collapse of the Empire (in the sense of a greater economic and political unit), on the other hand. In so far as political control of the territories and populations is taken up by a new social group of a different psychomental complex—first a secret society and later a political communistic party—the latter acts, quite unconsciously, as a regulator of two movements —the centripetal and the centrifugal—manifested in the creation of new local equilibria and expressed in a new slogan: "communistic constructive work" and "self-government of nationalities" (viz. ethnical units). Considering this as an ethnological phenomenon, nothing new is observed in this respect, except a great uncertainty of steps, their tentative character, poor theoretical justification and lack of experience in the art of government, owing to which privileged groups and oppressed groups are formed, resulting in a general weakening of these populations, taken as a unit (empire),

and a further disintegration of these populations. The position of the Tungus groups is especially difficult.

Strong units, like the Buriats and Yakuts, who are numerous enough to oppose the pressure of the central government and to maintain their independence, have given rise to unfavourable conditions among the Tungus groups, owing to which the Tungus had to submit to their assimilation by these strong units. Moreover, when the Tungus leave their territory, the Buriats and Yakuts try to occupy it, and when they meet with opposition, they refer to the principles of equality, rationality etc., owing to which they cannot be prevented from penetrating* into that territory. The effect will soon appear—the strong units will multiply quicker and will eventually occupy the Tungus territory. With the increase of the economic difficulties the exploitation of the Tungus populations has already become unbearable for the Tungus. In spite of the stopping of the extermination of fur-animals by hunting, characteristic of a long period of "civil war", and notwithstanding the lack of munitions among the Tungus, the former level of the fur production cannot be attained. Thus, economically the Tungus are no more interested in maintaining their ethnical independence. But the cultural disintegration of the Tungus goes still deeper. Here the pressure of the communistic party and their agents is especially important. From the theoretical point of view the Morgan-Marxian attitude is simple: the clan organization, barbarian econmic methods, and ideological superstructure are doomed to perish in the face of a "new society", therefore everything must be done for facilitating this process. Practically, first the clan organization must be destroyed; modern methods in the economic exploitation of the territory must be applied and "superstitions" must be exterminated. As regards the destructive part of this work, it is not difficult to carry it out, for the Tungus cannot resist it and defend themselves; but the economic reorganization is senseless for the Tungus as such, for they will simply perish as an ethnical body. In the process of this activity, the Tungus will receive a new administrative system, the soviets, with a great number of officials, and, on paper, the right to their territory etc. For bringing up the new system, naturally opposed by the old generation, the young generation—which has not yet been trained for the hard work of the hunter and which does not yet know the technique of this profession— is supposed by the government to suppress the resistance of the old generation. In the preceding chapters I have already pointed out that in former times the young generation often opposed the old generation and only owing to the existence of the clan organization it was possible to maintain the Tungus complex and particularly the oral traditions concerning the technique.

With the help of the government the whole Tungus organization will be split into two halves, in which state it

* A few interesting facts are scattered e.g. in V. N. Vasiliev's report concerning the Yakuts. I have also similar facts from my informers familiar with present conditions in Transbaikalia. Very interesting facts are communicated by Kai Donner who had an opportunity to work with an Enissei Ostiak in Finland. This group is not numerous and has rather strong neighbours—the Yurak and Tungus. These groups made attempts at the occupation of Enissei Ostiak territory. The territory was saved, because the Enissei Ostiaks were well armed. (Kai Donner, "Ethnological Notes about the Yenisey Ostyak", Mémoirs de la Société Finno-Ougrienne LXVI, 1933, Helsingfors, pp. 14 et seq.). Naturally, if the Tungus were numerous enough, they would not hesitate to act as the Yakuts and Buriats.

will become paralyzed and the old professional experience will be lost. The loss of their cultural complex by the Tungus will evoke no regret in the leaders, for they are theoretically prepared for the fact that "backward" ethnical groups must give place to "advanced" groups, as they consider themselves (a curious case of ethnocentric manifestation within a not yet completely formed ethnical unit —the communists). This process is helped by giving special education to the Tungus youth. Some of them are selected among the Tungus groups, sent to the present surrogates for middle schools or the universities, and to special schools for political education, and later they may be given a higher education. The first aim to be reached is the appropriation by the pupils of the communistic teaching, after which they must go further and become propagandists of marxism among their own people in order to fight "superstitions" and to prepare their people for the joining of "free mankind, liberated from the capitalistic oppression". In the psychology of these representatives of the Tungus groups the most important point is that, in looking at the wealth accumulated for centuries, which resulted from the former cultural adaptation of the Russians, they believe it to be a communistic achievement—they are impressed by it; secondly, after learning the elements of marxism they assume a special vulgarity of mind of half-educated people, who believe themselves strong enough to discuss any given problem (a state which is characteristic of the culturally low classes of population in so-called democratic countries) ; thirdly, they lose their ethnical consciousness and do not want to return to their people. In reality, even in this respect, there is nothing new as compared with the attempts at the introduction of another alien complex among the Tungus—Christianity. There is a difference in the quantity, namely, the missionaries and Church authorities were not permitted to spend too much for the individual education of the Tungus in their schools, and the number of Tungus involved was not very large; with the communists, who have no administrative experience and are not satisfied with experiments on a small scale, the idea of the re-education of the Tungus is very strong and they want to attract the greatest possible number of them.[*] The effect is evident: those who do not return to their own people will become petty officials of low ranks in the communistic centres of activity, and in this way the Tungus will lose them; and those who will return to their own people will continue the unfinished work of the disintegration of the Tungus and complete their assimilation by the communists (chiefly Russian speaking communists), i.e. exactly the process induced by the missionaries before the old government realized the undesirability of the complete ethnical extinction of the Tungus, as an important economic factor in the scantily peopled regions of the taiga. However, a change of this policy on the part of the communists is impossible, for it would mean the denial of all theoretical background of communism and the abandoning of this population as being beyond control. On the other hand, this measure will come too late, for other ethnical groups,

like the Buriats and Yakuts, are now relatively stronger than they were before, and they will overwhelm the Tungus.

Such are the present conditions of the existence of the Tungus and there is no doubt that the Tungus ethnical units, which may survive the economic collapse, will not survive cultural disintegration. Since the clan organization can be destroyed and replaced by the common sovietic administration, the Tungus will be gradually incorporated into the mixed population of Siberia which, because of its numerousness will absorb the inherited Tungus complex, and the Tungus, as a group, will perish for ever and shamanism too will perish with this physical extinction of the Tungus groups and with a cultural distintegration of their remains.[*]

The present position of the Tungus groups in Manchuria has also changed, for they are now found deprived of their rights as a privileged group, as they were in the Manchu military organization. The influx of the Chinese population into the regions of the Tungus territory continues. For instance, the Xulun region, formerly occupied by the Birarčen, is now an important agricultural region peopled by Chinese. Regions of the taiga are overfilled by Chinese hunters who exterminate local animals, so that the Tungus who live on hunting, e.g. in the Little Khingan mountains, sixteen years ago already found it difficult to earn their living and, now it has probably become impossible. The Chinese migration into remote regions will not stop, because of the almost inevitable economic development of Manchuria, now covered with railways, navigation along the rivers, a new system of roads and a net of business organizations. The Tungus will be compelled to leave their mountains and settle in villages amid a mixed population. Since the fur bearing animals are decreasing in number and will soon be extinct, there will even be no economic stimulus to maintain the Tungus as good hunters—they will meet with no assistance from any government. When they settle in villages, they will be first of all disorganized in respect to their clan

---

[*] Many facts regarding Tungus disintegration and even physical extinction are found in special sovietic publications. However, the analysis of these facts is not easy, because they are sometimes represented so as only partially to reflect the actual situation. On the one hand, a great body of facts is not published at all, because the facts are compromising; on the other hand, the organisers of the disintegration are interested only in some facts, directly concerning them as professionals. Moreover, for understanding the meaning of the facts, one must be familiar with the conditions of the groups before the collapse of the national government. I give here a quotation which is rather typical of the justifications of the Tungus disintegration and which also deals with shamanism. An analogous attitude can be found in reference to the family, the clan and the ethnical units of several other aborigines. "Pointing out that the fighting against shamanism and other religious cults in the North" (the northern regions of the territories controlled by soviets) "is one of the sections of class struggle, a struggle for a socialistic construction, for a cultural revolution, the VIIIth plenary meeting of the Committee for the North" (i.e. the regions chiefly peopled by non-Russian groups; the Committee was organised by the government in order to introduce the socialistic system within these groups) "has decided: to introduce in the North a deep, systematic anti-religious propaganda as an inseparable part of all politico-enlightening work, showing to the working masses the counter-revolutionary activity of the shamans, the sectarian propagandists and other servants of religious cults". (Cf. "Materials of the First All-Russian Conference on Development of Languages and Writing among the peoples of the North", edited by J. P. Alkor (Koškin) and I. D. Davydov, Moscow-Leningrad, 1932, pp. 35-36, and repeated on p. 74.) Indeed, these desiderata, as many other great schemes and plans of communists, will remain only on paper.

---

[*] As to the psychology of the actors, it is interesting that this side of the ethnical disintegration of the Tungus is carried out by the group of sentimentalists-ethnographers who want to save these groups from their enemies, but by their interference only accelerate this process. The point of interest is the psychomental reactions of this group of "benefactors" on the process and their own idea as to their part in it.

system, which is the back-bone of shamanism, and the functions of the shamans will be taken up by the Chinese professional doctors, in so far as treatable diseases are concerned. The process of loss of shamanism will be accelerated by the adoption of Chinese schooling, quite indispensable under the new conditions. So the Tungus language will soon be forgotten, as it has already happened with Manchu.

Naturally, under these new conditions, there is no chance for the survival of shamanism in Siberia, in Manchuria and in Mongolia. It seems to me that the material gathered by myself and presented here in an analysed form will become the last trace of shamanism. Even at my time signs of an approaching end could be seen. Perhaps, in some remote regions, some remains of it are still preserved, for since my visit to those regions from fifteen to twenty-two years have already elapsed, which, under the present circumstances, is a very long period with regard to changes. However, a reserve must be made, namely, as a Tungus told me one day (*vide* SONT), the ethnical units, which are now in play, will perhaps perish, as a great number of them have perished before, and the Tungus will be able to survive, and grow up again. What will be left of shamanism as a self-regulating psychomental complex after all these eth-

nical cataclysms, is difficult to say. But one thing is evident: should the Tungus really survive, shamanism will not be the same as it was observed by me and there will be a new complex to be investigated from beginning to end, element by element, and in a new ethnical complex.

Since I have recorded here analysed ethnographical facts almost accidentally—my choice of the Tungus as a material for ethnological observations was more or less incidental—and since there were hundreds, and thousands of similar complexes which perished and which will never be repeated, I am inclined to see in my investigation into shamanism chiefly one side, namely, *that of a study of the function of the psychomental complex under the variable conditions of an ethnographical complex in a variable ethnical and interethnical milieu*, which can be studied, perhaps even with better success, on some other ethnographical material. Therefore, I shall not particularly emphasize the great loss for science, should the end of shamanism actually occur. I always have in mind that perhaps in the past there were phenomena still more complex and more interesting from the ethnological point of view than shamanism. Perhaps, if ethnologists turn their attention to similar mechanisms in other cultural and ethnical complexes, they will find still richer material for their deductions.

CONCLUSION

CHAPTER XXXII

DIFFERENTIATION AND FUNCTION OF COMPLEXES

149. TUNGUS MENTALITY IN GENERAL In Section 1 of Chapter VIII of my study "Social Organization of the Northern Tungus" I have given a general characteristic of the Tungus from the point of view of their mentality and psychology. I needed this characteristic as an introduction to a description of some social customs; but the chief material used for it was that expounded in the present work. Since the facts are now given, I need not repeat what I formulated there as a general characteristic, and I shall merely refer to the above indicated section. However, some particular points ought now to be stressed.

Reviewing the first chapters of Part One, one may see that the Tungus are very good observers and their method of drawing inferences is not lacking any element of logic, as compared with that of Europeans. More than this, when the inference may have a vital importance, the Tungus become more careful—they always check up their inferences and remodel them, when needed—than the Europeans are with regard to subjects of not vital (or seemingly a not-vital) importance.* The question as to how quick the Tungus are in arriving at sound and correctly made conclusions and how long they may remain in a state of trying their inferences, naturally depends on the frequency of opportunity of observation, the importance of the inference, and perhaps the natural state of the Tungus mental process and their reactions on it. When the inference is made and can successfully work, it has all chance of being, at least for a time, stabilized as a fixed acquisition of knowledge, regardless of whether it is wrong or correct from our point of view. If the inference comes into a conflict with newly observed facts and if the inference has a vital importance, it will be immediately modified. The Tungus very often remain critical as to their inferences and they are not afraid to say: "I do not know", when they are not certain. It is thus natural that facts of vital importance, gathered in great numbers, i.e. practically facts directly relating to the sources of victuals and maintenance of life, such as animals, plants, topography, etc., guarantee the correctness of the inference. In fact, the Tungus ideas about these facts are more reliable than some "scientific" inferences, say, of the last century. Indeed, there may be no question that most of these inferences, in so far as the process of their establishment is concerned, are arrived at by the Tungus

---

* Cf. "Aspects", pp. 176 et seq. in which I demonstrate a case when the method of Europeans is much inferior to that of the Tungus.

through the same mental process: observation→hypothetical generalization→trial of this generalization→fixation of the generalization.

It may be pointed out that some Tungus have even come to the idea of classification of animals according to "clans" (*vide supra*, p. 72) which presumes a common origin of some animals, i.e. a further step of an analytical generalization. Such an idea ought to be regarded as a scientific conception not implied by the practical interest of an immediate satisfaction of need. This fact alone may suffice for demonstrating the existence of "science" as a product of inquisitiveness and unrestricted motion in the process termed thinking.

However, I have shown several instances of this kind, among which I wish to draw attention to the hypothesis of micro-organisms, which is particularly interesting because of its being recognized to be a hypothesis and because we can quite clearly see the process of its creation. The Tungus solve the problem of infection by going from the analysis of facts. The fact of deep wounds in which larvae of insects and worms may appear, seen by the eye, leads them to the idea that, since worms and insects originate from germs, which are different, there may be other "*germs*" which do not grow big and which cause inflammations, swelling, secretions and the physiological reaction of fever. In the general setting the analysis and the way of approaching the problem are correct. The next step is to find the specific micro-organisms which are responsible for different kinds of diseases. That the micro-organisms are different is known to the Tungus: they give instances of different insects, worms and even seminal liquid which contains "germs". The point of importance is a really ingenious hypothesis: there are small organisms which do not grow and thus cannot be seen. Moreover, *the whole construction is regarded by the Tungus as a hypothesis.* I do not see any difference between this Tungus construction and, for instance, the modern approach to particular problems such as cancer, which by some investigators was hypothetically believed to be caused by a micro-organism, the latter remaining undiscovered because of an inadequate technique.

This case is demonstrative of the same mental character of the Tungus: a realistic approach to a new problem by gathering of facts, by analysis, and by inferences temporarily accepted as a hypothesis. However, in this case a utilitarian stimulus may be suspected, namely, the treatment of certain diseases.

403

In a great number of Tungus hypotheses shown in Part Two we find all stages of the formation of stable theories, accepted as established truths and beginning with sceptically adopted suppositions liable to immediate rejection, should contradictory facts be disclosed. Indeed, there are some hypotheses which have not yet received general recognition, even hypotheses just formed by individuals as suppositions, and there are hypotheses generally recognized. Some of the hypotheses are merely the result of a further logical reasoning about facts known and analysed; some other hypotheses have a conscious stimulus in the wish to find a practical solution of a faced problem; finally, there are hypotheses the exactness of which is not cognized and which are not even observed to have been formed. Again, in this respect no difference between the European complex and the Tungus complex can be seen. However, in so far as quantity and spheres of mental work are concerned, there are very essential differences. In fact, for instance, a great number of facts created by the existence of new relations between the European ethnical units and their milieus are totally lacking as subjects of the Tungus thinking process; the existence of a comparatively rudimentary technical culture eliminates a great number of problems too; on the other hand, problems of primary milieu, in connexion with the hunting complex of the Tungus, are better developed in the Tungus complex; perhaps, the same may be said in reference to the complex connected with shamanism, as a method of regulation of psychic equilibrium. Yet, the total amount of knowledge of the Tungus is naturally much smaller than that of the European groups.

I have already pointed out that the distribution of knowledge among the Tungus is much more even, than it is e.g. among the groups living in big cities and farmers confined to a limited area and to a limited sphere of interests. As a matter of fact, the Tungus enters into contact with a much wider milieu than any citizen or any farmer. In the first group, consisting chiefly of workmen of big factories, the mental interest is naturally reduced to the necessary minimum of what is seen in the factory and in the poor quarters in which the workmen live, and this lasts, without any essential change, during their whole life and even for generations. The position of a farmer is slightly better, for he still deals with nature and must know, at least automatically, the conditions of the primary milieu. However, being confined to a limited area, the farmer greatly narrows his interest and knowledge. The Tungus, who lives on hunting, has to come in contact with all elements of the primary milieu of a large area sometimes covering millions of square kilometres. He must also come in contact with other ethnical groups, his neighbours—Tungus and even non-Tungus groups. He runs much more risk than the citizens and farmers. This produces a beneficial effect upon the selection and acts as an imperative stimulus for individual adaptation. Indeed in so far as the mass of the population is concerned, this is so, but living in large groups, which possess complex forms of technical and social adaptation, greatly facilitates the creation of a selected group of individuals whose function is based upon the division of work.* However, even this "thinking ap-

paratus" of the ethnical unit is affected by the same conditions of division of work and the still deeper process of biological selection. Indeed, one may treat ethnical units as a whole and refer to the group of selected "thinking apparatus", as though it were itself an "ethnical unit"; but that would not give an idea as to the mental state of the mass of the population. For all these reasons the individual Tungus, in the poorness of his technical culture, sometimes with periods of hardship and even starvation, which occur after epizooties, is much more broad-minded and much better adapted for acquiring new knowledge; he is in a much lesser degree affected by an obstinate opposition to an appeal to the reason and logic, than the farmers of "civilized nations" and especially the low working classes of the cities, who in a great number of cases must be watched and compelled by special organs of the authority to function as useful and sufficiently productive members of the units to which they belong.

I have touched (vide SONT, p. 310), with a great caution, upon the problem of "inherited" conditions of mental ability of the Tungus. Apparently the Tungus themselves are conscious of the fact that these conditions are, at least partly, inherited. Indeed, it is impossible to abstract different aspects of the Tungus psychomental complex, namely, the factor of selection, that of favourable milieus, and automatic transmission of physical conditions by the mechanism of inheritance, as well as the always possible mutations and new combinations of inherited elements, for they are only different aspects of the same complex phenomenon—the existing psychomental complex.

* There seems to be no way out of this situation, which is a consequence of the division of work and of the agglomeration of people on limited spaces of land. This is brought about by two factors: firstly, by an increase of the population which cannot be stopped by the ethnical unit without the risk of being absorbed by its neighbours (in which case the unit would perish and cease to play its part in the interethnical equilibrium); secondly, by an increase of the production per working individual, which is also caused by the growth of the population and the interethnical pressure. This condition is realized by most of thinking men, but it cannot be helped, for it exceeds the power of individual ethnical units. The minds of sensitive people may be allayed by apparently practical solutions, such as the effort of philanthropists to raise the intellectual standard of the population; as a socialistic dream of increasing productivity by means of a further mechanization of the industry and thereby allowing free hours for the intellectual development of the masses. However, the philanthropic work and an "artificial" education during the hours of leisure will not stimulate the yearning for knowledge which in the mass of the population is always created by the conditions of life, more precisely by the struggle for existence. Another very unfavourable condition is the decrease of natality and accordingly a reduction of the natural selection, both of which combined affect populations, chiefly in the sense of giving more chance to the weaker and the more specialized part, while the upper layer, as soon as selected from the brutalized part of the population, shows a further decrease of power of self-reproduction, and thus this mechanism acts like a continuous pumping. The ethnical units which try to interfere with this process are very likely to spend their energy without any effect and to make way for other ethnical units which do not waste their energy. There remains another dream—that of reaching an agreement among all strong units, in order to carry out a definite policy. But this is nothing more than a manifestation of a leading ethnos under the conditions of a varying interethnical milieu, which, as a practical way, is in a sharp conflict with the process of variations generally observed. As far as I can see, this is a process which inevitably leads to the collapse of the present species of man and perhaps to the creation of new biological species of man—but to change the course of things is impossible. Density of population and, as a form of adaptation, its settling on a very limited territory cannot be regulated for all mankind. The immediate consequence thereof is the reduction of the biological functions, as is typical of sedentary animals.

150. DIFFERENT COMPLEXES In the description of the T u n g u s psychomental complex we have seen a great difference between the complexes observed among the various Tungus groups. In reality, these differences are great only when they are analysed on Tungus soil and the complexes are compared with one another. However, if one compares the Manchus with the Reindeer Tungus of Transbaikalia, the difference will be great, even as compared with other ethnical groups. In the analysis of different complexes I have occasionally shown the difference of the origin of various cultural elements, some of which might be traced back to the Chinese, Tibetan and Mongol complexes, in some rare cases even further, both historically and territorially. For instance, in the Manchu complex we meet with a great number of cultural elements, particularly that of the technical complex, unknown among the Tungus, but responsible for differences, viz, the agricultural complex which imposes a settled life with all its consequences, as well as a strong Chinese influence, also the professionalization of shamanism and mafarism. Among the Reindeer Tungus we meet with elements like the reindeer breeding, the hunting complex as a basis of the economic system, the rich complex of ideas borrowed from the Buriats and Yakuts, all of which are lacking in the Manchu complex and all of which are responsible for the existence of a different psychomental complex. The other groups may be put between these two groups with an evident deviation where the "nomadic complex" and the Mongol (Buriat and Dahur) influences appear.

In spite of elements of distinction there are many elements which are common to all groups here described. First of all, there is doubtless a common Tungus language which reflects a certain similarity of the psychomental complex of all groups, a great number of ideas borrowed probably at different historic moments from the neigh-·bouring ethnical units, perhaps some elements which have originated among the Manchus and later spread over other Tungus groups—e.g. the elements of social organization—and finally some elements which may be supposed to have been preserved from the time of the pro-Tungus. With a lesser certainty we may also suppose that there are some common elements of reactions which are connected with inherited physiological conditions and which, in so far as they are associated with the common anthropological types, may be preserved among different Tungus groups.

Combinations of distinct elements and common elements in the Tungus groups are responsible for the creation of different local and technical complexes in various degrees similar and distinct when compared. The psychomental complexes of all these groups are thus not similar.

Naturalistic knowledge among the Tungus groups covers a very wide range of phenomena, but it is as variable as its contents and methods of approach. We have seen, for instance, that the Manchu complex is impregnated with modern Chinese elements and at the same time is poorer in so far as this knowledge depends on the chance of facing naturalistic problems. However, in so far as fundamental conceptions are concerned, the groups here treated do not show any essential differences. On the other hand, the naturalistic knowledge of the Northern Tungus, as far as I know, remains in some respects quite undisseminated. The chief cause of this is the fact that these Tungus live in the midst of nature which they must know and in which they are interested, both from the utilitarian point of view

and from the point of view of seeking pure knowledge. In the case of the theories regarding the structure of the world, we can see that the Tungus ideas are seemingly not their own invention and can be easily traced to the original sources of borrowing. However, there remain some elements which are found in some Northern Tungus complexes, about which we cannot definitely say whether they never existed among other groups, or were forgotten. That the elements of the complex of naturalistic knowledge may be lost is beyond any doubt. This may be seen from a great number of instances and particularly in the knowledge concerning animals. The latter, known to the Tungus from the point of view of their anatomical features, psychic and mental characters, geographical distribution and general habits, do not remain the same. Yet, this knowledge is most intimately connected with the hunting complex; it may be even better included in this complex as one of its components; and to be maintained this knowledge must be carefully transmitted from one generation to another. When a Tungus group migrates to another region, it may easily forget its biological knowledge of the animals not found in the new. area. The same would undoubtedly happen, should the animal become extinct or the knowledge be lost, if the hunting complex is replaced by any other complex—by that breeding of cattle, agriculture, etc. Such cases may now be observed. For instance, the Birarčen, after their final settlement in their present area, did not find the elk (Alces) and their knowledge of this animal has lost its vividness. Some clans of Reindeer Tungus of Transbaikalia, which migrated from Manchuria in recent time—apparently two or three centuries ago—have only a very faint remembrance of the tiger, which is common in Manchuria. This faint idea will soon be lost altogether. The Manchus formerly used to be familiar with hunting and practised it. It may thus be supposed that their knowledge of methods of hunting and of animals was not like those expounded in their books, which are chiefly translations from Chinese. At the time of their brilliant career in China, hunting had to be given up, and naturally together with it the knowledge of Manchurian animals. After their political collapse they returned to Northern Manchuria and at least partly resumed their hunting. However, this time they had to learn it from the Northern Tungus from whom they again learnt important facts regarding local animals. This case is interesting, for the Manchus, after having forgotten this element of the old complex, restored it with the help of another ethnical group, which had been the keeper of the ancient knowledge.

The present naturalistic knowledge among the Tungus groups is thus very variable, and it may be supposed that in former time some of the Tungus groups possessed a much richer knowledge than that of the present time, and this knowledge was not rich in elements of scholastic theoretization and speculation recently obtained chiefly from the neighbours.

The Tungus complexes receive a special character owing to the configuration of the area occupied by them. These regions impose a special complex of means of communication and offer a special material for observation. The degree of their development depends on several other conditions, e.g. the chief source of food supply, the draught animals, the density of population which in turn may impose a different degree of movement. Different means of communication greatly affect the psychomental complex of the groups. While sedentary groups, like the Manchus, who use carts and do not leave their small area crossed by a system of roads, naturally confine their interest to local phenomena and form a rather confused idea as to the mountainous regions adjacent to their arable land, while their neighbours, the Northern Tungus, on horseback and especially on reindeer back, can freely move where they wish and gradually become acquainted with a variety of conditions of milieu and populations—other ethnical groups, animals, little accessible mountains, etc.—so all natural phenomena lose their enigmatic character in the Tungus complex. A third type of means of communications is that created by the navigable rivers. In fact, the river populations are more free in their movements than the Manchus, but they greatly depend upon the direction of the rivers and thus they are less free than the Tungus who use horses and reindeer. A fourth type is that of nomadic groups, like the Nomad Tungus of Transbaikalia, who live in the steppes and use horses. They are relatively free, but while the conditions of the steppe complex offer excellent means for communication, they give less material for the psychomental complex. As it is with the naturalistic knowledge, concerning means of communication, the loss of ability of movement may here occur. So, for instance, the Tungus, who have lost their reindeer and adopted horses, are not so free in their movements as the reindeer breeders, for, as I have shown (SONT), the horse can be used only during certain seasons. It should be noted that the settled Birarčen group, who no longer practise hunting, differ greatly from those who still maintain the hunting complex and go to the mountains. The difference is due not only to the incorporation of alien elements. There is also a marked difference in the attitude, a definite "unrealistic" trend of ideas, and an evident loss of the original Tungus mental vivacity and naturalism. Seemingly a certain loss of the original complex has also occurred among the Manchus, which is especially evident in females, who have entirely lost their independence of movement; so they are usually carried on carts like a load, while in former times they used to go on horseback. A Northern Tungus woman is not embarrassed if she has to go alone, without men, sometimes even to travel in an unknown region, while the Manchu woman has no ability of orientation and adaptation necessary in travelling; the narrowing of the psychomental complex is only natural. The Tungus, who first lost their reindeer and later their nomadic complex and who adopted the settled mode of life of a simplified Russian agricultural complex, greatly differ from their neighbours who live on reindeer breeding. Their original psychomental complex changes in the same sense, i.e. in the sense of its impoverishment. Since the elements of the psychomental complex, which are connected with and depend on means of communication, may disappear altogether, there is no possibility to restore the old complex, as it was at the time of the better ability of movement. This remark applies also to the naturalistic knowledge, which can be lost without leaving any trace of its existence.*

The complex of technical culture, as a whole, is greatly responsible for the character of the complexes observed among the Tungus. After what has already been stated in reference to the naturalistic knowledge and the means of communication this needs no emphasizing. When the Tungus is brought to a region where there are no hunting possibilities and where he must become a fisherman, cattle-breeder, or agriculturist, he has to remodel all his technical culture and to transfer his main interest to the new field of activity. If the group fails to adapt itself, it perishes. We may observe the interesting phenomenon of how the old remembrance of a former technical complex is gradually assuming confused form and the former psychomental complex gives place to a new complex. Since the transition from one complex of technical adaptation to another is made in imitation of the local groups, the "theoretical contents" of the complex are gradually adopted. However, some elements of the old complex may be temporarily preserved, sometimes in a complex composed of contradictory elements. Such is the case of some Tungus of Manchuria, e.g. of a group of settled Birarčen, who have partly assimilated Dahur and Manchu complexes, who have forgotten a great deal of the Tungus elements and increased their complex with alien elements, so that sometimes two hypotheses, two theories, two opinions exist about the same subject, just as in the complex of technical culture. From this point of view the decorative art is very characteristic.

In the analysis of the social organization of the Northern Tungus and Manchus, not to speak of the administrative system usually imposed by the alien groups, we have seen certain differences in the complexes of various Tungus groups. In fact, in the system of clan organization, in so far as it is reflected in the terms of relationship, different types are distinguished, i.e. the Reindeer Tungus of Transbaikalia, the Tungus of Manchuria, whose system is a fusion of three distinct systems, the Nomad Tungus who reproduce the Buriat system, and the Manchus whose system bears elements of an old complex and of those borrowed from the Chinese. The same we have seen in the complexes of marriage, of wedding and of family which are liable to a marked adaptation, for instance, to the mode of dwelling. All these complexes include various percentages of alien elements. However, the social organization, as I have shown, is not always cognized, so that in the psychomental complex it occupies no place of importance. By this remark I do not mean to say that the social organization does not also condition a certain diversity in the psychomental complex. Indeed, such two distinct complexes as, for instance, the Manchu system, with its seclusion of the woman within the family in which she is allowed to have a certain freedom of sexual relations with juniors, and the Northern Tungus system in which the woman is practically free to arrange her sexual life as she likes, must have a great influence upon the functioning psychomental complexes.

An attempt at the restoration of an old Tungus social complex is confronted with the same, and even still greater, difficulties than that at the restoration of other complexes. However, some forms may be restored with some degree of probability; such are e.g. the dual clan organization, perhaps the matrilineal system and the matrilocal marriage. The theories of spirits are more or less identical in the

---

* It is very common to look for "survivals" in the folklore. However, it seems to me that this method is extremely risky, for the elements of folklore may be easily borrowed, and together with them hints as to the formerly existing elements may have crept in which in reality never existed. Still more risky is the operation with the linguistical material. In fact, borrowings, semantic changes, phonet-

ic similarity and dissimilarity and loss of terms may produce quite an artificial picture of what had never existed.

sense of their formation and the evidences brought in their support; but as to the hypotheses regarding different individual spirits, they present a great diversity, even in different clans of the same ethnical units. The diversity of hypotheses is still greater when the complexes of ethnical units are compared. We have seen that a great number of spirits may be traced to the original sources, as, for instance, the group of *burkan, fučk'i, enduri*, perhaps the *sèvèŋ*, and individual spirits, such as *Ilmunxan—Irlinkan, jol, n'ayn'aŋ*, and others. However, there remain some spirits which are met with among a great number of groups and which seem to have no parallels as to their names and sometimes their functions among the near living neighbours. Such are, for instance, *buga* and *buni*. A careful analysis of spirits, their names, history and present functions in the complexes offer a certain possibility for the restoration of the old Tungus complex. However, as in all other cases, it ought to be kept in mind that some old elements might disappear without leaving any vestige in the present complexes. It is thus evident that we can easily define the psychomental complexes according to the recognized spirits, every one of which is connected with a certain idea, a hypothesis, or at least with some ethnical groups, as source of borrowing. Indeed, hypotheses expressed in spirits are very demonstrative of the character of psychomental complexes, so that a list of spirits alone may be sufficient for giving a short characteristic of the Tungus ethnical complexes. However, as shown, differences in the lists of spirits in the clans, and even in different families are common—there are no two absolutely similar complexes.

Practical methods of managing spirits and souls show the same range of variation in ethnical units and even clans, but there are some fundamental methods which are common to all Tungus groups and to some of these groups. Certain methods may be historically traced to their original inventors. Such is, for instance, the complex of mafarism which has grown in the Manchu soil, being stimulated by the opposition to shamanism and by the imitation of the Chinese. As another instance I may give the mechanical methods of trial of the shamans with fire, water, etc. which, in so far as the Tungus are concerned, are met with only among the Manchus and groups directly influenced by them. However, the formal source of these methods is not certain—it might be the old idea of "fire-proof" and "water-proof" spirits. On the other hand, there are methods like the sacrifice, which is universal, the only difference being in that which is sacrificed—the physical matter, or its immaterial substance. But even in the sacrificial ritualism there are elements which may be classified according to the ethnical units, e.g. the methods of slaughtering by perforation of the chest and the pressing of the aorta, by pricking of the cerebellum through the foramen magnum, by cutting the throat; the mehods of exposition of the sacrifice on dishes, on the table, on the platform, on the trees etc. There is still more differentiation in the prayers. Much less variation is seen in the burial complex and the deviations are not enigmatic. The method of burial in the earth, practised by the Northern Tungus, can be easily traced to its source of borrowing—the Russians. The same is true of the mound burial borrowed by the Tungus from the Chinese. On the other hand, there are elements, such as the carrying of the souls of dead people on the dog, practised by both the Manchus and Tungus, both the horse-breeders and reindeer-breeders. If it is not a "custom-idea" of the type of the

"lame brother" who transports the souls in his canoe across the river into the lower world in the West (WNW and NW), which may have been borrowed by the Tungus groups, then the dog's part in the disposal of the souls may be regarded as a very old element, now incorporated into distinct complexes.

What has been stated in reference to the practical methods of managing spirits and souls may also be applied to the particular elements of this complex, namely, the paraphernalia and particularly the placings for spirits, the most attractive for the investigators and collectors of ethnographic specimens. It should be noted that besides the conditions of life which sometimes require a reduction of the size of the placings and a special choice of material, there are actually distinct complexes, as for instance the use of ribbons for the clan spirits by the Manchus, of which I know no good parallels, and of pictures for shamanistic spirits which have been created by the Manchus in imitation of the alien iconography. The placings-pictures of the same origin have penetrated into the complex of the Tungus of Manchuria, but they have not been incorporated into the complex of the Reindeer Tungus, although they might see them among the Buriats and in the hands of lamas. Shamanistic paraphernalia also may show great diversity as to the distribution of elements among the Tungus ethnical groups. In fact, e.g. the drum, although slightly varying in shape, is known among all groups, while the headdress is very variable, as well as the coat, and the full dress, including moccasins, apron and trousers, is confined only to some Tungus groups of Transbaikalia; the belt with conical trinkets and skirt are confined only to the Manchus, Goldi and some other neighbours; the "implements", such as swords, tridents etc., are met with only among the Manchus. Some of these paraphernalia can be easily connected with the original sources, as for instance, the Manchu costume, while the others remain enigmatic, as for instance, the reindeer head-dress of the Tungus.

Shamanism, as a whole, observed among different groups, presents a great variety, so that it may be formulated that there are no two absolutely similar complexes, in so far as formal elements are concerned. However, this complex possesses a characteristic similarity among all groups, namely, the idea of spirits mastered by the shamans and its functioning as a regulator of psychic troubles, of individuals and in masses. In some cases we can historically trace the origin of shamanism, as it is, with the Manchus, but in some other cases only suppositions may be made as to the imitation of the whole of complexes and their elements known among the neighbours, such as the Manchus, Buriats and Yakuts. Yet, it is evident that the shamanism of different groups consists in complexes composed of elements of various and chiefly quite recent origin. The psychomental basis, in the form of a disturbed condition, is also not similar in all groups, whence there are differences of shamanism in the ethnical groups, conditioned by the psychomental functioning of units. For instance, the degree of spreading of "olonism" is not the same among the Manchus and other groups; the mass psychosis which affects clans is more common among the Northern Tungus than among the Manchus. However, when the clan organization is shaken, the mass psychosis may not affect the mass of the clan, but may affect territorial groups. In the last case the spreading of a psychosis will not be intensive, if there is no presumption that the spirits are confined to the clansmen.

151. FORMATION AND FUNCTIONING OF COMPLEXES

From the above review of different manifestations of cultural adaptation, as they are reflected in the psychomental complex of ethnical groups, we can see that the complexes may be very distinct and that there is no absolute similarity of two complexes, although there may be common elements, which may give an idea of a common origin of the complexes. Naturally, the question comes to that of the formation of complexes. Although the observer may receive the impression of an incidental character of all complexes studied here, this impression will not be correct. First of all, the creators of complexes are themselves bearers of complexes who put together elements found in the milieu, so that every complex strictly depends on the historic moment at which it is created, and on the milieu from which bearers of the complex draw the elements. Secondly, there are great limitations as to the possibility of the incorporation of new elements into an existing complex. Thirdly, when no ready elements are found, they are invented; but the possibility of invention is limited by the fact of the smallness of the Tungus groups.

The first condition is evident from the observed facts. The Tungus who live in different ethnical milieus, even though being beyond the control of their neighbours, are liable to borrow distinct elements. For instance, the Reindeer Tungus of Transbaikalia, now living in contact with the Buriats, and formerly with the Yakuts, are found in a position different from that of the Birarčen Tungus who were in contact with the Goldi and Dahurs. Still greater is the influence of the groups which controlled the Tungus in the past or control them now, such as the Dahurs, Manchus, Chinese and Russians. When cultural influence is reinforced by political pressure, the alien milieu becomes a very intensive source of borrowing of elements, from which the Tungus draw whatever suits their complex. The same is true of the Tungus ethnical milieu from which it is still easier to borrow elements that are needed. As a matter of fact, no understanding of the Tungus complexes is possible without the consideration of the historic and present conditions of the ethnical milieu.

Limitations of borrowing depend, in the first place, on the existing complex of primary milieu. It is evident that the elements directly connected with agriculture, which is impossible in some Tungus regions, are automatically rejected. It should be noted, that sometimes also elements only indirectly connected with agriculture, but to some degree dependent upon it, as for instance, the agricultural calendar, spirits held responsible for the success of agriculture etc. may be rejected. The same is true of other cultural complexes which depend on the primary milieu. For instance, means of communication and modes of orientation and topographical terminology therewith connected, as well as the complex of technical adaptation may depend on the primary milieu. It is evident that in a locality where the cart cannot be used and where there is no food for horses the elements of the locomotion complex by means of horse-drawn vehicles and their reflection on the psychomental complex will not be borrowed.

The conditions (structure) of the cultural complex may also be responsible for rejection. Although some technical inventions are very useful, they cannot be adapted and therefore they are rejected. For instance, the modern rifle is much "superior" to the flint or piston gun, but since the bullet is too large, this weapon cannot be used for hunting squirrels—the animal is too small and the cartridges are too expensive. Therefore guns of the oldest type, but of small calibre, are preserved as particularly precious. The Tungus sometimes manufacture such guns, the rough specimens of which produce on ethnographers an impression of "primitiveness". Indeed, although a rapid-shooting automatic rifle is superior to the common one-cartridge Berdan rifle, the latter will be preferred by the Tungus, because with a modern gun of small calibre big game, such as the Alces, the tiger and the bear often cannot be killed by one shot and, being wounded, may run away. A great number of elements which presume the existence of an extensive division of work, "class organization" etc. will not be borrowed, for the Tungus are not numerous and cannot afford to have specialists. The small number of the population in small ethnical groups greatly restricts the borrowing of new elements. In fact, it is very often forgotten that small ethnical units cannot assimilate some complexes at all because of the need of a certain number of population for the introduction of these complexes; and the failure of the ethnical units to assimilate alien complexes of this type is attributed to the inborn lack of mental and psychic ability. Owing to the limited population in the Northern Tungus groups the idea as to the social distinction of individuals, according to their economic position, is not accepted and, even being known, is greatly adapted and naturally distorted, as compared with the original models. There is of course a possibility of "learning" an alien complex and of teaching the Tungus, but these instructed Tungus would not be in a position to apply the learned elements to their own complex. Such a knowledge will be merely a "Tungus knowledge about other ethnical groups", which cannot be practically applied, and if there is a too great number of Tungus familiar with it, it will become a simple burden. The practical uselessness of the elements to the borrowers is generally a cause of rejection of alien elements. The elements which are not useful may be borrowed, but only in a limited number. This principle, though very simple, may sometimes be wrongly applied. In fact, the decision of rejection does not need to pass through the consciousness of the ethnical unit. In this case the mechanism is that of a trial. If the element does not bring any practical effect and if the unit is not particularly inclined to keep it, it will be dropped. However, if the unit wishes to keep it at any price, another mechanism, that of the loss of badly adjusted elements comes in play; the unit loses its adaptive ability and enters into a series of negative impulses of variations, or still more commonly, it is pressed by the neighbouring groups and the element perishes together with the unit. Certainly, a limited number of such elements may be preserved for a long time, sometimes at a high cost, but this cannot occur with a great number of elements. Among all Tungus groups we have observed the introduction of cultural elements which were tried during a certain period and rejected. Probably thousands of Tungus were attracted by the watch, but this instrument, very useful in city conditions, is practically a burden in the Tungus conditions, and is not given "recognition". · However, water-proof and half water-proof canvas, e.g. for tents, are greatly appreciated and when received from foreigners, they may be included into the Tungus complex, which one may observe among several groups. The same is true as regards the accumulation of knowledge. Although the high mathematics is a very useful method, in the conditions of Tungus life it is useless, like the theory of electricity, the history of the Greek philosophy etc. Should the Tungus spend their energy on this knowledge, they would lose their time needed for the training in hunting, shooting, migrating, and practical knowledge of the milieu. The process of elimination—i.e. rejection—of this knowledge is very simple. The individual Tungus who possesses such a knowledge, useless for the Tungus, (1) will not be considered as worthy of imitation, (2) will come into a conflict with his Tungus milieu, and (3) will leave his people and settle among those from whom he learned the new elements. This is the most common occurrence among the Tungus, some cases of which I have already quoted (vide Chapter XXXI). The Tungus are naturally no exception—this is the most common occurrence which may sometimes cover even a social group that would be rejected on the first suitable occasion, which, in this case, would take the form of a "social movement" and under certain conditions even that of a "revolution".*

When the change of language is connected with the psychomental disrupture, the process of rejection may also assume a form of ethnical conflict (chiefly in "nations"). Owing to the action of this mechanism among the Tungus, useless elements of knowledge borrowed from the interethnical milieu are rather seldom met with. However, when we introduce the principle of utility, important corrections must be made. First of all, the utility may be weighed when expenditure and benefit are taken into account. There are elements which being useless, as such, require no expenditure for their maintenance, so their existence is not protested. For instance, we have seen some customs in the wedding ceremony which are not Tungus and have no visible practical importance, but which are maintained, because there must be some complex of custom to mark the fact of wedding, i.e. the obligations imposed by marriage. Sometimes the "utility" cannot be understood by the Tungus, and only our analysis of the function of the element (or complex) may give us an idea of the practical "utility". There are also elements which are useless, but are not rejected, because their rejection is difficult and moreover they must be cognized. Such is the case of a great number of spirits borrowed by the Tungus from their neighbours. They are not always rejected because of the fear of coming into conflict with these spirits. However, we have also seen the mechanism of their rejection, i.e. the forgetting of the function of the spirits, the loss of the ritual connected with the management of the spirits and lastly, the throwing of their names to complete oblivion. We have also seen what a burden such a complex may become, when it is fixed in a written form, as it is among the Manchus. So that the overgrowth of such a knowledge may result in its disfunction and the disequilibrium of the psychoment-

al complex as a whole* with all the consequences resulting from such a state.

The psychomental complex itself may present obstacles to the including of new elements. Here I have in view some fundamental conceptions, the lack of which may cause the rejection of a new element. Let us suppose for a moment that the idea of mastering spirits is not accepted, then the whole system of shamanism and its elements would be rejected. However, when some of these elements included in shamanism are not in conflict with the existing complex, they may be adopted; but at the same time they will be adapted in a new function.** I shall revert to the problem of readaptation, but I shall now dwell upon some concrete cases observed among the Tungus. For instance, among the Tungus the idea of "master-spirits", which means "master" of a region, mountain, animals etc., is not very common and it is not very important, as compared with what we know of other ethnical groups. Indeed, there are some spirits of this type, but most of them are of alien origin, as we have seen from the analysis. It is not easy to introduce among the Northern Tungus a new master-spirit, for the realm of natural phenomena among the Tungus is not so "misty" as it is among the groups which are not living in the forests and mountains; moreover, as shown, there is a mechanism which checks the spreading of these ideas, viz. the fear of these spirits which would make life impossible. For this reason the Tungus unconsciously reject the ideas disturbing their economic activity. Should such a spirit be adopted, it would lose its "power" on the Tungus soil. Should too many spirits be introduced, the Tungus would be obliged to change their mode of life, or they would not be able to maintain their existence and in the psychomental complex it would be reasonable to expect a condition of disequilibrium with mass psychosis.

On the other hand, the Tungus will not accept the idea of the soul as a function, for their complex is lacking in theoretical premises—the physico-chemical principles of physiology—while a great number of facts points to the existence of an "immaterial" substance and a "soul" as independent phenomena, which can be separated from the body. Indeed, the idea of an ideal world, as it is pictured by the philosophers of the idealistic complex, might be easily accepted by the Tungus, but it will receive a more "material" interpretation—it will thus be adapted and remodelled.

We have seen that the Northern Tungus here treated have the idea of a supreme power lacking anthropomorphic features, which, however, is a "being". This idea seems to be very old and, owing to its existence, the Tungus very easily accept the idea of God, as professed by Christians. However, the real difficulty is met with when the Tungus must accept the idea of Jesus Christ, as well as his being born from a human being, Saint Mary. Those of them who are familiar with the complex of spirits, with its numerous manifestations,

---

* When a group is affected, then a strong centripetal movement is naturally formed within it, which has its effect of increase of the centrifugal movement in the greater unit as a whole. Such a differentiated unit may also easily become a foreign body within the greater unit. Such seems to be the case, when interethnical pressure in the form of "cultural influence" affects only a part of the population.

* The same may happen with the knowledge of the European groups and it seems to have happened in formerly prosperous ethnical groups of Western Asia, and perhaps in Egypt.

** For this reason shamanism cannot be assimilated, e.g. by the Russians, who oppose the idea of mastering spirits. In exceptional cases, when this idea is accepted by Russians, the latter present a typical picture of psychopathologically affected individuals (I shall revert to this question). The same relates to the Chinese, in whose complex this idea leads to professional magic.

very easily accept the idea of the Trinity as independent of God, but a human being, Jesus Christ, turns into a "shaman" whose soul has become a spirit. This difficulty is due to the lack of important elements in the Tungus complex, namely, the intense interest of *buga* in human affairs, the idea of the saving of souls of sinners, and the possibility of *buga* descending to Earth in the form of a human being born of a human being because of a miraculous conception.* Some of these elements, in their remodelled form, may be accepted and adapted by the Tungus, but on the whole, the adoption of Christianity would mean the loss of the mechanism that regulates the Tungus psychomental life and the inevitable loss of their vital equilibrium, for the Tungus complex lacks specialists in psychiatry and special regulations of psychic phenomena by an intelligent government. The final effect would naturally be the absorption of the Tungus by other ethnical groups.

Thus, the assimilation of new elements is greatly limited. It depends on the primary milieu, the existing cultural adaptation, the density of population and especially on the existing psychomental complex. All these conditions of the Tungus ethnical units are the more resistant to the introduction of new elements, when they are well adjusted and the ethnical unit is stable in its equilibrium.

It may thus be formulated as follows: *every cultural element* (and complex) *has its potential power of diffusion varying according to the milieu* (primary and ethnical) *in which it is spreading*. Thus, potential power of diffusion varies from zero to an absolute and immediate acceptation of the element (and complex). In some of the above given instances we have seen that the elements of the psychomental complex are not always accepted in the form in which they are received, but are modified and adapted to the Tungus complex. The forms of adaptation are different, namely, there may be a formal change of the element (or complex), and there may be no formal change, but only a change of function in a different (Tungus) complex. Naturally both changes may also be combined. Here I give for illustration some examples. The modern army rifle is a weapon used for war, but when it is adopted by the Tungus it is used for hunting—which is a change of function. The same rifle may be made lighter by a reduction of its wooden parts and by removing some metallic parts—which is a formal change. In the adaptation of the elements of psychomental complex we may observe all degrees of changes. In fact, when for instance, the Tungus adopt Russian standards of measurement, they do not change them either in form or in function; the same is true in the extension of biological knowledge of animals, and practical methods of fighting diseases, for instance, by vaccination. The Chinese complex *n'ayn'ay* preserves its function in the Tungus complex, but the list of manifestations is shortened. The Chinese prestidigitators' tricks are used in theatrical performances for amusement; the Manchus borrow them as a component of shamanistic performance in which they assume a new function, especially in the trial of a new shaman, the same complex is shortened among the Tungus, but it preserves almost an identical function in their shamanism. The Mongol complex of *oygun*, which is a shamanistic spirit, equivalent to the Manchu

* The last idea has no success among naturalistically minded Tungus, but it may be easily adopted by the Manchus who, at least theoretically, accept the idea of conception from the class of *enduri.*

vočko and the Northern Tungus *sèvèy*, is reduced in the Northern Tungus complexes to the term designating domesticated animals used as carriers of placings for spirits, seldom as riding animals for the clan spirits which are not mastered and are not connected with shamanism. Thus there are changes in form and function—so that only a term and a very vague connexion with spirits in general may actually remain. We may observe variations of formal and functional changes of elements even when they are borrowed by the Tungus groups from other Tungus groups. When there is no formal change, but merely a functional change, the latter may be discovered only when the whole complex is very carefully investigated from the point of view of the respective groups, for as soon as a complex is transferred into a new ethnical milieu, it may lose altogether its former function. Indeed, every one of the above indicated conditions of the existence of elements, after their being borrowed, may be illustrated with a great number of facts found in the present work, but a really bottomless source are the phonetic and semantic changes of sounding starters ("words") which are well known to the linguists actually dealing with the ethnographical material which is the language as a functional phenomenon.

From the great number of facts discussed and expounded above it is evident that elements may be borrowed singly, or in groups and only very rarely as a large complex. The reason why the elements are not borrowed in large complexes is that the incorporation of a new complex is seldom possible; for such an incorporation of complex with a complete reconstruction of the whole cultural complex, save in exceptional cases, results in the loss of ethnical equilibrium, the further loss of ethnical independence and assimilation by other ethnical groups. Practically, elements of an alien complex are borrowed one by one, sometimes being accepted only by a small group of individuals of the ethnical unit and being at least slightly modified, and sometimes entirely changed in the process of adaptation. The process of fusion of groups of elements into a finished complex may last a very long time, and it may very often be left incomplete. Instances of this kind may be found among Tungus groups. The extensive complex of Buddhism began its penetration among the ancestors of the Manchus (the Manchus began to incorporate it into their complex) nearly ten centuries ago and it did not succeed in winning all Manchus. Another extensive complex, Christianity, began its spreading among the Tungus nearly three centuries ago and there is now not a single Tungus group which can be considered as having perfectly assimilated Christianity. However, as shown, a great number of Buddhistic and perhaps even Christian elements have been included in various Tungus complexes, sometimes in an unrecognizable form. Moreover, it has been shown that it was probably Buddhism which was directly responsible for the psychological stimulation of a new complex of shamanism, which was partly supplied with Buddhistic elements. In the complex of social organization the Northern Tungus clan, as it can be observed in Manchuria, was built up with the elements of the Manchu complex, but only a part of them, e.g. some terms, clan chief, etc. were incorporated. It may be noted that in this respect the Birarčen clan had more Manchu elements than the Kumarčen clan and the latter more than the Khingan Tungus clan. Some elements were doubled: the earlier Tungus elements were used beside the Manchu-Chinese elements, which is indicative of a process of further incorporation of new alien elements one by one. Still, there were very essential differences between the Birarčen clan and the Manchu clan.

I must dwell upon the problem of invention as a source of new elements in the Tungus complexes. Indeed, in the course of the present exposition of facts we have always been meeting with elements invented by the Tungus. In fact, every generalization further applied as an analytical instrument is an invention; any newly formed sounding starter is an invention. These inventions are so common, and they are sometimes made simultaneously by so different persons, that their origin is even not noticed. It is especially true of those inventions which do not greatly affect the existing complexes. We have seen that every Tungus group has its own spirits ("inventions", "hypotheses") which have no parallels in other groups, and we have met with hypotheses individually proposed and sometimes accepted by more or less larger groups. In the process of formation of a new complex dealing, for instance, with the explanation of psychic phenomena, a great number of elements may be borrowed from the neighbours—interethnical milieu—while the lacking elements may be invented. Such are e.g. the shaman's own spirits that are supposed to influence the other spirits which affect a person. As in the case of formation of new "words" from the known components, practised by every child, and as in the case of formation of new "words" for new phenomena (vide supra e.g. ičenki,—"binocular") in similar psychological conditions of individuals treated by the shamans, the latter naturally come to similar new methods, whence absolutely similar situations and attitudes of the patient and the shaman will appear, about which it would be impossible to say, whether they are invented or borrowed, if we have no definite historical record,* or evidences of the geographical distribution. The importance of the diffusion of cultural elements and complexes, and that of the parallelism of invention were over-estimated to make of them the great ethnological problems, only because facts were selected to prove one or another aspect in the formation of complexes and because the attention of theoreticians was chiefly attracted by striking (for them) elements and complexes, while the greater mass of facts was omitted altogether.** Both,

* Even a term by which the new invention is designated may be misleading, for the term, even an alien one, may come later, i.e. after the cognition of the new phenomenon, and it may create an impression of borrowing of the element.

** There are special psychological conditions which perfectly explain why this question attracted so much attention and sometimes produced animated discussions. If we observe these phenomena in a great number of units, we may notice that the great inventions are usually connected with the ethnical units which in the interethnical milieu play a very important part at certain historic moments. They are usually connected with the leading ethnical units and with those which are so potentially, or which recently were so. We have seen that an ethnical unit which shows comparatively a great increase of population and a great change of the cultural adaptation has a greater chance of becoming a leading ethnos. For such a unit the change of cultural adaptation and consequently continuous invention is the primary condition of success, for of all units it must be the best adapted. Therefore the psychomental energy is naturally directed towards invention. As a matter of fact, without invention there is no possibility of adaptation to the new condition of an increased population. Among thousands of ethnical units a few of them usually spend their efforts on inventions, while the other units imitate them, when the inventions are of adaptive interest or when they are attractive for various reasons. Since the stimulus of becoming "leading" is great and since the benefits of invention are quite clear, more attention of the investigators was attracted to the

diffusion and parallelism of invention are the most common phenomena of similarity of elements in different Tungus groups.

However, among the Tungus the part of invention requires some additional remarks. I have now not picked out cases of Tungus invention that would be *striking* in the eyes of Europeans, for such are not needed to demonstrate the mechanism of variations and formation of the Tungus complexes. Besides, the selection of such cases would by no means be easy, because the European eye can be struck only by inventions which could be used in the European complex, and the number of such inventions is certainly restricted, because of the difference between the complexes. One condition more is to be taken into account, namely, the potential power of invention among the Tungus cannot be very high because the Tungus are not numerous. In fact, inventions are produced when needed or when incidentally made by individuals, so that the greater number of people, the greater the potential power of invention. On the other hand, inventions of a disturbing type ("striking" in the observer's eye) are made when the ethnical unit is found under conditions of a rapid tempo of variation stimulated by positive impulses and, as shown, greatly conditioned by the interethnical milieu. This is not the case with most of the Tungus groups. One realizes the importance of invention, when one considers the limited number of the Tungus, their cultural complex (well balanced and perfectly adapted to the size of the population and the conditions of primary milieu) and even the minutely worked out system of regulation of psychic life which is greatly disturbed by a comparatively powerful interethnical pressure.

If now we remember what has been said above in reference to the limitations of adoption and to the adaptation of cultural elements, it will be evident that the Tungus, who derive their cultural elements from the same source, e.g. Chinese or Mongol, may sieve and modify them to the point of complete impossibility to recognize these elements. It is especially so when the borrowed elements are added to the previously existing complex and then, or even later, a new complex is supplied with the elements created on the spot. In fact, a series of complexes within different units may be formed which may have the appearance of "common origin", or at least of being copied from a pre-existing model, while actually they may be merely the product of in-

phenomenon and the function of striking inventions than was actually deserved in the life-history of ethnical units and particularly in the formation of new complexes. It may also be pointed out that for some time "invention" was especially attractive to those theoreticians who were puzzled by their own idea of "progress" and all practical consequences resulting from it as to the policy and behaviour to be adopted for better achievement of "progress". Naturally the investigators who were dealing with leading ethnoses (this is the common case with historians particularly attracted by leading ethnos) were inclined to over-estimate the invention-factor; those who were dealing with the "backward", "primitive" ethnical units or merely non-leading units were more inclined to see elements of diffusion, borrowing etc. The phase of the process ethnos manifested in "leading ethnos" was taken for inherited genius, so that this idea greatly handicapped further penetration into the ethnological process in mankind. Indeed, such a belief becomes especially natural among the leading and potential leading ethnical units, for it justifies their attitude of aggression towards other "inferior" units and it further spreads among the non-leading ethnical units which accept their position of being led and influenced by the leading ones. This, in its turn, facilitates consolidation of leading ethnical units and thus such an attitude belongs to the mechanism of interethnical equilibria.

dividual adaptation to the complexity of conditions of milieus—the primary milieu, which fixes its limitations and imposes definite forms, the secondary or the cultural milieu, created by the unit, which is always changing, the tertiary milieu, from which new elements are borrowed, and the inherited morphological and physiological complexes, first of all formed in individuals and cognized by the reaction of individuals. Hazardous and responsible is a further step in the classification of the observed phenomena, namely, the association of formed complexes with groups of individuals—firstly, among the individuals of the closest . grouping in the natural unit of the family; secondly, among the individuals grouped into.clans; thirdly, in still larger ethnical units and other units, when they are markedly differentiated. Some of the cultural elements are not correlated at all with these units, as such, while other elements are not only correlated, but may be a form of adaptation of these units. For instance, within certain limits the knowledge of the primary milieu may be confined to the family in which it is found and transmitted;* shamanism is essentially a clan or a territorial function, and all of its theoretical background is transmitted to and found in these larger units;** the complex of reactions and positive knowledge, with the theoretical background, as to other ethnical units is essentially a function of ethnical units. However, as I have shown, the ethnical units themselves are only the visible manifestations of a process which I have called ethnos. Therefore, when the complexes are separated from the concrete units, with which they are functionally "correlated"—it must be emphasized that the existence of units may be recognized from the fact of these functions only—these become meaningless abstractions with which . one cannot operate. However, *such abstractions may serve as a method of rough classification, chiefly for the memorizing of observed facts,*

Thus the complexes, as they are treated here, ought to be also distinguished from the point of view of their connexion with the concrete units within which they are created

* A similarity of these complexes observed in different units within a clan or territorial or ethnical unit is not a character pointing to their functional connexion with these larger units.
** A similarity of shamanism in different clans and even in different ethnical units is not indicative of its functional connexion with the larger units.

and for which they are needed. Indeed, such a larger complex as shamanism includes elements functionally connected with individuals, families and clans (or territorial units), and the same elements may enter into different complexes. For instance, the knife carried by every Tungus may be used: (1) for cutting food (food-utensil complex), (2) for hunting, when there is no other weapon (hunting complex), and (3) for self-defense and attack from and on human beings ("war" complex). The same is true of some elements of the psychomental complex which may have different functions in different complexes within the same ethnical unit. However, there are some elements which have only one connexion, i.e. with one of the complexes.

Thus, from the point of view of the history of formation of complexes and from the point of view of their function in ethnical units, the complexes cannot generally be regarded as entities which exist by themselves. They are chiefly a scientific method of classification of facts for the convenience of exposition and memorizing. One cannot arrive at a clear understanding of the existence of the Tungus ethnical units by an abstraction of such complexes.*

* Indeed, the operation of investigators with the complexes greatly facilitates the recording of facts and their exposition. The idea of regarding complexes in their abstractions has been common in other sciences as well. For instance, formally different physiological functions, such as reproduction, blood circulation, metabolism, high nervous activity etc. were regarded as complexes, but at present one is more and more inclined to regard these "complexes" as functions which depend on the whole of the animal organism. For instance, a definite correlation between the constitutions, which themselves are expressions of several "complexes", and the character as an average common behaviour of the individual, seems to be a fact; so that since character is the most complex manifestation of adaptation, one turns one's eyes to the constitution, as to the primary condition of the character, and to the ethnical milieu in which it is manifested. A "psychological" approach to the problem of character is impossible, unless one gives a new meaning to "psychological". The "complex" of reproduction, intimately connected with a series of organs, like glands of internal secretion, nervous (central and peripheral) nervous systems, and even ethnical milieu, can be no more regarded as a complex by itself. The same is true of the thinking process which is done by the whole organism and cannot be confined to the brain alone. Limitations as to the use of complexes put new requirements for the investigator, much greater than before, but it does not mean that these limitations must be rejected on the ground of the difficulties involved by the limitations.

CHAPTER XXXIII

EQUILIBRIUM OF THE COMPLEXES

152.   COGNITION AND
        CULTURAL COMPLEXES

In the course of the exposition of facts, concerning the psychomental complex we have seen that certain phenomena of the Tungus culture remain unnoticed by the Tungus—they are not cognized. In fact, even such an evident fact as the social-economic-biological unit—the family—is cognized only partly, as a household, chiefly associated with the "wigwam". Indeed, it may appear in Tungus eyes in its other function, e.g. the biological function; but still there will be no full cognition of the phenomenon. The same is also true of units, such as

the "clan" and the ethnical unit, which are very important realities and which are not fully cognized. Still less are cognized important elements of the psychomental complex and their regulation. For instance, such an important mechanism of regulation of psychic life as shamanism is functioning without being cognized. Although some elements which constitute shamanism may be cognized and even termed, other elements remain unnoticed altogether, while third ones are noticed in their non-shamanistic functions, e.g. as an aesthetic phenomenon, and the like.

The fact of non-cognition of these phenomena is not

surprising, for it is known to, be so among other ethnical groups, which have been the subject of an ethnographic analysis. However, such a non-cognition has always been explained as due to a condition of low mentality of the "primitive" groups. Since the question of mentality for its serious discussion ought to be put on different ground and since as a simple explanation of psychomental differences it cannot be used any more, we have to approach the problem of non-cognition from another side. That the question is not as simple as it seems to be at first, is evident from the fact that such a lack of cognition of existing and functioning phenomena is characteristic even of the ethnical groups which are supplied with methods of modern science. The same is true of the earlier ethnical complexes, such as that of the Greeks and Romans, who were groups which cannot be regarded as "primitive". Those who have an absolute faith in the scientific methods may say that even though the Greeks and Romans, as well as the Europeans of the eighteenth and even nineteenth centuries, could not raise themselves up to the height of self-cognition, it does not mean that this state will never be reached by other ethnical units (and groups) which will perfect their scientific methods so much that anything will escape from the analytical eye of scientists. Indeed, such an attitude of certainty is perhaps the only one which is possible for a psychomental complex adapted for a continuous change of the cultural complex, and chiefly along the line of positive variations (conditioned by positive impulses). It is not my idea to deny its existence or to diminish its functional effectiveness. It exists as a part of the mechanism which maintains the function of the psychomental complex in any ethnical unit (or group). However, facts are facts. They show that the cognition of all phenomena of cultural adaptation was never complete. The description and analysis of relatively simple forms of social and economic organizations were always much more successful in respect to the past than to the present, supposing the material was available. The same social and economic contemporaneous systems were usually neither described nor understood, could not be cognized in all their varieties. This was due not only to the defective methods, but apparently to some deeper reasons. As a matter of fact, we have only one method which may be used, namely, the comparative method. It is used in application to the same unit at different historical moments and to different groups studied simultaneously. No methods exist which permit to distinguish immediately a new form and even a new element, and still less to foresee them as forms and elements of the future.* So that even the description of the existing forms meets with difficulties, for these forms become noticeable only in their historical and ethnographical aspects, and the cognition of new forms is always behind the facts. However, the question of cognition of forms is very intimately connected with the tempo of variations. When the tempo is rapid the comparative material is abundant; when the tempo is slow the material is limited, or there is none, especially if two changes are separated by several generations and no written records exist. A relative increase of interest in these problems observed among the ethnical units (and groups) of the European cultural cycle is chiefly conditioned by the tempo of variations of

observed phenomena and not by the special cleverness of the bearers of the complexes, or the special properties of these complexes.* There is another condition which is also responsible for the process of cognition. This is the variation of the pressure produced by the interethnical milieu. Let us remark that these two conditions are especially typical of the psychomental complexes of leading ethnoses and therefore, in the given conditions of cultural adaptation, it is likely to expect a growth of science in the leading ethnoses, quite independent of the inherited thinking ability of the population which forms the leading ethnical units.** By this remark I do not want to deny the possibility of the existence of favourable and unfavourable conditions of "inherited" predisposition for productive mental work in general. In so far as the groups possessing a complex cultural adaptation are concerned, another and new condition appears, namely, a selection of the elements better adapted for thinking. This may have a positive effect upon the thinking power of the unit as a whole. In fact, the destruction of this element and of the mechanism of selection may cause general lowering of the thinking power of the unit, whence a decrease of its power in the interethnical milieu. In the history of ethnical units (and nations) these facts are so numerous that some observers considered the condition of selection to be the only one which is responsible for the variations observed in different ethnical units, while others believed in an equally distributed inherited mental ability. Very closely connected with the above mentioned conditions is a third one, namely, the numerical power of the unit, especially in growing units, for the mental work is carried out and handed over to the coming generations by individuals: the more numerous the individuals, the greater the chance of producing thinking individuals. Indeed, both a special mental endowment and an organized selection are important conditions, but if there is no change within the units and if there is no interethnical pressure, the mental power will remain unemployed or confined to the aspects of special adaptation, which may even not be noticed by other ethnical units and which will not contribute anything to the cognition of the milieus.***

Therefore the process of cognition of milieu must be regarded as a function of quantity of population and of changes which occur in the interethnical pressure and in the cultural adaptation of the ethnical units, the latter being physically more or less adapted (inherited condition) and organized (selection, both cognized and not cognized).

Besides these conditions of cognition there is a still deeper reason for arresting at a certain point the cognition of milieu, and especially the psychomental complex of the

---

* Various theories regarding future forms of the social and economic activities are merely justifications of conscious and unconscious desires. As such they belong to the mechanism of variations and not to that of cognition of the present forms.

* This success is ascribed by the historians to the special development of scientific methodology, while the latter is nothing but a component of the complex. Indeed, to explain the progress of science expressed in an accumulation of knowledge and generalizations through that of methodology is equivalent to a tautology.

** The conviction of mental superiority, also characteristic of leading ethnoses, has its biological (ethnological) function, without which the leading ethnical unit may lose its ability of being "leading" for other ethnical units.

*** In some instances of ethnical units we may guess a practical application of mental power, for instance, along the line of penetration into the psychology, a kind of self-cognition, also a scaffolding of religious teachings in their ethical aspect and operation with an imaginary world of abstractions. In such cases the psychomental complex may lose altogether its function as a component of ethnical equilibrium, but it will be rather a fruitless discharge of mental energy of the ethnical unit.

unit itself. Namely, the psychomental complex of a unit as shown, cannot be abstracted. When new elements are introduced into the complex, the complex is already not the same as it was and there is a change of the whole complex of cultural adaptation, be it small or great; any newly acquired knowledge as to the milieu or particularly the psychomental complex produces such an effect upon the whole complex, and a further step is automatically done for its rebuilding. In its new form it must be again cognized. Here I have in view a cognition which is reached by the whole unit, or at least by the leading section of the unit. Indeed, there may be individuals who possess full cognition, but they will have no influence on other members of the unit and thus they will not exactly be members of the same unit.

It is evident that this limit cannot be overstepped by the unit.

What has been said above was referred to ethnical units being in a state of variation produced by positive impulses. However, the situation is different with the units which are in a state of decline, especially at the period of a decline at a rapid tempo of variations. In fact, such a unit, with every new step of its decline, has to simplify its complex, and the latter will be easily cognized and understood. However, it may be so only in case the process of decline is noticeable within a short period, practically less than a generation. The decline may remain without producing any cognizable comparative material should the process be very slow. The second condition is that of at least relative preservation of the thinking element, if it is found in a selected group. In the first case, when the thinking selected group is affected, the process of cognition may be arrested still earlier, so that the unit will produce a picture of a complete psychomental decline—a rather frequent occurrence in the life of highly differentiated units—which will not be a psychomental decline of the population; in the second case, when the group is not destroyed, the process of cognition will not be arrested and the unit, in spite of its actual decline, may produce an impression of great brightness.* The last case is rare, for under the conditions of negative variations the unit usually becomes disorganized, in which state it cannot function as before, and thus the psychomental functions are also curtailed. It should be noted that this refers to the ethnical complex and not to individuals who may preserve a perfect cognition in all conditions and therefore will be still more separated from the bulk of their ethnical unit.**

I note here that, when an ethnical unit comes to a clear understanding of its own social organization, economic system, and psychomental complex "acting" at the given moment—by the way, this is a great ambition of educationalists and science*—it usually means that the unit has already reached its state of decline.** In fact, this can also be recognized from other signs of biological order, the movement of the population, and the change of interethnical pressure.

A particular case of decline, which may remain unnoticed, is that when there is a general decrease of the interethnical pressure connected with a partial, particularly selected, loss of population, occurring during important wars and "revolutions", which affect large groups of the "population". Such a decrease is not much noticed, because the process affects all units bound by the given interethnical pressure. The lucidity of thought after wars is only partly conditioned by the increase of experience, but it closely depends on the temporary decline and relative simplification of relations*** which occur within a short period.

As I have already pointed out, the comparative material for the cognition of one's own complex may be received from the interethnical milieu. However, this cannot be done by the ethnical units, but only by the scientists who may transmit their knowledge still further—to the bulk of the population. However, there are great limitations too, namely, the time required for cognition (at least one generation) and for transmission (at least two generations), during which the complex undergoes further changes. The application of this method becomes more or less hopeless when the self-cognizing unit is in the process of leading ethnos, and must create a new form, naturally unprecedented in its own history. The complex may be cognized only hypothetically, by extrapolation of the pre-existing forms, and it will not be fully cognized even by scientists, who again will have no time to transmit their knowledge to the bulk of the population prior to the occurrence of new changes, sometimes very essential in the life of the unit. Such an impossibility of cognition of the complex of the leading ethnical units thus resides in the nature of the psychomental complex.****

---

* Such is the state of leading ethnical units at the period of the first steps in the decline and also at the periods of a stationary state.
** Ethnical units which are strongly affected by the process of social differentiation, followed by a formation of new potential ethnical units (a strong centrifugal movement) receive on the spot a great deal of material for the cognition of the milieu. This is the comparative ethnographical material which becomes available for all differentiated groups. It is not incidental that the units, which undergo this process before their final collapse (disintegration), very often produce "thinkers". In so far as cognition of milieu is concerned the case of a unit affected by the process of social differentiation is similar to that of the units being under an increase of interethnical pressure. Indeed, what has been said in reference to the ethnical units holds good for differentiated social groups before and especially during the process of disintegration. This is, of course, natural, because the nature of the social groups is the same as that of the ethnical units. Vide supra Section 6, p. 19-20.

* Indeed, such ambitions are of a professional character without which the profession cannot exist. As I have shown, the function of educationalists is much more moderate than it is usually believed by this profession—to transmit the past knowledge to the coming generation, the present knowledge being beyond the reach of professional educationalists and especially that of the bulk of the population which constitutes the ethnical units (and groups), when they undergo a process of change at a rapid tempo.
** Within the units that are in such a state one may notice a very curious phenomenon of "clear thinking", "cynism" and other attributes of supposed to be "modernism". They are also indicative of the same process. Practically this process is easier to be understood when studied in differentiated ethnical groups (especially "nations") dissolving into changing social groups which attain a state of ethnical differentiation. In small and simply organized ethnical units all these processes are too slow for being observed.
*** It is very risky to speak of one's own time, but the present psychomental state of the masses of the European populations (in nations and ethnical units) is undoubtedly due to both factors, namely, to experience and to a significant cultural movement backwards, in the sense of "simplification" of the complex. Still stronger is the lucidity of thought among the individuals who at the same time realize the impossibility of regulating the process and are only "functioning".
**** Poor cognition of the existing complexes was always explain-

In thinking over and over again the problem of self-cognition of ethnical units (and groups), one naturally comes to the idea that perhaps such a complete cognition and understanding is generally impossible—as soon as such a state would be achieved, a free readaptation of the cultural complex and the interethnical equilibrium would be lost and the unit, possessing such a knowledge, would become a permanent leading ethnical unit. This would gradually annihilate all other ethnical units, or the leading ethnical unit would perish in the struggle with the whole interethnical milieu. In the first case, should no new differentiation occur, there would be almost an immediate arrest of further readaptation (no impulse produced by the interethnical milieu) and a general decline, first of all affecting the psychomental complex; should the process of further differentiation occur, there would be a loss of the former cohesion and the benefits resulting therefrom, and the psychomental complex would suffer at once. The idea of the limitless power of science seems to belong to the psychological mechanism of the leading ethnos among the groups of the European complex, without which it could perhaps not function at all. Indeed, the same idea among the non-leading ethnical units is a mere reflection of the interethnical milieu.*

When the problem of cognition of the cultural complex is put on this basis, we may easily approach the situations

ed by a reference to "poor development" of science. It is true that, for instance, the present investigations of rather simple aspects of cultural complexes, such as social organization, political organization (which is only an aspect of social organization), also economic systems, are far from being able to give a full description of a formal organization and functioning. So in books on "political science" outer forms are usually given, almost nomenclature of some easily perceived facts, like "constitutions" etc., but the actual mechanism is neither seen nor shown. The best approach to the social phenomena—the psychological aspect—fails even to describe this mechanism, though the latter is only a minor part of the task. The best approach to the economic system—mathematical and statistical—is psychologically based on the hope that in the material of the past, laws, good for the present and the future, will be discovered. But even with this approach no description of the present complex is possible. The creation of a science which would permit to foresee the present and future forms of these complexes, is perhaps a mere dream, for actually the rôle of these sciences is functioning as "applied sciences" or as a justification of the past, the present being beyond the cognition and understanding, if the unit is in a process of positive variations. This becomes still clearer if we remember that besides these complexes, always changing, there are also very important changes in the physical characters of the peoples—a factor which affects other complexes, which cannot be noticed at once and will be so in the future. An interesting instance is that of Russia, where under the conditions of great simplification of the whole complex, attempt was made to create a premeditatedly elaborate system. When it was produced, seemingly according to a certain plan, the inventors lost control of the process, and now special investigations into the problem of social differentiation of the creators themselves and their psychomental complex etc. are required. It is thus that in spite of the relative simplicity of the existing complex, they find themselves in a more difficult position than anybody else among the experimentators, for they have eliminated, as far as possible, thinking elements of the controlled ethnical units; they require a rigid, simplified approach to the actuality and prohibit scientific inquiries into the problems. Among other ethnical groups (nations) such a tendency exists too, but those nations are not so much affected by the belief in the system practised, so that the complexes are merely functioning, while in the case of Russia they are paralysed.

* This idea is also maintained by the professionals, who are living on science, for making themselves more important in the society, but in this case there is no relation to science, as such, nor to the motives underlying the activity of the scientists.

found in the Tungus psychomental complex. First of all, under the present conditions, the Tungus groups are not leading units, but probably some of them were so in the past; secondly, as shown, some of them are found in a state of decline and complete disintegration; thirdly, the lack of cognition is not a particular character of the psychomental complex of the Tungus, but it is a general phenomenon; fourthly, since the Tungus complex is not very voluminous, it may be better understood than the complexes of greater quantitative volume; fifthly, there are some aspects of the psychomental complex, as for instance psychic life, which is well studied by the Tungus and expressed in elastic hypotheses and in the symbolization of spirits.

153. SELF-REGULATION OF THE COMPLEXES We have seen in a great number of instances that the psychomental complex does not remain the same among the Tungus groups and Manchus. All the complexes that have been described have been found to be in a state of changes. The latter have been explained as due to the multiple conditions of milieu, especially the interethnical milieu, also as due to the internal causes residing within the ethnical units and principally connected with the fluctuations of the population. Such changes of a psychomental complex are, so to say, normal, while a rigidity, a petrifying of a complex becomes a great hindrance for a smooth functioning of the reactions produced by the ethnical unit, in consequence of which the complex itself is usually replaced by a new one, if the unit does not lose its adaptive ability.

A readaptation, an adjustment of the psychomental complex, expressed in a series of changes, practically observed in the manifestation of the difference of opinions, the uncertainty about some particular problems or aspects etc., is not a sign of lack of equilibrium in the complex and ethnical unit, but is a sign of a condition which may be termed "moving equilibrium". To distinguish where there is a condition of "moving equilibrium" and where there is a real condition of disequilibrium, is very important for forming a correct idea as to the state of the ethnical unit and that of the psychomental complex. An analysis of the mechanism of the psychomental complex particularly and the cultural complex in general shows the character of the moving equilibrium, as distinct from that of disequilibrium.

Indeed, there are two movements—a movement towards a further complication of the complexes and of the elements of which they consist, and another movement towards a simplification of the complexes and the elements, both movements being an expression of adaptation. Such an adaptation may be beneficial for the preservation of the bearers—the ethnical unit—or it may be pernicious, or may have no influence at all.

The most important source of changes in the psychomental complex, as in any other cultural complex, is the process of its transmission to the coming generation, i.e. the preservation of the complex. It is especially important in the sense of re-adaptation, for in the process of transmission it may lose some elements, it may give a new interpretation to some other elements, owing to a change of some third elements of the same complex. Even a minor disfunction of the transmitting apparatus—the family system, the differentiated organization of school education, the social groupings, etc.—may be responsible for a partial loss of the complex, and even for its complete loss. In ethnical units (and groups) which possess written records this eventuality is greatly reduced, but it is not so when the unit possesses both oral and imitative tradition.* A transformation of elements may also be due to the refusal of the coming generation to accept (or the teaching generation may abstain from transmitting) some elements, because of their impracticability in their old form or function, so that these elements are modified, formally or functionally. In so far as the transmission of a complex may act as a factor of change, it belongs to the mechanism of readaptation of the complex in its function of self-regulator of the complex.

We have seen some instances of loss, because of the disintegration of the educational system, as it happened among the Manchus with the abolition of Manchu teachers. A refusal to accept the old system could be observed among the Reindeer Tungus of Transbaikalia, when the young generation began unregulated hunting, as a new form of adaptation to the supply of food by the Russians and to the extension of the market for hunting spoil. The same is particularly common when the Tungus adopt Christianity. The old generation among the Tungus of Manchuria did not hand over their art of shooting the bow, for the latter was replaced by fire-arms; the old generation explained its non-insistance upon learning this art because of its uselessness under the present conditions. Among the Reindeer Tungus of Manchuria, together with the disintegration of the clan, the whole complex of clan spirits was omitted, for the clan organs had perished.

However, the most interesting mechanism of adaptation of the complex is the retardation of the process of changes. This mechanism is very rich in forms, on some of which I shall now dwell.

The most common forms are: (1) a lack of understanding of a new element or complex; and (2) a negative reaction of the ethnical unit. In fact, when new hypotheses or even facts are proposed and if their understanding requires a great effort, they may be left aside, practically unnoticed. This is especially likely to happen when these hypotheses and facts are in a conflict with the existing ideas. In this respect, the greatest number of facts is supplied by the history of discoveries, particularly scientific discoveries, for which we have records. However, even Tungus complexes give some facts of this class, especially observed in individuals of an unusual mental ability. Naturally these facts are not recorded. Indeed it is at present impossible to say how far the work of Aristotle was understood by his contemporaries. However, his ideas, for instance in the field of embryology, could be understood by the Europeans only in recent years. Of course, in this instance there was no continuity of the ethnical unit in which Aristotle was born and lived, and the unit has shown a marked cultural decline, while the European complex was for a long time behind the achievements of the Greek science. A well known case is that of Mendel's discovery of inheritance which for a long time remained "unknown", chiefly because of its relative "prematureness" in the com-

plex which existed during his lifetime. Then, Darwinism was a revolutionizing teaching which could hardly be digested by Mendel's contemporaries. The Malthusian theory of population, debated during more than a century, could not receive due recognition and needed perfection until very recent time. The Belgian mathematician Verhulst's mathematical theory of population, first published in the forties of the last century, was not noticed at all, and only recently was brought to life by R. Pearl. There is a very interesting example of a great Russian scientist of the middle of the eighteenth century, Lomonosov, very little known abroad, who, as it was recently discovered from his manuscripts preserved in the archives of the Academy of Sciences (at St. Petersburg), came to the formulation of some physico-chemical principles which could be understood only in the light of most recent discoveries.* Such creators of new ideas are found in almost all branches of human mental activity, and it must be admitted that a great number of similar facts remain still undiscovered, for the distance between the present achievements of cultural adaptation and great discoveries of the past is still not bridged. Here we have in view only those discoveries which have been recorded (published), while there remain a great number of discoveries which have never been published. There are two reasons for this, namely, financial difficulties met with by the authors, when they proposed to publish their works which were not understood and therefore rejected; and some of them realized the prematureness of their ideas and did not publish anything which could not be understood by the contemporaries—they are human beings and not all of them believe into the practicability of working for "mankind of the future". Such an attitude may be seen in works of some of the greatest scientists who do not pronounce their last words. The fact of not being understood by the contemporaries is so frequent a phenomenon that the above given illustrations suffice for making a generalization, namely, that only those ideas and facts are adopted which are on a level with the living generation, and when the difference is too great, these ideas and facts remain unnoticed. Still among the ethnical units which have writing, such discoveries may sometimes be recorded, but a great number of them remain unpublished, while among the ethnical groups which have no writing all these discoveries perish together with their authors. This is a great factor in the mechanism of retardation of the process of change of the psychomental complex in general. As shown before, the psychomental complex is in correlation with the existing social and technical adaptation, and the tempo of change of these complexes has its very strict limits (vide Introduction p. 17)

The form of the regulation of change of the psychomental complex through the negative reaction of the ethnical unit may assume two principal forms, namely, conscious and unconscious rejection. In the first form the situation is relatively simple: the ethnical unit does not accept the new idea because it does not want it for different reasons, e.g. the new element may be in conflict with the existing complex. In a very common and simple case, when the complexes are sharply outlined—e.g. ideas harmful for a religion, or a conflict of two religions, or any two elements which exclude one another—the rejection comes almost automatically. However, when the complexes are not so

---

* However, even the written records may perish, as it happened, for instance, with the Manchus, so that the process of the loss of a complex may only be accelerated because of the existence of writing.

* In so far as I know his works will soon be published.

defined, the rejection may even take the veiled form of a justification of the impossibility of an acceptation, by means of considerations lying far from the real reasons. For instance, the rejection may take place because of the source of the element or complex—a person who is not trusted, an ethnical unit which is not "friendly", the form in which it is presented, etc. The elimination of these causes would create a more favourable condition for the acceptance of the new element, but most probably some other reason for the rejection at any price would be found.

One of the particular conditions of the mechanism of rejection is the existence of written records of the elements of the psychomental complex. In fact, if the record is handy and if it is recognized as "correct", a simple reference to it may suffice for an automatic rejection of new elements which are not in conformity with the written records. So that the ethnical units which possess writing, which is also a powerful means of propagating new elements, also create a special condition for neutralizing the destructive influence of this new means by increasing the authority of some written records up to the recognition of their sacred character. The influence of a great genius may last a very long time, owing to the belief in his superiority, and thus the introduction of new elements may be retarded. On the other hand, an increase of written records tends toward the annihilation of their restraining character, because of the physical impossibility of reading a great mass of records and their vulgarization by the new generations, in whose hands the old complex is naturally adapted to the new requirements of the existing complex.*

We have seen the effect on the Tungus soil of written records made among the Manchus, which has resulted in a further adaptation of shamanism and its visible functional decline. The unconscious rejection, as a mechanism of retardation of variation of the psychomental complex, is much more complicated. For illustration, I shall now give only some of these forms. Among the units with a great differentiation of groups one of the most common cases is the differentiation of a special social group, the function of which is to carry out definite sections of work. Naturally there may originate professional groups which would not be inclined to admit outsiders who do not share their opinions. A particular case is that of "schools" which monopolize institutions, periodicals etc., and "sects" which take hold of religions and institutions. As a working mechanism of particularization the following may be mentioned: e.g. the conviction of being right, the utilitarian calculus of having a secure income, a mere ambition to control other human beings, and the necessity of maintaining the unity of groups differing in opinion as to the preservation of efficiency of the centripetal movement within the whole of the ethnical unit. Any new idea, element or complex may be rejected by depriving the authors of the possibility of propagation of their ideas, elements or complexes. Still greater is the power of the mechanism of unconscious rejection, when other social groups are involved, e.g. industrial and commercial groups, when they invest their capital in concerns connected with scientific discoveries, or elements such as, e.g. new medicines, literary works, theatrical pieces etc. Under this condition, everything which may diminish their income is rejected without further consideration.

In these ways an ethnical unit quite unconsciously retards the process of change of the psychomental complex produced by the introduction of new elements. In an extreme expression of particularization such groups may assume a form of legally fixed castes with all consequences resulting therefrom, i.e. the formation of potentially differentiated ethnical units as an effect of strong centrifugal movement within the greater unit and the natural disrupture of the intimate connexion between the bulk of the population and the particularized group.

Among the Northern Tungus we meet with this phenomenon only as a tendency, while among the Manchus there were already differentiated professional groups of monks and later mafas (*vide* mafarism) not to speak of scholars who, however, did not reach a state of perfect isolation. Tendency towards isolation may be observed among the shamans who oppose themselves to the "common" people and in rare cases try to keep shamanship in some definite families. However, as shown, this tendency is strongly opposed by all systems of shamanism connected with other clan functions.

As to the general reaction on the new elements, it is very often referred to the fundamental psychomental condition generalized as "conservatism", "liberalism" and "radicalism". These are very complex phenomena manifested under certain political conditions of some countries in the form of political parties. However, the condition is actually much more profound than it is manifested in political parties, especially since the time when politics became a professional occupation. In fact, first of all, certain psychological conditions may be distinguished, perhaps connected with the physiological complexes of individuals and even with the constitutions, whose bearers give different reactions on innovations—i.e. new elements. There may be a negative reaction in general, expressed in a bold opposition to any new element; an indifferent reaction, and a continuous desire of change and introduction of new elements. These fundamental types of reactions may be reinforced, in their manifestations by the conditions of the psychic complex in the system of their working equilibrium. When the individuals are not psychically stable, the reactions of the above indicated types may turn into acts which go beyond the limits of normal phenomena, while in the case of reduced reactions—an indifferent attitude—the reactions will also not be normal. It is well known which physiological-constitutional (and psychological) types are more inclined for psychic instability or reduction of reactions, whence there may be a disproportional increase of unstable and dull elements in the above indicated types. So that the frequency of instability in these types to some degree depends on their physical complexes.*

The second condition is that of the degree of knowledge regarding practical possibilities of changing the complex,

---

* Instances of this kind are numerous: the Malthusian theory in the hands of vulgarizers in its new adaptation has turned into an enumeration of practical means of contraception; the Darwinian theory in the hands of vulgarizers has turned into a "struggle for existence"; the Marxian theory of class struggle has turned into a justification of robbery; the theory of relativity, into "all is relative". In such forms the theories are merely adapted to the existing complexes, which may incorporate new elements without any consultation of the works of the original creators. A bottomless source of facts may be found in the work of commentators.

* This aspect of the problem assumes a great importance when there is a substitution of anthropological types, constitutional types or merely an influx of immigrants. A partial desturction of selected groups in a war may have the same effect.

which in rare cases may be calculated on the basis of a profound knowledge of the realities and when one has sufficient imaginative power for pondering all effects of a new element on the whole complex; but in most cases they may be only guessed, with the help of the thinking mechanism known as "intuition". The degree of positive knowledge, foresight, and power of intuition are very variable in individuals.

The third condition is that of the tempo of variations taking place in the ethnical unit at the present moment and at a certain moment of cyclic growth (*vide* Introduction, p. 17), if there is any. This is an important condition which helps to extend the visual power and psychologically in a different degree prepares for the possibility of changes, already experienced.

The fourth condition is that of the existing psychomental complex and the general cultural adaptation as point of departure for variations and reactions on them.

The fifth condition is that of the interethnical pressure which, as shown, may reinforce and accelerate, as well as produce all reactions going on within the unit.

The sixth condition is that of variations of primary milieu, particularly produced by an energy received from the sun and perhaps from other sources lying beyond the earth.

When all the above indicated conditions are considered an exact idea of the behaviour of individuals in reference to the changes may be formed. It is evident that the issue of a serial variation of the psychomental complex may be accelerated and retarded by this mechanism, for an outcome of changes depends on the average psychomental ability of the whole unit, in which a change of percentage of individuals who react differently affects the average of the ability of individuals in the units. In the life of ethnical units the elasticity of the mechanism of change of the percentage is an important condition for a smooth functioning of the ever changing psychomental complex. If the mechanism is not elastic, the unit may come to a differentiation into parties (particularly political ones), with a further differentiation of ethnical units—an occurrence which is usually prevented, because a complete collapse of the larger unit* might take place.

* The above given scheme of conditions of differentiation of groups with different reactions must not be directly transferred to the political parties. First of all, in a great number of instances, they are not indigenous inventions (adaptation), but a simple imitation of other ethnical units, and so they do not reflect at all the actual grouping of similarly reacting individuals. Secondly, all political parties, in so far as they are represented by leaders, do not actually reflect groups of the population. In fact, the requirement of a leader is that he must be a good speaker, very often a journalist; he must possess the special ability of a "leader", in which the place of sincerity is taken by a special art of simulation. Thus this complex is connected with a certain degree of insolence, cynism and amorality. Thirdly, under concrete conditions of the European complexes, a large number of politicians have become professionals who are living on this profession, as do lawyers, journalists who adapt their opinions to the source from which they derive their means of existence. These rather unfavourable conditions of selection are confined to a very limited group of active politicians. Should additional requirements be introduced, for instance handsomeness, the selection would become still less favourable for the best elements, from the point of view of normality and mental ability. It may thus be supposed that the ethnical groups which by a long process of adaptation adopted the present costly system of governing themselves, are not well repre-

The work of this delicate mechanism of readaptation of percentage of groups of similar reactions among the Tungus and Manchus could not be observed for two reasons, namely, most of these groups, as shown before, were investigated under the condition of final or temporary disintegration, due chiefly to the interethnical pressure; secondly, the earlier records of the psychomental state of these groups were too scanty for risking an analysis of the process of shifting. However, the direct observation of a great number of individuals in different groups and situations shows that, due to the variable conditions, all types in their many varieties may be discovered and that a large group of individuals remains at the shifting point.

One of the practical consequences of this analysis is that a general characteristic of the Tungus as "conservative" or "progressive" loses altogether its scientific meaning. Within a short period a Tungus group may change its behaviour concerning changes of the psychomental complex, even without being affected by a mass psychosis.

The above discussed conditions, which I have included under the heading of self-regulating mechanism of the psychomental complex, are responsible for maintaining the change of this complex at a certain tempo corresponding to that of the change of other components of the cultural adaptation. This mechanism is naturally not cognized by the Tungus, nor by other ethnical units, and its "normal" fluctuations must not be mistaken for a real disequilibrium of the psychomental complex.

154. DISEQUILIBRIUM OF THE PSYCHOMENTAL COMPLEX By the term "disequilibrium" of the psychomental complex I designate a condition of this complex which, on the one hand, cannot satisfy the need of the ethnical unit for a necessary cognition of the milieu and the establishment of relations with the milieu which may assure the survival of the unit; and on the other hand, the lack of working balance in the psychomental complex itself. The first condition, as a case of disequilibrium, may be understood only from a historic point of view, i.e. when the same unit is compared at two different moments. In fact, such a disequilibrium may

sented by their political leaders, who do not represent the best which may be selected from the ethnical units and nations. Indeed, such a sudden change of opinions which may be seen in political elections does not correspond to the actual change in the percentage of psychological groupings, for the mass of the population adapts itself to the overgrown apparatus and very often takes temporary advantage to pass through the political machinery certain concrete pending measures. What is actually going on in these groups is little known, for the usual policy is only to prevent the outburst of general dissatisfaction, instead of to govern—selected political professionals are not prepared to govern. Owing to this, unexpected situations are always created, whence "misunderstandings" and costly changes of government with an enormous loss of ethnical energy. For all these reasons the above given scheme may be referred only to the populations which form ethnical units. However, with all necessary precautions the analysis of a complex ethnographical phenomenon, as the political parties, is possible and the above given scheme ought to be considered as an actual condition of populations with which existing political systems may come into conflict. Rejection of the parliamentary system in several countries is not due only to the post-war conditions in which cultural decline is a fact, but it goes much deeper. This analysis is indeed very difficult, for the ethnography of the so-called civilized groups is not yet carefully investigated, and too many interests are involved in this problem.

occur only when there is a change in the conditions of milieu, or when there is a sudden negative change in the ability of cognition. Such a condition of the psychomental complex may produce the impression of a great stability of a complex well balanced within itself.

It may be supposed that after migrations, when the old psychomental complex cannot satisfy the needs of a new adaptation to the new conditions of the milieu, a great number of ethnical units perishes through a direct extinction, disintegration, absorption and assimilation. The same would happen in the case when the ethnical unit is put in a new interethnical milieu, but the way of its perishing may be different, namely, through the change of the psychomental complex under the influence of a milieu to which the old complex is not adapted, while the cultural complex, as a whole, is not sufficient for an effective resistance. This is the most common case among the Tungus groups here discussed, especially in the past. The same effect may occur in case of the diffusion of a new element and a complex which is only a particular form of interethnical pressure. Indeed, when the pressure is gradually increasing, the unit has time for adapting itself. It assimilates a new element or even a complex and produces at the same time the necessary modifications and adaptations in the old complex. However, if the mechanism of self-regulation fails to operate, an introduction of new elements may be quite fatal for the existence of the unit.

The case of a sudden change of the ability of cognition may occur in case of a partial destruction of the thinking elements, due to a war with the neighbours, or to their extermination in the process of an internal struggle (the particular case of "revolutions"). A substitution of anthropological types, which possess different ability, may also occur (this is a rather slow process, so that usually there is a sufficient period of time for readaptation) and an influx of alien elements incorporated in a too great number. When such an incorporation takes place without affecting the differentiated groups of the thinking apparatus, more lowering of the average may occur, while should it take hold of this apparatus as well, the effect may assume a form of ethnical collapse of the former unit. Such cases are observed among the Nomad Tungus.

Disequilibrium of the psychomental complex may also occur because of a defective self-regulating mechanism. In fact, if it is in a state of disfunction, two cases may occur, namely, the efficiency of the psychomental complex may be below the needs of the unit and it may be above these needs. In the first case the effect will evidently be a retardation of the cultural adaptation in general, and thus a reduction of the interethnical value of the unit; but if its working capacity sinks below the needs of maintaining the functioning of the cultural complex in general, a general reduction of the cultural complex may result.* In the second case various situations may occur, e.g. the disruption of the specialized group from the mass of the population; a change of the direction of adaptation, e.g. in the form of a confinement of oneself to the problems of secondary

importance from the point of view of the adaptation of the unit as a whole; in the form of a psychic condition of general dissatisfaction among the thinkers, due to the conflict between the reality and the theoretical imagination; and other forms. The general effect is the same as that in the first case, namely, a loss of adaptative power of the unit, as a whole, with a reduction of its interethnical value, although in the last case the unit may produce the impression of great "brilliancy". However, such occurrences will remain within the range of fluctuations of the psychomental complex and after a certain period a temporary disfunction will be removed, the internal equilibrium being preserved. Thus a disfunction of this mechanism may occur without any important change in the normal psychology of the ethnical unit, or without any change of the interethnical pressure, but only as a defective condition of a continuous readaptation and adjustment.

We have seen that the psychomental complex depends on inherited conditions as defined by the constitutions and the behaviour, i.e., from the functional point of view, on the physiological complex. However, the latter may smoothly function only in case the conditions of the milieu do not go beyond the limits within which the physiological complex was formed.

Unfortunately, at the present time it is impossible to speak of the conditions of the physiological complex disturbed by the change of general conditions. However, there are certain facts indicating that the physiological functions may show important deviations in case of such changes. Continuous deficient nutrition—one of the common occurrences—produces important changes in the physiological behaviour, as manifested in an arrest of the growth process, in the lowering of the production of useful energy, and in a general reduction of biological activity; it seems to have quite a definite influence upon the determination of the sex in children. On the other hand, overfeeding which does not exceed a certain limit produces its effects in the sense of the increase of biological activity, while an excessive overfeeding may also result in the decrease of this activity. The same is true in reference to the supply of solar energy, not only in the form of heat, but also in other forms, such as light—a complex phenomenon—and rays of electrically charged particles, also air and water. Although the elasticity of the physiological complex, considered in earthly conditions, is relatively great, it deviates from the optimum only within the limits typical of the region when the organism appeared as a by-product of a long adaptation. It is evident that in the adaptation of human ethnical groups the cultural complex is only a further extension of the possibilities of milieu, a complex, the volume of which, as shown, depends first of all on the density of the population. As shown, it possesses also certain limits of variations, although much less stable ones than those of the primary milieu. Indeed, in the process of reaching an adapted form the physiological complex depends on the cultural complex with its deviations from the optimum characteristic of a given adaptive form. Naturally, the cultural complex is only one of the conditions of the milieu which cannot be omitted from the consideration of the conditions responsible for the existence of the physiological complex. This becomes perfectly clear when ethnical units (and groups) find themselves under the conditions of disfunction of the cultural complex, as it

---

* Such an occurrence is common e.g. when the unit partially loses its organized system of transmission of the complex, when this group loses its efficiency, e.g. owing to a strong "professionalization", interference of other groups etc.; when the grouping of types of similar reactions is petrified, but the process goes in a cyclic way, and so forth.

happened, for instance, with several European groups during and after the last war.*

It would now be superfluous to insist upon the fact that any change in the physiological regime of any *populatio* has its effects upon the psychological complex. Not to speak of specific chemical ingredients found in the food, which may greatly influence the physiological and psychological behaviour, the most common ingredients, such as salt and fat, have a direct influence on the behaviour. Since individual behaviour depends on these conditions, the population composing ethnical units cannot be indifferent to the individual changes in behaviour.

We are much more familiar with the conditions and effects of starving groups which may sometimes produce quite opposite social reactions; namely, (1) a dull indifference and concentration of attention on an immediate search for food, and (2) revolt against a real or an imaginative cause of starvation. Both of them will not be normal for a smooth existence of the unit and they will be responsible for a temporary disfunction of the psychomental complex. However, not only a change in the supply of these common and important ingredients of the food regime can be responsible for a disturbance of the psychomental complex, but also a lack of some much less important ingredients, and even a change of the form to which the unit is adapted may produce their effect. The experiments with various prohibitions, particularly with that of alcoholic drinks, show that in a few years the unit may feel the effects in the form of either a decrease or an increase of criminality, of a change of interests etc. Indeed, such revolutions in the food regime also have their social effects and the latter also affect the psychomental complex.**

Finally it should be noted that the psychomental complex may be affected by mass psychoses due to imitation. We have already observed that among the Tungus some ideas or a complex behaviour of individuals may appear which may be imitated. I do not enter now into the discussion of the question in *what conditions* these ideas and imitation may appear. Indeed it is very likely that these ideas and harmful imitation are impossible, when the unit is perfectly stable,*** when it has not been previously brought to a state of instability, e.g. by an unfavourable change in the chemical regime; but since fluctuations of conditions are common and the Tungus include all varieties

* Although periodical famines, due to climatic fluctuations, may greatly affect units, the latter may become more or less adapted to the periods of abundance and starvation, sometimes resulting in great irregularities of birth-death ratio; so their influence is much less effective than that of a sudden change of an usual equilibrium.
** For instance, such was the case of the Tungus, when after the prohibition of selling alcoholic drinks in Russia (at the beginning of the Great War) there was an interference with important ceremonies, like weddings and partly with shamanism. This created a kind of psychic unrest. Still stronger was the effect upon the Russian population, both physiologically and socio-psychologically. Seemingly the population of the United States was still more affected, when prohibition was enforced.
*** In fact, I. Pavlov has failed to produce neurosis in the well-balanced type of dogs, while he was successful with other types. Here it should be noted that types well-balanced, from the point of view of the mechanism of conditioned reflexes, and strong, are those which formerly were called "phlegmatic" and "sanguinic", although their behaviour differs; while badly-balanced types are "choleric" and "melancholic" types which produce weak reactions. Cf. "Physiology of Higher Nervous Activity", in "Priroda", 1932, Nos. 11-12, p. 1151 et seq.

of the classical types of characters, the disturbing influence of imitation is possible, if not probable. When a certain group of the population is affected, a mass psychosis of different extent results.*

The conditions pointed out above, namely, (1) the disfunction of the psychomental complex which cannot master a newly created situation of the unit; (2) the reduction of the thinking apparatus; (3) the defectiveness of the self-regulating mechanism; (4) physiological-psychological disturbances, and (5) psychoses, are conditions which may be produced within the unit by the unit itself, without any outside influence. However, in the life of ethnical groups, disturbing influences produced by the interethnical milieu are perhaps more common than those produced by the internal influences.

The disturbing influence of the interethnical milieu on the psychomental complex can be direct and indirect. In the first group various forms of pressure may be included, especially a military pressure, which must be clearly perceived and, when necessary, opposed. In fact, any danger of this kind requires a great nervous and mental effort and, as such, it produces its effect upon the psychomental complex which is deprived of its normal smooth functioning.**

A still more disturbed condition is created, when opposition is to be formulated and the unit must enter into a war. Indeed, directly and indirectly it endangers all members of the community, which reacts upon the psychomental complex. Among the Tungus the period of wars has ended long ago, but in the past—i.e. before the stabilization of the Russian and Manchu control over the territories occupied by the Tungus, which took place only in the seventeenth century—this was a common occurrence.

Alien pressure on the territory with its partial occupation may also have had an indirect influence upon the stability of the psychomental complex. In fact, the occupation of a part of the territory by an alien group imposes a readaptation of the cultural complex either of one of the populations, or even of both of them. If there is a readaptation of the cultural complex, and moreover with a sudden change, a disequilibrium of the psychomental complex is very likely to occur, for such a change requires an especially great effort of the unit. In case of loss of population there may be only a slow loss of the former complex, and a psychomental disequilibrium is not likely to occur, if no essential change in the initial tempo of variations is connected therewith.*** The loss of popula-

* A great number of similar facts are collected by V. M. Bexterev, cf. his "Collective Reflexology".
** One day I observed the psychic state of a Tungus unit which intended in entering into an armed conflict with another group. It was due not to an accidental loss of psychic equilibrium, but to a continuous and long condition of disturbed psychomental complex, justified by reference to the past and rationalized in reference to the violation of a certain practice—marriage. Vide SONT, p. 221.
*** This is a special case, when the ethnical unit not only loses its territory and population, but also suddenly changes its tempo of variations. In such a case, because of the inertia of movement, energy has no application, no discharge, and a psychomental disequilibrium is almost certain. This is exactly the case of units, the movements of which are impeded by interethnical pressure. Since this usually occurs during or after a war, the unit is liable to a continuation of an internal war between the differentiated units, to an internal struggle, to a psychic condition of "defeat", sometimes "revolution", and a great movement and readaptation of the whole psychomental complex. Quite wrongly this is often explained as only due to the loss of the war.

tion is therefore dangerous only when it is connected with the change of the tempo of variations. However, a "defeated" unit may also manifest various signs of a disequilibrium produced by the fact of the defeat and the loss of hope for the future. This is much more dangerous in the sense of producing psychomental disequilibrium for leading ethnical units or those which may soon become so, than for, so to say, ordinary ethnical units. These phenomena may be observed among the Tungus groups too, namely, among the Manchus who failed to meet Chinese pressure.

Alien pressure may be manifested in an introduction of certain cultural elements which may directly and indirectly produce their effect upon the stability of the psychomental complex. The most common case is that when the actual cause of the instability is due to the acceleration of the tempo of variations. In fact, the introduction of a new technical invention which imposes a corresponding readaptation of the social organization—i.e. the creation of new professional groups—and their subsequent further change do create a new attitude towards changes in general, the essential of which is the weakening of traditions and "rationalization". In consequence thereof, any other cultural element may be subject to a new re-rationalization, which may not always be satisfactory for maintaining the existence of these elements. In such a state several Tungus groups have been found which had adopted modern firearms and came into new relations with powerful ethnical groups.

Still clearer are the cases when new ideas are introduced and accepted. They may produce a real revolution in the psychomental complex.

A consecutive loss, at least a temporary one, of functional efficiency is therefore a common occurrence. It is especially true of those ideas which come into conflict with the existing complex. For instance, the penetration of a new religious system, of a new social teaching, of a new artistic fashion may produce a sceptical attitude toward the formerly existing complex, so that the latter as a whole, will fall under suspicion and will cease to function as an adaptive phenomenon. The history of mankind gives us a great number of such instances, but one of the most interesting ones, which is being recently observed, is that of the socialistic teaching that affected in various degrees, one after another, the ethnical groups, or at least some parts of the groups. Such was the case among the Tungus with the introduction of Buddhism and Christianity. The introduction of Buddhism has even resulted in an increase of psychoses, which began to spread over the Tungus groups in the form of mass and individual psychoses as a secondary reaction on the new ideas. However, there is nothing particularly Tungus in it. The case of psychoses, especial-ly mass psychoses, by which ethnical groups are affected one after another, is well known from the history of mystic teachings which periodically spread over mediaeval Europe. There may have been especially favourable conditions, perhaps physical, physiological in their nature, which facilitated the penetration of these psychoses, but this supposition is even superfluous. For instance, during the last great war the psychosis of fear of enemy spies was quite common, but it was due to the general psychic instability during the war and, at the beginning of the war, not to any special physical conditions, which were created much later. Something of the psychopathological order can also be seen in the recent spreading of sexual exhibitionism and manifestations as expressed in nudism, American dances (adapted Negro complex), etc. which have affected almost all countries of the world after the Great War. No doubt, mediaeval mass hallucinations, mania of persecution (spies), mass sexual exhibitionism and other similar phenomena do not leave the psychomental complex, as a whole, undisturbed. The rôle of simple imitation in all these cases is evident, and the imitation itself is subject to the same regulating mechanism as any other cultural phenomenon.

I have not directly observed the spread of such mass psychoses among the Tungus groups, with the exception of the above mentioned "spirits", particularly connected with Buddhism, as the latter was adopted and understood by the Tungus. It is difficult to say at which moment "olonism" began to spread among the Tungus, but its gradual spreading may now be observed. When it assumes very distinct forms and affects numerous groups of the population, it may produce a real disequilibrium of the complex. The same is true of hysteria. However, in this case, as in other similar cases, the individual susceptibility to these conditions is first to be considered. If the number of susceptible individuals is great, then the unit may be affected much stronger than when the number of such individuals is limited. But this must be accepted only with reserves, as a probable supposition, for in the presence of phenomena of mob psychology whose duration may be short or long, even well-balanced individuals act as if they were with the crowd and thus affected by the mass psychosis. Apparently there are some deeper causes behind these phenomena than the simple mechanism of imitation.[*]

* An interesting case is that of sudden changes in the psychomental complexes during the so called revolutions, when opinions change suddenly and decisions most inconsistent with the safety of the unit are taken, and the unit is generally deprived of the ability of acting in the adaptive sense. The leading of the masses, in such cases, does not present a great technical difficulty if the tendency of the psychoses is understood or, better to say, guessed. It can be done by individuals who are not particularly prepared to such leadership, but who are naïve enough to imagine themselves to be "leaders", while the real leaders of the ethnical unit are rejected.

CHAPTER XXXIV

REGULATION OF THE PSYCHOMENTAL COMPLEX

155. SELF-REGULATION I have shown that the present psychomental complex of the Tungus groups is a product of the adaptation of these groups to the complex milieu in which they lived before. If one wants to understand it, not only the positive knowledge of these groups must be considered, but also the whole of the cultural adaptation, tempo of variations, ability of reactions, inherited and ontogenetic physiological complex of individuals, of which these groups are built up, and above all the interethnical milieu as a source of borrowing and a factor of pressure must be taken into consideration. This is so in so far as the composition of the psychomental complex is concerned. However, this is not enough for a complete understanding of the complex—one must be acquainted with the mechanism of self-regulation of the complex, in the sense of the maintaining of its equilibrium, which is necessary for the survival under the conditions of interethnical competition and theretofore, to a great degree, under the conditions of interspecies pressure.* But one will meet with great difficulties in following these processes, especially among the units which have no written records. In fact, as I have already stated, ethnical units, which cannot maintain their psychomental equilibrium, perish. Thus we may observe a condition of disequilibrium only in the units which are so found at the moment of observation, for those which have been affected and disintegrated have left no reliable documents as to the causes of their collapse, while, in such cases, the restoration of their complexes and that of the conditions of the interethnical milieu is uncertain and therefore cannot be used as established facts.

In a great number of instances we can see how the Tungus readapt their hypotheses which have become burdensome. The importance of a spirit may, little by little, diminish, so that this hypothesis will not harm the unit; in another case, when the condition corresponding to a certain hypothesis—usually in the form of a spirit—is not often repeated, the spirit may be forgotten; in a third case formalization, especially an elaboration of the ritualism of conventional performances and their written record may reduce the effectiveness of a hypothesis up to its complete inefficacy. If the psychomental conditions which called a hypothesis in existence are not entirely eliminated, even if the hypothesis is forgotten, hypotheses will appear, sometimes being borrowed from the neighbours. So that, for restoring the process of the change in the psychomental complex, in so far as it is expressed in hypotheses and practical consequences of these hypotheses, the investigation must be directed along the line of the mechanism which underlies these hypotheses and practices.

The most finished in form and in function is undoubtedly the complex of shamanism, so I shall now give a summary of my inferences drawn from studied facts.

* Such a pressure does exist even at the present time but its forms are different. When man, as a numerous and characteristic species of the late quarternary, increased, there were essential changes in the interspecies equilibrium—a great number of species, especially mammalians have perished.

I have advanced the hypothesis that shamanism, as it is known among the Northern Tungus and Manchus, was stimulated by the spreading of Buddhism. However, it does not mean that this was so among all Tungus groups. In fact, some of these groups have adopted the complex of shamanism in a ready made form, as it had been created by other units.

Shamanism is very intimately connected with the psychic troubles observed in individuals and masses of ethnical units (sometimes even of regional groups). These conditions are the cause, in the sense of being stimuli, of the existence of shamanism as a complex, the treatment of psychic troubles being the practical aim of shamanism. The latter, in so far as it requires performers, can come into being only on the condition of the existence of individuals affected by various psychic troubles. This is the reason why shamanism has often been identified as a psychopathological phenomenon, a point of view which as shown, I do not share. Shamanism, as I have stated, is a secondary complex which has resulted from the process of a long self-regulation of the psychomental complex.

This secondary complex has been gradually formed, but probably began at the moment when the ancestors of the present Tungus groups met with the new cultural current of Buddhism, and a new complex in general, which undoubtedly produced its psychomental effect upon the Tungus. We have seen that among the ancestors of the Manchu Buddhism was actually introduced under the Nuichen, and not without opposition. The reason of the opposition was the preservation of the original cultural complex and the protection of the unit (Nuichen) from alien groups. It is of course impossible to reproduce all details of the process, but it is not difficult to understand its nature and character among the Nuichen, for we can observe it in a great number of instances in other units. This was a case of a difficult assimilation and adaptation of a new complex which, as shown, resulted in the creation of a new complex—that of shamanism. We have also seen that the chief function of shamanism is the regulation of the psychic life of the units, whence we may suppose that a "need" of such regulation appeared simultaneously with the spread of a new complex, i.e. Buddhism. The question whether Buddhism was the cause of the shaking of the psychomental complex, or such a shaking was due to other causes, cannot now be answered. In fact, after the Nuichen victory over the Kidans and a sudden numerical and territorial growth—a great number of new units, such as the Northern Tungus, and perhaps some Palaeasiatics, having been incorporated into the new unit—the Nuichen may have been affected by a certain psychic instability, which may have appeared independently of Buddhism; but it is evident that it was Buddhism which supplied the Nuichen with certain patterns on which elements now observed in the Manchu shamanism were modelled.

Unfortunately we have no information as to the history of shamanism among the Dahurs, except that it is not an old complex and has Buddhistic elements, i.e. that we find the Dahur shamanism in nearly the same situation as the Manchu shamanism. It may be supposed that the shamanism of the Dahurs has some connexion with that of the Manchus. If we remember that the Dahurs are off-springs of the Kidans, that the latter were "converted" to Buddhism at about the same epoch as the Manchus, that they lived southwest of the ancestors of the Nuichen, that they were the first to face the Buddhistic movement, both from China and from Central Asia, that the Kidans might have been affected even a little earlier—it may be supposed that the Dahur shamanism is perhaps parallel to that of the Manchus. I speak of parallelism, for the Dahur and Manchu shamanistic complexes have a certain typical difference, at the same time possessing some elements in common. The Dahur shamanism is important to us, because it influenced the Northern Tungus, a part of whom—the Solons—were for a long time satellites of the Dahurs (Kidans)[*] and another part, namely, the Kumarčen, the Birarčen, the Nomad Tungus of Transbaikalia,[**] and a part of the Reindeer Tungus of Transbaikalia,[***] were under a strong cultural and political influence of the Dahurs. Most and perhaps all of these groups received their shamanism through the Dahurs. All these groups were not in similar conditions. If it is true that the Solons shared with the Dahurs their political functions, they naturally adopted shamanism under the same conditions as the Kidans-Dahurs, i.e. at the period of great variations connected with the change of interethnical pressure and milieu. At such moments the psychomental complex is subject to at least a temporary, disequilibrium. Perhaps the Tungus groups which much later moved with Gantimur from Manchuria were found in similar conditions. Other Tungus groups were in a different position. At the moment of their coming into the southern regions they apparently met with half-settled and firmly settled groups of Dahurs and Tungus. They soon lost their reindeer and had to adapt themselves to the new conditions of existence. During the migrations and during the change of the cultural complex the psychomental complex was naturally not very stable. All of them may have been badly affected by disequilibrium. This ground was good for an implantation of the shamanistic complex, the importance of which was still great in the eyes of the Northern Tungus, because it was a cultural achievement of a culturally superior group, the Dahurs.

Theoretically, there may have been another source of borrowing by the groups of the Northern Tungus who lived between two ethnical belts, namely, the Yakuts in the North and the Mongols in South-West (Dahurs in South-East). As far as I know the history of the Mongol and Yakut shamanism, these sources are not certain. As I have pointed out during the analysis of the Tungus complex, there are some elements in the Mongol shamanism which are met with in the Tungus shamanism. This is especially true of the Buriat complex. However, a great number of these elements reveal a secondary origin, i.e. their incorporation into shamanism as a complex which already existed prior to the establishment of a contact with the Mongols. Yet the Buriat cultural complex, in general, does not seem to be identical with that of the Mongols. Moreover, the Buriats themselves are more likely a group of a mixed origin, so that in respect to Buddhism they might

have been in a position similar to that of the Tungus. The Yakut shamanism might have played the rôle of stimulus at least for some Tungus groups. These groups found themselves greatly pressed by the Yakut intrusion and were probably not reluctant to adapt shamanism as a complex, if the Yakuts had it. These groups were not in a condition of having a well-balanced psychomental complex for two reasons, namely, they had to migrate under the Yakut pressure and they were influenced by a culturally "superior" group, the Yakuts. This becomes especially evident when we take into consideration the final outcome of this ethnical clash. However, it ought to be remembered that prior to the first appearance of the Russians in the basin of the Amur River there was a rather frequent intercourse between the Dahurs and the Yakuts. The source of the Yakut shamanism might have been not only the ethnical groups of their former area about the Lake Baikal, but also an infiltration from the South-East. In this case there might have been the same source of shamanism among the Northern Tungus and the Yakuts—the Kidan-Dahur-Nuichen groups.

It should also be noted that the Yakuts are particularly affected by the variations of hysteria, olonism, and other conditions of evident psychomental disequilibrium. They might have been imitated by the Tungus, who at present are not as strongly affected as the Yakuts.

Finally, the Tungus and Palaeasiatic groups of regions, lying to the North-East from the area of the ancestors of the Manchus, may have received their shamanism from the Manchus. These Tungus groups, such as the Goldi, Oroči, Udehe, Oroki, and Gilaks, were already strongly influenced by the ancestors of the Manchus, whose political organization brought them into a close contact not only with the Tungus groups, but also with the Chinese and Mongols. Seemingly a great number of these groups have perished under these conditions. Indeed, we know the psychomental state of ethnical units, when they are in the process of decline, or in a process of assimilation of an alien complex. It is impossible to suppose that there might be any stability of the psychomental complex, and this was a favourable condition for the adaptation and further formation of shamanism.

For all these Tungus groups the system of shamanism was a practical solution of two problems, namely, the assimilation of an alien complex—either Buddhism or shamanism—and the regulation of the psychomental disequilibrium stimulated by the conditions of a fast varying cultural complex, which in some cases might be due even to the sudden changes of the whole complex.

From the description of the actual conditions and the discussion of existing complexes it was seen that the chief function of the present shamanism is the regulation of the psychomental troubles, individual and especially those affecting groups of population. However, the whole situation may be treated differently if we regard shamanism as a continuous cause of psychomental disturbances among the groups practising it. Indeed, if we approach shamanism from this point of view a great number of facts may be brought forth for showing that (1) the theory of spirits is greatly responsible for the possibility of accepting any new hypothesis which may disturb the minds; (2) the practice of public shamanistic performances is greatly responsible for the reproduction (imitation) of a certain behaviour which manifests psychomental instability and which in

---

[*] Cf. SONT pp. 62 et seq., 84 et seq.

[**] They were brought by Gantimur from the Dahur territory in Manchuria, vide SONT p. 62

[***] Vide SONT.

certain conditions may be responsible for the troubles; (3) the existence of shamanistic methods of curing and checking some troubles leaves a possibility of practising a show of hysterical and pseudo-hysterical conditions. However, such an approach to the problem of shamanism, i.e. an explanation of the shamanism by means of shamanism itself, is not of much use for an understanding of the phenomenon from the point of view of its functional rôle in the Tungus complex and from that of quantitative expression among different ethnical units. Undoubtedly if there be no theory of spirits, shamanism in its present form would be impossible. But we have to accept, as a matter of fact, the existence of this theory as a preliminary condition, somewhat independent of the shamanism. The public performances are stimulated not only by the conditions characteristic of shamanism but, as shown, by a complex mechanism of attractiveness. Moreover, besides shamanism other methods of curing and checking psychomental troubles may also exist, as observed among other ethnical groups. On the other hand, shamanism may decrease in its intensity, but psychomental stability is not visibly restored. Such are the cases of Tungus groups which give up shamanism, as it is with the Russianized Tungus of Transbaikalia, and partly with those of Manchuria and the Manchus who reject shamanism and practise mafarism. Undoubtedly behind the shamanism there are much deeper psychomental conditions which are responsible for the existence of disturbances.

E. Huntington put forward the supposition that the actual cause of the psychic instability of the Siberian groups is the environment. Indeed, this point of view is worthy of consideration for, as a matter of fact, psychic troubles are common among different ethnical groups of that area. However, this implies another hypothesis, namely, that the groups in question had all migrated from the south, for if they were aborigines, they should be perfectly adapted to the climatic conditions and particularly to the long dark season which theoretically must affect the psychic complex. Thus migration must be accepted for all groups, such as the Tungus, the Yakuts and the Russians. However, there remains a large group of other ethnical units which are not newcomers, and the area of psychic troubles of the type of "hysteria arctica" is much wider than the region of the rigourous climate. So shamanism was practised by the populations of South Manchuria, North Korea and the South Ussuri region which can be regarded as "rigourous" only by reason of subtropical regions.

In the same line of ideas is a suggestion made by M. Czaplicka, namely, that all "unfavourable" conditions—those of Siberia and those of the tropical area—may be responsible for conditions similar to hysteria arctica, observed e.g. among the Malays. Indeed, the *change of environment* may affect the psychic complex of migrating units, but this cannot be regarded as the only cause of the condition, for the units are sometimes affected without leaving their original area. As shown, psychic disequilibrium is likely to occur in all cases of lack of adaptation, be it of internal origin, or brought about by the interethnical milieu, or, lastly, be it conditioned by the primary milieu, particularly by climatic changes, due to the actual change and to the migration of ethnical units. Therefore we need no hypothesis as to an "unfavourable environment" for our understanding of the conditions in which shamanism can appear.

It may now be asked what existed among the Tungus before the introduction of shamanism as a regulator of the psychic life of the units. In fact our knowledge of the psychomental conditions of the Tungus prior to the introduction of shamanism is very limited. It would be very risky to re-establish the old complex by a substraction of elements which constitute the shamanism, for the latter might take the place of some other complex. However, it may be supposed that the psychomental conditions of the units prior (chronologically) to the spreading of Buddhism were different. Probably the difference was that the interethnical pressure was much smaller; the influx of new ideas was much more limited than later; the process of cultural changes was rather slow. On the other hand, the important condition of adaptive stability of the psychomental complex, the ethnical adaptation to the tempo of variations may also have been lower, and the process of migrations imposed by and resulting in the change of milieu was continuously going on. Under such conditions the occurrence of instability can be as frequent as it was at the moment of the spreading of Buddhism.

From the pre-shamanistic period of the Tungus we have some facts which indicate that there were changes in the cultural complex and in the interethnical milieu, as well as in the primary milieu, due to migrations. Such important change of the cultural complex occurred with the transition from the matriarchal clan organization to the patriarchal system. In the Tungus complexes we can see the incorporation of alien terms of relationship connected with this process. The change of interethnical milieu is also known as a historic fact concerning the territories of Mongolia and Manchuria with the adjacent areas of the forest regions of the Amur and Lena basins. In fact, the Tungus groups, which were in contact with other groups, could not be indifferent to the changes of the interethnical milieu: first the Palaeasiatic groups and after them the Turkic and Mongol groups, and later the Chinese groups, the Yakuts and the Russians produced the pressure on the Tungus. A great number of Tungus groups perished altogether and a still greater number of them included new elements in their complexes and adopted new cultural complexes. The Southern Tungus—the ancestors of the Manchus—were the first to be formed as a result of the overlapping *populationes* and cultural complexes. It is natural that in almost every case of collapse of ethnical units, of their extinction, or absorption and remodelling, conditions of psychomental instability occurred. Under these conditions new hypotheses were created to explain the fact of individual and mass instability, and in the process of regulation of the psychomental complex new methods were also created or merely introduced. The greater part of these hypotheses and methods are now forgotten and a great number of them perished together with the ethnical units. However, some of them have survived among the present ethnical units. The establishment of the identity of their original inventors is quite impossible.

I have again dwelt upon shamanism as on a specimen of the by-products of self-regulation of the psychomental complex when the latter is in a state of instability, brought about by the interethnical milieu and adapted for "internal use" of the units. Under the existing conditions we can observe how this complex is formed, how it changes and how it perishes. From this point of view mafarism is not less interesting than shamanism, for it is also a by-product of self-regulation of the psychomental complex among the units which have failed to maintain the adaptive function of the old complex. Indeed, the function of shamanism, as a complex of formal elements, may be quite different in other ethnical groups, and for this reason I am particularly opposed to the idea of a scholastic generalization concerning shamanism treated as a "primitive religion". This was good at the time when we did not know shamanism in its *original Tungus form* which was, as a matter of fact, the starting point of the generalization.

In these cases the adaptation of alien elements and the formation of complexes proceed without being cognized by the populations as a functioning psychomental complex. However, it can be observed, at any moment, among the ethnical groups of the earth, especially those which are undergoing a process of cultural change and which are found under a strong interethnical pressure. A functioning psychomental complex, as a whole, is not cognized, but the elements of which it consists are usually understood as, for instance, a "literary movement", a "religious movement", an "art movement", a "political movement", "fashion", "ideas", "public opinion". In case of a disturbance of smooth functioning there would be an increase of insanity, psychoses, especially mass psychoses, which usually take a strongly veiled form of violent "movements" resulting in riots, rarely "civil wars", and "revolutions". Indeed, in such forms of disturbances, conditions of disequilibrium of centrifugal and centripetal movements under varying interethnical pressure are involved. The condition of disturbed psychomental complex results in an increase of criminality of different types, beginning with simple cases of disobedience and breaking of social order and ending with murder and banditry. An increase of the number of psychically affected individuals and criminals may result in a further disturbance of the psychomental complex of the affected unit. Such a condition of units is usually understood as due either to the biological condition of individuals,* or to the ill-temper of individuals, who must be punished and isolated, or to the influence of the social environment, and lastly to all the above indicated "causes", attention being attracted by these manifestations of disturbance of the psychomental complex of the whole unit, i.e. in just the same manner as the attention of a Tungus is attracted by certain individual conditions and hypothetic spirits.

156. PHENOMENON OF REGULATION   One of the interesting conditions of the equilibrium of the psychomental complex is that the ethnical units believe in the possibility of the regulation of the psychomental complex.** I have already pointed out that the idea of regulating this equilibrium appears chiefly in the leading units. In fact, this question is closely connected with that of the "leading ethnos". Therefore we have again to revert to this question.

Although the problem of the leading ethnos is rather simple in its historic aspects, it is greatly handicapped by the fact of the existence of a moving interethnical equilibrium. In fact, owing to this condition, colonies of ethnical units may appear as units opposing themselves to other similar colonies and single ethnical units. Such is the case of a great number of "nations", also of units grouped by common cultural complex, as for instance "religions", etc., and such is the case of overgrown ethnical units which have undergone a long process of internal differentiation and finished with the creation of several ethnical units, one of which may assume the functions of the leading unit. "Nations", and other groups of the same type as well, and overgrown ethnical units may have a short and a long existence. Naturally, only a long existence may result in the creation of functionally distinct ethnical units which become leading ethnical units and make the process of leading ethnos concrete.

As in the formation of ethnical units all the potential units do not become ethnical units, so in the process of formation of leading ethnical units a great number of potential leading units appear, but by far not all of them attain a functional crystallization. In my definition of a leading unit I have put stress upon the adaptation which permits the unit to become a leading unit.* Indeed, every invention requires a readaption of the psychomental complex and when the process of variations of the whole complex is too fast, there appears a necessity of restoration of the equilibrium of the psychomental complex and thus a continuous readjustment and variation of the complex. The ethnical groups which do not play the part of a leading unit have to perform absolutely the same operation with their complex, especially when the interethnical pressure varies and when it is strong. They may borrow new cultural elements from the leading ethnical units, and therefore they do not perceive the process of readaptation of their psychomental complex as their own active direction of the process, while the leading ethnical units believe into their directing of the process of changes.** As a matter

---

* The theory of inherited complexes is of great assistance for a justification of the situation. Moreover, the attention may be attracted to this side of the situation and no other aspects will be seen.

** Another question is how far the fact of regulation is cognized; in a great number of cases it is not cognized at all, but the readaptation proceeds as it has been shown before, i.e. by the special mechanisms of change. Indeed, there are two entirely different situations, namely, when the need of a change is cognized and when it is not so. At present we are concerned only with the first group of cases, namely, the groups which believe in the possibility of regulation.

---

* It should be noted that under the variable conditions of primary and interethnical milieu the cultural complex changes, as it changes under the pressure of an increasing population within the given unit. Such a change may be "positive" and "negative" in the sense of the increase of the complexity of cultural adaptation and its simplification. However, both of them require a certain readjustment of the whole complex, including the psychomental complex. Theoretically at the historic moments of loss of the former cultural adaptation and its simplification, the ethnical unit, which finds new "simplified forms", may also become leading in a direction of general fall of the former cultural adaptation. There are some historic facts of this order which usually occur at the periods of the collapse of larger colonies of ethnical units and "nations" of the empire-type. The emotional condition of disdain among the survivors and the general disapproval of the actors during the periods of decline and collapse—let us add quite natural in biologically strong units—always hinder a full understanding on the part of "leading ethnical units". Indeed, the function of the leading ethnical units is very often, and yet quite unconsciously, connected with the "progress" which is given an objective contents but which is usually a mere justification of the processes.

** Such a distinction of behaviour in the leading and non-leading ethnical units disappears at the historic moments when there is a change of leading ethnical units and when there is a temporary readjustment of the interethnical pressure and equilibrium.

of fact, if the process of change is cognized, without such a belief the leading ethnical units would not have "nerve" for carrying out the changes of the cultural adaptation, imposed either by an increase and decrease of the population, or by a change of the interethnical pressure. This response to the impulse of variations, if cognized, is perceived as a voluntary regulation of the process; when it is not cognized, it is not perceived as a voluntary act, but is carried on, for otherwise the unit perishes. In the case of units which are not leading ones the change, if cognized, may be accepted as one enforced by the interethnical pressure (influence). However, even if it is not cognized, it is carried on. The cognition of the process of changes is not an indispensable condition of the changes, most of which are carried out by the mechanisms heretofore described and are made step by step, element by element, reactions on which are naturally variable. It is evident that when the process of changes is zero, the element of cognition is lacking, while it increases with the increase of the tempo of variations. However, in the leading ethnical units, when the tempo of changes is high, the element of cognition is of great importance, for such units, in order to be able to survive, must *invent* new cultural elements and the elements must be *recognized*.

––––––

To exhaust the discussion concerning the cognition and regulation of the psychomental complex in leading units, as well as in other units by the leading units, is now impossible. I therefore end herewith my conclusions. Although they are clear, I feel that a part of them may not appear so, if some general principles of variations of ethnical and ethnographical phenomena are not thoroughly discussed. I hope to revert to them in my further publications where I shall prepare the ground for answering question as to whether an actual "regulation" can exist or whether there is a mere "justification" created by functioning units which assume a new form of rationalization in conformity with the new complex of Science.

THE END

GLOSSARY

1. PRELIMINARY NOTE

This Glossary contains only Tungus material, both Northern and Southern Tungus. Unfortunately, it was impossible to include in the Glossary all the non-Tungus comparative material used in the present work. The spirits are also not included in the Glossary being presented in a special Index. The refrains, used in shamanizing, and Tungus proper names are entirely omitted. However, some proper names are included in General Index.

From the text of this work it is seen that I did not "standardize" Tungus words and terms. In fact, I have reproduced variations of pronunciation and phonetic peculiarities met with in different dialects and even among individuals, as seen in the same "words". For this purpose I have used my original records. My aims were to show that, on the one hand, no standard pronunciation, nor uniform phonetic system exist, and that, on the other hand, such a fidelity to the original record does not hinder the reader in his following the text. However, some additional remarks, especially concerning the Manchu material, are needed.

As I have shown (cf. my paper "Reading and Transliteration of Manchu Lit." in Rocznik Orjentaлистyczny, Vol. X, pp. 122-130, 1934) there are at least four different ways of rendering Manchu lexic material, namely: I. A transliteration of Manchu Writ. (tr. Man. Writ.) which I use here not having heard the reading myself; 2. A phonetic (approximate) transcription of the present reading, as used among the non-sinicized Manchus of the Aigun district (Manchu Writ.); 3. A Phonetic (approximate) transcription of the former reading practised by the Manchu "purists" (as used by P.P. Schmidt); 4. A phonetic (approximate) transcription of the Manchu language spoken chiefly in the Aigun district (Man. Sp.). However, in so far as the standardization is concerned, in Man. Sp. we meet with great difficulties, namely, with various individual phonetic peculiarities which, in fact, are not fixed at all. For instance, the series *b~ѣ~p*, in the same "words", is commonly met with. So we have *bigan* = *ѣ'igan* = *p'iyan*. In the same line of variations the series *g~ǥ~k*, as well as other series are found. Moreover, the alternations of the type *z~ž*, *g~γ*, *l~ĺ~l* and others, make the standardization quite impossible. In Manchu and in most of the Northern Tungus dialects we meet with the phenomena of variability of "voiçedness", bilabialization. palatalization and aspiration, so that in the same dialect the individual phonetic systems accept, for instance, palatalized and non-palatalized consonants, narrowing and widening of vowels, etc. There are some peculiarities in the phonetic systems of different sexes, e.g. the females show a quite definite tendency for palatalization. Here some simplifications of the transcription have appeared indispensable. It was also necessary to omit the musical contents in all transcriptions, which are evidently beyond the means of the present methods of record. The present transcription

may be only approximate and to some degree artificially "standardized". Owing to these considerations I have omitted the distinction of some vowels, which, as a matter of fact, form series only with some "centring" about *a* type, *e* type, *è* type, etc. In fact, since in a spoken language no individually used fixed sounds exist,—as any other natural phenomena, they range with their variations about certain centres which as a system, with the course of time, may shift as well,—it is obvious that a simplification of the symbolization may produce a false impression of the existence of firmly fixed sounds. Of course, the idea of existence of fixed phonetic systems in languages was necessarily postulated because of the practical need for the creation of *written languages*. But as soon as they were created, a secondary process of phonetic theoretization originated, i.e. the written languages were taken as the starting point of a new construction, while the fundamental fact of a conventional fixation was, so to say, forgotten. From this point of view it is interesting to note that such a written language, with its secondary theoretization, may have a great chance of having an uninterrupted continuity, and that it may also be responsible for a burdening of the ethnographical complex and a subsequent petrifaction. We have observed this phenomenon in the instance of Manchu shamanism. Although the historians soon realized the situation, the idea of fixed sounds in a language still continued, and in the languages, the history of which was not yet clear, it sometimes brought the linguists and philologists on the wrong tracks. In so far as the living material is concerned, I do not think that this idea is needed. I therefore with great reluctance accept simplifications of the dialectal and individual phonetic systems which, unfortunately, by means of the existing methods cannot be symbolized. Perhaps, this is impossible altogether. However, it must be noted that for the ethnographical treatment of cultural complexes such a simplification is not very harmful.

The transcribed Chinese words, met with in Man. Sp., are given in Manchu forms. However, in the list of spirits (Index) I also give some Chinese spirits. Their transcription is based upon the Manchu pronunciation, chiefly of the Aigun District, but sometimes it is rendered in the conventional form of foreign transcription of the Chinese reading of the Chinese characters. I was also compelled to omit the special symbolization of "tones", partly for the reason that the Manchus do not strictly observe them and partly for the same reason as in the case of the Tungus tonality. It must also be pointed out that the Chinese characters given in the body of this book have been received by me from the Manchus. Thus, some errors here will be only natural. However, not being versed in Chinese, I do not venture to discuss possible corrections, which though quite evident, may also distort the ethnographical fact, namely, the Manchu familiarity with the Chinese characters.

2. ABBREVIATIONS

A. THE NORTHERN TUNGUS DIALECTS ACCORDING TO THE AUTHOR

Amur — the dialect of the Reindeer Tungus living in the eastern part of the Amur Government also spoken by a Tungus group in Sakhalin Island

Barg. — the dialect of the Reindeer Tungus of Transbaikalia living in the Barguzin taiga

Bir. — the dialect of the Tungus of Manchuria living in the regions lying between the Amur, Sungari, and left tributaries of the Nonni (Birarčen)

Borz. — the dialect spoken by the Nomad Tungus living in South-Eastern Transbaikalia, in the basin of the Borz'a

Khin. — the dialect of the Tungus of Manchuria (Mongolia) living in the Khingan Mountains, chiefly in

Hulun Buir

Kum. — the dialect of the Tungus of Manchuria living in the basin of the Kumara, Panga, Albazixa, and Upper Nonni (Kumarčen)

Mank. — the dialect of the Nomad Tungus living in South-Eastern Transbaikalia, in the Mankova region (volost')

Nerč. — the dialect of the Reindeer Tungus (partly settled) living in the Nerchinsk taiga

RTM. — the dialect of the Reindeer Tungus of Manchuria living in the basin of the Bystraia and Albazixa, also Upper Kumara

All dial. — all the above-mentioned dialects

B. THE NORTHERN TUNGUS DIALECTS, ACCORDING TO UNPUBLISHED MATERIAL GATHERED BY OTHER INVESTIGATORS

Enis. — the dialects of the Enisay Tungus gathered by the missionaries, brought by I. P. Tolmačev, and put at the author's disposal by W. L. Kotwicz

Lam. — the dialect of the Reindeer Tungus of the Yakutsk Government included into Lamunxinskii rod (cf.

S. K. Patkanov, Essai), gathered, and put at the author's disposal by P. V. Olenin

Tum. — the dialect of the group above-mentioned included in the Tumunxanskii rod; cf. Lam.

C. THE NORTHERN TUNGUS DIALECTS KNOWN FROM OTHER PUBLICATIONS

Ang. Tit. — the dialect of the Reindeer Tungus of the Angara region in Northern Transbaikalia, according to E. I. Titov

Enis. Ryčk. — the dialect of the Tungus of Enissy (Enisei) Gov., according to R. M. Ryčkov

Irk. Tit. — the dialect of the Tungus of Irkutsk Gov., according to E. I. Titov

Kal. Tit. — the dialect of the Reindeer Tungus living in the basin of the Kalar and Kalakan rivers, according to E. I. Titov

Mank. Cast. — the dialect of Mankova Tungus (vide supra), according to M. A. Castrén

Neg. Sch. — the dialect of Negidals, according to P. P.

Schmidt

Nomad Barg. Poppe — the dialect of the Nomad Tungus of Bargusin District, according to N. N. Poppe

Oroči (Leon.) (Marg.) (Sch.) — the dialect of the Oroči of Maritime Gov., according to S. Leontovič, V. P. Margaritov, and P. P. Schmidt

Solon. Iwan. — the dialect of the Solons, according to A. O. Ivanovskii

Udehe, according to S. Brailovskii

Ur. Cast. — the dialect of the Urulga Nomad (and settled) Tungus, according to M. A. Castrén

There are used some other abbreviations for various dialects, according to A. Schiefner and W. Grube

D. THE SOUTHERN TUNGUS LANGUAGES AND DIALECTS

Man. Sp. — the Manchu Language as spoken by the Manchus of the Aigun District in Manchuria, according to the author

tr. Man. Writ. — according to the Manchu sources, I. Zaxarov, P. P. Schmidt, and other published material

Man. Writ. — reading of the Manchu Written, as recorded in the Aigun District, according to the author

Nuichen — according to W. Grube, and P. P. Schmidt; W. Grube's transcription sometimes is preserved.

Goldi (Lop.) (Grube) (Sch.) — according to I. A. Lopatin, W. Grube, and P. P. Schmidt

Olča (Grube) (Sch.) — according to W. Grube and P. P. Schmidt

E. THE NON-TUNGUS LANGUAGES

Mongol (Kow.) (Rud.) (Podg.) — according to O. Kowalewsky, A. D. Rudnev, P. A. Podgorbunskii; also rarely according to other authors (not abbreviated)

Buriat (Podg.) (Rud.) vide Mongol

Dahur (Ivan.) (Poppe) — according to A. O. Ivanovskii and N. N. Poppe, rarely (Dahur), — according to the author

Yakut (Pek.) — according to E. K. Pekarskiĭ rarely according to V. L. Sʼeroševskiĭ
Gilak — according to W. Grube

Chinese — according to various sources, including some records by the author from the Manchus, Tungus and Nikan

3. APPROXIMATE PHONETIC EQUIVALENTS OF TRANSCRIPTION

(in alphabetic order)

a — *a* as in "father"
ä — *a* as in "man"
b — *b* as in "boot"
b̃ — almost voiceless *b* (in Manchu and Chinese)
c — *z* as in German "zwar"
č — *ch* as in "chair"
d — *d* as in "door"
d̃ — almost voiceless *d* (in Manchu)
j — *j* as in "joke," an affricate: *dž*
e — *e* as in "get"
ė — *e*, very backed
f — *f* as in "foot"
g — *g* as in "good"
ĝ — almost voiceless *g* (in Manchu and Chinese)
h — an aspirate, slighter than h in "hope"
γ — a voiced *x* (see below)
i — *i* as in "bit"
j — *y* as in "yellow"
k — *k* as in "kind"
l — *l* as in "ful," Slav *l* (e.g., in Polish)
l — las in "land" (in Manchu when followed by labials, dentals, and gutturals, the tongue touches neither palate nor alveolæ i.e. near to *l̦*, see below)
l̦ — *l* cerebralized

m — *m* as in "moon"
n — *n* as in "noon"
ŋ — *ng* as in compound "ng" in "ring"
o — *o* as in "rope"
ö — *ö* as in German "König"
p — *p* as in "pipe"
r — *r* as in South French
s — *s* as in "sale"
š — *sh* as in "shop"
t — *t* as in "top"
u — *oo* as in "moon"
ü — *ü* as in German "müssen"
v — *v* as in "vote"
w — *w* as in "wood"
x — *ch* as in German "Bach," and *x* as in Spanish
y — *y* as in Polish and Russian in "myło"
z — *z* as in "zone"
ž — *j* as in French "jamais"
ʒ — an affricate: *dz*
diacritic signs:
¯ (*ā*) — designates long vowels
˘ (*ă*) — designates short vowels
ʹ (*á*) — designates accent, both musical and expiratory
ʼ (*n'*) — designates palatalization and "mouillement"

4. TUNGUS GLOSSARY

abači (Enis. Ryčk.) [Etym. p. 81]—the bear
abdanda (var. dial.) vide *abdanna*
abdanna (Bir. Kum.), *abdahda*—the leaf of a tree
abdu (n) (RTM) (Ur. Cast.) vide *adun*
abka (tr. Man. Writ.); cf *apka* (Man. Sp.)—the heaven
ačin (Bir. Khin. RTM)—"is not", "not" (cf. p. 107)
adali (Bir. Kum. Khin. Mank.) (Man. Writ. Sp.)—like, similar, equal to, the same
adasun (Bir.) vide *adun*
adun (Bir.) (Man. Writ. Sp.); cf. *abdu(n)*, adasun [Etym. p. 71]—the cattle, herd
age (Man. Writ. Sp.)—the brother, the male spirit (of a secondary importance)
agjulan (Man. Sp. Writ.)—a kind of bird
ayakakun (RTM) [Etym. p. 81]—the father, the male bear
ayiltana (RTM)—the moment about one hour and a half before the sun

set
ailn'i (Bir.)—of village
aiman (Manchu)—the clan (formerly used), administrative unit (later used)
ais'in (Man. Writ.), *alžin* (Man. Sp.)—the gold; cf. *anču* (Nuichen)
aitere (Man. Sp.) vide *eitere* (Man. Writ.)
aižin (Man. Sp.) vide *ais'in* (Man. Writ.)
aja (all North. Tung)—good, good-hearted, handsome
aja (+suff.) (Bir. Nerč) (Neg. Sch.)—to like
aja (stem) and derivatives vide p. 105
ajaki (Bir. RTM. Nerč.)—down stream, with the stream
ajam'i fan'alko (Goldi, Lop.)—a special placing for the soul, p. 217, 367
äjen-x'jen (Man. Sp.) [Etym. 201]—the Chinese incense
ajega (Amur)—a precious thing, amulet
ajige (Man. Writ. Sp.)—small, little,

petty
afiratkan (Bir.)—the sturgeon
ajor buni (Bir.)—the souls of Lower World whose names are not remembered; vide *ojor* and *buni*
aki-noku (all North. Tungus)—"senior-junior", the clan
akipču (Bir.) — tabooed, prohibited (females); cf. SONT
akfan (tr. Man. Writ.)—the thunder
aksinn'i (RTM) [Etym. p. 58]—the name of the month which follow *satin'i* (RTM)
ala (=*ala*) (Nerč. Barg. RTM. Bir.)—tasty, sweet
alban (Man. Sp.)—public, non-private
alda (Mank.) (Ur. Cast.)—the "fathom" (cf. p. 61)
alimb'e (Man. Sp.)—to attend
alin (Man. Sp.)—the mountain
alin'i (RTM) [Etym. p. 58]—the name of the month which follows *boy'in'i* (RTM)
aljamb'e (Man. Sp.)—to be angry (in reference to the spirit); cf *aljambi*

(Man. Writ.)—to separate, to leave a position, etc.

àlla (Bir) vide *olo*

aḷxa (Man. Sp. Writ.)—piebald

ama (Bir.)—the father, the grand father, the senior, the bear

ama (+ suff.) (Bir.)—to return, to be back

amasar—the name of a river—[Etym. p. 67]

amaskan děṛ'i (Bir.)—the swastika; vide *děṛ'i*

amba (Man. Sp. Writ.)—great, big, large, important

am'i (all North. Tung.)—the father

amiran (Nerč. Khin.) (Ur. Cast.) [Etym. p. 98]—the father

amnuli (RTM)—the source of a river

amnunnali—the name of a river—[Etym. p. 67]

amzun (Man. Writ.), *amzun* (Man. Sp.)—the sacrifice

amtasal (Bir.) [Etym. p. 166]—the forefathers

amuji (Khin. Bir.)—the lake

amujija—the name of a river—[Etym. p. 67]

amun (Kum. Bir. Khin. Nerč. Barg. Mank)—the fecae

amun (+ suff.) (Kum. Khin. Nerč)—to "evacuate"

amzun (Man. Sp.) vide *amsun* (Man. Writ.)

an'a (Man. Writ. Sp.) vide *aygan'i*

anači (Udehe, Brail.)—the "evil spirit"

an'akan (Barg. Nerč.)—the soul

an'akan (Bir.)—the placing (anthropomorphic) for spirits; vide *an'an*

anam (RTM. Bir. Kum. Khin. Nerč.) (Ang. Tit.), *anami* (Man. Writ)—the elk (Alces Alces)

anami (Man. Writ.) vide *anam*

anan (Lamut, Klap.) vide *aygan'i*

an'an (Bir.) [Etym. p. 52]—a special placing for the child's soul; originally "the soul"; cf. *an'akan*

anču(n) (Nuichen)—the gold ; cf. *ais'in* (Man. Writ.)

ančulan (Man. Writ.)—the owl

anpá (Bir.)—the four fingers together, as a standard unit of measure

an's (Nuichen, Grube) vide *aygan'i*

an'ikan (= *an'akan*) (RTM. Bir. Kum.)—an anthropomorphic placing for spirits; cf. *an'an*, *an'akan*

ant(a) (stem) [Etym. (N.T.T.O.) p. 62]—the "south"

anyn (Oxot. Klap.) vide *aygan'i*

ayani (Bir.) (Mank. Cast.) vide *aygan'i*

ayaptun (Bir.)—a strip with ball-bells attached to the shaman's costume

ayga (Manchu Sp. Writ.)—the mouth;

ayga ban'jimb'i (Man. Sp. Writ.)—to speak

aygan'i (Khin. RTM. Barg.), *ayyani* (Bir. Kum. RTM), *ayani* (Bir.) (Mank. Cast.), *ayyini* (Lam.), *anyn* (Oxot. Klap.), *anan* (Lamut, Klap.), *an's* Nuichen, Grube), *an'a* (Man. Sp. Writ.)—the year

ayyani (Bir. Kum. RTM.) vide *aygan'i*

ayyini (Lam.) vide *aygan'i*

apkaĭ (*endur'i*) (Man. Sp.) vide *abka*

ar (stem)—to revive; cf. p. 138

ar (Bir.) (Sam. Tit.)—to come to life; cf. *ori*

arba (Bir. Kum. Khin. Nerč.)—the dry river, shallowed

arbukakta—the name of a river—[Etym. p. 68]

ārča (Bir.), *arca* (Mank.), *arči* (RTM) [Etym. p. 201]—the juniper

aroa (Mank.) vide *ārča*

arči (RTM) vide *ārča*

āri (Ur. Cast.) vide *ori*

orkalan (Nerč. Barg.)—a component of the shaman's costume; cf. p. 288

arkaptun (Bir.)—a large *tǒli* with additions, put on the back, over the costume, by the shamans

ark'i (Man. Sp. Writ.)—the wine, brandy

ark'ivun (Mank.)—a stick (for grilling meat)

ariksa (Enis.)—the life; cf. *ori*

āriksan (Ur. Cast.)—the breathing; cf. *ori*

arsulan (Man. Writ.)—the lion

asaran (Bir.)—the "common people", as opposed to the shamans

asaran (Bir.)—a big bell with silk (and other kinds) kerchieves hung up on the shaman's costume; cf. p. 291

asi (all North. Tung. with variations)—the wife, female

asu (Man. Sp. Writ.)—the net, coat of mail; code of law, of regulations

atirkan (Bir. Kum. Khin. RTM. and others) — madame, the bear-female (hon. name for)

ātirkān (Bir. Kum. Khin. RTM and others)—monsieur, the bear-male (hon. name for)

atirkaya (Kum. Barg. RTM. Khin. and others)—the bear; vide *atirkan*, *atirkān;* (emphat. sympath.)

atirku (Nerč. Barg.)—the bear (hon. name, sympath.) ; cf. *atirkan*

axa (Man. Sp. Writ.)—the slave

axa mafa (Man. Sp.)—a specialist dealing with some spirits.

axas'i gurun (Man. Sp.)—"the kind of slaves", the slaves; cf. *axa*

axundo (Man. Sp.) = *axun do*—"seniorjunior", the clan; cf. *aki nokun*

ĭ'a (Man. Sp. Writ.)—the moon; the month (Man. Writ. Sp.) (Bir. Kum) ;

cf. *b'ja* (Man. Writ.)

ba (Man. Sp. Writ.)—the place, locality ; cf. *bua*, *boa*.

ba (*mbi*) (Man. Writ.)—to become inefficient, weak, exhausted

bāda (Barg. Nerč.)—the face, the placing in the form of a face

baita (Man. Sp. Writ.)—the business, affair

bajan (all North. Tung.) (Man. Sp. Writ.) [Etym. p. 126]—rich

baka (Bir. Kum. Khin. Barg. Nerč.) (Ur. Cast.)—to find; cf. *baxa* (Neg. Sch.), *bǎka* (Mank.), *baxa(mbi*) (Man. Writ.)

bakaja (Neg. Sch.) [Etym. p. 81]—the bear, "the one who is found by the hunter"

balan (Man. Writ. Sp.)—fearless

balbuka (Bir.) vide Index of spirits

bālin (Bir.) vide *bělči*

balju (Man. Sp.)—bald, hairless

bǎm'i (Bir. Kum.), *bǒm'i* (Mank.)—a special placing for spirits of right road

bana (Man. Sp.)—of the place

ban'ji (*mb'i*) (Man. Sp. Writ.)—to beget; *ayga ban'jimbi*—to speak

banjibu (*mbi*) (Man. Sp.)—to make, to produce

bao ejen (Man. Writ. Sp.)—the house (family) master

bargila (Ur. Cast.) (var. dial.)—the opposite side of the river

bargǒsun (Mank.) [Etym. p. 70]—the midges

baron julaski (Mank.)—"the right southern", a form of shamanizing

batur'i (Man. Sp. Writ.)—the hero; cf. *baturo*, *baturu*

baturo (Man. Writ.) vide *batur'i*

baturu (Man. Writ.) vide *batur'i*

bega (with variations all North. Tung.)—the moon; cf. *b'a*

beĭse (Man. Sp. Writ.)—the prince; a special spirit (Man. Sp.)

bějü (Bir.) vide *bojo*

bějü osekta (Bir.)—a constellation, cf. p. 43

běje (Man. Sp. Writ.) vide *bojo*

bělči = *bālin* (Bir.) [Etym. p. 244]—a person affected by a non-violent insanity, idiot; cf. *beli*

bělči kǒdu (Bir.)—a person affected by violent olonism, cf. p. 244

beli (Man. Sp.)=*belen* (Man. Sp. Writ.)—a person affected by olonism; vide *bělči*

b'i (all dial.)—I, me

b'i (+ Suff.) (all dial.)—to be

bibä (Man. Sp.) [Etym. p. 131] vide Index of Spirits

b'iyǎn b'igan (Man. Sp.)—the wilderness; cf *bigan* (tr. Man. Writ.)

b'ilän (Tum.) —the wrist, the fourth month of the year

bilen (Lamut)—April, cf *b'ilän*

b'ira (all North. Tung. dial.)—the river; cf. *bira* (Man. Writ.)

b'iran'i—of river

b'iran'i foto (Bir.)—the river pebble

b'irge (Bir.)—the place where *buga* permanently stays

b'itxe (Man. Sp. Writ.)—the book; cf. *bitze* (tr. Man. Writ.)

b'ja (Man. Writ.) vide *b'a*

bo "(Bir. Kum.)—the measure of length (about a half of kilometre) equal to a Chinese li

boa (Goldi, Grube) vide *ba*

boa (Oroči) (Goldi, Grube)—the world; cf. *buya*

boa (Oroči) (Goldi, Olča, Grube)—the heaven, sky; cf. *buya*

boani (Samar, Sch.)—the sky, heaven; cf *boa*

boaw (Enis. Czek.) vide *buya*

bôbai (Bir.) [Etym. p. 180]—the talisman

boborowki (Tung. Transb. Tit.)—the bear

bočoyo (Man. Sp. Writ.)—bright, many coloured

boga (Neg. Sch.) vide *buge* (Neg. Sch.)

boga vide *buya*

bogdo (RTM.)—the subject of China (under the Manchus)

bogo (Udsk.) vide *buya*

boya (Kum. Iw.) vide *buya*

boy'ija (RTM) [Etym. p. 58]—"the pine bark can be separated", the name of the month which follows *omija* (*buyustar*)

boy'in'i (RTM) [Etym. p. 58]—the name of the month which follows *boy'ija*

boyu vide *buyu*

bôigon (Man. Writ)—of house, of clan; cf. *poizun, p'oyun*

bôigun (Man. Sp. Writ)—the house; whence "the clan people"

bôigun (Man. Writ) vide *p'oyun*

boiyga (Mank. Bir. Kum. RTM)—the wild mammalians of large size, beast; cf. *bojun*

boixon (tr. Man. Writ.)—the earth, soil-ground, country, etc. cf. *buya, pühhuô* (Nuichen, Grube)

boixun (Man. Sp.) vide *bôigon*

bojeyga (Bir.)—the beast, Cervus Elaphus; cf. *boiyga*

bojo (with variations all North. Tungus dial.), *bèje* (Manchu) [Etym. p. 72] —the man

bojuja (Nerč. Barg. Khin.)—the wild animal, the tiger (Nerč. Barg.), the leopard (Khin.); the wild man deprived of organization

bojun (Mank. Bir. Kum. RTM.) (Neg.

Sch.) vide *boiyga*

bolen'i (Ehis. missionaries)—the spring (? S. Sh.); cf. *bolo*

bolo (stem) (all Tungus dial.)—the autumn.

boloni (Bir.) vide *bolo*

bolor'i (Man. Writ) =*polor'i* (Man. Sp.) vide *bolo*

bolor(i) (Bir.)—autumnal

bôm'i (Mank.) vide *bàm'i*

borel (also *boren*) (Khin. Nerč.)—the Buriat

boror (RTM)—the moment after the sunset

boško (Bir. Kum. Khin.)—a lower grade of militar rank; cf. *bošoku* (Man. Writ.)

boso (stem) [Etym. p. 62]—the northern slope of the mountain, North

bova (Samagir, Sch.)—the sky-heaven

bu (+ Suff.) (all Tungus dial.)—to give

bǔ (+ Suff) (all Tungus dial.)—to die

bua (Bir.) vide *ba*

buačin (Bir.)—the prayer

buayi (Bir.)—of taiga

buarin (Bir.)—a place on the high mountains covered with the burned cedar

bučexe (Man. Writ)—dead; cf. *pučèye* (Man. Sp.)

bučo (part. perf.) vide *bǔ*

budiya (Bir.)—the internal organs; "inside"

bug (Lam.) vide *buya*

buge (Neg. Sch.) = *boga*—the world; cf. *boa, buya*

buy (Kum. Bir. Khin. RTM) = *buyu*, [Etym. p. 72]—the male Cervus Elaphus

buya (all North. Tungus dial.) [Etym. p. 122]—the place, the world, the God, the heaven, the locality; the universe—*buga, boya, boga;* cf. *boa, buge, bogo, buha, bug, boaw*

bɩˈya (Ang. Irk. Tit.)—the earth, locality

buyadulin (RTM)—the Polar Star, the middle of the universe

buyu (Bir. Kum. Khin. Nerč. Barg.) (Ur. Cast.) (Ir. Aug. Tit) cf. *boyu, buy; buxu* (Man. Writ.) [Etym. p. 72]—the Cervus Elaphus

buyustar (RTM) [Etym. p. 58]—"the ice (river) breaks", the name of the month which follows *kuluntutar*

buyutuna (Mank.) [Etym. p. 70]—the midges

buha (Udsk.) vide *buya*

buku (Man. Sp. Writ.) (Barg. Nerč. Mank. Bir. Kum. Khin.)—strong

bukulJin (Bir. Kum)—a race of strong, now extinct people

buleku (tr. Man. Writ)—the mirror; *gisun buleku*—a dictionary

bulen (Bir.) vide *buloy*

buloy (Barg. Nerč), *bulen* (Bir.) *bulän* (Ur. Cast.), *bulun* (Man. Sp.) —the war; especially between the shamans and between the spirits

bulôr (Bir.)—the marshes

bulun (Man. Sp.)—the heap, crowd; the war between the shamans and between the spirits; cf. *buloy*

bumbo (Bir.) [Etym. p. 617]—the cylinder

buni (*bǔ*-stem) (Barg. Bir. Kum. Khin), *buno* (Barg. Nerč), *bunil* (Nerč.)—the dead people; the world of dead; the Lower World

bunil (Nerč. Barg.) vide *buni*

buno (RTM. Barg. Nerč.) vide *buni*

buyče (+ Suff.) (Bir.)—to cry (ref. to animals)

burgu (Bir. Kum. Khin. Mank.) (Ur. Cast.)—fat

bur'imb'i (Man. Sp.)—to shadow, to cover with dust, etc

burkan (Barg. Nerč.) (Ur. Cast.) (Nerč. Tit.) [Etym. p. 148]—God (Christian)

burkan (Barg. Nerč.)—a placing for spirits.

buškulèmb'e (Man. Sp.)—to send *bušku* (vide Index of Spirits)

buta (Stem) (Bir.)—"the idea of harpoon"

butam'i (Bir.)—to harpoon

buxu (Man. Writ.) vide *buyu*

čaka (Bir.)—the articulation of calcaneus and tibia

čalbon (Kum. Mank. Nerč. Barg.), *čolpon* (Bir. Khin), *ǒolbon* (RTM), *čalbon* (Aug. Tit.) [Etym. p. 56]— Venus, Evening and Morning Star

čalbon (Ang. Tit.) vide *čalbon*

čarg'i (Barg.) [Etym. p. 310]—a birch-tree used in shamanizing

čargi (Man. Writ) vide *čergi*

čark'i (Man. Sp.)—the castanets used in shamanism

čaru (m'be) (Man.'Su.)—to fry (in oil)

čaruya èfen (Man. Sp.)—the fried cakes (in ritualism)

čejèn (Man. Sp.)—a part of chest (of sacrificial animal) offered as sacricfie to the spirits; cf. *tuyan bokto*

čefin (Man. Writ.)—the gullet

čergi (Man. Sp.), *čargi* (Man. Writ.) —preceding

čergi foieyo (Man. Sp.)—the soul which precedes (the second soul)

čiga (Bir.)—the needles of coniferous trees

čiya (Bir.)—the animals good for their fur

č'ikta (Bir.), *č'ikti* (Nerč. Bir.)—the small beads

čiléakuma (Bir.)—a place rising up in

a valley, or steppe and covered with forest

činaka (Bir.)—a small bird (mostly passerers)

č'ipkanin (Nerč. Barg.)—a special wooden apparatus for purification; cf. *s'ipkan*

čirda (Bir.)—the war arrow, the comet

čok! (Barg. Nerč.)—"good!", used as an exclamation in approval (in shamanism)

čōka (Mank.) vide *čuka*

čoka (Lamut)—August

čoko (Man. Writ. Sp.)—the chicken

čoko fatka (Man. Sp.)—the chicken's foot, the name for an ornament

čokomokta=čokomukta (Bir.)—the midges

čolbo (Nerč. Barg.)—the birch-tree; the tree used in shamanising

čolbon (RTM) vide *čalbon*

čoto (Man. Sp. Writ.) [Etym. p. 169]—the list of spirits, of names

čolpon (Bir. Khin.) vide *čalbon*

čotorga (Bir.)—to become green

čuaŋ (Man. Sp.) [Etym. p. 211]—the bed

čuka (Nerč. Barg.) (Neg. Sch.), cf. *čoka, čōka, čúka*—the grass

čūka (Ur. Cast.) vide *čuka*

čukalaya (RTM)—the season of an intensive grass growth.

čuk'ita (Bir.)—the snail

čuŋeka (Bir.)—a land surrounded by the sinuosities of a river

čuŋuka (Bir.)—a place, near the river, covered with good pasturage

čurakta (Bir.)—the shaman's mask, vide p. 293

čuza (Man. Sp.), *čooza* (tr. Man. Writ.)—the troops, soldiers

da (tr. Man. Writ.), *da* (Man. Writ.), *da~ta* (Man. Sp.)—principal, chief, great

da (Neg. Sch.) (Man. Writ.) vide *dar*

dayačan (Barg. Nerč.)—the spirit master, cf. Index of spirits

daimin (tr. Man. Writ.)—the eagle

dajeje (Man. Sp.)—the great grandfather

daktá (Bir.)—the tick (in general)

daligdi (Bir.)—taste of fat

dalkon (Khin. Nerč.)—a platform erected for the sacrifice to be exposed; and in general

dandakka (Lam.)—the elk

dan'ǐe (Man. Sp.)—near by nearer than *xan'ǐo* cf. *xanči*

dayšan (Man. Writ.) vide *daŋs'i*

daŋs'i (Man. Sp.) (shaman. express.)—the charcoal, remainders, what is left; corr. to *dayšan*

dapkur (Bir. Khin. Mank.) (Ur. Cast.) [Etym. Mong.]—double, two-walled

dar (Bir. Khin.), *da* (Neg. Sch.) (Man. Writ.)—the fathom; cf. *dari, darambi*

darambi (tr. Man. Writ.)—to stretch the arms

dari (Goldi)—to measure

dǎril (Bir.)—the type of spirits of "night-road"

dasa (+ Suff.) (Bir.)—to improve, to correct; to treat by shamanizing (Bir. Khin.)

davak (RTM) vide *daviksa*

daviksa (Nerč. Khin. Kum.)—the mineral colouring (blue, red, etc.) matter, the ochre; cf. *davak, davuk* (RTM.)

daviksa—the name of a river—[Etym. p. 68]

davuk (RTM) vide *daviksa*

dèyi (Bir. Nerč.) (Lam.)—the bird

dekta (RTM)—the needles of coniferous trees

dělača (Mank.) vide *dilačá*

delača (Nerč.) (Enis. Czek.) vide *dilačá*

deliksan (Bir. RTM.)—the name of the ornament,—"swastika in a circle"

delim (Bir.) [Etym. p. 61]—a half-fathom

dèrègde (Bir. Kum. Khin. Mank. RTM.)—a special placing for spirits (in the form of a face)

derikan (Tum.)—the bear

d'idin (Bir. Khin.) also *didin*—a high mountain range, a watershed

diyinmajen (Bir.) [Etym. p. 72]—the Cervus Elaphus with four branched antlers

dilačá (Bir. Kum.), *dilača* (Nerč. Barg.) (Ang. Tit.), *delača* (Nerč.) (Czek.), *dělača* (Mank.) [Etym. p. 57]—the sun

dilača (Nerč. Barg.) vide *dilačá*

dil (with var. all North. Tung.)—the head

dō (Bir.) (Man. Sp. Writ.) [Etym. p. 52]—the complex of mental and psychic activity, "inside", "internal organs"

dobkur—the name of a river—[Etym. p. 67];

dobkur (→*dapkur*) vide *dapkur*

dog'i (with var. all North. Tungus)—the bird; cf. *dèyi*

doyi (+ Suff.) (Bir.)—to fly like a bird

dolbo(n) (with var. all Tungus)—the night

dolbondulin (Bir. Kum. Khin. Barg. Nerč. RTM)—the midnight

dolbor (Bir.)—of night (spirits' roads)

don (Nerč.) vide *dō*

doy (Khin.) vide *dō*

dōna (Bir. Kum.) = *don'i* (Bir.)—foreign, alien, out clan (in reference to the spirits)

doygnoto (+ Suff.) (Bir.)—to freeze

don'i (Bir.) vide *dōna*

ǎorg'i (Man. Writ.) vide *torg'i*

ǎoro—ǎor'i (Man. Sp. Writ.)—the custom, practice, law, regulations

doroyon (Bir.)—the rule, law, "faith"; cf. *ǎoro*

dosimbi (tr. Man. Writ.)—to be, to stay, to come into (ref. to the spirits); to be, to live (ref. to the men)

doveš (Bir.)—the shaman (called so by another shaman when shamanizing together)

doxolo (Man. Writ.)—lame

diúgun'i (Lamut) [Etym. pp. 58, 59]—July

dun (Man. Sp.)—four

dúnda (Barg. Nerč) (Ang. Tit.) [Etym. p. 125]—the earth, Earth, the middle world; cf. *dunna* (RTM)

dunna (RTM)—the earth, the soil, the elevated locality; vide *dunda*

durō (Bir.)—the mode, manner; the regulations; perhaps corr. to *ǎoro*

durōv'i dasača (Bir.)—the saint, the just man (woman), "godly"

duša (used by some Tungus) (Russian)—the soul

dux (used by some Tungus) (Russian)—the spirit

ebiko (Enis. Ryčk.) [Etym. p. 81]—the bear female, the grandmother

eča (Lamut)—March; cf. *iečan*

èfen (Man. Sp.)—the cake

efimbi (tr. Man. Writ.), *èvemb'e* (Man. Sp.)—to play, to joke

eitere (tr. Man. Writ.) vide *aitere* (Man. Sp.)—to cheat

ejakat (Bir.)—anything

eji (Neg. Sch.) vide *ori*

ejan (Bir.) = *èjan* (Bir.) vide *ojan*

èjèn (Man. Sp.) vide *ojan*

èjin (Goldi, Grube) vide *ojan*

èla gurun (Bir.)—the world beyond *buni*

elan (Tum.), *elann'i* (Lam.)—the month

elann'i (Lam.) vide *elan*

èlèn (= *elen*) (Man. Sp. Writ.)—the house people, clansmen; the family, house

èlxe (= *èlxe*) (Man. Sp. Writ.)—the peace, safety (in a moral sense)

èlxe taif'in (Man. Sp. Writ.) [Etym. p. 203]—"the peace"

emana (Bir.)—the snow

èmǒ (+ Suff.) (Bir. Khin.)—to come, to arrive; vide *omo*

eya vide *iya*

endu (Man. Sp.) (Man. Writ.?)—"sacred", "holy"

endur'i (Man. Sp.) vide Index of Spirits; also used as a polite address to different spirits; saint, wise; God (Chrisian) (Goldi) *enduri* (Man. Writ.) [Etym. p. 123]— a class of spirits; vide Index of Spirits

enduripa (Man. Sp. Writ.)—"saint, holy, god-like"

enen buxu (Man. Writ.)—the female of Cervus Elaphus; cf. *ènin, onin*

ènin (RTM) vide *enen buxu*

èr (Man. Sp.), *ere* (Man. Writ. Sp.)— this

er(u) (+ Suff.) (Tum. Mank.)—to pull, to draw, to carry

ère (Man. Sp.) vide *èr*

èrga (Bir. Kum. Mank.) [Etym. p. 51] —the life

èrga sudala (Bir.) [Etym. p. 51]—the life, the blood vessel (arteria)

ergan (Lam.) vide *èrga*

erge (Tum.) vide *èrga*

èrge (mb'e) (Man. Sp.)—to breathe

èrgen (Man. Writ. Sp.) vide *èrga*

ergeni (Goldi, Lop.)—the life (S. Sh.); cf. *èrga*

èrgin (Bir.)—the Middle World; the living one; vide *orgu bojen*

èr'in (Man. Sp.) (Man. Writ.)—the time, hour, period

erèembi (tr. Man. Writ.)—to take care of

erów (Bir. Kum.) [Etym. p. 329]—the assistant shaman

èsači ilga (Bir.) [Etym. p. 112]—"the eye having ornament"

ètku (Man. Sp. Writ.)—the dress, clothing

euri'i (Tum.)—left (used as a component fer distinction of the names for months; p. 58)

èvemb'e (Man. Sp.) vide *efimbi*

evenki (with var. most of North. Tung.) —the Northern Tungus (p. 103).

fača (mbi) (Man. Writ.) (Man. Sp.)— to split, to divide

fayun (Man. Sp.), *faxun* (Man. Writ.) —the liver

faidan (Man. Writ)—a row of soldiers, a line of soldiers

fajanga (Man. Writ), *fojeyo* (Man. Sp.) [Etym. p. 52]—the soul

fan (Man. Sp.) [Etym. p. 214]—a long piece of red cloth used in the ceremony of burial

fan'a (Goldi, Lop.) [Etym. pp. 52, 53] —a special placing for the soul; cf. *an'a*

faykara (Man. Sp. Writ.)—one falling down

faryun (Man. Sp.)—the carrying on forward

gasa(mbi) (Man. Writ.)—to sorrow, to cry

fart (some Tungus) [Etym. p. 90] (Russian dialectal)—the luck

fasimbi (Man. Writ), *fažemb'e* (Man. Sp.)—to stangulate (?), to hung up

fatka (Man. Sp. Writ.)—the foot (e.g. of a chicken)

fè (Man. Sp. Writ.)—old, ancient

fè doro (Man.)—the old faith, law

fèn (Man. Writ), *f'in* (Man. Sp.) [Etym. p. 146]—a section

f'ičx'alaya (Man. Sp.)—burnt, burned

f'ikurem'e (Man. Sp.), *fekurembi* (Man. Writ)—to jump in

f'in (Man. Sp.) vide *fèn*

fisiku~fisixe (Man. Writ.) vide *fus'ixe*

fojeyo (Man. Sp.) vide *fajanga*

fos'ixun (Man. Sp.), *fusixun* (tr. Man. Writ.)—inferior

fuč'k'i mafa (also *mama*) (Man. Sp.) —the Buddhistic monk (*mafa*) and nun (*mama*)

fudere (←fudèmb'e) (Man. Sp.—"bringing out"

fulg'an (Man. Sp.)—red (colour)

fulo—fulo (Man. Sp.)—full, plenty

funske (Man. Sp.)—the plate (oval)

fus'ixe (Man. Sp.), *fisixe, fisiku* (Man. Writ.)—the millet flour

gā (+ Suff.) (all Tung.)—to take, to take up, "to marry"

gajamei (Bir. Kum.)—the name of a prayer to the Lower World; refrain in the same

galbu (Bir.) [Etym. p. 126]—the world change (theory of)

gale (stem.) vide *yale*

gálegda (Bir. Kum. Khin.) [Etym. p. 79]—the things, men, places touched by a tiger or a bear

gálenk'i (Bir.) [Etym. p. 79]—the act in consequence of which *gálegda* appears

gēn—the name (of a foreign origin) of a river

gani (Barg. Nerč.) [Etym. p. 243]— mad

gan'uya (Man. Sp. Writ.)—marvelous, unknown, strange, ominous etc. (Zax.) ; "unknown marvelous things which are pernicious"

gaoli (Bir.) = *gauli, gōli, goli* [Etym. p. 190]—the brass, bronze

gara (Nerč.) vide *gèrèn*

gargan (Man. Writ. Sp.)—the "branch", the branch of a clan, exogamic unit

garku (Barg.)—the spouse, a couple

gāsa (Goldi) vide *gasxa*

gasa (Goldi, Grube) [Etym. pp. 217, 309,]—to be in sorrow

gasa doro (Man.)—the custom of sorrow (in the complex of "liquidation of the soul")

gaskan (Man. Sp.) (Writ.)—a short sickness; an epidemic disease (Zax.)

gasxa (Man. Sp. Writ), *gāsa* (Goldi) —the bird;

gātá (Kum.)—the Polar Star

gauli (Khin.) vide *gaoli*

gaza dor'i (Man. Sp.) vide *gasa doro*

gè (Khin.)—an exclamation in approval

gebu (Man. Sp. Writ.)—the name

gèdènèkta (Bir.)—the gad-fly (white, heavy one)

gègè (Man. Sp.) = *xexe* (Man. Writ. Sp.), also *xèxè, gèxe, gèxè*—the sister

gehun (Lam.) vide *giss*

g'eiču (+ Suff.) (Bir.)—to shamanize, (to go) to the Lower World

gemu (Man. Sp.)—all, whole

gènè (+ Suff.) (with var. all Tungus) —to go, to proceed

gèrèn (Bir. Kum.)—a violent insane person; cf. *gara*

gèrèn (+ Suff.) (Bir.) [Etym. p. 244] —to become insane

g'es'il (Goldi, Lop.) vide *giss*

g'eva (Bir.)—the shaman's head-dress (imitation of Lama's head-dress)

gèxè (Man. Sp., rarely Writ.) vide *gege*; a group of female shamanistic spirits

g'ida (RTM)—the name of a river— [Etym. p. 68], a spear

g'idamb'e (Man. Sp.)—to push, to press on, to turn to; corr. *gidambi* (tr. Man. Writ.)

g'ilbaun (RTM. Nerč. Barg.)—a component of reindeer harness and loading complex; cf. p. 110

g'ildena (Enis. missionaries)—January and February

g'iligdi (Bir.)—cold

g'ingne (mb'e) (Man. Sp.) (Writ)—to sacrifice

g'ingun (Man. Writ.)—the attention

g'ingun (Man. Sp.) (in shamanistic texts)—"pure"

g'ira(n) (Stem) (Barg. Nerč. Khin. Bir. RTM.) (Ur. Cast.)—the bone

g'iramk'i (Bir. RTM.)—the coffin, the burial

g'iramk'iči—the name of a river— [Etym. p. 68]

g'iramk'ivun (Bir. Kum. RTM.) [Etym. p. 211] vide *g'iramk'i*

g'iramna (Bir.)—the bone; varely, the burial, tomb, cf. *g'ira(n)*

g'irās'ikta (Bir.)—a stride, the unit of length

g'irg'iwlan (Bir.)—the trinkets, e.g. on the shaman's drum

g'iš (Ang. Tit.) vide *giss*

g'isavun (Bir.) vide *giss*

g'is'ivun (Kum. Khin.) (Neg. Sch.) vide *giss*

gisivun (Mank.) vide *giss*

giss (Nerč. Barg.) = *g'iš* (Ang. Tit.), *g'isavun* (Bir.), *g'is'ivun* (Kum. Khin) (Neg. Sch), *gisivun* (Mank.), *g'es'il* (Goldi, Lop.), *gehun* (Lam.), *fehun* (Tum.), *g'ixun* (Man. Sp.)

gisun k'exe (Man. Writ.) [Etym.

p. 298]—the drum stick (used for shamanizing

gisun (tr. Man. Writ), *g'izun* (Man. Sp.) [Etym. p. 298]—the word; cf. *giss*

gisun k'eze (Man. Writ.) vide *giss*

g'izun (Man. Sp.) vide *giss, gisun*

ĝ'jo (Man. Writ.)—the roe-deer

ĝ'joxun (Man. Writ.)—the falcon

gočun (Bir.)—the moccasins, long, light, used during dry weather

golema (Nerč.) [Etym. p. 190]—golden

gōli (Mank.) vide *gaoli*

goli (Ur. Cast.) vide *gaoli*

golima (Ang. Tit.)—of brass; cf. *golema*

gonin (Man. Sp.)—the thought

gonom (Bir.)—long

gosi (Nerč. Barg.), *goti* (Khin.) (Ur. Mank. Cast.)—bitter

goti (Khin.) (Ur. Mank. Cast.) vide *gosi*

goxon ilxa (Man. Writ.), *koxon ilya* (Man. Sp.)—the hook (horn-like) ornament; cf. p. 112

guan (Man. Sp. Writ.) [Etym. p. 222] —a special yard for domesticated animals

gula (Barg. Nerč.), *guļa* (Barg.)—the house (square), storehouse, dwelling in the Lower World, the coffin

ĝun'imb'i (Man. Writ.)=*gonimb'e* (Man. Sp.)—to think

ĝun'in (Man. Sp.)—the heart (the organ of thinking)

guran (Man. Sp. Writ.)—a male roe-deer

ĝuran k'jo (Man. Sp.)—a male roe-deer

guran'i ikeè (Man. Sp.)—a special shaman's head-dress; cf. p. 295

gurgakta (Bir. Kum. Khin. Barg. Nerč. and others) — the beard, wiskers, moustaches

gurgu (Man. Sp. Writ.)—a quadruped animal

gurun (Man. Sp. Writ.) (Bir.)—"state", nation, power, people, species, kind, kingdom, ethnical unit

gusaida (Man. Sp.) = *gusa i da* (Man. Writ.)—the chief of a regiment

gusin (Nerč. Barg. Mank.) Bir. Kum.) (with variations)—the mother's brother and senior in general

gusin—ina—the mother's clan

haja (RTM)—the saint, the souls of people which remain in this world, a special kind of spirits

halanjan (RTM)—the elk, "the one with the antlers forked in a sperial manner"

hamayik (Lam.) vide *samas'ik*

haman (Lam.) (Kirensk, Czek.; Vilui, Maack) vide *saman*

hamanda (Lam.) vide *samda*

han'inn'i (Lam.) [Etym. p. 53]—the soul

heŭnni (Lam.) [Etym. p. 160]—the placing for spirits

hewu (Lam. rest. S. Sh.) vide *heŭnni*

h'ira (RTM) [Etym. p. 72]—the elk, during the period of mating

hobal (RTM)—the bear (humiliating name), "the one who has an ugly (hideous) appearance"

homoko (+ *kan*) (RTM)—a special anthropomorphic placing for spirits

hunni etann'i (Tum.)—the third month of the summer

ï (+ Suff.) (all North. Tung.)—to go, to proceed

iča (Bir.)—the elbow; the unit of length (foot)—from the root of fingers to the elbow

ičan (Bir. Kum.) (Neg. Sch.) (with var. most of Tung.)—the elbow

ičan (RTM) [Etym. p. 234]—the vizard

ičaptun (Bir.)—the ornamented band on the sleeve of the shaman's coat (on the height of elbow)

iče (Stem) (with var. all North. Tung.) —to see

idägä (Ur. Cast.) [Etym. p. 288]—the shaman's costume

idakon (Mank.) (Ur. Cast.) [Etym. p. 270]—the female shaman; cf. *odakon, idokon, odoyan*

idokon (Barg. Nom. Poppe) vide *idakon*

iečan (Tum.)—the elbow; cf. *ičan*

iyay (RTM)—a stony slope of a mountain

ikeè (Man. Sp.)—the head-dress (crown) of the shaman

ilan (with var. all Tung.)—three

ilan kirči (Bir.)—"triangular"

ilanmájen (Bir.)—the Cervus Elaphus with three branches (of the antlers)

ileli buni (Bir.)—the souls (in the Lower World) whose bearers' names are remembered

ilga (Bir. Kum.), *ilya* (Man. Sp.), *ilxa* (Man. Writ.)—the flower; an ornament; the small pox, the chicken pox, and some other diseases in children manifested in spots on the body and face

ilguka (Bir.)—the tibia

ilya also *ilya* (Man. Sp.) vide *ilga*

ilxa (tr. Man. Writ); *ilxa* (Man. Sp.) vide *ilga*

ilxa mo (Man.)—"the bluming tree" used in shamanizing; cf. p. 309

imaxa (Goldi)—the fish.; cf. *n'imaxa*

imči—imčin (Man. Writ.) vide *jimčin*

imtoï (Nerč.)—a person speechless

in—in' (stem) vide *inji*

in (Ang. Tit.)—to live, to exist

ina (+ Suff.) (With var. all Tung.)— "my sister's progeniture", "my

mother's clan junior group"

inan (with var. all Tungus)—the day; cf. *inoyi, in'i*

inandulin (Bir. Rum. Mank. RTM and others)—the midday

iyb'e (Man. Sp.)—a screen in front of the house (in the yard), used as placing for spirits

indaxun (Man. Sp.), *indaxun* (Man. Writ.)—the dog; cf. *ninakin*

indaxun (Man. Writ.) vide *indaxun*

ineyi (Man. Sp.) (Bir)—the day; cf. *inan*

iyga vide *ipa*

ingali—the name of a river—[Etym. p. 63]

in'i (Goldi)—the day; vide *inan*

in'i (Man. Sp.)—her, his, its

inji (RTM). (Enis. Mission.)—to live

inji (Lam.)—the arteria, pulse

irakta (Nerč. Barg.) (with var. all North. Tung.)—the larch tree

ireldu (Enis. Missionaries)—the summer (? S. Sh.)

irgakta (Bir. Kum. Khin. RTM. Mank. Nerč.) (Ur. Cast.)—the gad-fly

irg'i (with var. all North. Tung.)—the tail

irg'ivlán (Bir.) [Etym. p. 292]—a special part of the shaman's coat, on the back

isela (Bir. Kum.)—the lizard

isö (+ Suff) (Bir.)—to attain, to reach

itik (RTM)—a reindeer reserved for the spirits; cf. p. 198

ixan (Man. Sp. Writ) [Etym. vide "Bilab". and "Aspects"]—the cattle, cow

jaba (Bir. Kum.) (Man. Writ) [Etym. p. 244]—a speechless person

jabumb'e (Man. Sp.)—to send

jačin (Man. Sp.)—dark coloured

jafan (Man. Writ) = *java* (Man. Sp.) [Etym. p. 158]—the kitchen garden

jaga-ja (Man. Sp.)—a refrain used when Tungus spirits come

jaya (Man. Sp.) = *jaxa* (Man. Writ.)—the fire

jajayku (Bir.)—a bird-like piece attached to the collar of the shaman's coat

jakso (Bir.) = *jaso, joso* (Bir.)—the place where spirits are permanently staying

jali (Man. Sp. Writ.)—the meat, flesh

jambot (Man.) [Stym. p. 112]—an ornament (Chinese→Manchu) on tobacco bag

jamj'i (Man. Writ. rarely Sp.) vide *jemji*

jay (Ner.)—a treeless peak

jaysan—jaysan (Man. Writ)—the sickness cf. *jays'i*

jayse (Man. Sp. Writ.) = *jayseya*—

"handsome" in reference to the horse when it has an even and glossy hair

jaŋs'i (Man. Sp., whence Writ.)—a small sickness, "smell of sickness", "agent of sickness" cf. *jaŋsan~ jaŋšan*

jasil (Nerč. Barg.) [Etym. p. 198]—a reindeer reserved for spirits

jaso (Bir.) vide *jakso*

jatka (Man. Sp.)—"tabooed"

java (Man. Sp.) vide *jafan*

jaxa (Man. Writ.) vide *jaɣa*

jeŋin (with var. all North. Tung.)—nine

jemj'i (Man. Sp.)—the evening, night; of evening, of night; cf. *jamj'i*

jimčin, jemčin (Man. Sp.) ; *imči, imčin* (Man. Writ.), *unčufu* (Goldi, Lop.)—the drum (shaman's)

joko' (Bir. RTM.)—the Yakut

jorko (Nerč. Barg.)—the earth, soil, land, Earth

joso (Khin.) (Ur. Cast) (Man. Writ.) [Etym. p. 91]—the rule, law, faith

joso (Bir.) vide *jakso*

jû (with var. all North. Tung.)—to come me out

jús'ik (Barg. Nerč.)—an ornament on moccasins; cf. p. 290

ja (RTM)—the birch bark canoe; *also jaw*

jabjan (Bir. Kum.) (Man. Sp. Writ.), *jabdan* (Neg. Sch.), *javdan* (Nerč. Barg.), *tavj'an* (Bir. Kum.)—the boa-constrictor

jag (stem) vide *jVgd* (stem)

jaɣda (*mo*) (Man. Sp.)—the pine tree

j'aɣj'i (Goldi, Lop.) [Etym. p. 217]—the performance of burning a sacrifice after the settlement of the soul in the Lower World

jai (tr. Man. Writ.)—second

jaka (Man. Sp. Writ.) (Bir.)—the thing, piece

jakáptun (Bir.)—the collar used by the shamans

jal (RTM)—the companion in hunting, comrad

jalen (Man. Sp.)—the class (generation)

jalāva (Bir.) [Etym. p. 52]—the thought:—(+ Suff.)—to think; cf. *jalva*

jalva (Nerč.) vide *jalāva*

jam (+ Suff.) (RTM)—the hydrophites

jamku (Kum.) [Etym. p. 68]—a place in the rived visited by elks

jampan (Khin.)—the mosquito-net covering the bed

jangrin'ama (Lam.)—"ten hundred", one thousand

jaŋin~jaŋglin (Man. Sp. Writ.)—the commander (of a regiment)

japu (Man. Sp.) [Etym. p. 143]—"the ancestors", the clan list

jăr'i (Bir. Kum. RTM.) (Man. Sp.) [Etym. p. 329]—the assistant shaman

jar'imb'i (Man. Writ.)—to sing prayers

jatuŋa (Man. Sp.)—sharp

javdar (Barg. Nerč.)—a strip (chamois) symbolizing the Earth (in shamanism) ; cf. *jabjan*

javo (Bir.) (with var. all Tung.)—to take

jawraltan (RTM) [Etym. p. 68]—a river good for using birch bark canoé

jehun (Tum.) vide *giss*

jekse (Man. Writ.) [Etym. p. 166]—the section of the steppe or forest burnt

j'erɣá (Mank.)—red (-haired horse)

jerɣ'i (Man. Sp.) (Bir.)—the kind, sort, "so an so spirit"

j'ia (Bir.) [Etym. p. 154]—the happiness, luck

jiŋgel (Man. Writ.)—a kind of parrot

jiŋjil (Man. Writ.)—"the golden hen"

jo (Goldi)—the house

joyun (Man. Sp.)—the road, path, way

joii (Nerč. Barg. RTM. Kum. Khin.)—the taimen (Salmo)

joliŋgra (RTM) [Etym. p. 68]—a place in the river good for hunting taimen

jolo (all North. Tung.)—the stone, stone-matter

jolo amunin (Nerč. Barg.) [Etym. p. 50]—the "purgative stone"

joloy (Bir. RTM.)—the stony slope of mountain

jon (with var. Nerč. Bir. Khin. Mank.) (Ur. Cast.)—to think

juan (Man. Writ.)—ten

judu (Bir.)—at home

juɣa (Stem.)— the summer; *juɣani* (Nerč. Bir.), *juven'i*, (Man. Sp.), *jua* (Goldi), *duɣan'i* (Neg. Sch.)

jugun (Man. Writ.) vide *joyun*

jûru (Man. Sp.)—a fairy story, an imaginative story

jukā (Bir.)—the ice

jukte(n) (Man. Sp.)—the spirit *vočko* when introduced into a placing

juktembi (tr. Man. Writ.)—the sacrifice

jûldu (Bir.)—the place where the spirits are when sent in a ring along the "road"; cf. p. 351

julexen (tr. Man. Writ.)—the evenness, equality

jun (Man. Writ. Sp.)—the opening of a stove

jur (with var. all North. Tungus)—two; cf. *jure*, *jua*

jure (Man. Sp. Writ.)—a couple

jurmájen (Bir.)—the Cervus Elaphus which has antler with two branches

juve (*mb'e*) (Man. Sp.) — to spend the summer .

jVgd (var. dial. all Tungus)—to burn, the fire, etc.

kačin (Bir.), *xačin* (Man. Writ.)—the kind

.kadar (with var. all Tung.)—the rock

kaidun (tr. Manchu Writ.)—"the rider going on alone or ahead of a group"; "usual", "permanently used"

kaikari (tr. Man. Writ.)—the ammonite

kais'i (Bir.)—the early spring when the snow is off

käkta (Tungus, Sch.), *k'axta* (Oroči. Olča, Goldi, Sch.)—the shell fish

kala (Bir. Kum. Khin. RTM.), *xala* (Man. Sp. Writ.)—the clan, species, group

kalbaykan'i tikanin (Bir.) [Etym. p. 293]—the ribbons attached to *jajaŋku* (shamanism)

kallá (+ Suff.) (Bir.) —to change (the world)

kalta (Mank.), *kaltaka* (Bir. Nerc.) (Neg. Sch.) (Ur. Cast.)—a half

kamniŋa (RTM. Khin.)—a narrow valley (gorges) which leaves but a narrow passage

kan (Nerč. Barg. Bir. Kum. RTM.), *kân* (Ur. Cast.)—the khan

kaŋan (Bir.) [Etym. p. 52]—a special placing for woman's spirits; also vide Index of Spirits

kandaya (Bir.), *kandaxan* (tr. Man. Writ.) [Etym. p. 72]—the elk (Alces)

kandaxan (tr. Man. Writ.) vide *kandaya*

kapči (Man. Sp.)—"connected", twins, etc.

kara (Bir.)—to look out

karaŋa (Man. Sp.*Writ.)—black

karavu (Bir.)—to look out for

karma (Man. Sp.)—to watch

kasatē (*ra*) (Goli, Grube)—to shamanize (? S. Sh.)

kavila (Bir.)—the turtle

kaza taor'i (Goldi, Lop.) vide *ɣaza dō-r'i*

keyapti (Lam.)—the bear

keksere (Man. Writ.)—joyful

kes'ida (Man. Sp.)—the favour

ketta (Khin.)—the river bivalves, mollusks

k'ilerčan (Man. Sp.→Writ.) vide *k'ilerɡ'i*

k'ilerɡ'i (Man. Sp.→Writ.)—the Northern Tungus, a modification of *k'ilin*

kilxu (Man. Sp.)—the heron

k'imun (Man. Sp. Writ.)—a mischief, hostility

kir (*i*) (Bir.)—the peak

kirči jaŋg'i (Bir.) [Etym. p. 352] — a tally for spirits

k'iran (RTM)—the eagle

k'iraŋ (Man. Sp.), *giran* (Man. Writ.)

—the bone

k'irbu (Bir.), *kirfu* (Man. Writ.) —a kind of fish, like sturgeon

kirfu (Man. Writ) vide *k'irbu*

kitat—the Chinese, vide SONT

koĉo (Bir.)—a piece of land surrounded by sinuosities of a river and covered with a good but not thick forest; "cozy"

kognor'jo (Mank.)—the bear, "blacky"

koyon ilya (Man. Sp.) vide *goxon ilxa*

koira (Mank.) [Etym. p. 244]—insane

koklo (Ang. Tit.) vide *koklon*

koklon (Nerĉ.)—the path followed by celestial bodies

kolboyku (Bir.)—the ribbons on the shaman's head-dress; cf. *kalbaykan'i tikamin* .

köli (Man. Sp.) = *kooli* (tr. Man. Writ.) —the written rituals

kolomtan (RTM) [Etym. p. 129] — "what is found under the fire"

koltoko (Kum.)—a narrow line laid between the river and its former bed, periodically under water

komĉoki (Bir.)—the gad-fly (black one)

komna (+ Suff.) (Bir.)—to wriggle

konin (Mank.) [Etym. p. 71] — the sheep

kukku (Bir.)—the cuckoo; a wooden piece on the shaman's dress (collar)

kulikan (Bir. Kum. Khin. Nerĉ.) (Neg. Sch.) (Ur. Cast.)—the suake, the worm; (Bir.)—the micro-organism; vide *kulin*

kulin (with var. all North. Tungus)— the snake

kulin elann'i (Tum.) [Etym. p. 58]— the second month of the summer

kulinda—the name of many rivers · [Etym. p. 68]

kulla (RTM)—a place where there was a fire (in the steppe or forest)

kuluntutar (RTM) [Etym. p. 58]—"to keep the kolt"; the name of the month which follows *olon'o*

kulura (Nerĉ.) vide *kulla*

kuma (Khin.), *kumay* (Bir.)—a treeless peak

kumay (Bir.) vide *kuma*

kumaka (Bir. Kum. RTM. Nerĉ. Barg.) (Ang. Tit.) (Neg. Sch.) (Goldi, Oroĉi, Sch.)—the Cervus Elaphus (in general)

küm'i (Bir. Kum.)—the hemispherical hunting hut

kurakan (Mank. Bir. Kum. Khin.) [Etym. vide SONT]—the husband of junior female (of the clan)

kuri (Man. Sp.)—dark brown

kurume (Man. Sp. Writ.)—a short coat, the shaman's coat

labdu (Man. Sp. Writ.)—much, many

lama (+ Suff.) (Bir.) —to carry out a lamaistic service; "to lamaize"

lamu (Khin. Nerĉ. Barg.) (with var. all Tungus) —the sea, ocean; rarely a big lack (e.g. Lake Baikal)

lavu (Kum.) [Etym. p. 82]—the tiger; cf. *lawda*

lawda (Bir.)—the tiger; cf. *lavu* '

lawda ujá (Bir.)—the tiger's foot print; an ornament

lebĝere (Man. Writ. Sp.)—fierce

lefu (Man. Writ.) (Sp?)—the bear

linpay (Man. Sp.) [Etym. p. 214]—the shading made of mats

lorin (Man. Sp. Writ.)—the ass

luk(ü) (Bir.)—to throw away, to leave away

lnyur (Nerĉ.)—the moment (of the day) at the sun-set

lusè (Man. Writ.) vide *luzä*

luzä (Man. Sp.) [Etym. p. 169]—the pagoda

mafa~mava (Man. Sp.)—senior males, ancestors; also ref. to the monks and specialists (not shamans) dealing with the spirits; also vide Index of Spirits

mafa (Bir.) [Etym. from Manchu]— the tiger

mafar'i~mavar̆i (Man. Sp.)—the ancestors; the specialists; vide *mafa*

mayin (Barg. Nerĉ. Bir.) [Etym. p. 128]—the hunting luck; cf. *mahin, majin, main*

mayun (Nerĉ. Barg.)—the saint, the soul admitted to the Upper World; vide *mahun* (RTM)

mahin (Barg. Nerĉ. Bir. Kum. Khin.) vide *mayin;* (RTM.) vide *mahun*

mahun (RTM) = *mayun* = *mahin* — the spirit of taiga

maikan (Man. Sp.)—the tent

main (Enis. missionaries)—God, "master" (? S. Sh.) (Transb. Tit.) — "god", Jesus Christ (? S. Sh.)

majin (Bir. Kum. RTM.) vide *mayin*

malo (Goldi, Lop.) = *malu* (Goldi, Grube) ; vide *malu;*—a special place in the house

malu~malu (RTM. Nerĉ. Barg. Bir. Kum. Khin.)—the place in wigwam (house) in front of the entrance

mama (Man. Sp.) cf. *mafa*, but referred to the females

maya (Ur. Cast.) vide *mayga*

mandi (Bir. Khin.)—hard, difficult, strongly; cf. *manni, mani, man'i*

manga (Neg. Goldi, Oroĉi) (Sch.) vide *mayga*

mayga (Bir. Nerĉ.) (Man. Sp.) — the strong one, whestler, hero; cf. *manga*, *maya, mayyu*

mayga (mo) (Man. Sp.)—the oak (tree)

mayya (Nerĉ.) vide *mayga*

manju (Man. Writ. Sp.)—Manchu

man'i (Nerĉ. Barg.), *mayi* (Ang. Tit.) —the bear

mayi (Bir.)—the Orion (constellation)

mayi (Bir.) [Etym. p. 178] —the extinct strong race

man'i~mani (Bir. Kum) vide *mandi*

manmäkta (Bir.)—the mosquitoes; *manmaktá* (Nerĉ.)

manman'i (Enis. missionaries)—June

manni (RTM.) vide *mandi*

mayn'i (Man. Sp.)—the badger; cf. ? *maygigu, dorgan* (Man. Writ.)

m'ao (Man. Sp.) [Etym. p. 243]—the temple, shrine

mar (most of North. Tung.)—the forest of shubs, a locality covered with ... (often marshy)

mar'ikta—the name of many a river— [Etym. p. 67]

maro (Khin) = *malu*

megdu (Khin.)—the leopard

mẹgẹ (Man. Writ.) vide *mögo*

mei̇tẹ̈rä (Man. Sp.)—"cutting" (part. pres.)

men'i (Man. Writ.)—ours

mentexun (Man. Sp. Writ.)—a stupid person

m'er'ir'in (Bir.)—"stripped", the tiger

metere misprint; should be *medere* (Man. Writ.)

m'in (Stem) (all Tung.)—me, my, mine, I

m'ir (Lamut), cf. *m'ir'i* (Tum.) [Etym. p. 58]—February

m'ir'i (Tum.)—the shoulder, the second month of the year

mo (all Tung.)—"wood", "tree"

moĉo (Man. Sp. Writ.)—a person mentally dull, blunt (by birth)

moduje (Bir.)—one on the tree; [Etym. p. 80] the bear (small species)

modumoĉo (Bir.)—"stupid like wood"; cf. *modu + moĉo*

mögo (Bir.), *moko* (Khin.), *mẹgẹ* (Man. Writ.)

moi faksi (Man. Writ.)—the carpenter

moko (Khin.) vide *mögo* (Bir.)

mokun (Man. Sp.) . (Bir.)—the exogamic unit, clan

mokunda (Man. Sp.) (Bir.)—the elected chief of a clan

mŏma ι(Nerĉ. Khin. Bir.) — wooden, "possessing quality of wood"; placings for spirits (made of wood)

mŏmate (Man. Kum.)—the wooden placing for spirits

moygoraku (Man. Writ.)—the ribbon, strip facing the edges of a dress

moyyavdaptin (Nerĉ.) [Etym. p. 112] —an ornament (in form of strips) of a dress ·

monyojin (RTM. Bir.)—the Cervus Elaphus over one year old

mon'i (Man. Sp.)—my, mine (also ours)

monmaktá (Nerč.) vide *manmákta*

monnaya (RTM.)—the elk (Alces) over one year old

mont' akli (Tum)—the fourth month of the summer, (Lam.)—the summer

morin (all Tung. with var.) [Etym. p. 71]—the horse

morin (Nerč. Barg.)—the staff (like "horse") used by the shamans

moritin (Nerč.)—an ornament on the reindeer boxes; cf. *on'o* (RTM), p. 112

moro (Man. Sp. Writ.)—the cup

moroskun (Man. Sp.)—a kind of spirits produced from the souls of killed people. Addition: ? Etym. *moro* (*mbi*) (Man. Writ.)—to keep wide open eyes

mosapka (*mo* + *sapka*) (Man. Sp.)—the chopsticks (Chinese)

moza (Enis.) [Etym. p. 132]—the forest

mudan (Man. Writ.)—stoping, with round back

muduje (Bir.)—one in the water (analogous to *moduje*

muduje činaka (Bir.)—a kind of bird which can go under the water

mudur (Bir. Khin.)—the dragon

muxa (Laŋ.) [Etym. p. 132]

muxan jarya (Man. Sp.)—the leopard

muxonn'i (Lam.)—the soul (corresp. to Yakut *sür*)

mujan (Man. Sp.) [Etym. p. 169]—the carpenter

mujuxu (Man. Writ.)—the carp

muke (Man. Sp. Writ.)—the water

muktexen (Man. Writ. Sp.)—the temple

mun (Stem) (all Tung.)—oûr, we, etc. cf. *min*

muni (Nerč. Khin.) = *munu*—to become rotten, to smell

munm'ikta (Nerč.)—a kind of mosquito

munuči—the name of a river—[Etym. p. 67]

mureŭl dèyi (Bir.)—a special placing for spirits: "horsed bird"

muxan (Goldi) [Etym. p. 132]

muxan fiisu (Man. Writ.)—the male leopard

mudiya (Man. Sp.) a misprint; should be *wudiya*, vide infra

na (Man. Sp. Writ.)—the earth

nadan (with var. all Tungus)—*seven*

nadan unii (Bir.) [= *unat* (Kum.)]— "Seven girls", Pleiade

nayan (Man. Sp.)—the stove bed; *amba nayan*—the great stove bed facing the entrance

nai (Man. Sp.→Writ.)—of earth, earthly

nai ikse (Man. Sp.)—a special shaman's head-dress used for a special spirit, *naijulan*

n'aigda (Bir.)—the kind of gad-fly (with white head)

naixan (Man.)—the khan of Earth

najil (Bir.) [Etym. p. 153]—the relatives of the wife

nakču (Man. Sp.)—the senior of the mother's clan

nálki (Ur. Mank. Cast.) vide *nVl*

n'alma (Man. Sp. Writ.) vide *n'aḷma*

n'aḷma (Man. Sp.) [Etym. p. 72]; cf. *n'ama*, *n'alma*, *n'ijalma* (Man.), *n'i* (Goldi)—the man

n'ama (+ Suff.) (Bir.)—to get warm

n'ama (Man. Sp.) vide *n'aḷma*

n'amen (Man. Sp.)—the heart; the circle

namu (Man. Sp. Writ)—the sea, ocean; cf. *lamu*

n'anĵan (Kum.)—an ornment on the slash on the side of a coat

n'anmakta (Nerč.)—vide *monmakta*

n'ayŋla∼n'ayŋna (Bir. Nerč. RTM.) (Ang. Tit.) (Man. Writ.)—the sky, heaven

n'ayŋ'ako (Kum. Maack) vide *n'on'oko*

nantkun (Bir.) [Etym. p. 244]—stupid

napčin (Bir.)—the leaf (of a tree)

n'ari (Tun. Sch.) vide *n'irai*

nar'igačan (RTM.)—the Cervus Elaphus below one year of age; *neir'iyä* (Bir.)

narxun (Man. Sp.→Writ.)—thin, "insignificant"; (Writ.)—small

nataragdi (Transb. Tit.)—the bear

natolorg'i (Man. Sp.) [Etym. p. 126] —"the Earth outside"

nejavi (Neg. Sch.) vide *n'irai*

neir'iyä (Bir.)—the Cervus Elaphus one year old; cf. *nar'igačan*; cf. *ner'iga*

nëlki (Mank.) vide *nVl*

nelki (Tum.) vide *nVl*

n'eyn'er'i (Man. Writ.) vide *noy* (*ja*)

n'éng'in'i (Lamut) [Etym. pp. 58-59] vide *neun'in'i*

nerčugan (Nerč. Barg.)—the Nerčinsk Tungus

ner'iga (Bir.)—the embryo, fetus. very young (animal)

ner'igači (Bir.) [Etym. p. 72]—pregnant

neun'in'i (Tum.) [Etym. pp. 58-59]— the first summer month

n'i (Goldi) vide *n'aḷma*

n'ič'ikun (Bir. Kum. Khin.)—small

nijalma (tr. Man. Writ) vide *n'aḷma*

n'ikan (Man. Sp. Writ.)—the Chinese incorporated into Manchu military organization

n'ik'i (with var. Bir. Kum. RTM.) (Tum.) (Ur. Cast.) (Manchu)—the duck

nilki (Transb. Tit.)—March (? S. Sh.)

nilki (RTM) vide *nVl*

n'imaxa (Man. Sp. Writ.)—the fish; *imaxa* (Goldi)

n'imeku (Man. Sp, Writ)—the sickness

n'imagan (Goldi, Lop.) [Etym. pp. 217, 309]—the bringing (by a shaman) of the soul to the Lower World

nimya (Nerč. Barg. Bir. RTM.), *nimyana* (Ur. Cast.)—to shamanize

nimyayk'i (Nerč. Barg.)—the (shaman's) drum

nimnakawn (Nerč.)—the "true story"

n'inakin (with var. all dial.)—the dog; cf. *indaxun*

n'inan (RTM. Bir. Kum. Barg. Nerč.) —the elk (Alces) below one year of age, sometimes the fawn of Cervus Elaphus

n'inanan (Kum. RTM.) [Etym. p. 72] —the one with a fawn, ref. to the Cervus Elaphus (female)

n'iŋg'ar'i (Man. Sp.)—the spring

niŋgun (Man. Sp. Writ.)—nine

n'irai (Bir. Kum.), *n'iravi* (Mank.), *nejavi* (Neg. Sch.) *n'ari* (Tun. Sch.)— the male; cf. *n'aḷma*

n'iyavi (Mank.) vide *n'irai*

n'irugan (Man. Writ.) vide *n'urgan*

n'joxun (Man. Writ.)—"blue sky"

nmnatta -a misprint; should be *umnattan*; p. 351

nmua -a misprint; should be *umna*; p. 351

n'ogen'i (Enis. missiouaries) [Etym. p. 59]—April

nölk'ini (Bir.) vide *nVl*

nöltki (Neg. Sch.) vide *nVl*

noy (*ja*) (stem)—the spring (when the grass appears); *noyja* (RTM), *nöuyi* (Lam), *n'ongun'on*, *nöngnön* (Neg. Sch.), *n'öngn'ö* (Goldi, Sch.) *n'eyn'er'i* (Man. Writ.)

n'oyŋ'in sog'i (Man. Sp.)—the so-called "Chinese cabbage"

n'öngn'ö (Goldi, Sch.) vide *noy* (*ja*)

n'ongn'on (Neg. Sch.) vide *noy* (*ja*)

nöngnön (Neg. Sch.) vide *noy* (*ja*)

nongnön'i (Ang. Tit.)—"June-July" (? S. Sh.)

noyja (RTM) vide *noy* (*ja*)

n'on'o∼nonó (Bir. Kum. Khin)—the babe

n'on'oko (Bir. Kum. Khin.) [Etym. p. 81]—the bear, "a grand babe"

nonokon (Bir.)—early, before

n'opti (Bir.)—"what was in earlier time"

n'opti (Barg. Nerč. Bir. Kum. Khin. RTM. Mank.)—old, early

nordojar'i (Barg. Nerč.)—one who is singing prayers; "he who is praying"

nöuyi (Lam.) vide *noy* (*ja*)

nulki (Khin.) vide *nVl*

n'últan (Lamut) vide *n'ultin*

n'ultin (Lam. Tum.), *n'últan* (Lamut) —the sun

n'upn'ak'i (with var. all Tung.)—the goose

nura (Man. Sp.) *nure~nurǝ* (Man. Writ.)—a light, millet wine

n'urgan (Man. Sp.) = *n'uryan; n'urxan* (Goldi, Lop.), *n'irugan* (Man. Writ.) —the picture, particularly one representing spirits

n'uxu° (Man. Sp. Writ.)—*n'oxu*—the wolf·.

nVI (+ Suff.)—the Spring; *nolk'i* (Bir.), *nulki* (Khin.), *nèlki* (Mank.), *nälki* (Ur. Mank. . Cast.), *nelki* (Tum.) (Neg. Sch.), *nilki* (RTM), *nöltki* (Neg. Sch.)

ɣala (Bir.)—to fear, to be frightened

ɣalaɣa (Bir.)—the tiger; "the fear exciting one" ·

ɣale vide *gale*

ɣaleɣa (Transb. Tit.) [Etym. p. 81]— the bear

ɣukata (Neg. Sch.)—the bear

o (with var. all North. Tung.)—"to do not"; an auxil. verb

ō (with var. all Tung.)—to do

obdowǒa (Bir. Kum.)—"broken"

oboči (Transb. Tit.)—the bear; "one who has fear"

obon (Mank.) [Etym. p. 201]—the tumulus (a heap of stones) erected on the tops of mountains and passes

odakon (Nerč.) vide *idakon*

od'en (Khin.) vide *ojan*

odin (Bir. Khin. Mank. Nerč.) (with var. all North Tungus)—the wind

odoɣan (RTM) vide *idakon*

ogdeu oǒikta (Ang. Tit.) — the Polar Star

ogdi ·(with var. all North. Tung.)— great, grand

ogdi dulga (Bir.)—the period of the day, between the morning and midday

oɣekat (Lam.)—the star; cf. *os'ikta, toɣuǔiɣa*

oɣōvun (Nerč. Barg.)—the singer, "the shaman"

ôigōn (Neg. Sch.) vide *ǝrga*

ojo (Man. Sp.→Writ.)—the immaterial substance of sacrifice

ojan (RTM. Bir. Kum. Nerč.), *od'en, ojon, ǝjan, ǝjǝn, ǝjin, ɣdi* [Etym. p. 126]—the master, the master—spirit, the ruler, husband, etc.

ojon (Nerč.) vide *ojan*

ojor (Bir.)~*ajor*—early, old

okto (with var. all North. Tung.)—the road, way, path

okugdi ,(Bir.)—hot

oldo (also *ollo*) (with var. all North. Tung.)—the fish

olen' (Mank.) [Etym. p. 72]—the Cervus Elaphus

olgo (Stem) (with var. all North. Tungus)—the idea of "dry"

olgo (+ Suff.) (Bir. and others)—to dry, to get dry

olgokta—the name of a river—[Etym. p. 67]

ollo (Bir.) vide *oldo*

olo (Bir.)—every, all; vide *alla*

olo (l) (+ Suff.) (Mank.)—to jump aside (ref. to a frightened horse)

olo (+ Suff) (Bir.) — to be suddenly frightened

olo (mǒi) (tr. Man. Writ.)—to tremble from fear

olon (Barg.)—a rectangular piece (usually skin) attached to the shaman's costume

oloɣ (Bir.) [Etym. p. 244]—a person affected by a special condition of olonism

olondokon (+ Suff.) (Bir.)—to be affected by olonism

olorgi (Man. Sp.)—external

olorgi foɣoɣo (Man. Sp.)—the external (third) soul

olon'o (RTM) [Etym. p. 58]—the name of the month which follows *toksun'u*

oltarga (+ Suff.) (Bir.)—to appear

om'i (Bir. Khin. Kum.) [Etym. p. 531] —the soul (in children)

om'i (Ur. Cast.)—the soul

omija (RTM)—"the season when the grass appears"; the name of the month which follows *olon'o*

omiija (Goldi, Sch. Lop.)—"the soul"

omo (with var.· all North. Tung.)—to come

omo (= *omok*) (Barg. Nerč. Mank.) [Etym. p. 198]—the clan

omugda (Enis. missionaries)—the soul

ōmule (Bir.)—a kind of gad-fly (large one, brown-yellow)

omuts (Bir.)—the hook; a special placing for envoys, spirits

ŏn (all dial.)—"rule", "law"

onin (RTM. Bir. Kum.), *on'in* (Khin) —the female Cervus Elaphus; cf. *enen buxu* (Man. Writ.)

on'in (Khin.) vide *onin*

oni(n) (with var. all Tung.)—the mother

onma (Lamut)—May; vide *unm'i*

on'o (RTM)—the ornament on the re-·indeer boxes; cf. *moritin* (Nerč.)

on'o (Bir.)—the bear female; the mother, the grandmonther

onŏl! (sev. dial.)—an interjection: to express pain.

oɣgo (Bir. Kum), *oɣgun* (Khin. Mank. Barg. Nerč. Bir. Kum.), allo *oɣrun* [Etym. p. 197]—the horse, also reindeer reserved for the spirits

oɣgun vide *oɣgo*

oɣɣun vide *oɣgo* ·

oon'i (Bir.)—a special aperture under the arm in the shaman's costume (for spirits)

or (Vr, Stem) vide *ori*

orgi (as a component) (Bir. Barg. Nerč. and others)—lower

orgidunda~ŏrg'idunda (Barg. Nerč.)— the Lower World

ŏrgisk'i (Barg. Nerč.)—downwards; a form of shamanizing

orgo (Man. Sp.→Writ.) vide *oryo*, and *orxo*

ŏrgö (Goldi, Sch.) vide *ǝrga*

orgu bojen = *ǝrgin* (Bir.)—the lower (living) people

orɣo (Man. Sp.)—the grass (dry), straw

ŏr'i (Bir.) vide *ori*

or'i (Bir. Mank.) vide *ori*

ori (Khin. Nerč.), *ori, ŏr'i, or, ôri* (Ur. Cast.), *eji* (Neg. Sch.)—to breathe

or'i (Man. Writ.)—the male sexual element

ormu (Khin.)—a special ornament on the moccasins; cf. *orumus*

oroč̌o (Nerč. Barg.)—the stony slope of mountain

orokto (with. var. all North. Tungus) —the grass

oron (Man. Sp.) (several North. Tung. dial.)—the throne, place, seat; the place of a star.

oron (Nerč. Barg. RTM) (Ur. Cast.) [Etym. vide SONT]—the reindeer

oron (Nerč. Barg.)—the staff used by the shamans (in form of reindeer)

oru (Enis.) vide *ar* (Bir.)

orū (all dial.)—bad, the bad thing

orumus (Nerč.)—the knee protector

orun (Man. Sp.)—the place; cf. *oron*

orxo (Man. Writ) vide *oryo*

osekta (Bir.) vide *ŏs'ikta*

ŏs'ikta (Mank.) (with var. all Tungus) cf. *oɣekat, wuǔiɣa*—the star

oǒikta (Ang. Tit.) vide *ŏs'ikta*

oskun (Man. Sp.), *osukun* (Man. Writ.) —small

oskunči (Man. Sp.→Writ.) = *eskunj'i*

ovilasani (Nerč.), *ovilassa, ovilašani, ovelakšani* (Ang. Nerč. Tit.)—the spring

owlan (Bir.)—a constellation; corr. *dolowon* (Dah.) cf. p. 46

panâgo (RTM)—a plank with thongs for carrying a load on the back by hunters

p'iɣan (Man. Sp.)—the taiga; cf. *bigan*

pŏdǝ (Man. Sp.)—"house, clan, family"

p'oɣun (Man. Sp.) vide *boigon;*—family, clan, house ·

polori (Man. Sp.) vide *bolori;*—the autumn

puǒǝɣe (Man. Sp.) vide *buǒexe;*—dead

puĉѐγe gurɪn (Man. Sp.)—the World of dead, the Lower World

puĉѐγe joγun (Man. Sp.)—the "road" (of spirits) of dead

pud (Goldi, Grube) [Etym. p. 277]—to shamanize (? S. Sh.)

pùhhuŏ (Nuichen, Grube) vide *boixon*

rikŝa (*urikѕa*) (Enis. missionaries) vide *arikѕa*, cf. *ori*

. ѕa (+ Suff.) (with var. all Tungus)—to know

sagdas'i (Man. Sp.)—the old people, ancestors, spirits of ancestors

sagdas'i voĉko (Man. Sp.)—the clan list

sagdikikan (Khin.) [Etym. p. 80]—the old (man), the bear

sägi (Bir.)—the whirl

sayale (Man. Sp.), *saxalin*, *saxalan* (Man. Sp. Writ.)—black

sajaka (Bir.)—a treeless space in taiga

ŝajan (Man. Sp.→Writ.)—white, gray (hair) ; = *ŝajen* (Man. Sp.) ; cf. *ŝan'jan* (Man. Writ.)

ŝajen (Man. Sp.) vide *ŝajan*

saja (Bir.)—a flat place near the mountain pass

sakal (Mank.) [Etym. p. 74]—the beard

sakha (Udehe, Brail.)—the "evil" spirit

salpa (Bir. Khin.), *s'ilpa* (Bir.), *selpe* (Kum.), *selfe* (Man. Writ.) [Etym. p. 112]—an ornamented slash in the side of a coat

salu (Man. Writ.) [Etym. p. 74]—the beard

sama (+ Suff.) (RTM), *samada* (Mank.), *samda* (Bir.), *xamal* (Tum.), *samda* (*mbi*) (Man. Writ.), *xamandal* (Lam.) [Etym. p. 304]—to shamanize

s'ama~ŝama~sama (Goldi, Schrenk, Sch.) (Oroĉi, Sch.) vide *saman*

samalda (Mank.) vide *sama*

s'aman (Barg. Amur, RTM) vide *saman*

saman (with var. all Tungus) [Etym. pp. 269-270] *haman*, *xaman*, *s'aman*, *ŝama*, *s'ama*, *sama*—the shaman

saman'i ĕtku (Man. Sp.)—the shaman's costume

saman'i g'evan'i ilga (Bir.)—the swastika on the shaman's head-dress

samás'ik (Bir. Kum. Khin. Nerĉ. Mank. Barg.)—*s'amás'ik*, *ŝamaŝik*, *hamaγik* (Lam.)—the shaman's costume

ŝamaŝik, vide *samás'ik*

samda (*mbi*) (Man. Sp. Writ.) vide *sama*

ѕamdame tarimbi (Man. Writ.)—to be distributed with interruptions

samdo (Bir.) vide *sama*

samna (Nerĉ.)—to wear out

samnakon (Nerĉ.) [Etym. p. 68]—a placing with grass destroyed and shrubs cut off

sän (Man. Sp.) *saŋ* (Man. Sp.)—good, well!

saŋ (Man. Sp.) vide *sän*

saŋga (Man. Sp.)—a hole, aperture

saŋgnan (Bir.) vide *saγγur*

saγγur (Bir.)—a tally

ŝaγin (Man. Sp.)—white; cf. *ŝajan*

saŋk'ira (Bir. Nerĉ.), *saŋkra* (Nerĉ.), *saŋk'ir'i* (*x'jan*) (Man.)—laedum palustrum

saŋk'ir'i (*x'jan*) (Man. Sp.) vide *saŋk'ira* [Etym. p. 201]

saŋkra (Nerĉ.) vide *saŋk'ira*

sapil (Bir.)—the colour of hourse: very light brown with dark mane and tail

säpsäku (Transb. Tit.) (Ur. Cast.)—the bear

satimar (RTM) [Etym. p. 81], *ŝatimar* (Nerĉ. Tit.)—the male bear

ŝatimar (Nerĉ. Tit.) vide *satimar*

satin'i (RTM) [Etym. p. 58]—the name of the month which follows *atin'i*

savak'i (Bir. Kum. Khin. Nerĉ.), *sѐvek'i*, *savaki*, *ŝavak'i*, *s'avak'i*, *sevoki*, *sewek'i* [Etym. p. 160]—the placing for spirits

ŝavak'i (Barg.) vide *savak'i*

sävak'i (Bir. Kum. Khin) vide *savak'i*

s'avak'i (Barg. Nerĉ.) vide *savak'i*

savak'iĉan—dimin. from *savak'i*

saxalan ula (Man. Writ.)—the Amur River

sebѐγa (Man. Sp. Writ.)—the blood vessels, arteria and veins; life

sebu (Bir.) vide *sѐfu*

sĕĉѐ (Man. Sp. Writ.)—the sock of plough; the turtle

sѐfu (Man. Sp. Writ.), *sebu* (Bir.) [Etym. p. 147]—the teacher; the teacher-shaman

sekan (Bir. Khin. Kum. Nerĉ. Barg.)—the ear-ring

sekta (all dial.)—the shrub

sѐlѐ (Man. Sp. Writ.)—the iron

selfe (Man. Writ.) vide *salpa*

sѐmde (Man. Sp.) = *sendexen* (Man. Writ.) [Etym. p. 377]—the place in the house where placing for spirits are preserved

sѐn (Udehe, rest. S. Sh.) vide *syn*

s'ena (Bir.)—the mourning clothes

s'en'ŝan (Bir.) [Etym. p. 235]—the specialist dealing with some spirits

s'erä (Bir.)—the rain bow

ŝeri (*mb'e*) (Man. Sp.) = *ŝere* (Man. Writ.) — to become hot red, white face; to have the high fever

sѐsѐre (*mbi*) (Man. Writ.)—to put in disorder

s'euwa (Goldi, Grube) vide *seven*

seva (Goldi Samagir, Schrenck)—the idol (? S. Sh.) also vide Index of Spirits

sѐvѐk'i (Mank.) vide *savak'i*

sѐvѐn, *sѐvѐŋ*, *sewo*, *seva*, *s'euwa*, *sevo,* *sѐn*, *syn* vide Index of Spirits

sevenkan, etc. dimin. *seven* etc

sevo (Olĉa, Sch.)—an idol, god (? S. Sh.)

sevoki (Goldi, Oroĉi, Olĉa, Sch.) vide *savak'i*

sѐwѐk'i (Bir.) vide *savak'i*

sewek'i (Nom. Barg. Poppe) — "idol made of rugs"

s'i (all Tungus)—thou

ŝifu (Man. Writ.)—as transcription of a Chinese word; cf. *sѐfu*

siγilaya· (RTM)—the season good for hunting squirrel

s'ihun (RTM) vide *s'ivun*

s'ij'im~s'id'im (Bir.), *sit'im* (RTM.), *siji* (Man. Writ.)—the rope, string

s'iksä (with var. all Tung.)—the evening

s'iksän'i (Bir.)—the moment about one hour and a half before the sunset

ŝilbe (Mank.) [Etym. p. 74]—the tibia

s'iliksä (Bir.)—the dew

silkir—the name of a river (Šilka, Amur)—[Etym. p. 67]; "stressed"

sillä (+ Suff.) (Bir.)—to change colour (green cover of plants)

s'ilpä (Bir.) vide *salpa*

s'iрkan (Barg. Nerĉ.) vide *ĉipkanin*

s'ira (Nerĉ.)—the threads

sirg'i (RTM.)—the sand

sirg'idika (RTM)—the sand-worm

sirg't is misprint; should be *sirg'i*

s'irinan (Nerĉ.) [Etym. p. 112]—an ornament made of threads

.s'iŝa~s'iŝa~siŝa (Man. Sp.→Writ.) — the shaman's belt with trinkets

siu (Oroĉi, Sch.) vide *s'ivun*

s'iun (Neg. Sch.) (Goldi, Grube) vide *s'ivun*

s'ivak (Nerĉ.)—the water grass

s'ivak—the name of a river—[Etym. p. 68]

sivar (Bir.)—a marshy place, "mud"

sivartu—the name of a river—[Etym. p. 68]

s'ivun (Khin.), *s'ihun* (RTM), *s'ivn* (Neg.) (Goldi, Grube), *s'iu* (Oroĉi, Sch.), *sun* (Neg. Sch.), *ŝun* (Man. Sp. Writ.)—the sun

ŝoforo (Man. Sp.)—a sickness (contagious) ; cf. p. 232

soyon (RTM) (Ang. Tit.), *soyonon* Nerĉ.) [Etym. p. 72]—the female Cervus Elaphus

solbar dѐvi (Bir.)—the "Chinese Phoenix" on the shaman's costume

solimb'e (Man. Sp.), *solimbi* (Man. Writ.)—to invite, to invite a spirit during the sleep (shamans), to sacrifice (invite for)

solo (+ Suff.) (Bir. Nerĉ. RTM)—to go up to stream by water *solo* (+ Suff.) (all dial.)—"up stream", against the river's current

,solox'i (Man. Writ.) vide *solx'i* (Man. Sp.)

solx'i (Man. Sp.)—the polecat

sovčoxo (Man. Sp.)—odd, odd-days—happy days

soor'i (Man. text), corr. *soorin* (Man. Writ.)—the place (e.g. of a spirit)

soptoran (RTM.)—"the one who empties himself with berries"; the bear

sorgon (Man. Sp.)—the ribbons (attached or used by spirits); cf. *sorgun*

sorgun (Man. Writ.) vide *sorgon*

šovok'i (Enis. missionaries) vide *sav-ak'i*, *zovok'i*

sozatyi (Mank.) [Etym. p. 72]—the elk (Alces)

eudala (Bir.) (Man. Writ.) vide *èrga*

sudala (Bir.)—the venal system

sudur'i (Man. Sp. Writ.)—the history

sugdun (Man. Sp.) (Bir.), *sukdun* (tr. Man. Writ.)—the vapour, steam; the sickness

suixa (Man. Sp. Writ.)—a kind of grass good for animals; "wormwood" (?)

sujara (Man. Sp. Writ.)—leaning, pressing against

sujen (Bir.)—the narrow space, near the river, covered with sand and pebble

s'uk'a naï ikse (Man. Sp.)—a special shaman's head-dress

sukdun (tr. Man. Writ.) vide *sugdun*

suks'i (Man. Sp.→Writ.)—the air saturated with sickness

sula (Man. Sp.) [Etym. p. 316]—a. spirit of unknown origin, free

šulen (Man. Sp. Writ.)—the lynx

sum (Bir.)—the unit of meassure: a distance between the stretched thumb and the articulation of the first finger; cf. p. 61

sun (Neg. Sch.) vide *s'ivun*

šun (Man. Sp. Writ.) vide *s'ivun*

sun'Ja (Man. Sp. Writ.)—five

supkoit—the name of a river—[Etym. p. 67]

supkta (Nerč.)—"deep" (river)

sünesun (Ur. Cast.), *sunusun* (Mank.) [Etym. p. 53]—the soul

šurdèrè (Man. text)—"revolving"

surei (Man. text)—wise

sus'i~sus'e (Kum. Bir.)—the soul

syn (Udehe, Brail.) = *sèn* (S. Sh.)—a "good spirits" (? S. Sh.)

sVvV (all North. Tungus) — stem for *seven*, etc

ta (Man. Sp.) vide *ča*

ta jár'i (Man. Sp.)—the chief shaman assistant

ta saman (Man. Sp.)—the chief clan (*p'orun*) shaman

taa (~*tã*) (+ Suff.) (Bir.)—to do; to

produce; to pull

tabjan (Bir.) vide *jabjan*

tabu (*mb'i*) (Man. Sp. Writ.)—to put, to put a sacrifice

tači (*mb'i*) (Man. Sp. Writ.)—to teach, to learn

tagila (+ Suff.) (Man. Sp.)—to come, to arrive (e.g. guests)

tai (Man. Sp.) vide *ča*

taif'in (Man. Sp.→Writ.) [Etym. p. 222] —the peace, condition of peace

taim'in (Man. Sp.), *tamin* (Man. Writ.) —"erected hair", in oxen considered as a sign of health

taišima èfen (Man. Sp.)—a special kind of cakes, covered with beans, used as sacrifice

taize (Man. Sp. Writ.) analogous to *be-ise* used in the names of spirits

tãka(n) (Nerč. Bir, RTM. Khin.) also *taka*—the trunk of a tree, beam, bridge

taka (+ Suff.) (Man. Sp.)—to recognize

takaoi—the name of a river—[Etym. p. 57]

tak'ira (Bir. Kum.)—the river mollusk with a shell, cf. *tazura*

taktikaydi (Transb. Tung. Tit.)—the bear; "the one who is living in cedar forest"

takto (Man. Sp.)—the house of Manchu manor located left from the main house

tãl (Nerč.) vide *töli*

tala (Bir. Kum. Nerč. Barg.)—the salty ground

tala—the name of many a river—[Etym. p. 67]

talmen (Man. Sp.)—a kind of short, tender grass, good for animals at certain seasons

talman (Man. Sp.) = *talman* (tr. Man. Writ.)—the fog

tãm (Bir.) vide *tiyan*

tamnV (var. Tung. dial.) (Stem)—the fog

tan (Bir.)—to stretch, to pull, to teach

tãnã (Bir.), *tünäy* (Mank.) *tänäk* (Ur. Cast.) *tanag* (Bir. Mank.) [Etym. p. 244]—a person weak-minded, idiot, insane

tänäg (Bir. Mank.) vide *tänä*

tänäy (Mank.) vide *tänä*

tänäk (Ur. Cast.) vide *tänä*

tan'čin'i (Man. Sp.), *dančin* (Man. Writ.)—of wife's clan people

tangu (Man. Sp. Writ.)—one hundred

tar(V) (with var. all Tungus)—that

tara (Man. Sp.)—to stop, to arrest

targa (Man. Sp. Writ.) (Bir.)—a tissue, fabric; taboo: a piece of fabric hung up in order to indicate tabooed place or house

targidula (Mank.)—thither

tarin tasza (Man. Sp.→Writ.)—the male tiger

tarkin (Man. Sp.) = *talk'an*—the lightning

tasíya (Khin.) *tasza* (Man. Writ.) [Etym. p. 82]—the tiger;

tasza (Man. Writ.) vide *tasíya*

tavjan (Bir. Kum.) vide *jabjan*

tazura (Man. Writ.) vide *tak'ira*

tebu (*mb'i*) (Man. Sp. Writ.)—to put straight

tèdu (*mb'e*) (Man. Sp.)—to lie down

tèya (Bir.) = *tèyačen*—the Tungus non-incorporated into military organization

te'ifun (Man. Writ.)—the cane for old men; staff; cf. *tijavun*

tèmgètu (Man. Sp.)—the certificate

tet (Stem) (all Tungus, with var.)—(to) dress

tetu (Goldi, Lop.)—the shaman's dress; cf. *tet*

texè (Man. Writ.)—sat, was sitting

texe (*mbi*) (Man. Writ. Sp.)—to seat, to occupy the throne, etc

texeren (Man. Writ.)—the similarity, comparison

tiyan (Bir.)—a place under the high river bank

tiy'ika (RTM)—a place (locality) good for horse riding

tiyir'if'ki (Bir.)—the tick (one which deeply penetrates the skin)

tijavun (Bir. Nerč.)—the staff used by women when riding reindeer (Nerč.), by men when using ski (Bir.), the shaman's staff (Bir.); cf. *teifun*

tik (+ Suff.) (with var. all Tungus)—to fall, to seat

tikanin (Bir.)—the root

tiru vide *turu*

to (Oroči, Sch.) vide *töki*

toyo (with. var. all Tungus)—the fire

toyolga(n) (Bir.)—the pillar, post, axis (celestial)

toyoljin (Bir.)—the one living in fire

töki (with var. all Tungus) [Etym. p. 72]—the elk (Alces)

tokso (Man. Sp. Writ.)—the village

toksoko (Nerč.)—a mountain covered with a good forest

toksun'u (RTM.) [Etym. p. 58]—"the cold weather is over"; the name of the month which begins from the end of January

töli~joli (Barg.)—the taimen (salmo lenok); a special placing in shamanizing

toli (Goldi, Olč.) (Man. Sp. Writ.) vide infra, *töli*

töli (Bir. Kum. Khin.), *tãl*, *tolo*, *toli*, *tölö* [Etym. p. 278]—the brass mirror

tōló (Barg.) vide tōli

tolo (Nerč. Barg.) vide tōli

toloɣeï (Mank.)—an isolated mountain

tōlungu (Neg. Sch.), tōlum (Neg. Sch.), tōlungu (Olča), tolingu (Goldi), tōlumčī (Oroči, Sch.)—a story

tome (from tolome) (Man. Sp.→Writ.) cf. p. 222

toɲdo (Man. Sp.)—straight

toɲdo mo (Man. Sp.)—the erected (straight) post for spirits

toɣɣolkon (Bir.)—"true story"

toɣor (Bir.)—a unit of measure; the distance between the stretched thumb and the little finger

tor (Oxotsk) vide tur

torgadan (Nerč.) [Etym. p. 112]—an ornament: strips sewn upon the coat

torg'i (Man. Sp.) = ɗorg'i (Man. Writ.) —"inside", "inner part"

torgomó (Nerč. Barg.)—"ornamented with some fabric"

tōril (Bir.) [Etym. p. 156]—a group of infectious diseases

tōril (Bir.) [Etym. p. 156]—the dust

torun mo (Man. Sp.) vide turu

totti (Lamut)—"rising" (? S. Sh.), used as a component of the names for months

toxo (Man. Writ.) vide tōki

toxoli ɛ̌en (Man. Sp.)—a special kind of small cakes used for sacrifice

tua (Man. Sp. Writ.) vide toɣo

tub'ize (Man. Sp.)—fruits (in general)

tučimbu (Man. Sp.)—to bring out, to make to come out

tuga (with var. all Tungus)—the winter

tuɣan'i (Bir.) vide tuga

tuɣə (Man. Sp.) = tugi (Man. Writ.)— —the heavy clouds

tui (Neg. Sch.) vide tur

tuk (V) (Barg. Nerč. Bir. Kum. Khin.) —to bring up, to lift, to erect

tuki (Bir.)—to fall; cf. tik

tuksa (Bir.)—the fog, cloud; also tuksu (all North. Tung.)

tuksa (Bir. Khin. Nerč. Mank.) (Ur. Cast.), tuks'i (Bir.), tuɣa (RTM), tuč (Tum.), suju (Man. Writ.)—to run

tuksak'i (Barg. Nerč.)—the hare

tuksaɣ'i (Barg. Nerč.) [Etym. p. 311] —a special form of shamanizing

tukš (+ Suff.) (Bir.)—to freeze, to become cold

tukuɗon (RTM. Nerč.)—the elk when it is "thin" in the spring

tulilaɲi (Bir.)—of outside

ʈunɣan bokton (Man. Sp.) vide ɗejèn

tunga (with var. all Tung.)—five

tunɲanmajen (Bir.)—the Cervus Elaphus with antlers with five branches

tuŋkä (Bir.), tuŋken (Man. Sp. Writ.) —the drum in general; (Bir.) in refence to the shaman's drum (rarely)

tuŋken (Man. Sp. Writ.) vide tuŋkä

tuɣo (Bir.)—to bend

tuɣor'in (Bir.) [Etym. p. 61]—ellipsoid

tur (Kum. Bir. Khin.)—the earth soil; tor (Oxotsk), tui (Neg. Sch.) ; cf. turu, turi

tura (Bir.)—to talk, to speak (particularly birds)

turi (Bir.) vide tur

turil (Bir.)—to blow dust

turn'i (Bir.) [Etym. p. 80]—the large bear; "one of earth"

turtan (Bir.)—the coldst period in winter

turá (Nerč. Barg.) (Nom. Barg. Poppe) also tur, rarely tiru—the universe

turu (Nerč. Barg.)—a post erected during the shamanizing; cf. toru, toro

turukan (Barg.)—a small turu

učikan (Transb. Tit.)—the bear

uɣalaɣin (RTM)—the moment about three hours before the sun set

uɣi (RTM)—narrow

uɣi (with var. all Tungus)—"upper"

uɣidunda (Barg. Nerč.)—the Upper World

uɣikon (Bar.)—the ladder (partic. in shamanizing)

uɣikta—the name of a river—[Etym. p. 67]

uɣila (Mank.)—a form of shamanizing

uɣillan (Bir. Kum.) [Etym. p. 126]— "upwards", the Upper World

uɣisk'i (Nerč. Barg.)—a form of shamanizing

uju (with var. all Tungus)—to boil

ujá (with var. all dial.)—the footprint

ukóptun (Bir.)—a special component of the shaman's costume, cf. p. 292 .

uksa (with var. all North. Tungus)—the sleeve

uksáptun (Bir.)—an ornament of the cuff in the shaman's costume

uks'i (with var. all North. Tungus)— the swan

ukur (with var. all dial.) [Etym. p. 71] —the cow

uláɣir—uliɣir (Bir.) [Etym. p. 43]—an imaginative story

ulda (with var. all Tungus)—the meat, flesh

ulōki (with var. all North. Tung.)—to lie

umčufu (Goldi, Lop.) vide jiměin

umna (Bir.)—to review the spirits by a new shaman, also by a shaman periolically

umun (with var. all Tungus)—one

una (Bir.)—to speak

unaka (Bir.)—the finger; the unit of mesure

unat (with var. all North. Tung.)—the girl, daughter

unen (Man. Sp. Writ.) [Etym. p. 71]—

the cow

unengi (tr. Man. Writ.) vide wuneɣi

unil (Bir.)—the girls

unit—a misprint; should be unil; p. 56

unm'i (Tum.)—the fingeɪ

unm'ikta (Nerč. Barg.)—the midges

untuɣun (Khin.) vide uptuvun

untun (Man. Writ.) (Lam. Tum.)—the drum; cf. uptuvun

untúvun (Ur. Cast.) vide uptuvun

uɣilivla (Bir.)—the tick; one which moves forwards with its back

uptuvun (Bir.); untŭvun, untun, untuɣun—the shaman's drum

urgulikkan (Bir.)—the bear; "the heavy one"

urō (with var. all North. Tungus)—the mountain

urokono (Khin.)—a big sea animal which can swallow a man

uru (Nerč. Bir. Kum. Khin. Barg.) vide urō

uruptun (Nerč. Barg.)—the apron; partic. a component of the shaman's costume

ušito (Barg.)—the lasso

utačt (Bir.) [Etym. p. 82]—the tiger; "one who has children"; "father, grandfather"

vagana (Bir.)—the "Tibetan" bear (small, black)

valjamb'i (Man. Sp. Writ.)—to throw ritually a small sacrifice

vălu (RTM. Man. Sp.)—a low mountain with slight slope

veče (mbi) (Man. Writ.)—to offer sacrifice to vočko (spirits), to perform rites, to shamanize

věčěku mafai těmgětu (Man. Sp. Writ.) —the list of ancestors; the clan list

večen (tr. Man. Writ.)—the sacrifice

večun (Man. Sp.)—the apron used by women for cooking, etc.

věɣe (Man. Sp.)—the stone

veïxumb'i (Man. Sp.) = veïjumb'i (Man. Writ.)—to ressurect, ref. to plants, animals after the hibernation

věrèn (Man. Writ.)—the wave

ves'ixundě (Man. Writ.)—"on the rise"

wa (Bir.)—a bad smell

weiɣun (Man. Sp.)—living one, alive

wuče (Man. Sp.)—the door

wugdun (Man. Sp.)—the underground house, sty for pigs

wujun (Man. Sp. Writ.)—nine

wujíma (Man. Sp. Writ.)—the domesticated animals

wuju (Man. Writ.)—first

wukun'ju (Man. Writ.)—the spleen [the bladder, bile, acc. to I. Zaxarov]

wuɣg'imb's (Man. Sp.)—to send

wuneɣi (Man. Sp.) = unengi (tr. Man. Writ.)—true

wuneɣi fojeɣo (Man. Sp.)—the true

soul; the first soul
wur'i (Man. Sp.)—a row
wuri (Man. Sp.)—gray (colour)
wuzer'i (Man. Sp. Writ.)—all
wuzer'i texêr'i (Man. Sp.→Writ.)—all equal
wušiya (Man. Sp.) [Etym. p. 56]—the star; cf. *usixa* (tr. Man. Writ.)
wušin (Man. Sp.) =*usin* (tr. Man. Writ.) —the bed for plantation
xačin (Man. Sp.)—the kind; cf. *ǰerg'i začin*
xala (Man. Sp. Writ.)—the clan (formerly used)
xaman (Tum.) vide *saman*
xan'alambi (Man. Sp. Writ.)—to go (the shaman) to the Lower World
xanči (Man. Sp.) = *zan'ǎe*—near by
xandu (Man. Writ.)—the rice; also a kind of tree
xǎnšin (Man. Sp.) [Etym. p. 309]—the Chinese gaolan wine
xaúki (Lamut, Schiefner) vide *xovok'i*
xeǰǎ (Tum.) [Etym. p. 58]—the top of the head; the name of the month, which begins at the end of January
xeja (Lamut)—January; cf. *xeǰǎ*
x'eyečin (Lam), *x'ieyečin* (Tum.)—the evening
xèǰèn (Bir.)—the Goldi

xele (Man. Writ. Sp.) [Etym. p. 244] —a speechless person
xelen aku (Man. Writ.) = *xele*
x'ieyečin (Tum.) vide *x'eyečin*
x'jan (Man. Writ.) = *x'jen* (Man. Sp.) [Etym. p. 201]—the incense
x'jaxa (Man. Sp. = *xijaxe* (tr. Man. Writ.) [Etym. p. 236]—a special receptacle; also used as a unit of volume
x'jen (Man. Sp.) vide *x'jan*
x'jenči (Man. Sp.)—the stick incense; cf. *x'jen*
xobo (Man. Sp. Writ.)—the coffin
xoboi maïkan (Man. Sp.)—the tent for coffin
xŏdu~kodu (Bir. Kum) [Etym. p. 243] —a violent insane person
xogŏxa (Man. Sp.) [Etym. p. 354]—a special Chinese dish; cf. p. 354
xoïtaxa (Man. Sp.)—attached
xolboko (Man. Sp.)—the earthen accomodation for char-coal (burning) in the house
xon'ǒ'ix'in (Man. Sp.) also *xon'čx'in*— of my mother's clan people
xoygo (Man. Sp.)—the brass bell
xorxodai (Man. Writ.)—bald, hairless
xos'i (Man. Sp.) = *xošo* (Man. Writ.) —the corner

xoškan (Man. Sp.), *xúsixan* (Man. Writ.) *xoz'a* (Goldi)—a skirt, used by the shamans; cf. 294
xošo (Man. Writ.) vide *xos'i*
xošoka (Man. Sp.)—a part (section) of the Earth
xovak'i (Enis. missionaries) vide *xovok'i*
xovok'i (Enis. missionaries) [Etym. p. 123]—God (Christian); cf. *xovak'i*, *xaúki*, *šovok'i*
xoz'a (Goldi) vide *xoškan*
xuašèn (Man. Sp.)—flowery, with flowers
xula(mò'e) (Man. Sp.)—to fall down
xulg'in (Bir.) = *xulxi* (tr. Man. Writ.) —a stupid person
xulxi (tr. Man. Writ.) vide *xulg'in*
xum'in'i (Enis. missionaries)—"July"
xuse (Man. Sp.) [Etym. p. 74]—the beard
xusi (Stem) (Manchu)—(to) wrap, cover
xutur'i (Man. Sp. Writ.)—the happiness, luck
ydi (Udsk, Middendorff) vide *ojan*
zuyga mafa (Man. Sp.)—the master of ceremony

LIST OF WORKS QUOTED

Note: The present list does not comprise all the works which I have used. Moreover, when using my old notes, I was unable here to find bibliographical details about some publications and for this reason they are omitted. Those readers who are interested in the Tungus bibliography are kindly asked to refer to my foreword (p. XII) to "Social Organization of the Northern Tungus" (SONT) and to consult the lists of works given in my other publications.

ABBREVIATIONS:

A. A.—American Anthropologist
A. U. L.—Acta Universitatis Latviensis
J. A.—Journal Asiatique
I. R. G. S.—Imperial Russian Geographical Society
J. N. C. Br. R. A. S.—Journal of the North China Branch of the Royal Asiatic Society
M. A. A. A.—Memoirs of the American Anthropological

Association
M. A. M. N. H.—Memoirs of the American Museum of Natural History
P. M. A. E. R. A. S.—Publications du Musée d'Anthropologie et d'Ethnographie, de l'Académie Russe des Sciences
R. O. Rocznik Orjentalistyczny

A g a p i t o v, N. N. and M. N. X a n g a l o v, "Materials for the Study of Shamanism in Siberia" (in Russian), East-Sib. Sec. I. R. G. S., 1883, Irkutsk
A l e x e i e v, B. M. "Notes from the Domain of Chinese Temple Syncretism" (in Russian); in "Oriental Memoirs" (Vostočnyje Zapiski), Vol. I, pp. 283-296; 1927, Leningrad (St. Petersburg)
A l k o r, J. P. (K o š k i n) "Projet d'alphabet pour la langue des evenkis (toungouses)" (in Russian); 1930, Leningrad (St. Petersburg)
„ "L. J. Sternberg as Tungusologist" (in Russian); in "At the Memory of L. J. Sternberg 1861-1927" published by the Academy of Sciences "Sketches on History of Knowledge", Fasc. VII, 1930, Leningrad (St. Petersburg)
„ and J. D. D a v y d o v, edited by ... "Materials of the All-Russian Conference for development of the languages and writing of the peoples of North "(in Russian); Moskow-Leningrad (St. Petersburg)
A n o x i n, A. V., "Materials concerning Shamanism among the Altaians" (in Russian); in P. M. A. E. R. A. S. vol. IV; 1924, St. Petersburg
A n u č i n, V. I., "An Outline of Shamanism among the Enissy Ostiaks" (in Russian); in P. M. A. E. R. A. S. vol. II; 1914, St. Petersburg.
A r s e n i e v, V. K. "Dersu Uzela. Travelling in the Ussuriland" (in Russian; there is a German translation of the same work); 1921, Vladivostok
B a n g K a u p, W. "Türkologischer Brief aus dem Berliner Ungarischen Institut", in Ungarische Jahrbücher, vol. V; 1925 Berlin
„ "Türkische Turfantexte" in Sitzungsberichten der Preussischen Akademie der Wissenschaft; 1929-30, Berlin
B a n z a r o v, D. "The Black Faith, or Shamanism among the Mongols" (in Russian); in Mem. of the Kazan University; 1846, Kazan; the second edition, 1891, St. Petersburg
B e n e d i c t, R. F. "The Concept of the Guardian Spirit in North America"; in M. A. A. A., No 29; 1921, Lancaster
B e x t e r e v, V. M. "Collective Reflexology" (in Russian) [there are a German and an English translations]; 1921, Petrograd
B i č u r i n, vide H y a c i n t h
B o a s, Fr. "The Mind of Primitive Man"; 1916, N. Y.
„ "Anthropology" an article in "Encyclopaedia of Social Sciences, Vol. I; 1930, N. Y.
B o g o r a s, W. "The Chuckchee"; in M. A. M. N. H. Vol. VII; 1909, Leiden—N. Y.
„ "Einstein and Religion. An application of theory of relativity to the investigation of religious phenomena" (in Russian); 1923, Moscow—Petrograd (St. Petersburg)
„ "Ideas of Space and Time in the Conception of Primitive Religion"; in A. A. Vol. 27, pp. 205-267; 1925
„ "L. J. Sternberg" (in Russian); in Etnografia, Vol. IV; 1927, Moskow
B r a i l o v s k i i, S. "Tazy, or Udihe. Essay of an ethnographical Investigation" (in Russian); in Živaja Starina, Fasc. 2; 1901, St. Petersburg
B u s s e, Th. Th. "Sketch of the Land Tenure in the Amur" (in Russian); in Biblioteka dla Čtenija, Aug.—Dec., 1869, St. Petersburg
C a s t r é n, M. A. "Grundzüge einer tungusischen Sprachlehre, nebst kurzem Wörterverzeichniss" (published by A. Schiefner); 1856, St. Petersburg
C h a v a n n e s, E. "Voyageurs Chinois chez les khitans et les joutchen"; in J. A., 1897 and 1898, Paris
„ et P. P e l l i o t "Un traité manichéen retrouvé en Chine" traduit et annoté par; in J. A., Mars-Avril, 1913, Paris
C z a p l i c k a, M. A. "The Aboriginal Siberia. A study in social anthropology"; 1914, Oxford
C z e k a n o w s k i, A. vide A. Schiefner
D a v e n p o r t, C. B. "Human Growth Curve"; in Journal of General Physiology, Vol. X, 1927
D a v y d o v, J. D, vide J. P. A l k o r (K o š k i n)
D e n i k e r, J. "Les races et les peuples de la terre", Second ed.; 1926, Paris
D o n n e r, Kai "Ethnological Notes about the Yenisey Ostyak", in Mémoires de la Société Finno-Ougrienne, Vol. LXVI; 1933, Helsingfors

445

Doré, H. "Recherches sur les superstitions en Chine"; 1911-19, Shanghai. (English translation, 1914-1926)

Eliot, Sir Charles "Hinduism and Buddhism. A historical Sketch", 3 vols; 1921, London

Frazer, Sir. J. G. "The Golden Bough; a Study in Magic and Religion", 12 vols; 1907-1915, London

Gabelentz, C. von der "Mandschu—deutsches Wörterbuch"; 1864, Leipzig

Gapanovich, I. I. "The Tungus, Negidal Tribes of the Amgun Basin: their Future" (in Russian, a summary in English); in Memoirs of the Manchuria Research Society, Section History and Ethnography, Series A, Fasc. 20; 1927, Harbin

Gennep, A. van "L'etat actuel du problème totémique"; 1920, Paris

Georgi, J. G. "Beschreibung aller Nationen des russisches Reiches" 4 Vols; 1776-1780, St. Petersburg
„ "Bemerkungen einer Reise im russischen Reich im Jahre 1772"; 1775, St. Petersburg

Gluzdovskii, V. "Catalogue du Musée de la Société pour l'Étude de la Région de l'Amour" (in Russian); in Memoirs of the same society, Vol. X; 1907, Vladivostok

Gmelin, J. G. "Reise durch Sibirien von dem Jahre 1733 bis 1743"; 1751-1752, Göttingen

Gräbner, F. "Methode der Ethnologie"; 1911, Heidelberg

Granet, M. "Fêtes et chansons anciennes de la Chine"; 1919, Paris
„ "Dances et légendes de la Chine ancienne"; 1926, Paris
„ "La civilisation chinoise; la vie publique et la vie privée"; 1929, Paris

Grebenščikov, A. V. "A Short Sketch of Manchu Literature" (in Russian); in Bulletin of the Oriental Institute, Vol. XXXII; 1909, Vladivostok

Grube, W. "Die Sprache und Schrift der Jučen"; 1896, Leipzig
„ "Giljakisches Wörterverzeichniss ... mit grammatischen Bemerkungen"; 1892, St. Petersburg
„ "Goldisch-deutsches Wörterverzeichniss"; 1900, St. Petersburg

Grünwedel, A. "Mythologie du Buddhisme au Tibet et en Mongolie basée sur la collection lamaïque du prince Oukhtomsky"; 1900, Leipzig

Halde, J. B. du "Description géographique, chronologique, etc. de l'Empire de la Chine et de la Tartarie Chinoise, etc." Vol. IV; 1730, Paris [English translation, 1735, London]

Hankins, F. H. "The Racial Basis of Civilization"; 1926, N. Y.

Harlez, Ch. de "Histoire de l'Empire de Kin ou Empire d'Or"; traduite du mandchou par; 1887, Louvain
„ "La religion et les cérémonies impériales de la Chine moderne"; in Mémoires de l'Académie Royale, Vol. LII; 1893-1894, Bruxelles
„ "La religion nationale des Tartares orientaux, mandchous et mongoles, etc."; 1887, Bruxelles

Hatt, C. "Moccasins and their Relation to Arctic Footwear"; in M. A. A. A., Vol. 3; 1916

Hemmes, D. vide Roberts, H. H. and

Hikisch, C. "Die Tungusen"; 1882, Dorpat

Holmberg, Uno "The Shaman Costume and its significance"; in Annales Universitatis Fennecae Aboensis, Series B, Vol. I, No 2; 1922, Turku (Finland)

Hsieh, E. T. "A Review of China Anatomy from the Period of Huangti"; in China Med. Jour., Anatom. Suppl.; 1920, Shanghai

Hyacinth, (Bičurin) "China in her civil and moral conditions", 4 Vols. (in Russian); Second ed. 1912, Peking

Ionov, V. M. "Spirit Master of the Forest among the Yakuts" (in Russian); in P. M. A. E. R. A. S., Vol. IV; 1916, Petrograd (St. Petersburg)

Ivanovskii, A. O. "Mandjurica. I. Specimens of the Solon and Dahur Languages" (in Russian); 1894, St Petersburg

Jameson, R. D. "Three Lectures on Chinese Folklore"; 1932, Peiping

Jastremskii, S. V. "Specimens of the Yakut Folk Literature" (in Russian); 1929, Leningrad (St. Petersburg)

Jochelson, W. "The Koryak"; in M. A. M. N. H., Vol. VI; 1905-1908, N. Y.
„ "The Yukaghir and Yukaghirized Tungus"; in M. A. M. N. H., vol. IX; 1910-1924, N. Y.

Karlgren, B. "Analytic Dictionary of Chinese and Sino-Japanese"; 1923, Paris

Klaproth, J. "Asia Polyglotta, Sprachatlas"; 1823, Paris

Köhler, W. "The Mentality of Apes"; 1925, N. Y.

Kohtz, N. "Investigation of the intelligence of Chimpanzee" (in Russian); Moskow-Petrograd (St. Petersburg)

Koppers, W. "Der Hund in der Mythologie der zirkumpazifischen Völker"; in Wiener Beiträge zur Kulturgeschichte und Linguistik, Jahrg. I; 1930, Vienna
„ "Tungusen und Miao. Ein Beitrag zur Frage der Komplexität der altchinesischen Kultur"; in Mitt. der Anthrop. Ges. in Wien, Vol. LX; 1929, Vienna

Koškin vide J. P. Alkor

Kotwicz, W. L. "Sur le mode d'orientation en Asie Centrale"; in R. O., Vol. V; 1927, Lwow
„ "Sur le besoin d'une bibliographie complète de la littérature mandchoue"; in R. O., Vol. 1928, Lwow

Kowalewski, O. "Dictionnaire Mongol-russe-français"; 1844, Kazan

Kroeber, A. L. "Anthropology"; 1923, London
„ "Historical Reconstruction of Culture Growth and Organic Evolution"; in A. A., Vol. 33; 1931

Langlès, L. "Rituel des tatars-mantchoux, etc."; 1804, Paris

Laufer, B. "Burkhan"; in Journ. of the Amer. Orient. Soc., Vol. XXXVI; 1917, N. Y.
„ "The Decorative Art of the Amur Tribes"; in M. A. M. N. H., Vol. IV; 1902, N. Y.

„ "Origin of the Word Shaman"; in A. A., Vol. 19; 1917
„ "Skizze der manjurischen Literatur"; in Keleti Szemle (Revue Orientale), Vol. VIII; 1907, Budapest
L e r o y, O. "La raison primitive. Essai de refutation de la théorie du prélogisme"; 1928, Paris
L é v y-Bruhl, L. "Les fonctions mentales dans les sociétés inférieures"; 1918, Paris
„ "La mentalité primitive", 1922, Paris
L i p p e r t, J. "Kulturgeschichte der Menschheit in ihrem organischen Aufbau"; 1886-1887, Stuttgart
L i u, C. H. "The Dog Ancestor Story of the Aboriginal Tribes of South China"; in Journal of the Royal Anthropological Institute, Vol. LXII; 1932, London
L o o n, F. H. G. van and R. Thurnwald "Un questionnaire psycho-physio-morphologique"; in Revue Anthropologique; 1930, Paris
L o w i e, R. H. "Primitive Religion"; 1924, N. Y.
„ "Primitive Society"; 1920, N. Y.
L o p a t i n, I. A. "The Goldi of the Amur, Ussuri, and Sungari Rivers. Essay of an Ethnographical Survey" (in Russian); in Memoirs of the Society for the Investigation of the Amur Region, Vol. XVII; 1922, Vladivostok
L o t k a, A. "Elements of Physical Biology"; 1925, Baltimore
M a a c k, R. "A Journey to the Amur in 1855" (in Russian); 1859, St. Petersburg
„ "The Viluisk District of the Yakutsk Gov."; 1883-1887, St. Petersburg
M a x i m o v i c z, C. vide W. Grube
M a l i n o w s k i, B. "The Sexual Life of Savages in North Western Melanesia"; 1929, London
M a r g a r i t o v, V. P. "On the Oroči of Port Imperial"; 1888, St. Petersburg
M e i l l e t, A. "Le tokharien"; in Indogermanisches Jahrbuch, Vol. I; 1914
M i d d e n d o r f f, A. Th. "Sibirische Reise" in 4 Vols; 1848-1875, St. Petersburg
M i r o n o v, N. D. "Aryan Vestiges in the Near East of the Second Millenium B. C."; in Acta Orientalia, Vol. XI; 1933, Leiden
„ "Kuchean Studies. I. Indian loan-words in Kuchean"; in R. O., Vol. VI; 1929, Lwow
„ and S. M. S h i r o k o g o r o f f "Šraman-Shaman. Etymology of the word «Shaman»"; in J. N. C. Br. R. A. S., Vol. LV; 1924, Shanghai
M i x a i l o v s k i ï, V. M. "The Shamanism" (in Russian); in Mem. of the Soc. of Friends of Nat. Sc., Anthr. and Ethn., 1892, Moskow
M ö l l e n d o r f f, P. G. "Essay on Manchu Literature"; in J. N. C. Br. R. A. S., Vol. XXIV; 1889, Shanghai
M o r g a n, L. H. "Ancient Society"; 1877, N. Y.
M o s t a e r t, A. vide A. de Smedt
M ü l l e r, F. W. K. "Uigurica"; 1908, Berlin
M ü l l e r, G. F. "A Description of Siberia with a Complete History of Events there, etc" (in Russian); 1750, St. Petersburg
„ "Sammlung Russischer Geschichte"; 1732-1764, St. Petersburg
N a d a r o v, I. "South Ussuriland and its Present State" (in Russian); in Bull. I. R. G. S., Vol. XXV; 1889, St. Petersburg
P a l l a s, P. S. "Reise durch verschiedene Provinzen des russischen Reiches" in 3 Vols; 1771-1776, St. Petersburg [a French translation here is used,—nouvelle édition, l'an II de la République, Paris]
P a r k e r, E. "A Thousand Years of the Tartars"; 1895, Shanghai (republished 1925, London)
P a t k a n o v, S. K. "Essay on the Geographical and Statistical Distribution of the Tungus" (in Russian); in Mem. I. R. G. S., Vol. XXXI; 1906, St. Petersburg
P a v l o v, I. P. "Physiology of Higher Nervous Activity" (in Russian); in Priroda (Nature), Nos. 11-12; 1932, Leningrad (St. Petersburg)
„ "Twenty-Five Years' Experience, etc. Conditioned Reflexes" (in Russian); 1925, Leningrad (St. Petersburg)—Moskow (translated into English)
P e a r l, R. "Studies in Human Biology"; 1924, Baltimore
„ "The Biology of Population Growth"; 1925, N. Y.
P e k a r s k i ï, E. "Dictionary of the Yakut Language" [with collaboration of D. D. P o p o v and V. M. I o n o v] (in Russian); 1917-1930, St. Petersburg
„ "The Russian-Yakut Dictionary"; 1916, St. Petersburg
„ and V. N. V a s i l i e v "Coat and Drum of the Yakut Shaman" (in Russian); in Materials Concerning Ethnography of Russia (Russian Museum of Emperor Alexander III), Vol. I; 1910, St. Petersburg
P e l l i o t, P. "Sur quelques mots d'Asie Centrale attestés dans les textes chinois" in J. A., Mars-Avril; 1913, Paris
„ "Les mots à ķ initiale, aujourd'hui amuie dans le mongol des XIIIe et XIVe siècles"; in J. A.; 1925, Paris
„ E. C h a v a n n e s et vide C h a v a n n e s, E.
P e t r i, B. E. "Ornament among the Kuda Buriats" (in Russian); in P. M. A. E. R. A. S., Vol. V; 1917-1925, St. Petersburg
P o d g o r b u n s k i ï, I. A. "Russian-Mongol-Buriat Dictionary"; 1909, Irkutsk
P o n i a t o w s k i, S. "Materials to the Vocabulary of the Amur River Gold"; in Bibliotheca Universitatis Librae Polonae, Fasc. 10; 1923, Warszawa
P o p p e, N. N. "Dahur Dialect" (in Russian); 1930, Leningrad (St. Petersburg)
„ "Material for the Study of the Tungus Language: The Dialect of the Barguzin Tungus" (in Russian); 1927,

Leningrad (St. Petersburg)

Priklonskii, V. L. "Three Years in the Yakutsk Gov." (in Russian); 1890, St. Petersburg

Radin, P. "The Method and Theory of Ethnology. An Essay in Criticism"; 1933, London—N. Y.

Remusat, Abel "Recherches sur les langues tartares"; 1820, Paris

Richards, A. I. "Hunger and Work in a Savage Tribe. A Functional Study of Nutrition among the Southern Bantu"; 1932, London

Roberts, H. H. and D. Hemmes "Songs of the Copper Eskimos"; in the Report of the Canadian Arctic Expedition 1913-18, Vol. XIV; 1925, Ottava

Robertson, T. B. "The Chemical Basis of Growth and Senescence"; 1923, Philadelphia and London

Rosenberg, F. "On Wine and Feast in a Persian Epic Poem" (in Russian); in P. M. A. E. R. A. S., Vol. V; 1917-1925, St. Petersburg

Rudnev, A. D. "Materials for the Dialects of Eastern Mongolia" (in Russian); 1911, St. Petersburg

" "New Data as to the Living Manchu Language and Shamanism" (in Russian); in Mem. of the Oriental Section of the Imp. Rus. Archaeol. Soc., Vol. XXI; 1912, St. Petersburg

Ryčkov, K. M. "The Enissy Tungus" (in Russian); in Zemlevedenie, Vols. III-IV; 1917—1922, Moskow

Salemann, K. H. "Manichaica", Fasc. V; 1913, St. Petersburg

Sanžeev, G. D. "Darxaty. Ethnographical Report on a Journey in Mongolia in 1927" (in Russian); 1930, Leningrad (St. Petersburg)

(Sandschejew) "Weltantschaung und Shamanismus der Alaren-Burjaten"; in Anthropos, Vol. XXIII; 1928, Vienna·

Saussure, L. de "Les origines de l'astronomie chinoise"; 1930, Paris

Schiefner, A. a series of publications [in "Mélanges Asiatiques" published by the Imp. Russ. Acad. of Sciences, Vol. III (1859); Vol. VII (1874), Vol. VIII (1876)] of Tungus materials gathered by A. Czekanowski, Bar. G. Maydell and others

" vide M. A. Castrén

Schmidt, P. P. "Chinesische Elemente im Mandschu"; in Asia Major, Vol. VII, Vol. VIII; 1932, Leipzig

" "Der Lautwandel im Mandschu und Mongolischen";in Journal of the Peking Oriental Society,·Vol. IV; 1898, Peking

" "Essay of the Grammar of the Mandarin Language" (in Russian); 1915, Vladivostok

" "The Language of the Negidals"; in A. U. L., Vol. V; 1923,·Riga

" "The Language of the Olchas"; in A. U. L., Vol. VIII; 1923, Riga

" "The Language of the Oroches"; in A. U. L., Vol. XVII; 1928, Riga

" "The Language of the Samagirs"; in A. U. L., Vol. XIX; 1928, Riga

Schmidt, W. "Der Ursprung der Gottesidee. Eine historisch-kritische und positive Studie" Vol. III; 1931, Münster

Schott, W. "Wohin gehört das Wort Schamane"; in Altajische Studien; 1831, Berlin

Schrenck, L. von "Reisen und Forschungen im Amur-Lande in den Jahren 1854-1856"; 1858-1900, St. Petersburg

" "On the Natives of the Amur Region" (in Russian); 1883-1903, St. Petersburg

Shirokogoroff, Elisabeth N. "Folk Music in China"; in the China Journal of Science and Arts, Vol. II; 1924, Shanghai

Shirokogoroff, S. M. "Anthropology of Eastern China and Kwangtung Province"; Extra Vol. IV, J. N. C. Br. R. A. S; 1925, Shanghai

" "Essay of an Investigation on General Theory of Shamanism among the Tungus" (in Russian); in Mem. of the Hist.—Phil. Faculty, Vol. I; 1919, Vladivostok [a German translation, 1935]

" "Ethnical Unit and Milieu. A Summary of the Ethnos"; 1924 Shanghai

" "Ethnological and Linguistical Aspects of the Ural-Altaic Hypothesis"; 1931, Peiping

" "Ethnos. General Principles of Variations of Ethnographical and Ethnical Phenomena" (in Russian); 1923, Shanghai

" "Function of Folklore and Science of Folklore" a note in R. D. Jameson's "Three Lectures"; vide R.·D. Jameson

" "Northern Tungus Migrations. The Goldi and their Ethnical Affinities"; in J. N. C. Br. R. A. S., Vol. LVII; 1926, Shanghai

" "The Northern Tungus Terms of Orientation"; in R. O., Vol. IV; 1928, Lwow

" "Notes on the Bilabialization and Aspiration in the Tungus Languages"; in R. O., Vol. VII; 1930, Lwow

" "Phonetic Notes on a Lolo Dialect and Consonant L"; in Bull. of the Inst. of Hist. and Phil., Vol. II; 1930, Peiping

" "Process of Physical Growth among the Chinese", Vol. I; 1925, Shanghai

" "Reading and Transliteration of Manchu Lit."; in R. O., Vol. X; 1934, Lwow

" "Social Organization of the Manchus. A Study of the Manchu Clan Organization"; Extra Vol. III, J. N. C. Br. R. A. S.; 1924, Shanghai

" "Social Organization of the Northern Tungus with Introductory Chapters concerning Geographical Distribution and History of these Groups"; 1929, Shanghai

" "What is Shamanism?"; in the China Journal of Science and Arts, Vol. II; 1924, Shanghai

" N. D. Mironov and; vide N. D. Mironov "śramana-Shaman"

„   G. F r o m m o l t and "Anthropologische und gynäkologische Beobachtungen an Chinesinnen der Provinz
        Kwantung"; in Zeitschrift für Geburgthülfe und Gynäkologie, Vol. 99; 1931, Stuttgart
S i e r o s z e w s k i, W. L. "The Yakuts. An Essay of an Ethnographical Investigation" (in Russian); 1896, St.
        Petersburg
Š i m k e v i č, P. P. "Materials for the Study of Shamanism among the Goldi" (in Russian); in Mem. of the Amur
        Section I. R. G. S., Vol. I; 1896, Habarovsk
„   "Some Moments in the Goldi Life and Superstitions connected with Them" (in Russian); in Etnograf'ič'eskoje
        Obozr'en'ije; 1897, Moskow
S m e d t, A. de and A. M o s t a e r t "Le dialect Monguor parlé par les Mongols du Kansou occidental. Dictionnaire
        monguor-français"; in Publications de l'Université Catholique de Pékin; 1933, Peiping
S o l a r s k i i, V. V. "The Present Legal and Cultural Position of the non-Russian Groups of the Amur Region" (in
        Russian); in the Material for the Study of the Amur Region, Fasc. 26; 1916, Habarovsk
Š o s t a k o v i č, V. B. "Historico-Ethnographical Value of the Siberian Rivers' Names" (in Russian); in the Mesc.
        of the East-Siber. Sec. I. R. G. S., Fasc. 2; 1925, Irkutsk
S t e r n b e r g, L. J. "The Cult of Eagle" (in Russian); in P. M. A. E. R. A. S., Vol. V; 1917-1925, Leningrad (St.
        Petersburg)
„   "Divine Election in Primitive Religion"; in the publ. of XXIe Congrès International des Américanistes, Ses-
        sion de Göteborg, 1924, Göteborg
„   "Materials for the Study of the Gilak Language and Folklore" (in Russian); Vol. I; 1908, St. Petersburg
S t e r n b e r g, S. A. "Matériaux du Musée concernant le chamanisme des Tlinghits" (in Russian); in P. M. A. E.
        R. A. S., Vol. VI; 1927, Leningrad (St. Petersburg)
S u m n e r, W. G. and A. G. Keller "The Science of Society"; in 4 vols; 1927, New Haven
T h u r n w a l d, R. F. H. G. van Loon and
T i t o v, E. I. "Some Data on the Bear Cult among the Lower Angara Tungus of Kindigir Clan" (in Russian); in
        S'ib'irskaja živaja Star'ina, Vol. I; 1923, Irkutsk
„   "Tungus-Russian Dictionary"; 1926, Irkutsk
T r o š č a n s k i i, V. F. "The Evolution of ‹Black Faith› among the Yakuts" (in Russian); 1902, Kazan
V a s i l i e v, P. V. "Note on the Inscriptions" (in Russian); in Bull. of the Imp. Acad. of Sciences, Vol. IV; No 1;
        1892, St. Petersburg
V a s i l i e v, V. N. "Preliminary Report on the Work among the Aldan-Maja and Ajan-Oxotsk Tungus in 1926-1928"
        (in Russian); publ. Acad. of Sciences; 1930, Leningrad (St. Petersburg)
„ ·   vide E. K. Pekarskii and V. N. Vasiliev
V ' e n ' u k o v, M. "Travels along the Frontiers of Russian Asia" (in Russian); 1868, St. Petersburg
V i t a š e v s k i i, N. A. "From the Observations on the Yakut Shaman's Actions (Behaviour)" (in Russian); in
        P. M. A. E. R. A. S., Vol. V; 1917-1925, Leningrad (St. Petersburg)
X a n g a l o v, M. N. Vide N. N. Agapitov and
Y a s s e r, J. "Musical Moments in the Shamanistic Rites of the Siberian Pagan Tribes"; in Pro-Musica Quarterly,
        March-June; 1926, N. Y.
„   "Theory of Evolving Tonality"; 1932, N. Y.
Y e r k e s, R. M. "Genetic Aspects of Grooming, a socially important primate behaviour pattern"; in Journal of
        Social Psychology; 1933
Y e r k e s, R. M. and Yerkes, A. W. "The Great Apes. A Study of Anthropoid Life"; 1929, New Haven
Y s e b r a n t e s, Ides E. "Three Years' Travels from Moskow Overland to China, etc."; 1706, London
Ž a m c a r a n o, C. Ž. "The Ongons of the Aga Buriats" (in Russian); in Mem. of the Imp. Russ. Geogr. Soc., Vol.
        XXXIV; 1909, St. Petersburg
Z a x a r o v, I. "Grammar of the Manchu Language" (in Russian); 1879, St. Petersburg
„   "The Manchu—Russian Dictionary"; 1875, St. Petersburg
Z e l e n i n, D. K. "Les mots tabous chez les peuples de l'Europe Orientale et de l'Asie du Nord" (in Russian); in
        P. M. A. E. R. A. S., Vol. VIII; 1929, Leningrad (St. Petersburg)

INDEX OF AUTHORS AND INVESTIGATORS

Names of the authors of various dictionaries, used in the present work, are included into this Index, but the pages on which these names occur are not indicated when the dictionaries are used only for a comparative purpose. In such cases after the names of the authors there is made a remark [Ling. Par.], i.e. linguistical parallels.

INDEX OF SPIRITS

INDEX OF ETHNICAL UNITS AND GROUPS

GENERAL INDEX

(Abbreviated)

Note: Foreword and Conclusion are not included. Vide the conclusive sentence of the Foreword, p. XII.

459

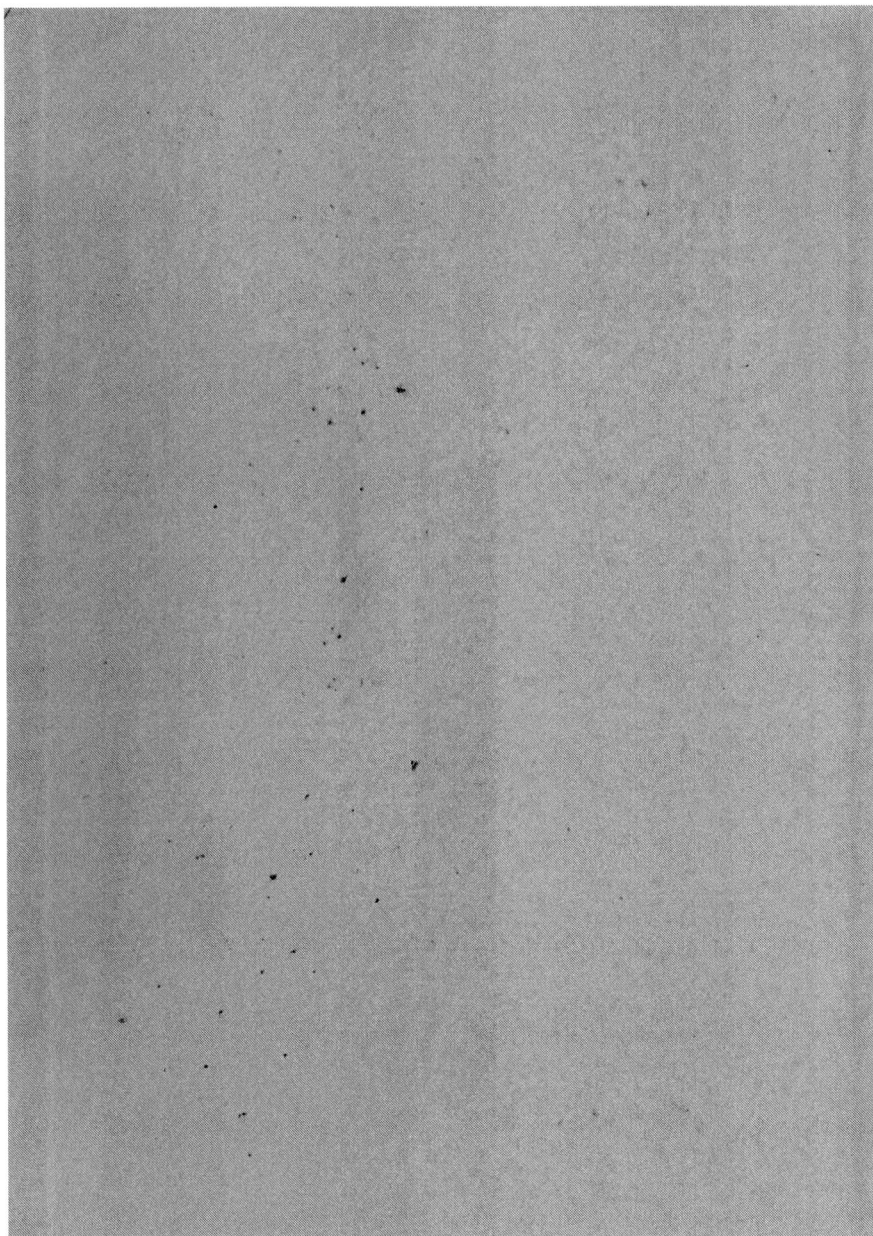

Printed in the USA
CPSIA information can be obtained
at www.ICGtesting.com
LVHW012312261024
794816LV00001B/16

9 781013 498701